Community Energy in Germany

Jörg Radtke

Community Energy in Germany

A Social Science Perspective

Springer

Jörg Radtke
Research Institute for Sustainability – Helmholtz Centre Potsdam
Potsdam, Germany

ISBN 978-3-658-39319-9 ISBN 978-3-658-39320-5 (eBook)
https://doi.org/10.1007/978-3-658-39320-5

The translation was done with the help of artificial intelligence (machine translation by the service DeepL.com). A subsequent human revision was done primarily in terms of content.

This Springer imprint is published by the registered company Springer Fachmedien Wiesbaden GmbH, part of Springer Nature.
The registered company address is: Abraham-Lincoln-Str. 46, 65189 Wiesbaden, Germany

Preface

When I wrote this book between the years of 2010 and 2015, I would not have thought that the topic would become a permanent challenge for the energy transition in Germany, Europe and worldwide. In the beginning, I doubted that community energy participation could be of any overall public interest.

More than ten years later, it is clear that community energy can still be regarded as an essential problem-solving approach for ensuring the success of the sustainability transformation. In Germany, the *Energiewende* was proclaimed in 2011, when it was politically decided to phase out nuclear power. But community energy projects had already experienced a boom in previous years, triggered by the introduction of the Renewable Energy Sources Act in 2000. This motivated me to carry out this work. I wanted to know whether and to what extent community energy is more than just the acquisition of a financial participation certificate (just like a share). I also wanted to know to what extent community energy constitutes a new form of sustainability-oriented participation, which includes a political dimension for issues of community action and climate protection, despite these perhaps not being obvious at first glance. The sometimes unapparent nature of this political element was made clear to me in many conversations, through statements like: "This is just a financial investment and that's it!"

My work was triggered by the close observation of the planning and construction of a community wind park in my hometown at the end of the 2000s. Around 2010 community energy was a big topic in public debate in Germany. Since then, the number of start-ups has dropped significantly. Community energy stakeholders have constantly emphasized that politics must finally respond with stronger support schemes to give the movement more impetus. So far, this has not happened. However, with the recently introduced federal government which took office in

2021, a new legislative package has been initiated (in April 2022), which vows to significantly strengthen its support of community energy. Meanwhile, in its Clean Energy Package, the European Union has encouraged the promotion of energy communities in all member states. However, the model has yet to achieve a breakthrough in Germany and Europe, let alone worldwide. In Germany, the energy transition is now expected to gain momentum partly due to a shift in energy production (accelerating the expansion of renewables and importing liquefied natural gas) through substitutes for reduced energy imports from Russia as a consequence of the Russia-Ukraine war in 2022. This expected momentum is also caused by the goals of the Green Party's Minister of Economics and Climate Protection of the new German government. Community energy could be a crucial silver bullet for the acceptance and participation of renewable energies, especially for the ongoing *Energiewende* in Germany, if energy systems become more numerous and get closer to local communities in the future. In a new decision by the Federal Constitutional Court of Germany from May 2022, the Court stated that the obligation of financial participation by local residents and communities close to wind farms is permissible in principle. In other words, wind energy companies could be obliged to share a portion of their financial earnings with local, affected residents. This creates a new, fundamental and forward-looking basis for municipalities, cities and districts throughout Germany to mandate financial participation in renewable energy. Therefore, the relevance, challenges and the essential principles of community energy participation explored in this book have not changed.

The basic findings of the book are therefore still of interest to the scientific community, even though the empirical data are now several years old. Since conducting those earlier investigations, I have carried out further evaluations of the data material and, in doing so, have performed analyses that were rather too complex at the time of writing and contextualized the findings within newer research study results (see Radtke and Bohn 2023; Radtke et al. 2022; Radtke and Ohlhorst 2021). This probably does not address all, but most of the study's findings. The finding of greatest relevance in this study is that the levels of participation between social groups, within community energy projects, is unbalanced. Too few younger and female people as well as non-academics and people with lower incomes are involved. This remains the biggest challenge of realizing a just and democratic community energy transition in the coming years. Closing this gap through establishing more social diversity in community energy projects is therefore the most crucial task.

For the readers of this book, the summaries of research papers in the literature review chapter are certainly no longer sufficient, as they are outdated. Therefore, I would like to provide some references for new aspects from recent literature so that readers can bring themselves up to date in a timely manner:

1. What does community energy mean and encompass? In this regard, following the well-known definition of Gordon Walker and Patrick Devine-Wright (2008), a number of papers have emerged that summarize all research findings and empirical realities (Azarova et al. 2019; Bauwens et al. 2022; Baxter et al. 2020; Brummer 2018; Campos and Marín-González 2020; Coy et al. 2021; Creamer et al. 2018, 2019; Devine-Wright 2019; Magnani and Cittati 2022; Mey and Hicks 2019; Saintier 2017; Wyse and Hoicka 2019).
2. What are the community aspects and principles in community energy projects (Broska 2021; Coy et al. 2022; Dóci 2021; Goedkoop et al. 2021; Hamann et al. 2022; Hicks and Ison 2018; Islar and Busch 2016; Koirala et al. 2018; Kooij et al. 2018; Lode et al. 2022a; McGookin et al. 2022; Ryszawska et al. 2021; Sadik-Zada and Gatto 2022; Tricarico 2021; van der Schoor et al. 2016), what is the role of gender and diversity for the engagement in projects (Berka and Dreyfus 2021; Eras-Almeida and Vásquez-Hernández 2022; Johnson et al. 2020; Kooijman et al. 2018; Lane et al. 2021; Łapniewska 2019; Lazoroska et al. 2021; Maduekwe and Factor 2021; Osunmuyiwa and Ahlborg 2019; Tsagkari 2022)? What is the relationship between energy democracy, justice and community energy (Droubi et al. 2022; Forman 2017; Goedkoop and Devine-Wright 2016; Hanke et al. 2021; Jenkins 2019; Johansen and Emborg 2018; Lacey-Barnacle 2020; Melville et al. 2018; Mundaca et al. 2018; Simcock 2016; Stewart 2021; Tarhan 2022; van Bommel and Höffken 2021; van Veelen 2018; Wahlund and Palm 2022; Wittmayer et al. 2022)? To what extent are social and sustainable innovations promoted (Dall-Orsoletta et al. 2022; Grignani et al. 2021; Grimley et al. 2022; Hewitt et al. 2019; Magnani 2021; Mihailova et al. 2022; Otamendi-Irizar et al. 2022; Schmid et al. 2022; Wittmayer et al. 2022) and what redistribution of benefits can be demonstrated (Norbu et al. 2021)? How is the concept of community energy criticized (Kumar and Taylor Aiken 2021; Rommel et al. 2018)?
3. What motivates individuals to join community energy projects (Bauwens 2016; Brauwer and Cohen 2022; Cohen et al. 2021; Conradie et al. 2021; Dóci and Vasileiadou 2015; Fischer et al. 2021; Hackbarth and Löbbe 2022; Hanke and Lowitzsch 2020; Kalkbrenner and Roosen 2016; Karasmanaki 2021; Kracher 2021; Romero-Castro et al. 2021; Sloot et al. 2019; Standal and Feenstra 2022; Wu et al. 2022)? What are the projects trying to accomplish (Holstenkamp and Kahla 2016), what are success factors (Ahlemeyer et al. 2022; Germes et al. 2021)? What are the attitudes of members of community energy projects (Bauwens and Devine-Wright 2018) and what are the effects on the individual level (Sloot et al. 2018)?

4. Which influencing factors affect the emergence of community energy projects, which governance and policy challenges arise (Bauwens et al. 2016; Busch et al. 2021; Ehrtmann 2021; Araveti et al. 2022), which instruments and policies can support community energy (Hoicka et al. 2021; Krug et al. 2022; Leonhardt et al. 2022; Lupi et al. 2021; Meister et al. 2020; Schmid et al. 2020; Spasova and Braungardt 2021) as well as the implementation of the concept of energy communities in the European Union (Caramizaru and Uihlein 2020; Coenen and Hoppe 2022; De Lotto et al. 2022; Lode et al. 2022b, c; Löbbe et al. 2022; Verde et al. 2020; Vernay and Sebi 2020)?
5. To what extent can new business models revitalize community energy and what are the success factors (Herbes et al. 2021; Mahzouni 2019; Manjon et al. 2022; Mishra et al. 2022; Romero-Castro et al. 2022; Sperling 2017)? Do smart energy systems play a role in community energy (de São José et al. 2021; Radtke 2022; van Summeren et al. 2022) and to what extent can energy storage be a new field of activity for community energy (Barbour et al. 2018; Biggins et al. 2022; Dong et al. 2020, 2021; Gährs and Knoefel 2020; Koirala et al. 2018; Parra et al. 2017)? What is the future of community energy in Germany (Benedettini and Stagnaro 2022; Broska et al. 2022; Chudoba and Borges 2022; Fernandez 2021; Holstenkamp 2021; Punt et al. 2022; Wierling et al. 2021)?

With the help of the automatic translation software DeepL, this work was translated by Springer Nature. I would like to express my sincere thanks to Jan Treibel from Springer Nature for this opportunity as well as to Snehal Surwade for assisting with the process. My very special thanks go to Sabrina-Maria Anderson, who did an excellent job of proofreading and editing this text and also critically reviewing these lines. Despite all the effort spent editing, some errors are probably unavoidable and may remain in the text, for which I would like to apologize to the reader. I would also like to thank Emily Drewing, Lars Holstenkamp and Franziska Mey, Dörte Ohlhorst, Lucas Roth and Özgür Yildiz for their inspiring thoughts on the topic of community energy in endless conversations. Finally, my heartfelt thanks go to my life partner Anja Link, who has always patiently followed the writing process from the very first second and supported my scientific work with every conceivable form of support.

By the way: The community energy wind park, which once triggered my research interest, has been waiting for a "big brother" in the form of a second wind park in its immediate proximity since its commissioning in 2007. It is likely to be built in the coming years, after a fifteen-year (!) planning and approval phase. If the enthusiastic initiator of the project had not persevered for so long, this wind farm would certainly not exist. What is more, this is absolutely typical for community energy as this study has shown: Without the civic engagement of active citizens, numerous projects would not have been born. These engaged citizens will certainly continue to play a crucial role in the future, shaping the *Energiewende* collectively. This will open up numerous research perspectives as further characteristics of community action continue to be discovered, creating a better understanding of participation *in* and democratic legitimation *of* sustainability transformation processes.

Jörg Radtke

References

Ahlemeyer, K., Griese, K.-M., Wawer, T., & Siebenhüner, B. (2022). Success factors of citizen energy cooperatives in north western Germany: A conceptual and empirical review. *Energy, Sustainability and Society*, *12*(1), 29. https://doi.org/10.1186/s13705-022-00354-4

Araveti, S., Quintana, C. A., Kairisa, E., Mutule, A., Adriazola, J. P. S., Sweeney, C., & Carroll, P. (2022). Wind Energy Assessment for Renewable Energy Communities. *Wind*, *2*(2), 325–347. https://doi.org/10.3390/wind2020018

Azarova, V., Cohen, J., Friedl, C., & Reichl, J. (2019). Designing local renewable energy communities to increase social acceptance: Evidence from a choice experiment in Austria, Germany, Italy, and Switzerland. *Energy Policy*, *132*, 1176–1183. https://doi.org/10.1016/j.enpol.2019.06.067

Barbour, E., Parra, D., Awwad, Z., & González, M. C. (2018). Community energy storage: A smart choice for the smart grid? *Applied Energy*, *212*, 489–497. https://doi.org/10.1016/j.apenergy.2017.12.056

Bauwens, T. (2016). Explaining the diversity of motivations behind community renewable energy. *Energy Policy*, *93*, 278–290. https://doi.org/10.1016/j.enpol.2016.03.017

Bauwens, T., & Devine-Wright, P. (2018). Positive energies? An empirical study of community energy participation and attitudes to renewable energy. *Energy Policy*, *118*, 612–625. https://doi.org/10.1016/j.enpol.2018.03.062

Bauwens, T., Gotchev, B., & Holstenkamp, L. (2016). What drives the development of community energy in Europe? The case of wind power cooperatives. *Energy Research & Social Science*, *13*, 136–147. https://doi.org/10.1016/j.erss.2015.12.016

Bauwens, T., Schraven, D., Drewing, E., Radtke, J., Holstenkamp, L., Gotchev, B., & Yildiz, Ö. (2022). Conceptualizing community in energy systems: A systematic review of 183 definitions. *Renewable and Sustainable Energy Reviews*, *156*, 111999. https://doi.org/10.1016/j.rser.2021.111999

Baxter, J., Walker, C., Ellis, G., Devine-Wright, P., Adams, M., & Fullerton, R. S. (2020). Scale, history and justice in community wind energy: An empirical review. *Energy Research & Social Science*, *68*, 101532. https://doi.org/10.1016/j.erss.2020.101532

Benedettini, S., & Stagnaro, C. (2022). 21 – Energy communities in Europe: A review of the Danish and German experiences. In S. Löbbe, F. Sioshansi, & D. Robinson (Hrsg.),

Energy Communities (S. 363–384). Academic Press. https://doi.org/10.1016/B978-0-323-91135-1.00015-8

Berka, A., & Dreyfus, M. (2021). Decentralisation and inclusivity in the energy sector: Preconditions, impacts and avenues for further research. *Renewable and Sustainable Energy Reviews, 138*, 110663. https://doi.org/10.1016/j.rser.2020.110663

Biggins, F., Ejeh, J. O., & Brown, S. (2022, April 25). *Going, Going, Gone: Optimising the Bidding Strategy for an Energy Storage Aggregator and its Value in Supporting Community Energy Storage.* SSRN Scholarly Paper. Rochester, NY. https://doi.org/10.2139/ssrn.4092281

Brauwer, C. P.-S. de, & Cohen, J. J. (2022). Citizen preferences for co-investing in renewable energy. In F. Karimi & M. Rodi, *Energy Transition in the Baltic Sea Region* (S. 61–89). London: Routledge. https://doi.org/10.4324/9781032003092-7

Broska, L. H. (2021). It's all about community: On the interplay of social capital, social needs, and environmental concern in sustainable community action. *Energy Research & Social Science, 79*, 102165. https://doi.org/10.1016/j.erss.2021.102165

Broska, L. H., Vögele, S., Shamon, H., & Wittenberg, I. (2022). On the Future(s) of Energy Communities in the German Energy Transition: A Derivation of Transformation Pathways. *Sustainability, 14*(6), 3169. https://doi.org/10.3390/su14063169

Brummer, V. (2018). Community energy – benefits and barriers: A comparative literature review of Community Energy in the UK, Germany and the USA, the benefits it provides for society and the barriers it faces. *Renewable and Sustainable Energy Reviews, 94*, 187–196. https://doi.org/10.1016/j.rser.2018.06.013

Busch, H., Ruggiero, S., Isakovic, A., & Hansen, T. (2021). Policy challenges to community energy in the EU: A systematic review of the scientific literature. *Renewable and Sustainable Energy Reviews, 151*, 111535. https://doi.org/10.1016/j.rser.2021.111535

Campos, I., & Marín-González, E. (2020). People in transitions: Energy citizenship, prosumerism and social movements in Europe. *Energy Research & Social Science, 69*, 101718. https://doi.org/10.1016/j.erss.2020.101718

Caramizaru, A., & Uihlein, A. (2020). *Energy communities: An overview of energy and social innovation.* Brussels: Publications Office of the European Union. https://doi.org/10.2760/180576

Chudoba, C., & Borges, T. (2022). 22—Platform-based energy communities in Germany and their benefits and challenges. In S. Löbbe, F. Sioshansi, & D. Robinson (Hrsg.), *Energy Communities* (S. 385–397). Academic Press. https://doi.org/10.1016/B978-0-323-91135-1.00003-1

Coenen, F. H. J. M., & Hoppe, T. (2022). Renewable Energy Communities as a New Actor in Home Energy Savings. *Urban Planning, 7*(2), 108–122. https://doi.org/10.17645/up.v7i2.5088

Cohen, J. J., Azarova, V., Kollmann, A., & Reichl, J. (2021). Preferences for community renewable energy investments in Europe. *Energy Economics, 100*, 105386. https://doi.org/10.1016/j.eneco.2021.105386

Conradie, P. D., De Ruyck, O., Saldien, J., & Ponnet, K. (2021). Who wants to join a renewable energy community in Flanders? Applying an extended model of Theory of Planned Behaviour to understand intent to participate. *Energy Policy, 151*, 112121. https://doi.org/10.1016/j.enpol.2020.112121

Coy, D., Malekpour, S., & Saeri, A. K. (2022). From little things, big things grow: Facilitating community empowerment in the energy transformation. *Energy Research & Social Science*, *84*, 102353. https://doi.org/10.1016/j.erss.2021.102353

Coy, D., Malekpour, S., Saeri, A. K., & Dargaville, R. (2021). Rethinking community empowerment in the energy transformation: A critical review of the definitions, drivers and outcomes. *Energy Research & Social Science*, *72*, 101871. https://doi.org/10.1016/j.erss.2020.101871

Creamer, E., Eadson, W., van Veelen, B., Pinker, A., Tingey, M., Braunholtz-Speight, T., … Lacey-Barnacle, M. (2018). Community energy: Entanglements of community, state, and private sector. *Geography Compass*, *12*(7), e12378. https://doi.org/10.1111/gec3.12378

Creamer, E., Taylor Aiken, G., van Veelen, B., Walker, G., & Devine-Wright, P. (2019). Community renewable energy: What does it do? Walker and Devine-Wright (2008) ten years on. *Energy Research & Social Science*, *57*, 101223. https://doi.org/10.1016/j.erss.2019.101223

Dall-Orsoletta, A., Cunha, J., Araújo, M., & Ferreira, P. (2022). A systematic review of social innovation and community energy transitions. *Energy Research & Social Science*, *88*, 102625. https://doi.org/10.1016/j.erss.2022.102625

De Lotto, R., Micciché, C., Venco, E., Bonaiti, A., & Napoli, R. (2022). Energy Communities: Technical, Legislative, Organizational, and Planning Features. *Energies*, *15*, 1731. https://doi.org/10.3390/en15051731

de São José, D., Faria, P., & Vale, Z. (2021). Smart energy community: A systematic review with metanalysis. *Energy Strategy Reviews*, *36*, 100678. https://doi.org/10.1016/j.esr.2021.100678

Devine-Wright, P. (2019). Community versus local energy in a context of climate emergency. *Nature Energy*, *4*(11), 894–896. https://doi.org/10.1038/s41560-019-0459-2

Dóci, G. (2021). Collective Action with Altruists: How Are Citizens Led Renewable Energy Communities Developed? *Sustainability*, *13*(2), 507. https://doi.org/10.3390/su13020507

Dóci, G., & Vasileiadou, E. (2015). "Let's do it ourselves" Individual motivations for investing in renewables at community level. *Renewable and Sustainable Energy Reviews*, *49*, 41–50. https://doi.org/10.1016/j.rser.2015.04.051

Dong, S., Kremers, E., Brucoli, M., Rothman, R., & Brown, S. (2020). Improving the feasibility of household and community energy storage: A techno-enviro-economic study for the UK. *Renewable and Sustainable Energy Reviews*, *131*, 110009. https://doi.org/10.1016/j.rser.2020.110009

Dong, S., Kremers, E., Brucoli, M., Rothman, R., & Brown, S. (2021). Establishing the value of community energy storage: A comparative analysis of the UK and Germany. *Journal of Energy Storage*, *40*, 102709. https://doi.org/10.1016/j.est.2021.102709

Droubi, S., Heffron, R. J., & McCauley, D. (2022). A critical review of energy democracy: A failure to deliver justice? *Energy Research & Social Science*, *86*, 102444. https://doi.org/10.1016/j.erss.2021.102444

Ehrtmann, M., Holstenkamp, L., & Becker, T. (2021). Regional Electricity Models for Community Energy in Germany: The Role of Governance Structures. *Sustainability*, *13*(4), 2241. https://doi.org/10.3390/su13042241

Eras-Almeida, A. A., & Vásquez-Hernández, T. (2022). Addressing the Gender Gap in the Energy Sector: The Case of Energy from Women. La Energía de las Mujeres. In A. K. Ghosh & C. Rixham (Hrsg.), *Proceedings of the American Solar Energy Society Na-*

tional Conference (S. 103–109). Cham: Springer. https://doi.org/10.1007/978-3-031-08786-8_11

Fernandez, R. (2021). Community Renewable Energy Projects: The Future of the Sustainable Energy Transition? *The International Spectator*, *56*(3), 87–104. https://doi.org/10.1080/03932729.2021.1959755

Fischer, B., Gutsche, G., & Wetzel, H. (2021). Who wants to get involved? Determining citizen willingness to participate in German renewable energy cooperatives. *Energy Research & Social Science*, *76*, 102013. https://doi.org/10.1016/j.erss.2021.102013

Forman, A. (2017). Energy justice at the end of the wire: Enacting community energy and equity in Wales. *Energy Policy*, *107*, 649–657. https://doi.org/10.1016/j.enpol.2017.05.006

Gährs, S., & Knoefel, J. (2020). Stakeholder demands and regulatory framework for community energy storage with a focus on Germany. *Energy Policy*, *144*, 111678. https://doi.org/10.1016/j.enpol.2020.111678

Germes, L. A. M. H., Wiekens, C. J., & Horlings, L. G. (2021). Success, Failure, and Impact of Local Energy Initiatives in The Netherlands. *Sustainability*, *13*(22), 12482. https://doi.org/10.3390/su132212482

Goedkoop, F., & Devine-Wright, P. (2016). Partnership or placation? The role of trust and justice in the shared ownership of renewable energy projects. *Energy Research & Social Science*, *17*, 135–146. https://doi.org/10.1016/j.erss.2016.04.021

Goedkoop, F., Sloot, D., Jans, L., Dijkstra, J., Flache, A., & Steg, L. (2021). The Role of Community in Understanding Involvement in Community Energy Initiatives. *Frontiers in Psychology*, *12*, 775752–775752. https://doi.org/10.3389/fpsyg.2021.775752

Grignani, A., Gozzellino, M., Sciullo, A., & Padovan, D. (2021). Community Cooperative: A New Legal Form for Enhancing Social Capital for the Development of Renewable Energy Communities in Italy. *Energies*, *14*(21), 7029. https://doi.org/10.3390/en14217029

Grimley, M., Shastry, V., Kânoğlu-Özkan, D. G., Blevins, E., Beck, A. L., Chan, G., & Rai, V. (2022). The grassroots are always greener: Community-based organizations as innovators of shared solar energy in the United States. *Energy Research & Social Science*, *90*, 102628. https://doi.org/10.1016/j.erss.2022.102628

Hackbarth, A., & Löbbe, S. (2022). 9 – What motivates private households to participate in energy communities? A literature review and German case study. In S. Löbbe, F. Sioshansi, & D. Robinson (Hrsg.), *Energy Communities* (S. 153–166). Academic Press. https://doi.org/10.1016/B978-0-323-91135-1.00026-2

Hamann, K., Bertel, M., Ryszawska, B., Lurger, B., Szymanski, P., Rozwadowska, M., Goedkoop, F., Jans, L., Perlaviciute, G., Masson, T., Hofer, A., Held, J., Gutschi, C., Grosche, C., Fritsche, I., Favaro, T., Eisenberger, I., Corcoran, K., & Athenstaedt, U. (2022). *Energy Citizenship as a Viable Concept: An Interdisciplinary Understanding to Unfold the Potential of Legal, Economic, and Psychological Perspectives on the Citizenship-Based Energy Transition*. University of Leipzig.

Hanke, F., & Lowitzsch, J. (2020). Empowering Vulnerable Consumers to Join Renewable Energy Communities-Towards an Inclusive Design of the Clean Energy Package. *Energies*, *13*, 1615. https://doi.org/10.3390/en13071615

Hanke, F., Guyet, R., & Feenstra, M. (2021). Do renewable energy communities deliver energy justice? Exploring insights from 71 European cases. *Energy Research & Social Science*, *80*, 102244. https://doi.org/10.1016/j.erss.2021.102244

Herbes, C., Rilling, B., & Holstenkamp, L. (2021). Ready for new business models? Human and social capital in the management of renewable energy cooperatives in Germany. *Energy Policy*, *156*, 112417. https://doi.org/10.1016/j.enpol.2021.112417

Hewitt, R. J., Bradley, N., Baggio Compagnucci, A., Barlagne, C., Ceglarz, A., Cremades, R., … Slee, B. (2019). Social Innovation in Community Energy in Europe: A Review of the Evidence. *Frontiers in Energy Research*, *7*. Abgerufen von https://www.frontiersin.org/article/10.3389/fenrg.2019.00031

Hicks, J., & Ison, N. (2018). An exploration of the boundaries of 'community' in community renewable energy projects: Navigating between motivations and context. *Energy Policy*, *113*, 523–534. https://doi.org/10.1016/j.enpol.2017.10.031

Hoicka, C. E., Lowitzsch, J., Brisbois, M. C., Kumar, A., & Ramirez Camargo, L. (2021). Implementing a just renewable energy transition: Policy advice for transposing the new European rules for renewable energy communities. *Energy Policy*, *156*, 112435. https://doi.org/10.1016/j.enpol.2021.112435

Holstenkamp, L. (2021). Community Energy in Germany: From Technology Pioneers to Professionalisation under Uncertainty. In F. H. J. M. Coenen & T. Hoppe (Hrsg.), *Renewable Energy Communities and the Low Carbon Energy Transition in Europe* (S. 119–152). Cham: Springer International Publishing. https://doi.org/10.1007/978-3-030-84440-0_6

Holstenkamp, L., & Kahla, F. (2016). What are community energy companies trying to accomplish? An empirical investigation of investment motives in the German case. *Energy Policy*, *97*, 112–122. https://doi.org/10.1016/j.enpol.2016.07.010

Islar, M., & Busch, H. (2016). "We are not in this to save the polar bears!" – the link between community renewable energy development and ecological citizenship. *Innovation: The European Journal of Social Science Research*, *29*(3), 303–319. https://doi.org/10.1080/13511610.2016.1188684

Jenkins, K. E. H. (2019). Energy Justice, Energy Democracy, and Sustainability: Normative Approaches to the Consumer Ownership of Renewables. In J. Lowitzsch (Hrsg.), *Energy Transition: Financing Consumer Co-Ownership in Renewables* (S. 79–97). Cham: Springer. https://doi.org/10.1007/978-3-319-93518-8_4

Johansen, K., & Emborg, J. (2018). Wind farm acceptance for sale? Evidence from the Danish wind farm co-ownership scheme. *Energy Policy*, *117*, 413–422. https://doi.org/10.1016/j.enpol.2018.01.038

Johnson, O. W., Han, J. Y.-C., Knight, A.-L., Mortensen, S., Aung, M. T., Boyland, M., & Resurrección, B. P. (2020). Intersectionality and energy transitions: A review of gender, social equity and low-carbon energy. *Energy Research & Social Science*, *70*, 101774. https://doi.org/10.1016/j.erss.2020.101774

Kalkbrenner, B. J., & Roosen, J. (2016). Citizens' willingness to participate in local renewable energy projects: The role of community and trust in Germany. *Energy Research & Social Science*, *13*, 60–70. https://doi.org/10.1016/j.erss.2015.12.006

Karasmanaki, E. (2021). 5—Understanding willingness to pay for renewable energy among citizens of the European Union during the period 2010–20. In G. L. Kyriakopoulos (Hrsg.), *Low Carbon Energy Technologies in Sustainable Energy Systems* (S. 141–161). Academic Press. https://doi.org/10.1016/B978-0-12-822897-5.00005-5

Koirala, B. P., Araghi, Y., Kroesen, M., Ghorbani, A., Hakvoort, R. A., & Herder, P. M. (2018). Trust, awareness, and independence: Insights from a socio-psychological factor analysis of citizen knowledge and participation in community energy systems. *Energy Research & Social Science*, *38*, 33–40. https://doi.org/10.1016/j.erss.2018.01.009

Koirala, B. P., van Oost, E., & van der Windt, H. (2018). Community energy storage: A responsible innovation towards a sustainable energy system? *Applied Energy*, *231*, 570–585. https://doi.org/10.1016/j.apenergy.2018.09.163

Kooij, H.-J., Oteman, M., Veenman, S., Sperling, K., Magnusson, D., Palm, J., & Hvelplund, F. (2018). Between grassroots and treetops: Community power and institutional dependence in the renewable energy sector in Denmark, Sweden and the Netherlands. *Energy Research & Social Science*, *37*, 52–64. https://doi.org/10.1016/j.erss.2017.09.019

Kooijman, A., Cloke, J., & Clancy, J. (2018). *Needs, wants and values: Integrating gender with energy access. Briefing Paper 3. Low Carbon Energy for Development Network.* Loughborough University.

Kracher, A. (2021). Renewable Energy Communities—Exploring behavioral and motivational factors behind the willingness to participate in Renewable Energy Communities in Germany. *(2021)*. Abgerufen von http://lup.lub.lu.se/student-papers/record/9058633

Krug, M., Di Nucci, M. R., Caldera, M., & De Luca, E. (2022). Mainstreaming Community Energy: Is the Renewable Energy Directive a Driver for Renewable Energy Communities in Germany and Italy? *Sustainability*, *14*(12), 7181. https://doi.org/10.3390/su14127181

Kumar, A., & Taylor Aiken, G. (2021). A Postcolonial Critique of Community Energy: Searching for Community as Solidarity in India and Scotland. *Antipode*, *53*(1), 200–221. https://doi.org/10.1111/anti.12683

Lacey-Barnacle, M. (2020). Proximities of energy justice: Contesting community energy and austerity in England. *Energy Research & Social Science*, *69*, 101713. https://doi.org/10.1016/j.erss.2020.101713

Lane, L., Dhal, S., & Srivastava, N. (2021). Gender Empowerment and Community of Practice to Promote Clean Energy Sustainability. In W. Leal Filho, A. Marisa Azul, L. Brandli, A. Lange Salvia, & T. Wall (Hrsg.), *Affordable and Clean Energy* (S. 689–698). Cham: Springer. https://doi.org/10.1007/978-3-319-95864-4_151

Łapniewska, Z. (2019). Energy, equality and sustainability? European electricity cooperatives from a gender perspective. *Energy Research & Social Science*, *57*, 101247. https://doi.org/10.1016/j.erss.2019.101247

Lazoroska, D., Palm, J., & Bergek, A. (2021). Perceptions of participation and the role of gender for the engagement in solar energy communities in Sweden. *Energy, Sustainability and Society*, *11*(1), 35. https://doi.org/10.1186/s13705-021-00312-6

Leonhardt, R., Noble, B., Poelzer, G., Fitzpatrick, P., Belcher, K., & Holdmann, G. (2022). Advancing local energy transitions: A global review of government instruments supporting community energy. *Energy Research & Social Science*, *83*, 102350. https://doi.org/10.1016/j.erss.2021.102350

Löbbe, S., Sioshansi, F. P., & Robinson, D. (Hrsg.). (2022). *Energy Communities. Customer-Centered, Market Driven, Welfare-Enhancing?* London: Academic Press.

Lode, M. L., Coosemans, T., & Ramirez Camargo, L. (2022a). Is social cohesion decisive for energy cooperatives existence? A quantitative analysis. *Environmental Innovation and Societal Transitions*, *43*, 173–199. https://doi.org/10.1016/j.eist.2022.04.002

Lode, M. L., Heuninckx, S., te Boveldt, G., Macharis, C., & Coosemans, T. (2022b). Designing successful energy communities: A comparison of seven pilots in Europe applying the

Multi-Actor Multi-Criteria Analysis. *Energy Research & Social Science, 90*, 102671. https://doi.org/10.1016/j.erss.2022.102671

Lode, M. L., te Boveldt, G., Coosemans, T., & Ramirez Camargo, L. (2022c). A transition perspective on Energy Communities: A systematic literature review and research agenda. *Renewable and Sustainable Energy Reviews, 163*, 112479. https://doi.org/10.1016/j.rser.2022.112479

Lupi, V., Candelise, C., Calull, M. A., Delvaux, S., Valkering, P., Hubert, W., Sciullo, A., Ivask, N., van der Waal, E., Iturriza, I.J., Paci, D., Della Valle, N., Koukoufikis, G., & Dunlop, T. (2021). A Characterization of European Collective Action Initiatives and Their Role as Enablers of Citizens' Participation in the Energy Transition. *Energies, 14*(24), 8452. https://doi.org/10.3390/en14248452

Maduekwe, M., & Factor, A. G. (2021). Gender assessment in energy projects: Perceptions, practices and the role of a regional directive in ECOWAS. *Impact Assessment and Project Appraisal, 39*(3), 251–261. https://doi.org/10.1080/14615517.2021.1904711

Magnani, N. (2021). Community Renewable Energies Between Social Enterprises, Social Movements and Hybrid Networks. In N. Magnani & G. Carrosio, *Understanding the Energy Transition* (S. 71–96). Cham: Springer. https://doi.org/10.1007/978-3-030-83481-4_5

Magnani, N., & Cittati, V.-M. (2022). Combining the Multilevel Perspective and Socio-Technical Imaginaries in the Study of Community Energy. *Energies, 15*(5), 1624. https://doi.org/10.3390/en15051624

Mahzouni, A. (2019). The role of institutional entrepreneurship in emerging energy communities: The town of St. Peter in Germany. *Renewable and Sustainable Energy Reviews, 107*, 297–308. https://doi.org/10.1016/j.rser.2019.03.011

Manjon, M.-J., Merino, A., & Cairns, I. (2022). Business as not usual: A systematic literature review of social entrepreneurship, social innovation, and energy poverty to accelerate the just energy transition. *Energy Research & Social Science, 90*, 102624. https://doi.org/10.1016/j.erss.2022.102624

McGookin, C., Mac Uidhir, T., Ó Gallachóir, B., & Byrne, E. (2022). Doing things differently: Bridging community concerns and energy system modelling with a transdisciplinary approach in rural Ireland. *Energy Research & Social Science, 89*, 102658. https://doi.org/10.1016/j.erss.2022.102658

Meister, T., Schmid, B., Seidl, I., & Klagge, B. (2020). How municipalities support energy cooperatives: Survey results from Germany and Switzerland. *Energy, Sustainability and Society, 10*(1), 18. https://doi.org/10.1186/s13705-020-00248-3

Melville, E., Burningham, K., Christie, I., & Smallwood, B. (2018). Equality in local energy commons. A UK case study of community and municipal energy. *Rassegna Italiana di Sociologia*, (2/2018). https://doi.org/10.1423/90582

Mey, F., & Hicks, J. (2019). Community Owned Renewable Energy: Enabling the Transition Towards Renewable Energy? In P. Newton, D. Prasad, A. Sproul, & S. White (Hrsg.), *Decarbonising the Built Environment: Charting the Transition* (S. 65–82). Singapore: Springer. https://doi.org/10.1007/978-981-13-7940-6_4

Mihailova, D., Schubert, I., Burger, P., & Fritz, M. M. C. (2022). Exploring modes of sustainable value co-creation in renewable energy communities. *Journal of Cleaner Production, 330*, 129917. https://doi.org/10.1016/j.jclepro.2021.129917

Mishra, R., Naik, B. K. R., Raut, R. D., & Paul, S. K. (2022). Circular economy principles in community energy initiatives through stakeholder perspectives. *Sustainable Production and Consumption, 33*, 256–270. https://doi.org/10.1016/j.spc.2022.07.001

Mundaca, L., Busch, H., & Schwer, S. (2018). 'Successful' low-carbon energy transitions at the community level? An energy justice perspective. *Applied Energy, 218*, 292–303. https://doi.org/10.1016/j.apenergy.2018.02.146

Norbu, S., Couraud, B., Robu, V., Andoni, M., & Flynn, D. (2021). Modelling the redistribution of benefits from joint investments in community energy projects. *Applied Energy, 287*, 116575. https://doi.org/10.1016/j.apenergy.2021.116575

Osunmuyiwa, O., & Ahlborg, H. (2019). Inclusiveness by design? Reviewing sustainable electricity access and entrepreneurship from a gender perspective. *Energy Research & Social Science, 53*, 145–158. https://doi.org/10.1016/j.erss.2019.03.010

Otamendi-Irizar, I., Grijalba, O., Arias, A., Pennese, C., & Hernández, R. (2022). How can local energy communities promote sustainable development in European cities? *Energy Research & Social Science, 84*, 102363. https://doi.org/10.1016/j.erss.2021.102363

Parra, D., Norman, S. A., Walker, G. S., & Gillott, M. (2017). Optimum community energy storage for renewable energy and demand load management. *Applied Energy, 200*, 358–369. https://doi.org/10.1016/j.apenergy.2017.05.048

Punt, M. B., Bauwens, T., Frenken, K., & Holstenkamp, L. (2022). Institutional relatedness and the emergence of renewable energy cooperatives in German districts. *Regional Studies, 56*(4), 548–562. https://doi.org/10.1080/00343404.2021.1890708

Radtke, J. (2022). Smart energy systems beyond the age of COVID-19: Towards a new order of monitoring, disciplining and sanctioning energy behavior? *Energy Research & Social Science, 84*, 102355. https://doi.org/10.1016/j.erss.2021.102355

Radtke, J., & Bohn, N. (2023). (forthcoming). Beyond ownership: What means "local" and "community" in community energy? How community energy projects are viewed by their members. *Energies. Special Issue Renewable Energy Systems and New Regimes of Ownership.*

Radtke, J., & Ohlhorst, D. (2021). Community Energy in Germany – Bowling Alone in Elite Clubs? *Utilities Policy, 72*, 101269. https://doi.org/10.1016/j.jup.2021.101269

Radtke, J., Yildiz, Ö., & Roth, L. (2022). Does Energy Community Membership Change Sustainable Attitudes and Behavioral Patterns? Empirical Evidence from Community Wind Energy in Germany. *Energies, 15*(3), 822. https://doi.org/10.3390/en15030822

Romero-Castro, N., Miramontes-Viña, V., & López-Cabarcos, M. Á. (2022). Understanding the Antecedents of Entrepreneurship and Renewable Energies to Promote the Development of Community Renewable Energy in Rural Areas. *Sustainability, 14*(3), 1234. https://doi.org/10.3390/su14031234

Romero-Castro, N., Piñeiro-Chousa, J., & Pérez-Pico, A. (2021). Dealing with heterogeneity and complexity in the analysis of the willingness to invest in community renewable energy in rural areas. *Technological Forecasting and Social Change, 173*, 121165. https://doi.org/10.1016/j.techfore.2021.121165

Rommel, J., Radtke, J., von Jorck, G., Mey, F., & Yildiz, Ö. (2018). Community renewable energy at a crossroads: A think piece on degrowth, technology, and the democratization of the German energy system. *Journal of Cleaner Production, 197*, 1746–1753. https://doi.org/10.1016/j.jclepro.2016.11.114

Ryszawska, B., Rozwadowska, M., Ulatowska, R., Pierzchała, M., & Szymański, P. (2021). The Power of Co-Creation in the Energy Transition—DART Model in Citizen Energy Communities Projects. *Energies, 14*(17), 5266. https://doi.org/10.3390/en14175266

Sadik-Zada, E. R., & Gatto, A. (2022). Civic engagement and energy transition in the Nordic-Baltic Sea Region: Parametric and nonparametric inquiries. *Socio-Economic Planning Sciences*, 101347. https://doi.org/10.1016/j.seps.2022.101347

Saintier, S. (2017). Community Energy Companies in the UK: A Potential Model for Sustainable Development in "Local" Energy? *Sustainability, 9*(8), 1325. https://doi.org/10.3390/su9081325

Schmid, B., Meister, T., Klagge, B., & Seidl, I. (2020). Energy Cooperatives and Municipalities in Local Energy Governance Arrangements in Switzerland and Germany. *The Journal of Environment & Development, 29*(1), 123–146. https://doi.org/10.1177/1070496519886013

Schmid, B., Serlavós, M., & Hirt, L. F. (2022). 10 – Community energy initiatives as a space for emerging imaginaries? Experiences from Switzerland. In S. Löbbe, F. Sioshansi, & D. Robinson (Hrsg.), *Energy Communities* (S. 167–181). Academic Press. https://doi.org/10.1016/B978-0-323-91135-1.00006-7

Simcock, N. (2016). Procedural justice and the implementation of community wind energy projects: A case study from South Yorkshire, UK. *Land Use Policy, 59*, 467–477. https://doi.org/10.1016/j.landusepol.2016.08.034

Sloot, D., Jans, L., & Steg, L. (2018). Can community energy initiatives motivate sustainable energy behaviours? The role of initiative involvement and personal pro-environmental motivation. *Journal of Environmental Psychology, 57*, 99–106. https://doi.org/10.1016/j.jenvp.2018.06.007

Sloot, D., Jans, L., & Steg, L. (2019). In it for the money, the environment, or the community? Motives for being involved in community energy initiatives. *Global Environmental Change, 57*, 101936. https://doi.org/10.1016/j.gloenvcha.2019.101936

Spasova, D., & Braungardt, S. (2021). Building a Common Support Framework in Differing Realities—Conditions for Renewable Energy Communities in Germany and Bulgaria. *Energies, 14*(15), 4693. https://doi.org/10.3390/en14154693

Sperling, K. (2017). How does a pioneer community energy project succeed in practice? The case of the Samsø Renewable Energy Island. *Renewable and Sustainable Energy Reviews, 71*, 884–897. https://doi.org/10.1016/j.rser.2016.12.116

Standal, K., & Feenstra, M. (2022). Engaging the public for citizen energy production in Norway. In F. Karimi & M. Rodi (Hrsg.), *Energy Transition in the Baltic Sea Region* (S. 135–154). London: Routledge. https://doi.org/10.4324/9781032003092-11

Stewart, F. (2021). All for sun, sun for all: Can community energy help to overcome socio-economic inequalities in low-carbon technology subsidies? *Energy Policy, 157*, 112512. https://doi.org/10.1016/j.enpol.2021.112512

Tarhan, D. (2022). Community renewable energy's problematic relationship with social justice: Insights from Ontario. *Local Environment*, 1–17. https://doi.org/10.1080/13549839.2022.2077713

Tricarico, L. (2021). Is community earning enough? Reflections on engagement processes and drivers in two Italian energy communities. *Energy Research & Social Science, 72*, 101899. https://doi.org/10.1016/j.erss.2020.101899

Tsagkari, M. (2022). The need for gender-based approach in the assessment of local energy projects. *Energy for Sustainable Development, 68*, 40–49. https://doi.org/10.1016/j.esd.2022.03.001

van Bommel, N., & Höffken, J. I. (2021). Energy justice within, between and beyond European community energy initiatives: A review. *Energy Research & Social Science, 79*, 102157. https://doi.org/10.1016/j.erss.2021.102157

van der Schoor, T., van Lente, H., Scholtens, B., & Peine, A. (2016). Challenging obduracy: How local communities transform the energy system. *Energy Research & Social Science, 13*, 94–105. https://doi.org/10.1016/j.erss.2015.12.009

van Summeren, L. F. M., Breukers, S., & Wieczorek, A. J. (2022). Together we're smart! Flemish and Dutch energy communities' replication strategies in smart grid experiments. *Energy Research & Social Science, 89*, 102643. https://doi.org/10.1016/j.erss.2022.102643

van Veelen, B. (2018). Negotiating energy democracy in practice: Governance processes in community energy projects. *Environmental Politics, 27*(4), 644–665. https://doi.org/10.1080/09644016.2018.1427824

Verde, S., Rossetto, N., Ferrari, A., & Fonteneau, T. (2020). *The Future of Renewable Energy Communities in the EU: An investigation at the time of the Clean Energy Package*. Fiesole: European University Institute. https://doi.org/10.2870/754736

Vernay, A.-L., & Sebi, C. (2020). Energy communities and their ecosystems: A comparison of France and the Netherlands. *Technological Forecasting and Social Change, 158*, 120123. https://doi.org/10.1016/j.techfore.2020.120123

Wahlund, M., & Palm, J. (2022). The role of energy democracy and energy citizenship for participatory energy transitions: A comprehensive review. *Energy Research & Social Science, 87*, 102482. https://doi.org/10.1016/j.erss.2021.102482

Wierling, A., Zeiss, J. P., Lupi, V., Candelise, C., Sciullo, A., & Schwanitz, V. J. (2021). The Contribution of Energy Communities to the Upscaling of Photovoltaics in Germany and Italy. *Energies, 14*(8), 2258. https://doi.org/10.3390/en14082258

Wittmayer, J. M., Campos, I., Avelino, F., Brown, D., Doračić, B., Fraaije, M., Gährs, S., Hinsch, A., Assalini, S., Becker, T., Marín-González, E., Holstenkamp, L., Bedoić, R., Duić, N., Oxenaar, S., & Pukšec, T. (2022). Thinking, doing, organising: Prefiguring just and sustainable energy systems via collective prosumer ecosystems in Europe. *Energy Research & Social Science, 86*, 102425. https://doi.org/10.1016/j.erss.2021.102425

Wittmayer, J. M., Hielscher, S., Fraaije, M., Avelino, F., & Rogge, K. (2022). A typology for unpacking the diversity of social innovation in energy transitions. *Energy Research & Social Science, 88*, 102513. https://doi.org/10.1016/j.erss.2022.102513

Wu, H., Carroll, J., & Denny, E. (2022). Harnessing citizen investment in community-based energy initiatives: A discrete choice experiment across ten European countries. *Energy Research & Social Science, 89*, 102552. https://doi.org/10.1016/j.erss.2022.102552

Wyse, S. M., & Hoicka, C. E. (2019). "By and for local people": Assessing the connection between local energy plans and community energy. *Local Environment, 24*(9), 883–900. https://doi.org/10.1080/13549839.2019.1652802

Contents

List of Figures

Introduction: Community Energy and Democracy

1

1.1 Participation and Democracy

Conceptions and practices of democracy are currently discussed on the one hand under the aspect of threats (Brodocz et al. 2009) and crises (Streeck 2013; Wöhl 2013; Merkel 2015a), predominantly negative diagnoses are theoretically summarized by the catchword of Colin Crouch (2004) as post-democracy and practically promoted by citizen protests (Butzlaff 2016).

On the other hand, new, creative and innovative democratiniaic (participation) forms are constantly being discovered and disseminated; there is talk of a (new) participation revolution (Nanz and Leggewie 2016). This concerns in particular the inclusion of citizens in public affairs and political decision-making processes in connection with the use of virtual forms of participation and co-decision-making (Kubicek et al. 2009; Oxenfarth and Obermayr 2011; Klages and Vetter 2013; Vortkamp 2013; Voss 2014); but also the invention of new collective forms of design through commons – and thus the establishment of new forms of community, based on free-wage activities (open source, sharing, urban gardening, etc., see Ostrom 1990; Helfrich 2014; Felber 2012; Welzer 2013; Adloff et al. 2014; Sommer and Welzer 2014; Welzer et al. 2014; Adloff and Heins 2015; Kirwan et al. 2016). This goes hand in hand with alternative approaches in response to "accelerated" (consumer) societies (Rosa 2005, 2013a, 2013b; Brettschneider 2012; Hellmann 2013; Baudrillard 2015; Habermann et al. 2015) such as a "slowed down" democracy (Clark 2012) and degrowth society (Jackson 2016, 2021; Blätter für deutsche und internationale Politik 2015; Latouche 2015), by emphasizing communal and communicative action and closeness to individuals, ultimately therefore local unity again (Sennett 2012; "roots of modern democracy": Pinzani 2009). The currently exercised democratic concept seems to be increasingly con-

J. Radtke, *Community Energy in Germany*,
https://doi.org/10.1007/978-3-658-39320-5_1

troversial (see Nolte et al. 2014), the criticism often refers to the economic system (Rosa et al. 2014; Bertelsmann Stiftung 2016) as well as ecological challenges (keyword sustainability, see Gesang 2014).

In addition, there are increasing social demands, or rather approaches to increased citizen influence ("citizen power": Roth 2011a, "courage instead of anger": Leggewie 2011), more citizen participation (Coelho and von Lieres 2010; Beck and Ziekow 2011; Roth 2011c, 2013c), direct democracy (Roth 2013b), integration of citizens into the state (Geiger 2012), consumer democracy (Lamla 2013), more civic engagement (Hessel 2011; Roß 2012) and individual as well as collective empowerment to influence decision-making processes (Pratchett et al. 2009; Gershon 2011) – consequently an increasing focus on the possibilities of individuals to influence and act in politics and society ("the new power of citizens": Marg et al. 2013; overview in Sommer 2015, 2017), which affect both rural-communal (Wolf 2012; Bühlmann 2013; Roth 2013d) and urban spaces ("We are the city", Rauterberg 2013; "Participation makes architecture", see Hofmann 2014; "Right to public space", see Hoidn et al. 2016). Support from the state is critically discussed here: a contradiction is said to exist between "mission statement rhetoric" and actual engagement policy action (Sandberg and Embacher 2014). Overarching, the discourse may well be aptly summarized by the question of a "resurrection" of democracy (Bretherton 2014),[1] because democratic practices, especially in civil society, may be nothing more than the other side of the coin of a post-democratic society and negatively interpreted value synthesis (Roßteutscher 2004; Pasqualoni and Treichl 2012; Freise and Hallmann 2014). In particular, the newly activated or reactivated civil society associations are supposed to serve the modernization of democracy in the twenty-first century (Freise and Hallmann 2014). However, a serious paradox is emerging with regard to participation opportunities: Jan van Deth points out that while on the one hand numerous opportunities for participation exist, on the other hand they are predominantly not taken up – he therefore speaks of a difficult relationship between participation and democracy (van Deth 2014b: 10). Non-participation in particular, combined with social exclusion, therefore poses a serious challenge to modern democracies (Gabriel 2013a: 181).

Criticism of Participation

However, while the calls for more participation in democracy are increasing, increased offers of participation are exposed and criticized as "sham participation" (Wagner 2013) to conceal underlying, technocratic-economic principles

[1] A similar idea is formulated by della Porta, according to which participation, deliberation and social movements can contribute to saving democracy (della Porta 2013).

("Nightmare Participation": Miessen 2012; see also Walter 2013). In addition, there is the reproach with regard to the (participatory) basic problematic in the form of unfulfillable claims to legitimacy, protection of minorities and elite rule that prevail here too, as well as paradoxes that arise between incompatible system logics of democratic approaches and social milieus or rather systems. For instance, there is a conflicting parallelism between representative and direct democracy (or participatory elements), in which relevant decisions remain with the polititical elites and only insignificant issues are up for discussion (Miessen 2012; Blühdorn 2013; Michelsen and Walter 2013).[2] A democracy "light" or forms adapted to prevailing market conditions (consumption, leisure time compatibility, individual benefit drawing) are also diagnosed. Therefore, new possibilities of citizen influence in the sense of a "consumer democracy" (Lamla 2013), a "civil capitalism" (Lotter 2013) or social capitalism (Barber 2013), as well as ideas of social entrepreneurship as a transformation mechanism (Bornstein 2007) are critically discussed (see Mason 2015).

Empirical evidence shows that membership figures for conventional forms of engagement (e.g., party and trade union work) are declining, but that beyond this, alternative forms of involvement in particular (often subsumed under the terms civil society activities, such as citizens' initiatives, working groups like urban gardening, sharing actions, etc.) are increasing, as these are apparently more attractive (see Olk and Gensicke 2014). Thus, high engagement rates can be demonstrated especially in these unconventional areas beyond party and committee work in Germany (see study results in Alscher et al. 2009; Gensicke and Geiss 2010, 2015; Enste et al. 2012; Statistisches Bundesamt/WZB 2013; Statistisches Bundesamt 2015; Zentrum für zivilgesellschaftliche Entwicklung 2016), although engagement in Western Europe as a whole decreased between 1999 and 2009 (Hooghe and Oser 2015).

However, as the empirical findings of the last decades continue to show "unequal and rather low participation despite growing opportunities", the essential challenge is to "mobilize socially marginalized groups" in particular; for only in this way will "democracy have a good chance of leaving the age of post-democracy behind in the long run" (van Deth 2014b: 20).

[2] See also Luhmann (2009: 159 ff.) for a fundamental critique of the concepts of participation and the achievement of legitimacy. In his fundamental critique, Luhmann outlines an overall paradox of participation, which is caused on the one hand by logical incongruities of the approach itself, but on the other hand also in the undesirable consequences such as increasing bureaucratization. Jason Brennan is currently very prominent in his fundamental critique of the ideal of political participation and also questions (Western) democracy as such (see Brennan 2016).

1.2 Participation in Renewable Energy Projects: Decisions, Investment and Planning

For several years, community energy initiatives have been forming in Germany to collectively raise funds to operate renewable energy systems in the local area (trend research and Leuphana University Lüneburg 2013; Yildiz 2014; Yildiz et al. 2015; Hall et al. 2016).

The question of the present work is whether, beyond monetary participation, civic engagement unfolds in these communities and whether discourse and co-determination are practiced – in other words, whether democratic practices can be found. Common forms of action such as cooperation, discursive exchange and consensual decision-making are indicators of this (Weißeno and Buchstein 2012). In this way, the question of whether community energy initiatives are examples of active civil society, participatory democracy and contemporary, project-based engagement and volunteering in the technology sector is explored by balancing self-interest and common good motives through the mode of participation and discourse (see Knierim et al. 2013; Bogner 2014; Böschen and Pfersdorf 2014; Petersen and Klauer 2014). Since an extension of political participation to social practices in the context of civil society has recently been discussed (van Deth 2014a), a classification of community energy initiatives, which can be located at the intersection of private sector ventures, civil society and political claims, will finally be made against this background. Of particular interest are innovative practices of participation and cooperation both within community energy projects and in exchange with local actors and publics (in the sense of citizen proximity, see Gramke 1978). For if political participation also extends to hybrid-structured social spaces, the "emergence of the new in politics" could unfold at these points of connection (Rosa 2012b).

The central pivot within current debates about the weakness of representative democratic procedures (such as elections) is the importance of participation (e.g., through more direct procedures such as voting), which can be understood on the one hand as a basic democratic principle (bringing in the vox populi), and on the other hand as a corrective to the representative proxy system (Harles and Lange 2015). Thus, in politics and society, demands for an increased involvement of citizens in matters of public interest are becoming louder. The energy transition in Germany (so-called *Energiewende*) is an example of this desire for participation. Since the energy transition is a new phenomenon, fields of action and options for participation are still relatively unencumbered by societal and scientific influences and extensive and long-term scientific research and evaluation (see on citizen participation in renewable energies, e.g., Dunker and Mono 2013; Degenhart and Schomerus 2014; Yildiz et al. 2015).

The question of how the actual participation of citizens in this segment unfolds is therefore of great interest. From the perspective of democratic theory, it would have to be observed whether patterns of post-democratic participation (individual self-interest motives leading to segregated patronage projects) or optimization; or expansion of representative democracy through the development and establishment of new forms of democratic procedures and processes (see Reder et al. 2014) lead to additional citizen influence, inclusion, transparency and legitimation and "democracy learning" (see on this Ullrich et al. 2014). Concisely, the question can be summarized as by Pohl, Massing and van Deth: "More participation – more democracy?" (Pohl et al. 2014).

The central objective of the present study is to investigate and typologize practices of participation (use of participation offerings, civic engagement in the sense of personal initiative) in the form of joint action within community energy initiatives.

The aim is to provide an insight into participation cultures in the form of the use of participation offerings, the formation of participation structures and exchange processes. In this context, dominant practices and procedures as well as commonalities and differences of different participation formats are to be elaborated. In addition, individual definitions and perceptions of those involved in the energy participation projects will be recorded and related to the contextual conditions of the participatory arrangements.

The empirical study follows a mixed methods approach. The qualitative method approach consists of conducting interviews with initiators, members and involved actors (administration, cooperation partners, consultants). This is complemented by a document analysis of records and minutes of the community energy initiatives and in the case of public participation procedures of the administration; participant observation of meetings and working groups.

The quantitative approach of the empirical survey consists in the use of an electronic survey among the members of the community energy initiatives in order to close research gaps. The social structure of the members, evaluation of the energy project and individual participation in the form of discursive expression are recorded; in addition, qualitative input is also included. By interweaving the results of both methodological approaches in the sense of the mixed methods approach, a mutual complementation and gap-filling method is to be achieved to compensate for weaknesses of the respective approach.

A subsequent category-guided and typology-generating analysis of the empirical material serves to reconstruct the structure, course, conflicts and problems of the community energy initiatives. In addition, discourses and conflicts in meetings and working groups are characterized. The results of the qualitative interviews will be compared with the information provided by the members of the online survey. Basic modes of participation and specific participatory arrangements of individual engagement development, creation of participation options and development of community and collaborative approaches are elaborated.

The chosen empirical approach allows a closer insight into the participation of citizens in these groupings. In addition, an assessment of the members with concrete, newly added aspects is provided by collecting additional qualitative data. Finally, a condensed picture of community energy initiatives or civic engagement and public participation in the field of energy will be made possible. On a theoretical level, references are made to approaches of democratic theory in the field of participation and a classification of the forms of participation is made against the background of findings of empirical participation research (Radtke and Schaal 2018).

The present study is based on the assumption of a requirement for explorative, situationally specific and openly interpreted empirical investigations. The development of fixed typologies is avoided, rather findings derived from empirical data material are interpreted on their own and with limited validity value.

The guiding dimensions of the study concern the analysis of actor networks (emergence of community energy initiatives in the context of local politics, civil society and economy); modes of action, forms of organization and participatory arrangements of community energy initiatives and procedures of public participation; characteristics of individual and collective engagement, collaboration and co-determination; effects and modes of impact on the local context.

Downsizing of Technology and the Chance for Collective-Creative Design: Vitalizing Democracy Through Technology Design?

The establishment of renewable energies is an exceptional example of how society can find a creative-collaborative way of dealing with technology (in contrast to the industrialization of the eighteenth and *nineteenth* centuries and the centralized technology allocations of the *twentieth* century) mainly due to the increasing fragmentation of technology resulting in better integration into routines and everyday forms (downsizing process) (see Murphy 2007; Pietschmann 2009; Markandya et al. 2011; Becker et al. 2014b; Lüdeke-Freud and Opel 2014).[3] This results in a far-reaching socio-spatial-technical transformation process both of landscapes and of political and social forms of action, design and coordination/control, which consequently affects society as a whole (see descriptions and analyses of the new energy landscapes in Becker et al. 2012; Brühne and Tempel 2013; Gailing and Leibenath 2013; Stremke and van den Dobbelsteen 2013; Lindquist 2014; Bruckner and Oswalt 2015; Frolova et al. 2015; Radtke 2015; Apostol et al. 2016; Pollet et al. 2016; on the social and political dimension Jänicke and Jacob 2008; Rifkin 2011; Verbong and Loorbach 2012; Brown et al. 2015). However, only individualswithin the framework of a certain degree of fit are able to intervene in a formative way themselves: power plants can only be built by large companies or controlled by state institutions. But actors in the private sector and the public sector are also changing their forms of action as a result of the transformation movement of the energy transition with regard to decentralization (Ekardt 2014; Maubach 2014; Schmid et al. 2016). The social spheres and actors influence each other here (reciprocal character). This newly discovered and still to be explored scope for design and action can in this way contribute to the vitalization and renewal of the relationship between democracy and technology, which tends to be difficult and fraught.

The Energy Transition as a Transformation Process for Society as a Whole
Since a transformation in energy production – from conventional energy sources to renewable energy sources – has been taking place, the question of what social effects this energy production transformation generates has been discussed in parallel. In addition, there are changing ways of handling, perceiving and using energy: how do technology and society influence each other? This results in social science questions from the technical context: in the sociology of technology, energy, environmental and technology policy, as well as the "technology and society" research strands, a wide variety of effects of mechanization and ways of dealing with technology have been discussed for decades.

The debate about a conversion of the energy system to renewable energy sources, which has been taking place since the beginning of the twenty-first century, is assumed to be a serious upheaval of technology and society (see current

[3] On collaborative approaches and practices in the literature see Booher 2004; Skelcher et al. 2005; Ansell and Gash 2008; Armbruster and Lærke 2008; Donahue and Zeckhauser 2011; Hemetsberger 2012; Koontz and Newig 2014; Reuter 2015; Challies et al. 2016; Gailing and Röhring 2016; Hutter 2016. Römmele speaks of collaborative democracy in the context of citizen participation in the energy transition (Römmele 2013).

report of the Club of Rome: Randers 2014; see also Rogall et al. 2014). The process known as the Third Industrial Revolution (Bäcker 2008; Jänicke and Jacob 2008; Rifkin 2011; or also as the "Green Industrial Revolution"; see Clark and Cooke 2015a, 2015b, 2015c), accompanied by far-reaching societal effects and in connection with other profound impact processes such as climate change and the Digital Revolution (Bostrom 2014; Brynjolfsson and McAfee 2014; Floridi 2015), is referred to as the "end of the world", as it is known from the recent past (Leggewie and Welzer 2011) and can be equated with the dawn of an age of sustainability (see on the sustainability turn Grin et al. 2010; Cohen et al. 2015).[4] Also due to this scope, a requirement for citizen participation can be derived: "The transformation of the energy sector does not go hand in hand without social debates and conflicts. Questions of distributive justice arise, for example, how the costs of the transformation of the energy infrastructure can be distributed fairly in society, but also how conflicts of values and interests can be resolved" (Schippl and Grunwald 2013: 6).

One level below this overarching reflection, there are three aspects in particular that require closer examination and form the larger contextual framework of the present study:

1. **The fundamental conflictual nature of the energy transition**, triggered, among other things, by the clash of population and technology, policy implementation, diversity of interests of the actors (see Reiche 2009; Feindt and Saretzki 2010; Welzer et al. 2010; Forschungsjournal Soziale Bewegungen 2014; Rule 2014; Kuzemko et al. 2016).
2. **Criticism of forms of representative democracy and indications of vitalization**, threats and crisis of democracy as well as renewal through direct-democratic-participatory elements (see Dalton 2004; Hacker and Pierson 2006; Hay 2007; Brodocz et al. 2009; Russell and Sossin 2009; Posner 2011; Roth 2011b; Graeber 2013; Papadopoulos 2013; Poguntke 2015; Sebaldt 2015; Neunecker 2016); social inequality problem (Fratzscher 2016).
3. **The idea of using the energy transition to create democratic modes of energy generation and distribution**, inclusion of citizens in discourse and decision-making processes, and a socially acceptable transformation of the energy system ("community energy transition", see Peters 2010; von Braunmühl 2010; Vaze and Tindale 2011; Herrmann and Gatzweiler 2012; Töpfer et al. 2013; Kreß et al. 2014a; Schröder and Walk 2014; Walk 2014; Embacher 2015;

[4] See also Brown and Brown 2009; Boyle and Open University 2012; Dincer 2012; Everett and Open University 2012; Kataki 2012; Tester 2012; Halff et al. 2014; Brown et al. 2015; Dhar Chakrabarti and Energy and Resources Institute 2015.

Müngersdorff et al. 2015; European Economic and Social Committee 2015; David and Schönborn 2016).

These three aspects outline the radius of questions for the structure and approach of the present work. Beginning with the theoretical starting point of the current discussion about democracy and the use or supplementation of participatory elements, a look is taken at the regional development processes in the context of the expansion of renewable energies and the question is pursued as to what input and activity emanates from the citizens. At the core are the questions of the extent to which citizens can actually participate in the establishment of renewable energies and what possibilities and tests of democratic, consensual and communal practices arise; in short: what formative power of citizens unfolds.

Community Energy Between Self-interest and the Common Good

This study deals with the specific issue of so-called community or citizen energy,[5] in which citizens in Germany build energy plants on their own ("energy by citizens for citizens", see Thüringer Energie- und GreenTech-Agentur 2012). At first glance, this circumstance may appear to be of little political or sociological relevance. However, if one takes a closer look at these local measures and strategies for the use of renewable energies that have been taking place in Germany for several years – initially still often in the form of community initiatives in smaller rural communities, later developed into a partially organized (social) movement – it becomes apparent that the construction of quite a few renewable energy plants is due to the local commitment of many citizens. Citizens have come together for a variety of motives – be it ecology, sustainability, a good deed for the community or local community, or even profit-making – with the aim of financing, building and operating energy plants themselves for years to come. Some of these community energy initiatives are based on civic engagement and emerge from the midst of the citizenry. By building energy plants, citizens are achieving more than just electricity production: they are actively promoting environmentally friendly and sustainable

[5] In comparison to "citizen energy", "community energy" is the more general, umbrella term and is mostly referred to in research and literature. The term citizen energy focuses more on the individual level, which means that citizens are participating in or have founded the community energy project at hand. The term commnity energy includes projects with diverse ways of founding, operating and participating in renewable energy facilities by individuals, communities, organizations, public institutions or joint ventures, but excludes purely marked-based private enterprises. Therefore, in the following, the more common term community energy is used to address and include all forms and variations of citizen- or community-driven, participatory energy projects.

technologies; they are creating a momentum for action and a concrete product that they themselves have initiated and that benefits the general public – thus, they are generally also serving the common good. Other reasons for engagement may include a belief in energy self-sufficiency. Moreover, by generating energy in a decentralized way, it is in the hands of local communities; independence from large energy companies is achieved. The motivations may also stem from long-term sustainable and intergenerational ideals, in that energy technology should provide energy and profits for future generations. Finally, it can also be argued in the sense of a common good economy that local investments strengthen regional value creation and that profits or benefits from the investments primarily benefit local communities.

However, another perspective on community energy could also come to the conclusion that some citizens in Germany, by setting up energy plants, merely want to grab subsidy sums that result from the sale of the generated electricity through the remuneration rates of the Erneuerbare-Energien-Gesetz (Renewable Energy Sources Act) in force in Germany and thus enrich themselves personally. Through private initiative or in a community, for example by founding an energy cooperative, a primarily economic activity is pursued. The founding of participatory enterprises such as energy cooperatives, civil law partnerships (GbRs) or limited liability companies and partnerships (GmbH & Co KGs) promotes citizens to entrepreneurs who must make profits within their community energy company. In this view, the citizens involved are merely shareholders and have corresponding expectations of returns, as they have deliberately not invested their money in classic forms of investment such as savings accounts. Ecological or public-spirited ideals may then play only a secondary or tertiary role, or perhaps no role at all, in the founding of the company or project and the participation. The use of renewable energies is intended to generate profit, the environmental friendliness of the technology is a welcome side-effect and serves the positive external presentation and public relations.

Participation in the Energiewende: Top-Down and Bottom-Up Approaches

Community energy initiatives in Germany show a wide range of activities: they try to buy electricity grids and operate them themselves. They install photovoltaic systems on roofs, erect wind turbines, build their own local heating networks and use geothermal energy. They make use of biomass and fire combined heat and power plants. In the case of hydroelectric power, cooperative forms of operation have long been a successful model in rural areas, for example, in Baden-Württemberg. Thus, there is almost no form of renewable energy where there is no known civic activity in terms of promotion and operation.

The energy transition in Germany means major changes and technical-societal upheavals. Some of this is clearly visible, such as large offshore wind farms at sea, but the majority of these socio-technical transformations are taking place on a small scale – with citizens installing solar panels and investing in energy saving and efficiency measures, or founding community energy projects or companies to operate renewable energy plants and heat and power grids (see Schmid et al. 2016).

In order to achieve social compatibility – that is, acceptance of the technologies – among the population, governments and administrations in Germany rely on the participation of citizens by promoting participation procedures and measures. A wide variety of approaches are possible here: from discussion events to financial compensation payments to virtual suggestion schemes.

Participation has become a social buzzword – not only in the context of the energy transition – and often serves as a problem-solving key for diverse social conflicts and unequal distribution effects. Expectations of its solving power and efficiency are correspondingly high. But participation does not necessarily mean acceptance, nor does it necessarily promote better (i.e., majority supported) decisions and processes. It is not so much a question of "whether" participation is important, but rather of "how" in the sense of meaningful, fair, transparent and broadly inclusive procedures.

This study aims to analyse the ways in which participation unfolds in the context of renewable energy at the local level. The empirical survey aims to take stock with the goal of capturing some of the characteristics, contextual conditions and effects of participation in the context of the energy transition. As already indicated, different approaches to participation can be distinguished here (see Koontz and Newig 2014):

- **Participation top-down**: In this case, participation offers are addressed to the population. On the one hand, this can take place on the part of the public administration within the framework of public participation, in the case of renewable energies in the planning of wind turbines or other larger technical facilities (see Renn et al. 2014; Schweizer et al. 2016). On the other hand, participation offers can be created by founded community energy companies or projects (initiated by individuals, banks, investors, project developers or even larger energy companies). The aim is to investigate which offers for participation exist, how participation processes run and function, and how they can be characterized.
- **Participation bottom-up**: This refers to the activity of citizens and initiative power of citizens' associations. Community energy initiatives are often initiated by individuals, (citizens') groups (citizens' initiative, local agenda, etc.), civil society actors (clubs, associations, etc.) or public institutions (schools,

universities, etc.) (see David and Schönborn 2016). A look into the black box of civic activity to contribute to the community, the articulation and organization of interests and of individual as well as collective decision-making processes represents a core concern of the present study.

- **Effectiveness of participation**: By looking at the individual (citizen), the aim is to understand what individuals achieve in their environment within the framework of participation by taking part. The aim here is to clarify what formative power emanates from citizens, what degree and extent of the development of commitment and cooperation is evident.
- **Individual perception of participation and effects**: How are participation (in participation offerings) and activities (within participation processes) assessed by the citizens themselves?

Culture of Civic Engagement and Support Structures

It seems obvious that simplified participation via purely monetary incentives or the provision of information is not sufficient to meet the (idealistic) demands and expectations of citizen participation. In addition, there is the need to coordinate and involve groups of actors and the population, which entails taking into account widely varying demands, interests and motivations (see e.g., Rommel et al. 2015, in relation to ecological action). Therefore, relying solely on a single approach cannot suffice for a successful participation strategy. For example, a study by the German Environment Agency (Alcántara et al. 2014: 129) emphasizes the future importance of early dimensions of participation such as problem definitions and agenda setting, alongside the later phases of decision-making, implementation, evaluation and response/re-definition. Local processes in particular suffer from the problem of providing very singular and selective access and integrating only certain stakeholders and individuals. Thus, the central challenge is to represent as many social groups and actors as possible and, at best, a broad cross-section of the population. These demands can best be achieved on the one hand through targeted integration strategies, and on the other hand through adapted participation approaches in combination depending on the target group (Olk et al. 2010; Roth 2010; Klein et al. 2013).

Overall, permanent participation processes, voting on important issues, and possibly also a permanent citizens' council in municipalities in the sense of a permanent culture of participation would be an ideal of participatory democracy that is unlikely to be realistic (see Vetter et al. 2013). Beyond ideas of an engagement-promoting municipality, individual activities at the micro level should not be disregarded; an activity of citizens and communities that often remains hidden without direct public access (*stealth democracy*, see Hibbing and Theiss-Morse 2002) (see critical discussion in Clarke 2008a and Staeheli 2008). This tendency towards privatistic, semi-public action (e.g., in neighbourhoods, urban districts and networks) can have advantages in that negative effects of the public sphere are absent, which are criticized precisely in the formats of representative democracy.[6]

Civic activities, as in the case of community energy, tend to depend on financial support from the public sector, cooperative municipal administrations, an active local civic structure as well as some prominent, committed actors, advisory support from administrations or associations, initiators or management of the projects, and numerous interested and, at best, committed members. These seem to be very many conditions that are difficult to achieve. In fact, however, practice in Germany shows that many community energy initiatives have emerged in recent years and that a wide variety of commitment cultures obviously exist in Germany.

For the further expansion of renewable energies in Germany, the achievement of climate protection goals as well as a civically engaged participation culture, further areas of engagement, fields of activity as well as support and cooperation conditions will probably have to be intensified and activated in the future (thus referred to in the literature as participation landscapes: see Gottschick and Ette 2014).

Due to the vast, imminent expansion of renewable energies in Germany, contacts, discourses, disputes and protests will most likely intensify considerably (see expansion plans of the German government: increasing the share of electricity from renewable energies to 50% by 2030 and 80% by 2050, see BMWI 2010: 5; on an environmentally and socially compatible expansion of renewable energies, see Krug 2014). This is also due to the path of decentralization (i.e., local operation of energy technology), which has been adopted in some areas, as this results in spatial disparities (in the sense of distributive inequality) (see Johnson and Hall 2015).

Even if a "local solution" is entirely in line with the principle of subsidiarity in basic law, negotiation processes with other political levels are probably the greatest challenges (see Müller 2014; Rademacher and Lintemeier 2015). Dialogue procedures – as practiced in the case of grid expansion (see Kamlage 2013a, 2013b;

[6] See The *Politics of Small Things* (Goldfarb 2007), *Democracy in Small Groups* (Gastil 1993) and *Grassroots Democracy* (Kaufman and Dilla Alfonso 1997; Nunes and de Sousa Santos 2006; Stout 2013); experiences with Small *Change* at the local level in urban planning (Hamdi 2004) as well as *Small-scale Research (*Denscombe 2010) and *Do It Yourself Citizenship* (Ratto and Boler 2014), also ideas on making things visible: *Making Things Public: Atmospheres of Democracy* (Latour and Weibel 2005), in an ecological context, *Small is Beautiful* (Schumacher 1973), Banks et al. 2013 speak of *Everyday Ethics* in the case of community participation, Marres 2012 of *Everyday Publics* in the case of material participation; *Lifestyle Politics* are described by de Moor 2017.

Kamlage et al. 2014) – promise to prevent a drift into separate spheres. Here again, challenges lie in the interplay of too many actors and interests ("joint decision trap", see Scharpf 1994; Bauer 2015) as well as an inevitable subordination of municipal interests in the multilevel federal system (Ohlhorst et al. 2014). The creation of stakeholder forums to hold discourses at common tables can in turn bring the levels together (e.g. energy dialogues, round tables, dialogue forums). An explicit example of this is the "conflict dialogues in the approval of energy transition projects" already developed (see Ziekow et al. 2015). The inclusion of the population via financial, discursive and voting instruments therefore appears to make sense (see Frey 2013; Kamlage 2013a, 2013b; Ruppert-Winkel et al. 2013; Buchholz and Huge 2014; Kamlage et al. 2014; Witte 2014; Alcántara et al. 2014; Renn et al. 2014), as well as an exchange about a possible technology design as a possible solution (see Grunwald 2003), in order to achieve acceptance of the technology and especially of the decision-making processes and procedures (see Bentele et al. 2014). In the present study, therefore, local support structures are also taken into account and evaluated in terms of their effectiveness in supporting community energy projects.

1.3 Democracy and Technology

Why are democratic aspects important in technical projects and infrastructure measures (see Thießen 2012)? In the case of planning and subsequent implementation in the construction of technical facilities (whether of commerce, industry or trade) and infrastructure facilities (roads, railways, networks, etc.), people are always affected – whether indirectly or directly through immediate proximity to the technical facilities (see Sherry 2000; Johnson and Wetmore 2009; Bijker et al. 2012; Goeke et al. 2015). In politics as well as in science, consideration has therefore been given for some time to a "socially acceptable" design of technology, which, following rather negative experiences with technology in the course of and after the industrial revolution (such as environmental pollution, health hazards, disfigurement of cities and landscapes, etc.)[7] would allow a control and design of the use of technology that appears "compatible" with the population – that is, that generates acceptance. Especially in the planning of technology, local knowledge and attitudes of the population can be included (referred to in the literature as *Material*

[7] For example, the literature (Byrne and Toly 2006) points out that "threats" to the environment have been and continue to be perceived: climate change, acid rain, pollution, loss of biodiversity, etc.

Politics (Barry 2013), *Material Participation* (Marres 2012) and currently discussed with regard to more recent participation practice as *Remaking Participation* (Chilvers and Kearnes 2016). For this reason, the German energy transition is also seen as a social challenge (besides the technical one) (Grunwald 2003; Töpfer et al. 2013; see for an overview of the German energy transition BMWi 2014; Schmid et al. 2016). However, this is old news for sociology, as here the sociology of technology basically assumes that "technology is a cognitive system" and "technology is therefore also a social product and part of a social system" (Weingart 1989: 114). Here, the effects of new technologies in different spaces and their acceptance have already been considered for some time.[8]

The theoretical question of technology as a social product and the way society deals with technology has been discussed in the humanities and social sciences for some time.[9] A social science approach focuses in particular on the actions, motivations and ideal systems of thought of actors.[10]

In practical disputes, too, the awareness has been created for some time that such technology design is at best considered, planned and controlled with the population – which represents a democratic starting point for this approach. In the Federal Republic of Germany (FRG), for example, the Office of Technology Assessment at the German Bundestag was founded in 1990. In addition, numerous state institutions such as ministries and offices at local and national level are concerned with the issues of technology design (Grunwald and Kopfmüller 2021).

In publications and research, the field of "democratic technology design" has found expression parallel to these developments (Grunwald 2003; Abels and Bora 2004), with opportunities for participation (especially of the population and civil society organizations) being discussed in particular (Baron 1995; Gottschalk and Elstner 1997; Holeschak 2000; Riehm 2009). From a theoretical point of view,

[8] See Friedrichs 1987: 335 ff.

[9] See Berger 1991: 328 ff; Passoth 2008: 219 ff; also Weingart 1982, 1989; Rammert 1993, 2007.

[10] According to Rammert, the analysis of techniques is (1982: 39) essentially about:

- identify the initiating, participating and affected groups as social actors,
- to find out about their interests, their objectives and their values,
- their power positions, their chances for the success of enforcement or prevention strategies, their disposal of power resources or coalition building. However, as Rammert (ibid.) points out, in many cases the technology implemented is not the intended strategic result of an actor: "Since a large number of actors with different objectives intervene in the mechanization process at different points in time, unintended effects and new development dynamics arise that can no longer be traced back to individual actors and their intentions".

various analyses have also been carried out which outline the influence of technology on social and political changes (Simonis and Saretzki 2001) and attempt to uncover influences with regard to democratic structures. Martinsen and Simonis (2000: 12 f.), for example, attempted to summarize the larger developments in the social discourse surrounding technology. According to them, especially discussions about genetic engineering in the 1990s, technology assessment[11] as well as new possibilities of participation through new media such as the internet were of crucial importance: "As a result, it can be stated that after the debates on the "technical state" (1960s), the possibilities and limits of state technology policy (1970s), the opportunities and risks of the information society (1980s), the steering capacity and control of the state in the multi-level system (the late 1980s/early 1990s), we have entered a new phase of discussion of the relationship between politics and technology since the mid-1990s, in which questions of democratic theory have once again gained greater importance" (ibid.: 139).

In recent years, conflicts over the use of technology in particular have been a core topic in social science research. Thus, protests by the population against buildings, energy sources and infrastructure are now also in the increased focus of scientific interest (see e.g., Roth 2011a; Marg et al. 2013). Feindt and Saretzki (2010) address an interesting difference between consensual demands on politics and transversal levels of conflict: "The emphasis on consensus and cooperation-oriented politics, however, often refers to past conflicts that have been overcome, to latent conflicts, or to anticipated future conflicts. A historical longitudinal analysis shows that neither environmental nor technology policy has developed without conflict" (ibid.: 9). The authors illustrate this with the examples of nuclear power use, the BSE crisis, genetic engineering, as well as "numerous local settlement and land use conflicts", which makes it clear that "the introduction of new technologies and the socio-economic growth process lead to conflicts centered on the perception, assessment, prevention and distribution of risks". These conflicts can, in turn, be seen as representative of larger, society-wide discourses: "In many cases, these conflicts are linked to a fundamental dissent about the societal and technological development path [...]" (ibid.).

Such a disagreement about the development path can be observed in the German energy sector: This runs between the prevailing conventional system of the energy

[11] Accordingly, technology assessment attempts to "respond to technology blockades by well-organized critics as well as to the growing multiperspectivity of technology assessment by developing and implementing moderation and discourse procedures and by attempting to open up new potential for action and innovation through negotiations with stakeholders" (Martinsen and Simonis 2000: 12).

industry (which has so far been oligopolistic at the actor level in Germany) and a transformation (energy turnaround) towards a decentralized system[12] with a multi-actor structure or various future scenarios[13] (Schmid et al. 2016). In Germany, a discourse around the *Energiewende* could already be observed for quite some time until it was officially adopted by the federal government in 2011.[14] The ideas of a locally situated and decentrally organized energy supply go back – internationally – to the 1970s. In 1977, Amory Bloch Lovins published the book "Soft energy paths – towards a durable peace" (see Lovins 1977). In this volume, Lovins turned against the conventional, centrally organized energy companies and propagated small, alternative energy projects. In this way, he brings the idea of "energy for everyone" into play and points to the social and civic dimension, which he reinforces with the idea that enthusiasm for such projects could serve to bring other projects into being (domino effect). This idea of decentralising energy systems has

[12] See on the decentralized, self-sufficient energy system approach Teske 2005; Alanne and Saari 2006, Hiremath et al. 2007; Moser 2011; Müller et al. 2011; Watson and Devine Wright 2011; Eiselt 2012; Gailing et al. 2013; Klagge and Brocke 2013; Ruppert-Winkel et al. 2013; Gailing and Röhring 2014; Goldthau 2014; Ruppert-Winkel and Hauber 2014; Funcke and Bauknecht 2016. On the relationship between decentralization and acceptance of renewable energies, see Hildebrand 2015.

[13] In this context, there is therefore also talk of a "revolution". Such considerations also exist with regard to a "Third Industrial Revolution" (see Bäcker 2008; Jänicke and Jacob 2008; Rifkin 2011). This refers to an overall social upheaval - triggered by environmental problems - towards an ecological state, which includes changes in all areas of life. The authors of these works usually venture towards a conceivable future, whereby the descriptions are to be understood as suggestions and demands for an ecologically oriented reorientation of society. Leprich and Rogall (2014), for example, speak of a social transformation process in the case of the energy transition.

[14] Skeptics of conventional forms of energy are mostly open to the alternatives of this in the form of renewable energy, which results in a discussion about possible use, visions and ideas for the future. This "euphoric" strand proclaims not only the "pure" establishment of renewable energies, but also small-scale, decentralized options for the construction of an alternative energy system that is to be autonomous and connected with ecological balance (Eiselt 2012). In this interpretation, the greening of the energy system is linked to social ideals and overcoming the imbalance between the users of the energy system and those societies and social classes that cannot participate in energy. Thus, the politician Hermann Scheer, as a solar pioneer, advocated a solar age and mass application of renewables throughout his life (see Scheer 2010).

been taken up again and again and is still a core idea in the further development of energy systems today.[15]

In addition, the more fundamental question is addressed as to what extent "environmentally harmful" technology should be replaced by "environmentally friendly" technology at all, and whether a renunciation of such technology (or savings and reduction in the use of technology) does not represent the more promising approach – which can be found within the so-called degrowth debate (see Kallis et al. 2010; Martínez-Alier et al. 2010; Klitgaard and Krall 2012; Paech 2013; Schneidewind et al. 2013; Sekulova et al. 2013; Welzer and Wiegandt 2013; Schneidewind and Zahrnt 2013; D'Alisa et al. 2015; Kallis et al. 2015; Kerschner et al. 2015). The idea of a degrowth society is also linked to questions about the future of a democracy that is compatible with these sustainable-community conceived social designs (Cattaneo et al. 2012; Deriu 2012; Ott 2012; Romano 2012). In Germany, historically, the development path of investing in environmentally friendly technologies has prevailed – based on the conviction that this can solve environmental problems (in contrast to degrowth thinking). Thus, (especially from the 1980s onwards) the term "ecological modernization" became established. This refers to the formula introduced at the beginning of 1982 to underline the common intersections of economy and ecology (Jänicke et al. 2003: 435). It is aimed at innovation-oriented environmental protection, in which technical progress is primarily focused on reducing the consumption of natural resources (while working conditions remain untouched). Later uses of the term also include non-technical modernizations (see also various ideas on the further development of ecological modernization such as eco-effectiveness of circular economy in McDonough and Braungart 2009; Braungart and McDonough 2011, 2013, as well as critical discussion in Wegner 2013; on Green Economy see Williams 2010 and Pollin 2015). Also more recent is the development of so-called "Transition Towns" (Hopkins 2008; Scott-Cato and Hillier 2010; Merritt and Stubbs 2012; van der Schoor and Scholtens

[15] According to this approach, energy should be generated and consumed locally without transmitting complications (Eiselt 2012). The advantages of this are the elimination of electricity transmission masts and the associated transmission losses, financial benefits for the local population, as well as local tax revenues and regional value creation through companies that build and operate the energy plants. In addition, higher acceptance and trust of the local population towards the energy plants could be generated. Close to this decentralized energy generation idea is the approach that these local energy plants are built and operated by citizens themselves or municipal companies (municipal utilities) (community energy). This would mean that the energy plants would no longer be concentrated and of large scale, but small-scale and distributed throughout all regions. This would tend to exclude a "threat factor" such as from a large power plant.

2015), which attempt to implement a changed way of living, housing and working in terms of energy conservation measures. A similar approach is represented by the so-called "transition management", which describes a pragmatic-analytical approach that has also become more prominent in science in recent years (see Elzen et al. 2004; Geels and Schot 2007; Loorbach 2007, 2010; Meadowcroft 2009; Grin et al. 2010; Borras and Edler 2015). In theory, the focus is on broad participation of many actors (multi-actor approach), long-term further development and change of systems with milestones ("system change"), learning processes at the level of the (technological or societal) "niche" (Junginger et al. 2010) and system-relevant factors (societal levels and actors). In particular, the development of technological niches is of great importance here, which also plays a major role in energy technology fields, as they can promote experimental-creative innovations (see Groß 2014; Stehr 2015). In addition to the micro level of the "niche" (here of energy technology, also entrepreneurial niches such as "grassroots" energy projects), a meso (regime) (e.g., energy policy) and a macro level (landscapes, i.e., spatial level) are also considered. However, the approaches developed so far mostly describe sectoral transition strategies, as in the field of energy transition (see Verbong and Loorbach 2012).[16] A British group of researchers tries to relate these approaches to community energy initiatives, as these can generate innovations of a special kind (technical, economic, social) through their "grassroots" activity (Seyfang and Haxeltine 2012; Smith and Seyfang 2013; Hielscher et al. 2013a, 2013b; Seyfang et al. 2014). Closely related to the transition approach is the idea of a degrowth or degrowth society. Starting from the basic economically influenced idea of a vision of society without inherent growth rates, thoughts develop here that critically question the organization of work and life imprinted in Western welfare nations and propagate a model of society that relies more on sufficiency (i.e., quasi renunciation) and less consumption of resources (time, financial means, work, etc.) (see Seidl and Zahrnt 2010; Jackson 2016, 2021; Rydzy and Griefahn 2014; Jakob and Edenhofer 2015; Latouche 2015). Within the theoretical concept, the commons and new social communities, also concepts of power, space and subjectivity, play a prominent role (see Jeffrey et al. 2012; Kirwan et al. 2016). The individual perspective is decisive here: what should the life of the individual look like (how much time and resources will be spent on what? How should work and leisure time be organized and designed? What ideal is taken as a basis, what is the measure of the idea of a "good life"? – see discussion in von Hauff 2014) – whereby the consider-

[16] In Germany, most likely represented by the 100% renewable energy regions approach as well as bioenergy villages, where municipalities aim for a complete coverage of their energy demand by renewable energy resources (see Moser 2011; Ruppert-Winkel et al. 2013; Grundmann and Ehlers 2016).

ation is admittedly fed by macroeconomic as well as macrosociological considerations (in the sense of the "limits to growth", which can lead socially, ecologically as well as economically to diverse problem situations worldwide, as the Club of Rome has repeatedly stated since 1972, see Meadows et al. 1972; Randers 2014).

On the meso-organizational level, the spark of hope again falls to civil society communities in the degrowth society: starting from individual people who want to work less, consume fewer resources, etc., the next step would lead to organization in degrowth communities, which, for example, as sustainable neighborhoods, take the vision of a life of renunciation into their own hands. It is not surprising that in this train of thought the aspects of "democracy, equal citizenship and participation" (von Braunmühl 2010) play a key role.

This is accompanied by ideas for other forms of living together (see Adloff and Heins 2015) of a freer, communal use of goods ("commons", see Helfrich 2014; Helfrich and Bollier 2015; Kirwan et al. 2016 related to urban contexts see Baier et al. 2013), as it is also discussed in the degrowth-society debate (see Elsen 2015), whereby questions of the extraction, use and distribution of energy are up for discussion (see idea of energy democracy, Kunze and Becker 2015b).

Citizen energy or community energy can be seen as an example of this conceptual approach of collective ownership, combined with alternative forms of organizational, work and corporate structures (Welzer et al. 2014; Kunze and Becker 2015a; critical discussion in Rommel et al. 2016b, 2018). Similarly, democratic implications play a crucial role in the degrowth society (von Braunmühl 2010; Kallis et al. 2012; Bonaiuti 2012; Cattaneo et al. 2012; Deriu 2012; Johanisova and Wolf 2012; Ott 2012; Romano 2012; Andreoni and Galmarini 2014). Within the discussion, cooperatives are seen, for example, by Elsen as forms of civic appropriation as well as organizations of social innovation and as "transformative forces on the way to the degrowth society" (see Elsen 2004, 2009, 2014).

The traditional path of the "environmental state" in Western democracies is, above all, held responsible for solving environmental problems by counteracting environmental pollution through restrictions (requirements, laws, regulations) and relying on technical solutions and improvements (e.g., filter systems, catalytic converters, technological efficiency; so-called ecological modernization, see Jänicke 2000). In contrast, the approach of sufficiency (a core degrowth concept) implicitly doubts the strength of ecological modernization, as it is not considered genuine sufficiency on the one hand (without corresponding sufficient lifestyles), and on the other hand it is not deemed as effective, because the supposed improvements are in turn countered by higher overall consumption (rebound effect) (Otto et al. 2014). Armin Grunwald, for example, considers the idea of "ecomodernism", that is, ecological modernization, to be "untenable in terms of responsible ethics" (Grunwald

2015b). The example of community energy, however, shows overall rather a model of ecological modernization (in that in essence through new technology again the environmental problem is to be met), rather than sufficiency and renunciation. Both this study and other studies (Rauschmayer et al. 2015) suggest that community energy members are, on the whole, more ecologically minded and active people, but there is no discernible shift towards a more sufficiency-oriented lifestyle. Nonetheless, community energy initiatives can range widely between "conservative modernism" (support through local-limited investment of a site-specific project for homeland security motives or the like) and creative-experimental real laboratories that develop and test new or alternative forms and innovations in the fields of technology, social affairs, work, organization, participation, communication and economy and bring them into society (see discussion in Rommel et al. 2016, 2018).

A New Governance Regime for the Energiewende

The energy transition could unfold a new governance regime (Benz and Dose 2010; Sack 2013) in that governance modes have changed more towards local and remunicipalized (i.e., state) as well as private-civil society and purely private sector structures (Sack 2018). This more open mode of governance in the energy sector can presumably be more conducive to social innovations, which in turn can be key drivers for the development of creative modes of operation, organization and action in the energy sector, particularly concerning the emergence of social or ecological entrepreneurships ("Ecopreneurs": Schaper 2010, "Civil Entrepreneurs": Stein 2015). This leads to the question of which governance and organizational patterns emerge in these constructions of social innovations (on this, see a first conceptual framework of social innovations in research, which includes extremely diverse aspects of governance, social learning, financing, monitoring, narratives, game changers, systemic changes and micro/meso/macro levels, in Haxeltine et al. 2013, 2015).[17]

[17] Social innovation research has become more prominent just recently, see Taylor 1970; Henderson 1993; Kanter 2000; McElroy 2002; Mumford and Moertl 2003; Mulgan 2006; Regalia 2006; Taatila et al. 2006; Leadbeater 2007; Martin and Osberg 2007; Maruyama et al. 2007; Moulaert et al. 2007; Mulgan et al. 2007; Drewe et al. 2008; Heap et al. 2008; Jegou and Manzini 2008; Phills et al. 2008; Moulaert and MacCallum 2009; Pol and Ville 2009; Westley and Antadze 2009; Goldsmith 2010; Goldsmith et al. 2010; Howaldt and Jacobsen 2010; Lettice and Parekh 2010; Moulaert 2010; Moulaert et al. 2010a, 2010b; Murray et al. 2010; Howaldt et al. 2011; Moore and Westley 2011; Nicholls and Murdock 2011; Young 2011; Beck and Kropp 2012; Faaij et al. 2013; Moulaert 2013; Rückert-John 2013; Cajaiba-Santana 2014; Howaldt et al. 2014; Rückert-John et al. 2014; Kopf 2015; Nordic Council of Ministers and Nordic Council of Ministers Secretariat 2015; Wittmayer et al. 2015b.

Political Strategies of the Participatory Energiewende

Although civil society-private sector solutions, as in the case of community energy, have some advantages, such as the possible direct influence of members, they also suffer from disadvantages, such as a lack of representativeness of the entire population and thus limited legitimacy and possible dominance of elites – which the results of the present study suggest in part. A state-institutional solution, on the other hand, would have advantages, especially in terms of public control and indirect representation of the common will. However, an analysis of German energy policy concludes that "the restructuring of the energy industry associated with the energy transition with the aim of compensating for the electricity gap resulting from the nuclear phase-out" led to "rising economic costs" (Illing 2012: 264). Now, in Illing's view, "it is up to the federal government to decide which shares of the gross domestic product should be invested in the goal of the energy transition. In doing so, it is also up to it to decide whether the market or the state should drive the energy transition" (ibid.).

Ultimately, a mix of public-civil society-private sector forms of operation and multi-level arrangements of different actors seems convincing. In this way, the most diverse forms of development can be expressed, and several forms of participation and influence can coexist, which better accommodates the heterogeneous structure of less and more engaged citizens (see overview within the *Energiewende* in Maubach 2014). Without a doubt, cooperative discourse in energy policy will continue to be of great importance in the future in order to harmonize the various interests of the actors – as Ortwin Renn put it some time ago (Renn 1999).

Furthermore, the pressing question for the future is how community energy participation can also be designed, managed and promoted in the transnational context of the European Union – as a supplement to, support for or competition with local and national strategies (see European Institute for Public Participation 2009; Bruninx et al. 2013; Müngersdorff et al. 2015; Kamlage and Nanz 2015; Neuhoff et al. 2016; Strunz et al. 2016). As an example of this, a European participatory budget is being discussed, which should simultaneously create participatory democracy, administrative modernization and social justice (Sintomer et al. 2010). However, since the sustainability policies of EU states are not synchronized (Göll and Sie 2004) and attitudes as well as ideas on environmental behavior can vary greatly across Europe (Telesiene and Groß 2016), the literature discusses "how much Europe needs the energy transition " (Gawel et al. 2014b) and even brings the idea of a foreign policy for the energy transition into play (Tänzler and Müller 2014). While at the lobby level in Germany the *Bündnis Bürgerenergie e. V.* ("Alliance for Citizens' Energy") has been founded, at the European level the initiative "Community Power (for people's ownership of renewable energy)" exists, which is supported by 12 European organizations (e.g., *Friends of the Earth*). However, the numerous practices, initiatives and support programs in the EU area are so numerous that they are aptly described as "Sustainable Energy United in Diversity" (Squitani et al. 2014); a European energy transition thus certainly exists in this respect.

Irrespective of this, "collective action for climate protection" (Jaeger-Erben/Walk 2014) by citizens and civil society will continue to be important and shape the political agenda (discussed in the literature, for example, under the term *Politics of Green Transformations,* see Scoones et al. 2015). It still remains uncertain whether stronger state or civil society significance can be assumed for the management of the energy transition, even if the former can currently be considered more likely. This is because overarching, strongly state-controlled measures such as the expansion of offshore wind power dominate, and this is legitimized by the implicit demand of the population for state control, which overwhelmingly defines the energy transition as a task for the state (see surveys: Wolling and Arlt 2011; Schack and Gellrich 2015: 28 ff.). However, the future of community energy would most likely be conceivable as a more integrative model, which is rooted in and connected to the overall energy and mobility system as well as the political, social and cultural landscape of climate protection strategies and policies (suggested by Koirala et al. 2016).

A Review of the Literature

2

2.1 Participation

2.1.1 Research on Participation: A Review of the Literature

Participation seems to have become a catchword since the turn of the millennium ("age of participation", see Harles and Lange 2015; participation in the twenty-first century, see Nabatchi and Leighninger 2015; Roberts 2015; Chilvers and Kearnes 2016),[1] a greater (direct) involvement of citizens in decisions and modi operandi in democracy and the promotion of participatory bottom-up activities of citizens seems to represent an overarching consensus (Ullrich et al. 2014; Bentele et al. 2014; Düber et al. 2015). Praxis and research on participation may now look back on more than 40 years of experience in the Federal Republic of Germany (FRG).[2]

Since the so-called participatory revolution in the 1970s, a wide variety of procedures and methods of citizen participation have been developed and tested in the Federal Republic (see Roth 2013a), including, in part, utopian ideas from today's perspective: such as the planning cell (Dienel 1978), the joint participatory budget and the citizens' municipality (Bogumil and Holtkamp 2011; Masser et al. 2013; Neunecker 2016), various procedures of public participation in the context of public planning projects (Schluchter 2002; Renn 2013a, 2013b; Steinberg 2014a;

[1] On the concept, idea and history of participation see Boss-Stenner et al. 1970; von Alemann and Studiengruppe Partizipationsforschung 1975; Kaase et al. 2000; Gerhardt 2007; Roy 2013.

[2] For an overview see Boss-Stenner et al. 1970; Hendler 1977; Kohout 2002; Geißel 2004b; Kersting 2008; von Alemann 2011; Roth 2011e, 2013a; Nanz and Fritsche 2012; Kersting and Woyke 2012; The Bertelsmann Stiftung and Staatsministerium Baden-Württemberg 2014; Gabriel 2014; Geißel and Kersting 2014; Newig 2014; Denecke et al. 2016.

J. Radtke, *Community Energy in Germany*,
https://doi.org/10.1007/978-3-658-39320-5_2

Drazkiewicz et al. 2015), conference procedures (Future Conference, Citizens' Conference, Planning Conference), scenario developments, citizen juries, dialogical approaches (see the citizen dialogues of the Federal Government in the context of the energy system transformation, most recently the analysis of Erhard et al. 2013, and also in the context of network expansion Lietzmann 2013; Kamlage and Fleischer 2014; Kamlage et al. 2014); furthermore also mini-publics (Goodin and Dryzek 2006), deliberative polls (Fishkin and Luskin 2005), etc. (for an overview, see Kersting 2008; Kersting and Woyke 2012; Hebestreit 2013; Bertelsmann Stiftung and Staatsministerium Baden-Württemberg 2014; Straßburger and Rieger 2014, on discursive participation Fishkin 2009).

However, none of these instruments was able to assert itself in the long term; disillusionment in society, politics and research became particularly apparent in the 1990s and 2000s, until recently demands have been made for increased citizen participation (e.g., in the context of infrastructure planning such as Stuttgart 21 or in the context of the energy revolution) and in some cases also realized (see Römmele and Schober 2013; van Deth 2014b; critically, see Thießen 2012). These new approaches are usually referred to using the term participatory *democratic innovations* (Saward 2000; Karch 2007; Smith 2009; Cheema and Popovski 2010; Geißel and Newton 2012; Geißel and Joas 2013; Bußjäger and Gamper 2015). The basic conditions and effects of participation have not changed; participation processes and procedures still face a number of challenges (see Parsons et al. 1965; Pateman 1970; Rosenau 1991; Creighton 2005; Wilkinson et al. 2012):

- Overloading of the organizers and participants.
- Input and inclusion: only certain clientele participate (repeatedly), problem of inequality.
- Result and decision making: lack of influence.
- Cost-benefit ratio.
- Frustration and "fraying" (multiplying) of procedures.

In this way, citizen participation becomes a fragile concept in view of the legitimacy gap, the demands of the population and the perceived gap between real involvement in decision-making and "sham participation" (Merkel 2015b) (on the issue of inequality see Klatt et al. 2011; Linden and Thaa 2014; Lee et al. 2015).

For some time now, therefore, consideration has been given to how public participation could be carried out in a higher quality, more effective and more goal-oriented manner. Many procedures are currently being tested, developed and applied – an overall assessment will only be possible in a few years.[3] Trends are already emerging, particularly in connection with the use and linking of digital participation opportunities via the internet.[4] Here, an overarching, online platform would be combined with selective access. The advantages of electronic participation are that the internet is now available nationwide, broad inclusion is theoretically possible (even for people who do not appreciate a physical presence or for whom the effort involved is too great; younger people can be reached better, see De Vreese 2007), but older people without internet access would be excluded and would have to be given participation opportunities via alternative methods. Previous studies suggest that it is, in turn, the participation – oriented milieus of offline space that participate here – at least in formal procedures and forums (Schlozman

[3] See recent research on alternative forms of participation (Ganuza and Francés 2011b; Ganuza et al. 2014), material participation (Marres 2012) and new forms of participation in civil society in van Deth (2011), Theocharis and van Deth 2018 and van Deth and Maloney (2012), Micheletti and McFarland (2011) discuss "creative participation"; central questions are the modes of action with regard to democratic inclusion in Merkel and Petring (2012) and critical comments on "checkbook participation" in Stadelmann-Steffen and Traunmüller (2010).

[4] See approaches that reflect recent trends in citizen participation procedures in Germany (Baumann et al. 2004; Hartwig and Kroneberg 2014), electronic forms of participation (Kubicek et al. 2009; Märker and Wehner 2011; Seckelmann 2014) and electronic-cooperative forms (Holtkamp and Bathge 2013), under the term of extended citizen participation, mostly innovative-creative processes and cooperative action using modern forms of communication (so called Citizen Participation 3.0, see Oxenfarth and Obermayr 2011 – Citizen Participation 2.0, however, understood as the inclusion of electronic processes, see Masser et al. 2013). Back in 2003, when the internet did not yet have the omnipresence it has had since the beginning of the 2010s, Claus Leggewie and Christoph Bieber spoke of a "democracy 2.0" and meant a "democratic renewal" with the help of new media (Leggewie and Bieber 2003; see also Leggewie and Bieber 2001 and the discussion in Imhof 2015). On internet and participation and political action, see also: Wesselmann (2002), Heigl and Hacker (2010), Bundeszentrale für politische Bildung (2012), Gräßer and Hagedorn (2012), Lamla (2012), Lutz et al. (2012), Banse (2013), Dahlgren (2013), Dolata and Schrape (2013a), Kneuer (2013), Voss (2014), Send et al. (2014), Baringhorst (2015), Coleman and Freelon (2015), Merkel (2015b: 64 ff.), Trottier (2015), Fries et al. (2016), Lindner et al. (2016); critically, Schrape (2010). It is still unclear what effects electronic forms of participation generate. The theoretical possibility of easier access and a broader circle of users has so far been rather doubtful: "In contrast, decision-theoretical approaches tend to expect greater participation through the use of modern means of communication such as the internet, e-mail and mobile communications. These technologies considerably reduce the information and participation costs for all participants. However, experience with these new technologies shows neither a remarkable increase in participation nor a strong expansion of the circle of participants" (van Deth 2009: 156; see also Schlozman et al. 2010; Kersting 2014; Vowe 2014: 43 f.).

et al. 2010). Post-democratically conceived, however, there is a danger here of staging participation; media sensationalism in the sense a short-lived event without sustainable involvement and support of the population over a longer period of time (on mediatized forms of participation see Biermann et al. 2014; Hepp and Pfadenhauer 2014).

Ultimately, the question is whether citizen participation can be reinvented at all, which does not seem very likely. Nevertheless, an intelligent combination of online and offline participation can certainly produce something new, and it is not only the instrumental level that is decisive, but also the "how", that is, the qualitative level of participation. According to the current state of research, it seems to be important for participation processes that procedures are limited in time, with not too many participants, a targeted problem and question formulation, exclusion of excessive demands and overload as well as intelligent linking of certain participation tools, taking into account the specific context and the participatory objective (situational participation).

In this way, small-scale solutions can be found which, taken together, would have the potential to increase the overall quality and legitimacy of decisions. It remains to be seen how these possibilities will be dealt with in the twenty-first century. At any rate, lessons could be learned from certain mistakes of the past: overall, a higher degree of professionalization can be measured today, but at the same time this very fact harbors a great threat of social exclusion, which also persists electronically. Participation continues to be just a makeshift means for the influence of citizens, it cannot change fundamental constellations, and a realistic understanding of participation has become increasingly accepted in recent years. All in all, a pluralization of forms of participation is thus discernible, both in the real and the virtual realm; above all, a trend towards electronic instruments can be observed.

Parallel to this development, an expansion of the concept of political participation can also be observed through the delimitation of the concept of the political or political subject area and political sphere (see Fox 2013; van Deth 2014a). An interweaving of social and political participation is particularly decisive in adjacent areas, such as civil society activity and the expanded forms of political participation (e.g., discursive forums and processes of encounter/exchange between different actors, see Bartels 2015).[5] Added to this is organizational participation as a special case of internal participation within organized communities, through which members are to participate in internal decision-making processes (co-determination, participation). It is possible that this form of participation is currently being reactivated and more strongly emphasized again, as associations and organizations such as political parties are once again devoting more attention to this form of participation (e.g., *community work*, see Larsen et al. 2013).[6]

On the one hand, this increased participation in society can tend to increase the legitimacy of decisions – also within organizations through the internal participation of members, etc. (see assessment by Steinberg 2014b: 415) – on the other hand, the decisive criterion here also continues to behow strongly the input side can be represented. However, the hope of virtual "expansion" of the participatory space does not seem to be fruitful: Studies on liquid feedback in parties have already shown that the usage rate is rather low (Bullwinkel and Probst 2014: 400 f.). Jan van Deth also adheres to the extended forms of participation (van Deth 2009: 149): "The citizens of democratic societies obviously limit their political activities mainly to going to the ballot box regularly and signing petitions. It is remarkable that the enormous expansion of the repertoire of political participation forms in recent decades has obviously not led to a similarly strong increase in the use of these possibilities".

The starting position and discussion about political apathy can be clearly countered empirically. The political-public interest is generally very high in Germany compared to Europe as a whole (72% of those surveyed) (Gensicke and Geiss 2010: 310). The findings of the 2004 Volunteer Survey also indicate that the self-

[5] On the transformation of participatory practices see Jan van Deth (2009: 156 f.): "Due to the close connection between democracy and participation, the continuous expansion of the repertoire of political participation can certainly be seen as a strengthening of democracy, despite the persistent social and political inequality. Moreover, a stabilization or perhaps even a decline in the level of political participation need not necessarily be interpreted as harmful to democracy. Increasing prosperity and higher education have obviously contributed to the fact that politics is no longer seen as a necessary part of social conflicts, and citizens can therefore increasingly turn to other occupations. Moreover, a lack of participation in modern societies can also be attributed to the success of traditional politics – and not to the defeats, incompetence, inability, alienation or frustration caused by politics. Politics has made the lives of many citizens considerably easier and safer in recent decades. It is precisely because politics has been so successful that citizens can devote themselves to the more enjoyable things in life (…)".

[6] Kersting and Woyke assume, however, that in the end it is the social movements that lead to less solid membership and that sporadic activity leads to a crisis in voluntary work and causes the legitimacy of organizations to decline (Kersting and Woyke 2012: 16).

image of voluntary activities relates primarily to volunteering and honorary work, and less to civic engagement, initiatives and project work (Gensicke and Geiss 2010: 313). Among the population, 30% stated that they were not engaged, 36% said they were engaged, and even 34% said they were active (but without taking on voluntary/honorary tasks). In 1999, 36% were still not committed (see also Gensicke and Geiss 2015). Although this means that far more people are interested and committed to politics than ever before, the nature and depth of involvement must also be taken into account, which, at least in Europe, empirical surveys show is not very pronounced (Gabriel 2013a: 180).

The positive finding that civic involvement has increased over the last 10 years, especially in unconventional forms (less so in the context of political parties and trade unions, for example), contrasts with the question of social structure: Which parts of the population participate at all? Three relevant questions can be derived from this: on the one hand, which forms, intensities and changes in participation (type of participation) can currently be identified in society, which persons participate (social structure) and which forms of action they take (practice of participation).

In the literature, it is assumed that a change in social values (change in living conditions) is taking place and that as a result there will be changes in engagement practices (Holtkamp et al. 2006: 100 ff.).[7]In principle, it can be stated that there is an imbalance, an "unequal distribution of political and civil society participation" (Böhnke 2011; see also Schäfer 2013a) and that political activities are generally weak in the population (Böhnke 2011: 19). The core problem here is that it is precisely those strata that are particularly affected by the consequences of politics that show little activity and little interest: "Educational and high-income strata of the population participate most frequently. It is here, and not among the socially disadvantaged, for whom improving their situation should be a particular concern, that representation of interests takes place" (ibid.). Unconventional forms of participation (in addition to the ballot, such as citizens' initiatives) exacerbate this problem even more, since these represent even less socially disadvantaged strata. The new forms of participation, in which citizens are involved in public planning, for example, demand "a high level of competence with regard to negotiating skills, stra-

[7]Current data can be found in particular in the Engagement Reports for the German Federal Government of 2012 and 2016 ("First Engagement Report", see Enste et al. 2012; "Second Engagement Report", see Zentrum für zivilgesellschaftliche Entwicklung 2016) and the 2009 study by the WZB Berlin (see Alscher et al. 2009). Finally, the so-called Volunteer Survey (Gensicke and Geiss 2010, 2015) collects a wide range of findings on civic engagement and the backgrounds of volunteers.

tegic thinking, eloquence, self-confidence" (ibid.) – which plays particularly into the hands of the highly educated. Böhnke (ibid.) also sees the problem that low "life and realization chances" reduce confidence in democracy, which in turn leads to less interest in participation due to the onset of disappointment and pessimism: "Not protest and commitment, but resignation and apathy go hand in hand with precarious life situations, if these are personally responsible for them as blows of fate in accordance with the individualized zeitgeist and appear less and less accessible to social and political shaping" (ibid.: 21). Böhnke is thus not critical of the new forms of civic engagement, such as citizens' initiatives, but in his opinion actual progress of a "broad" participation would only be achieved if topics of overall social importance and "broad sections of the population" were integrated into the engagement groups (ibid.). Otherwise, there would be a primarily self-interested "representation of interests for one's own clientele" through civic involvement (ibid.).

Finally, concrete data from the Socio-Economic Panel (SOEP) can clearly demonstrate the unequal distribution. Voluntary commitment, political participation and political interest are much more pronounced among "fully employed" and "affluent" than among "poor" and "unemployed": Since 1992, the figures have fluctuated between 15 and 20% of activity in the case of voluntary work and political participation for the former and 5–10% of the other two population groups. Similarly, political interest is also differently pronounced with 20% for the latter group and 35–50% for the first group (ibid.: 21). While political interest rose slightly overall in the 1990s, it has been falling again since the mid-2000s. Voluntary commitment has risen slightly overall, while political participation has fallen (with more pronounced fluctuations). Most recently, political participation has risen slightly again: Böhnke suspects that this may be the "beginning of a new understanding of participation"; in fact, the latest SOEP data in the two areas of "volunteer work" and "political activity" point to a further general increase among all population groups.[8] Finally, Böhnke (ibid.: 22–25) was able to prove that when negative life events in the form of unemployment and impoverishment occur, all three factors (interest, commitment, and activity) decrease. There is also a second finding that suggests a strong influence of the level of education: "Higher education goes hand in hand with stronger political interest" (ibid.: 25). In addition, there are personality traits such as "conscientiousness, openness to experience and belief in the meaning of influence and the ability to shape things", which promote "interest

[8] In the SOEP monitor (from 2012), see the two questions "Proportion of persons who are "active as volunteers" at least once a month" and "Proportion of persons who are "politically active" at least once a month", last survey for 2011; see Goebel and Haas 2014: 26 f.

in political events" (ibid.). From this perspective, it is concluded that "political interest is to a large extent based on consolidated attitudes and socialization-specific coinages and is a characteristic that can be changed only in the long run" (ibid.). This insight thus leads to the socialization environment of "family, school and friends", an integration of political education into "everyday life of families and schools" (ibid.). This is again a reminder of the school of democracy: according to the view of the representatives of "democracy learning" (see Beutel and Fauser 2001; Edelstein and Fauser 2001; Detjen 1999, 2000; Beutel and Fauser 2011; Hill 2015) democratic principles must be learned and practiced in social institutions (public as well as private), hence, they are understood here as the foundation of democracy. This consideration in turn supports the thesis of "non-citizens" by Michael Greven (Greven 1997, 2000, 2009), who sees the only way out of a democracy of self-interest and egoism entailing an "enormous effort" to "socialize and also consciously educate the citizens necessary for democracy to an unprecedented degree" (Greven 2009: 221). Ultimately, Greven sees "no real practical alternative to socialization and also conscious political education for democracy" (ibid.).[9]

Participation on the Local Level

The perspectives on participation sometimes differ. Civic participation usually takes place at the local-regional-communal level, and accordingly the focus is directed, for example, at cities and communities (Roth 1997; Holtkamp 2001; Beckmann 2012; Klages and Vetter 2013; Kost 2013; Vetter et al. 2013; Gabriel and Kersting 2014).

In addition, participation is also understood as an additive of representative democracy in the sense of alternative ideas in the form of direct democratic procedures and cooperative democracy (e.g., through joint forms of action and decision-making, see Kuhlmann 2010, as well as dialogical procedures, see Lietzmann and Mittendorf 2011; Rohland 2011).

The idea of expressions of direct democracy, for example through local or municipal self-administration (Hoffmann-Axthelm 2004; Holtkamp 2010; Bürgerkommune, Bogumil and Holtkamp 2011), is also frequently problematized in terms of insufficient financial resources for German municipalities (Holtkamp 2011; Holtkamp and Bathge 2012). Using the example of participatory budgeting, Klages (2011) speaks here of a "door opener" and "drive for a new participation culture in the municipalities" (see critical analysis in Neunecker 2016). There are also other

[9] See the view of Jason Brennan, who only wants competent citizens to have a say in democracy, as less competent citizens are more likely to contribute to negative, that is undemocratic, effects in elections (see Brennan and Hill 2014).

examples, such as planning cells (see Dienel 1978), in which citizens are to be integrated as "planners" into the shaping of the municipality and the environment; Lietzmann et al. (2013) even see this as a "new separation of powers" (see also Lietzmann 2012).

But also, more comprehensive, very far-reaching participatory measures in the sense of joint design in the field of urban and regional development are envisaged (Maas and Madrazo 2013; Selle 2013; Blandow et al. 2014; Huning 2014; Klages 2014; Wade 2015). These stock-takings ultimately led to the discussion of overarching issues, for example between "participatory change or the end of local self-government" with regard to the tasks of the welfare state (Holtkamp 2011) or the question of municipal scope for action and the associated democratic legitimation by citizens (Holtkamp 2013).

Empirical findings suggest that the local level plays a significant role in the feeling of satisfaction with political institutions and democracy in the municipal sphere, particularly with regard to the context factors that have a strong impact here (political, social, economic environment) (Vetter 2013). Accordingly, the impact of citizens' initiatives, as in the case of community energy, should not be underestimated.

2.1.2 Explaining Political Participation: The Standard Socio-Economic Model (SES)

The factors influencing participation (whether and how participation occurs) are still largely unclear, only the so-called standard socio-economic model has become accepted as a simple way of explaining,[10] the finding that a high socio-economic status (education, income, occupation, social contacts, etc.) leads to more commitment, interest in participation and involvement in associations (see in particular Verba and Nie 1972, this is known as the middle class bias and is described in the *standard socioeconomic model* (the causal connection between higher socioeconomic status (SES) and political participation) and *civic voluntarism model* for the explanation of political participation, see Almond and Verba 1963; Milbrath 1965; Nie et al. 1969a, 1969b; Verba and Nie 1972; Verba et al. 1978, 1995; Zipp et al. 1982; Brady et al. 1995; Putnam 2000; Almond and Verba 2001; Hooghe and Quintelier 2013, 2014; see also the evidence in the context of consumption and activity or dissatisfaction of citizens in Pfaff and Blivice 1977), which applies to both con-

[10] See Keil (2013b: 54).

ventional and unconventional forms of political participation.[11] In addition, there is the effect of other factors such as (local) networks of individuals and/or actors.[12] Even if the findings in the form of the socio-economic standard model are older, they still hold true today, as Oscar Gabriel notes:

> The findings on the influence of the social position of people on the nature and extent of their political activity are not new (…). However, they have become more relevant in recent years, because empirical research provides evidence of an increase in social inequality in modern democracies. These findings not only contradict the hope that the ongoing modernization of European societies will lead to a long-term reduction in socio-economic inequality. They also challenge the self-understanding of democracy, because persistent or even growing social inequality may undermine the idea of equal participation of all citizens in shaping the political community. (Gabriel 2015: 68)

Of particular interest are the more recent studies on the impact of (local) contextual factors on participation behavior (as a facilitating or an inhibiting factor). Oscar Gabriel and Silke Keil (see Keil 2013b) refer to incomplete knowledge about extended participation activities, but theoretically assume a strong influence of socio-structural factors (Gabriel 2013b: 406 f.): "Our knowledge about the significance of contextual factors for people's decision to become actively involved in politics is relatively incomplete. Does the complexity of the political situation reduce participation, while the abundance and relevance of local authority competences promotes it (…)? Are there participation-friendly institutions that encourage individuals to engage in political activity and what do they look like (…)?" Empirical research has provided far less reliable answers to questions of this kind than to the question of what role individual resources and motives and integration into social networks play in citizens' political participation. In this respect, it makes sense and is important to pay more attention than before to the role of contextual factors in the emergence of political engagement and to focus this analysis on the local level of the political system, where the contexts of action are presumably more cognitively present to people than in national politics. The result of these efforts is sobering at first glance. Yet, The direct effects of the context, here of socio-economic modernity and community size, on political participation cannot be proven.

Gabriel's own research results see a greater individual influence in relation to local contextual conditions, which would invalidate the thesis of an activating culture of engagement (ibid.: 407): "For participation in traditional political activities and in legal protest actions in the 28 Hessian towns and communities investigated

[11] See Schultze (2005: 676).

[12] See Keil (2013a: 186).

here, it is completely irrelevant whether the citizens live in a large, medium-sized or small community or whether this community has a high, medium or low level of socio-economic development. Quite different factors are important: the more the citizens are involved in associations, the better they are equipped with socio-economic resources and the more they identify with a party, the more they are likely to participate in traditional activities and protest actions (…). The influence of socio-economic resources on political participation challenges the democratic ideal of political equality, because due to their active involvement in politics, the higher status groups have a better chance of being noticed by the political leadership. This increases the probability that their preferences will be taken into account in the decisions of the political leadership (…). The traditional intermediary organizations thus continue to play an important role in mobilising individuals for individual political activity".[13] However, Gabriel attributes a possible reinforcing role to the context.[14]

Silke Keil (2013a), on the other hand, considers the local context to be an essential criterion: "The fact that people in medium-sized and large cities are mainly active locally, but that people in smaller communities visit clubs in neighboring communities more often, is an indication of the importance of the size of the community, which is supported by the consideration of non-institutional social participation. In small communities, friends and acquaintances meet more frequently and neighborly contacts are more intensive than in large cities" (186). However, Keil's study shows that the individual characteristics of those involved are "far more explanatory" than the contextual effects (ibid.). High income is by far the "most important determinant" (ibid.). In addition, there are further indicators: "On the one hand, the unemployment rate exerts an influence, i.e. social participation in communities differs according to the level of the respective unemployment rate". In communities with a low rate more people are active in associations than in communities with many unemployed. In addition, the frequency of church attendance plays a role, but not in the expected positive direction: "If the proportion of fre-

[13] See also Gabriel (2013b: 407).

[14] See Gabriel's further argumentation according to which the structural local context can have a positive influence on individual political involvement (Gabriel 2013b: 407 f.): "The socioeconomic modernity of a community plays an important role in how strongly individual resource endowment influences participation in traditional political activities. Socioeconomic development promotes political equality because it weakens the resource dependence of political participation. Social engagement also has different effects on political participation in different contexts. Its political mobilization effect is particularly strong in highly socioeconomically developed communities. These results convey a positive message for the future of participatory politics, because as modernization progresses, political engagement is increasingly linked to social engagement and less to access to socioeconomic resources".

quent churchgoers is lower in a municipality, its parishioners are more likely to be active in associations" (ibid.) (on the commitment of socially disadvantaged people see Klatt et al. 2011).

However, there are other factors of organizational participation which play a decisive role for an evaluation, especially against the background of ideals of participation theory (such as the connection to the community, see Bühlmann 2013). In this context, Silke Keil focuses on the question of which factors can counteract the bias that "the interests of resource-strong groups and individuals have a greater chance of being accepted and heard in the political process than those of resource-weak groups" (Keil 2013b: 54). From this, the "democratically relevant question" is derived, "whether certain organizations exist that can counteract this bias and thus contribute to the social engagement of all people, regardless of their income, education, gender and age" (ibid.: 55). For this reason, Keil explicitly includes organization-specific characteristics (size, degree of professionalization, financial resources, dependencies on donors, structure of voluntary work, content orientation) in an evaluation of the social structure of local engagement structures: these should have an influence on "whether and to what extent an individual is socially engaged" (ibid.: 67).

Keil therefore assumes that "small voluntary organizations are more likely to have a balancing effect on the social bias than large voluntary organizations and less professionalized voluntary organizations are more likely to have a balancing effect on the social bias than highly professionalized voluntary organizations" (ibid.: 58). In small organizations the probability is said to be greater "that socio-economically less well-equipped individuals come into contact with other people and are more likely to acquire the norms and values that are important for democracy" (ibid.: 57). In large organizations, it should be more difficult to establish contact. Furthermore, with a lower degree of professionalization or institutionalization the probability is supposed to be greater "that citizens with fewer resources are more likely to find access to other people" (ibid.). The size and degree of institutionalization of an organization should correspond: "For above a certain size, an association can no longer cope with the tasks at hand without the appropriate personnel and rights and obligations and goals formulated in writing. A professional organizational structure becomes indispensable in order to meet the demands of the association members" (ibid.).

Some study results thus point to a significant influence of local context factors such as the size of the municipality; Keil also assumes that the size of the organization plays a role (small, less professional civil society associations have a more balancing effect than larger organizations).[15] Here, a research deficit is assumed to exist for taking these factors into account. Ultimately, a wide variety of conditions

[15] See results of Dahl and Tufte (1973), Oliver (2000) and Keil (2013a, 2013b).

such as the size of the community, the type and structure of the participatory association and the situational environment have a certain influence on local engagement structures, even if Keil has not been able to substantiate this: "If organizations have many members and have a highly professionalized structure, the social bias remains. However, it is *not* observed that the influence of the social bias is reduced by small and less professionalized organizations. (...) Organizational characteristics do not have the expected balancing effect on the social bias" (ibid.: 67).

Despite the problem of empirical verifiability, the thesis of an influence of local contextual conditions is maintained. In particular, the size of the municipality and organization-specific structures and arrangements are attributed a key role with regard to an influence on socio-structural characteristics:

> Individuals maintain contact with their fellow human beings and the frequency and intensity of contact depends on the size of a city. In the context of participation in voluntary organizations, it can be expected that participation is less socially determined when cities are very small. In a village community, all individuals are more likely to participate than in a large city. (...) The clearer the objective, the more likely it is that people will meet who are similar in their socio-structural composition. A small environmental protection association is more likely to have a homogeneous composition of its members than a large leisure association, which in turn can have an impact on whether and how organizational characteristics work. This means that both the size of a city and the orientation of the organization and the interaction of both factors can have an effect on whether and how organizational characteristics can have a balancing effect on the social bias. (Ibid.: 67 f.)

The crucial question in the form of a "social question of democracy" with regard to the effect of income and education (Bödeker 2011) is a recurring theme in the literature,[16] with regard to the hopes for participation by Geißel (2011b) it

[16] Thus Nolte (2011) also addresses the issue of middle class bias. Finally, he points to the (long known) problem that the "new, post-representative dimensions of democracy" favour above all the middle class, which is educated and articulated – the "working and lower classes, the formally less educated, often also migrants" are missing, since they cannot overcome "material and cultural entry thresholds" (ibid.: 11 f.). Nolte concludes: "Now mistrust and withdrawal of the lower classes, who have difficulty finding their place in multiple democracy, are increasing" (ibid: 12) – Walter (2013) comments on the "law of the middle class": "For this reason alone, members of the middle class with academic titles and degrees populate the citizen petitions, but hardly any people from the precariat. And in collective engagement, the expansion of competence continues once again among those who are already abundantly supplied with knowledge, information, oratory skills. For in the organization of collective commitment, skills also accumulate. The active members must be able to build up organizational structures, maintain contacts with the media, exert pressure and make an impression on the authorities with solid justifications for their concerns, and be knowledgeable in the details of jurisdiction".

is summarized in the following: "Chance or danger for the political representation of the poor and foreigners?" Silke Keil (2012: 205) still considers the old explanatory model (*Standard Socioeconomic Model of Participation* and *Civic Voluntarism Model*) to be valid in an analysis of social and political participation of European states in Germany (as well as other Western European states). Interestingly, the "active social participation of the West German population is relatively strong in all sizes of municipalities" compared to Europe and East Germany (ibid.: 203). Within West Germany, on the other hand, it is noticeable that particularly in the large cities there is a high level of active participation, which cannot be found anywhere else in Europe to the same extent (ibid.). Particularly strong use is made of participation in parties or citizens' initiatives (see also Geißler 2014b: 393). The validity of the standard model for the extended forms of participation is also assumed[17]: "(…) The better the socio-economic resources available to citizens are, the greater, ceteris paribus, their probability of participation. This quasi-lawfulness has also been confirmed for the non-constitutional forms of participation and thus, because of their voluntaristic nature, again raises the question of political equality (…). Here, political and political science questions of the institutionalization of unconstitutional forms of participation are addressed, which should serve the goals of expanding the participation possibilities of citizens and at the same time prevent the slide into a pure democracy of being affected" (Kaase 2000: 469).

Recently, influences of the social milieu and status such as gender and migration background have also been noted: "The reasons why an individual is politically active also result from his or her social position. Political involvement grows with income, educational level and professional status. Participation often has a 'middle class bias' (…). By contrast, citizens from poorer social classes stay away from politics. This often overlaps with other socio-economic indicators such as education and migration background. Population groups with a migration background show weaker political commitment in almost all generations" (Kersting 2014: 59). "Furthermore, gender-specific differences are evident in all groups. Women tend to be in the minority in a variety of forms of participation. However, younger women generally show an equally strong or even stronger political commitment. In particular, the

[17] Hoecker cites the socioeconomic standard model (after Verba and Nie 1972) as an important determinant of participation, according to which the rule should apply: the higher the level of education, the more qualified the profession and the higher the income, "the greater the chance for conventional political participation" (Hoecker 2006: 12). The same rule should apply to the unconstituted forms of participation (ibid.: 13).

time-consuming participation instruments are used significantly less often by women in the middle generation (30–50 years) than by men. This lack of commitment is not fully compensated for in old age either (...)" (ibid.).

There is also an influence of the age structure: "There are also serious differences between the generations. Whereas only decades ago unconventional forms of participation were used, especially by young people or the younger generation, and conventional forms, such as voting, were favored more by the older generation, participation patterns are changing. It was stated that the electoral norm (voting as a civic duty) is more firmly anchored in the older generation, whereas for a long time it could be assumed that protest actions were initiated and supported primarily by younger population groups. In contrast, the most recent protest around Stuttgart 21 in particular shows a strong commitment of the older generation between 40 and 65. The group over 65 in particular is considered to have a lot of time on their hands and is therefore involved in both conventional and unconventional participation processes. In the group between 40 and 60, a very high level of dissatisfaction with the political system is becoming increasingly apparent, resulting in an increased need for participation" (ibid.: 60).

In addition to the socio-structural characteristics, an overarching dynamic of participation behavior can be observed. This is the remarkable phenomenon of "waves of participation". Apparently, there are periods of increased interest in participation, followed by more passive periods of abstinence. In addition, there seem to be cycles in participation behavior: Phases of major public engagement are followed by a retreat into the private sphere for many (...). These changes also characterize participation behavior in the FRG, which is determined by the increase in unconventional and direct-democratic participation since the 1970s and the sharp decline in conventional participation since the 1980s, especially in voter turnout, party identification and membership, in which the loss of confidence of citizens in the political class finds its most visible expression (...) (Schultze 2005: 676) (see also Hirschman 1982).

2.1.3 Criteria of Participation

Procedures and instruments of participation must be evaluated in terms of their quality – participation as such is relatively insignificant on its own, a participation process is only an added value if it is of high quality. On the one hand, quality inevitably results from the reversal or avoidance of the risks and dangers of participation (e.g., an open, integrating climate versus closed, excluding practices). In addition, general quality criteria are also described in the literature (Kersting names here openness and political equality; power control and legitimacy; rationality and transparency as well as efficiency and effectiveness, see Kersting 2008: 33; see also Dienel et al. 2014).

The criteria are fundamentally reminiscent of claims to political procedures and processes. Here and there, the core issue is the possibility of freely exchanging opinions (openness), preventing opinion leaderships (power control), allowing minorities to have their say, conducting all discourses in public (transparency), and ultimately making binding and accepted decisions (effectiveness). However, the criteria of rationality, efficiency and effectiveness can also be too much. Purely rational procedures would be those of technocracy, participation processes always include "empty loops", possibly unproductive phases, which however usually contain other qualities of exchange of opinions and voting (seeCraig 2014). It is clear that a participation process should move between the poles: the scales should never experience massive imbalances, a balancing of procedures is probably the "golden road" – that is neither too little discourse, nor too much discourse, etc.

Jan van Deth examined the delicate question of whether participants are the "better democrats" at all and tried to answer this empirically by examining the acceptance of democratic civic virtues among participants (van Deth 2013b: 49 f.).[18] In doing so, he came to two incisive conclusions. The first point concerns differences in the individual: according to this, very active citizens are also the better democrats: "Their acceptance of democratic virtues is clearly above average levels" (ibid.: 50). But also politically-passive persons agree with the "basic principles of a democracy" (ibid.). Large differences can be observed, however, among those involved in conventional forms of participation (e.g., party work). Here, the acceptance of civic virtues and agreement with democratic basic rights is significantly lower, which is a surprising result (ibid.).

[18] See on the classification of the van Deth study (2013b: 49 f.) and on democratic civic virtues Abendschön (2013).

Another point refers to the well-known inequality problem of participation (resource-poor population groups participate less) as a "threat to democracy", which is put into perspective after these results: "However, these findings should be considered with caution when assessing the viability of democratic political systems. Despite the clear differences in socio-economic characteristics and political and social orientations, support for democratic virtues is hardly characterized by such profile deviations. It is particularly important that citizens who do not participate politically support democratic civic virtues" (ibid.). From this van Deth concludes that although politically active citizens are "better democrats", "the viability of democracy is also guaranteed by politically inactive citizens" (van Deth 2013b: 51).[19]

2.2 Political Participation: Changing Participation and Changing Effects of Participation

In the context of public participation procedures and participation via civil society associations or public forms of action and participation procedures in the context of energy system transformation, it is of particular interest from a scientific perspective to examine more closely the question of which forms of participation and modes of action are based on applied forms of participation.

For a long time, political science research concentrated on political participation. However, the overview of theories of political participation is difficult to grasp (see Behr 1999; Connolly 2006; overview of procedures can be found, for example, in Nanz and Fritsche 2012 and in general on civic participation in Dienel 2011; for a comparative perspective see van Deth 2015 and the more recent conceptualization of Hooghe et al. 2014). Although a fundamental distinction can be made between a normative and an instrumental understanding of participation

[19] Van Deth explains: "(...) Activists are relatively highly educated, count themselves among a higher class and have a higher level of internal political self-confidence than other citizens. For passives and citizens who limit their participation to voter participation, the reverse is true. We therefore see violations of the democratic principle of equality especially among very active and passive citizens. Above all, the profile of citizens who do not participate at all differs significantly from the profile of the 'average citizen'" (van Deth 2013b: 50).

(Hoecker 2006: 9),[20] two mechanisms – the theoretical expansion of the concept of the political and the increasing differentiation of civic activity in society (i.e., also

[20] The former sees participation as a goal and value in itself, the function is seen as self-determination and self-fulfilment of the individual, direct democratic forms are preferred, political-social participation is seen as meaningful in as many areas of society as possible (see on this and in the following Hoecker 2006: 9). The intensity of participation is understood to be processual; the acquisition of political competences is to be achieved through education and participatory practice, and finally, the aim is a "self-transformation" of society through participation. Political apathy results in this way of thinking as a result of concrete power relations; a reduction of this is to be achieved through the expansion of participation. The instrumental understanding of participation, on the other hand, sees participation primarily as a method and means to an end; its function is the regulation of social conflicts through representation and elite rule. Representative democratic forms, especially elections, are emphasized here. Participation is considered to be limited to the political sphere; the intensity of participation is only perceived as selective. Political competences are supposed to counteract the lack of knowledge and lead to insight and possible willingness to engage. Political apathy is seen here as an empirical fact and is perceived functionally in terms of system stability. Hoecker also describes a taxonomy of political participation (Hoecker 2006: 11). According to this, the dimensions of political participation are, on the one hand, conventional and constitutional procedures with the forms of citizenship (elections) and party-oriented participation (activity in parties). On the other hand, there are unconventional and unconstituted forms, which are divided into legal and illegal forms. The former is understood as problem-oriented participation (participation in citizens' initiatives, participation in demonstrations, collection of signatures, participation in assemblies in public discussions, etc.) (ibid.).Similarly, Schultze (2005: 675) divides political participation into an instrumental and normative understanding: "Instrumental or purpose-rational are all those forms of political participation that citizens undertake voluntarily, individually and/or collectively in association with others in order to influence political decisions directly or indirectly in their favour. It is about participation, value consideration and the assertion of interests". The addressees of political participation are institutions and decision-makers in the political system. In contrast, in the "normative understanding, participation is not only a means to an end, but also an end and value in itself. It is not about exerting influence and asserting interests, but rather about self-realization in the process of direct-democratic cooperation and political-social participation in as many areas of society as possible. Such a normative concept of participation is consensus-oriented, communitarian and expressive, whereas the instrumental concept of participation, closely related to the market-liberal understanding of rationality, is conflict-oriented" (ibid.: 675 f.). Direct democratic forms of political participation such as citizens' initiatives would indeed "allow participation graded according to intensity, but would also be associated with a (in part far) higher level of commitment and costs" (ibid.: 676).

changing or gaining new forms of participation[21]) – have on the one hand broadened the definition of political participation or made it more complex.[22] On the other hand, however, this results in an overlap with the descriptions of other forms of participation (social, monetary, organizational, etc.), which have been investigated for some time independently of the debate on political participation. At first, it seems obvious that analogous to the expansion of the sphere of the political (into all social and life spheres), the definition of political participation is also being expanded (see Fox 2013). The literature is still divided on this point.

Definitions of political participation have not been uniformly established in the literature; although some similarities can be found, some striking differences can also be identified. Overarching are definitions of political participation across areas (representative, direct, deliberative and demonstrative and symbolic participation)[23]as well as definitions of political participation about a form of influ-

[21] This includes all activities of citizens that go beyond classical political participation via elections and parties, for example, events, initiatives, etc.: "The change in the political behavior of Germans can be seen above all in the great increase in the importance of topic-related activities, which since the 1970s have played an increasingly important role as forms of political influence and for some years have been more widespread than party and election-related activities" (Kersting 2014: 58).

[22] See on the extended forms of political participation, which for example go beyond elections Christensen 2011, on methodological distinctions Pfenning and Benighaus 2008 and on the question of increasing democratic quality through extended procedures Erhard et al. 2013.

[23] According to Kersting, political participation can be subdivided into four areas of democratic participation, each of which contains different instruments and logics: representative (invited space, e.g., elections), direct (e.g., referendum, petition), deliberative (e.g., forum, citizens' assembly, planning cell, advisory board) and demonstrative (invented space, e.g., demonstration, letter to the editor) or symbolic participation (Kersting 2014: 60). Elsewhere, Kersting and Woyke distinguish between the following forms of political participation (Kersting and Woyke 2012: 21 ff.): "indirect/representative – direct/theme-oriented; numerical – dialogical/deliberative; mobilized (invited space) – spontaneous (invented space); real – virtual".

ence of individuals on political decision-making processes.[24] The question remains here, however, as to what should already constitute an influence and in which case a political decision-making process can be identified.[25] Finally, according to the more recent understanding, individual actions to achieve political goals are used as a defining characteristic of realistic empirical theory of democracy as opposed to the normative variant, which would regard participation more as an (integrative) principle of life (see Hoecker 2006).[26]

The frequently cited defnition of Max Kaase, proposes a simple and broad definition of political participation as being any (voluntary) activity which aims to in-

[24] In 1978 (p. 46), Verba et al. defined political participation as "legal activities by private citizens that are more or less directly aimed at influencing the selection of governmental personnel and/or the actions they take". Verba et al. (1995: 38) further expanded this definition to include "political participation can be understood as every kind of behavior of the citizen, taken individually or as a group, with the goal to influence a political decision". Barnes and Kaase (1979: 42, see also Kaase 1992: 339) spoke in a similar way of "behaviors of citizens (…) that they voluntarily undertake, alone or as a group, with the goal of influencing a political decision".

[25] Max Kaase (2000) attempts to concretize political participation further as "all actions that citizens undertake voluntarily, individually or in groups, with the aim of influencing and/or making decisions at the various levels of the political system (municipality, state, federal government, possibly supranational units). This instrumental definition of participation does not mean that in reality there cannot also be cases in which participation takes place in the context of, for example, group activities without a political objective of their own (expressive participation)" (Kaase 2000: 466). However, he also puts attitudes into perspective: "By limiting the focus to concrete actions, attitudes toward participation are initially excluded. On the one hand, this makes sense in the interest of a clear delineation of the subject matter. On the other hand, research has shown that action-related attitudes also contain important information about the action orientations of societies as a whole and about the conditions under which concrete acts of political participation take place" (Kaase 2000: 466 f.).

[26] Beate Hoecker derives from the previous definition that only actions that are explicitly aimed at the achievement of a political goal are covered; moreover, it indicates individual use, primarily guaranteed by elections (Hoecker 2006: 4). Hoecker classifies such an approach into the realistic-empirical theory of democracy, which is distinguished from a second direction, the normative theory of democracy, which regards democracy not primarily as a method, but as a form of rule and life (ibid.: 6 ff.).

fluence the political system[27]: "*Political* participation refers simply to activity that is intended to influence government action-either directly by affecting the making or implementation of public policy or indirectly by influencing the selection of people who make those policies. *Voluntary* activity means participation that is not obligatory-no one is forced to volunteer-and that receives no pay or only token financial compensation" (Kaase 2011: 1781). However, it becomes more difficult with a defnition of social participation that could cover up or integrate political inclusion. Kaase focuses on activities that go beyond the private sphere: "Other than political participation, social participation has not yet achieved the status of a well-defined social science subfield. Analogous to political participation, social participation can be defined as all activities by individual citizens in soical contexts going beyond the inner circle of family and friendship relations that are not primarily directed toward influencing political outcomes. As such, social participation constitutes a core elment of civil society" (Kaase 2011: 1786). The importance of social participation has increased through the "discovery" of civil society, based on studies on the importance of social capital (Putnam 2000) (ibid.).

Oscar Gabriel agrees with Kaase's definition, which in this way also seeks to include an expansion of forms of participation that goes beyond classic forms of political participation such as elections and parties (conventional forms as opposed to unconventional forms of participation such as demonstrations, petitions for sig-

[27] Max Kaase (2011: 1777) finally attempts a fundamental approach to participation in general with regard to the possibilities of influencing different levels of society: "(...) each domain encompasses individuals (the microlevel), an intermediary structure (the mesolevel) linking individuals and institutions in that domain, and systemic elements crystallized in rules and institutions regulating the particular domain in question (the macrolevel)". There is also an overarching transnational level. Kaase now describes the participation options that may arise depending on the level, whereby individual influences (participation is sought "from below" by individuals) and institutional arrangements (participation is made possible "from above") are conceivable: "Participation refers (...) to activities by individual members of any given mesoor macro-unit of analysis. Secont, in the core of participation is the action itself -that is, individual behavior-even if attitutes as the antecedents of such behavior (...) may also be of interest. Third, individuals never act in a social void; therefore, to understand why people act at all and in the way they do, one has to consider the embeddedness of individuals in a context conducive to action. This context can also be the institutional arrangements on the macrolevel (e.g., for voting, the electoral law in a given country) or the social environment that an individual is part of. Fourth, modern social science is (...) also about dynamics and change (...). Fifth, and returning to the concept of domains as subunits of sociopolitical systems resulting form processes of differentiation in in contemporary societies, participation for the purpose of this entry is divided into a part on political participation and a-smaller-part on social participation (ther are other fields worth looking at, e.g., cultural participation (...)" (ibid..: 1777 f.)

natures and citizens' initiatives): "all voluntary activities by means of which citizens – not the holders of political or administrative positions – attempt to influence personnel or material decisions at various levels of action in the political system or to participate directly in them (...). Since the beginning of empirical participation research, the activities carried out by citizens for this purpose have multiplied and structurally become more and more differentiated (...). As a result of the expansion and differentiation of the participation system, traditional forms of political influence, especially voting in elections and membership in political parties, have declined sharply in Germany in recent decades. Even though voting in elections is still by far the most widespread form of political participation, it has lost weight in contrast to other forms of political influence" (Gabriel 2013b: 383).

Dieter Rucht (2010: 2) also refers back to Kaase's definition and defines political participation rather broadly but dissociates it from personal interests and commitment "(...) from mere political interests and forms of social or charitable commitment (such as neighborhood aid or donations for disaster victims)". Rucht, however, would like to link political commitment to motive and benefit, which, however, are defined individually and subject-centered: "Political interest is generally a necessary but not sufficient condition for political participation. In order to trigger real participation, a motive for a concrete commitment is additionally required, and usually also the hope that the chosen activity will have some kind of benefit. This may consist of the satisfaction of having expressed one's anger, it may be aimed at maintaining or obtaining an individual or collective advantage, or it may also consist of the moral satisfaction that may result from a commitment to underprivileged groups or to the common good" (ibid.).

Another fundamental examination of political participation can be found by Jan van Deth. He initially composed political participation from four basic conditions (van Deth 2009: 170 ff.):

- Activity as a citizen and not as a politician (amateurish/non-expert?).
- Action, not only attitude (intentional action or motiveless activity?).
- Voluntary action (voluntary/optional or obligatory?).
- Related to the sphere of government or politics and the public (locus: politics/government/state), not limited to specific levels or issues of the political decision-making process (target: politics/government/state or problem/community).

Moreover, van Deth considers the distinction between the instrumental and normative concept of participation to be of little use (ibid.: 143 f.); he sees the two perspectives as "setting priorities" rather than as "dividing lines" (ibid.: 144). Participation thus serves in particular "certain purposes within the framework of democratic decision-making processes" (ibid.). Van Deth sees three central purposes of participation, namely influencing, having a say and forming opinions and wills (ibid.: 145). Ultimately, he asks, especially on a subjective level, what purposes would be pursued by the participants: "Well-hidden self-interests, attempts at rationalization and legitimization, but also ignorance and false perceptions do not make it easy to reliably recognize the purposes of participation" (ibid.).

Therefore van Deth distinguishes between different forms and levels, he considers terms such as "unconventional forms of participation" to be outdated (ibid.: 146); furthermore, a constant expansion of forms has taken place (ibid.: 146): "The gradual dissolution of the boundary between the political and the non-political sphere in modern societies and the revival of the Tocquevillean and the communitarian approach led to an expansion of political participation through 'civic' activities such as volunteer work (...). Until then, participation in 'voluntary associations' or 'social participation' was conceptualized as analytically and empirically different from political participation. The result of this gradual expansion was that the field of political participation became almost every conceivable form of non-private activity. Even if one classifies all forms of political participation used in various studies very loosely and roughly, one arrives at a list of about 70 activities (...). The repertoire of political participation has obviously grown enormously in the last decades". Based on classifications of previous research, van Deth himself distinguishes four dimensions of political participation (ibid.: 147): voting, campaigning activities, contacting authorities or politicians, and activities in voluntary organizations (it is still unclear whether it is a separate type).

2.2.1 New Definitions of Political Participation: Introducing an Individualized, Subject-Centered View on Political Participation

More recently, some authors have developed innovative, newer approaches to systematizing and classifying participation.

New questions, for example concerning the space and scope of participation ("where does political participation take place?", e.g., private, public or virtual spaces, function and structure of spaces, etc.) can be addressed[28] and participation channels[29] can be found.

---

[28] de Moor (2017).

[29] Thus, Jan van Deth refers to typological approaches that distinguish between structural channels (van Deth 2009: 147): channels of representation (such as elections, party activities or even citizens' initiatives that want to influence members of parliament) as well as other channels beyond democratic institutions (such as the use of product boycotts or attempts to influence public opinion, another new form is consumption).

However, the debate focuses in particular on the question of whether and to what extent the concept of political participation should be expanded to include activities that are not directly related to political affairs (political content in the sense of policies) or spheres (political system in the sense of polity) or processes and procedures (political instruments in the sense of politics). This means in particular activities of civil society (e.g., in the form of civicengagement[30]) that are

[30] See on the debate about the exclusion of civic engagement from political participation versus inclusion of civic engagement Norbert Kersting, who explicitly advocates a separation: "First of all, a fundamental distinction must be made between political participation as participation in decision-making and civic engagement as participation in the implementation of self-help projects oriented towards the common good. (…) Civic engagement (co-production) plays an important role in society (e.g., for building social capital). However, this civic engagement should be fundamentally distinguished from political participation, i.e. participation that is primarily aimed at influencing decision-making" (Kersting 2014: 60). See elsewhere also Kersting and Woyke, who define civic engagement as participation in the context of implementations or (public welfareoriented) self-help, which could be found in privatized, self-responsible organizations (such as associations) (Kersting and Woyke 2012: 20 f., and Kersting 2008: 20). Political participation, on the other hand, is exclusively "participation in the decision-making process" (ibid.). Klaus Koopmann takes a contrary view by explicitly speaking of civic participation. He refers to the influence on political processes and combines participation with high qualitative, in particular individual demands, in relation to "voluntary, reflective, responsible, cooperative and not for personal material gain related participation of citizens in public, community-related, democratically legitimized negotiation and decision-making processes involving state political actors and institutions under the conditions of written democratic rules and public, conflicting constellations of interests and public use of power" (Koopmann 2012: 1). In the form of a combination, Koopmann defines civic participation as follows: "Civic participation (…) is the voluntary, reflective, self-directed and at the same time cooperative and responsible participation of citizens in public, community-related, usually problem-solving oriented, democratically legitimized negotiation and decision-making processes involving state policy actors and institutions under the conditions of written democratic rules as well as public, conflicting constellations of interests and the public use of power" (ibid.: 6 f.).

related to public space and matters of public interest (e.g., community-based activities[31]).

Susanne Pickel (2012: 43), for example, expands forms of political participation of the classical grid by further, mainly social and virtual forms and thus takes a contemporary classification: (1) formally and conventionally as fulfilment of duty (citizenship role) or personal initiative (as party-oriented participation, participation in political discussions, social participation with voluntary work or as online participation), (2) informally either unconventionally and legally as problem-specific participation (and thus again connected with social participation and voluntary work) or informally changing the system and thus – in the sense of a revolution – illegally.

A prominent representative of the expanded understanding of political participation is Jan van Deth. To justify this, he refers for example to a correlation between contact with politicians and political consumption in terms of motivation and type of influence. Individual, non-organized forms of civil society involvement are thus also to be seen as political participation in the sense of a supplement to the repertoire of political participation (van Deth 2009, 2014a, 2014b; van Deth and Maloney 2012, on the broad initial consideration see van Deth 2013a as well as on the classification of lifestyle politics as political participation de Moor 2017).

According to this understanding, the character of activities in particular becomes a decisive factor in classification: "Following Alfred Hirschman's (...) distinction between 'exit' and 'voice', one can break down forms of participation into forms of influence that citizens can or cannot use (such as elections) and activities that are used to draw attention to certain preferences or interests (such as citizens' initiatives or signature campaigns)" (van Deth 2009: 147). It can also be broken down into which addressees the forms of participation have: "Within this last group

[31] Thus Wichard Woyke defines political participation as "those behaviors of citizens who, as a group or on their own, voluntarily seek to exert influence on political decisions at various levels of the political system (local, state, federal, and European). A distinction is made between conventional (written, legally guaranteed and regulated) and unconventional (not written) forms of political participation (Woyke 2009: 549). Woyke defines community-related activities of political participation as "institutionalized, but temporary forms of political participation (...) such as, for example, temporary participation in local problem solving (...)" – which presumably means citizens' initiatives and the like (ibid.: 550). Woyke, in turn, distinguishes these forms of political participation from social participation, which "includes above all voluntary and civic engagement" (ibid.).

The distinguishing feature here should be volunteerism, although this can also be an explicit component of political participation: "Although these activities aimed at social integration can certainly achieve a political character, they are usually to be found in the voluntary sector" (ibid.).

of forms of participation, a difference is also possible on the basis of the objective of the activities. Some forms of political participation are aimed at specific actors, groups or institutions (such as a blockade of the town hall shortly before an important local council meeting is addressed to the council members), while other activities have no clear addressees and mostly try to influence the public (such as the publication of future projections)" (ibid.: 147 f.).

In this grid, community energy initiatives would be classified as exit-based and extra-representative channels analogous to the mode of participation in the form of political consumption, whereby a threshold to the voice-based character of the activities would be found (not specifically through activity in the grouping, but specifically through contact) when members switch from passive financial participation to active use of their participation opportunities. Analogously, the idea that both alternative consumption practices and alternative-economically oriented forms of action such as community energy generate innovations of participation and collaboration is likely to be true (Jäckel 2014).

The expansion of the classification of newer, individualized and participatory practices to political participation makes a concrete classification of participation procedures and practices increasingly difficult, if not impossible. According to Jan van Deth, an almost endless number of terms have developed (van Deth 2014a, 2015). This is due in particular to the fact that the integration of civil society activities, that is civic engagement, is increasingly being addressed (inclusion of civil society participation discussed in Cornwall 2002; Macedo 2005; Zukin et al. 2006; Cornwall and Coelho 2007; Dalton 2008; Woyke 2009; Koopmann 2012; Whiteley 2012; Fox 2013; de Moor 2017). Van Deth points out the inaccuracies that arise here: for example, according to Macedo (2005), influencing public life can ultimately mean anything, and the same applies to the characteristics "voluntary" and "related to problem solving and assistance" (van Deth 2014a: 350). Such definitions would result in a very general and superficial description of political participation. Van Deth, on the other hand, would like to maintain a link between the newer individualized forms of participation in political and state affairs as a minimum requirement for attribution to political participation; however, civic activities can be explicit as a form of political participation: "Political participation is an abstract or general concept that covers voluntary activities by citizens usually related to government, politics or the state" (ibid.: 353).

A solution to the dichotomy between a very broad interpretation and more precision could lie in a tiered understanding of political participation, dependent on four decisive criteria (ibid.: 354 et seq.) – similar to van Deth's definition mentioned above (van Deth 2009):

- Criterion 1: Do we deal with intentional action or motiveless behavior?
- Criterion 2: Is the activity voluntary?
- Criterion 3: Is the activity carried out by citizens?
- Criterion 4: Is the activity located in the sphere of government/state/politics?

Based on these criteria, van Deth developed seven conditions and four forms of political participation (van Deth 2014a: 354 ff.). The first condition consists of an action or activity which must represent a concrete intention (if 'no': an orientation/attitude/opinion). The second condition refers to the existence of voluntariness (voluntary/optional, if 'no': obligatory action/authoritarian rule). A third condition describes the activity of citizens, which does not have to be carried out professionally or paid for, but refers to amateurish/non-expert citizen action (amateurish, if 'no': professional activities). Finally, a fourth condition requires that the action be located within the sphere of politics, government or state; van Deth understands this as the general institutional architecture of the political system (sphere of the polity dimension) (ibid.: 356). If these four conditions are met, they will lead to a first, minimal definition of political participation (Var. 1 of political participation) (ibid.).

The fifth and sixth conditions focus on the objectives and intentions of the participation. They must either directly concern the political sphere (target: politics/government/state) (Var. 2 of political participation) or community action and serve as an overarching problem-solving approach (target: problem/community) (Var. 3 of political participation). In the latter case van Deth further distinguishes between whether political or non-political activities follow from this and whether they are politically motivated (non-political activies, but politically motivated: Var. 4 of political participation). What is meant by participation that serves an overarching problem-solving approach are those of civic engagement within the sphere of civil society (such as citizens' initiatives or neighborhood councils with ecological motivation or similar) (ibid.: 358), which must additionally fulfil the already mentioned conditions of concrete goal-oriented actions, voluntariness and amateurish (as in non-expert) citizen action. This field of political participation includes so-called "individualized collective action" (ibid.), which means a newer variety of singularized political participation in combination with practices which are based on the handling of material goods. These forms of community action are collectively organized, but oriented on individualized practices of participation (e.g., urban gardening, repair cafes or food sharing), which are part of an overarching community problem-solving strategy (Micheletti 2003; Shirky 2008; van Deth 2011; van Deth and Maloney 2012).

In the case of the parallel existence between non-political modes of action on the one hand and political motivation on the other hand, the last possible variant of political participation means very individualized and less community-oriented forms of political participation (Var. 4 of political participation). This includes various creative, expressive, personalized and singularized forms of participation. An example of this can be politically motivated consumption (van Deth 2014a: 358 f.). What is decisive here is the conscious and targeted form of action as well as the aspect of self-realization, as expressed in the ideas of do-it-yourself citizens, politics and democracy (Willis and Schor 2012; Bennett 2012; Ratto and Boler 2014; Lee 2015).

Finally, van Deth also demands the presence of (individually shaped) political motivation in the case of the previous three types of political participation, which only makes the classification final. Van Deth treats this dimension of motivation in isolation in order to be able to proceed more precisely with the method of determination (van Deth 2014a: 360). This approach of classifying and defining characteristics attempts to integrate the most diverse participation practices by not teleologically assigning characteristics to conditions, "the question is *how to include such aspects consistently*" (ibid.: 358).

However, van Deth's four definitions can again be based on the classical ideas of political participation (ibid.: 361): The first variant corresponds to the conventional forms of political participation (elections, party work, etc.), the second variant to the unconventional forms (petitions, political activism, etc.). The fourth and last definition of expressive political participation, on the other hand, describes individualized community action and personalized influence (political consumption, boycott) (see further typology of lifestyle politics in de Moor 2017, which divides into individual and collective forms and direct and indirect strategies).

Participation in the context of community energy initiatives would be part of the third variant of community problem-solving, which includes social and organizational participation. Here, however, comes the problem of the imprecision of the definition of civic engagement in civil society, as mentioned by van Deth, because it can include all kinds of actions. It remains unclear what exactly the terms "problems" and "community" mean, these would have to be specified. For example, they could be problems of public concern, such as climate protection. The effects of climate change as well as the use of renewable energies are felt by the entire public. The community approach to problem solving would also apply to the phenomenon of community energy initiatives in the form of a collective commitment by citizens. However, this is opposed by the private sector status, which is already excluded in van Deth's basic conditions. Therefore, this concept would particularly cover smaller amateur community energy initiatives without professional management, which are based on voluntary work and volunteerism.

In summary, the integration of civic engagement can be recorded. Civil society activity can be of a political or social nature and take place via conventional or unconventional forms. The concrete place of participation is irrelevant, but the sphere of the "institutional architecture of the political system" (polity level) must be affected (ibid.: 356).

This could possibly represent an interface between political and social participation that could be described as a "vastness of the political pre-space" (von Alemann and Strünck 1999). This would be an obvious model for thinking, since in the extended forums of political participation, such as Local Agenda groups, climate protection initiatives and forums, political issues are explicitly addressed. Community energy initiatives and environmental clubs and associations active in this field are often in contact with these forums in the local environment, and in some cases these initiatives even take the role of organizers and promoters. This would make highly probable an influence on political decision-making processes through proximity, exchange and contact with the political system and would likely widen the scope of discussions within the public sphere (see hypothesis by Hälterlein 2015).

In the context of community energy, a step towards sustainably motivated consumption is not far off. Those involved in community energy projects primarily make a financial decision to purchase. So they do not "consume" a product or the like directly. However, the starting position is very similar: here and there, a financial decision should primarily be made to achieve an idealistically motivated goal (climate protection, ecology, common property, strengthening the community and region, etc.) (in the sense of green or sustainable consumption, see Kinnear et al. 1974; Roberts 1996; Straughan and Roberts 1999; Zarnikau 2003; Goldblatt 2005; Kühling 2014). In some cases, there may even be a link between consumption and community energy participation. By setting up and operating their own heat or electricity networks, citizens can become consumers of the heat or electricity they produce themselves (prosuming), thus closing the circle of independent production and individually controlled consumption (see Rifkin 2014: 135 ff.; Hellmann 2018). Both community energy and sustainable consumption thus have the potential to generate social, economic and technical innovations (Cohen et al. 2013b). Finally, for this study the question remains open whether, analogous to politicized consumption (Lamla and Neckel 2006), community energy also represents a politicized form of, in this case, civil society-economic action.

The proximity of conscious and reflected consumption and production practices and diverse participation possibilities in this context is thus clearly evident. The significance of the citizen role and shaping power in the area of consumption and related topics has meanwhile been described in a differentiated manner in the literature (see Kreß et al. 2014a, 2014b; Rubik and Kreß 2014; Rubik et al. 2014). The committed climate citizens can assume different roles in the case of community energy. According to Rubik and Kreß (2014: 4), these relate on the one hand to the private (energy consumption in the household) and the public sphere (influence on the development of renewable energies as an investor or producer, as in the case of community energy, and as a political actor in the context of local energy policy); on the other hand, in addition to the two roles of energy consumer and investor/producer, they also play "through (social and political) support/commitment" and "social effects (education, finding public opinion)" (ibid.: 2 f.). The latter two roles in particular would imply a clear proximity to political participation, since the initially monetary participation is in unity with further social and/or political participation in the energy or climate protection topic area (e.g., participation in local climate protection initiatives), as well as spillover effects on the environment (demonstration effects, inciting further participation of acquaintances, neighbourhood, creation or use of further participation opportunities, etc.) and can form a starting point for further participation in other areas (see Kreß et al. 2014b; Rubik et al. 2014).

In the case of the community energy construction, a collaborative chain of action in the sense of prosuming is also possible (Toffler 1980; Hanekop and Wittke 2010; Juntunen 2014; Rifkin 2014: 135 ff.; Hellmann 2018). This makes it possible to individually shape production and consumption, starting with an idea-finding phase, through the development and financing of (energy) production, to independently controllable use and consumption. Particularly noteworthy is the individualistic character of these participation and design patterns. To a considerable extent, the individual can decide on questions of design (e.g., organization of a production community), the type and amount of financial participation, the placement and type of technical equipment and the consumption of the energy produced (type, use and intensity).

The starting point of sustainable consumption and financial, social and organizational participation in community energy initiatives is therefore a very individual willingness to act for conscious consumption, as well as membership and design of community projects. Motivation and impetus for action are individually determined and defined; thus, from a research point of view, they can only be determined individually, which could be complicated. As the motivations of a person will probably fluctuate and be ambiguous, they are often not concretely ascertainable. Further problems may arise from the phenomenon of social desirability in the case of information on motivation in the case of surveys (ecology appears more desirable than return). Furthermore, motivations are often hybrid and represent a conglomerate of different ideas, wishes and conceptions. Therefore, a coupling of measured motivations and concrete individual courses of action could be useful for determining and classifying forms of participation (de Moor, for example, only refers to courses of action, see de Moor 2017: 6).

Ultimately, it remains questionable whether the new individualized – whether web, consumption or monetary based – forms of participation can be classified as political. Sigrid Baringhorst refers to van Deth's new understanding of political participation, according to which this attribution is based on the assessment of the participants themselves (see Baringhorst 2016a, 2016b). However, it is precisely this self-definition of political sphere and activity that is apparently still conventionally undertaken by participants: political space is perceived as that of parties and parliaments, individual consumption is not itself experienced as political action (Baringhorst 2016a, 2016b: 52 f.). The relevant question here, however, is whether this self-attribution should be decisive at all. Rather, it can be considered obvious that in the case of an activity by citizens that is in some way tangential to public concerns (e.g., dealing with issues of public, not purely private or economic relevance), its attribution to political forms of participation and engagement seems obvious. Independently of this, the question of the place of participation addressed by van Deth seems to be answerable: Whether the citizen's action takes place in private or public space may make a difference with regard to its mode of action, but it does not change anything about the assignment to the political (e.g., a political statement that is disseminated in private space via online media does not lose its political location). Nevertheless, private or public spaces can also be identified on the internet, such as public or closed member forums. The boundaries here are very fluid and seem to be a question of public access and dissemination. Content, form as well as context (private or public) are therefore relevant for the classification of political participation.

The possibilities of virtual participation and exchange also exhibit a strongly individualistic and privatistic character. In the case of online participation, the individual has a very strong and self-determined influence on any input and output of expression; the degree of possible control and steering exceeds any form of non-electronic communication. At the same time, control can also slip away if personal statements made can no longer be taken back; moreover, manipulations are possible.

Furthermore, individualized forms of participation exhibit characteristics of capitalization, market conformity and the individualized forms of life of liberalism, as post-democracy theorists argue. In contrast, however, it is precisely collective forms of action and forms of joint exchange and cooperation that are emerging, which, as it were, exhibit an interweaving with individualized practice, e.g., individually regulated use of energy/heat with simultaneous joint forms of operation in the case of community energy (see Dolata and Schrape 2013b; Baringhorst 2016a, 2016b). Thus, fundamentally opposing forms of a privatistic component of participation (see on this Papacharissi 2010 and Sennett 2014: "tyranny of intimacy") would be combined with less individualistic-private-spatial forms of public participation and living together as described by Adloffet al. (2014) ("convivialism" as forms of living together "beyond the growth society") and Welzer ("communities of practice", e.g., cooperatives: Welzer 2013: 185 ff.; Welzer et al. 2014) as well as Sommer and Welzer (2014) described, coincide. Therefore, in terms of motives, demands, uses, organizational constructions and social modes of action, a hybridization of forms of action and participation can be stated.

For there is a multitude of ambiguities in these hybrid forms, such as in the area of consumption: "Sustainable consumption, for example, is often embedded in complex forms of self-production or of exchanging, recycling or repairing products. (…) In solidarity farming, organic farmers and consumers find new forms of direct networking bypassing trade; repair cafés become popular places where consumers exchange technical knowledge and support each other to extend the life of electronic devices and thus avoid e-waste" (Baringhorst 2016a, 2016b: 56). Above all, practicality and a direct reference to application are typical expressions of the experimentation of exchange and collaboration: "Sustainable prosumers and produsers are trying to work together on practical solutions to the major challenges of climate change and a future with dwindling raw materials, especially fuels. They create experimental niches for participatory innovation, which, according to republican understanding, are considered neither political nor conducive to democracy" (Baringhorst 2016a, 2016b: 56 f.). While community energy initiatives, like consumption practices, contain strong monetary-economic components, they also offer their members opportunities to influence internal decision-making and will-forming processes (co-determination, organizational participation). In conjunction with virtual and local networking opportunities, an independent pattern of participation can therefore emerge. Consequently, in this context, the adoption and application of the idea of an integrative way of looking at and recording different forms of participation seems to make sense (integrative theory of participation, see Vilmar 1977).

This reveals a closeness to creative and experimental democratic forms of participation, as discussed in various facets in the literature (Micheletti and McFarland 2011; de Nève 2013; Lamla 2013). The idea of "Do-It-Yourself-Citizenship" aptly captures this manifestation of a strongly self-aware citizen role in the form of civic influence as an independent form of action (Ratto and Boler 2014), as does "Do-It-Yourself-Democracy" (Lee 2015). However, this idea of creative participation cannot be stated in the creation of purely monetary participation options as in the case of community energy initiatives. As has been shown, a kind of creative individual participation arrangement can be achieved through linked, neighboring forms of participation and modes of action as well as social effects (e.g., simultaneous membership in community energy initiative, environmental association, climate protection initiative and green electricity consumption). To what extent this linkage of different forms of participation and perception of several citizen roles in different contexts could be given and which individual motivations and practices of "collaborative problem solving" are present in community energy initiatives, will be investigated in the present work. Previous study results already point to the linkage of citizen roles, social effects and the presence and benefits of multiple modes of participation in the thematic field of energy (see Kreß et al. 2014b: 17; Rubik et al. 2014: 17).

In summary, in the case of activities such as community energy, urban gardening and car sharing, a new form of participation with an individualistic character and a flexible structure in its form and practice can be identified, which presumably results on the one hand from the individual practices (e.g., a wide variety of monetary and, in particular, virtual modes of influence and contribution) and the differentiation of the structures of the scopes of application (e.g., varying consumption practices depending on the context, project character of community energy initiatives, etc.).

Hereby, a subject-centered view of participation becomes concise, which is strongly characterized by intrinisic motives and views of the participants (individualistic participation in bottom-up mode, more creative, creation of *invented space*). This would have to be distinguished from externally animated motivations and suggestions for action, which, for example, can often be initiated by social movements and organizations (NGOs), campaigns and initiatives, and which already offer concrete, already established steps and instructions for action, which can be directly taken up and adopted by the subject (more top-down participation offers, less creative, creation of *invited space*). Of course, it cannot be ruled out that the individualized form of participation is also due to stimulation from outside. These stimuli and linkages would in turn have to be determined individually at the subject level. The significance of the social structure ("who participates?") and the individual understanding of participation ("how is participation perceived and described?") move into the focus of research interest.

2.2.2 Financial Participation

In addition to the classic-conventional and unconventional types of participation, financial participation can also be considered, which represents participation through financial shares, for example through donations, foundations, etc., where a financial contribution is intended to serve a "good purpose". The decisive factor here is the recipient of the benefit: securities tend not to be counted as monetary participation, but support for a local association, a local initiative (saving an indoor swimming pool, etc.) or a direct measure (purchasing school books, etc.) is likely to be similar to local involvement – in a more or less passive form. Monetary participation does not exclude active engagement, but as a single aspect it is likely to correspond more to "silent participation" in the majority.

Stadelmann-Steffen and Traunmüller speak here of a "chequebook participation" and emphasize an upheaval of classic social and political forms of participation towards individualized, non-binding and thus sometimes also monetary forms, such as in the field of donation culture (Stadelmann-Steffen and Traunmüller 2010: 345). The authors stress: "Although this development is definitely viewed critically and such 'chequebook participation' is often regarded as an inferior form of civil society participation (…), the positive side of this form of participation is also increasingly being discussed" (ibid.). Such activities as donations would not be directed "primarily at official representatives of the political system" ("extra-representational"), moreover, financial support could be terminated at any time ("exit-based") (ibid.). Such a commitment represents a "highly effective use of community energy", the giving of money can "despite little effort, often be more effective than active cooperation or participation in an interest group or in a local association" (ibid.: 345). Moreover, it has the advantage of being easily accessible to large groups of the population, "it seems to attract a group of people who would not otherwise participate politically" and is therefore to be considered better than no involvement at all, it can even lead to a "formation of a sense of community" (ibid.: 345 f.).

2.2.3 Organizational Participation

Organizational participation means participation, involvement and influence of persons, that is, members in associations, organizations and companies, for example, through group work and co-management (Blümle et al. 2012), traditionally guaranteed through co-determination opportunities (organizational democracy).[32] A recurring research question relates to the proof of actual participation channels and use by employees (see critically on this Hoffjann et al. 2013, who speak of a participation myth; similarly on meaninglessness and instrumentalization Steger and Kranz 2014).

For a long time now, people have been thinking about participation in organizations such as business enterprises on the one hand and clubs and associations on the other, discussing a wide variety of ideas and concepts and finally often evaluating them against the backdrop of overarching social developments and policies. Organizational participation in both sectors of business and civil society has a longer tradition (see on participation in clubs and associations Hoffmann 2003; Zimmer 2007). Particularly since the formative processes of industrialization, with the jobs created in new workplaces and workshops, the participation and co-determination of the worker or employee played an essential role with regard to the social question (working conditions), but also the democratic demand (and the genuinely democratic basic idea) for participation and the possibility of involvement beyond a mere work for the purpose of earning money, without any ties to the company ("workplace democracy": Weber and Höge 2009). A research strand of industrial democracy or organizational democracy, *workplace democracy* and co-determination extended in the post-war period into the 1980s and 1990s (see Crouch and Heller 1983; Wilpert and Sorge 1984; Stern and McCarthy 1986; Dew 1997; Heller 1998, 2000). With the legal anchoring of co-determination, perhaps also justified by other zeitgeisty motives, the orientation of scientific research increasingly dried up. Such fields of research – including cooperative research with a long history – seem "dusty" in today's scientific research systems (as well as in other areas of society), hardly capable of being taken up; which is why the question arises as to whether a renaissance is possible under changed conditions or whether completely different research approaches are developing, perhaps even this branch is not directly capable of continuation. In fact, some questions have recently been taken up

[32] See co-determination research: Schaffer and Eidherr 1973; Ahlbrecht 1976; von Mitschke-Collande 1977; Barthel and Dikau 1980; Wilpert and Rayley 1983; Diefenbacher et al. 1984; Kißler 1989; Greifenstein et al. 1991, 1993; Wilpert 1997; Frick 1999; Kommission Mitbestimmung 1999; Niedenhoff 2005; Herbert 2008; Andersen 2009; Greifenstein and Kißler 2010; Kißler et al. 2011; Weninger 2011; Kolbe 2013; Rügenhagen 2013; Lowitzsch et al. 2014; Lowitzsch et al. 2014; Wilkinson 2014; Owetschkin 2016.

again by researchers (see, for example, contributions by Philip Pettit on democracy and learning in organizations in Griffin et al. 2015).[33]

Parallel to the very concrete and practical question of co-determination of employees in a company or organization as a basic principle, it can be discussed on a theoretical level to what extent principles of democracy can in principle also be applied to associations, organizations and companies – this can be seen in the frequently discussed concept of economic democracy and organizational democracy alone. Broken down again to the individual level, the (state) citizen would become active in civic role thinking as an economic and organizational citizen, or adopt such a self-image, which would attempt to reconcile both democratic ideals and principles and logics of economics and organizationalism. This view is again reminiscent of the different spheres of shifting involvements: between private action in the private sphere and action in the public sphere as a citizen of the state – extended by action as an employee at the workplace in the interest of the company and organization. Different logics of action, structure and system confront the citizen, who can adopt uniform patterns of action in a citizen role, but also strongly divergent modes of action in different roles depending on the context.

A perspective of organizational democracy approach would

- focus individually on the employee's rights and opportunities for action;
- collectively consider the actions and strategies of the organization in terms of equity, influence, fairness, transparency, etc.;
- reveal dynamics and effects of power, interests, conflicts and tendencies such as oligarchic developments;
- understand participation as co-determination, collaboration and (procedural as well as process-related) justice;

[33] See on recent research of participation in business: Rothschild and Whitt 1986; Arlt 1999; Baglioni 1999; Weber 1999; Weber et al. 2003; Vilmar and Weber 2004; Weber 2004a, 2004b; Demirović 2007; Weber et al. 2007, 2012; Weber et al. 2008; Moldaschl and Weber 2009; Schmid 2009; Weber and Höge 2009; Weber et al. 2009; Weber and Lampert 2010; Wegge et al. 2010; Unterrainer et al. 2011; Fricke 2012; Hemetsberger 2012; Lind 2012; Ostendorf and Thoma 2012; Weber and Moldaschl 2012; Weber and Unterrainer 2012; Verdorfer et al. 2013.

- define the individual citizen role as a synthesis of community responsibility and the interests of the organization as well as economic modes of action.

Organizational participation basically describes participation within the organization, in terms of opportunities for participation and co-determination, but especially in terms of its effects within and outside the organization. In the past (and so also today), "internal" participation primarily represented co-determination (opportunities) within the company or the constituted organization.

Within research, the effects in terms of increasing effectiveness and efficiency as well as satisfaction (of the participants) have been studied for a long time (Wilpert 1994: 295). In essence, it is about participation in decision-making processes and to what extent participation here includes the delegation of decision-making powers (ibid.). Bernhard Wilpert advocates a rather broad understanding of organizational participation, which in turn contains the distinction between direct vs. representative as well as self-determined modes of action: "Participation is the totality of forms, i.e. direct (personal) or indirect (through representatives or institutions), and of intensities, i.e. ranging form minimal to comprehensive, by which individuals, groups or collectives secure their interests through self-determined choices among possible actions" (ibid.). Thus Wilpert emphasizes the distinctive features contained:

- safeguarding interests through various courses of action,
- goal-oriented courses of action by individuals or groups,
- direct-personal or representative representation of interests,
- varying efficiency in safeguarding interests.

Furthermore, the relevance of informal participation processes is pointed out; interestingly, the higher relevance is given to the outcome of decisions compared to the process of decision-making. Motivational foundations and participative competence are named as prerequisites for organizational participation, social prerequisites consist of the organizational value system, organizational structures, technology, participative structures, organizational processes and the organizational environment. Concerning the participative structures, Wilpert points to the definition of the International Research Group "Industrial Democracy in Europe" (IDE): "the totality of all formal (i.e., written down) operational rules and regulations that prescribe a certain involvement of various groups in intra-organizational decision making" (ibid.: 300). Of perhaps greater importance, however, are the effects of participative structures with regard to de facto participation, which, according to studies in various countries, show a clear correlation: "participative structures have proved to be among the best predictors of de facto participation" (ibid.: 300). Accordingly, the will to participate also generates actual participation processes: "This is an important finding, since it illustrates the phenomenon of participation to be a result of socio-political will" (ibid.). Moreover, it can be confirmed that the commitment of leaders to participation and active membership of members in participatory bodies in turn generates de facto-participation, moreover, essential knowledge and skills are acquired, which in turn are necessary for further participation (ibid.). In this respect, Wilpert supports the older, individualistic theory of Mulder (1977, "the daily power game"), according to which what matters is the reduction of power differences at the individual level (Wilpert 1994: 299, 305).

In this definition, a distinction is made between two modes of participation at a process level:

- direct participation (participative management, firmly anchored working group participation) and
- indirect (representative) participation ("indirect participation encompasses both intermediate decision making and reaching these decisions without prior consultation with those represented, but viewing their perceived needs") (psychologically with regard to communication, interactions and modes of perception, structurally with regard, for example, to oligarchic tendencies through the design of elections, rotation principles and periods of office, inter-organizationally with regard to networks of organizations) (Wilpert 1994: 303).

Finally, Wilpert identifies different kinds of effects of organizational participation (ibid.: 304 ff.):

- Individual level (rising expectations versus demotivation, personal development and acquisition of competences as well as transfer of competences into other areas of life. Wilpert emphasizes the question, which is difficult to answer, of whether participatory competence or participatory experience must first exist and suspects a reciprocal double interaction in the sense of a circular process (ibid.: 308): “the exertion of power, being associated with positive sentiments, leads to increased motivation to reduce power distance form upper hierarchical levels with, in turn, implies gaining further experience through exercise of power, leading to higher levels of aspirations, etc.”).
- Organizational level (significance of conflicts, represents an old question in participation research, for which there is mutual evidence; Wilpert himself assumes a general (i.e., positive as well as negative) increase in conflicts, which is in the nature of participation; organizational climate/culture/identity/image; productivity; quality of decisions).
- Social level: with regard to spillover effects of a democratization of the whole society (Wilpert differentiates here “this will depend mainly on the factual degress of learning transfer from organizational participatory experience to the other life roles of individuals”, he also points to little empirical confirmation) (ibid.: 307).

Organizational research continues to emphasize the importance of organizational justice, group dynamics and commitment (identification with the organization), as well as questions of power (Coleman 1979); in addition, (economic) ethical considerations with regard to prosocial behavior,[34] democratization,[35] economic citizenship ethics,[36] etc. In addition, there is the associative-organizational aspect: participation in more or less organized groups of civil society (clubs, associations, citizens' initiatives, etc.). In the case of the implementation of democratic principles such as equality through internal organizational instruments of co-determination, the creation of opportunities for influence, principles such as transparency, fairness, equal treatment, etc., this is referred to in research as organizational democracy. The Chicago School in particular dealt with participation via social organization (Vortkamp 2003).

---

[34] Weber (2004b: 466) names as research desiderata of organizational research:

- Social perspective-taking at a higher level (willingness to take into account socio-economic concerns of the community, also beyond the current interaction situation and one's own interests under a far-reaching time horizon, including valid maxims of action).
- Socio-moral judgement competence and readiness for communicative action.
- Work- and community-related humanistic value orientations.
- Pro-social, civic work behaviour towards other company members (including willingness for mutual support, solidarity, knowledge sharing and building of common resources as an extended concept of organizational citizenship behavior.
- Organizational commitment, especially affective commitment to socially responsible companies.

In his own study of research cooperatives, Weber (ibid.: 468) first found a positive correlation between "the extent to which cooperative members (…) were involved in decision-making (…) and the willingness to act pro-socially towards the cooperative and its members (…) reported by respondents" (ibid.: 468). Second, a relationship exists between "the level of democratic participation and affective commitment (…)" (ibid.). "The more the cooperative members surveyed can have a say in their operational concerns, the more likely they are to identify with the values and goals of their company, the more they are committed to its concerns, including publicly, and the more likely they are to feel part of a community" (ibid.). On this question of the transformation from individual-utilitarian to pro-social action through cooperative behaviour, see also Weber 1998.

[35] Moldaschl and Weber (2009), for example, investigated the extent to which organizational participation can contribute to social democratization and came to the following conclusion (ibid.: 104): "Decision-making participation of employees and the sociomoral atmosphere are positively related to work-related solidarity and helpfulness, humanistic orientations and the willingness to get involved in democratic and social concerns in society. The same applies to the affective and normative commitment of employees towards their company".

[36] For a theoretical concept of integrative business ethics, see for example, von Ulrich (2008).

2.3 Social and Civil Society Participation

Social and civil society participation refers to any form of participation by citizens in semi-public or public space that cannot be assigned to the state or private sector sphere.[37] Typically, these are more or less organized activities in neighborhoods and districts as well as more formalized in citizens' initiatives, clubs and associations (subsumed under the collective term civil society associations: see Roßteutscher and van Deth 2002; Vogt 2005; Zimmer 2007, 2011; Zimmer and Speth 2009; Maloney and van Deth 2010; Priller et al. 2011; Böschen and Pfersdorf 2014; Zimmer and Simsa 2014). In participation literature, this broad range of civic activities is commonly circumscribed as social participation. The attribution "civil society" usually suggests that these are more or less organized modes of action within the framework of civil society associations. Roßteutscher, for example, defines social participation as the "myriad of opportunities for participation offered to the individual in a wide variety of groups in society: the football club, the singers' association, the self-help group or the welfare organization. Social participation always extends beyond purely private concerns, "but involvement in the family or circle of friends is not enough" (Roßteutscher 2009b: 162). Finally, Roßteutscher distinguishes between forms of participation that are directed at collectives ("volunteers running a soup kitchen") and those that are exercised collectively ("as a member of a station mission running a soup kitchen") (ibid.). She draws the line to political participation through the target dimension of explicitly influencing "decisions or decision-makers at different political levels" (ibid.). Social participation therefore means "as a rule public, collective action without direct political motivation", which "extends beyond the private sphere" (ibid.). Under the term public participation, Gensicke and Geiss also describe all activities that unfold within the framework of a civil society infrastructure (Gensicke and Geiss 2006: 311). Accordingly, political participation refers to "political purposes, in particular the exer-

[37] See on the discussion of questions of demarcation between political and social participation van Deth 2001 and on the connection with local participation Bühler 1997; Detjen 2000; Wollmann 2002 and Vetter 2008.

tion of influence on political decisions", while social participation refers to the "whole range of other purposes around which civil society revolves, e.g., sporting and cultural activities in clubs and associations, help for the socially disadvantaged and the weak in institutions and initiatives, involvement in the voluntary fire brigade and rescue services, for environmental protection" (...). Social participation is understood here in the sense of van Deth (2004: 297), who focuses on influencing decision-making within the various organizational forms of civil society. He defines social participation as "all activities that citizens undertake voluntarily within social organizations" (van Deth 2001: 208).[38]

The question of demarcation between political and social participation seems to be increasingly problematic due to the expansion of the concept of political participation. It seems unclear where extended political participation in the area of civil society activity should end and where social participation should begin. Keil refers here to the arguably inseparable amalgam of political and social participation: "What is defined as social participation today depends to a large extent on individual motivation, because in the meantime the boundaries between social and political participation are becoming blurred due to the enormous expansion of participation opportunities" (Keil 2013a: 159, see also Keil 2012).[39] Therefore, Keil takes a specific definition of social participation in organizations (Keil 2013b: 55):

[38] Jan van Deth (2001) considered the relationship between social and political participation ("alternatives, complements or twins?"). He argues that "both types of activities are closely linked and support (or inhibit) each other. The two forms are therefore seen as complements rather than alternatives or twins" (van Deth 2001: 195). Van Deth therefore assumes that participation generates participation (thought of in both directions).

[39] Silke Keil increasingly sees the "boundaries between political and non-political disappearing and citizens choosing the appropriate means to achieve their goals" (Keil 2013a: 177). These goals of citizens' political action "do not in principle have to be disposed of by political means", "which means that participation nowadays has to be defined broadly". Following Jan van Deth (2009: 141), Silke Keil suggests that ultimately, actually everything a person does can be considered political participation at some point (Keil 2013a: 176 f.). In her way of thinking and arguing, Keil explicitly refers to the areas of political consumption and boycott.

"What is social participation?" As mentioned above, the study of social activity in voluntary organizations forms a classic object of investigation in participation research. Despite the large number of studies, there are few systematic considerations, but a variety of different conceptualizations of the term social participation. Often, the context or the research question determines the definition and delimitation of the term. If, for example, the connection between social and political participation is the focus of research interest, the delimitation or the similarities and differences between these two forms are formulated. Keil limits social participation to organizations: "Accordingly, the term refers exclusively to organization-related activities and does not include other forms of collective action in informal groups. (…) And regardless of whether participation is passive membership, occasional activity, or regular active volunteering, all activities have the following characteristics in common: They are unpaid, voluntary and carried out together with others; they serve to participate in the shaping of collective affairs and are not directed at political addressees (…)" (ibid.: 55 f.).[40] Despite this limitation to civic engagement in civil society associations, however, it remains unclear when an orientation towards political addressees should be present and when not: the sphere of the political can also be reached by an association or federation if this does not explicitly correspond to the specified content orientation.[41] This would result in a

[40] Furthermore, Keil emphasizes that social participation does not have to be related only to formalized structures: "Social engagement can have many manifestations and not only take place in associations. In informal terms, there is also a broad field of activity: people help other people, family members stand by each other in emergency situations, people meet with friends and get involved in projects together, they work in professional contexts to solve various problems, etc. However, formal involvement in clubs and associations is usually considered to play a more significant role in civil society than informal participation. Particularly in the context of theories of social modernization and social integration, they are seen as a necessary link between primary groups and state institutions" (Keil 2013b: 53).

[41] On the connection of civil society associations to local politics and democracy see Hallmann 2005 and on the networking function of cooperatives between municipalities, citizens and business Bauer et al. 2014; on the one hand, functions of civil society associations as a "democratic productive force" (Rucht 1997), on the other hand as a counterforce to representative elements of democracy are discussed ("check the parliament", Paulsen et al. 2008).

case-by-case approach, which also corresponds to the newer approach to political participation (which must be determined concretely in each individual case, e.g., on the basis of motivations).

Social participation is further associated with the transmission of social competences, democratic values and norms, political mobilization (due to diverse contacts to the political sphere, Roßteutscher 2009b: 167) and the formation of social capital. Roßteutscher divides social capital here into system capital, which refers to institutions (their number, activity, cooperation) and relational capital (referring to the social relations of individuals, with conditions of trust, solidarity and cooperation). However, the negative dimension of social capital should not be ignored. Roßteutscher describes this primarily in terms of in-group effects: "Why should people who have learned to trust each other in the close-knit small group pass this trust on to unknown people outside the group? Is it not at least as plausible to expect that precisely because trust is based on regular cooperation in the group, it will initially be withdrawn from people who are outside the group?" (ibid.: 175). Already since the studies of Robert Putnam, a distinction has been made between *bridging* and *bonding* social capital (see Putnam et al. 1993; Putnam 2000)[42]: bridging effects between associations (positively evaluated because of presumed higher orientation towards the common good) and bonding forces between members, which can lead to encapsulation and exclusion (clientelism). In the second

[42] Following Pierre Bourdieu (see Bourdieu 1983) and Robert Putnam (see Putnam et al. 1993; Putnam 2000), social capital is defined by Westle and Gabriel (2008: 5) "as a construct consisting of three elements: 1) social relationships, as they arise primarily from activities in associations and other types of networks, 2) a fundamental trust in one's fellow human beings and 3) certain values and norms that support thinking and acting in solidarity with the community. (…) This is postulated: The more social capital (i.e., the more involvement in associations, the more trust and the more community values and norms) there is in a society, the better democracy and the welfare state function, and the more likely it is that the manifold evils and distortions of modernity can be avoided." See also Coleman 1988; Baron et al. 2000; Dekker and Uslaner 2001; Gabriel et al. 2002; Klein et al. 2004a; Smith et al. 2004; Franzen and Freitag 2007; Maloney and Roßteutscher 2007; Castiglione et al. 2008; Häuberer 2011; Badura et al. 2013; Li 2015.

case, there are strong *trust* effects (*thick trust*), which then result in the exclusion of all individuals who do not fit into the tightly woven network of the included. This also leads to negative external effects, in that the ability to "receive resources and information from outside the group" is hardly formed; the opposite is true in the case of associations with bridging social capital (Roßteutscher 2009b: 175).

Social capital effects can also be applied to the external and internal space of associations, in the case of inclusive social capital through "generalized trust and norms of reciprocity arising from social networks with a collective goods orientation", and in the case of exclusive social capital through "personalized trust and specific norms of reciprocity arising from interactions in social networks with a private goods orientation" (ibid.: 176).

The part of civil society that is active in the public sphere thus consists of associations (groupings of individuals, more or less organized) and – either within the framework of this or outside it – committed citizens (civic engagement) (Roßteutscher and van Deth 2002; Maloney and van Deth 2010). The spectrum ranges from less or more organized and formalized organizations (small initiatives often weaker, large associations more formalized and organized), the time horizon can be limited (as is often the case with citizens' initiatives to achieve a single goal) or unlimited and long-term (organizations such as associations and cooperatives).

There is a wide range of research desiderata on civic engagement (engagement research) and the modes of action and structures of civil society associations (association and federation research), from which an overall picture of activities and processes of institutionalization can, however, only be depicted with difficulty due to the complexity. In recent years in particular, the importance of civil society associations has been emphasized time and again: Sebastian Braun coined the phrase "rediscovery of associations in the slipstream of social crises" (Braun 2006). Civil society associations have long been studied in the social sciences in association and organization research (Koch-Baumgarten 2014). In the context of the present study, civil society associations play a role in the form of citizens' initiatives,[43] cooperatives[44] (especially energy

[43] See Ebert 1974; Hättich 1978, 1984; Gabriel 1983, 2000; Simon 1983b; Guggenberger and Kempf 1984; Schneider-Wilkes 2001; Dachwitz 2002; Pappi 2004; Guggenberger 2009; Wolling and Bräuer 2010; Klausen and Winsvold 2012.

[44] Research on cooperatives is very complex, describing, among other things, the following topics (for an overview, see Michie et al. 2015):

- Avoidance of yield orientation (Purtschert 2013).
- Function as a link between market and civil society and promoter of community transformations (Alscher 2011, 2012).
- Function as an organizational form of civic engagement (Alscher and Priller 2007).
- Function with a socialist claim (Altvater 2012).
- Function as an alternative form of economy (Bierbau 2008), sustainable and socially just way of doing business (Münkner 2012), form of social market economy (Schmale 2012), as "responsible entrepreneurship" (Emmelius and Krönlein 2012).
- Place of generation of social innovation and sustainable development (Elsen 2012).
- Place of cooperation (Flieger 1996, 2008, 2011; Göler von Ravensburg 2012) and participation (Mori 2014).
- Place with democratic decision-making and (member) participation (Flieger 2002, 2006).
- Shaping internal issues: collaborative business operation (Kober 2010), member orientation and closeness to the member (Nonn 2012; Zeuch 2012), corporate culture (Schaumann 2011), value-based organizational form (ex. trust, Steiner and Schütt 2011 and Ringle 2007 and common good orientation Malowitz 2002, transparency and values Ringle 2012a), issue of conflict and compatibility between shareholder value and member value (Ringle 2012b), cultural core and value concepts (Ringle 2012c, 2012e, 2013b), communication (Ringle 2012d).
- Idea of member orientation: promotion mission (Ringle and Göler von Ravensburg 2010; Ringle 2010), member promotion and member values (Gmür 2011; Ringle 2013a; Suter 2013; Theurl 2013), member retention (Ringle 2005) active membership (Ringle 2003, 2006) contradiction between member retention and economics (Horsthemke 2002).
- Commitment of the cooperative idea in the present (Thiemann and Armbruster 2000), summed up by Warbasse (1926) as "cooperative democracy achieved by voluntary association of people as consumers".
- Link to the local context of the municipality and neighbourhood (Cordes 2003; Brachmann 2009), as promoter of social urban development (König 2004).

cooperatives[45]), and environmental associations.

It tends to be difficult to distinguish civil society associations from other social organizations. At first glance, a separation of state and civil society is easy to identify – however, there are known cooperations, jointly managed enterprises, etc., where one must speak of a mixed or hybrid arrangement (as in the case of public-private partnerships); especially since many cases are known in which the state is at least a silent partner or supporter. In some cases, it is even more difficult to draw a precise distinction between civil society and the private sector. In principle, a distinction can be made in such a way that a "classic" civil society association cannot pursue purely economic principles (such as the exclusive generation of profit/return) and that neither the purpose nor the meaning can be derived exclusively from economic criteria (nonprofit organizations).

There is no doubt that such (mostly voluntary) associations can be found – such as the traditional association, in which people with common interests meet to exchange ideas with a rather subordinate or even no economic purpose. However, the following must be considered here: on the one hand, all social actors are dependent on fundamental economic principles that have an effect on society as a whole (e.g., incurring and covering costs). On the other hand, civil society associations have to operate in order to maintain a sustainable structure (to an ever-greater extent as structures grow and differentiate). Here, a clear scale phenomenon emerges (see Keil 2013b): the larger the association becomes, the more economic issues come to the fore. The explanation for this is obvious – on a small scale, activities can be fulfilled on the one hand through the voluntary principle (i.e., free of charge), and on the other hand, costs can be kept within limits (e.g., meetings in private rooms,

---

[45] Research now covers the following aspects and areas:

- General descriptions/analyses (Degenhart and Holstenkamp 2010, 2011; Volz 2011a; Weismeier-Sammer and Reiner 2011; Wieg 2011; Maron and Maron 2012; Bayer 2013; Holstenkamp and Müller 2013; Staab 2016; Yildiz 2014).
- Overview (Hielscher 2011; Weismeier-Sammer and Reiner 2011), scientific research perspectives (Yildiz et al. 2015).
- Approach for the successful establishment of renewable energies (Viardot 2013) as well as for structural change (Klemisch 2014a, 2014b), remunicipalization measures and for securing services of general interest (Klemisch and Maron 2010; Klemisch and Boddenberg 2013).
- Findings on financial-economic-organizational conditions (Debor 2014).
- Benefits (Flieger 2011, 2012; Klemisch and Vogt 2012), multiplication and spillover effects (Volz 2012a, 2012b).
- Implementation of the funding mandate (Volz 2011b).
- Often rural reference, but also challenge and solution urban areas (Bär and Thunecke 2011; Müller and Rommel 2011).
- The place of social innovation through grassroots, bottom-up activity (Seyfang and Haxeltine 2012; Smith and Seyfang 2013; Hielscher et al. 2013a, 2013b; Seyfang et al. 2014).

etc.). However, as the association grows, costs will increase, for example, for the administration of members, paid staff (if the effort exceeds the level of voluntary leisure activity), for communication (letters to members, etc.) and for events and activities. It is true that for a long time many associations have been supported by membership fees, donations, etc. Recently, however, a further increase in economic orientation has been observed, which involves increasing economization and monetization.

The focus of this study is on civil society participation. In this respect, the research on the one hand highlights positive characteristics (e.g., of nonprofit organizations) as well as negative aspects of the organizations and their spread ("dark sides of civil society"). On the other hand, associations with regard to specific characteristics (internal principles, mechanisms and behaviors as well as communication in external relations with other actors, etc.) are subjected to deeper analyses. Through their networking function, associations and organizations can form social capital: here a distinction is made between positive and negative social capital,[46] recently functions are also discussed under the term sustainability (Theuvsen 2013).[47] The thematic orientation and objects of investigation of social capital and civil society research are in many respects congruent.

[46] Dark sides of community and civil society associations such as corruption, exclusion, oligarchy, imbalance in the overall social influence, clientelism, cronyism, etc. are discussed in the literature by Fiorina (1999), Nullmeier (2002), Roth (2003, 2004, 2008), Adloff (2005), Munsch (2005), Stecker and Nährlich (2005), Zimmer (2003, 2007), Clarke (2008b), Fehren (2008), Geißel (2008a), Staeheli (2008), van Deth and Zmerli (2010), Klatt et al. (2011), and Gmür (2013b), Schäfer (2013a), Simsa and Zimmer (2014), and Wilde (2014).

[47] Sebastian Braun examined a wide variety of social aspects in associationism, such as solidarity, community and common good (Braun 2004), as well as voluntary associations "as catalysts and producers of social capital" (Braun 2003, 2007), similarly "associations as catalysts of social and political competences" (Braun et al. 2007) and "associative lifeworld, binding social capital and communities of choice of taste" (Braun 2009) (see on this already Simon 1983a). In addition, Vortkamp was able to make contributions to the question of "integration through participation and participation through citizen engagement in associations and associated civil society potential" (Vortkamp 2005, 2008). – See further studies on the question of whether civil society associations can serve as carriers of solidarity, community and common good (Braun 2004). Further topics concern the creation of associative lifeworlds, binding social capital and communities of taste (Braun 2009; Bühlmann and Freitag 2007), the question of the connection between social inequality, social capital and subjective quality of life (Oshege 2002; Jütting et al. 2003; Geißel 2004a; Geißel et al. 2004; Hartmann 2009; Hellmann 2004; Kern 2004; Stecker 2005; Diekmann 2007a; Diewald and Lüdicke 2007; Franzen and Freitag 2007; Kriesi 2007a; Gabriel 2010), creation or equalization of inequality (Lüdicke 2007; Manske 2007; Keil 2013b) as well as formation of social capital in the context of entrepreneurial activity (Preisendörfer 2007) and an exclusionary effect of social capital (Vogt 2009).

In this study, community energy projects or companies are analyzed as (more or less distinct) nonprofit organizations. The research on these associations mainly emphasizes questions regarding

- positive and negative effects and conditions of civil society structures in terms of "aspiration and reality" (e.g., volunteerism under pressure, dangers of monetization and economization, generation of social capital and action for the common good, see Erlinghagen 2003, 2013)[48];
- internal modes of action within the associations are also mostly measured against a hypothetical ideal (e.g., formation of cooperative and collaborative structures, formation of communication processes and trust, emergence of reciprocal behavior and conflict, etc.).[49]

2.3.1 Discussion: Financial and Material, Organizational and Civic Participation in Community Energy Projects as a New Type of Political Participation?

Monetary and organizational forms of participation initially describe an economized form of participation, which only acquires membership or participation in a company through the acquisition of a financial share, which empowers co-determination. In this way, political participation is not yet achieved. According to van

[48] Effects such as organizational learning are analysed by Hansen 2008; Bono 2012 and Trumann 2013, as well as educational processes by Naumann 2010, local value creation by Flieger 2010, and innovation potential and trust-building through active co-determination by Kädtler et al. 2013 and Scholl et al. 2013; further effects relate, among other things, to communication in neighbourhoods (Danner et al. 2007), creation of community (Immerfall et al. 2010) and socialization services (Nobis 2012). On the importance of volunteering, see Janning and Bartjes 1999; Dettling 2000a, 2000b; Klages 2000a; Notz 2000; Erlinghagen 2003; Nitschke 2005; Zimmer 2005b; Priller 2010; Ehrhardt 2011 and Stricker 2011; for descriptions of parallel developments in civic engagement, gainful employment and organizational development, see Birkhölzer 2002 and Sprengel 2007.

[49] Examples of this can be conflicts between committees (Bürgisser 2011, 2012a, 2012b, between honorary/official (Bürgisser and Helmig 2009). See further criticisms such as "participation myth": Identifying lofty participation ideals and low (participation) supply in Hoffjann et al. 2013; in addition, a lack of willingness to take on responsible positions and their work between civic engagement and management (Zimmer 2005a; Beher et al. 2008; Deicher 2010; Wolf and Zimmer 2010; Liebig 2011) as well as problems regarding gender-specific aspects (Weg 2005) and power issues (Zimmer 2003) are described.

Deth's (2014a, 2014b) participation model, the decisive factor would be the location to which the form of participation refers; it would have to be assigned to the political sphere. This would be the case for community energy initiatives if they are not purely private-sector oriented companies, but there is a link with civic-voluntary engagement as well as a certain orientation towards the common good (i.e., no exclusive return orientation); possibly supplemented by political-social activities, e.g., in the context of local climate protection initiatives (see Walker and Devine-Wright 2008; Holstenkamp and Degenhart 2013). In addition to this determination of the actor characteristic, there is also the individual participation of the subject: purely monetary participation would not be sufficient for the existence of political participation, nor would the active use of co-determination opportunities in the organization's internal decision-making process (voting, etc.). First, politically motivated courses of action would have to be discernible (e.g., participation for climate protection, not for profit motives), which, secondly, would have to be related to topics, discourses or measures or projects that affect the public space (e.g., construction of a wind turbine, installation of a local heating network, operation of photovoltaic (PV) systems on non-private roofs – material participation, see Marres 2012). If these two conditions are met (firstly, the community energy initiative's orientation towards voluntarism, honorary offices and a certain degree of public interest orientation, secondly, subjective motivation from political public interest motives and individual understanding of the community energy initiative as a local political actor and not as a private business enterprise), the form of participation could be evaluated as an outflow of political participation (in the sense of *lifestyle politics,* related to the politicized everyday actions of citizens, see de Moor 2017). It can be assumed, however, that both the actor orientation and the individual motivation are heterogeneously composed. The decisive factor would then be the primary, action-guiding orientation of the project and individual motivation.

Civil Society Participation: Empirical Findings

According to a study on civil society associations by the Berlin Social Science Center (WZB), membership development of the associations studied is characterized by dynamism. Most of the civil society organizations surveyed reported rising membership figures (Priller et al. 2013: 5). For associations, cooperatives and foundations, engagement is a means of securing their existence (ibid.). Young people are thus underrepresented (ibid.), very many organizations work together with state institutions, companies and other civil society associations (ibid.: 6). This is mainly about exchanging information and carrying out joint actions, rather than jointly recruiting volunteers (ibid.). Rather little is done for transparency: "To promote transparency, more conventional instruments, e.g., targeted media work or public access to documents, are still used. Organizations rarely participate in concrete transparency initiatives" (ibid.).

Accordingly, financial support from the state is decreasing, while a "large proportion of organizations are registering an increase in competition. (…) Above all, the increase in performance-based forms of financing is relevant here. The spread of business management instruments, e.g., cost and performance accounting, quality management as well as further controlling measures, speaks for an increased economic orientation" (ibid.: 7). However, the authors counter this: "Despite these tendencies towards economization, the orientation towards the common good retains a high value. This is both an expression of the traditional involvement of the organizations in social contexts and of the adherence to their ideal mission" (ibid.). The biggest problems are those with the state (in the first place, resulting from financial dependence), in addition to a competitive relationship with private-sector companies for tasks and fields of activity (ibid.). In addition, "ageing and the declining sense of community are major problems of associations and cooperatives" (ibid.). Nonprofit limited liability companies "complain in particular about the increasing pressure for efficiency and competition as well as the lack of planning security due to unclear revenue developments" (ibid.).

According to the 2013 Data Report, the number of association members has been stagnating at around 600,000 for several years (Alscher and Priller 2013: 350). Central problems of civil society organizations (as also shown in the WZB study of 2009, see Alscher et al. 2009) are a lack of planning security due to unclear revenue development, increasingly market-like structures, as well as efficiency and competitive pressure, ageing and a declining sense of community in the organization (Alscher and Priller 2013: 353). Cooperatives name the last three points to a pronounced degree.

Overall involvement has been rising slightly since the 1980s: currently around 36% of the population are socially involved (of which 15% are involved to a lesser extent with organizations), almost 20% at least monthly, 13% less frequently (ibid.). At 40%, men are somewhat more committed than women (32%), and commitment is more pronounced among younger people and the middle-aged; the employed (40%), pupils/trainees/students (38%) and housewives/husbands (36%) are also more committed than the unemployed (26%) and pensioners/retirees (30%) (ibid.: 354). Similarly, higher levels of education (45%) and middle levels of education (37%) are more engaged than those with basic levels of education (23%). This trend has intensified over the years: in 1999, the figure was 25% for those with a basic level of education and only 41% for those with a high level of education. In western Germany (37%), commitment continues to be more pronounced than in eastern Germany (30%).

Alscher and Priller conclude from this in the data report (ibid.: 356): "Civic engagement in Germany has become a permanent feature of society. The number of civil society organizations in which engagement is frequently exercised has increased over the years. Nevertheless, or perhaps precisely because of this, these organizations are having increasing problems finding committed individuals. In the different forms of engagement: organization-bound, less organization-bound or donations, individual population groups are more strongly represented than others. People who are involved in an organization or donate are usually at least middle-aged, employed and economically secure. In comparison, people who are involved in less formalized associations tend to be young and not employed. Thus, on the one hand, not all people have the same opportunities to access civic engagement forms, but on the other hand, the different engagement opportunities enable a broader range of people to get involved. ".

Political interest is just under 30% in West and East Germany, reaching higher peaks in 1990 and 2002, since when it has been relatively stable (ibid.: 364). Among the non-institutionalized forms of participation, signature collection is still the most popular (around 50%, although falling from over 60% in 2002, but higher than in 1998 when it was under 40%), demonstrations are also only used by around 20%, citizens' initiatives have seen the same jump: from 9% (West)/6% (East) in 1998, to 20% (West)/13% (East), membership fell to 11% (West) and 8% (East) (ibid.: 365). Total activity in citizens' initiatives is put at 2% in 2010 (1% of which is as an active member/volunteer), this figure was stable at 1% from 1976 to 1998 (rising to 2%). By comparison, political parties had a figure of 3% in 2010, and nature conservation organizations 7% (ibid.).

The empirical data thus clearly show that conventional forms of political participation have lost importance, while unconventional formats remain of interest: "In summary, the results indicate on the one hand that the degree of political integration in relation to traditional institutionalized forms of participation has declined significantly over the past two decades. Politics no longer attracts as much interest among citizens as it did in 1990; interest groups and parties are losing membership appeal. On the other hand, non-institutionalized forms of political participation have not lost importance. Politics still plays a major role for citizens; there is no complete withdrawal. The fact that the differences between East and West Germany, as well as those between younger people and the population as a whole, seem to be diminishing or even disappearing altogether is a positive development. However, it should be noted as a warning signal that traditional forms of politics and political participation are becoming less attractive to citizens and that the extent of political integration in institutionalized politics has weakened" (Weßels 2013: 369).

While the participation role of "informed citizen" can be demonstrated less and less, the type of "issue-specific participant" is expanding strongly (Stark 2015: 163). Thus, in Germany, the importance of unconventional forms of participation continues to increase (ibid.: 166 f.; they were used by 65% of respondents in 2008), which has also been noted in other countries (see the studies by Putnam (2000) for the USA as well as Whiteley (2012) for Great Britain, international comparison in Putnam (2001)).

Civil Society Associations as Schools of Democracy?
From a normative point of view, civil society associations are supposed to assume important functions for democracy: democratic values are supposed to be experienced and learned in the voluntarily united groups, at least (bridging) social capital is supposed to be formed, social cohesion, identity and a sense of community are supposed to be experienced (see Roth and Olk 2010).[50]

For a long time now, two views (supplemented by a differentiated one) have been opposed to each other: the positive pro-civil society perspective already mentioned, a critical-doubting one, which, on the other hand, recognizes exclusionary tendencies, oligarchic traits, privatist-self-benefit-oriented views and motivations up to undemocratic manifestations (extremist, radicalizing, etc.). A differentiated approach would assess civil society associations neutrally, without benefit or harm to democracy – although there are often slightly graded oscillations between democracy-promoting and democracy-damaging.

Oscar Gabriel assessed both civil society associations and citizens' initiatives more in the latter sense of being at least not conducive to democracy. In addition, he names important functions of associations:

- Behavioural influence (socialization) (Gabriel 1983: 244 ff.).
- Consequential effect in the form of political participation (here Gabriel assumes cumulative influence, in that members of associations are closer to political participation, i.e., a strong relationship exists between association membership and political participation, ibid.: 247).

[50] Thus van Deth (2001) assesses the consequences of participation in clubs and associations as consistently very positive. Accordingly, empirical analyses show that especially voter turnout and participation in so-called conventional forms of political participation are promoted by citizens' social involvement. In this sense, social participation should be regarded as a "school of democracy". On the evaluation of civil society associations as schools of democracy in the sense of democracy-promoting learning and democratic practices, see Simon 1983a, and on the acquisition of competencies through voluntary engagement Hansen 2008 and Düx et al. 2009.

- Democratic training and role models in clubs (ibid.: 252 ff.).
- Individual-psychological motivational factors (willingness to participate) (ibid.: 255 ff.), – meso-societal function of associations as actors of civil society (political participation through associations as elements of local pluralism, creation of local power positions, e.g., through personal union, circulation of offices and density of contacts).
- Indirect additional participation opportunities for members (e.g., contact with politicians).
- As well as the integration function of associations with regard to political participation (e.g., community spirit, integration) (ibid.: 257 ff.).

Ultimately, it may find above all an overarching integrative function, in the sense of "integrating citizens into their local environment and into the community" in order to serve community cooperation (ibid: 265). "It stands to reason that those citizens are more likely to take part in local politics who feel an attachment to, are proud of, and have an interest in their community of residence. Thus, to the extent that associations contribute to this local attachment, they would indirectly increase citizens' participation in local politics" (ibid.). But to Gabriel it seems questionable "whether associations have any effect at all in this direction". Empirical results of the time did not seem to him to confirm this function (ibid.). Rather, Gabriel assumes a depoliticizing effect of associations, possibly even that "the association even discourages its members from the little political activity outside the association that most of them are just willing to do (…)" (ibid.: 268). Finally, Gabriel assumes only very limited positive, democracy-strengthening effects: "As a training ground for political or even democratic activity, the clubs come into question only for the core of active people who run them. For this limited group of people, their functions in the association open up additional opportunities for political participation in local politics that go beyond the opportunities offered by local parties and institutions: easier access to politicians, political offices, political decisions" (ibid.: 269).

Due to the principle of representation, which in turn applies, direct influence for members remains more of an illusion for Gabriel: "The broad membership of the association has at most an indirect share in these possibilities of participation via the associations, in that they can try to use 'their' association leaders in political questions. A general indirect influence of the members, for example by participating in the internal formation of the association's will in order to determine the local political influence of the association's leadership, does not take place, both as a result of political member apathy and as a result of oligarchical tendencies in the association" (ibid.). For Gabriel, this leaves only contacts and networks and thus more information, less influence: "Both together also prevent the main hope that associations, as a school of democracy, would better enable and stimulate their members to political participation from being an illusion. It remains that associations offer their members opportunities for contact with politically active personalities and thus, in addition to political influence, also provide political information and perhaps a kind of role model for political activity" (ibid.).

In an empirical study of East German associations, potentials for the promotion of democracy could not be identified either: "In summary, it can be stated that mere membership in associations does not offer any indication of higher integration or increased civic engagement compared to non-association members. On the contrary, in various areas membership serves to maintain social-cultural or political niches in which members seal themselves off from the society around them. This isolation can ultimately lead to social disintegration and reduce the willingness to engage in civic engagement insofar as it goes beyond self-interest, for example in sports clubs" (Vortkamp 2005: 81).

From this, Vortkamp concludes that the "level of integration of individuals on the secondary or social macro-level depends on the socio-political positioning of the respective institution" (ibid.). Thus, in the future, one will no longer be able to attribute the generation of civic engagement to associations as such, but will have to distinguish between different types of associations. Whether associations are civil society institutions and have a democratising function (…) is therefore essentially dependent on the political-social location of the organization in question, its structures and the norms and values on which they are based (…). Furthermore, it is not the willingness (as in the case of potentially active people), but participation itself that has a positive effect: "It is active action and direct participation in the respective social and political processes that have an integrating effect, and this is true even in system-refusing niches. Lack of participation, on the other hand, correlates highly with disenchantment with politics" (ibid.: 81 f.). Undoubtedly, the function of the associations remains to play an integrative role at the municipal level in a network of actors between business, politics and society at that meso level, which is likely to have a positive effect on the members (as assumed by Gabriel) (see Hallmann 2005: 101; Zimmer 2007, 2011).

Roßteutscher analyses both positive and negative views: according to this, civil society associations are to be understood as ambivalent, on the one hand they are an "important and indispensable building block of democratic systems", on the other hand they can be derided as a "hoard of provincial thinking, stuffy attitudes and German small-mindedness", and even "take on characteristics detrimental to democracy" (Roßteutscher 2009a: 61). The author assumes a strong link between associationism and practiced democratic culture in general ("mirror image of state and society"): "If the state is democratic, if its dominant political culture is characterized by love of freedom, tolerance, willingness to compromise and openness, then free associations make an indispensable contribution to the reproduction and reinforcement of these basic democratic virtues" (ibid.: 73). In addition to this positive cycle, however, a negative variant is also conceivable (ibid.: 73 f.):

The associational system receives the socially dominant mood and feeds it into its inner workings. Here democratic association remains marginal. (…) While quite normal clubs in the consolidated democratic system undoubtedly strengthen the nature of the democratic structure, their role as a savior and solution to all problems must nevertheless not be overestimated. The hope that through involvement in sports or hobby clubs, more educationally distant, less competent citizens could be introduced to the political system in order to make their voices heard in the future is deceptive. Social participation is similarly stratified as political participation. Also, a not inconsiderable number of associations are socially extremely homogeneous and do not perform the bridging function that is so central to the production of collective goods of the most diverse nature. Civil society is an important foundation of democratic systems, but to expect it to solve all problems is clearly mistaken. In both non-democratic and democratic systems, there can and will always be associations that live in closed, self-contained environments and can thus cultivate their own attitudes that are resistant to the social mainstream.

2.4 Civic Engagement

Closely linked to the activity of citizens – whether in the context of political participation or in civil society associations – is the significance of the civic engagement that unfolds in them. This represents the driving force behind citizens' action. Individual commitment, forms of civic action and associated effects such as the formation of social capital, democracy learning, etc. have been examined in particular in studies that have received international attention (Putnam et al. 1993; Skocpol and Fiorina 1999; Putnam 2000).[51] The forms of civic engagement show different structures, lines of development, traditions and conditions of development

[51] See study results on Germany in Alscher et al. 2009; Gensicke and Geiss 2010, 2015; Enste et al. 2012; Statistisches Bundesamt and WZB 2013; Statistisches Bundesamt 2015; Zentrum für zivilgesellschaftliche Entwicklung 2016.

(see Zimmer 2000). The citizenry and its manifold expressions of civic engagement can basically be regarded as a "bearer of civil society" (Kocka 2002).

However, it is initially difficult to define engagement precisely, since it touches on the boundaries of privacy, the public sphere, interest-based or public interest-oriented motivation, and political and social spheres – analogous to the definitional approaches to the concept of civil society and participation.[52]

Klie and Stemmer (2011b: 84) seek to define civic engagement as "unpaid forms of engagement with a civic quality". Civil society should emphasize stubbornness, norms of solidarity, and activism beyond a profit and market logic. Accordingly, monetized forms of engagement also include "cooperative and public service activities", which generate "common basic needs", "meeting needs and securing livelihoods" and aim at "social integration". "Cooperatives (…) are not gratuitous insofar as they are integrated into a logic of economic activity or the "common own"" (ibid.: 83).

Bühler (2010: 83) assumes that voluntary engagement must go beyond a private environment; he defines it as "productive, individual activities carried out within the framework of an organization or association, which are not or only slightly remunerated, which are not based on a coercive situation and not primarily an intention to generate income, and which are intended to benefit exclusively or also third parties, but not only strangers, relatives, the family or the household community". In addition, research analyses "we-relations" (Ortega 2010) as well as an economic-ethical significance (Ulrich 2008) of engagement.

The evaluation of civic engagement varies greatly in the literature. While on the one hand it is widely regarded as an important prerequisite for the democratic community, Ulrich Beck, for example, sharply attacked the emphasis on engagement and civil society: "Civil society is a repetitive middle-class event, civic engagement

[52] Helmut Schoene (Schoene 2011: 248) defines civic engagement as "citizens access to and participation in information, decision making, and implementation of public policies broadly construed; taking part in democracy – individually or as a part of organized groups – through communication and public actions (including electoral campaigns and elections) where public interests prevail over private ones; the act of becoming involved in the political process and working to better the community; and a means to guarantee the credibility of institutions, through articulation of citizens' demands and holding public officials accountable". In the definition, the emphasis on civic education becomes visible, also the input side, decision-making and quality of engagement are emphasized, in particular the accesses of individuals to decision-making processes are focused (ibid.). See also further definitions in Evers (2009) and Olk and Hartnuß (2011) as well as reflections on guiding principles of the concept of engagement by Maaser (2010).

only the garnish of political helplessness" (Beck 2001; see also Keupp 2010b on the discussion).

Roland Roth, on the other hand, is a proponent of strengthening and emphasizing civic courage (Roth 2000: 44) and more positive effects of engagement (Roth 2010, 2013c). Finally, attention is also drawn to the increasingly strong individualistic component of civic engagement ("What can I achieve in society?"), in contrast to the classic collective-community approach ("What can be achieved with a movement?") (Heinze and Strünck 1999).

Finally, the question of and reference to the local level also comes into play in the area of civic engagement: a strong representative of the local politics school ("all politics is local") is Jörg Bogumil (together with Lars Holtkamp), who fundamentally sees municipalities as having a duty to create convincing offers for the development of civic engagement (Bogumil 1999: 167; see also Holtkamp et al. 2006; Keupp 2010a; Bogumil and Holtkamp 2013). He sees the self-interest of citizens in the context of this as legitimate; it is an essential empirical yardstick for strengthening civic engagement. Interests of the common good should be secured through contracts, incentive systems should support this (Bogumil 1999: 167). Accordingly, a fixed contact person in the municipality could also promote the perception of interests of articulately weak circles; the municipalities should also offer suggestions, take the initiative, and create support services (ibid.: 168).

Finally, civic engagement can also find its forms of expression in economic activity, mostly oriented towards ideals of the common good and the social market economy (see Hollstein 2013; Bertelsmann Stiftung 2016), in that the economic form pursues a specific common good-oriented purpose, as can be characterized in the case of community energy.

Typologies of Civic Engagement

Typologies have also been attempted in the area of civic engagement. First, a distinction can be made as to the structure and context of the engagement. Karl et al. (2008: 43 f.) distinguish here four basic types of engagement: Type 1: networking-based engagement; Type 2: institution-based engagement; Type 3: engagement diversity based on personal relationships; Type 4: independent development of a service offering (see also a typology on the civic engagement of socially disadvantaged groups: Meusel 2016).

In addition, different types can be derived from the sources of motivation for civic engagement. Gensicke (2010a: 91) derives from the results of the 2010 Volunteer Survey the most important motives for involvement as shaping society on a small scale, sociability and social duty orientation (see also Gensicke and Geiss 2010: 12; Gensicke 2010a, 2010b). The self-interested motive of remuneration is weighted least here: only 22% of respondents would like it. For qualified evaluations, however, further contextual conditions and effects must be included. In this context, Klie and Stemmer point to the problems of deprofessionalization and dequalification; due to financial scarcity, often only poor design is possible (Klie and Stemmer 2011b: 82). In addition, there are financial risks and legal imponderables due to tax and insurance obligations. First and foremost, qualification secures access to engagement resources; inequalities are further deepened even within organizations: the importance of money is definitely emphasized in this context (ibid., Gensicke and Geiss 2010: 148 ff., 251 ff.). In an overall view, the question of justice thus gains crucial importance: higher educated classes benefit particularly strongly from voluntary engagement.

2.5 Typologies and Scales of Civic Participation

In the literature, ladders of civic participation have been developed: For example, in the well-known "ladder of citizen participation" by Sherry R. Arnstein (1969) from low level (e.g., information) to participation in events to adoption and self-control of issues by citizens.[53] More recently, this idea of a typology of participation levels has been taken up again and again.[54] There are also typologies of forms of engagement (e.g., Rowe and Frewer 2005; Sliep 2010).

Heike Walk (2011) and Erhard et al. (2013: 37) criticized that such subdivisions do not make much sense. For example, Fung (2006: 67) questions whether the more or less implied goal of "full control" should really be valued so highly than, for example, an advisory role or similar. Attempts have been made to form other

[53] Arnstein (1969: 217) divided into "Manipulation", "Therapy", "Informing", "Consultation", "Placation", "Partnership", "Delegated Power" up to "Citizen control".

[54] Lüttringhaus (2000, 2003) distinguishes between "granting participation" and here the levels "information", "exchange, dialogue, discussion", "cooperation in partnership", "delegation of decisions" as well as "participating" with the levels "observation/information", "participation", "co-decision", "self-responsibility" and "autonomy". Further classifications can be found in Arbter et al. (2005), Abels (2007), Zschocke (2007) and Fishkin (2009).

ladders with different emphases (e.g., Connor 1988),[55] with a focus on the effect of social learning (Collins and Ison 2009). In fact, however, the intrinsic weighting of different types of participation seems very problematic. It hardly seems justified why one particular mode should rank above another. The participatory paths and effects should rather be placed horizontally next to each other; moreover, generalizations can blur the manifold specifics of participation forms here as well and neglect individual contexts – some of which presumably have a considerable influence on the type and mode of effect of the participation form.

This also seems to be the case with participation in the context of the energy transition. In individual cases, it always depends on how, for example, community energy initiatives are structured (a) and what framework conditions exist, for example, other forms of participation (citizens' meetings, events), associative local context (actor networks, influence of the municipality, community life, etc.) (b). Overall, therefore, different degrees of participation are possible from case to case, and a general classification would thus be primarily theoretical in nature.

In one study, community energy initiatives were tentatively classified in a ladder analogous to the highest form of "self control", although this is also considered to make little sense here (Rau and Zöllner 2011: 18). In the context of an extended understanding of participation, welfare production by civic actors is integrated alongside participation in opinion and decision-making processes; alongside decision-making, (service) participation is assumed in the context of community energy initiatives, which is simply supposed to represent civic engagement (self-or-

[55] Connor (1988) presented a ladder of stages with a different understanding, citing the three stages of "education", "information feedback" and "consultation" with regard to public participation, "joint planning", "mediation" and "litigation" at the level of the "leaders" and finally, at the highest stage in the reverse understanding (i.e., starting from citizens themselves), the introduction of "resolution" and "prevention". On the one hand, Connor thus goes more into the ideas of public participation (i.e., how citizens can at best be involved from the user perspective, see Connor 1988: 256), on the other hand he emphasizes the perspective of learning influence and cooperative co-creation, which was still rather excluded in Arnstein's work and in a rather radical way of thinking can only be achieved through autarky. However, whether one stage can and must always only necessarily build on the other, as Connor (1988: 257) indicates, seems very questionable, even if he concedes that processes can run synchronously and approaches must always be adapted to the specific context (ibid.).

ganized and self-managed) (Rau and Zöllner 2011: 18).[56] "While classical citizen participation takes place in the context of planning and decision-making phases, the service participation of citizens in the sense of civic engagement is found quite predominantly in phases of implementation (…), that is, in the implementation of very concrete projects and activities. Examples include associations that take over formerly public institutions or community foundations that launch projects and actions (…)" (ibid.). These forms of participation "cannot easily be categorized in the classical participation thinking". "On the one hand, the traditional conceptual pair of participants = politics/administration on the one hand, participants = citizens on the other hand, makes less and less sense in a context of action in which different actors jointly influence regional processes and developments (…). On the other hand, citizens are also in demand as active co-creators within the framework of governance and, besides the economy, are the second potential private partner of public actors (…), so it is not only a matter of decision-making but also of performance participation. In fact, the latter is even in the foreground and political control through forms of regional governance is said to be in danger of reinforcing existing democratic deficits, since new elites can emerge within this framework that are neither democratically legitimized nor accessible to public control" (ibid.) (see also Geißel 2009).

Within the framework of the above-mentioned study, a model of its own was developed (Rau and Zöllner 2011: 19, taken up from the previous study Schweizer-Ries et al. (2008: 30) as well as theoretical preliminary considerations in Keppler (2010)), which is said to have the advantage that it includes "both two-sided and one-sided communication", thus also "sham participation" or "token activity" (ibid.: 19). Although "at first glance it strongly resembles the more traditional ap-

[56] The pyramid is also applied to e-renewable energies in another study (Carmen 2014: 13), whereby the lowest level of "information" is supposed to mean informing, "consultation" is supposed to mean thinking, "cooperation" is supposed to mean co-deciding and shaping, and the highest level of "responsible action" is supposed to mean initiating projects on one's own initiative (ibid.). This highest level of acting on one's own responsibility as well as the lower level "cooperation and co-determination" should lead to financial participation and, with regard to this, to "active acceptance, support and commitment", which could also be given in the other cases, but here there is also the possibility that only "passive acceptance" and "advocacy" will develop (ibid.: 14).

proaches, it is open enough to be able to take into account the newer forms of, for example, civic engagement" (ibid.: 19).[57]

2.6 Effects of Civic Participation

Advantages and Positive Effects of Civic Participation

Studies and research have demonstrated various positive effects of participation:

- Impacts and effects of participation, for example, participants as better democrats (van Deth 2013b), learning effects, uncertainty and (half) knowledge

[57] The model distinguishes between "participants" with "information: providing information", "consultation: obtaining opinions", "cooperation: granting co-decision", "acting on one's own responsibility" and "participants" with "informing themselves", "thinking and expressing opinions", "co-deciding", "self-responsible action". It is related to three different perspectives: "local / facility-based participation", "financial participation" and "Regional participation". An acceptance and commitment/participation dimension are linked in a matrix (Schweizer-Ries et al. 2008: 30). An acceptance dimension is combined and related to the strategy or commitment of the operating company, resulting in four criteria:

- Advocacy (analogous to: moderate commitment of the operating company on site, advocacy of the plant (no committed advocacy), participation of the population
- takes place within the legally prescribed framework as well as no direct engagement of the population against the plant, but also no rejection).
- Rejection (analogous to: lack of commitment of the operating company on site, rejection of the plant (passive), citizens are seen as hurdles in the implementation process as well as no direct commitment of the population against the plant, but also no endorsement).
- Active engagement (analogous to: active engagement of the operating company on site, active engagement for the plant on the part of the municipality, participation of the population beyond the legally prescribed framework as well as citizens' initiative for the plant).
- Resistance (analogous to: requested commitment by the municipality remains unanswered by the operating company, active commitment against plants on the part of the municipality, population is actively prevented from participating in decision-making processes, and citizens' initiative against plant).

Accordingly, a positive evaluation can lead to advocacy or active engagement, a passive evaluation to acquiescence or active action, and a negative evaluation to rejection or resistance (ibid.). Finally, the levels of participation in a scale are: informing, questioning, involving, cooperating, participating. It can be seen that implicit normative criteria such as "self control" are dispensed with. Nevertheless, the meaningfulness of a hierarchical subdivision remains questionable (Rau and Zöllner 2011: 115).

(Westle 2012), acquisition of democracy competencies (Reinhardt 2004, 2011) and political skills (Ferris et al. 2005).

- Participation leads to increased acceptance, social learning, conflict resolution and, in the case of corresponding actor preference, also to increased output, that is, the achievement of environmental goals (Newig and Fritsch 2009: 219). Furthermore, the process design, interests and contextual conditions are essential for successful participation (Newig 2011: 495). In the successful case, it is possible to resolve conflicts, build trust and make appropriate, environmentally relevant and better accepted decisions (ibid.).
- Newig et al. summarize the positive effects as follows: decisions in participatory processes reflect public values, they are robust, problem-solving oriented and contribute to confidence building and education of the population (Newig et al. 2011: 41). Process design is more intensive, successful and contextual difficulties can be compensated. It also helps to resolve conflicts, builds mutual trust, and ultimately leads to more appropriate, better accepted and more environmentally relevant decisions.
- There is a qualifying effect in that through information and discussion people can develop differentiated thinking, learn and better understand contexts, acquire problem-specific knowledge and broaden their horizons; democratic values and principles are also realized and democratic convictions strengthened (Gundersen 1995: 6, 112; Renn et al. 1995; Geißel 2008a: 38).
- Personal and social qualities should improve, a higher level of commitment and tolerence should be strengthened, and the pursuit of egoistic goals should be transformed into responsible action. In addition, marginalized groups of people are to be given the opportunity to bring in their interests and lend weight to their voices (Pateman 1970; Barber 1984: 232; Mansbridge 1999; Fung and Wright 2001; Delli Carpini et al. 2004).

Empirical research can also show concrete results on the positive effects of associative action on the individual and society. Sebastian Braun investigated civic associations, to dertermine whether there are spillover effects of community action at the individual level (social and democracy learning, etc.) and meso level (enhancement of local social capital, etc.). Braun raised two elementary questions here: on the one hand, why one should actually acquire civic skills in voluntary associations that one could acquire elsewhere, and on the other hand, the ambiguity of what is going on in the "black box" of the voluntary association (Braun 2005: 150). After all, these associations would lack authoritatively defined goals and the certainty of a predetermined membership as in a family (ibid.: 150 f.). Beyond idealized notions, it is still unclear how the mechanisms are supposed to work to transfer acquired social and political orientations to other areas of life (ibid.: 151). In the end, he could rather not confirm the assumption whether internal integration of members leads to cross-border external integration (ibid.: 150). He argues that the common notion that every voluntary association would mark the same integration achievements in terms of internal and external integration is distinctly questionable (Braun 2005: 150). Finally, Braun questions the social capital approach as such, arguing that "individual trust is generalized through involvement in voluntary associations, thereby also improving the overall socio-economic performance of a society" (ibid.: 178). The generated resources could in fact have a suboptimal effect, because they could lead to misallocation or negative allocation effects resulting in an overall failure of civil society compared to market and state systems (ibid.). Finally, Braun (ibid.: 194) also questions the idea of the function of a "school of democracy" of civil society (referring to negative effects, see Stecker and Nährlich 2005), in addition to a lack of selectivity and precision of the terminology (Braun 2005: 195): "What are 'civil' or 'non-civil virtues'? Is everything that does not endanger or violate the rights of others to be valued positively or merely neutrally? If it is to be valued merely neutrally, at what point does it become something positive?" – At least in the case of the sports clubs studied, this was questionable.

Furthermore, Hansen (2008) investigated to what extent associations are suitable for creating structural contexts of action for learning. In principle, associations are suitable places for this, since "interaction and negotiation conducive to learning represent an important pattern of action in them" (ibid.: 134); in addition, opportunities can be opened up to "personalize tasks and activities, i.e. to align them with objects of interest or learning content" (ibid.: 135). On the other hand, entrenched routines have an obstructive effect, that is, it must be possible to make choices according to interests (i.e., self-determined), or also a benefit that goes beyond the association (ibid.: 134, 136). According to this, however, the association is also conducive to learning "because the voluntarily engaged, out of fear of informal sanctions and due to their emotional attachment to the association, perceive their activities as demands which they try to meet with the help of self-directed and formal learning processes" (ibid.: 135). In the unfolding of civic engagement, a development of identity can take place in the individual, which can be of importance in terms of social pedagogy as well as didactics of democracy in the sense of education for democracy. Steinfort examined possible potentials in the exercise of civic engagement and worked out some concise features (Steinfort 2010: 213 ff.).[58]

Disadvantages and Negative Effects of Participation

On the other hand, the following negative effects of participation have been demonstrated in research:

- Problems with participation are essentially seen in a possible equity gap, lack of knowledge and responsibility, power structures, risk-taking and peer pressure (Kersting and Woyke 2012: 26 ff.).
- According to Newig and Fritsch (2009: 219 f.), a particular problem lies in the complexity of problems: In the case of high complexity, the process itself is crucial and the input variables such as information and interest aggregation; in the case of low complexity, the focus is on promoting the output of the procedures. Another problem arises, according to the authors, regarding the effectiveness of the procedures due to the increased number of decisions (*clearance points*) and counter-movements (veto players), lack of compatibility in communication (communication barriers) and flexibility, and regarding the extent to which legitimate interests are represented. Too many veto players also tend to lead to immobilism (Lijphart 1999: 258 ff.; Tsebelis 2002; König et al. 2010). There are also problems with the increasing size of procedures and the involvement of too many actors in decision-making processes, for example if there is ultimately only a small influence on the actual objective (output, outcome) (Newig 2011: 493 f.).
- There is a dilemma between system effectiveness and citizen participation, since many problems can only be solved on a larger scale, while participatory procedures are bound to manageable and thus local conditions (Dahl 1994).

[58] Enumerated are: Coherence (meaning of individual action), self-location (living out personal idiosyncrasies), significant others (making new contacts), productivity (e.g., dealing productively with frustration, individual concerns, meaningful time management), "experiencing competence" (building on one's own strengths), recognition (private/public, self-acknowledgement, subjective valuations, social recognition). Possible competencies that play a special role in civic engagement are thus personal and social competencies, methodological and emotional competencies, and communicative and technical competencies (Steinfort 2010: 230).

- Ineffectiveness can be observed in location decisions (Bogumil et al. 2003; Holtkamp et al. 2006).
- There is hardly any measurable influence on output and outcome in participatory processes (Newig et al. 2011: 41).
- Individual interests prevail to the detriment of the common good (Raymond 2002: 183).
- Grassroots elites and organizationally strong groups that are already active also adopt these procedures, leading to pseudo-democratic elite rule and the dominance of material interests (Papadopoulos 2004: 220).
- There is a lack of legitimacy as in the case of elected representatives, political laymen do not have sufficient contextual and overview knowledge (Fraenkel 1974: 139).
- In the case of social or organizational participation, tendencies towards oligarchy (power and domination issues[59]), exclusion, lack of inclusion (Thaa 2009), importance of the knowledge dimension in the sense of knowledge formation (knowledge for action) and competence transfer (Gohl and Wüst 2008).

[59] See research on power and domination issues in associations and organizations: Städler 1984; Alvesson 1996; Abell and Heller 2000; Wex 2004; Clegg et al. 2006; Jäger 2011; Imbusch 2012; Jörke 2012; Richter 2013.

As early as 1975, Paul Kevenhörster listed a variety of possible negative implications and problems associated with the increased use of participation.[60]

Critics continued to fear a "tyranny of participation", that it would be used as a moral imperative or that it would be assessed as a Christian and neo-colonialist approach from a development policy perspective (Cooke and Kothari 2001, see also Miessen 2012). The normative impetus is thus repeatedly at the center of criticism.

In this context, Geißel points to voices in the literature according to which participation harbors dangers in that "individual interests prevail to the detriment of

[60] Kevenhörster summarized here (Kevenhörster 1975: 35 ff.):

1. Stratification-specific participation barriers.
2. Potentially extremist and stability-threatening content of high participation rates.
3. Crisis and disfunctionality of high participation rates.
4. Privatization and apathy of the citizens.
5. Political apathy due to unfavorable cost-benefit ratio in the provision of information.
6. High degree of role differentiation and interdependence in modern industrial societies, which inhibits participation.
7. Anticipatory decision-making by political elites in response to potential citizen action, making continued participation seem superfluous.
8. Limited information processing capacity of organizations.
9. Frustration of citizens that their preferences are repeatedly ignored in decision-making processes.
10. Impairment of the renewal capacity and agility of complex organizations.
11. Creating rigid attitudes that make it difficult to negotiate compromises.
12. Risk of political participation becoming a vehicle for pathological needs and the release of frustration and aggression.
13. Possible totalitarian consequences if initial enthusiasm for activity leads to a refusal to participate and promotes minority rule.

According to Kersting (2008: 17 ff.), further points of criticism concern:

- Lack of knowledge and responsibility of the participants.
- "Empowerment for what?"
- Strong external influence such as "framing" by (consulting) agencies.
- The idea of change management (as a process of change towards a participatory culture) is described as brainwashing (Schein et al. 1961), in that coercive persuasion is assumed to be involved.
- Successful group cooperation is doubted (group dysfunctionality) (Cooke and Kothari 2001).
- Risk-taking can be due to a lack of seriousness, but can have fatal consequences.
- Danger of the Abilene Paradox: Target approach, which, however, is not supported by the participants at the core.
- Building peer pressure (and other suboptimal group effects such as exclusion/marginalization, suppression of opinions, etc.)

the common good" (Geißel 2008a: 31). "This is because politically already active segments (men, the educated, the middle class), groups with strong resources and organization, and grassroots elites also adopt participatory procedures. They have the time, money and know-how to participate in the relevant processes and thus ensure that their preferences are taken into account. Such forms of participation would involve the risk of pseudo-democratic elite rule and the dominance of special interests" (ibid.). There are similar critical voices from supporters of the existing representative democratic system: "The result of such co-determination by political laymen, who have hardly any contextual and overview knowledge, would be decisions that would ultimately harm all citizens" (ibid.). Moreover, a high number of veto players could prevent effectiveness and generate immobilism – according to this, participation would rather generate "political dissatisfaction, legitimacy deficits and inefficiency" (ibid.: 31).

Drawbacks of Participation Within Civil Society Organizations
In the context of these considerations, the drawbacks of civil society organizations are of particular interest. Beyond the normative ideal of a positively connoted image, another civil society world is obviously in parallel existence, which can be subsumed under the umbrella terms of particular interests, economization tendencies, mediatization, eventization and exclusion mechanisms. According to Roland Roth (see Roth 2003, 2004, 2008), there are many dangers in relying on civil society as a learning ground for democracy: these include clientelism, exclusion, neglect of weak interests or issues, support for further market expansion and corruption. This raises the possibility that civil society produces inequalities or exacerbates existing social imbalances – but these processes would take place covertly, as the

other side of the coin of the "disguised" stealth *democracy.*[61] Roth (2003: 70) summarized these critical diagnoses as follows: "This necessitates the abandonment of two fictions: the far-reaching independence and the genuine democratic substance of civil society associations" (see also Klatt et al. 2011 on the involvement of socially disadvantaged people).

The same could presumably apply to the community energy initiatives examined here: Indeed, it does not seem unlikely that these dark sides can be found. However, it remains questionable, also in the sense of the considerations of Stecker and Nährlich (2005), what alternatives remain in this case, since apart from municipal enterprises (public utilities) only large corporations serve the energy supply. Nevertheless, the fundamental question remains whether municipal enterprises represent a better, more public welfare-oriented solution due to public supervision and control as well as the associated legitimacy (see the idea of municipal utilities as "good citizens" in Schönberg and Jost 2011). However, dark sides such as cor-

[61] Nolte points to these solidifying tendencies of social inequalities (2003: 38): "Civil society is a beautiful dream, the design of a better society. For this reason alone, it is not surprising that the project of civil society is often associated with a relatively egalitarian society: a society not only of citizens with equal rights, but also of relatively equal economic privileges and opportunities. In contrast, however, is the reality of entrenched social structures, the reality of socio-economic inequality. In a reversal of the secular egalitarian trend that prevailed for many decades, social inequality has actually worsened in most Western societies since about 1980; gaps have grown again." – Two tendencies are central for Nolte in this context: the decline of the labor movement and the lack of integrative power of the new culture of engagement (ibid.: 44): "Can we infer from this, conversely, that civil society can be produced solely with a middle class that is politically engaged? This question has become more explosive in recent decades in all Western countries in an unsuspected way. The traditional working-class movement culture, and with it the lower-class organizations that had largely adapted to the bourgeois model of civil society, are increasingly dissolving or losing their power to shape society as a whole; new lower classes beyond the classical industrial workforce are withdrawing from organizations and, as the class-specific decline in voter turnout shows, tend to behave politically indifferently or apathetically. On the other hand, the new forms of civic engagement that have gained in importance in recent decades over the classical culture of clubs, associations, and organizations (e.g., citizens' initiatives, protest movements) are characterized to a conspicuous degree by a post-educational middle class and are in many cases far less capable of cross-class integration than was the case in the traditional pattern."

ruption and nepotism are likely to be a general phenomenon that can be found in all areas of society. Protection of minorities does not necessarily have to be ensured either. Finally, in addition to the eradicated negative effects of citizen enterprises, their positive effects would also be lost if other forms of operation were preferred.

In his summary of the international comparison of social capital in different countries ("Society and Public Spirit"), Robert Putnam already emphasized a dark side of social capital with regard to new forms of engagement (Putnam 2001: 781), in that "the new individualistic forms of civic engagement are less able to contribute to the pursuit of common goals. The older forms, now on the wane, combined individual pleasure with collective purposes and guessed at different spheres, such as Catholic trade unions or party-affiliated sports leagues. In contrast, the newer forms of social engagement are narrower, less bridge-building, and less focused on collective or public-spirited purposes. The important hypothesis that emerges from our initial investigation is that the newer forms, while they may be more liberating, are less solidaristic – they mark a kind of privatization of social capital". In the context of these considerations, these "dark sides" of civil society are of particular interest.[62] Beyond the normative ideal image, another civil society world is obviously unfolding, which can unfold in the spheres of particular interests, nepotism, economizing tendencies and exclusion mechanisms.

In connection with the emergence of new social movements and NGOs, Münkler speaks of the emergence of new oligarchies, due to the "combination of expertise and media competence" (Münkler 2002: 173), he also criticizes a "moral monopoly" and sees their purpose for the population, which supports the organizations financially to calm their consciences (ibid.). Democratic control here, he argues,

[62] Walter (2013) also describes the dark sides of civil society as a well-known phenomenon: "Civil society, i.e. the space between the state and individuals that is organized by citizens themselves, is not only a proven fertilizer for the praiseworthy virtues of liberality, tolerance and humanity. Civil society is also a nesting place for pathological fears and aggressions, social and ethnic exclusion and repression, cynicism and contempt for the democratic process. (…) A civil society fragmented in confrontational world views and individual worlds, moreover heated up by agitation and confronted with weak state institutions and representative bodies, cannot consolidate parliamentary democracies, but only undermine them". See also the résumé of Gmür (2013b: 32), who speaks of the limits of civil society, it "does not only stand for free engagement, orientation towards progress and the common good or social integration, but it can also mean: particular interests, exclusion, developmental delay or patriarchy".

only takes place "through the new participatory form of bank transfer" as opposed to the classical form of voting (ibid.). In addition, there is the question of who participates in these forms: "Of course, there is no question that the middle class or the "new middle" gains a relatively greater influence as a result of these new forms of political participation than is provided for and the case in the classical electoral process. First of all, the notoriously greater political commitment and, in particular, the better education in the middle social strata play a decisive role, but of course also, due to higher incomes, a greater availability of funds to be paid in return for tax-reducing donation receipts. While political participation through voting has been organized according to the principle of radical equality (one man – one vote) since the introduction of universal, free and equal suffrage, in the case of participation through commitment or donation the 'votes' are weighed rather than counted" (ibid.: 174).

Roth (2003) summarizes four core problems as downsides which he identifies in civil society:

1. Dilemma between dilettantism and professionalism: associations can act as professional lobbyists, be nationalistic and fundamentalist in orientation, and thus not serve as associations of responsible citizens.
2. Importance of private companies as a pillar of civil society: corporate citizenship, public-private partnerships and the moralization of markets serve solely to open up new markets (also the core criticism of Colin Crouch 2004).
3. Devaluation of the state: overestimation of self and lack of legitimacy of civil society organizations, high own share of actions (self-referential) and uncritical approaches.
4. Civil society's creative power is limited in the system itself due to functional differentiation.

In addition, for Roth, there is "increasing intensity of corruption" (Roth 2004: 53 ff.) in connection with market expansion, state failure, failure of civil society ("cliques, cronyism and patronage structures are also social networks that generate social capital" (ibid.: 56), referred to as out-of-date social capital or anti-modern social capital, ibid.) as well as right-wing radicalism, right-wing populism and xenophobia. Such objections can also lead to a fatalistic view: Frank Nullmeier (2002), for example, provocatively asked, "Forget civil society?"[63]

Stecker and Nährlich (2005) arrived at differentiated results in their analysis of nonprofit organizations, stating that although doubts about the beneficial effects were justified, these should not be evaluated overly critically in comparison with

[63] Nullmeier (2002: 18) identifies the penetration of economic principles as a central problem: "These external influences, but also internal efforts of civil society organizations to adapt to new social developments of individualization and competitiveness, lead to a creeping transformation of civil society. Resources specific to civil society are increasingly being procured in ways that conform to the rules of competition, the services of civil society are being extensively marketed, and the internal organization obeys the latest management concepts." As a solution, Nullmeier proposes a strategy of politicization and transformation of the citizen role from economic to political citizen (ibid.: 19): "A continuation of the civil society debate would have to produce both a less euphemistic analysis of reality and develop a more offensive strategy towards the market and economic competition. The citizen in his role as a committed person, donor, volunteer will be of secondary importance if his possibilities as a political citizen are weakened and he is confronted with an overpowering economic citizen. It would therefore be important to attack the citizen in the role of the economic citizen. Such a task cannot be left or assigned to state politics alone. From within society, the market must be made the object of intervening activity. Civic engagement must also extend to economic decisions. Of course, this implies a politicization of civil society, a shift from helping, active to participatory engagement, towards a self-image as a political actor in society – towards a politics beyond the state. Thus, the word should be spoken of a political civil society that is able to actively intervene in market events, that sees itself as an expression of social control and correction of economic events, whose commitment does not shy away from intervening in the economic cycle and thus offers a counterweight to the state and the market.

other social spheres (since, for example, hardly any more positive effects could be expected in the private sector).[64]

New Tendencies: The Economizing and Monetizing of the Voluntary Sector
Klie and Stemmer (2011a, 2011b) called "voluntarism in the field of tension of economic calculations" the (new) basic problem in civil society associations and civic engagement. For some years now, research has been trying to answer the question of whether, on the one hand, such tendencies of economization and monetization are measurable and how communities and organizations deal with these influences. The following tendencies can be identified:

- influence of money on the motivation to engage, but monetary amounts are too small for this (Klie and Stemmer 2011b: 80);
- Stubbornness and specific potentials of voluntary engagement are lost, "money flow brings economic logic" (ibid.: 81);

[64] Stecker and Nährlich (2005: 162) point out the empirical deficit of the initial consideration: "At this point, however, it becomes conspicuous that the socially integrative effects for the macro-level of society have not yet been conclusively demonstrated, although they are also used to justify the resources allocated to the nonprofit sector. But what if the resources merely produce a suboptimal effect (misallocation) and the voluntary associations are overburdened by the positive characteristics often attributed to them?" The authors see advantages above all in comparison with other areas of society: "These diverse claims, hopes and objectives raise the question of whether voluntary engagement and the nonprofit sector can actually achieve what is expected of them. For it is to be feared that the nonprofit sector is overtaxed in the face of these complex challenges. Doubts are also raised as to whether voluntary engagement and nonprofit organizations even possess the positive qualities attributed to them. In order to answer these questions, (…) the dark sides of the functions located on the meso level of the organizations and the effects acting on the macro level of society were examined. In this context, in terms of institutional choice, it is only in comparison with the institutions of the state, the market and the family that the comparative advantages, if any, of the third sector emerge. The existence of comparative competitive advantages at the level of nonprofit organizations does not automatically indicate more efficient economic production and economic allocation". – For this reason, there is a plea to differentiate more strongly between functions and effects and to include the emergence of external effects (ibid.: 176): "It is considered imperative to turn away from the largely one-sided positive evaluation of nonprofit organizations and civic engagement. Neither is nonprofit status under tax law a (sole) guarantee for the fulfilment of certain positive functions and the occurrence of positive external effects, nor do commitment and the third sector represent a 'general solution' for all social problems. Here it is necessary to come to a realistic assessment of the performance of the third sector and – in comparison to the market, the state and the family – to refer more strongly to its comparative advantages" (ibid.).

- one-sided promotion of commitment and competition for financial incentives: it is only a question of economic benefit calculations (ibid.).

In the meantime, empirical results are available on the development of economization and monetization tendencies, assuming an increasing influence of economic ways of thinking and acting. Although the research results have basically confirmed these presumed tendencies, they come to very differentiated conclusions.

In addition, the following findings are available in this context:

- Monetization and economization tendencies in the field of tension between *voluntary work and gainful employment* (Knopf 1983; Sozialministerium Ba. -Wü. 2000b; Jakob 2001; Grehn and Kumpf 2002; Kühnlein and Böhle 2002a; Schumacher 2003; Farago and Ammann 2006; Hessisches Sozialministerium 2007; Stadt Frankfurt a. M. 2007; Roß 2008; Klie et al. 2010; Adloff and Roose 2011; Klie and Stemmer 2011a, 2011b).
- Challenges posed by individualization and globalization (Sozialministerium Ba.-Wü. 2000a; Siegenthaler 2006; Evers and Zimmer 2010; Gmür et al. 2011), motivational and structural change (Heinze and Strünck 1999; Klages 2000b; Beher et al. 2001; Dathe and Kistler 2002; Kühnlein and Böhle 2002b; Klages 2002; Rucht 2010; Rauschenbach and Zimmer 2011), modernization trends (Klein et al. 2004b).
- *Economic challenges* (Priller et al. 2013) and entrepreneurial action (Badelt 2004).
- *(Value) change in* nonprofit organizations, in volunteering and in (traditional) volunteering (Weng 2003; Cattacin 2006; Zimmer and Priller 2007; Salamon 2010), "reinvention" of old associations (Roß et al. 2006), motivations and recognition (Schürmann 2013)
- Analyzed monetization and economization tendencies (mercantilization, bureaucratization, technocratization) (Frey and Jegen 2002; Seibel 2003; Knittlmayer 2004; Ammann 2006a, 2006b; Balbo 2006; Evers 2006; Gmür 2011; Droß 2013), threats posed by monetary incentives (Güntert and Wehner 2006), relevance of the culture of recognition (Jakob 2006), normative aspects of monetization (Landert 2006), combination of gainful employment and voluntary commitment (Schumacher 2003).
- *Torn* between commitment, gift economy and money, power, market (Horch 1992; Bürgenmeier 2006)

Oligarchy in Civil Society Associations and Organizations
A basic problem of civil society, but also of any organized association in politics, economy and society, is the formation of oligarchic tendencies (see Bluhm and Krause 2012; Schaal 2012). While "unorganized citizens" may not yet have leaders and hierarchies, these organized structures usually form over time in any social association. Negative consequences of these structures can be exclusion mechanisms, disempowerment of members, discrimination of minorities, and lack of transparency with co-determination (on power structures of actors see Sandner 1993).

The oligarchic problem within civil society associations was already vividly described 30 years ago by Oscar Gabriel in the context of citizens' initiatives. Despite the deliberately loose organizsational structure, the leadership of the initiatives is ultimately seen as extremely influential due to their personal orientation: "The leadership groups of the initiatives act as the crystallization and communication nucleus: As a result of the largely absent stabilizing organizational elements, (…) the functioning of the group depends largely on the coordination and integration skills of the leadership group (…). In this way, the separation of leadership and membership roles takes on a new and much greater significance than one might initially suspect: although participation in the leadership group is in principle accessible to everyone, it presupposes relatively great political and social skills, a circumstance that may be the cause of the occasionally criticized academization of the leadership group. The great time and organizational burden on the leadership personnel is presumably also the reason why this group remains quite small and is often limited to the founding members (…), i.e., that the offer of participati'n 'cooperation in the leadership group of the initiat've' is taken up only by very few people who, moreover, do not differ in their social characteristics from other groups of participa"ts" (Gabriel 1983: 290).

Especially the newly emerging citiz'ns' groups and initiatives are accused of adhering to oligarchic tendencies per se (Jörke 2011: 17": "The paradox of the current situation is that, on the one hand, a lively democratic practice can certainly be observed, which is not least manifested in unconventional forms of participation. On the other hand, however, the social basis of this new democracy tends to have oligarchic features, with the consequence of a decline in egalitarian political cont"nt" (ibid.: 17). Thus, these civil society possibilities of participation would not represe"t "a way out of post-democr"cy" (ibid.). Especially from classical organizations of political will formation these hierarchies have been known for a long time. While one ideal is described by Offe (within parties) as"a "lively process of discussion supported by collective ident"ty", this is contrasted wi"h "preferences of 'n 'oligarc'ic' body of functionar"es" (Offe 2003b: 70).

Domestic democracy in organizations, associations and clubs can therefore obviously only ever be guaranteed with difficulty. Robert Michels has pointed out the problem of oligarchic tendencies that almost inevitably develop over time (Michels 1908). He saw little possibility of democratic control within organizations: Members were left only wi“h “adherence to the path of insta”ce” (Michels 1911: 42–) – he therefore conceded control possibilities only“a “pseudo-existe”ce” (Michels 1911: 34). T“e “iron law of oligar”hy” coined by Michels was subsequently characterized as“a “basic problem of democratic leadership in organizati”ns” (Grunwald 1980).

The topicality of–the problem has changed little to this day (see Bluhm and Krause 2012); Bender and Wiesendahl (2011) address Mich’l“’ “iron law of democr”cy” in relation to the current political system. According to them, the basic oligarchic structures have not changed much, only more direct participation can be a solution, but even this does not change the elite rule as suc”: “Representative democracy has an inherent tendency to oligarchization and independence of elected politicians. This raises the question of how the rule of the elected over the voters could be limited and tied more closely to the will of the voters. In this context, there are calls to limit the representative democratic rule of professional politicians or to replace it with more direct democracy in the sense of an authentic self-government of the people and a self-organization of citizens. (…) More direct democracy, according to the quintessence, does not necessarily bring less elite rule, if this is not limited in the accumulation of offices and the durat”on” (ibid.: 24).

Cooperative Participation

In an extensive study of opportunities for more cooperative forms of participation, it was found that democratic opportunities for members to exert influence are very limited: “The salient democratic position of members shrinks in reality, however, to accepting the board’s annual report and exonerating the board” (von Blanckenburg 2014: 261).

On the other hand, a link to traditional values of cooperatives could be analysed, “the essence of the ‘cooperative idea’, namely the community and the solidary value orientation ‘revived’” (ibid.). However, this is again strongly dependent on the participatory organization and structure of the cooperative (ibid.: 281). According to these findings, participation does not lead to a learning effect among the members in the sense of competence building: “Overall, however, (…) the participation function in the sense of a ‘learning platform for climate-protecting behaviour and climate-protecting measures’ is hardly perceptible, although the cooperatives we studied are active in climate protection” (ibid.: 276).

Von Blanckenburg nevertheless draws a positive conclusion for cooperatives compared to other forms of enterprise, despite the empirical finding of only limited available and partially used participation opportunities: "Despite the conditions, which may not be easy in reality, it must be emphasized that every cooperative member has the opportunity to contribute his or her own interests. Within the participatory organizational structure of cooperatives, climate protection can be discussed and measures decided and implemented in a way that goes beyond what is possible in other forms of enterprise" (ibid.).

Above all, overarching positive effects of participation are emphasized, which could be proven: "Participation (…) ensures effective climate protection, first by finding solutions that integrate as many positions as possible, second by ensuring that the decisions taken meet with a high level of acceptance, and third by building up competencies within the framework of the participation processes and by promoting awareness-raising" (ibid.: 277).

Participation in the Critical Perspective of Systems Theory: The Hegemony of Democratic Bureaucracy

Niklas Luhmann, in his system-theoretical view, does see possibilities for the creation of "legitimation through procedures"[65] but fundamentally problematizes the idea and expectations of participation and legitimation of political action, since hopes of the 1960s quickly faded and were disappointed in the following period: "But the loud dramatization of the problem of legitimacy only made sense as long as one saw possibilities of creating legitimacy – above all through better participation. The expectation, strange as it may seem in retrospect, was that more participation would lead to more consent – rather than more disappointment. In this respect, the two issues, participation and legitimation, were closely related and consequently faded into each other" (Luhmann 2009: 159 f.).

In terms of the basic principle and based on previous experience, he sees hope in participation as inflated. He attributes this to an excessive belief in education and an ignorance of social class differences, leading to an absurdity of Habermas' original idea "It is on these tensions that the old idea of participation breaks down. If new hopes are placed on *procedures as a* result, these hopes are designed from the outset in far too small a format – without a sense of proportion and without a sense of realities. This applies to voice regulations within organizations, but also to the lofty idea of a possibly effective 'discourse free of domination'" (ibid.: 161). Finally, he

[65] See Luhmann 1983, who has already pointed out the problem of disappointment in participation procedures (Luhmann 1983: 233 ff.) and paradoxical processes within the administration (ibid.: 203 ff.).

even rejects the term legitimation; it only obscures the fact that it would only be about governmental practices, which is what it is all about in essence: "One should not be seduced into illusionary ideas by the choice of the term legitimation. It is only about prognostic and practical-rhetorical problems of re-election or non-re-election of governments – about nothing more and nothing less" (ibid.). Luhmann wants to overcome these conceptualizations and instead deal with political processes in a more concrete and at the same time abstract way, for instance by analyzing "social system, communication, action, complexity, selection, evolution, self-reference, etc." – that is, in line with the analytical grid of systems theory (see ibid.: 162). "Historical concepts such as participation or legitimation cannot be adopted uncontrollably; otherwise, with the help of these concepts, one places expectations in contexts in which they cannot be fulfilled, and thus provokes disappointment" (ibid.). In his view, formulas such as legitimacy reduce complexity too much, since "it is easier to communicate about values than about realities" (ibid.: 164).

He recognizes the main problem in the fact that more participation subsequently also leads to more bureaucracy (so-called demo-bureaucracy): "Like a puppet in a puppet (note: what is meant is a Russian matrjoschka puppet), participation develops into an organization within the organization, a bureaucracy within the bureaucracy. The result can be censured under the name of bureaucracy and praised under the name of participation. The double evaluation then has an immobilizing effect: one affirms for reasons of principle what one considers bad in implementation. The individual resigns and settles for individual strategies of getting along, of increasing influence or even of defence and self-immunization" (ibid.: 163).[66] Luhmann points out that due to this structural logic, original goals of participation with regard to changing the mode of the system are lost: "Insofar as this result itself has been a goal of structural reforms, one has achieved the goal. Insofar as it was intended to set structural reforms in motion, the procedure has not been successful. Apparently, even demobureaucracies are subject to the general law of bureaucracy

[66] Luhmann explicitly explains his idea of bureaucratization through participation elsewhere: "Democratization already means in itself: Multiplication of the burden of decision. One decision becomes many decisions. Whoever participates in committees, commissions, conferences, senates, councils, must decide how to cast his vote. Often he has to take part in further meetings, which are supposed to ensure a coordinated voting, because otherwise the aggregability and the connectivity of the decision-making would be endangered and random majorities would rule. Voting, for its part, requires preparations, some at random meetings, some at arranged ones; and it requires specially elected organizers in each case. Democracy means the resolution and recombination of factual decision-making, and the organization required for this inevitably takes on bureaucratic, pre-regulated, formalized structures" (ibid.: 226).

to minimize change" (ibid.). Luhmann tries to substantiate this with examples of practiced participation: "Everywhere where results have to be achieved within a certain time, recognizable ineffectiveness, overload and nonsense have admittedly prevented the full realization of the principle of participation. Especially in industrial enterprises which have experimented with participation, the hoped-for participation in power, the intended decentralization, has not materialized. This is shown by studies from Yugoslavia, but also from Chile" (ibid.).

Ultimately, for Luhmann, participation has to struggle with paradoxes of society as a whole, "against which old postulates such as participation or orientation towards values with which one can earn legitimacy break down" (ibid.: 165). Modern society, he argues, endangers itself through the structure of its rationality in economics, science, medicine, education, and politics, "by producing an environment in which it can no longer sustain and perpetuate itself. For this means that if you act right, you act wrong" (ibid.). Welfare state policies create problems simply by "solving problems, and can only solve problems by creating problems" (ibid.). The idea, in turn, of solving problems through political planning and control, would result in solving only residual problems and unintended side effects, which would, however, remain "within the framework of acceptable costs or tolerable inconvenience" (ibid.). From this Luhmann immediately concludes, "Today it looks rather the other way round: that the work on many small-scale daily problems leads into large-scale problems that can no longer be solved. Could it be, then, that our society is a paradoxical system, or at least that its self-reflection forces it to describe its unity as a paradox? If this were so, it would be obvious that such a structural problem cannot be dealt with by demanding more participation or by noting that society constantly disregards the values to which it feels bound" (ibid.: 165 f.). Instead, Luhmann returns to the republican political system and sees only the work of government and opposition, and specifically democratic influence through elections, as a solution to the legitimacy-participation problem. However, this leaves open how he intends to address the issue of citizens' lack of influence in society merely through the act of voting, the inadequacies of the political system, as well as dissatisfaction and lack of trust in the citizens' political system and disenchantment with voting. Luhmann's frustrated walk away from the individual acts of direct participation, which can certainly be seen as problematic and paradoxical, seems quite understandable, but refocusing on the political system does not change its weaknesses and lack of citizen influence on public issues. But for Luhmann, a hope for participation ultimately remains pure illusion, a belief and value system that simulates democracy, since one ultimately encounters an "underlying paradox": "One wants to democratize operations and preserve their autonomy, that is, one wants to realize co-determination and self-determination at the same time. This has a double consequence: on the one hand, the individual is resigned to *illusions as* far as democracy and autonomy are concerned. The bearer of this illusion is the group or, as one likes to say: the team. The team can be both at the same time: co-determination and self-determination. It is created, praised and defended in order to maintain this illusion. But this requires a renunciation of feeding back experiences with one's own decisions into the organization. The team is irresponsible" (ibid.: 228). While on the one hand irresponsibilities of the group are created, on the other hand decision-making processes are initiated which spread uncontrolled and thus self-referentially follow their own dynamics and logics, and in the end only cost resources: "On the other hand, the contradiction of co-determination and self-determination becomes *productive.* Every move in favor of one principle forces compensations for the other. Since decisions can be arbitrarily decomposed, pulled apart and related to each other, the 'material' of which the organization is made does not resist this. It is not impossible, so it does not refute the principles. Only time and money become perceptibly scarcer" (ibid.: 229). Thus, Luhmann calls for "more restraint" in the face of this paradox of a "productive illusion" (ibid.).

It is not surprising that Luhmann also rejects ideas of a stronger consideration of civil society for the further development of society (Luhmann 2008: 8), especially since he points to effective inclusion and exclusion mechanisms within networks (ibid.: 227 ff.; 233 ff.), which in their structural descriptions essentially correspond to the analysed dark sides of social capital and civil society (see above) (see on this also Fuhse 2010).

Facing Future Challenges: What Role Will the Overburdened Citizen Play?
Oscar Gabriel focused on the problematic expectation in the participatory approach of the individual in the sense of "excessive expectations of the interest, the level of information, the readiness to participate, the ability and willingness to compromise of the famous 'average citizen'" (Gabriel 1983: 102). Thus, Gabriel recognizes a binding of participation and quali fication ideas: "For this reason, the demand for extended participation often occurs together with the desire for more or less far-reaching changes in political consciousness. According to these ideas, the functioning of participatory democracy depends on the existence of politically informed, interested, active citizens who are willing and able to engage in discussion and who prove capable of seeing through the manipulative contexts that supposedly exist and of recognising their 'objective' interests" (ibid.: 102).

Gabriel objects: "Normatively, of course, there is nothing wrong with the model of the responsible citizen. For the social scientist (…), however, this textbook citizen has about the same usefulness as 'homo oeconomicus' for the design of economic policy strategies. It seems more appropriate to start from the empirical facts that the normal citizens of Western democracies divide their scarce time between a number of different spheres of activity, among which politics, although increasing, still plays a subordinate role. According to all the information available to us, continuous participation in politics is currently of interest to a numerically small group of the population whose social background is unrepresentative. As long as these conditions do not change, additional opportunities for participation primarily create additional opportunities for the already active to exert influence. This does not have to be negative, but it runs counter to the expectations of the expansion of participation opportunities" (ibid.). Therefore, Gabriel also sees advantages of representative democracy: "Representative institutions can currently even help to protect the interests of the non-active to some extent" (ibid.). Therefore, Gabriel cannot automatically assume a "more" of democracy through participation: "'More participation' does not automatically lead to more democracy, if only because conflicts are conceivable between the individual goals aimed at with the expansion of participation" (ibid.: 103).

Reinhard Hendler pointed out the problem of apathy as early as 1977: "On the one hand, the extremely widespread political apathy among the population could lead to many citizens not making use of the opportunities for participation at all" (Hendler 1977: 24). But Hendler counters: "It is true that one can hardly speak of a general interest in urban development in larger circles of the population at the moment. For it is difficult to overlook the fact that at present, as a rule, increased attention is only paid to questions of the structural-spatial design of the place when the corresponding measures affect the personal, especially economic, sphere of interest of the citizen" (ibid.: 25). However, urban planning arouses increasing interest, since it concerns "the design of the closest spatial environment of each individual person", whereby "public administration begins to intervene to an ever greater extent in the personal sphere of life of the individual with serious consequences" (ibid.). Hendler also continues to assume increasing interest, since the "structural-political conditions of the local area require an intensification of urban planning" (ibid.). From this, Hendler deduces for concrete participation instruments that these should not presuppose "permanent, active participation based on one's own initiative by all citizens called upon here in each case (the urban public or those affected)" (ibid.: 25). They would simply fail due to apathy, instead the administration was obliged "to establish direct contacts with the citizen", the municipality had to take the initiative and seek dialogue with the citizens (ibid.: 25.). Since activity by citizens could not always be expected (such as citizens' initiatives etc.), the administration had to provide constant support to the citizen, "and here in particular to those who have not learned or are for other reasons unable to articulate and effectively represent their interests" (ibid.: 26). "It must, as far as this is necessary in each case, give suggestions, provide assistance, if necessary also actualize an only potentially existing readiness to participate, in short: it must provide 'participation assistance' within the framework of its possibilities" (ibid.). Under no circumstances should this lead to manipulation, paternalism, the imposition of participation or the creation of a "people of participants", but everyone who is willing to participate must be given the chance to "realise this willingness" (ibid.). The administration must also champion the interests of citizens who "do not want to get involved in the planning of the local area in the context of civic participation, or at least not to the same extent as others" (ibid.). Ultimately, Hendler counters the apathy argument with the high interest of the population as well as the possibility of controlling participation procedures with regard to the group of participants (ibid.). Even 36 years later, Walter (2013) sees a possibility precisely in the fact that frustration leads to "real" and not simulated participation: "The accumulation of frustration must first have gone beyond a tolerable limit before new insights break through and behaviors that have become routine change. Then, however, this often happens violently and fundamentally. Then it would no longer be possible to speak of merely simulative participation" (ibid.). On the other hand, Walter addresses a problem of overload and a problem of disappointment or frustration in participation, which result from the increasing complexity of social issues and limited political problem-solving potential (ibid.).

As participation advocates, Adalbert Evers and Roland Roth assume that the power of citizens it fundamentally underestimated, stating firstly that it is a prejudice that citizens and civic engagement have only limited capacities and secondly arguing that they cannot be managed by politics (e.g., municipalities delegate mainly unrewarding tasks such as outdoor facilities to citizens, but no substantial issues) (Evers and Roth 2005: 104). Citizens should therefore not be planned as "gap fillers", but the opportunity should be used "to test the resilience and productivity of civic engagement in times of austerity" (ibid.). The potential of civic engagement is therefore underestimated, citizens are underchallenged (ibid.).

In addition to the advocates of participation, critical comments and findings have long existed,[67] for example addressed by Sauer (1994): "What does it mean

[67] On the question of enhancing legitimacy and accountability, see Abels (2007) and Bringenberg (2013); on the failure of participation processes, Avenhaus et al. (2006b); on conditions for political participation (socio-structural, etc.), Baum (1978) and Buse et al. (1978); on experiences and evaluations of various participatory instruments Bertke et al. (2005) and Blakeley and Evans (2010); on the staging of participation Burchardt (2008); on the establishment of participation standards Avenhaus et al. (2006a).

and for what purpose do we participate?". Basically, the biggest problem (analogous to the findings of civil society research) is the creation of inequalities and the lack of democratic standards (such as minority protection), Schäfer and Schoen (2013) speak here of "more democracy, but only for a few" in the sense of the conflict of goals "between more participation and political equality", since not all population groups participate to the same extent (on further criticism of participation see Klatt et al. 2011; Miessen 2012; Schäfer 2011, 2013a; Blühdorn 2013; Michelsen and Walter 2013; Wagner 2013; Merkel 2015b)).

Chantal Munsch addresses the problem of inequality in the engagement debate in more detail: "The reproduction of social exclusion processes in the area of civic engagement functions both through the forms and the topics of the engagement of socially disadvantaged population groups" (Munsch 2005: 112). Access barriers, for example, the language and availability of people, but also personal contacts are particularly tricky: "People who, for the most part, have no personal relationship to each other apart from their involvement or did not know each other before their involvement, also work together beyond personal sympathy for a specific, limited purpose" (ibid.). Dealing with the problem of access as a matter of course leads to exclusion; it "also excludes population groups that cannot or do not want to participate in this defined way because they are not familiar with this framework due to their biographical experiences or milieu affiliation, associate negative experiences with it, or prefer other frameworks for their engagement" (ibid.). In this context, Munsch also questions whether the "organizational connection really means a public sphere and thus access to engagement for all residents". She rather assumes "that the understanding of the public sphere underlying political and civic engagement conceals the life references of socially disadvantaged population groups as private" (ibid.).

Finally, the gender issue also plays a role, because the necessary resources (time, knowledge, skills, self-esteem, etc.) for an engagement development fall especially to men in higher professional positions: "The male-attributed ideal of the active citizen, who can engage in public structures, free from the concern for daily life, excludes women and men who remain trapped in this concern for a secure existence. Thematically, the social structures underlying poverty and unemployment hardly play a role in the political discussion about civic engagement" (Munsch 2005: 112 f., on this also with reference to civic see energy Fraune 2015).

These problems could result in a pessimistic view of the democratic theoretical potential of participation. A prominent representative of this attitude is Oscar Gabriel, who sees neither empirical-realistic nor normative arguments as tenable with regard to the advocacy of participation (Gabriel 1983: 98). Thus, he argues, participation neither leads to a destabilization of the democratic order, nor can it be understood as an "instrument of the 'emancipation of the underprivileged'" (ibid.). Also, expanded political participation "has so far tended to solidify rather than reduce existing social inequality" (ibid.). Beyond democratic-theoretical normative considerations, practical questions of practicability are therefore ultimately relevant for Gabriel: "which goals are actually to be realized through participation, what motives support it, what the relationship between individual and system goals looks like, what solutions are envisaged for conflicts of goals that arise, and what institutional form extended participation should take" (ibid.).

2.7 Summary

In summary, the following questions and problems of significance for the study can be derived from the theoretical research approaches presented:

- **Effects of participation**: schools of democracy or practice in democracy (Leser 2011) or post-democratic participation as covert elite rule and underpinning of marginalization and exclusion of certain milieus (Blühdorn 2011, 2013)?
- **Politicization and depoliticization, divided role of the citizen**: do new political-social and civic modes of action, civic participation and intervention represent examples of increased politicization of society (Beck 1996; Gatens 2006; Zürn and Weidner 2009; Gehrau 2014) or, on the other hand, is depoliticization taking place in the form of undemocratic-economic-individualistic ulterior motives and principles (Hay 2007; Hay and Stoker 2009; Mouffe 2011)? Do informed, politically-interested and engaged active citizens emerge in this way (Detjen 1999, 2000; Münkler and Krause 2001; Boeser and Schnebel 2013), competent citizens (Münkler 1997), critical citizens (Geißel 2011a) or "politicized non-citizens" who no longer represent civic values despite commitment (Greven 1997, 2000, 2009; Salomon 2010)?
- **Fluctuation and oscillation of participation**: more and more forms and ideas of participation are emerging, demarcations between political, social, organizational, associative participation as well as civic engagement are becoming increasingly difficult (Kersting and Woyke 2012), while the idea of participatory spaces (*invented* and *invited space,* Kersting 2014) and the expansion of the political sphere also emerge on social – and thus almost all spaces of action. The dissolution of boundaries and hybridization through networked worlds and multiple subject areas make it difficult to define them more precisely.
- **Darksides of civil society and social capital**: civil society action can also have dark sides – nepotism, patronage, exclusion and oligarchy, accompanied by in-

creased inequality and marginalization, are core problems, democratic principles and "practicing democracy" need not necessarily be promoted by civil society action (Roth 2003, 2004; Nullmeier 2002; Klatt et al. 2011; Schäfer 2013a). In the variant of binding social capital, social capital can lead to strong internal group cohesion – to the detriment of bridging external ties (Putnam 2000; Geißel 2008a, 2008b).

- **New subject-centered variant of political participation**: a new individualized, project- and subject-centered variant of political and social participation is increasingly being found (Pickel 2012; de Moor et al. 2013; van Deth 2013a, 2014a, 2014b, 2015; Baringhorst 2016a, 2016b; de Moor 2017), which is strongly based on civil society activities and exhibits both professionalized forms and is characterized by individualized forms of collective action (van Deth and Maloney 2012). Here, less formalized engagement without ties to organizations is preferred (Shirky 2008); instead, specialized topic-based participation on changing issues is practiced, avoiding fixed, established, highly structured, and long-term ties. Participation practice is more pragmatic and spontaneous, with more creative-experimental and collaborative components, which can be adapted to the situation and flexibly supplemented in a fragmentary and multimodal way (*hybrid participation*), thus enabling individualized, self-centered participation (Micheletti and McFarland 2011; Ratto and Boler 2014; Lee 2015). Overall, this creates a fluctuating, erratic and dynamic mode that allows for a more open and relaxed participation which is less fixed in terms of time, content and organization, more flexible and much less connected with social or political, ideological or dogmatic values or other higher normative (e.g., ethical or moral) motives (*Lifestyle Politics*, see de Moor et al. 2013; de Moor 2017). Even seemingly contradictory motives are compatible in a pragmatic sense (and often linked to technology-based practices) such as material and common good aspects (Marres 2012). Online-based forms of communication play an essential role in networking and activation (Baringhorst and Yang 2014; Baringhorst 2015, 2016a, 2016b). Although this changes patterns of individual political communication (Vowe 2014), this does not alter the importance of socio-economic resources in the intensity of participation (van Deth 2009; Schlozman et al. 2010; Kersting 2014).

3 Study Design: Analysis of Community Energy Participation

In this explanation of the research approach, in addition to relevant questions, the methodological approach is described and justified. Current research results and theoretical approaches are taken into account, and the limits of the study are defined.

Starting Point: Methods of Qualitative Social Research

In qualitative social research, the research question is often open-ended and describes process or status issues (Krumm and Westle 2009: 118). In this research approach, both process and status dimensions are captured through the elaboration and analysis of social phenomena.

In addition to the research question, the formation of presuppositions and justification of methodological procedures, the definition of individual stages of the investigation (descriptive, classificatory and case-reconstructive, see ibid. 118 f.) are part of a concept specification that takes place here. At its core, the specification first concerns preliminary assumptions, which are derived from research findings and the object of investigation itself. Subsequently, several analytical dimensions are formed and discussed, and contextually adapted questions are developed. Finally, the process leads to the formulation of analytical goals in the form of the development of typological models and the presentation of exemplary characteristics of empirical cases.

The Energiewende in Germany and Opportunities for Citizen Participation

The primary research question of this thesis aims at the forms and intensities of citizen participation processes in the context of renewable energy development in Germany. This concerns three dimensions: first, modes of action in the context of renewable energy at the local level, for example, energy policy measures; second,

J. Radtke, *Community Energy in Germany*,
https://doi.org/10.1007/978-3-658-39320-5_3

Local Energy Policy	Public Participation	Community Energy
Example: Designation of sites for wind energy	*Example:* Participation in wind energy planning	*Example:* Operation of energy facilitiesby community energy projects
Decision-relevant institutions: Political authorities, administrative bodies, working groups	*Decision-relevant institutions:* Political authorities, administrative bodies	*Decision-relevant institutions:* Project management boards, meetings, members
Citizen participation: Discussion, commitment in political parties	*Citizen participation:* Discussion, input of proposal, petition	*Citizen participation:* Membership, public discussion
Type of participation: Political participation	*Type of participation:* Political participation	*Type of participation:* Organizational and social participation, political participation(?)
POLICY SECTOR	CIVIL SOCIETY SECTOR	PRIVATE SECTOR

Fig. 3.1 Participation patterns in the context of renewable energy systems

the involvement of the population through participation processes (in the context of public participation, e.g., in wind power use); and third, civic engagement of citizens in the form of self-initiative to establish community energy initiatives (see Fig. 3.1).[1]

The idea guiding the study is the approach leading to a differentiation of participation and acceptance by the population, either initially unstructured through citizen action (*invented space*, in the sense of a bottom-up initiative) or in the form of targeted measures to involve citizens (*invited space*, in the sense of top-down participation) can result in opportunities for shaping the local space through the use of renewable energies.[2] The starting point of the question in this study is therefore the participation and activity of citizens in the context of the development of renewable energies in Germany. Here, the empirically relevant core question in the foreground is, how the participation and bottom-up initiative movement of citizens takes place and to what extent leeway is created and exploited through contextually

[1]Less attention is paid to the role of the citizen as energy consumer, and especially roles as independent investor and energy producer as well as political actor in (renewable) energy policy offer a direct participation in local energy projects (see Kreß et al. 2014a, 2014b; Rubik et al. 2014). An exception to this is the combined role as investor or energy producer and consumer in the case of prosuming (i.e., purchasing energy produced by an energy company in which the citizen themself is involved as an investor) (see Juntunen 2014; Rifkin 2014: 135 ff.; Hellmann 2018).

[2]The terms invented and invited space are taken from von Kersting (2014).

shaped and application-related opportunities for participation and citizens' own initiative (types, forms and specifics of participation processes). From this, a kind of blueprint of participatory arrangements is to be derived.

Participation in Community Energy Projects

Community energy initiatives offer interested citizens participation in the form of financial participation, membership in the association, and opportunities for co-determination and collaboration.

Disadvantages of participation, such as the lack of a goal-oriented commitment, are largely avoided in the case of community energy through strongly goal-oriented action with a time-limited radius. In addition, there is also the possibility of dominant management in this case, which does not create a participation-friendly climate. The internal structures of corporations, which are formed in the case of community energy projects, tend to promote this orientation in the sense of shifting decision-making processes to the management board. Despite the fact that the community energy company has a "citizen management" (e.g., in the case of members working on a voluntary basis) means that the classification of Keppler, Rau and Zöllner towards a high level of participation ("citizen control") tends to be satisfied (see Keppler 2010; Rau and Zöllner 2011: 19; Carmen 2014: 13 f.), the transfer of design tasks to citizens in conjunction with the establishment of a civil society does not automatically result in broad participation.

In addition, in cases of wind energy use in municipalities, it is also possible to make use of state-initiated procedures within the framework of participation opportunities in planning procedures for wind energy plants. Here, there are classic possibilities of information, (written) submission of criticism, suggestions, etc. to the competent specialist administration and the citizens' assembly, as well as within the framework of protest procedures, in particular petitions and the formation of citizens' initiatives (in addition to other forms of protest). While these participation procedures and options are likely to correspond to the predominant application in practice, there are also other possibilities for participation, such as in the context of planning cells, (citizens') workshops, deliberative forums such as climate protection circles, etc.

In addition, some other aspects play a role that seem rather unusual for a private-sector enterprise: On the one hand, this concerns the fact that in a lot of energy projects work is done on a voluntary basis. On the other hand, the members of the energy project can also participate in the sense that they are actively involved within it, contribute their own ideas and participate in the shaping and activities of the project (e.g., working groups can be founded, etc.). In addition to these forms of collaboration, the members also have a certain degree of co-determination, which is secured through voting rights at meetings. In the case of energy cooperatives, the rule here is that each member has one vote, irrespective of the level of financial participation. Furthermore, internal processes and procedures as well as external actions are characterized on the one hand by a certain degree of transparency and openness and on the other hand by a joint and diverse external presence – provided that the goals and ideals of the energy initiatives are taken as a basis. In addition, there are cooperative and networking activities of the energy project, which relate not only to contacts in the private sector, but also with civil society and government institutions. Finally, other activities of the energy initiatives stand out, which may relate to a social and/or ecological commitment that goes beyond the ordinary activities of the project (e.g., events, participation in ecological activities).

3.1 Analysis of Forms of Participation

3.1.1 Forms of Access to Participation

The combination of general participation research and specific energy participation research results in three dimensions, which relate to the specifics of participation (how people participate, what does participation mean?), social conditions (formation of communities: participation cultures) and effects of participation (social capital, identification, acceptance).

Form of Participation: How Is Participation Carried Out?

Questions

- What forms of participation are designed, made available and used?
- How are participation terms understood, interpreted and applied?
- What do participation processes look like in detail? What comparisons can be made between participation mechanisms and models? Does a step-by-step formation of structures take place (bottom-up initiated), or does a project create participation offerings (top-down driven)?

- How is participation defined, what forms are used, invented and filled (*invented/ invited space*)?[3]

Participatory Practice: Who Participates?

Questions

- In which role do the individuals see themselves, how do they define themselves? What activity develops among the participants, to what extent is participation or the use of participation options pronounced? What are the "popular" participation instruments and mechanisms?

Participation Effects: What Influence Does Participation Have on Individuals, Social Communities, Local Discourses and Publics? What Social Dynamics Emerge and Are Initiated?

Questions

- What different cultures of participation are formed in different social contexts, in different forms of participation and in connection with varying forms of technology use?
- Which social processes run synchronously with the formation and establishment within new social communities ("internal processes"), how do they influence participation?
- What mechanisms of participation (such as co-determination, engagement, collaboration) are found within the communities? How do the communities relate to their environment externally ("external processes" such as cooperation, partnerships, conflicts)?

Participation and Motivation

In this context, a distinction must be made between three forms of activity: independent of the community, within the community and collectively by the community (at the societal micro and meso levels). First, an individual level can be recorded, which includes the motivation and activity of the members (on the one

[3] Wesselink et al. (2011: 2699) summarize the following questions in this regard: "What are we trying to achieve? Is this legitimacy, effectiveness, efficiency, or representation? Do all relevant actors agree? Is participation necessarily the best way to realize these goals? What if actors have different purposes and resources? Conversely, while participation is considered a solution by many, the existence of separate participation rationales indicates that the problems they are trying to solve are very different".

hand, individual motivation of the participants, e.g., return-oriented or common good-oriented; on the other hand, collaboration of the members within the enterprise collaboration). In addition, an organizational level is found, which refers to the organizational-institutional arrangement (influence of the members in the form of co-determination; voting rights of the members at meetings; entry threshold of participation; open, participative and transparent procedures within the company, association or project). Finally, associative action unfolds within the community energy projects, companies or associations (through entry, within or through the association itself; cooperative action of the project, voluntary activities as well as further engagement of the project).

3.1.2 Forms of Participation in Community Energy Projects

In this context, modes and possibilities of participation concern different (communicative, structural and procedural) access channels of discursive arrangements, which can show different degrees of formalization and levels of activity.[4] Instead of vertical ladders or pyramids, modes of participation are to be depicted in a horizontal orientation:

1. ***Informative-exchanging***: (a) Communicating information (uptake) about renewable energy, planning procedures, design, sites, installations, technology, etc.; (b) Local exchange within neighborhood, district, municipality or residential area.
2. ***Participatory-involving***: (a) Informative participation in briefings, walk-throughs, policy committee meetings, etc.; (b) Formal participation in formal proceedings, submissions, hearings, meetings, etc.
3. ***Actively shaping-involving***: (a) Discourse participation in forums for shaping municipal and regional energy policy, for example, agenda group, active group, forum, planning cell, etc.; (b) Protest participation in the form of rallies, events, petitions, etc.; (c) Associative participation in citizens' initiatives, associations, federations; (d) Monetary participation through financial shares and membership in community energy projects.

[4] This study primarily considers associative participation within community energy initiatives. Other, accompanying participation activities are only dealt with in the empirical part in the case of contact and exchange with community energy initiatives.

Starting points for participation in the context of local arrangements such as citizens' initiatives or public forums arise on the one hand through associations of citizens via accession or membership, and on the other hand through public procedures in the form of the targeted use of special participation procedures (in the case of concrete planning procedures). In addition, dialogical-discursive instruments (such as forums and dialogues) can bring together several groups of actors and citizens (see Table 3.1).

Essentially, therefore, a distinction is made between three modes of participation:

- First, **state-initiated procedures** of participation and political framework conditions (public). These include participation in planning procedures in the case of wind energy at the local level through public participation (citizens' meetings, citizens' submissions to the administration, etc.).
- Second, **participatory arrangements** for group-internal participation and collaboration (non-public). Within this framework, organizational participation through co-determination and input of ideas (meetings, elections, voting rights) (formalized) as well as individual intra-organizational participation and collaboration are possible (e.g., public relations, drafting of a constitution, etc.) (non-formalized).
- Third, **discursive forms of interaction** for the exchange of involved actors, politics and the population (e.g., climate protection forum) (public, not formalized).

Table 3.1 Modes of participation in renewable energy decision making processes

	Public participation	Climate protection or energy forum	Community energy project
Involved	All	Stakeholders, citizens	Members
Participation mode	*Formal*: statements *Non-formal*: town hall meeting	Panel discussion, round table, dialogue event	General meeting, working group
Format	Public	Public or semi-public	Non-public
Classification	Political participation	Political, social, civic participation	Associative-organizational participation *Political, social and civic participation in individual cases*

In the literature, organizational, social and political participation are distinguished from each other. Political participation is classified as institutionalized/non-institutionalized, authored and non-authored, and conventional and unconventional (see Barnes and Kaase 1979; Widmaier 2011). Political participation is present in renewable energies, especially in wind power: Here, citizens participate in the context of public construction planning, through individual input, meetings, appeals, etc. (Involvement in decision-making, planning processes and construction or ongoing operation, although the latter is rarely the case or even possible; in the case of companies, influence is only possible for the shareholders).

There is also the opinion in the literature that community energy initiatives themselves mean political participation, which is made dependent on certain conditions (e.g., orientation towards the common good, see Holstenkamp and Degenhart 2013) – however, this would have to be differentiated from case to case. In terms of the general classification of political participation, community energy initiatives would be non-institutionalized and offer unconventional forms of participation, the procedures are partly formalized (e.g., voting), partly not formalized (working groups). According to van Deth's (2014a, 2014b) recent view, participation within community energy initiatives could belong to an extended form of political participation; this question will be discussed finally at the end of this study.

In addition, community energy projects could offer social participation within the project community. According to Jan van Deth, this means forms of participation that do not arise directly in the political system, but in the social system. Community energy initiatives stand at the interface between private enterprise and civil society association. From case to case, depending on their structure and orientation, they may be closer to civil society associations or private sector enterprises. In any case, they offer organizational participation within society; social participation through the formation of working groups, events and open discourse forums can be added. Jan van Deth assumes an entanglement of political and social participation in that background variables do not lead to a division into political or social participation, but are complementary in an exchange relationship. This leads to the assumption that both modes of participation behave like twins to each other (van Deth 2001: 200), in that "social participation and political involvement are almost always directly and positively related. Social and political participation thus behave as mutual complements or like twins to each other" (ibid.: 202). However, van Deth, after his own research, qualifies that the general thesis "cannot be supported unreservedly": "Political and social participation are indeed closely related, but both the forms of political participation and the forms of social participation have to be considered in their specific cultural context" (ibid.: 216). This insight makes it clear that in this question, too, connections must be analyzed on a case-specific and context-dependent basis, which is why, in the context of the present study, participatory forms must first be considered in principle and with an open impetus – without a previously definitionally restricted approach. Consequently, this leads to an application specific research perspective on participation, initially considering the disclosure of the participatory arrangement in the specific case context, it is then necessary to assess which features can discovered and which mappings of participation modes can be made.

Based on the methodological research approaches presented above, three dimensions of participation – including the questions derived from them – will be addressed (derived from Erhard et al. 2013: 39)[5]:

1. **Inclusiveness of the participation offer**: how many local citizens participate in community energy projects and connected participation processes and options on the local level in energy transition policy?[6]
   - Is the participation process and participation time in the initiatives characterized by the criteria of proximity, transparency, fairness, discursivity and openness? In the case of organizational participation, how is the internal organization and governance structured: important here are voting rights, inclusion and exclusion mechanisms, deliberation, independence, openness, inclusion, construction of the participation option and organization, modes of action and effectiveness of the management.
   - Are solutions developed that create acceptance and trust among the population?[7]

[5] In a study on community energy initiatives, the effects of "legitimising decisions" (democratic legitimation), "making procedures and control objectives more efficient or achieving them" (control efficiency) and "mobilizing citizens to act on their own responsibility" (emancipatory aspect) are named (Rau and Zöllner 2011: 134 f.).

[6] According to Kubicek (2014: 287), examples of the input dimension are: personnel and material resources, organizational procedures, legal requirements, political commitment. Criteria here are (ibid.): legitimacy, connectivity, bindingness; extended: deliberative-discursive legitimacy of the throughput dimension.

[7] According to Kubicek (2014: 287), examples of the output dimension are: information and communication offerings, for example, newsletters, forums, polis, meetings, focus groups, telephone surveys. Criteria here are (ibid.): appropriateness, acceptability, usability. Examples of the outcome dimension are according to Kubicek (ibid.): use: number of participants, retrievals; quality of participants, especially representativeness; quality and relevance of contributions. The consequential effect describes the decisions made; the criterion here is comprehensibility (see ibid.).

2. **Equal and unequal participation requirements**: social characteristics, access, formal and informal barriers to participation, options for contributing opinions.
   - Specifics of the participation offers: only those who clear the financial entry hurdle can become members of a commmunity energy project. In some cases, members are no longer accepted after a short time, and there are also completely closed structures. The minimum duration of membership can also lead to an indirect reason for exclusion, for example for younger and financially weak persons.
3. **Effects of participation**[8]: learning democracy through action in discourse and through deliberation (contacts, exchanges and networking), procedures such as fairness, transparency, dialogue, acquisition of knowledge and skills and development of trust, dealing with conflicts, problem-solving skills and strategies (development of social capital).
   - Negative tendencies due to the community's handling of clientelism, exclusionary modes of action, minority discrimination, informal agreements, intransparency and suppression of discourse.

Assessing the Democratic Quality of Community Energy Projects

From the preliminary considerations for the present study, the results of recent participation research (see Fox 2013; van Deth 2014a; Baringhorst 2016a, 2016b) as well as criteria for evaluating participatory arrangements from the literature (see Rowe and Frewer 2005; Geißel 2008a, 2008b; Vetter 2008; Erhard et al. 2013), concrete questions can be derived regarding the democratic quality of community energy projects:

- **Places of democracy and associative-organizational democracy**: Are community energy projects perceived as compatible with democratic principles, or are such projects organized on the basis of private-sector principles are evaluated as non-democratic in general?

[8] Examples of impact according to Kubicek (2014: 287) are: substantive goal achievement in the subject area, leading to (a) changes in attitudes (e.g., trust in political institutions), (b) changes in behavior (e.g., future participation, voter turnout). Effects, according to Kubicek (2014: 288 f.), are first on the individuals involved: building and strengthening trust, expertise, commitment, etc.; second, on the community (district, neighborhood): efficiency, traction, social capital and cohesion; third, on the decision-making processes: greater influence of citizens in general and of previously excluded population groups in particular.

- **Understandings and ideas of democracy**: Are there various understandings and ideas of democracy to be found by members of community energy projects? This could be in the sense of concrete inclusive social action in everyday life (through institutionalization in participatory formats and processes), or in a representative sense through delegated power or in a pragmatic sense through financial and material participation.
- **Decision-making**: What does co-determination mean in community energy projects? How is the principle of co-determination evaluated in the context of energy democracy?
- **Schools of democracy and learning democratic norms**: What basic democratic principles can participatory procedures and community energy projects teach?
- **Invited and inventend spaces of participation:** Are there bottom-up or top-down approaches which are enabling community energy participation?

Furthermore, analytical levels can be derived for an empirical investigation. On a process level, the establishment phases of energy projects can be examined with regard to internal social processes and modes of action and procedures. In addition, on an organizational level, a structural analysis of the individual actor constellation can be used to assess the structural characteristics and set framework conditions of the organization with regard to a suitable and conducive framework for participation. Finally, a spillover level is captured by mapping the possible creation of acceptance of the energy systems through social effects (generation of community, discourse, trust, inclusion, social capital, democracy learning).

Working Hypotheses of the Study

Community energy initiatives offer the opportunity for participation, collaboration and the possibility to formulate and contribute ideas and actions of individuals. In this way, they serve the idea of citizen participation and co-determination in democracy and fulfil direct democratic principles. In this sense, the participation of citizens in renewable energy systems goes hand in hand with an increased socio-political engagement of citizens and an active contribution of members within society.

The participatory arrangements of the energy initiatives depend on both internal organizational structures and external framework conditions. Internal structures concern strategies, personnel and management of the energy initiatives. The external framework conditions relate to cooperation with other actors (cooperation potential), the local environment and political framework conditions. Over time, there is increased cooperation with various actors, and a specific network of actors is formed. This increases the degree of cohesion between civil society, private sector and state actors, and at the same time tends to reduce the potential for conflict. Within this, specific *story lines* of the initiatives can emerge (in the sense of *policy narratives* as well as identification/commitment with the community energy project and a sense of belonging/social cohesion), which have the potential to hold different views together. In this way, challenges, hurdles and conflicts can be addressed collectively. This can lead to spillover effects in that further community energy initiatives are formed or learn from each other (learning effects for initiators, members, involved actors, see Junginger et al. 2010), but also other actors change their strategies (multiplier effects through the onset of commitment by involved persons and actors).

The research objectives are, in particular, to work out the typical characteristics of citizen participation in renewable energy projects on the basis of cases and in this way to create a situationally and flexibly applicable as well as modifiable typification of participatory arrangements of community energy initiatives.

3.2 The Empirical Approach to the Study of Community Energy

Through an analytical-empirical view of the processual level, which is oriented towards specific and individual modes of action of the actors, overarching patterns of subjective views, motivations, modes of action are to become visible. This empirical-analytical approach is oriented towards the participation groups and tries to elaborate certain subjective modes of action that occur repeatedly (independent of collective affiliations) and their specifics in order to capture the different logics in the generation of collectivity (see Pias 2016). Here, two dimensions of participation are of crucial importance:

- **Energy communities**: How are the energy communities structured and motivated? What subjective patterns of community action occur? Which action-specific orientations of the communities emerge? (***ways of community action***).
- **Participatory process**: Which dynamics evolve into specific forms of participation concerning community energy? What are the relationships between them (overlaps, parallels, reciprocal relationships)? Which spaces of participation and specific modes of creating community spaces open and close? What are the modes of access to these spaces like? What is the relationship between participants and upstream discussion spaces (*invited space*) and self-created forms of community action and participation (*invented space*)? (***spaces of participation***).

An example of participatory dynamics can be the already mentioned problem of the possible trade-off within communities between professionalization and self-interest (Does the common good or return motivation constitute a vehicle function for engagement? To what extent does individual motivation shape individual understandings of participation and democratic principles? How do individual motivations and perceptions influence the participatory process and space)?

Another point of inquiry is the internal processes of participatory communities and procedures. In this context, research has differentiated various areas (Ison 2010): power and accountability, networking and organizational structure, decision-making processes and management of opposition and conflict, public and private spheres, and performance criteria and outcome.

A reconstruction of the internal governance structure of community energy initiatives is of particular interest here with regard to participation options, decision-making processes and co-determination (Ison 2010: 11 ff.).[9] Within the internal governance arrangements, Ison distinguishes between meta-governance (of the members), strategic governance (of the management) and day-to-day governance (of the project, departments, partners, local actors).

In particular, community practice, which is based on the convergence of community goals, criteria and knowledge (which should lead to awareness of mutual expectations and the formation of social capital), as well as co-generation of knowledge and behavioral change through practical experience, is of outstanding importance (Ison 2010: 32). With regard to decision-making processes, the importance of unilateral decisions by only one person, majority voting and consensus decisions are emphasized (Ison 2010: 33).

The effects that result from organizational design of community energy projects are decisive for the conditions of all types of community action, such as:

- Public image of the project, formation of community, spillover effects on the local and regional level, energy production despite low profit margins (common good orientation), ecological motivation or community motivation (members' identification with all parts of the project strategy and community goals).
- Sharing of knowledge and learning effects: Support for further initiatives and actions within the project.
- Personal-individual evaluation, commitment and values of experience (self-efficacy).

[9] In the case of energy cooperatives, Kneußel (2014: 221) assumes participatory and representative coordination within the organizational form with predetermined governance rules.

- Sense of community, support structures, trust and social cohesion (in the sense of social capital), overarching motive of sense of community, identification and commitment to the project.

Based on these considerations, central research questions regarding participation through community energy initiatives can finally be derived:

1. Internal governance mechanisms and structures: How are community energy projects managed? Who is involved in organizational governance and decision-making processes? What instruments and practices of associative-organizational democracy and democratic forms of co-determination exist?
2. Patterns of cooperation: Why are the social procedures and community structures used to include (or exclude) individuals and actors? What modes of cooperation emerge? Why and in what way are certain actors integrated and others not?
3. Democratic effects: To what extent are social effects such as the acquisition of competencies and qualifications (learning democracy) generated? Do overspill effects on other spheres of social life, community action and influences on other local community members occur? And, in addition, are indications for the creation of binding and bridging social capital through participation apparent? What understanding of democracy is found among members of community energy projects?
4. Drawbacks: What negative tendencies of associative dynamics within the community energy projects such as oligarchy, nepotism, hierarchical power structures, opinion leadership, frustration, disappointment, exclusion and enforcement of particularistic interests are found in internal organizational structures and external ways of action within the local and regional policy networks and climate protection governance?

4 Community Energy Research

4.1 Framing the Debate

New Social Science Methodologies for Energy Research?
"Closing the gap between energy research and modelling, the social sciences, and modern realities" is how Jefferson describes the necessary closing of the gap between (technical and scientific) energy and social science research and real conditions (Jefferson 2014). Despite a long tradition of energy and technology research, renewable energies represent a new challenge for the social sciences (see Groß and Mautz 2014).

As a cross-cutting issue, the energy transition thus represents a transdisciplinary challenge in scientific terms (Heinrichs et al. 2011a; Radtke and Hennig 2013; Schweizer-Ries et al. 2013; Grunwald 2015a, 2016a; Schweizer-Ries et al. 2016; von Weizsäcker et al. 2016), from which the need for cooperation between natural, social and human sciences in the climate and energy field can be derived (Christ et al. 2012; Holm et al. 2013).

However, in the course of this, there is also a shift in thinking from disciplinary boundaries to a more holistic approach, because by linking to the concept of sustainability, ecological, economic and social aspects are increasingly being thought of integratively in the energy context (Santoyo-Castelazo and Azapagic 2014, also for example with regard to the acceptance of energy systems, see Upham et al. 2015).

One core aspect of social science energy research concerns the current sustainability paradigm (Heinrichs et al. 2011b). However, research is still unable to determine exactly what sustainability is in the first place (see on the definition and

J. Radtke, *Community Energy in Germany*,
https://doi.org/10.1007/978-3-658-39320-5_4

history of the term Grunwald and Kopfmüller 2021; Grober 2013; Pufé 2014; Stolze and Petrlic 2016). In the political system, a shift from environmental to sustainability policy or governance is clearly visible (Stark 2006; Voß et al. 2006; Leach 2007; Pesendorfer 2007; Heinrichs and Biermann 2016), which is more concerned with socio-ecological resilience and transformations (Smith and Stirling 2010a, 2010b). In the thematic field of community energy, a step towards the concept of sustainability in the context of business and economy is not far (Radke 1999; Langer 2011), neither is a step towards sustainability-oriented municipal enterprises (Sandberg 2011), the use of sustainability indicators (Rösch et al. 2016), sustainable corporate governance (Fellner 2015), holistic life cycle management (Herrmann 2010) as well as the topic of corporate social responsibility (see Hardtke 2011) in connection with cultural social responsibility (Steinkellner 2015). Although the processes of the emergence of new markets and the institutionalization and legitimization processes of new forms of organization and economy as well as technology can be regarded as current phenomena (see on the Fairtrade phenomenon Doherty et al. 2014, on biotechnology Markard et al. 2016, within companies Müller-Christ 2012), well-known questions of business ethics remain topical in the context of sustainability (see Beschorner et al. 2015).

Community energy initiatives are in every respect an example of "sustainable investing" (Schaefers 2014) as well as the implementation of the idea of socially shaping demand management (Breukers et al. 2013) and promoting the communication of sustainability (Michelsen and Godemann 2007; Prexl 2010; Fischer et al. 2016). Also, a connection between smaller-scale projects like voluntary energy initiatives led by local citizens and the current trend of enterprises can be assumed: thus, small and medium-sized enterprises are described as a business model of the Anthropocene (North 2015). Finally, the nexus of energy, entrepreneurial context and gender evidenced in the present research is of importance that should not be underestimated (Sovacool et al. 2013). In the context of community energy, however, the basic economic orientation also raises the question of the extent to which civil society can promote sustainability at all (Renn 2012; Frantz and Fuchs 2014). In this respect, the private sector and civil society are often no (longer) viewed in opposition to each other, but are rather considered integratively in terms of "management perspectives for civil society in the 21st century" (von Müller and Zinth 2014).

In the future, social science aspects of sustainable development (see Michael 2015) will continue to play a major role, especially related to topics such as resilience (Barr and Devine-Wright 2012; Becker 2014; Kegler 2014; Schaffer et al. 2014), human–space relations in the field of technology (on this, see Bailey and

Devine-Wright 2013; Radtke 2015) as well as at the urban neighborhood level (Berardi 2015).

Questions of "energy and society" (see Calvert 2015) thus have a considerable impact on the tasks of the social sciences, which already analyze numerous individual topics in the environmental and sustainability sector (Renn 2001; Berkhout et al. 2003). Recently, therefore, a social science research agenda for the energy sector has been drawn up, bringing together the findings of the last 15 years (Sovacool 2014). Critical, reflexive and exploratory questions about contributions of the social sciences to energy research have been repeatedly addressed (Shippee 1981; Rochlin 2014; Ryan et al. 2014), often including a call for the integration of the social sciences into energy research (Sovacool et al. 2014). Recent research developments and findings appear to be leading to an overall strengthening of social science energy research, for example, emphasizing an intervention and importance of social science as a critical science in global challenges of the Anthropocene (Lövbrand et al. 2015; Trachtenberg 2015a, 2015b), developing deconstructionist perspectives regarding the demystification of energy facts (Sovacool and Brown 2015), and making connections of social science to energy policy (Stirling 2014). Further examples of the interaction of social and ecological-scientific factors of influence can be found in the context of marine energy use (Bonar et al. 2015) or with regard to the importance of communities in the hydropower sector (Bracken et al. 2014).

On an overarching level, the socio-scientific-political research agenda concerns the governance of socio-technical systems, which often serves as an explanatory model, especially for transformation processes (Borrás and Edler 2014). The starting point is the idea that the energy transition represents a regime change (Strunz 2013). Here, the energy transition can be viewed from both a socio-technical and a multi-level perspective (Verbong and Geels 2007). The analysis of energy use as a socio-technical system also explicitly considers social factors such as norms, social capital and cooperation (Bock et al. 2015). Another, actor-centered perspective can be found in network research approaches in the energy (policy) sector (Poocharoen and Sovacool 2012; Parag et al. 2013), there are also approaches to building frameworks that can explain energy infrastructure decisions and make them comprehensible (Whitton et al. 2015). The newer and innovative actor-network approach can also be applied in the field of energy research (Wong 2016).

On the level of political policy research, with regard to the linkage of community energy initiatives, political governance and design, and contextual actor constellations, political strategy analyses (Tils 2005) and interpretative policy analyses (Münch 2015), but also laboratory experiments (Zieseniß and Ernst 2013), can generate promising insights into influences and interactions as well as mechanics and modes of action of energy policy styles; new perspectives of policy research can expand this in the future (Wenzelburger and Zohlnhöfer 2015).

The systemic analysis of transformation processes has led to a separate branch in research in the form of transition research, which analyses sustainability transformations as a societal challenge (Hübner et al. 2015) and often analyses temporal dynamics such as of energy transition processes (Sovacool 2016). In the case of sustainability transitions, the importance of social modes of action is emphasized (Pant et al. 2015; Rauschmayer et al. 2015; Rauschmayer and Omann 2015), which overall exhibit a greater range and diversity in their forms of action and modes of impact (Stirling 2011).

From this perspective, the majority of the literature explains the governance of energy systems in terms of flexible – that is, learning, reflexive, knowledge-based, participatory, collaborative and transformative – forms of governance and transition management, which tend to lead to greater sustainability, although this is certainly controversial in detail (Voß et al. 2006; Kemp et al. 2007; Smith and Stirling 2007; Walker and Shove 2007; Jacob et al. 2015; Challies et al. 2016; Newig et al. 2016; Stirling 2016; van der Arend and Behagel 2016) and analyzed in the case of the energy transition as an example (Gailing and Röhring 2016; Kuzemko et al. 2016). With regard to the energy transition, the question of the extent to which changes to rigid structures are possible through mediation processes in the case of energy system transformations is of particular importance (for the case of Denmark, see the transition to decentralized small-scale solutions in Eikeland and Inderberg 2016 and overview in Mattes et al. 2015). Transitions are also being studied at the micro level, for example through experiments in real-world laboratories (*Reallabore*) for sustainable development (Schäpke et al. 2015; Wagner and Ertner 2016), in order to find out "what works" (Grunwald and Wagner 2015). Here, not only the question of "what" (happens), but also the "how" of transformation processes is crucial (Kristof 2014). Another branch focuses on social processes of "abolishing" and "renewing" (so-called innovations and exnovations) in sustainability transformation (Arnold et al. 2015); similarly, it addresses the extent to which social situations of crisis and disintegration can be the starting point for sustainable processes by launching social innovations in the form of social, political and economic alternatives (Newig 2013). This points to an evident connection between energy innovations and social science research (Cohen et al. 2013b), both in terms of new aspects and challenges of energy innovations (Fri and Savitz 2014), and more recently through greater inclusion of spatial and landscape issues (Coles and Millman 2014; MacGillivray and Franklin 2015), which are of great importance in the energy transition.

In addition to numerous empirically based studies, a normative branch of social science energy research has also emerged, analysing social norms and values in particular (Allcott 2011; Künneke et al. 2015), with the concept of energy justice becoming a buzzword (Sovacool and Dworkin 2015; Fuller and McCauley 2016). This perspective often focuses on the issue of energy poverty in a wide variety of global contexts (Bazilian et al. 2014; Halff et al. 2014; Tews 2014) and access to energy supply (Magnani and Vaona 2016). Here, too, a link can be drawn to community energy, where the idea has developed that overspill effects can generate participation in the energy sector which has a positive impact on rural areas (El Bassam 2001; Belmonte et al. 2015). For example, there is the possibility of involving Indigenous as well as local communities (Kerr et al. 2015), such as by using self-sufficient off-grid energy solutions with renewable energy (Ranaboldo et al. 2013, 2015).[1] Incidentally, this idea of linking community participation with rural energy supply as a special development path was created long ago (Shivakumar 1996).

In the case of opposition, resistance and protest against renewable energy, both emotional and rational factors can also be examined in more detail from a social-psychological perspective (Cass and Walker 2009). In the context of community energy, the importance of social norms and personal responsibility (Dwyer et al. 2015), knowledge acquisition and learning aspects (Gluch et al. 2013; Lane et al. 2014; Martin et al. 2014; Southwell et al. 2014) as well as material culture and social organization in energy use practices should be further emphasized (Shove et al. 2014).

At the social micro-level, a variety of issues have been analyzed so far regarding the conditions of civic engagement, for example, in relation to energy behavior (Bull et al. 2015), procedural justice in the establishment of renewable energy (Knudsen et al. 2015), as well as in terms of its mode of action in different publics and social representation in the context of its impact on implementation effectiveness (Cotton and Devine-Wright 2012). The influence of engagement on (or conditioned by) energy infrastructure (Cotton and Devine-Wright 2011) as well as in individual case studies such as high-voltage power lines (Cotton and Devine-Wright 2013) and offshore energy projects (Devine-Wright and Devine-Wright 2009b; Wiersma and Devine-Wright 2014b), but also engagement in the context of public opposition (Devine-Wright 2011e) and in the case of community energy (Devine-Wright and Devine-Wright 2009a) have already been studied. In sum-

[1] See, for example, the activities of the International Network for Sustainable Energy (INFORSE), a network of NGOs that has been promoting the establishment of renewable energy worldwide since 1992.

mary, it seems reasonable to conclude that social and political engagement or participation should also be extended to this topic area of renewable energy. An analogy can be drawn here with the long-running critical discussion regarding the development of political commitment (sustainable or non-sustainable) and citizenship or civic role in the context of consumption,[2] which, for example, places the conscious decision to consume in the vicinity of the act of voting or links it to learning democracy (Stevens 1994; Shaw et al. 2006).

Contextual, especially cultural and psychological aspects play a considerable role in the energy transition ("energy cultures", see Stephenson et al. 2010; Sarrica et al. 2016; Matthies 2013 on user behavior in the energy system), which can, for example, generate the acceptability of energy use alternatives in the first place (Perlaviciute and Steg 2014).

British researcher Patrick Devine-Wright has analyzed the latter aspects in a wide range of studies with regard to socio-psychological influences, internal structures and effects in the context of community energy and renewable energies in the field of tension between people, the environment and technology (see on social and psychological effects of climate change and environmental issues Wall et al. 2007; Irvine et al. 2009; Clayton et al. 2015a, 2015b). Concrete models and derivations can be found, for example, with regard to the visualization of technology-human-organization relationships (Devine-Wright et al. 2010) as well as public discourses (Cotton and Devine-Wright 2011), local inclusion of the population in the expansion of renewable energies (Devine-Wright et al. 2001) and emphasis on local specifics to increase acceptance (Devine-Wright 2011a). A particular focus is on the analysis of the modes of emergence and effects of engagement, with a particular emphasis on aspects of the operation of place (place or local attachments, people-place relations and place change) (Simmons and Walker 2004; Agyeman et al. 2009; Devine-Wright and Howes 2010; Devine-Wright 2011d; Bailey and Devine-Wright 2013; Devine-Wright 2013b, 2015; see also Walker et al. 2015b; Moore and Hackett 2016), identity (Devine-Wright and Clayton 2010) and communities and their resilience (Barr and Devine-Wright 2012) have been elaborated in relation to psychological effects of climate change and other factors affecting energy

[2] See the manifold literature: Lewinsohn-Zamir 1998; Parker 1999; Blühdorn 2000; Batley et al. 2001; Curtis and McConnell 2002; Irving et al. 2002; Dryzek 2003; Micheletti 2003; Spring 2003; Couldry 2004; Keum et al. 2004; Micheletti et al. 2004; Slocum 2004; Soper 2004, 2007, 2008; Barnett et al. 2005; Lang and Gabriel 2005; Berglund and Matti 2006; Baringhorst et al. 2007; Lamla 2007, 2008; Livingstone et al. 2007; Nelson et al. 2007; Lockie 2009; Mol 2009; Adams and Raisborough 2010; Devinney et al. 2010; Kneip 2010; Defila et al. 2011; Heidbrink et al. 2011; Barry 2012; Stolle and Micheletti 2013; Bossy 2014; Pratt and Luetchford 2014; Weller 2014; Wilson and Swyngedouw 2014; Meyer 2015.

supply. For example, community-based "localism", that is, locally centered motivated ways of acting (Walker et al. 2007) and negative attitudes towards renewable energy can be better explained by personal, place- and project-specific factors (Devine-Wright 2013a); Similarly, public attitudes and responses to energy transition issues are more comprehensively understood and critically discussed (Devine-Wright 2005b, 2008, 2009; Sherry-Brennan et al. 2010; Batel et al. 2013; Bridge et al. 2018; Devine-Wright and Batel 2013; Batel and Devine-Wright 2014). Landscape context continues to play a major role in the establishment of renewable energy, and a comprehensive study on power line development confirms this assumption (Batel et al. 2015).

If, therefore, the energy transition is or will be inscribed in landscapes (and, conversely, this has an effect on the perception and handling of energy supply), then a stronger consideration of narratives in the context of the energy transition must also be considered as a consequence. Thus, in system transformations such as the energy transition, narratives of the future ("what should the world look like in 2050?"; see Welzer and Wiegandt 2011) are of importance that should not be underestimated (Miller et al. 2015a). Thus, a whole history of the energy transition can be drawn (see on the history of the energy transition Mautz et al. 2008; Bruns et al. 2009; Ohlhorst 2009; Bruns and Ohlhorst 2011; Hellige 2013; Hake et al. 2015; Quitzow et al. 2016; Schmid et al. 2016), including cultural implications (Sarrica et al. 2016). Also of importance here is the effect of the creation of the idea of man carried by the energy transition (Rauschmayer 2015), or even more hopeful the creation of innovation narratives, as has been elaborated in the case of smart grids (Vesnic-Alujevic et al. 2016).

Meanwhile, the importance of political narratives is also recognized in the literature (Shenhav 2005, 2006; Gadinger et al. 2014), especially in the sustainability field (Leach et al. 2010), in the context of social innovations (Wittmayer et al. 2015a, 2015b) and in socio-technical transformations such as the energy transition (Hermwille 2016) and smart energy technologies (Raimi and Carrico 2016). Political narratives that transport social concepts can be found as a meta-narrative form throughout society, they can form identitarian building blocks of social movements and can also be observed within energy cooperatives ("narrative cooperatives", see Flieger et al. 2015: 1 f., who name an identity, democracy and solidarity principle; see also Nelson et al. 2016 on identity formation and patterns in cooperatives). The dynamics and modes of emergence of political narratives have only recently been examined in more detail (Gadinger et al. 2014); in the case of energy cooperatives, too, an in-depth analysis is still pending, although they presumably represent a fundamental backbone of this form of organization (Flieger et al. 2015).[3]

Possible further social science research perspectives in the community energy sector may include holistic approaches to climate-friendly regional energy development (Cosmi et al. 2015), organizational research in the energy sector (Deline 2015), public attitudes regarding an energy transition (Demski et al. 2015), gender issues (Ding et al. 2014; Fraune 2015; Sundström and McCright 2016), engagement in smart grid projects (Gangale et al. 2013), and scenarios for energy and societal development (Crabtree et al. 2014). In the context of citizen energy/community energy research, there are also still numerous white spots on the map. These concern, among other things, the significance of "experimental non-knowledge" in innovations located here (Groß 2014), the question of the importance of key figures (Kern 2006; Leistner 2013) in the context of community energy and climate protection cooperatives (Walker 2008; Volz 2012b; von Blanckenburg 2014; David and Schönborn 2016: 48 ff.) as well as capturing the overarching phenomenon of the construction of technology and space by local *communities* in the case of renewable energy (Radtke 2015; Moore and Hackett 2016); tracing energy geographies (Brücher 2009; Goshn 2009; Zimmerer 2013; Schüssler 2014; Calvert 2016; Sovacool and Ryan 2016) and giving more consideration to socio-ecological and resilience aspects (Hodbod and Adger 2014).

The analysis of energy transition landscapes thus leads to a technological perspective which, in the context of community energy, can reveal a strong fixation on the use of photovoltaics by community energy (especially in energy cooperatives). However, the future of community energy will presumably lie in the fact that its members use the generated energy themselves, if possible, in spatial proximity to the plant (Flieger et al. 2015). This can be described as a further development in the direction of "prosumer community energy" (ibid.). In addition, there is the increasing importance and use of wind power (see Smith Stegen and Seel 2013; Goetzke and Rave 2016). For community energy initiatives, this use still poses a considerable challenge, both in financial-organizational and spatial-conflict terms. The conflict potential in municipalities can be considered very high in this respect: quite a few citizens' petitions stop wind power projects in Germany (Löhle 2012; Geißler

[3] See, for example, initial approaches to the analysis of social construction performances in the context of energy and stakeholders involved in Montefrio et al. (2015), with regard to creative construction performances of spatial worlds in the context of entrepreneurship Jähnke et al. (2011) and McKeever et al. (2015).

2014a), the future increased expansion will aggravate this problem.[4] Surprisingly, however, studies have shown that the expansion of onshore wind turbines does not reduce acceptance among the population; a resulting preference of the population for (more distant) offshore sites cannot be derived either (Ladenburg 2015a, 2015b; see also Ladenburg and Dubgaard 2007, 2009). In line with the idea of more urban energy strategies, the use of wind energy in the city may also be an option in the future (Khorsand et al. 2015). Nevertheless, in the case of wind energy, there is a need to weigh more strongly the advantages and disadvantages for the environment (Sovacool et al. 2015b), wind energy basically represents a very complex energy policy (Toke 2005; Szarka et al. 2012; The European Wind Energy Association 2012). Here, influences of spatial-political levels and narratives (such as meta-narratives) are also of considerable importance in managing conflicts in the form of *framings,* as Jürges and Newig have already demonstrated in the case of wind energy projects in Lower Saxony and Rhineland-Palatinate (Jürges and Newig 2015). However, geothermal energy as a possible alternative energy use can also be assessed rather critically in terms of risks (Kunze and Hertel 2015), which is why conflict field analyses, as applied in the context of *fracking, can* be particularly useful in these areas (Saretzki 2010; Becker et al. 2016a; Bornemann and Saretzki 2018). In the future, alternative uses of renewable energies will therefore be of great importance for community energy in technical, economic and social terms (Ekardt et al. 2012; Austel 2013).

Due to the ambitious expansion targets of both the federal government (see expansion plans of the federal government: increasing the share of electricity from renewable energies to 50% by 2030 and 80% by 2050, see BMWI 2010: 5; see on the further restructuring of the energy system Plenz et al. 2015) and the federal states, the question of the social compatibility of the further expansion of renewable energies will be decisive in the future (see Jones et al. 2011; Krug 2014; Gawel et al. 2016). Since the goal of expanding renewable energies as such is not up for discussion, local weighing and balancing processes ultimately remain, which offer the opportunity for a balance of interests, acceptance and integration of many voices – and can thus contribute to distributive and procedural justice (see van Wynsberghe 2001; Zöllner et al. 2005; Cass and Walker 2009; Cowell 2010; Cowell et al. 2011; Sovacool and Dworkin 2012; Walker and Day 2012; Johnson and Hall 2015; Fuller and McCauley 2016).

[4] In this context, Einig and Zaspel-Heisters speak of a "wind energy expansion controversy" (see contributions on land potential, wind energy control, regional planning, project planning and protests in the corresponding special issue on this topic in Herrmann et al. 2015).

The energy transition is leading to a multifaceted and complex penetration of space with energy technology (process of hybridization of technology and landscape, emergence of "energy landscapes", see Bruckner and Oswalt 2015; Küpper et al. 2014; Knaut 2015), with wind turbines being integrated into forests, seas and mountain landscapes ("engineered lifeworlds", see Adam et al. 2015). Implications for the future of energy transition scenarios discussed today still remain ambiguous (see Dieckhoff et al. 2016), but the intensification of engineered lifeworlds (Adam et al. 2015) will also raise questions of a socio-political nature, such as with regard to the dominance of ecological modernization and possible "losers" of this transformation process (in the sense of a hegemony project, see Krüger 2015) – despite all efforts of participation and integration, which is precisely characteristic of these approaches (see on previous considerations with regard to a discursive-deliberative and collaborative design of the energy transition, i.e., active design by citizens and organized groups, Beinke et al. 2012; Mans and Kayser 2013; Töpfer et al. 2013; Alcántara et al. 2014; Renn et al. 2014; Kamlage and Nanz 2015; Reuter 2015 speaks here of collaborative infrastructures). These issues and new approaches of collaborative action are widely considered in ongoing debates and therefore enable a broad and enhancing perception and discussion of the influence of technology on society.[5] In this context, community energy projects – as envisaged from the outset in this approach with regard to the upgrading of marginalized spaces – could play the role of a bridge to the possibility of connecting materially worse-off areas and population groups to technology,[6] which can develop potential especially in times of crisis (Findlay and Findlay 2013; Gmür 2013a) and make a contribution to rural development (Poisat et al. 2013; Kaphengst and Velten 2014).[7]

[5] This is explicitly assumed by Ingolfur Blühdorn, who assumes that sustainability policies lead to the exclusion of marginalized population groups and thus, as a paradoxical result, to non-sustainability (see Blühdorn 2013).

[6] In a similar way, this idea is formulated in terms of a "compassion economy" (see Projektgruppe Neue Mitleidsökonomie 2016) or also discussed as the New Social Economy as well as a cooperation model of economy and society using the example of cooperatives (Glöckner et al. 2013; Götzl 2013).

[7] The basic idea of this approach is that cooperatives can provide better access to technology and services (Schelisch 2013), including intelligent linkages such as housing and electric mobility (Struber 2013). All in all, cooperatives have a wide range of options for action with regard to climate change beyond the community energy variant (Schröder and Walk 2013). The fundamental advantages of the cooperative model are that education can be imparted (Goldmann 2013) and social capital can be generated (Lang 2013); in addition, self-determination and the development of skills and abilities can be promoted (Schmale and Degens 2013).

The Triad of Social, Ecological and Economic Dimensions
In research, three thematically overarching categories can be found, which form the context for economic-civil society action in renewable energy (Rogers et al. 2008: 4222):

1. **Social** (benefit, strengthen community, make an example of community action, educational, better living conditions enable more people to stay).
2. **Environmental** (preserve environment for future generations, conserve energy and resources, benefit environment, use local resources).
3. **Economic** (local employment, benefits for individuals are good for whole community, save money, economic benefit, attract visitors).

This overall context gives rise to different, possible levels of inquiry for social science research and scholarship (Devine-Wright 2005a: 134)[8]:

- **Local contexts** (macro and meso levels: influence on community energy projects and local community climate action, manifold interactions between levels, actors, physical objects (e.g., energy plants) and subjects).
- **Acceptance** (macro and meso level: spill-over effects of participation on communities, population, regional and national levels).
- **Participation** (meso- and micro-level: participation of citizens (Var. 1: top-down process based on public participation and consultation) or activity of citizens and community action (Var. 2: bottom-up process based on civic engagement, associative-organizational participation) in planning procedures, social influence processes, associations and organizations, citizens` initiatives, enterprises and projects.
- **Conflicts** (meso- and micro-level: within local communities or community energy projects, between local actors or groups of the public).

Participation in the energy and environmental sector relates in particular to public opinion-forming and concrete forms of action (see Marquart-Pyatt 2013). This can result in the inclusion of actors and stakeholders, the promotion of actor diversity and approaches to action, legitimacy and acceptance, knowledge transfer, democracy learning and empowerment, the inclusion of individuals in consumption patterns (prosuming), and democratic organization and co-determination (Viardot 2013; Kaphengst and Velten 2014; Sagebiel et al. 2014).

[8] Devine-Wright differentiates between physical, contextual, political and institutional, socio-economic, social and communicative, symbolic and ideological, local and personal categories (Devine-Wright 2005a: 135).

Overall Findings in Community Energy Research

At a higher level, Walker and Cass (2007) analyzed various types of community energy in their work and attempted to categorize socio-technical systems. According to this, it is possible to first make a rough distinction between "hardware" and "software" (ibid.: 459 f.). In the case of hardware, on the one hand the types of energy are dealt with (e.g., wind, biomass and solar) and a scaling of sizes is undertaken – a distinction is made between macro, meso, micro and pico levels.

By the "software", the authors refer to the types of social arrangements and the organization of the infrastructure. These types of internal structure result from the combination of different interacting arrangements and relationships between actors and institutions. Here, the authors distinguish four types: function and performance (concerning the energy assets), ownership and return, management and operation, infrastructure and network formation (ibid.: 460). In their research, the authors also analyzed five types and immanent system logics of renewable energy implementation (ibid.: 461 f.). These concern public use (principle: general supply), private use (principle: market logic) or community use (principles: neo-communitarianism, participation, sustainable communities), households (principles: individual environmental responsibility, self-sufficiency, autonomy) and companies (principles: corporate social responsibility, efficiency criteria). Accordingly, ownership models and types of organization can vary: public, private and economic; in the community sector, partnerships, cooperatives and user-led models.

Finally, the different roles of the public (types and factions) and the links with the implementation models were analyzed (ibid.: 465 f.). According to this, active and passive consumers (e.g., the former consciously opt for a green electricity tariff), users of green electricity, financial investors, local recipients of benefits and subsidies from renewable energies (e.g., due to the technology, infrastructure or education), project opponents and project supporters, participants in the project as well as owners of land and buildings, and energy producers who directly generate electricity from renewables and own the plants can be distinguished as the main groups of actors.

For the purposes of this study, it is noteworthy that a wide variety of influences can be observed in the system as a whole through an enormous range of "hardware" and "software", principles guiding action, as well as publics and actors. Difficulties can then arise in empirical analyses in drawing boundaries and isolating certain categories in terms of their characteristics. This problem is to be countered here with the approach of thematically narrow fixation while at the same time keeping the empirical survey open.

Initially, financial participation in energy production and community energy projects appear as economic and entrepreneurial actions. However, many references and even foundations of action are of a social and political nature, especially due to the unusual contexts of origin, motivations and orientations of these hybrid forms of organization and enterprise.

International research shows that community energy initiatives are essentially a social phenomenon, they generate social innovations, produce various complex social effects and contexts, and influence contextual conditions (networks).[9] This also focuses on a kind of empowerment of individuals through ownership, self-management and control of energy production ("power to the people": van der Schoor and Scholtens 2015), at the same time implying a decentralization of energy production and operation (Chmutina and Goodier 2014; Wiersma and Devine-Wright 2014a). Devine-Wright (2014) structures the different approaches (social, spatial, technical) of the research according to social levels with actors, effects and conditions of action:

Energy from Communities (Meso-Level)

- Actors: Grassroots volunteers (in the sense of community energy initiatives led by local citizens and other mainly volunteer activities), municipalities and local organizations (e.g., public utilities, see Schönberg and Jost 2011; Weller and Funk 2014).
- Effects: Process and outcome levels.
- Process: Who initiates the energy projects? (Citizens, banks, organizations, associations, clubs, energy companies, investment groups, project developers, etc.).

Energy Near Communities (Macro-Level)

- Actors: Large-scale renewable energy projects.
- Effects: Acceptance issues (conceived as a multidimensional construct capturing different dimensions of acceptance, resistance and protest, see Ellis et al. 2007).

[9] See descriptions in the literature such as "Energy as a Social Project": Byrne and Toly 2006, "Community Energy: A Social Architecture for an Alternative Energy Future": Hoffman and High-Pippert 2005 and "Integrating Social Science in Energy Research": Sovacool et al. 2015c. See also Bolton and Foxon 2015a, 2015b for a socio-technical perspective, West et al. 2010; Walker et al. 2011; Kerr et al. 2014; Miller et al. 2015b; Schweizer-Ries et al. 2013; Schweizer-Ries et al. 2016 for social and cultural science conceptualizations.

- Process: Reframing protest: environmental citizenship (Dobson 2003; Dobson and Bell 2006; McClymont and O'Hare 2008), place protection (space and landscape protection), place making and trust building processes (Fast and Mabee 2015).

Energy in Communities (Micro-Level)[10]

- Actors: Individual (individual persons), interpersonal (households) and smaller groups.
- Effects: Diffusion of innovations in the energy sector and local energy action.
- Process: Formation of trust and reciprocity (Ricci et al. 2010; Walker et al. 2010) or, on the other hand, its fragility or non-existence; leads to challenges especially in intra-community decision-making.

The salient features of community energy are thus the importance of networks and situational knowledge (Catney et al. 2014), understood as a counter-model to top-down participation approaches and information-led behavioral change in favor of "silent" learning and lay knowledge in existing networks (Parag et al. 2013). Virulent here is also the equity dimension (fairness, justice, injustice distributive and procedural (van Wynsberghe 2001; Zöllner et al. 2005; Cass and Walker 2009; Cowell 2010; Cowell et al. 2011; Sovacool and Dworkin 2012; Walker and Day 2012; Johnson and Hall 2015) because there are varying capacities of communities present in the space to get involved in renewable energies (Devine-Wright 2014).

Furthermore, it must be taken into account that actors' actions, such as the construction of energy plants, are always embedded in (local) space (and therefore questions of the significance of *place attachments* and *place identity* are virulent (see Vorkinn and Riese 2001; Devine-Wright and Clayton 2010; Devine-Wright and Howes 2010; Nash et al. 2010; Raymond et al. 2010; Devine-Wright 2011d, 2013b; Devine-Wright and Wiersma 2013), which means that there are multiple contacts between the actors (actor networks, exchange processes, mutual influence) (McLaren Loring 2007).

The key hurdles in the processes are between the spatial dimensions (local, regional and remote) and the connections between micro, meso and macro levels,

---

[10] See on the micro-level of renewable energies related to the use in and on buildings as well as in the immediate environment of households, smaller communities and neighborhoods and urban quarters: Keiner and Kim 2008; Friedman and Cooke 2011; Hoppe 2012; Xu et al. 2012; Rydin et al. 2012; Ellis et al. 2013; Verbong et al. 2013; Wiedenhofer et al. 2013; Chmutina et al. 2014; Naus et al. 2014.

which is why feelings of place identification are crucial (Devine-Wright 2014). Devine-Wright therefore distinguishes between communities of locality and communities of interest, where, for example, citizens build energy systems out of a sense of place to promote and support the local area (e.g., environmentally oriented) or primarily interest-based, for example, for profit.

Community energy is summarized as a local, collective and participatory approach (ibid.). In a closer examination and classification, a distinction can therefore be made between individual and collective approaches, different modes of participation and approaches to participation and sharing, underlying (flexible) values and ideal motivations, as well as the concrete benefits (who profits?) (ibid.). Of paramount importance here are questions of social integration and identification as well as the building of interpersonal trust, on the other hand also social deficits and discrepancies (see Bell et al. 2005; Ricci et al. 2010; Bell et al. 2013).

Finally, as a summary of the considerations, questions harden on the two points of: the extent to which energy participation can be regarded primarily as rhetoric due to the small number of participants (see Catney et al. 2014) and which exclusively small-scale solutions are being sought by the citizens' communities and participation projects, that is to say, less a complete system change, which can be assumed according to the state of knowledge to date (Hargreaves et al. 2013; Devine-Wright 2014). However, global reference points (e.g., climate change) are considered as motivations for action in addition to local references (Rogers et al. 2008). Bauwens (2014b, 2016), for example, distinguishes 15 different motivations between community responsibility and financial incentive, as a financial incentive is also thought of multidimensionally here.

What is striking is the strong qualitative orientation of the studies, often the focus is on the creation of categories, variables, core criteria, for example, purpose and goals of the projects, external influencing factors (political, social, etc.), innovative strength and character,[11] potential for changing the energy system; the

[11] According to Hielscher et al. (2011: 17), community energy projects (here mainly related to bottom-up approaches) are characterized by the fact that they include different strategies to shape energy production and consumption and include the possibility to generate behavioral change through individual mechanisms. Similarly, they can change contexts themselves and bring about higher levels of engagement in the processes of participation in new energy systems – in contrast to traditional, conventional top-down approaches. By attempting to put ideas of a "new economy" into practice, the potential to generate change in society could also be generated in the process. In this way, community energy would create spaces where other rules of everyday life and socio-economic conditions and citizenship exist. The authors thus establish a proximity to the approaches of social entrepreneurship and the common good economy.

internal social science analyses of the communities are particularly interesting here. The qualitative research approaches here are mostly exploratory, which is due to the low level of knowledge and diversified illustrations (see on the diversity of methods Armstrong and Bulkeley 2014).[12]

Walker and Devine-Wright (2008) point out that a characteristic of community energy initiatives is precisely their diversity and complexity. This can be a challenge when conducting a targeted, methodical study of case studies. The roles of project participants also need to be distinguished in advance (Walker and Cass (2007: 465) define the basic constellation as follows: "membership of organising group, attending meetings or hands on installation and maintenance") – however, this membership is only achievable for "public" members of a community-based approach. Public institutions (such as public utilities), households and private energy producers, on the other hand, are usually based on an exclusive, small group of people, which is not accessible to a larger community.

4.2 A Closer Look at Community Energy Research

In the international research literature in particular, the phenomenon of citizen participation in renewable energies (in the sense of the less commonly used term "citizen energy") has been described predominantly as *community energy* (or community renewable energy (CRE)) (see Walker and Devine-Wright 2008; Walker and Simcock 2012; Creamer et al. 2019; and Bauwens et al. 2022).[13] The participation of citizens in community energy initiatives or the energy transition is a recurring

[12] Lang et al. emphasize the importance of situationally adapted qualitative research approaches: "context-sensitive qualitative research" (Lang et al. 2013: 227). For further research, the need for descriptive analyses of organizational forms is emphasized: "context-sensitive research that goes beyond merely descriptive governance analysis is needed, taking into account the historical trajectories of public-citizen partnerships" (ibid.).

[13] "Community energy" is the most common category in research, followed by "energy community," "community renewable energy", "community solar", "community wind", "solar community" and "renewable energy community" (Bauwens et al. 2022). The German term *Bürgerenergie* (which translates directly as citizen energy) cannot be equated with community energy, as citizen energy in German generally means individual participation by individuals, which cannot always be assumed in the case of community energy, which includes also forms of associative and institutional activities without explicit individual (financial) participation. In both cases, however, participatory arrangements concerning renewable energies are addressed. For a definition of the term, see also Walker and Devine-Wright 2008; Hielscher 2011; Holstenkamp and Degenhart 2013; Hicks et al. 2014; Kunze and Becker 2015a and the discussion in Sect. 4.4.

theme in the research literature (see overview in Schweizer-Ries 2011). In the research literature, the explicit aspect of participation through community energy initiatives is addressed, related topics are empirically investigated as well as put into relation with social science explanatory models. In this context, numerous investigations and studies have been conducted in recent years. Some important findings from the social sciences and humanities are now summarized here. First of all, three research perspectives or approaches can be distinguished:

- **Attempts to define** and identify the different interpretations of community energy initiatives (Walker and Devine-Wright 2008).
- Emergence of local-regional **publics** generated by community energy projects and civic or actor-based public engagement forms in mediatised interplay with (individual) actors, individuals and organised interests from politics, business and civil society in (sub)publics (Devine-Wright 2011b, 2011c, 2011e, 2011f).
- Differentiation of the various **functions** that individuals or actors can assume in the renewable energy landscape (Walker and Cass 2007).

In the literature, the perception of participation in the internal structure of associations, organizations or initiatives by members is fundamentally regarded as the "key to trust and commitment" (Österberg and Nilsson 2009). This brings community energy initiatives close to the idea of social entrepreneurship, social or civil entrepreneurships and social networks in the sense of social innovations (Gliedt and Parker 2007; Huybrechts and Defourny 2008; van der Horst 2008; Huybrechts and Nicholls 2012; Huybrechts 2013a, 2013b; Dufays and Huybrechts 2014; Stein 2015; Dorniok 2016; Dorniok and Lautermann 2016). According to this, community energy initiatives are to be understood as hybrid organizational forms and economic enterprises (Huybrechts 2012), whereby questions of internal organization and governance (organization, structure, set-up, design) of community energy are frequently addressed (Ison 2010). Furthermore, aspects of the economic inclusion of stakeholders in the organizational structure of social enterprises to increase legitimacy are important here (Huybrechts et al. 2014), as are viacross-sector *collaborations* (i.e., collaborations with other civil society actors). According to the results of the study, the following factors are decisive: the firm decision to collaborate, the choice of partners or collaborators and the form of the partnership; in addition, the emergence and development of the collaborative activity. In this context, the importance of legitimacy and a non-functionalist perspective continue to be emphasised (Huybrechts et al. 2014). Beyond simple explanations (such as function), the authors describe in this respect individual specifics of collaboration and the contexts of emergence, which can be of multiple origins – beyond an orientation towards utility and function. Furthermore, the generation of legitimacy through collaboration is relevant (Huybrechts and Nicholls 2013). Here, two research perspectives are described to explain legitimacy and to find causes of its generation: on the one hand, focusing on strategies of organizations (here internal governance/organizational structures), which depend on certain resources. On the other hand, the organizational structure is seen as a social construction, which is only one part of a broad network of social relations. For the authors, this results in the need for a complex and multidimensional view as a research approach (Huybrechts and Nicholls 2013). Furthermore, a possible de-legitimation through the assumption of ascribed roles of the actors and players must also be taken into account (Navis and Glynn 2010, 2011).

With regard to the effects of community energy, three effect dimensions of energy cooperatives are distinguished in the literature, which can generally be applied to community energy initiatives (Lang et al. 2013: 227):

- **Practical implications** ("If regional government representatives are supporting a bottom-up initiative, they are more inclined to provide crucial resources for the public–citizen partnership and tensions between different stakeholders involved are weakened"),
- **Social implications** ("Co-operative public-citizen partnerships might enhance participatory democracy and seem to strengthen solidarity and social cohesion on the neighborhood level") and
- **Democratic implications**: ("In showing that co-operatives are a suitable governance structure for community organizations, which enhance democratic decision making and foster social innovation in public service delivery, we support the findings of other studies").

For a sociological analysis, the following sub-areas of the social phenomenon "community energy" can be found in the literature (see Hielscher 2011: 51; Yildiz et al. 2015):

- **Social movements** (founding initiation, identities and imaginaries, resource mobilization, opportunity structures and influence).
- **Partnerships/collaborations** (with local authorities and decision makers, business, advice, support, promotion, and advocacy).
- **Energy initiatives** (organization and ownership models, resources and returns, forms of energy production and distribution: consumption and service models).
- **Policy goals** (drivers and barriers, general energy/environment/climate protection policies, specific community energy policies).

- **Capabilities, skills and competencies** (individual and group, cohesion, commitment and trust).
- **Participation** (inclusion, exclusion, representation and power relations).
- **Innovative space** (adaptable forms of energy service, diffusion of elements, system effects).
- **Normative claims** (collective returns, scope and sustainability, system effects, modes of exemplarity and legitimacy).
- **Social enterprise** (business models, entrepreneurship, leadership).
- **Normative claims** (collective rewards, reach and depth, power of demonstration, legitimacy).
- **Performance** (generation, reduction, awareness, distribution).
- **Measurement** (metrics, definitions, monitoring processes, performativity of research).
- **Aspirations and values** (asset/means to other goals, local resilience/community, alternative energy).
- **Localities and scales** (geography of community energy, distribution of consequences, communities of interest).

In the context of the present study, it is possible to draw in particular on research findings that address questions of participation, acceptance, inclusion and exclusion, personnel and governance of community energy initiatives:

- Emergence and effects of **participation and civic engagement** (Hoffman and High-Pippert 2005, 2010; Adams et al. 2011; Devine-Wright 2011b, 2011c, 2011e), learning effects (Junginger et al. 2010); meaning, agency, creation of publics (Walker and Cass 2007).
- Importance of **communities and community action** (Walker 2011; Wirth 2014), equity between communities (Park 2012), emergence of conflict, trust and social capital (Ricci et al. 2010; Walker et al. 2010), deliberation (Fast 2013) and community capacities and power factors (Middlemiss and Parrish 2010), resources of mobilization and volunteerism (Bomberg and McEwen 2012), knowledge and skill acquisition (Gluch et al. 2013; Heiskanen et al. 2013; Kandpal and Broman 2014), characterization as a protest movement (Dorniok 2014).
- Modes of **governance** (in terms of internal organization and structure) (Ison 2010; Höfer and Rommel 2015), ownership and ownership structures (Walker 2008; Warren and McFadyen 2010; Woodin et al. 2010), responsibility and accountability (Herbert 2005).

- Influence of **local civil society structures** (Hargreaves et al. 2013; Boon and Dieperink 2014), requirement of involving local groups in the initiation and development phase of community energy initiatives (Hathway 2010), links to political system and public (Cass et al. 2010), support and cooperation with local politics, municipalities and regions (Peters et al. 2010; Peters and Roberts 2010; Holstenkamp and Rückheim 2013; van der Horst 2015), and highlighting network structures of local communities, politics, businesses, civil society organizations and energy initiatives (Parag et al. 2013; Bird and Barnes 2015; Tweed 2015).

Social Innovations Through Community Energy

Community energy projects as social community processes within civil society in the context of energy, climate and environment (called "climate cultures" by Welzer et al., see Welzer et al. 2010), can in certain cases develop forms of "connective action" and thus grow beyond a purely technical-material purpose (of operating energy plants) (Bennett and Segerberg 2013) – and thus generate innovations for sustainability (Leach et al. 2012; David and Schönborn 2016).

Participation in the context of community energy can be described in this line of thought with the idea of "collaborative infrastructures" with the help of technology design (Reuter 2015), whereby practices of collaboration and cooperation of "epistemic communities" are now increasingly becoming the focus of research interest (Wray 2015). Thus, it can tend to be assumed that the modes of action of such energy communities are close to the field of social innovations (see Howaldt and Jacobsen 2010; Rückert-John 2013; Kopf 2015; Kersting 2017), as creative forms of organization, enterprise and participation are sometimes found and tested (see on innovative approaches in the energy field, e.g., crowdfunding Vasileiadou et al. 2016, see on creative forms such as *grassroots campaigning* Speth 2013). In such cases, community energy can therefore certainly be seen as a form of social entrepreneurship (in the sense of "ecopreneurs" (Schaper 2010), "civil entrepreneurs" (Stein 2015) or "public entrepreneurship" (Hjorth and Bjerke 2006)). Moreover, since operating and supply solutions such as energy cooperatives also serve employment and thus overall a social variant of work, service, supply and technology access, there is a certain proximity to social work approaches that can be explicitly oriented towards the ideal of democracy (Geisen et al. 2013). From this perspective, in the case of the community energy projects in which citizens participate in the form and structure of enterprises and community, a kind of "creative participation" (Micheletti and McFarland 2011) in the sense of a "democratic experimentalism" (Brunkhorst 1998) can be assumed, as described long ago by John Dewey as "democratic experimental communities" in civil society (Kettner 1998; Honneth 1999; Bernstein 2000; Jörke 2003; Kadlec 2007; Dewey 2008; also Hans Joas 1992, 2000) and was also concretely tested and theoretically founded by Jane Addams in local projects (Addams 1902; Fischer et al. 2009).

Participation Through Community Energy

In the research, references can be found to topics such as democracy, participation, civic action and social capital.[14] Participation and civic engagement are discussed in some studies, and the concept of democracy is used explicitly. In this context, the question of social forms of action and organization is of fundamental interest. Communicative action, in this context especially collaborative-cooperative action, is emphasised here (Mc Morran et al. 2014). In addition, there are possible close links with social movements, such as environmental and climate protection groups.

In the case of community energy initiatives, a basic distinction is made between *grassroots initiatives* (the initiation of the community energy initiative comes from individual or several citizens) and formalised, organised forms (associations and organizations such as environmental associations create participation options through their initiation of energy projects) (Seyfang and Haxeltine 2012; Hargreaves et al. 2013; Seyfang et al. 2013; Smith and Seyfang 2013; Feola and Nunes 2014; Seyfang et al. 2014; David and Schönborn 2016).

The civic engagement of community energy initiatives has been studied in depth by Devine-Wright and Devine-Wright (2009a). Here, the authors deal with an energy project by analysing discussions with local residents. The researchers find that in the project there is rather a passive role of the residents in individual and collective terms regarding energy production. Some residents are very disappointed

[14] Kneußel (2014) describes energy cooperatives as "places of cooperation and participation" in the sense of civil society participation with references to deliberative democracy, participation in civil society and participation in organizations. A social reference through cooperation and participation (social action and cooperation, participation through collective action as well as a change in motives and values for participation) is assumed. Furthermore, a framework of community energy is set, including organizational theoretical references (design of the organizational form, governance and participation structures, values, will formation processes, conflicts, leadership design, founding motives), structure and modes of action (in the form of organizational structure and typology of energy cooperatives, organizational action, goal formation of participation, actor reference to participation as well as participation and its orientation), structure and action of new social movements (civil participation in the energy sector, social complexity of the energy transition, commons cooperations and energy ecological goals).

with the compensation paid by the operators. Cooperative action can therefore only be achieved if all actors (developers, consultants and residents) are clear and agree on how energy production should be designed and communicated (both visually and verbally) (Devine-Wright and Devine-Wright 2009a: 303).

In another study, Hoffman and High-Pippert (2005) choose studies on civic engagement in the USA (Skocpol 2003) as the starting point for their reflections; the theoretical concept here is about the revival and activation of an active civil society. The authors identify links to theoretical approaches from the literature in the form of social capital (Putnam et al. 1993; Putnam 2000), *stealth* democracy (Hibbing and Theiss-Morse 2002) deliberative democracy (Habermas 1977, 1992, 1998, 2011a, 2011b) and strong democracy (Barber 1984). In another paper (Hoffman and High-Pippert 2010), the authors find through qualitative analysis that members of community energy initiatives are often enthusiastic about getting involved because of potential (financial) community gain, appreciation or emphasis on location, or sense of social obligation or responsibility, less dominated by self-interest. In this way, an initiative brings together people who have different "backgrounds", giving the initiative experiences in very different ways (ibid.: 7572). The phenomenon of community energy initiatives therefore contradicts the argument that civic engagement is currently declining or dissolving: "what some argue is an era of declining civic engagement" (Hoffman and High-Pippert 2010: 7572). Such participatory community energy projects are thus possibly examples of Benjamin Barber's approach to participatory democracy (1984), in which community groups participate in the form of innovative institutions through self-governance (decentralized in small units). They ideally involve discourse and debate on issues that are precisely not mutually shared; as well as developments for an agenda based on participation and matters of public interest (public goods, public good oriented). While such initiatives do exist, Hoffman and High-Pippert (2010) found that the number of those that incorporate these practices of participatory democracy is very small.

Finally, in the literature Walker et al. (2010: 2661 ff.) critically evaluate interpretations that assume a certain stability and solidity between the social connections within the community of a community energy initiative, whereby often only the positive characteristics and abilities of the groups would be focused on (similar assessment also in Hoffman and High-Pippert 2010). Many of these positive attributes that would be associated with the term "community", however, would appear problematic if these relationships were examined more closely in everyday life. Communities that appear inclusive from the outside may be perceived as exclusionary by the local population, marginalising individuals who see themselves as not fitting in or unable to join the community or its ideals and goals. Such rifts can occur not only between local people and members of the initiative, but also within the initiative itself. Future plans and decision-making processes may unite, but they may also cause communities to break apart; likewise, individuals may join or leave the community, or they may separate themselves from the group. Communities are therefore not "static", they evolve and so do the relationships between individuals. Therefore, they are described by the authors as dynamic and volatile.

A topic that is particularly relevant in terms of democratic theory in this context, and which has so far been underexposed academically, concerns social cohesion and proximity (community cohesion) between citizens, community members and activists (see Devine-Wright 2014), as well as the internal structure and organization with regard to the question of democratic modes of action ("democratic governance in communities": Mori 2014). The participatory practices and social exchanges of individuals in this field seem to be highly heterogeneously structured according to the available findings. Participation in a community, such as a group of citizens running an energy project, further describes not only those factors of the actor that distinguish the concrete project, but also those that keep it alive – that is, sustain the engagement of citizens. In order to find out which different factors have an impact on the participation level of individuals, Rogers et al. (2008: 4224 f.) highlight that especially the role of the initiator of the project plays an essential role for the existence and success of the project (see also David and Schönborn 2016: 48 ff.).

Trust and Social Cohesion Versus Social Exclusion and Marginalization
Walker et al. (2010) have analyzed the potential interrelationship between the degree of participation and the gradations of social cohesion in a community. The starting point of their considerations is the embodiment of effects and preconditions of the type and quality of relationships between individuals and organizations that are part of a community; as well as the social arrangements under which energy technologies are implemented.

The notion of "trust" is central in this argument (borrowing from Luhmann 2014; Misztal 1996 and Metlay 1999; see also Ricci et al. 2010; Yildiz et al. 2015: 69 f.). Further sub-areas can be (procedural) justice or conflicts (Yildiz et al. 2015: 68 f.). Walker et al. refer here to Robert Putnam (Putnam et al. 1993: 171), who sees interpersonal trust as an elementary characteristic for citizen participation and engagement, since trust leads to cooperation and cooperation in turn builds trust (similarly, the term *thick trust* according to Williams 1988) (Walker et al. 2010: 2657). This relates to individuals and local institutions within communities. According to the authors, this could be a rationale for why community energy appears attractive and distinctive to those individuals who defend its deployment and development. Trust in social connections thus supports and generates cooperation, communication and engagement in such a way that projects are more likely to be developed consensually and with community benefits, and technologies are built appropriately, that is, accepted, in the local space. Being engaged within community energy initiatives can thus improve trust between the individual and the organization, which both secures local resources for the future and generates further community action – ultimately leading to increased societal trust in renewable energy from the grassroots level (acceptance generation). However, the authors also qualify that cooperation, social cohesion and trust are not specific characteristics of community energy initiatives, but should be seen as an outcome of local activities, which brings benefits for the future of rural and local areas.

Thus, in their research, the authors received both positive feedback ("working together to achieve something good") and skeptical reviews ("most people are focused on themselves") (ibid.). Accordingly, these skeptical voices reflect opinions in scientific literature which contend that real-world conditions exist behind community discourses – beyond only basic, theoretical assumptions of positive aspects of community spirit. Thus, the communities considered to be inclusive may also be highly exclusive in character, marginalising individuals who are deemed not to fit.[15] In addition, it is also important to consider that different communities exist in a common place and extended communities of interest can cross physical boundaries.[16] In this sense, communities can also be short-lived and dynamically structured and sometimes break up – in which case community energy emerges as a solitary event and does not form any relationships. This perspective problematiszes the normative meaning and claim attached to the community aspect of community energy, as well as the extent to which the implications and preconditions of trust and conducive social connections actually exist in practice.

In one case, for example, an ideal situation exists in which there is a broad basis of trust and a highly participatory, cooperative and consensual process could be analyzed in the development and realization of the project. Also, social capital formation, capacity building and learning processes were identified, so that in this case further community activities can be expected in the future. However, it is also pointed out that the projects that were studied are usually very specific in character, which is why generalizations can hardly be made (ibid.: 2662).

Moreover, the authors are certain that a "community label" is not sufficient to imply trust and social cohesion in all cases. Thus, the rhetorical figure of close-

[15] Effects described, for example, by Williams 1976; Young 1990; Harvey 1996.

[16] See Willmott 1987; Lave and Wenger 1991; Delanty 2003.

knit rural communities must face the realities that fractures and disputes can arise, especially when individuals find that projects have been misunderstood or that some individuals have enjoyed fewer benefits than others or have been harmed as well. Ultimately, this boils down to the question of what fundamentally defines community energy. For example, there is partial approval of a community energy project, but at the same time there is criticism that not everyone is included in this project. Community energy projects are therefore characterized by a high degree of indeterminacy and ambiguity. In parts, however, the particular strength can be seen in the fact that many interests can be integrated and different projects can take into account a wide variety of accompanying circumstances appropriately and in advance. The authors basically assume that a particularly "positive" implementation – that is, when many people are active, directly involved and act with "heart and mind" – also produces better outcomes: both in financial terms and with regard to the fact that people develop a more positive attitude towards renewable energies, learn to know and appreciate their scope for action, and are involved in the production of energy and decisions regarding energy consumption (ibid.: 2663). Nevertheless, the replicability of the projects remains doubtful.

Such trust-building processes occur more during the development phase of the initiative. Walker et al. (2010) argue that such initial trust-building processes can help in the process of promoting a highly participatory development overall. In contrast, however, it is possible that in community energy initiatives where there is only a small group of active individuals, it is important to consider that only a few individuals in the community act in a very select grouping ("exclusive") and therefore social segregation (inclusion/exclusion) is produced (see Agarwal 2001).

Internal Governance and Organization

Ison (2010) examined internal organizational structures ("governance") of community energy projects with regard to power relations, opportunities for co-determination and possibilities for members to influence and shape (see on governance in cooperatives furthermore Nolte 2013). Here, the theoretical concept of associative democracy (according to Hirst and Bader 2001; Hirst 2013; Bader 2014; Klein and Olk 2014), social learning (Collins and Ison 2009) and the concept of organizational structures of heterarchy and autonomous accountability (Fairtlough 2005) are linked. In this regard, Ison (2010: 7) refers to Stoker (1998) and Hirst (1997) by defining governance as political structures: "that is concerned with creating the conditions for rule and collective action in accordance with established social standing". Governance thus involves processes of decision-making, conversation and action (after Barber 1984). Governance arrangements are shaped in particular by three different, central layers of relationships:

- Local group of citizens and professional renewable energy company.
- Ownership structure (either in the hands of a local community or professional renewable energy company) combined with local community members.
- Civil society or private sector organizations promoting and supporting the community energ project (both the local community and the professional renewable energy company).

According to Ison (2010: 9), such an understanding also underlies the theories of organizational democracy. Here, the basic approach is to shift power and control from the larger macro-levels to small, local micro-levels and to decentralize them (see Hilmer 2010). A typical form of organization in this field is the cooperative (see Rothschild and Whitt 1986). Finally, the idea of heterarchy is invoked, which, in contrast to hierarchy, embodies the idea of "multiple rule, a balance of powers rather than the single rule of hierarchy" (Fairtlough 2005: 28). Thus, with autonomy in its own right, a grouping decides who is responsible for the outcome of a decision. Ison considers this to be a connecting point to associative democracy as it relies on alternative approaches to governance and management. Also, this approach reflects the three basic conditions of governance: discourse, decision-making and action. Accordingly, Ison (2010: 10 f.) can categorize the organizational forms of community energy initiatives as social enterprises (following Smith 2005b). Thus, the initiatives would be best located with the help of the concepts of associative democracy and social economy.

Ison's basic consideration is now based on the fact that some participatory processes can exist in a "disempowering or hypocritical manner" (Ison 2010: 5). The author argues that the designation of participation is in part insufficient for an initiative to be considered genuinely community-initiated or having the effect of increased social cohesion. Power and influence of participants must therefore be thought of in addition to the participatory role.

Following an analysis of these processes within community energy projects, it was possible to distinguish between two different governance typologies. While the bottom-up mode (citizens set up an energy project themselves) is described as highly participatory, the top-down participation model is seen as having less potential for participation and co-determination, since essential power and control options are exercised by the community energy project in which the citizens participate (ibid.: 46):

> The first (governance typology) is highly participatory, with a significant degree of community power; this is typically possible for smaller scale projects and requires significant commitment on behalf of a few local acitivists. (...) ...this arrangement tends to produce benefits such as increased community cohesion and pride, trust and even tourism. The second model entails differentiated responsibility of different organisations at different levels of governance, less community participation and power, with an expert renewable energy company having the majority of responsibility and power. These arrangements tend to produce expediently developed projects that provide dividends to its membership and to the local community through a trust fund.

Both governance typologies attribute power or voice to group members by either expressing consent or using the option to leave the initiative (exit option). Both models thus offer the possibility of exercising control or achieving consensus through an exit and by using the individual voice of the members (ibid.). As in most cases, the ability to influence decision-making, discourse and action varies between these two typologies depending on frequency and influence. Accordingly, both governance models are democratic to some extent, which can mean "stronger and weaker acts of democracy" as well as "higher and lower acts of participation and commitment" (Ison 2010: 46). The greatest barriers to community energy initiatives are seen to be in the form of time, dependence on stakeholders and access to knowledge and expertise, as well as financial resources. Within the first model of governance, practice and learning facilitates the development of an initiative, and potentials for community resilience exist.

In a further study on the internal governance of energy cooperatives, Höfer and Rommel (2015) point out that there are many different internal governance structures in energy cooperatives and that causal links between internal governance structures and member characteristics are difficult to establish, as the members themselves determine their influence within the organization. However, with the help of a game-theoretic experiment, it was possible to prove that a significant influence emanates from the level of education, knowledge and information of the members. The authors also point out that there is still no scientific research on the relationship between the distribution of participation rights and the performance of energy cooperatives.

Community Energy Projects as Energy Policy Actors in the Public Space
Hibbing and Theiss-Morse (2002: 2) speak of a form of democracy which they call *stealth* democracy. According to this, democratic practices do exist in society, but they are not visible and obvious at first glance. The decisive factor is therefore ultimately a participatory option for citizens: the possibility of participation must exist, as must influence on political representatives through elections – the potential option, rather than the actual exploitation, is decisive. Under a guise or in secret, it is then also possible that beyond the obvious participation structures (e.g., elections or the formation of a citizens' initiative) activities of citizens take place (e.g., close to the private sphere in neighborhoods, rural communities, neighborhoods, districts, etc.), which, do not appear on the screen of society, politics or science.

Hoffman and High-Pippert take up this approach for the classification of community energy initiatives: accordingly, the idea of such a civil society, which is based on a low basic level of participation, is commonly assessed as problematic in the literature (Hoffman and High-Pippert 2005: 389). Jürgen Habermas, for instance, argues that social and political systems consist of different parts (civil society, public space, organised political system and constitutional state, see Habermas 2011a, 2011b). From this, Hoffman and High-Pippert, referring to Jane Grant (2003), deduce that a network mediates between institutionalised problem-solving processes and issues of public interest within organised public spheres. Alongside this internal network is the public sphere where discourses of public interest are conducted and opinions are specified and focused. This sphere is described as open and reflexive as well as – from a democratic theory perspective – the place of emergence of processes where overarching social norms and collective decision-making processes are formulated, agreed upon and decided upon. This sphere is thus a communication and information space, albeit determined by the media; however, it also contains public forums that serve discussion, deliberation and participation.

Stealth or Strong Democracy?
Hoffman and High-Pippert refer to various models of community energy initiatives, which according to them correspond best to the intermediary role in the theory of *stealth democracy* (Hoffman and High-Pippert 2005: 399), according to which the largest part of the population does not share the commitment, which is lived out by a small group of citizens very intensively, actively and constantly in an exhaustive, democratic debate and is hardly visible from the outside ("camou-

flaged"). For this part of the population, the factors of time and what has been achieved or what is to be achieved (= output/outcome dimension) are more important than in other participatory arrangements such as citizen juries. There are always only a few citizens who have the necessary interest and knowledge to participate in the discourse. The interactions with the population are then primarily characterised by messages such as: "Wind is good, nuclear energy is bad". Only very few citizens would get involved in the topic area or the political discourse in a strong way.

High demands on the individual according to Barber's concept of strong democracy (Barber 1984) could therefore not be expected by making participation a full-time task. Rather, it is about a very broad inclusion of all social groups. In this conception, the participants of community energy initiatives do not act in a public sphere between the state and the population, but rather a bilateral exchange takes place with policy makers. This decisively shapes the ideas and ways of thinking (e.g., on the functions of the public sphere, democracy, business, etc.) of members of the community energy initiative. This idea corresponds to the "vehicle function" according to Skocpol (2003), according to which political activity is not only based on social interaction, but is determined by an active role of the individual in shaping policy or political content.

In the case of guaranteed grid integration of the electricity generated by community energy initiatives (guaranteed in Germany by the Renewable Energy Sources Act EEG), the *stealth* version is said to be sufficient in the covert for achieving a status conducive to democracy. In the other case of a "robust" form of community energy in the sense of strong democracy, many problems are to be expected:

- How citizens can be involved in the process.
- Better living conditions enable more people to stay.
- Activating dynamic forms to organize and manage grassroots initiatives.
- Promote education for sustainable development and create awareness.
- Present complicated issues to an audience without technical expertise.
- Establish appropriate professional expert and technical networks.
- Striking a balance between being an expert and being close to the people.

Before community energy can become a comprehensive model, the authors (ibid.) believe that these problems must be solved in the culture of civil society (Hoffman and High-Pippert 2005: 399 f.): "If communities, however defined and operationalized, are to be given authority over their energy system; that is, if communities can decide whether they prefer wind over nuclear power and then put that decision into effect, decision-making authority must rest in the hands of the community and not in the hands of an external body. How to structure the sorts of democratic relationships required under such a scenario is a daunting task".

From the perspective of creating economic benefits in terms of regional value creation, this means that democracy is defined in particular by the possibility of creating equal opportunities to share the financial benefits. The limits of community participation are reached where a financial mechanism is developed to attract as many local shareholders as possible as well as an approach which, under these conditions, distributes the energy gained to this community (i.e., prosuming) (meaning an overload of voluntary work). Similarly, there would be limits in terms of ownership and those who derive financial benefits from subsidies (selective benefits for a few people).

According to Hoffman and High-Pippert (2010: 7572), community energy as a whole means more than that citizens can only be seen as economic actors in the field. According to Benjamin Barber's ideas, this would be the exchange of shared interests as well as the negotiation of interests that are not shared by the community, agenda setting and other political activities. The goal is participation and self-governance, which ranges from neighborhood to national issues. A minimal prerequisite for this would first be issues of citizen groups that can establish a sense of community that forms a collective identity which transcends pure selfishness and self-interest. In group-based projects, this function of participation could be fulfilled by the multiplicity of tasks and projects, also by the fact that the activities build social connections between individuals who are otherwise very different from each other in terms of their experiences and backgrounds (in the sense of unifying moments and themes). Now, in order to establish a deliberatively conceived public sphere according to Jürgen Habermas, Hoffman and High-Pippert (ibid.) consider such activities that can generate basic patterns of trust and reciprocal action as well as sustainable and long-term associative behavior as crucial (Coleman 1990; Edwards et al. 2001). Community energy initiatives would thus be a counter-example to the stated decline of civic engagement and an erosion of social capital, as often assumed in studies (such as by Robert Putnam, see Putnam et al. 1993; Putnam 2000).

According to Hoffman and High-Pippert (2010: 7572), the community energy initiatives they studied are precisely a real model of "lived" strong democracy.[17] They argue that the ingredients for a vital civic culture were indeed measurable (sustained enthusiasm for the issues; stable forms of deliberation; extended social connections through information sharing with other members; the perception and belief that actions lead to success). However, the authors also have to qualify that the number of participants is very small (a few hundred) and for long-term projects the number is much smaller still. Similarly, the number of participants in projects resulting from such initiatives is extremely small.

[17] The authors examined six very heterogeneous community energy projects (Hoffman and High-Pippert 2010: 7568 f.):

- The Clean Energy Resource Team (CERTs) initiative. began in 2003, the CERTs project is a collaborative of the Minnesota Department of Commerce, the University of Minnesota, and the Minnesota Project, a nongovernmental organization. Six regional CERTs teams have been created, with each team bringing together people from various cities and counties, farmers and other landowners, industry, utilities, colleges, universities and local governments. The initial outcome of the project was a strategic vision and a renewable and energy conservation energy plan for each region; and
- Linden Hills Power & Light (LHP&L), a community-based organization located in the lakes area of the city of Minneapolis. LHP&L is defined entirely by specific neighborhood boundaries whose work includes a variety of energy-related and waste reduction activities, including the development of a neighborhood anaerobic digester.
- Metro CERTs, a Twin Cities-based version of CERTs created by the state legislature in 2007;
- Greenstar Cities, a statewide program to designed to engage, support, and reward communities that meet and exceed the state goals for energy efficiency and global warming emissions reductions;
- RENew Northfield, a 2003 initiative in a community about 1 hour south of the Minneapolis-St. Paul city proper; and
- The Phillips Community Energy Cooperative (PCEC), a program of the Green Institute, a local nonprofit organization based in a largely low-income, minority neighborhood of Minneapolis.

On the other hand, community energy projects can show how bottom-up initiatives can succeed[18]:

[18] In an analysis of other studies, Hoffman and High-Pippert found that participation was not the focus of members' interest. Only the criterion of local ownership could be found (Hoffman and High-Pippert 2005: 392). The authors subsequently examined three community energy initiatives with regard to participatory aspects. They used criteria from the study by Verba et al. (1995), in which four types of motivation for political activity were developed (*selective benefits, material benefits, social gratification and civic gratification, desire to influence policy outcomes*). The first case study corresponds to a large extent to participatory ideas and implementations in practice as a "real" grassroots initiative. The following characteristics were analyzed in this project:

- Process dimension: The initiative is concerned with its future development and options, it conducts dialogues on energy use, community leadership and decision-making.
- Internal structures: The members harmonize very well with each other and enjoy working together; exchange and thus networking are very strong.
- Behavioral changes: Members have changed and adapted their attitudes and behaviours in the process.
- A high degree of *social gratification* can be observed.

In contrast, the following characteristics were present in the second example:

- The co-op is located in a low-income urban area.
- There is a migration background of many members.
- Although the focus is on *social* and *civic gratification*, only low levels are achieved.
- There is good cooperation, but there is also a lack of exchange and networking and a low level of involvement.
- In addition to *civic gratification,* material benefits are also in the foreground.

Finally, the third case study describes a Minnesota state program:

- *Material benefits* and advantages for the career of the members.
- Interest in renewable energy and links to jobs.
- Participation in events, as well as electronic participation, which, however, tends to be leads to low *social gratification* and social connections.

Overall, the survey also found that participants consider a high level of information (about technologies and renewable energies) to be very important (ibid.: 397 f.). Other points highlighted by participants included the development of "strong" communities, energy security, construction of energy technology, opportunity for participation, identification and transparency of energy production costs, staff involvement, local jobs, small-scale energy technology, threats from climate change, change in public discourse topics, and the structure of locally owned energy projects. Less important to the participants were lower electricity costs and the possibility of owning their own energy project; of particularly low relevance was the possibility of own financial benefit, which is in line with other findings in the literature.

1. The programs attract interested parties in particular through personal incentives, by recruiting them through people they know, for example.
2. Individuals remain in the initiatives because the benefits they receive flow back into the community. Thus, the motive is less about the direct benefits they receive personally.

While the authors do not wish to exclude other influencing factors altogether, the idea that it is the image of and the community itself, and less the purely individual advantage, which is the decisive causal motivation for participants, has been strengthened.

The authors describe the combination of recruitment strategies and the construction of participatory incentives, which are characterized by the connection to and appreciation of a place (such as a neighborhood, school or similar, where the energy plant is built), as a decisive condition for success (ibid.: 7572). The initiators would themselves face the unfavorable conditions of "hidden democracy", individualized action and hardly available time resources for civil society action (ibid.: 7572 f.). Thus, the central challenge would ultimately be to change the behavior of uncommitted members, since ultimately only a few well-informed and active citizens act in a highly dynamic public sphere (ibid.: 7573).

However, according to the authors, community energy initiatives can be an example of how the transformation from individual to collective or communal action can succeed (ibid.). This picture can also be maintained, although many citizens do not make any efforts with regard to participatory procedures (ibid.). However, this finding is less in line with the preconditions of deliberative processes according to Benjamin Barber. In addition, there are some very strongly committed citizens in the initiatives who, although they are in the absolute minority, have the ability to incite less committed citizens and integrate them into the community program.

According to the authors, a successful approach to community energy must first and foremost be realistic about the different understandings of engagement and actual framework conditions (ibid.). Thus, they can lead less to expertism and expectations than to the fact that a large number of engaged people will participate. The ultimate goal, he argues, is well-informed citizens, a few of whom will also invest a higher level of time and effort, thereby fulfilling normative demands for a democratic community. Successful recruitment strategies would need to be structured in a tiered fashion, as well as exude commitment and enthusiasm, in order to attract citizens who are only willing to participate with a low or medium level of engagement. The authors cite information from stakeholders interviewed as success factors for this (ibid.):

- high number of decision-makers are aware of the community energy project;
- dialogue and exchange with public, governmental and local authorities, educational institutions, business and industry;
- small number of members leaving the communit energy project;
- unsuccessful projects are traced to personal contacts and networks of the project;
- change of living habits, spillover effects on environmental behavior in the neighborhood;
- strong social cohesion as well as a sense of energy ownership.

The definition of the policymakers, who understand participation both politically and economically, is seen as problematic by the initiatives surveyed (ibid.). This explains why opposition to wind energy projects can come from a community that is also a beneficiary of the project. These oppositions are said to be explained by an overused concept of community, as such projects are often financed in a more benefit-oriented way and do not address local concerns.

In summary, community energy initiatives organized bottom-up can be seen as supporting pillars of a civic culture in the energy sector, where the majority of citizens are willing to engage in order to reduce the impacts of the conventional energy system. In this sense, community energy initiatives are a valuable complement to institutional approaches.

4.3 Community Energy in Germany

Tradition of Cooperatives in the Energy Sector

After the emergence of the first fossil fuel and renewable energy (hydro power) electricity plants at the end of the nineteenth century, long-distance electricity suppliers were established in rural areas in Germany at the beginning of the twentieth century, which were also operated in cooperative form (electricity cooperatives (see Wolterstorff 1919; Stier 1999; Heinrich-Kaufmann-Stiftung 2012; Hellige 2013; Holstenkamp 2014, 2018; Holstenkamp and Stier 2018). As late as the 1930s, close to 6000 of these plants existed in the German Empire (Faust 1977; Holstenkamp 2012: 6), but rural areas were uninteresting for the larger energy companies that had emerged in the meantime. However, in Württemberg, for example, many hydropower energy cooperatives with a corresponding tradition still exist today. The electricity cooperatives remained a temporary phenomenon, because the supply was increasingly taken over by the large energy companies and the rural areas were also connected to the supra-regional electricity grids. It should be noted that this form of operation has an alternative rural character (see Klemisch and Maron 2010; Klemisch 2014a, 2014c).

The phenomenon of community energy is therefore not new. Even before the Erneuerbare-Energien-Gesetz (Renewable Energy Sources Act) came into force in 2000, which established a 20-year guaranteed tariff for the feed-in of electricity from renewable energy sources, thus making the use of renewable energies attractive, community energy plants already existed.[19] Thus, a few citizens set up wind turbines and PV plants, partly as a reaction to and signal for the possibility of a transformation of the energy system, also spurred on by the anti-nuclear movement and emerging ecological movements. Here, however, apart from the traditional cooperative hydropower plants, it remained with a few plants for demonstrative purposes. The boom in the expansion of renewable energies and community energy can therefore be attributed to a large extent to the subsidy policy of the Renewable Energy Sources Act (*Erneuerbare-Energien-Gesetz: EEG*), but other influencing factors must also be taken into account as explanations, which have not yet been scientifically analyzed (Kalkbrenner and Roosen 2016).

Finally, it should be noted that community energy initiatives are not evenly distributed across Europe (see Becker and Kunze 2015). A list or mapping of many energy cooperatives in Europe shows that this is a phenomenon of wealthy countries in the north and center of Europe; in the south and east of Europe there are apparently much fewer community energy projects (Bauwens et al. 2016: 139; thus referred to in the literature as the "Nordic welfare model" as a basic condition for energy transition activities, see Westholm and Beland Lindahl 2012)[20] Since energy cooperatives predominantly use PV energy sources, this represents a paradox. An obvious explanation seems to be the justification as a welfare characteristic, since citizens with higher incomes show a stronger investment power and a stronger environmental awareness as well as affinity for civic engagement.

[19] See on the development of energy policy in Germany in recent decades Saretzki (2001), Illing (2012), Sohre (2014) and on the influence of the Renewable Energy Sources Act (EEG) and the expansion of renewable energies Hirschl (2008), Mautz et al. (2008), Bruns et al. (2009), Ohlhorst 2009, Bruns (2011), Brunnengräber and Di Nucci (2014), Hake et al. (2015), Quitzow et al. (2016), Schmid et al. (2016), Strunz et al. (2016).

[20] See map of energy cooperatives in Europe at: http://rescoop.eu/rescoop-map

Community Energy and Energy Cooperatives in Germany

The turning point, as already mentioned, was the introduction of the Renewable Energy Sources Act in 2000. In fact, over time, the Act was able to have an effect: more and more investments were made in renewable energies. Private households decided, for example, to install PV systems on roofs, and more and more ideas and first projects of citizens' initiatives emerged. While these associations initially experimented with different legal forms of organization (and often founded several GbRs), cooperatives finally prevailed at the peak of the founding of community energy projects. In addition to democratic principles, the inclusion of members, no profit for the management and voluntary commitment, the legal form offers further advantages in terms of limited liability and the possibility of growth (possibility of constant membership and construction of further energy plants under the umbrella of a single company or project).

There are no exact data on how many citizens in total are financially involved in renewable energy installations.[21] In terms of installed renewable energy capacity in 2012, the share of community energy in the broader sense was 47% (this includes cases where citizen participation accounts for less than 50% of the total share of the investment) (in terms of electricity generation: 43%, in terms of net investment in renewable energy: 31%), and of community energy in the narrow sense 34% (in terms of electricity generation: 32%, in terms of net investment in renewable energy: 28%) (see on this and the following: trend research and Leuphana University Lüneburg 2013: 42 ff.). In the case of the latter, however, individual owners account for 25% (of total output, 24% of electricity generation, of net investment in renewable energy: 26%), and only 9% is accounted for by community energy companies (of electricity generation: 8%, of net investment in renewable energy: 2%). In terms of energy types, in the case of wind energy (onshore), community energy companies can account for 20% of output (of net investment in renewable energies: 10%), in the case of photovoltaics it is only 0.8% (of net investment in renewable energies: 10%), and in the case of bioenergy 0.2% (of net investment in renewable energies: 10%).

[21] For example, the current share of private individuals who own renewable energy plants is 35%; furthermore, 14% of the plants are owned by project companies, another 14% by industry, 13% by investment funds and banks, and 11% by farmers; the four large energy corporations RWE, E.ON, Vattenfall, and EnBW hold only 5% (Hall et al. 2016: 10). Nevertheless, the installed capacity of energy groups in renewable energies amounts to 33%; smaller plants with a capacity <10 MW also account for 33% (ibid.: 9). See also trend research and Leuphana University Lüneburg 2013; Leuphana University Lüneburg and Nestle 2014.

In the case of energy cooperatives, however, relatively precise findings are available: currently, more than 900 energy cooperatives are recorded in Germany, more than 130,000 private individuals are involved here with 470 million euros of equity capital; in the process, around 1.35 billion euros were invested (DGRV 2014: 12; DGRV 2015: 15; Yildiz et al. 2015: 63).[22] Since 2007 and 2008 in particular, many new energy cooperatives have been founded (see Yildiz et al. 2015: 63).

In the meantime, however, a "slowdown of the foundation boom" can be observed (Engerer 2014); in 2014, only 29 new energy cooperatives were founded (Müller and Holstenkamp 2015, see also DGRV 2015). Overall, this can be attributed to the decreasing funding quotas of the Renewable Energy Sources Act (EEG), but possibly also to limited potentials or exploitation of civic engagement in the municipalities. However, the planned special support for community energy in the 2017 version of the Renewable Energy Sources Act (EEG) amendment could counteract this (see BMWi 2016). In an overarching view, "mostly small(er) photovoltaic companies with a high equity ratio" were established (Engerer 2014: 2). Although there are some examples of the use of other forms of energy than photovoltaics (especially wind energy, biomass, hydropower and geothermal energy, as well as energy distribution, e.g., the provision of electricity and the operation of electricity/heating networks), such energy projects involve considerably more effort and financial volumes.[23] The number of such initiatives is therefore also lower,

[22] The average minimum participation in an energy cooperative is 738 euros (see on this and in the following: DGRV 2014). In almost three quarters of the cooperatives, participation with less than 500 euros is possible. However, the actual average participation is 3298 euros. In two thirds of the cooperatives, the average participation amount is between 1000 and 6000 euros. In a quarter of the energy cooperatives, participation is already possible with an amount of less than 100 euros. Energy cooperatives are founded by an average of 43 people. The spread ranges from 4 to 427 founding participants. In most cases, the number of members increases very quickly. At the time of the survey, the average number of members had already increased almost fivefold to 198. About 60% of cooperatives have between 50 and 200 members, and only 16% have fewer than 50 members. More than 90% of the members are private individuals. The energy cooperatives have an average start-up capital of just under 686,000 euros and invested an average of just under 1.9 million euros in renewable energies at the beginning of 2014. The equity ratio is 54% on average. Almost every fourth cooperative invests completely without outside capital. The cooperatives generate an annual turnover of about 337,000 euros on average and distribute a dividend of 4.26% on average. However, half of the cooperatives did not distribute any dividends at all in 2013. Often, distributions do not begin until a few years after the founding.

[23] In the case of wind power use (community wind farms), the limited liability company and partnership (*GmbH & Co KG*) legal form is often used in Germany; see on challenges for energy cooperatives in wind power use Holstenkamp and Degenhart 2014.

and the potential, while theoretically considerable, is limited in practice due to these inhibiting factors (Yildiz et al. 2015: 62).

The investment volume of energy cooperatives is often between 200,000 and 2 million euros, the equity ratio often between 10 and 30% as well as 100% (Volz 2012b: 517; see also Debor 2014; Yildiz et al. 2015). The infrastructural location is predominantly rural (two-thirds of all cases), predominantly urban are only 9% (Volz 2012b: 517). In most cases, there are only 7–20 founding members (45%), and only 4% have more than 100 people (ibid.). The number of people later involved is between 50 and 200 (ibid.). Initiators are often Volksbanks, private individuals and citizens' or environmental initiatives, sometimes in combination with municipalities, energy companies, public utilities and cooperative associations (ibid.: 518). The proportion of voluntary work is very high (94%) (ibid.: 519). The network of actors (promoters, multipliers, key actors) is often composed of local banks, other cooperatives, municipal utilities, churches, regional politicians, municipalities and mayors (ibid.). Supra-regional project developers also play a significant role in community energy.

As crucial success factors of community energy, energy cooperatives state in particular the amount of the dividend, as well as the number of members and earnings development. Less important are the effects on CO_2 reduction (ibid.: 521). With regard to the self-image (own definition and interpretation of the energy cooperative), respondents named renewable energy production as the main objective. In addition, also contribution against climate change, avoidance of CO_2, strengthening the feeling of "we", public perception for the region, role model function, keeping added value in the region, providing for future generations, taking on a pioneering role, feeling of doing something good, enabling environmentally compatible capital investment, self-sufficient energy supply, counter design to the large energy providers, increasing the quality of life, good dividend payment, security of supply, low-cost energy supply as well as creation of jobs (ibid.: 522). The advantages of the legal form mentioned in the first place are the principle of democracy and the possibility to participate with small amounts of money; it is also stressed that it is not a capital-oriented approach (ibid.). Future challenges are seen in the reformation of the regulations of the Renewable Energy Sources Act (EEG), finding land, regulations and hurdles in the construction of new plants and ensuring the satisfaction of the members; in addition, "from honorary to full-time office", winning volunteers for the board, gaining own expertise, institutions and citizens as members, networking with actors in the field of renewable energies and partly low public awareness (ibid.).[24]

Further research results show that energy cooperatives serve a stronger orientation towards the common good, which goes beyond the traditional principle of mutuality and has a "proximity to citizens" (Huybrechts and Mertens de Wilmars 2014), but also has problems in terms of viability and replicability.[25] For Huybrechts

[24] See Yildiz (2013), and Engerer (2014), Poppen (2015) and Tarhan (2015) for further overview of findings on energy cooperatives in Germany.

[25] See further empirical findings on energy cooperatives (overview in Schreuer and Weismeier-Sammer 2010; Weismeier-Sammer and Reiner 2011; Volz 2011a, 2012a; Holstenkamp and Müller 2013; Yildiz 2013; Müller and Holstenkamp 2015; Poppen 2015; Tarhan 2015; Yildiz et al. 2015) and on citizen energy (trend: research GmbH and Leuphana University Lüneburg 2013) in the literature. See Schreuer and Weismeier-Sammer (2010) on the characteristics of energy cooperatives in Europe.

Kaphengst and Velten (2014) and Wirth (2014) investigated the wealth of experience of cooperatives and the associated conservative character as well as the importance of regional networks and local conditions. Viardot (2013) analyzed effects in the form of increased acceptance of renewable energy, transfer of knowledge and expertise and cost reduction of technology introduction. Kaphengst and Velten (2014) demonstrated learning effects in the form of reflection on energy consumption and capital investment behavior; Sagebiel et al. (2014) were able to show that transparency and opportunities for co-determination increase willingness to pay. Further research topics in this context concern:

- Increasing land use conflicts (Bosch and Peyke 2011; Radtke 2015), overriding issues of spatial planning (Kufeld 2013).
- Local level as a place for shaping the energy transition (Droege 2014; Kamlage and Fleischer 2014).
- "Citizens as the bearers of the energy transition" (Kreß et al. 2014a).
- Citizens' willingness to pay for green electricity from energy cooperatives (Sagebiel et al. 2014).
- Importance of the cooperative model in the field of renewable energy use (Huybrechts and Mertens de Wilmars 2014).
- Systematization and definitions of participation opportunities in the energy sector (Kreß et al. 2014a/b; Degenhart and Holstenkamp 2013; Holstenkamp and Degenhart 2013; Kneußel 2014).
- Systematization of energy cooperatives (Holstenkamp 2012; Huybrechts and Mertens de Wilmars 2011).
- Funding principle in energy cooperatives: ranks in the middle according to a survey (Volz 2012b: 522), energy cooperatives hardly comply with the approach, but do not violate it either, as they are not exclusively profit-oriented (Volz 2011b).
- Actor network: for example, cooperation with municipalities (Holstenkamp and Rückheim 2013), cooperative fulfilment of municipal tasks (Karner et al. 2010)
- Acceptance generation: Carmen 2014, foundation 100% renewable/Haug and Mono 2012.

and Mertens de Wilmars (2014), this basic orientation illustrates why this organizational model is very attrattive for community initiatives. Overall, energy cooperatives offer the potential to support the dissemination of renewable energies – especially in spaces and contexts where conditions are rather unfavorable for the operation of these energy sources (Viardot 2013).

Flieger et al. see energy cooperatives not only as economic organizations, but also as social organizations, which can be regarded as business associations (Flieger et al. 2015: 4). They thus form a kind of "hybrid organisation", between a partnership (e.g., association) and a corporation (ibid.). In addition to a material participation, however, an immaterial participation is also assumed, which arises via co-determination rights within the organization. "These immaterial participation rights cannot be withdrawn from the general assembly – the supreme body of the cooperative as an assembly of members (…). These decision-making rights include the election and deselection of supervisory board members, the direct appointment of board members or, in most cases, indirect appointment via the supervisory board members they elect. Likewise, all decisions on the amendment of the articles of association, the adoption of the balance sheet, the adoption of resolutions on profit or loss, the discharge of the board of directors and the supervisory board as well as comprehensive information rights on the business affairs of the cooperative cannot be withdrawn" (ibid.). Despite these comprehensive co-determination rights of each individual member (which also include a parity weighting of votes, in that each member has one vote regardless of the amount of the shareholding) the following is limited: "(…) energy cooperatives are organised bi-democratically, but not self-governing. This is because the individual bodies have clearly allocated competences. This includes the fact that the board of directors manages a cooperative on its own responsibility. The members or supervisory boards are only involved in operational decisions to the extent that this is laid down in the articles of association for specific decision cases (unless decisions are explicitly delegated, e.g., to working groups). Accordingly, the founding statutes set the decisive preconditions for a more participatory decision-making structure or a decision-making structure that is more in the hands of the management" (ibid.).

Apart from the Renewable Energy Sources Act EEG remuneration scheme, there is no explicit state support for community energy production in Germany. Occasionally, indirect support can be found, for example, support measures by the BMU, for example in the case of the 100% renewable energy regions or bioenergy villages, also by the EU (e.g., European Energy Award) (see Moser 2011; Ruppert-Winkel et al. 2013; Müller 2014; Grundmann and Ehlers 2016). Federal states and municipalities can also offer isolated funding and assistance (see Renewable Energies Agency 2015). However, there is no comprehensive or support framework program at federal or state level for community energy initiatives.

The Renewable Energy Sources Act (EEG) is therefore an essential steering instrument, which has indirectly promoted and allowed the emergence of community energy, in particular through the feed-in tariffs and the grid connection obligation. With further reductions in feed-in tariffs, the phenomenon of community energy may dwindle even further; however, overarching support is quite conceivable in the future and is being sought in the 2016 amendment to the EEG (see BMWi 2016). Political discussions about the EEG often focused on the possible large profits thanks to the EEG remuneration and the high costs of support, while the topic of community energy hardly made it onto the political agenda. For a long time, community energy initiatives in Germany were not organized in terms of a common representation of interests. Since the founding of the Alliance for Citizens' Energy in January 2014, a certain representation of interests has been created, which, however, cannot be equated with other associations. Indirect interest representation continues to arise in the case of community energy through cooperative associations and the renewable energy associations. In other countries such as Denmark, Austria and the UK (here e.g., Community Energy Strategy, see Cass et al. 2010; Department of Energy and Climate Change 2014; The Scottish Government 2013), stronger overarching political support for community energy is known.

Public Participation and Planning in Infrastructure Management

At the regional level, community energy is embedded in the political program of holistic municipal climate protection (Ekardt and Hennig 2014; Behr and Kamlage 2015), whereby participatory processes are of outstanding importance in municipal planning anyway (Benighaus et al. 2007, see on municipal assemblies in the context of climate protection Mittelbach and Schemske 2015). Planning processes, as in the case of renewable energies, are fundamentally of interest to citizens, and public participation makes sense here because of its significance for the concrete living environment; moreover, many options for participation are now known and can be combined (see McAfee 2013; Renn et al. 2014; Schweizer et al. 2016; Leshinsky and Legacy 2015).

Meanwhile, location-related acceptance problems in German industrial and technology policy have already been identified by associations (see Raven et al.

2009; Verein Deutscher Ingenieure 2014), recommendations for early communication and public participation in the planning and construction of infrastructure projects and grid expansion have been developed (see Verein Deutscher Ingenieure 2013, 2014; Brennecke 2015; critically on this from the perspective of politicians: Rademacher and Lintemeier 2015). However, early consideration and approach cannot solve all problems, as Bauer (2015) has clearly shown using the example of public participation in the context of grid expansion. This is because participation entanglement traps can occur here: due to the different intentions of participating administrations and participating citizens, which are also brought in at different times, possible positive effects (i.e., taking up and utilising suggestions, creating alternatives, "involving" the population in the process) cannot be developed due to these diverging logics (see Bauer 2015). However, since spatially relevant decisions are conflict-ridden anyway, planning approaches that promise more participation can even be counterproductive if the "disappointed hopes for effective participation only contribute to further exacerbating the conflicts" (Wolsink 2002: 17). The idea in the context of community energy and energy transition, "plan acceptance, shape citizen participation, gain legitimacy" (100% renewable foundation/Haug and Mono 2012; see also Dunker and Mono 2013) can therefore probably not be fully effective. According to the results of the present study, participation cannot serve the lofty purpose of being a "silver bullet" for acceptance (Rau et al. 2012), but tends to create good conditions for it. Of outstanding importance is presumably also the ability of any planning initiatives to integrate conflicting interests already in the planning phase (Sovacool et al. 2015a).

In the case studies of this study, however, many cooperative administrations and local political representatives could be found. State support structures thus exist (see analysis of administrative initiatives to promote photovoltaics in Sweden in Palm 2016 as well as on the connection of civil society action with state action in de Moor et al. 2013; de Moor 2015), also at regional district and state level (see Renewable Energies Agency 2015; Mattes et al. 2015), but they face a differently oriented federal regime (see Radtke 2018a), which tends to weaken approaches at local level. In particular, excessive demands and congestion will weaken the *grassroots variant of* community energy in the future and, in all likelihood, also reduce it; larger interconnected projects are then more likely to remain.

The idea of "green electricity from the region for the region" (Bettinger and Holstenkamp 2015) with the associated hope of small, locally fixed participation projects with great proximity between energy project and participants will then tend to take a back seat, especially without state support. On the one hand, the stabilization of community energy depends on state support (see the example of the "Baden-Württemberg participation portal" (*Beteiligungsportal*)), and on the other hand on the professionalization and self-help of the initiatives (see the examples of the "Civic Plants" (*Bürgerwerke eG*), a joint venture of multiple cooperatives in South Germany, and the public network of community energy cooperatives in Hesse and the public network of voluntary energy initiatives in Baden-Wuerttemberg). However, both are fragile and unevenly distributed; professionalization processes and strong links with state institutions in turn harbor disadvantages – but so does pure independence (excessive demands, being left on one's own). A more balanced system would be a task for the future. In addition, there are the financing hurdles for community energy, which will presumably also continue in future with more focused smart microgrid approaches, in which electricity production and distribution are to be intelligently combined (see Holstenkamp et al. 2015; Scheiner et al. (2015) speak here of "intelligent infrastructures" across the board). Despite the compelling logic of smart, intelligent and flexible models of (community-focused) energy supply, Moss et al. question of whose energy transition it is in terms of organization and ownership seems justified, since, for example, the shares of private investment in the population are not equally distributed. In this respect, too, a conclusion in the direction of the ideas of remunicipalization in different variants and degrees seems obvious (Becker et al. 2015a; Blanchet 2015; Becker et al. 2016b; Blanchet et al. 2016).

Public Participation in the Context of the Energiewende

Public participation procedures in the context of the energy transition have also become a topic for research. Here, all approaches are of interest in which citizens are involved in the planning and approval of renewable energy plants, whether formally or informally, whether through classic submissions to the administration or in discursive discussion events, walk-throughs or virtual forums (see on citizen or public participation in the wind energy sector Bell et al. 2005; McLaren Loring 2007; Wright 2012; Bell et al. 2013; Jami and Walsh 2014; Leibenath et al. 2016). Dialogue processes have already been studied, for example, in the context of grid expansion (Kamlage 2013a, 2013b; Lietzmann 2013; Kamlage et al. 2014) or urban development (Kuder and Ritzi 2013). Fundamental considerations and approaches, mostly connected with recommendations for action and highlighting advantages and disadvantages of procedures, can be found in Renn (2013a, 2013b,

2014, Renn et al. 2014), Gawel et al. (2014a) and Schweizer et al. (2016). Ortwin Renn (as well as Kuder and Ritzi 2013) represents here the deliberative approach in the sense of deliberative democratic theory, which basically assumes that deliberation through exchanging discourses between citizens, administration, stakeholders, civil society organizations, etc. represents the best approach to solving problems and conflicts that arise, as well as to exchanging interests. Procedures of public participation should therefore primarily create such open spaces of deliberation, which are bound to certain standards (e.g., fairness, temporal-thematic manageability, etc.). In contrast, community energy research emphasizes direct participation in the sense of participatory democratic theory, for example in the sense of Benjamin Barber (Hoffman and High-Pippert 2005, 2010; Ison 2010) as well as the importance of the formation of social capital (Walker et al. 2010).

4.4 Definitions and Typological Approaches

Various attempts have been made in the literature to define, classify, typify and taxonomize community energy projects (see section above) (see on various citizen participation models Degenhart and Schomerus 2014; Holstenkamp and Radtke 2018). Walker et al. (2007: 64 ff.) argue that, on the one hand, it is not at all possible to provide an exact definition of the term "community" or "communal" in the context of renewable energy projects. This could embody any collective communitarian principle, which in practice can include both a high-involvement project and a collection of buildings. On the other hand, available analyses suggest that a wide variety of environmental and energy policy demands, controls, and targets have led to a decentralized energy landscape. Instead of a fixed classification, the authors emphasize the characteristic of the confluence of interests and actors. Within new discourses, innovative approaches to action and ways of thinking would be formed. However, these individual success stories ("policy narratives") and approaches to solutions could only be considered individually and are not transferable to a generalized modeling.

Finally, Walker et al. (2011) developed an open framework as a rough analytical grid that is able to show actors, exchange relationships and effects.[26] A very common framework for classification differentiates between process and outcome dimensions (remote/private and closed/institutional vs. open/participatory and local/collective) (Walker and Devine-Wright 2008).[27]

---

[26] In order to be able to classify the phenomenon of community energy from a social science perspective in society, Walker et al. (2011: 11) developed a framework that is essentially composed of two circuits (in exchange relationship). The first circuit refers to effects of initially public, social actions:

- The focus is on interactions (meetings, discussions, letters, exhibitions, media reports, petitions, protests, flyers, etc.).
- The interactions led to expectations of the public or the process.
- This brings actors and groups into network, which in turn leads to engagement strategy and actions, which in turn can lead to interactions.
- These processes are influenced by economic and political contexts. The second cycle describes the effects of project activities.
- Interactions lead to expectations of the project and the process.
- This in turn leads to engagement strategies and actions (actions of actors in public space). These in turn lead to high-profile interactions. This process is now strongly linked to the local context: the place and the community as well as the regional-local policy.
- The whole process is influenced by local strategies, technology design and incoming proposals and ideas (e.g., by whom and where should the energy project be built?).

Finally – flowing out of the open circuits – there are consequential effects: The interactions, engagement strategies and actions lead to formal decision-making processes and finally to an outcome (decisions).

[27] In the field between the points "open and participatory" (process level) and "local and collective" (outcome level), the authors now categorize three interpretations of the term "community renewables "76. The first point of view (A), described by participants, refers to the process dimension and sees community projects as characterized by a high degree of involvement of local people in the planning, creation and ultimately also operation of the project. Typical representatives of this viewpoint are advocates of alternative forms of energy and those experienced with participation projects, strongly influenced by normative principles of empowerment, participation and capacity building.

The second view (B) focuses on outcomes and is less concerned with questions of who participates, but rather how revenues or returns are shared. In particular, interviewees emphasized that the projects were essentially designed, built and managed by local actors – as long as they serve parts of the community, such as creating jobs, strengthening local regeneration or contributing to education (alongside broader goals such as reducing greenhouse gas emissions). The third control room (C) is described as an open space, open to different project forms and orientations. In these cases, stakeholders place less emphasis on the "right" community concept, but emphasize progress in general and productivity and usefulness of the project. With this objective, a wide variety of combinations for the design of process and outcome are acceptable to the initiators.

It remains questionable how helpful these classifications are for a scientific debate – here, too, the definitional-classificatory approach depends on the individual (researcher's) perspective; the classifications vary accordingly. Other definitional and typological approaches attempt to specify and limit the terminology (citizen energy, participation in renewable energies, community energy, etc.) in more detail (Holstenkamp and Degenhart 2013) or to differentiate according to individual ways of accessing opportunities for participation and action (Kreß et al. 2014a).

But here, too, the question remains as to what is meant by the underlying concepts: they appear variable, interchangeable and not very precise. The author's typology (Radtke 2013, 2014), which is based in particular on structural forms and "participation-friendly" conditions (e.g., the type of small, participatory energy cooperative), also seems questionable. Such cases may be empirically verifiable, and the detection of accumulations and thus generalizations also seem possible to a certain extent. But it remains doubtful what can be achieved with such abstract-theoretical models in view of the enormous heterogeneity of empirical cases and thus great accumulation of deviations and variabilities (complex, diversified characteristics and structures of community energy projects).[28] Even the model-like small, participatory energy cooperative addressed here can exhibit completely unexpected practices and dynamics in concrete cases that deviate entirely from the model conception.

Definitions of Community Energy

Community energy is shaped by different characteristics such as the use of different types of energy, economic (financing, forms of enterprise), political (energy policy), social (user and confronted communities) and spatial (specifics of the place of energy use) structures (Walker and Devine-Wright 2008; Creamer et al. 2019; Bauwens et al. 2022). These characteristics are mirrored in the orientations of the research.

[28] Thus, another, social-psychological model was developed by Schweizer-Ries (2011: 191), which focuses on options and barriers of action, influenced by physical, media, economic, legal-political and administrative conditions. The options and barriers of actions, perceptions and assessments can be influenced by a "change system" – both at the individual and organizational level. Again, context is emphasized (through nature, social, cultural, objects and processes), overall again the model is not thought of as linear but as a developmental process. The authors also emphasize the relevance of permanence (conceived as an ongoing process, requiring time), commitment (related to the process and proximity to the local, requirements and goals) and communication (between groups and actors) (ibid.: 197). This model also focuses on exchange processes and reciprocal relationships, and is designed to be very open and flexible: Barriers and options are likely to arise for any project. Whether such simplistic model formations make sense here at all may be doubted – it is precisely individual specifics that distinguish projects and represent the essential, the really relevant conditions.

The term "Bürgerenergie" is used exclusively in Germany (or German-speaking countries) and has become widely accepted in linguistic usage and scientific literature. The term is usually derived from compound words such as citizen wind farm or citizen solar. The term is somewhat misleading and imprecise, as it suggests that the renewable energy plants are owned or operated by citizens or that they are involved in planning. However, community energy projects are not always founded by citizens and are not always fully owned by citizens (e.g., citizens often have a small financial stake in plants). Moreover, the term suggests that the owners or shareholders are exclusively citizens. However, often times this is not the case. Other ownership models (with other co-operators and shareholders such as companies, municipalities, public utilities, associations, etc.) would be excluded, which would have the disadvantage of inadequately reflecting the complex actor structures. The English-language concept of "community energy" (see definition in Walker and Simcock 2012 and Bauwens et al. 2022)[29] offers a broader scope. It

[29] In this study, the German term "Bürgerenergie" is translated to the most common word in scientific literature, community energy. Actually, several terms (e.g., citizen or civic energy, energy community, community renewable energy) are used in literature, sometimes synonymously. Although this does not do justice to the distinction between the German definition of "Bürgerenergie" and community energy presented here, the multiple terms are not uniformly defined in the literature (see Walker and Devine-Wright 2008; Hielscher 2011; Holstenkamp and Degenhart 2013; Hicks et al. 2014; Kunze and Becker 2015a; Holstenkamp and Radtke 2018; Creamer et al. 2019; Bauwens et al. 2022). As a consequence, different terms are sometimes used in reference to the same phenomenon (as well as vice versa). Here, "Bürgerenergie" is understood as a kind of sub-concept of community energy, as citizen energy initiatives can predominantly be summarized as an individual-participative approach under the collective term community energy (which also covers associative or institutional engagement or participation of actors without explicit individual participation of citizens). In other words, the term "Bürgerenergie" in Germany is generally attributed to individual participation of independent persons. Conversely, community energy research thus refers to energy projects that do not involve (direct) citizen participation by individuals. In the version of the Renewable Energy Sources Act (EEG) from 2017, community energy is classified as a privileged actor protected by special regulation. For this purpose, the Federal Ministry of Economics defines community energy as follows: At least ten members of the company must be natural persons. Each member of the company may exercise a share of no more than 10% of the voting rights and the natural persons must have at least 51% of the voting rights. At least 51% of the voting rights must be held by members of the company who have been registered for at least one year in the district pursuant to § 17 of the Federal Registration Act (Bundesmeldegesetze) (as their primary residence) where the renewable energy plant is to be located. By linking the company to the district, the company's location in the district is ensured (BMWi 2016: 11). The basic problem of this privileged position of community energy in German energy law lies in the fact that to meet these requirements, they can be simulated, by using fake identities or "letterbox companies" to take advantage of this market access.

emphasizes the principle of community (e.g., also a community of actors or the commitment of an institution (usually public or intended for the common good, as in the case of public institutions, clubs, associations or churches that pursue an energy project in the interest of their members or the public), in which individuals (citizens) do not necessarily have to be involved) and is thus more open than the concept of citizen energy. There is less emphasis here on the process of inclusion (of citizens and other civic persons) and more on the orientation of a community energy production of actors, individuals. This makes sense in some respects, since the basic aim of many initiatives is to act collectively. However, such initiatives are not always based on a community or collective action, as in the described cases of financial participation of citizens in renewable energy limited liability companies (top-down participation mode). Here, there is neither an initiative character (bottom-up mode), nor is there in many cases a far-reaching inclusion of citizens (beyond financial shares via discursive and jointly shaping community).

In the English-language literature, the term community energy (or community renewable energy: CRE) is therefore interpreted differently and used more openly and flexibly to describe and include different types of participatory energy initiatives, e.g. institutional public investments (Walker and Devine-Wright 2008; Creamer et al. 2019; Bauwens et al. 2022). Moreover, the special term "intermediary" in this context refers to organizations and networks that build links between specific community energy groups and share experiences, good practices, expertise and advice (including lobbying policy makers). Not only is the term community energy interpreted flexibly, as is the term "community" itself (Hielscher 2011: 11). As such, a broad range of definitions of community exist in sociological literature (Bauwens et al. 2022). Hielscher considers the aspects of social capital, "community capacity", social learning and norms, as well as social networks to be essential (Hielscher 2011: 11).

In the literature, different emphases are placed on the degree of community involvement in the initiatives, geographic boundaries, ownership structures, and modes of profit-making when attempting to define community energy. For example, Hathway (2010: 44) defines community energy projects as a local model: "Community projects involve local groups developing low carbon energy solutions appropriate to local situations and with community groups having ownership over the outcomes. Examples include solar water heating clubs, or insulation clubs, which provide mutual support for system installation, energy awareness and behavior networks, which provide guidance and reassurance to neighbors on energy matters relevant to them; and co-operatively owned small-scale renewable energy systems such as micro-hydro and wind".

Interpretations not only define the meaning of community energy in terms of the different initiatives, but also provide evidence of the diversity of community activities. The initiation, management and construction of the project can arise from grassroots actions, but also from partnerships between community energy groups, NGOs, local governments/municipalities or from companies and institutions/organizations – all of which share the motivation of wanting to share their income with a community. Such a definitional differentiation and classification is based on the origin of the grouping and the resulting variable levels of autonomy and independence (see Steward et al. 2009). These delimitations already imply various innovative procedures of community energy initiatives (Hielscher 2011: 12), related to:

- **Organizational structures** (social organizations refer to values, norms, processes and behaviors to organize and manage member interactions, as well as the level of participation and internal governance methods).
- **Legal forms of projects** (the choice of legal form has an impact on the way money is collected, bonuses and risks are assessed, and links are formed. Some groups are likely to have more informal structures and may therefore vary the degree of formality).
- **Financial structure** (e.g., project developers, credit institutions, municipalities, organizations, individual actors).
- **Partnerships and networking activities** (voluntary, public, private social groups. Initiatives can emerge through three modes: bottom-up and top-down mode or partnerships).
- **Basics of human resources** (tends to limit commercial activities, financial support and mutual exchange of energy projects).
- **Ownership structures** (ownership models consist, for example, of actor cooperations, public ownership, nonprofit organizations and joint ventures, funds, local companies, private ownership, non-commercial energy companies).
- **Development models and business plans or models** (development projects, group projects from existing resources or new initiation).
- **Functions of members** (members of the group can assume the roles of financial investors, project participants, project supporters or local beneficiaries (Walker and Cass 2007). The relationships can be either personal or obscure, ongoing or sporadic, and direct or indirect (Steward et al. 2009).

Involving communities in energy initiatives can thus take different forms of project initiation, administration, development, decision-making and financial support (Rogers et al. 2008). In addition, community energy initiatives may differ in terms of the conditions of development, in the support of the initialization and continuation of the initiative, and in the degree of support they receive from local communities. This support often depends on the distribution of economic, social, and contextual revenues, especially when groups seek to implement energy systems (Walker and Devine-Wright 2008). However, the diversity of community energy initiatives is not exclusively shaped by social, legal and organizational arrangements, but also by the nature of community involvement in community groupings (which may be based on interest, spatial reference or socio-demographic background) and the form of technology used (e.g., difference between solar and wind energy).

Hielscher (2011: 3) defines community energy projects as composed of people and non-human actors.[30] "Initiatives" means that they are focused on the production of energy and "activities" characterize the steps that are necessary to implement the project. The term initiative is meant to emphasize the processual nature: "The word 'initiative' is used to indicate that these are ongoing processes and are not time-limited" (Houghton 2010: 9). Community energy (resp. "CRE initiatives"), is then characterized by a wide variety of activities, which relate to three areas: energy, (especially) renewable energy and climate change (Hielscher 2011: 4).

Another definition targets the energy use and operation context (Seyfang et al. 2013: 978): "Community energy is a diverse field of activity and includes both energy generation and conservation projects such as (…). They are typically instigated or run by a diverse range of civil society groups, including voluntary organisations, cooperatives, informal associations etc, and partnerships with social enterprises, schools, businesses, faith groups, local government or utility companies".

Seyfang et al. continue to emphasize the difficulties of a concrete definition of the term (ibid.): "Defining 'community energy' precisely is somewhat problematic: there is no consensus over the term, and policymakers, intermediary organisations, practitioners and academics infer varying degrees of community involvement (…). Walker et al. (2007) reviewed a number of different CRE projects to investigate the variations in community ownership and outcomes across the range, and to examine the diversity of interpretations of 'community energy' in use amongst different actors. While offering a slippery concept for analysis, the 'flexibility' of interpretations did work in favour of wide acceptability of the concept of community energy".

[30] Hielscher thus refers to Bruno Latour, who in his actor-network theory explicitly considers non-human actors (such as energy plants), for example in his idea of a parliament of things (see Latour 2001, for a discussion of Latour's concept in the context of the energy transition Radtke 2015).

The extended definitional approach is also preferred by the authors (ibid.): "(...) we follow Walker and Devine-Wright's (2008) lead and consider community energy to refer to those projects where communities (of place or interest) exhibit a high degree of ownership and control, as well as benefiting collectively from the outcomes, and we include both supply- and demand-side sustainable energy initiatives".

Overarching assumptions in the literature are that revenues from community energy projects promote greater public participation in terms of local empowerment and increased income for local people, increase a diversity of skills, generate jobs, and strengthen social cohesion and inclusion.

The decisive factor in the case of community energy, in contrast to conventional operator approaches, is community, which in the literature (Steward et al. 2009: 143 ff.) is related to the following elements:

- "Doing things together".
- "Reaching the parts others can't reach").
- "Increasing the visibility of personal behaviour".
- "Acting holistically".
- "Local not parochial".
- "Developing and demonstrating".

In addition, a community energy project can increase the capacity of individuals to develop innovative organizational forms and legal structures (and thus promote social innovation) and to build and influence network flows (Walker 2008; Capener 2009; Houghton 2010). In addition to overarching goals of transforming the energy system and reducing greenhouse gas emissions, community energy projects should have the effect of increasing public support for and acceptance of renewable energy and therefore mitigate the NIMBY effect ("not in my backyard"). Community energy initiatives also offer municipalities and citizen communities the opportunity to be financially independent, while raising awareness of renewable energy among the population (Walker et al. 2006, 2007; Walker 2008). However, both aspects are controversial, the NIMBY idea has already been criticized as an overly simplistic concept that does not take into account the many influencing factors regarding oppositional behavior (Krohn and Damborg 1999; Wolsink 2000; van der Horst 2007; Devine-Wright 2005a, 2005b, 2009, 2013a, 2013b – see critical discussion in Mcclymont and O'Hare 2008; Haggett 2010, 2011 and Feldman and Turner 2011, 2014). The links between local action and the environment do not always underlie the actions and motivations of community energy initiators (see Gamel et al. 2016). Local needs and demands (e.g., regional value creation) seem to be in some cases the stronger driving motivation of community energy initiatives compared to global thinking (climate change, ecology).

In addition, Graf and Fuchs (2015) emphasize the political science dimension of community energy by talking about local transformation processes and their normative embedding in governance structures of the multi-level system. This aspect of the interaction of community energy initiatives within local governance structures in exchange and interaction with numerous actors has received little attention in the literature so far. Mostly, analyses are focused on internal structures and mechanisms or on effects of community energy, which are concretely affected by projects on the ground and can therefore also be studied.

Three Attempts to Define Community Energy

In the literature, various definitions of community energy can be found, which attempt to explicitly determine individual dimensions and characteristics.[31] Three approaches will be presented here, which illustrate the different perspectives and approaches to the phenomenon.

First Approach: An Organizational and Structure-Centered View – A Tiered Definition of Community Energy

In an approach by the Leuphana University Lüneburg, reference is first made to different uses of terms, such as citizen participation model, citizen wind farms, citizen energy (cooperative), in English terms such as *community ownership* and *community energy* are used, with regard to cooperatives the terms *co-operative ownership,* in addition also *local ownership* or *grassroots power* (and some more terms) (trend: research GmbH and Leuphana University Lüneburg 2013: 14 f.[32]).

[31] On the structure and action of energy cooperatives in the form of organizational structure and typology of energy cooperatives, organizational action, goal formation of participation, actor reference to participation as well as participation and its orientation, see the presentations in Kneußel (2014).

[32] The authors point out that there is still a lack of clarity in the definition and use of terms but assume that this will become established in the course of further research: "It is not the aim here to present a fully comprehensive analysis of all these terms or even to order the field of terms. Rather, this illustrative list is intended to illustrate that in order to scientifically analyze the contexts of interest and communicate the findings, it is necessary to outline the precise meaning of the terms used. Depending on the approach and theoretical perspective, the choice of terms and explication may vary. In this respect, the proposal presented here should be interpreted as one that must prove fruitful in empirical studies" (trend: research GmbH and Leuphana University Lüneburg 2013: 15).

First, according to Holstenkamp and Degenhart (2013: 9), a distinguishing feature results from the distinction between

- involved citizens (in a renewable energy investment model): top-down model
- and actively engaged citizens, "capital giving citizens": bottom-up model.

These two basic mechanisms of citizen participation can be extended to include a combination of participation approaches, which can compete with each other (ibid.: 21)[33]:

1. **Bottom-up initiative**: citizens` or civil society initiatives or associations initiate a community energy project from the bottom up (*grassroots approach, invented participation*).
2. **Top-down participation**: the energy company or project involves citizens by offering them the opportunity to join the company (*grasstops approach, invited participation*).
3. **Linking of bottom-up and top-down participation**: an energy company co-operates with bottom-up initiatives or creates a joint venture project.

Within the participation constructions, the influence of other actors in decision-making structures is of great importance: "The share of municipalities and local banks in civil partnerships is likely to be small overall, so that the allocation to community energy can be made unambiguously. At the same time, the influence on decision-making in the society can be deviatingly large. It is questionable whether this has an influence on the acceptance of concrete projects. Against this background, a classification into top-down vs. bottom-up initiatives would be interesting for data collection, but very time-consuming" (ibid.).

[33] Similar to these mechanisms as well as the definitional approach of participation according to Kersting (2014), Lang et al. (2013: 227) additionally distinguish between a *contested* and *invited space* of participation in energy cooperatives:

- the bottom-up self-organization of citizens (co-operative as 'contested space');
- the top-down organization to canalize citizen participation (co-operative as 'invited space'). Co-operative public-citizen partnerships therefore represent a balancing act between dependency through public funding and autonomy through community-based decision making.

See also Ison 2010; Seyfang and Haxeltine 2012; Hargreaves et al. 2013; Parag et al. 2013; Seyfang et al. 2013; Smith and Seyfang 2013; Feola and Nunes 2014; Seyfang et al. 2014 for the distinction.

In addition, there are further participatory mechanisms, which can be demonstrated by means of energy cooperatives (Bauwens 2013a[34]):

- The transfer of property rights results on the one hand in being involved in the decision-making process via equal voting rights in the assembly, and on the other hand in benefiting from a financial share of the profits.
- Bauwens sees as effects, on the one hand, a limitation of the principle of profit maximization, establishment of trust, perception of justice and also, through participation in the decision-making processes, an increased social acceptance of the technology.
- In addition to "passive consent", there are other ways of actively participating in an energy cooperative, which for Bauwens results in the description of an "energy citizen" (in the sense of a citizen, i.e., in this case a "climate citizen"), in that these concrete activities also go hand in hand with increased environmental awareness and citizen participation in the energy sector in general.

Of interest now is the closer definition of the concept of participation. According to one view in the literature, the concept of participation refers to the relationship between actors, from which an actor-specific view is derived (Holstenkamp and Degenhart 2013). In this context, the concept of citizen roles is used. Accordingly, definitions of the concept of citizen can be made via the classic distinction between citizen of the state (*citoyen*) with a common good orientation, economic citizen (bourgeois) with reference to economic action and cosmopolite as a way of reacting to global challenges. In addition, the financial-economic concept of the public (in the sense of a public offering) can be added (Holstenkamp and Degenhart 2013: 16). In the course of time, the concept of citizen has been further extended, an example of this is the more recent extension to legal persons (companies as citizens, so-called corporate citizens) (ibid.: 10).

The authors see above all, the territorial reference of the bourgeois and citizen concepts as a possible point of contact and apply this idea to the concept of community energy (ibid.: 15): "Here it is rather assumed that we are dealing with private individuals who are resident in a place or region. It would be conceivable and, when it comes to regional or local identities, understandable to extend the concept of citizen also to those inhabitants who come from this region or place and still feel connected to the region or place".

[34] See also Bauwens (2013b, 2013c, 2014a, 2014b, 2014c) on the context of energy cooperatives and decentralization, and Johnson and Hall 2015 on the problem of inequality in terms of distributive justice in decentralized energy use through community energy projects.

Following the communitarian discourse, Holstenkamp and Degenhart define the citizen via political participation rights and orientation towards the common good, the bourgeois via the classical definition according to the liberal model of thought in the form of defensive rights against the state (ibid.: 10). The authors now want to extend the opposition between citizen and state and another dimension of the economic sphere (ibid.): "Thus, the concept of citizen can also be placed in opposition to the state and the market. The call for increased civic engagement, the focus on cooperative forms of organization, the development of an *économie sociale* (*et solidaire*) – all this is an expression of the search for alternative governance mechanisms, a tertium beyond market and state, not least as a result of the recent financial crisis. Such a demarcation would also seem quite plausible against the background of historical developments in the energy sector: renewable energy technologies were initially further developed not least by solar and wind pioneers who explicitly opposed the large energy corporations and state energy policy." Applied to the notion of citizen participation in the context of renewable energy, the authors argue that the consequence would be to exclude ownership via public entities. However, with regard to hybrid operating models consisting of public, private sector and civil society actors, this would be of little help. It is concluded from this that attempts to delimit, define and conceptualize the location and motivation of the actors and participants are not useful in advance, but should be "included in the research program as a question to be decided empirically" (ibid.: 11).

Community energy initiatives can also be classified by further, more closely defined characteristics of ownership structure and local connection. In the literature, a narrow and a broad definition of the term is used. Accordingly, community energy in the narrow sense means: "Counted among community energy are all those cases in which private individuals and/or local commercial or agricultural sole proprietorships or legal entities (other than large corporations) individually or jointly invest equity in (renewable) energy plants, provided they hold at least 50 % *of* the voting rights and come from or are located in a region" (Leuphana University Lüneburg and Nestle 2014: 3). The authors break this down further into (ibid.):

- Projects of individual citizens (e.g., installation of a PV module),
- Community energy companies and projects (e.g., a cooperative operates a solar plant) and
- Projects of small or medium-sized agricultural business or other local enterprises (e.g., farmers or companies use roofs for solar power generation, biogas plants, etc.).

Beyond this narrow definition, however, there is also talk of community energy in a broader sense (ibid.): "In a broader sense, community energy could also include projects where the investors come from different regions ('communities of interest') or where less than 50% *of* the voting rights are held by citizens ('minority shareholdings')".

Overall, three decisive sets of criteria are thus found: Regionality, form of participation (equity) and participation rate. From this, a classification grid with four possible types of community energy can be formed (trend: research GmbH and Leuphana University Lüneburg 2013: 28 f.):

1. **Community energy in a narrow sense**: high regional reference and participation rate in the form of an equity share of more than 50%.
2. **Minority participation**: also high regional relevance, but equity ratio of less than 50%.
3. **Community of interest**: little regional reference, but high equity ratio of over 50%.
4. **Community of interest with minority participation of citizens**: low regional reference and equity ratio of less than 50%.

The definition of community energy in the narrow or broad sense includes three possible groups of actors (private individuals, individual agricultural enterprises and legal entities), excluding large corporations; these can invest in renewable energy either individually or jointly.

Discussion

It remains questionable with this rough distinction to what extent this is helpful in individual cases or also offers a really well-founded discriminatory power. The authors illustrate this with a self-selected example of the determination of the participation quota of 50% chosen here (trend: research GmbH and Leuphana University Lüneburg 2013: 28): "Insofar as certain decisions require a qualified majority, these can also be significantly influenced by a minority, as long as the necessary quorum is reached (often 25%). This could be used as an argument to set the limit further down in terms of the participation quota. Similar arguments can be made for the other criteria. Which terminology is chosen therefore depends on the question posed for investigation." The other characteristics also remain vague: with regard to the form of participation, it is noted that there must be a "financial participation with equity" which guarantees voting and control rights "so that control of the projects by the citizens is possible". In various organizational forms such as cooperatives this may clearly be the case, but in other constructions (in the case of loans it would not be given) the classification could turn out to be more difficult (if, for example – as it represents a case in the empirical part of the present work – a cooperative is affiliated to a GmbH and thus has fewer voting and control rights).

The characteristic of regionality is also described here by the fact that members of a community energy project come from the region or are resident there, "whereby, with regard to the borders of a region, reference is made to common identity formation processes" (ibid.). Although the unit is clearly to be located below federal states as a sub-national unit, "the common identity can, however, transcend the borders of federal states". Here, too, it can be seen that the concept of region can hardly be used in a clear-cut way. The obvious option of using the unity of counties, or even establishing municipal boundaries on a smaller scale, hardly comes close to the reality of the orientation of citizen energy projects. The closest that can be done to delineating larger units is to make these projects non-national in scope. Among these, it must then be decided on a case-by-case basis whether the project is predominantly focused on

- the municipal district,
- refers to a county, region (as a district), city-state or similar, or
- is designed on a cross-regional basis (e.g., covering several counties).

Second Approach: The Subject-Centered View – Roles and Possibilities of Community Action

Another classificatory approach focuses on civic participation via different channels, that is, the participation opportunities from the perspective of the individual (see overview by Kreß et al. 2014a: 15 – the presentation is taken up below, but modified):

- Citizens in the role of consumers in their everyday actions: for example, consumption of electricity (in the sense of saving and efficiency), heat as well as other consumption and mobility (related to ecological-climate-friendly consumption patterns).
- Citizens in the role of consumers in strategic consumption choices: for example, consumption of electricity (conscious choice possible through consumption of electricity from renewable energy sources), heat efficiency measures, etc.
- Citizens in the role of prosumers: own generation (or consumption) of electricity from their own energy systems (e.g., PV system).
- Citizens in the role of investors: investing in renewable energy investment opportunities (e.g., funds) or community energy systems.
- Citizens in the role of entrepreneurs: founding a community energy company.

- Citizens in the role of political actors and planners Var. 1 (participatory and/or direct democracy): as participants in formal procedures and participation mechanisms: urban land use planning (in the case of wind energy plants, etc.).
- Citizens in the role of political actors and planners Var. 2 (participatory in the representative political system mode): as stakeholders in formal and informal institutional arrangements and participation mechanisms: local council, inquiries, etc.
- Citizens in the role of political actors and planners Var. 3 (participatory and/or-direct democracy): as participants in informal procedures and participation mechanisms: Citizens' initiatives and civic engagement in the energy and climate protection context.
- Citizens in the role of political actors within the framework of the representative political system: electoral citizens and expression of opinion.

In a similar way, a definitional approach is possible with the focus on involved actors and their characteristics (trend: research GmbH and Leuphana University Lüneburg 2013: 20). In community energy systems, four groups of actors are distinguished:

- Community energy consisting of citizens, network actors and initiatives, and civil society associations.
- Municipal energy utilities consisting of administration and politics as well as diverse municipal companies.
- Conventional or established energy industry consisting of financial enterprises, trade companies and industry, agricultural investors and industry, energy systems manufacturers, project developers as well as other energy suppliers.
- Links with civil society: The authors see a proximity of civil society actors to the alternative and ecologically oriented "green" social movements with spheres of community energy systems, from which community energy projects have evolved (ibid.). According to this, the civil society associations are less owners, but rather in the role of initiators, knowledge brokers and supporters for projects, partly also active in the operational management (ibid.).

With regard to the degree of professionalization, a proximity of the citizen concept to the layperson concept is rather rejected. Due to acquired expertise, incipient professionalization, proximity of the committed persons to the energy industry and assistance provided by professional service providers, a higher level of competence is assumed. An equation with private individuals is suggested here ("who have a public effect through their investment", ibid.: 21), but a great heterogeneity of this group of actors is pointed out.

In the context of community energy, Holstenkamp and Degenhart point to the concept of community as a further classificatory feature.[35] This is derived from the term "community energy", which is frequently used in the English-language discussionand refers to processes of identity formation (Holstenkamp and Degenhart 2013: 11 ff.). A congruence with the German concept of citizen (energy) is not seen; the concept of community is identified as rather vague and complex.

The authors first distinguish three community variants (ibid.: 11)[36]:

- relational community (professional, intellectual, spiritual),
- territorial community (neighborhood),
- engagement community (political, social engagement).

The concept of community always implies an external demarcation between community members and outsiders (inclusion and exclusion) (ibid.). In social-psychological terms, the following characteristics of a "sense of community" can be taken up in this respect (ibid.; see Obst and White 2005: 128 ff.)[37]:

- Feeling of belonging and identification, of being part of a collective from which you derive emotional safety ("membership").
- Bi-directional need, for a group to exert influence of its members to promote cohesion, and also for members to feel they have some control and influence within the community ("influence").

[35] See also a study on the potential of community in the case of citizen energy, which highlights a high and clearly measurable importance of community (Burchell et al. 2015: 171 f.):

1. The idea of community was expressed in a variety of ways, both positive and negative.
2. More broadly, many project members expressed the broader significance for them of what we can call a sense of being part of something (though this was not necessarily being part of a community specifically).
3. Being part of something remained important for people even when they were not directly interacting with others.
4. The local and non-commercial characteristics of the project were very important for project mmembers.

[36] The distinction is borrowed from Gusfield (1975).

[37] Adopted from McMillan and Chavis (1986) and Obst and White (2005).

- Need for the individual-group association to be rewarding for the individual members, and places importance on common needs, goals, beliefs and values on achieving this ("fulfillment of needs").
- Sense of shared history and identifica- tion with the community and the bonds developed over time through positive interaction with other community members ("shared emotional connection").
- Members' attachment to their community ("identification"), cognitive accessibility of membership in particular groups ("salience"), split into chronic accessibility and situational accessibility.

Based on these assumptions, Holstenkamp and Degenhart (2013: 12 f.) finally form four community dimensions, which include in particular a community of locality and a community of interest[38]:

- Association of several persons to form a group.
- Existence of spatial proximity (community of locality) or connection between persons or actors (community of interest), whereby the group should involve stronger interaction between the members beyond a gathering of people.
- Shared identity via community commitment. This can result from a common project history, in any case the possibility of participation must be open to all members of the community, "at least a substantial number of the group constructed via this identification".
- A public space is not presupposed within decisions are made. Interests in the common good are not sufficient as an essential characteristic, but "trust and (common) influence or control" are crucial.

Incidentally, an equation of shared facilities (i.e., energy facilities operated by several persons or actors as common property) and citizen participation is rejected (ibid.: 12) – which seems easy to understand, as the concept of participation encompasses other theoretical and practical features that clearly go beyond common or shared ownership.

Third Approach: The Dimensional View – Process and Outcome Model

A grid for classifying community energy initiatives that is frequently taken up and disseminated by research differentiates between two dimensions (Walker and Devine-Wright 2008: 498):

[38] Here, the authors draw on Ferdinand Tönnies' concept of community, which distinguishes between kinship, neighbourhood and ideal community (Tönnies 1991).

- Process dimension (distant and private versus open and participatory).
- Outcome dimension (closed and institutional versus local and collective).

In the ideal model, for example, a community energy initiative can be characterized as highly participatory and open in its participation approach and as local and collective in its structure and orientation. The opposite, in the form of closed, purely private-sector structures, would be a conventional energy company. Between these poles, community energy initiatives can fluctuate between being more or less openly oriented, more collaborative, or more firmly formalized in their governance and boards. It seems obvious that community energy initiatives can indeed be more or less open and participatory. But two crucial questions arise:

- How should characteristics such as "open" and "participatory" be defined in concrete terms?
- What research findings are supposed to be capable of making these determinations? It is true that qualitative analyses can suggest a certain degree of participation. But it seems more realistic that even in the case of positive participatory practice, there may also be ways of acting that could be characterized as non-participatory (e.g., strongly controlling management bodies that stage participation and collaboration). This would counteract the formal classification as "participatory" and thus make the classification contradictory. A holistic view without committing to specific features might therefore be more useful. The authors point out this problem themselves and warn against ignoring diversity (ibid.: 499 f.). As long as such definitions of characteristics remain relatively unspecified and only serve to clarify rough differences between approaches, they seem permissible. However, the inadequacy becomes clearer when they are concretized in more detail.

Discussion

Although the subject-centered and dimensional perspectives have some advantages in terms of an initial, superficial classification, it also seems questionable to what extent this approach can provide more detailed information about the individual ways of acting and thinking as well as the different orientations of the community energy projects. The division into citizen roles makes it clear that citizens cannot be thought of one-dimensionally in terms of just one function ("role"), and different actor references can also be identified, but neither of these classifications say anything about the concrete structure and dynamics of a community, which would, however, have to be used for a more concrete assessment against the background of political participation, characteristics of commitment and actor construction. A more promising approach seems to be an analysis of community structure as presented by Holstenkamp and Degenhart, which can reveal different functions and characteristics. However, by combining the models discussed here, a more consistent picture of the characteristics of community energy initiatives could be achieved. In principle, the models offer the advantage of at least being able to depict overarching tendencies. Thus, the overarching classification of more or less participatory and open as well as local-community structured and shaped community energy initiatives by Walker and Devine-Wright seems comprehensible and applicable. Nevertheless, there is a danger of strongly standardising different structures (e.g., the participation behavior in a project), which creates a homogenized picture that is then, however, no longer connected to the concrete phenomena, that is, can no longer be directly traced back. This clear comprehensibility and direct traceability to empirical phenomena should always be guaranteed.

4.5 Summary: Defining Community Energy

On the basis of selected characteristics, an attempt can be made to assign energy investment companies to the concept of community energy. Holstenkamp and Degenhart have established various dimensions for this, which are taken up and discussed here (see Holstenkamp and Degenhart 2013: 22 ff.).

1. Participation as a provision of equity capital
   (a) Inclusion in the project, company or association including rights of co-determination (type 1: company/project/association member).
   (b) Passive participation model without rights (type 2: financial investment) (see ibid.: 22).
2. Equity functions and characteristics
   (a) Co-determination or control or management function (voting rights, information and control rights).
   (b) Administrative rights (participation in shareholders' meetings/members' meetings, right to vote, right to challenge, right to information, right to control) (ibid.: 23)
3. Voting rights, information asymmetries and principal-agent problems.
   (a) Equal voting rights in the parity model (in cooperatives, "one member, one vote", cooperative democracy principle) (1).

   (b) Unequal distribution of voting rights according to the size of the shareholding in a company/project/association (2).
   (c) Problem of an asymmetrical distribution of information due to the function of a management board.[39]

4. Transparency, discourse and control.

   (a) Creating spaces for discourse.
   (b) Presentation of reports by the board of directors, supervisory board or management and discussion in general meetings.
   (c) Individual practical arrangements are decisive.

5. Openness of participation to a wide range of citizens.

   (a) Is participation in principle open to all?
   (b) Relationship between the minimum investment amount, the duration of the existence and the success of the project.
   (c) The problem of setting a limit value.[40]
   (d) Tendency of increasing coordination effort and costs for decision-making with higher membership numbers vs. claim of participation (trade-off).
   (e) Increase in the amount of participation and representative assembly leads to problems of indirect-representative influence and principal-agent problem.
   (f) Option of virtual participation in meetings and discussions (possible problem of admissibility).

---

[39] The question remains open here "whether different degrees of influence yield different results in terms of acceptance effects" (Holstenkamp and Degenhart 2013: 25); empirical verification seems difficult. In principle, participating citizens as limited partners are excluded from the possibility to participate in the management – in cooperatives, on the other hand, members of the board of directors and supervisory board often come from the ranks of participating citizens (ibid.).

[40] Although Holstenkamp and Degenhart discuss the difficulties of establishing a definition at this point, they nevertheless want to use a certain level of minimum participation as an indication of openness: "One could therefore make the minimum participation a criterion for defining citizen participation. In doing so, however, the problem arises of having to give factual reasons for setting the threshold value if the typology is not to turn out too arbitrary. In the case of closed-end funds, the minimum investment is usually between EUR 5000 and EUR 10,000, sometimes considerably more. This means that closed-end funds are primarily aimed at wealthy private individuals. In this respect, it is obvious to use a minimum investment amount of (significantly) less than 5000 euros as an indication that the investment offer is designed to include as many people as possible" (Holstenkamp and Degenhart 2013: 26).

   (g) Riskiness of the financial investment; investment requires sufficient equity capital
   (h) Hurdles to entry and exit (losses).

6. Direct vs. indirect participation

   (a) Indirect participation: for example, municipal utilities participating in renewable energy project companies, presumably with similar acceptance effect.
   (b) Municipal institutions such as public utilities are indirectly controlled and legitimized by the municipal political system and thus within the framework of representative political procedures; on the other hand, there is less direct influence of citizens through direct financial participation.

7. Differentiation of multiple project levels and extent of citizen participation

   (a) Special problems in the case of several companies at different project levels.
   (b) Citizen participation in the narrow sense in the case of shares held by the operating company in the community energy project company, including co-determination rights (e.g., participation of a cooperative in a wind farm).
   (c) Co-determination rights of the participating cooperative may vary: in the case of debt or mezzanine capital shares, they are limited (citizen participation in the broader sense).

8. Public offering of the shares (e.g., by means of a prospectus)

   (a) Problem of effort for smaller projects.
   (b) Through repeated reproduction of the participation offer, many people can nevertheless be reached.

9. Citizen participation in the form of debt capital

   (a) Influence of outside capital (e.g., through a financial company).
   (b) Option can be deliberately restricted, influence is de facto irrelevant as long as information flows to citizens, consultation opportunities and control rights remain in place.

10. Citizen participation through financial investment (citizen participation in the broader sense)

   (a) Possibility of so-called silent partnerships, which enable citizen participation through loans, bonds, savings certificates or similar.
   (b) In most cases, no say in corporate decision-making possible for stakeholders.
   (c) The actual degree of co-determination depends on the concrete corporate law structure of the participation model and the contractual structure of the financing variant.

11. Other features

   (a) Ratio of the number of participants to the relevant community.
   (b) Amount of the share held by citizens.
   (c) Character as a bottom-up movement in contrast to top-down organized initiatives.

In summary, Holstenkamp and Degenhart (2013: 33 f.) identify six definitional characteristics that must be present in order to be classified as community energy:

1. Provision of capital for renewable energy projects.
2. Territorially defined group: Members must come from a limited spatial unit, for example, a municipality or a county. It remains questionable whether this limitation must be given.
3. Adequate representation: Theoretically, access to participation must be open to all without a high barrier to entry. Even if only a few people are involved, the criterion is fulfilled if a "replication of the participation model is, however, envisaged from the outset" (ibid: 33).
4. A certain orientation towards the common good: not only return and risk, but also "non-financial objectives directed towards the common good" should be given "possibly accepting certain discounts on return or risk premiums" (ibid.). It remains unclear what these should be in concrete terms; a proximity to ecological goals – among other motivations – seems to be obvious. However, it hardly seems possible to verify this, even in surveys.
5. Co-determination and control rights: "Citizens can participate in decision-making on important issues and have control rights over the actors they appoint for day-to-day business", in the case of equity constructions and thus membership in a company this is regularly the case (ibid.). However, it remains a question of the concrete individual case "how great the possibility of exerting influence actually is with the chosen organizational structure" (ibid.: 34).
6. Majority shareholding: The citizens involved must own more than 50% of the total shares; simple and qualified majority participation as well as inclusion and

sole participation are possible. The determination of 50% seems understandable due to the internal majority relationships of the participating citizens. Nevertheless, it seems questionable that community energy companies that do not have a majority participation of citizens should not be counted as types of community energy corporations. Further influencing factors would be decisive for a classification.

Finally, the application of the characteristic criteria suggests a distinction between four possible types of community energy projects in the narrow sense:

(a) **Democratically organized community energy projects.**
(b) **Capital-oriented community energy projects.**
(c) **(Founding) initiatives with a bottom-up process and grassroots context: citizens' initiatives.**
(d) **(Start-up) initiatives with top-down participation offers.**

In addition, the type of citizen participation in the broader sense is described with five constructs:

(a) **Financial participation**: in contrast to equity capital, capital is provided through loans, profit participation rights or savings bonds.
(b) **Community of interest** (e.g., county or municipality, interaction of members with common history).
(c) **Typical investment vehicle** (investment solely for risk-return considerations).
(d) **Minority participation** (less than 50% citizen participation).
(e) **Limited membership**: employee or customer participation model (*closed shop design*, e.g., employee cooperative), "however, with a locally or regionally broad customer base, the difference to citizen participation becomes blurred" (ibid.: 35).

In addition, a typology of energy cooperatives can be found in the literature (Volz 2011a, 2012a: 146 ff.), which forms four clusters according to the characteristics "self-directed energy supply" (here: motivation for energy in the hands of citizens), "solidarity-based action" (here: social factors), "ecological sustainability" (here: motivation for ecological) and "ecological capital investment" (here: motivation for returns):

- "**Avant-garde**" (focus on the first three characteristics, objective: self-sufficient energy supply) (share: 30% of energy cooperatives).

- "**Sustainable PV traditionalists**" (focus on "solidarity-based action", "ecological sustainability" and "ecological capital investment", objective: sustainability contribution and long-term preservation of livelihood), (share: 23% of energy cooperatives).
- "**Active ecologists**" (focus on "self-directed energy supply" and "ecological sustainability", objective: contribution to climate change), (share: 18% of energy cooperatives)
- "**Investment-oriented**" (focus on "ecological capital investment", objective: return on equity) (share: 29% of energy cooperatives).

Discussion

Holstenkamp's and Degenhart's definition of the characteristics appear to be useful for a rough characterization; in the case of individual points (in particular the definition of public interest orientation and majority shareholding), the realistic possibility of a more detailed definition and actual usefulness for a definition can be doubted. Here, too, it seems that the characteristics may be more suitable as guidelines for a classification.[41] When used for classification, however, important individual contexts could be pushed into the background, which could possibly have a considerable influence on a classification. The term community energy can thus be defined along certain characteristics and dimensions, but so many variations are possible within this that an individual arrangement would only be inadequately represented.

The situation is similar with typologies, as presented by Volz: it seems understandable that different motives of the participants can be identified and a focus of the prevailing motivation can be formed according to the statistical data. However, on the one hand distinctions remain imprecise (e.g., difference between "self-sufficient energy supply" and "energy supply on one's own" is insignificant), on the other hand categories such as "investment-oriented" and "ecological" act rather as basic motivations, which are complemented by further attributes. Nevertheless, differences can obviously be measured in the characteristics of the motivations – participants orient themselves more strongly to a certain category as a guideline for action. Accordingly, individual participation can also be shaped by specific prevail-

[41] For example, the grid is already adopted elsewhere, in that a citizens' wind or community wind definition is based on three characteristics (1. individual (citizen) participation >50% of equity, 2. voting sovereignty with civil society, 3. majority of value creation remains in the region), of which two characteristics should be sufficient for the existence of a citizens' wind project (Landesverband Erneuerbare Energien NRW and World Wind Energy Association 2016: 5).

ing motivations, whereby participation as such can be determined more closely via the individual-subjective approach according to the more recent take on things (van Deth 2014a).

In addition, a linking of the various definitional and typological approaches and perspectives on the phenomenon of community energy (financial, spatial, socio-political, actor-oriented classification) as well as an expansion and concretization of further characteristics seems sensible. At best, each arrangement should be analyzed individually on a situational basis, taking into account the specific context, and evaluated in terms of the individual motivations and modes of action of those involved.

4.6 Effects of Community Energy and Open Research Questions

In the literature, community energy is associated with forms such as bioenergy villages or zero-emission communities (Burch et al. 2012; Walker et al. 2015a), which are treated under labels such as *(smart) sustainable* or *green communities* and *eco villages* (Conrad 1996; Clark II and Eisenberg 2008; Rodger 2008; Clark 2010; Clark II and Cooke 2015a, 2015b, 2015c; 2016) and combine sustainable lifestyles with community organization (*community building*, see Chitewere and Taylor 2010; Chitewere 2016). Likewise, connections to technical-digital approaches ("smart" solutions, derived from the smart city discussion, cf. to smart grid interconnections (idea of a "social smart grid", see Skopik 2014; see also Servatius et al. 2012; Lund et al. 2014; Ruiz-Romero et al. 2014) in combination with sustainable and community approaches can be found.

While the former *community approach* is more characterized by ecological motives, the smart city/smart grid approach has a strong focus on technology. Finally, a third variant can be found, which is characterized by self-sufficiency efforts of spatial units (Morris 1982; Mather 2009; Gehring 2012; Cassell 2013) and promotes independence from the electricity grid through self-production (*off the grid* model, see Ryker 2007; Bode and Schmidt 2008; Rosen 2010; Reid 2011; Davis 2015; Jakes 2015; Vannini and Taggart 2015; Woods 2016). In the already independence-oriented USA, for example, a decoupling of rural regions into self-reliance and independence (also with regard to energy, among other things) is sometimes strongly propagated (for example, by the Institute for Local Self-Reliance, see. Farrell 2008, 2010; Farrell and Morris 2008). In fact, the self-sufficiency motive is inherent to all approaches, as both sustainable communities and smart cities aim to achieve self-sufficient energy production, control and use.

However, the motives of the three approaches are fundamentally different: Sustainable communities produce their own electricity because this is part of the global approach to environmental protection and sustainability; from the point of view of smart city advocates, intelligent forms of use and control can be derived from decentralized energy production, which in turn are part of the overarching idea of more technically oriented approaches to solutions; in the case of the *off the grid* movement, self-sufficient electricity supply is intended to be a conceptual building block of a completely self-sufficient form of living and working (subsistence), with independence as such from the state and corporations being the main driving force.

Interestingly, community energy is compatible with all of the above approaches; it can be part of a wide variety of concepts. The results of the present study have even shown that the motivations presented here can also be found in a similar form among the members – with one exception: an exclusive profit orientation is conceivable among community energy participants but is not a component of the approaches presented. Smart city advocates may also be strongly return-oriented, but the technology aspect is more prominent. Nevertheless, this research has also shown that initiators can often be driven more strongly by ideational motives such as ecology, self-sufficiency, strengthening rural development and social community than members. Members, on the other hand, share several motives, also with different weightings, but presumably one central, dominant impulse stands out less.

In some cases, however, community energy or citizen energy initiatives are also linked to ideas or visions of a sustainable society ("Green Energy Community with Smart Society for Sustainable Living", see Rodprasert et al. 2014); increasingly, they are also being analyzed from the perspective of resilience (Sircar et al. 2013), in that regional vulnerabilities, for example, with regard to energy shortages and climate change, are to be reduced through decentralized energy production (Radinger-Peer et al. 2015). The self-sufficiency idea with a focus on individual citizens and village development resources with regard to the use of renewable energy has been mooted for some time (Thompson and Laufman 1996); the mobilization and discussion of the idea of community energy has been found in the literature for some time,[42] but in recent years it has been increasingly taken up (Bomberg and McEwen 2012), diverse concepts are controversially discussed (Chung et al. 2012). In other countries, the idea of civic energy/community energy

[42] The idea is first found in the context of development policy (Bulgarian Academy of Sciences 1900; Golding and Thacker 1956), later it becomes better known, being used and disseminated in a peace policy context, for example, by Amory Bloch Lovins (1977).

is discussed from a perspective other than as "social capitalism" (e.g., in the country comparison between China and California, see Clark II and Li 2010).

In addition, related aspects such as community planning and management of energy production and supply play a major role in the community energy discourse (see. Anderson and Doig 2000). In the field of energy infrastructure planning, concepts such as *community energy planning* are discussed, focusing on the inclusion of the local population in the planning phase of energy facilities, which is reminiscent of public participation in Germany, for example, in the context of wind energy (Huang et al. 2015). However, much of the research focuses on *sustainable energy communities* (Schweizer-Ries 2008; Romero-Rubio and de Andrés Díaz 2015), which often also have links to public institutions such as schools, universities, and civil society associations and organizations (McComas et al. 2011).

Other aspects that are very close to the phenomenon of community energy concern the purchase of solar systems by private households at the individual level (Sonnberger 2015), stakeholder participation in the broader (i.e., not only related to citizen participation projects) community energy sector ("energy labs", see Dvarioniene et al. 2015) or experimental-creative local communities that are committed to climate protection and are referred to as *low-carbon labs* (Heiskanen et al. 2015). Increasingly, questions of equality/justice and risks of local energy projects are coming into focus (Adams and Bell 2014; Fuller and McCauley 2016).

A British working group on *science, society and sustainability studies* is primarily dedicated to so-called *transition pathways* (as in the context of the energy transition) and researches phenomena such as community energy, but also processes and effects such as democratic implications, engagement, social practices, political strategies, and the handling of knowledge and the influence of intermediary actors (see Chilvers 2012a, 2012b; Hargreaves et al. 2012a, 2012b; Hulme 2012; North and Longhurst 2012; Seyfang and Longhurst 2012a, 2012b; Seyfang et al. 2012; Barton et al. 2013, 2015; Hauxwell-Baldwin 2013; Jensen 2013; Chilvers and Longhurst 2014).

In another branch of research, economic and monetary aspects are investigated, such as questions of willingness to pay for community energy participation via shares (Hobman and Frederiks 2014; Sagebiel et al. 2014; Rommel et al. 2015), financial linkages of energy projects (Rydin et al. 2015) as well as financing solutions for community energy projects (Saunders et al. 2012) and possible economic effects for the local community in the case of wind power (Aitken 2010). Here, the motivations for why citizens are interested in such investments in the first place play a significant role. Previous research results show that, beyond pure return expectations, overriding values such as community and trust are emphasized (Kalkbrenner and Roosen 2016).

The literature also contains a wide range of recent analyses on community energy, which show that more and more topics are being developed in the broader context of citizen energy/community energy (see Bagdanavicius et al. 2012):

- Community energy in the power grid sector (Domenech et al. 2014): Grid connections of community energy projects have been discussed for a long time (Holtz 1977), currently considered possibilities are for example, energy sharing with the help of smart grids (Rathnayaka et al. 2015) or the development of community microgrids (Ravindra and Iyer 2014).
- Community energy in the wind energy sector (in Canada, see Girvitz and Lipp 2005; in Australia, see Gross 2007; in Oregon, see Yin 2012; in Nova Scotia, see Mudasser et al. 2013; on wind energy cooperatives in Europe, see Bauwens et al. 2016).
- Community energy planning projects (in Canada, see St. Denis and Parker 2009).
- Importance of social networks (Bale et al. 2013).
- Analysis of diverse socio-economic impacts of community energy projects, for example, in northern Scotland (Okkonen and Lehtonen 2016); citizen engagement in the context of geothermal energy use in southern Italy (Pellizzone et al. 2015) and in the field of combined heat and power (Schubert 2014, 2017).
- Bottom-up diffusion of photovoltaic systems in society (Reinsberger et al. 2015).
- Influence of civil society contexts in the renewable energy/energy transition sector, for example, grassroots initiatives (Blanchet 2015; Blanchet et al. 2016).
- Support from governments, administrations and local authorities of local energy initiatives (Hoppe et al. 2015).
- Question of equal participation of the local community in community energy projects: to what extent is the local population adequately represented here? (e.g., investigated in Scottish community wind farms, see Slee 2015; see on German community wind farms Alle et al. 2015 and on the financing practice of wind farms Beery and Day 2015).
- Limits to civic engagement due to high demands in terms of desired goals, social action and resilience (Parkhill et al. 2015).

In addition to the function of shaping local space and ecological commitment, community energy is also seen in the literature as an alternative to the resistance of renewable energies, rural structural weakness, conventional financial investment forms and thus is understood as as a stimulation of a small renewable energy market (Walker et al. 2007: 64 ff.). If this approach is combined with high participatory shares as well as sustainable grassroots initiatives of citizen groups, discourse coalitions can emerge. It is precisely this display of community that promotes the initiatives in their status as a grouping associated with positive connotations (generating acceptance, trust and legitimacy among the population and in the community of actors) (ibid.). Within the framework of an empirical study, three groups of motives for participating in community energy projects were identified via surveys as an explanatory framework for the emergence of community energy (Walker et al. 2007: 72 f.):

- First, there is a **social learning and expert knowledge motivation** with regard to renewable energies, which arises almost as an inevitable effect through participation in community energy initiatives and local exchange.
- The second motivation is the **political claim** to promote the market for renewable energies against the background of climate protection and energy saving targets.
- A third motivation concerns the **social and economic outputs** that can be derived from the community energy projects. This concerns in particular the hope for a strengthening and activation of the (predominantly rural) area: income generation, creation of jobs (regional added value) against the background of the decline of other economic sectors, the rural exodus and the decrease of economic power.

These factors tie in with social and political themes of the late 1990s (emphasis on economic and local agency). In addition, the authors point to an influence of the principles of normative-ideal communitarianism and participatory democratic theory. Accordingly, there are links to learning processes within the framework of cooperative approaches (see Junginger et al. 2010), such as those developed within the framework of Local Agenda 21 strategies, as well as to the principles of strengthening the public sphere and promoting civil society involvement, which have been pushed in government programs.

In addition, measuring outcomes in this field is considered to be very difficult, as they vary greatly and are perceived differently (e.g., renewable energies are generally regarded as positive by the population, but this does not necessarily coincide with the perception of energy plants on site). A more detailed determination of acceptance and processing of the topic on site by the population and local actors can probably only be made by a broad- based quantitative-qualitative long-term study.

Of central importance is the formation of communities and the associated social effects. Community energy initiatives and accompanying participation processes could be examples of the formation of social capital in the sense of social cohesion, trust, acceptance and commitment. Here, the focus is on how a group identity is formed and maintained, how group cohesion is generated and built, and the extent to which a sense of group purpose is critical to ongoing participation and coalescence (Seyfang and Haxeltine 2010: 18). This aspect of bonding social capital within communities relates to a core research question regarding the formation of conducive conditions for participation.

In addition, there is the importance of bridging social capital (according to Putnam et al. 1993), which can form through trust, networks and norms of reciprocity not within a group but between communities (see Geißel 2008a: 39 f.). In the case of successful cooperation between actors and networking services, this is probably often the case. However, the extent to which this bridging social capital is now responsible for the success of engagement, participation and functioning communities could be an important but at the same time difficult to measure variable. As an initial condition, citizens' trust in local politics, regional operators and local administration is said to be already quite high (Kreß et al. 2011: 28). Furthermore, it has been proven that positive effects occur when actor networks are included at local level (Hoppe et al. 2011). However, a problem arises with regard to the competitive relationship between "soft" deliberation in discourse and "hard" factual issues and logics. While actors in the energy system adopt the rhetoric of deliberative engagement, they lack clear rationales and effective means to provide citizens with perspectives on long-term development processes or to address issues of specific infrastructure and incorporate proposals for siting into strategies (Devine-Wright 2013a; Cotton and Devine-Wright 2013). When it comes to the siting process of renewable energy plants, citizen participation may occur at an early stage during what is considered to be a lower level of the decision-making process where citizens have little influence over decision-making practices. Here, risk of frustration, disappointment and disengagement arise within apparent participatory processes, particularly when aspects of procedural justice are affected (e.g., access to information and actual opportunities for participation or influence) (Devine-Wright 2013a: 778). For this inquiry, it seems relevant which constellations and effects can be observed in several case studies concerning these issues.

Local value creation and renewal or innovation, local acceptance and obtaining planning permission, local control, low energy costs and secure grid feed-in, ethical and environmentally oriented commitment, and management of the electricity grid are cited in the literature as further drivers and positive framework conditions for community energy projects (Walker 2008). Economic (mainly costs) and legal (mainly permits) factors are named as barriers (Walker 2008: 4403). In addition, funding programs, empirical knowledge, expert support, technical issues and contact intensities, networking and cooperation are of considerable importance. In addition, individual initiators and supporters (promoters) play a key role (see David and Schönborn 2016: 48 ff.). The importance of these promoters will be given special consideration and analyzed in more detail in this study.

In summary, the following **advantages** of community energy can be derived from the literature:

- Identity creation, strengthening the community.
- Influence of and opportunities to participate and collaborate for citizens.
- Education, social, technical-economic, political and environmental or sustainability learning, knowledge acquisition and diffusion.
- Practice and experience of different citizen roles (political citizen, active and engaged citizen, competent citizen (related to dealing with technology, economy, bureaucracy, organizations, local policy networks, etc.), informed citizen.
- Social learning in the group, acquisition of group-specific skills.

Disadvantages of community energy, on the other hand, relate to the following factors:

- Inequality: procedural and distributive justice, social structure, access to resources.
- Minority protection based on selective co-determination principle.
- Overstraining of community action and exhaustion of volunteers.
- Lack of involvement of party concerned in energy planning and measures.
- Economization and monetization effects.
- Oligarchy, nepotism, informal leadership and power circles.
- Unequal gender distribution and diversity.

Findings on Local Acceptance of Renewable Energies and Community Energy

From the current research of recent years on renewable energies, citizen participation and acceptance of the population, it is known that there is a connection between involvement of the population in planning processes as well as financial participation or compensation and acceptance of energy plants (see in particular Zöllner et al. 2011; Rau et al. 2012).[43]

Participation in renewable energies should also have an effect on society as a whole: To strengthen the acceptance of the population regarding the establishment of renewable energies in general.[44] On the one hand, acceptance can be strengthened by the project itself, as the members of the societies are highly convinced of this type of energy generation and its socio-ecological compatibility – in addition, multiplier effects complement the process, as the mostly locally-based participating citizens spread their attitudes, convictions and views. On the other hand, the longer establishment phase and the handling of the issue by the community initiatives create the chance for the projects to take place through a better exchange with the local population and in this way there will be better coordination (especially since affected local residents can get involved in the procedures and processes themselves). In this way, the energy project itself can be planned and implemented by people – who admittedly have different individual interests, motivations and levels of concern – in a way that is acceptable to the majority of all those involved. The extent to which this balancing process actually occurs depends on the type, extent and scope of participation: For example, projects with a high degree of early discourse and participation can be expected to have a higher level of acceptance than those with exclusively financial participation options by unknown, external companies.

---

[43] See on this from the broad literature the insightful and substantial summary by Patrick Devine-Wright (2005a) as well as recent results and overviews: Sørensen et al. 2001; Sørensen et al. 2002; Wüstenhagen et al. 2007; Zöllner et al. 2008; Firestone et al. 2009; Wolsink 2010, 2012a, 2012b, 2012c; Musall and Kuik 2011; Schmid and Zimmer 2012; Wunderlich and Vohrer 2012; Zöllner et al. 2012; Batel et al. 2013; Cohen et al. 2013a; Hall et al. 2013b; Hitzeroth and Megerle 2013; Hübner and Löffler 2013; Tiwary et al. 2013; Viardot 2013; BMWi 2014: 170 f.; Carmen 2014; D'Souza and Yiridoe 2014; Karlstrøm and Ryghaug 2014; Olsen and Anker 2014; Ruggiero et al. 2014; Songsore and Buzzelli 2014; Stigka et al. 2014; Walker et al. 2014; Walter 2014; Cronin et al. 2015; Firestone et al. 2015; Enevoldsen and Sovacool 2016; Petrova 2016.

[44] See acceptance surveys by the German Renewable Energies Agency, according to which 93% of Germans support the expansion of renewable energies (https://www.unendlichviel-energie.de/mediathek/grafiken/umfrage-akzeptanz-erneuerbare-energien-2015). Local expansion is also supported even in the case of wind power (60% approval, compared to 77% for solar parks, but only 39% approval for biogas plants and 25% for gas power plants, 7% for coal power and 4% for nuclear power. Incidentally, respondents with corresponding plants in their own neighborhood always show higher acceptance values (solar park: 86%, wind power 72%, biogas 53%, gas power 40%, coal power 22%, nuclear power 16%). See also more detailed results from the Agentur für Erneuerbare Energien (2014).

These questions of acceptance have already been investigated in various studies (Zöllner et al. 2007, 2008, 2012; Rau and Zöllner 2011; Kortsch et al. 2015). Accordingly, acceptance differs substantially between the energy sources: in the case of solar use, acceptance is very high, as expected, while in the case of wind energy, the conflicts are much greater. In the case of geothermal and hydropower, the resistance is less high. A study determined how the importance of various participation measures and models is assessed by the population (Rau and Zöllner 2011: 93). According to this study, information opportunities in the form of visits, information through the media and information events are of crucial importance. Round tables, websites, brochures and expert discussions are also rated as having a high priority. In contrast, financial participation is given the lowest priority by the respondents. According to the authors of the study, financial participation is a particularly context-dependent pattern in that "financial participation is subject to certain framework conditions and individual prerequisites, and must therefore always be examined and adapted in the specific case" (ibid.). Experience is still considered to be limited, and the probability of spillover effects, for example, in the form of the founding of associations, is even considered to be very low. It becomes clear at this point that participation cannot automatically be equated with increased acceptance. In addition, a local energy initiative can only ever include part of the population (input-legitimation problem) and can therefore only represent a partial approach.

Further studies have already provided information on the internal relationships between actors, contextual conditions and the effects of participation processes in the context of the German energy transition. For example, a wide range of findings have been obtained in studies on the initial conditions and attitudes of the population towards the acceptance of renewable energies. In principle, research assumes that there is a connection between the acceptance of renewable energy plants and a joint form of operation in which citizens can participate (see Warren and McFadyen 2010). This has been proven to be very likely in various studies, at least in several cases: "The project results emphasize the relevance of comprehensive participation opportunities for the acceptance of renewable energies, especially with regard to the activation of groups of actors in the sense of active acceptance: Numerous practical examples prove the positive effects of public planning participation as well as financial participation opportunities for the further expansion of RE" (Rau and Zöllner 2011: 2). However, financial participation is not sufficient for the formation of acceptance; the solution is seen in a coupling of (deliberative-discursive) participation in planning procedures and financial shares in the energy plants: "equally the participatory involvement of residents in the planning and design of the technology introduction process through information, consultation and co-design" as well as "the financial participation of regional actors in RE plants at local level". In addition, there are further qualitative aspects: "experience of justice in the participation process", "trust in the competence and credibility of those responsible for planning" and the "transparency of the process" (ibid.). Furthermore, "institutionalized participation structures for the sustainable and lasting implementation of participation processes" are considered to be very important – in the planning practice found, however, it is precisely "comprehensive participation strategies" that are largely dispensed with, "whereby, among other things, a lack of knowledge and know-how about the implementation as well as the perceived effort or feared additional costs are the main reasons" (ibid.). The qualitative analysis of participation processes can reveal here the extent to which such standards are actually achieved and which problem situations, conflicts, but also unexpected constellations arise in practice.

The establishment of renewable energies in the context of the German energy transition in particular offers a special opportunity for citizens to be involved in the planning and technical installations themselves and thus actively shape their technical living environment (see Kreß et al. 2014a; Kamlage and Fleischer 2014). However, according to Beinke et al., who call for a collaborative design of the energy transition in Germany, a main danger is that there is a sole "focus on formal procedures" – a way out is seen in dialogue procedures (Beinke et al. 2012: 6). In a model for participation-oriented infrastructure planning, the authors suggest providing information as consistently as possible, giving dialogue a central place (dialogue forum), clarifying and evaluating facts, planning jointly and involving citizens financially (ibid.: 7 ff.). The evaluation of dialogue procedures in the context of the grid expansion of the energy transition has shown that even conflicts that were conducted "without compromise" for years could be resolved in the end in a consensual and trust-building manner (Kamlage 2013a: 12). In contrast, another study of dialogue processes in the context of grid expansion came to the conclusion that resulting positive effects were more on the side of technology and nature than on the side of the population: "the planning and coordination processes for the grid expansion project" had "little positive effect on the fundamental acceptance of the infrastructure project" (Schnelle and Voigt 2012: 32). Overall, deliberative participation formats such as dialogues, forums, etc. are emphasized in particular as part of the formal or informal public participation procedures (see Renn 2013a, 2013b; Renn et al. 2014).

The present study focuses in particular on formal and informal participation procedures in the context of meetings and events as well as input from citizens in the context of planning wind energy plants. These procedures are to be assessed in addition to the citizen activities for the establishment of the energy plants (by community energy projects) with regard to their

- guaranteed influence and de facto impact on decision making,
- feedback with and impact on community energy action, and
- development of innovative and creative potentials of participation is analyzed.

Research gap: While several research results on deliberative public participation formats are available, little is known about exchange and decision-making processes as well as the formation of social capital within participating communities (such as community energy initiatives). Similarly, more detailed findings on social structure are lacking, and a review of the middle-class bias thesis has yet to be conducted.

Negative Participation: When the Promotion of Civic Engagement Fails
Another analytical aspect is the traceability of "negative" participation: why participation processes do not unfold, why an involvement of citizens in discourses and group formations does not take place.[45] In research, categories have been formed for the reasons why people do not want to or cannot be involved in community energy projects (Rogers et al. 2008: 4222):

1. **Personal reasons** (e.g., no time, no interest).
2. **Lack of accountability, responsibility and motivation** (e.g., community approach is not practicable; preference for individual action; individual contribution to the community already existing or made; environmental problems perceived as global, not local challenges).
3. **Institutional framework** (e.g., no influence on the project possible, not enough information available, insufficient financing solutions, non-existent formation of a community)

Rogers et al. (2008: 4225) found in their research that while community energy is a popular concept and people find the role of participant attractive, local control over projects in this way is not a realistic option for many rural areas.[46] Although two-thirds of households in the survey had shown themselves to be interested in participation, not a single person had identified with the role of project manager. It was also stated in interviews that "community control" was not identified as a possible solution. The reasons for this are seen as the limited success of other local initiatives

---

[45] See Chatalova and Valentinov (2014), who point out that community energy initiatives only offer participation for a few and especially wealthy individuals. See also Eadson and Foden (2015) for critical perspectives on the community energy phenomenon.

[46] See also Walker 2008; Barry and Chapman 2009; Sovacool 2009; Richards et al. 2012; Szatow et al. 2012; Byrnes et al. 2013; Viardot 2013.

and the fact that interested residents do not know where to access specialist knowledge and skills or how this is to be generated. These are also seen as legitimate reasons: For example, it has been noted elsewhere (Letcher et al. 2007) that community initiatives need access to a "trusted source of resources" that has expertise regarding community development and technical issues. Support in coordinating and managing a project would also be helpful in advising interested communities on this. However, there is often a lack of skills, experience, confidence or time to develop projects independently. Such support could include assistance in structuring opportunities for involvement as well as in advising community members.

Ultimately, the considerations focus on the benefits of support for the development of renewable energy initiatives. It is assumed that there is no lack of enthusiasm for participation, but that there are structural hurdles that could be overcome by more institutional support from organizations or local political institutions. In contrast to Walker and Devine-Wright (2008) and Walker et al. (2010, 2011), the authors therefore advocate the development of concrete, standardized guidelines and recommendations for action or options.[47]

In addition, there is the significance of negative manifestations such as nepotism and corruption (Geißel 2008a: 40). The question that arises in connection with the dark sides of civil society is primarily the extent to which these are pronounced in community energy initiatives and hinder participation. Such tendencies can be linked to the question of the emergence and termination of involvement (see the concept of *shifting involvements* by Albert Hirschman[48]). Here, too, no detailed research findings are available (research gap).

[47] Walker and Devine-Wright (2008) and Walker et al. (2010, 2011) cast doubt on any sense of recommended action due to the widely varying local contexts and structures of energy projects.

[48] In a first step, Hirschman starts from disappointments that the individual experiences as a private person; these can be the impetus to enter the public sphere and to engage in concerns that have led to frustration, disappointment or anger (motive of improving living conditions) ("collective action"). However, when it comes to engaging in public concerns, frustrations can again lead to personal engagement and participation in the public sphere, which is related to pre-emptive attitudes and excessive demands on the part of individuals. This can then again result in privatization tendencies ("retreat into the private sphere") (see Hirschman 1982; on this also Ritter 2008). Hirschman describes above all disillusionment processes in public engagement, which force a return to reality ("down-to-earth usefulness and practicability") and thus lead directly into the private sphere ("cultivate our garden") (Hirschman 1982: 129). Hirschman sees the main cause for this development to be the increase of one's own prosperity, that is, self-interested motives (ibid.). Thus, in the end, the commitment leads again to disappointments of the consumer society – and thus to a more individualistic-liberal view (ibid.).

4.7 A Summary of the Research Findings

Integrative Model and Understanding of Renewable Energy Communities
In the present study, the empirical survey and analysis focus on the aspects of citizen participation and activity.

Combined with the findings of the implementation models and actor structures, it is striking that especially in the case of community energy, users of green electricity, renewable energy investors, local benefits and participants coincide. In this mode, a high number of actors, utility functions, participation types and discourse communities thus come together.

Within the framework of the empirical survey, community energy initiatives linked to their local contexts are to be reconstructed and described in more detail in order to reveal interrelationships and thus gain an integrative understanding of the process and dynamics of the longer-lasting discourse and course of planning procedures, participation processes and network exchange.

According to the understanding of participation represented here, participation as such can never be considered in isolation, but must always be assessed contextually, situationally and in interaction with other, parallel processes. On the basis of this integrative-open understanding and with the help of methodological surveys that are kept open, an analysis, reconstruction and classification on an overarching level can become possible.

Research Focus: Associative-Organizational Participation
Internal participation in associations is an important effect and mode for member participation. A first question is what the entry requirements and barriers are and to what extent communities are more open or closed in structure. In principle, it is true that every community has an exclusionary effect, since in most cases not everyone can enter. In the case of community energy initiatives, enrolment often stops after some time because, in terms of a financing mode, they enrol as many people as are needed to accumulate finance. Still other community energy projects leave their access open as a matter of principle and focus on broad and long-term integration of the local population.

While public participation requires certain resources to participate, membership in a community energy project may be possible without any other activity. The initiatives can also take measures themselves to increase or create legitimacy: inclusion, transparency, information, active involvement in the local community, openness, inclusive and collaborative ways of acting are some examples here. Finally, it can even be achieved that the energy project is recognized and supported by the majority of the local population. In addition, citizens can develop collaborative practices in the process. Also the community can be involved in the community energy project, many different social constructions are conceivable here.

Ideally, a community energy initiative would practice membership proximity and promotion, offer many participation opportunities, grant co-determination, and establish local citizen and public proximity. This would make the initiative part of an overarching approach in the sense of a municipal climate protection strategy and a climate protection network. However, the governance and participation models may collide: while the representative principles of the elected representatives apply in the municipality, the community energy projects act independently, autonomously and on their own responsibility. This can lead to a feeling of powerlessness vis-à-vis the energy project on the part of the local population, which could, however, be countered by involving and delegating power.

Thus, the freely acting initiatives and the approach of *citizen control,* which was highly valued by Arnstein (1969), are ultimately opposed to the fact that there are no legally anchored and controlled standards and fewer responsibilities (e.g., not obligated to the community). Instead, structures and modes of action can be arbitrary; a community energy project is not subject to the principle of "participatory governance". For example, leaders can develop oligarchic tendencies, and members can be excluded and discriminated against. Although legal regulations apply (e.g., company law) and voluntary commitments can be formulated (such as orientation towards the common good and members), individual practices, for example, failure to take members' interests into account, lack of transparency and power-securing practices can have undemocratic features that are not very conducive to participation. Formal channels do exist for members (e.g., submitting applications), but these can be blocked, prevented or not taken seriously. This would also be possible in public procedures, but in the case of community energy projects there are no directly accessible higher (control) authorities (apart from associations with only limited possibilities). This reveals a fundamental problem of the civil society association system.

In summary, it remains to be stated that an empirically founded analysis of the new and expansive forms of participation in the form of community energy projects can provide information on whether this form of citizen participation can represent a gain for democracy through social effects (positive modes of action of social capital, democracy learning, spillover effects, see explanations above). For a balanced evaluation, in addition to the positive effects, a look at negative tendencies, which could be taken from the state of research, is indispensable for integration into the empirical survey.

Key Aspects in the Democratic Evaluation of Community Energy Projects
In summary, the following aspects can emerge as neuralgic points in the unfolding of participation processes in the context of community energy initiatives:

- Problem of the **protection of community minorities, recognition and protection of affected persons and parties** (in conjunction with the participation roller paradox).
- **Public good and return paradox** between return-oriented motivation and public good as well as ecological oriented action.
- **Professionalization-economization and participation trade-off** between small, participatory initiatives and large, professional managed participation companies.
- **Inclusion and output trade-off**: increasing participation and members` involvement leads to decreasing effectiveness and output of community energy projects.
- **Oligarchy and inclusion trade-off**: increasing power of boards leads to less inclusion of members and weakening the principle of checks and balances.
- **Conflic potential of members` collaboration**: involvement of members leads to conflict and downturn of activities, engagement and momentum.
- **Trade-off between decision-making participation and seriousness**: as decision-making participation increases in quantity and contents concerned, the relevance of decisions and the weight and influence of votes decreases.
- **Trade-off between discourse and effectiveness**: increased discourse and many discussions lead to decreased effectiveness and efficiency of the project.
- **Overlapping roles for citizens**: citizens can participate simultaneously in three spheres: in the context of public participation, associative-organizational co-determination in community-owned companies or projects and involvement through membership in associations, organizations and initiatives. This can lead to an overlap of contradictory interests: either citizens act opportunistically or mutually contradictory depending on the specific context.

For this study therefore, the central insight from the literature review of community energy research is the distinct necessity to evaluate participation patterns as individually and case-study-related as possible. Ultimately, according to this micro level perspective, a wide-ranging kaleidoscope of patterns and structures of community energy participation can be compiled, which can in a second step be condensed to identify a typology of different forms of participation in community energy projects in Germany.

5 Methodological Considerations for Data Collection and Analysis

The essential feature of the chosen research design is a mixed methods approach that combines both quantitative and qualitative survey instruments and different procedures and analytical methodologies (see Kuckartz 2014a). At its core, this approach has the following characteristics:

- **Open, exploratory conception** due to less available research evidence.
- **Qualitative case study analysis** based on data from **expert interviews**: gaining detailed insights into individual aspects of various cases.
- **Online survey**: collection of quantitative and qualitative data from members of community energy projects in Germany.
- **Methodological approach**: elaboration of differentiated **typologies** of multiple community and local participation processes in renewable energy systems.

Mixed Methods Approach: Combination of Case Study Analysis and Online Survey

The empirical approach chosen here is composed of various methodological approaches and building blocks. On the one hand, a comparative case study with selected case studies is conducted with the aim of elaborating participatory arrangements with regard to organizational and institutional structures as well as practices. On the other hand, methods of typology will be applied by carrying out a reconstructive typological procedure to depict participatory designs.

The overall methodological conception is further substantiated by the chosen empirical approach. The overall methodological orientation of the research design is characterized by a mixed methods approach, combining qualitative and

J. Radtke, *Community Energy in Germany*,
https://doi.org/10.1007/978-3-658-39320-5_5

quantitative methods of data collection (see Kuckartz 2014a).[1] The qualitative data collection is carried out with the help of expert interviews; in addition, qualitative information is collected through open text entries from an online survey. The quantitative data collection are carried out by means of an online survey with the help of standardized selection questions.

The methodological embedding of the approach results from three perspective levels, which shape both the societal actor level (scope of the actors' actions on socio-political levels), the spatial level (scope of the actors' actions in spatial units) and thus the empirical access (see Donges 2012).[2] It is not unproblematic to carry out such crude level differentiations (see Mayntz 1999), but a staggering is recommended in this context due to the clarity achieved.

Macro-Scale (Culture-Level)

This level describes all external factors that influence the object of study (here, civil society associations and participation procedures). These can be a wide variety of political, economic, legal, social, etc. conditions of influence (e.g., effects of political decisions on a national level). In addition, the spatial reference must be taken into account, which is important in the case of the use of renewable energies (see Bosch and Peyke 2011). Recently, qualitative social research approaches have also been evaluated against the background of the spatial reference level (see Rothfuß and Dörfler 2013; Goeke et al. 2015). Participatory, spatially bound planning and design processes are part of this approach. Here, it can first be a matter of individual spatial constructions, interest-dependent objectives and strategic spatial images in general; in particular, a conflict orientation (conflicts of distribution, use and interests, conflicts of values and social relations) and participation perspective (e.g., thematic framework and objective of the participation process) can be analyzed (Uhlendahl 2013: 149 ff.). In this research context, the focus is on the impact of social forces and effects on the individual actor or groups of actors ("impact").

[1] The approach is particularly emphasized in the context of community energy research, see Rogers et al. 2008; Seyfang et al. 2013; also in relation to the sustainability context see Browne et al. 2014.

[2] Donges (2012: 217) describes from an organisational sociology and systems theory perspective a macro-level as "society and its subsystems", meso-level composed of the organisations and micro-level as "social action of individuals". In between he determines a "macro-meso area" in which the organisations move in society as well as a "micro-meso area" in which the individuals and groups act in organisations. See in relation to community energy also the micro-, meso- and macro-division in Devine-Wright 2014.

Meso-Scale (Actor-Level)
At this level, the acting collectives (actors) are focused. This level describes the collective action of individuals as a collective actor to the outside world. Through certain actions, such as entering into partnerships, representation in public, etc., the actors move in a public, shared interdependence space, whereby a wide variety of effects, such as the formation of social capital, can be observed (see Seubert 2009). Of interest here are specific modes of action and exchange relationships among the actors. Since the focus of the study is on the level between the individual on the micro level and the collective actor from the meso level, a core question from organizational sociology can be used here. This refers to the basic problem of every organization, "how individual interests and collective interests can be brought together" (Wilkesmann 2007: 163; Widmaier 1978). Here, a reference to the process-oriented methodology of sociological organization and process research suggests itself. According to Baur and Ernst (2011) as well as Ernst (2010: 75), an empirical approach is concerned with the relationships between individual and figuration (interdependence network between individuals) in order to finally determine and analyze the "specific interdependence network" (Ernst 2010: 75). The methods of organizational research here coincide with those of empirical social research in general (see Kühl et al. 2009).

Micro-Scale (Individual-Level)
The central point of reference of the study is the action of individuals in participation procedures and civil society associations (see Neuberger et al. 1985). Here, the focus is on individual modes of action and the resulting engagement structures as the basis for characterizing participatory arrangements. From an action-theoretical perspective of empirical-analytical political science (Braun 1997), the practices of individuals (e.g., related to the formation of social capital, see Bühlmann and Freitag 2004) are of interest. The reference to organizational theory asks about institutional structures and framework conditions, which can be understood as guidelines for modes of action.[3] From a democratic theoretical point of view, reference points can be formed to the democratic order, motivations of democratic action, processes of democratic action and selected problems of democracy (see Schubert

[3] Social (emergent or latent) patterns of interaction and interpretation, geneses of meaning, and social dynamics of interaction are not of interest, or recorded (see e.g., Przyborski 2004; Deppermann 2008; Lamnek 2010; Przyborski and Wohlrab-Sahr 2008; Medjedović 2014; Reichertz 2014). A level of content is covered, which mainly concerns procedural-systematic dimensions (e.g., course/process of an assembly or modes and forms of action such as working groups); see on the political science perspective Patzelt 2012.

2005). In detail, communicative action (discourse communities, see Yang 2012) as well as creative-testing action (experimental communities), which serve the inclusion of individuals, are in the foreground in the sense of deliberative, pragmatic and participatory democratic theory (Lembcke et al. 2012). The starting point is empirical democracy research (Pickel and Pickel 2006), which more recently has also been taken into account by political culture research. According to Pickel, political science initially ignored the individual in addition to the analysis of political systems: "The citizen was often only marginal in these considerations and played a subordinate role in political events" (Pickel 2010: Abstract). This changed increasingly since the 1960s due to the influence of Anglo-American researchers, for example in the context of civil society research, which "assigned citizens a greater influence on the stability and change of political systems" (ibid.). Methodologically, this view is represented today in particular by the approaches of qualitative social research and is widely applied (see Keller 2012).

Derivation of Research Criteria for Civic Participation in Community Energy
Specifically, for the empirical research approach of this study, findings from empirical civic participation research (Geißel 2008a, 2008b; Kersting 2008; Vetter 2008; Erhard et al. 2013; Kubicek 2014), in particular also research on public participation (Renn et al. 1995; Arbter et al. 2005; Arbter 2009, 2010; Rhodius 2012: 255 ff.; Renn 2013a, 2013b; Kamlage et al. 2014) can be drawn upon. Core aspects of the present study in the form of individual subject relations and modes of action are captured in particular by empirical deliberation research (Delli Carpini and Shapiro 2002; Mutz 2008: 530; Schaal and Ritzi 2009: 21). Various dimensions are described in the analysis of discourses (Mutz 2008: 530):

- **Dimensions of action research**: public vs. private sphere, individual vs. collective action, and links to political action.
- **Mechanisms of community action**: control mechanisms, group procedures, and joint modes of dealing.
- **Discourse conditions**: meaning of information in discourse, disagreement, and interactivity of discourse.
- **Principles of civic participation** such as reflection, change of perspective, face-to-face exchanges, equality and equity of participants, and learning effects.

In an empirical study, dimensions, mechanisms and conditions of discourse in particular can be concretely investigated (e.g., transition from private to public form of action, group procedures, organization). Principles of discourse, on the other hand, are more difficult to analyze; these usually remain at a level of conjecture.

In addition, effects of the participation procedures can be recorded in an analysis (Mutz 2008: 530):

- **Social forms of action and their effects**: consensual decisions, formation of social capital, sense of community, social trust, trust in democratic processes, change of perspective towards public spirit, civic engagement.
- **Cognitive effects**: knowledge and information gain, learning effects.
- **Social and habitual behavior, procedures and perception**: empathy, ability to compromise, awareness of counterarguments, political tolerance, consideration of the legitimacy of other point of views, consistencies of different worldviews, efficiency and effectiveness, mutual recognition regarding other opinions and mindsets.

It is assumed that various social effects can be analyzed within the framework of individual case analyses and evaluation data, in particular assessments of community spirit, identification, information gain, knowledge acquisition, acquisition of procedural and habitual competences, and reflective ability (Weißeno 2010b). The recording of these effects is a primary goal of the study.

With regard to the typological approach, it is possible to fall back on existing classifications, which are to a certain extent traditional in participation research (Arnstein 1969 and differentiations based on this such as Lüttringhaus 2000; furthermore Connor 1988; Fürst and Scholles 2008; Arbter et al. 2005; Zschocke 2007; Collins and Ison 2009; Keppler 2010). There are also specific typologies in the context of renewable energies and citizen participation (Schweizer-Ries et al. 2008; Rau and Zöllner 2011; Carmen 2014; participation structure in Kreß et al. 2014a). In addition, typological differentiations were made in the context of civil society associations (Stricker 2007; Sliep 2010; Keil 2013b) and civic engagement (Alscher 2008; Karl et al. 2008; Nobis 2012). Above all, suggestions can be taken from these results to avoid problematic effects such as oversimplifications and imprecise definitions.

The aforementioned works draw on different empirical approaches. In the field of empirical analysis of participatory modes of action, engagement research, and civil society and social capital research, qualitative approaches are predominantly used. Here, different research design constructs can be found, from narrative individual case studies to representative surveys in the form of standardized electronic surveys. The empirical approach is thus an essential criterion for subsequent analytical procedures.

5.1 Research Design

5.1.1 Overview

The empirical data collection methods of the present study follow the mixed methods approach in the form of a comparative case study combined with an online survey (see Mayring 2001; Johnson and Onwuegbuzie 2004; Creswell and Clark 2011; Johnson et al. 2007; Bergman 2008; Kelle 2008, 2014; Tashakkori and Teddlie 2010; Creswell 2013, 2015; Kuckartz 2014a; Mertens 2014; Sreejesh and Mohapatra 2014). Qualitative data from expert interviews and document analyses are supplemented by quantitative data from a representative online survey, with additional qualitative survey data (see Mayring 2001; Kelle 2008). The intended comparison of contents and results is primarily intended to reveal similarities and differences of social phenomena (here: actions, perspectives and assessments of the individuals surveyed) (Muno 2009: 113).

The chosen survey approach allows the existing three options for case analysis to be considered in terms of the mixed methods approach: Single Case Study Analysis and Quantitative and Qualitative Analysis of Multiple Cases.

Comparative Analysis of Case Studies

The task of the comparative analysis is in particular to first inductively condense the data material. Subsequently, overarching patterns and characteristic features are elaborated in order to achieve an analytical overview on the basis of which a typification is to be made (see Bohnsack et al. 2013). The results of the qualitative case study are compared with the quantitative-qualitative data of the online survey and result in a thematic-analytical description and discussion. On the one hand, a mutual complementation of information is hoped for, on the other hand, contradictions can also arise, which can offer a deeper understanding through a comparatively designed discussion of results (see Kopp and Lois 2014).

5.1.2 Combining Case Studies and an Online Survey: A Mixed Methods Approach

The methodological approaches used relate to each other cumulatively in the sense of a supplementary addition, not in the form of a replacement or comparison. Both forms are combined in such a way that the respective approach captures dimensions that are not given by the other. In doing so, the two approaches reflect two different perspectives on the research field to be covered. On the one hand, a detailed case analysis reconstructs and condenses individual perspectives, while on the other hand, a broad survey generates an extensive and representative, but at the same time less specific picture.

The possibility of comprehensive mapping, complementing and contrasting these two approaches is the primary motivation for the chosen combination. Recourse to only one information channel is more likely to promote one-sided views, monocausal patterns and distorted perceptions. Thus, it is assumed that behaviours, attitudes and motivations of involved citizens will remain obscured until they can be appropriately integrated by the research approach. The use of the methodology is thus primarily deductively based and oriented, as the appropriate approach to gathering the relevant information is derived from the situation encountered. To this end, findings from one methodological area are used to develop the other methodology, in that the qualitative interview phase precedes the survey. Finally, the respective partial results can be discussed and mutually evaluated against the other findings.

In principle, a combination of methods today no longer represents a scientific controversy between quantitative and qualitative advocates. In the sense of defusing the discourse, the duality of the two approaches is replaced by a third paradigm of the mixed methods movement (Kuckartz 2009: 353): "It is true for both methods that they are by no means monolithic, but encompass a large spectrum of heterogeneous approaches. Striking juxtapositions hide this diversity of approaches found in reality in favor of an apparent dualism." In combining methods, "both types of data, qualitative and quantitative, are combined in a meaningful way" (ibid.). Frequently, this combination can be found in studies that have the construction of a typology as an objective: "The construction of types is generally a field of method combination (…)" (ibid.). Kuckartz further assumes that in the method-integrative approach, each stage of the investigation influences the one that follows. In this approach, initial findings or links between the various forms of action or behavior and the context in which they are embedded are obtained in an initial investigation (via document analysis). From this, questions are generated and the qualitative sample is constructed (ibid.: 361). After patterns of interpretation and action orientations have been identified in this way, these in turn flow into a modified instrument development for the second, actual qualitative sub-study (ibid.).

Using Triangulation in Mixed Methods Studies

In a mixed methods approach, the procedure corresponds to a parallel design in which the methods stand side by side on an equal footing and are applied in parallel (as opposed to a sequential order). This approach can be reconciled with considerations of triangulation, as it is primarily concerned with "validation" or "enrichment of perspectives" (ibid: 360). Triangulation means "taking different perspectives on an object under study or more generally: in answering research questions" (Flick 2004: 12). In method triangulation, the same phenomenon is captured with different methods (Kuckartz 2009: 355). In other words, it is a method-external combination, as it is not differentiated and combined within one approach, but, as in this case, quantitative-qualitative survey data with qualitative interviews (ibid.: 355).

In triangulation, it is crucial that there is a "concentration of all the procedures and follow-up analyses used on the same substantive research topic" (Pickel 2009: 518). The aim is to "compensate for assumed weaknesses of the respective data collection and analysis method by means of information and analysis techniques of the other collection method and, by combining the advantages of the methods, ideally by means of between-method triangulation, to achieve a higher validity of the investigation and a further gain in knowledge by illuminating as different aspects of the phenomenon as possible" (ibid.). In the broader "triangulation of perspectives", there should be an independent analysis of the data collected in each case using their own methods and their recognition as independent and equally relevant findings (ibid.; Flick 2004: 79). A pure triangulation, on the other hand, would use "different methods and their results merely to improve the interpretation of only one dominant form of collection and analysis" (Pickel 2009: 519) by "misusing interviews as a hypothesis generator" (ibid.). The chosen combination approach corresponds to the complementarity model of triangulation, in which different subject areas are surveyed with the respective method, which are then worked on in a complementary manner to answer the (common) research question (Pickel 2009: 520). Here, the research approaches are applied "in a complementary manner" and serve "to explain the results obtained with the respective other method" (ibid.: 521). For example, information from interviews can be helpful in designing and developing questions for a large sample (ibid.: 522). As has been shown, the methodological approaches serve to capture different target groups and characteristics (reflecting different perspectives). In a complementary way, collected information from a first phase (individual case analysis) flows into the design of the second step (online survey).

Triangulation and the mixed methods approach are considered pragmatic approaches (Kuckartz 2009: 354, 362). Advantages of method combinations are seen in the fact that weaknesses of the respective other method are compensated; results can be more comprehensive and not bound to the limits of only one method and different scientific-theoretical perspectives can be included (see Pickel 2009: 522). Disadvantages, on the other hand, can be that overarching core knowledge is required; a high expenditure of time and money arises; there is a danger that standards of the individual methods "are undermined with regard to the linkability of the results" and the "urge to link results" can mask structural incompatibilities of different results (ibid.).

Fundamental criticism has also been levelled at the triangulation approach. Naïve realism is assumed through the simplified assumption of objective positions and, in particular, the fundamental assumption is called into question "that different methods have the same explanatory power for the research question" (Kuckartz 2009: 361). In this regard, Kuckartz notes that a situation can produce completely different results with different methods, depending on the topic (ibid.). This criticism seems to be justified with regard to the last two arguments. Therefore, it must be taken into account that not the same explanatory power is given depending on the approach and method, and that results can also vary. In this respect, it ultimately seems to be the task of the researcher to differentiate the results, to discuss them critically and to reflect on fundamental discrepancies in the underlying methodological approaches.

Discussion

While it is true that in the combination of methods one methodological orienta tion should meaningfully complement another, the case described in the literature of a cannibalization of certain results is not the goal of a complementary use of different methods. The aim here is not to cannibalize individual methodological building blocks and use them exclusively to provide additional support for a priori research assumptions, but rather to bring to light results and information that could not be developed and uncovered by a singular methodological approach. The starting point for this consideration is the change of perspective described above, in which an expert perspective is supplemented by a research-theoretically and practically relevant perspective of the individuals involved. For an adequate representation of the participatory arrangements found, this supplement appears to be of well-founded value.

Finally, the various survey techniques, whether in-depth or generalized, can in principle be used in all phases of the research project (Pickel 2009: 520). Results of expert interviews, for example, can be used "to concretize, narrow down or formulate a research question" (ibid.).

5.2 Comparative Case Studies

5.2.1 Deductive Versus Inductive Exploratory Studies: Using a Combined Approach

With the help of qualitative case analysis, generalizations are to be achieved through an inductive approach, via the analysis of specifics of the cases (Muno 2009: 119). Conversely, findings from the research also flow into preliminary assumptions, which are also obtained from the research material through initial (document) analyses (in the sense of theoretical sampling of grounded theory). This combines deductive and inductive approaches, which is a regular process in the form of assumption-checking and gaining new assumptions through analysis of cases (ibid.). When used correctly and with considered research design, case studies can "specify and measure complex variables", "inductively identify new variables and develop new hypotheses", and "formulate contingent generalizations or typological theories" (Muno 2009: 123). In this study, the focus is particularly on the attempt at generalization through the formulation of typologies.

A central problem with case-oriented qualitative comparisons is that too many questions and variables are collected for too few cases (Ebbinghaus 2009: 203). However, the problem can be countered by the fact that, with careful case selection, just one case can be sufficient to refute a hypothesis (via the difference method) (Ebbinghaus 2009: 204). In the present study, the findings of the survey are intended to help examine what participatory motivations and modes of action depend on and whether these vary under fixed framework conditions (e.g., location and form of organization), for example, whether forms of participation and degrees of use change with different forms of association.

It is admittedly unrealistic that all relevant conditions can be covered and controlled by case selection (ibid.: 205). However, this need not be a problem if the aim is only to test assumptions or to gain knowledge at all: "In this case, it is not the number of cases that is the limiting factor, but the discovery of actual contradictions between the predicted and the actual event" (ibid.). In the literature, therefore, the inductive-exploratory approach, with the help of which hypotheses are to be generated from very complex data material, is criticized above all in the sense of "blindly poking around" (ibid.). Despite a certain openness and exploratory character of the present study, the orientation of the research process (objective) must therefore be explicitly defined to a sufficient degree in advance. A problem is already hidden in the initial phase of the investigation. While the purely inductive-exploratory approach is criticized in the literature for its lack of goal orientation and instead, in the sense of qualitative content analysis, preliminary deductions of categories from the state of research and theories are preferred, grounded theory deliberately seeks to avoid prior, "fixed" assumptions and categorizations that restrict the free view. Kuckartz, in his type-forming procedure, attempts a mitigated alternative in the form of initial minor analyses for category formation (see above). In this way, an attempt is made to pursue neither one direction nor the other exclusively (see Meinefeld 1997)[4]; instead, in the sense of a flexible approach, partial areas are considered in each case:

- Generation of first rough categories from structural data through document analysis of the framework conditions as well as consideration of previous research (here: organizational-structural conditions of the participatory arrangements).
- Final generation and definition of the category system in the sense of grounded theory only during the analysis process (qualitative content analysis with parts of open coding).
- In a final discussion and evaluation, the categorization is checked again and all the findings generated are compared with the data from the survey and the results of the case analysis in the sense of a critical questioning. Subsequently, the three strands of knowledge (formal-structural data from the document analysis, case analysis data based on expert interviews and participant observation, and quantitative-qualitative survey data) are brought together in a deliberative discussion process for a characterization and typologization of the participatory arrangements of the community energy initiatives and participation processes studied.

[4] Meinefeld sums up by noting: "Qualitative methodology cannot stop at fundamentally rejecting the prior formulation of hypotheses and only allowing ex-post facto hypotheses for the interpretation of the collected material; it must also assign an independent place in its methodological justification to the control of the researcher's prior knowledge. This does not mean that qualitative social research must always be preceded by elaborate hypotheses oriented towards theories (…). In particular, it cannot be a matter of narrowing social research to the testing of hypotheses. Qualitative methodology, however, cannot continue to adhere to the self-image of having at its disposal a specific access to social phenomena which is free of prior knowledge and which is fundamentally different from the guidance of perception by ex-ante hypotheses. It must develop communicable possibilities to reflect and make explicit the pre-structuring of the object area that also occurs in it" (Meinefeld 1997: 32).

5.2.2 Assessing Sample Representativeness and Focussing on the Individual Level

Initially, specific cases are sought for analysis in order to be able to carry out a comparative review of assumptions (Muno 2009: 116 f.). A comparison here is intended to highlight different ways of acting in order to provide a broad basis for typologization. However, qualitative case analysis has the disadvantage that, due to the small number of cases, it is not representative and therefore less meaningful. The addition in the form of the results of the online survey therefore has a favourable effect on validity. It is precisely this addition that supports representativeness and closes open questions or gaps in the case analysis. The disadvantage that quantitative approaches do not provide "adequate explanations" due to "inherent reductionism" and that "generally valid generalizations" sacrifice complexity and concretization in favor of "abstraction and simplification" in qualitative-statistical approaches (Muno 2009: 122) is to be countered here by a mixed methods approach.

Both case analysis and survey serve the particular purpose of enabling the inclusion of the individual or the citizen in order to include his or her "value orientations, behaviours as well as elements of civil society" (Pickel 2009: 297). This is where the exploratory part of the research approach comes to light, by empirically "searching for signals that are not known in advance", "which are significant for the actors in the given situation" (Diekmann 2007b: 536). This is indispensable for developing a typology and gaining knowledge of actor perspectives and modes of action at the individual level in the sense of capturing epistemic practices. At the same time, however, the dangers of the aimless inductive search process must be counteracted by an explicit content-analytical methodology.

In addition to the survey method of expert interviews in the qualitative field, a broad-based survey also has "the invaluable advantage for comparison that it can depict society in its breadth, taking into account the idea of representativeness" (ibid.). In this way, "it succeeds in making the subjective side of politics (…) usable for comparative macro-analysis, but at the same time does not lose sight of the individual" (ibid.).

Comparative case analysis, on the other hand, can provide more depth for the evaluation and typological approach by taking into account individual (actor) perspectives. Case studies generally offer the advantage of providing "accurate knowledge about a case" (Muno 2009: 121) and providing a "depth and density of understanding" (Sartori 1994: 24). On the other hand, however, there is a danger that details and particularities are overstated, established categories of general theories are ignored, and ultimately only ad hoc explanations are produced, which Sartori points out (ibid.: 19). A relativization can be achieved by interweaving qualitative with quantitative data.

5.3 Data Collection and Methods of Analysis

5.3.1 Using Expert Interviews with Community Energy Stakeholders

The literature on the use of expert interviews in qualitative social research is diverse. Here, we draw on various findings by Meuser and Nagel (1991, 2009, 2013), Bogner et al. (2009, 2014), Westle and Krumm (2009), Gläser and Laudel (2010), Helfferich (2011, 2014), Nohl (2012), Kaiser (2014) and Kruse (2014), some aspects of which are relevant to this research.

In the research, expert interviews are used to generate knowledge about the energy initiatives by interviewing the following people:

- Initiators and board members of the community energy projects.
- Representatives of public or state authorities, administrations and institutions involved in the procedures and in contact with the community energy projects.
- Persons from energy agencies and consultants who have accompanied the procedures
- Representatives of citizens' initiatives or civil society associations, organizations and groups (e.g., Local Agenda 21 groups).
- Members of the community energy projects.

In addition to the online survey for the citizens involved and a document analysis of documents from the energy initiatives and state energy programs, the expert interviews represent a central survey instrument in the present study. The interviews are therefore of great importance because, due to the lack of scientific knowledge in this area and the limited informative value of written documents without contextual knowledge, it hardly seems possible to develop and generate relevant information. For example, the chronological sequence of the processes in detail, including hurdles and accompanying circumstances, as well as motivations, assessments, etc., can only be reconstructed in this way, since written documents do not exist. The aim of this approach is to reconstruct the course of community energy initiatives (from the initial idea to implementation and the subsequent period) as well as to uncover the interrelationships between the actors involved in them. Positive (in the sense of successful cooperation and progress of the energy initiative) as well as negative (in the sense of conflicts and problems in terms of personnel and material) aspects mentioned by the interviewees are also recorded.

Meuser and Nagel note a double meaning of the term expert and define as experts (Meuser and Nagel 2009: 466):

- who is in any way responsible for the design, development, implementation and/or control of a problem solution,
- and thus has privileged access to information on groups of people, social situations, decision-making processes, policy issues, etc.

The expert interview should generally cover a broad spectrum of relevant aspects and offer the interviewee the freedom to introduce his or her own aspects (see Kremer 2010: 13). The inclusion of independently contributed thematic aspects of the interviewee is of particular relevance in the present study, since due to the intended genesis of the development course of the energy initiative, important topics of the interviewee himself should be included as broadly as possible, so that the interviewee himself initially addresses possible particularities, such as problems with the initiation or also successful and conflict-laden phases, in a biased manner (see on the recording of political narratives Gadinger et al. 2013).

In this context, the exploratory aspect of expert interviews is crucial (Westle and Krumm 2009: 253; Bogner et al. 2009). It serves the thematic exploration and sharpening of problem awareness. In the study, expert interviews are conducted in a knowledge-generating manner for thematic probing with an exploratory-narrative orientation.

With regard to the interview forms, a wide variety of procedures are conceivable: from very open to standardized approaches. In most cases, a guideline is used. Meuser and Nagel advocate an open guided interview (Meuser and Nagel 2009: 472), as the researcher wants to learn more than just "statements" as answers to standardized questions. Therefore, if the interview is designed exploratively, this "can only succeed in open interview situations" (ibid.). "For conducting the interview, this results in the necessity of a thematic guide and its flexible handling". However, the interview should not be conducted without a guideline (and thus structuring), since on the one hand the researcher would appear incompetent, and on the other hand "the strategies of acting and criteria of decision-making related to a specific functional context" (ibid.) should be adequately recorded. The interviewer's competence is very important for the acquisition of knowledge in expert interviews (ibid.: 473).

Narrative passages pose a challenge in expert interviews with open-ended guidelines. "If the content of the narrative is an episode from the professional field of action, these certainly prove to be key passages for the reconstruction of orientations guiding action" (ibid.). Narratives should be challenged through interviewing. Meuser and Nagel see the decisive justification in an implicit knowledge of the expert, which is to be detected through the interview in the first place: "Narratives provide information about aspects of the expert's action, which the expert himself is not fully aware of, but rather only becomes aware of step by step in the course of the narrative". This aspect is also of particular importance in the study, as the experts' "narratives" can provide a good insight into how and under what circumstances the idea of an energy project was pursued.

In the evaluation, the "thematic units, in passages that belong together in terms of content and are scattered throughout the texts" are decisive (ibid.: 476). In this way, "the functional context of the experts" is to gain weight: "the experts' utterances are located from the outset in the context of their institutional-organizational conditions of action, they receive their meaning from here and not from where they fall in the interview".

A delicate aspect in this context is the problem of the openness of questions. Maximum openness offers little influence of the interviewer, which is welcome, but this contradicts the task of guides to procure specific information on several different topics in "limited time" (Gläser and Laudel 2010: 131). Therefore, Gläser and Laudel (ibid.: 133 ff.) rather suggest imputations in which "the interviewer formulates his knowledge about the subject of the question or his assumptions as an implicit prerequisite" (ibid.: 133). The advantage here is that the interviewer's level of knowledge becomes apparent and a thematic orientation is established, since the interviewee now stays within the topic and does not digress.

Basically, many different types of questions can be distinguished, which can be structured according to content or functional aspects (ibid.: 130). In this case, the focus is on content-related questions, that is, opinion, fact and reality-related questions. In addition, narrative prompts and detailed questions are used as control questions in order to obtain more detailed information and assessments from the interviewer about the process of initiating community energy initiatives. When conducting the interviews, particular use is made of the concept of open guides, which are not strictly applied, according to the ideas and suggestions of Meuser and Nagel.

5.3.2 Document Analysis of Formal and Informal Records

In addition to the expert interviews, the study also requires information to be extracted from documents that describe and present the facts in more detail. In particular, the following documents are used for this purpose:

- Documents of the community energy projects, such as audit trails, statutes, reports, presentations, advertising material, etc., which reveal their community actions and participation strategies.
- Documents of the involved specialized administrations, for example, audit trails of meetings, submissions by citizens, statements by the administration, etc., which provide information on participation procedures.
- Press and media documents (reports) documenting participation processes.

The first two types of documents are particularly important for the reconstruction of processes within the community energy projects and of citizen participation processes in the context of the approval and planning phases in the case of wind power use in the municipalities. Press articles are also consulted, but are not a central source of information. This is due to the fact that, on the one hand, they offer less relevant information and, on the other hand, they tend to convey opinions and moods, which are not part of the research interest within the present study. In order to grasp the working methods and interrelationships within the community energy projects as well as their participation models and to be able to understand the citizen participation procedures in the municipalities, those documents which are directly connected to the procedures and offer a direct as well as rather objective description in terms of both time and content are most suitable for evaluation. These are, in particular, minutes of meetings and assemblies that have been produced in a timely manner, describe the content and process of the procedures, and reproduce statements in a meaningful way.

Of greater interest are the stages of analysis of individual documents (Noetzel et al. 2009: 330). First, formal characteristics are classified: text type, text origin, text producers as well as addressees must be able to be determined exactly. With regard to the interpretation, the text structure (composition and structure), the text content (statements, central arguments, key terms) and linguistic features (language style, rhetorical devices and phrases, etc.) are to be classified and addressed. Finally, a final evaluation takes place: this involves a possible detection of contradictions in the document, intentions and interests of the author, (un)intended effects on the recipient, an anticipation of possible criticism and finally a classification of the significance of the document for the initial question of the investigation.

In the present study, the document analysis is intended to obtain factual knowledge in particular. With the help of the information, the following aspects are to be developed:

- Reconstruction of the day-to-day operations of community energy projects.
- Comparison of participation models of community energy projects.
- Reconstruction of the planning, approval and public participation procedures.
- Substantive issues and aspects of meetings, sessions, comments and submissions from citizens and other stakeholders (concerning the community energy project).

Finally, it is necessary to discuss the limits that document analysis can encounter and the problems that can arise with this procedure. Noetzel et al. (2009: 333) see possible limits in the "processuality and especially in the orality and informality of many decisions": "About many decision-making processes in politics, only minutes of the results are available, but not records of the path of decision-making and the behavior of the actors in the process. Oral and informal modes of decision-making are particularly prevalent in policy-specific networks. Such policy networks often consist of informal patterns of relations between different governmental and nongovernmental actors within a policy field" (ibid.: 333 f.). Furthermore, it must be taken into account that a network is often connected to another actor network, which is more likely to be revealed through interviews or observation (ibid.: 334).

Nevertheless, the written documents and information play a role that should not be neglected: on the basis of these documents, meeting procedures, topics mentioned and discussed, as well as formal legal regulations (e.g., statutes of the community energy companies or projects, which determine the forms of participation) can be recorded in a comprehensive and mostly complete manner. In addition, the written documents offer insights into thematic areas and processes that either do not come up in interviews (e.g., because they are critical issues) or are omitted or incompletely presented. Thus, document analysis forms an important third pillar in the development of relevant information: While the interviews record the temporal processes of the community energy projects and the motivations of the initiators, the survey depicts the structure of the citizens involved and their motivations and assessments, written minutes, reports and statutes document important factual data of the community energy projects (types of participation, number of members, costs, etc.) and the contents of meetings, written submissions from citizens and administrative processes (permits, funding programs, energy concepts).

5.3.3 Online Survey: Questionnaire Survey Design

The survey of the participating citizens in the energy projects was conducted through a so-called online survey. For data protection reasons, it was not possible for all persons to be contacted directly by the researcher. However, such contact was made possible by the initiators and boards of the projects, who forwarded a notice to the participants in the community energy projects. Since many energy projects have contact details of their members and often use the internet for notification or information forwarding, this access is obvious. However, there is a recognizable problem that older members do not have internet access and were therefore excluded from the opportunity to participate. Ebert et al. (2012: 2) point out these problems especially in nationwide surveys of the population.

The criterion of targeting is met in the context of this survey in the way that members are reached in a targeted manner via key persons (initiators, project managers, board members). However, misuse cannot be ruled out entirely. Such a case would, however, be verifiable, as one survey was placed per project. On the one hand, this is advantageous for a differentiated evaluation; on the other hand, the participation in each survey can be explicitly traced by the electronic administration program of the survey (number and time of participation, so-called audit trail).

Differing practices in the dissemination of the survey can only be countered by adopting a comprehensive approach with the highest possible number of cases. By covering as many projects as possible and achieving high participation rates, different accompanying circumstances and dispersions of the survey in the population can have less influence (see Wagner and Hering 2014). Based on these considerations, the online survey was distributed throughout Germany and ultimately covered 84 community energy projects with 2826 individual responses. Within the framework of the evaluation, it is also possible to assign the respective participating energy project to the various clusters.

The design of the questionnaire is based on the mixed methods approach: "In addition to standardized questions with prescribed answers, open questions can also be asked" (Ebert et al. 2012: 3). This approach also offers a research pragmatic advantage: since the answers are entered by the participants, the "normally arduous work of transferring handwritten answers into the computer program" is not necessary (ibid.).

In this survey, both standardized (quantitative data-generating) and open-ended (qualitative data-generating) questions are used. In the case of the former, predefined answer options exist if a certain knowledge about the aspect is assumed and "consequently all important answer options can be anticipated" (ibid.: 5). With open questions, a high gain in knowledge can be achieved when "motives, justifications, contextual information or emotional aspects are involved" (ibid.). These questions are particularly recommended when "subjective contexts of meaning or patterns of interpretation" (ibid.: 6) are to be recorded – in this case, for example, positive or negative assessments of what is happening in society. One problem with open questions can be the increased time required for evaluation. Similar to the handling of other qualitative data, it is necessary here to make a selection and to record relevant passages by means of content analysis procedures via electronic evaluation.

The design of the questionnaire is further guided by findings from Kallus (2010), Kirchhoff et al. (2010), Mayer (2012), Raab-Steiner and Benesch (2012), Latcheva and Davidov (2014), Klöckner and Friedrichs (2014), Hoffmeyer-Zlotnik and Warner (2014), Franzen (2014) and Porst (2014a, 2014b). Although it is difficult to establish general rules for the design of questionnaires, it is possible to draw on some contextually significant rules of experience from research (Porst 2014a: 95 f.).[5]

With regard to the evaluation of the data, there are a number of possibilities. Ebert et al. (2012: 14 f.) recommend an exploratory data analysis, which in this case would take place across cases, as a basic count is carried out and evaluated according to individual characteristics (cross-case exploration). This is also necessary due to the high number of responses.

The qualitative data from the open questions can be evaluated category-based by "developing categories along the lines of the research question and from further research-relevant ideas that arose during the exploration" (ibid.: 15). Corresponding text passages are then classified into the categories as if they were containers (similar to coding, as is known from qualitative content analysis and can be carried out with the help of qualitative data processing software) (see ibid.).

---

[5] Porst (2014a: 95 f.) mentions here: "use of simple, unambiguous terms that are understood in the same way by all respondents; use of questions with a clear temporal reference; use of answer categories that are exhaustively free of overlap; definition of unclear terms; avoidance of long and complex as well as hypothetical questions; avoidance of double stimuli and negations as well as of insinuations and suggestive questions; avoidance of questions that aim at information that many respondents presumably do not have; the context of a question should not have an (uncontrolled) effect on its answer."

5.3.4 Analysis of Qualitative and Quantitative Data

The evaluation procedure of the qualitative data should be uniform in the present study. This has the advantage of comparability, but also of a coherent and not fragmentary processing of partial data, which are ultimately summarized under one category. The information should complement each other within these processes, merge and offer different perspectives, assessments and facts on a topic. In this way, a comprehensive, coherent picture should be drawn, although missing information (puzzle pieces) should also be pointed out at appropriate points and actively included in the analysis.

For the evaluation of expert interviews, Meuser and Nagel recommend transcribing relevant passages (Meuser and Nagel 2009: 476) as well as paraphrasing (sequencing the text according to thematic units) and coding (thematic order of the selected passages), which serves to condense the data. "In doing so, the approach is close to the text, the terminology of the interviewees is taken up. In favourable cases, a term or a phrase can be adopted directly. Whether one or more codes are assigned to a passage depends on how many topics are addressed in each case." The course of the text may be broken up. "Condensations, typifications, abstractions remain within its horizon" (ibid.). After these steps, a thematic comparison of text passages is possible by "bundling thematically comparable text passages from different interviews" (ibid.). The authors also favour textual categorization, which is reminiscent of the grounded theory approach (ibid.). Within a category, "the particular of the shared knowledge of experts is condensed and made explicit" (ibid.: 477). On the one hand, passages are thus collected and subsumed under a term, on the other hand, this is also intended to promote a reconstruction of the term. This should serve the empirical generalization, but always remain close to the available statements (ibid.: 477).

Finally, through a "theoretical generalization" the categories will be "theoretically ordered in their internal context" (ibid.). "The presentation of the results is done from a theoretically informed perspective on the empirically generalized 'facts'" (ibid.). Finally, through a meaningful reconstruction, "contexts of meaning are to be linked to form typologies and to form theories" "where addition and pragmatic juxtaposition have previously prevailed" (ibid.). The evaluation should also be recursive, by flexibly going back and forth within the steps and possibly correcting them (ibid.).

Meuser and Nagel's approach is similar to the now widely used coding method of qualitative content analysis, for example, according to Gläser and Laudel (2010: 44 ff.; see also Kuckartz 2014b, Mayring and Fenzl 2014; Mayring 2015). Here, an analysis grid is used, but extracted information is then "further processed relatively independently of the text" (Gläser and Laudel 2010: 46). While the conception of a grid seems sensible for effective processing, the wider process of tearing apart the contextual-teleological context is not followed. Rather, an approach of conversation analysis that captures the context is followed (see Przyborski 2004).

Combination of Multiple Methodological Approaches

By combining different approaches in the sense of an intelligent linkage, some methodological problems can be addressed. Approaches of an object and process orientation of the problem-centered interview according to Witzel (2000; Witzel and Reiter 2012), a flexible category formation according to Gläser and Laudel (2010) as well as the application of the permanent comparison of the grounded theory according to Glaser and Strauss (2010) can be helpful here (see Strübing 2014b). Object and process orientation, category formation according to Gläser and Laudel, and open coding have in common that they offer a high degree of flexibility.

In this context, it is also important how a category is found or a category system is constructed. In principle, two approaches are possible: inductive and deductive category formation (see Kuckartz 2009: 340). In this case, deductive and inductive elements are mixed – as in most cases of empirical surveys of social data. On the one hand, categories are developed from the material itself, on the other hand, categories are derived from an existing theory or previous research, in that the categories serve to test hypotheses formed from theories or existing research without first sifting through the material.

According to Mayring (2015: 3, 6), the procedures are essentially similar anyway. Admittedly, category definitions are first established in different ways in the inductive case and structuring dimensions in the deductive variant. Eventually, however, categories are derived from the material in the former case, and a coding guide is formed from established definitions, anchor examples and coding rules in the latter. In both cases, the categories are then revised and a second pass through the material and an evaluation are carried out.

On the one hand, this procedure is reminiscent of grounded theory approaches, but it is also reminiscent of classical content analysis in both deductive and inductive respects (see Mayring and Fenzl 2014 and Strübing 2014a). This procedure of mixing survey approaches is not uncommon in research practice: Kuckartz (2009: 340) speaks of the fact that the two types are rarely found in their pure form: "In fact, one often finds mixed forms in such a way that one starts with a relatively rough deductive category system that is refined through inductive category formation" (ibid.).

Discussion

A flexible approach is of particular importance in the context of the present study. Mayring (2015: 8) sees limits and restrictions in content analysis procedures "where either the research question is more open, exploratory, variable and the reference to fixed categories would appear to be a limitation, or where a holistic, not dissecting-step-by-step analysis process is desired".

On the other hand, a complete neglect of any category formation and structuring of the procedure would also be fraught with several disadvantages (including unsystematic, confusing, imprecise, etc.). Therefore, the approaches of object and process orientation, flexible category formation as well as coding and conducting comparisons in the sense of grounded theory seem to be appropriate here. Thus, on the one hand, the approach is very similar to the basic procedure of a content analysis, as described by Kuckartz (2009: 338 ff.), for example, in that after a category system has been created, a material run-through including coding takes place, which is followed by a category-based evaluation and a cross-category context analysis. In detail, however, different evaluation approaches are used in a flexible and appropriate manner.

Such a flexible approach was also recommended by Glaser and Strauss in their grounded theory. According to them, categories are found at different stages in the evaluation process: "Categories of a rather low level of abstraction emerge rather quickly during the early phase of data collection. Overarching and integrating conceptualizations at higher levels – as well as the properties they specify – usually emerge later, during the simultaneous collection, coding, and analysis of data" (Glaser and Strauss 2010: 54). For the formation of a new theory or, in this case, a characterization and type formation, the authors see a generation from data in particular as indispensable: "To underpin an external category with data tends to distract from the generation of new categories. The work then consists primarily in collecting data and not in generating it".

Moreover, such categories are also judged to be advantageous because they are "usually the most relevant and best applied to the data" (ibid.). In the way they emerge from the data material, "they are formulated as generally as possible, nevertheless specified in their meaning and examined for their relevance" (ibid.). This means that there is no further question as to whether indicators are also appropriate to the chosen categories. However, if in the inductive case a category is to be taken out of another theory and modified, this could become problematic in finding suitable indicators (ibid.: 54). Such an approach attempts to "'squeeze round data' into 'square categories'", moreover "elaborately and prolifically" (ibid.: 54 f.) to justify. The authors explicitly emphasise that "anyone who tries to fit data to categories or properties with coercion can be sure to raise doubts from the outset among colleagues and laypersons alike" (ibid.: 55). Moreover, "borrowed" categories are "harder to find", "rarer and not as rich", "because they are not made (and ultimately may not even be relevant) to our particular project". By placing "emphasis on the emergence and development of new categories", "problems of fit, relevance, constraint, and richness" are solved (ibid.).

The approach chosen here is essentially in line with the considerations of Glaser and Strauss. Essential insights are to be gained and generated from the data, a superimposition of categories and approaches from the literature is to be avoided. Nevertheless, various approaches from the literature are used in parts to build models where this seems appropriate. This seems to make sense, as it does not seem realistic to reinvent the wheel of data collection and to completely ignore existing approaches. However, models from the literature are used in the form of a suggestion and not as a direct template for evaluation. A compulsive insertion into existing models would probably be dysfunctional and would also lead to less coherent results. A flexible use seems to be the more appropriate approach here. The evaluation of the empirical data is carried out against the background of type and category formation. These are – as has been explained – obtained in particular from the empirical material itself in the sense of the inductive approach. Findings from other studies are used as a supplement.

5.4 Empirically Grounded Construction of Types and Typologies in Qualitative Social Research

The essential intention of a type-building procedure is to "create classifications and typologies on the basis of several or many cases" (Krumm 2009: 313). The procedure is strongly related to qualitative content analysis and grounded theory approaches through the formation of categories (questions asked of the text) and coding of text units (selection of relevant content) (ibid.). "To understand the method, it is useful to keep in mind that categories are basically the questions used to collect the relevant data" (ibid.). In addition to a flexibly understood reference to application, the approach also makes it possible to deal effectively with larger amounts of data.

From a theoretical point of view, the planned typification is based in particular on considerations by Kelle and Kluge (1999), Kluge (1999) and Kuckartz (2010a, 2010b) (also based on de Haan 2001; Fleiß 2011; Przyborski and Wohlrab-Sahr 2014). Kelle and Kluge (1999: 82) describe a sequence of four steps, which is taken up here.

First Step: Developing Comparative Dimensions and Characteristics

First, relevant comparative dimensions are developed on the basis of the available data material (Yankov 2010: 19). According to Kelle and Kluge, this involves "identifying those characteristics or comparative dimensions that are to form the basis for the subsequent typology" (Kelle and Kluge 1999: 83). The aim should be "to find such categories or to dimensionalize categories in such a way that the cases assigned to a particular combination of characteristics are as similar as possible to each other, but there should be maximum differences between the individual groups or combinations of characteristics" (ibid.). In summary, the rule here is that "the typology should be maximally 'internally' homogeneous at the level of the types, but maximally 'externally' heterogeneous at the level of the typology" (ibid.). In this case, this is done in a first step by a rough characterization of the case studies and further comparative cases with the most important key figures on general data and participatory arrangements. For the analysis of the expert interviews, first (a priori) categories are formed by structuring and assigning text statements (coding) (ibid.: 20). Here, categories are generated from the analysis of the characteristic data of the energy initiatives as well as from the research questions and knowledge interests.

Second Step: Grouping Cases and Analysis

A second stage describes the grouping of the cases and analysis of empirical regularities: "For this purpose, the cases are grouped on the basis of the defined comparative dimensions and their characteristics, and the groups determined are examined with regard to empirical regularities. The grouping of cases on the basis of combinations of characteristics, i.e., the combination of different categories (characteristics) and their subcategories (characteristic values), represents the actual transition from dimensionalization to type formation" (ibid.: 86). With the help of the comparison dimension (based on the research question) and the formulation and identification of characteristics, a comparison dimension (based on the data analysis) can be created, which corresponds to a certain type with the "typical" characteristics existing there (ibid.: 89). After carrying out the classification, it is recommended to "return" to the text material in order to follow interpretative evaluation steps (ibid.: 90).

Third Step: Creation of Types and Cluster of Cases

In a third stage, an analysis of the contextual meaning and the actual type formation or characterization of the types is carried out. On the one hand, this is based on the search for contextual connections between the categories or characteristics (ibid.: 91 f.). In the analysis of content-related connections of meaning, the conditions and causes that led to the coincidence of certain characteristics must be determined (Yankov 2010: 29). "On the basis of the qualitative data material, this step therefore examines what caused or facilitated this coincidence in the more or less numerous cases of a group. The researcher returns to the interviews and first examines each case, and then compares the cases to identify the various conditions and causes" (ibid.: 29). This step has not been systematized much so far (see ibid.), Kelle and Kluge (1999: 82) recommend here the theoretical sampling of grounded theory (as one possibility besides case contrasting based on counter-examples as well as the construction of qualitative sampling plans, see Kelle and Kluge 1999: 40).[6] Furthermore, comparisons and contrasts of the cases within the groups of characteristics must be carried out in this phase, which may then produce a different picture (Yankov 2010: 29).

Successive Creation of Types: Theoretical Sampling

The step for the construction of an initial typology is now of particular interest: the foundations for this can "already be laid by a criterion-guided case selection", in that the "cases studied are systematically selected on the basis of characteristics that are significant for the research question" (Kelle and Kluge 1999: 83). The various forms of criteria-guided case selection can then already be used for type formation. There are different possibilities here: On the one hand, "the categories and features that form the basis for the construction of a feature space (...) can be developed successively in the process" (ibid.), as in the procedure of "searching for counterexamples" or "theoretical sampling" according to Glaser and Strauss.

Theoretical Sampling in Grounded Theory Research

Theoretical sampling of grounded theory, in contrast to the method of counter examples, is particularly helpful when no preliminary hypotheses can be made because there is no knowledge about the cases and data and from the literature. In this case, therefore, analysis of the data material and case selection take place synchronously (Kelle and Kluge 1999: 44). The first cases are selected "on the basis of a general sociological perspective and certain local concepts of the problem field under investigation" (ibid.: 44 f.). These initially developed theoretical categories then justify the case selection and can also be changed in the further course, as they were developed from the material itself.

Finally, cases are compared that "have one or more categories of interest in common" and show either relevant differences or great similarities. In the course of the process – searching for new findings and examples, modifying and reformulating the hypotheses – differences are then either minimized or maximized through this targeted procedure (see ibid.). This process is continued until no more relevant

[6] See Fleiß (2011) on the use of grounded theory in connection with the typological method.

similarities or differences can be found in the data material (theoretical saturation) (see ibid.: 46).

In the present study, the first part of the "theoretical sampling" approach is used in particular. In order to formulate initial theses, questions and assumptions, a rough initial review and superficial analysis of the data material is necessary. This is necessary because research findings on the chosen topic and specific research question are lacking (research gap), and it also seems sensible to coordinate assumptions and case selection from the outset. Relevant criteria are initially determined by systematic framework data of the cases (e.g., size, investment volume, level of participation, etc.). This mutual, synchronous influence of research process and research design seems to make sense in the first phase of the study in order to incorporate as many initial findings as possible into the formulation of assumptions and category formation. However, after completion of the phase this process should end in order to carry out a comparison with the results of the subsequently taking place extensive content analysis of the qualitative data.

The Use of Grounded Theory Methods

Grounded theory is basically a method for discovering theories on the basis of empirical data evaluation, with the aim of enabling an object-based, material-supported generation of theory (Krumm 2009: 317 f.; Mey and Mruck 2011; Strübing 2014a).

Fundamentally, the inventors of grounded theory, Barney Glaser and Anselm Strauss, assume that a theory "proves itself to the extent that it has been developed inductively" (Glaser and Strauss 2010: 23). In addition, they also consider other criteria, which are not directly related to the methodology, to be very important, such as "logical consistency, clarity, parsimony, density, scope, integration, as well as suitability and manageability" (ibid.). Therefore, for the authors, the adequacy of a theory is inextricably linked to the process by which it is generated (ibid.). The crucial point, then, is processuality in order to generate a theory or typology.

Crucial to grounded theory is the fact that no linear procedure is recommended in the research process, but rather a "simultaneity of collection and evaluation of data, with the respective evaluation guiding the next collection step (theoretical sampling) until saturation is reached and new material no longer brings any new information to the case" (Krumm 2009: 318).

Initially, therefore, to collect data, theoretical sampling is envisaged in that the first survey is derived directly from the research interest in a subject matter, the further survey steps are then decided on a case-by-case basis (ibid.).

In a first step, the so-called open coding is applied, whereby one subdivides the text into individual parts and highlights similarities and differences therein (ibid.: 319). "The individual parts of the text are named by generaliszable concepts, which in turn are linked to provisional categories with characteristic properties and their arrangement on a continuum (dimensioning)" (ibid.). Within this stage, initial findings can also still be incorporated into the formulation of hypotheses (ibid.). By exploring the characteristic properties, groups and subgroups or clusters are formed, which are immediately compared with each other (comparative analysis) (ibid.).

Open coding is to serve as an approach to qualitative evaluation in the present study. An important aspect to note here is that concepts and categories are derived from the data material itself and – in the spirit of deduction – this forms the starting point for creating the categories. "Similarities and convergences with the literature can still be identified later, after the analytical core of categories has emerged" (Glaser and Strauss 2010: 55). This allows for the inclusion of information that only comes to the researcher's awareness from the data. With regard to the hitherto scarcely studied topic field, this is of great importance for the research approach to the analysis of member activities and participatory strategies and action approaches of community energy initiatives.

Finally, grounded theory distinguishes between material and formal theory in the educational process: in this case, formal-theoretical considerations are developed on a "conceptual or formal area of social research" (Krumm 2009: 320) (socio-political engagement and citizen participation), since, for example, it is not about a specific political subject area, which is the focus of formal theories.

In the analysis of the data material, content-related correlations are then substantiated or refuted by concrete text passages, for example by finding cases that deviate from the typology, which may indicate new, previously unknown factors (Kelle and Kluge 1999: 278). Finally, for a new analyzed type, sufficient "conditions and causes for the coincidence of the characteristics in many cases must be found" (Yankov 2010: 30).

Coding Qualitative Data: Combining Three Coding Procedures

In addition to defining characteristics via theoretical sampling, three other approaches can also be used. First, "if the investigators have knowledge or working hypotheses about relevant structural influencing factors in the field under investigation, characteristics can be determined a priori and incorporated into the construction of a qualitative sampling plan" (Kelle and Kluge 1999: 83). By means of a specially designed sampling plan, which contains the scope as well as the selection criteria, it is to be guaranteed that "carriers of certain theoretically relevant combinations of characteristics are represented in the qualitative sample" (ibid.: 83 f.). A second possibility is the development of an interview guide in order to "determine those central comparative dimensions that lead to the formation of typologies" (ibid.). Finally, the third possibility is a classical coding of the data material using a category scheme combined with a dimensionalization of this category scheme in order to determine comparative dimensions (see ibid.). The categories are often supposed to be the starting point for a dimensionalization: "They can be abstract sociological concepts with little empirical content (…) or everyday concepts (…). The subcategories for these categories can be explicated on the basis of prior conceptual knowledge and thus formulated before the data analysis (…) or elaborated through a comparative analysis of the text passages belonging to the categories (…)" (ibid.). The subcategories, in turn, can be used to code the data material one more time (see ibid.).

In the present study, in addition to the approach of theoretical sampling for type generation, interview guidelines are used within the framework of the expert interviews as well as the coding procedures of qualitative content analysis – extended by the open approach of grounded theory.

Fourth Step: Arrangement in Groups of Cases

In a next step, the cases are grouped according to their characteristics (Yankov 2010: 24). This is done here, for example, by clustering the case studies as well as the survey cases. Clustering has the particular advantage that a large number of variables are grouped into "blocks" (see Voß and Studierende 2010: 43). In the process, those variables are pushed into the background which "cannot make a significant contribution to the intended typifying classification" (ibid.). Finally, essential statements and characteristics of a cluster are presented, which were mentioned or found more frequently than average (ibid.: 48). After this first classification, the step in which "a detailed descriptive characterization of the typological classification found is carried out with recourse to the transcribed interviews, i.e., with recourse to the statements of the interviewees" (ibid.: 52 f.) remains important.

In Kelle and Kluge's fourth stage, a characterization of the types formed is undertaken. In this regard, Kelle and Kluge (1999: 94) note: "Since the cases of a type will not be alike in all characteristics, but only similar, the problem arises as to how the 'common' of the types can be aptly characterized. In research practice, so-called 'prototypes', i.e., real cases that best 'represent' the characteristics of each type, are often selected (…). In this way, individual characteristics of individual cases can be distinguished from the 'ideal type'" (ibid.: 95). For the effectiveness in the concrete procedure of data analysis, Kelle and Kluge recommend in the case of expert interviews the isolation of individual thematic aspects in order to be able to analyze them specifically (ibid.: 97).

Udo Kuckartz also links the formation of prototypes with the construction of "ideal-typical constructs" or a "representative case interpretation" (Kuckartz 1988:

221 f.; Kelle and Kluge 1999: 95). For this purpose, ideal cases of individual clusters are determined, which can then be considered "classic" for a cluster (ibid.). However, if a type should be very heterogeneous, the determination of a classic case would be problematic, so in this case an ideal-type construct composed of several prototypical cases should be created (Kuckartz 1988: 224). An "ideal case" is constructed from cases with as many typical characteristics as possible (ibid.). For this purpose, qualitative text material must also be intensively consulted (Kelle and Kluge 1999: 95).

A particularly problematic aspect of this method is the fact that the contrasts and "exaggerations" ultimately create differences between the cases which are possibly larger or perceived as being distorted compared to reality and precisely that ideal type cannot be found in reality at all (ibid.: 96).

Construction of Different Types of Cases Using Computer Assistance: The Quantification of Qualitative Survey Data

Udo Kuckartz bases his typological analysis in particular on a computer-assisted evaluation of verbal data (e.g., through programs such as MaxQDA or Atlas ti) (see Kuckartz 1990, 2010a; Spennemann and Stempka 2010: 35 ff.).

Here, type formation takes place in four steps: definition of a feature space, construction of the typology, description of the individual types and assignment of the interviewees to the types formed (Spennemann and Stempka 2010: 39).

In type-based case analysis, a text interpretation is carried out with the aim of assigning it to the typologies that have already been formed. Only with this step are the "empty" types "filled with life" through a recourse to the subjective meaning established in the individual case (Spennemann and Stempka 2010: 40; Kuckartz 2010a: 100, 106). Here, Kuckartz refers to Max Weber's approach of ideal types (concept of "understanding sociology") with regard to social regularities (see also Kelle and Kluge 1999).

Kuckartz also assumes that not "all cases can be presented in full detail" (Spennemann and Stempka 2010: 40), so either a representative case interpretation or the construction of a model case should take place (Kuckartz 2010a: 106 f.). While the model case results from a compilation of text segments that together form an "ideal case", in the case of representative case interpretation a prototype is identified that represents a particularly suitable case and represents the center in a cluster to which all cases come very close (see Spennemann and Stempka 2010: 41).

In this way, Kuckartz's approach differs from other type-forming procedures to a greater extent than it might at first appear: "In contrast, Kuckartz pursues a completely different strategy in his procedure of 'typological analysis' with the coding of the data material. Thus, by means of a dimensional analysis of the coded text passages, he also arrives at subdimensions; but in the next step he uses these subcategories to define variables with the help of which the persons under investigation are to be compared and finally typical constellations of characteristics are to be found with the help of computer-aided procedures." In this way of "'quantifying' verbal data, i.e., the formation of variables" a considerable data reduction is also to be achieved (Kelle and Kluge 1999: 85). However, it is pointed out that this procedure runs the risk of entailing "considerable losses of information" (ibid.: 86). "In addition, there is the danger that characteristics are excluded (only because of missing values), although they play a significant role for the analysis of the data as well as the type formation" (ibid.).

Within the framework of the evaluation of the online survey used here, quantification with the help of qualitative data evaluation software is necessary due to the amount of qualitative data obtained. In addition, classical coding procedures in the sense of qualitative content analysis, combined with the open, comparative approach of grounded theory, are used in selected fields of the survey. Both evaluation methods in combination seem to offer a favourable complement.

Discussion

Kuckartz's method represents a suitable framework for typologization in the present study, particularly with regard to the use of clustering. However, the question arises as to whether the computer-assisted evaluation makes sense, since Kelle and Kluge (1999: 212 f.) also note that due to the qualitative analysis that ultimately takes place, the results of the electronic evaluation do not have sufficient significance. In this case, both a pure electronic evaluation and the possibly problematic construction of a model case are dispensable. The summary to a model case is considered as extremely problematic, since important and partly outstanding differences between individual cases would have to be omitted. However, it is precisely these differences that are to be discussed in the comparative analysis of the case studies and clusters. The relevant different characteristics can relate both to the clusters among themselves and within the clusters. It is true that homogeneity within the clusters is to be aimed for, but homogeneity, which is guaranteed in the present study by certain fixed characteristics (here, for example, the form of energy and size of the community energy initiatives), also leaves heterogeneous characteristics, which are to be worked out precisely through the comparison. Only at first glance are certain cases outwardly similar to each other through the same, especially descriptive and quantitative data, which is to be further substantiated through a more in-depth, qualitative and exploratory analysis and thus then rather confirmed or refuted.

In contrast to Kuckartz's method, the stage model of empirically based typification according to Kelle and Kluge has "a much greater openness and flexibility" (Kelle and Kluge 1999: 8). In contrast to Kuckartz's method, which is strongly influenced by electronic procedures, the model is open to different evaluation methods and techniques and therefore "accommodates the diversity of qualitative questions and the varying quality of the data material very well" (ibid.). Here, it can be decided openly from case to case (or cluster) which methodological approach is suitable: "Depending on the research question and the type of data material, it makes more sense, for example, to leave the case context as far as possible when working out comparative dimensions (…) or rather to 'isolate' individual thematic aspects in order to be able to analyze them specifically (e.g., in the case of expert interviews)" (ibid.: 8 f.). The four evaluation stages also guarantee "that the central sub-goals of the type formation process are realized (elaboration of relevant comparative dimensions, grouping of cases and analysis of empirical regularities, analysis of content-related contexts of meaning and type formation, characterization of types)" (see ibid.: 9).

Kelle and Kluge further emphasize that "due to the openness of the stage model" it is possible to "compare different procedures with each other" as well as to enable a connection of the different evaluation techniques and thus to "overcome the separation between the different approaches" (ibid.). In the context of the analysis of content-related contexts of meaning, procedures of coding according to grounded theory are combined with approaches of content analysis in this case. What both approaches have in common, however, is that a systematic uncovering of connections between categories via a search for meaning in terms of content is unavoidable (see Kelle and Kluge 1999: 98 ff.). This common core again places the researcher at the center.

5.5 Conclusion

In the present study, the empirical analysis primarily serves the goal of uncovering characteristics with a subsequent typologization of individual modes of action, motivations and effects of the heterogeneous participation processes studied in the community energy associations and related contexts.

In particular, the stage model of Kelle and Kluge (1999) will be used and four typology-generating procedures will be applied under the conditions of the interweaving of quantitative and qualitative data of the chosen mixed methods approach.

- **Step 1 (Creation of comparative dimensions)**: Preparation of initial variables or dimensions of typologies of clusters through a combination of theoretical aspects and initial, quantitative and descriptive data of the case studies (following the theoretical sampling of grounded theory).
- **Step 2 (Arrangement in groups of cases)**: Elaboration of clusters of community energy types and initial assignment of case studies and survey cases based on congruent quantitative-descriptive data (regularities).
- **Step 3a (Analysis of contextual meaning of individual cases)**: Type-based comparative case analysis through qualitative evaluation of expert interviews and document analysis using a combination of the procedures according to Kelle and Kluge (1999), the coding procedures of grounded theory (Krumm 2009; Glaser and Strauss 2010; Mey and Mruck 2011; Strübing 2014b) and computer-aided analysis according to Kuckartz (1988, 2001, 2010a, 2010b, 2014a).
- **Step 3b (Analysis of quantitative survey data and contextual meaning of qualitative survey data)**: Cluster analysis using a larger sample of survey data for further grounding, validation and detailed specification of previously generated features of the types (underpinning and matching).
- **Step 4 (Defining and configurating the types found in the analysis)**: Determination of relevant comparative dimensions and other salient features based on interview and survey data, comprehensive presentation of the contextual meaning of the case studies, as well as recording of the typical characteristics found in the analysis (prototypes, ideal types, extreme types, etc.).

In summary, the combined approach presented here offers several advantages for the empirical analysis of the present work. On the one hand, a flexible application of the chosen methods in the sense of an object and process orientation can take place. On the other hand, the formation of categories is also possible during the evaluation of the material, which guarantees a flexible way of reacting to new findings. With the help of open coding and a permanent comparison of individual passages, an appropriate handling of the material is made possible, in which new adjustments can be made without additional effort. Finally, the combination of deductive and inductive approaches offers integration and comparison of existing research findings as well as case information. This combines modes of capturing epistemic practices and formalized information, which are essential for type formation.

To analyze and classify community energy participation it is necessary to combine and match formal information about community energy governance structures (through document analysis of local energy policy programs, community energy corporate governance frameworks and the participatory observation of meetings), detailed information from exploratory interviews with initiators of community energy projects, as well as the findings from survey data (see Hartmann and Lengerer 2014; Helfferich 2014; Küsters 2014; Meyermann et al. 2014; Salheiser 2014; Thierbach and Petschick 2014).

6 Empirical Analysis of Community Energy Projects in Germany

6.1 Framework of the Empirical Analysis

6.1.1 Selection of Case Studies

In the following, various case studies are analyzed on the basis of qualitative interview data, which represents different local community energy projects or citizens' community energy initiatives for community energy.

A total of eight projects from different regions of Germany were included. In accordance with the objective and methodological orientation of the work, the projects were selected according to various criteria in order to ensure the greatest possible coverage of different local and specific constellations. In the further course, according to the developed research question and the methodological conception, the energy projects are examined with regard to different groups of criteria (e.g. participatory arrangements and political framework conditions), which contain further individual categories. In the following, six selection criteria related to the case selection are presented in advance. The criteria capture the structure and context of the projects and break down essential categories, which are decisive for the subsequent analysis, classification and typification.

Renewable Energy Source

Five projects were selected that operate solar energy plants. In addition, two wind farms and one geothermal project were added. This covers three major renewable energy sources; two major remaining forms of energy (hydropower and biomass) are often not implemented as equity projects in the first case, and in the second case such plants are operated by farmers in particular.

J. Radtke, *Community Energy in Germany*,
https://doi.org/10.1007/978-3-658-39320-5_6

Legal Form of Community Energy Projects

The projects include six community energy cooperatives, one community energy limited liability company (GmbH) and one hybrid form that is still in the planning stage. Cooperatives are a predominant legal form in community solar projects; in addition, a community energy private company (civil law partnership: GbR) form is also widespread, although this is more likely to be used for individual plants. In one selected project (case study 3), an energy plant is operated in GbR form. In the case of wind power plants, on the other hand, the organizational form of a GmbH is found in many cases. However, in order to contrast the typical organizational form of community wind farms in Germany (limited liability company and partnership, GmbH & Co KG) with another model, a wind farm in the legal form of a cooperative was added. In the case of the geothermal project, a combination of a GmbH, the municipality, and a cooperative is planned. This differentiates this model from the other legal form structures. Finally, in one case (case study 5), the energy plants are operated as a project-oriented spin-off by an environmental association; the participation here takes place in the legal sense through a loan agreement.

Overall, this covers a wide range of legal forms of community energy projects in the renewable energy sector. In Germany, there are also profit participation rights, often used by larger companies and associations, which are reminiscent of the loan model in their indirect form of participation, as well as a case of a stock corporation.

Location of Community Energy Projects

Of the selected projects, three are located in Bremen, one in Lower Saxony, two in North Rhine-Westphalia and one each in Bavaria and Baden-Württemberg.

Due to the feedback of the projects with the local context and the interconnectedness with local political and civil society actors, it is advantageous in an investigation if these conditions are related to a location in order to keep these variables constant. This is possible in the case of the three energy projects in Bremen, which are located within a small federal state and urban area.

This option was not available for the other projects. However, this also has the advantage of allowing other contexts to be included in the analysis. In the case of the two wind power examples and the geothermal project, there is a strong local embedding and interconnectedness, which can be represented accordingly. The supra-regional energy cooperative has fewer such connections due to its overarching approach.

Finally, there is also comparability between a rural and urban area: While three case studies are located in a large city, four are located in a rural area; the supra-regional energy cooperative is not limited to a specific location due to an overarching approach.

Overall, this structuring makes it possible to represent a diversity of structures – while at the same time keeping the number of different contexts manageable.

Structural Approach and Context of Community Energy Projects

The selected projects are embedded in different local contexts, have different trajectories and have emerged from different motivations and, in some cases, specific action program. In this area, too, the aim is to present as heterogeneous a range of variants as possible, while at the same time ensuring comparability and manageability.

Four projects (case studies 2, 3, 6, and 7) are very strongly linked to civil society action program and initiatives that were either precursors of the energy projects (in case study 2 a community initiative, in case study 6 the Local Agenda 21) or are both precursors and running concurrently (community initiative "pro Geothermie" and active group "Energiewende" in case study 7, the "SaHNE" association in case study 3).

Such a link to associations or groups in the sense of an initiating force also exists to a certain extent in case studies 4 and 5: In the first case this is the environmental committee of a university, in the second case a large environmental association (BUND) – in both cases the energy project is a concrete spin-off company. In case studies 1 and 8, on the other hand, there is no such "accompaniment" or initiation by a civil society group.

In summary, the present structuredness of the case studies has the advantages that, on the one hand, different initiating and accompanying civil society groups can be analyzed; on the other hand, comparability with projects without such embedding can be achieved and made the basis of further analysis. With regard to the two leading overarching research questions and clusters of projects in the form of conditions for success and participatory arrangements, direct conclusions can be drawn about the influences of these accompanying civil society processes.

Size of the Community Energy Projects

The energy projects differ from each other in terms of size. The size results from various factors such as the number of members, the investment volume of the energy plants and the range of the projects. In terms of investment volume, wind farms tend to be larger than solar plants, which is also the case in the wind farm examples. The planned geothermal project also has a large investment volume. However, the solar cooperatives in the other case studies are quite different from each other: While the solar project at the university is only related to this location, expansions are planned in case study 3. In case study 8, there is a large scope in the form of various energy projects in Germany, but each individual project is limited to only one or a few solar installations.

Overall, a wide range can be covered in this landscape of community energy projects as well; what is not covered, however, are larger energy companies, which is due to the fact that here, in most cases, participation takes place only in an indirect way and therefore such companies tend to have less participatory arrangements.[1]

Participation Type and Participation Options: Participatory Arrangements
Citizens and individuals can participate in the energy projects in different ways and to different extents. In principle, a distinction must be made in the projects as to whether participation is possible and practiced within the framework of the energy project itself, or in the upstream or parallel action program or associations (Local Agenda 21, associations).

In case study 1, the citizens involved are members of a limited liability company and partnership (KG), the project itself is managed by a limited liability company (GmbH). The other wind farm (case study 2) is owned by a cooperative, which was preceded by a community initiative. A similar situation applies to the planned geothermal project in case study 7, and the energy cooperatives in case studies 3 and 6. The case studies mentioned have a strong local connection, since the energy plants are built at the local site and there is a connection to local communities. Case study 4 is a special case in this respect, as this cooperative is only open to members of the university (in the sense of an employee cooperative).

In the case of the energy cooperative in case study 8 on the other hand, people from all over the country can participate; moreover, the cooperative has no local ties, there are no "accompanying" local communities.

Within this framework, the core of the study analyses which explicit participation opportunities are available to individuals: on the one hand, internally within the community energy project (in working groups, discussion forums, advisory

[1]This question is explored in more detail in the following chapter through an analysis of the survey results.

boards, etc.), and on the other hand, externally within accompanying sustainability groups (Local Agenda 21, association, club, etc.).

Another point of influence in technical projects is public participation in the planning of energy plants. This point is particularly relevant in the case of wind energy plants, as the local community has an interest in participating in the planning on the one hand, and on the other hand, public concerns are also affected in the form of the use of a public site. In the case of case study 1, there is such input from citizens to the municipality, which is presented here as part of the social factors in the external conditions for success.

Political Energy Policy Conditions for Community Energy

Political influences emanate from the national level in the form of federal energy policy and the central control instrument in the form of the Renewable Energy Sources Act (EEG), but are also set by control mechanisms of state policy and municipal policy decisions. With regard to the effects of the federal government's renewable energy policy, it is relevant to ask to what extent the energy projects are dependent on the feed-in tariffs to the extent that they would not be able to operate plants if the tariffs were lowered, for example. At the state level, the wind energy sector is particularly affected by the case studies, as state decrees have an impact here. However, the local level is at the core of the analysis, as this is where the main framework conditions for energy projects are defined and have an impact. In the case of wind energy, too, important decisions are made here in the form of designations of priority zones; in the area of solar energy, solar roof exchanges and solar cadastres provide opportunities for the allocation of suitable roof areas. The approvals of the plants also play a further role.

The impact of state government decrees is analyzed in more detail in case study 1, and the influence of authorities at the district level is also included in this case. In case studies 3 and 5, the energy policy of the state and the city of Bremen plays a significant role. The same applies to case studies 6 and 7. With regard to case study 4, the role of the university is of interest, whereas in case study 8 there are effects of several local framework conditions, which cannot be analyzed in more detail. In the second wind farm example, the influences of state ministries on the planning of energy plants are discussed.

The approach of several levels (multilevel) makes it possible to highlight various interactions between the levels and to identify essential influencing factors. However, due to the problem of complexity, it is advantageous on the one hand to highlight only individual essential modes of action and on the other hand the constellation that case studies 3, 4, and 5 are located in a federal state or a municipality which has a favorable effect. Overall, an adequate representation of different framework conditions can be achieved through the wealth of variants. Both possible different dependencies of the energy projects on the framework conditions and the consideration of the circumstance of different modes of action can be represented in this way.

Organizational Structure and Configuration of Actors

Community energy initiatives have individual architectures of their organizational structure. Thus, they can be based on different actor associations and cooperations and develop certain characteristics of their radius of action and their networking with the local context. Four different approaches could be identified in the case studies examined here:

- **Approach 1: Local coalition building** (community energy initiative in cooperation with a bank, local municipality and politics; found in case studies 6 and 7).
- **Approach 2: Civil society support structures** (clubs and associations as initiators and promoters of community energy projects; found in case studies 3 and 5).
- **Approach 3: Community energy project as a full-time managed company** (professional processing by full-time management, strongly interested in expansion, as well as citizen-oriented, flexible, transparent and open-minded organization, but less as a solitary project of a local community; found in case studies 1, 2 and 8).
- **Approach 4: Closed employee cooperative** (participation possibility is only directed at members of an organization, public institution, company etc., strong fixation on this delimited space; found in case study 4).

Context of Origin

In addition, the contexts of emergence of community energy initiatives can be summarized and categorized. The contexts of emergence refer to the activities of civil society associations (such as citizens' initiatives) that have led up to or preceded the founding of community energy projects, or the personal circumstances and characteristics of the initiators (see Gamel et al. 2016). Local networks and social structures also play a role here. In the case studies, the following characteristics of community energy initiatives could be identified[2]:

[2] As this categorization is oriented towards the cases under investigation, other types of community energy projects in Germany are missing, such as those initiated by Volksbanken (people's banks), ecological groupings, associations of an associative nature with other defining characteristics, which (often) have a connection to sustainable energy production (clubs, associations, etc.), e.g. a women's energy cooperative.

Type A: Grassroots project with a civil society background

Type A1: Citizens' initiative

(preliminary stage for the foundation of a community energy company)

- Case studies wind energy cooperative (2) (here community of interest pro wind energy) and citizens' community geothermal energy initiative (7) (here community of interest pro geothermal energy)

Type A2: Local Agenda 21

(preliminary stage for the foundation of a community energy company)

- Case studies rural energy cooperative (6) (here sub-group on energy topics of Local Agenda 21) and citizens' community geothermal energy initiative (7) (here active group on energy topics)

Type B: Spin-off project with associative-institutional background: civil society association or community (association, organization, private or public organization, nonprofit company, etc.).

Type B1: Environmental association

(Own project of the association)

- Case study environmental association community solar project (5).

Type B2: Workforce

(Completed own project of an institution)

- Case study employee cooperative (4) (here: university).

Type C: Individual initiative project: Isolated, independent background (idealistically motivated seniors or progressive young entrepreneurs – start-up project)

Type C1: Individual initiation: Idealistic motivation

(Founded by individual initiators)

- Case study community wind energy in North Rhine-Westphalia (1)

Type C2: Individual initiation: Start-up company

(Founded by individual initiators)

- Case study supra-regionally acting energy cooperative (8)

6.1.2 Comparison of Project Size and Participatory Arrangements

An initial comparison of the case studies on the basis of key figures reveals a number of differences, which relate in particular to the size of the community energy project (persons involved and investment volume) and the share of participations in the total investment sum:

- **Community wind case studies**: Due to the cost-intensive use of wind turbines, the two case studies 1 and 2 have high investment volumes in the millions (3.6 and 15.5 million euros), but have different levels of participation: while only 88 citizens are involved in case study 1, there are 362 citizens in the wind energy cooperative, who have also provided a high proportion of the total sum (80 percent) (compared to only 20 percent in the wind farm limited partnership).
- **Community solar cooperatives**: Apart from the very small cooperative in case study 3 with only 19 people involved, the cooperatives have membership numbers of around 100 to 150 people (between 90 and 140). The investment sums range between 200,000 and one million euros. Apart from one cooperative (case study 3 with only 19 participants), the numbers of persons involved are also in a similar range between 90 and 140 persons. However, it is not possible to draw any conclusions about the percentage shares from either figure: these vary between 30 and 100 percent. Presumably, the number in case study 3 is low because the cooperative has not succeeded in attracting additional members. However, an increasing size of the project (high investment amount) does not necessarily mean that the share of citizen participation has to be low: both the wind cooperative (case study 2) and case studies 4 and 8 have high shares. In the case of the "100 percent projects", however, a differentiation must be made: In case studies 5 and 8, the high shares are due to the fact that in one case the plants are completely financed by loans from citizens and in another case the solar modules are purchased individually by citizens. Only in case study 6 has full coverage been achieved in a conventional way (founding a cooperative and receiving contributions from members).
- **Citizens' community geothermal energy initiative**: The planned investment sum in case study 7 is exceptionally high at 40 million euros. Presumably, the amount of equity capital from citizen participation cannot be very high here – for this reason, the initiative is also trying to attract local and/or energy companies and other larger actors as financiers.

6.1.3 Regional Distribution of Community Energy Projects[3]

Case Study 1: Community Wind Farm
Name of the energy initiative: Rothaarwind GmbH/Bürgerwindpark Hilchenbach
Legal form: Limited liability company and partnership
Location: Hilchenbach, North Rhine-Westphalia

[3] Status of 2012/2013 data.

Citizens involved: 88
Investment sum: 15.5 million euros
Percentage of citizen participation: 20

Case Study 2: Community Wind Cooperative
Name of the energy initiative: Energiegenossenschaft Ingersheim und Umgebung eG
Legal form: Registered cooperative
Location: Ingersheim, Baden-Württemberg
Citizens involved: 362
Investment sum: 3.6 million euros
Percentage of citizen participation: 80

Case Study 3: Urban Community Solar Cooperative
Name of the energy initiative: Solar Popular eG
Legal form: Registered cooperative
Location: Bremen
Citizens involved: 19
Investment sum: 300,000 euros
Percentage of citizen participation: 30

Case Study 4: Employee Community Solar Cooperative
Name of the energy initiative: UniBremen Solar eG
Legal form: Registered cooperative
Location: Bremen
Citizens involved: 130
Investment sum: 700,000 euros
Percentage of citizen participation: 50

Case Study 5: Environmental Association Community Solar Project
Name of the energy initiative: Bund für Umwelt und Naturschutz Deutschland (B.U.N.D.) (Friends of the Earth Germany) BUND Bremen Bürgersolaranlagen
Legal form: Registered association (BUND), participation via loan
Location: Bremen
Citizens involved: 140
Investment sum: 271.000 Euro
Percentage of citizen participation: 100

Case Study 6: Rural Community Solar Cooperative
Name of the energy initiative: Bürgerenergie Syke eG
Legal form: Registered cooperative

Location: Syke, Lower Saxony
Citizens involved: 110
Investment sum: 210.000 Euro
Percentage of citizen participation: 100

Case Study 7: Citizens' Community Geothermal Energy Initiative
Name of the energy initiative: Geothermie Initiative Markt Schwaben
Legal form: Joint limited liability company connected with a registered cooperative (planned)
Location: Markt Schwaben, Bavaria
Citizens involved: -
Investment sum: approx. 40 million euros (estimated)
Percentage of citizen participation: -

Case Study 8: Supra-Regional Community Energy Cooperative
Name of the energy initiative: Energiegewinner eG
Legal form: Registered cooperative
Location: Cologne, North Rhine-Westphalia
Citizens involved: 90
Investment sum: 985,000 euros
Percentage of citizen participation: 100

6.1.4 Case Studies

In the following, an overview of the main chronological developments and characteristics of the case studies is presented. Each brief description is followed by central research questions, which will be analyzed in more detail with regard to the respective energy initiative and taken up later.

Community Wind Energy Projects (Case Studies 1 and 2)
The topic of wind power is relevant in a different dimension with regard to the questions of acceptance by the population, protest, media influence and symbolism than is the case with the energy carrier solar energy and related efforts of application. For this reason, examples of these special (participation) processes and characteristics (of wind energy) will be presented here, which are fed by the two wind farm examples: the focus is on the temporal acceptance process and the symbolism of the wind turbines in case study (1) (community wind farm "Bürgerwindpark Hilchenbach", North Rhine-Westphalia) as well as the wind energy cooperative Ingersheim (case study 2, Baden-Württemberg), where there was public resistance

to the wind turbine and great media attention. In both case studies, a focus of the analysis is on the political framework conditions at local and regional level as well as on the public participation procedures in the context of the wind turbine planning processes.

Case Study 1: Community Wind Farm, *Hilchenbach* (North Rhine-Westphalia)

In 2008, a community wind farm was put into operation in the Siegerland region (Siegen-Wittgenstein district, North Rhine-Westphalia) near the town of Hilchenbach (population 15,000). The five turbines were the tallest in North Rhine-Westphalia at the time of installation, with a height of 138 m (hub height) and 180 m (incl. Rotor blade). Due to their dimensions, they have a significant impact on the townscape, as they were installed on a hilltop (at a height of 600 m) for reasons of efficiency. The total output of the park (five wind turbines spread over 30 hectares) is ten megawatts. Around 20 million kWh of electricity are produced annually – more than the inhabitants of neighboring Hilchenbach consume. In this way, about 21,000 tons of CO_2 are avoided each year. In addition to the environmental benefits, the wind farm also brings economic advantages for the region: profits benefit the co-owners due to the community wind farm concept. The operating company has also deliberately moved its headquarters to the municipality where it is located, so that the town of Hilchenbach also benefits from any trade taxes incurred. In addition, the wind farm creates jobs through the production and installation of the five wind turbines. 88 persons participated in the wind farm within the framework of citizen participation (of which one "person" is the municipality itself), which represents a percentage share of 20 percent of the investment sum (15 million Euros).

Case Study 2: Community Wind Energy Cooperative, Ingersheim (Baden-Württemberg)

In the small municipality of Ingersheim (6000 inhabitants) in Baden-Württemberg, a community initiative (Windkraftinitiative WKI) had been active since around 2001, and had already made efforts to realize a wind turbine in the 2000s. In 2004, a first building application was submitted, but the project failed the following year. A second attempt was made in 2009, which finally led to successful approvals, the founding of a cooperative, the construction of the wind turbine in 2011, and the commissioning in 2012.

The wind turbine generated investment costs of 3.6 million euros, which were raised by the energy cooperative with a very high equity ratio of 80 percent, which has 365 members. Seventy-five percent of the members come from the community of Ingersheim and the surrounding area.

Initially, as with most initialization processes for wind turbines, the aim was to measure the wind conditions and have the municipality designate a wind priority zone. After the designation of the priority zone, the second attempt could finally be undertaken due to increased planning security. The installed wind turbine is of the same type as in case study 1 with a hub height of 138 meters. In contrast to case study 1, however, there is a greater proximity to residential development in the form of two agricultural farms, which are located at a distance of a few hundred meters. Due to the small distances, expert opinions on noise emissions and shadow impact of the plant were therefore prepared in this case. The expert opinions came to the conclusion that there is no significant interference with regard to noise emissions; one agricultural farm is affected by the shadow for 19 hours in a year, and the plant is to be stopped during this period.

Case Study 3: Urban Community Solar Cooperative, Solar Popular (Bremen)

In the case of the solar cooperative in case study 3 (state of Bremen), the focus is on discussion and participation processes within the cooperative. In addition, there is the specific feature of a solidary distribution of a part of the profit for social projects.

The solar popular cooperative is a solar energy cooperative that was founded in Bremen in 2011. The cooperative emerged from the project "Soft High Technologies in Food and Energy Production" ("Sanfte Hochtechnologien in der Nahrungsmittel- und Energieproduktion") (SaHNE), which discusses issues related to food and energy production at the Center for Solidarity Economy in Bremen. The cooperative counted 19 members at the beginning of 2012, the investment volume is planned for the year 2012 in the amount of 350,000 euros. The members' shares in the investment sum would then amount to 30 percent. In 2009, the first community solar plant was designed and put into operation at an agricultural business, which is run in the legal form of a civil law partnership (GbR). At that time, the investment sum of 100,000 euros required for the installation was acquired within five weeks.

After another project finally failed in 2011 following lengthy preparation and planning periods, the cooperative succeeded in erecting the first three systems in 2012 in Bremen Hemelingen on the roof of a recycling company. The use of a roof of a primary school is also in preparation. The cooperative is planning further activities and an expansion in investments and plants by searching for more roofs and recruiting new cooperative members.

Within the framework of the cooperative – which, in contrast to a civil law partnership (GbR), can operate several energy plants – it is planned to lease roof areas in Bremen and the surrounding area in order to install solar plants on them. The roofs can come from private as well as public sources, a possible access to this can be made by the solar roof exchange NordWest operated by the city of Bremen and personal contacts. In addition to deposits from members of the cooperative, loans are used to a large extent. From the annual surplus, a dividend is paid out to the members – as is also customary with other energy cooperatives.

A special feature of this cooperative is the promotion of social and ecological projects ("solidarity transfer"), which are supported annually in the amount of 20 percent of the annual surplus. One third of this donation goes to the Center for Solidarity Economy in Bremen. The remaining share flows to collectively determined projects in that the cooperative's board of directors proposes four additional projects each year with the invitation to the general meeting, whereupon the members select two of these proposals. The initiators justify this by saying that they do not want to stop at generating clean electricity, but also want to provide some form of support. For example, a solar installation on a newly built school library in Cameroon was financed by the contribution from the first solar project. In this way, a contribution is to be made to the use of modern and sustainable technologies in a structurally weak region of the world.

In this case study, an attempt is thus made to make a contribution to social or ecological projects that goes beyond this through the so-called solidarity transfer. In this way, an attempt is made to achieve a community benefit in addition to an individual benefit. In addition to participation in the annual general meeting, members' involvement in the cooperative and the association beyond this is expressly desired and encouraged accordingly.

Case Study 4: Employee Community Solar Cooperative, UniBremenSolar (Bremen)

In case study 4, members of a university (state of Bremen) founded an employee cooperative and formed working groups from the ranks of the members during the founding process, which worked on various issues.

The preparations for the founding of the UniBremenSolar cooperative in 2011 were a project of the University of Bremen's environmental management, with the university's Center for Environmental Research and Sustainable Technologies being the starting point for the commitment. In this area as well as in the environmental committee of the university, the idea was developed to found a cooperative organized and financed by and for employees and students, which would use the roofs of the University of Bremen for the operation of solar plants. Within three months a growing team, which formed working groups and consisted of employees from different departments of the university, worked on the preparations for the foundation of the cooperative. The goal was to complete the plants by the end of 2011 and feed the electricity into the grid. One justification for this approach is the feed-in tariff based on the Renewable Energy Sources Act, which was set to fall at the turn of the year.

One motivation for founding the solar cooperative was to cover the university's electricity consumption, but this is not directly possible in practice due to the fact that only a general electricity grid exists. As part of an investigation process, the university's roofs were examined for their suitability. Seven particularly suitable roofs (owned by the university) were identified, of which three could eventually be used. The roofs were made available to the cooperative by the university at very low cost. The investment volume was one million euros, and the members of the cooperative were able to accumulate equity capital of approximately 350,000 euros.

The cooperative finally incorporated in the fall of 2011, and the working groups were increasingly able to cease their work and were essentially replaced by the cooperative's elected bodies in the form of the board of directors and supervisory board.

The model of this case study thus corresponds to a kind of staff cooperative, as membership is only open to members of the university (students and staff). Within the analysis, the discourses within the cooperative can be analyzed in more detail through minutes of the meetings. Another interesting object of analysis arises from the question of inclusion and exclusion, on the one hand with regard to the fact that the cooperative is not open to the entire population, but on the other hand also on an internal level with regard to the inclusion of committed members in the founding process.

Case Study 5: Environmental Association Community Solar Project, BUND (Bremen)

Participation in the community solar plants of the BUND environmental association (Bund für Umwelt und Naturschutz (BUND) (Friends of the Earth Germany) e. V., Landesverband Bremen) in case study 5 represents an example of passive participation without member involvement in the energy project. Of interest are the formed collaborations of the environmental association with civil society actors in order to be able to carry out energy projects.

In 2012, the regional association of BUND in Bremen, operated a total of six solar plants in the city and surrounding area of Bremen. This can cover the electricity consumption of 32 three-person households, which corresponds to an annual

CO_2 saving of over 80,000 kg compared to electricity generation from conventional energy sources. Of these six plants, three are citizen solar plants, in that citizens have participated financially in these plants. The first system was erected in 2006 on a machine hall of the Bremen Dike Association (Bremischen Deichverbandes) on the right bank of the Weser.

This first project was based on a "sun bet" between BUND Bremen and BUND Hannover. 85 people from Bremen and the surrounding area were involved in the installation. In addition, the project was financially supported by a local energy supplier.

In 2010, a second community solar plant was erected on the roof of a Protestant parish in the city center. The church congregation itself is involved with 22,000 euros, in addition to private individuals with a share of 60 percent and a further 20 percent through the local energy supplier. In this case, the parish was both the initiator of the system and the owner of the roof space; in addition, the parish extensively advertised for participation in the parish and in the district. At the end of 2011, a community solar plant could be realized, which is located on a barn roof of an agro-ecological BUND farm on the outskirts of the city. The photovoltaic plant fits well into the concept of the project Hof Bavendamm, because the solar plant is only one part of a project in which ecological agriculture, nature conservation and environmental education are pursued. The solar system is integrated into further regenerative energy use concepts in the form of a wood pellet heating system with solar-assisted water heating and a rainwater harvesting system.

In this case, in addition to a 20 percent subsidy from the local energy supplier, the solar plant could be financed exclusively through citizen participation, which indicates greater interest and resonance among the population. In the case of BUND Bremen, however, citizens do not participate in the legal form of a cooperative or civil law partnership, but through loans, by concluding a corresponding loan agreement with BUND Bremen.

In contrast to the legal form of a limited liability company and partnership (GmbH & Co KG) and the cooperative model, this case study shows another way in which an association can become active and enable participation without the special establishment of a corporate form. The subject of analysis here is in particular the conditions for success in connection with the specific actor connections, which are to be presented and analyzed in more detail for the second solar plant in connection with the church congregation.

In addition, due to the bundling of different case studies in the federal state and the municipality of Bremen, local energy policy is presented in more detail and examined in terms of influence and control (also related to the concrete case studies) through interview data and document analysis. Thus, a second dimension of political steering in the context of renewable energies is taken up. Finally, there is another dimension related to the planning area of wind energy. Linked to this is a third dimension regarding acceptance. In this context, the possibilities of citizens to influence, modify or prevent the construction of energy plants will be examined more closely (protest and influence possibilities in the planning process in the wind case studies).

Case Study 6: Rural Community Solar Cooperative, Syke (Lower Saxony)
The local solar cooperative in case study 6 (Lower Saxony) has a civic background, where the foundation of the energy cooperative was preceded by the work of a Local Agenda 21 group. This link between the Agenda group and the energy cooperative, as well as the participation of citizens in the Agenda work, are in the foreground in this case study.

The cooperative Bürgerenergie Syke emerged from the Local Agenda 21 group "Building, Living, Energy and Climate Protection" in Syke in the summer of 2008. Here the idea arose to build a solar plant collectively, which was then carried out through the founding of the cooperative in the same year with the participation of 90 citizens. The cooperative is therefore primarily an association of several citizens. It was founded in 2008, and the first project was realized in the same year in the form of a solar plant on the roof of a sports hall. A second solar plant would be put into operation in 2009 on the roof of a primary school, whereby the bank loan could be kept low due to high participation, which was the intention of the initiators. In 2011, a third system was to be installed on the roof of a municipal fire station, but the application for this was initially rejected by the municipality. At the same time, the city of Syke, together with two neighboring municipalities, founded a public energy company with the aim of setting up municipal utilities, which could establish itself as a municipal energy supplier after buying back the electricity grids. Due to this, a competitive situation may arise between the municipal energy company and the energy cooperative.

In the end, however, the municipality was able to provide the energy cooperative with a third roof in 2012. The energy cooperative itself has found a different strategy due to the situation in which it was temporarily no longer able to realize new projects with the municipality: It planned to cooperate with two other energy cooperatives in the vicinity in order to jointly realize a larger project in which greenhouses with solar panels are to be built. Since the investment volume here is much higher than for the pure installation of solar systems on public roofs, this project is only feasible for Bürgerenergie Syke through a cooperation with two other energy cooperatives. Due to the temporary barrier of the first way (equipping public roofs in the municipality with solar systems), a second idea was thus developed, which finally – independent of the first way – led on the one hand to a cooperative, and on the other hand opened up another field of activity.

According to the statutes, the object of the cooperative is "the construction and maintenance of plants for the production of regenerative energies, in particular solar plants, and the sale of the energy obtained in the form of electricity/heat". The vision of the members and thus the primary purpose of the cooperative is to promote the ecological commitment of the local citizens in order to be able to put further plants into operation. The cooperative is explicitly not limited to the operation of a plant, but is also intended to include citizen engagement. Of further interest in this case, is the development of civic engagement from a Local Agenda 21 group to the establishment of an energy cooperative. For this purpose, documents of the Agenda 21 group and interviews with the cooperative and representatives of the Agenda group can be evaluated.

Case Study 7: Citizens' Community Geothermal Energy Initiative, Markt Schwaben (Bavaria)

In case study 7, a citizens' group tries to initiate a geothermal project in a municipality in Bavaria. In doing so, it is supported by a civic, local active group (similar to an Agenda 21 working group). The approach of the citizens' group to initiate a very ambitious energy project as well as the cooperation with the active group are of particular interest here.

In the small municipality of Markt Schwaben (12,000 inhabitants) in Bavaria near Munich, initial considerations were made 15 years ago as to whether and how geothermal energy available there could be used. However, these initial efforts failed in 2002.

Then, in 2008, 13 citizens of the community founded the association "Interessengemeinschaft pro Geothermie Markt Schwaben e. V. ". Since then, the association has been weighing strategies and ideas to develop the geothermal resources and to develop business and financial models. The association sees itself as an information medium towards the citizens as well as a link between political decision makers, investors and consumers. In order to realize this idea, the association, in contrast to solar cooperatives, for example, has several problems that make implementation difficult: On the one hand, it involves a very high investment volume, which is estimated at about 40 million euros. Secondly, the use of geothermal energy can only make sense if it is used in the form of thermal energy. From this follows the construction of an own local heating network, which requires further planning. In neighboring municipalities, such a geothermal energy utilization with a local heating network has already been realized (e.g. by the public utility company). In Markt Schwaben, the construction of such a local heating network would lead to a competitive situation with the large energy company E.ON, which operates a heating network there. Therefore, the association has developed a strategy in which financial resources and competences are bundled through the association of several actors in the form of the municipality, local companies and citizens and through the foundation of different legal company forms. In this way, the plan could be realized in the future.

To implement their plan, the initiators have designed a so-called citizen model, which is to be built into a three-stage expansion of legal company structures. Basically, it is assumed that many citizens invest in wind power and solar plants and are therefore interested in participating in energy plants for ecological reasons, return expectations and tax reasons. Geothermal energy is seen as advantageous compared to wind and solar power, as it is permanently available and there is no problem with regard to storage.

The use of heat energy through geothermal energy should be done by replacing the current providers of the heating network, which would bring the advantage of being able to break away from the operating conventional companies and the associated dependence on the world energy market. The decisive factor for the use of geothermal energy is primarily the initial investment, as the operating costs are not high.

The basic idea of the citizens' model is that the customers of the local heating network should also become investors for the geothermal plant at the same time. In this way, the investment volume could be raised, and at the same time, customers of the heating network would exist. The initiators also point to added value for the community and a return for the investors. As in other community energy projects, the financial hurdle of the overall project is to be taken on by the financial help of participating citizens.

The planned legal company structure should take into account the interests of both, the future customers of the heating network, and the investors. For citizen participation, an energy cooperative is to be founded in which the customers of the heating network (if they also participate financially) are assembled and represented with their shares. In addition, there should be a supply company in which the cooperative holds a majority stake and therefore has a great deal of influence, also with regard to energy pricing. However, the entry into geothermal energy can only take place if an investment sum of approximately 32 million euros is available for a core network. This requires equity capital of around nine to ten million euros. Finally, the model is to be implemented in individual stages. In the first stage, a heating company is to be founded independently of the geothermal energy use in the form of a limited partnership. Here the municipality with its own existing capital of one million euros is to create a heat supply company, which will set up a heating network, into which geothermal energy can be integrated. So-called "heat islands" are also to be used for this purpose (buildings such as schools, municipal facilities, new buildings and renovation objects which already have a heat supply). This should generate income that will benefit the further development. In 2009, there was already a unanimous decision by the municipal council to implement a district heating network. If the necessary equity structure is achieved in this way, the company can be developed into a geothermal supply company or participate in the company.

In a second stage, an investment company is to be founded, also in KG form, in which interested citizens can already participate in the heat supply company. This financing company is intended to provide the necessary equity capital to be able to carry out the expansion of the heating network; ultimately, the financing is to flow into the use of geothermal energy.

The first two stages are independent of geothermal energy use: the companies would exist and the heating network could be used even if geothermal energy is not used. In a third stage, a community cooperative is to be founded, which, is to be linked to the use of geothermal energy. The participation possibility for the population is planned as exclusive monetary investment and is to fulfill a function similar to a savings investment. The cooperative itself should only participate in the utility company at a time when the financing and use of the geothermal energy has been secured. The community cooperative is then supposed to have a share of more than 50 percent in the equity of the utility.

The realization of geothermal energy requires a high level of investment, including equity capital, which is to be financed by public and private investors. On the one hand, there is to be a municipal participation by the municipality, which has already provided budget funds of one million euros. This amount is to flow into the network company of the first stage.

On the other hand, a limited partnership serves the financing, which results in a further participation possibility for citizens and tradesmen of the municipality. These persons can also become heating customers at the same time. The investment company also has a direct share in the heating company's profits. Since the investors' participation is commercial in nature, pro rata results of the investment company (initial losses and later profits) can be claimed for tax purposes.

Finally, citizens in particular, and thus large sections of the population with even small financial shares, can participate in (financing) the cooperative, whereby an equity capital volume of five million euros is required. Here, too, the subscribers can also be heat customers at the same time. The form of participation is laid out as a financial investment with appropriate net yield (about 3–5% are planned). The distributions of the cooperative represent income from capital assets for the investor, which are subject to the final withholding tax. Commercial investors can also participate in the cooperative model. However, their share in the equity capital is to be limited to a maximum of 25 percent, since the basic idea of the "citizen model" is to be maintained. Finally, this financing and investment model should also serve factors of security and flexibility. On the one hand, the municipality of Markt Schwaben stands behind the project without reservation, which is made clear by unanimous municipal council resolutions and its own financial participation. On the other hand, although cooperative shares can be subscribed to before the geothermal energy is put into operation, they are not due until its use is guaranteed.

The special feature of the geothermal initiative's phased model now is that adjustments can be made to the design and corporate structures depending on the specific course of development. An increase in the subscription volume can, for example, be used for equity increases or shareholder loans, allowing debt capital to be reduced more quickly.

In addition to this particular model of building up community energy participation companies, there is also a high level of civic engagement in this case study, which can be found on the one hand in the community of interest, and on the other hand in a so-called "Energiewende" active group. In addition, a Local Agenda 21 group also worked on energy issues some years ago. For an analysis, interviews with representatives of the community of interest and the active group can be evaluated. This should be of particular relevance with regard to the question of the extent to which cooperation between actors can be found and through which strategies and approaches the realization of a participation project can be achieved – even with high investment costs.

Case Study 8: Supra-Regional Community Solar Cooperative, Energiegewinner (North Rhine-Westphalia)

The eighth case study represents a rather unusual case, as this energy cooperative has a supra-regional orientation and has energy projects at various locations. The question here is how the energy cooperative forms cooperation with actors for the implementation of energy projects, as well as a closer look at the innovative participation approach.

The Energiegewinner cooperative was founded in 2010 by 10 young individuals in Cologne, as an energy cooperative. The cooperative sees itself as a democratic enterprise, as the members are supposed to be participants and decision-makers, which is possible by subscribing to a comparatively small business share of 50 euros. The concept is to operate solar plants together with municipalities, associations, civil society initiatives and common projects (as well as religious communities), and the workforces of companies, either jointly or by using roof surfaces. For this purpose, the cooperative has developed a special participation model, which differs from that of other solar cooperatives. By the end of 2011, the number of members had increased fivefold and 900 solar modules had been installed. So far, more than 500,000 euros have been invested, which refers exclusively to direct participation. A total of five solar plants have been built, three of which are located in Cologne, Hanover and Hesse. In addition, five further plants are planned in North Rhine-Westphalia, Lower Saxony and Saxony.

The cooperative participation model, which specifically takes into account the requirements of community solar projects, is characterized by the fact that the establishment of new legal forms for community solar projects is no longer necessary and direct participation in the solar plants themselves is possible (instead of, for example, closed-end funds). In this way, there is also no mixing of projects. As a result, a precisely-calculated disbursement of the yields can also take place according to the tariffs based on the Renewable Energy Sources Act, and there are no fluctuations. As in other energy cooperatives, there is also local cooperation with different actors. The joint cooperative form saves organizational effort, since a company does not have to be founded for each plant, and finally there is also networking and exchange of experience within the community of the cooperative and participating actors.

Participation in the Energiegewinner cooperative can take place in three different ways. On the one hand, it is possible to participate with a very small amount of only 50 euros, which corresponds to a cooperative share. A dividend of about 3 percent is paid out annually. On the other hand, it is possible to purchase one's own solar modules, whereby a solar module costs about 700 euros and the yields are then paid out annually in relation to this module. The third participation option is the pre-financing of projects, which is possible upon request.

Furthermore, it is possible that under the umbrella of the cooperative, every person can initiate his own project. If, for example, a company, a club or an association, but also an individual has an interest in installing solar systems, this can be done via the cooperative, which takes care of the process and construction, makes its participation options available and can thus integrate several projects under the common roof. This possibility is feasible due to the separation of the participation with regard to the solar modules. Since a direct participation takes place in this case, a module can be installed theoretically everywhere, which is entitled to the participant directly.

It becomes clear here that this cooperative differs in some respects from other energy cooperatives, since on the one hand it operates very flexibly in terms of location and on the other hand it offers a special participation model, which involves the direct participation of people in concrete energy plants.

6.1.5 Online Survey

In order to gain more insight into the social structure and inner workings of community energy projects,[4] a representative survey was conducted in 2012 and 2013 among 85 participating energy projects in Germany, which generated a total of 2826 responses (these also include the case studies examined in more detail in this study). In essence, the data collected will be used to further investigate the research gap regarding the characteristics of community energy projects in terms of the following dimensions:

- Social structure of the members
- Participation activity and use of participation and co-determination opportunities
- Identification and commitment with the project/company/initiative/association
- Learning effects, attitude changes and acceptance ratings
- Positive and negative feedback from members

The focus of the survey is on the participatory aspects with regard to the actual input of the members. The aim is to enable an assessment of the level of participation and activity of the communities.

The participation of members of the community energy projects in the survey can be estimated as high overall. It is not possible to give precise information on the percentage of participants per project. However, in various cases a percentage of at least 30 percent is met, and in some projects the rate is significantly higher. The numbers of participants within the projects of the case studies show a very high percentage overall. In the case of the largest participating community energy

[4] In the studies on civic engagement in Germany, the engagement field of community energy presumably falls into the thematic field of "environmental protection and nature conservation", which with a rate of 4.5% in 2004 (compared to 3.1% in 1999) (Alscher et al. 2009: 29) is an area of engagement that is not pronounced, but which seems to be gaining importance (other sources cite 2.8% for "environment and animal protection" in 2009 (1.8% in 1999 and 2.6% in 2004) (Statistisches JahrbuchBundesamt 2013: 203; Enste et al. 2012: 12). The environmental sector is strongly dominated by organizations (77%), initiatives account for 17% here, governmental/municipal activities are only 6% (Alscher et al. 2009: 31). The Volunteer Survey (Gensicke and Geiss 2010: 93) indicates 2.8% for nature and animal conservation (up from 1.8% since 1999), and 1.9% for local civic engagement (1.3% in 1999, but 2.1% in 2004) (data from 2009). Nature and animal conservation as well as local civic engagement have a high potential among people interested in engagement, a strong increase since 1999 was observed (for nature conservation from 9 to 17%, for local engagement from 1 to 7%) (ibid.: 136).

company (Green City Energy), a percentage of around 20 percent was achieved (out of 3000 investors participating in the company).

Structuring of the Questionnaire

The questionnaire captures different dimensions of the research project and key issues of community energy companies or projects by dividing them into broad thematic clusters and arranging different question groups within them. A total of five question groups were designed.

The first group of questions relates to personal information. This includes the following questions in detail:

- Form of participation (individually/ with family members/with other citizens)
- Gender
- Age
- Educational qualification (e.g. apprenticeship, high school diploma)
- Occupation
- Occupational status (e.g. worker or senior civil servant)
- Gross income
- Residential housing location (e.g. city center of a large town or small town)
- Residential housing area (e.g. single-family house or apartment block)
- Number of persons in the household
- Distance to the nearest energy facilities of the community energy project in which the participant is involved
- Perception of the energy facilities of the community energy project in which the participant is involved
- Medium through which the participant became aware of the participation opportunity

With the help of these socio-structural data, it should be possible to draw conclusions about the individual characteristics of the people involved in the community energy projects. In addition, the factor of distance to the energy plants in particular is taken into account.

The second group of questions covers dimensions of people's actual involvement in the projects. This includes the following information:

- Financial amount of the investment
- Motivation for participation (three questions: financial incentive, ecological interest, self-sufficiency "energy in the hands of citizens")

- Special reasons for participation (special knowledge of the energy plants, initiators and locations)
- Reason for commitment (two questions: connection to the workplace and similar (world) views within the community energy project)
- Necessary expert knowledge for participation (about renewable energies, cooperatives, etc.)
- Existing personal experience with community energy projects, cooperatives, etc.
- Own definition of a community energy project

Within this group of questions, in addition to questions concerning the actual amount of financial participation, inquiries were also made into motivations for participation as well as existing knowledge and required know-how. An individual description and definition of the community energy project, company, association or initiative were also sought.

The third group of questions relates to the respondent's participation within the community energy project in both a theoretical and a practical sense. This group includes questions about:

- Participation in general meetings
- The desire for discussion forums and co-determination on further topics
- The call to actively play a role in the project
- Input of members' ideas
- Dealing with opposing opinions and conflicts
- Assessment of the democratic potential of the project
- Acceptance of the statutes and evaluation of the contents of the statutes
- Scope of information on the project

This group of questions specifically touches on the core of the research approach. The answers can provide more detailed insights into whether participation takes place through deliberation, whether various opportunities for this exist, and whether the members would like to have further opportunities for discourse and co-determination. In this way, information on the subjective opinion-forming processes and assessments of the members can be obtained, which is only possible through direct questioning.

A fourth group of questions deals with topics that address the handling of and relationship to renewable energies as well as their acceptance:

- Sense of community within the energy project
- Local anchoring of energy project and return expectations of investors
- Interest in further participation in another community energy project
- Interest in participation in an unknown community energy project (e.g. fund)
- Identification with the community energy project
- Support of further renewable energy plants and expansion of the community energy project
- Support of the expansion of renewable energies in the neighborhood
- Change in attitude towards renewable energies since participation in the community energy project
- Assessment of the acceptance of the energy plants of the community energy project by the local population
- Aspects of the implementation of energy projects (involvement of the population, added regional value, etc.)

Through these questions, more detailed information can be collected on the attitude of the people involved in renewable energy projects in general, and the energy plants in which the respondent is directly involved. The questions on acceptance, in contrast to other questions, are based on the respondent's assessment of larger contexts (sentiment), i.e. the perceived acceptance in the population, which expresses a highly subjective view. Even if this information must be interpreted with particular caution, it is likely to reflect an overarching picture of opinion in the aggregate.

Finally, a last group of questions deals with evaluation questions regarding the energy project and the respondent's further civic engagement. These include the following questions:

- Positive feedback and criticism of the energy project
- Civic and political engagement and proactive participation
- Evaluation of the survey

The selected topics and the structuring should make it possible to record the most important criteria for assessing the structures of the people involved: Statements about the socio-structural background, the concrete participation in the energy project, possibilities of co-determination and factual use, the use and acceptance of renewable energies as well as an evaluation of the energy project. Here, different types of questions were combined: Besides factual information, there are evaluation questions and weighting questions. Some of these questions are problematic in their nature with regard to a suggestive effect and require a cautious and differentiated evaluation, which will be pointed out in detail in the context of the evaluation. A fundamental distinction is made between factual questions and evaluation, and assessment questions in the evaluation. This differentiation is taken into account accordingly in the presentation of the results. Individual questions differ from case to case, which is due to the individual characteristics of the different energy projects and a modification of the questionnaire in the initial phase of the survey. These specifics are also referred to in the course.

Conceptual Characteristics of the Survey

One main reproach and a basic problem with the participation mode of community energy projects, which relies on civic engagement and personal initiative[5] and includes monetary participation as an entry condition and at its core, is that community energy initiatives by no means include the entire local population ("clientele project"), and are primarily initiated by wealthy and thus mostly middle- and upper-class citizens from the point of view of returns, and these people thus represent the main group of members. This form of participation would thus suffer from a lack of population representativeness, a problem familiar to participatory contexts and community initiatives, in that financially weak and educationally disadvantaged population groups are not involved and do not participate.

Furthermore, it is still completely unclear within the research to what extent the activity and commitment of members goes beyond purely financial participation, i.e. silent and passive membership. In addition to the individual contribution of members, offers and requests of the associations themselves and wishes of the members are thematically relevant. Finally, this raises the question of whether feelings of belonging and sense of community (commitment to the association) arise in the case of actively engaged communities, and how the association itself is assessed, defined and criticized by its members, for example with regard to (internal) democratic aspects, dealing with conflicts and criticism or feedback, the degree to which it is informed, and approval of organizational regulations and structures.

Of further interest are the effects and spill-over effects of participation with regard to individual behavioral changes, perceptions and assessments of the acceptance of one's own energy system as well as an overall acceptance of renewable energies.

[5] According to their own definition, the committed in Germany describe their activities predominantly as voluntary work (42%, tendency decreasing), volunteering (35%, tendency increasing), less than initiative and project work (8%, tendency unchanged) or civic engagement (9%, tendency increasing) (Gensicke and Geiss 2010: 112).

Finally, additional qualitative information is taken into account in the form of statements on criticism or feedback, which on the one hand represent concerns of outstanding importance to the members and on the other hand can integrate aspects that were not captured in other items.

In order to obtain a differentiated and meaningful overall picture of information and data, both quantitative and qualitative information was made possible in the standardized questionnaire section. This procedure primarily takes into account the fact that so far there is little or no knowledge of community energy initiatives from other studies, which is why it is primarily a matter of generating exploratory knowledge; furthermore, the low level of initial knowledge is to be taken into account by keeping it flexibly expandable. These free text fields can either concern exclusively qualitative individual answers (open text fields) or represent additional information on quantitative questions in order to supplement them if necessary. In the following, on the one hand, the qualitative information is presented and quantified according to the number of mentions; for this purpose, characteristics were formed from the information and then coded.[6] On the other hand, in some selected cases, the qualitative data material is analyzed in more detail and presented comprehensively within the framework of a content analysis.

For the evaluation and subsequent implementation of comparisons, overarching characteristics are determined to structure the overall sample (clustering). The formation of comparison groups serves the purpose of variance control: The aim is to isolate the selected characteristics more strongly and thereby increase the probability of eliminating or minimizing other causes. While the average values of the total sample contain valuable but more general information in the sense of trends (e.g. participation levels), it is only through the formation of groups that it is possible to determine the extent to which certain characteristics differ from one another depending on the variable (e.g. by type of enterprise or gender). These breakdowns and comparisons provide particularly valuable information which is only revealing and meaningful when viewed relationally (inter-group comparison of characteristics), (e.g. gender distribution by type of the legal form of the community energy project). The greatest problem here is the potential lack of representativeness (due to the number of respondents) of the specific category, due to a lack of coverage (see below for more detail on the characteristics).

[6] The coding was done with the program MaxQDA. A large amount of qualitative data made this form of analysis necessary. A more detailed content-analytical evaluation follows in parts (see below). Open coding was used (flexible category extraction from the material), which is based on considerations of grounded theory.

The clusters to be compared are formed from both formal organization-specific and socio-structural characteristics.

Types of the Legal Form[7] Classification into three types of legal forms cooperative, limited liability company and partnership (GmbH & Co. KG), and limited liability company (GmbH). The largest group are the energy cooperatives, the total sample includes 67 cooperatives with a total of 1872 responses. A second large group is formed by the community energy limited liability companies (GmbHs), consisting of only two projects, but containing 615 responses. These two GmbHs represent two larger community energy companies that citizens participate in either via profit participation rights (i.e. without voting and/or other participation opportunities), or as limited partners in an affiliated limited partnership. In the context of this study, the community energy limited liability companies and partnerships (GmbH & Co. KGs) are exclusively community wind farms; the survey includes five wind farms with 178 responses. These three types are presented separately in the survey analyses. However, there are three other company types, the private company (civil law partnership: GbR) (eight cases, 117 responses), the registered association (one case, 22 responses), and the (environmental) organization (one case, 22 responses), which are not included in the following comparisons. All these three types refer to small community solar projects, while the association is a larger nature conservation association. In terms of type, these three types could be classified as small solar cooperatives in terms of structural characteristics. Nevertheless, participatory practices and structures can vary greatly here as well. For a simplified presentation of comparisons, in particular in order to reveal possible special features of the legal form types, the three groups of cooperative, GmbH and GmbH & Co. KG mentioned above are placed next to each other. At this point it should also be pointed out that the number of responses shows a strongly varying representativeness and significance of the values: while the cooperatives are shown with a high representativeness, and the GmbHs also have a higher significance, the GmbH & Co. KGs as community wind farms with only 178 responses are less representative in comparison. The informative value here is already considered critical, which is why the values should be viewed with a cer-

[7] In Germany, 907 energy cooperatives are currently recorded (as of 2013/2014), of which 495 are in the photovoltaic sector, 200 in the biomass sector, 76 in the wind energy sector, 29 in the hydropower sector and 8 in the solar thermal and geothermal sectors (Yildiz et al. 2015: 62 f.). Concrete numbers of community wind farm companies and other participation projects that are not organized in the cooperative form are not known. In 2016, the number of energy cooperatives will probably be at least 1000.

tain degree of caution in the following. However, since a very low threshold was exceeded and at least a trend statement is of interest for the comparison, this group is mapped. For the handling (as well as the scientific use) of the presented results, it is important to note at this point that the values for the cooperatives show a strong representativeness and therefore also validity, while the values for GmbH & Co. KGs are rather to be understood as indicative and trend values; they do not adequately represent community wind farms in Germany. To give a concrete example: Community wind farms in this survey have, on average, higher participation levels than cooperatives. This general statement can be classified as relatively valid in the sense of a trend statement – the specific figures, on the other hand, have only very limited significance. Further comparison in the context of general project sizes can then put these values into further perspective: The GmbH & Co. KGs in this survey are classified as medium-sized companies – values in this characteristic group are then more meaningful in comparison.

Project Size Three different classes were formed with regard to the size of the community energy project: small, medium and large projects. Small projects (a total of 61 projects, surveyed members: 1012, mostly cooperatives) are usually PV plant investment projects that usually only operate a few energy plants in the local area. The investment sum here remains below one million euros, up to one hundred people are usually involved, sometimes much fewer, sometimes slightly more people. Medium-sized projects (eleven projects, surveyed members: 587, mostly cooperatives and community wind farms) represent companies with an investment amount of more than one million euros in renewable energies and a more far-reaching participation approach; mostly more than one hundred people are involved (sometimes much more, in a few cases also less). Usually, these projects are active in the field of wind energy or several types of energy, also in combination with local heat generation. The large community energy projects (eight companies, surveyed members: 1227, consisting of larger cooperatives and wind farms as well as two community energy limited liability companies (GmbHs)) form companies with investments in renewable energies beyond ten million euros (as a rule); they offer financial participation opportunities throughout Germany and can therefore be assessed as nationally significant players in the energy market that also act very professionally. The two community energy limited liability companies are still to be assessed as significantly larger in terms of investment sums, persons involved, and plant portfolio, than other community energy projects within this group – these are shown under the characteristic type of a limited liability company (GmbH). The main problem with this subdivision lies in the difficult demarcation in borderline cases: If borderline or threshold values of the categories are present, an allocation must be made according to further indications (expansion efforts, supra-regional orientation, membership strength). A certain arbitrariness and lack of information cannot be completely ruled out here. Information from the community energy projects can also be outdated or misleading, and membership figures can vary considerably. While the membership figures cannot be high for very small community energy projects, and likewise for large projects at least very low membership figures are ruled out, there is a possibility that the range here is very wide for medium-sized community energy projects. The use of this classification must therefore again be evaluated critically. In combination and by comparison with the characteristic type "project type", however, the informative value can again be increased. Here, too, the results should be understood primarily as trend values.

Medium-sized projects are weaker represented in this sample by response numbers, which is due to many smaller solar cooperatives and the two large community energy limited liability companies (GmbHs) that participated in the survey. It is possible that such a medium size project is generally more a rare case among community energy projects, which at least this data collection suggests.

Gender Within the framework of the social characteristics, a subdivision into genders is made. There is a strong imbalance in the overall sample, with a total of 2079 people being male, but only 545 people being female (the difference is due to no information provided by the respondents). By highlighting this categorization of characteristics, it is intended to examine more closely the extent to which differences exist between the genders, particularly with regard to participation practice, perception and motivation, as well as identification.

Educational Level As a further social dimension, a highly simplified distinction is made between academics and non-academics. Academics include all persons who have a university degree and/or a doctorate.[8] 1441 persons stated that they had a university degree, 209 persons a doctorate (1650 persons in total). However, as it appears that some people have indicated both a university degree and a doctorate (i.e. are counted twice when the university degree and doctorate are added together), the number of academics is reduced to 1602 (56.7%). The number of non-academics is correspondingly lower (1224 persons, 43.3 percent). Due to the distribution, both groups have a high degree of representation.

[8] Due to the possibility of multiple answers, the respondents were able to make different statements, e.g. to indicate only a doctorate or a university degree and a doctorate.

Income Another expression refers to the different (gross) incomes of the participants (individual, not household income), which are divided into three classes (low, middle and high income). Low income is composed of the range from zero to 2500 euros, middle income from 2500 to 5000 euros, and high income from over 5000 euros. Low-income individuals ($n = 622$) are relatively equally distributed as high-income individuals ($n = 501$). The middle income represents the largest group within the characteristic with 1102 persons.

Energy Type For some variables, it is examined in more detail whether the participants provide different information for different types of energy used by their civil enterprise. A simplified distinction is made here between wind energy, PV/solar energy and several types of energy (e.g. by using wind and solar energy, but also biomass, geothermal energy or hydropower). While the large community energy limited liability companies in the survey invest exclusively in several types of energy, the other large community energy projects predominantly use wind energy (often in combination with solar installations); the same applies to the medium-sized projects. The small energy projects predominantly operate only solar plants. Solar and wind energy are the almost exclusively used forms of energy of the community energy projects represented in this survey, in addition there is the approach of biomass energy production for the operation of a local heating network or for electricity generation. Hydropower and geothermal energy are not represented as used forms of energy in this survey (apart from the investments of the two limited liability companies). In the sample, projects with PV/solar energy use represent the largest group ($n = 1206$). Larger community energy projects using several forms of energy (e.g. wind plants, PV plants, biomass use, hydropower) include 1005 responses in the survey. Wind energy projects form a smaller proportion with 601 respondents. Finally, two energy cooperatives participated, which are active in the field of heat supply in combination with a biomass power plant ($n = 14$ persons).

Finally, some weaknesses of the survey and survey conditions should be pointed out. For example, it was not always possible to use the same questions in the surveys, and in exceptional cases the number of questions was reduced at the special request of the participating energy project. In addition, minor modifications had to be made after the survey had been used by the first participating energy projects. A uniform data set was created for the evaluation. In the results presented here, there is only one marked case of a question that was not included by the community energy limited liability companies because it did not make sense. However, this problem is inherent within the overall survey: some questions and answer options make less sense in the specific context of a community energy project, e.g. in the case where the projects have only just been founded and therefore have no experience of meetings. This can lead to bias and distortion of the results. However, on the one hand, qualitative information can be used to check more closely where the significance is reduced; on the other hand, as has already been mentioned, the results as a whole should at best be understood as trend and guideline values. Only in this way can errors in the survey be put into perspective and a differentiated picture drawn up by adequately taking into account problems of the fit of questions and representativeness.

There is also the problem that some questions contain more or less socially desirable answers, so suggestive effects can also arise. For example, respondents might be inclined to emphasize their own activities more strongly and present them optimistically, as this makes a more positive impression. The same applies to questions about motivation and assessments of the community energy project in which one is involved. Information given by respondents can vary extremely or contradict each other, also certain questions can be misunderstood as they are not clear enough. Some questions were less suited to the community energy projects or the companies were still too young and there was hardly any experience available. Due to these phenomena, a very critical and comparative discussion is necessary, weak points are therefore highlighted in the respective question and in the comparison. Important clues for further differentiation are provided by consulting the qualitative data. In this way it is possible to make more general statements with a high degree of validity, for example by stating that meetings of smaller energy projects are more frequented than those of large ones and that the main criticism of the participants concerns a lack of information flow. In contrast, it is not possible to make very specific statements, such as whether there is a low financial motivation in every case.

The combination of questions through matching and detailed evaluation with critical-reflective discussion can therefore address these problems and thus generate an overall picture whose informative value can at least be increased. In essence, trend statements are produced in this way; the range depicted here is always very wide (example: small cooperatives can contain very high and very low membership activities). It was the explicit aim of the present study to collect such trend values. A more valid survey in detail would have required a different design and a more standardized and rigorous procedure as well as a different survey design (e.g. further runs, longitudinal analyses, etc.). The low level of prior knowledge, little empirical research knowledge, and the wide variances in the subjects of the study (community energy projects) necessitated an overall flexible and open-exploratory design here. The evaluation is carried out according to these guidelines in a correspondingly open, differentiated and critical manner.

The individual categories, clusters and groups are discussed in detail in a comparative manner below. A summary overview first shows central results of the survey:

Social Structure

- *Age*: 54 percent of respondents are 45–64 years old.
- *Gender*: 80 percent of the respondents are male.
- *Education*: 57 percent of respondents are academics (university graduates).
- *Income*: 49 percent of respondents earn over 3500 euros (gross).
- *Civic Engagement*: 80 percent of respondents are members of a civil society organization.

Motivation

- *Ecological Motivation*: 93 percent of respondents say they participate primarily for ecological reasons.
- *Financial Incentive*: 56 percent of respondents say they participate primarily for reasons of return.
- *Knowledge*: 36 percent of members know the locations of the energy plants connected to the community energy project in which they are involved.
- *Experience*: 52 percent of respondents had experience with community renewable energy projects at the time of participation.
- *Informedness*: 95 percent of respondents reported being well informed about the community energy project in which they are involved at the time of becoming a member.

Participation

- *Total investment amount:* 52 percent of respondents have invested more than 3000 euros in the community energy project in which they are involved.

Attendance

- *Meeting attendance:* 76 percent of respondents say they always or rarely attend general meetings of the community energy project in which they are involved.
- *Verbal Expression:* 89 percent of respondents express themselves "frequently to occasionally" at general meetings and sessions of the community energy project in which they are involved.
- *Issues Discussed:* 11 percent of respondents emphasize the importance of organizational issues over other issues being discussed.

Dialogue

- *Request for Contributions:* A call for ideas from members occurs 46 percent of the time.

- *Input:* 19 percent of respondents say they have already contributed at least one idea.
- *Discussion:* 14 percent of respondents would like to see more discussion within the community.

Energy Democracy

- *Definition of energy democracy:* 69 percent of respondents consider the community energy project in which they are involved to be democratic.
- *Explanation of energy democracy:* 54 percent of the respondents explain the attribution of a democratic community energy project with the existence of voting rights.
- *Codetermination:* 60 percent of respondents are unsure whether they would like to have more of a say.

Community

- *Sense of community:* 60 percent of the respondents can describe a sense of community within the project.
- *Criticism:* 47 percent of the respondents are not aware of criticism within the project.
- *Conflicts:* 15 percent of the respondents stated that conflicts in the project have not been resolved.

Effects of Participation

- *Identification:* 85 percent of respondents can identify with the community energy project in which they are involved.
- *Acceptance:* 53 percent of the respondents, rate the acceptance of the energy plants (connected to the community energy project in which they are involved) by the local population as positive.
- *Joint activities:* 41 percent of the respondents stated as an effect of participation that they are in favor of more collaborative and participatory projects in society.

6.2 Contextual Conditions and Social Structure

6.2.1 Political Framework Conditions

Political framework conditions are understood to be those measures at the political level that relate directly and immediately or indirectly in their effects to the energy projects under investigation. Essentially, this refers to the local renewable energy policies of the federal government, state governments, counties and municipalities. The influence of the political regulations depends in each case on the selected type of energy used by the energy project (e.g. solar or wind energy). While the Renewable Energy Sources Act (Erneuerbare-Energien-Gesetz, EEG) is of decisive importance at the federal level, as it sets the feed-in tariffs for the different types of energy, the state governments and parliaments only have an indirect influence. The energy companies depend on obtaining local permits for their plants, on the ability to meet conditions and on the availability of sites. This varies from one type of energy to another: for example, projects with solar plants depend on roofs for installation, while wind power plants require sites that demand extensive planning and land-use designation procedures. Municipalities alone are responsible for these procedures. However, a possible influence of municipalities, city councils, counties and the state governments is possible through the design of these procedures (in the form of simplifications or consideration of the interests and requirements of the energy projects), or through a support policy (for example, decrees of the state government with the character of recommendations and special programs and catalogs of measures as well as financial assistance and consulting services). Finally, city councils and municipal administrations have a key position in that they can make concrete decisions on the designation of areas in the case of wind power. The counties and state governments exert only indirect influence on this practice of the municipalities. In this way it already becomes clear that the use of renewable energies cannot be ordered by the state, but can at best be encouraged and supported. The energy projects are ultimately responsible for their own concerns as independent undertakings, and the role of the state is therefore twofold: on the one hand, state administrations are legally responsible for approving the installation and operation of energy plants; on the other hand, in addition to the specialist administrations, political actors and institutions pursue the goal of promoting renewable energies, for example by promoting energy projects in the sense of cooperation or partnership, or even by integrating a municipality into an energy project.

In terms of the subdivision into levels of government, the following areas are covered by the study:

Influence of Renewable Energy Policy at Federal Level

The Renewable Energy Sources Act (Erneuerbare-Energien-Gesetz, EEG) is the key funding instrument used by the German government to promote renewable energies. There are other, mostly flanking measures, such as measures for the expansion of electricity grids, regulations of the Federal Building Code, immission protection and regional planning law. However, the guaranteed remuneration over a period of 20 years granted by the Renewable Energy Sources Act is of decisive importance for the community energy projects, as they are financed by these amounts over a fixed period, and thus make the project possible in the first place.

Influence of Renewable Energy Policy at State Level

At the state level, there are also actors and regulations that are of some relevance for renewable energy projects of citizens. On the one hand, there are the actions of the state governments and their administration in the form of the ministries, which can form a political framework by either directly influencing the energy policy of the districts and municipalities through certain decrees or other regulations, or indirectly through a support policy (in the form of financial grants or through the establishment of advisory agencies, etc.). Like the federal government, the federal states are also pursuing the goal of increasing the share of renewable energy sources in many cases in Germany. Support for local community initiatives is often an obvious choice, as the state governments place particular emphasis on the aspects of acceptance and regional value creation. However, in the case of wind power, but also in the case of solar energy and geothermal energy, the planning sovereignty and the main decision-making points at local level lie with the districts and municipalities. For this reason, state policy primarily has an indirect effect on energy policy with regard to the control of renewable energies in the state. The study highlights influences particularly in the area of wind energy in North Rhine-Westphalia, and the promotion of solar energy in the state of Bremen.

Renewable Energy Governance at Local Level

As already mentioned, the main focus of the control of renewable energies lies at the local level. Regions and municipalities have a whole range of possible control options with regard to planning and intervention:

- In the case of **wind power,** a key aspect is the designation of priority zones by the local authority in the spatial planning and building sector. Here, a municipality can specifically designate a certain area as a zone for the use of wind power. A wide variety of interests must be taken into account, such as agricultural or forestry use, distance from residential areas, nature conservation concerns (nature conservation areas), proximity to infrastructure such as roads, airfields, etc.
- In the case of **solar energy,** the energy initiatives are dependent on areas for the solar plants. These are gladly taken up by public authorities, as it is a comparatively uncomplicated arrangement for the energy companies and, in addition, large roof areas can often be offered. The municipalities, for their part, have an interest in brokering, as they sometimes earn leasing income from this (although

in some cases they are also made available free of charge), and this can also support the municipalities' efforts to strengthen renewable energies. In many cases, the municipalities operate so-called solar roof exchanges or solar registers, which provide an overview for interested parties with all relevant information. In this context, the environmental agencies also accept roofs from other actors, such as businesses and industries, who are interested in brokering their roofs. However, once roof areas have been brokered, there are still further steps for the energy initiatives to take: On the one hand, a permit is required for the plants, on the other hand, this area also involves a check of the statics of the buildings, which must be suitable for installation. The general condition of the roof is also relevant if it needs to be renovated.

- In addition, permits are required for the **construction of energy plants –** on the one hand with regard to the aspects mentioned for priority zones, and on the other hand also with regard to the technical plant itself. Various offices and specialist administrations are involved here, which are also located in the district and in some cases also in the state. The involvement of the specialist departments depends on the respective concerns on site (e.g. in the case of a forest site, forestry authority and nature conservation authority).
- At the **political level** in the municipalities, the city council and the specialist committees are involved in the procedures. On the one hand, fundamental decisions are made here (e.g. whether the city council is generally in favor of the use of wind energy and the designation of priority zones), and on the other hand, specific issues are discussed (e.g. specific siting issues). Citizens' concerns can also flow into the political bodies and thus into the planning and decision-making processes – on the one hand indirectly via the city councilors as elected representatives of certain electoral districts, and on the other hand there are opportunities for direct input through municipal petitions or in the form of a reactive procedure by lodging objections to notices of approval (or similar). The last form would also be all forms of protest. Within this municipal political system, various groups of actors or individual actors are relevant, such as the mayor himself (who in many federal states heads both the administration and the city council), various parties or factions of the city council, as well as individual representatives of the administration such as the heads of the specialist departments, councilors, advisors and commissioners for special topics, such as the environment and energy sector. These stakeholder structures were taken into account in the selection of interview partners.

Wind Energy Policy of the Federal States of Baden-Württemberg and North Rhine-Westphalia

North Rhine-Westphalia: Political Objectives in the Wind Energy Decree

In North Rhine-Westphalia, the preface to the state government's wind energy decree already refers to the importance of wind energy and the encouragement for municipalities in their aim to support this energy source (Windenergieerlass NRW 2011: Vorwort):

> The state of North Rhine-Westphalia wants to be a pioneer in climate protection and will therefore be the first federal state to adopt binding climate protection targets in the form of a climate protection law. The promotion of renewable energies and also the expansion of wind energy use are part of this strategy. (…) At the municipal level, the state government wants to support the efforts of the cities and municipalities to develop their own climate protection concept, in which the municipalities can decide to what extent the use of wind energy can be part of such a concept for the promotion of renewable energies. The state will (…) provide a package of measures for this purpose: This includes support in identifying wind energy potential, the creation of a clearing house to assist in resolving conflicts in advance, and a comprehensive advisory package for municipalities.

In the guideline "Framework conditions for wind turbines on forest areas in North Rhine-Westphalia" (page 4) of the Ministry for Climate Protection, Environment, Agriculture, Nature Conservation and Consumer Protection, the state government's goal of increasing the share of renewable energies is also explicitly referred to for wind energy:

> The state government of North Rhine-Westphalia has set itself the goal of significantly reducing CO_2 emissions. This necessarily means an increase in electricity generation from renewable energies. Wind energy in particular will play an important role in this, as without its more efficient expansion the climate protection targets in North Rhine-Westphalia cannot be achieved. The share of wind energy in North Rhine-Westphalia is to be increased from the current 3% of electricity generation to at least 15% by 2020. This target will be achieved on the one hand by repowering, i.e. replacing old turbines with newer, more powerful ones. On the other hand, new priority areas and concentration zones for wind energy use will have to be designated.

The new priority areas and concentration zones also refer to those areas where the use of wind energy takes place or is made possible in forest areas and has led to controversial discussions with regard to nature conservation and species protection (in the updated version of the wind energy decree of 2015, the state government maintains the possibility, even if forest locations are linked to certain conditions and compensation for the interference is provided for wind turbines and early public participation is recommended and suggested).

In fact, the impact of the 2011 decree is considered by community wind energy actors in North Rhine-Westphalia to be very positive and even decisive for their activities (Landesverband Erneuerbare Energien NRW and World Wind Energy Association 2016: 2).

Baden-Württemberg: Political Goals in the Wind Energy Decree

The wind energy decree of Baden-Württemberg begins by commenting in detail on the objectives of the state government and the importance of wind energy, similar to the formulated climate policy objectives of the wind energy decree of North Rhine-Westphalia, but with additional emphasis on the importance of regional value creation.

For example, reference is made to the Federal Government's decision to phase out nuclear power (Windenergieerlass Baden-Württemberg 2012: Ziffer 1.1.): The expansion of wind energy use has become considerably more important as a result of the final phase-out of nuclear energy by 2022. This applies to Germany as a whole, but also to Baden-Württemberg. While hydropower has so far been a major factor in energy generation from renewable energy sources, this, like biomass, "will foreseeably reach its limits in the near future" (ibid.). "In contrast, there is still considerable potential for expansion in photovoltaics and in the use of wind energy" (ibid.). From these federal policy implications combined with the local circumstances, the political objectives of the state government as well as a public interest are derived. (ibid.):

> The energy supply with renewable energy and in particular the expansion of wind energy use is thus a central objective of the state government and is thus in the special public interest.

Accordingly, a wind atlas designed by the state of Baden-Württemberg makes it clear, "that the state government's goal of providing at least 10% *of* the state's electricity from domestic wind energy by 2020 is feasible" (ibid.). "In order to achieve this target, it is necessary to build around 1200 new wind turbines in the state, each with a capacity of around 3 MW" (ibid.).

In order to be able to achieve this ambitious goal, the government seems to be aware that this will not be possible without the use of forest areas: "The designation of areas for wind energy use is therefore also necessary in forest areas in order to ensure the expansion targets of the state government by 2020" (Windenergieerlass Baden-Württemberg 2012: Section 1.1). "Forest areas are fundamentally suitable for wind energy use" (ibid.).

Finally, the state government also points to the economic importance of wind power. First of all, reference is made to the wind power industry: "The use of wind energy has become a significant economic factor" (ibid.: 1.2). "Although the state is not yet a location of any manufacturer of wind turbines that has series production, there are a lot of companies active in the state as suppliers to the wind energy industry" (ibid.). Apparently, there is even reason for a special justification: "Wind energy creates and secures jobs, also in Baden-Württemberg" (ibid.). In addition, however, effects at the regional level are also emphasized under the point "Regional and municipal added value" (ibid.: 1.3): "Local use of wind energy can also be economically beneficial for municipalities and their citizens". In another point, reference is made to the particular importance of participation, consensual procedures and acceptance of wind power (ibid.: point 2):

> The wind energy decree forms an important basis for the implementation of the energy policy objectives for the use of wind energy. These targets, in particular to achieve 10% of electricity generation from wind energy by 2020, cannot be implemented without a broad social consensus. According to current surveys and the results of very specific votes in individual towns and communities in Baden-Württemberg, the vast majority of citizens welcome the expansion of the use of renewable energies and specifically the use of wind energy in the state.

In order to achieve this goal of a citizen-friendly and accepted, but at the same time massive expansion of wind power, a broad participation of citizens on many levels and with different procedures is seen as an instrument. However, the government does not see government agencies as having a particular duty in this respect, but rather the project sponsor, i.e. the plant operator: "The decisive prerequisite for a broad social consensus on the use of wind energy is the early involvement of citizens, all relevant interest groups and associations, in particular through citizens' information events already in the very early planning phases. Completely new methodological approaches, such as moderation or mediation procedures, are also suitable for this purpose. In any case, the initiative for this should come from the project developer. Here, too, the energy transition is defined as a joint task (ibid.): "The use of wind energy requires the joint cooperation of all stakeholders".

Regulations on Public Participation in the Wind Energy Decree of Baden-Württemberg

The application of public and citizen participation in the planning process can also be found in case study 2, the community wind turbine in Baden-Württemberg.

The wind energy decree of the state of Baden-Württemberg in the 2012 version under the Green-Red state government regulates "public participation" under point 1.4, which is very extensive in this new version. Among other things, it states:

> In the expansion of wind energy, the state government attaches great importance to the participation of citizens. This applies not only to public participation in the preparation of wind regional plans, in urban land use planning, and in a formal immission control licensing procedure, but also includes the recommendation to the developer to make use of the many opportunities for public participation on a voluntary basis, regardless of the type of licensing procedure.

The state government thus recommends participation procedures beyond those provided for in the law, which go beyond an ordinary level. Furthermore, community energy plants are explicitly recommended:

> In addition, the construction and operation of community wind turbines/community wind farms is supported. These are wind energy plants in which local citizens can participate conceptually and/or financially. They are often the result of civic engagement in the community concerned.

This recommendation is justified by the higher acceptance of the turbines among the population and the planning process itself: "Local initiatives at the municipal level are very well suited to creating a positive basic mood in favor of the use of wind energy. Skepticism and reservations can be reduced much more easily if local citizens are directly and immediately involved in the project. Of course, this applies to all phases of the planning process, from the beginning of the planning itself to implementation and operation".

Furthermore, the following points relevant for community energy projects are named:

- Possibility for a municipality to participate in a project itself
- Use contracts between municipalities and land owners with the help of "pool solutions" (owners benefit from lease payments) should offer project sponsors (e.g. citizens) optimal implementation through municipal coordination.
- Recommended exclusion of liability for involved citizens in the community wind farm
- Provision of suitable land by the state government and the state forestry authority and preferential treatment of citizens as well as consideration of regional and municipal value creation in the allocation of land

In addition, a concrete design and control of citizen participation is recommended:

> In view of the primary objective of increasing acceptance, the articles of association should specify the maximum number of shares that each citizen can acquire in order to enable as many citizens as possible to participate financially and to prevent the accumulation of many shares in the hands of a few participants. It is also conceivable to precisely define the group of potential participants and to limit this, for example, to the citizens in the immediate vicinity of the wind farm who are primarily affected by the actual impact of the turbines.

Finally, an overriding preference for community projects is guaranteed by the state government in all relevant matters. Overall, it is clear that the state government is massively strengthening and encouraging the promotion of citizen projects in the wind energy sector. The municipalities are required to back and promote citizen projects before all other interested parties. However, it remains questionable how municipalities are to manage this support without concrete support from the state (lack of budgetary and human resources). In addition, there are possible obstructive effects due to overarching political levels (e.g. EU regulations on award procedures (principle of the highest bidder), which can lead to community energy initiatives being left out of competition in the allocation of land).

Community Energy Commitment of the State Governments

In addition to the recommendation to municipalities to give preference, the state governments of the two federal states also show further commitment with regard to the promotion of community energy projects: although there are no explicit and financial support mechanisms, consultations are offered, various brochures on the topic are intended to provide information, education and impetus through recommendations for action. Municipal forums and forms of collaboration are also suggested as a framework, for example:

- Climate protection working group
- Community solar initiative
- Local Agenda 21 working group on energy issues
- Climate protection working group with multipliers
- Community solar association as co-initiators of cooperative and citizen participation mechanisms

In addition, evaluative-exploratory instruments (preparation and implementation of surveys, interviews, expert opinions and project checks) are also suggested. In addition to the considerable importance of the decrees (especially with regard to usable areas), such climate protection or renewable energy initiatives by individual municipalities as well as community wind networks and information platforms are highlighted by community wind actors in North Rhine-Westphalia at the local level (Landesverband Erneuerbare Energien NRW and World Wind Energy Association 2016: 2).

Solar Energy Policy of the State of Bremen

In the federal state of Bremen, the control of renewable energies (in this case photovoltaics) faces similar challenges in terms of a more passive approach in the form of information systems, recommendations and advice, rather than measures for active promotion and support.

For example, the state of Bremen launched a solar initiative: "At the suggestion of 'Bremer Energie Konsens GmbH', the 'Solar Initiative Bremen' was founded in 1999, a community of interest of over twenty institutions at the time, which, in addition to senatorial departments, included associations of the skilled trades, research institutions, consulting agencies and energy companies" (Bremische Bürgerschaft Drucksache 17/741: 3). The initiative was supported by the senatorial authority for the environment and carried out "publicity campaigns" such as "Solar Action Weeks", organized trade fairs and developed the "Solar Roof Exchange Northwest", "an internet-based platform for the procurement of large roof areas for use for large photovoltaic systems", in the development of which the state of Bremen was "significantly involved" (Bremische Bürgerschaft Drucksache 17/741: 3). "Since the start of the project in 2004, Bremen has regularly made large suitable roof areas of public buildings available for solar energy use on a contractual basis" (ibid.).

With regard to the number of solar systems on public roofs, the Senate puts this figure at "a total of 20 photovoltaic systems" (ibid.). The "share of photovoltaic systems on public buildings" in the state of Bremen is 19.5 percent (ibid.: 5). The share of electricity generation from photovoltaics in the final energy consumption (electricity) of the state of Bremen is put at 4.8 percent in 2005 (ibid.: 6).

The Senate attributes the expansion of solar installations since "the discontinuation of Bremen's investment subsidies at the beginning of 2000 (…) primarily" to "federal subsidies including the Renewable Energy Sources Act (Erneuerbare-Energien-Gesetz)" as well as to the "solar advisory program" (ibid.: 8). Finally, the Senate discusses the benefits of program such as a solar potential analysis, which is used in Osnabrück and provides more detailed information on the existing solar potential (ibid.: 9). The use of larger areas, or indeed the further expansion of renewable energy in the state of Bremen, is seen as fundamentally limited (ibid.: 10): "The amount of land available in a city state like Bremen is limited. The cities of Bremen and Bremerhaven are therefore obliged to handle their land with care. Priority must therefore be given to the possibility of installing photovoltaic systems on roofs". With regard to the promotion of solar systems, the Bremen Parliament also dealt with the development of a roof area register, which can provide information on the solar potential of roof areas on the internet (cf. Bremische Bürgerschaft Drucksache 17/1365). In the case of the application of such a cadastre, there were doubts on the part of the Liberal Party (FDP) parliamentary group as to whether the collection of data (e.g. by Google Street View) would meet data protection requirements. This exemplifies additional problematic situations in a case in which the state authorities are seeking to facilitate access to suitable roof areas for interested parties (such as citizens' groups).

An inquiry by the Green Party (Bündnis 90/Die Grünen) parliamentary group on 15.6.2010 aimed to find out to what extent the city and state of Bremen actually exploit the "solar potential of public land" (Bremische Bürgerschaft Drucksache 17/620 S). The Senate sees the possibility of using roof areas in the city of Bremen as ambivalent (ibid.: 1): "Due to the high building density in a city state like Bremen, there is a very large potential of roof areas which – theoretically – could be suitable for solar use. Since a number of other boundary conditions must be met for actual solar use, above all the structural condition, the statics, the extensive freedom from shading and the interest or consent of the property owner, only a fraction of this is practically usable".

With regard to the procurement of roof areas, the Senate refers to the Solar Roof Exchange Northwest, where suitable roof areas can be identified via the internet. Finally, it is stated that overall, in a positive case, "the roof areas are being leased to interested companies or persons with increasing success" (ibid.: 2). So far, "roof leases have been granted for 13 public buildings" (as of mid-June 2010) (ibid.). In addition, support at federal level is provided by the Renewable Energy Sources Act (EEG), which is seen as a sufficient support measure for solar systems – also in the north of Germany (Bremische Bürgerschaft Drucksache 17/620 p: 2): "In the opinion of the Senate, the legal framework and the support instruments at federal level are attractively designed, particularly for solar use for electricity generation by PV systems, and in many cases enable economic operation also in the north of Germany".

In addition, free solar advice is emphasized, which the Senate has been offering "together with the nonprofit climate protection agency (energiekonsens) for ten years as a supplement via external task bearers", "in order to give interested citizens, but also businesses and associations, well-founded advice on the use of solar energy in their own area" (ibid.: 2). This state energy agency offers "public events", "press work", provides "information material" and arranges "contacts to further advisory services" (ibid.: 2). For the future, the development of larger areas by merging several actors is being considered (ibid.: 2).

In summary, the political attitude in the state of Bremen appears to be positive towards participatory approaches – concrete participation measures have also been adopted, which could have an impact on the construction of energy plants. However, it is not clear how the state of Bremen intends to stimulate and strengthen civil society involvement in the field of renewable energy. Despite all other efforts, this does not seem to be a direct political objective.

The main instrument, the solar roof exchange, was originally formed out of a working group and covers not only Bremen but also the neighboring metropolitan region: "(…) the solar roof exchange is not limited to Bremen, but to Bremen and the surrounding area. This exists in the metropolitan region Bremen-Oldenburg. Originally, the solar roof exchange was only conceived for Bremen and in the course of the metropolitan region, a specialist working group was founded a few years ago, which is called 'Energy Network Northwest', where the colleagues from various municipalities, districts and also from the cities, who have to do with energy issues in the area of 'public buildings', meet two to three times a year" (I 9: line 793 ff.).

Another advantage is that the platform is open to anyone who is interested – but de facto it is mainly used by the municipalities: "(...) it is an offer, nothing more. And it is also open in principle to private homeowners or building owners. (...) In principle it is open to everyone, but it is mainly used by municipalities." (ibid.: line 811 ff.).

The success of the instrument is, however, clearly measurable: a strong expansion of PV has indeed taken place (however, the presumably heavier influence of the Renewable Energy Sources Act (EEG) remains unconsidered here): "(...) in the metropolitan region we have mediated a total of about thirty roofs through this solar roof exchange – and in the meantime the total output is over one megawatt. I am so proud and claim that without the solar roof exchange none of this would have come about (...)" (ibid.: line 823 ff.).

Once initiated, the solar roof exchange should eventually profit from its popularity, and information about it should spread further and further (snowball principle): "Then it will become more and more a matter of course. So – you do not have to advertise it anymore, but it is known in specialist circles and then they look in from time to time: what have we got that is new in the northwest? Lives of course from the offer..." (I 9: line 830 ff.).

However, even if a case were to arise in which a public institution showed interest in installing PV systems, the core problem of financing would still exist here. Such investments would apparently not be counted among the core tasks of public administration: "Only, as a rule in Bremen – and not only in Bremen – it fails when someone says: I will do it myself – as a building construction office, for example (...) – but first I need a million. No one will give it to you because it simply is not there, and according to the motto 'We have many more wishes and no money. Why PV of all things? We have much more urgent things: renovation of roads, of schools, of all infrastructure, where the money is needed much more urgently'. PV may be worthwhile, but it is not necessarily one of the tasks of municipal services of general interest. They have to be satisfied first and they cannot be satisfied decently almost everywhere in Germany" (ibid.: line 894 ff.).

In this context, the administration asks itself whether more support should be provided by the state – this even seems possible if the impetus comes from elsewhere, such as the energy agency or the local electricity provider: "The question would then also be: Is it the task of the authorities to get more involved, or is it rather the task of the authority, for example, to say to others: 'We will somehow create structures where these people can be helped. It does not always have to be the direct work of the authorities. As I said, the SWB with its 'Pro Natur Fonds', the 'Bremer Energie Konsens' are in themselves the born initiators for something like this. Of course we would also support them" (ibid.: line 1321 ff.).

However, since there is no initiative from either side, this situation presents itself as a vicious circle in which the call to action is passed on from one actor to another. The employee sees the general demand for state action and initiative as too simplistic: Accordingly, the state cannot do the work of ensuring that citizens ultimately earn money from (again, state) funding above all else. It defines the field of activity in particular through criteria of classic entrepreneurship – composed of know-how and a willingness to take risks: "Only if everyone always expects: 'So, the state should do something' – or: 'The city, the municipality should do something' – and then, when everything is ready, we lie down in bed and earn our money. – I have to be honest, I think that is a bit too easy. Everybody always likes to earn money, but nobody likes to do a bit of work themselves and take on an economic risk … nothing comes of it! Or if it does, then only on a small scale. But then, please, nobody should complain that the big ones do the big projects and earn the big money. It requires expertise and a willingness to take risks, and if that is not there, then it cannot work" (ibid.: line 1327 ff.).

Summary

The state of Bremen has been committed to the promotion and expansion of renewable energies in the state for years. There is an expansion plan for renewable energies for the year 2020, in which no additional photovoltaic and hydropower is planned, but more wind power and possibly more biomass use. In the photovoltaic sector, the state of Bremen operates a solar roof exchange as a third-party operator promotion program, in which suitable roof areas of public buildings can be called up via a database (which is operated by the state of Bremen) and, if necessary, a lease agreement can be signed for their use. The state of Bremen has deliberately decided against the operation of PV systems by the public sector itself. The Social Democratic Party (SPD), as the governing party, is in favor of a municipal company that would independently construct and operate PV plants. Despite government activity, the initiative has not yet been followed up by a resolution in parliament. Although advisory agencies for the energy sector exist, no explicit promotion of community energy is implied or carried out.

6.2.2 Social Structure of the Members of Community Energy Initiatives

Types of Participation Individuals are the main participants, with a quarter of the participants being families. However, the idea of citizen participation does not lead to many community associations with a share of only 2 percent. Nevertheless, this participation mode is interesting for people with low incomes (and is also used to a certain extent), to be able to take the option of being able to achieve larger minimum participation sums. Strong (financial) "participation community" is thus not triggered by energy shares. However, the high family participation rate is striking.

Gender Community energy projects are in fact dominated by men, with a share of 80 percent. Participations in larger community energy projects with a supra-regional focus are more likely to attract women – in contrast to locally anchored, smaller participation projects that are more part of an association culture. Civic involvement in Germany is often male-dominated, and this also applies to certain civic associations (e.g. sports clubs, etc.).[9] In this case, it is probably the combination of technology, economic activity and connection to local engagement culture that is associated with greater interest for men. Participations in the larger com-

[9] While men are not very active in the area of working hours with a low time interval (vice versa for women), this then rises sharply for time intervals from 30 to 55 hours per week (for women it decreases correspondingly sharply); the critical area where the ratios overlap is at 30 to 40 hours per week (related to couple households with children) (Alscher et al. 2009: 48). Men who work a lot are thus very committed, women on the other hand very little – and the reverse is true when working hours are low. In the area of sustainable consumption, on the other hand, there are high participation rates among women (see Baringhorst 2016a, 2016b). – In Germany, the distribution between the sexes is: male 49 percent to female 51 percent (Statistisches Bundesamt 2013: 26). In the case of volunteering, according to the Federal Government's Engagement Report (Enste et al. 2012: 73), the engagement rate for men is 37.9%, while for women it is 31.6% (overall rate: 34.3%). This is reported consistently by the Volunteer Survey (Gensicke and Geiss 2010: 19); an overall rate of 36% is formed (Statistisches Bundesamt 2013: 203). The 2013 data report distinguishes between general civil engagement (men: 40%, women: 32%) and engagement tied to organizations as an integrative component, where women are more involved (men: 12%, women 18%) (all data from 2009, Alscher and Priller 2013: 354). The Volunteer Survey (Gensicke and Geiss 2010: 19) also presents the differences in terms of age: among young people and in the case of 40–44 year olds, there are hardly any differences between the sexes; strong differences are present in the age spectrums of 20 to 40 years and 55 to 75 years (ibid.). It should be noted that the engagement rate varies greatly in different studies, for example in a survey by the WZB in the 2000s between 18 and 52% (Alscher et al. 2009: 21). In the environmental field, too, there is a gender difference in engagement between 35 and 64%, and in professional advocacy the difference is also 26 versus 74% (ibid.: 38; see also Kersting and Woyke 2012). "In 2010, 5% of men but only 2% of women in West Germany were members of a political party" (Geissler 2014: 392). "West German women are also considerably less likely (8%) to be members of a trade union than men (20%), and they are also less likely to participate in community initiatives (men 2% – women 1%). Instead, their involvement in cultural and charitable activities is more pronounced than for men, and they are also more frequently involved in the environment, nature, health and self-help" (ibid.).

munity energy limited companies, on the other hand, exclude such local integration; the participation is more anonymous and has less connection to local regulars' tables. Although participation without contact to the community energy project and meetings would be conceivable here as well, participation offers without any previous involvement seem to be more obvious.[10]

Age Many people in community energy projects are of advanced age: the core is made up of 45–65 year olds.[11] Forty-seven percent are between 35 and 55 years old, while those over 55 form a strong group with 42 percent. This can probably be explained by the fact that people of this age are less involved in their careers and families, and also have enough money to invest. Older persons, however, are not as strongly represented as one might expect (since persons aged 65 and over are sometimes more involved due to greater time resources): from 65 to 75 years of age, 13 percent are still involved; from 75 onwards, participation decreases significantly. Older persons are involved just as little as younger persons: only 10 percent are under 35 years of age, and very few participate under 25. The age distribution thus corresponds very well to the data on education and income: Since especially persons with higher, completed education and higher income are active, this corresponds to middle-aged persons. It is only difficult to explain the not very high values of persons over 65 years of age: especially for conscious pensioners and retirees such an investment or engagement may seem attractive. It is possible, however, that this form of participation is too complicated and costly for some older people – this explanation is supported by the fact that older people take up the offers of the large

[10] The distribution found here is confirmed by other survey results (survey limited to the region of South Westphalia), in which a share of 20% was determined in the case of wind energy use and a share of 30% in the case of PV use (Fraune 2014; Fraune 2015: 60). In this study, it can be confirmed that in the community wind farms there is an increased share of 85% male gender, the lowest share being in the members of the community energy limited liability companies with 76%. However, a breakdown into energy types (PV, wind, multiple energy types) yields very small variations (PV: 79%, wind: 81%, multiple: 78%). Bauwens (2014b, 2016) investigated in a survey two energy cooperatives in Flanders (number of participants: about 4000). Here, too, the proportion of male members was found to be over 80%. In another study of energy cooperatives in Germany, a male share of 74% was also determined (Rauschmayer et al. 2015: 5).

[11] Bauwens (2014b, 2016) determined an average age of 50 years in energy cooperatives. In Germany, the age distribution is: 0–18 years 16.1%, 18–25 years: 8.2%, 25–40 years: 18%, 40–60 years: 31.1%, 60–65 years: 6%, > 65 years: 20.6% (Statistisches Jahrbuch 2013: 33). In another study of energy cooperatives in Germany, an average age of 59 years was determined (Rauschmayer et al. 2015: 5).

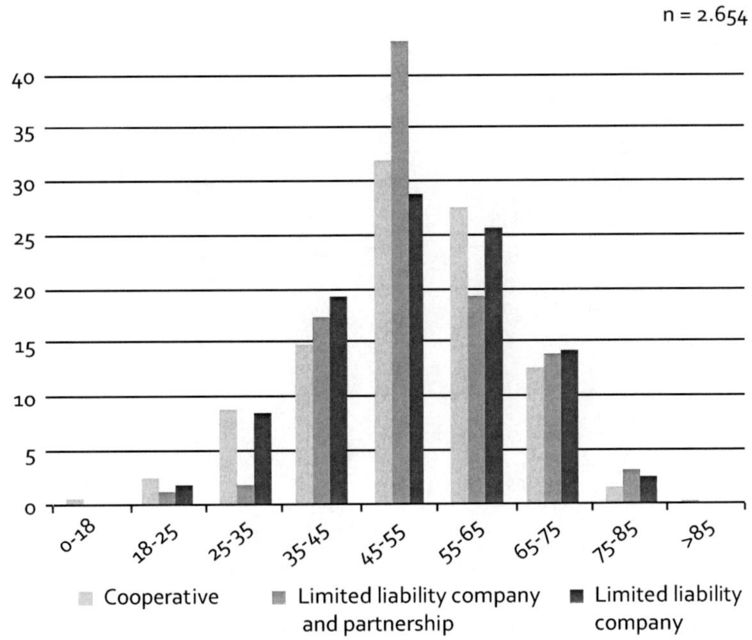

Fig. 6.1 Age by type of legal form

community energy projects, as participation here is less complicated and appears to be more of a pure financial investment (e.g. for descendants). Younger people are more involved in cooperatives – this is possibly due in particular to the fact that cooperatives offer low initial investment amounts (Figs. 6.1 and 6.2).

Education, Income and Occupational Status Academics in community energy projects slightly predominate with 57 percent.[12] This means that the people involved are almost evenly divided between academics and non-academics, but only 7 percent have a secondary school leaving certificate, and there is also a low proportion of trainees. The gross incomes are correspondingly high: 72 percent earn over 2500 euros a month, 23 percent over 5000 euros alone. Only 9.5 percent earn

[12] Bauwens (2014b, 2016) determined a share of between 73 and 76 percent of university graduates in energy cooperatives. In another study of energy cooperatives in Germany, a similar figure of 70 percent of university graduates was also found (Rauschmayer et al. 2015: 5).

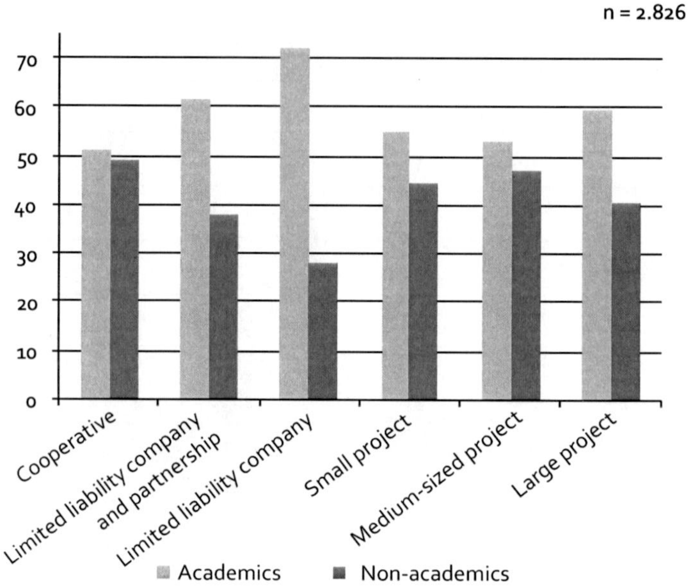

Fig. 6.2 Distribution of academics by type of legal form

less than 1500 euros, and only 1.7 percent have no income of their own.[13] Thus, this finding also fits into the picture of predominantly highly qualified middle-aged to older persons with higher incomes[14] . This is also clear from the data on salaried employees and civil servants in managerial positions; these two groups alone ac-

[13]The average gross income in Germany is 3900 euros (Statistisches Bundesamt 2013: 164). In terms of income, socio-political engagement also shows that people with high net incomes are more engaged than people with low incomes on a graded basis (over 4000 euros net: engagement rate 47%, 2500–4000: 43%, 1500 to 2500: 36%, 750 to 1500: 26%, under 750 euros: 24% (Alscher et al. 2009: 44). Bauwens (2014b, 2016) identified in energy cooperatives a share of about 20 percent with a household income, which is below 2000 euros, 49 percent earn between 2000 and 4000 euros, about 20 percent have over 4000 euros per month. In another study of energy cooperatives in Germany, a net household income of over 2500 euros was determined for 66 percent of the members (related to photovoltaic/heat energy cooperatives; Rauschmayer et al. 2015: 5).

[14]The WZB puts the proportion of committed people among the middle class at 55.3%, among those with high incomes at 26.5%, and among those at risk of poverty at 18.2% (based on the year 2007, Alscher et al. 2009: 56).

count for 19 percent. Salaried employees are strongly represented with a total of 44 percent, civil servants are slightly overrepresented with 12 percent[15] . In line with the age groups, 17 percent are pensioners and retirees. The high proportion of freelancers and self-employed persons with 17 percent is most likely due to the fact that, on the one hand, it is precisely the self-employed (such as engineers and energy consultants) who create energy initiatives, and on the other hand, these persons

[15] In Germany, 44% of the population is employed, of which 11% are self-employed (Statistisches Bundesamt 2013: 339). 5.5% are registered as being in economic inactivity (ibid.: 348), 7% as unemployed (ibid.: 355). Pensioners and people who draw their income from assets make up 23% (ibid.: 342). In terms of occupational positions, white-collar workers make up 67%, civil servants 10% and blue-collar workers also 10% (ibid.: 94). Apprentices make up 1.7% (ibid.), pupils make up 10.5% (ibid.: 82) and students make up 3% (ibid.: 88). The engagement rate of employed persons, pupils and students as well as housewives/husbands is generally higher than among the unemployed and pensioners/retirees; it is slightly lower among the inactive (Alscher et al. 2009: 43, as also in the survey of volunteers, see Gensicke and Geiss 2010: 103). The same picture emerges for the activity requirements (from simple to high level, with sharply rising values for the engagement rate in each case) (Alscher et al. 2009: 44). The 2013 data report distinguishes between general civil engagement (employed: 40%, unemployed: 26%, pupils/trainees/students: 38%, housewives/husbands: 36%, pensioners/retired: 30%) and as an integrative component organization-bound engagement, where persons in training as well as housewives/husbands are more engaged (employed: 13%, unemployed: 15%, pupils/trainees/students: 21%, housewives/husbands: 17%, pensioners/retirees: 14%) (all data from 2009, Alscher and Priller 2013: 354).

have a higher affinity to the basic orientation of community energy, based on the self-sufficiency approach.[16]

While the proportion of academics and non-academics is relatively balanced in the cooperatives, the difference is greater in the community wind farms ("Bürgerwindparks", organizational form: GmbH & Co. KGs) and the community energy limited liability companies (GmbHs) (50 percent compared to 60 and 70 percent). Small and medium-sized community energy projects are still relatively balanced, but the strong difference is again noticeable in large projects. While non-academics are more likely to decide to participate in a smaller energy project that is presumably located nearby, it is academics who are interested in participation offerings such as those from Greenpeace. This means that locally anchored energy participation projects are actually in a much better position to address and involve people from less academic backgrounds (this corresponds to the circumstances and

[16] In Germany, 39% of the population have a "low-level" secondary school-leaving certificate (*Hauptschulabschluss*), 24% have a "mid-level" secondary school-leaving certificate (*Realschulabschluss*), 30% have a "high-level" secondary school-leaving certificate (*Abitur*), and 4% have no qualifications (Statistisches Bundesamt 2013: 76). 73% of the population have a vocational qualification (accordingly, 27% of the population have no vocational qualification (ibid.: 78). Of the graduates, 69% have completed an apprenticeship, 10% technical college, 7% have a university of applied sciences degree, 11% have a university degree, 1.5% a doctorate (ibid.). With higher education, civic engagement tends to increase, and in the context of environmental protection and community initiatives/civic associations to an even larger extent (Gensicke and Geiss 2010: 54). The involvement of people with a high level of education is much higher (rate: 43%) than for those with a medium level (37%) and basic level (26%) (Alscher et al. 2009: 43). The Volunteer Survey (Gensicke and Geiss 2010: 54) reports that members in non-profit organizations are composed of 32% persons with simple education, 35% persons with medium education, and 43% with higher education. Again, persons with higher education are more represented in environmental organizations (7% compared to 3% simple education and 5% medium education) and community initiatives and associations (5% compared to 3% for simple and medium education) (2009 data). The same applies to activities through participation in citizens' meetings (total 41%, high education 44%, low 36% and medium 41%) and community initiatives (total 27%, high education 32%, low 18% and medium 27%) (2009 data) (ibid: 55). This is equally true for differences between "low-level" secondary school (*Hauptschule*) and "mid-level" secondary school (*Realschule*) students and "high-level" secondary school (*Gymnasium*) students, as well as students at universities versus those in company-based training or vocational schools (ibid.: 150). The 2013 data report distinguishes between general civic engagement (simple educational level: 23%, medium educational level: 37%, high educational level: 45%) and engagement tied to organizations as an integrative component, where the values are more levelled (simple educational level: 11%, medium educational level: 14%, high educational level: 15%) (data from 2009, Alscher and Priller 2013: 354).

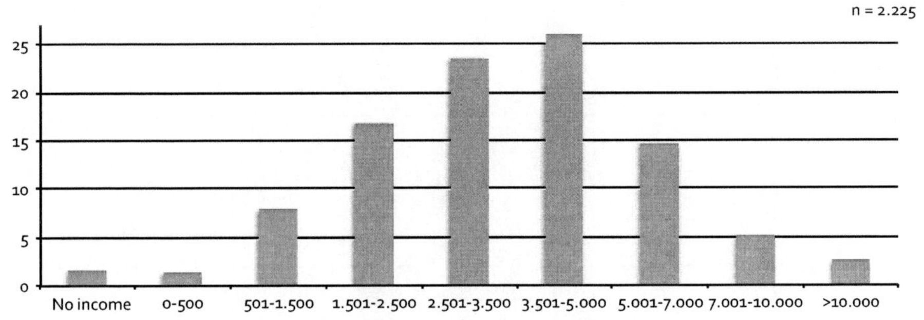

Fig. 6.3 Individual gross income (per person, no household income): total sample

information that lower participation amounts are possible here, and the attitude is more pronounced that an explicit level of knowledge is not necessarily required, as the project is closer and clearer, cf. below) (s. 6.3, 6.4, and 6.5).

Household Size and Residential Location The majority are two-person households and families – remarkably, the number of single households is low (12%).[17] This distribution tends to coincide with the data on higher incomes, which are less likely to be distributed among single households and shared apartments in the population. Added to this is the fact that long-term financial investments are likely to appeal in particular to people in this type of relationship (couples and families). However, it is not possible to draw a direct conclusion, as the survey asked about individual income. Presumably the smaller rural energy projects explain the high values of the very strong representation of villagers (37 percent). Together with small towns, this rural group accounts for 56 percent, compared to 34 percent for

[17] By way of comparison, 40.5% of the population in Germany live in one-person households, two-person households make up 35%, households with three or more persons form 24%, and the average is 2.01 members (Statistisches Bundesamt 2013: 48 f.). Overall, 28% live in families (ibid.: 51). People in large households are more active communally than those in 2- or 1-person households (80% participating actively in civil society infrastructure among 4- and 5-person households, 72% among 3-person households, 69% among 2-person households, and 65% among 1-person households (total: 71%) (Gensicke and Geiss 2010: 76).

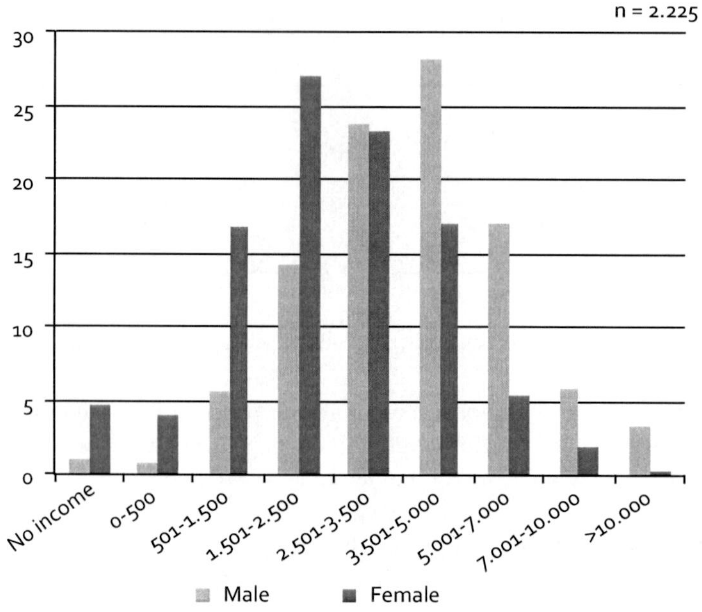

Fig. 6.4 Individual gross income: by gender

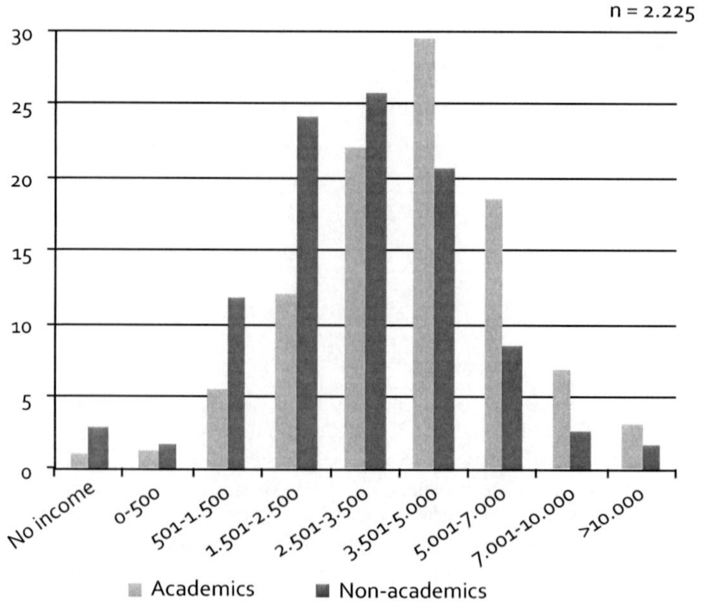

Fig. 6.5 Individual gross income: by level of education

large cities.[18] Medium-sized towns are severely underrepresented.[19] In both medium-sized towns and large cities, there are also some smaller energy initiatives, but these are not in proportion to the population; this is strikingly true of Germany's largest cities. Here, there are fewer opportunities for people who want to invest small amounts to participate in a smaller energy project.

Distance to Energy Plants and Perception The majority of stakeholders do not live near the energy plants of the community energy project in which they are involved. Only 25%are within a maximum distance of five kilometers, 12 percent see the turbines every day. Those involved in community wind energy projects also hardly notice their wind turbines acoustically themselves, as they do not live in the vicinity. Nevertheless, there are still 5 percent who notice the energy plants on a daily basis. This means that community energy projects also integrate people who are in the direct vicinity of the turbines and are confronted with possible adverse effects. Here, too, the wide range becomes apparent: 25 percent of the participants living in the vicinity is not a negligible size, which is presumably represented by smaller projects. At the same time, there are also the larger community energy companies, whose participants come from all over the country and thus complement the overall picture and participation opportunities.

Civic Engagement The civic engagement of community energy is very strong, with only 17 percent of respondents not being committed.[20] Of these, 55 percent are even active, i.e. not passive payers of membership fees or similar. Those who are active are less likely to be found in large community energy projects and among people with high incomes. Similarly, participants in community energy limited liability companies and large community energy companies generally have fewer committed individuals, and the same applies to income differences. This illustrates

[18] This is reflected in the engagement of Germans: especially in rural towns (2000–5000 inhabitants), small towns (5000–20,000 inhabitants) and among village populations (less than 2000 inhabitants), engagement is more pronounced than in medium-sized and large cities (engagement rates of 38 to 42% compared to 30%) (Alscher et al. 2009: 37). According to the Volunteer Survey (Gensicke and Geiss 2010: 26), engagement is higher both in the densely populated surrounding areas of cities and in rural areas than in the core cities.

[19] In Germany, 35% of the population live in cities or densely populated areas (more than 500 inhabitants per km^2), 23% in rural areas (less than 100 inhabitants per km^2) and 42% semi-urban (100–500 inhabitants per km^2) (Statistisches Bundesamt 2013: 29, 2011 data).

[20] This finding is consistent with the results of a study of energy cooperatives in Germany, according to which 52% of members are also members of an environmental protection organization (referring to photovoltaic/heat energy cooperatives; Rauschmayer et al. 2015: 10).

that participants in smaller energy initiatives (which in turn increasingly include people with low incomes) are somewhat more committed to social policy than high-income participants in large participation projects.[21]

The civic engagement relates primarily to associations (40%), with associations, religious communities and political parties ranking in the middle at around 15 percent.[22] Less involvement relates to local community associations (Local Agenda 21, neighborhood groups) and trade unions. It is not surprising that

[21] In 2009, the Volunteer Survey counted 36% voluntarily engaged (taking on tasks, work or functions in civil society over the longer term), 35% publicly active (only participating in events, for example) (i.e. a total of 71% engaged) and 29% not publicly active among those engaged (Gensicke and Geiss 2010: 6). Engagement has increased slightly over the last few years, with only 27% of the population not engaged (ibid.: 8). The proportion of committed people has risen from 23% in 1985 to 33% in 2011 (Alscher and Priller 2013: 352). Regular engagement (at least monthly) has increased (19% in 2011), with 11% engaged on a weekly basis (ibid.). The 2013 data report distinguishes between general civic engagement (overall rate: 36%) and engagement as an integrative component of organizational commitment, which is much less pronounced (overall rate: 15%) (all data from 2009, Alscher and Priller 2013: 354).

[22] Associations are also the most pronounced organizational framework within the nationwide commitment (number in 2011: 580.000, strong increase since 1960, stagnating since 2001, Alscher and Priller 2013: 350), quantified in 2004 at a share of 43%, followed by churches and religious associations (15%), self-help groups, initiatives and projects (15%), state and municipal institutions (12%), associations (7%), private institutions and foundations (3%), political parties (2.8%) and trade unions (1.8%) (Alscher et al. 2009: 30). Other studies with data from 2009 state: clubs (46%), church/religious association (14%), groups and initiatives (13%), state or municipal institutions (9%), associations (7%), parties and trade unions (4%) and private institutions, foundations and others (7%) (Enste et al. 2012: 16). Similarly, data from the 2009 Volunteer Survey: clubs (47%), church/religious association (14%), groups or initiatives (13%), state or municipal institutions (9%), associations (7%), parties and trade unions (3%), and private institutions, foundations, and other (7%) (Gensicke and Geiss 2010: 28). According to the data from the Survey of Volunteers, membership figures in associations, state or municipal institutions, and parties and trade unions are declining slightly (also according to Alscher et al. 2009: 51, 69), remaining constant in churches/religious associations and federations, but showing growth in groups and initiatives as well as private institutions, foundations, and other (ibid.). Civil society organizations cite ageing, a declining sense of community, a lack of planning security due to unclear revenue trends, and increasingly market-like structures, efficiency and cost pressure as the main problems (Alscher and Priller 2013: 353). While the first two points are essential for associations and cooperatives, the latter two aspects play a greater role for nonprofit community energy limited liability companies (ibid.).

association memberships are more pronounced among the locally anchored, mostly smaller cooperatives, and also attract more men. The fact that there are more young and old people on lower incomes is also unsurprising, as people on higher incomes are often less engaged during the middle-aged working years.[23] However, it is surprising that active membership is most pronounced in the low-income group.

On the other hand, the association-related involvement of the cooperative members means that there is less involvement in associations in contrast to those involved in community energy limited liability companies (which are partly supported by an association). In conjunction with the result that academics are much more active here than non-academics (20 compared to 9%), membership in a larger association (e.g. environmental protection such as Greenpeace) leads to joining a supra-regional participation opportunity (represented in the case of the survey by the case of members of Planet Energy, the energy investment company of Greenpeace e. V., interviewed here). Memberships in churches and religious communities are equally distributed, which is due to the fact that this affiliation repre-

[23] The Federal Government's engagement report (Enste et al. 2012: 73) states that high engagement rates exist in the age ranges 30–45 years (37%) and 45–55 years (40%) (average: 34%). People between 16 and 30 engage less (especially among 25–30 year olds the rate is 29%), also people over 65 engage less (26%) (see in agreement Gensicke and Geiss 2010: 20, where it is shown, however, that the engagement of older people increased strongly from 2009 compared to 1999: among 65–69 year olds from 29 to 37%, among 70–74 year olds from 24 to 30%. It also points out that the high engagement from 35 to 49 year olds is due to family status (ibid: 17)). The 2013 Data Report distinguishes between general civic engagement (14–29 years: 35%, 30–69 years: 40%, 60 and older: 31%) and engagement tied to organizations as an integrative component, where younger people are more engaged (14–29 years: 19%, 30–69 years: 14%, 60 and older: 12%) (all data from 2009, Alscher and Priller 2013: 354). The rate of engagement has been increasing slightly overall in Germany since the 1980s, which mainly concerns regular engagement (Alscher et al. 2009: 34). The involvement of older people aged 60 and over has risen sharply overall since the 1980s (ibid.: 41). In terms of age cohorts, it can be seen that it is the so-called '68 generation (1939–1950), the baby boomers (1951–1969) and also the younger people (from 1983) who are disproportionately committed (ibid.).

sents a dimension that is comparatively independent of other characteristics.[24] It remains unclear how the respondents interpreted their involvement in a church congregation or faith community: whether as pure membership or an involvement that goes beyond this. Measured in terms of the total number of members in Germany, the value is low, but in terms of active church members it would presumably be high.[25] The characteristics of political party members (overrepresented in GmbH & Co. KGs, small and medium-sized community energy projects, higher age groups, academics, and people with medium and high incomes) seem to reflect the overall German member characteristics in the political party landscape (higher age and high-income academics) quite adequately.

In the local citizens' groups, people in small and medium-sized community energy projects are more active, which is easy to understand due to the proximity to local initiatives that often exists here (if, for example, the energy project arose directly from an Local Agenda 21 group). Here, academics, women and older people are more involved, but at the same time also people with low and middle incomes, which reveals an interesting structure. Apparently, these initiatives also manage to address women and to integrate people with low incomes – this is an important finding for the work and assessment of such initiatives. Consequently, if

[24] More recent findings on engagement in the context of civil society activities related to the environmental field can be found in relation to protest movements (Marg et al. 2013). According to these findings, more than 25%of participants in these groups are between 46 and 55 years old, and even more than 30% between 56 and 65 (ibid.: 304). Almost no participants are found in the range between 16 and 25, only 2.5% are between 25 and 35 years old. However, only a few older people are also found (13% between 66 and 75, 4% over 75). The 35 to 45 age group is not well represented at 16%. Walter points out, however, that in the past no older persons were involved at all (ibid.: 305). The social structure is strongly characterized by academics: 45.8% have a university degree, 9% even a doctorate (ibid.: 308). Only 0.6% do not have a degree and 0.6% have a "low-level" secondary school-leaving certificate (*Hauptschulabschluss*). At 16%, the "high-level" secondary school-leaving certificate (*Abitur*) is more strongly represented than the "mid-level" secondary school-leaving certificate (*Mittlere Reife/Realschulabschluss*) (5.4%). 14% have completed vocational training, pupils and students are not strongly represented (8.4%). Significantly more men are active (68.6% are male), and a conspicuously large number of people are non-denominational (61.5%) (ibid.: 314, 316). Among the study groups, one third are active in the field of energy and urban development, and the education/school sector is the most pronounced (75%) (ibid.: 315).

[25] According to the extrapolation of fowid (Forschungsgruppe Weltanschauungen in Deutschland 2015), 34% of the population in Germany are non-denominational. The 2013 data report indicates 18% non-denominational for western Germany, 68% for eastern Germany (2012 data, Statistisches Bundesamt and WZB 2013: 347). People with a denominational affiliation are much more committed than those without (73% compared to 27%) (Alscher et al. 2009: 45).

energy participation projects are linked to these initiatives, hypothetically these otherwise less represented population groups could be addressed directly.

In trade unions, more people from small community energy projects, and also with low incomes, are members and fewer persons from GmbH & Co. KGs – this correlates with the data that in small community energy projects people with low incomes tend to participate; the community wind farms (as GmbH & Co. KGs) integrate fewer of these groups due to the higher membership amounts. The male predominance and higher age correspond to the general picture of the membership structure of trade unions, but the lack of difference between academics and non-academics is surprising.

Finally, the qualitative data confirms the picture that the interviewees primarily make use of conventional forms of engagement, non-conventional engagement is cited but touched upon less here (4.5% of the data, 22% on the other hand, refer to conventional forms).[26] This is surprising, since it is precisely the locally anchored community energy projects that are partly interpreted as reactions to anti-nuclear power movements and the like. A certain proximity to unconventional forms of engagement and participation would therefore have been expected, but according to the available data – although unconventional engagement was not explicitly queried in the quantitative selection list – participation can be assumed to be rather weak overall (Figs. 6.6, 6.7, 6.8, and 6.9).[27]

Overall View

The data confirms the law of the standard socio-economic model, as it is mainly academics with higher incomes who participate in community energy initiatives: The whole of society is not mirrored, in particular socially worse-off strata tend to

[26] The data also suggests that the respondents understand commitment here primarily as membership. In this sense, the question on active membership puts actual engagement beyond silent membership into perspective (44 percent of respondents).

[27] Unconventional engagement is usually not recorded in studies, and the attribution and definition is still unclear in some cases, which is why a wide variety of forms can fall under it – however, according to data from 2008 (ALLBUS), the WZB assumes that, for example, 23% of respondents are members of informal groups (such as discussion groups and regulars' tables) (Alscher et al. 2009: 32). Informal participation behavior is supposed to be complementary to formal involvement, as this is presumably strongly influenced by the social middle classes.

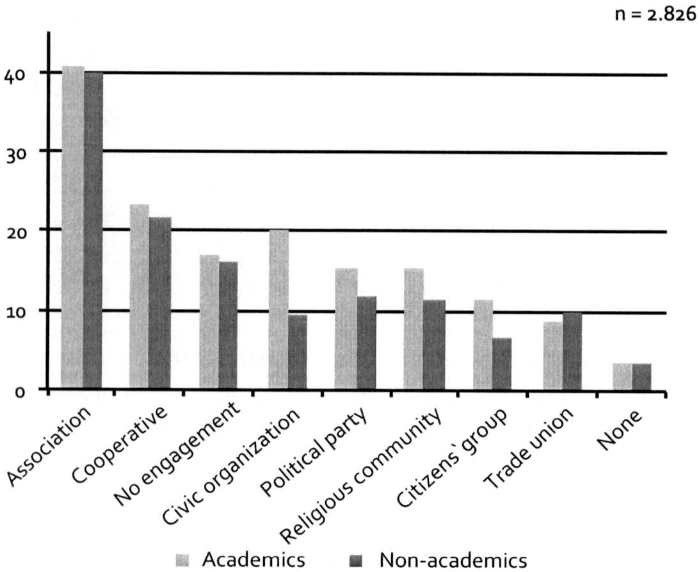

Fig. 6.6 Civic engagement: by level of education (multiple answers possible)

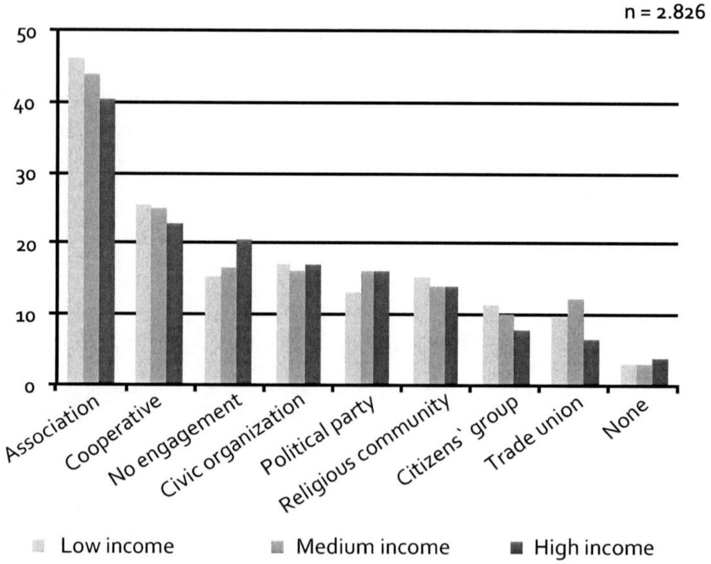

Fig. 6.7 Civic engagement: by income

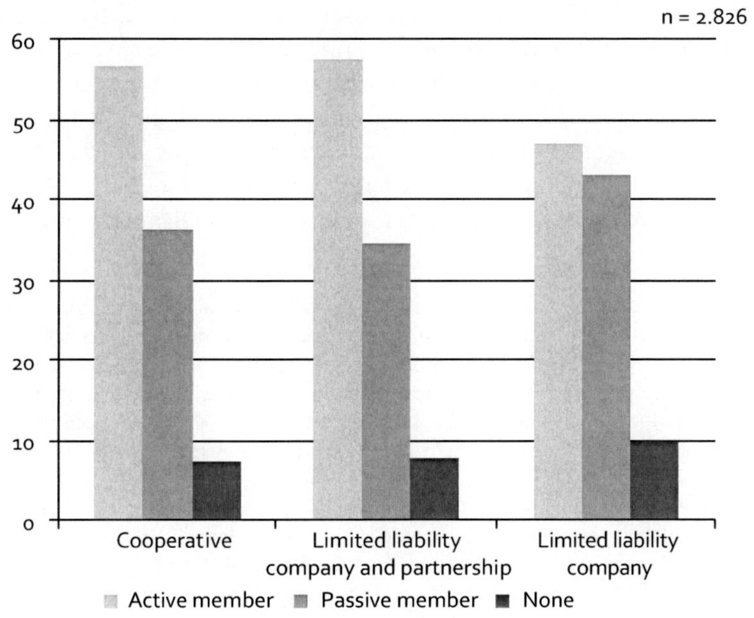

Fig. 6.8 Active membership in the context of civic engagement: by type of legal form

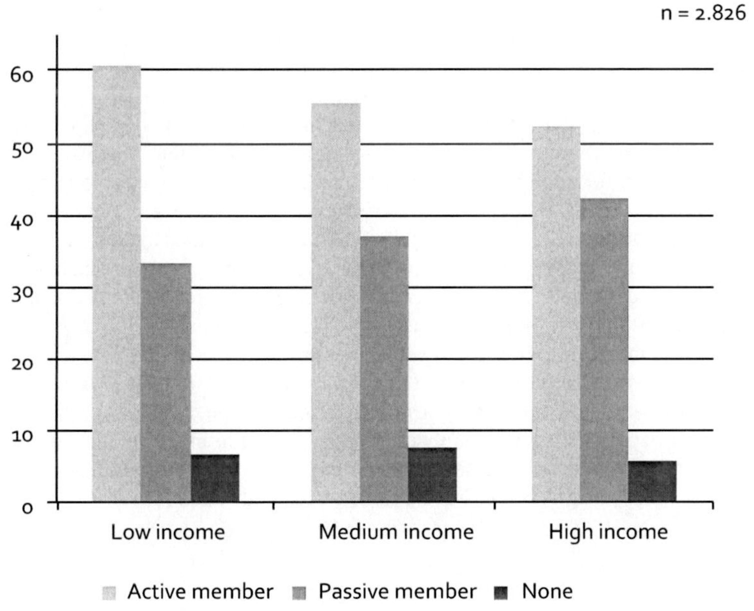

Fig. 6.9 Active membership in the context of civic engagement: by income

represent a minority.[28] However, the other assumption that non-academics and low-income earners are excluded cannot be confirmed either – there are also opportunities for participation for these people, which interestingly are provided by small cooperatives (with the option of a low participation sum) on the one hand, and by large community energy projects (non-academics) on the other, and therefore complement each other. Thus, community energy projects offer a variety of participation options. However, the constellation is unfavorable in relation to city dwellers:

[28] See also similar results of a survey in Heidelberg by Kreß et al. (2014b: 15): "The results of the questionnaire survey show: 11% of the respondents from Heidelberg state that they own their own RE system. Owners are more likely to be found in the middle age segment, often have a middle to higher level of education and a net household income of over 3500€. Of those who say they do not own a RE system, about a third (31%) of respondents say they are interested. A further 19% are 'partly' interested, while almost half (44%) express 'little' or 'no' interest (...). Interest is mainly expressed by younger people; citizens with low household incomes tend to be negative. Only just under 3% of respondents have a financial stake in a community RE system. Of those who do not currently have a financial stake, 4% are 'fully' interested, 11% are 'fairly' interested and a further 21% are 'partly' interested in participating in a local community scheme in the future. Trends emerge here depending on the gender, age and income of respondents: the lower the income, the lower the interest of respondents. Women and older people are also more likely to express a negative opinion. 9% of the citizens surveyed have or had money invested in renewable energies in general. This does not apply to 87%. Of those who have not yet invested, 11% would be interested, and a further 25% 'partly'. Older people tend to be opposed to the idea". – Similar results emerged from the same survey in the district of Steinfurt (Rubik et al. 2014: 13 f.): "The results of the questionnaire survey show: A quarter of all respondents say they own their own RE system (...), although these tend to be middle-aged respondents, while older people are the least likely to own their own system. Moreover, the tendency to own a RE system increases with education and income. About a quarter of non-owners would be 'quite' interested in owning their own RE system; for another 11% this is 'completely true'. Younger people and those with a higher level of education and income were the most likely to express interest. Only 7% of respondents are or have been financially involved in a community RE system. Of those who are not yet involved, 20% are interested in participating in the future, just over 19% are interested to some extent, and 55% of all respondents reject possible participation altogether. There are tendencies here depending on the gender, age and income of the respondents: the lower the income, the more likely the respondents are to reject participation; women and older respondents were also more likely to reject participation. 8% of the citizens surveyed have or had already invested money in renewable energies in general. However, this does not apply to the majority, 14% of this group would be interested in investing their money in renewable energies, the approval increases here with the level of education and income, women and older people tend to express themselves rather "reserved" again.

if there are no cooperatives (and similar initiatives) here that allow small participation sums, it would be difficult to realize a wish to participate. Especially ecologically-oriented younger people are probably a missed potential here. Citizen wind farms, on the other hand, do offer participation opportunities in rural areas, but often with high entry sums. Therefore, high-income (mostly male) middle-aged and older people are to be found here, fewer non-academics and fewer young people. In all cases, however, it is already socio-politically engaged people who participate. Community energy is obviously difficult to address and reach strata that are far removed from engagement – and therefore hardly ties up any new social capital here.

6.2.3 Personal Qualifications for Participation and Motivation

Knowledge and Experience Many people involved know the locations of the energy plants and the initiators of the community energy projects in which they participate (about 40% each); people involved in larger community energy projects know the energy plants and locations less, but even here the initiators are well known. Given the distance and dimensions, this is to be expected. Among all participants, one fifth know the energy plants personally, i.e. through direct visits or similar. Here, too, the figures are below 10% for community energy limited liability companies, and somewhat higher for large community energy projects. However, the community wind farms stand out, because the initiators, locations and energy plants are best known in the GmbH & Co. KGs (community wind farms): the strong involvement with the wind energy plants and the high relevance of the locations (for participants and the local population) probably leads to this high level of information.

Relatively unanimously, many participants (over a third) are of the opinion that little knowledge is sufficient for a participation (but especially in smaller projects), the participants in large community energy companies and GmbHs emphasize much more strongly the relevance of knowledge about renewable energies, the financial investment as well as specifics of the community energy project compared to cooperative members and members in small projects – the latter, on the other hand, are much more (a quarter) of the opinion that even no knowledge at all is necessary. Again, this seems to reflect the investment nature: As stakeholders in large societies are further away, they mostly have to use information materials – the installation as such (i.e. a wind turbine somewhere in Germany, for example) is much less easy to grasp and evaluate than if the wind turbine were located in a well-known place nearby. Nevertheless, there seems to be a difference in understanding even beyond that, possibly because of the valuation as a financial investment (about which a lot of knowledge is required, often associated with very high investment sums for those involved in the GmbHs), or as an investment in the environment and sustainability, where the principle as such is sufficient beyond investment data.

The sources of information through which the respondents became aware of the participation opportunity were mainly related to advertisements of the energy project, friends and acquaintances, as well as information in the daily newspaper – this indicates a strong direct link in that the participants became aware of the energy project in a very targeted manner. Thus, for 15 percent of the respondents there is a concrete connection to the workplace with regard to participation in the energy project. The internet was named as a more general source of information by only 12 percent. Local associations, federations, initiatives and clubs are only minor sources of information. As many as 10 percent of all respondents are themselves initiators of the energy project. Among the respondents, just over half were already involved in an energy project (which does not have to mean explicit membership) before using the participation through which they took part in the survey. People in medium and large community energy projects have more experience – presumably these are people with more of an "investor character" who use different participation options, as opposed to people who may only participate in a project once due to local proximity, for example because they know it specifically, there is a close connection, etc.

Motivation The main motivation among the respondents is the ecological motive (93 percent agree overall, only 3.7 percent disagree), followed by the participation and self-sufficiency idea of "energy in the hands of citizens" (82 percent agree overall, only 13 percent disagree) and finally the financial incentive (56 percent agree, 37 percent disagree) (Figs. 6.10, 6.11, 6.12, and 6.13).[29]

The latter point of financial motivation is a more important participation aspect among the participants in GmbHs or large community energy projects. However, more members in cooperatives agree with full conviction compared to the GmbHs – obviously there is a group here that emphasizes this aspect very strongly – just as a larger group completely rejects this motivation. In cooperatives, the discrepancy

[29] This finding is consistent with the results of a survey of energy cooperatives in Germany, according to which the most important motives for a decision to join were contribution to independent energy production (81 percent), environmental protection (79 percent), contribution to the community energy transition (78 percent), contribution to long-term cost-effective energy (73 percent); less important, however, was contribution to strengthening the regional economy (57 percent) and making a difference in society (56 percent) Rauschmayer et al. 2015: 7 f.). At the same time, the motives were queried with regard to general agreement, whereby the motives of making a difference to society (67 percent), participation in the energy transition (63 percent), strengthening the regional economy (68 percent) and contribution to long-term cost-effective energy (66 percent) are particularly striking. In contrast, the values for the two highly rated motives contribution to independent energy production (84 percent general agreement) and contribution to environmental protection (77 percent) are similar. Apparently, the immediate effects of community energy on site are less essential for concrete participation. Incidentally, non-members rated the motive of making a difference in society by far the highest with regard to the decision to join, which is the least relevant motive among cooperative members. Apparently, this motive represents a kind of starting point, which, however, plays less of a role with regard to topic-specific reasons (such as environmental protection and energy transition) with regard to concrete participation. For non-members, just as for members, the community energy turnaround and environmental protection are the most important motives for a possible decision to join (ibid.). With regard to the evaluation of the return on investment, interestingly enough, the results are reversed for members and non-members: While members assess energy cooperatives quite predominantly as profitable (69 percent), only 5 percent of non-members do so. Accordingly, 5 percent of members rate energy cooperatives as very or somewhat low in terms of return on investment, but 38 percent of non-members do. Fifty-seven percent of non-members guess a return on investment as partly-somewhat, while only 27 percent of members do so (ibid.: 9). Accordingly, cooperative members indicated that for 28 percent the return aspect is rather or very unimportant, 34 percent consider it to be partly important and partly unimportant, in contrast to 38 percent who consider it to be rather or very important. Also, 75 percent of non-members state that the return aspect does not play an outstanding role (ibid.).

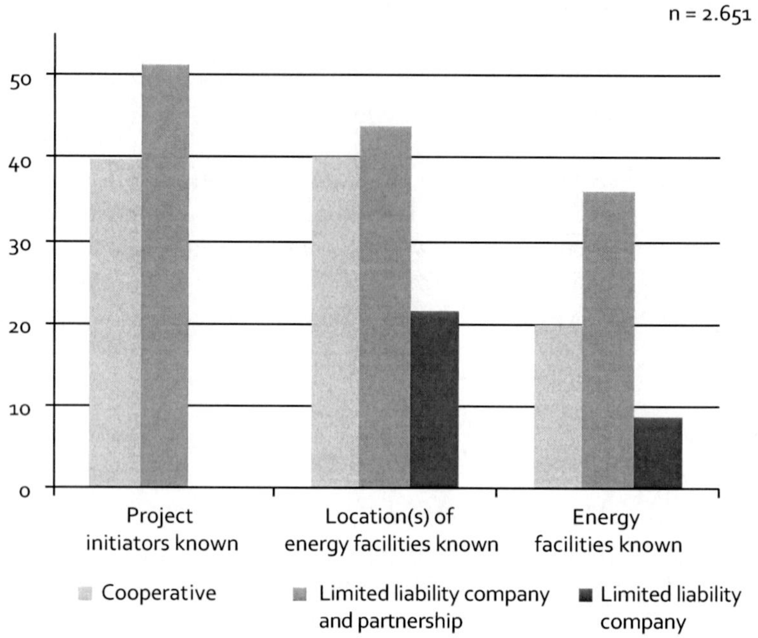

Fig. 6.10 Specific reason for participation: by type of legal form (The answer option "initiators personally known" was not included in the answer catalogue for community energy limited liability companies)

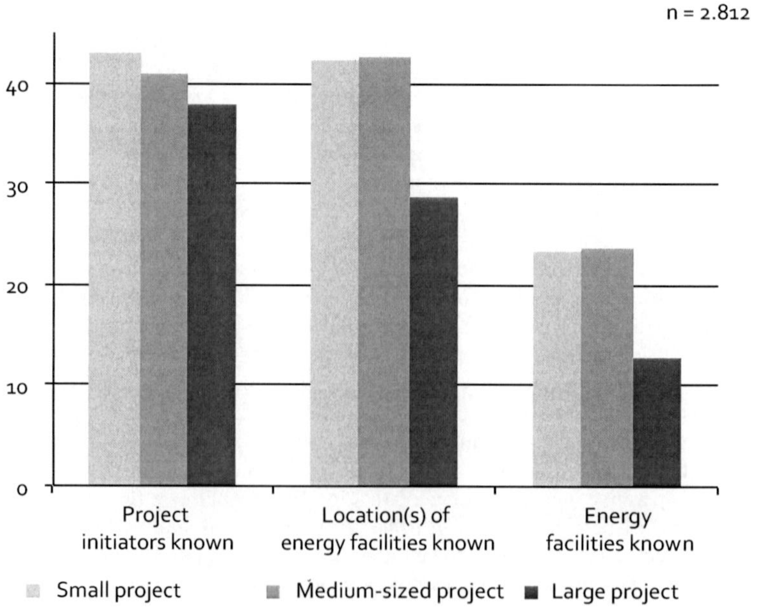

Fig. 6.11 Specific reason for participation: by project size

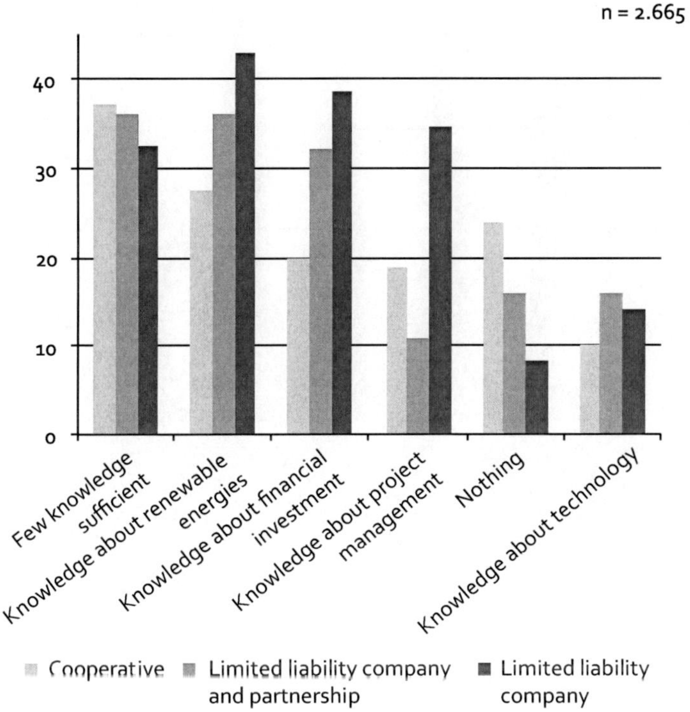

Fig. 6.12 Required knowledge for participation: by type of legal form

between strong approval and rejection is thus greater, and the orientation is more extreme here.[30]

Men agree with this motivation significantly more than women, academics reject it more strongly, and people with low incomes reject this point more decisively than those with higher incomes. For women, the return aspect is obviously unim-

[30]The main motivation for socio-political involvement is shaping society, at least on a small scale, and getting together with other people (60% fully agree); acquiring qualifications, prestige and influence, and professional advancement are seen as less important (Gensicke and Geiss 2010: 12). Above all, the activity should be fun, help other people, serve the common good, serve the community and offer input as well as the development of knowledge and experience (ibid.: 13). The Volunteer Survey therefore summarizes these statements under three types of motivation: Common good-oriented (strongly increasing tendency, especially among older persons), sociability-oriented (strongly decreasing tendency, similarly distributed in all age groups) and interest-oriented (slightly increasing tendency, especially more pronounced among younger persons) (ibid.: 122).

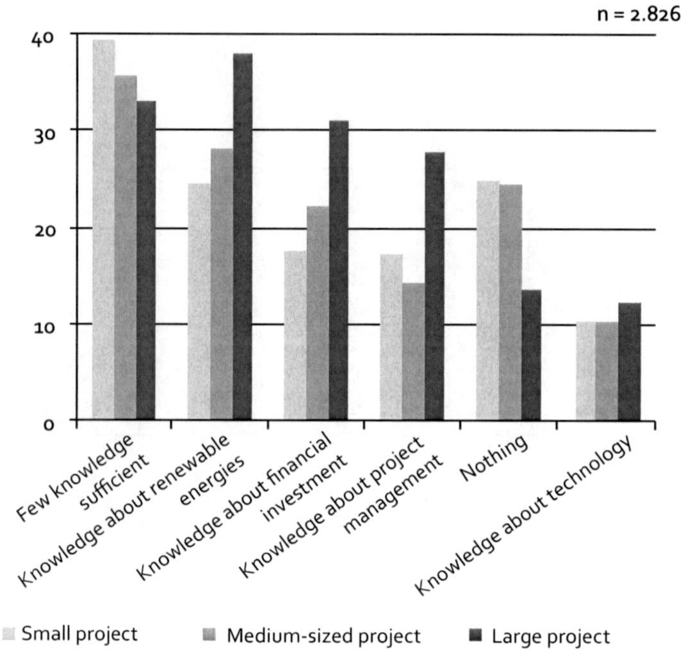

Fig. 6.13 Required knowledge for participation: by project size

portant, and the approval ratings for ecological motivation are correspondingly much higher than for men. The idea of "energy in the hands of citizens" (energy self-sufficiency) is shared equally by both men and women. Academics similarly reject the return point more strongly and emphasize ecological motivation somewhat more strongly; here, too, the "energy in the hands of citizens" idea is balanced. While people with high incomes emphasize the return aspect somewhat more strongly, those with low incomes reject it more decisively, the latter emphasize the other two motivations more strongly. Non-academics and people with high incomes are thus more inclined towards the return orientation, while academics and low-income earners agree more strongly with idealistic motives. However, it should ultimately be pointed out that the differences between the groups represent more tendencies – extreme differences cannot be ascertained in this area.

With regard to the ecological aspect, all participants in all types of community energy projects strongly agree, in small projects the agreement is somewhat stronger with full agreement, in the large projects a disproportionately large number of people partially agree. Here, participants in community energy limited liability companies and community wind farms outvote those in cooperatives in terms of full agreement. For these groups, the ecological aspect seems to be the decisive criterion, possibly due to the overall attitude: due to the ecological attitude, participation in community energy is a form of expression of this; in the case of cooperative members, participation seems to be more specific in that it is linked to a wide variety of individual aspects (e.g. meaningful project for the community, etc.). This corresponds to the social structure in the form of generally committed academics among the community energy limited liability company participants and the broader spectrum of population groups in cooperatives, who have arrived at participation on the basis of a wide variety of motivations.

Finally, the community energy projects differ more on the "energy in the hands of citizens" motivation: cooperative members agree very strongly, but it is medium-sized projects in particular that agree here. Those involved in community energy limited liability companies, on the other hand, reject this motivation somewhat more strongly, which is not surprising since they themselves represent this idea less with their approach, which corresponds to the previous consideration and supports it. Nevertheless, higher agreement values are also present here.

Interestingly, the size of the shareholding affects the motivational strength: Financial incentive motivation increases with increasing share (10.5 percent full agreement and 4 percent full disagreement for a share amount of more than 5000 euros, versus only 6 percent full agreement and 20 percent full disagreement for a share amount of less than 2000 euros). In contrast, ecological motivation decreases as the share increases (56 percent fully agree for a share of less than 2000 euros, compared to 45 percent fully agree for a share of more than 5000 euros). Likewise, the "energy in the hands of citizens" motivation rates drop with increasing share (44 percent full approval with a share of over 5000 euros, compared to 54 percent approval with a share of under 2000 euros).

Co-founders or initiators show a comparatively lower financial motivation, but a stronger ecological and slightly higher "energy in the hands of citizens" motivation (cf. Gamel et al. 2016). These results are also confirmed by the findings of another survey, in that the return motive is more pronounced for community wind farms (in the legal form of a GmbH & Co. KG) compared to cooperatives, wind energy compared to photovoltaic and biomass use, community energy projects in the north compared to the south of Germany (wind power factor), members compared to management staff and higher compared to lower participation amounts (cf. Holstenkamp and Kahla 2016; in addition, also building on the same data Leuphana University Lüneburg and Nestle 2014: iv. The results of Rauschmayer et al. 2015 and Bauwens 2016 at least tend to indirectly confirm these trends) (Figs. 6.14, 6.15, 6.16, 6.17, 6.18, and 6.19).

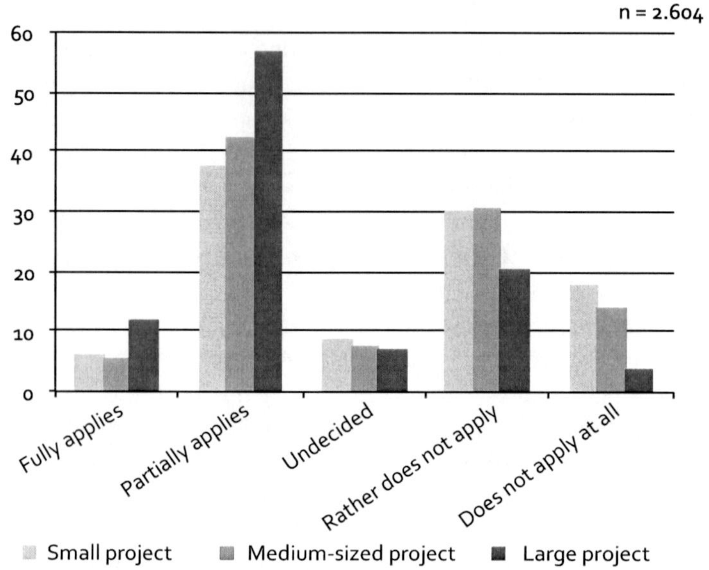

Fig. 6.14 Financial motivation: by project size

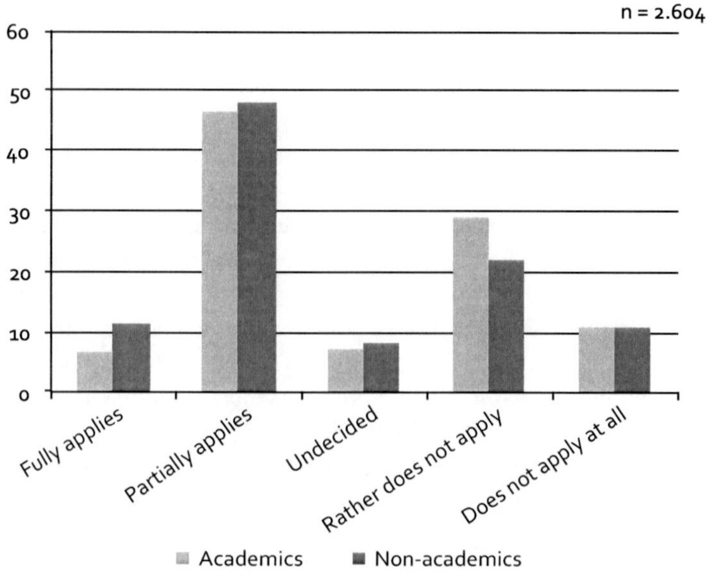

Fig. 6.15 Financial motivation: by level of education

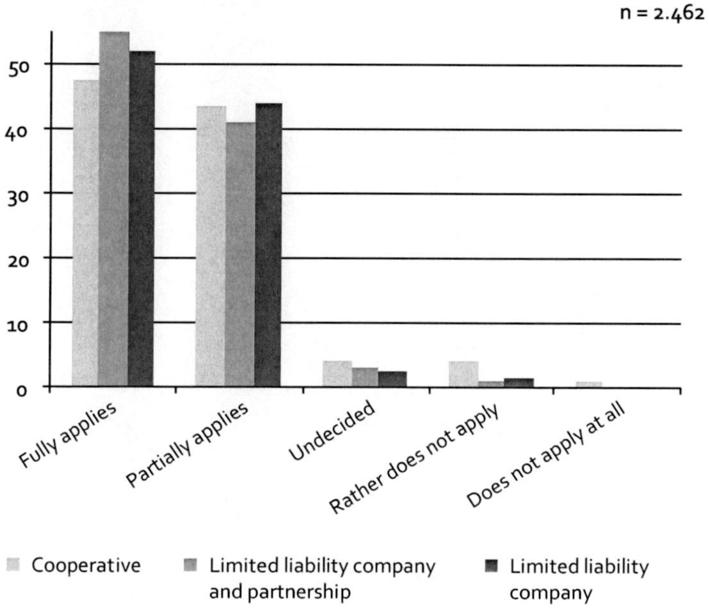

Fig. 6.16 Ecological motivation: by type of legal form

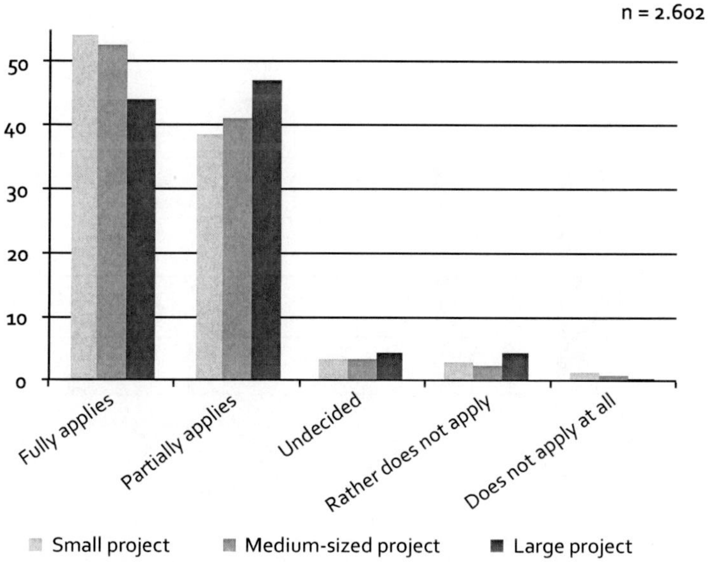

Fig. 6.17 Ecological motivation: by project size

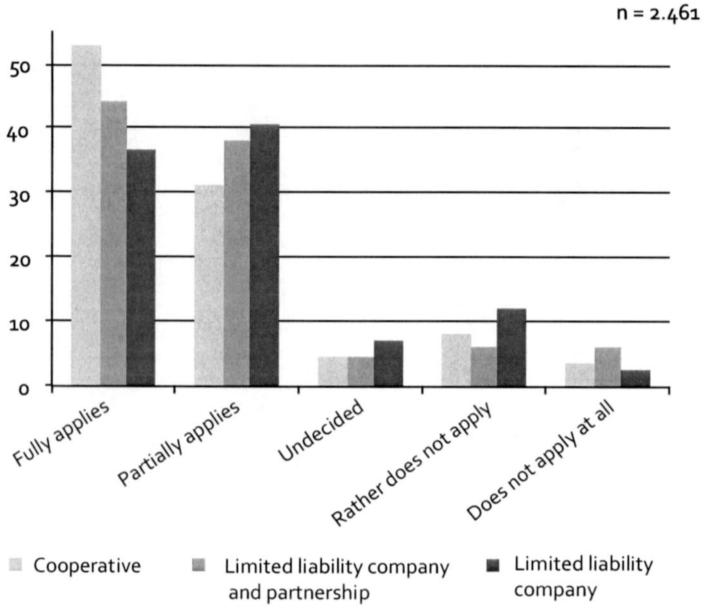

Fig. 6.18 Self-sufficiency motivation: by type of legal form

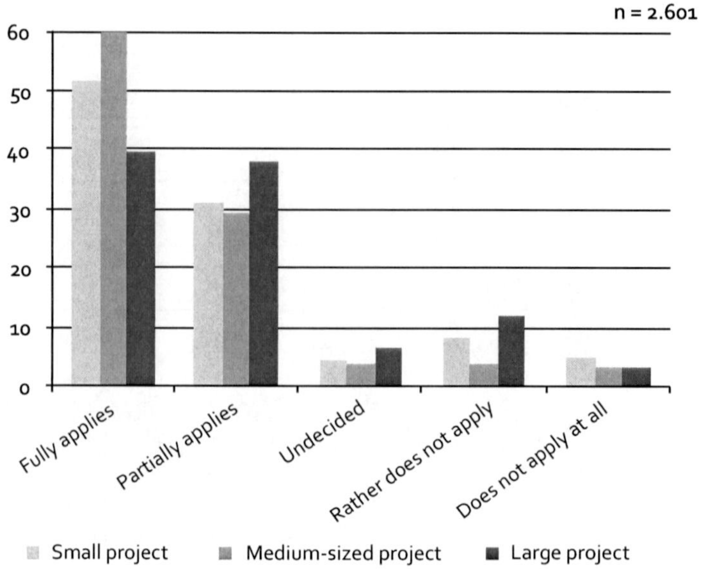

Fig. 6.19 Self-sufficiency motivation: by project size

Overall View

Community energy provides more proximity to renewable energy through increased engagement in the form of knowledge and competence acquisition (regarding technology, locations, participation offers, involved actors, implementation procedures, energy policy), and creates a high level of knowledge about the energy project and energy plants.[31]

Although many participants do not live near the energy plants, they know the plants, locations and initiators. Many participants already have experience with renewable energy participation projects, and most of them learned about the participation directly. The interviewees were mainly motivated to participate due to ecological reasons; the idea of energy in the hands of citizens is also decisive; less

[31] Bauwens (2014b, 2016) distinguishes as motivational conditions for participation in an energy cooperative on the one hand public benefits (1. reduction of CO_2 emissions, 2. reduction of commodity dependencies), and on the other hand private benefits (1. Monetary benefits: Return on investment or discounted electricity tariffs, 2. Non-monetary benefits). It was found that in two of the energy cooperatives studied, non-monetary motives for participation were decisive, in particular ecological orientation as well as interpersonal trust and social identification. Distributive justice/fairness (i.e. the enjoyment benefits of energy use) and procedural justice/fairness (procedures and processes of implementation and administration of energy use) were analyzed as not decisive. Again, social identification and distributive justice are the main explanatory factors for the level of contribution. The financial incentive is also in this study only a partial factor for the participation decision, here high values are in the midfield between strongly shaping the decision and not shaping at all. In this case, however, the two differently oriented energy cooperatives studied differ considerably from each other in terms of the maximum deviating approval or disapproval values (in the case of the energy cooperative with many small participations (on average 2000 euros, 47,500 participants), the value of low return orientation is about 12 percent (9 percent full approval for return orientation), while in the case of the energy cooperative with fewer participants (on average 4000 euros, 2400 participants), it is about 27 percent (18 percent full approval for return orientation), see Bauwens 2014b: 6). Similarly strong differences from case to case can also be found within this survey (especially with regard to size, participation orientation/distribution (many small vs. a few large shares), bottom-up initiatives or top-down participation offerings).

so is the yield aspect, which can, however, be assessed as a thoroughly relevant partial condition, as will be discussed in more detail below.[32]

6.2.4 Characterization of the Case Studies

Through an initial analysis and compilation of relevant information, data and facts from the case studies and comparative cases, it is possible to characterize and describe the cases on the basis of this information. Against this backdrop, a deeper analysis can take place using data from the expert interviews and results of the online survey, and possible similarities and contradictions can be uncovered.

The number of members of the case studies of community energy companies and projects basically shows a very wide range. The amount of investment also varies greatly.[33] In an overview (see "Overview of energy initiatives" in the

[32] See also similar results of a survey in Heidelberg on motives for investing in renewable energy systems by Kreß et al. (2014b: 15): "The main motives for investing in renewable energy systems are to make a 'contribution to climate protection' and to 'protect the environment'. More than 70% of the respondents agree with these motives. 58% of the respondents want to be 'independent of energy suppliers' through RE systems or give financial motives. Slightly more than one third would like to 'strengthen the regional economy'. The interviews and the focus group came to similar conclusions: investments in community renewable energy systems are seen as financially secure by active citizens. Other important motives are self-determination, ecological and technical interest as well as regionality, because it is "a nice thought that this is close by". In the case of investments in their own plants, ecological or normative motives are more prominent among those involved, but are also linked to financial aspects: 'not only to take account of the energy transition now or to be part of it, but of course return considerations also play a role'." – Similar results – albeit with a stronger emphasis on the return aspect – emerged from the same survey in the district of Steinfurt (Rubik et al. 2014: 14 f.): "The main motives for investing in RE systems are to 'contribute to climate protection' and to 'protect the environment': more than 60% of respondents agreed with these motives in each case. 68% of respondents would like to gain financial advantages through RE systems and 62% would like to be 'independent of energy suppliers'. Slightly more than one third would like to 'strengthen the regional economy'. The interviews and the focus group came to similar results: In addition to the need to do something for the region, the advancement of the local energy transition and the real practice of citizen participation are further motives. In addition to financial gains, these aspects also convey a good feeling: 'You are a member and that just feels very good!' The participants in the focus group were more focused on financial gains. When it comes to investing in one's own investments, financial motives come first among the committed, but they are also linked to normative aspects: 'for my children I have to do something someday.' That was an investment in the future. That wasn't about money'."

[33] The data used here is based on the status of 2012.

appendix), various key figures of the case studies and four community energy companies used for comparison are presented. The four additionally presented community energy projects represent, on the one hand, large supra-regional energy cooperatives ("Jurenergie" and "Norddeutsche Energiegemeinschaft") and, on the other hand, large energy companies with the option of participation rights. ("Planet Energy" as a participation company of "Greenpeace e. V." and "Green City Energy" as a participation company of an environmental association ("Green City e. V.")).

These four cases are presented as a comparison to the case studies, because on the one hand they represent types of community energy initiatives which are not covered by the case studies that are analyzed in more detail, and on the other hand, with the help of the key figures and the survey results, they should enable a review of the extent to which size, distance and type of participation lead to less participation and member activity than in smaller, local community energy projects (large vs. small community energy projects). The two community energy cooperatives and two community energy limited liability companies selected are of such a size on the one hand, and on the other hand they are part of specific survey clusters ("limited liability companies" as well as "large companies").

Project Size

To determine the size of the community energy projects analyzed here, key figures on the number of members in the community energy projects, investment volumes and the number of energy plants are compared.

Wind Energy Case Studies The largest community energy project in the wind sector as well as within all case studies is the community wind cooperative in Baden-Württemberg (case study 2) with 362 members. In case study 1, the community wind farm has 88 participating citizens (as limited partners). The two wind energy examples are therefore of different sizes and can be assigned to a medium size in the wind energy sector, since they neither represent a community energy project with fewer than 100 members nor a project with at least 1000 members.

The relative shares describe the percentage that the members' investments represent of the total investment amount. In the wind sector, there are major differences between the two projects: While in the case of the cooperative 80 percent of the investments are borne by the members, in the case of the community wind farm it is only 20 percent. This corresponds with the total investment sums: These are very high in the case of community wind farm (15.5 million euros), while in the case of the cooperative they are significantly lower at 3.6 million euros. The members of the community wind farm have thus provided almost three million euros in equity capital, which is not far from the amount provided by the cooperative. Accordingly, the cooperative installed a single wind turbine, while the GmbH & Co KG built a wind farm with five turbines. The wind turbine of the cooperative is identical in construction to the turbines of the wind farm.

Medium-Sized Solar Energy Cooperatives and Community Solar Projects Among the solar cooperatives in the case studies, the UniBremen solar cooperative (case study 4) has 130 members, Bürgerenergie Syke has 110 members and the Energiegewinner cooperative has 90 members. A total of 140 people are involved in the community solar plants of BUND Bremen. Thus, these case studies represent a medium size with about 100 members. In all cases, the relative shares of members are very high: in the case of the University of Bremen cooperative, they are 50 percent, in all other cases even 100 percent. Compared to wind energy plants, the investments are lower and usually amount to several hundred thousand euros, since about 50–100,000 Euros have to be calculated per plant. The solar plants of the UniBremen and the Energiegewinner cooperative represent the highest values with a total sum of about one million euros. In the first case four plants could be erected, in the second case eight plants. In the other cases, there are one to four plants.

Small Community Solar Cooperative One solar cooperative differs from the others because it is significantly smaller: The solar popular cooperative has only 19 members and one solar plant. The few members have a comparatively small 30 percent share of the total investment.

Community Geothermal Energy Project This project has not yet been realized, which is why no information can be provided on participations. However, a total of 40 million euros would have to be raised for the construction of both a local heating network and a geothermal plant, which is why the local heating network is being targeted first. For the three million euro necessary for this, at present approximately one million euro would be available, which is made available, however exclusively, by a few partners of a project company created first. The further investments are then to be funded by the contributions of the members of an investment cooperative.

Energy Cooperatives of the Comparison Cases The two supra-regional energy cooperatives used for comparison have almost the same number of members (726 and 753 persons). However, the investment sums differ significantly: In the case of Jurenergie it is 2.3 million euros, in the case of the Norddeutsche Energiegemeinschaft it is seven million euros. Of greater importance, however, are the relative membership shares, which also vary greatly. In the first case it is almost 100 percent, whereas in the case of the Norddeutsche Energiegemeinschaft it is only 20 percent. While the latter operates ten solar plants, Jurenergie has solar plants on 22 roofs and stakes in two wind energy plants.

Community Energy Projects of the Comparative Cases The two larger community energy companies, in which several thousand people are involved (a total of 4000 in the case of Green City Energy and 5000 in the case of Planet Energy), are on a different scale again. The sums invested here are in the hundreds of millions (108 million euros for Planet Energy and 150 million euros for Green City Energy). The relative shares of the members are comparatively very small here: in the case of Planet Energy, 12 million euros, which corresponds to about eleven percent. In the case of Green City Energy, however, this conversion is not possible, as information is only available on the amount of holders of profit participation rights (eight million euros out of 1000 people), but the holders of KG shares must be added to this (a further 3000 investors).

Renewable Energy Plants

The use of renewable energies is presented here on the basis of the energy performance figures, the locations of the energy plants and planned expansions of the community energy projects. As expected, the energy outputs differ according to the energy types and the size and number of energy plants. While the single solar plant of the case study 4 cooperative produces 25,000 kilowatt hours of electricity per year, the larger energy cooperatives already produce about 400,000 and 750,000 kilowatt hours. The wind turbines, on the other hand, produce 3.5 million kilowatt hours of electricity per year in the case of a single turbine (case study 2), and 18 million kilowatt hours in the case of the wind farm with five turbines. The two large community energy companies produce 105 and 160 million kilowatt hours per year, respectively.

The locations of the energy plants depend on their type and the orientation of the community energy project. The two community wind case studies installed their wind turbines near the place where the community energy companies are also located. Thus, the citizens involved mostly live in close proximity to the turbines. In the case of case study 1, the five wind turbines are located on a mountain in a forested area above the town – and thus also relatively far away from residential areas. The single wind turbine of case study 2, on the other hand, is located much closer to the residential area, and there is no distance between it and the surrounding forest and mountains. Two farms in particular are directly affected.

Such proximity of the energy installations to the citizens involved can also be found in the energy cooperatives, which in case studies 3, 4, 5, and 6 operate the solar installations in the city where most of the people involved live. For this purpose, the cooperatives use roofs of larger buildings to which they either have direct access through known actors or use the offer of the municipality to use urban roofs. In the case of the larger and supra-regional energy cooperatives, this proximity to the stakeholders no longer exists: the plants are built somewhere in Germany. In the case of the larger cooperatives in the case studies, there is still a certain proximity within a region, but this is no longer the case for the two larger community energy companies. Accordingly, a rough rule can be formulated here: The larger a community energy project becomes, the further away the energy plants are from the homes of the people involved.

Expansion is generally planned for most community energy projects and projects. Expansion is a common goal and part of the enterprise. Both the solar cooperatives and the larger community energy projects are almost all aiming to build more plants. On the other hand, this situation is different for the community wind energy projects: in case study 1 as well as in case study 2, no further plants are planned for the time being. This is probably due to three reasons: On the one hand, the investments and the effort for the initiators were so high that a further commitment is not possible. Secondly, there are usually only a few sites available for wind turbines in the vicinity of the community energy companies' headquarters. Finally, case study 1 is a closed project, as the founded limited partnership only pursues one goal – the operation of the five wind turbines. Nevertheless, the managing director of the community energy limited liability company can found a new holding company if further areas and interested citizens can be found. Expansion into other regions and districts is not an option for these community energy projects due to their regional approach. A supra-regional approach is only present in case study 8 in the form of a medium-sized cooperative whose concept is also based on this orientation. Finally, there is one case study that is no longer planning any further expansion: The environmental organization "BUND Bremen" in case study 5 is not planning any more expansions, as the individuals here were directly involved in the financing of a plant by means of a loan, and due to the association's approach of using the roofs of actors close to the association, this represents a limitation of possible areas. However, all solar cooperatives (apart from case study 8) are subject to this limitation due to the regional approach.

Organization and Structure of Community Energy Projects

First of all, based on a document analysis, the legal forms and governing bodies of the associations, the number of members in the board of directors and supervisory board, number of initiators in the management as well as information on meetings, voting rights and voluntary structure can be presented.

- Case study 1 organized as a **limited liability company and partnership (GmbH & Co KG):** In case study 1, there is a GmbH acting as operator, including a management board, and a limited partnership as the holding company, in which the citizens participate as limited partners. The management body is therefore the GmbH with a management board; there is no management board or supervisory board here. The initiator of the wind energy project is also the managing director of the GmbH. The limited partnership holds a partners' meeting once a year, whereby the participating citizens have voting rights depending on the amount of their financial shares. It is also possible for members to propose topics for the meetings and to table motions. The managing director does not work on an honorary basis; his remuneration is set out in the partnership agreement and can be classified as low.
- Case studies 2, 3, 4, 6, 8; comparative cases 1 and 2 organized as **cooperatives**: In the case of cooperatives, a general meeting is held once a year for all members. Unlike a limited partnership, each member has one vote at the meetings when votes are taken, regardless of the level of financial participation. Again, agenda items can be proposed and motions can be introduced. In all of the cooperatives in the case studies, the members of the boards are volunteers; likewise, in all of these cooperatives, the initiators of the energy projects serve on the boards. The management of a cooperative consists of a board of directors and a supervisory board. However, in some of these cases the size of these boards varies: It is noticeable that two persons always form the management board. The supervisory board, on the other hand, is made up of three to eight people. These descriptions also apply to the Jurenergie cooperative in the comparison cases. However, the situation is different for the larger cooperative: Here, the two board members also work on a voluntary basis, but they come from an energy company on whose initiative the cooperative was founded together with banks. It is also striking that the supervisory board here is unusually large, with ten people.
- Case study 5 organized as an **association**: The citizen participation of the environmental association "BUND" differs fundamentally from the other participation models: here, no separate company was founded, but the energy plants were built by BUND. To finance the plants, citizens could invest in the plants through loan agreements. Therefore, there are no committees and meetings of a separate energy company. The persons involved have made a pure financial investment through loan agreements, which does not include any further partici-

pation or co-determination. An influence would only be possible in an indirect way through an activity within the BUND regional association.

- Case study 7 organized as a **combination of a limited liability company (GmbH) and a cooperative**: In this case, a management acts as in case study 1, but on a voluntary basis. The planned cooperative would then be a holding company, so that this construction is also reminiscent in this respect of the combination of a GmbH with a limited partnership in case study 1. However, there is a difference here: in contrast to the limited partnership, the cooperative has a management, which means that the interests of the members are presumably represented more actively. The limited partnership, on the other hand, is excluded from management. How the joint interaction of a community energy limited liability company and an associated cooperative would proceed, cannot yet be estimated.

Community Engagement

A joint commitment of the community energy initiatives means here a possible existence of "supporting" initiatives and further civic engagement of the community energy projects. Sponsoring initiatives are those institutions and organizations from which the community energy projects have either emerged as spin-off projects or which accompany them. These civil society groups can take the form of clubs, associations or citizens' initiatives.

Type 1: No Civil Society Background Case studies 1 and 8 have no civil society background in the form of any organization. These energy projects were initiated and founded by individuals or several private persons (in both cases there were two persons each). In the case of the cooperative of case study 8, there is also no further, e.g. social commitment of the community energy project. In the case of the community wind farm, the commitment consists of opening up the wind farm to the population and interested persons and institutions: For this purpose, guided tours and conferences are offered, the projecct is very present among the population and at events, and in addition, interested persons and actors are given advice free of charge.

Type 2: Citizens' Initiatives Case studies 2 and 7 emerged from citizens' initiatives. In both cases, these initiatives had been pursuing the idea of how a community energy plant could be built for many years. The wind energy cooperative also shows a high level of commitment in the form of a diverse presence in the community, events as well as special citizens' meetings. The information policy of the cooperative can also be classified as very extensive. The same applies to the citizens' community geothermal energy initiative in case study 7, which is currently still trying to win over broad sections of the population as well as political groups and local companies to the idea.

Type 3: Local Agenda 21 Groups The community solar cooperative of case study 6 is the sole result of the work of a Local Agenda 21 group. Even after the foundation of the cooperative, the Agenda work was continued, which then focused on other ideas. However, the cooperative does not show any other outstanding commitment. A similar grouping in the form of an "active group" also exists in case study 7, which, however, accompanies and supports the energy interest group – and thus cannot be equated with it.

Type 4: Associations and Clubs In case studies 3, 5, as well as in the comparative cases of the large community energy companies, associations and clubs are the origin of the establishment of community energy projects (energy project as a concrete spin-off). This ranges from rather small to very large organizations: The association in case study 3 is a very small, specialized association, while in the other cases large environmental protection organizations initiated the energy projects (regional association of BUND, Greenpeace Germany as the sponsor of Planet Energy, and the environmental protection organization Green City in the case of Green City Energy). In the first case, the further motivation and commitment of both the association and the cooperative can be regarded as very high: Within the framework of a so-called solidarity transfer, 20 percent of the annual surplus of the cooperative is donated to charitable projects (e.g. development aid). The commitment of the larger environmental protection organizations is correspondingly large and varied. However, the community energy projects are not active here themselves, apart from a municipal energy advisory service provided by Green City Energy, which is, however, only offered for a fee.

Type 5: Public Initiative A direct or indirect initiative by public institutions can be found in case study 4 as well as in one solar cooperative of the comparative cases. In the first case, it is the university's environmental committee that developed the idea of founding a solar cooperative at the university. As this is a staff cooperative, i.e. it is only open to members of the institution, the further involvement of the cooperative only relates to this framework – in the form of exhibitions, presentations and by involving academic departments and research. In the case of the Jurenergie cooperative, a district as well as a development company (which is supported by state institutions and banks with a public mandate) initiated the energy project. In this case, there is also a further form of involvement on the part of the cooperative: Local "sponsorships" are to be used to recruit people who are to establish a "closeness" to the energy project in the population and region. This form of engagement clearly stands out among the cases of a larger cooperative. In addition, consultations and the (direct) sale of electricity are planned.

Type 6: Private-Sector Initiative The North German Energy Community, the second comparative case in cooperative form, was the only energy project initiated by a regional electricity company and five cooperative banks (Volksbanken). This comparatively large cooperative thus differs from the other cases in one decisive point. There is no further involvement of the cooperative.

In summary, it is noticeable that especially the wind energy projects as well as smaller cooperatives show a high, more far-reaching commitment. In the first case, this is probably due to the problem of acceptance of wind energy among the population, and in the second case to the high motivations and demands of the initiators and members of the small cooperatives.

Financial Participation

As purely quantitative indicators and formal conditions, the minimum amount and fixed upper limits of the investment amount for a financial participation, as well as possibilities of withdrawal from the community energy project or termination of the participation, can be taken into account in the first instance.

Community Wind Energy Case Studies The community energy projects in the wind sector have comparatively high entry sums: In the case of the wind energy cooperative it is 2500 euros, in case study 1 it is varied: for the local population 3000, for people living further away as much as 10,000 euros are required. The further increments here are 1000 euros, in the case of the wind cooperative the amount of 2500 can only be multiplied. Financial upper limits of the participation do not exist here, thus even very high, individual participation sums are conceivable. Due to their high investment sums, these projects are also not designed for an early withdrawal of the invested sums: In case study 1, the earliest possible termination date is 31.12.2023; in case study 2, termination is possible at the end of a financial year after a period of two years. However, in the case of the wind cooperative, it is possible to terminate parts of the shares at the end of a year. This is not possible with case study 1, here only one share can be transferred in its entirety to other persons, which is also possible with case study 2 – here even partial transfers are possible.

Community Solar Energy Cooperatives In the case of the solar energy cooperatives, financial participation is possible with very small amounts: in the cooperative of case study 8 it is only 50 euros, in case studies 4, 5, and 6 it is 100 euros; a share of 500 euros is possible in case study 3 as well as in the two solar cooperatives of the comparison cases. The highest entry sum of 1000 euros is required in case study 6. The increases in the shares are also different at 100 euros (case studies 3, 4, 5, 6), 250 euros (comparison case 2), and a maximum of 500 euros (comparison case 1). Case study 8 is a different case: Here, a person becomes a member of the cooperative by paying in an amount of 50 Euros. However, this does not mean that the person has a direct stake in the energy systems, as the members each purchase one solar module (or several).

The upper limits of the participation amounts are also set differently: In the case of case study 4, the maximum participation amount is 25,000 euros, while in case study 3, an agreement is required for an amount of 25,000 euros or more. In case studies 6 and 8 there are no limits. Interestingly, the two solar cooperatives in the comparison cases both have a limit of 100,000 euros.

Leaving a solar cooperative is generally possible by selling or transferring the shares or terminating the membership. The transfer of shares is always possible at any time. In case study 4, however, this is possible for the first time after four years. In case studies 3 and 4, notice periods of two years each also apply. In case study 6, shares are initially fixed for one year; notice of termination can then be given at the end of a financial year with a period of notice of 12 months. However, repayments by the cooperative are only possible here if at least 90 percent of the cooperative capital is retained. Withdrawal is less problematic in case study 8: Here the share in the cooperative (which in this case is only 50 euros) can be terminated annually. However, the investments acquired in this case can only be resold to other members or persons. This makes it comparatively difficult to exit in this case.

Community Energy Projects of the Comparative Cases and BUND Community Solar Project While a participation in the BUND solar plants is possible from as little as 100 Euros (as well as further increments of 100 Euros each), the minimum amount in the case of Planet Energy is 1000 Euros and varies between 1000 and 10,000 euros in the case of Green City Energy. Further increases are 1000 euros in both cases. While the maximum loan amount in case study 5 is limited to 5000 euros, which is the lowest maximum amount of all cases, there is no upper limit for the two larger community energy projects.

In case study 5, there is a fixed term of 20 years – due to the loan agreement. The same applies to the investment forms of profit participation rights in the two larger community energy projects: Planet Energy has a fixed term of 20 years, but the situation is more differentiated in the case of Green City Energy: the term of profit participation rights varies here between three and 20 years, and in the case of shares through membership in a limited partnership company (GmbH) it is between eight and 20 years – depending on the project in which a person actually participates.

In summary, it is noticeable that the community energy projects obviously want to use the regulations to prevent the member shares from being redeemed at an early stage, which could affect the liquidity of the company. Since the projects have acquired the plants from the members' shares and mostly also through external financing and pay out the profits generated through the sale of electricity to the members in the form of a return, they do not have an accumulation of capital (only reserves for the dismantling of the plants, for example). The smaller cooperatives and projects in particular have limits of comparatively small amounts, as there is obviously a concern here that there will be large imbalances in the distribution of shareholdings. The two larger solar cooperatives in the comparison cases take a middle course with a fairly high limit, as they have formulated a limit in contrast to the larger societies. Surprisingly, however, no limits existed for some of the smaller cooperatives. This may also be due to the fact that very high investments are not expected.

6.3 Organization and Structure

6.3.1 Organizational Framework Conditions for Social Inclusion and Participation

Structural-Organizational Conditions Due to the Legal Form of Community Energy Projects

Within the case studies, different legal forms of the founded community energy projects occur: In case study 1, the community wind farm is managed in the form of a limited liability company and partnership (GmbH & Co. KG), in case study 2, a wind turbine was installed by a cooperative. Case studies 3, 4, 5, 6, and 8 are organized as cooperatives in their legal form. In case study 7, a combination of different legal forms is sought. In case study 5 (environmental association community solar project), people participate through loans. Finally, in case study 3, the first energy plant is managed in the form of a private company (civil law partnership: GbR).

In summary, the majority of the case studies use the cooperative form, which is also favored for future activities in the case of two case studies (urban community solar cooperative and citizens' community geothermal energy initiative). The legal form of a limited liability company and partnership (GmbH and Co. KG) is a typical legal form for operating community wind farms in Germany. Cooperatives, with lower investment volumes, are mainly represented in the solar energy sector. However, exceptions to this rough distinction can be found (case study 2: wind energy cooperative) as well as hybrid forms such as in case study 7 (citizens' community geothermal energy initiative).

An important question from the perspective of the citizens involved in this context is liability. In the first case study, a limited liability company (GmbH) acts as the managing director of the limited partnership (Kommanditgesellschaft, KG). Within the limited partnership, the citizens are involved as shareholders (limited partners). As a limited liability company, the GmbH is legally a corporation, whereas the limited partnership is a private company. Corporations are independent legal entities, i.e. the company itself is capable of doing business and acting legally under its corporate name. In contrast, partnerships are not legal persons; only the persons participating in the partnership have legal capacity. For this reason, a GmbH is capable of being the general partner of a KG.

The two legal forms of a limited liability company and a limited partnership also differ in terms of liability, which is also relevant in the case of the other forms of company (private company (civil law partnership: GbR) and cooperative). In the case of corporations, such as a limited liability company (GmbH) or a joint stock company (AG), the company is only liable with its own capital. In the case of a GmbH, it is liable with its share capital, which must amount to at least 25,000 euros. An exception for a limitation of liability can only be gross negligence and intent. In the case of partnerships, such as a private company (civil law partnership: GbR) or a general partnership (Offene Handelsgesellschaft (OHG)), the partners are liable with their entire private assets. The limited partnership (KG) also belongs to the private companies, but here a distinction is made between the so-called general partners and the limited partners of the KG. The former include the management of a limited partnership, which is liable for the KG with its entire assets. The assets of the GmbH consist however only of the share capital as well as possibly from further assets of the GmbH. The limited partners are liable however not with their private fortune, but only with their contribution registered in the trade register. Therefore, no natural persons – in this case the participating citizens – have to bear the entire risk. In practice, in the case of a community wind farm, the limited liability company (GmbH) as managing director takes care of the day-to-day business, organization, accounting and decision-making of the limited partnership's day-today business and is responsible for all services. The limited partners of the KG therefore do not play an active role in the organization and running of the business, but they do participate in important company decisions as partners, and have a right of control over the GmbH which is regulated in the partnership agreement.[34] While with the GmbH and Co. KG the liability for the persons involved can be excluded, then this represents a problem with the organizational form of a private company (civil law partnership: GbR), particularly since it is not possible to exclude the liability by a legal form addition (thus as a GbR with limited liability). The liability is joint and numerous, i.e. in the external relationship the individual partner must initially be liable for all debts of the GbR also with his private assets, in the internal relationship they can then subsequently demand the money back from their co-partners. In the case of the urban solar cooperative (3), due to this problem, an association stopped operating energy plants through the civil law partnership model and decided to form a cooperative.

In the case of cooperatives, liability is limited as a matter of principle. It follows that the members of the cooperative are not liable with their personal assets. In addition to the shares they have subscribed to, members are liable in the event of bankruptcy or liquidation for at least a further amount (depending on the articles of association also a certain multiple) equal to the amount of the shares they have subscribed to. However, the liability is only to the cooperative; there is no direct liability of the members to the cooperative creditors. The legal regulations do provide for a so-called obligation to make additional contributions on the part of members, but this can be limited or even completely excluded in the articles of association. Thus, in practice, the cooperative is only liable to its creditors with its own assets.

Finally, other participation models exist in that persons participate through so-called profit participation rights (first cluster of GmbHs) or a loan agreement (case study 5). In the first case, the liability issue is problematic, since in the event of insolvency or liquidation the repayment of the profit participation certificate holder's contribution is only made after all other creditors have been fully satisfied. Therefore, a total loss of the contribution is possible. A direct liability of the participation certificate holder does not exist by law, as far as the nominal contribution and the premium (agio) have been paid. The investor is liable only in accordance with the participation right conditions of the enterprise. There is normally no obligation to make additional contributions.

[34] The issues of the right of control and possible influence on shareholders' meetings will be discussed further in the next section, "Participatory Arrangements".

In terms of liability, profit participation rights can be structured as equity capital or as subordinated liable capital – and thus economically as debt capital. The liability position of the participation right holder and the participation right capital is structured in accordance with the position between the company capital and the fixed-interest liability. It is subordinate to debt capital, but remains senior to the voting equity of the full shareholder. In the event of insolvency, all outstanding claims of creditors providing outside capital are satisfied first, and only then are the profit participation capital investors reimbursed for their invested capital by the owners of the company, provided there are still free assets. Profit participation capital is therefore to be regarded as liable capital. However, there is no obligation to make additional contributions if the agreed profit participation capital contribution has been made. The profit participation capital investor is therefore only liable internally to the company within the scope of his obligation to make a contribution. He is not personally liable in the external relationship to the creditors of the company, so there is no joint liability and no direct external liability. Therefore, the profit participation rights provider cannot be held directly liable by third party creditors if he has paid the profit participation rights capital to the company on the basis of the terms and conditions of the profit participation rights. There is no liability in case study 5 through a loan agreement, since in this case the borrower (environmental association) is liable with its assets.

Participatory Arrangements: Models and Approaches of Community Energy Projects in Detail

Community Wind Farm (Case Study 1)

The total costs amounted to 15.5 million euros, 18% of which was financed from equity, and the rest from loans (I 1.1: line 36 f.). It was thus possible to buy the equity shares amounting to 2.9 million euros (ibid.: line 37 f.). A limited partnership was founded for this purpose, whereby an entry threshold of 3000 euros was levied (ibid.: line 38 f.). The managing director justifies this by saying that on the one hand the amount is kept low enough so that every citizen and not only large investors can acquire shares, but on the other hand not everyone (e.g. opponents of wind power) can buy in, who could then use their share in the shareholders' meetings to hinder constructive cooperation (ibid.: line 39 ff.). Nevertheless, the sum seems comparatively high.

The citizens of Hilchenbach had a pre-emptive right to buy the shares (ibid: line 46 f.). At the beginning, the mood had been very restrained, but this quickly changed according to press reports, as analysts there rated the investment as very attractive (ibid.: line 47 f.). Finally, much more equity could have been gathered, but this was not realized for reasons of relative profit (I 1.1: 49 ff.).

In the regularly convening shareholders' meeting, in which the course of business is presented, the shareholders are entitled to vote and profit according to the amount of their share (ibid.: line 44 ff.).

The participation of a newly joining limited partner is possible from a sum of 10,000 euros (§ 4 para. 5 partnership agreement) – a significantly stronger hurdle for a participation. The citizens of the nearby municipality, on the other hand, were given an advantage: for them, the entry sum was 3000 euros. The same applied to cooperatives of various forest cooperatives in the vicinity or in the municipality. However, on the other hand, the fact that no maximum participation sum was set precisely made it possible for financially strong people from the wider area to participate.

However, it must be borne in mind that at that time it was more difficult to obtain sufficient deposits at all. One citizen involved commented on this as follows: It had been difficult for the community wind farm to generate the required investment sum in the surrounding area (ibid.: line 89 f.). Due to this fact, it can be assumed that more than 50 percent of the investment sum comes from people who live more than 50 kilometers away (ibid.: line 90 ff.).

At a later stage, an exclusive or predominant participation of local people would have been conceivable. Nevertheless, it remains questionable to what extent it is possible to speak of a wind farm belonging to the community, if only a few people from the local community are actually involved. There also appears to be a large bias due to high proportions of citizens from other parts of Germany. However, this may seem negligible if the basic possibility of participation has been granted.

An ordinary partners' meeting is held once a year (§ 8 (1)); in addition, limited partners with 25 percent of the limited partnership capital may convene an extraordinary meeting. In addition to the "usual" partnership matters (annual financial statements, amendments to the partnership agreement, exclusion of partners, discharge, legal transactions requiring approval and dissolution of the partnership), "each partner has the right to submit motions to the partners' meeting" (§ 8 para. 4), which must be submitted to the management at least two weeks before the meeting.

In addition to the management, there is no supervisory board in this case, in contrast to a cooperative, as it is a limited partnership (M 1.2: line 40). According to the managing director, an advisory board assumes functions similar to those of a supervisory board in a limited partnership (ibid.: line 40 f.). According to the partnership agreement there is also the possibility to establish an advisory board (§ 10), which would be possible with a majority of 75 percent of the votes. However, due to a lack of interest and commitment on the part of the shareholders themselves, for whom the advisory board would act as a representation of interests, it was not possible to set up an advisory board (ibid.: line 41 ff.): "The election of an advisory board is possible under our KG agreement, I have proposed the election of such a body to the shareholders several times. So far, however, there has been no interest in this, probably because they always feel well informed about all processes".

Urban Community Solar Cooperative (Case Study 3)

In the cooperative in case study 3, the focus was on the approach of involving as many people as possible, even with low contributions: "But we also wanted to give many people the opportunity to participate. That is why we had such a low limit" (I 3.1: line 90 f.).

In addition, an upper limit was defined to prevent very large investments and thus the dominance of a few large investors: "We did not want the project to be dominated by a few individuals, hence a maximum limit of ten thousand euros" (I 3.1: line 91 f.).

However, in this case it quickly becomes apparent that the activity of the members is not necessarily guaranteed, but rather that they can acquire shares without any personal contact and then remain in the community energy company as silent partners under certain circumstances: "Then the interested parties could send the subscription form to us by post. We then countersigned it, and then they were partners" (I 3.1: line 182 ff.). The cooperative or the longer established private company (civil law partnership: GbR) can thus be characterized as comparatively open and participatory: The entry threshold is comparatively low, the board of directors is elected by the general meeting, there is a rotation principle in the supervisory board, there are also forums for exchange, and the initiators are open to ideas and suggestions from the members.

Environmental Association Community Solar Project (Case Study 5)

The environmental association is confronted with the question of whether a social commitment through the use of profits would be appropriate, as practiced by another local energy cooperative: "(…) it starts with (…) the surpluses, that one can then decide, (…) what to sponsor here, so that a project in this area or that they have a solar plant in some African country, I don't know, with it, (…) they have (…) a more overall social approach" (I 5.2: line 786 ff.). However, the environmental association also invests in other charitable or ecological projects. For the citizens, the BUND participation is also attractive in the sense that it is "convenient" for them: "Well, we say that the (…) surpluses do not go to the lenders, but we also want to use them to launch other projects. (…) So, another goal perhaps. Of course, this appeals to other people (…), so people do not have to work with it. They decide once for a loan, then they give a thousand euros and then they get, so to speak, an annual distribution and that is of course very convenient (…) I do not mean that negatively at all" (ibid.: line 790 ff.).

The latter point is justified by the fact that it would not be reasonable for the entire population to spend their free time on energy projects: "(…) you do not necessarily want to have something to do with work all the time, so to speak, but you have other projects that you find important, or hobbies or work, or whatever and you say: 'But I would like to do that too, but others will do it for me, so I do not have to put a lot of time into it myself'". (I 5.2: line 797 ff.). Thus, this participation approach corresponds to a need of the population: since they are overloaded with tasks, they would also want to achieve something with little commitment: "(…) That is why I find our approach, to some extent, to be quite satisfying(…) where you are sometimes also overwhelmed, where you always have to take care of it first and familiarize yourself with it and read into it and decide. It is very simple, very manageable, very clear and involves very little effort for both sides" (ibid.: line 801 ff.). The concept of the environmental association is therefore interesting for a larger group of the population, the SaHNE association has higher demands and relies on more commitment: "I would say that of course this simply appeals to more people. (…) SaHNE has very high demands, very high goals, there is nothing at all against it, but it definitely also requires a lot (…), definitely also a lot of commitment, in order to (…) participate in things (…)" (ibid.: line 814 ff.). "No, so with us the participation (…) or the work that goes along with this participation is very low. And with that, of course, you can address a lot more people (…)" (ibid.: line 818 ff.).

Just Pools for Financial Investment?

Despite the lower commitment, the personal investment approach is understood as being different to an investment via securities in a community energy company that can also build renewable energy plants. This is attributed to the local connection of the projects and regional value creation: "(…) has this very strong environmental idea, to say I also have added value in the region. (…) I know what I am participating in. I can see and look at it here on site. It is not somehow (…) a share investment in some wind energy company that is building wind turbines in France or something like that. (…) you could also say: '(…) ecological aspect (…) is also fulfilled and the return is also within the framework that I can imagine and is good'" (I 5.2: line 820 ff.). This local attachment not only had something to do with the local position of the energy plant, but also with the emotional attachment of the citizens involved with the energy project: "(…) but there is also more to it, it is local, and I have a connection to it. Emotionally and also in reality" (ibid.: 826 ff.). In the end, this approach could simply address a larger target group in the population than only through a citizens' group: "And I think that at the same time (…) the effort I have to put into it is very, very manageable and very clearly defined, and think you can of course address a lot of people with it. More than (…) in another circle perhaps. But I think it is also more appealing to a different group of people, who, for example, belong to this community initiative" (ibid.: line 828 ff.).

Rural Community Solar Cooperative (Case Study 6)

In another case of rural solar cooperatives, the importance of a broad participation of the population is also pointed out – in order to ensure an integration also of citizens who cannot build a solar plant themselves (community idea). Thus, this case study focuses on the locally anchored community project and the idea of a democratic community enterprise characterized by co-creation and co-determination (similar to case study 7), in contrast to more economically oriented (case study 5), occupancy-oriented (case study 4) or ethically motivated approaches (case study 3). The confirmation of a commonly expressed interest of the citizens is ensured by two principles: Firstly, through regular feedback (evaluation), and secondly, through openness to alternative or even new proposals from within the cooperative.

In addition, there is the aspect of achieving possible acceptance of the energy plants among the population: among the possible usable forms of energy, the energy cooperative wants to focus on those that also meet with a high level of interest and acceptance among the population. Here, too, the principle is emphasized that the energy project should have additional benefits beyond pure energy production (spillover effect) and – in a democratic-legitimizing sense – be supported by a large majority. A concrete co-determination and co-design of the members should be possible by the fact that they themselves propose topics and discussion points, and finally also common votes on these can take place. Furthermore, the members decide on the meetings, elect the members and discharge them. Another principle, which is addressed for the first time in this case study,[35] is the active inclusion of interested members (integration and inclusion) and admission or integration into committee work.

In addition, there is the specific aspect in this case of the close interlinking of Local Agenda 21 work and the energy cooperative, which is expressed both di-

[35] Information on this was also found in the minutes of meetings in case study 3 (urban solar cooperative), where one member showed interest in serving on a committee; this aspect was also discussed in case study 8 (supra-regional energy cooperative).

rectly and indirectly: the Agenda group serves here as a source of ideas, provides space for higher-level principles, secures local anchoring and support, can use resources of the municipality, and thus create more local community (social capital and legitimacy).[36]

On the one hand, the energy cooperative needs financial resources, on the other hand it can make financial profits by selling electricity, which amounts to an economic justification: "So we can have money, and we can also put money to work again. Then the citizens are quite willing and say: Mayor, give me all the available land, I'll install it (note: the solar panels) (…) and hopefully everyone will not forget that I am making the only real money with what I have sold in electricity (…) (I 6.1: line 192 ff.)".

The special orientation towards citizen participation and the inclusion of citizens is seen here (similarly in other cases), in the two principles of limiting the amount of shares as well as the low minimum amount of participation (and the associated potentially high number of participations): "(…) and it is due to citizen acceptance that we say: If we give ourselves a statute, the use of funds should be limited. A certain amount must be put in. However, not too much should be put in, so that there are many users. And thus there are citizen ideas that come to fruition" (I 6.1: line 197 ff.).

In this case study, too, a further component is indicated in the form of a long-term financial investment, which can also serve later generations and thus (in addition to ecological sustainability) also offers financial sustainability or a long-term perspective. Interestingly, a deliberative component is also referred to, in that citizen participation leads to a debate and discussion of the issue among citizens: "And then it is quickly done that you say: grandpa or a grandchild, grandma or a granddaughter – all that. And there is quickly an acceptance, because a little money is given here; a family that talks about it together" (ibid.: line 201 ff.).

The cooperative is also distinguished from other legal forms of community energy projects, as this legal form offers "participation" and flexibility of investment: Entry and exit into the cooperative are classified as uncomplicated, and thus citizen- or participation-friendly: "(…) not a civil law company, which is usually so dominant there. Instead, they said: let us make a cooperative: The comrades are shareholders. And then I have an acceptance. Because I (…) have noticed: The cooperative idea, that is, participation within this cooperative, in that you put the

[36] The function of a "think tank" or advisory function is known in almost all case studies: this is the case in case studies 3 (socio-ecological association), 4 (environmental working group), 5 (environmental association itself), 7 (local active group of committed citizens) and 8 (cooperation with local civil society groups).

capital in and can also take capital out again in part (…)" (ibid.: line 204 ff.). It is precisely this flexibility that is seen as a particular advantage: the solar cooperative is outlined as an ideal model in conjunction with the long-term investment perspective as well as the acceptance of the energy plants by the population: "And that is the beauty. That is to say, to participate part-time, so you can accompany the system for a period of time. (…) deposit money there and not devalue it, take money out again, no longer be a member. That also means a dynamic that does justice to the citizen. You can say: People, put the money in and, if I want, I will the amount out again and have all the money. And put a fixed rate here – 3 or 4 or 5 percent- for the children, for example. And there we have acceptance. Sun. Wonderful. We will do that. And done" (ibid.: line 211 ff.).

The Rural Community Solar Cooperative from Its Own Perspective: Following a Project-Oriented Approach

Compared to a purely discursive approach of the work of the (parallel) Local Agenda 21 group, from which the energy cooperative developed, the concrete implementation of a small holding company is understood as a factual, project-oriented model in contrast to a more discursive, political approach: "It is more issue-oriented, that is, it works value-oriented. The aim is to solve, work through and organize problems that are now pending in Syke in a sensible way. Therefore, not so much from a political standpoint, but to solve and organize project-related problems in the region for people (…)" (I 6.2: line 40 ff.).

This civil society Local Agenda 21 group sees itself less as a supplement to political design processes, but would like to pursue certain goals in the long term: "(…) but we all actually know that the parties tend to move in their own traps, that is, they orient themselves in a certain direction, considering four years within a process, political decision-making process, that is as long as the attitude of the legislative period continues. In Syke-Plus, we all now look twenty years into the future and want to work piece by piece on the city here to develop positively. Local Agenda 21 work was not supported in Syke in previous years. By the politics rather even hindered (…)" (ibid.: line 45 ff.).

However, the commitment did not lead to success, but ebbed away again, because the grouping did not see itself supported by local politics and the city administration, but instead as a competing association – with some exceptions of committed employees of the administration: "Everyone else rather hindered it. The Greens have been rather neutral. Then Mrs. X or Mrs. X in general are people in the city of Syke who have a positive attitude towards this whole Agenda process, who have also tried again and again to involve people who are not politically organized in this Agenda process, i.e. they have regularly invited people. We have had various starting points. We have already been to the town hall with ninety people, but it has never worked. This process always crumbled or failed because there was simply no political will behind it. Nobody was really interested. We did not have the feeling at all in the city of Syke or other municipalities that they really support such an Agenda process. The politicians saw us as competition, as an extra party (…)" (ibid.: line 53 ff.).

But the Agenda coordinator tried to promote the Local Agenda 21 process in the municipality, which at first also led to the hoped-for success: "That is why Ms. X invited everyone again, and 16 more people came. Then we dealt with it differently. We did some brainstorming, tried to sort ourselves out a bit more professionally" (ibid.: line 68 ff.).

At these meetings of the Local Agenda group, the idea of initiating a project with renewable energies finally arose (cf. also the section on the documented Agenda process), which had been considered within the group for some time: "That was in the spring/summer of 2008, and then there were also lively discussions. Everyone felt addressed, participated and then a neighbor said: 'Why do we not do something with a solar project on some Syke roof?' This was weighed back and forth and then we suddenly actually said: 'Yes, that would be a project, ´Bürger Energie Syke' [translated in this book to *Community Energy Syke*]. It was almost born with the name" (ibid.: line 73 ff.).

But the Local Agenda process led to a protracted process that proved unproductive for the particularly committed people (such as the initiator). But this in turn gave rise to the idea of an individual initiative: "Then it dragged on again, and then I got fed up, because it was already crumbling away again, and I said we should damn well do an event in the town hall, and found something there. (…) But that actually had nothing to do with an agenda, we just said we would meet there" (I 6.2: line 78 ff.).

The initiator attributed the great interest and the resonance of the idea among the population to the financial crisis at that time, which gives an indication of the economic calculation of an alternative financial investment (as also in case studies 4 and 5): "What happened in the autumn of 2008? That is when we had the big financial disaster. That means that a lot of people, and a lot of people from Syke lost a lot of money. At this event in Syke, that was exactly the time when this was discussed very intensively. Suddenly there were thirty or forty people at this event who wanted to understand what we had to say because we announced it in the newspaper. Why do you not invest your money in Syke before you throw it down the throats of hedge funds? Somehow it was in the newspaper" (ibid.: line 84 ff.). The initiator was convinced that local investments make more sense than anonymous, conventional investments: "But the core trigger was actually this dispute and this discussion about the financial disaster. My statement was at City Hall. ‘Does it not make more sense to invest here locally for infrastructure, for taxes, for everything, to have the win-win story regionally now, and not some hedge fund in America or somewhere else. What do you actually prefer?’” (ibid.: line 114 ff.). “For me, actually, the main reason for the financial story was this disaster. There people were disappointed, and lost a lot of money” (ibid.: line 147 f.).

This argumentation was therefore successful by focusing on the local reference. Nevertheless, there were initially arguments and discussions at a first meeting in the town hall: “Because of this, they were attracted, because they thought: ‘Man, many people are right about what happened there and we have to relate it more to us. Then there were big arguments and back and forth at the event. But then suddenly we were all of one mind. We really all disagreed. There were arguments among the audience as well. It’s like, ‘Yeah, it’s not even worth it with solar. ‘How is that. ‘You’re much too old anyway,’ ‘I’m doing it for my grandson’” (ibid.: p. 91 ff.).

Although the objective level was sometimes abandoned at this meeting (cf. discussion processes in case studies 1, 2, and 4), the decisive factor was a core group that wanted to implement the idea with vigor. It was precisely this that brought about the turning point, as the entire assembly came to trust this group of people: “There were really emotional arguments in the town hall about this topic and then very quickly there was a block of people who said: Now we actually want to do something here today. Then we held another event and so many people came again. Then we said: ‘We will think about how we are going to organize this technically, that is: What kind of community energy project do we want to make now or how do we want to regulate it?’ At that moment it was already clear to the people sitting there that something was happening now. With participation, with money, contribution and something like that” (ibid.: line 97 ff.).

In fact, the committed individuals took advantage of the positive momentum and immediately moved on to the process of founding the cooperative, forming the cooperative’s organs on the spot: “Then it was just a matter of, do we do a GbR, do we do a cooperative. What do we do at all? So we had already rammed our point, our arrow, so to speak, into the project and then it surprised everyone. Then suddenly it was said: Well, we decide on a cooperative. You are now a member of the board. Me? – Yes, you. Organize the board! Who wants to join? Harald, you join in, you join in, you join in. You were all for it. Come on, join in! Who’s on the board? (…) I am on the board. Two more! That was an emotional development that happened within an hour” (I 6.2: line 106 ff.).

The founding of the energy cooperative ultimately represents a concentration of what can be done concretely by citizens for the community as a contribution. In this case study, the basic economic idea of a financial investment is evident, but the energy cooperative was apparently not understood as a very profitable investment from the beginning: "So I have to do something for the place here – even if it is just a drop in the ocean – that makes the place more attractive. No matter what – what I can do and right now the only thing that comes to mind is: energy cooperative Syke. That sounds good. Everyone supported it, there was no more opposition. Then I (…) said: 'And whoever thinks they can get big profits from this cooperative now, when we are all working in it on a voluntary basis anyway. He was mistaken. He should please buy some hedge fund'. Everyone said: 'No, we do not expect that either.' That was the end of the subject for me. So that is the story of how Bürgerenergie Syke came into being" (ibid.: line 122 ff.).

In this way, this initiative also represents an antipole to political disenchantment. The concreteness and tangibility of the project is emphasized, as well as the possibility of citizen participation and collaboration, which apparently plays a greater role in this case study than in others: "On the one hand, a bit of resentment, on the other hand, financial disaster, maybe even disenchantment with politics somewhere, because many people say to themselves: 'Yes, you cannot make a difference there'. Now we have something tangible close by where we can get involved. Because we have already had two meetings in the cooperative. There were people who otherwise could never say anything about any topic. They could now say, 'Yeah, can't we do it better this way or that way, or I think it would be better if we had more yields, don't you?' They could get directly involved and dared to do so, because they said 'yes'. I own a piece of it, I would say something about it. (…) because suddenly they were in politics (…)" (ibid.: line 131 ff.).

The initiator also observed such initiative movements in other municipalities. He attributed the idea of solar energy to the great acceptance (in contrast to wind energy) and the comparatively problem-free feasibility (availability of roofs): "So this is our special case here in Syke. In parallel, of course, exactly the same thing happened in other localities at the same time. In addition, photovoltaics was perhaps more in the news somewhere, wind was criticized. Because of noise impact (…). Emotionally, it must have somehow gone in the direction of photovoltaics. Suddenly many roofs appeared" (I 6.2: line 142 ff.). Finally, the foundation of the cooperative was also supported by the municipality's advertising for the project: "Yes, the municipality also played a role, distributed information. Quite intensively, they then distributed their e-mails" (ibid.: line 1132 f.).

In this way, a project of their own developed without the involvement of politics and detached from the Agenda initiative. However, the Agenda process can be seen as preparatory and activating: "So it built up via the newspaper, via our founding activities, and politics had zero, nothing to do with it. Not even the city of Syke with the exception of (…), those who actually pushed the agenda processes." (ibid.:

line 163 ff.). "They have pulled the trigger, so to speak. That has to be said quite clearly" (ibid.: line 166 f.).

Another attempt was to be made, but under particular conditions, in order to avoid past mistakes: "The local authorities said to us: 'Under certain conditions we have formulated this in writing, as I imagine it, that we will be supported by the city and by the administration.' As a result, nothing happened at all at first. Then relatively quickly came an invitation (…) again on the subject of agenda work. They then organized themselves well and through a brainstorming session we once again formulated and wrote down our objectives for Local Agenda work" (ibid.: line 193 ff.).

This second attempt of the Local Agenda group was more successful, a joint brainstorming led to the idea of building and using renewable energies, but the interest threatened to wane again: "Everyone participated actively, stuck it on the wall with pieces of paper and sorted it again afterwards, so that we could get a structure. What do we want? Where do we actually want to go? In this context, we came to energy and regenerative energy, city and solar, and we soon deepened the topic at another event. But then it started to crumble again a bit. (…) Those who were invited became fewer and then (…) this financial disaster happened in 2008" (ibid.: line 199 ff.). This led to a meeting of particularly committed participants who decided to continue the project idea on their own responsibility: "We met in the town hall at exactly that point to seriously consider whether we should do a joint project here. A solid group of people got together. It was a solar project. The city said: 'Okay, we'll provide you with a roof. We support that'" (ibid.: line 207 ff.).

This initiative led to a higher response from interested citizens who came to the meeting: "In this context, there were suddenly forty people in the town hall and they had a heated discussion amongst themselves. Also, whether it makes sense at all to do solar and (…) from this fruitful dispute, then at the second meeting, where again so many people were there, our group formed, which then discussed, the legal form of the project, constellation – 'What do we want to do at all?'" (ibid.: line 201 ff.).

What in the case of the employee cooperative took a very long time and led to heated arguments, in this case took place in minutes: The election of the organs at the meeting (which apparently served directly as the founding general meeting), the vote on a constitution and determination of important points of content, such as the determination of the entry sum (I 6.2: lines 232 ff.). After the successful meeting, the mayor also joined in a supportive capacity, which is parallel to case study 1: "Our mayor supported us the moment he saw that the town hall was full of people. It is clear that he now also speaks positively about it" (ibid: line 167 ff.).

The initiator also emphasizes the reluctance of those involved in the project towards the outside world. Although there were newspaper reports, the project was not extensively presented to the public (which in other cases is nevertheless a decisive point in terms of gaining members): "But we never pushed ourselves forward. Instead, we said: 'Man, let's do something here for Syke and that's what we'll do now. We also meet, but we don't make a big fuss about it, but we want to see what we can achieve'" (ibid.: line 174 ff.). The financial participation was also very quick, a roof area could be acquired from the municipality: "At the next meeting, we prepared the contracts. Then they signed that they would subscribe so and so much and make the money available by a certain date. That set the process in motion. They got the roof from the city" (ibid.: line 241 ff.).

In addition to newspaper reports, the cooperative also set up a website to provide information. In addition, the young cooperative received many requests for reports on their experiences: "(…) via this website, which was then also very quickly clicked on by many, we were always very far ahead with community energy. Of course, we then received invitations from all directions, then we also received an invitation from Hanover to report on what we had done, how we had done it. Other communities have copied what we have done. We held counselling interviews in other communities, then gave information on how we did it. In the school here in Syke (…) we gave a lecture about electrosmog, to take away the fears" (ibid.: line 251 ff.).

Soon the energy cooperative also acquired a second roof from a school, which they included in the process. This led to exchange and information processes: "That was our next project with photovoltaics and then we brought the school into the process. We involved the school administrators. We involved the teachers. So they actively approached the people and they didn't know that. They were surprised. We had a parents meeting. Yes, we were able to get rid of all the 'ifs and buts', and then we were able to benevolently, how should I say, 'Do it with the plant technology on our roof'" (ibid.: line 260 ff.).

Local Agenda 21 Versus Community Energy Project

The initiating and accompanying Local Agenda 21 group ultimately suffered from a widespread phenomenon of increasing disinterest, and absence of the initially interested citizens: "But a large part of the Agenda movement was ultimately no longer present. You see, there was a continuous decline in interest" (I 6.2: line 300 ff.).

The problem of the Agenda group was in particular that ideas could not be implemented and there was a lack of support. The group did not feel that it was being taken seriously, and project ideas were not taken further into the committees of the city council, where concrete decisions could have been made in the first place: "Yes, I was the last one to leave. I held out for quite a long time until the end (…). But at some point they quit because they said: 'We can't find enough support for our consideration. We're tilting at windmills or our proposals are not being accepted or are not being discussed.' Would you continue working on this issue under these conditions? You can't have an open agenda process on the one hand and control it through an event on the other hand. There is this so-called steering group where people meet and compile the results from these events. The steering group is made up of people from politics, from the Local Agenda and from the administration, and they then have to take this to the Council and the individual committees, and discuss and debate it there. In many of our cases it did not get that far. We didn't have the feeling that we were being taken seriously. The overall attitude was like this: Do what you like and do not disturb us. As a result, the public interest has disappeared" (ibid., p. 309 ff.).

This is how the initiator describes ups and downs in the dynamics. In the end, the decisive factor was the concrete idea and a promised support by the municipality. At the same time, however, this also meant the end of the Local Agenda work: "We went down, there was this conversation with Mrs. X. We went up again. They had people again, had meetings again. But then it went down again. Then we (...) chose a project, a concrete project. Then the city said: I'll support it. That was the first time. Then the project was implemented. But the Local Agenda group is still no longer there" (ibid.: line 329 ff.). All in all, the initiator attributes the failure of the Agenda group to a lack of moderation, support and excessive demands on the responsible administrative staff: "(...) this pragmatic support, which an agenda needs from the city, is not there. Ms. X cannot provide it because she is completely overtaxed and overworked, because she is one of the most hard-working women in the whole town hall. Ms. X is also very much involved with democratic change at the moment. So that then gives us someone to help and support there. But that is again doomed to death. Citizens who don't know much about organizations (...) can't organize themselves. They have to be guided. There has to be a moderator" (ibid.: line 339 ff.). After the working group, which is also responsible for energy issues, became less and less frequented, the initiator considered the group to have failed: "Practically we left, of course. But there were only eight or nine of us left. That was the end of it" (ibid.: line 355 f.).

The second attempt, which resulted in the founding of the cooperative, was linked by the initiator to a firm promise of support from the municipality, which was in fact forthcoming: "Only, I did" set a condition. I said I would put it in writing what conditions I expected if we were to get an Agenda process going again. The condition was that the city supports us. That is what they did (...) (I 6.2: line 371 ff.).

The committed citizens also felt free after their own initiative and the success of their own citizens' project, and it seems that precisely this dynamic of founding a community energy project and the associated scope for action had a very positive effect. This probably corresponded to those aspects which were not present in the Agenda work, which was stuck in theory, and which were missed: "After we decoupled this project in Syke, we were also glad that it was decoupled in this way. With the foundation of the cooperative we were also intact. We had one hundred thousand euros and could start immediately. Give me a roof and we'll take the money and buy a photovoltaic system. We'll make a roof usage contract for 20 years with an option to extend and you'll give us the roof for free, as promised. That's what they did. At that moment we were able to act, to actively move the project. It was the same with the second roof. We then also ran advertising campaigns. We stood on the main street, we advertised, we collected signatures. We re-advertised share certificates. – 'Don't you want to do it again?' And so on and so forth" (ibid.: line 408 ff.). But the Local Agenda work has brought about an important experience and learning process for the initiator as well as a feeling for the interests of other citizens: "Yes, I finally got a feeling for what is possible and how the interests are and that, how shall I put it, citizens' feelings or citizens' thoughts are perceived as a danger. But that is also a reassurance (…)" (ibid.: line 426 ff.).

The great interest is attributed in particular to the local reference: a project by local citizens for local citizens: "They got a little sting somewhere and with the argument that we want to do it here in Syke, we live here after all. We also want to engage local companies that build the photovoltaic system. They buy their bread here. They let their children go to school here. I believe that a little bit of the message that we preached there has also arrived there" (ibid.: line 454 ff.).

Again, the initiator emphasizes the special feature of an energy cooperative in contrast to an Local Agenda working group: the concreteness and a range of participation from a passive to a strongly pronounced activity: "A tangible project, let us say it quite clearly and where you can now simply go – you can go there. You can get involved and none of them saw themselves as being in danger, I might have to do everything now. But I can get involved. That was, I think, a crucial point" (ibid.: line 462 ff.).

Thus, this case study focuses on the locally anchored community project and the idea of a democratic community enterprise of co-design and co-determination (similar to case study 7), in contrast to more economically oriented (case study 5), occupancy-oriented (case study 4), or socially-idealistically motivated approaches (case study 3): "The financial incentive was not there. I said, if you want to make profits, you cannot invest in the citizens of Syke, you have to invest in hedge funds. That means, don't expect us to make profits. Because I said right away, it could be that we support school projects or do this or that here. We don't know yet. I mean, that was presumptuous of me to say that. One of us is a comrade, so he can decide what we want. I can't decide that. They can tell me for a year, you're now a board member and may act. But if we don't like it, then we'll vote you out or something" (I 6.2: line 478 ff.).

Citizens' Community Geothermal Energy Initiative (Case Study 7)

Active Membership and Communication

An active involvement of members in the design of energy projects is also found in another case, the citizens' community geothermal energy initiative. Extensive investigations have to be carried out for this special type of energy. These technical questions are dealt with here by committed members who have special knowledge and experience in this field (diversification of members' fields of activity): "There have been problems, they have had collapses, but not now that anything has become dangerous. In any case, with us it looks a bit different. Although this is the start, so if you want to drill, geological investigations are made again. That is practically the prerequisite for knowing approximately where there are faults in the subsoil. Because where the faults are, that is where the water is. This is determined by geological investigations. But I am not enough of a technician. Because then we have our experts who deal with that. We are actually only the idea givers, in order to realize a citizen model" (I 7.1: line 62 ff.).

The employee also emphasizes the voluntary work of the members of the community of interest: "At the moment we are here only on a voluntary basis. There are experts who have already advised us. For example, there is a geologist (…), who has already accompanied many geothermal projects worldwide and he is therefore a very strong advocate for the Markt Schwaben area". (ibid.: line 75 ff.).

Many attempts to implement the project idea are reported, and the first initiative to use geothermal energy dates back to the 1990s: "In any case, initiatives have been taken up again and again. For example, at the end of the nineties I was approached by people in my profession and asked whether it would not be possible for citizens to participate here. There were already some interested people who wanted to participate" (ibid: line 116 ff.). These impulses originally came from the municipality itself, but they were not followed up: "It was originally the municipality, but the municipality pretty much let it fall asleep" (ibid.: line121).

In this case, too, there are parallel ideas and approaches of the Local Agenda 21 in the municipality, which presumably also promoted the idea of citizen participation: "The Agenda (…) was then founded. There was the kick-off event (…), then we heard nothing from the municipality for a long time. At this kick-off event, which was a moderated event (…), citizens were to be involved, i.e. ideas of the citizens etc., and how they could be realized. and how they can be implemented. At this kick-off event, the citizens' ideas were also in demand. At that time, I already suggested that we should consider pushing ahead with this geothermal energy project again. The citizens who took part were also asked. The most votes were actually cast in favor of pushing ahead with the project. That was quite positively received by the population. Then we tried to push the whole thing through these Agenda working groups. But then in 2002, the municipality again considered it to be too expensive" (I 7.1: line 129 ff.). "The kick-off event was in 1999. There it was brought back to life, and in the following years the working group on environment and energy was formed from this agenda (…) and an attempt was made with different people than at present to push this forward again. Economic efficiency calculations were carried out. I was also significantly involved in this. Forecasts were also made on how energy prices would develop" (ibid.: line 145 ff.).

Public Relations, Acceptance and Interest in Participation

A second phase of activities has occurred since 2008: Similar to the reports and developments in the case of the rural solar cooperative, the engagement was related to the global financial crisis at that time. Based on a worldwide consideration of energy supply, the use of geothermal energy was seen as a possible primary solution to achieve energy autarky and independence from the use of raw materials (and prices of the world market). The possibility of regional added value is also emphasized[37]: "Then there was a relatively long standstill, then in 2008 there was this big crisis again, the economic crisis, the banking crisis, etc. Oil prices rose again to infinity, although they later fell again, so some citizens, including myself, got together and founded an 'interest group for geothermal energy – a nonprofit association'. So now these new ideas have emerged. The aim of the community of interests was actually to develop the whole thing as a citizens' model in order to keep the subsequent added value from the energy in the region, because of the ever-increasing energy prices. We have done a complete calculation of the project. Every year, citizens pay around nine to ten million euros to the large energy companies for thermal energy. The idea was that if these nine million euros could be diverted to a citizens' project, then the added value would remain here (I 7.1: line 165 ff.).

In this context, the employee explains the further activities and procedures of the association: information events and concepts of realization models. However, the response from the population was not as great as had been hoped: "Then we started to develop models within the framework of this community of interest as to how this could be done. In this context, a financing model was developed, in which it was said that at entry, costs of thirty to thirty-five million, about one-third, would

[37] Thus, the theoretical approach of this case study is very similar to the community wind farm case study, which focused on similar motivations in a comparably costly energy project.

need equity capital and two-thirds could be financed through banks. Then we started to hold information events and also to distribute questionnaires, which of the citizens would participate with how much – so as a non-binding request –who could imagine participating and how much?" (I 7.1: lines 179 ff.). So far, only one million euros have been raised by the municipality (binding commitment), and one million euros by citizens (virtually through expressions of interest): "This has not been so successful. Within a very short period of time, we were able to ascertain that approximately one million people were willing to sign up, and approximately nine hundred thousand to one million would be ready. But if you imagine that this brochure was distributed to four thousand households, for example, and based on this brochure and the information event, only these nine hundred thousand to one million were collected. The municipality also said it would contribute one million. But it was unanimously decided in the municipal council that this would be funded" (ibid.: line 187 ff.).

With regard to the willingness of the population to invest, it is assumed that the potential is significantly higher than previous experience and feedback suggests: "It was the case that this one million people were willing to subscribe, there was actually only, I think, one percent of the citizens who expressed willingness to this one million. That actually means that there are many more who have capital available. That was a sign that many people did not register it that way. That we somehow have problems bringing the whole project to the citizens. That turned out later. When you asked people on the street: "Didn't you get this brochure? Then most of them said: 'No, we didn't get it. But it was sent to every household in the community anyway. So that means, in the end, everybody got it, but it was not registered as a project. It was even sent out by the municipality. We did not consider that the municipality had to be told that it had to be addressed to every citizen or every household. We just said: ´to all households´ in the letter and then distributed it to the mailboxes" (ibid.: line 199 ff.).

The direct contact with the citizens was the real problem. Various brochures were thrown away like ordinary advertising, the general public failed to be informed: "Our starting point was actually that: we had noticed, it also comes across in such a way that the address list is used to write to the respective household. That the letter would also include the family 'anyway'. Then, when it says: to all households, then they would say: 'It's an advertisement,' not even in an envelope of the municipality. That could well have been seen as an advertisement and that it then ended up in the letterbox. Our aim would actually have been to write to the citizens from the municipality, so that the citizen also notices that there is something serious behind it. It has turned out again and again that the difficulty is to establish contact with the citizens. There are many who are interested in it, we have always had relatively well-attended information events, we are also published on the internet (…), but these were then essentially always the same who had already registered and who simply wanted to know: 'How is it going?'" (ibid.: line 211 ff.).

The biggest problem for the community of interest is that many citizens are only interested in getting involved when certain structures already exist: "Many have said, 'We've already noticed, but nothing is happening. 'It's such a vicious cycle. If something progresses, then I think more would join in, but if nothing progresses, many say: 'Now I'll wait and see what progresses. That is our problem. Now we have said: something has to happen. Either the municipality already establishes a company and then expands it to a full supply at some point with geothermal energy – only it must be demonstrated that there is a seriousness behind it. This year there have been some …- we have got a new mayor, who has also formed such working groups or invited the citizens to form working groups" (I 7.1: line 227 ff.).

The founding of an associated citizens' investment company is justified by the fact that a GmbH with a very large number of shareholders would hardly be able to act: "But we want to distribute this among the citizens. The citizens could also participate directly in this GmbH & Co KG. That would lead to the fact that possibly the GmbH & Co. KG with one thousand participants is simply no longer so capable of acting. In this way, the capital would practically be collected in a financing company and the financing company would then participate as a shareholder in this GmbH & Co. KG" (ibid.: line 373 ff.).

In contrast to other case studies, not only a financial participation in the energy plant itself, but also the active use (in the form of a connection) to the heating network plays a major role here: "The acceptance must be on two sides. The first is the financial participation as a capital investment, and the second is the interest of the citizens in the connection. You cannot achieve both on your own. Only if the appropriate connections are created can the whole thing ultimately be financed. The financing must include current income, and one has a certain obligation, both to the shareholders and to the financiers, banks, etc." (ibid.: line 495 ff.).

Supra-Regional Energy Cooperative

Participation Model Through Direct Ownership of Community Energy

The energy cooperative in this case differs from the participation models in the other case studies in two key respects: On the one hand, the cooperative seeks to build energy plants throughout Germany. On the other hand, the citizens do not acquire "imaginary" shares in the energy plants, but clearly allocated solar modules that become their property. This allows them to freely dispose of their modules: They can trade them among themselves or even sell them. However, it remains to be seen what will happen when the term expires and the participating citizens have to sell, scrap or similar their modules in some way. Presumably, the cooperative will take care of this issue – however, this could represent an additional burden for the participants, which could deter citizens from participating altogether. Due to this configuration it becomes clear that this cooperative transports a strengthened, but furthermore also differentiated image of the participating citizen: On the one hand, the citizen themself should serve as a source of possible locations for energy plants, on the other hand, the citizen is also involved in the power generation in a very direct way through the direct purchase of solar modules. This means more transparency and identification of the citizen with "their" concrete participation – however, this presupposes an increased interest and an in-depth examination of the matter by the individual. On the other hand, there is the aspect that the energy plants themselves are distributed throughout Germany, which is why there is no concrete spatial connection here – in contrast to most other case studies.

This energy cooperative thus represents an example of a young, supra-regionally oriented energy cooperative, that aims to use an innovative participation concept to establish greater proximity and connection from the participating citizen to the technical facilities, and the management of electricity generation.

The Evolution of the Participation Model

After a phase of gathering the experience of the initiators, a new model for the cooperative to be founded was developed: "And then there were two intensive months where we just sat down together and talked through all the possible models. How we could organize it and how we could do it. And that then led to the participation model of the Energiegewinner cooperative (…)" (I 8: line 150 ff.).

In developing their own approach, the initiators were inspired by another energy initiative: "(…) The main idea was actually taken over from Ökostadt e. V. in Hanover. They have developed the model of not operating a PV system via (…) the share capital of a company, so to speak, but to divide the system into many small shares in terms of ownership. And to transfer ownership to the respective members of this company. Which has the advantage that…investment in the energy plant is basically taken out of the company, and in itself has a kind of seclusion. Through which the company, which is planning this plant, becomes free again to make new plants, which have completely different framework conditions, which perhaps also have different returns" (ibid.: line 153 ff.).

Although the initiators were convinced by the approach of the other project, they also saw a decisive disadvantage that they wanted to avoid with their own model in a further development: "That's the problem when you sort of throw everything into one pot and try to do something again two years later. (…) Especially if you work with outside capital, somehow you don't get a direct payout, that it would get mixed up. And the expectations that people had at the beginning can no longer be kept up with what comes along. (…) Yes, then you just start another company. Then, so to speak, every plant has a new GbR or GmbH. And that's what we do with the energy producers" (ibid.: line 162 ff.).

This newly developed approach of the cooperative is essentially based on a separation between the cooperative and the participation of the citizens in the solar modules: "So we have a cooperative, so to speak, where you become a member with fifty euros. So you can also put in more. But the projects themselves are financial, they have nothing to do with the cooperative capital. The corporate arrangement of the Energiegewinner cooperative itself is just a company that plans and implements participation projects. And then sells them among its members, so to speak, or has them financed by the members. That is the model…the idea of dividing a plant into individual modules and selling them (…)" (I 8: line 168 ff.).

In this way, the participating citizens actually become the direct owners of the solar modules, while the cooperative acts as the operator of the plants: "The cooperative operates the plant, and is officially the operator. It also receives the electricity remuneration from the plant and passes it on to the module owners in the form of a module lease. So we make purchase-lease agreements where the members can purchase modules. And then receive lease payments over twenty years" (ibid.: line 180 ff.).

According to the initiators, the acquisition of ownership of the modules creates a direct link between the members and their own solar systems: "(…) they already have them on rented roofs. But they just get a transfer of ownership. The serial number of the module is written on it. It also says where they can be found on the roof" (ibid.: line 189 ff.). "They are single owners of the modules" (ibid.: line 195). In this case, each PV project of the cooperative that carries it out stands on its own. It is economically independent, which is another difference to other energy cooperatives: "Well, we see ourselves as a nationwide cooperative and that is the charming thing, so to speak. The projects themselves are not only economically independent of other projects, but you can also, so to speak, decentralize them, but the cooperative itself can operate nationwide. That is just another special feature" (ibid.: line 649 ff.).

Return of Investment and Independence from Banks

In this case, the two initiators also form the board of directors at the same time[38] – which is highly comparable to a management in terms of tasks and fields

[38] This configuration is also found in all other cases examined, with the exception of the community solar plants of the environmental association, where, however, there is a participation approach that is not comparable with the other cases.

of activity: "So the two people who came up with the idea of the Energiegewinner cooperative are on the board. So we founded it last year on 10.10.2010 with ten people and have, so to speak, first looked in our environment of course, at who will be able to participate or who can we get in order to somehow first found the cooperative (…)" (I 8:line 693 ff.).

Despite non-local-community motivation, as in most other cases, there is no primary return orientation here either: "So certainly, if the maximum return somewhere wants to get out (…) then we have disadvantages, yes. With us, the return is perhaps not as high as with some other solar funds. That can be the case" (ibid.: line 969 ff.).

A low profit is accepted here mainly because (in contrast to all other cases) there is no credit financing at all, independence from credit institutions is seen as a very big advantage here: "(…) so you are simply much, much more independent without banks. (…) At information events where we are we then say: we do not work together with banks, but with members. At first they always say: 'Aha' and then their eyes glaze over – something like that. In the current situation, although you could leverage with loans and maybe get more return points out (…) it is not so bad that we do it without banks" (I 8:line 982 ff.).

This desired independence from banks is also a motivating reason for participation in the cooperative: "Especially when we (…) hold information events in schools and we have many people who have their money in savings accounts where they somehow have half a percent (…) and they just think: What can we do with our money that makes sense? And they don't want to make it available to the banks anymore. And if we say: We don't work with the banks anymore, then they don't look at the return points they want to achieve. I think we are addressing a completely different clientele. I think so, and it's not a small one. So especially nowadays it is not small" (ibid.: line 987 ff.).

Thus this participation represents a clearly delimited alternative to other forms of investment – similar to the approaches of the other case studies – here, however, still strengthened by the aspect of independence from banks: "Yes, you'd rather give up one or two percentage points, which you can obtain in net yield and know that the money is somehow independently invested" (ibid.: line 999 f.).

A very concise problem of this cooperative – in contrast again to all other case studies – is the spatial distance of the management of the cooperative to the members – this is due to the fact that the cooperative has PV projects all over Germany: "That is certainly a disadvantage that the management of the cooperative is located in Cologne and not, for example, in Witzenhausen, where we had our first project. That was also a frequent topic there. But at the end of the day, the question is, if there is no alternative or not enough people on the ground to set up their own project, so to speak, then it is certainly a good alternative to do it this way" (ibid.: line 1017 ff.).

On the other hand, cooperation with a local civil society actor (e.g. association) can create a certain local reference through this local community: "(…) We don't have to be represented everywhere with the Energiegewinner cooperative and do this in every region, and if there are already initiatives, it's great. So we don't have that claim at all, but we just notice that (…) in many places where project initiatives don't really make progress, can't get it going, that we could simply, yes often be the solution, (…) in order to be able to implement it" (ibid.: line 1021 ff.).

Future Challenges

The premise of the cooperative in the future will continue to be seen in particular in the implementation of PV projects: "Yes, that is, that is not a primary concern, so to speak, but we can do that. So we can simply implement the projects in those places and help to implement that, so to speak" (I 8: line 1030 ff.).

The greatest challenge is defined as being able to exist in the future. On the one hand, a very large theoretical potential is seen with regard to the idea of implementing energy projects together with other actors. On the other hand, the cooperative is still in its infancy and must implement further projects in order to be viable in the long term (in its existing form and structure): "Well, I would like to ensure that we have a sufficient size so that the company really remains. We are still in the start-up phase. (…) So we still have to grow a little (…). But I see that: everywhere we go, with initiatives, I see that somehow, without us knowing it at the beginning, that we really are a solution for initiatives that exist, that don't get anywhere – I notice that somehow what we have done, the whole idea, is actually huge" (I 8: line 1896 ff.).

For the future, the initiators and members still have a lot of ideas – which reach up to a larger vision: "(…) We still have so many ideas with energy accounts, which we still want to set up. We want to make such a login area where people, if they have their own electricity meter at home, which they feed in digitally, can see their electricity consumption, so to speak, and if they (…) own energy systems, (…) participate in solar modules or others, then they can see what energy they themselves need. So that the city dweller who (…) rents a house can see his own energy consumption and energy production for himself (…) and can bring it in. That's one idea. We want to bring that into such an internal area (…). And if we reach this association structure and a certain size (…) Yes, that (…) is a dream that will somehow come true. And it really has to have a basis so that it really lasts, that is very important" (ibid.: line 1902 ff.).

Trade-Off: Professionalization Tendencies Versus Inclusion, Activity and Co-determination of Members

Based on the previous findings, the presumption of a trade-off of member participation between a professionalized and less participatory and a less professional but open and member-inclusive community energy initiative seems very close. However, it is also quite conceivable that the members of a larger community energy project would be active and self-confident and organize themselves. However, this is not the case in the more "passively" organized case studies 1 and 5 (community wind farm and environmental association community solar project). But also in other cases the commitment of the members with regard to co-determination and co-design is not strongly pronounced. It can therefore be assumed that in many cases professional management does not encourage self-organized and active membership – and that it is therefore more a question of the management itself, to what extent it motivates members and encourages them to collaborate, actively promotes inclusion, and so on. Accordingly, a professionally operating community energy project can also be inclusive, collaborative, participatory and co-determination-friendly.

Deep Analysis: Fruitless Efforts in the Case of the Community Wind Farm

An important aspect with regard to the development over time, and the associated changes in the conditions for the success of community energy initiatives (dynamic development) is the process of increasing professionalism in dealing with the issues that arise in the development of energy systems (technical, economic, ecological). This can take place through the experience gained, through the involvement of other actors or exchange with them (expansion of existing know-how), or through the transfer of knowledge through specific, specialized institutions (e.g. state energy agencies) or consultancy services.

In the first case study, the representative of the district administration reports that "due to the experience gained (…) every actor in his area of responsibility (has) learned something new" (M 1.3: line 100 f.). In addition, "the technical competence of the offices entrusted with the preliminary investigations has also increased significantly" (ibid.: line 101 f.). In addition, "a mutual exchange/information takes place within the framework of joint events with the cities/municipalities belonging to the district as well as the specialist authorities (…)" (ibid.: line 105 f.). In contrast to this, however, there are "the increasingly extensive legal requirements (e.g. EU law on the protection of species, Natura 2000 …)" (ibid.: line 103 f.).

According to the managing director of the operating company, the most important point in the planned construction of a second community wind farm by the company is the motivation and attitude of the citizens and the municipal administration (M 1.1: line 68 ff.): "But above all: the conviction of the people of Hilchenbach that wind energy is good for the town". What differences can be found in the approaches and procedures of the initiators? Possible differences could be due to the speed of the processes, the number of contacts and closeness among the actors ("cohesion"), but also basic attitudes of the persons towards the matter, as well as the type and style of the procedures seem to be of importance. In the case of the community wind farm, these different modes are summed up as follows (M 1.1: line 132 ff.):

> Of course you become more experienced and more routine. Of course there is also an exchange of experience, but not very intensive. Some planners see each other more as competitors. In any case, I dislike some of the approaches of some planning offices. You probably develop your 'own style' of doing things. My 'methods' are perhaps slower than those of the big planning firms. But I am of the opinion that a wind project starts with thorough and patient information work. After all, the consensus created in this way has spread. Quite a few municipalities visit the wind farm and inform themselves about the community wind farm concept.

According to this, the situation can be described, especially for the initiators of wind energy projects, in such a way that proponents of joint citizen participation models act at a slower pace and without direct contact and feedback from the processes of the business field or the market. However, this "disadvantage" in terms of a condition of success for the energy project as a whole can be compensated for by gaining success factors in the area of public acceptance, and through coalitions with individual representatives from politics or other areas (including associations such as parties and federations). For the individual initiator or a grouping, therefore, no disadvantage need arise from this normative-ethical attitude – especially if the postulated goal is not to build up a series of plants with the highest possible profit margins.

The Importance of Organizational Issues in Community Energy Projects

A well-designed organization seems to be another important point in the implementation of community energy systems – as it is formulated on the part of the administration: "But you basically need doers who take matters into their own hands, who also put a small article in the newspaper and say: 'So, we're meeting next Thursday and everyone who wants to can come along, come along there. '- And that's how you have to organize it first. All the way to: 'How do we find out how much money we actually have' – long before a community energy project is founded" (I 9: 437 ff.).

In this case, the enthusiasm and motivation for the project also move in this area of planning and organization – it seems to be in particular the sense of community, the joint action and the pursuit of a common goal, which leads to the development of a collective identity, as the employee of the administration reports from his parallel private experience as a member of a community energy project: "Then they (…) get an idea of: How big can the plant become? How big is the roof area that I have in mind? Will it fit together? Can I manage with my money? Do I need more money? Or do I have to look for another roof because I have much more money than space (…)? (…) Those were always very exciting moments; to experience something like that. And this (…) group experience: 'Man, we're sitting here and suddenly there's fifty thousand euros virtually on the table'. That is of course also an incentive for the others (…): 'Man, I alone can't do it. But all together – we can do it. That was (…) certainly a key experience for some" (ibid.: line 449 ff.).

In Germany, some examples are known in which community projects were able to achieve a high degree of professionalism, which is interpreted here as a positive development with regard to a long-term perspective: "Well, I know of examples where such community associations or mergers have finally become something professional at some point. But at some point they also act in such a way that there is simply a company with a board of directors who has the authority to make decisions and who looks at things, can also judge them and can say: let's do it – let's not do it. And it doesn't need half a year for a discussion process and two extraordinary annual general meetings to decide something. You can do that with a sports club, whether you want to build a new changing room or not – or something like that. But not with a business like this, where the economic conditions change quite quickly …" (ibid.: line 1042 ff.).

In a community project, constant feedback processes with the members are common practice and also desired. However, these consultations are time-consuming, lead to controversial results – and, above all, do not allow for quick reactions and courses of action. Therefore, such a community – even with a high degree of know-how – can only carry out smaller projects with less risk, and larger project realizations are currently not conceivable[39] "When I think about how the current federal government has intervened in the Renewable Energy Sources Act (EEG), in some cases over-scheduling or changing things during the year – and each time the eco-

[39] Note: This assessment contradicts the practice of larger energy cooperatives in Germany. However, the employee presumably relates this view exclusively to the situation in the federal state of Bremen.

nomic situation is different, and each time you would have to ask your association members: 'Tell me, do we still want to do this or is this too stupid for us now? What do the economists say? It's a very lucrative business. In addition, a community association as a whole does not even have much expertise – I don't want to say overstretched, but they are not in a position to react quickly enough. In addition to the other handicaps that they bring with them. And that's why they're more likely to be active in the smaller 'sandbox' area. Ten KW of photovoltaics here on the kindergarten, or twenty there on a school. But six hundred KW of photovoltaics on the exhibition halls – I see that still in the far, far distance" (I 9: line 1050 ff.). This slow pace of the community projects also means that the return on investment is somewhat lower. According to these accounts, it is not a problem for the community project if less profit is made, since an ecological goal also plays a role. Therefore, community projects are not seen in a competitive relationship with larger, established societies, but a compatible coexistence of both approaches is outlined: "(…) and makes a lot of work … and brings little … that is a wonderful field of activity for such associations, where afterwards it does not matter that there is a five before the decimal point. It can also be a four, because it's a bit more difficult – and it takes a bit longer – and it's a bit more expensive. But a) it is for a good cause – b) you can still earn a little money, and you have done something good for the environment. I also believe that the smaller projects will tend to run in this direction. If the appropriate actors are found – and the big ones … you can either regret or welcome it – the big ones make the big money" (ibid.: line 1066 ff.).

In the case of the community geothermal energy initiative, the community of interest hopes for cooperation with the active citizen groups in the planning phase, although their creative power is considered limited (similar to the case of the rural solar cooperative in connection with the Local Agenda 21). This cooperation should primarily be about informing and convincing the population: "We already assume that in the development phase, the active groups will also become active. With the support of citizen surveys and data collection. You have to collect a lot of data: what is the structure of the buildings like? For example, the active group has now developed a form with us – also coordinated with the management – because originally there was a lot of data on it. Every citizen immediately puts it away and then the whole thing has been slimmed down (…)" (I 7.1: line 527 ff.).

Even if the community of interest and the active groups have so far developed their commitment purely on a voluntary basis, the representative of the community of interest sees this basis dwindling in the long term. However, in order to prevent a purely private enterprise from emerging from the project, it could be run by the municipality in the future after the construction is completed: "At some point, of course, a point will be reached where it must then continue professionally. Where even the managing director, who is also an expert, also does the management of the business for a fee. Mr. (…) is, just like me, quite busy with his job and of course it is not so easy to do the management on a voluntary basis in the long run – if it really becomes extensive. But now in the initial phase … sure, the active groups … of course we hope that they will remain active and also do some work. But that will probably run out of steam at some point, when the whole thing really becomes a commercial enterprise. I would have the goal to let the whole thing merge into public utilities or municipal utilities" (I 7.1: line 537 ff.).

This would mean that it would no longer be a "project by citizens", but an identification of the citizen with the project could still be possible: "I can imagine that the citizen still somehow identifies with his participation. If this runs, he'd say: 'I am also involved with ten thousand euros in the municipal utilities' (ibid.: line 558 ff.).

Fruitless Efforts of the Supra-Regional Community Energy Cooperative
If, in the end, too high costs (as well as too much effort) arise for community energy projects and they do not receive enough support, a successful implementation becomes rather unlikely for them: "In the end, they must also offer economic advantages for the people and, above all, for the people who initiate it. So if it (…) happens from nonprofit associations and where many work voluntarily, then it will only work to a certain extent (…)" (I 8: line 1483 ff.). Therefore, a professional approach to community energy projects and entrepreneurial thinking is emphasized in comparison to purely voluntary community initiatives: "The projects should bring a certain professionalism (…) and a certain economic basis for the people who initiate it. Then (…) it is more sustainable than if you have it on a voluntary basis and try to implement it. And there are far too many projects that are done on a voluntary basis" (ibid.: line 1486 ff.). "Perhaps a few entrepreneurial personalities are also needed to make it work," (ibid.: line 1495 ff.).

Another possibility of promoting community energy could also be active support by the municipalities: "But I could also imagine that municipalities simply support this with personnel (…)" (ibid.: line 1511 f.). "They could provide a business incubator or some people who are employed specifically for this purpose, in order to promote such developments, such initiatives" (ibid.: line 1517 ff.).

In current practice, it is mainly a few committed people in the municipal administrations who support community projects through their personal actions and initiative[40]: "But it also really depends on one person or two people who find this citizens' participation important" (ibid.: line 1533 f.). Another possibility would be

[40] This was found to be the case in all the case studies in this research.

an increased initiative of publicly owned public utilities, in which citizens could also participate financially – the task of the energy cooperative is simply taken over by the municipal public utilities at this point: "But I think it's just great to think about: the entire public utilities, which is still one hundred percent municipal property. Then by the majority, i.e. the founding cooperative, where the people participate in the project. But then it would be through the municipal utilities. So the public utilities run the projects and the city gives up its shares in favor of this company of citizens, which is worthwhile" (I 8: line 1547 ff.).

In this model, citizen shares could also make the municipal utilities more independent of the financially weak municipalities, and thus make them more capable of acting: "And they just have additional capital, which is not decided by the city council, so to speak. Not to simply invest more money and increase taxes, but rather the citizens can also participate, and can then decide for themselves how much they want to put in there now" (ibid.: line 1564 ff.).

The Idea of Founding an Association and Setting Up Advisory Boards

With regard to the problem that a larger project increasingly loses the proximity to the participating citizens and thus reduces their influence, the initiator of the cooperative points out that an increasing size also leads to a higher degree of professionalism: "(…) the larger a company becomes, the more professional it becomes – of course there is a conflict or it will also diverge. So we once had an idea to found an Energiegewinner association (e. V.) (…) 'We are part of this company and this community' – in order to build up a kind of local group, like a party" (I 8: line 1698 ff.).

This approach is based on the consideration that a community project needs a management capable of acting. Here too – similar to the situation in other case studies – discussion processes are seen as "paralyzing". However, an integrated association could offer space for discussion and at the same time serve the development of ideas[41]: "I noticed that with Mittelweser eG (energy cooperative), there were already fifty or sixty people at the beginning (…) when it was founded. That came out of the eco-village, and there were just so many people who (…) were too interested in such a company… I think if you have to run a company economically,

[41] Compare the similar consideration and practice in case study 3 (urban community solar cooperative), where the cooperative emerged from an association and this continues to function as a "think tank". In case studies 6 (rural community solar cooperative) and 7 (citizens' geothermal community energy initiative), a civic Local Agenda 21 group or a climate protection working group also represents a kind of ideal basis for the community energy projects.

it simply needs a management that can also implement and do things in the implementation or in the realization of the projects. So if there are too many people who have a say in it, then it is difficult, and (…) to equalize it by simply (…) integrating it into the economic operation… The cooperatives will perhaps have an association structure next to it… Where people can also discuss, where perhaps new projects can arise that can then be realized in the cooperative. I can imagine that very well" (ibid.: line 1728 ff.). In this way, the social cohesion of the community should also be strengthened: "We have just thought about it (…), in order to create even more proximity to the citizens, so to speak, or to create even more proximity to the members (…)" (ibid.: line 1749 ff.).

A similar idea would provide for the formation of advisory boards, in which, in addition to the board, some representatives of the members could represent their interests (vis-à-vis the management/board) in the form of an advisory board: "One could imagine something like advisory boards or something, so that (…) the management has advisory boards. These could be scientific advisory boards, but they could also be local group advisory boards or (…) project advisory boards, where you then write some mechanisms into your own statutes (…). But that doesn't exist in this form yet, I think" (I 8: line 1766 ff.).

On the other hand, however, they are convinced that such communities could at best grow "from below" and should not be imposed "from above": "Well (…) we are already thinking along these lines. (…) From a purely factual point of view, we are not doing this under the Energiegewinner association (e. V.), but we are doing it in the existing association. (…) However, if we had not implemented it together with them, I do not know how long the association would still have existed. So that is also a mutual story. Yes, when you initiate such an association from the outside, I don't know. I believe that these local groups must then also really come into being" (ibid.: line 1774 ff.).

The Limits of Voluntary Civic Engagement

The analyzed cases, which are mainly based on voluntary work, seem to suggest that the establishment of renewable energy plants poses great challenges for a voluntary office. In several case studies (2, 3, 4, 7), the persons from the leadership seem to be at the limits of their burden, in some cases excessive demands are recognizable and have been named several times. In case studies 1 (community wind farm), 5 (environmental association) and 8 (supra-regional energy cooperative) on the other hand, there is no voluntary commitment, but (quasi-)full-time work, which actually seems to lead to less excessive demands on those involved. These case studies are also particularly productive in terms of their output. A counter-example to this is the case of the wind cooperative, where a cooperative (based exclusively on voluntary work) has managed to erect a wind turbine and thus to manage a costly project than the operation of PV systems. Therefore, even under the conditions of volunteerism, enormous results are possible. However, limits to this commitment certainly seem to exist: If the goal were to set up many energy plants in a short time, a volunteer project would probably reach its limits very quickly. Voluntary community energy projects therefore need a lot of time to develop, to overcome lean periods and finally to get projects off the ground. This makes them less competitive and also leads to a collision with the ambitious expansion goals of the state governments, which want to build very many new energy plants in a very short time – such an implementation does not seem possible with community energy projects.

Emergence of Different Engagement Structures

In the cases analyzed, civic engagement can be found in different forms. Some overarching styles of engagement development can be found:

- Voluntary commitment of a core group, especially in the initial phase: employee cooperative (case study 4), rural community solar cooperative (case study 6) and citizens' community geothermal energy initiative (case study 7)
- Continuous voluntary commitment of a core group: community wind energy cooperative (case study 2), urban community solar cooperative (case study 3)
- Voluntary commitment of members, especially in the initial phase: employee cooperative (case study 4)
- Continuous voluntary commitment of members: urban community solar cooperative (case study 3)
- Voluntary commitment of an accompanying civil society group, especially in the initial phase: rural community solar cooperative (case study 6)
- Continuous voluntary commitment of an accompanying civil society group: citizens' community geothermal energy initiative (case study 7)

The Social Added Value (Solidarity Mechanism) in the Case of the Urban Community Solar Cooperative

In the urban solar cooperative, there is a special feature that distinguishes this solar project from all other case studies: The participating citizens donate a part of their return to social projects. This is a fixed regulation to which every participating person is bound: "(…) that is a deduction for social and ecological projects. Well, that doesn't have anything to do directly with the economies, but well/ yes it does. So we have also written it into the articles of association that we want to make a return possible for the shareholders with the community solar plants, so that they not only have their investment back after twenty years, but also a bit more. But we also want to promote not only quasi-individual wealth, but also, I say, social wealth" (I 3.1: line 462 ff.). In total, the so-called solidarity transfer is about twenty percent of the annual surplus (I 3.3: line 78). The value is set so high because it is believed that the sum must be large enough to be able to use it to advance sensible projects (I 3.3: line 78 ff.). In the first project, this amount was still flexible, which meant that in the end many projects were funded, but each with very little money (I 3.3: line 80 ff.). In this first scheme, the citizens involved were able to choose between different projects which they considered worthy of support and then support those projects in a targeted manner. Representatives of these projects could then promote their project at the group's meetings: "And that's why we said that at least thirty percent of the profits, that is, the profits that go beyond the system repayment, must be donated every year. (…) every shareholder has the possibility to choose between different projects in the subscription form, which we decided on at the beginning, and there are also, for example, many shareholder meetings, a round where we tell them what ideas we have. So the people responsible for these projects, some of them or most of them are also nonprofit" (I 3.1: line 468 ff.).

The funded projects suffer from underfunding, which is why profits from the solar system can ensure financing: "For the projects, however, it should not be in the first place that they somehow make a lot of money, but that they also do meaningful things, and then the idea was simply that such a donation via such a solar system could also simply help to support the center and support the work there. Also to present the work to a certain audience, and to finance certain activities in the center" (I 3.1: line 640 ff.).

The initiator admits frankly that this support is also an end in itself, since the projects originate from the superordinate cultural center, where the idea of a community solar plant had its starting point: "Of course, there is a certain stubbornness in the fact that we can finance certain things through it, but because of course we do not only do sensible projects at our place, but also in the warehouse, which also does not have much money to start projects or projects in ecological agriculture" (I 3.1: line 645 ff.). This regulation of the levy, however, also brings with it an option of co-design by participating citizens, and leads to overriding questions and discussions of the participants with regard to sensible investments: "There is always the possibility that ideas can also be given by the shareholders as to what can actually be done with this money and yes, I think that is a certain built-in mechanism that one is not only concerned with the purely financial questions, but also what can actually be done so sensibly with money in order to start innovative new projects (…)" (I 3.1: line 476 ff.).

In which projects does the group invest now? It is about the promotion of further energy projects, for example renewable energy projects in developing countries, which are to be supported: "So the planning of new energy projects exists, which could be promoted for renewable energies in Africa. There is also a project in the center, in which a working group is dealing with / two project partners in two villages in Cameroon have already been there several times, where fellow campaigners or people from the project have already carried out surveys and there are two weather stations on site to test the metrological conditions, and/or a solar kiosk is to be built in one of the two villages in order to bring light into the village via battery-operated lamps, i.e. into the houses of this village, which is not electrified" (I 3.1: line 560 ff.). A share of thirty percent is obligatory for the shareholders, but they can also donate their entire share. According to the initiators, this idea, which reduces the return for those involved, has been positively received and has not come in to criticism: "Yes, with at least thirty percent and the amount above that can then be chosen freely, so to speak. So it can also be a hundred percent/ Then this company would only get back the deposit in the twenty years and nothing on top of that, but/ We have already said that we also find it nice/ To promote projects with which most people can/ should also identify and that has actually been totally well received so far. So that there is this obligation, so to speak, to give at least thirty percent. Nobody has complained about it yet, but that's just the way it is, yes" (I 3.1: line 573 ff.).

In their second project, the group then put an emphasis on the promotion of local projects, which are also in connection with the cooperation partner (cultural center) and their own center (where the ideas working group is located): "(…) in the second system other projects were included, for example, projects in cooperation with the warehouse, which could promote this eco-office or the theater in the old office building, this is a cultural project. We try to include projects from the center, where we ourselves come from, because there is also voluntary work going on and new projects can be supported, which then have it easier. But we also try to integrate this into the active and vibrant everyday lives here" (I 3.1: line 594 ff.). This local connection should at best always exist with the cooperation partner – the group shows its ideas creatively and flexibly in its application: "So in the first project in this organic farm. In the second project in the warehouse or/ If we had done it with the school, we would have definitely offered for the school to include a school project in this funding catalogue, and there are always possibilities to include ideas" (I 3.1: line 594 ff.).

According to the new regulation, about one third of the twenty percent is now to be donated to the Center for Solidarity Economy, where the SaHNE Association is also based (I 3.3: lines 83 f.). The remainder is to be decided by the members at the

General Assembly, in what should be invested (I 3.3: lines 84 f.). Four proposals are to be submitted for this purpose, two of which are to be selected, each of which will then receive one third of the sum (I 3.3: lines 85 f.). The concept that more projects are proposed than can ultimately be supported is intended to encourage the projects to submit good proposals (I 3.3: lines 87 f.). The solidarity transfer thus leads on the one hand to the promotion of further projects, which is a clear added value of a solar cooperative, but on the other hand it restricts the cooperative in terms of its financial resources (e.g. expansion), and leads the community into the problematic situation of not being able to fall back on solar modules from Germany, which was actually the idea. Here, too, the picture is confirmed that the community cannot achieve all the goals together, which were originally in the conceptual planning phase.

6.3.2 Acceptance of Renewable Energy Systems

Perception of One's Own Energy Plants A majority of the respondents (40 percent) assess the energy plants of the community energy project in which they are involved, neither more positively nor more negatively than other renewable energy plants. A quarter of the respondents have a more positive perception, and just under a fifth consider their own assessment to be much more positive. On the other hand, only one fifth of the respondents do not consider the plants to be more positive. It is striking in this question that participants in the wind energy sector emphasize the perception of their own wind power plants as significantly more positive.

Acceptance at the Local Level Acceptance of the energy plants (in which the respondents are involved) by the population is predominantly assessed by the respondents as positive (53 percent), or as neutral, or slightly positive or negative (45 percent), but almost not at all as negative (1 percent).

In the case of community wind energy projects, the acceptance of wind turbines is assessed less positively and more negatively – however, overall as rather positive, in the case of community wind farms there are surprisingly increased values with extremely positive assessed acceptance. Apparently, some members here deliberately want to emphasize a high level of acceptance – contrary to the much-discussed acceptance problem of wind turbines.

Participants in community energy limited liability companies assume a high degree of positive acceptance, in small community energy projects the value "more positive" as well as "extremely positive" is stated more strongly. Here, it becomes

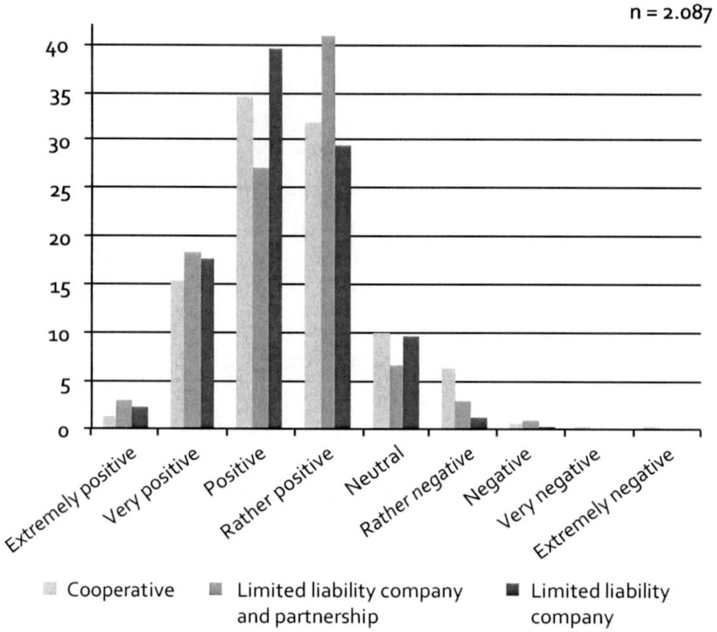

Fig. 6.20 Assessment of the acceptance of one's own energy plants: by type of legal form

apparent that the GmbH participants assume simplified positive acceptance more in a global way of thinking, while the members of small projects differentiate more strongly. In small community energy projects, less negative acceptance is also assumed, while the assumption of negative attitudes among the population increases for medium-sized to large community energy projects – this is presumably due to the fact that the various energy sources (possibly also the larger dimensions, especially in the area of biomass and wind power) sometimes generate more resentment, which may also include the participants themselves, who do not necessarily have to be in agreement with all the energy plants in their company's portfolio (Figs. 6.20 and 6.21).

Acceptance of Renewable Energies The respondents assume to a high degree that the acceptance of renewable energies in general has increased in recent years (80 percent).[42] Only six percent assume that the acceptance has decreased, few

[42] This is in line with the results of other surveys commissioned by the Renewable Energies Agency, where increased acceptance is also assumed (see Wunderlich and Vohrer 2012; Agentur für Erneuerbare Energien 2014; CARMEN e.V. 2014).

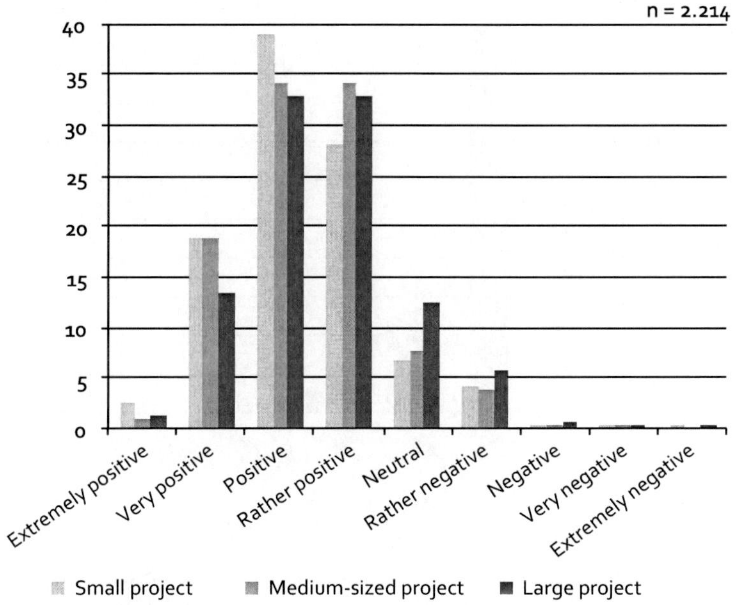

Fig. 6.21 Assessment of the acceptance of one's own energy plants: by project size

people assume an unchanged attitude (13 percent). Participants in community wind energy projects assume less of an overall increase in acceptance, which could apparently be due to their own concrete experiences. An increase in acceptance, on the other hand, is assumed more strongly in small and medium-sized projects than in large community energy companies. In the case of wind power, the increase in acceptance is apparently less of a given overall, while those involved in smaller projects "believe" more in the increase in acceptance of renewable energies in the whole of society – those involved in large projects presumably have several renewable energy types in mind, which is why it seems obvious that they assume less of an increase in acceptance for some energy types (Figs. 6.22 and 6.23).

Finally, the respondents were asked to give reasons for the acceptance value of their own energy system. Here, in the qualitative statements, a group formulated reasons related to the effect of their own energy project (*explanation ipso facto*): One-fifth expressed the assumption that the cause – in the positive case – lies with the energy projects themselves due to good information policy and transparency. A further 13 percent justify acceptance because of the alternative created to conventional energy production, 7 percent point to the contribution to climate protection and the regional

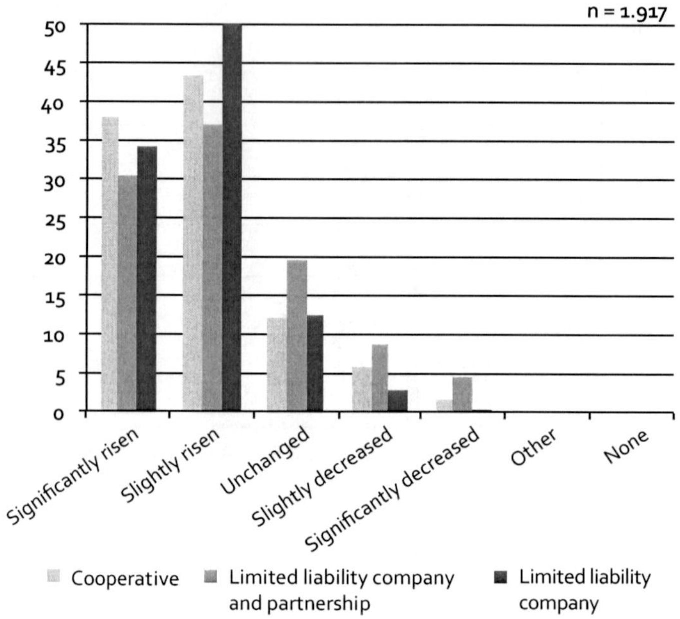

Fig. 6.22 Assessment of the acceptance of renewable energies in general: by type of legal form

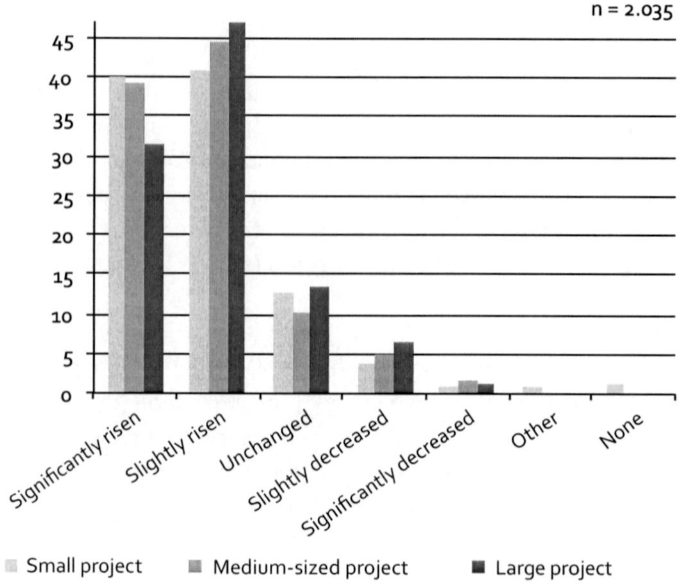

Fig. 6.23 Assessment of the acceptance of renewable energies in general: by size of project

location of the energy project, 2 percent refer to the cooperative form. Among the reasons given, the energy turnaround and the phasing out of nuclear power are frequently named as alternatives to the present (in relation to the finite nature of resource consumption and the risks of nuclear power plants), in the sense of a fundamentally new orientation towards alternative electricity and energy generation.

Another group finds causes in more general, societal context conditions (*general explanation*): 11 percent point to restraint and indifference of the population (which is also strongly criticized), 9 percent see causes in major, significant events such as the Fukushima reactor disaster in Japan in 2011 or due to the approach of broad citizen participation. A further 7 percent point to a negative portrayal in the media and the public sphere, while 6 percent more explicitly mention the portrayal of the financial burden of renewable energy sources. In this context, the participants frequently criticize communications from energy companies as well as representations by (federal) politicians with regard to a cautious to negative attitude towards renewable energies. The degree of information can be used as a reason for both high acceptance ratings (a lot of knowledge and discussions create acceptance), and low acceptance ratings (criticism of a lack of knowledge and ignorance). Respondents frequently refer to the statement "participation creates acceptance". In this context, reference is also made to the "St. Florian principle" or the "not in my backyard" mentality, according to which renewable energies are desired and accepted by the population, but specific disturbances caused by the energy plants in the immediate vicinity do not want to be accepted. Finally, a third, non-specifiable group (7.5 percent of those with qualitative statements) points to a need for acceptance; only 1.5 percent refer to general societal circumstances as a major explanatory factor. Instead, they emphasize the dependence on the degree of acceptance according to different energy sources (*differentiated explanation*). Here, the acceptance of energy plants is linked to the form of the energy plant. Wind power and biomass are considered unpopular, while PV systems are widely accepted.

Overall View

Stakeholders do not seem to have a much more positive perception of the energy installations in which they themselves are involved, compared to other installations. Acceptance of their own plants is assumed to be positive overall, but not extremely positive either. Wind plants have less high acceptance, but the degree of negative acceptance remains low. An even higher presumed acceptance of their own plants would have been conceivable, but obviously the members also take into account other views of the energy plants by the local population; furthermore a differentiation is made between the different energy sources. While PV has a very high acceptance, the acceptance of wind power is lower, but it is especially low in the case of biomass and biogas. The interviewees assume their own community energy participation model as the cause for the increase in acceptance or value, in addition to general societal influences such as the Fukushima reactor disaster and the overarching movement of the German Energiewende. They perceive negative reporting on renewable energies to a high degree, and in addition the not in my backyard phenomenon is observed among the population. Overall, the qualitative statements allow the conclusion that the members of community energy projects see themselves as part of a community energy movement; despite a lack of nationwide networking in the sense of an organized social movement, there is apparently an overarching idealistic common denominator as a uniform core of identification.

6.3.3 Perception and Assessment of Community Energy Projects

Information: Project Implementation Almost all respondents feel well informed about their energy project or participation at the time of their participation or entry into the project (95 percent). This very high value is in possible contradiction to qualitative statements regarding criticism of the energy project, where lack of information is a main point of criticism (see statements below). However, it should be borne in mind here that the feedback expressed relates to later developments, whereas this assessment relates to the time of participation, i.e. advance information. This very high value is given regardless of the type of community energy project. In the qualitative statements on this question, participants criticize above all the financial aspects as well as a lack of transparency, and a lack of information flow.

At the time of project implementation, two thirds express the desire to carry out public participation already at the time of planning renewable energies – in other words, public participation by the public administration is included and emphasized here. A further 45 percent consider a focus on climate protection in energy projects to be essential, a third are in favor of local companies carrying out the construction and operating procedures, and only a quarter emphasize tax revenue for the municipality. Participants in the community energy limited liability companies emphasize almost all aspects much more strongly; there is a balance between the projecttypes with regard to tax revenues and citizen participation in planning. This is possibly due to the fact that because of the lack of participation of the participants in these cases, other aspects, which are more related to the affairs of the community energy projects (and not the members), are focused on – which seems obvious due to the stronger delegation relationship. In community wind farms, surprisingly, less weight is given to the construction of renewable energy plants by local companies – which in this case has a higher relevance due to the larger dimensions. Overall, the strong emphasis on the participation aspect over all other points should be noted.

Definition of a Community Energy Project Three quarters of the respondents define a community energy project in particular by its contribution to the energy transition, and more than two thirds see the local-decentral energy supply as crucial. In addition, more than half state that small shares are possible, as well as the basic idea of financial participation, and an active role of the energy project in energy policy. The last point contradicts data above on thematic input by members, where a political role was indicated as less important. Apparently, the role of their community as an active social actor is quite important to the respondents, but it does not enjoy the highest priority.[43]

In the middle range of relevance are the points "citizen-initiated", "predominantly composed of citizen shares", "independence from the financial sector", and "led by citizens". These approaches strongly relate to some cooperative projects and idea-based communities. All points together result in the picture of an "ideal citizen-owned community energy project": founded by citizens, composed by them mainly from participations, managed and – due to the high citizen shares – acting independently from loans of the financial sector. This idea of "citizen-owned energy" thus represents a second-priority project approach – behind the general concern for ecological power generation with a citizen participation option. Finally, one third stresses the security of the financial investment, while one quarter advocates the active involvement of members as a "participatory core". The last value

[43] Hoffman and High-Pippert came to similar conclusions in a survey (Hoffman and High-Pippert 2005: 397 f.). Overall, the survey also found that participants consider a high degree of informedness (about technologies and renewable energies) to be very important. In terms of relevance, the development of strong communities, energy security, construction of energy technology, opportunity for participation, identification of costs of energy production, staff involvement, local jobs, small-scale energy technology, threats of climate change, change in public issue area, structure of locally-owned energy projects were highlighted in particular. Less important were lower electricity costs, the possibility of having one's own energy project, and the possibility of having one's own financial advantage was considered to be of particularly low relevance, which is in line with other results in the literature.

seems to reflect the committed share in community energy projects – the data on actual contribution support this assessment. Finally, the items "volunteerism", "design by members", "exclusion of large participation sums", "exclusion of fixed returns", "safe investment" and "openness to the inclusion of members' ideas", rank as less important. This suggests that the respondents attach less importance to the specific way in which their project is structured – whether it is volunteer-led, member-oriented, or has regulations concerning financial participation. At first glance, this seems to clash with the data on thematic involvement: the respondents here emphasized questions on the organization of the community energy project. However, these statements show that other aspects are meant by organizational matters – the statements on important regulations of the articles of association in the next point show them.

In the community energy limited liability companies, the aspects of energy transition, local supply, and enabling small shares are emphasized. Above all, an active role of the community energy project in energy policy and secure financial investment is strongly weighted – the larger community energy companies can actually also participate more as a publicly perceived player in supra-regional energy policy; financial investment is a more applicable perception of the participants here than in the other approaches (Figs. 6.24 and 6.25).

Furthermore, financial citizen shares, independence from the financial sector, and the inclusion of member ideas are more strongly focused on here – the participants obviously also express a desire for more member involvement. Accordingly,

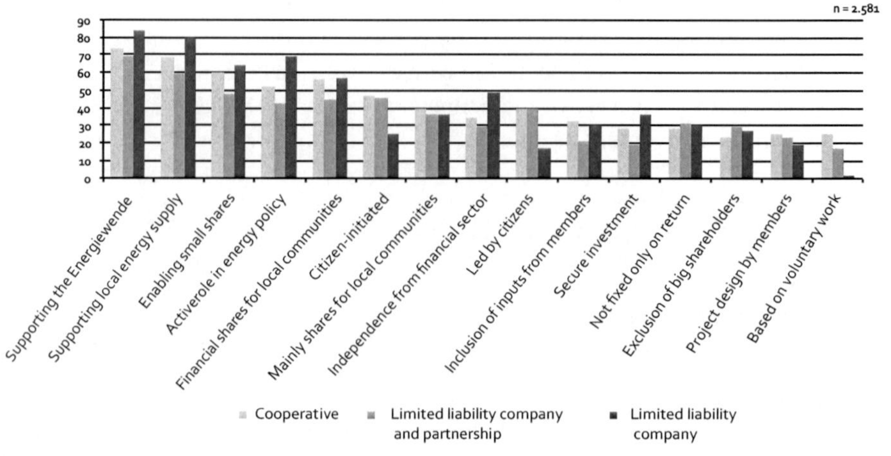

Fig. 6.24 Definition of a community energy project: by project type

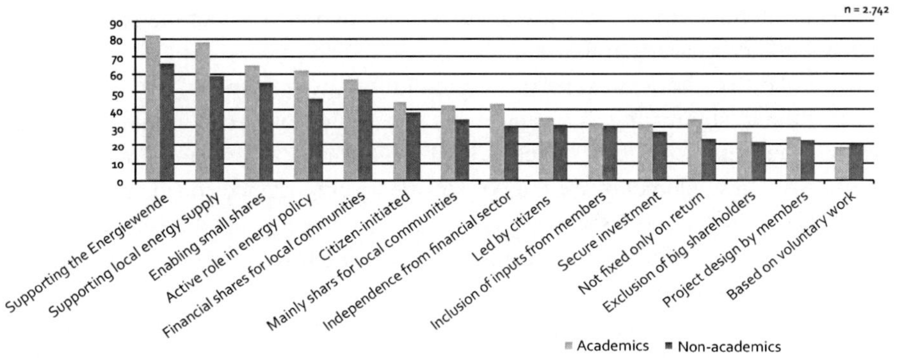

Fig. 6.25 Definition of a community energy project: by level of education

the participants of community energy limited liability companies define the issues "citizen-initiated", "managed by citizens", "design by members", and "volunteering" to a lesser extent – these are precisely the characteristics that do not distinguish their community energy projects. It should be noted that the members agree with the orientation of their projects and would rather see them as public NGOs; they also appreciate this role – at the same time, however, they would like more involvement, which also came to light in other questions.

In the cooperatives, the emphasis is on the categories of "local supply", "small shares", "active role of the community energy project in energy policy", "financial shares", "citizen-initiated", "inclusion of ideas", "secure investment", "member design", as well as very strongly on volunteer-work. The exclusion of large shareholdings is mentioned less, although it would seem obvious that capital concentrations should be avoided here.

In community wind farms, the issues of "citizen-initiated", "managed by citizens" and "exclusion of large investment sums" are named – it is extremely important to the participants here that outside investors do not install wind turbines; too high investment sums are presumably not welcome, as these often occur here on the one hand and can be associated with bad experiences on the other – investors of large sums can massively influence the fate of the limited liability company and partnership (GmbH & Co. KG), as they have voting rights depending on the amount of the investment sum. Altogether fewer persons agree here with most aspects – the relevance is consequently seen to be lower – and agreement is particularly low for the topics "independence financial sector", "inclusion of member ideas" and "secure investment". The latter value is surprising, as the wind energy sector in particular involves higher risks than the photovoltaic sector. And although the stakeholders are comparatively strongly involved, they do not consider the possibility of involvement to be overly important.

Regardless of the legal type of a community energy project, all respondents agree without significant fluctuations on the topics of "predominantly citizen shares", "not return-fixated", "exclusion of large participation sums", and "design members". These elements are thus of secondary importance for the members of community energy projects; however, a certain core seems to address these points in every project structure – this seems to be the "idealistic-participative" member subgroup already identified.

Academics emphasize all aspects more strongly, but agreement diverges strongly on the points "independence of the financial sector" and "not fixed in terms of returns" – these questions are much less important to non-academics. There is agreement on the questions of, "inclusion of members", "secure investment", "design of members" and "volunteering" – i.e. in areas of lower relevance.

Men endorse the topics "shares for citizens", "volunteering", "predominantly citizen shares", "safe investment", "independence of the financial sector", and "exclusion of large shareholdings". Women, on the other hand, prefer "shaping by members", "active role in energy policy" and "enabling small shares". Here, too, it is clear that women see much more community-participatory aspects as well as the political-public dimension in community energy. The gender statements are balanced for "citizen-initiated", "openness of member ideas", "design by active members", "contribution to the energy transition", "local supply" and "focus not on returns" – there is thus unanimity on the points with the highest relevance statements. The greatest differences, on the other hand, occur in the two characteristics "voluntary work" and "predominantly citizen shares". Women are thus more in favor of the ideal of a volunteer-led community energy project, which excludes higher proportions of credit financing.

Low-income individuals are more supportive of the attributes "created by citizens", "open to member ideas", "safe investment", "enabling small shares", "exclusion of large shareholdings", and "led by citizens" (the latter unites them with middle-income individuals). Thus, they affirm concerns of their group to a greater extent: with low income, the aspects of small and safe investment are more significant. At the same time, however, this group is also strongly influenced by ideals, in that participatory aspects and citizenship are placed in the foreground.

In contrast, "financial shares", "volunteering", "active role in energy policy", "contribution to energy transition", "return not the focus" and "predominantly citizen shares" are disproportionately pronounced in the middle-income group. This group thus combines, above all, characteristics that are highly valued by all respondents. In addition, the people imagine a volunteer-led association with a stronger idealistic orientation, which tends to reject a focus on returns – thus there is a great closeness to the cooperatives.

Among high-income individuals, the areas "led by citizens" and "design by active members" are emphasized only slightly, while "contribution local energy supply" and "independence financial sector" are emphasized strongly. This means that there are now major differences in the definition of a community energy project: High-income individuals place more emphasis on professional management and little on member shaping – they thus prefer a conventional company imprint. The only idealistic aspect is independence from banks, which they seem to distrust more. Local energy supply is presumably a matter of course for other groups, but the high-income group emphasizes its importance even more strongly from a far-sighted perspective. At this point, the gap between the perspectives becomes clear.

Statutes and the Rules of Procedure: Participation in Another Community Energy Project Almost all respondents state that they are in agreement (95 percent) with the statutes and the rules of procedure (or shareholder or loan agreement, design of the profit participation certificate) by their project, company or organization or community. However, it is clear from the qualitative data that very many people are not familiar with the articles of association, with one third explicitly stating this at this point.

Some people expressed criticism at this point, essentially relating to individual views on aspects of financial participation and risk/reward distribution, regulations on voting rights, entry conditions, notice period and lack of pre-emption rights. This shows that (at least) some participants would like to have more opportunities to exert influence on the one hand, while on the other hand information on financial participation is important to the participants in terms of transparency and information, which is also suggested by other qualitative information (see criticism below). In addition, more flexibility in participation is desired: in simple terms, easier entry and access to participation, as well as uncomplicated exit options.

The respondents continue to criticize conflicts of interest in the project (e.g. with regard to the orientation), acquisition of new energy projects, remuneration of staff, fixation of committees (and lack of committees, regulations on elections and the idea of rotation), exclusively regional reference, lack of obligation to provide information, voting procedures, rights of inspection, liability of the board of directors and audit procedures (e.g. by associations). General criticism refers to too strong a fixation on returns and economic orientation. Obviously, there are different views in the community energy projects regarding the orientation and design of the organizations:

- *Strategy*: social-ecological orientation without attention to maximum return vs. return-oriented orientation with focus on expansion
- *Management*: professional and remunerated management vs. volunteer staff without special expertise
- *Co-determination*: creation of many committees, working groups and voting procedures including strong involvement of members, granting of extensive rights of inspection, as well as comprehensive and regular briefings vs. reduction to prescribed procedures, handling of the agenda by management reporting

Furthermore, the respondents weighted individual, fundamental aspects of a constitution. More than half of them emphasized the basic ecological orientation of the project as an ideal goal (e.g. preamble). All other aspects were weighted in a fragmented way: reserves, investments, decision majorities, elections, determination of a maximum participation sum and termination of membership appear to be relatively important to the members. It is striking that very specific points of regulation concerning the business activity of the projectand financial participation are named. Undoubtedly, the members are thereby designating the essential cornerstones of the structure of their projects. The only other idealistic aspect concerns the exclusion of a fixation of returns. Moreover, these areas are apparently not subject to much criticism, as these aspects are hardly mentioned among the criticisms. Information with medium relevance is found in the definition of a minimum investment amount, the introduction of proposals, the size of the management board and supervisory board, the dissolution of the company, and the transfer of the company's assets. Finally, the transfer of voting rights, dismissal of management and exclusion of a member are rated as less important. These are predominantly issues which can be regarded as rather sensitive and unpleasant to deal with; they have an increased potential for conflict which, however, is not reflected to any great extent in all the member's feedback. Obviously, the overall relevance is rather low, although this may be different in individual cases.

Half of all respondents reject participation in an anonymous energy participation project that is not known in detail (e.g. only via prospectuses). Above all, people in community wind farms reject this mode of participation; they also emphasized aspects of a local anchoring under the information on the definition of a community energy project. Furthermore, the majority of respondents (84 percent) can imagine participating in another energy project. Conversely, however, this also means that not every person was convinced – but since criticism of participation as such is very low (see point "identification" below), it should be considered that further participation is not ruled out on the basis of negative experiences.

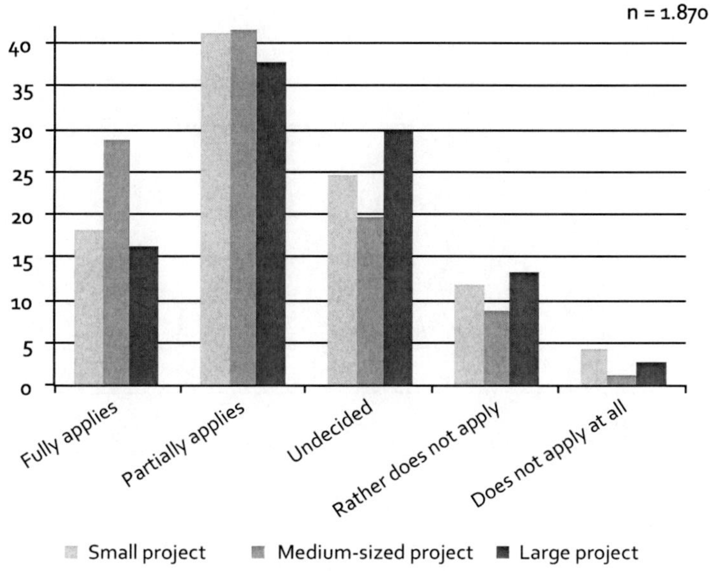

Fig. 6.26 Project creates sense of community: by project size

Sense of Community Almost two-thirds of respondents believe that the energy project has created a sense of community among those involved. Only 15 percent explicitly say no. Surprisingly, the values for full agreement are not very different between small and large societies (18 versus 16 percent).[44] It would have been expected that the feeling of "we" would be much stronger in small societies, since there is greater physical proximity between the participants. All the more surprising is the further circumstance that in medium-sized societies, however, there is significantly higher agreement, although fewer statements and contributions were mentioned here. The community wind farms and cooperatives represented here, which include many non-academics with strong local-centered "energy in citizen hands" motivations, are obviously projects in which there is de facto less discourse than in the smaller societies, but the sense of belonging to a locally welded community is strong. The type, "community wind farm" is not sufficient as an explanatory factor however, since the values here are not extraordinarily higher than those of the cooperatives and small projects. According to the affiliations of the groups of respondents to the medium-sized community energy projects, it is non-academics and people with lower incomes who feel a stronger sense of community (Figs. 6.26 and 6.27).

[44] The community energy limited liability companies are not represented on this issue.

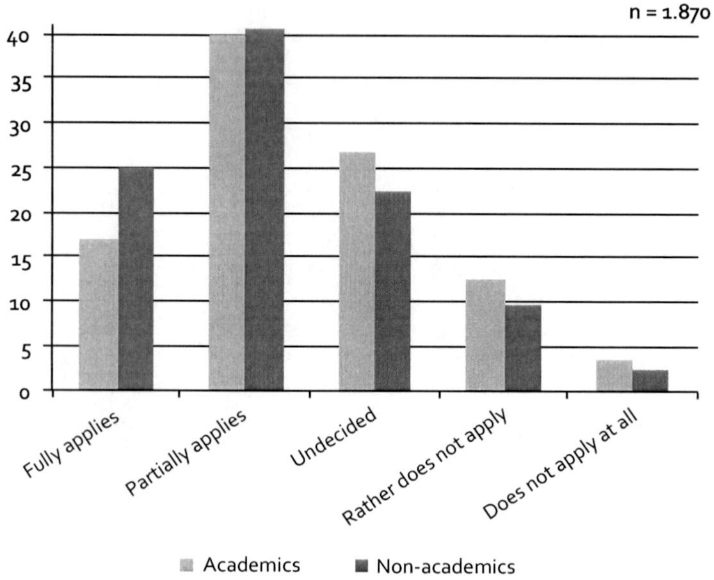

Fig. 6.27 Project creates sense of community: by level of education

Identification In contrast to the sense of community, many more respondents indicate a high level of agreement with the identification with the community energy project in which the participant is involved (80 percent).[45] Doubts about their own community energy project are expressed by 5 percent, and only 0.3 percent now reject the community energy project in which they themselves are involved.

Above all, members of community wind farms can express a strong identification with the energy project: here not a single person has stated that they now reject the energy project. This underlines the likewise pronounced sense of belonging, but also suggests that it is not so much the community spirit through contacts and exchange in the sense of active involvement and shaping that is pronounced on the one hand, and also not necessarily desired on the other (see statements on low involvement and little desire for more discourse).

In the large projects, there were more doubts overall, and there was also a lot less complete agreement. Many participants also expressed neutral opinions here –

[45] The two characteristics identification and sense of community were surveyed with the following questions:

- "To what extent do you identify with "XY Community Energy Project"?"
- "The XY community energy project created a sense of community".

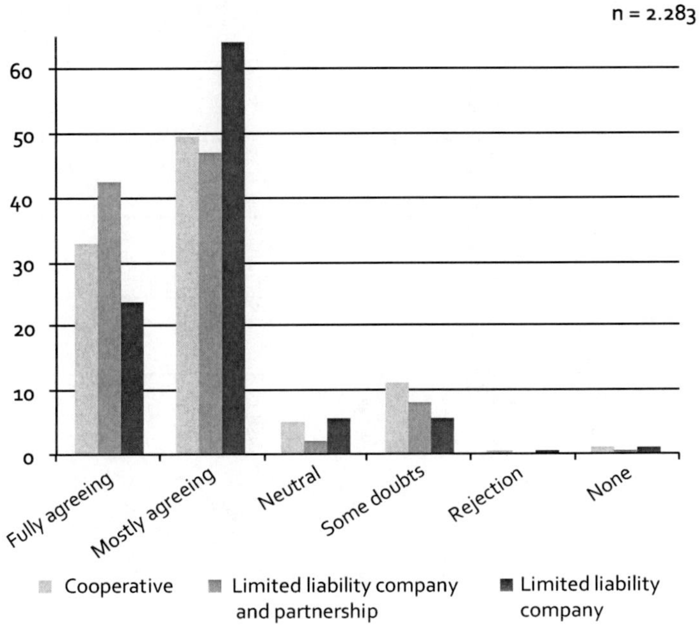

Fig. 6.28 Identification with the community energy project: by type of legal form

they were apparently not sure whether this should be a requirement for a community energy project at all. Interestingly, the cooperatives again present a split picture here: Doubts and concerns are most pronounced here (11 percent), while at the same time the approval ratings are high. Obviously, there is a core in the cooperatives that does not agree with this type of implementation.

Non-academics are conspicuously more likely to reject commitment, and approval is also somewhat lower overall among people with low incomes. This is surprising, since at the same time these groups are particularly involved in the societies and a stronger sense of community was indicated. Apparently, there is no direct connection between participation and identification, but there is one between participation and a sense of community (Figs. 6.28 and 6.29).

Identification is possible even if the distance between the participants and the meeting place is greater, and there is little or no physical presence. Identification can therefore be established through the mediated image of the community (i.e. the members of the energy project). However, identification is particularly strong when there is a local proximity combined with a local emphasis by the community itself, even if direct contact from member to community is weak. In principle, without contact to the community, there would be no difference to a community at a greater

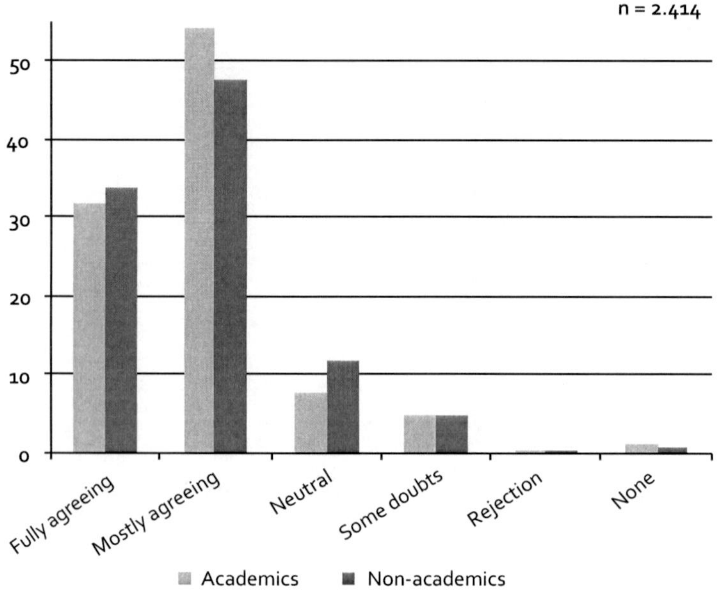

Fig. 6.29 Identification with the community energy project: by level of education

distance. The orientation of the community itself towards the local area (as a regional project for the local community) creates a stronger sense of belonging to the community in terms of local proximity of the member to the energy project.

Furthermore, it is striking that more disapproval is expressed by both low-income and high-income individuals, than by middle-income individuals. This is more difficult to explain: The middle-income member group expresses less interest in issues overall in other contexts and showed less input into concerns. Due to this rather neutral attitude, a less negative attitude towards identification could also result in this context, especially since the approval ratings are strong here. Stronger satisfaction and agreement are thus obviously related to less involvement and interest; less knowledge leads to less criticism.

Attitude Change and Learning Behavior Respondents overwhelmingly say they are more in favor of decentralized renewable energy supply since participation began (41 percent), and many participants are also more in favor of collaborative projects (such as cooperatives) (41 percent), and more citizen participation in the whole of society (36 percent).[46] A third also gained a more positive attitude towards renewable energy. Increased acceptance of disruption caused by renewable energy installations is also reported by 28 percent. Only one-fifth said they were more aware of their own energy consumption, and only 12 percent had a generally more ecological attitude. For 17 percent, participation has led to a greater rejection of large power plants. 38 percent of respondents indicated no change in attitude, and 1 percent even view renewable energies more critically since participating in the energy project. The strong emphasis on the community and participatory aspect is striking, which seems unusual due to the more restrained statements regarding internal organizational processes. Obviously, the basic motives of the participation option and foundation of joint energy projects are very important to the participants, whereas the internal design is rather secondary, which already became clear in the topics of contribution and relevance in project implementation. The relatively low values regarding individual behavioral change may also result from the fact that the individuals already had a high level of ecological attitudes and lifestyles at the time of participation. Therefore, the values are not necessarily evidence that energy participation does not lead to individual attitude change. In summary, the strongest effect of own participation is the access and stronger conviction of a possible realization of decentralized energy supply, similar to the idealistic approach of 100% renewable energy regions. This decentralized approach coupled with joint project implementation – and thus the respondents' own participation model – has become less of a utopia and isolated solution in the participants' imaginations, but rather a realistic concept of energy supply that is compatible with the majority (Fig. 6.30).

[46] A change in personal attitude since participation in the energy project was surveyed with the following question:

Ever since I joined XY Community Energy Project…

- I have a more positive attitude towards renewable energies in general.
- I am of the opinion that one also has to live with negative impacts of renewable energies (e.g. noise and appearance of wind turbines).
- I believe that a decentralized energy supply (without large power plants) can be achieved.
- I am more in favour of community projects (e.g. cooperatives).
- I have become an opponent of large power plants.
- I am in favour of more participation of citizens in the whole of society.
- I am paying more attention to my energy consumption.
- I have generally adopted a more ecological attitude.
- My attitude towards renewable energy has not changed.
- I have taken a more critical opinion on renewable energies.

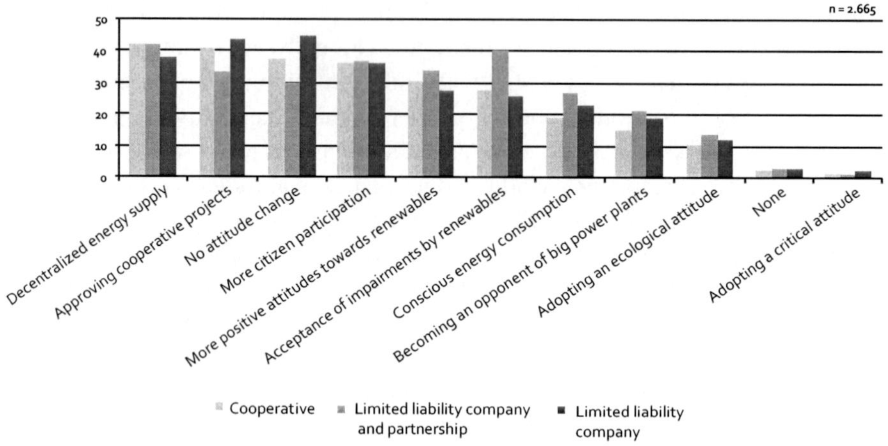

Fig. 6.30 Changes in attitudes since the date of participation: by type of legal form

In the community wind energy projects, a stronger positive attitude towards renewable energies is expressed, as well as more acceptance towards the disturbance that renewable energies generate. Obviously, this assessment refers primarily to wind energy plants, where disturbance and acceptance play a greater role than with PV plants. This shows that a certain transformation process regarding attitudes towards wind power is obviously triggered by participation; participation therefore generates – to a certain extent – more acceptance from those involved. Of course, this does not mean that a statement can be made about the acceptance of the energy plants by the local population as a whole.

Participants in community wind farms show a stronger awareness of energy consumption, rejection of large power plants, and a more ecological attitude, while at the same time they show comparatively low values for support of community projects and no change in attitude. These data further support the picture of participants in community wind farms in that there are no widespread overspill effects: Participation is understood very concretely and considered contextually meaningful, but in contrast to the basic cooperative idea of joint management of a wide variety of sub-areas, this idea can be described as follows: "Participation in a wind turbine on the doorstep makes sense, but that is why participation and joint use do not have to become the basic principle everywhere".

Participants in community energy limited liability companies, on the other hand, express less belief in decentralized energy supply and less positive attitudes towards renewable energies. In contrast, support for joint projects reaches the highest value among the legal forms, and a critical attitude towards power plants and attentiveness to energy consumption are also more pronounced. However, the highest values in the comparison are also seen with no change in attitude, and a more critical attitude towards renewable energies. These values make the participation structure of these energy projects even clearer: the two community energy companies themselves do not represent a local-decentral approach, as they operate supra-regionally, while power plants belong to the conventional energy production model. Due to a presumably more global view – as the community energy limited liability companies are involved in many different types of energy, the participants do not see all renewable energies in a consistently positive light (e.g. in some cases strong rejection of biomass and biogas use), critical attitudes can also be explained by this. However, the participants are strong supporters of the energy participation approach in general, they think less like community wind farm participants about the specific, locally noticeable participation in energy plants in the surrounding area, but rather about the principle that participation in renewable energies seems to make sense. Since a strong ecological emphasis was already shown in the question about motivation, an individual effect of energy saving is obvious. Since the participants cover a large spectrum of the total population, it might seem obvious that – in contrast to the cooperatives – there is less attitude change.

The cooperative members strongly emphasize decentralized energy use and joint operation – which corresponds to this approach. However, it would not have been expected that there would also be a high degree of no change in attitude, in addition to the lowest values for attentiveness to energy consumption, rejection of large power plants, and a more ecological basic attitude. Apart from the core effect of increased confidence in one's own energy project and the project idea, other effects (individually with regard to energy consumption and ideologically with regard to the rejection of power plants) are of secondary importance. A coupling in the sense of a mutual dependency cannot be determined.

Interestingly, one single effect is distributed more or less equally across all legal forms and types of energy used: the desire for more citizen participation in the whole of society. Here, all participants agree that their own participation has led to more advocacy of participation in general. However, advocacy is somewhat stronger in medium-sized societies, as is acceptance of interference. The latter is due to community wind projects in this group, and the other value is difficult to explain. This type is characterized by little participation in the community energy project but a very strong sense of community, there are many non-academics involved. Apparently, this is a group of participants who do not internally endorse intra-organizational participation, but define participation in a more formal sense like membership and emphasize it just as strongly. This understanding, vice versa, provides a further explanation for the strong sense of belonging. Thus, it is not the medium-sized societies, but the small and large societies in which a more critical attitude towards renewable energies is more widespread. While this seems understandable in the large societies due to the broad portfolio of energy types used, it is more difficult to understand in small societies. It is possible that the "critical core" of some members may be an explanatory factor, expressing a stronger social frustration not only towards their own energy project, but also in general.

Overall View

The members of the community energy projects feel very well informed about the energy project at the time of their participation, but at the same time there is some criticism regarding the decreasing flow of information over time.[47]

- In the **project implementation** of renewable energies, many respondents would like to see citizen participation at an early stage in the planning phase; an overarching effect of community energy is also the stronger demand for more participation in the whole of society as a general principle.
- In their own **definition** of a community energy project, many members emphasize above all overarching principles in the form of decentralized ecological power generation with a citizen participation option – in the sense of a contribution to the overarching energy transition.
- Many participants agree with the **statutes and the rules of procedure** (or the shareholder or loan agreement, the design of the profit participation certificate), but many members are not familiar with the contents. With regard to the content of the regulations, members are particularly concerned with specific questions of financial participation and risk/reward distribution, voting rights, entry conditions, notice period, and lack of pre-emption rights. Critical voices reveal different ideas of the members on the management of the community energy company, co-determination, and overarching strategy.

[47] In a survey of energy cooperatives in Germany, 82% of members expressed satisfaction with the participation opportunities, 80 percent also expressed satisfaction with the provision of information, and a further 78 percent stated that they were satisfied with the handling of conflicts (Rauschmayer et al. 2015: 6). However, 22% also reported back being only partly-satisfied with the handling of conflicts, and 10% were even rather or very dissatisfied (ibid.). However, this survey showed that significant differences exist in the environmental behavior of members of energy cooperatives compared to non-members: They buy more organic food, talk more with acquaintances about environmental problems, and obtain more information about environmental problems (ibid.: 10). Similar to the results of the present study, energy cooperatives generate for participants a strengthened sense of belonging among members (61 percent agree), a strengthened sense of belonging locally (52 percent agree), and a sense of being more a part of the local community (51 percent agree) (ibid.: 11).

- Both the **sense of community** within the community of participants and the **identification** with the community energy project are strongly pronounced; this applies above all to a high level of identification.
- The most important **effects** of community energy participation are a stronger conviction of ideas of decentralized energy supply, common project and enterprise approaches, as well as more citizen participation in the whole of society.

The members think in terms of the benefit to their community energy project (such as contribution to the energy transition) collectively as an actor, as opposed to an individual mindset (shaping through their own member contribution and individual participation in the community energy project). The energy transition has taken a firm place in the members' collective imagination as a common project for society as a whole (with which the members identify). For the members, the basic ideas of their energy projects in the form of citizen participation, community operation and decentralized energy supply have gone from being a singular idea to a model for every conceivable place. So, in simple terms, citizen energy increases confidence in community energy – but beyond that, members have found access to collaborative ventures beyond the energy field. To an extraordinary degree, projects have achieved a sense of belonging and personal identification that belies the notion of a silent, uninvolved membership. Thus, community energy apparently increases advocacy and trust in local community as well as local renewable energy deployment. Interestingly, however, participants are less likely to become opponents of conventional energy production, nor do they see an increased need for acceptance of the detriments caused by renewable energy. The values regarding the lack of attitude change and their personal energy consumption can probably also be explained by the fact that the participants already had an ecological attitude before joining the energy project.

6.4 Participation and Collaboration

6.4.1 Participatory Design and Engagement Structures for Intra-Community Participation and Collaboration

Participatory arrangements are understood to be those institutions, regulations, opportunities and forums within the community energy project, which are in some way suitable for offering the persons involved or members of the community an opportunity for participation, co-determination and co-design (see Fig. 6.31). On the one hand, these forms of participation can consist of people acquiring financial

Members` participation within a community energy project (var. A)	**Citizens` participation outside of community energy projects (var. B)**	**Members` participation of a community energy project through a parent civil society association (variant C)**
Influence through: • Voting • Discussion forums • Advisory boards • Meeting • Working groups	**Influence through:** • Information about planning procedures • Discussion forums • Input of proposals • Petitions • Protestactions	**Contextual factors:** • Local climate protection activities and regional cultures of civic engagement **Example:** Developing a climate protection concept
Influence on: • Internal and external development process of the project	**Influence on:** • Planning and development process of energy facilities and concepts	**Legal and administrative factors:** • Voting rights, meetings, forums
Legal and administrative factors: • Voting rights, meetings, financial shares	**Legal and administrative factors:** • Citizens` participation in planning and development process	**Personal factors:** • Hierarchy, Management, voluntary work
Personal factors: • Hierarchy, management, voluntary work	**Personal factors:** • Moderating, concept creation	**Members` factors:** • Internal participation
Members` factors: • Internal participation	**Example:** • Planning of wind energy plants	

Fig. 6.31 Three modes and types of participation in community energy projects

shares and thereby becoming members of the community energy project or association. This raises an initial question as to which access requirements must be met, and from what amount a share can be acquired. This status can give rise to rights with regard to participation in meetings and voting. In addition to such formal community meetings, other forums may also be established, such as member councils, clubs or regulars' tables, meetings of the sponsoring organization, etc., which often have a high level of participation and can often achieve a high level of input. Beyond the mere factual existence of such community forums (variant a), however, the individual, concrete contribution of individuals or groups through motions, draft resolutions, design proposals, ideas, etc. (variant b) is also relevant. Within these meetings and through design measures, conclusions can be drawn about existing discourses and deliberation within the communities.

In addition to participation conditions in this sense as an active process (variant I: participation through active shaping within the project or association in the context of organizational and social participation), participation activities on the part of the local population are also conceivable, in that they can participate in the planning processes of the energy plants, raise objections and discuss specific issues (variant II: participation through involvement in the planning and operational process in the context of public participation). While in the first case, the members of the energy project (and thus a smaller, possibly more homogeneous group) are responsible for shaping their own project, in the other case it is the local population as a large, heterogeneous group which influences the project-specific measures of the first group.

In the case of joint forums, events and exchange platforms, the population, stakeholders and members of community energy initiatives can meet and exchange ideas. Here, political participation would coincide with social participation; in particular, one could also speak of discursive participation. Such opportunities regularly arise through the establishment of climate protection forums, which can be founded on the initiative of a municipality or region, civil society associations or federations, or also through community energy initiatives, energy suppliers, etc.

In addition to the two variants of participation in the field of renewable energies, a third form is conceivable through internal participation in accompanying associations or federations. Similar to participation in a community energy initiative, there may be opportunities for shaping and contributing at the project level of associations which, for example, accompany or have initiated a community energy project (typical examples here are environmental associations, cultural associations, religious communities, etc.). If this grouping cooperates with the energy community energy project, it would be obvious for members to exert influence via this institution (variant III: participation at the higher level of a supporting institution). In this process, it is interesting to see to what extent participatory meta-control of the energy projectby the sponsoring institution is practically feasible and compatible with everyday routines. It should also be questioned to what extent such indirect co-determination also has direct effects on the energy project. An example of this could be decoupled levels of discourse (e.g. a working group on renewable energies), which apart from the possibility of exchange do not fulfil any function in terms of influencing decisions.

With regard to the engagement of members, the type of civic engagement involved in community energy initiatives will be examined in more detail. To this end, the structures of engagement and the specific fields of action and activity are to be examined and categorized. On the one hand, similar to the modes of participation, a distinction must be made between the extent to which the energy project itself develops a specific commitment to other actors externally, and the extent to which a commitment of the individual members takes place both internally in the community energy project and externally. On the other hand, with regard to contextual factors and individual characteristics of the persons involved (individual background, further engagement, etc.), it is necessary to scrutinize more closely which classification of engagement structures (question: How does engagement take place?), and which engagement characteristics can be found and categorized (question: How can engagement be described in terms of its characteristics?). In this way, different forms of engagement should be made visible and a classification made possible.

Blind Spots of Participation: Social Inclusion and Exclusion Capability of Community Energy Projects

Analysis of the Problem

To what extent are community energy communities designed to include many citizens in the communities? One measure of this may be the extent to which people with divergent opinions to the majority of members or project management can be successfully integrated. Some cases (case studies 1 (community wind farm), 4 (employee cooperative), 5 (environmental association community solar project)), are "closed" projects where citizens could only participate within a certain period of time or, in the case of the employee cooperative, they exclusively address a specific target group. In this case, it happened that some critical members could not be integrated. In the other case studies, however, it appears that many citizens were successfully integrated. In case studies 1 (community wind farm), 2 (wind energy cooperative), 3 (urban solar cooperative), 6 (rural solar cooperative) and 7 (citizens' community geothermal energy initiative) there were active and lively discourses, deliberation and discussion processes, which to a certain extent were also able to generate a problem-solving capacity.

Collaboration in a Community Energy Cooperative

Input Dimension: The Question of Number, Activity and Involvement of Members

In the case of the staff cooperative, a different participatory arrangement was chosen than in the other case studies, as only the members of the institution (university) were to be addressed here. This raised the broader question of who should and should not be included in the cooperative. Initially, the deciding factor was that the cooperative would also be provided with the roof space by the university, which enabled both the cooperative and the university connection: 'Quite clearly, the statement from the university management was that the roofs should be made available for our staff and our members. I think that would have been more difficult to conclude a lease agreement. Then the roofs would automatically have been opened to all people in Bremen. Then there is hardly any difference than if the savings bank had done it. I am actually quite happy that we only have our university people here" (I 4.2: line 270 ff.).

Opinions within the cooperative as to how many people should be included varied widely. The regulation that alumni (employees, students) should also be admitted led to a further stretching of the term: "Yes well, there are just opinions from the auditorium, you have to admit that. It's difficult to find a boundary. I find it totally difficult. I've got umpteen thousand, no umpteen thousand is an exaggeration now. I've received a few e-mails from people who live in Munich or somewhere else and have studied here for a year at some point and want to join in. You have to draw a line somewhere" (ibid.: line 278 ff.). With regard to the concrete individual question concerning the admission of a new member, the cooperative finally decided on a very pragmatic approach: "If we need money, I take in more and if we don't need any, I take in less. (…) Quite pragmatically. Someone was there all day and then we realized. As I said, he only studied here for a year and wanted to donate 10,000 euros. What should I do? If I had needed it urgently, I would have said: give me the money. But now I said: No, from Munich or something, that's too tricky for me. That's no longer a real member" (ibid.: line 289 f.).

In addition, the question was discussed from which financial amount a participation is possible and which maximum sum can be invested. Here, too, the initiators wanted to attract many members of the university and exclude too high a participation, which is also justified with their own commitment: "Yes, of course, they were deliberately chosen. We wanted to have here, I will say flippantly, the cleaning lady and the student. We also have some who have chosen the lowest limit and we also didn't want to have big investors there who pay half the plant. They actually profit from our work. They profit from my sweat and nerves, which I have to bring in here" (I 4.2: line 317 ff.).

Discouraging Discourse?

Within the founding phase of the cooperative, there was also criticism and failure of the cooperation in the course of the participatory process, when interested people got involved and dealt with the founding and possible tasks. After a few discussions, one interested employee decided not to join the cooperative. He later explained his reasons for this in more detail (see Communication M 4). On the question of the structure of the energy cooperative, criticism was voiced above all of the excessive discussion processes: "My idea was that once a year a general meeting would be called, the result and the distribution of the profit would be proposed by the main board and approved by the assembled members. Afterwards one goes over to a comfortable area with a beer or wine and talks more or less humorously about social, cultural, economic, ecological issues or whatever. In view of the course of the founding meeting, however, I rather expect endless general meetings where every detail is argued about. I have no desire for that" (M 4: line 16 ff.).

Individual Influence Within Nested Legal Constructions of Community Energy Projects

The equal voting principle of the cooperative does not play a major role in the case of the planned, more complex project structure of the citizens' community geothermal energy initiative, as the joint "voice" of the cooperative in the superordinate company is of greater relevance to business operations and decisions than the decisions in the cooperative itself, which does not hold the management here: "It will probably also essentially be smaller participations … one person may participate with two cooperative shares, but the voting rights in the cooperative are usually related to individuals. But that doesn't really matter either, because the people who are in it then form the uniform voting rights of the cooperative in this large extended operating company" (I 7.1: line 436 ff.). If a citizen wants to exert their influence here, they would first have to turn to the cooperative (management). Theoretically, a direct way to the management of the superordinate GmbH would also be possible, but ultimately the cooperative (management) would also have to be involved here – the mode actually used in practice, however, remains unclear in the conceptualization process: "In order to bring about decisions, he can only turn to the cooperative. So he practically has to bring his idea to the cooperative. (…) He can of course also turn to the management and say: 'I have a good idea. If the management then says: 'That would be a good idea', then they can put it to the vote. But then the cooperative will also have to make a decision: How does the cooperative then behave with its representative in the shareholders' meeting of this operating company?" (I 7.1: line 447 ff.).

The Knowledge of the Members as a Creative and Innovative Driving Force for Community Energy Strategy Development

The supra-regionally organized energy cooperative sees an advantage in the fact that it is very receptive to ideas regarding new photovoltaic plants, since for the initiators this also represents a full-time field of activity from which they profit. This leads to a double advantage: the initiators are interested in every idea, as it takes away project planning work from them. At the same time, the citizens involved are pleased that they can contribute their own ideas for new facilities and that these are treated seriously[48]: "And I don't know whether that is democratic, but

[48] This case is reminiscent of the urban solar cooperative case study, where the initiators are also interested in members' ideas for new projects.

at least it enables our members, where they are, to initiate things with the possibility of saying: Here, this just works in this place and we can do it relatively. So an individual with personal commitment can also implement projects (...)" (I 8: line 1056 ff.).

Social Cohesion and Social Capital

The social cohesion of the communities is an essential social factor: The "core" in the form of the members and their exchange with committees as well as within the communities must harmonize, constructive cooperation must be possible (in the sense of binding social capital) – the mostly limited resources of the communities due to voluntary work, heavy workload etc. require this basis all the more. The competencies of the project management also seem to be of essential importance: This is essentially about a targeted but at the same time inclusive style that does not suppress many voices within a community, but can nevertheless ultimately produce results that are capable of providing a useful basis for action. The other side of the coin refers to openness and connectivity to the outside: to interested parties, the local actor network and the local population (in the sense of bridging social capital). Finally, it is also about the community itself: to what extent is it able to contribute important competences and to generate new ideas or a broadening of perspectives? – In the case of the employee cooperative, conflicts arose between members and the board of directors, as well as between the supervisory board and the board of directors of the cooperative. Nevertheless, here too the cooperative benefited greatly from the competencies of the members, which impressively demonstrates the productive performance of member working groups beyond a mere discussion group. Similar findings can be found in the case studies of the wind energy cooperative, urban and rural solar cooperative, and the citizens' community geothermal energy initiative. Some case studies are less open to collaboration among members due to their professionalized and thus more shielded management, for example in the case studies community wind farm, environmental association community solar project, and supra-regional energy cooperative.

The collaborative achievements through the working groups in the case of the employee cooperative as well as the discussion rounds within the urban solar cooperative stand out among all the case studies. In the case studies of the rural solar cooperative and the citizens' community geothermal energy initiative, these processes are rather shifted "outwards" to the Local Agenda group and the active group, which, however, do not directly deal with the actions of the community energy project. In the case of the wind energy cooperative, a more far-reaching collaboration of the members is not known. Thus, collaborative processes probably remain rather a marginal phenomenon in community energy projects. However, the potential and integration power of working groups, i.e. possible problem-solving ability and binding of member interests, should not be underestimated. In the urban solar cooperative and employee cooperative case studies, negative effects of participation were noticeable, such as disagreement, complicated decision-making and a slowing down effect[49]- but this is countered by the design aspect as such: In this way, the energy projects also seem to have become their own business in the minds of the participants. In addition to a few critical voices, the management of the energy cooperatives supported this approach and consciously accepts negative effects. The findings from the case studies also suggest that it is crucial that the management itself initiates such forms of collaboration: a closed organized management creates a passive participation culture, an open-minded management can at least develop a breeding ground for collaboration, which would probably be used in most cases. However, the strategy of the leadership must contain more than a mere appeal; the active creation of forums, setting up of working groups etc. should be a minimum requirement.

Collaborative Activity of the Members

Urban Community Solar Cooperative

Citizen Collaboration, Design and Participation in Community Energy Projects

Within the urban solar cooperative, there were various discussion processes, cooperation between the people involved and the introduction of various topics and requests. Presumably, the association connected to the cooperative supports this exchange process. Already at the beginning, the grouping relied on exchange at frequent meetings: "Yes, we then called a shareholders' meeting at the beginning of February and coordinated and jointly decided on the further procedure" (I 3.1: line 196 f.).

Often the sequence of meetings (as in the other case studies) consisted of proposals for the sequence being made first, but also suggestions from the members: "It is regulated in our articles of association that the management makes a proposal

[49] Conflicts between working groups and the boards of cooperatives could also be observed in von Blanckenburg's study of climate protection cooperatives, according to which the "grassroots understanding" of the working groups could come into conflict with the board (von Blanckenburg 2014: 264). In the cases studied here, it was possible to identify a problem with regard to a competition of competences in particular, in that in one case study the board felt ignored by the working groups and restricted in its work as well as not supported; the problem ultimately amounted to a question of trust, as a result of which the working groups ultimately lose influence and motivations tend to be reduced.

for the agenda" (I 3.1: line 204 f.). "Then we reported how we wanted to build the plant and then made a proposal for the further procedure. Then, of course, there were also proposals from shareholders. This was discussed and a common way was found" (I 3.1: line 206 ff.). As in all other case studies, the possibility is basically given for members to contribute ideas and motions: "Every shareholder has the possibility to make motions also for the agenda at shareholder meetings. They can also convene the shareholders' meeting from a certain vote (…)" (I 3.1: line 496 ff.). The number of participants at the meetings is not very high: "It worked, there were about 12–15" (I 3.1: line 234). However, it must also be taken into account that the cooperative is rather small.

The written minutes of the meetings show which topics were of particular relevance at the meetings, and which led to discussions among the members. These included the following aspects and areas in particular:

- **Organization of the project:** Composition and size of the bodies (supervisory board and management board), admission and non-admission of members, amount of equity ratio and contributions (minimum and maximum amount), tax deduction of donations to social projects, amount of dividends (minimum and maximum amount)
- **Management of the project:** Preparation of a business plan for the establishment of the cooperative, lease agreements, amendments to the articles of association, preparations for the installation of new roofs.
- **Technical issues:** Advantages and disadvantages of roof sizes, integration of new roof areas, social and ecological standards for Chinese and German solar modules
- **Public relations:** Advertising for new members, press releases, setting up a Facebook page, events, information events
- **Social investment:** Support of social projects (solidarity transfer), possibilities of project selection ("Who is allowed to make proposals for projects?").
- **Stakeholder network**: Contact and exchange with other local energy cooperatives
- **Commitment and integration:** Interest of members of the cooperative in working in the affiliated project group of a nonprofit association

Different emphases on the topics become recognizable: Organizational issues, structure of the community energy project, public relations and questions about some design elements that generate a higher level of discussion. While most of the points also correspond to those in other case studies as well as to the results of the survey, differences exist with regard to social projects and standards for solar installations. Discussions regarding the question of minimum and maximum participation amounts, on the other hand, are also found in some other case studies.

Another point concerned the question of a limit on financial holdings. Originally, it was planned to set a maximum limit in order to prevent overweighting in the shareholdings. In the "expansion phase" of the cooperative, after lengthy deliberations, it decided not to set an upper financial limit on the shares (I 3.2: lines 72 f.). Even if a maximum limit was initially considered important and larger investors were to be prevented, it was recognized that larger sums were needed for implementation and that individual persons or organizations should not be deprived of the opportunity to invest larger sums (I 3.2: line 73 ff.).

Another discussion thread concerns the question of whether solar modules used by the cooperative should come from China (I 3.3: line 96 f.). Actually, the activists had always spoken out against this, but these modules are much cheaper than those from Germany (I 3.3: line 97 f.). The money saved from this could then flow into the intended social projects (I 3.3: line 98 f.). However, if German modules were chosen, the question would then arise as to whether investments in social projects could be dispensed with (I 3.3: lines 99 ff.). In one vote, the SaHNE group voted that social projects were indispensable (I 3.3: lines 101 f.). One initiator describes this question as a major dilemma for the cooperative and the SaHNE association (I 3.3: line 102 f.).

Regulations in the statutes are also an issue for increased exchange: The minimum contribution of 500 euros specified there is considered by some people to be too high, e.g. for students (I 3.2: line 91 ff.). Here it is discussed to possibly lower the sum to 100 euros (I 3.2: line 93 f.). The problem that is seen here is that the administrative costs would then rise sharply due to the larger number of members, although the cooperative would only grow slightly in terms of the investment sum and nothing else would be achieved apart from membership strength (I 3.2: line 94 ff.). There were also discussion processes in a previous solar energy project, where questions about which roof and which energy systems should be used were already a topic of discussion: "But now, for example, in the case of the warehouse, where everything has been delayed, there is of course already the possibility of saying: Well, if it is delayed so much, then we would rather not make a system, or we want the modules instead of them, or we don't want to have the local energy supplier (SWB) in it. Of course, there is already a vote on it or if, for example, a new project arises from such a private company (civil law partnership: GbR), if a company thinks there is a really great roof and whether SaHNE or shareholders of this private company (GbR) do not found a new private company (GbR), then of course there is also the possibility to co-determine this from the outset" (I 3.1: line 509 ff.).

Social Activities

Finally, questions and topics can also be brought into the group, which have nothing to do with the essential and business issues of the cooperative, but serve, for example, other activities and entertainment: "Otherwise, most things that go beyond this purely monetary participation are actually rather a bit out of a pulse. So once a shareholder approached us that she really wanted to go to an anti-nuclear demonstration, and if we would go there as well, and then it happened that somehow an email was sent to all shareholders asking if more would like to go, and it was suggested we go to the cinema together and watch this film, the fourth revolution" (I 3.1: line 481 ff.).

However, their own expectations of exchange, coordination and collaboration processes are also limited: "But I do believe that many people find it nice when there is such a fixed framework from the outset and no more fundamental things have to be decided" (I 3.1: line 516 f.). This applies in particular to the questions of planning the plants, which the initiators already take on in advance, in order to be able to present something on the one hand, and on the other hand, this preliminary work is also the basis of trust of the interested citizens in the project (see approaches of the wind case studies):

> (…) we have also made the experience that most of the shareholders find it nice when the planning of the plant is already completed in advance (…) If a flyer is created after the foundation, that is, if not SaHNE or the management or all those who were present at the foundation, also approaches the public, that then it can be directly advertised with concrete data. And for this, of course, modules have to be selected in order to obtain offers, and based on this, to make a profitability calculation, in order to be able to give a yield prognosis. In this respect, these initial questions are usually not quite so participatory, in order to be able to package everything nicely, so to speak, in order to then look for shareholders. (I 3.1: line 500 ff.)

In addition, there is the aspect that with many proposals it cannot necessarily be assumed that there is an interest in doing things differently. However, on the one hand, the open process as such is decisive, and on the other hand, there was actually a vote on the question of the financial support of the electricity provider: "Yes, there have always been questions like that / but on many points, I think they agreed to our plan. For the first system, for example, we looked exclusively at German modules and also thought about what technology we wanted to use. Well, there were a lot of questions / but then no one said directly: No, do it better this way, because we actually find that so much nicer. If there had been the possibility. Good. So in the case of the warehouse, there was definitely this discussion about the SWB and there was already a vote on whether it should be done this way or not" (I 3.1: line 541 ff.).

On the one hand it becomes clear that in this case study a comparatively high level of social cohesion and community feeling has been achieved, on the other hand the grouping had to say goodbye to its initially high ideational goals to a large extent, high expectations regarding activity, commitment and success were dampened. The learning processes of the community led to a perception of increased complexity in the realization of the social form, the construction of the facilities and the implementation of the demands for cooperation, committees and attitudes of the participants. However, since the grouping did not ultimately fail, it can be surmised that a gradual alignment of ideational goals and realistic courses of action occurred. Neither the one nor the other way of thinking therefore had to be completely revised, but the original expectations and idealistic goals weakened.

Employee Community Energy Cooperative

Initial Euphoria and Declining Activity

The engagement process was similar in the case of the employee cooperative. When the working group and collaboration were set up during the founding phase of the cooperative, there was initially a dynamic atmosphere and a high level of interest in discussion and participation:

> At first, there was probably a sense of optimism. Everybody, I say now, that is of course an exaggeration. There were a few people who wanted to help shape things. The group had to find itself a bit, of course. In the end, people motivated each other to move forward. Let's take X, for example, with the legal matters. If we hadn't had him. The cooperative association was also very important for me. It gave me a bit of legal certainty, how do you proceed, what do the articles of association have to look like? But on the other hand, there was also the fact that people wanted to discuss things and you have to take that on board first. You have to allow them to shape it. You are not allowed to present everything. (I 4.2: line 114 ff.)

The requirements for the founding of the cooperative structured the tasks and the distribution of these tasks among the members: "This all developed out of the necessity of what had to be dealt with" (ibid.: line 129 f.).

Areas such as public relations, economics, finance and law then emerged, but this was initially completely unstructured: "Then there was a very committed group here from the print shop around public relations, who made all the posters. Super, that too. Profitability and finances, that overlapped a bit. It was completely unstructured. Totally unstructured and messed up. But it was fine, it was all right. Was completely fine" (ibid.: line 134 ff.). "There was a small group that took care of insurance" (ibid.: line 142 f.).

The initial dynamic was inhibited by the establishment of the cooperative's organs (board of directors, supervisory board): "In the meantime, (…) we form the board of directors. There is also a supervisory board. There are then also two meetings and we simply manage the business by ourselves" (ibid.: line 138 ff.). The initiator can still fall back on the help of the committed members even after this phase: "I can still access the people again. Wonderful" (ibid.: line 149 f.)

In some cases, the cooperation took the form of interested persons approaching the initiators and becoming involved without any further motivation on their part:

> We didn't specifically approach the people, we simply had a meeting. We then had these various meetings to inform (…) He then (…) approached me and said: "I would like to work here and contribute my know-how". Wonderful, it doesn't get any better than that. (ibid.: line 414 ff.)

> (…) You can always be happy about that happening. With this dynamic that is in there, everyone wants to join and some people are sad that they can't join right away, because, for instance, we are full and cannot accept new members anymore. (I 4.2: line 1015 ff.)

The collaboration of the cooperative members in the working groups led to a higher identification with the institution (university): "They think it's great that you can shape the working world yourself. I think that is incredibly motivating. That's what I think is so great about this project. You also have to tell the management that it's great that they allow their employees to be so involved. This also leads to the fact that the employees identify more with their institution (…) they go to work with much more joy, I think". (ibid.: line 816 ff.).

In addition, there is the aspect of employee motivation: "(…) I praise them again and again and I also say in every lecture that I give, that it is great fun to work together with the colleagues. What kind of cohesion, what kind of motivation, what kind of dynamics exist. I have never experienced this in a research project as I have here in this project. (…) everyone is involved here. Here everyone is involved in shaping the project. That is something special" (ibid.: line 831 ff.). The commitment releases a high degree of creativity of the members: "Yes, that you can be creative. That is actually quite important in the working world. People who can be creative, such as self-employed entrepreneurs, are also creative. They have a completely different identification than when someone stands on the assembly line or sits at the cash register and just has to cash things in or something. They can't identify themselves, they just do their time. (…) Then ultimately, of course, the feasibility. That is also really fascinating" (ibid.: line 839 ff.).

In the university context, the project can also serve as an object for research: "We also want to make it possible to do a bit of research within the project, and we absolutely have to pursue that. That we bring in more and more young scientists or academics who use it here" (ibid.: line 422 ff.). The formation of various working groups (working groups: public relations and advertising, technology, economic viability, financing, organization) indicates that a potential lack of topics, as it was assumed at the beginning, is not demonstrable in a community energy project. Rather, the guiding question is to what extent the topics are available for collaborative processing. The conflict between members, supervisory board, and board of directors over agenda-setting illustrates this.

Rural Community Solar Cooperative

Deliberation and Collaboration Processes

Also in the case of the rural solar cooperative, discourse and collaboration of the members in the energy cooperative can be traced. Already at the beginning of the first meetings, a high degree of discursiveness was evident: "Yes, that was incredibly exciting and great. Because, there were different age groups there. People from 30 to 75, let's say. Of course, they all had different reasons for being there. Then an argument arose between the sceptics and the supporters among the audience. We were there with our six people in the front, where the mayor also sits in the town hall, and the spectators were in the room. They then partially turned to each other. So we were faded out and then they were talking to each other. Then a 75-year-old man stood up: 'You sceptics, you must have the courage to do something. I'm not doing this for me. I'm doing it for my grandson. He should also be able to say: 'Grandpa, you have done something for the environment and so on'. Such conversations arose and then one saw ahead" (I 6.2: line 518 ff.).

But there were also passive citizens in the meetings; after the discussions were over, the main topic was further progress: "The people who wanted to say a little less, they applauded. There were emotional arguments within this group. But this argument was just as good, that afterwards, after they had argued loudly, they sat down again and then actually, yes, the topic was clear. Then they were all more or less in agreement. Then they said, 'Yes, what do we have to do now? What happens now?'" (ibid.: line 528 ff.).

However, a thoroughly chaotic culture of conversation is reported, which is said to have been purposeful: "It was a motley mess. I think the characteristics of the people there were like that. Through this conflict, which they themselves had led, they somehow managed to get everything right, to jerk everything into place. Like a potato crate, suddenly everything sinks together and fits, and then they said: 'So, now we are in agreement, let's do it. And then we were back" (ibid.: line 544 ff.).

Here, the assembled citizens are clearly distinguished from politically-interested people: The project approach is described as less political and more factual (focusing on specific topics and goal orientation in the sense of project management): "There were many different impressions. They were all not politically oriented now. That is the point. They have nothing to do with politics, but have dealt with the purely factual circumstances there and this situation. Do we want this or not? I'm sure half of them came here and said: 'We're just interested in hearing what you have to say. In the end they said, 'We will sign. 'We didn't say anything. That was the genius of it. We didn't say anything. They worked it out amongst themselves, and you see it works. You don't always have to be the know-it-all or push your way to the front and say, 'Yes, you have to' or something like that (ibid.: line 555 ff.). "They weren't political, they were all normal citizens and everyone, as they sat there, as far as politics was concerned, they were fed up. (…) But they were people tired of politics. They sat there, the non-voters. We only held events with non-voters, and they were in favor" (ibid.: line 712 ff.).

This approach of project-oriented work is seen as a model of success. Another advantage is that decision-making processes are not based on interest groups, but on factual and substantive considerations: "This can perhaps also be transferred to other processes. Simply that one works in a project-oriented and factual way, and we have already done it in such a way that it is simple. (…) There could perhaps be more factual decisions and not so much globalization. Only the organizations are responsible for globalization. In the groups itself there are also different opinions, but they have a factional compulsion in part and this then does not come into effect. That is, it is no longer a living democracy" (I 6.2: line 730 ff.).

The orientation of the cooperative is clearly distinguished here from social initiatives or movements with a strong normative-ideal reference: "I don't have to act like an academic specialist here. I know that I know. I know that I think globally. I know that concerning energy or whatever, Germany has actually been in my grasp for 20 years, how it all works. But I would never bring that forward, I would just keep that to myself now" (ibid.: line 574 ff.).

Furthermore, in this case study – similar to most of the other cases examined – great importance is attached to the support of local companies (as plant manufacturers) and social-ethical aspects in the production of solar modules: "First of all, the company here in Syke, because it is closer, is preferred. It gets points. Yes, where do the modules come from? That's worth points. No modules from China. No modules from non-democratic countries, we said (…)" (ibid.: line 618 ff.).

However, this social-ethical component must also be supported by the members of the cooperative, especially since the cooperative must accept higher prices (see similar problem in case study 3): "I have to buy this openly for the cooperatives, cooperative members. The question is whether there is now an ethical component, and whether one will accept that. Because that certainly meant that the first plant was more expensive and so was the second plant" (ibid.: line 625 ff.).

Integration and Inclusion of Members

A concrete co-determination and co-design of the members should be possible here by the fact that they themselves propose topics and discussion points, and finally also communal votes can take place on these. Furthermore, the members decide on the committees, elect the members and relieve them: "Once a year we have a cooperative meeting and this cooperative meeting has an agenda that we propose, and this agenda goes to citizens and comrades, to members and then they can say: I would like the agenda item for this, or I would like the topic for this. Then the issues are worked through, the agenda items and then each agenda is voted on. A vote is taken on whether to approve the actions of the management board, and a vote is taken on whether to approve the actions of the Supervisory Board, and thus the citizens have an influence" (I 6.2: line 887 ff.).

Another principle is the active involvement of interested members and inclusion in committees[50]: "We had one who said: 'I think the distribution is too low. 'Then I said: 'Okay, we can't change that, but what do you do?' 'Yes, I'm an accountant and I do this and that. "It's wonderful, too. What do you think about joining the board? Maybe you can help us make it better.' He did. That means he can get directly involved. If someone says, 'I'd like to be on the supervisory board, or I'm interested in becoming a board member, too.' Then he can become a board member" (I 6.2: line 895 ff.). These possibilities, and in particular their actual application in practice are particularly emphasized: "That's a great possibility. (…) It's a nice responsible story and you can join right away. I can get you fully involved" (ibid.: line 903 ff.). "He can just come forward at a meeting. (…) After all, there is a vote. Every point is voted on, after all. He can propose a topic himself where he is against it. You are included in the agenda and then it is voted on" (ibid.: line 913 ff.).

The number of members attending the regular members' meetings is also estimated to be very high[51]: "Half of them are always there. Fifty, sixty people are always there" (ibid.: line 922). During these processes, the members of the cooperative obviously contribute a lot and help to shape the cooperative: "Suggestions are then made. Some things then come to nothing, as it is. Now we are in the process of looking into it: Let's do another photovoltaic system with the sports club, perhaps. We have several roofs and options there, or perhaps a small wind turbine. The district is considering whether smaller wind turbines (…) can be installed. There

---

[50] See the case of the urban solar cooperative, where one member showed interest in serving on a committee.

[51] High numbers of participants in some of the cases studied are known (community wind farm, wind cooperative and employee cooperative) and are evidenced by survey data, interviews, protocols and observations.

are several variants (...). Which are not yet fully developed. They are just there in the room and everyone is working on them a bit" (ibid.: line 948 ff.).

Acceptance and Evaluation

With regard to the possible usable forms of energy, the energy cooperative wants to focus on those that also meet with a high level of interest and acceptance among the population. Here, too, the principle is emphasized that the energy project should have additional benefits beyond pure energy production (spillover effect) and – in a legitimizing sense – be supported by a large majority: "That is, if the feeling arises that this form of energy is regarded as difficult here in Syke, then we would not necessarily push it to the front. We have the idea or sometimes it is just me, that we want to achieve synergy. We want to hold the city together here. We want to make ourselves positive for the city. We do not want to become a block. (...) We want to be something that moves positively and where the 111 members can say: That's o. k. They don't all have to say: that's great. But they have to say: Man, that's ok. what they are doing" (I 6.2: line 968 ff.).

It is precisely this confirmation of an expressed common interest of the citizens that is ensured here by two principles: On the one hand, through regular feedback (evaluation), and on the other hand, through openness to alternative or even new suggestions from the middle of the cooperative: "Ultimately, we always get the feedback. Every year, when we have our meeting, we ask again: Is that okay, the way it's going, the way we're doing it, or do you have another idea? Do we want to do it differently? They are challenged. And as it is in society. Most of them say: Gosh, no. Keep doing what you're doing. I don't have any ideas. It's not like I know any better.' That's a great thing, isn't it? That's when everybody came out of the closet. It can't get any better than this. We could have voted differently. But we didn't, so we go along with it every year. That is, this is still directly democratic, at least for these 111 people as our choice. They still have the influence that they could say: Stop, I want to have something taken into account. And this is not dependent on some politician putting it on the agenda, but they can do it themselves" (I 6.2: line 977 ff.).

Associative Versus Political Action

The structure of the cooperative is again distinguished from the shady sides of political action: "And now that there is also a clearer direction, board of directors, supervisory board, the people. That is a clearer structure. We work from this way to that and back. In politics it's like this, you have to lobby. Lobbies come from the outside. But you have to have my interest, you have to have an opinion, otherwise you don't get the vote, otherwise you don't get this, you don't get that. So it's a network of linkages that also exert undemocratic influence on the decision makers. You can't do that with us. At least it's damn difficult, especially since the right to vote stands in the way. If someone with ten thousand shares now had ten voting rights, then it would be possible again. But it's not really possible like that. And that's why I say there's a bit of socialism in it. That is a company with socialism" (I 6.2: line 1053 ff.).

However, limits to the potential of a cooperative are also clearly seen. This principle is suitable for individual projects, which can have a specific beginning and end point, less so for complex topics and tasks: "I don't believe that the cooperative is able to do complex things as an individual part. The cooperative is now here a model for concrete projects which have a project beginning and a project end. Then a new project can come" (ibid.: line 1066 ff.).

Finally, it should be ruled out that the cooperative is de facto dominated by a few individuals who have invested larger sums. However, some larger investment sums do seem to exist (which, however, due to the parity voting principle, do not have any significant meaning in the case of formal votes): "We have now said at the moment: so we don't want to have major shareholders (...). So we rather want – there are some who have given us eight thousand euros or even ten thousand euros – but that should not be the rule. We wanted to orient ourselves close to the people. Citizen-oriented means that we also take into account that the citizen can do it" (ibid.: line 1100 ff.).

In particular, the unity and the consensus found among the citizens who came together is a special feature in this case – in addition to the fact that the cooperative could be founded within an extremely short time: "We came together and we spoke with one voice and immediately founded a cooperative in the second event. You have to imagine that! In what time we took to set up, we had the first system on the roof. That was two months. I don't know if you know, when you found a company, how long something like that takes or what all has to be taken into account. But not two months" (I 6.2: lines 1185 ff.).

Preliminary Conclusions: The Challenge of a Lack of Topics in Discourse and Collaboration

The phenomenon of a lack of topics seems to be detectable in some case studies. In several cases, however, the members are apparently not even aware of which topics and contents might be up for discussion at all (as in the case studies of community wind farm, environmental association community solar project, rural community solar cooperative, and supra-regional energy cooperative). In other case studies, the topics seem to become superfluous after the successful establishment of the community energy project and the construction of the plants: In case studies 4 and 6, for example, the working groups have practically ceased their work. In the case studies community wind farm and environmental association community solar project, the question arises for the members in the completed projects, where no new members and energy plants are added, which topics could be relevant for discourse, exchange and cooperation at all. Only in the urban community solar cooperative case study do discourses continue, but they also seem to weaken.

The participatory monitoring of further general meetings after the founding of the employee cooperative (as well as partially in the case of the rural community solar cooperative) has shown, however, that topics of relevance to the members of an energy cooperative can certainly continue to exist, such as the design of the cooperative's organs, the question of further energy plants, the creation of reserves, the admission of further members, public relations, leaving the cooperative, collaboration with other energy projects, technical problems, etc., and so on.

In community energy projects, a kind of curve of activities can be observed, in that at the beginning a lot of questions and topics generate high interest at a foundation, members develop a strong commitment, animate other people to do so and a process of activity is set in motion – but after a relatively short time, motivation and commitment ebb away again and the ongoing business operations are finally maintained and secured by the formal-established management of the community energy project.

In summary, it can be stated that "completed" projects in particular suffer from a lack of topics and discourse, while "open" initiatives and associations (such as energy cooperatives, associations and project groups that would like to initiate further energy projects) suffer less. Here, discourse and collaboration are defined as components of a community energy project, combined with the hope of releasing creative-innovative potential through participation. In most cases, a certain repertoire of topics as well as a permanent, fluctuating discourse is maintained, which is open for the members to shape and, in the best case, can be worked on and shaped by them in a suitable framework (working groups). The decreasing willingness to engage is presumably a generally widespread phenomenon, as it is known from engagement research and findings on civil society associations, federations and organizations.

Deficits of Member's Participation in Community Wind Energy Projects

In the wind energy cases, too, the question arises as to the extent to which citizens actually participate in the community energy project and the assemblies and formulate motions, contribute ideas and suggestions, take a stand and ultimately actively help to shape and structure the processes and decisions.

In the case of the community wind park (case study 1), "the shareholders have so far been rather passive" (M 1.2: line 13 f.). Only participation in the wind energy association was proposed by one member as an item on the agenda (ibid.: line 12 f.). An interest in discourse and content-related participation is rarely expressed (ibid.: line 20 ff.):

"The only thing that was discussed intensively was the participation in the association, and there were also critical voices. Once there was a discussion about whether the wind farm was over-insured. Otherwise, there were only a few questions". In this case study, there seems to be no reference to discourse, involvement and co-design as a definitional inherent moment from the very beginning due to a different conceptual-organizational approach, possibly also due to different member structures and ways of thinking.

In the opinion of one of the citizens involved, a project that is rather large in scale provides little scope for establishing democratic forms (I 1.2: line 301 ff.). This could be more the case with a small solar cooperative (ibid.: line 302 f.). This is also justified by the fact that, due to the conditions, the many people involved, and the associated long, costly planning period and complex procedures, a form of operation is favored which creates little room for democratic principles (ibid.: line 306 ff.). In addition, it is assumed that cooperatives can become ineffective, as people with different intentions come together here: A person with a large investment volume pursues different interests than a person with only small sums invested, who may be pursuing more of a communicative goal, e.g. "drinking coffee together" (ibid.: line 313 ff.).

The larger the plans for energy plants are, the fewer community energy ideas are possible or present in this view (ibid.: line 310 f.). However, even in the case of a community wind farm, a few shareholders could be decisive for important votes (ibid.: line 319 ff.). The establishment of an advisory board is therefore seen as very sensible and beneficial for the interests of the participants (ibid.: line 325 ff.).

Other problems concerning member participation and co-determination relate to:

- **Unequal power relations:** due to high investment sums of only a few participants (I 1.2: line 13 f.), low chances of influence of other participants (ibid.: line 14 ff.).
- **Practice of participation as wishful thinking:** The guiding principle of citizen participation is considered more of a wishful thinking: Limited partnerships make more sense for large wind farms as opposed to cooperatives, the latter would be more suitable for small projects (ibid.: line 26 ff.). On a small scale (solar cooperatives), a "grassroots democracy" could rather be realized (ibid.: line 28 f.). In the case of wind farms, on the other hand, the planning and plant specifics are fixed from the outset – hence the question of what remains to be

decided (ibid.: line 30 ff.). The essential points cannot be influenced (I 1.2: line 33).

- **Co-design and co-determination in the case of project expansion:** However, important questions for the shareholders can always arise when a wind farm is to be expanded (ibid.: line 49 f.). Questions and thus discourse processes are linked to this, whether further external persons should be included through this additional investment or whether the sum should be raised internally (ibid.: line 50 ff.).
- **Personal qualifications for active membership and participation in dialogue:** An essential prerequisite for participation in discourse and contribution can be the requirement of specialist knowledge and competences. For example, it is emphasized that it is important for every investor to be well informed (ibid.: line 143). This is also against the background that for some members their financial investment can represent, for example, their old-age provision, therefore a high degree of trust, but also a willingness to take risks must be present (ibid.: line 192 f.). "Nice sales brochures" are considered to be of little use and are assessed as a poor basis (ibid.: line 143 f.). At best, interested parties would also always have to read the "small print" (ibid.: line 191). But even beyond that, it is difficult to grasp and understand all the relevant information – even local authorities cannot understand everything (ibid.: line 186 f.). Often many possible risks are presented, and then the whole project appears to be highly risky to an interested party with little prior knowledge (ibid.: line 238 ff.). On the other hand, important information was missing, such as objective expert opinions on the assessment of locations and technical plant specifics (ibid.: line 241 ff.)**:** Therefore, from this perspective, it could appear to make little sense to acquire only small financial shares in wind energy projects: The time required for intensive involvement with the project would then simply be too high to invest only a small sum (ibid.: line 144 ff.).
- **Advantage of advisory boards:** In projects where an advisory board exists in the form of a representation of interests of the participants, the cooperation within the project is perceived as more intensive (ibid.: line 100 f.).

Positive Effects of Participation in Community Energy

Positive Effects of Member's Participation and Motivations

In the case of the environmental association community solar project, two positive effects of the community solar plant are mentioned, which can arise both superficially through the immediate experience and superficially through a long-term financial investment: "(…) I also have frequent calls where they say: 'You know what, the display doesn't work at all. 'I drive by there every day and always look at it. So I already have that. And there's also this one case, which I think is really nice, of grandparents who have bought shares for their grandchildren. They don't think: 'Oh God, that's not worth it for me anymore', but they say: 'I think it's nice, I'm doing it for the future of my children, who will also benefit financially. 'So it's not only about what I leave for future generations, but also important that the children or grandchildren can hold their own shares in community energy projects" (I 5.2: line 837 ff.). So, on the one hand, this participation and the bond to the project is more direct and personal, on the other hand, special projects can also create a bond through a contextual background, as in the church community: "That's just more personal. That's very clear. You know, unlike a share package, where you don't even know where exactly what has been invested for (…) of course not all people are like that, that they drive past there every day. That is also clear. But there are a whole bunch of people who have a connection to it, so to speak, or who have this connection through the church, of course. Or are often at church (…) something like half to two thirds are parishioners. They will certainly look at it from time to time and say: 'My plant'. This feeling of 'my plant' produces so much. Of course that's the case. I believe that. You can say that quite clearly" (ibid.: line 850 ff.). Another source of motivation for the citizens involved is seen in the "energy in the hands of the citizens" idea: "But I think it is also very much about this idea of saying: 'No, no, we don't want four big companies to dictate our energy supply and the prices and all the politics that are involved, but we want to shape it ourselves. And of course, I would say, an incredible amount has happened in the last ten to twenty years" (ibid.: line 872 ff.).

Local Points of Reference and Motivations for Community Energy

The importance of the spatial and social proximity to the participating citizens is also emphasized in individual projects of the supra-regional energy cooperative (personal contacts, "investment to touch"): "But we have made the experience that that is not everything – that is not so important for many and there the cooperative form, I think, also plays a huge plus point that the people know us personally, that they can have a say at a general meeting, that it is with them locally. So especially in Witzenhausen many people took the money out of their savings accounts and they didn't want to put it into any funds, but they kept it at the school and some of the older people came by and visited us at the construction site and looked at where my money was going". (I 8: line 1139 ff.).

In an order of priority, the sustainability factor is mentioned first, followed by regional orientation and finally the return achieved (which is, however, seen as a *conditio sine qua non*): "And that is already important. So you certainly can't generalize. There is a different motive for everyone (…) The idea of sustainability and the local energy approach are quite important and on the other hand it is also important that: (…) a certain return must be yield, but it does not have to be/ It does not depend on two or three percent. So it has to be better than some call money accounts, I say. There it is somehow both. So somehow people don't give their money away for free. They want to invest it. It has to be an investment. So it has to pay off in the end, it has to be worth something" (ibid.: line 1150 ff.). Another essential aspect is added: the social cohesion, which is achieved through close exchange and non-business activities – here, however, a potential for improvement is also seen: "We actually celebrated the first anniversary on a larger scale and there were also relatively many people there. These are, so to speak, the personal acquaintance and the personal exchange, in order to know that this is our management board, our supervisory board. That is very important. I think it is very important that there is the possibility of exchange. We also want to intensify this a little more" (I 8: line 1179 ff.).

Finally, the information policy and public relations work of the cooperative towards its members as well as the stronger involvement of the members should be improved – obviously a deficit of the supra-regional orientation without a local anchoring moment: "So we don't only have the individual meetings, but that we also have regular newsletters and somehow information flowing via the internet, because we want to do more this year (…) than is taking place at the moment. There were no applications yet. We have (…) only had this one meeting so far. But at such meetings there are just (…) some voices saying: I could push another project and another… These people want to participate somehow (…) So, it goes in this direction that there are several collected ideas, that's for sure" (ibid.: line 1184 ff.). But members do also get involved in this cooperative in a concrete way: "There was one person who comes from Bottrop (…). There is an urban development program there. They have received funding. The program is called InnovationCity and he wants to do something within that program. So we get in touch with individual members who want to initiate projects with us. That is already happening more and more frequently" (ibid.: line 1195 ff.).

Economy for the Common Good

The Double Objective of a Cooperative Between Economic Enterprise and Personal Commitment to Ecology and Sustainability

In the case of the employee cooperative, an energy cooperative is basically defined more as a commercial enterprise: "I also see a cooperative first and foremost as a commercial enterprise and it is a question of finding the best possible equity ratio" (I 4.1: line 1200 ff.).

The preamble of the cooperative statutes, where an ecological objective of the project is claimed, is described in a relativizing way: "Yes, these are always the fair-weather clauses (laughing), and of course it also has this dimension that we all sit here and prepare this nonsense on a voluntary basis" (ibid.: line 1207 ff.).

On the other hand, the personal commitment is disproportionate to the return for each individual member: "If we were to see it purely as a capital investment, it would of course be stupid for us. The time I invest if I were to write expert opinions in that time/ Even if I could invest my money in a way that yielded less interest, which I still doubt. Elsewhere, one will certainly get similar returns, while of course, from a purely personal economic point of view, if we only see it as an investment, it's bullshit" (I 4.1: line 1213 ff.). In a certain respect, however, the ecological reference does play a subliminal role: "I had only mentioned the voluntary work, that (…) of course we also have more than just the return aspects in mind. Otherwise we would not commit ourselves to it. The commitment is just not paid economically accordingly. So of course these good-human clauses at the beginning have a certain significance. (…) Because of course there is a counter-argument somewhere: 'We do everything only from economic points of view'" (ibid.: line 1287 ff.).

Thus a dichotomy appears between the demand for a return on investment and the ideal of ecology and community, which are not necessarily mutually exclusive: "But of course (…) ideals are also involved somewhere. Otherwise this project wouldn't work. But you don't have to overdo it. (…) And then completely unnecessarily give up yield options""(ibid.: line 1297 ff.).

Changing Perceptions of Community Energy

In the case of the community solar plants of the environmental association, the motivation of the association to erect the plants has changed from exclusively ecological to more economic motives. This is explained by means of a comparison with the first solar plant erected, which was primarily intended to serve demonstrative purposes: "The photovoltaic energy train station project is an important showcase model, but I think we have actually said, okay, no, it isn't absolutely everything that the return or the economic viability sinks, as a result of the photovoltaic plants being shaded by the north station building, because we want it for ecological reasons (…) that is our first priority and it is then secondary that the plants are just not so optimal economically" (I 5.2: line 916 ff.).

However, since hardly any return can be expected from such projects, such plants would also not be suitable for citizen participation. Apparently, the relevance of the economic effect can be read from this negative argumentation: "I don't think that something like that really lends itself to such a participation. (…) in this respect it is somehow a bit different with every project and you have to decide a bit anew, see a bit, okay, why are we doing this at all and what was the background. (…) nowadays we would probably would not do that anymore, that we say, well, does such a location pay off at all, but at that time it was quite clear, no, we want renewable energies, it works" (ibid.: line 921 ff.). This is justified by the fact that in the meantime the demonstration effect is no longer given, because there are many solar plants and it is therefore no longer a special feature: "(…) I think, of course, you have to look at how the profitability is and if it is no longer so good, because solar energy has simply made a giant leap forward in the last ten years, that it is no longer so necessary to say, no, okay people look here, but there is simply already a lot (…)" (ibid.: line 934 ff.).

The Trade-off between Return and Ecology in Community Energy Projects

For the church congregation that cooperated with the environmental association, too, the broader question arose as to what motives were central to the commitment. Here, reference is made to an ecological background, which is related to an overarching ecological initiative "Green Rooster" of the Protestant Church in Germany (I 5.1: line 12 ff.). Thus, the project is classified in a course with energy saving, climate protection and opposition to nuclear power (ibid.: line 40 f.). It is assumed that about 70% of the people involved in the project were "convinced" (ibid.: line 102 f.). In the parish, an environmental group deals with environmental issues, which consists of about five people and holds three to four meetings a year (ibid.: line 67 f.).

Nevertheless, in this case, too, a combination of profit-oriented and public welfare-oriented participation is seen, whereby this is to be linked to a return that is not too low (similar presentations are also found in all other case studies):

> (…) from the people's point of view, of course, it depends on the returns that are there, but I would say that the interest of the people doing it, is huge. Of course, it's also a great opportunity to combine both, to say: 'I'm investing money', and I'll invest it – as I said, it was four percent a year ago, you wouldn't get otherwise. (…) So it's simply a good condition. It's not two percent and it's not 0%. But this: on the one hand, the money does not decrease and I also do something in the ecological area. Of course, that's a wonderful combination. (ibid.: line 302 ff.)

The citizens' community geothermal energy initiative has also experienced that ecological thinking alone is not enough to convince the population: "That is always the problem. You have to get on board now with a somewhat lower price, so to speak, because the price itself is of course also the basis: do I go for it or not? Purely the environmental idea: you can't get rid of that. If we now assume a moderate price increase – in gas prices – until geothermal energy is realized, then we will practically be back in about five years at a level where we can say that in five years, gas prices will definitely be as high as district heating can now be offered. The community of interests has been trying to get this across ever since it was founded" (ibid.: line 515 ff.).

Financial Participation and/or Democratic Participation?

The type and mode of participation is divided into two types in the case of the citizens' community geothermal energy initiative: On the one hand, a financial participation, on the other hand, a democratic participation in the form of contributing ideas and opinions. The financial form of participation is seen as a "simple" form of participation, and it also corresponds to the social model of a fixation on financial resources: "I think that nowadays everything can be weighed up in money, or must be weighed up in money, otherwise it is worth nothing. Otherwise it cannot be processed. Simply financial participation is a simple kind of participation. And it's one in which you don't even have to involve the people in a big way, I'd say it's just a form of participation in addition to the possibility of democratically involving them, taking their opinions, ideas and so on along with them. Simply to say: You are shareholders in such a project" (I 7.2: line 562 ff.).

However, the dimension of financial gain is put into perspective: High profits are not to be expected; instead, the investments are characterized by a long-term perspective and security. Here, the combination of financial advantage and ecological benefit is also pointed out: "But on the other hand, it also comes out: Well, the whole thing is a topic in which nobody earns anything stupid. Instead, there is a certain return on investment. It is somewhere in a reasonable range, but perhaps it has the disadvantage in comparison with some highly speculative investments that (…) build some dams in Brazil or something, that you don't get the promised twenty percent or whatever. On the other hand, you know that you are creating a double value here in the vicinity, both value in the sense of an investment good, which yields a return or which generates electricity, for example – and on the other hand an ecologically sensible thing" (I 7.2: line 577 ff.).

This openness and transparency of financial participation – that the project and the essential (business) framework conditions are open to all persons involved, in contrast to less transparent investments on the stock exchange, for example – represents a major advantage. It is therefore not the return that is exclusively in the foreground, but rather the multiple benefits that arise from the project – of which the financial gain represents a concrete, tangible, i.e. material effect for those involved: "I believe that in a certain way this represents it in a very simple way, about which one then does not have to discuss much at all. That's the benefit, I think, of having people financially involved. I don't think that the value or the advantage lies in the fact that people get a certain amount of money and say: Yes, that's great now. You can think of other value investments. But they have the feeling and they see that a reasonable return is achieved with it, reasonable in the sense of… it's global, I say. Overall with everything that you want to achieve like that: with sustainability, with a regional value creation, with a responsible approach simply to the environment – it's a good investment. That's what comes out of it, and it's also reflected relatively simply, so to speak, in a return that is neither astronomically high nor just as small, so that everyone says: 'Yes, all that is actually not practicable anyway, and it's only something for dreamers. I actually see an opportunity and an advantage in that" (ibid.: line 586 ff.).

Finally, the identification characteristics of the participants in the supra-regional energy cooperative in the form of the following aspects: sustainability, investment and local connection, confirm the existence of a hybrid motivational situation:

> So energy transition and sustainability are certainly in the foreground (…). But we have a statement right on our website, on the homepage: The first statement: that I am investing, so investment already plays a role. So under 'Investing' it says: 'Better in the neighborhood than on Wall Street. So the topic does play a role, but so does being close to the people on site (…) So I see the (…) equally weighted points. Whereby (…) for the people who then really participate, (…) this sustainability idea already plays the more important role. (ibid.: line 1659 ff.)

6.4.2 Financial Participation, Input of Ideas and Involvement[52]

Financial Amount of Investment The distribution of the amount of investment is widely spread: One fifth of the respondents invested high sums (over 5000 euros), another fifth even higher sums (over 10,000 euros). Likewise, a fifth invested 500–1000 euros, the same proportion invested 1000–3000 euros, fewer people (8 percent) took less than 500 euros in hand. While the cooperative members are those

[52] Hoffman and High-Pippert (2005: 399) were able to determine in case analyses that only a very small number of participating citizens in community energy projects were strongly involved in the topic area of renewable energy or the political process. At the same time, however, they found sustained enthusiasm for the issues, stable formats of deliberation, extended social contacts and information exchange, and a belief in success among the members (Hoffman and High-Pippert 2010: 7572). However, in the cases studied here, the number of participants is very low in each case, and particularly low in the case of long-term projects. In addition, in the projects studied there are very strongly committed citizens who, although in the absolute minority, have the ability to incite less committed citizens and integrate them into the community program (ibid.). Thus, according to the authors, community energy projects can be an example of how the transformation from individual to collective or community action can succeed. Based on the empirical results, this thesis is maintained by the authors, although many citizens do not make any efforts regarding participatory procedures. Community energy initiatives thus bring together people who have different "backgrounds", giving the initiative experience in very different ways (ibid.).

who have invested small sums (and offer such opportunities in the first place),[53] the higher sums are covered absolutely predominantly by the community wind farms and those involved in the community energy limited liability companies (GmbHs). In community energy limited liability companies and partnerships (GmbH & Co KGs) low investment sums do not exist at all, because they do not offer these opportunities. Medium-sized community energy projects tend to have characteristics similar to the larger projects, but somewhat more balanced. Interestingly, larger investment sums are untypical in cooperatives and small projects, although the opportunity of this does often exist. This shows that the citizens themselves are not interested in investing larger sums. Cooperatives thus not only offer the possibility of subscribing to smaller shares – citizens also make use of this to a very high degree. While the gender distribution is still balanced at low sums, and even more women invest sums between 2000 and 3000 euros as well as 5000 and 10,000 euros, men clearly predominate in investments above 10,000 euros. The amounts invested by academics and non-academics do not differ significantly; however, there is a discernible trend towards lower amounts being invested more by non-academics and higher amounts being invested more by academics. There are clear differences between income groups: People with low incomes invest more frequently sums below 500 euros, between 1000 and 2000 euros, and 3000 and 5000 euros. The middle income group is more strongly represented with amounts of 500–1000 euros and 2000–3000 euros. The higher sums above 5000 euros are dominated by the higher income peaks – but the proportions of low and middle-income people are also strongly represented here, comparatively balanced above 3000 euros for both low and middle income (each at around 15%).

However, this does not reveal an expected uniform picture: people with low incomes also invest higher sums. High-income individuals invest fewer low sums, but just as strongly in the middle segment, whereas they dominate in the higher segment. It is also noticeable that popular investment sums are those between 500 and 1000 euros and from 3000 euros upwards – sums below 500 euros and between 1000 and 3000 are less subscribed.

On the one hand, these results indicate that there are two types of participation (low sums and high sums), on the other hand, it is apparently also possible to invest lower sums in larger community energy projects (even if there is not much demand

[53] In a study of energy cooperatives in Germany, it was found that 56 percent of members subscribe to shares up to 2500 euros, another 15 percent subscribe to shares between 2500 and 5000 euros, and 13 percent subscribe to shares between 5000 and 10,000 euros, although 17 percent subscribe to shares above 10,000 euros (referring to photovoltaic/heat energy cooperatives; Rauschmayer et al. 2015: 6).

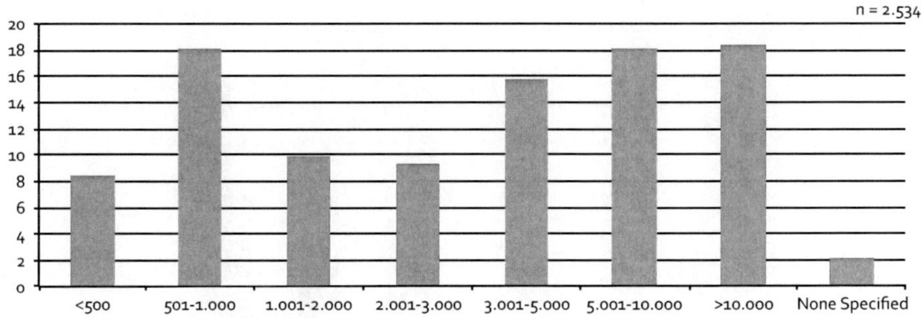

Fig. 6.32 Amount of investment: total sample

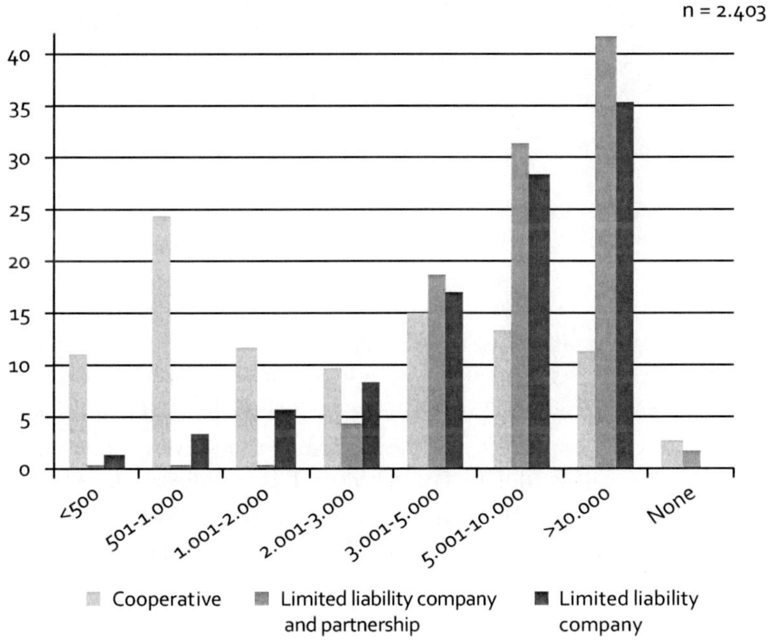

Fig. 6.33 Amount of investment: by project type

for this). The strongest statement remains that cooperatives are the actors that offer small sums and are essentially fed by these, whereas community wind farms and participants in community energy limited liability companies (GmbHs) place larger investment participation sums (Figs. 6.32, 6.33, and 6.34).

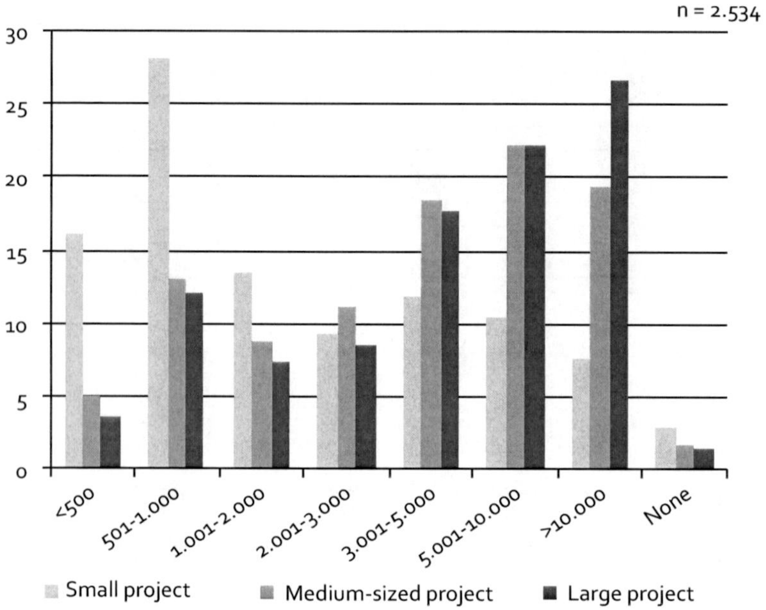

Fig. 6.34 Amount of investment: by project size

Input of Ideas[54] When it comes to the question of calls for ideas from members by the management, there is a split picture between small and large societies, in that the latter hardly know this.[55] In the case of cooperatives, a call for ideas has already taken place once in half of the cases, several times even in one third of the cooperatives, and no call at all in half of the cases. It is mainly smaller and medium-sized projects that have calls for ideas. In the qualitative data, two thirds of the data confirm that they are not aware of any calls (Figs. 6.35, 6.36, and 6.37).

[54]This aspect was surveyed with the following questions: Was anyone called to participate with their own ideas in the "XY Community Energy Project"? Have you already contributed an idea yourself?

[55]According to the Volunteer Survey (Gensicke and Geiss 2010: 34), the main content of activities in voluntary organizations are: organizing and running events (64%), practical work (58%), personal assistance (41%), public relations (39%), interest work and participation (37%).

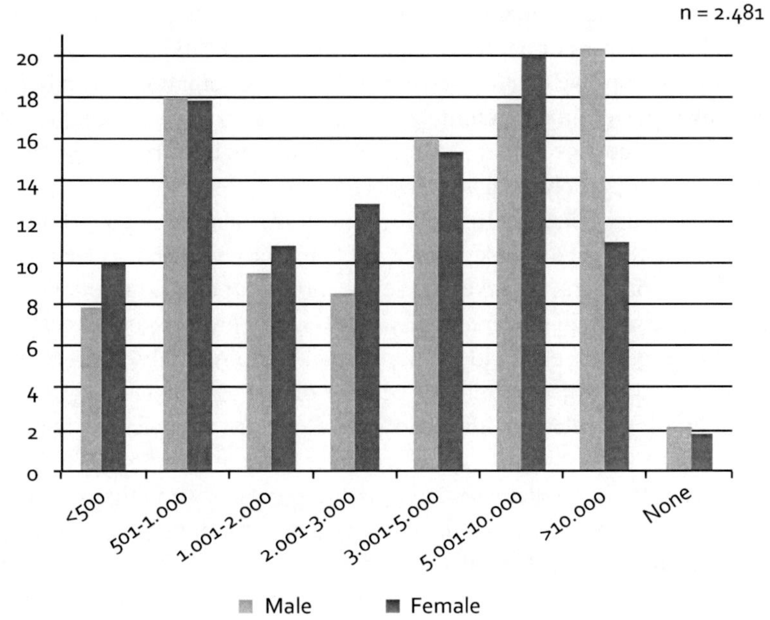

Fig. 6.35 Amount of investment: by gender

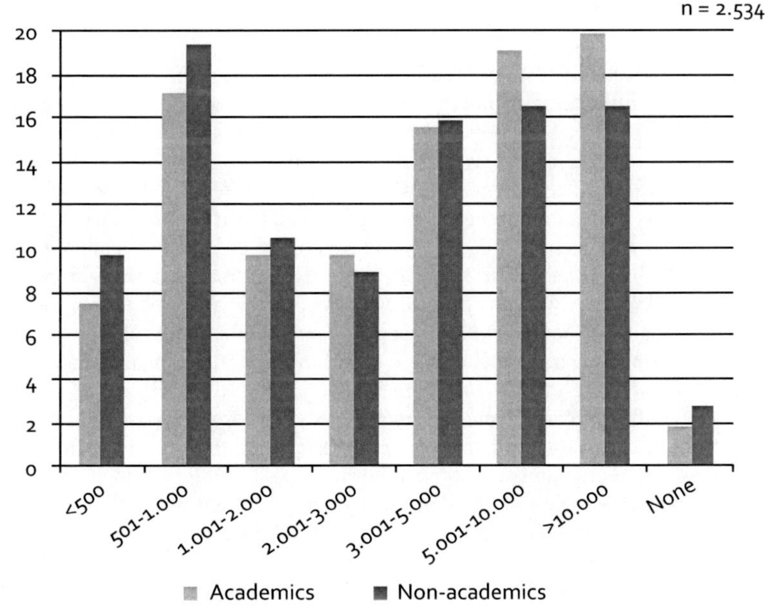

Fig. 6.36 Amount of investment: by level of education

Actual input of ideas by members is particularly widespread in small solar co-operatives: almost a third of participants have already contributed ideas here – this would essentially disprove the thesis that de facto no participation beyond financial investment takes place[56] in community energy projects. In large community energy projects, however, such idea input is marginal, which can be attributed to the orientation of the type of participation and the lack of local contact.

Again, it is mainly men and people with high incomes who get involved. Incidentally, involvement also takes place in community wind farms, and there are also calls for activity here; however, these are more pronounced in the PV sector, and there are fewer calls in the community wind energy projects and larger projects with several energy sources. Incidentally, such calls do not only take place in the start-up phase of the projects (only 10 percent of the cases). The degree of idea contribution is still not related to the share size. However, conspicuous features are found with regard to motivation: when financial motivation is only slightly pronounced, idea contribution increases strongly (16 percent several times idea contribution compared to 6 percent when financial motivation is not stated). The opposite effect occurs with strong ecological and citizen-owned energy motivation: A strong expression here goes hand in hand with stronger idea contribution (16 percent submitted contributions several times with strong ecological motivation compared to 3 percent with unspecified ecological motivation; likewise, 16 percent submitted several times a contribution with strong citizen motivation compared to 7 percent with unspecified citizen motivation) (Figs. 6.38 and 6.39).

[56] According to the results of a study on climate protection cooperatives by von Blanckenburg, there is usually little participation of members within the forums of cooperatives: "The opportunities for participation in cooperatives are largely evaluated positively by the members, even if in almost all cooperatives (...) they are limited to participation in the general assembly or the election of representatives for the general assembly. In fact, often only a minority exercises its democratic rights. This sometimes takes a contradictory form: people support participation and even see it as a special merit of the cooperative, but do not participate" (von Blanckenburg 2014: 263). – In case analyses, Hoffman and High-Pippert (2005: 399) found that only very few citizens were strongly involved in the issue area or the political process. At the same time, however, they found sustained enthusiasm for the issues, stable formats of deliberation, extended social contacts and information exchange, and a belief in success among members (Hoffman and High-Pippert 2010: 7572). However, in the cases studied here, the number of participants is very small in each case, and particularly low in the case of long-term projects. In addition, in the projects studied there are very strongly committed citizens who, although in the absolute minority, have the ability to incite less committed citizens and integrate them into the community program (ibid.). Thus, according to the authors, community energy projects can be an example of how the transformation from individual to collective or community action can succeed. The finding can be confirmed although many citizens do not make any efforts regarding participatory procedures. Community energy initiatives thus bring together people who have different "backgrounds", giving the initiative experience in very different ways (ibid.).

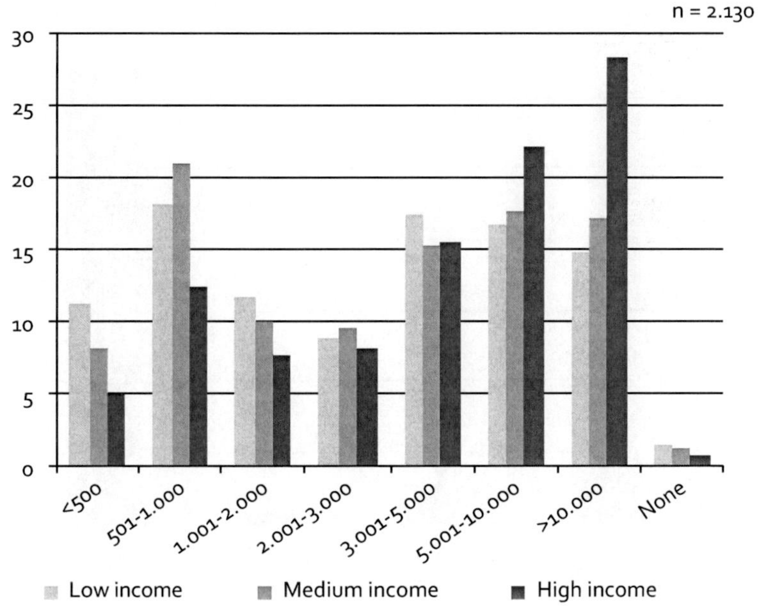

Fig. 6.37 Amount of investment: by income

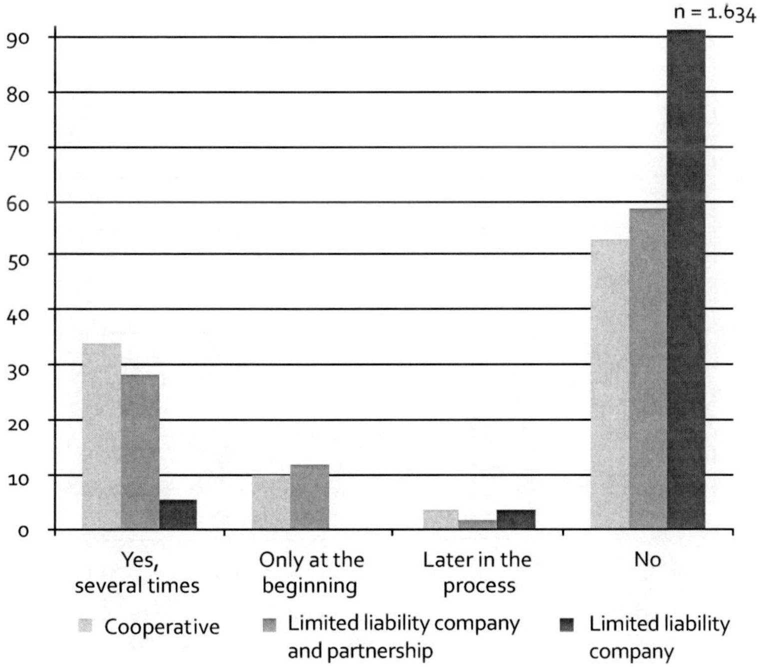

Fig. 6.38 Call for ideas: by project type

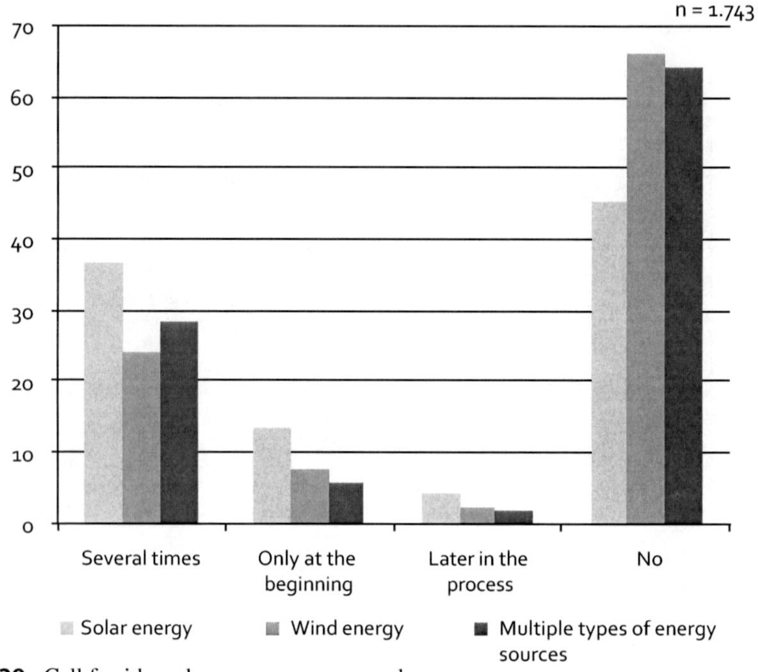

Fig. 6.39 Call for ideas: by energy source used

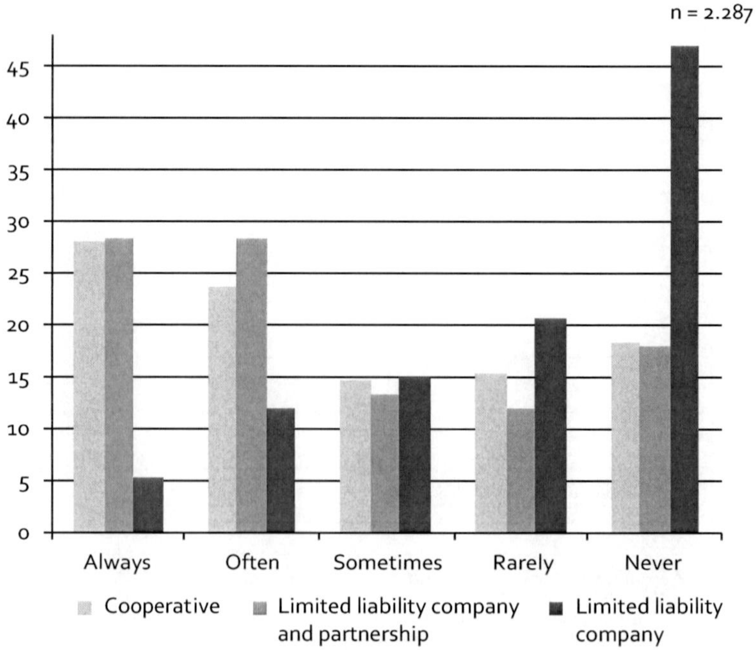

Fig. 6.40 Frequency of participation in meetings: by type of legal form

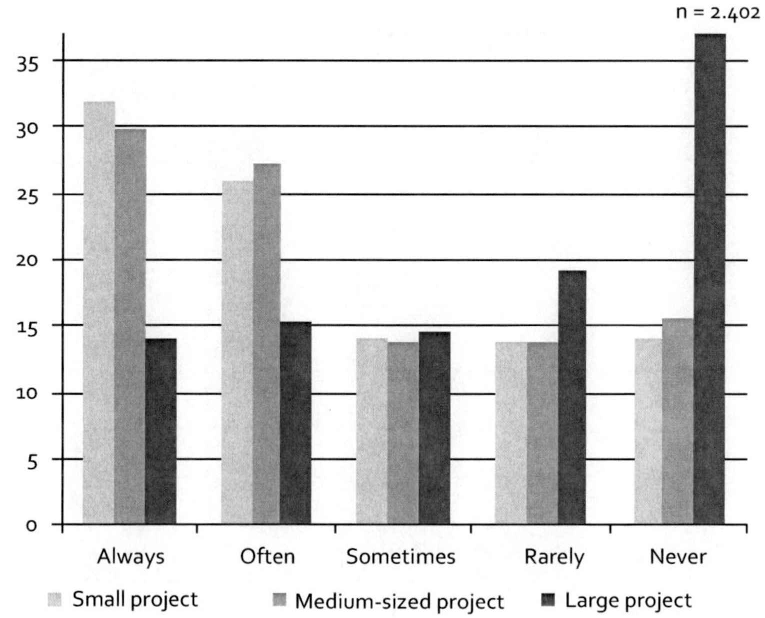

Fig. 6.41 Frequency of participation in meetings: by project size

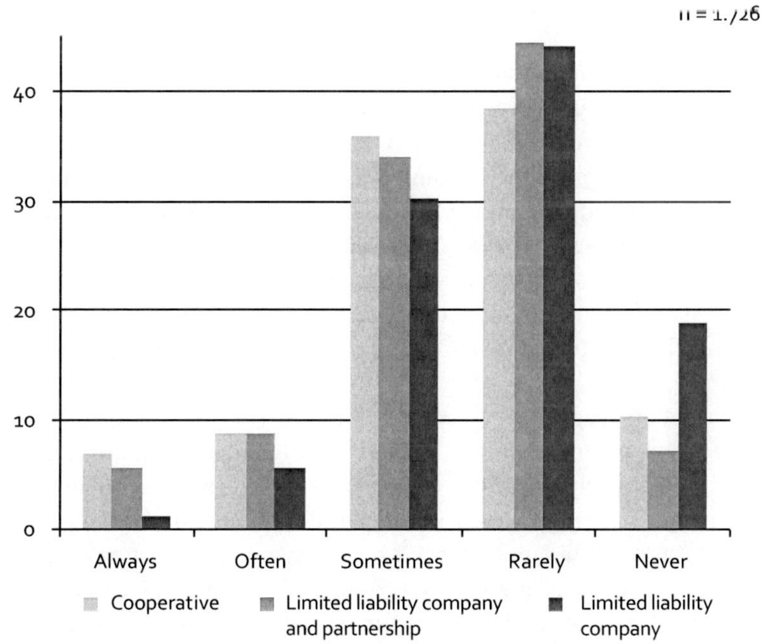

Fig. 6.42 Frequency of comments at meetings: by type of legal form

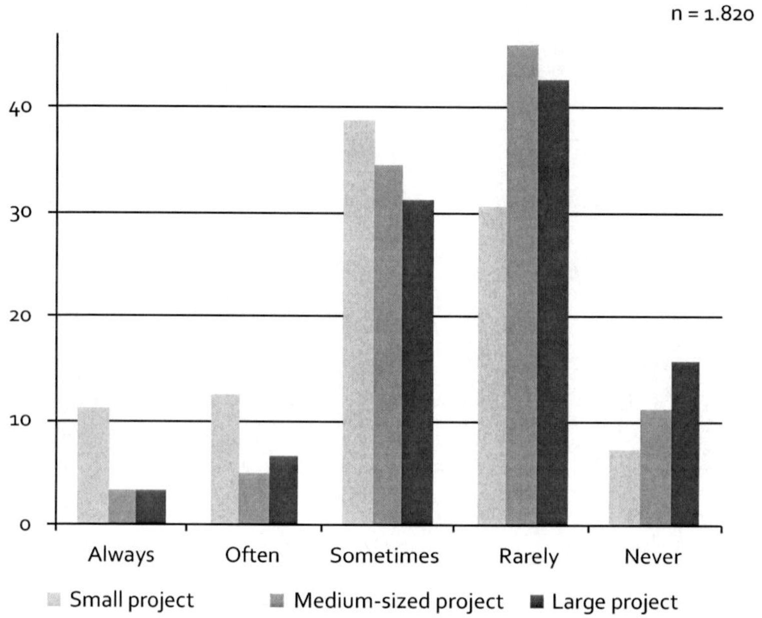

Fig. 6.43 Frequency of comments at meetings: by project size

Participation in Meetings and Activity Almost two thirds of all members are always, sometimes or rarely present at meetings of the community energy projects. Only a quarter never attend on average. In cooperatives, participation is somewhat more pronounced, whereas in community energy limited liability companies only a third of people attend meetings. Overall, more non-academics participate here, and women participate slightly less. The share level has no influence on the frequency of participation. Different degrees of motivation have a slight effect: Participation is somewhat more pronounced with low financial motivation and strong ecological and civic motivation (Figs. 6.40, 6.41, 6.42, and 6.43).

About half of the respondents speak out at meetings, again it is mainly the small societies where members speak out regularly. There is a big difference here compared to medium and large societies where expressions are less prevalent. Again, it is men and people with high incomes who participate more in debates.

It becomes apparent that not every cluster of energy projects participates in exchange processes to the same extent – after all, women and people with low incomes are also present, and non-academics even seem to be more interested, whereas academics behave more reservedly (Figs. 6.44 and 6.45).

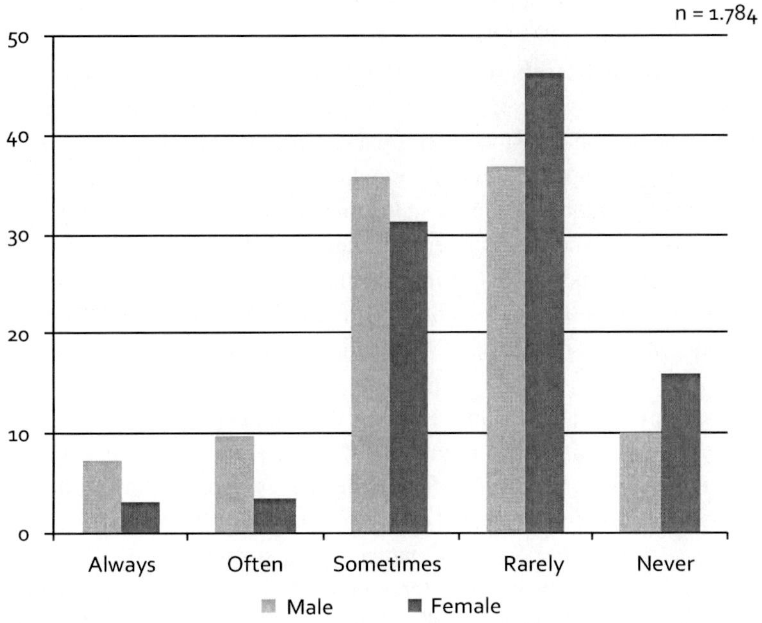

Fig. 6.44 Frequency of comments at meetings: by gender

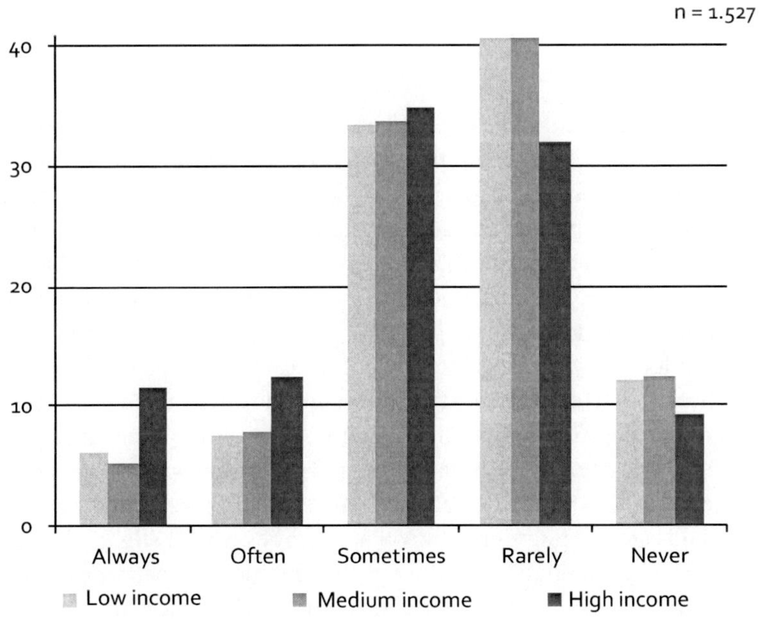

Fig. 6.45 Frequency of comments at meetings: by income

Topics Addressed by Members According to the respondents, particularly important areas concern the organization of the project, voting rights, (other) activities, and the locations and specifics of the energy plants. The political influence of the community energy project appears less important to the respondents. On the other hand, a quarter of the respondents explicitly stated that they did not perceive any opportunities for participation. The qualitative information confirms the high importance of location issues and the possibility of introducing thematic aspects: the importance of the choice of location and the possibility of introduction is also emphasized here – the latter is important to the respondents above all in a hypothetical respect.

All aspects are emphasized more strongly in small projects – this reflects the fact that there is generally more input here. The differences are particularly strong for the points "locations" and "specifics of the energy plants" – in smaller projects, strong influence is obviously exerted on these topics. No perception of contribution opportunities, on the other hand, is named more strongly in medium-sized and large community energy projects; interestingly, this value is most pronounced in medium-sized projects. In fact, a high value should be the result of the lack of opportunities for involvement in large community energy projects – on the one hand, the medium-sized community energy projects in the PV and wind sectors have obviously become too large for there to be a high level of member participation here in contrast to the small community energy projects – on the other hand, a certain degree of thematic involvement by members also seems to be possible in larger projects.

Questions of organization have a higher weight for men and people with high incomes (for the latter also the duration of the debt collection). For women, on the other hand, organization, but also voting rights and other activities are important, in contrast to men. The picture that emerges here is that men (who mostly represent the people with high incomes in this survey) are more interested in "hard" questions and facts. Non-academics emphasize voting rights and specifics of energy systems (similar to middle-income persons), whereas academics emphasize organizational and location issues as well as political influence much more strongly; other activities are also emphasized more strongly. However, there is little variation in the data on no contribution at all. Among people with low incomes, issues of facility type are considered rather unimportant. Lower values are found here for all topics – interest is thus lower overall. The highest values are found for locations, organizational issues, voting rights and other activities, with a slightly higher number indicating "no perception". In particular, the duration of operation and political influence are rated as rather unimportant. In contrast, people with a medium income give higher weighting to the topics of selection of certain energy plants, voting rights and political influence, while no relevance is seen for location issues, and the duration of operation is also rated as rather unimportant. For people with high incomes, the question of the duration of the operation is of very high importance – this group has also invested the highest sums. Organizational issues and other activities register the highest values among all income groups, and locations and specific investments are also emphasized; voting rights, on the other hand, register the lowest value among income groups. This clearly shows that there are very large differences between the income groups in terms of thematic relevance. These can be summarized as follows:

- **Low income:** Contribution rather unimportant, long-term nature not decisive, community energy project is not seen as a political actor.
- **Middle income:** Influence in community energy project important, specific issues are also relevant, classification of a community energy project as a political actor.
- **High income:** Long-term nature of the project very important, also organization and specific issues in the community energy project. Nevertheless, no reduction to business process, but emphasis on other activities.

It becomes clear that there are considerable differences in the ideas and relevance of topics of discourse – and thus in the overall orientation of the enterprise.

Desire for More Dialogue More than half of the respondents do not want any further discussion opportunities and forums. Only 14 percent would like to see more here – tending to be slightly more among cooperatives (15 percent), less among community energy limited liability companies, and surprisingly even less among members of community wind farms (9 percent). This would indicate a different membership structure. It is also particularly striking that members in medium-sized community energy projects would like fewer opportunities for discussion. Either forums and potential for discourse are available to a sufficient extent here, or the membership structures could differ, as in community wind farms, from the small, locally based projects and the large approaches in which academics are more strongly represented – which would seem to be the obvious choice. Small cooperatives and large participation projects are likely to have more "idealists", while medium-sized projects in particular are more likely to have "pragmatists" and "pure" investors. However, it is difficult to substantiate this thesis further. It is also striking that men feel the desire for discourse much more strongly than women (15 to 8 percent); they are also much more involved in discourse. Women, however, indicated a greater number of other activities among the topics of input – the interest here seems to be more in casual exchange (Figs. 6.46 and 6.47).

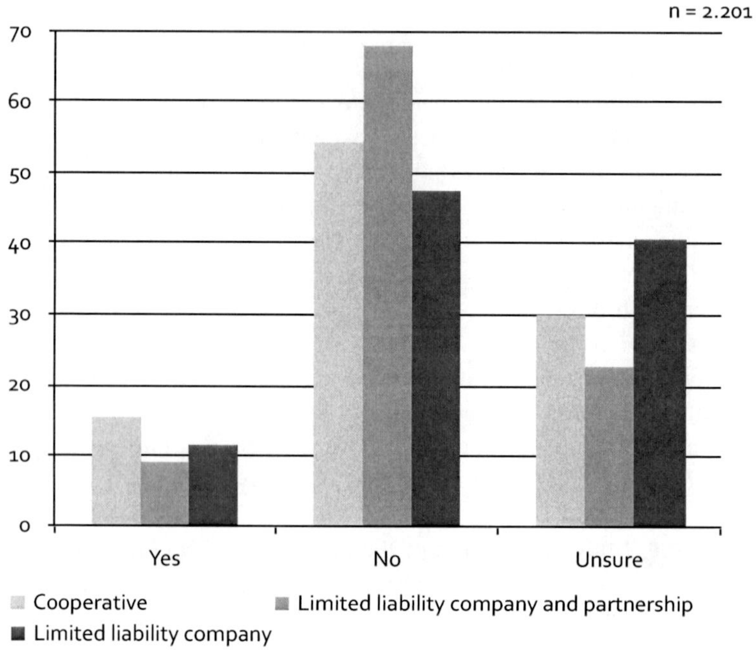

Fig. 6.46 Desire for discussion forums: by type of legal form

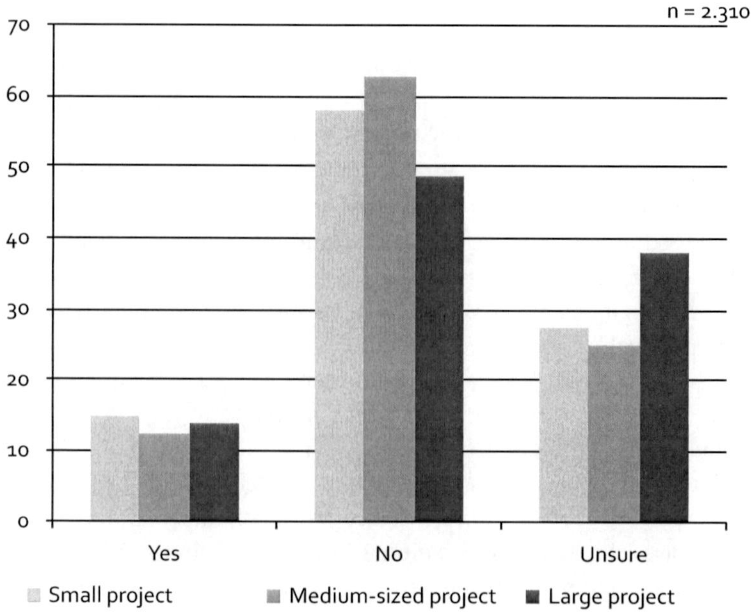

Fig. 6.47 Desire for discussion forums: by project size

Almost one third of the respondents are unsure whether more opportunities for discussion should be created – these statements are supported by qualitative statements: 21 percent of the persons do not consider them necessary or tie the creation to the condition that they should be goal and project oriented. Obviously, there is a fear of endless debates here. In addition, criticism of existing forums is voiced (6 percent), and wishes are also expressed with regard to improving or changing existing forms. These points essentially concern the establishment of internet forums, the inclusion of external expert opinion, online member surveys, strategy debates and theme evenings for discussion. This reflects the desire for an expansion of existing possibilities. Overall, further discourse is seen less as an absolutely necessary requirement and more as a pleasant addition that could be an enrichment.

Desire for More Co-determination Two-thirds of respondents are unsure about this question. One-third are against it, and only ten percent would like to have significantly more influence. This desire is much more pronounced in the GmbHs, as the participants have de facto no influence whatsoever via profit participation rights. It can be stated here that this is obviously only accepted – in fact, however, co-ownership would be preferred. The desire for more co-decision-making increases with the size of the community energy project; participants in small projects see the least need (Figs. 6.48 and 6.49).

Here, too, there is a striking difference between the sexes: only 0.6 percent of women compared to 11 percent of men would like to have more co-determination. There are also differences in the distribution of income: The desire is stronger with low incomes, and then rather weak with high incomes. The qualitative statements refer primarily to the desire for participation in content. There is little criticism of the status quo. Overall, the results suggest that there is a great deal of ignorance and uncertainty among members. Hardly any detailed, reflected and differentiated opinions are expressed, and those involved have so far given little thought to the issue – many have not yet become more deeply aware of the aspect of co-determination (Figs. 6.50 and 6.51).

Overall View

Most participants are involved with high sums – this finding coincides with the social structure of high-income population groups. The return aspect can only be

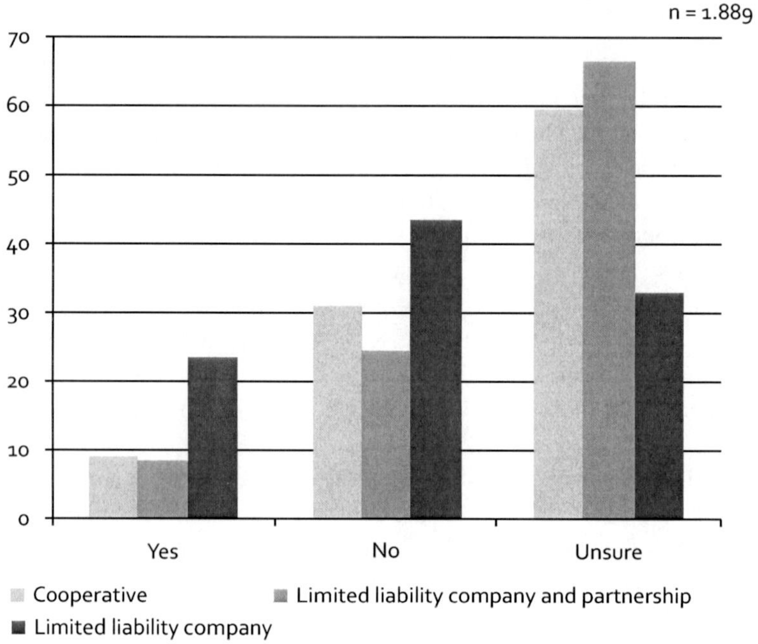

Fig. 6.48 Desire for more co-determination: by type of legal form

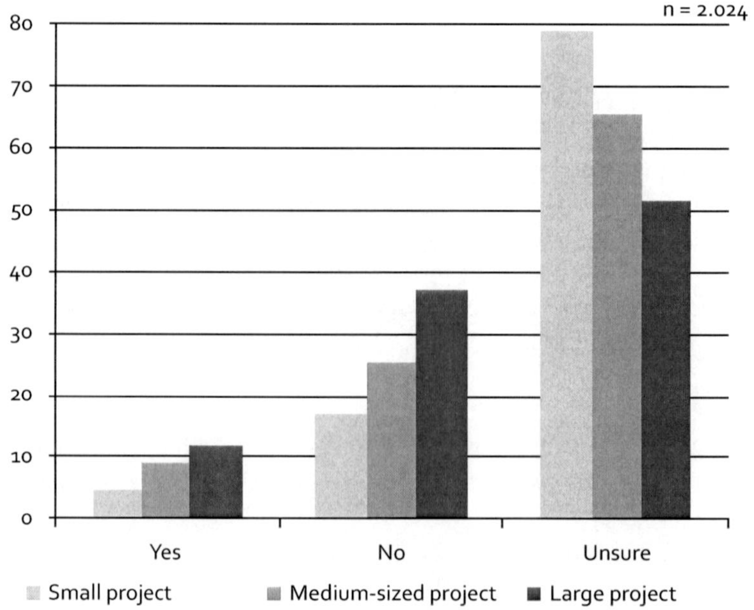

Fig. 6.49 Desire for more co-determination: by project size

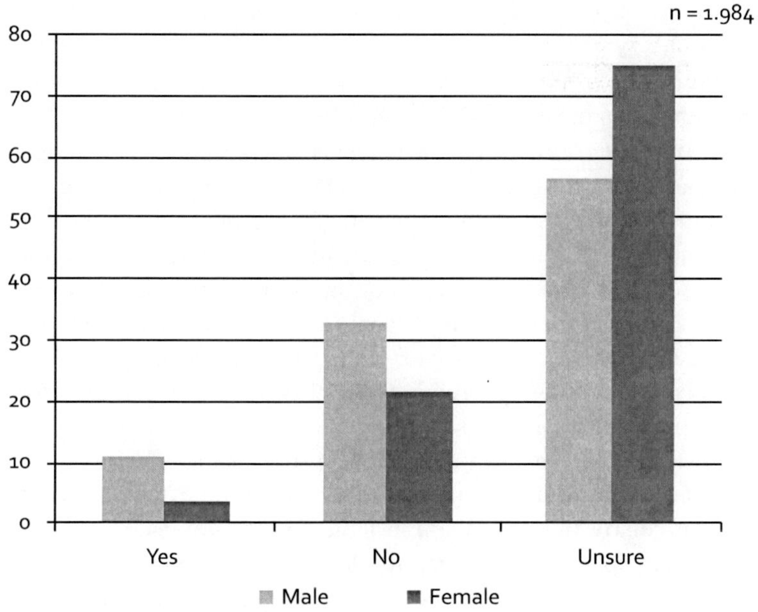

Fig. 6.50 Desire for more co-determination: by gender

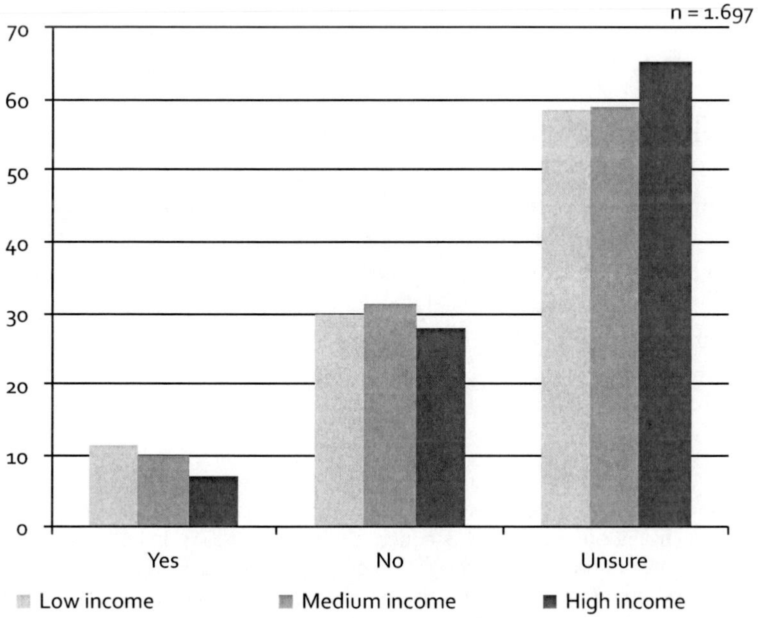

Fig. 6.51 Desire for more co-determination: by income

seen as a motivating factor alongside other aspects, with the ecological motive in particular, rather than the citizens' approach, being advocated.[57]

The level of participation and involvement is not exceptionally high in community energy projects as a whole, yet discussion does take place, members are often present at meetings and also often participate themselves. Only in one third of the cases do members call for ideas, and three quarters have never put forward an idea of their own. The topics of organization of the community energy project, voting rights and locations or types of energy plants are particularly important to them, but they see their association less as an actor in the political discourse. For the majority of participants, the existing opportunities for discourse are sufficient. However, a strikingly large number of people are unsure whether more discussion forums should be created – for many it would be conceivable, but not absolutely necessary. Even greater is the uncertainty regarding further opportunities for co-determination. Here it is particularly those involved in large community energy projects, who, beyond their participation right status, would like to have co-determination in the sense of co-ownership, and thus co-decision-making to a very pronounced extent. Ultimately, a proportion of one fifth of the participants who have already made at least one suggestion on the subject of contributing ideas cannot be classified as low (in relation to other internal organizational participation processes).

6.5 Democracy and Reflection of Community Energy

6.5.1 Criticism, Conflicts and Democracy

Dealing with Contrary Opinions Almost half of the respondents are not aware of any contrary opinions among the members of the projects. On the other hand, in just under a third of the cases are all opinions heard and taken into account. In just under a quarter, other views are only partially taken into account. Rejection of some aspects occurs in only 3.4 percent, complete rejection is found in only a marginal 0.2 percent.

[57] A further survey confirms these results. In a comparison between GmbH & Co. KGs and cooperatives, a stronger return motive is noticeable in the first case. In both forms of organization, the two most important motives are "energy transition" and "environmental protection": "The main motives of many citizens are environmental protection and the advancement of the energy transition, whereby financial motives cannot be completely neglected (Leuphana University Lüneburg and Nestle 2014: iv).

The case of consultation including consideration is more prevalent in community wind farms than in cooperatives, although more counter-opinions are known here overall. Participants in community energy limited liability companies, on the other hand, are much less familiar with counter-opinions. It is evident here that more counter-opinions are voiced in community wind farms – especially since the thematic subject matter in the case of wind turbines is likely to bring more diverse opinions to light. Obviously, the legal forms of community energy projects and the decision-making processes practiced are suited to adequately process other views. The qualitative data here suggest that, due to the decision-making processes, counter-opinions are overruled by the masses or do not really appear relevant to the majority of members because they represent minor opinions overall. As a rule, possibly unfavorable effects (such as exclusion, disappointment and frustration) cannot be assumed. Although there are negative reports of experience (see discussion below), measured against the totality the problem-solving competence of the community energy projects can be assessed as at least adequate.

Conflicts Are unknown in two thirds of all cases. Almost a quarter of the respondents state that all conflicts have been resolved. However, for 13.5 percent these are only partially resolved, and for only 1 percent they are stated as not resolved. In community wind farms there are higher values for the resolution of all conflicts than in cooperatives. In the latter, on the other hand, more conflicts are not resolved. Among the participants of the large community energy projects (which do not include the two limited liability companies in this question) and among cooperatives, conflicts are altogether less known. Thus, conflicts seem to occur more in the case of wind power use – in fact, in the wind sector there are higher figures for the assessment of partially unresolved conflicts. More unresolved conflicts exist in the photovoltaic sector – this is consistent with the indication that conflicts are more likely to be described as unresolved in small societies. However, it should be borne in mind here that members of larger societies presumably simply have less information at their disposal. The fact that lower values are also given here for the resolution of all conflicts seems to confirm this. For all types and sizes of community energy projects, the figures are the same in the case of "partly not resolved" – around one in seven can therefore report rather significant conflicts. Interestingly, people with high incomes are more likely to consider all conflicts resolved, while those with low and medium incomes are more likely to be unaware of them – this is not surprising, as it has already been shown that the former are more involved and participate and therefore have more knowledge. This circumstance in turn suggests that there are actually more conflicts in the committees than the overall picture would suggest. Non-involved people are not known to be able to assess this issue. Furthermore, the picture is confirmed that men and non-academics are more likely to perceive many conflicts as unresolved – both groups also have higher values for participation in the committees. Nevertheless, this does not change much in the overall assessment: a maximum of 14 percent describe conflicts as unresolved, and only 1 percent in these groups see all conflicts as unresolved (Figs. 6.52 and 6.53).

Democracy With a large majority of 70 percent, the respondents give their community energy project the attribute "democratic" – only 3.5 percent indicate a "no" here. The approval ratings are very high, particularly in the cooperatives and community wind farms; participants in the community energy limited liability companies can only partially agree here, but here too only around 10 percent indicate a "no". Non-academics agree somewhat more with the positive assessment, academics on the other hand more partially – obviously they would like to express themselves in a more differentiated manner. Among low- and middle-income individuals, agreement is stronger than among high-income individuals; the latter also frequently answer "no." Men also express a more negative assessment than women.

As reasons for the attribution of democracy in the project, the respondents predominantly named voting rights (54 percent), equal voting rights for all in the case of cooperatives (in all other cases a *request* to vote was named because no equal voting rights exist) (46 percent), possibility of small financial shares (42 percent) as well as joint voting (37 percent). The decisive criteria are thus voting rights, inclusion of groups of people who would like to become members through small amounts, and voting. This suggests a "classic" understanding of democracy: Voting rights, ballots and inclusion of broad segments of the population are decisive core criteria according to the prevailing view of republican-representative democracy. Less relevant are the option of financial shares (30 percent), the possibility for members to contribute ideas (29 percent), the inclusion of affected people in the project (29 percent), and discussions on various topics (23 percent). This illustrates that members are less likely to have a broader understanding of democracy, which would be expressed in broader member involvement and strong discursivity. As already suggested by the previous results, there is predominantly no rejection of spaces for exchange, but on the other hand there is also no strong demand and pronounced need for greater involvement and discourse.

The cooperatives emphasize very strongly the equal voting right, while community wind farms emphasize more strongly the general voting right – in the case of community energy limited liability companies and partnerships (GmbH & Co.

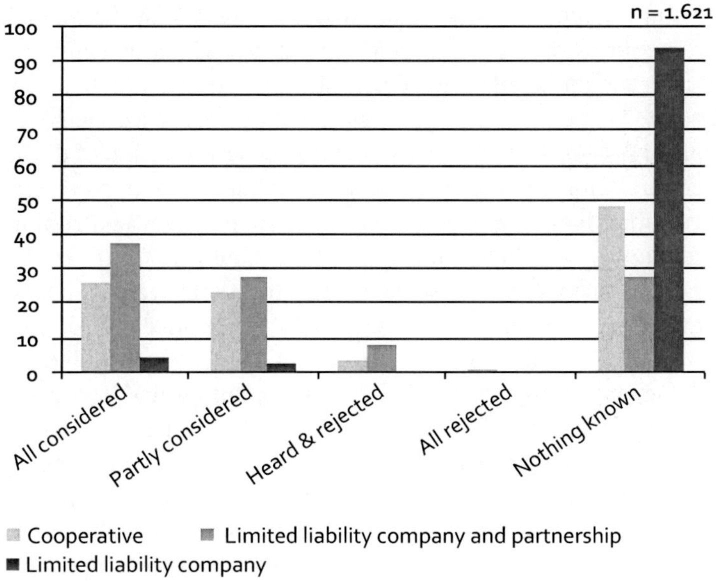

Fig. 6.52 Dealing with contrary opinions: by type of legal form

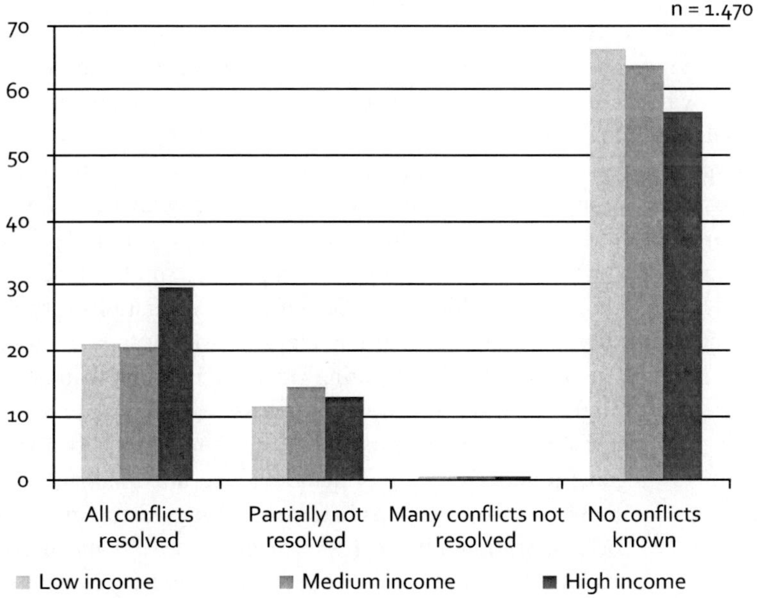

Fig. 6.53 Dealing with conflicts: by income

KGs), the voting weight is relative to the shareholding amount. The members here thus advocate more strongly the principles of their own participation models, in that the participants in GmbHs also emphasize less voting, which is lacking here again due to the lack of co-ownership. Instead, they emphasize the general possibility of financial shares more strongly, and the highest rejection of the attribution of a democratic community energy project is also found here (9.5 percent). This at least suggests that the participation models via cooperatives and community energy limited liability companies and partnerships (GmbH & Co. KGs) of the community wind farms should be classified as more democratic. All respondents, irrespective of the type of community energy project, agree on the possibility of small financial shares – although this is not possible in many cases with the community wind farms and community energy limited liability companies. This assessment is thus tantamount to a demand. The inclusion of affected parties is very strongly emphasized in community wind farms (40 percent). The importance here is context-dependent and therefore occurs specifically in the area of wind power. The need for discussion is also strongly present in community wind farms (34 percent compared to 24 percent in cooperatives and 17 percent in community energy limited liability companies) – this supports the assumption that there is a stronger need for discourse in this contrasting field. The possibility of contributing ideas is weighted slightly more heavily in cooperatives (34 percent) than in community wind farms (29 percent), and, as expected, less so in community energy limited liability companies (16 percent). The similar values for both questions in the case of the community energy limited liability companies indicates a certain core of participants, who have ideas about the wind farm represented far beyond the status of profit participation rights.

Academics emphasize more voting rights and voting overall – at the same time they value more strongly the rejection of the democracy aspect (4 percent). Unsurprisingly, academics are more critical and presumably also more differentiated in their opinion. Persons with low income emphasize small financial shares and financial shares in general, which is in line with the expectations for this cluster. High-income individuals, on the other hand, again turn out to be a group with solid ideas like academics, emphasizing voting rights and voting. Middle-income individuals, interestingly, indicate lower values across the board overall, and are most likely to emphasize the principle of equal voting rights. Thus, they appear to represent less of a general understanding of democracy in the organization. There is a clear gradation between income groups in terms of disagreement regarding the classification "democratic community energy project": Low-income individuals hold this view the least (2.8 percent), somewhat more strongly is middle-income individuals (3.6 percent), while high-income individuals hold it much more strongly (5.2 percent). Both low-income and high-income individuals agree on a stronger emphasis on the opportunity to contribute ideas – compared to middle-income individuals. In sum, this suggests that non-academics with low incomes are greater proponents of attributing to a democratic community energy project than other membership groups (Figs. 6.54 and 6.55).

The qualitative input here stems from the possibility of naming one's own ideas, conceptions and definitions of the aspect of practiced democracy in a community energy project. The persons who made textual statements felt compelled to reject or critically assess a positive association with a democratic community energy project, mostly in the form of a lack of necessity for democratic attributes. The supporters strongly emphasize co-determination and transparency as well as communication; the associations themselves and their reputation are also cited.

What is striking about the data is that

- The rejection of an analogous assumption of democracy in business is made with strongly generalized arguments ("business is not democratic") (separation

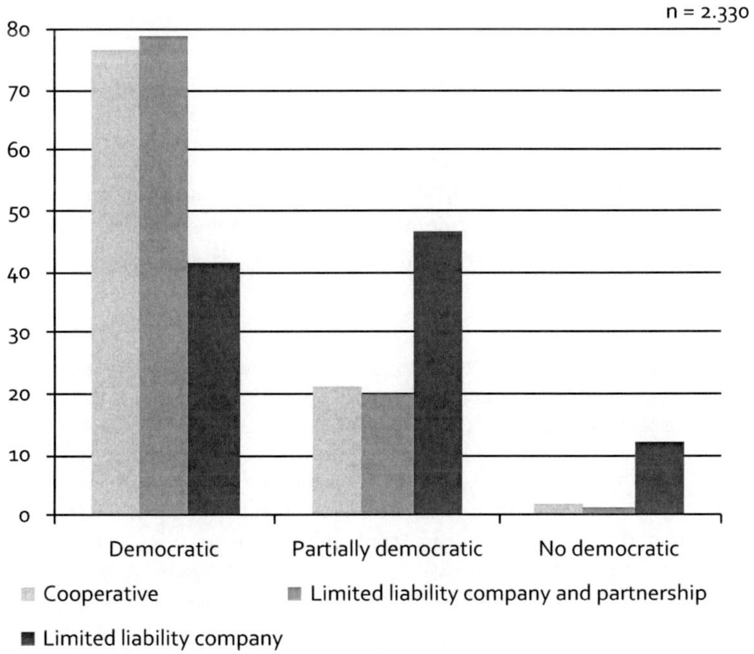

Fig. 6.54 Perception of community energy project as democratic: by type of legal form

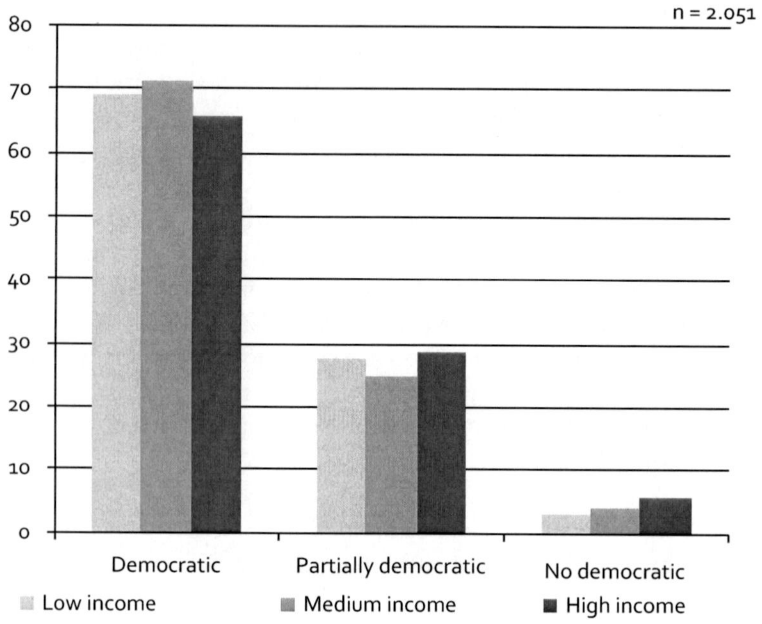

Fig. 6.55 Perception of community energy project as democratic: by income

of private business and community energy democracy – ***non-democratic interpretation of community energy democracy***).[58]

- Democracy is interpreted through a negative inversion of arguments: Instead of examples of democratic principles, practices and conditions are named that question the very existence of democracy and emphasize the "dark sides" of (democratic) organizations and institutions, such as nepotism, unequal distribu-

[58] Respondents' statements here are: "concept of democracy is hardly applicable to companies" (line 1585). "A company is not democratic" (line 1383). "I find it difficult to link a business enterprise with democracy" (line 1635). "overall hard to judge, in the end (...) [note: the community energy company] is a business" (line 1574). "democratic is an inaccurate term in this context" (line 1628). "(...) [note: the community energy company] is a limited liability company – not a cooperative or any other "democratic" company" (line 1767). "It is difficult to speak of democratic in the context of a business enterprise" (line 2348). "does a BSA [note: community solar system] have anything to do with "democracy"? I don't understand the question without discussion" (line 2460). "What does it have to do with democracy? But it makes sense" (line 2466).

tions of power and informal networks[59] (Critique of community energy democracy: dark sides as negative examples – ***critical understanding of community energy democracy***).
- An idea of "good leadership" is expressed, according to which an openly transparent and inclusive corporate management, as a "good representative", includes all member concerns in its actions and decisions – and therefore makes further-reaching democratic mechanisms and procedures as well as member involvement rather superfluous. A democracy-friendly management style should act as a guarantor of democracy in the community energy project. This expresses a strong trust in the management institutions, in a structural-formal sense[60] (Community energy democracy through democratic corporate governance – indirect interpretation and representative understanding of democracy. Emphasis of the definition ***on the polity dimension of community energy democracy***).
- The approval of community energy democracy, which on one hand confirms the attribute "democratic" for a community energy project, on the other hand, is supported with specific arguments. Here, the statements predominantly refer to instruments of co-determination and decision-making participation and the existence of bodies and assemblies for voting, which show an ***instrumental-procedural understanding of community energy democracy*** as a characteristic of democracy, in detail by:
- Votes and meetings (a),
- Voting rights (b),
- Bodies and structure (c),
- Balancing influences of affiliated civil society associations such as clubs, through which indirect influence can be exercised by means of co-determination instruments (d).
- In addition, there is the importance of discourse – the unfolding of discourse suggests the assumption of a democratic assignment, the absence of discussion,

[59] Particulars of the parties involved are here: "Banks and founders have the upper hand" (line 653), "there are also alliances and networks/advocacy coalitions" (line 1010). "however, I think it is difficult to exercise control" (line 1343). "was only at the beginning" (line 133). "partly democratic" (line 1804, second citation line 2593, third citation line 2708). "The democratization is not yet complete" (line 2429).

[60] Respondents' statements here are: "If the EC is run sensibly and responsibly, it may not need to be democratic" (line 109). "Doesn't need to be democratic" (line 1179). "I'm not in it to contribute. Employees are welcome to do that" (line 2471).

on the other hand, is perceived as an undemocratic feature (Democracy through influence and discourse: practical participation and consensual decision-making processes – active-direct interpretation, instrumental understanding. Emphasis of the definition on the ***politics dimension of community energy democracy***).[61]

- Another counter-assumption is based on the idea that a democratic component emerges through practices such as communication and principles such as transparency. Through a seamless flow of information and transparency of all processes and discourses, practical democratic practices and principles are likely or suggested to members. At the same time, this also means a definition ex negativo: nepotism, oligarchic tendencies and a lack of transparency stand for non-democratic tendencies (see also explicit information on this in 6.2.11) (Democracy through knowledge: Communication, information and transparency – ***passive interpretation of community energy democracy***).[62]

[61] Respondents' statements here are: (a: votes/meetings) "There are some areas / decisions that were not voted on, at these points the solar cooperative would not be democratic. Other issues were discussed and voted on, so it is (...) in some parts democratic and in other parts non-democratic (line 424)". "Not aware of any meeting" (line 657), "not participated in any meeting so far" (line 682). "I haven't found out about my voting rights, but think it's a good important thing – if anyone wants to get involved. But I also think it's good that you don't HAVE to do this" (line 973). "No public meeting yet" (line 2095). "I haven't thought about whether this co-op has democratic decision-making structures, and since I'm never at meetings, I can't say anything about that" (line 2688). "Haven't attended any meetings yet. New" (line 2728). – (b: co-determination) "Because limited partners have voting rights in the partners' meeting" (line 1595). "No cooperative shares, so no voting rights either" (line 1722). "The owner of the roof also became a partner" (line 300). "Because no shareholder can represent more than 10% of the votes" (line 2156). – Definitions are also made here ex negativo: "The EC not actually not typically democratic, no practical co-determination" (line 110). "because of proportional voting rights" (line 2202). One member also considers the partially applied rule of excluding high participation amounts because of the danger of dominance precisely as a non-democratic principle (equal treatment): "No upper limit on voting shares, because that is undemocratic" (line 2537). – – c: committees/structure) "there is a supervisory board" (line 132), "advisory board" (line 577), "haven't dealt with structure" (line 1549). "because the corporate law gives it" (line 2163). – (d: via club/association – community energy project as a spin-off) "Origin from and involvement of the association provide for a certain democratic effect" (line 1375). "Association in the background" (line 1290). "Don't know much about (...) [note: the community energy project], but the origin from (...) [note: a large environmental protection association] creates trust" (line 1677).

[62] Respondents' statements here are: "I have only been involved financially so far. But the communication about the project leaves me with the impression that (...) [note: the energy cooperative] acts according to democratic principles" (line 407). "Because management is transparent" (line 469). "Independence" (line 1415). "Transparency" (line 1276, 2nd mention line 1415). "Open and transparent communication" (line 2349).

- Democracy and democratic principles are considered by some participants to be a moral issue in the sense of a basic moral-ethical attitude. This understanding means less practical-action-specific guidelines, but rather ideal and normative attitudes, understood in this context as "good" (such as "just", "trusting", "weighing", etc.) ways of acting (democracy as a basic ethical and moral attitude – ***idealistic interpretation of community energy democracy***).[63]
- A trade-off is described between the exercise of democratic principles and success in terms of efficiency and effectiveness; in this view, democratic procedures and discourses hinder goal-oriented working methods and decision-making processes by causing delays or making it difficult for conflicting interests to pursue a streamlined strategy. Resources such as time, effort and communication are not used economically. (Trade-off democracy and success – ***efficiency-reducing interpretation of community energy democracy***).[64]
- The minority opinion is that the common good is served by the regenerative energy production of a community energy project alone. By involving citizens in energy production from which they themselves benefit, one can speak of a "democratization" of the energy system[65] (Participation in services of general interest in the energy sector as an outflow of democracy – ***global interpretation of community energy democracy***).
- Democracy is also perceived as a limited space that is not available everywhere. The idea is based on the consideration that a member who is not present at the "place of democracy" (assembly, place of decision-making) cannot enjoy democratic participation either (problem of location-based inclusion and physical exclusion). Democracy in this understanding is not available without boundaries –

[63] Respondents' statements here are: "it seems to me that "democratic" = morally good is set here. If that is what is meant, "morally good" or just "good" should be asked directly" (line 414). "I don't think this point is so important. More important to me is an ethical orientation" (line 1297). Similarly, "I haven't cared about participation so far, but the organization is probably not anti-constitutional "(line 1466). "Democracy is basic attitude" (line 1541). "I trust the cooperative. I trust the board of directors. Every cooperative in our society is the reflection of our democracy" (line 2827).

[64] Statements of the interviewee here are: "I don't want it democratic at all, I want it successful" (line 1455). "I consider professional and competent action more important than 'democracy' in a company" (line 1380).

[65] Statement of a respondent: "Because every participation is a contribution to the power supply in the country" (line 756). Another understanding suggests that a community energy project can be considered democratic through a wide variety of aspects: "because all points are probably possible" (line 2477). Another consideration is whether it is about the context of origin or processes in the organization, both are considered: "(...) the origin, the processes?" (line 2481).

many proposals for improvement therefore also envisage location-independent use of virtual participation opportunities (see below)[66] (Democracy as a real place of decision making – ***visibility and presence interpretation of community energy democracy***).

Overall View

Although community energy projects are strictly speaking private companies and therefore do not belong to the institutions of the political system, a very large majority of the members consider their association to be democratic. Voting rights, collective voting and broad inclusion of the population are the core aspects that reflect the basic democratic idea. Overall, three groups of divergent understandings can be filtered out:

- ***Classical understanding*** of community energy democracy in the project, based on voting rights, ballots and low barriers to entry – analogous to the basic principles of representative, republican democracy (**prevailing opinion**)
- ***Advanced understanding*** of community energy democracy in the project, based on active member input, discourse, communality and activities that go beyond regular organization – analogous to the ideas of participatory and collaborative democracy (**minority opinion**)
- ***Negative understanding*** of community energy democracy in the project, based on the assumption that commercial private-sector companies are not democratic – analogous to the liberal view of a strict separation of business and democracy (**minority opinion**)

The ability to resolve conflicts and deal with criticism in the community energy projects can be assessed as predominantly positive. Only a few significant conflicts and strong rejection of criticism and counter-opinions are known. However, conflicts and criticism are not unknown in the projects either, individual cases point to problems in some constellations, where presumably in particular a management with oligarchic tendencies or too little possibility of influence exist. A silent part-

[66] Respondent statements here are: "No participation so far..." (line 310), "I'm too far away to be able to get involved in present events, so I don't have the opportunity to participate democratically" (line 1186). "since I don't participate myself, I can't say anything about it" (line 1263). "Would like to participate personally, but too far away from me!" (line 1344). "No experience so far, having only been involved for a short time" (line 1532). "Assumptions, no experience of my own" (line 2184). "I haven't thought about whether this cooperative has democratic decision-making structures. and since I never attend meetings, I can't say anything about that" (line 2688). "Haven't attended any meetings yet. New" (line 2728).

nership via profit participation rights, which does not provide for the possibility of co-determination and influence, does not seem to be in the interest of the participants. The participation models of simultaneous membership including the granting of rights in the case of cooperatives and community wind farms correspond on the one hand more to the wishes and ideas of the members, and on the other hand, measured against objective circumstances, they come much closer to the requirements of internal organizational democracy (as is expressed, for example, in the parity voting principle in cooperatives).

6.5.2 Members' Feedback and Discussion

Of the qualitative information, a total of 1272 people (= 63 percent) provided additional information on positive aspects of their energy project, 369 people (= 18 percent) provided criticism, 15 percent provided neither praise nor criticism, and 4 percent provided no information. This means that 58 percent of all respondents gave their opinion on their energy project.

Positive Feedback

The respondents praise their projects above all for the local energy commitment (17 percent of the praise statements), the decentralized orientation of the energy project (16 percent), the commitment of the initiators and participants (11 percent), and the management's information policy, which is rated as positive (10 percent). It is striking that, in addition to the general criterion of decentralized energy generation, aspects relating specifically to the energy project are mentioned positively. Commitment and information policy thus represent important cornerstones for successful community energy projects, and the participants appreciate the actions of their management or committed members accordingly.

Other positive features, which relate to more general principles, are mentioned with regard to sustainable on-site energy production:

- Ecologically sustainable orientation of the energy project (8 percent)
- Direct local impact (regional value added) (4 percent)
- Increased local acceptance of renewable energy systems (achieved) (3 percent)
- Independence from conventional energy companies (2 percent)
- Manageability and small size of the energy project (2 percent)

In addition, positive characteristics of the community energy project and participation are presented:

- Democracy in the project, equality of members in the case of cooperatives (8%)
- Responsibility and sense of community (6 percent)
- Low financial barriers to entry (5 percent)
- Financial security of investment (4.5 percent)
- Personal connection, proximity, familiarity and acquaintance of the parties involved (2 percent)

The presentation of positive aspects thus essentially corresponds to the general positive aspects of public perception and presentation attributed to community energy projects:

- **Community energy "outward" (externalized view):** ecologically-independent as well as decentralized energy production, regional value creation and locally anchored.
- **Community energy "inward" (internalized view):** democratic internal organization and co-determination, vivid community, small financial shares, trust and proximity building activities.

Negative Feedback: Information, Participation and Co-determination in the Project

Since internal organizational practices are of great importance against the background of the research question, qualitative information from the interviewees regarding negative criticism or suggestions for improvement are listed here. In particular, the topic area of "participation and co-determination" is explained and discussed in more detail. Of particular interest is the question of which aspects are criticized in detail and which overarching categories can be derived.

Information Deficits The participants criticize to a pronounced extent lack of transparency and too little or missing information, which refers either to information on the current situation or with regard to future plans and developments (a total of 32 percent of all criticisms).[67]

As was already evident in other parts of the survey, there is a strong desire among members for more information – even though the majority of participants

[67] In the following, statements by participants are quoted on selected characteristics which are of particular relevance against the background of the focus of the study, e.g. lack of information, participation, activities, etc. The line references are taken from prepared MaxQDA documents.

considered themselves to be well informed at the time of their participation to a very high degree.

A key point here concerns the regularity of information:

> Regular information about projects, about critical issues (…). (line 271)

> Shorten the distance of information from cooperative work. (line 334)

In this context, members also have an interest in receiving an update on developments in their financial investments:

> Communicate information better and especially communicate financial aspects (return, losses etc.) more. (line 713)

A partial negative feedback here also refers to the information and disclosure of problems, obstacles and conflicts. This is related to a demand for transparency: the participants want to be able to better understand strategies, courses of action and arguments; here, too, more frequent and regular information is desired[68]:

> Difficulties should be presented in a more transparent manner and possible solutions be more clearly pointed out. (line 452)

> Even more transparency and information in the form of semi-annual info letters. (line 2451)

> Info, newsletter e.g. quarterly to members. An annual general meeting is not enough. (line 803)

One member gets to the heart of the matter, in that information and transparency create traceability and trust; in the other case, ill will is generated:

> sometimes the information is too little, e.g. why a payment does not come on time. if I know the reason, I can deal with it, otherwise I get annoyed. (line 1181)

The qualitative data also indicate that the flow of information increasingly dries up over time. Here it is important to point out the difference between information be-

[68] This is confirmed in the study on climate protection cooperatives by von Blanckenburg. According to this study, cooperatives are hierarchically organized, and there is also "the power imbalance typical of participation processes (or also information imbalance, imbalance in decision-making authority, etc.), but the promotion of members reduces the potential for conflict that often arises from such inequalities" (von Blanckenburg 2014: 278), as participation takes place in a specific framework.

fore participation and information after participation – the feedback refers in particular to the lack of information or the decline in the flow of information over time. In this context, it is particularly important to emphasize that members want information about future plans – if this is withheld, there is a danger of mistrust, suspicion and a loss of trust. This circumstance of knowledge or lack of knowledge alone can lead to disturbed relations between management and members (phenomenon and perception of "aloof" management), as the following statements make clear:

> Despite the implementation of improvement initiatives, investor communication/information, which has been highly commendable in the past, has slowed and reduced (e.g., confirmation of receipt, confirmation of payment, milestone information, delay information, etc.). (line 1401)

> Up-to-date figures could be published. The initial transparency in the planning and construction phase has now greatly diminished in the use phase. (line 1867)

The members also want to be informed about future plans and strategies – there is even a reference to identification with the energy project:

> Regular reports on planning and business development would interest me and probably increase interest. (line 113)

> Little to non-existent information flow after realization. Therefore, no identification possible. (line 404)

In this context, the idea of co-determination with regard to the future direction also comes up from having a say in strategic decisions: "More say and information on planned projects" (line 975).

Internet and Participation Many members would like to see greater use of information channels via the internet and virtual integration and networking opportunities. The respondents express many different ideas regarding the virtual use of information, discourse and co-determination opportunities.

In addition, the internet should also serve to provide information that is as up-to-date as possible, which requires a wide variety of communication channels in the new social media.

Media may include:

> Use of new media for communication (e.g. website, blog, forum…). (line 242)

There is also the idea of providing virtual information not only for members, but also for the external presentation of the energy project in the sense of public relations, by pursuing advertising at the same time:

> There could be better public relations, e.g. a Facebook account with daily news. (line 2784)

One suggestion of a member is that decisions could be brought about through the use of the internet via the website of the energy project ("co-determination e.g. by means of internet voting on projects", line 757), which could be achieved through "online voting" (line 1040) and virtual meetings ("online participation in meetings, voting", line 1186). The advantage of online meetings and voting would be the possible participation of members who live at a greater distance, which is not uncommon in community energy companies and is also formulated more frequently as a problem in the survey:

> Speed up decisions through website so that members at a greater distance can also participate. More information on the website and in the flyer (…). (line 462)

The interviewees also explain which positive effects could be achieved through virtual information and co-determination; it is in particular openness and transparency, the creation of a positive mood as well as social exchange beyond advertising or business activities that are addressed here:

> Internet connection of the plant where I am involved (…) would provide openness. (line 1296)
>
> Yield data of the wind farms etc. are certainly recorded 'live', relatively current insight into these values and e.g. forecast/expectation values for the plants in a protected area for investors would increase participation and enthusiasm. Furthermore, parents could use this to explain the plants to children or to arouse enthusiasm. (line 1685)
>
> Newsletter would be good even if 'nothing is going on' – to keep in touch. (line 2238)

Public Relations Another point of criticism with regard to information policy generally concerns external information, i.e. the public relations work of the organizations (11 percent of all criticisms). This point is repeatedly referred to in general:

> Generate public opinion for new projects. (line 36)

It is pointed out here that not all sections of the population are reached by "conventional" publicity ("clientele problem"). A stronger emphasis on positive aspects of community energy is called for; the dissemination and development of community energy in Germany is rated as low. The level of awareness of community energy is also considered to be low, and the communication of the benefits of the concept and public relations work by projects and associations to be underdeveloped:

> too little public relations work (the level of awareness is too low, which means that it is mainly the 'directly affected' politicians, public utility companies and people close to them who participate). (line 2532)

> Better marketing with regard to broad publicity in all strata of the population. Hints that even small money can do something for the regional energy supply, while doing something for climate protection and also brings everyone a return. (line 331)

> I have no criticisms, but the benefits of citizen participation are only dimly perceived by the public. We would have to 'infect' people so that projects are desired and demanded. (line 2426)

Another opinion points out that more members (from diverse segments of the population) could bring more ideas and perspectives to the energy project:

> More advertising so that even more members can be gained. From this I expect more opinions / ideas / project proposals and a higher financial strength. (line 2751)

Finally, there are ideas of getting more involved in the public sphere through actions and events, reminiscent of clubs, associations and social movements:

> Public relations, e.g. raffle at Stachus. (line 1587)

Professionalization and Management With regard to management, the members' ideas are divided: one group criticizes the lack of efficiency and professionalism (6.5 percent), the unfavorable working conditions of volunteers (5 percent), and the lack of regional economic cooperation (3 percent); occasionally, the desire for more or criticism of too little return is also expressed. Another group of members, on the other hand, sees the projects as being characterized by too much profit orientation and economic professionalism (6 percent), and calls for constructive solutions to criticism (2 percent). Conflicts between committees are sometimes mentioned.

The general criticism of unprofessional action essentially concerns efficiency, structuredness, speed and tight organization.[69] On the one hand, there is general criticism of the status quo:

> Site coordination. (line 2504)
>
> Amateurish management. Incompetence in matters of technology and finance! (line 1286)
>
> Professionalization at all levels. (line 1295)

On the other hand, concrete improvements are called for:

> A more structured, coordinated approach: Ideas are there, but in some cases they are not tackled consistently enough. (line 2571)
>
> Improve organizational structures, work more purposefully. (line 1362)

Of particular relevance to stakeholders here is the speed of processes (acceleration of procedures), sometimes coupled with too much and thus crippling bureaucracy, and more centralized and direct control and management:

> Overarching professionalism needs to be improved. Processes, contracts, management etc. should be centrally controlled and supervized. (line 1852)
>
> Clear organizational structure (…). Less bureaucracy. (line 1091)
>
> Faster decision making. (line 2753)
>
> Shorter realization periods. (line 2128)
>
> Some processes could possibly be accelerated (…). (line 1514)
>
> More professional/faster planning of further projects. (line 383)

Justifications can be found in the form of investor protection, i.e. conscientious handling of the invested sums, as well as communication, i.e. informing the parties involved:

[69] These assessments could also be found in the study on climate protection cooperatives by von Blanckenburg, in that direct channels of influence by members were problematized: "It is not the abandonment of direct democracy and the emergence of different ways of influencing decisions that requires explanation and classification, but conversely the direct and non-representative formation of opinion and influence is seen as a problem" (von Blanckenburg 2014: 269 f.). Furthermore, members' scepticism towards participation could be found: "It is interesting that some members are even skeptical about an expansion of participation opportunities" (ibid.: 262).

> Research backgrounds or contingencies in a more thorough manner and, in the interests of the members, i.e. to protect the entrusted funds, secure them contractually (…)! (Line 726)
>
> Communication with investors is not professional. (Line 1547)

Another point relates to demands for more know-how and expertise, which could also be brought in by setting up expert panels:

> Management should be 'broader'. Fewer politicians on the board, more experts. (Line 784)
>
> Advisory boards or expert committees could improve or increase the efficiency of existing renewable energy plants or new ones to be built through special expertise or contributions. (Line 1018)

Finally, the negative feedback can be summarized in two directions: a complaint about existing structures (especially related to uninformed staff) on the one hand, and ineffective processes that should be accelerated and streamlined on the other. At this point, the presumed trade-off between professionalization and democratic structures comes to light[70]: "too many opinions" and "doubters" thus stand in the way of efficiency and effectiveness:

> too much dreaming. (line 966)
>
> perhaps too naive about the sense and profitability of solar plants. (line 372)
>
> Too much red tape. Too many opinions. Too slow to act. (line 2437)
>
> Low speed of work. Low effectiveness. Doubting. (line 32)

The data also reveal some specific challenges of community energy projects. These are partly linked to the growth of the projects, which increasingly require more professionalization:

> (…) [note: the community energy project] is at a point where it is important to introduce a good management structure. This will be a switch for the future. Here you can do a lot right or wrong. (line 1433)

[70] In von Blanckenburg's study of climate protection cooperatives, it was shown that professionalization efforts lead to a consolidation of hierarchical structures, and thus tend to push back participatory patterns and "grassroots democratic elements" (trade-off between professionalization and participation) (von Blanckenburg 2014: 270). Accordingly, the strong formation of hierarchies can hinder the direct participation of members and working groups and therefore tends to lead to conflict.

> Grown very quickly. Therefore, organizational/personal need for improvement. (Line 1625)

The obvious possibility for smaller and voluntary community energy projects to obtain the expert knowledge for the management of business activities from outside, for example through tax consultants and the like, is also criticized – apparently the participants would rather have a professional management than, for example, a cooperative and voluntary board, which requires help from outside ("commercial knowledge must be obtained from external consultants" (line 2787)).

Instead, the stakeholders are convinced that cooperatives are also capable of professional business operations ("Tighter management: cooperative and maximally efficient!" (line 1713)). One member points out that a volunteer-run cooperative is the same as an association, but a community energy project is less close to an association than to a project (albeit formed and composed by citizens) – this makes professional management necessary. This approach is also linked to the idea of achieving high efficiency and effectiveness:

> The fact that the cooperative is run on a voluntary basis is disadvantageous. This gives it more of an association character. A "real" citizens' or community company needs a more professional management. Through this, the cooperative would certainly have achieved much more than it has so far. (Line 41)

Expansion of Community Energy Projects In addition to the idea of professionalization, expansion and growth of the energy projects is also suggested by participating members. On the one hand, they complain about the small size and lack of expansion opportunities (10 percent), demand more members (2 percent), and on the other hand criticize legal hurdles in project implementation (2 percent).

Here we find above all demands for growth and the development of new energy sources:

> Act more and faster, become bigger, invest more money and collect before, others are much faster !!! (line 1705)

> It is time to look for new fields of investment (e.g. wind power, CHPs, local heat supply). (line 1814)

This is justified, among other things, by the fact that more contributions from participants also mean more independence and less dependence on bank loans, which means that the idea of a citizens' or community company or project is more fulfilled. Beyond a small solar project, there are ideas of comprehensive and complex energy supply and service concepts through community energy projects, analogous to a municipal utility or larger energy supplier. According to the survey, some community energy projects are striving for this further development, and some of them have already implemented it:

> You have to attract more members. Also through promises of returns. (...) [note: The community energy company] must reach the critical mass of an 'alternative' municipal utility. Debt financing via banks contradicts the opportunities from citizen participation. (line 2402)

In addition, new topics and fields of activity are suggested: the ideas range from concrete proposals for the use of other energy sources to a completely different orientation of the fields of activity. Among the ideas and possibilities for other fields of activity of their energy project, there are many suggestions for the use of wind and water power, electricity storage and grid operation. This also includes suggestions for alternative, global strategies – which range widely.

Here, for example, it is voices from larger community energy projects that would like to see a "step back" again – for example in the direction of a cooperative organization – which is partly due to co-determination powers ("I would like participation in cooperative structures" (line 1249). In addition to the citizens' movement "from below", many energy cooperatives in Germany have also come into being through the initiative of the cooperative banks (Volks- und Raiffeisenbanken) – which, however, is not only met with approval, as the dangers of collusion and patronage projects are pointed out here ("it could be a citizens' movement and not a community of cooperative banks" (line 771)).

Finally, concrete practices are also questioned, in that a community energy project could also support smaller structures beyond the operation of larger energy plants, for example in the PV sector the use of roofs of private households (including the members themselves) ("possibly also smaller plants on private roofs" (line 2393)).

Criticism of Expansion of Projects and Professionalization Tendencies A group of members critical of professionalization warns of the negative effects of excessive growth and expansion (loss of closeness to members, economization) (3 percent).[71]

---

[71] According to the findings of von Blanckenburg's study on climate protection cooperatives, the existing understanding of participation by the management of cooperatives consists of "satisfying members", which is judged to be dysfunctional, as the management itself speaks of "customer management" (von Blanckenburg 2014: 275). Nevertheless, the cooperative principle of member promotion is taken into account: "on the other hand, however, it becomes clear how much the principle of member promotion leads to an active effort on the part of the management to take up the opinions and suggestions of the members and to integrate them into plans" (ibid.).

Here, too, there are two different orientations: On the one hand, concrete criticism is expressed, for example concerning a planned conversion into a public limited company ("I am critical of the conversion into a public limited company" (line 1566)). On the other hand, there is negative feedback that the focus on large and complex energy plant investments is at the expense of manageability:

> Offer again more participations in manageable individual projects instead of unnecessarily complicated corporate constructions with umbrella companies, etc. (line 1601)

> (…) [note: the community energy project] is growing: the projects are getting bigger, not so easy for outsiders to keep track of. (line 1585)

The use of certain energy sources is also criticized, with biogas (the controversial issue of "maize cultivation") being mentioned several times ("It's getting too big and we have to get rid of biogas" (line 1201)). On the other hand, the administration demanded by the proponents of professionalization is seen as unnecessarily costly ("the administration and operational structure is too costly" (line 2603)). Politicization in the form of a community energy project acting as a public actor is also seen as excessive by some members – while elsewhere it is precisely demanded by other members ("putting on airs is sometimes 'too thick', modesty would do better!" (line 1386), "political appearance" (line 968)).

Finally, some interviewees express negative feedback of economization, which sees a "commercialization" as contrary to cooperative models in particular:

> Growing at the price of 'professionalization' may be an economic necessity, but with the possible consequences of a mercantile streamlining. (para. 1517)

> Reduce the focus on existing financial market rules, reduce the focus on returns. Push cooperative models more, focus more on idealistic and social motivation. (line 1749)

Here, in turn, a higher proportion of citizen participation is emphasized, investments abroad are distrusted, and a "solid" and "sustainable" economy is demanded:

> Less debt participation in projects. Rather fewer projects and more citizen capital share! (line 1271)

> Please do not grow too fast, please be committed to solid management, i.e. returns with safety buffer. Expanding into foreign markets is questionable. Check market entry as an energy provider. (line 1454)

> Rapid growth can be or become economically problematic. (line 1576)

> Rapid growth – will there be enough substance left for sustainable development? (line 1508)

There is another contribution which criticizes the examination of the community energy project's growth, which is probably at the core of many statements: "(…) [note: the community energy project] seems to critically question its own growth and its speed too little" (line 1160).

However, there are also differentiated voices which, on the one hand, welcome the significant size and influence of the project, but on the other hand point to the presumed trade-off between professionalization and closeness to members:

> Do not forget where the roots are. Meanwhile, it is a proud medium-sized company that acts accordingly independently of its base. However, the strong bond between capital and the company is a central strength of the project. (line 1414)

Finally, one member finds himself caught in the dilemma of which objective of the energy project is more to be advocated: a maximum size for the benefit of energy transition and ecology or just the creation of investment opportunities:

> 'My energy cooperative covers a region with almost 1 million inhabitants, so it's not entirely clear to me whether the focus is on the opportunity for ecological investments or on co-responsible engagement in the energy transition'. (line 2420)

Another point concerns concrete criticism and suggestions for improvement, such as lack of flexibility, other forms of organization, negative feedback on location issues and plant operation, as well as concrete and practical ideas (e.g.: use of electricity by members).

Limits of Voluntary Action and Appreciation of Civic Engagement Closely linked to the criticism and demand for more professionalization is the diagnosis of some members that the voluntary management of cooperatives, associations and partly also in other constructions reach their limits due to the (administrative) effort:

> Through volunteer leadership, some actors easily reach the limits of their personal resilience. (line 26)
>
> Volunteer board members are at the limit of their endurance. (line 357)

The effects are, on the one hand, overstrain, frustration and abandonment ("Besides, I am worried that the protagonists will not use their own strength in a sustainable way, will not get paid (enough) and give up at some point exhausted" (line 1888)), on the other hand lack of organization, growth and support of the energy project:

> Investing more, at some point doesn't work as an honorary position. (line 151)

> Unfortunately, however, this can only be realized with more and better paid workers. (line 268)

This ultimately leads to a split pattern of opinion regarding the organization of a community energy project: on the one hand, the demand for a professional management, on the other hand, rejection of this due to the demand for a voluntary and down-to-earth character. In addition, there are expressions of encouragement in that the voluntary work could grow into structures, acquire competences and knowledge, and therefore a professional voluntary work could be an alternative:

> after initial enthusiasm, they let themselves be thwarted by bureaucratic difficulties. (line 2584)

In this context, some members feel compelled to express confidence in their volunteering; more trust and faith in the community energy project and the volunteering, as well as integration efforts are also called for:

> We need more trust in the activities of the cooperative. (line 263)

> The cooperative also stands and falls with the people who are involved there. The ability to work in a team is a prerequisite. (line 904)

> I trust the co-op. I trust the board of directors. Every cooperative in our society is the reflection of our democracy. (Z 2827)

Another approach assumes that the monetization of voluntary work in the form of paid work could be a promising solution:

> who value a lot of volunteer work more and pay for it in some cases. (line 469)

> One should perhaps try to 'reward' the commitment financially as well, in recognition of the many voluntary activities. (line 1877)

Local Cooperation and Networks Connections and links to the surroundings, i.e. cooperation with local companies, civil society organizations or state institutions, are in some cases seen as deficient. A group of members sees a dormant potential in this, which is at the same time defended against criticism regarding independence and nepotism:

> Networking with capital providers to be able to tackle larger projects. (line 27)
>
> - poor cooperation with the city (…) – too taken in by property owners. (line 2644)

One point of negative feedback here relates to the promotion of regional value creation by supporting local companies ("No regional companies are taken on for the construction of photovoltaic" (line 559)). Another point of criticism is that the failure to cooperate and expand may attract other actors who, especially in the wind power sector, will install wind turbines, which is something that the community energy project has failed to do:

> Honestly, nothing, except maybe the fact that not all the turbines in the region are ours, but now big energy plant operators and power producers are jumping on the bandwagon we created & investing themselves. So that blurs a bit the real point of wind turbines. We are and remain the HONEST ones. (line 2219)

Nepotism and Oligarchy Some participants criticize or fear oligarchic tendencies in the form of informal agreements and networks, preferential treatment (especially in terms of personnel), and power imbalances (power dominance).[72]

More often, oligarchic tendencies are complained about in the negative feedback, the project is "dominated by founders", there is only little participation (line 653). Relevant criticism of the project management is also illustrated by the following entry: "The board of directors does what it wants, I see citizen participation differently! An entrepreneur plans and manages everything and the board nods. No competitors!????! (line 1)". This point of feedback is reinforced by further disapproval of boards that have reduced member influence and promoted exclusionary tendencies, especially after the (often still very open) founding phase:

[72] Such tendencies could also be found in von Blanckenburg's study on climate protection cooperatives. Nevertheless, an individual member can exert influence on the co-determination channels. However, this possibility is linked to personal competences and resources, which cannot be assumed for every member (von Blanckenburg 2014: 281). From this it can be concluded that the potential for active participation for the individual member is to be classified as rather low overall: "The individual member has hardly any chances to set his own topics. Working groups acting as a community, on the other hand, can articulate convictions and proposals perceptibly and thus influence the formation of opinion, even if they tend to be perceived as a disruptive factor as soon as they exceed the service function" (ibid.: 270). According to this, extended forms of participation can also lead to conflicts with formal bodies: "The independent working groups come into conflict with the board above all (...) through a grassroots democratic understanding of participation" (ibid.: 264).

> since its foundation, everything has been in the hands of the board of directors and the supervisory board, the previously active project group no longer has any influence, there would still be potential there. (line 948)
>
> Ruled by founders (...). (line 653)

Similar to this is the description of non-transparent preliminary agreements without the involvement of the members:

> When the project was founded, everything had already been decided as to who would be on the management board and the supervisory board. There was no open discussion about this. (line 1110)
>
> Occupation of the posts/activities was agreed upon in advance! (line 2141)

Furthermore, conflicts and influence can apparently also arise between the boards: "Too much influence of the supervisory board in the management" (line 41). In addition, influence on the management of the project is criticized:

> It should not be controlled by party politics. (line 2312)

Further negative feedback concerns the awarding practice with suspicion of collusion and corruption – more transparency and information are demanded:

> That (...) [note: the community energy project] mainly uses companies of the acquaintances and friends of the leaders in projects. (line 1268)
>
> Project allocation is not transparent – suspicion of nepotism. (line 1077)
>
> Make awarding practices more transparent. (line 2377)
>
> Transparency of decisions-more information about the work of the executive board and supervisory board. (line 2457)

In addition to a lack of transparency, awarding practices and agreements, the communication style of the project management and committees is also seen as exclusionary and not open to criticism:

> Outdated discussion culture, partly know-it-all attitude. (line 956)
>
> Arguing more with doubters. (line 2566)
>
> Not capable of criticism. (line 2593)
>
> Minimal communication, no discussion, ability to criticize not given! (line 2602)

Furthermore, disclosure of the remuneration of the community energy project's management is demanded:

> There is no information about future payment models of the boards. (line 2257)

> Compensation scheme of founding commanders, and operating management. (line 2776)

Another point of view, on the other hand, assumes that a self-interested way of thinking and acting is not unusual and is human: "None – the interests of some mandate holders are simply sometimes subjective for their own benefit!" (line 2601).

Participation and Co-determination On the one hand, too few participation (opportunities) and co-determination are criticized (6.5 percent), on the other hand, participation in the project itself is seen as more difficult due to the selection of participants in the project (1.7 percent), as well as with regard to the financial hurdles for participation (4 percent). Here, too, reference is often made to possibilities of virtual participation (see discussion above, details e.g.: "online voting" (line 1040), "co-determination, e.g. by means of internet voting on projects" (line 757)).

Criticism of the lack of co-determination and influence is essentially that, on the one hand, no discourse at all is made possible, suggestions are not made possible or provided for on the part of the members:

> The members of the cooperative are confronted with accomplished facts, e.g. price increases, etc. (line 2828)

> (…) little say. (line 653)

> Even more information and participation of the citizens. (line 779)

> Improve suggestion system. (line 96)

On the other hand, there are also demands for participation from the members: "More members could participate actively" (line 352). In some cases, members are not even aware of the opportunities for participation and forums: "Opportunities to participate should be better communicated, many members do not know about the Future Workshop" (line 963). Another aspect concerns the lack of information exchange and the lack of response to members' enquiries:

> for a long time no reaction to critical inquiries (…). (line 1439)

On my inquiries (…) the information was not sufficient. (line 1375)

heard nothing since founding meeting. (line 2291)

A further point of departure concerns the timely internal participation of members: "earlier involvement of members in new planning" (line 889), as well as more involvement in decision-making: "Members should be more involved in decisions" (line 2111). As has already been mentioned, the involvement and co-determination of members in strategic planning and opening up for ideas concerning the future is the main issue for already established energy projects: "Implementation of a project successfully carried out – regular open forums about further orientation / activities are missing so far" (line 1865) as well as "earlier involvement of members in new planning" (line 889) are expressed and demanded here.

How could the inclusion of members look like, without them being only passive visitors of meetings or making motions in a formal framework, but on the other hand not only meeting for social exchange? One obvious possibility is the establishment of working groups and communities which work on specific topics and draw up proposals which can then be transformed into official courses of action through democratic decision-making in the general meetings. The members themselves emphasize the advantages of such collaborative practices: Broad knowledge inclusion and relief especially of volunteer leadership: "Prepare board decisions in working groups. Significant relief of the board width basis and know-how transfer to many members" (line 2064). "If necessary, distribute the workload over several shoulders (e.g. internal foundation of div. Working groups, or groups of interested parties)" (line 2430).

A definition of co-determination in a community energy project has already been presented, but this point is also taken up again in the open statements. Again, it is pointed out that co-determination through voting rights arises automatically: "because of proportionate voting rights" (line 2202). "Because no shareholder can represent more than 10% *of* the votes" (line 2156).

In cases where there is no cooperative organization, participants with high investment sums can have a correspondingly strong voting weight – some members would like to see compensatory measures implemented here: "Spread the holdings more widely, i.e. individuals should not 'hoard' so many shares" (line 2352). "Possibly reduce the amount of participation somewhat" (line 155).

One member, however, considers the partially applied regulation to exclude high participation amounts because of the danger of dominance to be precisely a non-democratic principle (equal treatment): "No upper limitation of the voting shares, because that is undemocratic" (line 2537). Likewise, it is demanded: "Increase of the max. business share" (line 774).

In addition, the already discussed circumstance that many community energy projects end the possibility of subscribing to shares after some time can develop as problematic, since they have either gained sufficient capital or the business construction also makes this necessary. This freeze on new memberships meets with criticism: "Too early member admission stop" (line 431). Due to the restrictions on the acquisition of shares, possibly also due to the lack of awareness of the energy project in certain parts of the population and in more distant areas, a participation structure can be created which only includes certain circles of acquaintances and networked population groups – one member points out this effect: "Lack of representation of different social milieus" (line 956).

The democratic claim of cooperatives with regard to strong member loyalty and strong co-determination thanks to equality of votes is contradicted. It is claimed that beyond theoretical influence, de facto co-determination is not possible: "The EC (...) actually not typically democratic, no practical co-determination" (line 110). Some members also urge that critical voices from the ranks of the members should be addressed: "Individual concerns should be taken more seriously" (line 2509). In this respect, more willingness to engage in discourse and debate is desired: "Argue more with doubters" (line 2566).

On the other hand, there is also a completely different way of looking at things: According to this, not every idea should be taken up, criticism of a lack of co-determination is invalidated in the sense that one's own initiative is first demanded:

> There is always room for improvement. However, one should not blindly run after every idea. Keep at it with moderation. (line 2623)

> Criticism, none, because yes we could change these points more member participation. (line 1826)

Also critically reflective is a member who complains about a lack of information, but at the same time suspects that the claim takes a back seat to not having enough initiative of one's own: "Feeling of lack of transparency → so far received a letter about planned projects. But it could also be that I have not informed myself enough" (line 549).

Following on from this, a remarkable paradox is observed between the impossibility of comprehensive information, low resources for taking in and processing information, and the simultaneous claim and requirement of being informed:

> Due to a lack of time, I have not yet paid enough attention to the essence of (...) [note: the community energy project]. But I also think that not every shareholder has to deal with everything personally. I read the emails I receive occasionally. But don't feel informed enough about the project. So how much money has been invested now, what

> is in the pipeline, when can I expect a return (I reported up front that I don't care about the return). Nevertheless, I would like to know of course, what happens with my money. Regarding this I have a not so good feeling. I just think that I will get my investment back if I need it (after a certain time). But I'm not sure. (line 407)

Access to Information and Barriers to Participation Some members criticize that for them access to information and thus also to discourse is more difficult due to a lack of expertise, and understanding of technical and business issues. The participants are therefore in favor of more simply structured and comprehensible information; they would like to see specific explanations and consideration of lower levels of knowledge in order to create more transparency and comprehensibility. This is mainly a matter of simplicity and understanding of complicated but important contexts as well as uncomplicated access to relevant information ("small print"). This point is closely linked to the issues of participation and co-determination, virtual opportunities, and the criticism of nepotism. The central pivot here is the creation of transparency and easily understandable information, which form the crucial basis for building trust and thus also more realistic use and equal weighting of co-determination. Conversely, it must also be stated that lack of transparency, informal agreements, incomprehensible information, the absence or prevention of co-determination in committees or via the internet mean that participation and co-determination are made more difficult or excluded in practice. On the one hand, members want simple explanations and information:

> More transparency and easier explanation for non-technical people who still want to support the cause. (line 33)

> - better marketing for educationally disadvantaged classes (simple explanations…). (line 155)

> sometimes too much expert language. (line 1149)

> Less official i.e. write more intelligibly. (line 2645)

On the other hand, more transparency, easy allocation, and breakdown of information and complicated facts such as calculations are desired:

> Too little information about the performance of the plant, and what it brings in terms of profit, etc. When you receive letters, they are usually so confusing that you don't even know what they are supposed to be. (line 496)

Improve the traceability of the operating companies' figures, which are included in the financial plans. (line 1446)

Formulate the risks of the capital investment in the investment prospectus more clearly, not only in a small print. (line 1624)

Dialogue and Inclusion, Activity and Community Among the statements of the participants there are some demands that a broader inclusion of the members should be created. More events, discussions, talks and exchanges beyond formal business processes and committee activities, as well as more activity on the part of the members, are suggested and demanded by various members, and in this context also backed up with concrete proposals.[73] A frequently expressed idea of some members concerns a vivid community in the community energy project or the organization by establishing activities and events besides the regular business operations and formal meetings and procedures. The initial criticism concerns a lack of discourse in community energy communities in that there is "too little discussion or interest in further ideas" (line 930). In essence, it is suggested to strive for more activities of the energy projects beyond the usual procedure: "broader basis for the activities, i.e. more active members that shape the image of the energy cooperative" (line 1133).

Additional Discussion Forums Another idea from the participants' reflections relates to the establishment of more informal forums alongside the regular bodies of the community energy projects, companies and associations. These meetings should primarily serve the purpose of social exchange and enable "informal" discourse on a wide variety of topics (both on "hard" issues, such as those relating to organization and management, and on "soft" topics such as events). For example, there are suggestions for "more intensive contact" and exchange with members "also between general meetings" (line 661), furthermore more "networking" is suggested (line 736). Concrete suggestions concern social events and meetings:

[73] This finding is consistent with the results of von Blanckenburg's study of climate protection cooperatives. According to this, members have little interest in formal meetings, but a preference for informal meetings and exchange (von Blanckenburg 2014: 280 f.). This also corresponds to the individual understanding of participation found among cooperative members, which refers primarily to communal practices and discursive formats (see ibid.: 274): "Strongly represented, on the other hand, is the awareness that participation creates social cohesion. A social, community-creating function is recognized above all in participation in discursive formats" (ibid.: 277 f.).

Some members see a solution in more internal activity, and exchange between members in non-formal forums and social events[74]:

> Annual exchange of experiences in summer, open day of a plant or other planned plants, with coffee and cake, small simple self-service party, (…) family cooperative care, information for further future cooperative projects. (line 795)
>
> every 2 months a meeting to get to know each other and exchange ideas. (line 970)

On the other hand, there are ideas for stronger networking with the outside world, organizing events with thematic references that do not have to do with organizational issues or formal rules and procedures:

> More communication! (line 406)
>
> Public presentation, e.g. at adult education centers. (line 657)
>
> More public relations work, such as lectures, e.g.: Where do I save electricity, fuel, waste? What does our world really look like? Films like Plastic-Planet or An Inconvenient Truth could serve as a basis for discussion for new ideas. (line 51)

Further suggestions concern the establishment of forums: "Regular open forums about further orientation / activities are missing so far" (line 1865), as well as the establishment of working groups (see above). According to this, a collaborative way of working can serve both the objective criterion of the organization-related inclusion of knowledge, support of voluntary work, improvement of the participation and co-determination climate as well as social exchange and togetherness. Further ideas and suggestions concern a "stronger networking with the comrades"

[74] The findings of von Blanckenburg's study of climate protection cooperatives indicate that not only the goal of material benefit, but also a high level of interest "in an exchange with one another" is clearly discernible (von Blanckenburg 2014: 279). Cooperatives apparently offer in principle the possibility of establishing a discursive basis beyond the principle of economic activity: "Cooperatives in particular, in which ecological economic activity is not one of the defined purposes, could however specifically expand their participation repertoire to include discursive formats in order to also develop orientation knowledge (...). In this way, a discussion would be initiated that would expand the justifications for climate protection investments, which are based on purely economic advantages, to include value orientations" (ibid.: 279). Thus, cooperatives can promote public welfare-oriented topics such as climate protection in the discourse (ibid.: 270), which is "inconceivable in this way with other forms of enterprise" (ibid.: 281). Internal organizational structures are crucial for the unfolding of such overarching discourses: "However, (...) in reality it has been shown that the hierarchical organizational principle frames participation, and is thus much more important for the thematization of climate protection" (ibid.: 270).

through regular "newsletter organization" and the establishment of a "comrades club" (line 139).

One concrete suggestion is to make wind turbines interesting for guests and visitors and attractive as a destination for excursions – according to this idea, technology can also fulfil other functions beyond pure energy generation: "Attach LED displays to the outside of the towers to show the current output. Build a viewing platform, thereby attracting even more (not only) wind tourists" (line 2783).

Topics and inclusion: Another problem in the development of discourse in the communities concerns the focus of topics, which does not always include all members: "The topics of discussion platforms such as the Future Workshop are very technology-heavy (how LEDs work) and uninteresting for the majority of members. More social topics should be addressed" (line 963). Other, more general discussion topics are also demanded, which the members themselves should also contribute: "The shareholders should participate more actively in information on the topics of ecology, climate protection, nuclear phase-out, energy transition" (line 1827). The demand for a more general, socio-political discourse is similar: "there is a lack of discussion on the current topic of the future of the Renewable Energy Sources Act and possible effects on investments in wind energy" (line 2721).

Trade-Off Distance and Inclusion in Community Energy In some wind energy and larger projects there is a problem of distance, which prevents concrete participation in the community energy project and even leads to resentment about decision-making without broad participation:

> The further away you live, the less contact there is. (…) [note: local participants] are in the majority and seem to settle many things among themselves. (line 2768)

> I don't know, because due to the spatial distance (…) I don't have the possibility to actively participate in (…) activities on site and therefore I haven't intensively dealt with (…) [note: the community energy project]. If I lived in Munich, I would definitely take the opportunity to participate in local activities. (line 1532)

In fact, some participants define their energy project primarily through participation in events and local proximity. Simply due to the fact that they live at a greater distance, they do not consider a (critical) statement on their energy project to be adequately feasible. Apparently, the information they have about their project and the knowledge they have gained through participation and observation of progress is not sufficient for them to actually make an assessment or comment on the participation, the project or the organization:

> It's far away for me, as I live in northern Germany. (line 1187)
>
> too little insight to be able to offer constructive criticism. (line 1224)
>
> I have not dealt with (…) [note: the community energy project] so intensively as to find fault with it. (line 1472)
>
> to be able to critically assess the work of (…) [note: the Community Energy project], I am not familiar enough with the matter. (line 1611)

In addition, there is another aspect in connection with local involvement, which is particularly important in the case of wind power: the involvement of those affected (people living in the vicinity of the energy plants) in the enterprise and joint exchange: "One should perhaps integrate those affected (residents where the plant is located) into the cooperative at an earlier stage" (line 2089).

Trade-Off Face-to-Face Meetings and Distant Home Interestingly, some members link a lack of personal ability to criticize not only to short membership, but also to physical presence at face-to-face meetings; information is not considered sufficient as a basis for criticism: "I can't say yet, because I haven't been around long enough and haven't been involved in any general meetings yet" (line 2012). "Since I moved away from the region a few years ago and thus no longer or rarely attend the meetings, my criticism would not be current" (line 2168). "As I have not yet been able to attend a meeting – was prevented due to association work – I cannot afford to criticize" (line 2229). "I have not yet attended any meetings. I'm new here!" (line 2728). Another member, however, considers absence from meetings to be unproblematic due to high trust in the community energy project: "I regret that I cannot attend meetings etc. for me due to distance. But on the other hand, it is not so important to me because I trust (…) [note: the community energy project]. The information I got about [note: the community energy project] led me to participate in it" (line 1216). "The further away you live, the looser the contact. (…) [note: local participants] are in the majority and seem to settle many things among themselves" (line 2768).

Further Development of the Financial Participation Mechanism In particular, participants in some community energy investment companies who have acquired profit participation rights that do not grant them any co-determination in the company are in favor of participation as co-owners as in the limited partnerships of the community wind farms or the "one-man, one-vote" cooperatives: "Instead of profit participation rights, better direct participation of investors as co-owners (e.g. as limited partners or cooperative members)" (line 1767). Similarly, another voice:

"Possibility to participate not only as a creditor, but also as a partner/co-owner" (line 2700).

Another point of contention with regard to financial participation models is the question of the minimum investment amount and the maximum investment amount (as already mentioned above). While one group is in favor of the possibility of small financial stakes and thus at the same time wants to prevent overweighting of large investors ("perhaps still smaller financial participations. (line 1308), "spread holdings more widely, i.e. individuals should not 'hoard' so many shares (line 2352)), another orientation pleads for the possibility of large business shares (line 774), which is even justified with the principle of democracy (line 2537, presumably based on a postulate of equality). Another argument aims at the fact that with many small shareholdings in combination with only a few shareholdings, the potential for the use of regenerative energies cannot be exploited, moreover, a high administrative effort arises with regard to the organization of many (small) participants – a complicated effect, which is also known from small cooperatives in the present study and represents an enormous challenge with regard to claim (offering many small shareholdings) and realization (volunteering overload):

> more financially strong citizens should have participated, then the roof would have been completely covered with modules. So there are many small participations, which increase the administrative effort. (line 2523)

Some members express ideas about participation models beyond the fixed and inflexible practiced forms via participation rights, and status as partners and owners: "I would also like to see other forms of financial participation: more flexible, also short-term – even if then less profitable" (line 1683). This points to a possible problem of community energy, which may have cost the movement many more interested citizens: due to the (required) strong and long-term commitment to the community energy project (for example, in many cases it may only make sense to be a limited partner in a community wind farm or cooperative member for a period of up to 20 years due to the long-term Renewable Energy Sources Act (EEG) subsidy, as only later a higher return, or any return at all, is achieved), a deterrent may have arisen. Through participation offers with shorter time limits and flexible models with regard to an exit, many more interested parties could possibly be won over.

The commitment to the terms specified by the Renewable Energy Sources Act (EEG) (20-year guaranteed fixed feed-in tariff) therefore represents a disadvantage for some participants – possibly also a major hurdle with regard to participation at all (which cannot be clarified in the present study). In fact, in the question area on the articles of association, the participants did not attribute any extraordinary relevance to the regulations on exiting the participation (e.g. transfer of business share, exit options from the community energy project, return of shares); presumably because this hurdle has already been taken. In some forms of organization, an exit is easier to realize than in others – it should be borne in mind at this point that participation in a community energy project often only makes sense over a longer period of time in terms of achieving a return, as initially no return is achieved due to repayments and then increasingly a certain bonus can at least be expected due to compensation payments that no longer exist. For this reason, it also becomes apparent at this point that alternative participation models (such as via loans and profit participation rights) can also bring great advantages for some participants (or population groups and milieus) despite the lack of co-determination opportunities and the absence of the formation of a community, as a long-term commitment is not possible or even desirable. For younger people in particular, the more flexible mode of participation is likely to be more attractive – in fact, only a few younger people are involved in the community energy projects designed for longer participation periods. Whereas it could be assumed that older participants may no longer be able to enjoy the profits themselves in the case of a "term" of 20 years, but will create and bequeath the investment to the following generations, this hypothesis is not necessarily true. An older member points precisely to the need to be able to dissolve the participation in an uncomplicated manner, which is made more difficult for him due to changes in the community energy company's regulations: "for me as a pensioner, it would be important to be able to return my shares without losses. This is not possible because the term has simply been extended" (line 2216).

A solution idea is formulated by a member, according to which small distributions could take place earlier and in this way a distribution and a higher attractiveness would be achieved at an earlier point in time (restrictive: if this is actually feasible, however): "Perhaps distribute a small return now and then" (line 2056).

Other Aspects Some members very openly express general negative feedback without reference to the energy project (1.5 percent); energy policy or the federal government as well as the socio-political framework conditions are also criticized (especially with regard to feed-in tariffs and lack of support) (1 percent). The general understanding of technology is rarely critically questioned (0.8 percent), male dominance in the energy project is disapproved of (0.4 percent), and legal inaccuracies are also criticized (0.2 percent).

Criticism of Energy Politics Some members criticize the lack of support from politics, the framework conditions set by higher-level politics (especially with regard to the Renewable Energy Sources Act (EEG)), but actually also local conditions caused by both associations and organizations, which therefore show little commitment to community energy:

> the framework conditions would have to be improved, especially in the start-up phase, which is very cost-intensive, e.g. compulsory membership of the Chamber of Commerce, of which we have none; the appreciation by the churches etc. could be better; one should be able to deduct one's voluntary expenses from taxes, etc. (line 36)

Other criticisms concern representatives of local politics who, according to these opinions, offer no support or even force the prevention of community energy: "there are still 'brakemen' in local politics. (mostly regulars' table opinions without factual background)" (line 2357). "the regional politicians give us a hard time, even though we want to bring money to the city. Funny, isn't it?" (line 2577).

Finally, some members conclude from the unfavorable framework conditions that the community energy projects themselves should exert an influence on federal as well as local politics and actively stand up for their interests: "More pressure should be put on local politicians to exert their influence in Berlin" (line 886). "more pressure on district administrator" (line 2588).

Return of Investment Among the negative feedback, there are some voices that simply demand a higher return of investment or are dissatisfied with the yield attainment[75]; here, various identical statements can be found (e.g.: "Poor yield, due to years with little wind. Very disappointing" (line 2330). One interviewee puts the core concern in a nutshell: "despite ecology, there could be more return" (line 1674). Another point concerns the disappointment about predicted returns and lower profits in actuality:

> Promises of returns are too high. (line 2161)
>
> Prices rise faster and higher than promised. (line 2835)
>
> Investment prospectus too optimistic. (line 2324)
>
> The yield calculation in the prospectus should have been calculated more cautiously. (line 2317)

[75] Evaluations of this are only carried out here by way of example.

Here, some members immediately formulate ideas on how to improve returns ("To improve returns, work less with borrowed funds" (line 2707).

Finally, the possible dependence of participation and enthusiasm for the energy project relative to the expected profits is pointed out ("I have my doubts as to whether the enthusiasm of the shareholders will continue even if interest rates change") (line 2442). Overall, however, the criticisms do not indicate that the participants would question the sense of their energy project in the event of a lower return (in some of the projects in the study, lower return values are known, but it is clear that with participant numbers of several hundred or even thousands of people, criticism of lower returns is isolated – thus supporting the participants' own statement that the monetary incentive is only a secondary source of motivation). In this respect, a proposal goes very far, which envisages that at best, only persons who are not primarily pursuing a monetary interest should participate – according to this, participation in a community energy project inevitably includes the fact that returns can fluctuate and the availability of the investment sum is limited, alternatives are admittedly not considered here:: "The cooperatives would have to be examined before entrance a little better. Those who see the whole thing exclusively from the point of view of returns (I also do, by the way) must then also live with the negative aspects (availability of the capital investment, etc.)" (line 238).

Male Dominance The imbalance in gender distribution is present in some projects and is explicitly criticized by female members. On the one hand, the predominance of men is pointed out, on the other hand, an increase in the proportion of women is suggested ("Strongly male-dominated" (line 956), "The proportion of women in the cooperative is far too low. Women in particular should be recruited for the cooperative", line 963).[76]

Acceptance, Ethical and Social Aspects In addition to the characteristic groups formed, there are further statements from participants which can be categorized less clearly. Essentially, these statements can be classified as idealistically ecological and socially democratic motivated criticism, in that fundamental attitudes or orientations of the energy projects are criticized or changes are proposed. This includes first of all the acceptance aspect, in that on the one hand more initiative for acceptance is demanded, and on the other hand integrating and socially compatible behavior and ways of dealing with things are urged. Here, it is exclusively the wind

[76] In Germany, there is one known case of an energy cooperative in which only women are eligible for membership.

energy sector that is affected; the turbines are obviously also sometimes critically assessed by the participants with regard to their aesthetic effects:

> promote more acceptance in the community and the population. (line 1075)
>
> The siting issues would need to be addressed more sensitively and with more lead time for wind farms/solar farms. (line 1101)
>
> More consideration for nature and citizens. (line 817)
>
> One should possibly integrate the affected people (residents where the plant is located) into the cooperative at an earlier stage. (line 2089)
>
> Less landscape blighting. (line 2772)

In addition, the use of biogas is critically questioned by some members, which due to the production conditions and ecological effects, is rather low on the agenda of the participants, as already revealed by another assessment of the energy sources elsewhere:

> Biogas plants require too much maize cultivation the landscape is thereby disfigured and appears monotonous. Wind turbines must only be built in very sparsely populated areas, must not cause noise pollution and have a visual, psychological and physical impact on humans and animals. (line 1167)
>
> Biogas is very damaging to nature, as a lot of arable land is still used. (line 1622)

Questions of regional value creation and the social conditions in the producing countries continue to lead some stakeholders to argue strongly in favor of energy plants that are produced in Germany, as well as in favor of commissioning German companies to build and install the energy plants:

> Please do not buy products in China!!! The overall (environmental) balance is important. (line 1247)
>
> pay more attention to regional added value, use of German products. (line 1258)
>
> Please give preference to German manufacturers for photovoltaics – I don't see why I should continue to support the Chinese policy that is destroying our solar industry! I will also no longer participate in plants with Chinese components – a little less return is acceptable! (line 1625)
>
> No foreign companies should be involved (…) Build a tower of a wind turbine, the rest is carried by foreign companies. I think we should therefore buy everything from Germany. (line 2029)

Finally, there are isolated voices that define (energy) self-sufficiency in their municipality as a goal, and therefore take the community energy project as a realizing actor of this orientation ("more for the self-sufficiency of the municipalities advocate", line 670). In addition, sustainability as a comprehensive approach to life and energy saving are referred to ("Further projects are: – saving energy – developing a sustainable lifestyle", line 2429). This aspect is one of the striking peculiarities of the survey: at first glance, it seems obvious that the use of renewable energies is only one part of a sustainability concept or corresponding idealistic attitude, and that other sustainability topics should therefore be present and addressed by the members. Surprisingly, however, there are rather few indications of this. The information on possible changes in (ecological) lifestyle and effects on behavior with regard to energy consumption tended to indicate a subordinate importance.

Summary: Criticism of Community Energy

Overall, the main criticisms are too little information for members, greater use of the internet, nepotism, and diametrically opposed ideas about the management of the project:

- **More professional management**, public impact and expansion in the form of acquisition of more energy facilities and members, and diagnosis of overstretched volunteers at the limits of their capacity as an impediment to progress.
- **Criticism of professionalization** in the form of profit thinking, economization, loss of closeness to members and drifting away of leadership, participation opportunities within the community energy project de facto not usable, hurdles to entry as well as emphasis on positive aspects and effects of voluntary work.

Obviously, these ideas point to two different modes of operation, according to which a community energy project can be defined in two ways:

- **Community project** with the attributes: small, open to ideas, discursive and creative (broad discussion of the most diverse approaches to action, which can also include lifestyles, behaviors and utopias), participatory-collaborative (e.g. organization of working groups and working or discourse communities such as forums etc.), collaborative, no profit orientation, volunteer management without special competences, no extraordinary growth intended (proximity to nonprofit association).[77]

[77] These forms are represented in the study by small community energy cooperatives (or in the organizational form of a private company (GbR), association or similar), see information at the beginning of the chapter on the definition of the criterion.

- **Business enterprise** with the attributes: large, expansive, professional management in the form of full-time employees with explicit know-how, generation of the highest possible return, concentration on practical, specific issues (e.g. construction of new energy plants, acquisition of new members) and efficient, effective action, presence as a public actor in energy policy, politics and the whole of society, role of members primarily limited to receiving information and notifications, and possibly exercising voting rights without significant personal initiative (proximity to a conventional energy company).[78]

However, the information provided by the participants does not necessarily indicate that critics of small association-like energy projects would like to see a highly professional energy company. In particular, the members want to draw attention to tendencies and wish for other design principles of their community energy project only in parts – after all, the degree of satisfaction of the participants with their energy project is extraordinarily high.

In addition, the participating community energy projects cover a wide variety, ranging from very small, association-like energy projects to large private limited companies. Some members of small projects would like to see a little more professionalism, while participants from larger community energy projects would welcome less formalized, economized and professionalized structures. The demand for more participation and determination or criticism of a lack of opportunities, on the other hand, seems to be a criterion that occurs relatively independently of the different types of community energy projects.

Transparency and information policy appear to be another issue within the community energy projects that is in need of strong criticism: many members criticize this point in their feedback statements. Overall, however, this does not apply to the majority of projects (see 95 percent value for the degree of information above), especially since this aspect is also explicitly praised by some members. Therefore, on the one hand, the impression arises that there are large differences in the information policy of the community energy projects (some projects succeed better in informing the members sufficiently), on the other hand, the members often feel well informed at the time of their participation, but later partly no longer. The newly emerging projects have to attach great importance to good information at the beginning – in order to win members, partly in the case of larger projects, but also because of regulations in the form of the obligation to publish a prospectus. The

[78] These forms are represented in the study by large community energy limited liability companies (or joint-stock companies or cooperatives), see information at the beginning of the chapter for the definition of the criterion.

criticisms now suggest that there seems to be a slackening of the flow of information over time. However, perceptions may also vary: in some cases, members of the same energy project expressed divergent views. Apart from this bias, there could also be more interest from members over time – it seems understandable that concrete knowledge about the whereabouts of the financial investment and the operation of the energy plants is demanded. Some projects provide a pronounced degree of daily information on values, such as the amount of electricity generated. Some provide such information on a monthly basis, the use of homepages on the internet as well as e-mail correspondence (newsletters) is common here – some members explicitly wish this for their project. The virtual possibilities can also be used to open up further subject areas: online discourse with members (forum), voting and surveys, information about activities and events, meetings between members (chat, forum) and multimedia contributions and networking (film contributions, podcasts, links, documentation such as photo galleries, etc.). Even meetings can sometimes be held virtually (see Klappstein 2013 on virtual general meetings in cooperatives). Especially the former forms are suggested by some members. However, the suggestions and thus presumably the actual potential in this area are not strong.

Another point of criticism concerns admission to the community energy project: in some cases, not everyone who is interested can become a member, which can be attributed to various causes (e.g. oversubscription, membership limited to one municipality, high minimum contribution). For the community energy projects there is a central challenge in this respect: On the one hand, there is a demand precisely to enable the local community to become participants in energy plants. On the other hand, the incorporation and thus enlargement of the project can quickly push the often volunteer management to the limits of its capacity. However, restructuring the project into a private enterprise would contradict the initial idealistic goal. For this reason, some energy projects stop the entry of further members. But even in the case of larger energy projects, such as the community energy limited liability companies (GmbHs) and large cooperatives, the participation potential is often limited – this is due to the project planning: if an energy project with certain energy facilities is planned, only a certain number of people should and can participate in it (which is sometimes also related to yield considerations). However, the ideas about the amount of such an equity share differ widely, as was often visible in discussions in the case studies.

Participation and Co-determination The input from community energy members regarding the issues of activity, participation and co-determination concerns the following overarching aspects in total:

- Online participation opportunities and more information
- More member and project activities, opportunities for dialogue and discourse, involvement of members and participation in decision-making
- Boards and committees that proactively include members
- More flexible financial participation instruments

In this respect, it remains questionable which problem-solving and further development potentials can be exploited in the projects, and which potentials exist here. With regard to online participation and the initiation of further activities, good will, commitment and initiating management bodies would be decisive pioneers. But the members themselves are also in demand – one member critically remarks: "Criticism, none, because we could change these points", but at the same time adds: "More participation of the members" (line 1826). This gives the impression that there is a double paradox here: On the one hand, a requirement of active and committed members is formulated, on the other hand, the inclusion of members by the management and committees is urged, without which a climate of participation could not arise. Apparently, only one characteristic is often present, while the other condition is not (committed members with closed leadership and open leadership with little committed members). The initiative of committed members or leadership then regularly reaches its limits.

Ultimately, it remains to be stated that more positive than negative feedback is expressed by the members. It is above all the commitment of the members and initiators, the local and decentralized as well as ecologically sustainable orientation of the energy projects, the transparency and information conveyed, values in the form of responsibility and a sense of community, a democratic attitude, opportunities for co-determination and low entry barriers that the members appreciate about their energy projects. Criticism focuses strongly on a lack of transparency and too little information (over time), on the one hand small size, lack of efficiency and lack of publicity, and on the other hand too little participation and voice, profit-orientation and economic professionalism, and too high financial entry hurdles. With regard to the management, in some cases a volunteering overload is observed, while at the same time in other cases too strong growth at the expense of the member orientation is criticized.

With regard to the external conditions for action, the lack of regional cooperation was criticized, more members were desired, and legal hurdles and a lack of political support were denounced. Other members praised the constructive handling of criticism with regard to internal conditions of action, but on the other hand criticized the questionable selection of participants in the project. The overarching point of criticism is nepotism, the most frequent demand is the use of the internet.

6.5.3 Summary of the Empirical Findings

Participation, Discourse and Co-determination

According to the findings of this study, the members of community energy initiatives would like more communication and information. This assessment is in line with the information provided by the project management.

On the one hand, members of the project leaderships sometimes feel attacked by members, on the other hand, they struggle with the overload of emerging tasks (often in connection with voluntary exercise). The offer of members' participation also leads the leaderships into distress: disclosure, lack of fit (exclusion of delegation) and additional effort in coordination, and agreement with active members lead to increased effort and strain.

Conflicts and escalations can occur at meetings, but usually it remains with this disclosure of critical voices, without further, deeper arguments or concrete consequences following from this. Some leaders want to create more discursive forums, but this is not the case, especially in projects where members are passive. Possibly this also represents a bogus motive: When the offer is created, this does not meet with any response. Therefore, a serious handling of membership matters is of high importance. Other phenomena found are mistrust of the leadership and fear of drifting in the direction of a closed clientele group that keeps to itself. In some cases there is no exchange at all, in which case there is completely passive participation, which is, however, also valued and expected by the target clientele. In other cases, the activity of members within the community was concealed at first glance.

Wind energy projects, on the other hand, gain cohesion and commitment in particular through a joint veto player position vis-à-vis the opponents of wind power. In still other cases, mediators, forums and open spaces of exchange without a formal character are missing. On the other hand, a high level of discourse, deliberation and discussion can lead to low output, dissent and paralyzing action.

An ideal model would presumably consist of constant communication and collaboration between bodies (executive board, supervisory board, management), members and member bodies (working groups, advisory board, thematic groups). Discourse, communication, exchange and deliberation are, with a few exceptions, rather poorly developed, as members and initiators complain in the cases studied.

Nevertheless, in all cases there are places of deliberation, which could be found above all in the members' meetings and citizens' meetings (in the case of wind power use). Here, however, there are also great obstacles, especially due to the formal character, the informal exchange then takes place in small groups without publicity. Of high relevance are therefore the spaces in between, i.e. face-to-face communication, which is roughly bilateral and has only minor communication barriers. Many meetings of the members actually also take place informally, the great deficit is the resulting exclusion, which is why a formalization of these forums seems sensible, which then leads to further strain on the leaders and initiators – yet seems unavoidable.

There were high numbers of participants in the citizens' meetings of the wind power case studies, and written submissions were also actively used. Finally, the main question is what the participation in these cases has led to. Here, above all, a gain in information and the achievement of closeness and trust through exchange are to be emphasized. In particular, the formation of a more realistic, objective picture can be achieved among all participants (enlightenment aspect). However, direct influence on the decisions of political bodies and administrations is often only possible to a limited extent. In the two cases investigated, it was at least possible to limit the height and temporarily shut down the plant. The influence (in terms of output and outcome of participation) is therefore clearly measurable. Nevertheless, the first-mentioned aspects appear to be of greater importance. Thus, the participation seems to have an overall positive impact. This affects less fundamental opponents of wind power, but in all cases an enormous increase in acceptance could be observed. In one case study, wind power opponents even turned into supporters and users of the effects of the energy plants (e.g. visitors, tourism, advertising).

Moreover, it can be considered favorable if possible sites for energy plants are discussed together with the population, since it is precisely the sites – like space and places in general – that are symbolically occupied by the population and associated with certain functions, meanings, and forms of use. In one case, for example, there was a transformation from forestry use to energy use, thus continuing the tradition of use. However, such descriptions of contexts of meaning and perception are more difficult in the case of recreational areas and leisure use.

Participatory Arrangements: Formal Participation Principles First, Informal Practices of Participation Second

Another finding concerns the structure of the participatory arrangements created: the constructions can be described as rather open or closed; if they are designed to be open-inclusive, they can have a legitimation-enhancing effect. While they only make up one piece of the puzzle in the local context, they certainly help shape the image of local, civic engagement culture. The representative potential of the construction is important: access for everyone is more likely to be possible due to low entry fees and simple-intuitive procedures. In addition, already the provision of different subject-bound options is important: at best, everyone can find "their place" in the community, whether more actively or passively shaped. Therefore, the existence of a variety of such offers is crucial and precisely this could be demonstrated on various occasions. In addition, it was also possible to identify constructions that de facto exclude strong member activity. Nevertheless, as a result of the investigation, the fundamental possibility of participation remains decisive, both theoretically and practically. A central problem here remains in the level of information: a lack of knowledge and too little education can lead to little interest among the population. Therefore, openness, transparency and going public are crucial steps for community energy initiatives. Finally, the participation structures themselves can have a strong legitimizing effect: through the factors of proximity, the emergence of discourse and representativeness through inclusion, trust is created in the public, and social capital is built up both internally and externally. The emergence of a positively connoted image of community can then be the consequence for members and the population.

From the findings, a rough categorization of participatory arrangements can be derived, consisting of formal ("hard") participation principles (e.g., legal regulations, organization-specific conditions) as well as informal ("soft") practices of participation (e.g., discourse, decision-making processes, etc.) (see Groddeck and Wilz 2015). The informal criteria are to be assessed as very significant with regard to an evaluation of participatory arrangements. They depend strongly on the individual design by the actors.

Participation in Practice: Diversity of Topics Rather Than a Lack of Issues

A pure labeling of participation in the sense of a postulate without content does not apply to the cases of community energy studied, but the actual possibilities of influence always depend on the respective participatory arrangement. Furthermore, no case is known in the present study in which there are no possibilities whatsoever for exerting influence and taking part in shaping the process. On the other hand, the motivation of the members to participate in shaping has a stronger effect. The assumption that community energy initiatives suffer from a lack of topics could be refuted. More decisive is the question of whether topics and channels of influence are of interest to the participants (keyword: attractiveness of participation). Presumably, the attractiveness can be increased by electronic participation options; participants explicitly express this wish. So far, such instruments seem to be used very little- again, commitment to the establishment and maintenance of such forums must be assumed.

Drawbacks: The Challenge of Avoiding Oligarchy and Solving Conflicts

Like any other civil society association, community energy initiatives are characterized by oligarchic tendencies (see von Blanckenburg 2014 op. cit.). Elected management can increasingly exclude members from influence and participation and shroud their own actions in an obscure background. But the analyzed measure of these tendencies remains average (within the framework of known dominance of individual persons and leadership figures), differences exist from case to case. The decisive factor is controllability, secured by a *checks and balances system,* which can be secured and granted by meetings, votes and additional bodies (supervisory board, advisory board, etc.). A further potential for conflict exists in principle in the relationship between members and committees (e.g. lack of trust, rejection of applications, ignorance), but the extent is also low according to empirical findings.

7 Conclusion: The Essence of Community Energy in Germany

Finally, a special focus should be placed on the specific contexts of democratic processes and modes, as their influence can be considered significant. For the inclusion of citizens, participation, deliberative practices, organizational processes, formation of social capital, etc. all take place at the local level (Roth 1994; Bogumil 1999; Kersting 2004; Mayer 2004; Evers and Roth 2005; van Deth and Tausendpfund 2013; Roth 2013d; pessimistic: Roth 2011d) and emphasize local and intuitive community spirit as a core principle (Wolin 1994; Little 2002; Taylor 2002; Pettit

J. Radtke, *Community Energy in Germany*,
https://doi.org/10.1007/978-3-658-39320-5_7

2008a) as well as the realization of democratic principles in smaller communities and groups (Gastil 1993; List and Pettit 2013).[1]

Finally, Michelsen and Walter formulate a kind of general suspicion of democracy by assuming that participation is instrumentalized: namely, they argue that participation is used and abused by elites (from the state, economy and civil society) to establish legitimacy for planned courses of action and measures (such as in the construction and infrastructure sector) and in this way is used to safeguard measures democratically ("simulation of democracy": Blühdorn 2013 and "participation trap": Wagner 2013; cf. also Miessen 2012; Hoffjann et al. 2013; Merkel 2015b). Here, however, the authors describe a basic dilemma: in essence, a problem is presented here that can hardly be conceptually invalidated. For the danger of instrumentalization described can be inherent in every type, form and application of participation – but whether this is the case, or even more so, whether it can

[1] Basically, local politics is closely linked to civil society, civic engagement and participation of the population (cf. Haus 2002). An active civil society is seen as a prerequisite for a Big Democracy (Trott zu Solz 1999) or Thick Democracy (Barber 1984). Archon Fung assumes a reinvention or rediscovery of local democracy and increased participation (local turn, cf. Fung 2006, combined with a public turn, cf. Mathieu 2005; Farmer 2013). What is striking about these approaches is the fact that the focus is always on the small political level, a local unit or specific sub-areas of state and society, and that here, beyond large framework conditions, it is supposed to form the breeding ground for democracy and the modern welfare state. Cellular democracy, for example, emphasizes a bottom-up structure based on small neighborhood districts that are supposed to solve their problems and assert claims independently (Foldvary 2002). Very close to these ideas is the grassroots approach, which originates above all in the ecological thinking milieu: motivated by environmental destruction, ecological problems and fragmented, meaningless modern societies, local communities are supposed to "grow from below", in that, starting with individual initiative and ending with group formation, forms of collective action are to be balanced out again and again according to the situation (Kaufman and Dilla Alfonso 1997). This way of thinking is again strongly reminiscent of principles of decentralized state building and social action in decentralized units: Known under the terms of subsidiarity (prioritizing the smallest level), devolution (transferring power to smaller units), localism and communalism (cf. critical comments on the democracy-promoting nature of the principle of devolution in Leach 2004). One could therefore also speak of *small-scale democracy* (Oliver et al. 2012). The authors' use of the metaphor of a "hidden" Leviathan (state) is again reminiscent of *Stealth Democracy* (Hibbing and Theiss-Morse 2002) and citizen engagement in the neighborhood.

develop, depends on the circumstances and the way in which participation is practiced in the specific case.[2]

Greven, on the other hand, assumes "deadweight effects" and the "enforcement of certain goals", thus arguing in terms of purely expedient motivation in the sense of patronage politics (Greven 2009: 219). What he misses is "the practical willingness to engage in the expansion of democracy or even against its partial restriction, beyond the pursuit of special interests" (ibid.). Greven sees community initiatives that advocate direct democracy or against surveillance rights, for example, in the minority and takes this as evidence of a lack of civic engagement to democracy – without ulterior motives. On the other hand, he says, such citizens' movements are strong, in which at times a large number of political members of society have represented their own interests with universalist pretensions, be it because of the demanded priority of ecological over short-term economic objectives of politics, be it against the dangers of the use of nuclear power, or be it in the women's movement for more equal rights. Greven wants to sharply distinguish between these two types of civic engagement; he assumes that the "actors of the 'new social movements' have a hybrid, moral self-awareness. In his view, ecological engagement also

[2] Beyond theoretical approaches in the sense of social designs, problems and social issues are discussed and resolved in small units (such as municipalities), which has recently been discussed under the term local governance (Schwalb and Walk 2007; Kersting et al. 2009), also regional governance (Giessen 2010; Böschen et al. 2014) or urban governance (cf. on urban governance and participation Schmidt 2014), thus taking up the governance perspective that has been increasingly discussed in Germany since the 2000s. This describes state action, albeit linked through exchange with civil society associations and business enterprises, which is no longer organized top-down (hierarchies), but is intended to enable horizontal strategies primarily through negotiation processes or market solutions in actor exchange (Benz and Dose 2010; Benz et al. 2012). Obviously, principles such as participation (Papadopoulos 2004; Walk 2008; Braun et al. 2007; Diebäcker 2008), cooperation (Papadopoulos 2003) and creativity (Schwalb 2011) are of great importance in collaborative work and intended joint decision-making. As a result, *soft skills* in the sense of mediation, joint discourse and coordination processes as opposed to purely executive action are increasingly taking center stage; in addition, there is also an increasing importance of (specialist) knowledge and specific competences as prerequisites for access to discourses (cf. Box 1997; Innerarity 2013). Meanwhile, Benjamin Barber (2013) also emphasizes the importance of cities in the 21st century; he speaks of a strengthening of urban communities against the background of increasing denationalization, which seems obvious with regard to the innovative and creative power of cities (cf. Kersting 2017). From a political science perspective, however, there remains a certain contradiction between the poles of size unit and democratic ideal, according to Robert Dahl this is the crucial question of size unit, the *Politics of Scale* (Dahl and Tufte 1973; Dahl 1984; Moss and Newig 2010), a gap between the valorization of the city and marginalized rural areas remains.

pursues self-interested interests: "The selective and temporary political engagement to ecological goals is quite consistent with the liberally interpreted representation of one's own selective interests, notwithstanding its 'universalist' character, which is not doubted here; after all, those who are committed would also have a share in the 'collective good' of a better environment, and it is evident that this is precisely their essential goal and the motivating driving force of their civic engagement. In the political commitment to such 'collective goods', universalism and egoism can easily be reconciled". And it is precisely this that Greven sees as a fundamental difference to a different kind of civic engagement to democratic values as such or to development policy goals. Greven now sees the resulting problem simply in the fact that due to the "small-scale nature", the question segmentation of issues and ideas, even larger social challenges can no longer be solved – small-scale and selective interests have a "narrow horizon". On the one hand, Greven thus assumes "increasing politicization" (ibid.), but on the other hand, the higher-order or superordinate context of meaning is missing – it is primarily the politicized non-citizens who get involved, for whom civic values sui generis are precisely not in the foreground.[3]

In the scientific climate change debate, a debate has recently arisen about the proposal of a "global citizens' movement" by the latest report of the German Advisory Council on Global Change (Wissenschaftlicher Beirat der Bundesregierung Globale Umweltveränderungen, WBGU 2014), which in the view of the Council is necessary to counter the global impacts of climate change. Criticism of the proposal concerns aspects such as eco-dictatorship, denationalized climate policy under neoliberal auspices, Eurocentric and market-compliant solution ideology, and a focus on people from the affluent North (cf. summary and discussion of the criticism in Mittler 2015). This discourse shows, firstly, that increasingly individualistic approaches to solutions are gaining in importance; secondly, the conflict over responsibilities between the market, the state and citizens or civil society; and thirdly, the basic problem of the fixation of educated, informed and materially (predominantly) better-off citizens (or active citizens, engaged citizens, etc., cf. Gabriel 2013a) – and thus an at least a tendency to ignore less (potentially) committed sections of the population. For this reason, Mittler (2015: 231) may also conclude to call for "more movement" and "less citizenship", but this does not change anything about the critical point of the participation bias, even in

[3] Cf. Also the debate about "critical citizens" as an effect of post-democratic-technocratic government, which leads to a critical attitude – between frustration and anger, activity and protest – and thus to a "danger or resource for democracy" Geißel (2011a), Norris (2011), Friedrichs and Lange (2012), Zürn (2013), besides Offe (2006) and MacDonald (2012).

the context of social movements. The idea of a "public entrepreneurship" that transforms the role of the citizen from social/consumer to public/citizen, as Hjorth and Bjerke (2006) argue, therefore seems to be valid only to a limited extent (see also Stein 2015 on civil entrepreneurs).

The citizen in its forms of expression and design is (perhaps surprisingly) still, even more than two hundred years after Rousseau's reflections, the subject of current research and may even be experiencing a renaissance in its attribution of meaning in politics, science and society. Whether a "new citizen" is coming (Brand 2010; Deichmann 2015), the citizen is becoming a partner in cooperative democracy (Foljanty-Jost et al. 2013), or even a changed citizen role in the digital age (Bennett 2008) with "digital active citizen" (Thimm and Bürger 2012) is dawning, the citizen in the roles of bourgeois and active citizen (and beyond) is ever-present[4] in academic discussion – even as citizen roles[5] and civic virtues[6] are constantly debated anew. While from an economic perspective it can be critically questioned whether it is more likely to find "hired hands" or "active citizens" in late modern capitalism (Rosa 2012a), on the other hand a focus on the increasing "digital mediation of politics" (Friedrichsen and Kohn 2015) and its effects of "networked publics" (Varnelis and Baer 2008) can be identified. Civic engagement is also becoming increasingly digitalized (Scammell 2000). Thus, online participation within organizations is becoming increasingly important; the participants in the survey of the present study also emphasize this, for example, and current trends and experiments by political parties further illustrate this (cf. Hanel and Marschall 2012). The idea that technology can serve democracy, even become an integral part of it, as expressed in the metaphor "using technology, building democracy", is obvious here, in that citizenship could be constructed through digital campaigning, for example (Baldwin-Philippi 2015). However, in addition to digital innovations for a digital citizen, serious problems, such as surveillance in the context of participation (Albrechtslund and Lauritsen 2013), may arise in the future with increasingly digital solutions to energy use and control.

Digitalization is accompanied by a further upheaval, which finds expression in the idea of consumer democracy (Lamla 2013): a "farewell to the average con-

[4] Cf. Kocka 1993; McCloskey 2006, 2011; Kocka 2012; Tenfelde 2012; Nida-Rümelin 2013; Moretti 2014; Pállinger 2014; Kocka and Merkel 2015; Poguntke 2015.

[5] See Plasser and Ulram 1993; Meyer 2003; Reis et al. 2005; Saward 2006; van Deth 2007; van Deth et al. 2007; Scherb 2008; Weißeno 2010a; Hanh 2012; Thorson 2012; van der Heijden 2014.

[6] Cf. Münkler 1994, 2000, 2001; Forndran 2003; Lohmann 2003; Pinzani 2003; Münkler and Loll 2005; Leggewie and Sachße 2008; Greffrath 2010.

sumer" (Bala and Müller 2015), which is apparently becoming a new way of seeing and practicing consumer and thus citizen research. This new, creative and multiple consumer (Hohnsträter 2015) can be found in the context of community energy especially in the examples of prosuming or prosumption (Toffler 1980; Blättel-Mink and Hellmann 2010; Hanekop and Wittke 2010; Juntunen 2014; Rifkin 2014; Hellmann 2018), similar to the idea of "product use" (Bruns 2009; Jun 2009). However, few members in the community energy projects presented in this study are also consumers of their self-produced electricity or heat; even fewer are likely to link their energy behavior or even "smart" control of electricity/heat/water consumption to this. Although, for example, actors of the community wind case study in North Rhine-Westphalia express interest in regional electricity marketing, electromobility, energy storage, energy efficiency as well as other renewable energies, the share of actors that already offer or are involved in regional electricity marketing is very low (Landesverband Erneuerbare Energien NRW and World Wind Energy Association 2016: 4).

Since questions of citizenship in the age of technology (Bulut et al. 2013) as well as (value) perceptions of the public with regard to the future design of the energy system in the sense of *Framing* and *Policy Making* (Butler et al. 2015) are becoming increasingly important, a closer examination of the "energy citizen" has also emerged in the meantime.

In this sense, specific citizen roles are described in selected contexts (e.g. sustainability, environment, energy and technology)[7]: Here, far-reaching, complex ideas and theoretical thinking of green citizenship exist (Dean 2001; Dobson 2003; Bell 2004; Smith 2005a; Dobson and Bell 2006; Flynn et al. 2008; Gabrielson 2008; Gabrielson and Parady 2010; Martinsson and Lundqvist 2010; Trachtenberg 2010; Arias-Maldonado 2012; Merritt and Stubbs 2012; Scerri 2012; Scerri and Magee 2012; Luck and Ginanti 2013; Bell 2014; MacGregor 2014) and an "energy

[7] The topic of citizens and technology in a wide variety of ascribed roles between design and protest can be found in the literature, for example, in Thomas Saretzki, who spoke of a "technological citizenship", "democratic compatibility of technology" and the "rediscovery of the citizen" (Saretzki 2001). In the context of energy cooperatives, Flieger (2010) described "energetic citizens"; with regard to engagement in climate protection, von Braunmühl (2011) addressed the ideal of equal citizenship Very specifically elaborated descriptions, considerations and characteristics can be found in Devine-Wright (2007), who explicitly described socio-psychological aspects of "energy citizenship", as well as Seyfang (2005, 2006), who related this specifically to the field of sustainable consumption ("Ecological citizenship and sustainable consumption"). In the field of community energy research, Walker and Cass (2007) also dealt with citizen roles in connection with engagement in community energy initiatives, as did Flynn et al. (2008) in the exemplary case of hydropower use.

citizenship" (cf. Morris 2001; Devine-Wright 2007), for example, in the sense of a "climate citizen" who actively engages in climate protection and environmentally-friendly energy use through individual action (e.g. energy efficiency in the household) and socio-political engagement (measures in local, national and international climate protection, engagement in action groups, organizations or energy cooperatives, etc.) (cf. on this Kreß et al. 2014a, 2014b; Rubik and Kreß 2014; Rubik et al. 2014). In the foreground of these theoretical considerations is often the question of the extent to which social learning, acquisition of knowledge and competencies, etc. take place through engagement and membership in these fields, which on the one hand prepares the citizen cognitively and makes them capable of action in the specific subject area (cf. on this Junginger et al. 2010), but on the other hand also conveys other positive effects such as social forms of action, group learning and democratic competencies. The crucial question here is probably whether individual resources and access to activities are available to each citizen. This raises more or less the same basic problem as with access to socio-political participation. In addition, in this particular case, there is a proximity to financial or also organizational participation, but also via special ways of co-designing in (work/action) groups, in addition via parties and organizations, but above all in the concrete and community-driven as well as issue- and action-related area: e.g. in the use and planning of renewable energies in a municipality. In turn, each approach harbors specific opportunities and risks: in particular, the financial-economic-technological component tends to harbor the danger of one-sided emphasis on and exploitation of, for example, returns under the guise of ecological engagement. On the other hand, this area of engagement represents a unique example of linking a wide variety of thematic and action-specific forms of contribution and engagement: The conscious integration of technical and economic issues can precisely represent an advantage and an upgrading compared to other fields of engagement, also against the backdrop of technocracy discourses (cf. idea of *Do-It-Yourself Citizenship* in Ratto and Boler 2014 and upheaval towards active citizenship in Dalton and Welzel 2014).

Ultimately, it remains questionable to what extent subdivisions within specific civic roles make any sense at all: Is "the citizen" not always a person with different roles, in society, in public, and in private? Can citizens not assume rather different, even contradictory roles in their lives? And even if an ideal of an active citizen, climate or the like should apply, to what extent does it then seem sensible to divide a highly diversified and differentiated citizenry again into fixed, clearly assigned roles? Therefore, a flexible approach to such conceptions of citizenship roles would be appropriate; most likely, certain types could be derived from empirical findings. On the one hand, these derivations would allow for an open framework, but on the other hand, each would be specifically dependent on the study context, which runs counter to any typification. At best, one should refrain from making generalizations that are crude and superficial, such as the type "climate citizen".

As early as 1977, Reinhard Hendler made fundamental observations on citizen participation in urban planning – in doing so, he noted that the precise definition and recording of participation on the one hand, and of those affected on the other, is difficult (Hendler 1977: 5 ff.). He did give a conclusive definition ("Participation is thus, in particular, the direct participation of the citizens concerned or the public in urban planning i.e., outside the general elections to the representative bodies and membership of the political parties. Since urban planning is mostly an administrative activity directed only at a single place at a time, the public (…) is to be understood only as the local public, which, although not exactly, is essentially limited to the entire citizenry of a municipality" (ibid.: 14 f). – but many questions remain open in detail. Hendler is above all certain about an emphasis on the active component of participation – in contrast to assumptions of participation research, which, for example, already classify information as a lower degree of participation: "From the word 'participation' it follows in this context that the public relations work of the municipal administration, insofar as it concerns the pure provision of information to the population, cannot yet be regarded as participation. For here the citizen is only in the role of a consumer; he is largely passive. His activity is limited to the receipt and – as far as this happens at all – the intellectual processing of the information supplied by the administration. It is true that a comprehensive administrative information and enlightenment work, which is imaginative in its technical implementation, is one of the most important prerequisites for an understanding and effective participation of the citizens in the decisions of the public administration, but it is not yet citizen participation itself. This only exists when a procedure is in place which allows the citizens' activity to be aimed directly at the administration with the aim of influencing the content of the decisions to be taken there. In a catchy formula (…): Participation is not given as long as the flow of information moves exclusively from the administration to the citizen, but only when it also takes the opposite direction – from the citizen to the administration" (ibid.: 15). Other forms of definition in this field also emphasize

- "basically **any kind of participation** of people in decisions concerning them" (Behringer 2002: 32);
- a **broad public** that feels affected by a political, social or planning decision (Fürst and Scholles 2008), in the narrower sense two-way or feedback communication between participants and those involved or those granting participation and those participating (Fürst and Scholles 2008; Lüttringhaus 2003), concerns both organized and unorganized publics (Zschocke 2007: 37 f.);

- **communication between citizens and administration**, not just coordination between interdependent actors or cooperation as collaboration between independent actors (Selle 2000; Selle and Beneke 2000);
- citizen participation as a **sub-category of public participation** includes both offering and outreach and activating participation, i.e. various communication channels in the planning process (Zschocke 2007: 37 f.).

According to one study, the prevailing understanding is that "there can only be talk of participation if it is a two-way communication or if co-decision rights are available. Accordingly, informing and other one-sided forms of communication do not represent genuine participation, but merely fulfil an alibi function. Everything else is sham-participation', for example – when decisions made by politics and administration are to be rubber-stamped (…)" (Rau and Zöllner 2011: 14; cf. also Keppler 2010: 6 ff.). In addition, there is the distinction between participation rights and decision-making rights. "Participation rights are the right to be informed (right to information), the right to be heard by the deciding body (right to be heard) and the right to 'put a matter on the agenda' (right of initiative)" (ibid.: 15). According to this, however, it remains open "to what extent the issues and information raised in this context are taken into account by the decision-makers" (ibid.). Decision-making rights would exist if those involved "can participate in the decisions themselves, for example by participating in committees or if a decision can even be taken by the grassroots instead of by political bodies, for example in the context of a citizens' referendum" (ibid.: 15).

Zschocke summarizes the goals of participation as legitimacy, procedural economy, identification and personal responsibility, transparency, acceptance, faster and better implementation, implementation orientation, and identification (Zschocke 2007: 80). A democratic theoretical perspective is summarized by Keppler in the way that "the increasing impact of regional decisions on individuals makes their participation more and more urgent, as people should have the opportunity to co-determine issues of their own quality of life (democratic theoretical minimum requirement). An active participation of citizens in political and social affairs is a necessary prerequisite for the realization of a democratic community and not only a means for the contribution and assertion of interests, but also for the self-realization of people" (Keppler 2010: 14).

In the meantime, however, the role of citizens in the energy transition can already be determined more precisely (Fleischer 2013; Ruddat and Sonnberger 2015: 124 f.). Accordingly, representative surveys show that "in Germany, both the approval of the restructuring of the energy system and the willingness to pay, one's own commitment and acceptance are present to a certain extent" (Ruddat and

Sonnberger 2015: 124). However, there are certain deficits in the areas of trust, autonomous action and fairness. For example, "the political system is perceived as a central steering institution of the energy transition", but trust is low (also towards the large energy companies) and is due to low perceived competence, a lack of fairness and a lack of "good will" ("only half-hearted implementation of the energy transition by politics") (ibid.). With regard to the aspects of autonomous action and freedom of choice, Ruddat and Sonnberger see a close connection with the principle of decentralized energy production, whereby they see the advantages of "personal experience of the energy turnaround", independence from energy corporations and control of this area of life, as well as an "opportunity to raise awareness with regard to the way in which energy can be generated and used" based on the data (ibid.). Fairness is understood to mean an "equal financial burden on industry and private households" in the sense of distributive justice, plus procedural fairness, i.e. procedural justice (ibid.). The overall societal perception of the energy transition is described as a "major societal project" that "should be implemented in a serious, consistent and carefully-planned manner by societal institutions (politics, business, science, citizens) in the sense of sustainable development" (ibid.: 124 f.). However, the authors also draw the evaluative conclusion from the mirror of the research results that significantly more needs to be invested in "trust and credibility (…)" than has been the case to date (ibid.: 125). In the context of the energy transition, knowledge and trust thus play essential roles that can be the starting point for individual courses of action. However, it may be a long way from a pure knowledge economy to an innovative democracy (Stirling 2015b).

This inevitably leads to the requirements of the citizen. Put simply: if they want to participate, what do they need to know and be able to do? To what extent is the well-informed and competent citizen in demand, especially for community energy investments? A particularly high level of resources in the voluntary sector is of course a matter here. The results of the present study show that participants feel very well informed, but many only want to participate financially as silent shareholders and hope for the goodness and quality of the project. Due to this problem of uncertainty for the interested citizen, a certification debate has recently arisen questioning whether certificates should be awarded to energy projects which offer "genuine" citizen participation and not to companies which camouflage dubious financial products under the label of a participatory energy project. In this sense, the Thuringian Ministry for the Environment, Energy and Climate Protection has been certifying "Partners for Fair Wind Energy Thuringia" since 2015. Another approach consists of a legally prescribed participation quota: As a pioneer, the state of Mecklenburg-Western Pomerania has presented the "Draft of a law on the participation of citizens and communities in wind farms in Mecklenburg-Western

Pomerania" (printed matter 6/4568 of 7 October 2015 of the Mecklenburg-Western Pomerania state parliament), which prescribes (financial) citizen participation in newly constructed wind turbines in the amount of 20%.[8]

In the future, however, the design of the Renewable Energy Sources Act will also play an important role for community energy; for years, there have been discussions about future reform (cf. Purkus et al. 2014; Umweltbundesamt 2014; Altrock et al. 2015). A central question here relates to a possible tendering model compared to the previous quota model (cf. Pankow 2014). An envisaged tendering procedure (Kohls and Wustlich 2015; Schulz and Möller 2015) would presumably pose a problem for community energy projects (as they would often not win the tenders), a special consideration of community energy projects in the law would therefore make sense (Hauser et al. 2014), as envisaged in the 2016 Renewable Energy Sources Act (EEG) amendment (BMWi 2016: 10 f.). Actors of the community wind case study in North Rhine-Westphalia estimate the effects of a tendering model for future activities exclusively as "negative" or "very negative" (Landesverband Erneuerbare Energien NRW and World Wind Energy Association

[8] The idea for the law was taken from Denmark, where financial support for associations of local turbine operators and interest groups, compensation payments to property owners for loss of value, and the obligation of operators to offer 20% of the shares to citizens within a 4.5 km radius of the turbine have been legally prescribed since 2009 (Bovet and Lienhoop 2015: 229). Experiences with this are viewed quite critically, according to which opponents of wind turbines are becoming stronger and organizing themselves more professionally; in the case of a few wind energy projects, only very few shares could be sold because local residents strongly opposed the project; compensation payments vary from region to region and provoke lawsuits; it is difficult to understand why compensation cannot also be paid for losses in value caused by other disruptive infrastructures (e.g. landfills) It is difficult for landowners to understand that the amount of compensation depends primarily on the value of the land and not on the intensity of the impact of the wind turbine (ibid.: 229). In addition, there are "wind energy nomads" who acquire land near the turbine simply to be able to buy shares (ibid.). Studies with focus groups would also question the assumption of increased acceptance, especially with regard to the purchase of shares (ibid.: 233). In Denmark, very few residents acquired shares when the project was already rejected in advance (ibid.). From this, the authors conclude, "It becomes clear that the option of economic participation alone does not lead to increased acceptance, but that there is a great need to have a say" (ibid.). They also argue that an increased right to information in the case of economic participation is not a particular advantage because it does not cover the whole planning process and it does not constitute a right to have a say (ibid.). Therefore, regulations are proposed to improve the whole planning process by working towards early public participation and using participatory processes such as planning cells at an early stage (ibid.). Other acceptance enhancing aspects introduced by interviewees relate to the way of operation, in that the promotion of regional operators is desired due to the lack of trust in external investors (ibid). The possibilities of regional use of regionally generated electricity are also viewed positively (ibid.).

2016: 3). In the future, therefore, a change in the use and new development of renewable energy business models will be of great importance for community energy projects (Energieagentur Rheinland-Pfalz and Landesnetzwerk Bürgerenergiegenossenschaften Rheinland-Pfalz 2015; Herbes 2015; Lawson et al. 2016; Ramos et al. 2016; Strupeit and Palm 2016).

However, even if a system such as the one in Thuringia can provide certification of participation offerings for interested citizens, the need for and problem of civic competencies remains. As was shown in the study, it is not only professional and methodological economic and technical knowledge (in the sense of declarative knowledge) that is advantageous, but also in social terms, further skills (social, personal and methodological competences in addition to professional, in the sense of procedural knowledge) are indispensable for active participation in the form of exercising participation rights. In this pre-political sphere of action at the interface between civil society and the economy, democratic competencies and political skills thus also play a significant role in the active participation of citizens (Reinhardt 2004, 2011; Ferris et al. 2005). An overarching political education for sustainable development would therefore be a logical consequence (Ohlmeier and Brunold 2015).

Robert Dahl sees civic competencies (representative of many) as the basis of a functioning democracy (Dahl 1992; cf. also Buchstein 2000; Reinhardt 2004, 2011; Ferris et al. 2005). Here, however, he not only recognizes the problem that the competences do not exist among the vast majority of the population, he also points out that they are usually assigned to a particular political entity or orientation – but today, multiple civic roles exist in manifold collective entities. For example, the energy citizen can simultaneously be a digital citizen on the internet as well as a committed organizational citizen in clubs and associations. The processes of attribution are therefore also likely to be more conglomerate in nature. The access requirements to the different civic roles, on the other hand, always seem to be similar, and resource endowment remains the key to moving away from a passive private role. However, even if the step from private citizen to community practice (Hoffman and High-Pippert 2010) is taken, this may ultimately involve "community versus society" (Gertenbach 2014), the problem of binding social capital. Here it then comes down to reciprocal integration forces, which depend on the sociomoral orientations of civically engaged people (Beetz et al. 2012) and thus touch on issues of political psychology (Zmerli and Feldman 2015). Although participation measures can tend to serve education and thus also promote integration and inclusion processes (Reichert-Garschhammer et al. 2015), there is presumably still a substantial need for research on the interactions and causal effects (also in relation to engagement in the field of ecology, see Perreault et al. 2015; Turner 2015).

7.1 Typology of Participation in Community Energy Projects

Starting from the initial question of how participation through community energy projects can be described and characterized and whether this is a form of political participation (analogous to the idea of political participation in the case of political consumption, cf. Stolle et al. 2004, 2005; Dalton 2008; Strømsnes 2009; Ward 2011; Stolle and Micheletti 2013; Yang et al. 2015; Baringhorst 2016a, 2016b; de Moor 2017), characteristics of the community energy constructs analyzed in the present study are finally summarized and mapped across different typologies.

In order to be able to make an assessment, the newer understanding of political participation according to Jan van Deth (2014a) is taken as a basis. According to this, political participation could be assumed in the case of community energy if certain conditions are met in the context of civil society activities. In the case of individual conditions, it must be decidedly discussed whether these can be determined as given (+) or not given (−):

1. Concrete action (+)
2. Voluntary work (+)
3. Honorary basis (+/−)
4. Place: Political sphere (−)
5. Civil society participation (+)
   5a. Goal: Collaborative problem solving (+/−): Politically motivated?
   5b. Non-political activities: Politically motivated?

In the case of a concrete form of action, van Deth first presupposes the characteristics of voluntary and honorary work (in the sense of "amateurish", i.e. non-professional action). The place or sphere of action must be assigned to the political public sphere. Since this is not the case in the instance of community energy projects shaped by private enterprise and civil society, the existence of a variant of political participation shaped by civil society would come into question if the goal of the action were oriented towards joint problem-solving of public concerns. Even if this is not the case, however, a "non-political" variant of political participation could be considered, as in the case of political consumption, provided – and this is ultimately regarded as a condition for the existence of any form of political participation – that the action is politically motivated by the individual. The concrete classification is thus ultimately made dependent in particular on subjective-individual modes of perception, i.e., how participants characterize their motivation themselves; this would have to be described as political. Therefore, the empirical results of the present study – in addition to the other characteristics described – will be analyzed in more detail with regard to motivational aspects.

First, four dimensions are distinguished for the evaluation of participation through community energy:

1. **Project size, organization and legal form:** Community energy projects can be described either more as a membership community or as a member-representative investment company.
2. **Offering participation options:** Community energy projects can offer varying degrees of co-determination, shared decision-making, member input and collaboration.
3. **Use and design of participatory tools:** Their use by members varies widely between passive participation and active contribution and engagement. Working groups, open forums and events can shape the image of a discursive community (counter-model to silent business operations).
4. **Members' individual definitions of participation:** Member attitudes in terms of role understanding vary between passive stakeholders, participation only within the processes of formal bodies and regular social exchange.

In the following, three dimensions are presented for the determination of action-shaping motivation. The designed representations, analyses and typologies are derived directly from the empirical results.[9] These dimensions are: motivation to found a community energy project (a) (cf. interview data in Sects. 6.2.4 and 6.3.1, survey data in 6.2.3), subjective motivation structure of the members (b) (cf. interview data in Sects. 6.4.1, survey data in 6.2.3 and 6.3.3), and in summary individual arrangements of community energy (cf. interview data in Sect. 6.4.1, survey data in 6.4.2–.6.5.2).

[9] In survey results as well as interview statements, the motivation characteristics "return on investment", "social-ethical", "ecological" and "energy self-sufficiency" were found. For the principle of local community, three characteristics were identified: "regional location", "community organization" and "local community". These characteristics fully merge into the motivational characteristics and types described below. Results of the qualitative and quantitative survey could therefore be interlinked and condensed more strongly and thus ultimately made more valid.

7.1.1 Motivation for Founding a Community Energy Project

In the initial phase of the project, a concrete, initiation-related motivation summarizes the context of origin and the sources of civic engagement with regard to specific goals and purposes: What original action-guiding ideas existed when the community energy project was launched? This motivation is also structurally and contextually shaped, as the impetus for the project can come from other spheres of action, for example. Different contextual spheres can be derived from the results of the study, from which community energy projects can arise. Basically, on the one hand, a context predominantly shaped by the actions of individuals can be found, which, starting from a bottom-up activity (action idea of individual citizens), builds up a top-down mode of participation (founding a community energy project and creating a participation opportunity for other citizens) (possible groups of people: young professional entrepreneurs, older ecologically motivated persons, technology-savvy persons and politically-ethically motivated Local Agenda/community groups). On the other hand, there may be a strongly organized collective context that, starting from top-down initiatives, relies on bottom-up activities of associatively involved persons (as possible groups of actors: Workforce, trade union, tenants' association, and club/association background).

1. ***New field of civic engagement: from private to public sphere or organizational participation***
   (a) **(Young) Professionals:** Young entrepreneurs (engineers, technicians, business professionals, singularly motivated persons) found community energy projects. This can be motivated by individual initiative or driven by ambitions for a business start-up. This type of initiation is represented by younger people without a local tradition-oriented background or ecologically influenced socialization. There is no strong ethical or moral motivation. The engagement is based on a weak political will. The initiators act independently in their own interest. Overall, this type follows an unconventional *grassroots character* with a top-down mode of participation.
   (b) **Local-individualistic engagement:** An individual commitment for local benefit, which simply means campaigning and is hardly based on political motivation. The focus and idealistic core of this type of engagement is based on a simple local kind of action without including a community driven motivation or orientation. This is why *grassroots activity* exists, but is usually combined with individual initiation in a top-down mode of

participation, however this is not the typical route of civic engagement movements.

2. ***Extended scope of civic engagement: public or organizational engagement creating additional civic engagement***
   (a) **Local politics:** The origins of this type of community energy engagement, which is often influenced by local politics, lie in communally active groups such as Local Agenda groups, associations or community initiatives. In the tradition of civic engagement and grassroots movements, community energy shapes an additional type of community engagement. This includes a specific *grassroots character* of community energy, which is, however, based on a vertical hierarchy within local politics and the community energy projects.
   (b) **Organization:** Through involvement within a civil society association or organization (club, association, workforce, etc.) or a private company, an opportunity of participation is created exclusively for involved members. The motivation is usually based on a social matter (e.g. improvement of conditions at the workplace). On the one hand, a bottom-up movement can arise from committed members through founding a community energy project, on the other hand, a top-down mode of participation is also possible through the initiation of management or committees; in either case, it is a closed-shop construction without opportunities for participation for non-members.
   (c) **Protest:** In this case, there is a strong, traditional attachment to environmental social counter-movements, such as the anti-nuclear movement in Germany. Strong ethical and moral motivation and political attitudes as well as mainly fragmented organizational structures characterize the engagement frameworks within these social movements. Links to traditions in the field of cooperatives and solidarity-based economy represented through other social movements are possible. Social movements in this field of civic engagement have mostly a *grassroots* character, however, informal top-down decision making within the leadership and administration of the initiatives or projects is possible.

Discussion

The overview makes it clear that, on the one hand, there can be spillover commitment based on local civic engagement, and on the other hand, organizational initiation is possible by addressing members of associations and organizations. In addition, individually driven initiatives with strongly individualistic motives can be found; social-ethical commitment of younger people can also be considered here.

The empirical findings suggest that the second mode prevails overall in all the cases analyzed. Accordingly, the finding according to "engagement generates engagement" seems to be true in the case of community energy. However, newly emerged fields of engagement in the form of change of activities of the engaged or complete reorientation of persons are remarkable, which implies a high degree of risk-taking and daring.

Interestingly, community energy is also a product of existing local engagement. After many years of consultation and deliberation, practical measures should follow in such cases, resulting in community energy projects. Community energy is thus an ideal field of activity in these civic engagement contexts such as Local Agenda groups, environmentally motivated local or community working groups, environmental associations or clubs. Goals should be manageable and realistic, and they should be achievable with existing manpower and volunteer work, serving the common good and supporting the local community. In addition, the activity should be tangible, i.e., it should be experienceable and discernible; the benefits should be directly perceptible and tangible. The emphasis on information boards about electricity generation is an example of this. In addition, there should be a time limit and a sense of achievement in that something tangible can be concretely realized.

Finally, the question arises as to when the civic engagement declines again. This is difficult to prove within the framework of the present study because the phenomenon of community energy is still very young. But possible tendencies can be inferred from various motives, such as overexertion or disappointment. However, frustrated members often stay with the community energy projects because of the organizational commitment, in contrast to public participation processes. Follow-up effects of public participation in the form of citizens' forums, as in the case of Local Agenda 21, can, however, also develop long-term commitment in the field of community energy, among other things. Local contextual conditions are therefore decisive; the environment of community energy projects can have a favorable effect through numerous, active civil society initiatives and associations, social movements and climate protection programs; in the other case, it can also reinforce negative tendencies (such as feelings of being overwhelmed, senselessness, helplessness and lone-wolfism) due to a lack of support and a lack of a sphere of trust.[10]

[10] In participation research, various references are made to the considerable influence of the local context: "What a number of the cases in this book show is that in such contexts, the introduction of new political practices, new spaces for the articulation of concerns and interests, and new opportunities for political apprenticeship can begin a process of change that may have broader ripple effects. They point to shifts that have begun to reconfigure democratic engagement" (Cornwall and Coelho 2007: 22).

7.1.2 Subjective Motivation Structure of the Members

In the following, different types of participation can be distinguished based on the different motivations and attitudes of the members. The typology is based on subgroups of participants, weighted according to the criteria of motivation, activity and definition of participation and member role (cf. Sections on survey data 6.2.3 and 6.5). Three overarching main groups of predominant motivation and activity can be distinguished, which can be found in all community energy projects:

1. **Ecological**
   - *Central motive for participation*: contribution to the energy transition and ecological climate protection motive.
   - *Participation within the community*: only of secondary importance.
   - *Individual definition of community energy*: primary focus on decentralized renewable energy generation.
   - *Distribution*: Largest group among the community energy participants, especially represented by members in larger and supra-regionally acting community energy projects, which offer a wide range of participation options, e.g. through large environmental organizations.
2. **Structural**
   - *Central motive for participation*: strongly varying motives.
   - *Participation within the community*: Influence only takes place in the case of far-reaching decisions. Other activities are seen as disruptive, unless they serve as a positive image in public or in the recruitment of members.
   - *Individual definition of community energy*: practicality and professional management.
   - *Distribution*: This type is represented in all community energy projects. Members of this type have a higher level of education and income.
3. **Investment**
   - *Central motive for participation*: financial incentives.
   - *Participation within the community*: little interest or rejection of participation offers. Indifferent attitude towards community activities.
   - *Individual definition of community energy*: efficiency, effectiveness, maximum return on investment.
   - *Distribution*: to be found within all community energy projects.

Building on the different contexts of origin described above, three further types of individual commitment motivation can be classified, which emerge in particular from the qualitative survey data (cf. 6.5.2) and interview statements (cf. 6.4, 6.5):

4. **Political and idealistic**

A first source of motivation goes back to political-idealistic attitudes, which can include a broad spectrum of social-ecological to liberal-individualistic value patterns. Often, a social-ethical-collaborative motivation (keyword: cooperative basic idea) or ecological-idealistic attitude (keyword: climate protection) can be found in community energy projects. In addition, however, there is also a communally influenced view based on conservative values. This civic engagement is often accompanied by strong activity in internal committees and a general interest in deliberation, contributing ideas and discourse.

5. **Pragmatic and action-oriented**

The second type of motivation involves a pragmatic, action-oriented way of thinking, which is characterized by project-related principles and feasibility considerations. This commitment can either be based on individual profit-oriented thinking or be entrepreneurial and economically motivated, but can also have a technocratic-pragmatic character (belief in technology). This type has no increased interest in discourse and deliberation; committee work is based primarily on efficiency criteria.

6. **Communicative and sense of community**

A third motivation can arise from interests in communicative and communal ways for living together in local communities. Here, the focus is on experiencing community, joint events, adventures and communicative exchange. Discursive activities are therefore supported, a content-related or thematic reference can sometimes be missing.

Particularly from the interview data (cf. Sect. 6.2), three further overarching subjective motivation factors can be formed which, in addition to the concrete-material motivations already described from the survey data (e.g. return on investment), also relate to ideational-abstract motivations (e.g. ecology, common good).[11] These consist of an attitude oriented towards self-sufficiency (a), a discursive attitude towards participation practice (b) and an associative attitude (c). The first source of motivation is found above all in locally anchored energy projects that are strongly supported by engaged local authorities and communities in climate protection (action-guiding idea of decentralized energy generation, e.g. 100% renewable energy regions).

The second motive is the assumption of being able to exert influence on decisions regarding energy supply through financial participation. Options for participation, opportunities for exchange and joint decision-making are basic prerequisites that are demanded for this. People with this attitude often have a high level of education and are primarily involved in energy cooperatives. The motivation is often linked to an ecological attitude.

A third source of impetus can come from civic engagement or membership of a civil society association or organization. By initiating an activity of the organization in the field of renewable energy, participation of the members in the targeted energy project becomes very likely. This energy participation project will then not be separated but perceived as part of the organization's commitment. Demands for a say and participation in the energy project can then be much less pronounced as a result.

In the literature, a similar typology has already been developed for energy cooperatives.[12] Here, four cluster types of energy cooperatives are distributed in relatively equal percentages. A percentage distribution of the types presented here is not undertaken, as this cannot be depicted by the empirical data. In comparison to the four energy cooperative clusters designed by Volz, two points should be noted:

Probably the most pronounced type exists in the "Ecological". The typology of Volz (2011a, 2012a, 2012b) underpins this: here, too, the characteristic "ecological sustainability" represents the overall strongly weighted value within all clusters.[13] In the present study, there is much to suggest that this type is also pronounced in all social models. It thus represents an overarching main motivation, which corresponds

[11] In the literature, a similar distinction is made between global motives (climate protection, ecology) and local motives (individual contribution, support of the region, local benefits, use of local resources) (Rogers et al. 2008: 4222). In addition, social motives (support for the local community, role model character, education), ecological/environmental motives (environmental protection for future generations, resource savings) and economic drivers (regional value creation, financial advantages for the local population, creation of local employment, benefits) are cited, which are also understood here as overriding ideal motives.

[12] Cf. Tthe typology of Volz (2011a, 2012a), presented on p. 195.

[13] See similar results in Bauwens 2014b, 2016; Leuphana University Lüneburg and Nestle 2014; Kreß et al. 2014b; Rubik et al. 2014.

to the motivation statement of over 90% with regard to ecological motives. Here, however, the motive falls less strongly on the cooperatives. Especially in the investment-oriented forms of participation such as profit participation rights, loans or similar, the main motivation is probably ecological energy production; other reasons, which are represented in the remaining types, are of secondary importance here. Thus, this type is also likely to account for the largest share in terms of the number of participants in the present study. While this characteristic represents a basic constant in all types, it is supplemented by two further types of "structural conservatives" and "investors". These are also found in all forms of participation but are probably less strongly represented because the motives were weighted less.

There are three basic motives in this typology, of which the ecological factor is outstanding. However, the community energy projects (case studies) examined here, which are differentiated according to legal and organizational form, are characterized to a greater or lesser extent by a number of outstanding features, which can be described as follows:

- **Ecological motivation** (e.g. climate protection, sustainability): Cooperatives (primarily in the community solar sector)
- **Energy self-sufficient motivation** (self-sufficiency, regional value creation): Community wind farms (legal forms: Limited liability company and partnership (GmbH & Co. KG), cooperative)
- **Loyalty to association motivation** (as result of a commitment beyond usual membership of an environmental organization): Participation offers of environmental associations in spin-off community energy projects (legal forms: limited liability company (GmbH), registered association (e. V.), mainly including profit participation rights, investment option, loan)

The basic subjective, action-guiding motivations based on the case study analyses can be supplemented by actor-related and project-oriented ideas, which are differentiated here under the principles of "local community" and "action radius". The action-guiding principle "local community" can be found in the form of the approach "regional localization" in case study 1, where a new, transformed local identity is attributed to the constructed wind farm at this location, in the sense of a "place attachment" and "place identity". The principle of "community organization" can be demonstrated through community initiative and organization in case study 2, where efforts of the citizens` initiative movement led to an integration of the energy project into the village-community. Similarly, in case study 6, where the energy project is a follow-up action (spin-off) to a civic Local Agenda group. Another principle found concerns the radius of action of the project: this can be rather delimited-closed (as in the case of an employee cooperative, case study 4) or expansive (example: citizens' geothermal community energy initiative in case study 7 and supra-regionally oriented energy cooperative in case study 8).

Principle of "Action-Guiding Motivation"

(a) Social-ethical (case study 3)
(b) Ecological (case study 5)
(c) Energy self-sufficiency (case study 7)

Principle of "Local Community"

(a) Regional location (case study 1)
(b) Community organization (case study 2)
(c) Local community (case study 6)

Principle "Radius of Action"

(a) Closed shop: Employee cooperative (case study B 4)
(b) Open shop: Strong cooperation with local implementation partners (case study 8)

Finally, the analyzed subjective motivation structures can be linked to the contexts and previously analyzed initial motivations of the community energy projects. This results in an interesting overall picture, as certain subjective motivations correlate with actor-related driving forces (e.g.: subjective energy-in-citizens' hands motivation with actor-related regional location motivation in the case of community wind farms, subjective ecology motivation with associative association motivation in the case of environmental association energy projects). This shows a close link between individualistic and collective demands and motivations, which is of interest for the assessment of participation in community energy initiatives – obviously, a separation of purely individualistic motivation from project-related driving forces cannot be made or would contradict the closely interwoven relationships found.

TYPE A: Regional Context – Local Identity – Community Energy as a Result of Place Attachment and Place Identity

- *Characteristics:* Regionally anchored and positioned energy project; participation option primarily for locally resident citizens ("by local citizens for local citizens"). Locally oriented motivation (emphasis on regional value creation and citizen initiation), in addition: safe investment motivation and energy self-sufficiency motivation.

- *Examples from the empirical study:* case study 1 (community wind farm), case study 6 (rural solar cooperative), case study 7 (citizens' geothermal community energy initiative).
- *Example 1:* The community wind farm (case study 1) is an example of a project that focuses on local place attachment and identity: The community wind farm is to be a regional wind energy project, which is to serve the local production of electricity for the local population and offers participation options especially for the local community.
- *Specifics:* Integration into the local community: idea of wind power as local enrichment promoting place attachment and place identity, great regional advantage, emphasis on the technical aspect (parallel case studies 5 and 7). Participation was no longer possible after the initial participation phase. The project is based on volunteering activities.
- *Example 2:* The rural community solar cooperative (case study 6) is strongly influenced by the Local Agenda 21 background, the focus is on the local place, the citizens primarily wanted to achieve something for their community through the implementation of the community energy project, it is highly a pure "citizen project": initiated by citizens, for the benefit of other citizens and the community.
- *Specifics:* Emergence from local engagement, emphasis on community action for the local community, open character, little member engagement beyond that. Participation open, low entry threshold. The project is not based on volunteering activities.
- *Example 3:* The citizens' geothermal community energy initiative (case study 7) is characterized by the idea of self-sufficiency, the independence of the heat supply from large energy companies plays a crucial role, similar to case study 6, it should also be a locally situated project that should primarily serve the local community.
- *Specifics:* Emergence from local engagement, emphasis on local engagement and the idea of technology (parallel case studies 1 and 5), fragmentation into managing GmbH and a corresponding, dialogue-oriented and more open group of active citizens. Participation is not yet possible for interested persons. The project is based on volunteering activities.

TYPE B: Associative Context – Community Energy as a Spin-Off Project

- *Characteristics:* Employee project or initiation by environmental associations, clubs, working groups. Frequently, the participants are motivated by a desire to secure a financial investment.
- *Examples from the empirical study:* Case study 4 (employee community solar cooperative), case study 5 (environmental association community solar project).
- *Example 1:* The employee cooperative (case study 4) represents a closed, exclusive project, a kind of "gated community", as only members of the university can become members of the energy cooperative. The formation of working groups resulted in a high degree of members` collaboration.
- *Specifics*: Closed community only for members of the institution, strong emphasis on acquiring benefits for volunteering persons, highly collaborative structures (very active working groups). Participation and inputs from members are possible on an individual level. Participation is open to all interested persons, but only short participation phase. The project is based on volunteering activities.
- *Example 2:* The environmental association community solar project (case study 5) is strongly ecologically motivated, since the participants are mostly members of an environmental association or have strong ties with it and invest in the PV projects primarily for ecological reasons. The form of participation is a passive investment, there are no meetings, options for co-determination or collaboration.
- *Specifics:* Closed shop, purely return-oriented project, emphasis on the practicability of renewable energy production (parallel between case studies 1 and 7) and the ecological idea. Participation is open to all interested persons, but only short participation phase. The project is not based on volunteering activities.

TYPE C: Professional Orientation – Community Energy as an Energy Company

- *Characteristics:* Supra-regional energy project, open for participation of citizens without local connection, mainly "safe money" and financial investment motivation for the participants.
- *Example from the empirical study:* Case study 8 (Supra-regional community energy cooperative).
- *Example 1:* The supra-regional community energy cooperative (case study 8) is the only supra-regional community energy project in this study. Due to the full-time and professionally acting board of directors, it shows parallels to the com-

munity wind case studies. This "young entrepreneurial" start-up energy cooperative is also characterized by its creative approach, in that the participating citizens become direct owners of the PV modules, which enables a very flexible course of action.
- *Specifics:* No local anchoring, focus on urban context, implementation of a business idea. Emphasis on the central project idea (orientation towards urban space), project realization in the foreground. Low entry threshold. Participation is open to all interested persons. The project is not based on volunteering activities.

TYPE D: Idealistic Orientation – Socially and Ecologically Driven Community Energy

- *Characteristics:* Idealistic and cosmopolitan motivation (ecological principle, social-ethical standards, idea of One World), collaboration of the members, predominant ecological and sustainability motivation (climate change, environmentally friendly energy production) among the participants, alongside social-ethical motivation (social effects through financial participation opportunities for the population).
- *Examples from the empirical study:* Case study 2 (community wind energy cooperative), Case study 3 (urban community solar cooperative).
- *Example 1:* The community wind energy cooperative (case study 2) represents a jointly organized energy project: as many citizens as possible in the proximity of the wind turbine should participate in the energy cooperative and thus become an energy project of all citizens.
- *Specifics:* Attempt at participation for all people, low entry threshold, broad anchoring in local community. Participation is open to all interested persons. The project is based on volunteering activities.
- *Example 2:* The urban community solar cooperative (case study 3) has a strong social-ethical motivation: By participating in the community energy project, not only green electricity should be produced, but also a benefit should spill over to other social projects – this social added value is a crucial effect of this approach. The project is linked to a cultural center and has a strong culture of discussion.
- *Specifics:* Parts of the profits flow into social projects, low entry threshold, idealistic aspects in the foreground. Participation is open to all interested persons. The project is based on volunteering activities.

7.1.3 From Pioneer Idea to Practice: Individual Arrangements of Community Energy Projects

In the following, several criteria are used to characterize community energy project in summary form. Here, very different ideas of democracy and participation of the participants, based on interview data (cf. 6.2.8) and survey data (cf. 6.2.10), are typologized. It becomes apparent that there can be considerable differences between community energy projects, especially in the form of deviations both between content-related and structural characteristics at the organizational level, as well as at the level of (majority found) motivations and attributions of the members.

Size of the Community Energy Project and Legal Form The main difference is between smaller energy projects, which can offer more co-determination and a higher level of activity and involvement of the members, and larger community energy investment companies, where co-determination is hardly possible and there is little activity of its members. The members of energy cooperatives and community wind farms perceive the energy project more in their role as shareholders (direct participation as part of the enterprise), while for passive participants the community energy project is more an independent, public actor, which is supposed to represent the members' interests (representative participation model).

Community energy project as a representative actor and the outcome of participation

Cooperative and collaborative	Partially collaborative	Focus on formal bodies	Exclusion of informal participation	Blockade
◀··				
························▶				
⊖		⊙		⊕

Use and Demand of Participation and Co-determination The participants understand and evaluate their way of individual participation in the community energy projects very differently:

- Participation in renewable energies: financial investment, contribution to climate protection, joint decision-making, privileged member of a community energy project.

- Expectations of membership: silent partners or active involvement in the community energy project, individual contribution of members to issues, sense of community.

Community energy participation and democracy as personal involvement and co-determination

Rejection	Neutral	Active use	Demand for extension
◀…………………………………………………………………………			
……………………▶			
⊖	⊙		⊕

Evolving Activities The individual role of membership is also interpreted differently by the participants – it can range from a negative or critical attitude towards any activity and participation, to limited perception, acceptance and tolerance of third-party activities, and up to a strong social formation and support of community projects, contacts, exchange and forms of cooperation and collaboration.

Members` activity in community energy projects as collaboration and co-creation

Rejection	Business	Topic related	Accepted	Community spirit	Social togetherness
◀…………………………………………………………………………					
……………………▶					
⊖			⊙		⊕

Motivation The motives for joining or becoming a member of a community energy project can vary from purely financial profit expectations to an undifferentiated, vague attitude (no predominant, but unintentional cause of motivation) to a strongly idealistic motivation based on overarching objectives (environment, common good and public spirit, sustainability, intergenerational justice, climate and energy justice, etc.). The motivational tendencies presented in the results of the study show that financial motivation leads to less activity and participation in the community energy projects (however not necessarily); idealistic, but also undifferentiated motivation can provide a basis for active membership. Presumably, very strong ideational motivation can lead to increased personal frustration over time, which is why the activity level can drop again over time.

Members' motivation as an incentive for participation and involvement in community energy projects

Mostly financial	Unspecified	Mostly idealistic
◀..		
........................▶		
⊖	⊙	⊕

Definition of Participation Based on the previous outlined aspects, overarching individual attributions of members' roles can be summarized. Silent partnership denotes a situation where uninvolved participation goes hand in hand with a lack of idealistic motivation and whereby motivation is strongly connected to specific expectations regarding the community energy project. Highly idealistic participation motivation (e.g. environmental protection) and the acquisition of ecological financial investments can be individually harmonized. A very active role through membership, on the other hand, is often connected to idealistic motivation in terms of hopes for building a social community and bringing about benefits through social exchange. In addition, between these poles there are less aspirations and expectations charged with high motivations, which is reflected in moderate activity (regularly within the scope of formal procedures, in individual cases also deviating for a limited period, e.g. in the case of a personal involvement); where motivation is not primarily focused on one specific purpose and both financial and idealistic motives can be identified.

Members' individual definitions of participation in community energy projects

Silent partnership (without idealistic motivation)	Moderate activity (and idealistic motivation)	Active role (with high idealistic motivation)
◀..		
........................▶		
⊖	⊙	⊕

7.1.4 Characteristics of a New Form of Participation Through Community Energy

The core of this thesis was to investigate the question of how participation can be defined in the context of community energy and renewable energies and how it can be scientifically classified. The investigation has revealed different forms of participation in the organizational, social and political context, as well as a heterogeneous sphere of action of the actors between economic, civil and political-public spheres of society.

Community energy projects are basically an example of an essentially economic activity that is very strongly linked to social and political spheres of society and subject areas.[14] On a societal-collective level, there may be differences in the assessment of a community energy enterprise (as Holstenkamp and Degenhart 2013 suggest to only assume a public welfare-oriented and thus genuine community energy enterprise if there are high citizen shares, voluntary work and rather nonprofit orientation, etc.) – on the individual level of the engaged citizens, this is less decisive, since the citizen is financially involved in any case and can participate in further public discourses (the questions of political and social participation on this level are thus a question of option). However, in the internal sphere – organizational participation – this question again plays a major role in procedural terms in the way the community energy enterprise is designed to be open, inclusive, collaborative and transparent.

In the literature, political and social or civic participation concepts are increasingly understood in an integrative way, the inclusion of aspects of social participation leads to a steady expansion of the concept of political participation, which can be attributed to the broad interpretation of the concept of the political (cf. recent, expanded ways of defining political participation in Zukin et al. 2006; Dalton 2008; Whiteley 2012; Fox 2013; van Deth 2014a, 2015). Thus, organizational participation can also be integrated into this sphere as an internal principle. However, at the same time, the concept of political participation is becoming increasingly blurred; it is also difficult to distinguish between the other forms of participation. Since political participation is broadly defined today, a local energy discourse would be included (e.g. erection of a wind turbine). Community energy projects are here on a threshold between financial, civil society and political participation; thus, extended inclusion and legitimacy can be generated via a connected local

[14] See also similar results in Bauwens 2014b, 2016; Leuphana University Lüneburg and Nestle 2014; Kreß et al. 2014b; Rubik et al. 2014. Cf. Characterization of the participation modes of community energy in Walker and Devine-Wright 2008; Walker et al. 2011; Holstenkamp and Degenhart 2013; Kreß et al. 2014a, 2014b; Rubik et al. 2014; Rubik and Kreß 2014. – See further for analogy to forms of participation in the field of sustainable consumption Stolle et al. 2004, 2005; Klintman 2009; Micheletti and McFarland 2011; Baringhorst 2012b, 2012c; Micheletti et al. 2012; Stolle and Micheletti 2013; Yang and Baringhorst 2014; Weller 2014; Rückert-John and Schäfer 2015; Baringhorst 2016a, 2016b.

discourse; the forms of participation can then hardly be considered separately from one another.

Social participation (here understood individually on a micro level: Involvement of the subject in various public/semi-public or private discourses, procedures, processes) can arise within community energy projects on the one hand and outside of the energy projects as a side effect of political participation in the broader sense on the other hand (associatively on the meso level through involvement of the actor in public-political discourses and procedures), e.g. in participation within the framework of public planning procedures.

In summary, community energy projects offer organizational as well as social participation within the communities. Social and political forms of participation can be mixed, however, if, for example, in the case of wind power planning, the community energy project participates as an actor in the public participation procedures and thus participates directly in the public-political decision-making and exchange process. However, this would describe an indirect mode of political participation, since as a rule some members (e.g. the board) are likely to represent the energy project.

First of all, three basic forms of participation by community energy projects can be distinguished in summary:

Financial, economic and material participation:
through financial shares, material benefits, partnership and entrepreneurship.

Civil society and organizational participation:
through co-determination via participation in decision-making (voting rights, election, assemblies, discussion, inclusion of ideas) as well as involvement in the local public sphere, energy governance, policy and politics, decision-making processes and cooperation in regional actor networks to impact on climate protection.

Cultural and social participation:
Through joint events, collaborative practices, community spirit and social exchange.

Participation within the framework of community energy projects can thus be thought of and defined both politically (in discursive participation procedures as well as through the action of community energy projects in local discourses and publics), and socially in the form of civic engagement as a source of community energy or organizationally (internal participation, involvement and co-determination of members). Presumably, the small-scale nature of some projects without inclusion in actor networks or external spillover effects is still an asset to local democracy and community. Robert Putnam's social capital thesis would confirm this assumption. The counter thesis of the CID[15] studies would assume that civic engagement does not spill over into public and political action. In this field, overspill civic engagement can be assumed, as ultimately energy policy issues and other meta-issues (ecology, sustainability, justice) are touched upon and find their way into the discourses of local publics (see, for example, Cox 2012). The survey results clearly demonstrate this spillover, as respondents indicated that they have become more interested in participation and community projects since the time of their involvement. Community energy projects can thus provide an entry point into socio-political engagement and insertion into discourses. At the same time, the individual behavioral level is much less affected.

In the community energy projects, however, there occurs also a problem of social inclusion and exclusion tendencies. The standard socio-economic explanation applies here, but with explicit exceptions. This is because population groups without an academic level of education are also integrated (the proportion of non-academics is 43%), although the academic level and the income level are very unequally distributed in contrast to the population as a whole. In terms of democratic theory, this represents the most significant deficit for community energy projects (lack of input legitimacy, insufficient creation of equality in access and use of participation options and rights).

Interestingly, although online communication is widespread (as an information pool for energy yields, notifications of events, meetings, etc.), community energy projects are essentially typical offline organizations. They thrive on face-to-face exchanges at events and meetings; real contact is precisely what makes them attractive to the local population. Many citizens also participate because of the community spirit they experience in the form of collective events.

Although community energy projects use various forms of collaboration and participation (working groups, meetings, voting, etc.), these are within familiar conventional formats. At this point, one of the central challenges for community energy projects arises: the establishment of balance and integration between formal forums (general meetings, etc.) and informal exchange forums (discussion groups, etc.). According to the available results, many community energy projects would like to establish more discursive forums, but at the same time there is a lack of concrete intentions for action. The citizen associations apparently do not want to exist out of pure business activity, but are unsure how to build and establish

[15] Research network "Citizenship, Involvement, Democracy".

discursive formats. An explicit desire, according to the results, is not strong.[16] Thus, in the end, not much would remain of the often highly ambitious aspirations at the beginning of the community energy initiative's founding (which usually go far beyond pure plant operation). On the other hand, concrete interest could still be aroused by those involved. A link with public formats such as Local Agenda groups, energy working groups and climate protection initiatives could have a double positive effect in terms of casual discourse and exchange with non-involved citizens. But the commitment resources are often exhausted with the establishment of the community energy project. There is no strength left to promote further formats, so it remains a silent wish and hope for the future.

Discussion: Political Participation as an Exceptional Phenomenon of Community Energy?

For a final evaluation of participation in community energy projects, the most important findings from empirical data and analyses can be summarized as follows:

- **Social structure and socio-demographics of community energy projects:** The majority of participants are higher income groups and highly educated classes. The ideal of integrating all sections of the population is not achieved, or is achieved only in individual cases; cooperatives in particular integrate socially weak milieus to a greater extent. The members are mainly people who are committed to social policy; it is hardly possible to include people who are not committed.
- **Members` participation:** Does not take place to a high degree, but opportunities and topics for diverse forms of involvement exist. People with low incomes and high participation sums participate more strongly, hence a possible dichotomy: participants with high sums and at the same time little interest in exchange

[16] This corresponds to the findings of the Volunteer Survey, according to which the "sociable-oriented" group, which was still very strong in 1999, regressed to become the weakest group alongside the "common good-oriented" and "interest-oriented" groups (Gensicke and Geiss 2010: 124). According to this, common good-oriented and interest-oriented issues have received a big boost in their importance in the context of civic engagement, which would include the phenomenon of community energy (keywords climate protection and communitarian-pragmatic problem solving) itself: "The big surprise of the decade, however, is that this particularly benefited the group of the common good-oriented. The group that places a particularly strong emphasis on the "we" and a lesser emphasis on the "I" in its commitment is thus the winner of the subjective changes of the first decade of the Volunteer Survey" (ibid.) (cf. also Gensicke and Geiss 2015).

and participants with low sums and high interest in social exchange and togetherness.

- **Effects of participation:** More interest in public participation in society as a whole is generated, but little individual behavior change occurs. One reason for this is that many participating citizens have already developed an energy-saving lifestyle before the time of their participation in the community energy project[17]; community energy participation can then be understood as an outflow form of precisely this ecological lifestyle. Other study results show that there are significant differences in the environmental behavior of members of energy cooperatives compared to non-members, but these relate primarily to the consumption of organic food, conversations with acquaintances about environmental problems, and information gathering on environmental problems (Rauschmayer et al. 2015: 10). Even from these data, firstly, it cannot be concluded that community energy members make significant changes in their en-

[17] Cf. Results of a survey in Heidelberg by Kreß et al. (2014b: 11 f.): "The results of the questionnaire survey show that the citizens of Heidelberg think it is important "that our society does something to ensure that industrialized countries save energy" (92%) and most (86%) say they are aware of several concrete ways to save energy in everyday life. The vast majority say they "always" save energy, which is reflected in activities such as switching off lights (63%), turning down the heating (72%) or consciously ventilating (61%) (…). Half of the respondents would also forego comfort in order to save energy, and only a few (above all older people, people with a low level of education or low income) feel that saving energy is costly (12%). Children should also be taught the importance of saving energy, according to 90% of respondents. Nevertheless, some respondents agree with the statement that they have little time in their daily lives to think about saving energy (18%). However, the majority of 54% disagree with this statement – of which older people and respondents with a higher level of education tend to be more likely. (…) The main motives for saving energy are ecological considerations such as "protecting the environment" (89%) and "contributing to climate protection" (87%) as well as the economic motive "saving money" (84%). 46% state that they are generally thrifty and can therefore imagine saving energy. Whether friends or acquaintances save energy plays a role for only 8% of the respondents". Similar results emerged from the same survey in the district of Steinfurt (Rubik et al. 2014: 12): "Reduction of energy consumption and conscious energy consumption are based on so-called motivational alliances of financial savings and ecological considerations. However, in the district of Steinfurt, there is also a very clear attitude that the quality of life should not suffer from saving energy, according to the principle 'You can also save yourself dead.´ Almost all of the role-playing citizens, however, see economic efficiency or financial advantages as a consequence of conscious energy consumption as the main motive; accordingly, the (foreseeable) lack of economic efficiency is the factor limiting their own commitment. If the savings efforts or expenditures for energy-efficient electrical and electronic devices were no longer economically worthwhile, this would be too great a sacrifice to continue to drive forward the energy transition".

ergy behavior; secondly, it is uncertain whether membership alone has led to the changes demonstrated. According to other study results, important motives for behavioral changes are, in particular, time and money resources, but also the belief that one cannot achieve much with a singular behavioral change alone. Obviously, behavioral changes often occur when this seems "practical" anyway, i.e. obvious (example: motivational alliances without having to do without something essential).[18] Obviously, there is always a complex, also irrational, and contradictory mix of motivations, which includes trade-offs as well as remote aspects and factors such as the aesthetics of energy-saving technology or self-initiative versus top-down order/recommendation in the case of energy consumption.[19] Other factors such as knowledge, attributions of meaning, habitus and physicality also play a role (Wallenborn and Wilhite 2014). Overall, moderate ecological lifestyles and behaviors are probably particularly promising compared to radical changes, as they can generate less resistance and more acceptance as well as integration potential in routines (Moser et al. 2015).

---

[18] Cf. results of Kreß et al. (2014b: 12): "A reduction of energy consumption and a conscious energy consumption are also based among the 'role-active' on so-called motive alliances of financial savings, ecological considerations and savings-related value orientations according to the principle of the "famous Swabian housewife". But socio-political efforts towards sufficiency can also be found: 'I simply want to consume little energy as a human being'. The active citizens still place the aspect of conscious consumption in the foreground. This combines motives such as responsibility for the environment, intra- and intergenerational justice, living in accordance with convictions or taking on a role model function. The committed citizens are aware that a powerful movement can develop from many activities of individuals, but that a critical mass is necessary for this and its absence can also lead to frustration (…). As important framework conditions and barriers to action, (…) financial resources (especially with regard to the purchase of energy-efficient household appliances), infrastructural framework conditions (e.g. technical equipment and type of construction of the house), but also social factors, such as the behavior of other household members (with regard to energy consumption behavior), were named. The interviewed citizens also mention 'good opportunities' as an encouraging factor, for example when defective appliances are replaced by more energy-efficient ones or when switching to green electricity in the context of a move. It is also clear from the suggestions for improvements in the framework conditions on the part of those involved that financing, as opposed to 'more time', is a significant part of the willingness to save energy: Various forms of cost reductions for the consumer, e.g. cheaper local and long-distance public transport or cheaper energy-saving light bulbs, are mentioned here first and foremost".

[19] See Kim and Choi 2005; Kim 2011; Tan and Lau 2011; Butler et al. 2014; Hildebrand et al. 2014; Stern 2014; Moser et al. 2015; Dumitru et al. 2016; Galvin and Terry 2016; Hansen 2016; Ruepert et al. 2016; Nachreiner and Matthies 2016; Sunikka-Blank and Galvin 2016.

- **Participation characteristics:** The community energy participation form is particularistic and individually motivated (synthesis of multiple motives), and in this sense very flexible. It is both self-interested and oriented towards the common good. Return on investment and financial aspects do not play a significant role here. Hybrid participation consisting of financial aspects, organizational participation and co-determination, social (individual contribution) and political participation (local players in the public and political spheres) is therefore present as a new type of participation. In the course of time, initiators experience the onset of dynamics of professionalization, economization ("business management") and monetization with a simultaneous weakening of idealistic initial motives for their actions since they are essentially active in the private sector.[20]
- **Conclusion:** Participation can be characterized as limited, mainly low-threshold and pronounced in less relevant social or project topics (on the other hand, stronger interest in social exchange), although the participants at the same time strongly emphasize the importance of organizational, financial and location issues. Comprehensive and above all profound discourses do not take place. Although these are considered to be frequently desired, they are empirically verifiable in only a few cases. Thus, despite the rather unconventional classification in the grid of political participation, community energy participation remains conventional in its characteristics, not very innovative and proceeds strongly along formal lines. Nevertheless, there is potential for more innovative and creative participation: Especially in electronic form and through the establishment of new formats; however, this rarely takes place in practice due to the increased effort involved. It also seems as if the participants do not know how to make concrete use of participation rights and exploit opportunities. Nevertheless, community energy participation remains an example of direct local shaping of the environment.

[20] This also takes up a consideration by Jürgen Habermas, in that a distinction is made between communicative and strategic action, the latter gaining more and more importance in modernity according to his thesis (cf. Habermas 2011a, 2011b). He refers to the penetration of economic ways of thinking and acting/principles in all areas of life as colonization of the lifeworld (Habermas 2011b: 470 ff.). The results of the present study indicate that originally indexed communicative action is indeed subject to strategic action, which is here attributed to a lack of fit (congruence) with other contextual spheres of society. In this way of thinking, the economized society forces resisting sections into its patterns of thought and action in the long run.

In the present study, there is no evidence to support the assumption that there exists a perfect incarnation of democracy that is realized through community energy projects on the basis of the survey data and the case studies. Nevertheless, there are empirically verifiable phenomena such as

- collaboration through group work (*collaborative democracy*),
- collective identity, sense of community and commitment (*associative democracy*),
- a strengthening of democratic awareness, principles and values (*learning effects*), and
- sense of direct influence, agency and self-sufficiency (*participatory democracy*).

Thus, learning about democracy can be concretely demonstrated to a limited extent with regard to the characteristics of participation in community energy pointed out in some cases. Local energy policy discourses and community energy projects can in a certain sense be considered as schools of democracy, insofar as the term school also includes dealing with challenges.[21] Crucial for the existence of practices conducive to democracy is the prerequisite that citizens come together in discourse and exchange and find local solutions, such as for the use of renewable energies, through exchange. It is conducive to democracy that various participation options are created for citizens or that they themselves create participation. Bottom-up activity by committed citizens (e.g. context of emergence via a community energy project as an outflow form of political participation) in the sense of an *invented space* of participation is to be assigned to political participation (creative handling of topics and modes of action could be found: Experiments with different participa-

[21] Cornwall and Coelho describe schools for democracy as follows: "Participatory sphere institutions can become 'schools for citizenship'- in the words of a Brazilian activist cited by Cornwall – in which those who participate learn new meanings and practices of citizenship by working together. The sheer diversity of actors and positions within this sphere offer opportunities for developing an 'expanded understanding' (…) that allows people to see beyond their own immediate problems or professional biases. As Rodgers, Barnes and Cornwall observe, participants in these spaces bring commitment to them and talk of getting an enormous amount of personal fulfilment out of their engagement. Interactions in this sphere can help change dispositions amongst bureaucrats as well as citizens, instilling greater respect, and enhancing their propensity to listen and commitment to respond" (Cornwall and Coelho 2007: 23). Baringhorst speaks in particular of the transmission of values of a substantial nature (liberty, equality, fraternity) and procedural values in the form of recognition and tolerance of dissenters, as well as the formation of an autonomous moral power of judgement and the formation of social and political trust (Baringhorst 2012a: 68 f.). On civic learning processes, see in particular Biesta (2014).

tion formats, inclusion of citizens, collaboration formats, exchange with other actors, politics and population). In these cases, the political motivations of participants and their participation in discourse within the public space can be demonstrated. Therefore, two fundamentally different types of participatory architecture within community energy projects can initially be differentiated here:

- Community energy as an outflow of **local political engagement** mainly organized in cooperatives or associated companies ("*invented participation*"), where the role intended to the participants is: *membership including the opportunity of active participation within the projects.*
- Community energy as an exclusively **financial mode of participation** in renewable energy investment projects ("*invited participation*"), where the role intended to the participants is: *passive financial investment without the opportunity for active participation within the projects.*

Finally, a crucial question is whether the community energy projects originally came together through the motives of "ecological profitability", but later developed other motives beyond the core idea of the project (shaping community and society, social-discursive togetherness, acting in public, social aspects) that have a more vague and far-reaching character. The survey data point to such dynamics, especially in the qualitative data. Participating citizens apparently learn further competencies, ways of acting and political skills beyond the explicit project through their membership and participation. A good example of this is a survey statement according to which a very large number of citizens are more in favor of community projects and more civic participation in general since their participation. Spillover effects are therefore clearly demonstrable. This could possibly also represent evidence of implicit learning about democracy or understanding, in that an acquisition of the "notion of democratic political action" (Thaa 2011: 17) is achieved through the discursive practices in the communities (cf. discussion of learning about democracy ("schools of democracy" in the context of civil society associations, networks and participatory procedures in Braun 2007; Braun et al. 2007; Fuhse 2010; Keil 2013b; van Deth 2011, 2013b; for summary see above).

This form of learning about democracy can encompass three dimensions here:

- **Acquisition of cognitive skills and professional expertise:** Learning about running small businesses (economic, legal, procedural, bureaucratic, technocratic expertise).
- **Action-oriented experience:** Group work, collaboration, creative co-operation, hierarchies, organizational knowledge.

- **Processual knowledge:** Experience and handling of asserting interests and balancing interests, voting behavior, dealing with resistance, diverging interests, cooperation and alliance or coalition building, consensus building, dealing with minorities and veto player constellations.

However, the learning about democracy that can be observed in this context relates in particular to individual ways of acting in the context of the organization (e.g. voting, putting one's own voice forward, reaching consensus, etc.). These forms of learning are, however, to be classified as context-bound and not necessarily transferable to the immediate environment. Based on the survey data, it is difficult to infer any penetration into individual lifestyles and concrete behavioral change (more environmentally conscious lifestyles). However, an overriding, undirected increased interest in participation in renewable energies and citizen participation among the public remains to be noted; in addition, it can be assumed that experiences with cooperation in community energy projects are taken up and passed on (spillover effects).

Beyond the passive-financial mode of participation, it is above all a communal-discursive type of participation that emerges here (cf. the understanding of participation in cooperatives analyzed in accordance with the study by von Blanckenburg 2014). Thus, the characteristic of collaborative problem-solving according to the framework of participation by Jan van Deth (2014a) would be existing in the case of community energy, provided that firstly voluntary activity and secondly no passive financial investment participation form are present. In these cases, the community energy participation form can be evaluated as a civil society variant of political participation. Assignment to the non-political forms of political participation such as consumption would not be appropriate here. This variant can, however, be stated for the passive financial forms of participation, provided that there is also a subjective political motivation – which can often be assumed on the basis of the survey data and interview statements (cf. statements on politically related motives such as ecology, common good, contribution to the energy transition, etc.; a political motivation would have to be ruled out in the case of a primary return motivation, but according to the survey data only for 8.5% of the participants).

Finally, in summary, following more recent conceptualization and definition of political participation according to van Deth (2014a), possible variants of political participation through community energy can be discussed (cf. van Deth's model in Sect. 2.2.1). In any case, the community energy participation type can be classified as a consumption-like variant of political participation as a kind of basic condition. Beyond that, however, it becomes difficult to make classifications. This is due to the wide range of engagement forms and the very heterogeneous styles and contexts of emergence of community energy projects: Thus, in some cases a civic-social participation can be analyzed, which can be characterized as a form of collaborative problem solving in the sense of the framework of participation by Jan van Deth (in the case of initiation based on civic activities as by a sponsoring association (e.g. environmental association/organization, cf. Fig. 6.31 above) or an initiative by local active citizens (Local Agenda group, energy working group, typical citizens' initiative, examples of cases in this study: citizens' initiatives in case studies 2 and 7, Local Agenda group in case study 6, associations in case studies 3 and 5) whose spin-off is the community energy project.

In other cases, there could also be unconventional political participation through localization in or close connection with the political sphere. In rarer cases, this classification as political participation would be possible if the community energy project (a) is (co-)supported by political actors and/or local political authorities (such as municipalities, regions) (e.g. as a shareholder) or (b) can be regarded as an official local political measure, for example as an outflow form of climate/energy policy programs (as a concrete component of a climate protection initiative, energy policy measure, etc.). However, these classifications are difficult to make both on a case-by-case basis and as a broad category for an entire case cluster: The crucial question here is what should ultimately be concrete criteria for when, for example, collective problem solving ("solving collective or community problems") or a political location/space ("locus: politics/government/state" or "target: politics/government/state") can be assigned. Are political contacts sufficient for this? How should hybrid constructions of actors from political, civil society and entrepreneurial constellations (e.g. joint project or initiative of community, association and company) and hybrid target constellations (e.g. political statement, ecology, return on investment, etc.) be evaluated?

Finally, the subjective-individual motivation for political action would have to be added as an overarching characteristic. Independently of the subjective motivations (cf. above) in the form of return on investment, ecology and energy self-sufficiency, the subjective motivations with regard to democracy and participation (cf. above) as well as the survey statements of the participants on the democratic assessment of their energy project (cf. Sect. 6.5.1) can be used to assess this question. This information confirms an overall rather political understanding of those involved in the role of a community energy project (70% share the attribution of democracy to their community energy project; here a conventional understanding of democracy prevails in the form of voting rights within the bodies of the project or company, etc.). The individual demands and guiding ideas of democratic, discursive and participatory design, however, show a very wide range overall and are also strongly determined by the social structure, i.e. dependent on milieu.

Therefore, a clear classification or definition is also difficult here. The example of community energy thus tends to show a hybrid nature of participation that is located between the spheres of politics, business and civil society, since forms of action – and thus also all individual and collaborative processes (such as communication, learning effects, co-determination) – are related to several spaces and are thus inseparable from one another. This makes unambiguous generalizations almost impossible.

Another finding confirms this assessment: when describing and defining the role of their community energy project, participants emphasize in particular a "contribution to the energy transition" (75% of respondents in the survey), which in turn confirms the classification of community energy as a community problem-solving approach, but also suggests a politically interpreted role of the participation contribution. This is because an "active role in energy policy" is also formulated by 55% of respondents as a requirement for a community energy project. However, it should also be taken into account at this point that a voluntary form of operation is seen as a relevant characteristic of a community energy project by only 19% and a bottom-up citizen initiation by 42% of the members surveyed. These findings condense into the overall impression that the participants themselves are obviously politically motivated and represent an understanding of the public mission (in the sense of the energy transition) of community energy. However, the concrete design is seen as much less significant both in terms of process, e.g. through participatory procedures, and in terms of action and actors, e.g. through roles in the public sphere. Thus, a very pragmatically oriented, subjective definition of community energy in the form of a collective, project-related problem-solving model, which is characterized by material and technology-related practicability, can be emphasized as the decisive characteristic of the type of participation within community energy.

Finally, participation in community energy projects can be seen as a form of expression of political participation in the sense of a multi-stage model:

- Starting with **consumption-like financial** participation (investment),
- via **civil society** (initiative based on civic engagement and voluntary operation)
- to **unconventional forms of political participation** (public actor in energy policy).

The thesis of a revitalization of democracy seems to be correct, based on the example of community energy projects through active engagement (politicization) with the topic of renewable energies. At the same time, participation formats of representative democracy tend to be questioned. Essential elements of community energy enterprises exhibit the character of the "new voluntary work" as well as forms of contemporary, project-related civic engagement. For on the one hand, from the point of view of the citizens involved (less so of the more idealistic initiators), community energy is an example of new forms of participation, voluntary work and civic engagement that flexibly combines (difficult to reconcile) motives of return on investment, energy self-sufficiency, ecology and social-ethical demands, which is primarily achieved through principles of objectivity, thematic fixity and time limitation (basic pragmatic-technocratic character). On the other hand, however, community energy is not an example of unconventional participation procedures and online participation. It mainly uses classical formats and face-to-face exchange (meetings, assemblies). In essence, therefore, the community energy approach serves the information, exchange and co-determination of stakeholders, consensual decision-making, joint opinion-forming, group learning and collaboration of the population, local actors, administration and politics in the context of the use of renewable energy. The members predominantly show a rather loose relationship towards their community compared to the traditional understanding of a strong associative bond, which corresponds to the loosened ties in the political culture diagnosed in the literature (Rudzio 2015).

A special feature is the wide range of civic engagement: from very passive to very active behavior, either emphasis on or suppression of discourse, integration of strongly divergent motives (exclusively profit-oriented or ecological), emphasis on cooperation between members and committees or suppression of members' interests, closed group activity or open project character are possible forms of activity and action in community energy projects.

In this way, community energy projects establish a new form of a specific expression of political participation which, in contrast to older conventional forms of political participation, can be characterized as multi-layered, heterogeneous and complex. In terms of democratic theory, this approach is close to some concepts of participatory and pragmatic democratic theory (Pateman 1970; Rorty 1982; Barber 1984; Dewey 1988; Hartmann 2003; Hartmann et al. 2013) than to deliberative and communitarian approaches (Sandel 1982; Habermas 1992; Walzer 1992; Etzioni

1995, 2009; Taylor 2002; Fishkin 2009; Jacobs et al. 2009; Dryzek 1990, 2000, 2012).[22]

[22] In addition to these more explicit ideas of the functions of democracy, there are also expansively conceived theories of democracy: The idea of inclusive democracy (Fotopoulos 1997), for example, pursues the inclusion and democratization of all areas of life (following ideas and approaches in economic terms from Karl Marx, as well as ecological ideas), this includes the private sphere as well as the economy in particular, and thus the workplace, as well as all social activities and forms of socialization. Consequently, these representatives based themselves on democratic ideas and procedures in the economy (industrial economic democracy, employee democracy, workplace democracy) and "democratic" forms of enterprise and ownership such as common ownership (cf. Ostrom 1990 approach) and "democratized" associations and non-profit organizations of civil society (organizational democracy) such as cooperatives, but also public/governmental institutions, political parties, trade unions and associations (cf. Pateman 1975; Weber 1999; Stohl and Cheney 2001; Cloke and Goldsmith 2002; Harrison and Freeman 2004; Moldaschl 2004; Smith 2009; Bode 2013). On the one hand, civic action is conceived here from intrinsic motives and sources – not republican or socialist top-down through the bestowal of civil rights or entitlements etc. but through the action and drive of the individual themself – i.e. bottom-up, legitimated by individual autonomous action. On the other hand, the idea consists in the firmly anchored institutional creation of democratic structures in organizations and institutions on the one hand, through rights of co-determination, and on the other hand, through the creation of additional bodies (such as advisory councils), working groups and representatives in committees. This "democratic design" is intended to stimulate and thus also make use of channels for co-creation and co-determination in companies, enterprises, public institutions, etc. – In a similar thrust, representatives of the concept of democratization (Vilmar 1973) and democracy education ultimately include everything in the democratic: The aim of democratization is to implement democratic practices and procedures in all spheres of society (economy, state, civil society, private sphere, etc.). But also a reinforcement of direct democratic elements of the representative form of government is discussed (democratization of democracy: Offe 2003a; cf. besides Schmalz-Bruns 1995; Decker 2012; Ante 2015; Öhlinger and Poier 2015; Solar 2016). According to the ideas of democracy education, from an individual perspective, a person who thinks and acts democratically must consequently do so in all areas of life (according to the democracy education or theory of John Dewey, cf. Dewey 1916; besides Bohnsack 2003; Ichilov 2009; Beutel and Fauser 2001, 2011, 2013; Nowak et al. 2013; Boyte 2015; Hill 2015). From this, a *democracy of everyday life* could ultimately be derived (Peterson 1990; Bentley 2005; Ginsborg 2005; Urquhart 2005; Chisholm et al. 2012; van Deth 2013a; de Moor 2016; Peterson 2009 and Banks et al. 2013 speak of *everyday ethics*, Marres 2012 of *everyday publics*). The difference between the schools of thought becomes recognizable: The pragmatic theory of democracy and democracy pedagogy thinks of democratization starting from the individual, in the sense of an influence through the sum of individual actions (bottom-up approach), the supporters of institutional democratization call for a democratization of the institutions, orders and processes already created (top-down approach).

7.2 Reflection on Community Energy

7.2.1 Development Model of Community Energy

In order to gain an overview of the activity of a community energy project and the participation of citizens, it is helpful to illustrate it with a phase model of the development process of a community energy project. The development of membership and the level of community activity and member participation can be modelled over time for community energy projects (Fig. 7.1).

Starting from an initiation phase, in which first ideas for an energy project are collected and concretized, via a start-up phase, in which the small community energy project is built up by the initiators, the community energy project increasingly gains members. An increasing activity of the members in the form of personal commitment and cooperation (collaboration) is particularly pronounced in this phase, as both the initiators and the members are busy building up the community energy project or company, which may include the establishment of working groups or circles, as well as cooperation in plenaries, joint events, promotional activities, strategy-finding discussions, etc. This peaks during the start-up phase, but membership numbers may continue to increase thereafter during the establishment phase, as most projects continue to accept members until they have reached a maximum or cannot accept any more people due to their planning. In some cases, the maximum is also reached earlier if only a limited number is admitted (different strategies of the projects regarding the equity share: as high as possible or only a certain share).

In the establishment phase, in which the community energy project is still being constituted in parts and processes are completed one after the other, as well as in the

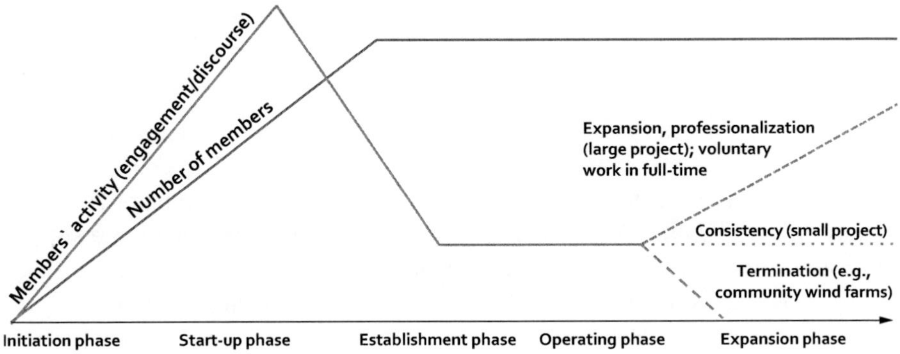

Fig. 7.1 Temporal phase model of a community energy project

operating phase, the number of activities is reduced, as the most important issues have been clarified, financing and business transactions have been carried out and the operation of the plants does not require any special effort. The number of members remains constant in most cases, and in some projects a long membership is also mandatory in order to avoid the enterprise no longer being profitable due to increased terminations. While the number of members usually remains stable until the end of the operation of the energy plants, the activity of the members can increase again in the further course. Three possible courses of events can be considered here:

1. The community energy project decides to **terminate** its enterprise. In this case, the energy plants are either uninstalled or sold on, and the members or shareholders are repaid the sums invested. This often takes place in the operation of wind turbines.
2. The community energy project operates its energy plants **beyond the originally planned period.** This is possible and also probable, especially in the case of the operation of solar plants by an energy cooperative. Possibly the energy plants will be replaced by new plants.
3. The community energy project decides to **expand** its enterprise. This case is also conceivable in the case of energy cooperatives, since here the legal form of the cooperative makes it possible to expand activities without any problems. In this case, the cooperative would plan and commission further energy plants or even in neighboring fields (e.g. operation of a local heating network, takeover of an electricity grid, services in the field of electromobility, electricity storage, energy efficiency, combined heat and power, combined heat and power plants, etc.). It can often be interesting for a solar energy cooperative to extend its activities to the field of wind power. In this case, the activities – similar to the initiation phase – would increase again, possibly becoming even larger if even more far-reaching planning is required (for example, the planning effort for wind energy is higher than for solar energy).

In such a case, the energy cooperative would take on additional members in order to obtain further capital and become increasingly professional. This could lead, for example, to the replacement or supplementation of the hitherto voluntarily active persons on the board by paid workers, and PR work would become more supra-regional in order to reach more interested citizens. The financial dimensions and business could then increase to such proportions that a “layman’s approach” no longer seems sensible. However, this process of professionalization may have a significant downside: Due to the more professional processing by permanent staff, the co-processing and participation of the members becomes increasingly obsolete. This can also be accompanied by a loss of openness and inclusion of the members in the planning, strategy formulation and business processes. This would mean that the cooperative would lose its original character of an open-participative project of a committed group of citizens – towards an community energy company which offers its members primarily financial shares and thus no longer represents a major difference to conventional energy companies (*trade-off between participation and professionalization*). Finally, however, this possible dynamic must also take into account that even smaller energy cooperatives with honorary boards can offer their members more open forums or pursue more closed processes and practices. Individual cases prove that a community energy project can also expand activities to a certain extent without losing its grounding in the members and an inclusive character – and thus manage the tightrope walk between size and professionalism on the one hand and participation and openness on the other.

7.2.2 Typology and Conception of Community Energy in Germany

The insights and characteristics gained can ultimately be combined into overarching, simplistic typological-conceptual models. Three models (actor-based, action-based, overall model) are presented below.

Action-Related Conditions of Participation: A Typological Spatial Model of Community Energy

From the individual motivations and attributions (e.g. ecological motivation and democratic aspirations) as well as pragmatic-material relationships (e.g. community activities), three types of community energy projects can finally be derived in terms of their predominant characteristics. Through the found definitions of community energy communities by the involved persons themselves (cf. 6.3.1, 6.3.3) as well as by including other survey statements (cf. 6.2.2, 6.2.3, 6.4.2–6.5.2) as well as characteristics of the participation modes (cf. 6.1.2, 6.1.4, 6.2.4), this model is generated, which is mainly shaped by similar ideas regarding a community energy project.

1. **Community energy projects as PLACES OF IDENTITY: Focus on regional anchoring creating local attachments and identity**
   - *Definition:* The energy project primarily serves the implementation of a local benefit strategy, benefits and profits should serve the local community.
   - *Energy projects:* Community wind farms and mid-sized community energy projects.

- *Characteristics of participating members:* Older members, regardless of income and gender, slight surplus of non-academics.
- *Criticism of participating members:* Lack of inclusion of the whole population in the community energy project, danger of nepotism.

2. **Community energy projects as SPACES OF COMMUNITY: Focus on vivid community creating social cohesion and social capital**
   - *Definition:* The energy project should be an outgrowth of collaborative action, it should enable community and exchange through cooperation and shared spirit of action.
   - *Energy projects:* Cooperatives and small projects.
   - *Characteristics of participating members:* non-academics, low income, greater emphasis on women.
   - *Criticism of participating members:* discourse without direction, lack of structure and coordination, tendency to inaction, lack of efficiency.
3. **Community energy projects as PLACES OF PROFESSIONAL DECISION-MAKING: Focus on efficient operation and management**
   - *Definition:* The energy project should be managed and controlled as efficiently and professionally as possible in economic and organizational terms. This includes the idea of "good leadership" (stakeholder orientation): Through transparency and openness, the management recognizes at best all the demands of the members and implements them in a balancing way.
   - *Types of energy projects:* All project types and sizes, increased interest among a group of cooperative members, strongly represented by large community energy investment limited liability companies.
   - *Characteristics of participating members:* mainly academics, high-income individuals, men.
   - *Criticism of participating members:* insufficient opportunities for co-determination and input by members, monopoly on information, nepotism, oligarchic tendencies.

Overall Model of Community Energy in Germany

In summary, based on the empirical findings in this study, an overall model of community energy in Germany can be drawn (see Fig. 7.2). The figure shows essential elements of a simplified version of a community energy project in Germany, including relevant groups of actors, core aspects in the use of renewable energies as well as individual goals of the participants in the project process.

Thus, different levels of action can be differentiated (organizational level of the community energy project, collective network level of the actors in the local area,

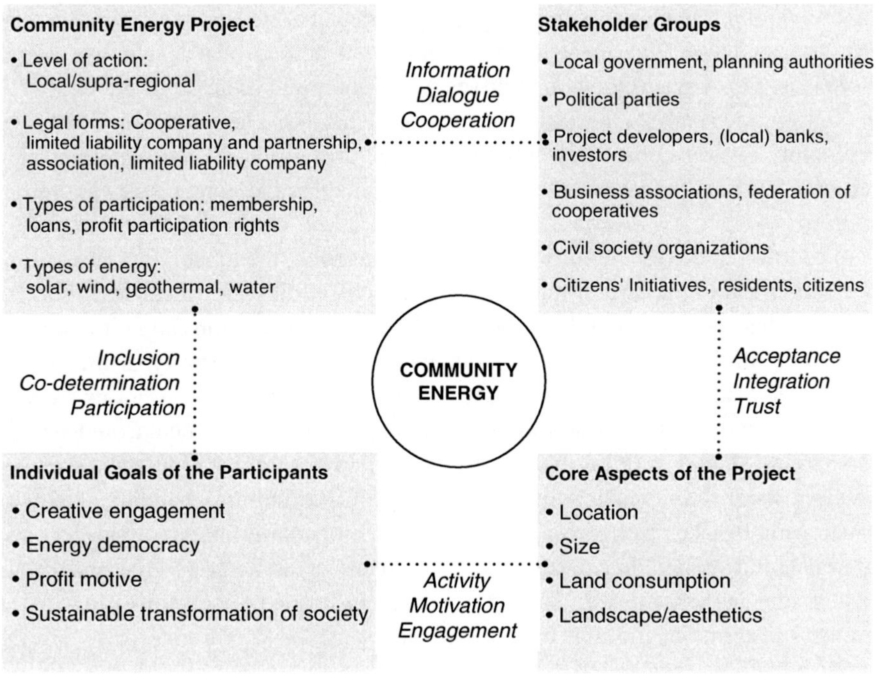

Fig. 7.2 Overall concept of community energy

internal level of the community energy project, thematic process level of the design and negotiation of the project issues, individual level of the members).

As has been shown, the radius of action of a community energy project can be local or supra-regional, which is usually also linked to the project size and intended scope of the project. In practice, the registered cooperative, the limited liability company and partnership (GmbH & Co. KG), the civil law partnership (GbR) or also registered associations and stock corporations are mostly used as possible legal forms of community energy projects. Smaller community energy projects are in most cases cooperatives (sometimes also GbRs), medium-sized projects such as community wind farms are run as limited liability companies and partnerships (GmbH & Co KGs), larger community energy companies are stock corporations or registered associations. The financial forms of participation result from membership in the cooperatives or as partners in limited partnerships or GbRs. In addition, participation through loans and profit participation rights is widespread among the larger community energy companies. The forms of energy used are predominantly solar energy, as well as local heating through combined heat and power plants (biomass) in the case of the cooperatives, wind energy in the case of the GmbH & Co KGs; geothermal energy and hydropower are used to a lesser extent. The larger community energy companies and some cooperatives operate various renewable energy plants (multi-MWs), mainly in the field of solar and wind energy as well as biomass.

In addition to the community energy project as such, the most important groups of actors are municipal administrations, political parties and local civil society groups such as environmental, energy and homeland associations and citizens' initiatives. Finally, the population or residents living in the proximity of the energy plants must also be taken into account. Other, supra-regional institutions such as the state governments and administrations as well as environmental and energy associations should also be mentioned. The main communication processes between the local actors result from the exchange of information, dialogue with individual institutions as well as cooperation (between community energy project and environmental association, municipality, or plant manufacturer). The individual goals of the participants can be differentiated in terms of the motivation of the members in terms of the will to shape (in the sense of a joint enterprise and the establishment of a registered cooperative or company), energy democracy (in the sense of a shift from conventional companies to projects owned by citizens), individual profit intention (in the sense of a return on investment) as well as with regard to the aspects of ecology and sustainability (in the sense of climate-friendly energy production) as well as common good orientation (in the sense of a joint project for the benefit of the general public). Overall, the actions of citizens' groups and local energy initiatives are characterized by activity, high motivation and strong commitment (civic engagement).

Finally, there are essential, substantive core aspects which relate to the energy plants as such and which are defined by the areas of "location" (Where are the plants to be installed?), "size" (What are the dimensions of the energy plants?) and "technology" (What are the risks associated with the technology used?), "land consumption" (How much land will the energy facilities take up?) as well as "landscape" and "aesthetics" (To what extent will the landscape appearance change, especially in the case of wind turbines?). The residents and members of the community energy project should gain influence and a say with regard to these essential questions through the inclusion of the population in the procedures (involving them in the procedures), (participation of the population) and enabling co-determination within the procedures.

In the best case, consensual procedures can be carried out and solutions found for possible problems and conflicts through the inclusion of key players, the population and members of the community energy project, by balancing interests and forming a common will in the procedures. It would then not be an exaggeration to speak of a project of the citizens, which is carried out in the interest of and supported by the general public. However, what is essential for this result is first and foremost the comprehensive involvement of the population and local institutions, as well as information, transparency and exchange. Even the exclusive provision of information would fall short if a certain degree of influence in the form of participation, consultation and co-determination were not also made possible.

Two central, positively valued consequences can be achieved: firstly, the acceptance of the population towards the new forms of energy; secondly, a shift and/or synthesis of individualistic profit-oriented motivation into a common good-oriented and communal-social variant can be brought about within the community energy projects.

In summary, community energy can have the following positive effects:

- ***Influence and actions in the local energy policy:*** Close collaboration, exchange and trust-building between the actors involved in community energy projects (local authorities, companies, associations, politicians, etc.).
- ***Participation:*** Informative, transparent and participatory procedures involving the local population in the planning process for renewable energies.
- ***Co-determination:*** Participation and co-determination of citizens within community energy projects
- ***Acceptance of renewable energies:*** by local actors and the population
- ***Energy citizenship and community spirit:*** Transforming individualistic return motivation into a community-spirited, collective and sustainable attitude
- ***Social capital:*** Creating social cohesion, trust-building, place attachment and play identity, and sense of community
- ***Lessons in democracy:*** Generating more interest in local participatory community projects, common goods, public participation and civic engagement

7.2.3 Citizen Roles and Citizen Action in Community Energy Projects: Pragmatic Climate Citizens

Citizens involved in community energy projects can neither be characterized as politicized non-citizens without civic virtues (according to Michael Greven, cf.

Greven 1997, 2009; see also Budde et al. 2010; Bude et al. 2010) nor as climate citizens who create legitimacy (cf. Kreß et al. 2014a; Rubik and Kreß 2014). Effects in the form of politicization and increased legitimacy through participation, input and discourse could be demonstrated in the present study. However, it remains open whether citizens have lost virtues (concept of "non-citizens" by Michael Greven) or whether they correspond to the ideal of an active citizen in accordance with the thinking of Jean-Jacques Rousseau[23] and the figure of engaged citizens in modern democratic theories. This becomes clear from the fact that even very committed citizens oriented towards the common good and social-ethical motives exhibit motives of self-interest thinking and are thus bourgeois at the same time. Simultaneously, citizens who think and act in an informed and politicized way carry within them the democratic virtues of the citizen. Citizen roles are thus multi-layered and to be understood as hybrid; they include both self-interested and common good-oriented ways of thinking and acting. The results of the survey and detailed qualitative statements have clearly demonstrated these closely interwoven patterns. Overall, it remains to be said that community initiatives such as community energy projects have the potential to change an original self-interest motivation with regard to returns, to a more common good-oriented and, in this case, especially community mindset. A good example of this is an increased willingness to forego returns in favor of investments in social projects and the community project (e.g. events, donations, construction of further facilities, etc.).

Overall, a higher interest of the participants in political and community-oriented topics can be observed, which is reflected in the participation and implementation of information- and discourse-oriented procedures as well as the contribution of various individual motives and interests. This leads to an unfolding of civic engagement, which contains the potential to qualify skills of action, discourse,

[23] Jean-Jaques Rosseau formulated the ideal of an active citizen ("citoyen") in contrast to a more passive citizen ("bourgeois"), whereby active citizens are involved in public affairs, engaged in the local or national public community oriented to the common good, politically interested and educated, and thus form the foundation of a vivid democracy. Contrary to this role of citizens in society, publicly passive, but at the same time wealthy and prosperous citizens are primarily interested in their own benefit, are selfishly active only in their private sphere and oriented to economic materialism and hedonism, not interested in politics and critical of government action. Rousseau was convinced, that active citizens can only be a result of conscious education and democracy will only work through this kind of social capital made by active citizens.

decision-making and conflict resolution (in the sense of political skills) and thus learning democracy. At the same time, the level and form of engagement show a very wide range, which also affects the effects of participation (e.g., increased engagement in the project or frustration). The results of the survey tend to confirm that community energy generates more interest in civic engagement, community action and the use of participation offerings.

A further fundamental question is the extent to which common good-oriented action is generated in community energy projects beyond a profit-oriented community of interests, for example through communal, common good-oriented activities, forms of open, inclusive cooperation and meeting and finally also through the generation of a communal identity as well as a "we-feeling" of the community (which tends to be perceived according to the survey data). Process-shaping characteristics such as openness, fairness, norms of justice in decision-making processes, transparency of procedures and processes are decisive criteria here as supports for trust-building, generation of legitimacy and formation of social capital.

Compared to other societal subsystems, another dimension comes to the fore in the environmental and energy sector: the overarching system benefit refers to ecological qualities that have a global character (climate change). According to Mayntz (2002), there is no normative priority of the overall system over the interests of its members between aggregated individual utility and system utility. In the case of community energy, however, the global benefit can coincide with the individual benefit, which is also the hope of the representatives of "ecological modernization". At this point, however, the gap opens up between purely profit-oriented self-interest and – interpreted negatively – only a superordinate, holistic system benefit in the sense of ecological and sustainable goals. Whether this action-guiding motivation leads to negative effects on an internal (concerning the community energy projects and their decisions) or external (concerning local communities) level is one of the overarching research questions of the field. However, it seems difficult to verify these assumptions with empirical case studies.

In the literature, Michael Greven contradicts the argument that ostensibly altruistic engagement is committed to the common good, while in reality it serves (rather self-interested) particular interests (cf. on this also Nolte 2011). He draws a clear line between alleged motivations that promote the common good and those that actually serve democracy (e.g. commitment to direct democracy), whereby the latter should be credible in contrast to diffuse (e.g. ecological) motives (Greven 2009: 219).[24]

In the participation of citizens in decision-making processes and in the described cases of linked forms of participation in civil society associations and public forums, this issue is reflected in the question of equality, in particular a sustainable assurance of equality in terms of access and representativeness as well as protection of minorities (representativeness question: representation of the entire population). A decision or a result can always be considered democratically legitimized if all individuals are involved in a certain process or procedure or vote and can at best contribute their voice (input).[25] A maximum, i.e. full input, is de facto impossible, but at least many individuals and actors must be represented so that sufficient input legitimacy is achieved. However, this is regularly not the case with participatory mechanisms and is hardly possible, especially with specific participation procedures, due to the effort and number of actors.

The decisive criterion is therefore to involve as many sections of the population and those affected as possible in procedures, to provide information as broadly and comprehensively as possible, without specific barriers and with as easy and intuitive access as possible, and to create options for participation, i.e. to make use of

[24] Cf. on the input problem Blühdorn (2013: 228): "On the input side, direct and representative participation transform into scientific objectivity, expert rule with maximum exploitation of forms of minimal participation. Deliberation and collective reasoning turn into strictly formalized, depoliticized procedures with criteria of transparency, information obligation and accountability. Finally, a subject-related effectiveness and efficiency is contrasted with a system-related variant with the help of service provider image and customer and service orientation." – It is thus assumed that civil society organizations only represent a "simulation of public legitimacy" (von Braunmühl 2011: 122), Petra Dobner similarly speaks of "legitimacy phishing" (Dobner 2008). Nolte (2011) describes a fundamental problem of legitimacy through particularism "in the guise of a supposedly irrefutable common good". On this problem, cf. Nullmeier (2002: 15), Schuppert (1997: 142 ff.) and Renn (2013b: 71) with regard to the participation of the population in the field of technology.

[25] See also Gabriel 1983: 98 f.; Scharpf 1999, 2005; Kraus 2004; Schäfer 2006a, 2006b.

diversity of involvement (internet, selective actions, face-to-face contacts, etc.).[26] The higher the representativeness achieved, the more likely the participation procedure or participatory measure is to represent a gain for democracy.

To summarize, in the proceedings

- the **broad inclusion** of everyone in the organization's decision-making processes,
- application of **democratic principles** (equality of votes, protection of minorities, right to be heard, etc.) and
- the attributes **open, fair, inclusive, deliberative, informative, decisive** (in the sense of openness to discourse, participation in decision-making) as well as proximity to the citizens involved are the most important criteria for achieving acceptance, representativeness and legitimacy.[27]

The primary objective is to create the highest quality, transparent, substantive and inclusive participation possible under given conditions:

Internal criteria

Openness, fairness, transparency, inclusiveness, non-discriminatory mode of operation, activating and informing member-based practices.

[26] For example, a study by the Federal Environment Agency (Alcántara et al. 2014) elaborates various dimensions of criteria for participatory processes. These include: Procedural rationality (important criteria: Input from the general public, fairness, openness to results, discussion atmosphere, deliberative quality, procedural reflection), power (roles in the process/ structural preconditions) (important criteria: Resources for the process, decision-making power, initiation, sanctions), inclusion (selection of participants, selectivity of participation, dismantling of access barriers, representation of different groups and interests), empowerment (for hard-to-reach groups in the process and beyond the process) as well as transparency (inclusion of the public, context, transparency about goals, explication of the participants' understanding of their roles, feedback of results). The point of inclusion in particular appears to be highly relevant from the perspective of democratic theory in private-sector civil society undertakings such as community energy projects.

[27] Michael Zürn, for example, emphasizes "zones of deliberation" beyond decision-making rules and majorities, in that arguments are not made in public space in a way that is determined by interests, i.e. deliberation is carried out in compliance with the rules of procedural qualities (fairness, equality, proximity, impartiality, reflexivity, etc.), which is supposed to have a legitimizing effect (Zürn 1998: 240 f., Zürn 2005, cf. as a further representative of the deliberative idea Pettit 2008a, 2008b; for discussion Rosanvallon 2010; Geis et al. 2012; Ritzi 2014).

External criteria

In addition, outwardly actor-related modes of action for the community and the public are conceivable, in that the community energy projects themselves actively strive for inclusion of the population, information and transparency as well as integration into the local actor network and social exchange processes.

In the discussion of the 'common good', Christoph Strünck warns against "unrealistic models" in consumer policy (Strünck 2011b) and speaks of the "myth of the responsible consumer" (Strünck 2011a). He also accuses political science research of having not developed quality criteria of the common good for political measures; consequently, the term, along with any concrete meaning, vanishes in various case studies (Strünck 2014: 21). Beyond vague descriptions, in his view, concrete criteria, e.g., certain results of negotiations and cooperation, must be able to be evaluated as promoting the common good. This could be interpreted in a utilitarian way: as "the greatest possible benefit for the greatest possible number of people" (ibid.: 22). Whether organizations serve the common good in an individual case must therefore be proven at least "plausibly in terms of content" (ibid.: 23); substantive criteria for the common good should therefore be possible for empirical-analytical political science (ibid.). In the context of the present study, such criteria could be (as shown above) in particular the openness of participation offerings, serious attempts to involve the population, cooperation and publicity efforts. This corresponds to the widespread understanding of inclusion-led participation in the literature: "Spaces for public involvement become sites for 'citizenship participation' only when citizens gain meaningful opportunities to exercise voice and hold to account those who invite them to participate" (Cornwall 2002: vii).

Against the background of the public good question, the question remains to what extent community energy projects are driven by expectations of returns and thus, on the one hand, do not make maximum use of the ecological potential and, on the other hand, are subordinated to this goal in all of the project's design options and courses of action. Empirical findings show that ecological motives for the common good take precedence over profit orientation and self-interest motives. This, however, is a contradiction to the survey data, which suggest a hardly increased sustainability orientation in other areas of life or also sustainable consumption. The empirical results have shown that the citizens involved are basically interested in participation and shaping their immediate local environment, which is confirmed by other study results (cf. Kreß et al. 2014b: 17; Rubik et al. 2014: 16). It has been shown that more participation offerings by public institutions increase the interest in participation and possibly also generate more participation (cf. ibid.).

The citizens who are strongly involved in the sense of committed climate citizens show idealistic motives in particular. The commitment has a self-reinforcing effect in that the citizens with greater self-confidence develop further activities.[28] It must be pointed out, however, that this only affects a certain clientele, namely milieus with a high level of education and income (cf. Social Structure, Sect. 6.2.2). It has been shown that the social environment in particular has a major influence: commitment can have a contagious effect by motivating personal acquaintances, activating neighborhoods and, in turn, influencing each other. In the process, civic roles can overlap, be expanded or undergo modifications.[29] For example, it has been shown that an overspill from the role of investor to the role of political actor

[28] Cf. results of a survey in the district of Steinfurt (Rubik et al. 2014: 17): "The interviews showed that the role-players volunteer in political debates and processes for idealistic reasons; they draw their motivation from their own interest in climate change and their own curiosity about renewables. For those who have successfully implemented actions, realized concerns and activated fellow campaigners, these successes have a self-reinforcing motivating and stimulating effect. In particular, they explicitly perceive time competition with other activities as a limiting factor for political engagement. In some cases, the lack of support from individual municipalities and municipal politicians (local councillors, mayors) delayed or prevented the establishment of new renewable energy community plants".

[29] Cf. results of a survey in Heidelberg by Kreß et al. (2014b: 17): "Across all three roles there are social effects as well as interactions, mutual influences between the roles. The social environment of citizens can have a great influence across all fields of action. Talking to acquaintances can convince friends and neighbors of the importance of the energy issue. (…) Especially when it comes to purchasing green electricity, the social network has a great influence. Investments in renewable energies can also be encouraged by friends or neighbors. By the mere visibility of their behavior, they influence the behavior of others and thus have a pioneering role (…). Citizens thus become aware of the possibility of political engagement through their environment". – Similar results emerged from the same survey in the district of Steinfurt (Rubik et al. 2014: 17): "The results of the questionnaire survey show: The social environment of citizens can have a great influence across all fields of action. (…) Energy-related behavior can also be influenced on a non-verbal level: With regard to energy consumption, the behaviors of other household members can have both an encouraging effect, e.g. by supporting energy reduction, and an inhibiting effect, e.g. when parents see difficulties in energy reduction by their children (…). Investments in renewable energies can be encouraged by friends or neighbors. They thus have pioneering roles, which influence behavior in the social environment through mere visibility".

is possible, and vice versa.[30] The role model function of the climate citizens as well as the entire community energy project as a role model can thus obviously have[31] effects on other citizens. On the other hand, Rubik and Kreß also explicitly emphasize that by gaining a good conscience ("green washing"), less ecological behavior can be justified in other contexts (cf. Rubik and Kreß 2014)[32] . In this way, the

---

[30] Cf. results of a survey in Heidelberg by Kreß et al. (2014b: 17): "These previous examples describe 'interpersonal' influences, i.e. influences between citizens themselves. However, there are also 'intrapersonal' (psychological) interactions between the different roles. On the one hand, the interaction of the different roles is perceived by the active citizens as mutually supportive. For example, some of the active citizens were initially only active in one role such as a political actor or exclusively as an investor. Later, these 'initial impulses' led to further activities in other areas. Being active in one role thus has an effect on behavior and becoming active in other thematic fields or on future activities. On the other hand, the activities in the different roles can also slow down or hinder each other: For example, it is a question of the personal time budget and the available financial means in which roles one becomes active. And there are other psychological effects that make engagement in one area an 'argument' against other activities. So-called 'licensing effects' can be seen, for example, in an increase in energy consumption legitimized by green electricity purchases". Similar results were found in the same survey in the district of Steinfurt (Rubik et al. 2014: 17).

[31] Cf. results of a survey in Heidelberg by Kreß et al. (2014b: 17): "From the interviews and the focus group it emerges: The active citizens see many commonalities in the roles and through the different ways participation opportunities are also perceived for different social groups, each with different backgrounds and resources (…)". – Similar results emerged from the same survey in the district of Steinfurt (Rubik et al. 2014: 17 f.): "Overall, the participants in the interviews and the focus group see many similarities in the roles and the idea of making a difference together encourages engaged citizens to remain active (…). Intrapsychically, too, the roles can usually be combined well; at best, it is a question of personal time budget and available financial means in which roles one becomes active. In addition to these positive interactions, negative interactions were also discussed. Possible licensing effects can be seen, for example, in an increase in energy consumption legitimized by the purchase of green electricity (…)".

[32] Cf. Rubik and Kreß (2014: 7 f.): "From a psychological viewpoint, the different roles seem to harmonize with each other. Existing time and financial resources might determine the degree of involvement. With the aid of projective methods (i.e. using symbols), participants in the focus group used particular items to show positive and negative entanglement of roles. Positive effects were described as spillover effects, insofar as one behavior impacted positively on another. However, participants mostly described negative effects such as classical rebound effects or licensing effects. Licensing effects occur for example, if people who produce their own energy show higher levels of consumption. Having solar panels on the rooftop does not legitimize underfloor heating, as one participant ironically noted. Others reaffirm that view, saying that acting sustainably does not free somebody to cause ecological damage in another context instead (in other words, that you use green energy, but still take a plane to your next holiday destination)".

seemingly contradictory statements of the participants in the survey can also be explained, in that few individual behavioral changes (ecological consumption and lifestyle) were indicated. Apparently, collective aspirations (global-ideal motives such as common good, ecology) and individualistic behaviors can diverge, but still be paradoxically linked as seemingly contradictory features like an oxymoron. This refers to both individual participation behavior (e.g. low interest in contributing something to society for the greater good) and individual lifestyles (e.g. sustainable consumption). This would confirm the paradoxical behavior in the sense of "separate waste but drive SUVs" that has been proven in other studies (cf. Wolling and Arlt 2011; Rückert-John et al. 2013). Interestingly, interest in cars has dropped significantly among younger people, but environmental awareness as a whole is assessed as significantly lower than it was a few years ago, "the environment and nature play a minor role in the everyday world of young people" (Gossen et al. 2016: 16). The newer degrowth idea tends to be rejected: Prosperity without growth is predominantly doubted, young people find themselves in a "dilemma between growth skepticism and prosperity worries" (ibid.: 12, 16). In concrete action, however, energy saving is of high importance for younger people, and there is also a pronounced inclination towards renewable energies: "In connection with energy issues, adolescents and young adults show particular interest in technical solutions involving renewable energies. Alternative power generation technologies such as solar plants, wind turbines or biogas plants have also arrived in the perception of young people, not least due to the energy transition" (ibid.: 43). In addition, organic food, vegetarian/vegan food, sharing and second-hand articles are of considerable relevance. However, according to the authors of the study, there is more knowledge than action with regard to green consumption (ibid.: 43 f.), so although half can imagine being actively involved in environmental protection, only 9% are actually active (ibid.: 14).[33] The commitment that actually exists is, in turn, primarily oriented towards a fit with everyday life; motives for this are described as mixed: "It is above all topics and activities that have a connection to one's own everyday life and that can be fulfilled within the framework of the individual time budget in which young people show interest. The motives vary greatly depending

[33] This result is also confirmed by the UNESCO Sustainability Barometer, according to which younger people (15–24 years) see hardly any opportunities to get involved in the energy transition. According to this, the most important fields of action that have already been tapped into are reducing energy consumption and replacing old appliances with energy-saving new ones; behind these are purchasing green electricity, familiarizing myself with the topic, getting politically involved in the energy transition, getting involved in regional energy projects (e.g. solar energy plants, wind power…) and using a hybrid car (cf. Michelsen et al. 2016: 173).

on the form of involvement and can be both altruistic and egotistical (ibid.: 14). These results thus show a clear parallel to community energy engagement: Here, too, everyday compatibility and mixed motives from egoistic and common good-oriented reasons are essential characteristics of this form of engagement.

In the context of community energy, an expansion of citizens' roles can be assumed in particular in cases where the community energy initiative encompasses several fields of action, such as the operation of a heat network or the provision of electricity.[34] In these cases, the prosuming level can be reached; it seems obvious that in these cases participating citizens perceive and deal with the consumption of heat or electricity from their own community energy project more consciously (cf. in the present study information in the citizen geothermal case study, where, in addition to the generation of heat, the consumption through connection of the participants to their own heating network also plays a decisive role).

Nevertheless, the motivations and behaviors of the individuals should be considered in a differentiated way: they contain several, even contradictory elements. However, the results also show that decision-making involvement, transparency and discourse are strongly weighted. At the same time, an excess of imposed exchange is rejected. A balance between efficient and discursive action seems to be an ideal. The same applies to the communality factor: social interaction and joint events are welcomed, but excess is rejected. Particularly relevant are constant information, transparency and participation in decision-making. The majority of community energy projects are considered democratic, which is primarily attributed to the existence of co-determination opportunities. Finally, evidence of democracy learning was found. Examples of this are cooperation, voting, consensus building, conflict resolution and regulation of responsibilities. In addition, involved citizens develop more interest in opportunities for participation and forms of joint public projects in society as a whole. On the other hand, however, interest in participation and activity by committed citizens within more professional organized community energy projects can be thwarted due to hierarchical and oligarchical tendencies as well as nepotism within the management team of such projects.

[34] Cf. in the field of renewable energies prosuming networking approaches such as the "buzzn" initiative, where private electricity producers and consumers are virtually connected. Although such possibilities exist in principle in the context of community energy, they are not used in the present study apart from the local heating examples. Suggestions from participants in the survey indicate that there is a high level of interest, but there are obviously hurdles in the concrete area of application. Overall, the potential for such intelligent networking in the area of generation and consumption ("smart grids") seems to be great, but the current actual dissemination of these forms of participation and networking in Germany seems to be only slightly developed (cf. Hellmann 2018).

These cannot be described as strongly pronounced, as they are partly due to the cooperative regulations and the still short period of existence. However, this aspect was observed and analyzed in the case studies and can also be taken from the survey results[35] .

Derived from the empirical findings of the study (social structure, cf. Sect. 6.2.2), the idea of the climate citizen only applies to very committed citizens of the high-income and high-education milieus. Critical questions here are to what extent community energy enables a large part of the population to participate, how well socially less advantaged strata are integrated, and which successful models and important factors can be analyzed for this. Some examples of energy cooperatives that enable very small shares as well as explicitly engage with low-income population groups are to be highlighted here. However, this is not a very broad approach. The very fact that many cooperatives (like the other participation constructions) do not accept any further participations after some or even a very short time (oversubscription) prevents broad and long-term inclusion.

However, the survey results have shown that people with lower incomes and lower levels of education are also integrated. A closer analysis also shows that some projects succeed better in this integration. This is mainly due to the structural framework conditions (amount of the membership fee, duration of the participation offer, strong presence of the community energy project in the local public community). This brings the relationship between civil society association and the environment into focus: overall, it is about the participation culture on the ground and the climate generated for such projects. A good reputation and level of awareness of the activities and initiatives can ensure a correspondingly large response and thus make the leap from clientele project to a common local community initiative. This is the responsibility of the initiators and strongly committed members, who can generate trust, bridging social capital and acceptance through their actions, social competences, and political skills. This forms the basis for perceived participation and new engagement. An independent citizen role in the sense of the climate citizen who creates engagement can thus be roughly characterized, but not as a firmly definable type. Rather, in the sense of an "equal citizenry" in energy and climate policy (cf. von Braunmühl 2011; also Mans and Kayser 2013), more

[35] Such undemocratic tendencies are considered an eternal dilemma in participation research: "An ever-present dilemma is how to insulate these spaces from capture by non-democratic elements, including administrations who simply use them for therapeutic or rubber-stamping purposes" (Cornwall and Coelho 2007: 24). – In a study on cooperative participation structures, the problem of (grassroots) democratic vs. oligarchic structures and processes at the level of members and management of a cooperative could be clearly demonstrated (cf. von Blanckenburg 2014).

empowerment and citizen action on an equal footing with politics and the private sector can be attested.

In summary, the essential building blocks for shaping both individual civic action and behavior are

- **formal criteria** (participatory arrangements, procedures, regulations),
- **informal processes** (informal processes through knowledge exchange, exercise of power, articulation of interests, inclusion and exclusion) and
- **procedural conditions** (practices, routines and type/quality of procedure)

The Promise of Participatory Democracy

Since her reflections on "Participation and Democratic Theory" (1970), Carole Pateman has considered the problem of how a high-quality discourse is to be achieved if it does not take place in public. More than forty years later, she still sees the greatest challenge in the goal of achieving such a participatory and deliberative public discourse (cf. Pateman 2012: 15). Similarly, Jürgen Habermas pursued thoughts about the effectiveness of discourse.[36] Today, however, the positive connotation with the term discourse seems to be under attack (cf. Buchstein 2013); the criticism also concerns ideas of participation and legitimation (see above). For instance, the propensity of the media and interest groups to influence opinions and gain attention through calculated or populist strategies, has eclipsed the attractiveness of and belief in the strength of public discourse and of achieving deliberative quality. These tendencies have therefore weakened the promises of deliberative and participatory democracy.

There are good arguments for the high importance and practice of deliberative discourse in a vivid and participatory democracy. In the cases studied here, discourse plays an essential role both within the community energy groups and in the public sphere. In particular, public discourse in the sense of a jointly conducted

[36] Philip Pettit also takes up Carole Pateman's approach and discusses old questions against the background of new insights and social developments. He comes to the conclusion that at the core it is always a question of changing from an ego-based way of thinking and acting in group discourse to an overarching, we-based perspective (Pettit 2008a: 202): "Participatory democracy requires people to cooperate, not just in the pursuit of common goals, but in the pursuit of common goals according to common judgements. And that sort of enterprise is more or less inevitably going to require members to adopt the group point of view and to be prepared, at least in certain contexts, to prioritize their group identity. Participatory democracy is not just a way in which individuals combine to satisfy their existing goals, according to their existing judgements; it is a way in which they combine to determine the goals and judgements that they will enact together".

debate on energy issues in a municipality – including a large portfolio of actors from the population, the economy and the state – seems to represent an optimum in terms of democratic theory (Radtke and Schaal 2018). Due to the opening of many administrations, e.g., through the joint development of energy concepts and climate protection plans, more discourse and community as well as the involvement of citizens' interests have become possible. However, these processes suffer from a lack of representative participation and/or are exploited.

However, it is precisely the discourses that take place in the local space ("grassroots") without much media attention that have great potential in the form of a debate without the serious influence of other actors from politics, the media, business, etc. In the cases of the present study, a comprehensive discourse was often achieved in a covert manner, which can definitely confirm the thesis of a *stealth democracy* by Hibbing and Theiss-Morse (2002).[37] The discourses within the community energy projects can be assessed as heterogeneous. On average, the survey results show a rather low level of exchange. Ultimately, this does not lead to a negative assessment, since the possibility of exchange and proven, practiced discourses alone can be considered beneficial for community, society and democracy. In this way, inclusive discourses generate both binding (within the community) and bridging (between communities, actors and publics) social capital.

7.2.4 Discussion: Community Energy as an Allegory for Contemporary Civic Engagement?

Making socio-political engagement "cross-country" in the current structure of society means creating monetary participation as well as flexible participation offers, as in the case of community energy. In this case, the special nature of the form of participation means that community energy projects can survive without the additional commitment of their members, but they can be upgraded as a result. In this, one could observe the emergence of a new type of bridging social capital: this could be characterized as having less social cohesion, but perhaps more "connecting

[37] Cornwall and Coelho also point to incremental, i.e. rather inconspicuous, processes of change: "The normative expectations of deliberative and participatory democracy find weak support in the findings of the studies of everyday experiences of participatory governance in this book. But despite considerable shortcomings, the cases presented here give some cause for optimism. Their very ordinariness tells other stories: of incremental change, of a growing sense of entitlement to participate, of slow but real shifts in political agency. They reveal glimpses of how opening up previously inaccessible decision-making processes to public engagement can stimulate the creation" (Cornwall and Coelho 2007: 21).

pragmatism" (described in a similar form by Galli et al. 2013 in the context of community governance and "social capital creation through collaboration").[38] This pragmatic way of thinking and looking at things, which is essentially based on collaboration (Sennett 2012), would emphasize the inclusion of citizens' knowledge ("Citizen Science", Finke and Laszlo 2014; cf. also Grunwald 2016b) and describe a kind of "civil capitalism" (Lotter 2013; Stein 2015); thus forming another example of economizing tendencies (Lessenich 2013). However, such civil society activities can in principle not achieve the legitimacy of formal procedures (especially due to a lack of guarantee of certain standards such as minority protection) but complement them in a positive sense.

Grassroots initiatives, in their function as supporters of community energy, are on the one hand themselves part of a transformation process of the energy system (cf. Sommer and Welzer 2014), and on the other hand they are confronted with overall societal transformation processes, such as economization, professionalization, mediatization, etc. (cf. Schimank and Volkmann 2008; Hepp and Pfadenhauer 2014; Schaal et al. 2014; Becker et al. 2015a, 2015b). According to the survey results, many members would like to see professional public relations work, which presents the community energy projects with the challenge of professionalization, because management is again not desired, according to the data. Stakeholders want both: professional management *and* participatory and voluntary grassroots civic engagements initiatives – this inevitably leads to ambivalence, discord, uncertainties and paradoxical challenges. Motivations (return on investment vs. climate protection), as well as the concrete actions (oligarchic vs. inclusive) and ideal aspirations (representation of local community by small groups vs. client projects) of the communities are ambivalent and amorphously structured.

The increasing processuality and technocracy appear as reflections of society and could be interpreted as signs of de-communalization (Sennett 2014; Vahsen 2014). But different developments are emerging: On the one hand, private-sector companies are emerging in the case of community energy, but on the other hand, social communities are also emerging. According to the empirical results presented here, democratic criteria, values and opportunities for co-determination are very important to those involved. Thus, a democratization process would be empirically

[38] In terms of theory and methodology, Pierre Bourdieu's theory of practice and approaches based on it could provide a link for research (Bourdieu 1979, 2014; Ebrecht and Hillebrandt 2004; Schäfer 2013b, 2016; Hillebrandt 2014; Schäfer et al. 2014). Max Weber spoke of a "reality science" here, and for years a "practice turn" has been emphasized (Soler 2014), but apart from the orientation towards empirical analyses, no separate approach or school for theory and method development has emerged from this.

verifiable. The question of communality, however, is only one example of developments in society as a whole that are caught in the dichotomy of professionalization and economization, technocratization and bureaucratization, as well as socio-cultural, emotional and strong commitment to a "strong" and "social" communality in groups, organizations and neighborhoods (described as bonding social capital by Putnam et al. 1993 and Putnam 2000). Interestingly, both extreme poles (gutted spaces without communality, predominance of pure factual logics and effective-economic modes of action vs. social-communicative spaces in which, apart from communication, processes of understanding and eventization, there are no longer any content-goal-oriented themes) are rejected. The solution would obviously consist of an attempt to balance these social mechanisms and power relations. This approach could represent a core aspect of contemporary civic action in today's democracies. It reflects the basic idea of the interaction of the social spheres of economy (economic action), civil society (social action) and state (bureaucratic-technocratic action) and in this sense corresponds to the guidelines of a new consumer democracy (Lamla 2013)[39].

Blühdorn (2013) and Michelsen and Walter (2013) assume a pure simulation of democracy and participation (cf. also criticism of participation in Miessen 2012; Wagner 2013 and Merkel 2015b). Such simulations may be part of real participation processes, but alongside this fundamental-existential critique of society, nuances are admitted, but in the end no meaning is attributed to them. When citizens come together to deliberate public affairs in discourse, a simulation diagnosis falls short. The examples of the present study do show that there are not always pronounced discourses and that motivations are not exclusively oriented towards the common good. However, it can be assumed that every action is based on egoistic-benefit-oriented motives (Becker 1976; Daniel et al. 1986; Batson and Shaw 1991; Wakefield 1993; Spieß and Nerdinger1998; Batson 2014; on the other hand, see Fehr and Fischbacher 2002; Schäpke and Rauschmayer 2014 for motive explanation approaches oriented towards the common good), as is also the case in civic engagement (Burns et al. 2001). Community energy projects are therefore good reflections of society and only one fundamental problem is revealed here: technocratization and expertocracy empty and gut any meaningfulness and deeper reason, community then becomes superfluous and no longer needed. But the crucial question then is

[39] A link to Max Weber and forms of social action can also be found here. Habermas' theory of communicative action (Habermas 2011a, 2011b) may lack this substantive factual aspect, which would have to be examined more closely in the future, to what extent social capital, participation as a basic social principle and collaboration are also dependent on this, what significance is attached to it and how strong the influences and meanings of this are.

how individuals react to these overarching tendencies. On the one hand, they desire communality and they make attempts to establish it; on the other hand, they are indifferent or apathetic, they accept existing forms or reject them. Again, democracy is about the synthesis of individual interests, claims and world views: democratic-community action builds on these negotiation processes. The further question then is: What develops from these interlocking interests and modes of action, what forms do they take? Here there are some indications of increasing integrated mechanization. However, this does not have to be interpreted negatively: For example, one approach to participation can be the use of virtual forms, which involves both opportunities and risks: Networking across distances becomes possible, an exchange with reduced barriers can emerge – but here, too, not everyone will use these forms of participation. Ultimately, however, social capital is formed in local and virtual contacts and communities, whereby various forms of cooperation hold communities together (Sennett 2012) and community energy projects build social capital which acts as a bridge to other social spheres and civil society actors on the local level. On the one hand, community energy projects are fighting against the global trend of increasing individualization and acceleration (Rosa 2013a, 2013b), but on the other hand, they are also fighting against the typical regularity of social communitization processes that the transformation requires, i.e. the challenges, strains and demands for each individual are particularly high in *do-it-together* approaches, since community projects require both a high degree of personal initiative and the active creation of community (Rückert-John et al. 2016: 85).

As seen from the previous descriptions, local voluntary work and an open-integrative approach are often coupled and show the weakness of being able to set up a few plants in the local environment with only small capacities – the output thus usually remains low. This suggests that such small-scale energy projects remain island phenomena that arise here and there (where the initiation conditions of the local context are favorable). The growth of such communities is not ruled out per se, but it would primarily be linked to the adoption of professionalization strategies through different management.

In the qualitative case analysis carried out here, considerably expansive strategies of the comparatively small community energy projects were not found. This has primarily to do with the fact that the community energy projects define themselves as part of a local community and want to "serve" the local environment – they would thus deprive themselves of their own existence if they were to act on a large scale. However, in the context of the countries' renewable energy expansion targets, it could be argued that many more energy plants should also be built in the local and rural environment than has been done so far. This goal could be hindered by the fact that the voluntary groups, whose level of competence and workload has certain limits, simply cannot offer the resources to implement many more energy projects. In addition, the citizens involved here may not even want to pursue this goal. In some cases of communnity energy, however, structural-organizational hurdles in particular stand in the way as decisive conditions for success, of which the following could be analyzed:

- Limited planning of wind power priority zones
- Lack of availability of public roof areas
- Lack of suitability of sites and areas for renewable energy facilities
- Economic and legal barriers in project organization and granted permissions

The primary criterion for any conceivable use remains the question of attractiveness through remuneration or use of the generated energy, which results either from the remuneration rates of the EEG or from the contexts of use (own consumption, etc.).

7.3 Outlook

7.3.1 Challenges and Future of Community Energy in Germany

In the literature, community energy and energy cooperatives are described with relative hope as a "socio-spatial phenomenon" to promote an "energy industry re-orientation" (Maron and Maron 2013) through a restructuring of the energy industry with the help of remunicipalization and energy cooperatives (Klemisch and Boddenberg 2013). After the promising start of community energy projects in the 2000s, however, the founding boom has slowed down considerably, and intensive thought is being given to future models for a further revival of community energy (Müller and Holstenkamp 2015; Müller et al. 2015). It is possible that specific support will be achieved for the first time through the 2016 EEG amendment (cf. BMWi 2016).

This study has shown that the range, variety and diversity of the forms of engagement in community energy projects is very large. In parts, community energy projects define themselves in clear distinction to open-discursive procedures such as agenda groups; in other parts, the focus is on discourse, ethics and social-communicative, collaborative action and transparent-participative procedures ("open" vs. "closed" approach). The same applies to political aspects of action: basically, in these cases, citizens come together, exchange ideas and find activities and fields of engagement themselves and shape them on their own responsibility, which is associated with diverse learning processes. The biggest challenge in this area is the negative perception of the political system (caused mainly by the influence of the EEG) Local political administrations can also be perceived negatively due to problems with permits and requirements. Such trends are recognizable on the one hand, but on the other hand many case studies are positive examples of successful and thus binding and bridging cooperation (in the sense of an advocacy coalition) between community energy projects and public administration, and in some cases also political bodies. The building of trust and positive feedback (e.g. further commitment) regularly goes hand in hand with this.

Community energy imparts diverse knowledge in the socio-political, communicative and technical fields (cf. Junginger et al. 2010). The visualization of possibilities for civic engagement and action, the creation of understanding towards technology, politics and economy are essential basic prerequisites here. The empirical findings confirm that participating citizens have developed more interest in community, participation and civic engagement in the local public space and thus in the shaping of or through democracy. Another advantage of this regional energy transition is that a balance of diverse interests is found through actor diversity and community action. However, simulations of procedures and processes can also take place, as a result of which the combination of the most diverse interests in a joint project can break down again into dualisms (state vs. civil society, etc.).

The already discussed possible development of increasing professionalization, which would form an alignment with conventional, purely private-sector energy providers as a trade-off against small discursive-participative units, is to be judged in a differentiated manner due to the most varied contexts. Such a development does not make sense at all in every case and is therefore not pursued. The result is therefore a diversified coexistence of small, medium-sized and large, more professional community energy projects alongside conventional energy suppliers.

Probably the biggest problem is the simulation of participation by community energy projects and participation in the context of public participation. Concerns and hopes of citizens regarding actual involvement beyond mere monetary investment and acknowledgement of input to the municipality should be taken seriously. Increased legitimacy through the procedures is achieved at best in the form of combined community energy participation with deliberative public discourse procedures.

It seems unlikely that large parts of the population will participate in community energy formats (cf. Müller et al. 2015). Many factors speak against it. Not only high minimum participation amounts and uncertain returns, but also low attractiveness of the forms of engagement due to a wide variety of factors (e.g. rejection of associations, mistrust, lack of interest in the energy sector) can be causes of this (cf. Painuly 2001; Walker 2008; Barry and Chapman 2009; Sovacool 2009; Bomberg and McEwen 2012; Martin and Rice 2012; Richards et al. 2012; Szatow et al. 2012; Byrnes et al. 2013; Eleftheriadis and Anagnostopoulou 2015). Perhaps it would be beneficial to decouple the debate with regard to a synthesis with financial return to a greater extent. In this way, a lifting of the veil of an exclusive return-on-investment orientation could be achieved. Close links between local working groups and community energy projects are positive examples of a kind of community energy forum in which financial participation can be only one component among many other activities and orientations. Participants in energy cooperatives are also more likely to express interest in investing in "soft" fields such as energy education and advice rather than focusing exclusively on the operation of energy carriers.[40]

In the case of the cooperative organizational form, the cooperative tradition is unlikely to play a role for many energy cooperatives. What seems congenial about this legal form is readily accepted by energy cooperatives, such as the principle of equal voting rights. Other basic cooperative principles such as member loyalty and the funding mandate, on the other hand, meet with less interest and resonance. The cooperative form was chosen primarily because it is well compatible with voluntary work and low expenditure as well as possible expansion. However, cooperative principles may be taken up in the further course after confrontation and discussion with these approaches. The innovative power of community energy projects beyond the rediscovery of cooperatives and citizens` initiatives in the energy sector through the establishment of new participation formats and procedures is therefore ultimately not yet assessable.

Various forms of community energy are also conceivable in the future (e.g. local heating, operation of electricity grids, integrative-combining solutions, etc.). In this context, community energy always means a diversity of approaches ranging from pure financial investment to a project anchored in the social community. Although state support through indirect support at the municipal and regional level could be proven in the present study, a discrepancy remains with regard to individual regional support on the one hand and only marginal or non-existent, non-structural support policies of state and federal policy on the other. In addition,

[40] For example, in a survey of energy cooperatives in Germany, the members of the cooperatives surveyed stated that energy education and awareness-raising were the most important new fields of activity for energy cooperatives (55%), followed by energy contracting (52%), energy consulting (43%) and energy refurbishment of buildings (Rauschmayer et al. 2015: 11). To this end, 67% of members would be willing to increase their investments (ibid.).

there are provisions under European law, e.g. with regard to tendering practices, which equate community energy with other forms of operation, but put it out of competition. Presumably, the community energy approach increases the local acceptance of energy plants in the vast majority of cases (see survey results). However, this effect can vary greatly from case to case.

Energy Transition and Democracy in the Twenty-First Century: From Fossil to Sustainable Democracy?

A major debate at the beginning of the twenty-first century refers to climate change in terms of implications for democracy ("The Future of Democracy in the Face of Climate Change": Ward 2012; economic development, climate change and governance as a central challenge for the European community: Fagerberg et al. 2015; populism and climate change as a sign of the apocalypse: Swyngedouw 2010). Concise questions are formulated here as to whether, on the one hand, climate justice is more decisive than democracy (Ren et al. 2015), or, on the other hand, capitalism is opposed to an intact climate (Klein 2014). Indeed, a certain radicality is inherent in the discourses around climate change, energy transition and sustainability (Lange 2008), and manifestos of innovation, sustainability and development can be found accordingly (Arond et al. 2008). However, it is not yet possible to assess whether we can actually speak of a "great transformation" (of society: cf. Held et al. 2015, of organizations and governance: cf. Avril 2013)[41] The focus on *Sustainable Development Goals* at UN level and the now newly formulated Agenda 2030 indicate, however, that a sustainability transformation and the development of sustainable concepts will be a central challenge in the coming years and decades (see the new UN Agenda 2030 for Sustainable Development, Beisheim 2015). At the same time, this is accompanied by a strengthening of degrowth thinking (Latouche 2015), especially since the green economy (Williams 2010; Pollin 2015) is being more strongly questioned and criticized (Fatheuer et al. 2015), which also affects renewable energies (see, for example, the discussion about increasing coal use and thus also carbon dioxide emissions (cf. Kunze and Lehmann 2015) and sustainability in the case of wind power (Ledec et al. 2011)). The belief in the solution capacities of ecological modernization (Jänicke 2000; Bornemann and Verlinden 2002) and technology assessment (Simonis 2013) is thus increasingly diminishing.

[41] Jeremy Rifkin, for example, is thinking of a "Zero Marginal Cost Society" in which the *internet of things* and the collaborative use of the commons herald the end of the era of capitalism (Rifkin 2014).

Due to the changed view of dealing with commons, which can also include energy, a "new politics beyond market and state" is being considered (Helfrich 2014). In fact, the energy transition itself is seen as a kind of (new) social contract (Banse and Fleischer 2013).

This raises fundamental questions about the foundations and conditions of democracy and the state, but also political economy (cf. Sovacool and Linnér 2015). Thus, in view of climate change, limits to growth, but also a new zeitgeist that is more critical of progress, it is being discussed whether "democracy can be sustainable" (Gesang 2014; cf. also Diendorfer and Welan 2016) or whether democracy's ability to solve problems in the face of climate change is being questioned (Saretzki 2011). At the same time, the exact opposite argument is made as to whether it follows from the human age of the Anthropocene that democracy must be kept on hold (Stirling 2015a).

In his study *Carbon Democracy*, Timothy Mitchell shows that the modern Western democracies in their present form could only develop in the nineteenth and twentieth centuries because of fossil fuels as the foundation of technical progress and modern labor and welfare societies. The current upheaval of the energy system can in turn have serious effects on the characteristics and structures of democracies. However, a positively hopeful claim of a revitalization of democracy contrasts with a sobering reality:

- On the one hand, hope is placed in the transformational power of socio-technical change, in that the design options associated with new technologies and their intervention in routines could be used, particularly at the spatial level, to promote social negotiation processes with regard to technology and sustainable neighborhood/urban or regional development (Drilling and Schnur 2012; Brühne and Tempel 2013; Becker et al. 2015a; Becker et al. 2014b, 2016a; Brühne 2015; Chapple 2015), at the individual level participation (Leggewie and Welzer 2011) and at the level of society as a whole to introduce more social aspects into working, economic and living conditions (Bundesministerium für Umwelt, Naturschutz und Reaktorsicherheit 2008; Jänicke and Jacob 2008). In fact, such opportunities are already increasingly emerging thanks to new technologies (e.g. smart energy use, cf. Servatius et al. 2012; Verbong et al. 2013; Lund 2014; Maubach 2014: 71 ff.), which could be further expanded in the context of an even broader Third Industrial Revolution (Rifkin 2014) with regard to digitalization (so-called disruption and *internet of things*, cf. Borell 2015; Miller 2015; Sidhu 2015; Gans 2016) as well as a possible agricultural and mobility/transport turnaround (cf. Appel et al. 2016; Canzler and Wittowsky 2016).

- On the other hand, the possibilities of shaping society socially with the help of technology existed even earlier: in the 1920s, the Bauhaus, among many other intellectual think tanks, propagated the approach of upgrading working and living conditions with the help of modern industrial mass production. Today, the Bauhaus Foundation Dessau is once again taking up utopian designs with regard to the energy transition by discussing scenarios of future energy landscapes (Bruckner and Oswalt 2015). However, the findings on the transformation currently underway point more in the direction of a degrowth society that is less collective-formalized and more individualized-pluralistic. But will this society lead to democratic and sustainable structures? – Ingolfur Blühdorn does not assume so, because due to fragmentation, individualization and pluralization, more patronage interests will prevail according to the Darwinian principle, which take sustainability into account primarily for themselves and also use it as an instrument of power (cf. Blühdorn 2013; alongside criticism in the form of loss of freedom through smart technologies by Welzer 2016). The present study tends to confirm this assessment, because not all population groups participate and benefit equally in the case of community energy. This reveals the core problem of selective participatory and civil society-based approaches: the inequality problem according to the standard socio-economic model also applies to the energy transition and thus remains the central problematic nexus of democracy, sustainability and participation (cf. on the energy transition Großmann et al. 2016; on unequal participation Gabriel 2014, 2015).

More democracy in connection with new technology is thus conceptually created through participation, which can be derived very directly, on a normative level, from the fundamental question "Why participation?": "Because participation offers personal development opportunities, (…) because it brings the opinions and preferences of citizens into the decision-making processes and (…) because participation legitimizes the decisions" (van Deth 2014b: 19). Only if the inclusion of all population groups is successful, however, can simulative, sham participation be countered (Merkel 2015b). A fatalistic conclusion against participation would nevertheless be mistaken, "because more participation does not automatically mean more democracy and more democracy does not necessarily mean more participation, the inevitability of the connection between the two should not be abandoned" (van Deth 2014b: 19). Therefore, in the future it will be important to consciously aim for a "barrier-free" form of participation for all parts of the population with the help of a regulatory variant (Düber et al. 2015). In the case of the energy transition, those directly (locations) and indirectly affected ("energy poverty", cf. Kopatz et al. 2013; Becker et al. 2014a, Hubert 2015; "energy and social inequality", cf.

Großmann et al. 2016) should be particularly in focus. The technological fixation of participation in the case of community energy and smart energy systems is inevitably linked to resources (Tauschek and Grewe 2015), which at the present time again lead to the creation or manifestation of unequal situations of advantage and disadvantage ("reproduction of social inequality", cf. Rehbein et al. 2015). This circumstance leads back to the problem of coupling to infrastructures that enable participation in the first place (Frischmann 2012; Kersten et al. 2012; Hirsch et al. 2013; Schüttpelz and Gießmann 2015). The energy factor, as a basic need, coincides with the housing factor, where a similar "ecosocial paradox" threatens, in that ecological upgrading can again lead to social disadvantage, as increased costs and processes of gentrification are often the result (Holm 2011). The serious discussion about a "right to the city" (Castells 1975; Mitchell 2003; Brenner et al. 2012; Harvey 2012; Lefebvre and Ronneberger 2014; Mullis 2014; Beveridge and Naumann 2015; Lefebvre and Schäfer 2016) highlights the problem of social inequality (Kronauer and Siebel 2013; Fratzscher 2016), which is taken up by social movements and civil society analogous to the community energy movement (Holm and Gebhardt 2011; Gestring et al. 2014). Not only "integration and exclusion in urban society" (Deutsches Institut für Urbanistik 2005a), but also "perspectives of regionalization" (Deutsches Institut für Urbanistik 2005b) beyond the core cities are central challenges of this century. Community approaches such as community energy can be starting points for decentralized measures against materially, infrastructurally and spatially conditioned social imbalances in urban and rural areas (cf. on political design possibilities Lemke 2012).

In summary, it is noticeable that democratic principles and models of application have increasingly become the subject of "debate" (Agamben 2012); there are demands that "democracy must change" (Nolte et al. 2014). Apart from this questioning and statement of a need for reform, however, it remains vague how this change or transformation is to be spelled out. The idea of an energy democracy may seem charming (Farrell 2011; Pfriem et al. 2014; Kunze and Becker 2015b; Weis et al. 2015; Angel 2016; Becker and Naumann 2017 Burke and Stephens 2017; Szulecki 2018; van Veelen and van der Horst 2018; Stephens 2019; Szulecki and Overland 2020; Droubi et al. 2022; Wahlund and Palm 2022), but it transfers normative principles into a multi-layered area of responsibility of politics, business and civil society, which presumably cannot simply be transferred as in the political system.

In recent years, political science has come to realize that at least a change in the political system can be observed, in that there is a "turning away from the parties" (Niedermayer et al. 2013; "Autumn of the People's Parties": Walter 2009)[42],

[42] More recent figures support the assessment that "a continuously decreasing social anchoring of the party system can be observed" (Niedermayer 2014a: 417; cf. also Niedermayer 2014b).

hitherto exercised modes of political participation are increasingly changing and apparently moving more towards individual and civically located activities (Dalton 2008; van Deth 2014a; Hooghe and Oser 2015; Yang et al. 2015). Research findings indicate that classical political participation (elections) is fundamentally and strongly linked to engagement in political associations such as parties, whereas political consumption is linked to political activism but less so to institutionalized participation in parties, clubs or associations (Bolzendahl and Coffé 2013).

In addition to these diagnoses, some views are (again) directed towards the state. For example, in the last report of the Club of Rome, Randers speaks of the state becoming more involved in the future (with regard to expected challenges such as climate change) (Randers 2014: 117 ff.). The transformations of the state have been extensively studied in research in recent years (Leibfried and Zürn 2006; Obinger et al. 2010; Voigt 2014; Leibfried et al. 2015; Voigt 2016), whereby after a "farewell", a "rediscovery" (Voßkuhle et al. 2013) or "reinvention" (Micklethwait and Wooldridge 2014) of the state is finally assumed again in recent times. In the context of climate change and energy transition, the state is therefore of crucial importance because guarantees of supply must be provided in the area of services of general interest; an almost ironclad link between the state and energy supply goes back to the emergence of the latter (Hellige; Radtke 2018b). After phases of privatization in the 1990s and 2000s, the pendulum has swung back again in recent years with remunicipalizations in the energy and infrastructure sectors (cf. Hall et al. 2013a; Sack 2018). In principle, state organization can generate a certain legitimacy and serve the common good via democratic influence and control (Schmitt-Egner 2015). In environmental policy, however, a conflict of goals between legitimacy and effectiveness has been known for some time (Hogl 2012; Newig et al. 2012), which has encouraged privatization tendencies in the past; but this is rather a question of individual legitimacy practice (Lemke et al. 2015).

Although the energy transition is primarily a transformation of the electricity system (Leprich 2014), it is also a social transformation process (Radtke and Hennig 2013; Leprich and Rogall 2014). Overall, it is therefore difficult to overview, analyze and evaluate the diverse, complex and sometimes paradoxical energy turns or transformations (Sarrica et al. 2016). In research, however, the *Energy & Society* debate has been demonstrable for some time (Rosa et al. 1988); currently it has been strongly reignited (Groß and Mautz 2014). Here, the system architecture is analyzed at a higher level, i.e. a broader governance of energy infrastructure. Here, effects of spatial levels as well as processes such as decentralization and polycentrism play a central role (Sovacool 2011; Watson and Devine-Wright 2011; Eiselt 2012; Goldthau 2014; Schmid et al. 2016), which emanate primarily from actors of the so-called third sector (civil society) beyond the state and private sector in the energy system (Wiersma and Devine-Wright 2014). Due to the linkage of different levels (local, regional and national), one can also speak of multilevel governance of renewable energies (Smith 2007). In addition, however, the concrete formulation and design of energy policies with regard to the initiation of energy transitions (Pollitt 2012; Sovacool 2013; Sovacool et al. 2016) and the promotion of community energy projects (Yin 2012) is also important. The literature emphasizes key principles of sustainable energy policies such as stability, participation and transparency (Mendonça et al. 2009). In addition, the idea of policy integration (the policy integration of sustainability is not grafted on, but transferred to all departments as an integrative policy strategy, cf. Bornemann 2014) and niche development of energy transition options has existed for some time, in that existing systems are not radically overhauled, but changes take place within the smaller framework of the large framework conditions that continue to exist (Ratinen and Lund 2015). From this, a potential for sustainable transformations of renewable energy communities (Dóci et al. 2015) can be derived. The political-administrative-economic *framings* of energy policies further create an initial condition to enable forms of participation and phenomena such as community energy, which as a possible outflow of this represent a concrete option for action, which are then again dependent on further variables ("filling the niche"). In this way, institutional change processes can possibly also contribute to the generation of technological legitimacy (Markard et al. 2016). Overall, the importance of political-economic governance of the energy transition is described in the literature as "key" to establishing sustainable communities (Clark II and Li 2014).

Another question concerns how local regions deal with energy transition goals and support for local (community) energy initiatives (Trutnevyte et al. 2011; Trutnevyte and Stauffacher 2012). Thus, the establishment of a socio-political space for renewable energies can certainly be assumed using the example of the impact of the EEG (Lauber and Jacobsson 2016). A potentially emerging energy governance in the sense of an energy community is already being spelled out (Buschle and Talus 2015). The energy transition in Germany, with the possibility of community energy or participation options, is now seen as a pioneering role worthy of imitation internationally (cf. Li et al. 2013); there is also talk of a German revolution in the decentralization of the energy system (Burger and Weinmann 2014). However, the German electricity market is currently "in a state of upheaval": a new market order is already being hotly debated (cf. Löschel et al. 2015).

In individual countries, targeted community energy governance strategies can be found, for example in UK (cf. for an investigation of policy strategies: Cass et al. 2010 as well as the government's community energy promotion strategy: Department of Energy and Climate Change 2014) and explicitly in Scotland (cf.

The Scottish Government 2013), where the operation of community wind farms is widespread (similarly in Northern Germany).[43]

For concrete implementation, however, small-scale, local *community-oriented* policies are required (Hain et al. 2005), which promote renewable energies and climate protection; these have been considered for some time in the form of a *community energy policy* or *community energy management* (Jaccard et al. 1997). The issues of *governing community energy* are already being discussed in pioneering countries such as the UK and Germany with regard to feed-in tariffs (Nolden 2013; Tveten et al. 2013; De Boeck et al. 2016; Hall et al. 2016; Winkler et al. 2016), while other contexts such as US energy monitoring and policy are being critically scrutinized (Gilbert and Sovacool 2016). Of particular importance for community energy projects are participatory, sustainable and inclusive local energy planning processes (Neves et al. 2015) and elaborations of policy options for community energy planning (Newsham and Donnelly 2013).

In local implementation, driving actors (local promoters and supra-regional project developers) and behaviors play a key role (Izutsu et al. 2012; Lopes et al. 2012, cf. on the role of municipal utilities Strasser et al. 2012); in this context, possibilities of new scope for action and a new understanding of the role of local institutions and administrations are considered in particular, e.g. in the sense of non-commercial corporatism (Lenhart et al. 2015; Argento et al. 2016; Di Giulio et al. 2016; Clifton et al. 2016; Marie 2016; McDonald 2016). The importance of promoters as initiators and project developers within the communities and outside in local networks and *epistemic communities* (David and Schönborn 2016: 48 ff.) as well as patterns of delegation of public tasks to public welfare-oriented actors such as community energy projects in the function as *group agents* (List and Pettit 2013) including feedback with the group/community as well as influences in local policies in the context of sustainability communities must be researched in more detail in the future.

Countries, regions and municipalities often pursue the principle of decentralization in their local climate protection policies (Eiselt 2012; Agentur für Erneuerbare Energien 2015; Funcke and Bauknecht 2016). This is usually accompanied by energy autonomy efforts of "sustainability communities" (Schweizer-Ries 2008; Rae and Bradley 2012), for instance via applied approaches such as road maps for decentrally organized *energy communities*, taking into account aspects of ownership and citizen participation, rural and urban contexts (cf. El Bassam et al. 2013; Lawson et al. 2016). The ideas of citizen energy or community energy operation, use and organization have, incidentally, been around for a long time (Bossel 1978:

[43] See at http://www.communityenergyscotland.org.uk

86 ff.; Hubbard and Fong 1995); concepts in the form of guidebooks on how to organize one's own or community-based local energy systems are also being formulated again today in a similar form (Pahl 2007, 2012). What all approaches have in common is that they focus on the regional level and its modes of action and solutions ("regional-innovative system perspective", cf. Mattes et al. 2015; also Mattes et al. 2015). Due to connections between the concept of community energy and fundamental aspects of participatory, deliberative, energy and climate democracy, however, normative questions are essentially included in empirical analyses of community energy, hence references to both the empirical and normative orientation of theories of democracy need to be discussed (Lembcke et al. 2012, 2015). This ultimately leads to a need for the theorization of participatory-environmental, energy and sustainability policies – yet these are still in an early stage of research (Gabrielson 2016).

The Wicked Problems of the Energy Transition

The Problem of Scale

Finally, the analysis of community energy projects leads to three trade-offs known in participation and organization research, all of which can be assigned to a scale problem:

- **Trade-off between project size and proximity**: large community energy projects are often more distant from members than energy projects located locally in a municipality, which can be attributed to both spatial and social distance, as professional management tends to have less direct contact with members.
- **Trade-off between participation and effectiveness**: member participation takes up resources of the organization and at the same time is not available for other tasks of day-to-day business and management, and ultimately efficiency and flexibility suffer.
- **Trade-off between project size and professionalization/economization**: larger community energy projects tend to optimize their technical and bureaucratic management to cope with the scale of activities and further expansion.

In the literature, these phenomena between participation and effectiveness have been described as a dilemma by Robert Dahl, who sees system effectiveness in conflict with citizen participation (Dahl 1994). Dahl also assumes that another democratic paradox exists: the ideal of democracy is highly valued by all individuals in democracies, yet there is little trust in state institutions (Dahl 2000). However, this paradox seems less demonstrable in the context of the energy transition: In this case, state and civil-society commitment tend to ally against the conventional energy suppliers of the private sector. In fact, however, a view of community energy members that is critical of the state has come to light in interviews and survey results of the present study; meanwhile, the criticism is intensifying as state remuneration for renewable energies has been reduced, which particularly affects community solar energy projects. This leads to the differentiation of state institutions vis-à-vis citizens: while local politics and administrations can become partners of community energy projects, the shadow falls on regulations of federal politics and thus reduces the overall reputation of the level.

Furthermore, the trade-offs between size, closeness to members and professionalization are described in the literature by Keil (2013b): The larger the association, the more economic issues come to the fore and the less closeness to members is achieved. This observation also seems to apply here (cf. also similar distinction in the model of community energy in Walker and Devine-Wright 2008). Increasing size seems to promote tendencies towards monetization, economization, bureaucratization, distance to members, shadow sides of social capital, less individual member participation and social exchange or togetherness. From this, one could simplistically deduce that increasing the size of an organization can be understood as a negative value. However, it should be noted that a certain organizational size may be necessary for the survival of the unit. In this way, more capacity to act can be achieved and thus more areas of responsibility tend to be served, which can also result in a member orientation (e.g. events, campaigns, programs and support for members). The survey results show that members are torn between the need for professionalism on the one hand and closeness to members, contact and influence on the other: On the one hand, professionalism is advocated and demanded, but on the other hand, closeness to members is also highly valued (cf. in particular qualitative survey data), whereby, conversely, small community energy projects emphasize professionalism more strongly, while large ones emphasize closeness to members – since there are obviously deficits in each case, but their elimination in turn causes the other loss.

The Multi-Level Governance Dilemma of the Energy Transition

Even if a local solution to the energy transition is entirely in line with the subsidiarity principle of the Basic Law, negotiation processes with other political levels are probably the greatest challenges (level dilemma, cf. Meadowcroft 2002; Moss and Newig 2010). Dialogue processes – as practiced in the case of grid expansion (cf. Kamlage 2013a, 2013b) – promise to prevent the drift into separate spheres. Here again, challenges lie in the interaction of too many actors and interests (entanglement trap, cf. Scharpf 1994) as well as in the possibly inevitable subordination of municipal interests in the federal system. Bauer speaks of participation entanglement traps in the context of participation procedures in the case of electricity grid expansion: Due to the different intentions of participating administrations and participating citizens, which are also introduced at different times, possible positive effects (i.e. taking up and utilizing suggestions, creating alternatives, "involving" the population in the process) cannot be developed due to these diverging logics (cf. Bauer 2015). The creation of stakeholder forums to hold discourses at joint "round tables" can in turn bring the levels together (examples: EnergyDialog. NRW, Grid Expansion in Dialogue, Citizens' Dialogue "Energy Technologies for the Future", Wind Energy Round Table, Renewable Energy Dialogue Forum), although the general population is not involved. An explicit example of direct citizen participation is the "Conflict Dialogues on the Approval of Energy Transition Projects" (biomass plants, geothermal energy, extra-high voltage power lines, pumped storage power plants, wind turbines) already developed on behalf of the Federal Environment Agency, although these have not yet been tested in practice (cf. Ziekow et al. 2015) as well as open, but less specific and therefore less suitable for solving concrete problems, citizens' forums (cf. Hohberg et al. 2014) and company dialogues on conflict topics such as fracking (Saretzki and Bornemann 2014).

According to Beinke et al. (2012), who call for a collaborative design of the Energiewende in Germany (similarly Töpfer et al. 2013; Reuter 2015 speaks of collaborative infrastructures in technology design), a main danger is that there is a sole "focus on formal procedures" (Beinke et al. 2012: 6). Therefore, there is a need to invest in dialogue. In a model for participation-oriented infrastructure planning, they propose to inform as consistently as possible, to give dialogue a central place (dialogue forum), to clarify and evaluate facts, to plan jointly and to involve citizens financially (Beinke et al. 2012: 7 ff.). Kamlage has already been able to analyze in dialogue procedures in the context of grid expansion that even conflicts that were conducted "without compromise" for years could be resolved in the end in a consensual and trust-building manner (Kamlage 2013a: 12; cf. also Kamlage et al. 2014, critically: Leibenath et al. 2016), which gives cause for hope. The results of the present study suggest that community energy projects can also make valuable contributions to conflict resolution in the establishment of renewable energies – though detailed studies and research results are still pending.

However, an overarching question arises as to whether larger societal challenges can no longer be solved due to the small-scale nature and fragmentation of issues and ideas, which is very close to the approach of systems theory (cf. Werber 2011). In political science, authors such as Michael Greven also assume that because all social actors think and act on a small-scale, selective and self-interested manner, they always remain in their narrow, limited spheres (scope for action) and do not go beyond them (Greven 2009: 219 ff.). Accordingly, a particularized society has lost overarching social ideas. Ultimately, however, what remains problematic with this view is that confusion, and an overload in discourse can threaten, interweaving traps of actors and strongly moderated formats (and thus limited in their possibilities for development) that suggest a simulation of participation (cf. Miessen 2012; Blühdorn 2013; Michelsen and Walter 2013; Wagner 2013; Merkel 2015b). The hope for discourse and a democratic force to resolve conflicts, overcome dualistic thinking and exclusively economic grabbing of benefits ultimately represents an (all too) large projection surface and could be overused. Especially in cases where citizens discuss a "when is enough enough" (Jones et al. 2011) in the face of proliferating technology in their immediate environment, it can be considered whether all the tools of coordination, participation and discourse do not change the fact that technology remains alien to people at its core and that symptoms (such as fears and dissatisfaction) can be treated, but not remedied at the root causes. The recipe for community energy here is to activate individuals who are confronted with new challenges (here the establishment of renewable energies), a kind of action therapy. As is well known, this is a very suitable means to counter feelings of powerlessness. After all, community energy promises ownership and thus, above all, control of events. Provided that this control then does not amount to just a few, the concept seems to be favorable for civil society. But precisely this transfer of acquired power would have to fall to the local sovereign in democratic terms. Niklas Luhmann (see above) also came to this conclusion, considering both this legitimacy deficit and the problematic side effects of participation in the form of fundamental pitfalls of expanding and counteracting bureaucracy of participation as well as inclusion and exclusion effects. His approach to solving this problem is therefore to change the mode of the system: he calls for a return to the representative republican system, which, despite the disadvantages of a lack of direct influence and involvement in processes of action, promises the advantages of legitimacy and direct responsibility as well as the decisive connection of citizens to the political system, who can otherwise develop an increasingly negative image and an exclusionfrom the democratic process, which in turn then erodes more strongly (Luhmann 2009: 165 ff.).

Making Community Energy Work: Negotiating and Deliberating Local Climate and Energy Policies as a Promising Solution?

One solution for the social management of the energy transition can be found in local negotiation processes, in which as many interests and concerns as possible are given a "voice" and in this way unequally weighted distributions of influence and power tend to be prevented. This local approach cannot be considered the exclusive silver bullet, but it promises a number of advantages in the sense of Bruno Latour's fundamental idea of "making things public" (cf. Latour and Weibel 2005).

According to Latour, such matters and discourses must first be made visible in order to find solutions through discussion, evaluation and joint, consensual negotiation processes. With this consideration, one can make links to Jürgen Habermas´ ideas of deliberative discourse from (idea of deliberation, cf. Habermas 1992, 2011). Ortwin Renn is a representative of the deliberative approach to procedures in the context of the energy transition (Renn 2012, 2013a, 2013b; Renn et al. 2014), which is also discussed in the current scientific debates (for example, the importance of participation and discourse is emphasized in the context of application examples such as the 100% renewable energy regions and numerous bioenergy villages, cf. deENet 2009; Rau and Zöllner 2011; Moser 2011; Zöllner et al. 2011; Rau et al. 2012; Ruppert-Winkel et al. 2013; Jami and Walsh 2014; Walker et al. 2014; Slee 2015; Grundmann and Ehlers 2016).[44]

Renn sees an analytical-deliberative discourse as a "promising method" to "integrate factual knowledge and values into a participation process" (Renn et al. 2014: 7). On the one hand, the possible consequences of different decision options should be determined analytically "to the best of our knowledge in all their complexity and interconnectedness"; on the other hand, there is a "deliberative task of finding an effective, efficient and fair solution to the initial problem on the basis of an exchange of arguments" (ibid.). First, Renn aims to assess the consequences in the form of opportunities and risks of the possible options for solving the problem in an "interdisciplinary forum with knowledge bearers" (ibid.). Finally, however, an "evaluation of the options for action" must be undertaken, which is to be done by representatives from "science, politics, business and civil society" (ibid.). Renn sees various possibilities for the selection of who may participate in the discourse in the case of non-organized interests, of which he prefers the random principle (i.e. random selection of representatives of the population) with regard to the democratic ideal, "because in theory this gives every affected citizen the same chance to actively participate in the discourse" (ibid.: 8). Thus, Renn sees the participation of citizens in a deliberative discourse as an opportunity to expand the knowledge base, provide important information for decision-makers, enable fair negotiations for resources, shape one's own lifeworld and promote a competition of arguments

[44] In the literature on the Energiewende, a distinction is made in the context of stakeholder and public participation between six different philosophical concepts (functionalist, neoliberal, deliberative, anthropological, emancipatory, postmodern), which are concretely translated with regard to the objective and approach of participation processes (Renn and Schweizer 2009: 180; Schweizer 2015: 28). However, it seems questionable whether these sometimes extremely complex and not self-contained systems of thought and theory can be broken down in this way.

"with the aim of placing collective decisions on a normatively secure basis on the grounds of justifications" (Renn 2013a: 15 f.). At the core is a discourse of "reasoned positions under the framework conditions of an examination of the arguments put forward in each case based strictly on logic and consistent derivation (claim to validity and proof of validity)" (ibid.: 16). For those involved, the focus is above all on "the question of the reasonableness of normative settings for all those affected (beyond the circle of those participating in the discourse)" (ibid.). According to Alcántara et al. (2014: 172), deliberative participation procedures "(…) serve the actual, factual discussion and consultation on the part of the population as well as the accumulation of knowledge, long before the decision on a state of affairs. Different sides are heard and given the opportunity to present their arguments, opinions and ideas. Mutual learning and opinion-forming processes take place, and the process leads to consensus or the disclosure of dissent". If one takes such an energy transition discourse between participating citizens as well as representatives of energy technology and participants from science, civil society, politics and administration as a basis, then not only questions regarding energy technology and its effects (e.g. nature conservation and health, cf. Songsore and Buzzelli 2014) flow in here, but locations of plants also become significant (Fast and Mabee 2015). However, not all discourse and participation formats are deliberative (overview in Alcántara et al. 2014: 157 ff.), and such procedures will therefore not "per se and under all circumstances represent progress towards a democratization of democracy" (ibid.: 4). Success depends on the "design of the procedures (according to normatively founded quality criteria)" and the "context of their implementation (in particular the situation of social inequality and asymmetrical power relations)", as problems of legitimacy can arise in particular by not including "disadvantaged groups" (ibid.).

In previously studied cases of wind energy (Jobert et al. 2007), grid expansion (Hoffmann 2014; Kamlage et al. 2014; Bauer 2015) and community energy (Devine-Wright 2005b; Walker and Devine-Wright 2008; Devine-Wright and Wiersma 2013; Yildiz et al. 2015), the importance of local references is particularly emphasized. In discourses, disputes and negotiations about the energy transition on the ground, the question of who negotiates there and how this takes place is thus central (cf. Brühne and Tempel 2013; Becker et al. 2015a; Brühne 2015). The "expert-friendly" perspective in Renn et al. (2014) can be critically questioned here: To what extent do experts represent marginal interests? Do hardly-noticed actors find their way into energy discourses? To answer these questions, it would be necessary to conduct more in-depth discourse analyses (cf. Fast 2013).

Alcántara et al. nevertheless hope, despite "the situation of social inequality and asymmetrical power relations", for "feasible possibilities of active empowerment of disadvantaged groups (…) as preconditions for successful legitimacy-generating procedures" (Alcántara et al. 2014: 4). They thus arrive at the positive vision of a "participation" of society, "(…) to dare more participation, indeed, to establish a 'culture of participation'" (ibid.: 5). Demanding prerequisites for this are "strict orientation towards high-quality procedures and processes, the institutional safeguarding of participation through the creation of clear and reliable framework conditions and the introduction of initiative rights, the provision of resources, the facilitation of democracy learning processes, the safeguarding of knowledge infrastructures as well as the further development of quality criteria and possibilities of linking participation processes with the representative system" (ibid.). All this, however, could only be achieved through an "institutional underpinning" of the "participation culture" in the form of "mainstreaming participation at all levels of politics and administration", a lofty goal. In the spirit of the idea of democratization in the 1960s and 1970s, participation mainstreaming is to be achieved by "gradually widening public participation" by "in perspective, greatly expanding the role of all people in the political process and increasingly transforming the representative system into the participatory one, thereby narrowing the gap between politics, administration and the population in favor of a cooperative atmosphere" (ibid.: 5). With the help of this "ambitious program", "democracy can be filled with new life again" and "challenges of the future can be mastered better, more democratically, more in the sense of the people" (ibid.: 5).

Even with these considerations, the path ultimately leads back to far-reaching and hitherto utopian demands on politics and society, where, due to the essential connectivity, more participation would have to be achieved in order to overcome isolated "islands of participation". However, the deliberative approach has also come under criticism in the meantime (cf. Flügel-Martinsen et al. 2014; Landwehr and Schmalz-Bruns 2014; Merkel 2015b: 42 ff. – for example, Leibenath et al. (2016) speak of a "talking shop" in the case of wind power public participation); possible alternatives to the strong emphasis on deliberation should be considered, which – as in the case of community energy – achieve positive results without foregrounding the deliberative paradigm. However, for comprehensive evaluations and comparisons of more or less deliberative participatory arrangements, more detailed information on socio-political contextual conditions would first be necessary (such as can be found in Baden-Württemberg through democracy monitoring, see Baden-Württemberg Stiftung 2015). In addition, the importance of informal politics (Bröchler et al. 2014; Bröchler and Lauth 2014) and its modes of action within governance arrangements and organizations should not be underestimated (von Groddeck and Wilz 2015). Finally, micro-phenomena and their interactions at the individual level must also be taken into account (for instance, individual motivations and modes of action within community energy groups), such as situational identity formation and social acceleration tendencies (Rosa 2013a, 2013b).

The Arithmetic of Community Energy in Germany: A Civil Society-Based Model in International Comparison?

Some countries' analyses suggest[45] that from a comparative perspective, in Germany a specific type of community energy is more popular than in other countries, as a result of the civil society background of many community energy projects in the country. This civil society pillar, on which many community energy projects were founded and which in turn is strongly grounded and dependent on already existing social capital in local communities, could be a specific German phenomenon (cf. analysis on this by Blanchet et al. 2016), although this grassroots variant can be found everywhere (see e.g. definition and analysis for UK in Smith 2012). Community energy is more or less linked to public engagement in every form and networked with civil society (see analysis on the influence of civil society in the energy transition in Italy in Magnani and Osti 2016), but in Germany it is mainly environmental clubs, associations, Local Agenda groups, climate protection initiatives, social movements such as Fridays for Future etc., from which the igniting engagement emanates. The characteristics and structures of civil society as well as dominant overarching motives for the establishment of community energy, such as climate protection or self-sufficient energy supply, presumably differ significantly between countries and regions as well as different community energy projects; a wide variety of constellations can be found in practice (see comparison in the area of fashion campaigns of social movements in France and Switzerland in Balsiger 2014; environmental attitudes and behavior in a European comparison in Telesiene and Groß 2016; on investment or participation motives in community energy Holstenkamp and Kahla 2016).

In many case studies, but also in numerous cases of the survey of the present study, it is mostly strongly pulsating, community-organized, discourse-intensive groupings of the grassroots variety from which community energy projects grow. A strong indication of the civil society base in Germany is the very high engagement value of 80% from the survey (and over 50% membership in environmental

[45] For example, for the UK: Seyfang et al. 2012, 2013; for Australia: Hicks and Ison 2011; Mey et al. 2016; Mey and Hicks 2015; for the USA: Hoffman and High-Pippert 2005, 2010; for Canada: Girvitz and Lipp 2005; see also overviews in Hielscher 2011 and Holstenkamp and Radtke 2018.

protection organizations according to the survey by Rauschmayer et al. 2015), in that the members are in any case predominantly also members of civil society or political associations and organizations in addition to their community energy engagement. In this respect, the Energiewende is indeed vibrating in German civil society, although further research is still needed in this field for a more detailed assessment and better classification. However, part of the phenomenon can probably be explained by the fact that in many other countries a strong use of wind energy is implied; in Germany, however, the civil society-based projects are particularly active in the photovoltaic sector, which is possibly more characterized by private individuals or commercial use elsewhere. Due to the high investment sums, wind energy often implies other organizational constructions, in which citizen participation then often makes up a smaller part of the total financing and thus also restricts co-determination and control. Nevertheless, the cooperative idea could also be transferred towards wind energy cooperatives (see case study 2 of the present study as well as for an assessment of the situation in Europe Bauwens et al. 2016). The results of this study suggest, however, that the technology used does not necessarily indicate the character of the operating community: In the case studies of the present study, civil society links are present in the photovoltaic sector as well as in the use of wind energy and geothermal energy. In percentage terms, however, civil society involvement or a civil society context of origin is probably less pronounced in the energy projects, which are associated with high expenditure and high investment sums. Findings from the literature and the present study also show that the predominant motives for establishing community energy differ contextually (e.g. in relation to types of community energy projects,, types of energy used, year of foundation, regions, initiators/leadership, members and amount of participation), e.g. in the form of a stronger return motive in the case of citizens' wind farms (cf. Rauschmayer et al. 2015; Bauwens 2016; Bauwens et al. 2016: 142; Holstenkamp and Kahla 2016). These findings can also be used as indications of differences between a less return-oriented civil society and a more return-oriented entrepreneurial variant of community energy. Another factor that decisively shapes community energy engagement is also the legal provisions on remuneration, operation, etc. (cf. analysis in this regard for France and Canada in Feurtey et al. 2015 and on the UK and Germany in Hall et al. 2016) as well as individual local support structures. Actors of citizen wind in North Rhine-Westphalia consider the guaranteed feed-in tariff to be absolutely essential with regard to the successful realization of community wind projects (Landesverband Erneuerbare Energien NRW and World Wind Energy Association 2016: 2).

Finally, two different types of communizy energy can be distinguished:

- **More citizen participation-oriented (community energy model with private participation mode):** Individual-citizen *grassroots approach* (cf. Seyfang et al. 2014), example: citizens' groups or associations found a community energy project.
- **Less citizen participation-oriented (community energy model with actor-based participation mode):** Collaborative, more actor- or institution-based approach (cf. Hoffman and High-Pippert 2005, 2010, cf. different models in Europe in Becker and Kunze 2014: 184), example: a wind farm is jointly financed by different investors (e.g. company, school, association, municipality); possibly a larger number of individual citizen participation is planned, but this share would not predominate within the total capacity of the project; further example: spin-off project of environmental associations.

This differentiation is also taken up by Walker and Devine-Wright (2008) in their description of community energy, and Holstenkamp and Degenhart (2013) distinguish between community energy in the narrower and broader sense (whereby a strong criterion here is the requirement of at least 50%citizen participation; adopted for the special regulation in the 2016 EEG amendment, see BMWi 2016: 11).[46]

In Germany, both community energy models can be found. In between are countless hybrid constructions, which in turn can be grouped into three larger types:

1. **Community solar energy cooperatives** (which make up the largest number in this study): These projects often have a strong grassroots character (which can also be the case with larger projects such as EWS Schönau (Sladek 2015), but members here are usually further away and tend to exert less influence).
2. **Community wind farms:** Here, individual actors (initiators are, for example, landowners/property owners such as farmers or banks, project developers, etc.) are more likely to be active founding investment in order to offer interested citizens top-down participation (cf. Gamel et al. 2016).
3. **Large multi-MW community energy projects:** These companies are quite similar to energy suppliers, but they offer shareholdings and often serve several types of energy, including electricity or heat supply, grid operation, etc. The representation and co-determination of participants is lower than in energy co-

[46] Cf. on the various financing models, organizational structures and systematizations: Enzensberger et al. 2003; Yildiz 2014; Holstenkamp 2015.

operatives, but even in this context there are positive effects on the participants, as the survey results suggest. Stakeholders in larger top-down projects, however, would like to have more opportunities for co-determination and shaping/influence.

Apparently, different clienteles of the population also feel addressed by the diverse community energy participation options: for example, the larger projects offer a more anonymous participation that also does not include further "obligations" (i.e. a further, obvious commitment that can at least be socially implied). However, since presumably not all participation options can appeal to all parts of the population, and since "democratization" can neither necessarily be assumed nor guaranteed, both within the community energy projects and through their influence on the energy system, state solutions could well be used, since guarantees can be created here (by applying public budgets and exercising legitimized control), which are not guaranteed in the private civil society sector (a state, transformative regulatory policy is called for, for example, by the German Advisory Council on Global Change in its 2012 report on financing the global energy transition, cf. WBGU 2012; on the topic, cf. further Argento et al. 2016; Clifton et al. 2016; Di Giulio et al. 2016; Marie 2016; McDonald 2016). The Basic Law, for example, provides for the provision of public services and infrastructure by the state (Art. 28, para. 2 Basic Law). For this reason, however, joint projects such as community energy structured by civil society and the private sector do not have to be fundamentally called into question; a plurality of forms of operation, stronger state involvement and more opportunities for the population to influence local energy policy beyond membership in a community energy project would be advantageous, at least from the perspective of participation, democracy and state theory, as is also being considered in the horizontal governance network mode (cf. Wolf and Pfohl 2014) – even if this is opposed by struggling municipal budgets. One conclusion that can be drawn from this is that greater emphasis must be placed on cooperation between actors (cooperative governance arrangements) in order to network and synchronize different approaches in the energy sector, such as municipal utilities, energy cooperatives, energy suppliers and climate protection initiatives; and thus to create a broader participation portfolio overall that is open to more actors and citizens and creates further alternatives for action and design (cf. on the need for coordination of the energy transition in federalism Schreurs and Steuwer 2015, on the topic Müller and Kahl 2015).

Finally, a four-field model can be sketched out that distinguishes between state-public (publicly owned municipal utilities) and civil society operation (citizen-initiated and financed: community energy cooperative) as well as more private-sector-oriented actors (e.g. Greenpeace Energy, Greencity Energy, solarcomplex AG). Greenpeace Energy, Greencity Energy, solarcomplex AG) and other actors that are hybrid in the form of public-private-partnerships or public-private-economy-civil-society (e.g. consisting of (high)schools, clubs, associations, workforces, individual investors and municipalities). In practice, a wide variety of arrangements can be found, which can be assigned to a field to a greater or lesser extent.

Based on the results of the study, the thesis is summarized here that the arithmetic of German community energy is strongly characterized by an active civil society. In particular, the mode in which bottom-up activity by engaged citizens and civil society groups is present seems to be disproportionately pronounced in an international comparative perspective. A comprehensive and targeted country-comparative study on this question is still pending. The question of the extent to which participation and community energy projects lead to an *empowerment* of citizens and individual actors and thus possibly feed alternative modes of action, social practices, forms of organization and more participation into society cannot yet be answered conclusively (see discussion in Schreuer 2016). However, these questions of *overspill* and *upscaling* are of fundamental importance for the future of the energy transition(s) and the idea of an emerging degrowth society. The increased interest in participation in general in public society expressed in the survey can be interpreted as an indication of a possible *empowerment of* the citizens involved.

As highlighted in the present study, the outstanding advantage of the community energy participation model is to involve citizens in a very direct way with their voice, but on the other hand, this variant of participation is also particularly vulnerable to social problems such as excessive demands, frustration, exclusions, rapidly declining commitment and low environmental support (similar findings are revealed by results of the survey in social innovation projects in Europe, cf. Pel et al. 2015). Institutionally created and secured conditions for engagement and action are thus essential for community energy (cf. Wirth 2014), but at the same time a backlash and concrete influence of grassroots community initiatives on local energy policies can be observed (cf. Blanchet 2015 and Becker et al. 2016b on community initiatives in Berlin and Hamburg that want to take over the operation of the electricity grid), which still needs to be investigated further.

The generation of social capital through community energy can ultimately be seen as a characteristic type of civil society, whereby the drawbacks of civil society contrast with the advantages of participation opportunities; there are also advantages and disadvantages in the case of public sponsorship (such as guarantees of existence, action on behalf of the public, political control functions, indirect democratic influence via elections).

Finally, mergers can make community energy projects sustainable, as in the case of Bürgerwerke, where forty community energy projects have joined forces, thus creating resilience for future challenges (e.g. with regard to new tendering procedures under the Renewable Energy Sources Act) and linking up with the idea of consuming, marketing and offering self-generated green electricity (prosuming idea). The larger associations are then likely to be faced with the challenge of internal democracy and participation opportunities for their members; on the one hand, the commitment and participation of the members is contrasted with a larger corporate format and a greater capacity to act and compete, effectiveness and professionalization of the holding companies on the other. The results of the present study indeed point to such a trade-off – however: a participatory culture can also be established in larger organizations. Smith et al. (2015) argue from the perspective of socio-economic niche research that, in addition to *strategic niche management* and *niche policy advocacy,* a consideration and analysis of *critical niches* with regard to social issues (keyword integration etc.) is also necessary to make the concept of community energy truly viable.

Seyfang and Haxeltine assume a growing number of *grassroots innovations*, especially in the field of sustainability, but the significance of social movements in this field of innovation, which are community-based, has hardly been researched yet (Seyfang and Haxeltine 2010) – which is why Seyfang et al. propose a special research agenda for the study of civil society influences in the energy transition or in sustainability transformations (Seyfang et al. 2010).

The Future of the Energy Transition: Participation Myth and Social Gap
According to the Ethics Commission, Germany's energy transition is "a collective work for the future" (cf. Ethik-Kommission Sichere Energieversorgung 2011, critically Rosenkranz 2014: 126). Although community energy projects can indeed create a form of community through collective action (Hardin 2015), the phenomenon is not sufficiently pronounced to be representative of the many local, regional and supra-regional energy turns (cf. Müller et al. 2015). In this respect, it remains questionable to what extent the energy transition can serve to create "more inclusive, just and sustainable spaces" (Jeffrey et al. 2012) beyond a few best-practice examples and not exacerbate existing social inequalities (Großmann et al. 2016). Hoffjann, Gusko and Sliwa speak of a "participation myth" in German associations, which intended to enable large-scale participation but offered little (Hoffjann et al. 2013). The "participation myth" also applies in part – as has been shown – to the community energy projects: Participation is important to every initiator interviewed, but enabling and actual take-up lag behind (in the literature this is characterized as a newer basic problem of civil society, Skocpol (1999) calls it "advocates without members").

The question of whether energy cooperatives "make green electricity more valuable" (Müller and Sagebiel 2015) or primarily serve a "growing green money" (Seyfang and Longhurst 2013) can remain open in conclusion, as both aspects are two sides of the same coin in the case of community energy. From the perspective of the population as a whole, on the other hand, a central question of the energy transition remains- to what extent energy consumption becomes a burden and a problem for citizens (Jamasb and Pollitt 2011). One approach to solving some of the problems (costs, resources, participation) could be "sustainability through region building" (Röber 2015). By facing up to challenges such as the energy transition, through bundled coordination and actor associations, regions and cities can think together in an overarching way about modern forms of citizen participation in municipalities (Hartwig and Kroneberg 2014), especially since sustainability initiatives at the local level definitely enjoy a high status and are thus also found (Rösler 2004). In this framework, numerous "options of modern citizen participation in infrastructure projects" (Albrecht et al. 2010) can be tested and coordinated, possibly also meeting requirements in large infrastructure projects (Schröter and Scheel 2015). Urban neighborhood cooperatives, which are *also* energy cooperatives (Müller and Rommel 2011), can also play a future role in this context by integrating them into the city or region as *integrated community energy systems* (Koirala et al. 2016), especially as they increasingly strive for energy self-sufficiency (cf. Moss and Francesch-Huidobro 2016). In this study, for example, the Local Agenda 21 approach, which has often been criticized and sometimes rejected, proved to be a very successful initiating factor for community energy projects. Similarly, potentials could be activated and tapped in the future at neighborhood level and through community solutions by households (Burchell et al. 2016). The model for this is holistic and integrative sustainable, participatory neighborhood and urban development[47] with city-wide management (Hölzinger et al. 2014), which includes urban sustainability initiatives (Barnebeck and Kalff 2015). The role of cities in the energy transition (Troglio and Haas 2013; Sauer et al. 2015a, 2015b) is being increasingly focused on as a whole, in terms of the possibility of "post-fossil urban development" (Hehn 2015), in which energy cooperatives also play a key role (Kooyman and Smit 2013). This could be one possible future for community energy as part of more integrative, decentralized energy system solutions in urban or rural districts (Adil and Ko 2016). Whatsmore, in this integrated

[47] Cf. Selle et al. 1996; Fritsche 2011; Mayer et al. 2011; Drilling and Schnur 2012; Bott et al. 2013; Selle 2013; Blandow et al. 2014; Klages 2014; Wilde 2014.

way, community energy could ultimately create more empowered participation (Fung 2006) for energy communities (Koirala et al. 2016), which completely participate and reap the benefits of the concept. At the same time, there is a risk that the community energy practiced so far will ultimately fail elsewhere: Those involved in citizen wind in North Rhine-Westphalia are already registering a decline in social interest in the energy transition as well as increasing opposition from nature conservation and species protection associations; in addition, there is increasing complexity in planning and operation and high lease levels (Landesverband Erneuerbare Energien NRW and World Wind Energy Association 2016: 3).

Nevertheless, the technology focus of this civic participation (cf. National Democratic Institute 2014) and the material character (Marres 2012) will persist – and thus appeal in particular to certain population groups and milieus. The critical comment that social cooperation can be seen as "commerce and community" (Garnett 2014) is perhaps going too far, however, the community energy examples in particular represent cases where an ecologically friendly financial investment and a little community do coincide. The sustainable neighborhoods as a solution to the community energy dilemma create more points of reference for a wider circle of residents, but in a global perspective, a problem of marginalization of rural areas could arise, especially as the expansion of renewable energies is more strongly pursued here.

The core problem thus remains a "participatory inequality" inherent in these forms of participation (Offe 2014; cf. also Lee et al. 2015). Lee et al. 2015), which Winfried Thaa summed up as an "unresolved inclusion problem in participatory reassessments of political representation" (Thaa 2009; Schäfer and Schoen (2013) speak of a conflict of goals between more participation and political participation ("more democracy, but only for a few"), furthermore inclusion problems and lack of possibilities for deliberation in participatory arrangements are addressed by Ganuza and Francés 2011a and the basic problem by Schlozman et al. 1999; Schlozman et al. 2012; van Deth 2014b and Gabriel 2013a, 2014, 2015). The hope that participation will act as a panacea ("Panakeia for the energy transition", cf. Schweizer and Renn 2013) can therefore not be fulfilled insofar as some population groups are so disproportionately represented in the forms of participation. This tends to create the danger that already existing social inequalities are further reproduced by a supposed solution measure in the form of engagement and participation (cf. Munsch 2005; Rehbein et al. 2015). In addition, there is the problem of minority protection: as long as community energy projects neither integrate certain minorities of the local community (e.g. also opponents of the energy project) nor map a representative average of the local population (which is why the projects can only offer a selective co-determination principle), minorities in the population have less representation and thus influence and therefore tend to be disadvantaged or marginalized (cf. on the fundamental problem of minority protection in the context of participation Kolbe 2013). The effect of local networks, in which community energy projects move and shape themselves, can also create or reproduce inequalities (cf. Fuhse 2010). This community energy dilemma can be characterized as a *social gap,* following studies on the expansion of wind power in Great Britain by Bell et al. (Bell et al. 2005; Bell et al. 2013). The social and equity problem in the establishment of renewable energies (both individually and collectively as well as distributively and procedurally) described by Bell et al. can thus be seen as a fundamental problem of the energy transition (Adams and Bell 2014; Johnson and Hall 2015; Sovacool and Dworkin 2015; Fuller and McCauley 2016)[48] .

How could these problems be solved in the future? What could happen on the participation services side? There are ideas in the literature that a special "design" (e.g. of technology) can already promote participation and sustainability (Stirling et al. 2007). In addition to *framing,* it is, above all, the quality of citizen participation processes that is most likely to generate acceptance and legitimacy, as Schröter et al. (2016) assume (fairness and competence in citizen participation have long been emphasized as essential prerequisites for successful participation processes, cf.). They distinguish between a wide variety of participatory arrangements after analyzing thirty different definitions of citizen participation. This allows them to finally determine three overarching criteria (Inclusiveness, Information exchange and learning, Influence on political decisions) as well as sub-criteria (Platform for communication and negotiation, Equal contribution, Exchange of knowledge, Common base of information, Transparency, Common understanding of the process, Effectiveness/Efficiency, Shared understanding of impact of results) (ibid.: 4). In order to be able to adequately capture these criteria in the research process, the authors believe that a recursive method (as is also advocated in the method section of the present study) including participant preferences in the design of evaluations is particularly revealing, in that the participants themselves may, for example, tend to emphasize procedural or output quality, which could be concretely demonstrated on the basis of a case study (ibid.: 9). According to this, the logical consequence is a flexible, situational and learning participation model in which changes can be made *during the process* with regard to the (temporally changing) attitudes and preferences of participants (ibid.). While this learning and adapting participation model seems quite coherent and convincing, it in turn places high demands on the *framing*, organization and concrete design of the participation measure. The

[48] Regarding the issues/aspects of the expansion of renewable energies: Who benefits? Who is adversely affected? Who supports or promotes? Who prevents or blocks?

learning process, which could certainly be found among citizens within the present study of community energy projects, at the same time leads to a heavy burden on the individual, which can tend to lead to dropping out of the participation path. One consequence that can be derived from this seems to be that participation opportunities are created that also provide low-threshold forms of participation. Analogous to the idea of the *ladder of citizen participation* (Arnstein 1969) and based on the didactic learning model of competence level development (Straka and Macke 2002; Fuchs 2003; Vonken 2005), there would thus be different levels that offer various points of contact for different preferences of the participants. Crucial for further analyses of social and political participation thus seem to be conditions and questions regarding the unfolding of collective action, the shaping of group behavior, underlying political socialization and socio-political attitudes that shape the arrangements of community forms of action (cf. Zmerli and Feldman 2015).

Beyond the participation debate, two current trends can be found that put the idea of participation in a different light and may even make it obsolete: the idea of more direct democracy on the one hand and community problem-solving approaches on the other. In combination, this could lead to a weakening of the importance of state-public participation procedures, in that direct influence via voting (in future more online-based) and concrete design through community initiatives (organization also online-based with selective, temporary actions) combine to form a new mode of participation. A current prominent example is the Tempelhofer Feld in Berlin, which on the one hand was put up for discussion via a direct-democratic vote regarding a possible building development, and on the other hand is being used by jointly organized and carried out civil society actions and projects (Dannenberg and Follmann 2015). The vote in 2015 actually led to a majority of the Berlin population speaking out against building on the site and wanting to preserve the character of an open space. However, this seemingly democratic character can be questioned critically: On the one hand, there was no direct participation of those affected, since not only the residents of neighboring districts, but all citizens of the urban area voted on the issue. On the other hand, it is noticeable that ideas for use that are oriented towards the common good (in this case, for example, social housing and the construction of a public library on the site) lose out in the direct-democratic procedure to interests that are also oriented towards the common good but are more immediate (in this case, the use of the open space). Apparently, a rejectionist attitude of the population towards the planned projects comes to light more often in infrastructure-related votes ("voting conservatism", cf. Montag 2011). It does not seem surprising that large-scale infrastructure projects (such as Stuttgart 21, cf. Bebnowski 2010; Brettschneider and Schuster 2013; Gabriel et al. 2014) have a threatening and drastic effect on the local population – even when they serve the common good. There are some examples of the mobilization of a certain clientele to prevent or implement certain measures, which can use the direct democratic instruments in their interest because milieus with a high level of education and income are more strongly represented in the votes and can presumably also be better mobilized (cf. Töller and Vollmer 2013: 310: f.; Kriesi (2009) asked in this sense whether votes can be bought). Grotz concludes from this: "Thus, the increased use of direct democratic procedures would further widen the participation differences between social strata that already exist in representative democratic procedures and would benefit the interests of the already privileged more – at least if substantive interests as well as the propensity to participate are related to socio-structural characteristics" (ibid.: 310 f.). This effect of a *hidden census* (Gaxie 1978; Passy 1993; Kriesi 2007b: 139) points to the importance of both socio-structural factors and campaign-related characteristics (Grotz 2009; cf. also Merkel 2015b: 24 ff.).

The problem thus falls back on the resources among the citizens, whereby on the one hand there can again be the problem of inequality, on the other hand the opportunity for education, as Schiller aptly summarizes: "What is certainly not easy to solve is the problem that social inequalities in individual resources for political participation can undermine the political equality of the right to vote. This imbalance in political interest, motivation to participate, knowledge or political expression is shared by direct democracy with all other forms of participation, be it voting, party memberships, participation in interest groups or civil society associations as well as in discursive participation procedures. Nevertheless, citizens' petitions and referendums open up opportunities for an issue-specific strengthening of motivation, political learning and 'empowerment' in practical participation in the 'political adult education center'. For this, appropriate procedures, institutions, parties, associations and media must make their contributions in order to facilitate access to the common and public 'political decision-making of the people' (Art. 21 GG) for socially and educationally weaker strata" (Schiller 2012: 205 f.). This brings us back to the starting point of education (or upbringing) for democracy, on which democratic participation – whether in direct democracy or via material participation – stands and falls (Majhanovich and Malet 2015), which has already been demonstrated in empirical studies, particularly with regard to a connection between education and *grassroots activism* (as well as elections) (Straughn and Andriot 2011). Thus, the "opportunities and risks of direct democratic participation" (Ante 2015) in general, but also direct democratic participation in cities in the context of urban development and conversion ("remeasuring citizen participation": Hummel 2015) remain in debate.

Another strand of scholarship, on the other hand, focuses on forms of public participation and living together, as summarized by Adloff et al. (2014) under the keyword “convivialism” as (new) forms of living together “beyond the growth society” (Adloff and Heins 2015) and similarly described by Welzer (“Communities of Practice”, e.g. cooperatives: Welzer 2013: 185 ff.; Welzer et al. 2014) or Sommer and Welzer (2014). The basis of these envisaged forms of community is usually an alternative-oriented and optimistic *sustainable thinking* with regard to shaping the future (Doppelt 2010). Community energy projects, if they are founded bottom-up by committed citizens, would be classic examples of such collaborative problem-solving approaches, which, however, suffer from the socio-structural specification. In conjunction with direct democracy, which also tends to be unequal, a future concept would thus emerge which, paradoxically, theoretically has considerable integration potential, but de facto cannot fulfil this promise due to too low participation rates and socio-structural inequality. Nevertheless, this diagnosis does not apply to every vote and every community project; integration and representativeness are certainly possible within the framework of targeted measures. The idea of convivalists and degrowth theorists, however, is more along the lines of first initiating a *Small Change* (Gladwell 2010) without a “Great Transformation” (Held et al. 2015). For example, there is the idea that private *philanthropists* in the sense of *philanthrocapitalists* could be a promising individualistic and market-compliant solution approach through meaningful investments (Brooks et al. 2009), which is reminiscent of the community energy approach. This would lead back to an “effective” altruism (MacAskill 2015), which is shared by a community due to a common characteristic (“green beard effect” derived from biology; here the green beard would be the common goal of climate protection), which, however, can also lead to *ingroup love* and *outgroup hate* as a flip side, which corresponds to bonding social capital (cf. Brewer 1999; Fehr and Fischbacher 2005; Weisel and Böhm 2015; on the importance of altruism and egoism in cooperatives, see Brazda and Schediwy 2013). Within small groups, civil society associations and joint projects, numerous pitfalls of collective action are known from research (Mills 1967; Olson 1992; Smith and Stephenson 2005), whether in internal participation in the corporate sector (cf. Lilge 1980), group work projects (Kühl 2001) or within clubs and associations (Zimmer 2003) – which is why Peter Feindt posed the question of whether the formation of social capital is rather the motor of democratization or exclusion (Feindt 2004). Ultimately, *community organizing* (Müller and Szynka 2010) is probably the most important factor in promoting the charming idea of *power to the people* as a transformation belt for sustainable electricity production by local *communities* for all parts of the population (van der Schoor and Scholtens 2015).

In summary, community energy in Germany has many links to social movements (e.g. with regard to the climate change challenge, cf. Nulman 2015), as well as to social entrepreneurship (cf. also references to social movements in the degrowth debate in Latouche 2010; Martínez-Alier et al. 2010; Seidl and Zahrnt 2010; Klitgaard and Krall 2012; Andreoni and Galmarini 2013; Johanisova et al. 2013; Sekulova et al. 2013; D'Alisa et al. 2015; Kallis et al. 2015; Kerschner et al. 2015). Like voluntary services, community energy projects are caught between state control and civil society design (Bibisidis 2015) and are at the mercy of the pitfalls of increasing professionalism (Wöhler 2015). In the context of self-managed forms of organization, there is therefore an enormous need for reform (Rixen and Welskop-Deffaa 2015).

Community-based and economically oriented associations such as community energy projects can serve to build social capital (Nabil and Eldayem 2015) and increase the resilience of rural communities (Skerratt 2013). Thus, in the field of community land use, the community wind farm example in the present study could tie in with the community forest management forms that are widespread in South Westphalia (tradition of so called *Haubergsgenossenschaften* (forest cooperatives), cf. Becker 1991; also discussed under the terms of community forests, forest commons and common-pool resources, cf. Späth 2015). On the other hand, some critical overarching questions remain as to the extent to which sufficient legitimacy, acceptance and public trust can be established through these new community-based, collaborative forms of participation (and thus also ways of living and working) (cf. Bentele et al. 2014; Dammayr et al. 2015); it can also contribute to the participation of young people (Tremmel and Rutsche 2015) and older people (Hanesch et al. 2014; Rießen et al. 2015) and to what extent this civil society engagement can also be reconciled with living conditions of people in precarious living situations (cf. Voigtländer 2015). The comprehensive potential of this form of *community innovation* in the niche field of renewable energies therefore still needs to be researched in more detail (Hielscher et al. 2011, 2013a, 2013b).

While on the one hand a virtually sacrosanct importance of civil society, participation and social capital for democracy is emphasized (cf. Nanz and Leggewie 2016), on the other hand one finds much more restrained assessments in empirical science (cf. Putnam 2002). This paper also concludes with a critical diagnosis. According to Putnam, locally oriented civic communities are most likely to generate social capital (Putnam 2000) and, according to Barber, to contribute to a *thick democracy* (Barber 1984), which is denied in a direct way at the overarching, e.g. national level (Berry 1999: 389). However, the deficits of inequality, marginalization of individuals and lack of legitimacy of civil-society-based community initiatives weigh heavily. Theda Skocpol argues that Alexis de Tocqueville would be surprised today that his idea of a vibrant and vivid civil society in Western societies has hardly become reality (Skocpol 1997). But perhaps this conclusion was drawn too hastily: For contrary to all defeatist assessments of a de-democratized post-democracy, in the case of the energy transition there are numerous examples of willingness to engage, offers of participation and collaborative modes of action. These local forms of development play an essential role in the citizens' understanding of democracy and their satisfaction (Vetter 2013). Looking to the horizon perhaps sometimes overlooks the movements at the grassroots.

Despite all post-democratic skepticism, the ideal of a democratically organized society remains valid ("democracy as the social bonding of a divided society": Klein et al. 2012; Pettit 2012). If and as long as the basic democratic principles are to be the guiding principles in the existing society, there is no way around taking into account and including the individual citizen as well as associations of civil society. However, since resources are not equally distributed, both materially and immaterially, in the participation of citizens in community decision-making and action processes, the democratic promise of participation opportunities will remain the core claim of a functioning democracy in the future.

7.3.2 Future Research

In the future, too, a continuing research task will be to examine the architectures of participatory-collaborative arrangements in the context of renewable energies and other infrastructure and technology discourses. The research claim postulated here is to look at communities and participation processes in a methodologically as well as analytically open, integrative and unbiased way. On a descriptive level, the most diverse manifestations of technology discourses can be outlined and documented. However, this should neither lead to an inevitable typification nor follow the corset of a certain method or the chosen analytical approach, but rather proceed in an open and provisional manner. Even in the case of typification, an elasticity should be the guiding principle of analysis in dealing with the uncovering of patterns, which allows typologies that have been made to be modified. In the sense of a dynamic and processual approach, it should always be kept in mind that all social phenomena are to be understood as provisional in the sense of a snapshot. Modes of action are fluctuating, certain patterns appear, but they can also fade away again. This in no way calls into question the meaningfulness of researching, uncovering, reconstructing and analyzing social structures, but it does open the claim to interpretation and puts the scope of the knowledge gained into perspective.

Social phenomena such as participation processes in the areas of sustainability, environment and technology are also immensely complex. Nevertheless, by combining many detailed analyses, certain patterns of action can be distilled, which allow a more comprehensible picture of the social dynamics of society to emerge (see, for example, the grid of overarching patterns of attitudes towards technology in Kerschner and Ehlers 2016: 143).[49] Through an expanded analytical penetration of both newly emerging and already established forms of citizen participation, forms of democracy can be better understood: "Assessing the potential of new spaces for citizen participation requires that we make sense of the dynamics of participation within these spaces. To do so, these spaces need to be located on a broader terrain, both with regard to their 'generative past(s)' and broader shifts in participation and development discourse" (Cornwall 2002: vii f.). Analyses of practiced participation can thus reveal the diverse modes and patterns of action of citizens and thus of democracy (cf. ibid.).

Possibly the unfolding forms of new civic forms of action such as community energy only stand like shadows on the wall in the platonic sense as blurry perceptible effects for the sustainability transformation of society at the beginning of the twenty-first century (similar to the thesis of Bellah et al. 2007). Just as pragmatically as the analyzed engagement in the present study, it can thus be concluded that neither an erosion of democracy and decay of public life (Sennett 2014; Vahsen 2014) nor a strong activation of citizens and revitalization of democracy can be assumed.

[49] Cf. on approaches to socio-ecological research in the field of energy and sustainability Holmberg 1995; Azar et al. 1996; Balzer and Wächter 2002; Jahn 2003; Young et al. 2006; Luks and Siebenhüner 2007; Fischedick et al. 2014.

Appendix 1: Overview of Community Energy Projects of the Case Studies

J. Radtke, *Community Energy in Germany*,
https://doi.org/10.1007/978-3-658-39320-5

3.1 Structural Data of the Community Energy Projects (Status of 2012)

No.	Name of the project	Location	Energy type	Number of energy plants	Locations of the energy plants
1	Bürgerwindpark Hilchenbach / Rothaardwind GmbH	Hilchenbach (North Rhine-Westphalia)	Wind	Five wind turbines in a wind farm, expansion in planning	On top of mountain near the town "Hilchenbach"
2	Energiegenossenschaft Ingersheim und Umgebung e.G.	Ingersheim (Baden-Wuerttemberg)	Wind	One wind energy plant	Near the town of Ingersheim
3	Solar Popular eG	Bremen	Solar	One photovoltaic plant on a roof, others in planning	Sandhausen (farm) near Bremen, commercial roofs in Bremen in planning
4	UniBremen Solar e.G.	Bremen	Solar	Four photovoltaic plants on several roofs	Roof surfaces of the University of Bremen
5	B.U.N.D. Bremen e.V.	Bremen	Solar	Three photovoltaic plants on several roofs	Parish "Friedenskirche" (Bremen); Dike Association Bremen e.V.; Hof Bavendamm, near Bremen
6	Bürgerenergie Syke e.G.	Syke (Lower Saxony)	Solar	Two photovoltaic plants on several roofs, third plant in planning	Syke (primary school and sports hall)
7	Geothermie Initiative Markt Schwaben	Markt Schwaben (Bavaria)	Geothermal.	District heating network in planning	Markt Schwaben
8	Energiegewinner e.G.	Cologne (North Rhine-Westphalia)	Solar	Eight photovoltaic plants on several roofs, two plants in planning	Cologne (four plants), Hanover (three plants), Witzenhausen (Hesse), Verl (North Rhine-Westphalia), Auerbach (Saxony)

Energy performance	Investment volume in Euros	Number of persons involved	Citizen shares (relative)	"Completed" project	Planned extensions (conc./gener.)
18 million kWh/ year	15.5 million	88	20%	Yes	Other buildings in the municipality/ yes
3.5–4 million kWh/year	3.6 million	362	80%	No	No/yes, also other renewable energies
25,000 kWh/year planned for 2012 one megawatt	300,000 in spring 2012 350,000 in the course of 2012	19	30%	No	Two roofs/ yes
375,000 kWh/year	700,000 (2012) + additional 300,000	130	50%	Yes	One roof/yes
10–15,000 kWh/ year 28,000 kWh/ year 20,500 kWh/ year	126,000 81,000 64,000	140	100%	Yes	No/no
58,000 kWh/year	210,000	110	100%	No	One roof/yes
–	Approx. 40 million in total, initially construction of district heating network for approx. 3 million	–	1 million euros equity capital available, 9–10 million euros anticipated	No	Complete heat supply for the whole local community of the town
293 kwP	985,000	90	100%	No	Several buildings/yes

(*continued*)

(continued)

No.	Name of the project	Location	Energy type	Number of energy plants	Locations of the energy plants
9	Jurenergie	Neumarkt (Bavaria)	Solar, Wind	22 photovoltaic plants on several roofs as well as two participations in wind energy plants	Various locations in Bavaria
10	Norddeutsche Energiegemeinschaft	Warin (Meck-lenburg-Western Pomerania)	Solar	10 photovoltaic energy plants	Various locations in Mecklenburg-Western Pomerania
11	Green City Energy AG	Munich (Bavaria)	Solar, Wind, Hydropower	Over 250 projects	Various locations in Germany
12	Planet Energy	Hamburg	Solar, Wind, Hydropower	Eight wind farms, three photovoltaic plants, several plants in planning	Various locations in Germany

Energy performance	Investment volume in Euros	Number of persons involved	Citizen shares (relative)	"Completed" project	Planned extensions (conc./gener.)
764,000 kWh	2.3 million	726	EUR 5.8 million (approx. 100%, partly debt capital)	No	Yes/three PV systems, one owned wind turbine
1800 kWp	7 million	753	3 million euros (20% equity share)	No	Yes/three photovoltaic plants wind energy plants
160 million kWh	150 million	1000 per profit participation rights, 3000 further investors	8 million euros through profit participation rights	No	Yes/yes
105 million kWh	108 million	5000 per profit participation rights	12 million euros through profit participation rights	No	Yes/yes

3.2

Over-
view
Energy

Initiatives: Participatory Arrangements

No.	Name of the project	Legal form	Governing bodies	Meetings	Voting rights	Volunteer leadership
1	Bürgerwindpark Hilchenbach / Rothaardwind GmbH	Limited liability company and partnership (GmbH & Co KG)	Management	Shareholders' meeting (once a year)	Relative to the amount of the share: 1000 euros gives one vote	No
2	Energiegenossen-schaft Ingersheim und Umgebung e.G.	Registered cooperative	Management Board + Supervisory Board	General Assembly (once a year)	Equal voting rights per person	Yes
3	Solar Popular e.G.	Registered cooperative	Management Board + Supervisory Board	General Assembly (once a year)	Equal voting rights per person	Yes

Civil society sponsoring	Members of the Executive Board/ Supervisory Board	Project initiators active in management	Minimum amount for participation	Upper limit of the amount for participation	Possibility of leaving the project	Further engagement of the project
None	One manager	Yes, completely	10,000 euros for non-residents, 3000 euros for residents of Hilchenbach, next investment levels by 1000 euros	No	Termination possible at the earliest on 31.12.2023 Shares can only be transferred in their entirety to another person	Regular visits to the wind farm, participation in conferences and meetings, consultations with other energy initiatives
Citizens' Action Group, which originally planned the project	2/5	Yes, completely	2500 euros next investment levels by 5000 euros, 7500 euros and so on	No	Invested for 18 years, at the end of a financial year subject to 2 years' notice In the case of several units: Termination of units at the end of a financial year subject to a notice period of 3 months Transfer of shares to other persons possible at any time	Wind turbine festival, various events/visits wide range of information on offer
Sa.H.N.E. e.V. within the Centre for Solidarity Economy Bremen	2/3	Yes, completely	500 euros	Open, from 25,000 euros agreement required	Sale of shares or termination of membership possible For the latter: Notice period of 2 years to the end of the year	Within the framework of a solidarity transfer, 20% of the annual surplus is donated to charitable projects

(*continued*)

(continued)

No.	Name of the project	Legal form	Governing bodies	Meetings	Voting rights	Volunteer leadership
4	UniBremen Solar	Cooperative	Management Board + Supervisory Board	General Assembly (once a year)	Equal voting rights per person	Yes
5	B.U.N.D. Bremen Bürgersolaran-lagen	Registered association	Board of Directors	None for parties involved	None for parties involved	No
6	Bürgerenergie Syke e.G.	Registered cooperative	Management Board + Supervisory Board	General Assembly (once a year)	Equal voting rights per person	Yes
7	Pro Geothermie Markt Schwaben WMS Wärmever-sorgung Markt Schwaben GmbH	Joint limited liability company connected with a registered cooperative (planned)	Management of the GmbH + Board of Directors of the cooperative	Shareholders' meeting and general meeting (once a year)	Relative to the amount of the share (GmbH) equal voting rights per person (cooperative)	No

Civil society sponsoring	Members of the Executive Board/ Supervisory Board	Project initiators active in management	Minimum amount for participation	Upper limit of the amount for participation	Possibility of leaving the project	Further engagement of the project
Environmental Committee of the University of Bremen	2/8	Yes, completely	100 euros	25,000 euros	After 4 years at the end of a financial year, notice period 2 years Transfer to others possible at any time Leaving university service is irrelevant	Exhibitions, presentations
Friends of the Earth National Association	–	–	100 euros, next investment levels by 100 euros	5000 euros	Fixed term of 20 years	No, indirectly via B.U.N.D. National Association
Local Agenda 21 in Syke	2/6	Yes, completely	100 euros, next investment levels by 100 euros	No	Business shares are fixed for a minimum of 1 year. Cancellations of membership at the end of a financial year, notice period 1 year Repayments only possible if at least 90% of the cooperative capital is maintained	No
Interessengemeinschaft "pro Geothermie" e.V. + Aktivkreis "Energiewende Markt Schwaben"	One manager	Yes, partly	Not yet determined	Not yet determined	Not yet determined	Not yet determined

(*continued*)

(continued)

No.	Name of the project	Legal form	Governing bodies	Meetings	Voting rights	Volunteer leadership
8	Energiegewinner eG	Cooperative	Management Board + Supervisory Board	General Assembly (once a year)	Equal voting rights per person	Yes
9	Jurenergie	Cooperative	Management Board + Supervisory Board	General Assembly (once a year)	Equal voting rights per person	Yes
10	Norddeutsche Energiegemein-schaft	Cooperative	Management Board + Supervisory Board	General Assembly (once a year)	Equal voting rights per person	Yes, but they come from WeMAG AG
11	Green City Energy AG	Stock company	Management Board + Supervisory Board	None (profit participation certificates)	None (profit participation certificates)	No
12	Planet Energy	Limited liability company (GmbH)	Management Board + Supervisory Board	None (profit participation certificates)	None (profit participation certificates)	No

Civil society sponsoring	Members of the Executive Board/ Supervisory Board	Project initiators active in management	Minimum amount for participation	Upper limit of the amount for participation	Possibility of leaving the project	Further engagement of the project
None	2/8	Yes, completely	50 euros plus costs for one/ several solar modules	No	Cooperative share cancellable annually and transferable Solar modules can be resold to other members at any time	No
District of Neumarkt and Regina GmbH (company of the municipalities of the county)	3/5	No information	500 euros next investment levels by 500 euros	100,000 euros	Termination excluded for the first five years, thereafter 1 years before the end of a fiscal year or Transfer of shares possible	Consultation and sale of electricity planned Local "sponsorship" by sponsors for the establishment of "proximity"
Founded on the initiative of WeMAG AG (regional electricity supplier) and five Volks- and Raiffeisen banks	2/10	No information	500 euros next investment levels by 500 euros	100,000 euros	1 year before the end of a fiscal year, or Transfer of shares possible	No
100% subsidiary of the Munich-based environmental protection organisation Green City e.V.	–	–	Varies, between 1000 and 10,000 euros next investment levels by 1000 euros	No	Term for profit participation rights between 3 and 20 years, for KG shares between 8 and 20 years, transfer possible	No, indirectly via Green City e.V.
Greenpeace Germany	–	–	1000 euros next investment levels by 1000 euros	No	Term 20 years, transfer possible	No, indirectly via Greenpeace e.V.

Appendix 2: Overview of Community Energy Projects Participating in the Survey

No.	Name	Energy type	Legal form	Size
1	BES Genossenschaft	Solar	Cooperative	Small
2	BürgerEnergiegenossenschaft Bergatreute	Solar	Cooperative	Small
3	Gemeindenützliche Genossenschaft Felsberg	Several	Cooperative	Small
4	UrStrom eG	Solar	Cooperative	Small
5	Bürgerenergie Pleichach-Kürnach	Several	Cooperative	Small
6	Sonnenkraftwerke Niederbergkirchen	Solar	GbR	Small
7	Sonnes – Genossenschaft der Mitarbeiter der Stadt Bad Neustadt eG	Solar	Cooperative	Small
8	BürgerEnergiegenossenschaft Bad Schussenried-Ingoldingen	Solar	Cooperative	Small
9	Energie-Genossenschaft Lindlar	Solar	Cooperative	Small
10	Bürger-Energie-Stuhr	Solar	Cooperative	Small
11	Bürgerenergie Stuttgart	Solar	Cooperative	Small
12	Ökumenische Energiegenossenschaft Baden-Württemberg e.G.	Solar	Cooperative	Small
13	SonnenSchein Mittelweser Genossenschaft	Solar	Cooperative	Small

(*continued*)

J. Radtke, *Community Energy in Germany*,
https://doi.org/10.1007/978-3-658-39320-5

(continued)

No.	Name	Energy type	Legal form	Size
14	Trierer Bürgersolarkraftwerke	Solar	Cooperative	Small
15	Bürgerstrom GbR Meckenbeuren	Solar	GbR	Small
16	BürgerEnergiegenossenschaft Illerrieden	Solar	Cooperative	Small
17	Energiegenossenschaft Mitarbeiter Unilever e.G.	Solar	Cooperative	Small
18	Sonnenwende Bürger-Energie-Harsewinkel eG	Solar	Cooperative	Small
19	Bürgerenergie Tübingen	Solar	Cooperative	Small
20	Bürger-Energie Zittau-Görlitz eG	Several	Cooperative	Small
21	Bürgerenergie Schelklingen	Solar	Cooperative	Small
22	DBE Deutsche BürgerEnergie eG	Solar	Cooperative	Medium
23	Bürger-Solar Barmstedt	Solar	GbR	Small
24	Bürgersolaranlagen in Rotenburg	Solar	GbR	Small
25	Sonnenland Genossenschaft	Solar	Cooperative	Small
26	Bürgerkraftwerken Berchtesgadener Land	Solar	GbR	Small
27	Bürger Energie St. Peter	Heat supply	Cooperative	Small
28	Energiegenossenschaft Bodensee eG	Solar	Cooperative	Small
29	Bassumer Energiegenossenschaft	Solar	Cooperative	Small
30	Bürgersolardach Kluftern GbR	Solar	GbR	Small
31	Bürger Energie Lenzkirch	Solar	Cooperative	Small
32	BürgerEnergieGenossenschaft Hochwald eG	Several	Cooperative	Small
33	BEG-SW Bürgerenergiegenossenschaft	Solar	Cooperative	Small
34	Solardach Ailingen GbR	Solar	GbR	Small
35	Sonne und Wind Stuttgart eG	Solar	Cooperative	Small
36	BürgerEnergieGenossenschaft	Solar	Cooperative	Small
37	BUND-Bürgersolaranlagen Bremen	Solar	Association	Small
38	BürgerEnergie Retzstadt eG	Solar	Cooperative	Small
39	Photovoltaik Genossenschaft Diekholzen	Solar	Cooperative	Small

(*continued*)

(continued)

No.	Name	Energy type	Legal form	Size
40	Energiegenossenschaft Starkenburg eG	Wind	Cooperative	Medium
41	Energiegewinner eG	Solar	Cooperative	Small
42	Nwerk	Several	Cooperative	Medium
43	Bürgersolaranlage in Bayern	Solar	GbR	Small
44	Heidelberger Energiegenossenschaft	Solar	Cooperative	Small
45	Solargenossenschaft Lausitz	Solar	Cooperative	Small
46	Bürgerwindpark Hilchenbach	Wind	GmbH-co	Medium
47	Bürgerenergiegenossenschaft BENG eG	Solar	Cooperative	Small
48	UniBremen Solar eG	Solar	Cooperative	Small
49	BERR-Genossenschaft	Solar	Cooperative	Small
50	Solargenossenschaft Essen	Solar	Cooperative	Small
51	Bürgerenergie Tauberfranken eG	Solar	Cooperative	Small
52	Volkswagen Belegschaftsgenossenschaft für regenerative Energien	Solar	Cooperative	Small
53	Bürgerwindpark Zöschingen	Wind	Cooperative	Large
54	Windkraft Diemarden	Wind	GmbH-co	Medium
55	Planet Energy	Several	Ltd	Large
56	Jurenergie eG	Several	Cooperative	Medium
57	Energiegenossenschaft Ingersheim und Umgebung	Wind	Cooperative	Medium
58	Norddeutsche Energiegemeinschaft eG	Several	Cooperative	Large
59	Green City Energy	Several	Ltd	Large
60	Solar-Bürger-Genossenschaft	Solar	Cooperative	Small
61	Ökostadt e.V.	Solar	Association	Small
62	Bürger-Energie Tübingen eG	Solar	Cooperative	Small
63	Energiegenossenschaft Odenwald	Several	Cooperative	Medium
64	West	Solar	Cooperative	Large
65	Raiffeisen Windpark	Wind	Cooperative	Large
66	Aufwind	Wind	Cooperative	Medium
67	Buxtehude	Solar	Cooperative	Small
68	Oberndorf	Solar	Cooperative	Small
69	Zukunftsgenossen	Solar	Cooperative	Small
70	Nahe	Wind	Cooperative	Small

(continued)

(continued)

No.	Name	Energy type	Legal form	Size
71	Maxwäll	Solar	Cooperative	Small
72	Lauter	Solar	Cooperative	Small
73	Arnstein	Solar	Cooperative	Small
74	Eifel	Solar	Cooperative	Medium
75	MIEG	Solar	Cooperative	Large
76	Westfalen	Wind	Cooperative	Large
77	Vogelsberg	Solar	Cooperative	Medium
78	Rhein-Sieg	Solar	Cooperative	Small
79	Erfurt	Solar	Cooperative	Small
80	BEGS	Solar	Cooperative	Small
81	Freudenberg	Wind	GmbH-co	Medium
82	Hohenlohe	Wind	GmbH-co	Large
83	Wotan	Wind	GmbH-co	Large
84	Kroppach	Wind	GmbH-co	Large
85	Emstal (only qual. Data recorded, $n = 24$)	Heat supply	Cooperative	Medium

In total: 85 community energy projects/energy cooperatives/companies with 2826 participants

Appendix 3: Overview of Interviews and Data Used

3.1 Case Study 1: Bürgerwindpark Hilchenbach / Rothaardwind GmbH

Interview I 1.1
Name: Günter Pulte
Function: Managing Director of Rothaarwind GmbH
Date. January 2009
Place: Kirchhundem-Rahrbach
Type: Interview

Interview I 1.2
Name: Martin Jatzkowski
Function: Shareholder in Rothaarwind investment company
Date: 31.1.2012
Type: Telephone Interview

Communication M 1.1
Name: Günter Pulte
Function: Managing Director of Rothaarwind GmbH
Date: 28.6.2011
Type: Notification

Communication M 1.2
Name: Günter Pulte
Date: 31.10.2011
Type: Notification

J. Radtke, *Community Energy in Germany*,
https://doi.org/10.1007/978-3-658-39320-5

Communication M 1.3
Name: Sylvia P. Heinz
Function: Head of Department Infrastructure, Transport, Regional Development and Economy, District of Siegen-Wittgenstein
Date: 27.10.2011
Type: Notification

3.2 Case Study 3: Solar Popular E.G.

Interview I 3.1
Name: Malte Zieher
Function: Member of the Board of Directors of the cooperative
Date: 25.5.2011
Place: University of Bremen
Type: Interview

Interview I 3.2
Name: Marcel Hecker
Function: Member of the Board of Directors of the cooperative
Date: 1.10.2011
Type: Telephone Interview

Interview I 3.3
Name: Marcel Hecker
Date: 16.12.2011
Place: University of Bremen
Type: Interview

3.3 Case Study 4: UniBremen Solar e.G.

Interview I 4.1
Name: Tobias Pinkel
Function: Member of the Supervisory Board of the cooperative and legal advisor
Date: 14.9.2011
Place: University of Bremen
Type: Interview

Interview I 4.2
Name: Dr. Doris Sövegjarto-Wigbers
Function: Chairwoman of the Board of Directors of the cooperative
Date: 30.11.2011
Place: University of Bremen
Type: Interview

Communication M 4
Name: Matthias Hohenfeld
Function: Employee of the University of Bremen
Date: 4.10.2011
Type: Notification

3.4 Case Study 5: B.U.N.D. Bremen

Interview I 5.1
Name: Ulrich Meine
Function: Employee of the Peace Church Bremen
Date: 6.5.2011
Place: Peace Church in Bremen
Type: Interview

Interview I 5.2
Name: Siecke Martin
Function: Employee of the Friends of the Earth Germany regional association Bremen
Date: 1.6.2011
Place: Friends of the Earth office, Bremen
Type: Interview

3.5 Case Study 6: Bürgerenergie Syke e.G.

Interview I 6.1
Name: Harald Behrens
Function: Mayor of the city of Syke
Date: 4.5.2011
Place: Syke, Town Hall
Type: Interview

Interview I 6.2
Name: Ralf Borchers
Function: Chairman of the cooperative
Date: 11.5.2011
Place: Syke
Type: Interview

3.6 Case Study 7: Geothermie-Initiative Markt Schwaben

Interview I 7.1
Name: Anton Hiermaier
Function: Head of Public Relations at Geothermie-Initiative Markt Schwaben e. V.
Date: 18.11.2011
Place: Markt Schwaben
Type: Interview

Interview I 7.2
Name: Andrä le Coutre
Function: Spokesman of the "Energiewende" working group in the municipality
Date: 18.11.2011
Place: Markt Schwaben
Type: Interview

3.7 Case Study 8: Energiegewinner e.G.

Interview I 8
Name: Kay Vosshenrich
Function: Chairman of the Board of Directors of the cooperative
Date: 20.11.2011
Place: Bremen
Type: Interview

3.8 City of Bremen

Interview I 9
Name: Hartmut Eichhorn
Function: Staff member of the Senator for the Environment, Building and Transport and Europe of the City of Bremen
Date: 18.5.2011
Place: University of Bremen
Type: Interview

References

Abell, P., & Heller, F. A. (2000). The Many Faces of Power and Liberty. Revealed Preference, Autonomy, and Teleological Explanation. In Heller F. A. (Ed.), Managing Democratic Organizations. Volume I (pp. 63–84). Aldershot u. a.: Ashgate.

Abels, G. (2007). Citizen Involvement in Public Policy-making. Does it Improve Democratic Legitimacy and Accountability? The Case of pTA. Interdisciplinary Information Sciences, 13 (1), 103–116.

Abels, G., & Bora, A. (2004). Demokratische Technikbewertung. Bielefeld: Transcript.

Abendschön, S. (2013). Demokratische Bürgertugenden. In J. W. van Deth & M. Tausendpfund (Eds.), Politik im Kontext: Ist alle Politik lokale Politik? (pp. 93–132). Wiesbaden: Springer VS.

Adam, M.-H., Gellai, S., & Knifka, J. (Eds.). (2015). Technisierte Lebenswelt. Über den Prozess der Figuration von Mensch und Technik. Bielefeld: Transcript.

Adams, C. A., & Bell, S. (2015). Local energy generation projects: assessing equity and risks. Local Environment, 20 (12), 1473–1488.

Adams, M., & Raisborough, J. (2010). Making a difference: ethical consumption and the everyday. The British Journal of Sociology, 61 (2), 256–274.

Adams, M., Wheeler, D., & Woolston, G. (2011). A participatory approach to sustainable energy strategy development in a carbon-intensive jurisdiction: The case of Nova Scotia. Energy Policy, 39 (5), 2550–2559.

Addams, J. (1902). Democracy and social ethics. New York: Macmillan.

Adil, A. M., & Ko, Y. (2016). Socio-technical evolution of Decentralized Energy Systems: A critical review and implications for urban planning and policy. Renewable and Sustainable Energy Reviews, 57, 1025–1037.

Adloff, F. (2005). Zivilgesellschaft: Theorie und politische Praxis. Frankfurt a. M., New York: Campus.

Adloff, F., & Heins, V. M. (Eds.). (2015). Konvivialismus. Eine Debatte. Bielefeld: Transcript.

Adloff, F., & Roose, J. (2011). Geld stinkt nicht? Zivilgesellschaft zwischen Abhängigkeit und Autonomie. Forschungsjournal Soziale Bewegungen, 24 (1), 3–6.

J. Radtke, *Community Energy in Germany*,
https://doi.org/10.1007/978-3-658-39320-5

Adloff, F., Leggewie, C., & Moldenhauer, E. (Eds.). (2014). Das konvivialistische Manifest. Für eine neue Kunst des Zusammenlebens. Bielefeld: Transcript.

Agamben, G. (Ed.). (2012). *Demokratie? Eine Debatte*. Berlin: Suhrkamp.

Agarwal, B. (2001). Participatory Exclusions, Community Forestry, and Gender. An Analysis for South Asia and a Conceptual Framework. World Development, 29 (10), 1623–1648.

Agentur für Erneuerbare Energien. (2014). Die Ergebnisse der AEE-Akzeptanzumfrage 2014 auf einem Blick. Renews Kompakt Nr. 23. Berlin. http://www.unendlich-viel-energie.de/media/file/383.AEE_RenewsKompakt_23_Akzeptanz-umfrage2014.pdf

Agentur für Erneuerbare Energien. (2015). Jahresreport Föderal Erneuerbar 2015. Berlin: Agentur für Erneuerbare Energien.

Agyeman, J., Devine-Wright, P., & Prange, J. (2009). Commentary: Close to the edge, down by the river? Joining up managed retreat and place attachment in a climate changed world. Environment and Planning A, 41 (3), 509–513.

Ahlbrecht, H.-J. (1976). Mitbestimmung und Mitbeteiligung. Technische Universität Berlin: Berlin.

Aitken, M. (2010). Wind power and community benefits. Challenges and opportunities. Energy Policy, 38 (10), 6066–6075.

Alanne, K., & Saari, A. (2006). Distributed energy generation and sustainable development. Renewable and Sustainable Energy Reviews, 10 (6), 539–558.

Albrecht, R., Grüttner, A., Lenk, T., Lück, O., & Rottmann, O. (2010). Optionen moderner Bürgerbeteiligung bei Infrastrukturprojekten – Ableitung für eine verbesserte Beteiligung auf Basis von Erfahrungen und Einstellungen von Bürgern, Kommunen und Unternehmen. Leipzig: Kompetenzzentrum Öffentliche Wirtschaft, Infrastruktur und Daseinsvorsorge e. V.

Albrechtslund, A., & Lauritsen, P. (2013). Spaces of everyday surveillance. Unfolding an analytical concept of participation. Geoforum, 49, 310–316.

Alcántara, S., Kuhn, R., Renn, O., Bach, N., Böhm, B., Dienel, H.-L., Ullrich, P., Schröder, C., & Walk, H. (2014). DELIKAT – Fachdialoge Deliberative Demokratie: Analyse Partizipativer Verfahren für den Transformationsprozess. http://www.umweltbundesamt.de/sites/default/files/medien/378/publikationen/texte_31_2014_de-likat-fachdialoge_deliberative_demokratie.pdf

Alemann, U. von, & Strünck, C. (1999). Die Weite des politischen Vor-Raumes. In K. Kamps (Ed.), Elektronische Demokratie? (pp. 21–38). Wiesbaden: VS Verlag.

Alemann, U. von. (2011). 40 Jahre Bürgerbeteiligung – Demokratie als Wagnis. In K. Beck & J. Ziekow (Eds.), Mehr Bürgerbeteiligung wagen (pp. 201–212). Wiesbaden: VS Verlag.

Alemann, U. von, & Studiengruppe Partizipationsforschung (Eds.). (1975). Partizipation, Demokratisierung, Mitbestimmung. Problemstellung und Literatur in Politik, Wirtschaft, Bildung und Wissenschaft. Eine Einführung. Opladen: Westdeutscher Verlag.

Allcott, H. (2011). Social norms and energy conservation. Journal of Public Economics, 95(9–10), 1082–1095.

Alle, K., Graf, A., Härdtlein, M., & Hinderer, N. (2015). Bürgerwindanlagen im Kontext der deutschen Energiewende. Eine Analyse des soziotechnischen Innovationsfeldes. LITRES Discussion Paper 2015-01. Universität Stuttgart, Institut für Sozialwissenschaften, Abteilung für Organisations- und Innovationssoziologie (SOWI VI), (01).

Almond, G. A., & Verba, S. (1963). The civic culture: political attitudes and democracy in five nations. Princeton, NJ: Princeton University Press.

Almond, G. A., & Verba, S. (Eds.). (2001). The civic culture: revisited (10th ed.). Los Angeles: Sage.
Alscher, M. (2008). Genossenschaften und Engagement: ein erfolgreiches Zusammenspiel zweier Konzepte. Saarbrücken: VDM Müller.
Alscher, M. (2011). Genossenschaften – Akteure des Marktes und der Zivilgesellschaft. Betrifft: Bürgergesellschaft Nr. 36. Bonn: Friedrich-Ebert-Stiftung.
Alscher, M. (2012). Cooperative Revolution. Cooperatives Can Change Our Communities and the World. Fabiana – The Fabian Women's Network Magazine, 18.
Alscher, M., & Priller, E. (2007). Selbsthilfe aus der Tradition in die Zukunft: Genossenschaften als Organisationsform bürgerschaftlichen Engagements. Stiftung & Sponsoring: Das Magazin für Non-Profit-Management und -Marketing, 10 (3), 15–16.
Alscher, M., & Priller, E. (2013). 12.3 Zivilgesellschaftliches Engagement. In Statistisches Bundesamt (Destatis) & Wissenschaftszentrum Berlin für Sozialforschung (WZB) (Eds.), Datenreport 2013: ein Sozialbericht für die Bundesrepublik Deutschland (pp. 350–356). Bonn: Bundeszentrale für politische Bildung.
Alscher, M., Dathe, D., & Priller, E. (2009). Bericht zur Lage und zu den Perspektiven des bürgerschaftlichen Engagements in Deutschland. Berlin: WZB. http://www.wzb.eu/sites/default/files/u13/zeng-bericht-engagement-2009.pdf
Altrock, M., Huber, A., Loibl, H. & Walter, R. (2015). Übergangsbestimmungen im EEG 2014. Kommentierungen und Materialien. Berlin: Erich Schmidt Verlag.
Altvater, E. (2012). Genossenschaft und gutes Leben – Der Sozialismus des 21. Jahrhunderts. Blätter für deutsche und internationale Politik, 57 (4), 53–64.
Alvesson, M. (1996). Communication, power and organization. Berlin: de Gruyter.
Ambruster, A., & Leach, W. D. (2008). Collaborative versus technocratic policymaking: California's statewide water plan. California State University, Sacramento, Center for Collaborative Policy.
Ammann, H. (2006a). Der Prozess der Monetarisierung – gespiegelt in der Interdependenz von wissenschaftlicher Neugierde und gesellschaftlichen Forderungen. Überblick. In P. Farago & H. Ammann (Eds.), Monetarisierung der Freiwilligkeit. Referate und Zusammenfassungen der 5. Tagung der Freiwilligenuniversität vom 30. bis 31.5.2005 in Luzern (pp. 179–183). Zürich: Seismo.
Ammann, H. (2006b). Der Prozess der zunehmenden Monetarisierung und seine Auswirkungen auf die Freiwilligenarbeit. In P. Farago & H. Ammann (Eds.), Monetarisierung der Freiwilligkeit. Referate und Zusammenfassungen der 5. Tagung der Freiwilligenuniversität vom 30. bis 31.5.2005 in Luzern (pp. 17–28). Zürich: Seismo.
Andersen, U. (Ed.). (2009). Handwörterbuch des politischen Systems der Bundesrepublik Deutschland. Wiesbaden: VS Verlag.
Anderson, T., & Doig, A. (2000). Community planning and management of energy supplies – international experience. Renewable Energy, 19 (1–2), 325–331.
Andreoni, V., & Galmarini, S. (2013). On the Increase of Social Capital in Degrowth Economy. Procedia – Social and Behavioral Sciences, 72, 64–72.
Andreoni, V., & Galmarini, S. (2014). How to increase well-being in a context of degrowth. Futures, 55, 78–89.
Angel, J. (2016). Strategien der Energiedemokratie. Brüssel: Rosa-Luxemburg-Stiftung Büro Brüssel.
Ansell, C., & Gash, A. (2008). Collaborative governance in theory and practice. Journal of Public Administration Research and Theory, 18 (4), 543–571.

Ante, C. (2015). Chancen und Risiken direkter Demokratie: direktdemokratische Partizipation auf kommunaler Ebene in Deutschland und der Schweiz. Baden-Baden: Nomos.

Apostol, D., Palmer, J., Pasqualetti, M., Smardon, R., & Sullivan, R. (2016). *The Renewable Energy Landscape: Preserving Scenic Values in our Sustainable Future*. Abingdon, New York: Taylor & Francis.

Appel, F., Ostermeyer-Wiethaup, A., & Balmann, A. (2016). Effects of the German Renewable Energy Act on structural change in agriculture – The case of biogas. *Utilities Policy, 41*, 172–182. https://doi.org/10.1016/j.jup.2016.02.013.

Araral Jr., E. (2016). Reply to: Design principles in commons science: A response to "Ostrom, Hardin and the commons" (Araral). Environmental Science & Policy, 61, 243–244.

Arbter, K. (2009). Öffentlichkeitsbeteiligung ja, aber wie? Standards für qualitätsvolle Beteiligungsprozesse. JeDEM-eJournal of eDemocracy and Open Government, 1 (1), 30–39.

Arbter, K. (2010). Öffentlichkeitsbeteiligung für nachhaltige Entwicklung wie qualitätsvolle Öffentlichkeitsbeteiligung bei strategischen Planungen zu nachhaltiger Entwicklung beitragen kann. In R. Steurer & R. Trattnigg (Eds.), Nachhaltigkeit regieren: eine Bilanz zu Governance-Prinzipien und -Praktiken (pp. 123–142). München: Oekom.

Arbter, K., Handler, M., Purker, E., Tappeiner, G., & Trattnigg, R. (2005). Das Handbuch Öffentlichkeitsbeteiligung. Wien: Österreichische Gesellschaft für Umwelt und Technik (ÖGUT) und Bundesministerium für Land-, Forstwirtschaft, Umwelt und Wasserwirtschaft.

Arend, S. van der, & Behagel, J. (2016). Training Participants. Building a Community of Practice to Negotiate Sustainability. In J.-P. Voss & R. Freeman (Eds.), Knowing governance: the epistemic construction of political order (pp. 193–214). Basingstoke, New York: Palgrave Macmillan.

Argento, D., Culasso, F., & Truant, E. (2016). Competing logics in the expansion of public service corporations. *Utilities Policy, 40*, 125–133. https://doi.org/10.1016/j.jup.2016.02.007.

Arias-Maldonado, M. (2012). Real green: sustainability after the end of nature. Farnham: Ashgate.

Arlt, H.-J. (1999). Bürger im Betrieb. Widerspruch in Sicht, aber keiner in sich. In U. von Alemann, R. G. Heinze, & U. Wehrhöfer (Eds.), Bürgergesellschaft und Gemeinwohl: Analyse, Diskussion, Praxis (pp. 149–158). Opladen: Leske + Budrich.

Armbruster, H., & Lærke, A. (Eds.). (2008). *Taking sides: Ethics, politics, and fieldwork in anthropology*. New York: Berghahn Books.

Armstrong, A., & Bulkeley, H. (2014). Micro-hydro politics: Producing and contesting community energy in the North of England. Geoforum, 56, 66–76.

Arnold, A., David, M., Hanke, G., & Sonnberger, M. (Eds.). (2015). Innovation – Exnovation. Über Prozesse des Abschaffens und Erneuerns in der Nachhaltigkeitstransformation. Marburg: Metropolis-Verl.

Arnstein, S. R. (1969). A Ladder Of Citizen Participation. Journal of the American Institute of Planners, 35 (4), 216–224.

Arond, E., Ely, A., Bell, M., Leach, M., Scoones, I., & Stirling, A. (2008). Innovation, Sustainability, Development: A New Manifesto. Brighton: STEPS Centre, University of Sussex.

Austel, N. (Ed.). (2013). Neue technische Perspektiven erneuerbarer Energien und ihre politisch-rechtliche Verarbeitung. Marburg: Metropolis-Verl.

Avelino, F., Dumitru, Adina, R., Longhurst, N., Wittmayer, J., Hielscher, S., Weaver, P., Cipolla, C., Afonso, R., Kunze, I., Dorland, J., Elle, M., Pel, B., Strasser, T., Kemp, R., & Haxeltine, A. (2015). Transitions towards New Economies? A Transformative Social Innovation Perspective. TRANSIT Working Paper #3, September 2015. Rotterdam.

Avelino, F., Wittmayer, J., Haxeltine, A., Kemp, R., O'Riordan, T., Weaver, P., Loorbach, D., & Rotmans, J. (2014). Game Changers and Transformative Social Innovation. The Case of the Economic Crisis and the New Economy. TRANSIT Working Paper. Rotterdam.

Avenhaus, W., Newig, J., & Fritsch, O. (2006a). Standards zur Öffentlichkeitsbeteiligung. Auf dem Weg zu effizienter und effektiver Partizipation. In J. Newig & O. Fritsch (Eds.), Effektivität von Beteiligungsprozessen. Beiträge des Instituts für Umweltsystemforschung der Universität Osnabrück. Beitrag Nr. 34 (pp. 54–67). Osnabrück.

Avenhaus, W., Newig, J., & Fritsch, O. (2006b). „When the dog doesn't bark" – Warum können Partizipationsprozesse scheitern? In J. Newig & O. Fritsch (Eds.), Effektivität von Beteiligungsprozessen. Beiträge des Instituts für Umweltsystemforschung der Universität Osnabrück. Beitrag Nr. 34 (pp. 54–67). Osnabrück.

Avril, E. (Ed.). (2013). New technology, organizational change, and governance. Basingstoke, New York: Palgrave Macmillan.

Azar, C., Holmberg, J., & Lindgren, K. (1996). Socio-ecological indicators for sustainability. Ecological Economics, 18 (2), 89–112.

Bäcker, D. (2008). Die dritte industrielle Revolution – Aufbruch in ein ökologisches Jahrhundert. Dimensionen und Herausforderungen des industriellen und gesellschaftlichen Wandels. Berlin: Bundesministerium f. Umwelt, Naturschutz u. Reaktorsicherheit.

Badelt, C. (2004). Unternehmerisches Handeln in Nonprofit-Organisationen: seine Rolle in Theorie und Wirklichkeit des Nonprofit-Sektors. In H. K. Anheier (Ed.), Zwischen Eigennutz und Gemeinwohl: neue Formen und Wege der Gemeinnützigkeit (pp. 175–202). Gütersloh: Verl. Bertelsmann-Stiftung.

Baden-Württemberg Stiftung (Ed.). (2015). Demokratie-Monitoring Baden-Württemberg 2013/2014: Studien zu Demokratie und Partizipation. Wiesbaden: Springer VS.

Bader, V. (2014). Sciences, politics, and associative democracy: democratizing science and expertizing democracy. The European Journal of Social Science Research, 27 (4), 420–441.

Badura, B., Greiner, W., Rixgens, P., Ueberle, M., & Behr, M. (Eds.). (2013). Sozialkapital. Grundlagen von Gesundheit und Unternehmenserfolg. Berlin u. a.: Springer Gabler.

Bagdanavicius, A., Jenkins, N., & Hammond, G. P. (2012). Assessment of community energy supply systems using energy, exergy and exergoeconomic analysis. Energy, 45 (1), 247–255.

Baglioni, G. (1999). Ist Demokratie möglich? Arbeitnehmerbeteiligung im Unternehmen – der schwierige Weg zwischen Demokratie und Effizienz. Baden-Baden: Nomos.

Baier, A., Müller, C., & Werner, K. (2013). Stadt der Commonisten. Neue urbane Räume des Do it yourself. Bielefeld: Transcript.

Bailey, E., & Devine-Wright, P. (2013). Varieties of people-place relations and place change: UK electricity transmission grid development. Estudios de Psicología, 34 (3), 335–338.

Bala, C., & Müller, K. (Eds.). (2015). Abschied vom Otto Normalverbraucher. Moderne Verbraucherforschung: Leitbilder, Informationen, Konsum und Demokratie. Essen: Klartext-Verl.

Balbo, L. (2006). Die Zukunft der Freiwilligenarbeit im Kontext der zunehmenden Monetarisierung. In P. Farago & H. Ammann (Eds.), Monetarisierung der Freiwilligkeit. Referate und Zusammenfassungen der 5. Tagung der Freiwilligenuniversität vom 30. bis 31.5.2005 in Luzern (pp. 80–95). Zürich: Seismo.

Baldwin-Philippi, J. (2015). Using technology, building democracy: digital campaigning and the construction of citizenship. Oxford: Oxford Univ. Press.

Bale, C. S. E., McCullen, N. J., Foxon, T. J., Rucklidge, A. M., & Gale, W. F. (2013). Harnessing social networks for promoting adoption of energy technologies in the domestic sector. Energy Policy, 63, 833–844.

Balsiger, P. (2014). The fight for ethical fashion: the origins and interactions of the clean clothes campaign. Farnham, Surrey, Burlington: Ashgate.

Balzer, I., & Wächter, M. (2002). Sozial-ökologische Forschung. Ergebnisse der Sondierungsprojekte aus dem BMBF-Förderschwerpunkt. München: Oekom.

Banks, S., Armstrong, A., Carter, K., Graham, H., Hayward, P., Henry, A., Holland, T., Holmes, C., Lee, A., McNulty, A., Moore, N., Nayling, N., Stokoe, A., & Strachan, A. (2013). Everyday ethics in community-based participatory research. Contemporary Social Science, 8 (3), 263–277.

Banse, G. (Ed.). (2013). Von der Informations- zur Wissensgesellschaft. e-Society – e-Partizipation – e-Identität. Berlin: Trafo.

Banse, G., & Fleischer, L.-G. (Eds.). (2013). Energiewende: Produktivkraftentwicklung und Gesellschaftsvertrag. 5. Jahreskonferenz der Leibniz-Sozietät der Wissenschaften. Berlin: Trafo.

Bär, T., & Thunecke, I. (2011). Participation in urban climate protection: answers of European municipalities. Potsdam: Heinrich-Böll-Stiftung Brandenburg.

Barber, B. R. (1984). Strong democracy: participatory politics for a new age. Berkeley: University of California Press.

Barber, B. R. (2013). If mayors ruled the world: dysfunctional nations, rising cities. New Haven: Yale University Press.

Baringhorst, S. (2009). Politischer Konsumerismus im Netz: Chancen und Probleme demokratischer Protestpolitik. In T. Groß, C. Bieber, M. Eifert & J. Lamla (Eds.), Soziale Netze in der digitalen Welt. Das Internet zwischen egalitärer Teilhabe und ökonomischer Macht (pp. 179–202). Frankfurt a. M., New York: Campus.

Baringhorst, S. (2011). Die Grenzen der webbasierten Konsumentenmacht: nachhaltiger Konsum im Netz. In Ökologisches Wirtschaften, (4), 15–17.

Baringhorst, S. (2012a). Bürgerkompetenzen der Zukunft – Politische Bildung in der digitalen Demokratie. In Pädagogik, 64 (7), 66–70.

Baringhorst, S. (2012b). Bürger als „Produser“: politische Beteiligung von Konsumentenbürgern im Social Web. In K. Lutz, E. Rösch & D. Seitz (Eds.), Partizipation und Engagement im Netz. Neue Chancen für Demokratie und Medienpädagogik (pp. 63–80). München: kopaed Schriften zur Medienpädagogik 47.

Baringhorst, S. (2012c). Politischer Konsum – eine neue Form kreativer politischer Partizipation. Neue Gesellschaft, Frankfurter Hefte, 59 (4), 38–42.

Baringhorst, S. (2015). Mehr Demokratie durch Online-Aktivismus? Zum Wandel politischer Partizipation im Netz. In L. Harles & D. Lange (Eds.), *Zeitalter der Partizipation: Paradigmenwechsel in Politik und politischer Bildung?* (pp. 76–85). Schwalbach/Ts.: Wochenschau.

Baringhorst, S. (2016a). Nachhaltigkeit durch politischen Konsum und Internetaktivismus – Neue Engagementformen zwischen postdemokratischer Partizipation und demokratischem Experimentalismus. In G. Diendorfer & M. Welan (Eds.), Demokratie als Beitrag zu einer nachhaltigen Gesellschaft. Herausforderungen, Potenziale und Reformansätze (pp. 43–60). Innsbruck, Wien, Bozen: StudienVerlag.

Baringhorst, S. (2016b). Mehr Demokratie durch Online-Aktivismus? Zum Wandel politischer Partizipation im Netz. In L. Harles & D. Lange (Eds.), Zeitalter der Partizipation. Paradigmenwechsel in Politik und politischer Bildung? (pp. 76–85). Schwalbach/Ts.: Wochenschau.

Baringhorst, S., & Yang, M. (2014). Kreative politische Handlungen im Social Web – Beiträge zur Demokratie? In M. Schröder (Ed.), *Politik und politische Bildung in der digitalen Welt: Chancen und Herausforderungen* (pp. 37–58). Reinbek: Lau Verlag.

Baringhorst, S., Kneip, V., März, A., & Niesyto, J. (Eds.). (2007). Politik mit dem Einkaufswagen. Unternehmen und Konsumenten als Bürger in der globalen Mediengesellschaft. Bielefeld: Transcript.

Barnebeck, S., & Kalff, Y. (2015). Urban Agenda and Urban Sustainability Strategies. Taking Stock of Policy Implementation and Policy Discussion. WWWforEurope Working Paper.

Barnes, S. H., & Kaase, M. (1979). Political action: mass participation in five western democracies. Beverly Hills, California: Sage Publications.

Barnett, C., Clarke, N., Cloke, P., & Malpass, A. (2005). The political ethics of consumerism. Consumer Policy Review, 15 (2), 45–51.

Baron, W. M. (1995). Technikfolgenabschätzung. Ansätze zur Institutionalisierung und Chancen der Partizipation. Opladen: Westdeutscher Verlag.

Baron, S., Field, J. W., & Schuller, T. (Eds.). (2000). Social Capital. Critical Perspectives. Oxford: Oxford University Press.

Barr, S., & Devine-Wright, P. (2012). Resilient communities: sustainabilities in transition. Local Environment, 17 (5), 525–532.

Barry, A. (2013). Material Politics. Disputes Along the Pipeline. Chichester: Wiley-Blackwell.

Barry, J. (2012). The politics of actually existing unsustainability: human flourishing in a climate-changed, carbon constrained world. New York: Oxford University Press.

Barry, M., & Chapman, R. (2009). Distributed small-scale wind in New Zealand: Advantages, barriers and policy support instruments. Energy Policy, 37 (9), 3358–3369.

Bartels, K. P. R. (2015). Communicative capacity: public encounters in participatory theory and practice. Bristol: Policy Press.

Barthel, E., & Dikau, J. (1980). Mitbestimmung in der Wirtschaft. Berlin: Colloquium.

Barton, J., Davies, L., Foxon, T. J., Galloway, S., Hammond, G., O'Grady, Á., Robertson, E., & Thomson, M. (2013). Transition pathways for a UK low carbon electricity system. Comparing scenarios and technology implications. Working Paper. University of Bath.

Barton, J., Emmanuel-Yusuf, D., Hall, S., Johnson, V., Longhurst, N., O'Grady, A., Robertson, E., Robinson, E., & Sherry-Brennan, F. (2015). Distributing Power. A transition to a civic energy future. Working Paper. University of Bath.

Bassam, N. El, Maegaard, P., & Schlichting, M. L. (2013). Distributed renewable energies for off-grid communities: strategies and technologies toward achieving sustainability in energy generation and supply. Amsterdam: Elsevier.

Bassam, N. El. (2001). Renewable energy for rural communities. Renewable Energy, 24 (3–4), 401–408.
Batel, S., & Devine-Wright, P. (2014). Towards a better understanding of people's responses to renewable energy technologies. Insights from Social Representations Theory. Public Understanding of Science, 24 (3), 311–325.
Batel, S., Devine-Wright, P., & Tangeland, T. (2013). Social acceptance of low carbon energy and associated infrastructures: A critical discussion. Energy Policy, 58, 1–5.
Batel, S., Devine-Wright, P., Wold, L., Egeland, H., Jacobsen, G., & Aas, O. (2015). The role of (de-)essentialisation within siting conflicts: An interdisciplinary approach. Journal of Environmental Psychology, 44, 149–159.
Batley, S. L., Colbourne, D., Fleming, P. D., & Urwin, P. (2001). Citizen versus consumer: challenges in the UK green power market. Energy Policy, 29 (6), 479–487.
Batson, C. D. (2014). The Altruism Question: Toward A Social-psychological Answer. New York, Hove: Psychology Press.
Batson, C. D., & Shaw, L. L. (1991). Evidence for Altruism: Toward a Pluralism of Prosocial Motives. Psychological Inquiry, 2 (2), 107–122.
Baudrillard, J. (2015). Die Konsumgesellschaft: ihre Mythen, ihre Strukturen. Wiesbaden: VS Verlag.
Bauer, C. (2015). Die Energiewende in der Politik- und Partizipationsverflechtungsfalle: Das Beispiel des Stromnetzausbaus. Verwaltungsarchiv, 106 (1), 112–154.
Bauer, H., Büchner, C., & Markmann, F. (2014). Kommunen, Bürger und Wirtschaft im solidarischen Miteinander von Genossenschaften. Potsdam: Universitäts-Verlag.
Baum, D. (1978). Relative Deprivation und politische Partizipation: sozialstrukturelle Bedingungen politischer Beteiligung. Frankfurt a. M. u. a.: Lang.
Baumann, F., Detlefsen, M., Iversen, S., & Vogelsang, L. (2004). Neue Tendenzen bei Bürgerbeteiligungsprozessen in Deutschland. Veränderte Rahmenbedingungen, Praktiken und deren Auswirkungen. Berlin: Rosa-Luxemburg-Stiftung.
Baur, N., & Blasius, J. (2014). Handbuch Methoden der empirischen Sozialforschung. Wiesbaden: VS Verlag.
Baur, N., & Ernst, S. (2011). Towards a process-oriented methodology: modern social science research methods and Norbert Elias's figurational sociology. In The Sociological Review, 59, 117–139.
Bauwens, T. (2013a). The contributions of renewable energy cooperatives to a socio-technical transition in the electricity sector. Working Paper. http://orbi.ulg.ac.be/handle/2268/154122
Bauwens, T. (2013b). Renewable Energy Cooperatives and The Decentralization of Electricity Production. Working Paper. http://orbi.ulg.ac.be/handle/2268/150414
Bauwens, T. (2013c). Le citoyen face au changement climatique. Working Paper. http://orbi.ulg.ac.be/handle/2268/157357
Bauwens, T. (2014a). Integrating the weight of history into the alignment framework: the case of distributed generation technologies. Working Paper. http://orbi.ulg.ac.be/handle/2268/161781
Bauwens, T. (2014b). What motivates members of renewable energy cooperatives? An econometric analysis. Präsentation Tagung 1st Symposium on Community Energy Systems. Lille, Frankreich.
Bauwens, T. (2014c). What roles for energy cooperatives in the diffusion of distributed generation technologies? Working Paper. http://orbi.ulg.ac.be/handle/2268/161780

Bauwens, T. (2016). Explaining the diversity of motivations behind community renewable energy. Energy Policy, 93, 278–290.

Bauwens, T., Gotchev, B., & Holstenkamp, L. (2016). What drives the development of community energy in Europe? The case of wind power cooperatives. Energy Research & Social Science, 13, 136–147.

Bauwens, T., Schraven, D., Drewing, E., Radtke, J., Holstenkamp, L., Gotchev, B., & Yildiz, Ö. (2022). Conceptualizing community in energy systems: A systematic review of 183 definitions. *Renewable and Sustainable Energy Reviews, 156*, 111999. https://doi.org/10.1016/j.rser.2021.111999

Bayer, K. (2013). Energiegenossenschaften – Träger der Energiewende? Eine Unternehmensform im Fokus gesellschaftlicher Veränderungsprozesse. In D. Gawora (Ed.), Energie und Demokratie: (pp. 141–153). Kassel: Kassel University Press.

Bazilian, M., Nakhooda, S., & Van de Graaf, T. (2014). Energy governance and poverty. Energy Research & Social Science, 1, 217–225.

Bebnowski, D. (2010). Stuttgart 21 und die Wutbürger. Politische Verschiebungen in der gesellschaftlichen Mitte im Licht empirischer Ergebnisse. In A. Drews (Ed.), Die Wiederentdeckung der Politik?! Perspektiven des Parteienstaates, Alternativen im Parteienstaat. Dokumentation einer Tagung der Evangelischen Akademie Loccum vom 6. bis 8. Dezember 2010 (pp. 135–143). Loccum: Evangel. Akademie Loccum.

Beck, G., & Kropp, C. (Eds.). (2012). Gesellschaft innovativ: Wer sind die Akteure? Wiesbaden: VS Verlag.

Beck, K., & Ziekow, J. (Eds.). (2011). Mehr Bürgerbeteiligung wagen. Wege zur Vitalisierung der Demokratie. Wiesbaden: VS Verlag.

Beck, U. (1996). Das Zeitalter der Nebenfolgen und die Politisierung der Moderne. In U. Beck, A. Giddens, & S. Lash (Eds.), Reflexive Modernisierung. eine Kontroverse (pp. 19–112). Frankfurt a. M.: Suhrkamp.

Beck, U. (2001). Zivilgesellschaft light? Die Gefahr wächst, dass die Reformidee verwässert wird – oder gar zu einer Parole des Neoliberalismus verkommt. Süddeutsche Zeitung v. 23.6.2001, pp. 15.

Becker, A. (1991). Der Siegerländer Hauberg. Vergangenheit, Gegenwart und Zukunft einer Waldwirtschaftsform. Kreuztal: Verl. Die Wielandschmiede.

Becker, G. S. (1976). Altruism, Egoism, and Genetic Fitness: Economics and Sociobiology. Journal of Economic Literature, 14 (3), 817–826.

Becker, P. (2014). Chapter 10 – Social Change for a Resilient Society. In P. Becker (Ed.), Sustainability Science (pp. 245–255). Amsterdam, Oxford, Waltham: Elsevier.

Becker, S., & Kunze, C. (2014). Transcending community energy: Collective and politically motivated projects in renewable energy (CPE) across Europe. *People Place and Policy, 8*(3), 180–191.

Becker, S., Gailing, L., & Naumann, M. (2012). Neue Energielandschaften – Neue Akteurslandschaften. Eine Bestandsaufnahme im Land Brandenburg. Berlin: Rosa-Luxemburg-Stiftung.

Becker, S., Kouschil, K., & Naumann, M. (2014a). Armut und Infrastruktur: das Beispiel Energiearmut. Geographische Rundschau, 66 (10), 10–17.

Becker, S., & Kunze, C. (2015). Transcending community energy: collective and politically motivated projects in renewable energy (CPE) across Europe. People Place and Policy, 8(3), 180–191.

Becker, S., & Naumann, M. (2017). Energy democracy: Mapping the debate on energy alternatives. *Geography Compass, 11*(8), e12321. https://doi.org/10.1111/gec3.12321

Becker, S., Beveridge, R., & Naumann, M. (2015a). Reconfiguring Energy Provision in Berlin. Commoning between Compromise and Contestation. In M. Dellenbaugh, M. Kip, M. Bieniok, A. K. Müller, & M. Schwegmann (Eds.), Urban Commons: Moving Beyond State and Market (pp. 196–213). Gütersloh: Bauverlag.

Becker, S., Beveridge, R., & Naumann, M. (2015b). Remunicipalization in German cities: contesting neo-liberalism and reimagining urban governance? Space and Polity, 19 (1), 76–90.

Becker, S., Bues, A., & Naumann, M. (2016a). Zur Analyse lokaler energiepolitischer Konflikte. Skizze eines Analysewerkzeugs. Raumforschung und Raumordnung, 74 (1), 39–49.

Becker, S., Bues, A., Naumann, M., & Betancourt, C. (2014b). Die Analyse lokaler energiepolitischer Konflikte und das Entstehen neuer Organisationsformen. Theoretische Zugänge und aktuelle Herausforderungen. Freiburg und Potsdam: Erkner.

Becker, S., Naumann, M., & Moss, T. (2016b). Between coproduction and commons: understanding initiatives to reclaim urban energy provision in Berlin and Hamburg. Urban Research & Practice, 1–23.

Beckmann, K. J. (Ed.). (2012). Bürgerbeteiligung in Kommunen. Anmerkungen aus der Stadtforschung zu einer aktuellen Herausforderung. Berlin: Dt. Inst. für Urbanistik.

Beery, Joshua A./Day, Jennifer E., 2015: Community Investment in Wind Farms: Funding Structure Effects in Wind Energy Infrastructure Development, in: Environmental Science & Technology 49, 2648–2655.

Beetz, M., Corsten, M., Rosa, H., & Winkler, T. (2012). Mitmachen und Mitreden. Sozialmoralische Orientierungen von bürgerschaftlich Engagierten im Ost-West-Vergleich. In Aufbruch der entsicherten Gesellschaft: Deutschland nach der Wiedervereinigung (pp. 328–330). Frankfurt a. M., New York: Campus.

Beher, K., Krimmer, H., Rauschenbach, T., & Zimmer, A. (2008). Die vergessene Elite. Führungskräfte in gemeinnützigen Organisationen. Weinheim u. a.: Juventa-Verl.

Beher, K., Liebig, R., & Rauschenbach, T. (2001). Vom Motivations- zum Strukturwandel – Analysen zum Ehrenamt in einer sich verändernden Umwelt. In R. G. Heinze & T. Olk (Eds.), Bürgerengagement in Deutschland (pp. 255–281). Wiesbaden: VS Verlag.

Behr, F., & Kamlage, J.-H., 2015: Kommunaler Klimaschutz – Handlungsmöglichkeiten und Rahmenbedingungen in deutschen Städten und Gemeinden. KWI-Working Paper Nr. 2, Essen: KWI.

Behr, H. (1999). Moderne Theorien der Demokratie und Konzeptionen politischer Partizipation. In H.-J. Lauth & U. Liebert (Eds.), Im Schatten demokratischer Legitimität: Informelle Institutionen und politische Partizipation im interkulturellen Demokratienvergleich (pp. 39–60). Wiesbaden: Wiesbaden: VS Verlag.

Behringer, J. (2002). Legitimität durch Verfahren? Bedingungen semi-konventioneller Partizipation. Eine qualitativ-empirische Studie am Beispiel von Fokusgruppen zum Thema „Lokaler Klimaschutz". Regensburg: S. Roderer.

Beinke, I., Bergmann, M., Bohne, M., Egle, C., Gohl, C., Heiny, A., Rucker, C., Simonic, B., Stern, M., & Wohlfahrt, A. (2012). Deutschlands Energiewende – Demokratie kollaborativ gestalten. Policy Brief der Stiftung Neue Verantwortung, 04.

Beisheim, M. (2015). Die „Agenda 2030 für nachhaltige Entwicklung": ein Ausblick auf ihre Weiterverfolgung und Überprüfung. Vereinte Nationen: Zeitschrift für die Vereinten Nationen und ihre Sonderorganisationen, 63 (6), 255–260.

Bell, D. (2004). Creating green citizens? Political liberalism and environmental education. Journal of Philosophy of Education, 38 (1), 37–54.

Bell, D. (2014). Environmental citizenship. Global, local and individual. In P. G. Harris (Ed.), Routledge handbook of global environmental politics (pp. 347–358). London: Routledge.

Bell, D., Gray, T., & Haggett, C. (2005). The "Social Gap" in Wind Farm Siting Decisions: Explanations and Policy Responses. Environmental Politics, 14 (4), 460–477.

Bell, D., Gray, T., Haggett, C., & Swaffield, J. (2013). Re-visiting the "social gap": public opinion and relations of power in the local politics of wind energy. Environmental Politics, 22 (1), 115–135.

Bellah, R. N., Madsen, R., Sullivan, W. M., Swidler, A., & Tipton, S. M. (2007). *Habits of the Heart. Individualism and Commitment in American Life*. First published in 1985. University of California Press.

Belmonte, S., Escalante, K. N., & Franco, J. (2015). Shaping changes through participatory processes: Local development and renewable energy in rural habitats. Renewable and Sustainable Energy Reviews, 45, 278–289.

Bender, C., & Wiesendahl, E. (2011). „Ehernes Gesetz der Oligarchie": Ist Demokratie möglich? Aus Politik und Zeitgeschichte APuZ, 61 (44), 19–24.

Benighaus, C., Oppermann, B., & Renn, O. (2007). Partizipative Verfahren in der kommunalen Planung. In G. Michelsen & J. Godemann (Eds.), Handbuch Nachhaltigkeitskommunikation. Grundlagen und Praxis (pp. 704–714). München: Oekom.

Bennett, W. L. (2008). Changing Citizenship in the Digital Age. In W. L. Bennett (Ed.), Civic life online: learning how digital media can engage youth. Cambridge, Mass.: MIT Press.

Bennett, W. L. (2012). The Personalization of Politics Political Identity, Social Media, and Changing Patterns of Participation. The Annals of the American Academy of Political and Social Science, 644 (1), 20–39.

Bennett, W. L., & Segerberg, A. (2013). The logic of connective action: digital media and the personalization of contentious politics. Cambridge: Cambridge University Press.

Bentele, G., Bohse, R., Hitschfeld, U., & Krebber, F. (Eds.). (2014). Akzeptanz in der Medien und Protestgesellschaft. Zur Debatte um Legitimation, öffentliches Vertrauen, Transparenz und Partizipation. Wiesbaden: VS Verlag.

Bentley, T. (2005). Everyday democracy: why we get the politicians we deserve. London: Demos.

Benz, A., & Dose, N. (Eds.) (2010). Governance – Regieren in komplexen Regelsystemen. Eine Einführung (2nd ed.). Wiesbaden: VS Verlag.

Benz, A., Lütz, S., Schimank, U., & Simonis, G. (2012). Handbuch Governance. Theoretische Grundlagen und empirische Anwendungsfelder. Wiesbaden: VS Verlag.

Berardi, U. (2015). Chapter 15 – Sustainability assessments of buildings, communities, and cities. In J. J. Klemeš (Ed.), Assessing and Measuring Environmental Impact and Sustainability (pp. 497–545). Oxford: Butterworth-Heinemann.

Berger, R. (1991). Politik und Technik: der Beitrag der Gesellschaftstheorien zur Technikbewertung. Opladen: Westdeutscher Verlag.

Berglund, C., & Matti, S. (2006). Citizen and consumer: the dual role of individuals in environmental policy. Environmental Politics, 15 (4), 550–571.

Bergman, M. M. (2008). Advances in Mixed Methods Research. Theories and Applications. Los Angeles: Sage.

Berkhout, F., Leach, M., & Scoones, I. (Eds.). 2003: Negotiating environmental change: new perspectives from social science. Cheltenham, Northampton: Edward Elgar.

Bernstein, R. J. (2000). CREATIVE DEMOCRACY – THE TASK STILL BEFORE US. American Journal of Theology & Philosophy, 21 (3), 215–228.

Berry, J. M. (1999). The Rise of Citizen Groups. In T. Skocpol & M. P. Fiorina (Eds.), Civic participation and the equality problem (pp. 367–394). Washington, D.C: Brookings Inst. Press u. a.

Bertelsmann Stiftung. (2016). Wachstum im Wandel. Chancen und Risiken für die Zukunft der Sozialen Marktwirtschaft. Gütersloh: Verlag Bertelsmann Stiftung.

Bertelsmann-Stiftung, & Staatsministerium Baden-Württemberg (Eds.). (2014). Partizipation im Wandel. Unsere Demokratie zwischen Wählen, Mitmachen und Entscheiden. Gütersloh: Verl. Bertelsmann-Stiftung.

Bertke, E., Hespelt, S. K., & Marggraf, R. (2005). Ein Regionaler Beirat als partizipatives Gremium in der Agrar-Umweltpolitik. In P. H. Feindt & J. Newig (Eds.), Partizipation, Öffentlichkeitsbeteiligung, Nachhaltigkeit (pp. 281–298). Marburg: Metropolis.

Beschorner, T., Ulrich, P., & Wettstein, F. (2015). St. Galler Wirtschaftsethik. Programmatik, Positionen, Perspektiven. Marburg: Metropolis-Verl.

Bettinger, C., & Holstenkamp, L. (2015): Grüner Strom aus der Region für die Region. Bericht des gleichnamigen Workshops im Rahmen des Energieforum 2015 an der Leuphana Universität Lüneburg, Lüneburg: Leuphana Univ.

Beutel, W., & Fauser, P. (2001). Erfahrene Demokratie: wie Politik praktisch gelernt werden kann. Pädagogische Analysen. Berichte und Anstöße aus dem Förderprogramm Demokratisch Handeln. Opladen: Leske + Budrich.

Beutel, W., & Fauser, P. (Eds.). (2011). Demokratiepädagogik. Lernen für die Zivilgesellschaft (2nd ed.). Schwalbach: Wochenschau.

Beutel, W., & Fauser, P. (Eds.). (2013). Demokratie erfahren. Analysen, Berichte und Anstöße aus dem Wettbewerb „Förderprogramm Demokratisch Handeln". Schwalbach: Wochenschau.

Beveridge, D. R., & Naumann, D. M. (2015). Unsere Stadt – unsere Infrastruktur! Standort, 39 (2–3), 108–111.

Bibisidis, T. (2015). Zivil – Gesellschaft – Staat. Freiwilligendienste zwischen staatlicher Steuerung und zivilgesellschaftlicher Gestaltung. Wiesbaden: Springer VS.

Bierbau, H. (2008). Renaissance der Genossenschaften? – Alternative zu finanzmarktgetriebener Unternehmenspolitik. Forum Wissenschaft, 3, 6–9.

Biermann, R., Fromme, J., & Verständig, D. (Eds.). (2014). Partizipative Medienkulturen. Positionen und Untersuchungen zu veränderten Formen öffentlicher Teilhabe. Wiesbaden: Springer VS.

Biesecker, A., & von Winterfeld, U. (2016). Wie regenerativ ist die Energiewende tatsächlich? Das Energiekonzept der Bundesregierung zwischen Aufbruch und nicht regenerativen Mustern. GAIA, 25 (1), 34–37.

Biesta, G. J. J. (2014). Civic learning, democratic citizenship and the public sphere. Dordrecht: Springer.

Bijker, W. E., Hughes, T. P., & Pinch, T. J. (Eds.). (2012). The social construction of technological systems: new directions in the sociology and history of technology. Cambridge, Mass.: MIT Press.

Bird, C., & Barnes, J. (2015). Scaling up community activism: the role of intermediaries in collective approaches to community energy. People Place and Policy, 8 (3), 208–221.

Birkhölzer, K. (2002). Erwerbsarbeit und bürgerschaftliches Engagement in der Sozialwirtschaft. In Bürgerschaftliches Engagement und Erwerbsarbeit (pp. 247–265). Wiesbaden: VS Verlag.

Bitzegeio, U., Mittag, J., & Winterberg, L. (Eds.). (2015). Der politische Mensch. Akteure gesellschaftlicher Partizipation im Übergang zum 21. Jahrhundert. Bonn: Dietz.

Blakeley, G., & Evans, B. (2010). Citizen Participation in East Manchaster: From Practice to Theory. Representation, 46 (3), 325–338.

Blanchet, T. (2015). Struggle over energy transition in Berlin: How do grassroots initiatives affect local energy policy-making? Energy Policy, 78, 246–254.

Becker, S., Blanchet, T., & Kunze, C. (2016). Social movements and urban energy policy: Assessing contexts, agency and outcomes of remunicipalisation processes in Hamburg and Berlin. *Utilities Policy, 41*, 228–236. https://doi.org/10.1016/j.jup.2016.02.001

Blanckenburg, C. von. (2014). Genossenschaftliche Partizipationsstrukturen als Teil der besonderen Handlungsmöglichkeiten im Klimaschutz. Partizipation in Genossenschaften und im Nachhaltigkeitsdiskurs. In C. Schröder & H. Walk (Eds.), Genossenschaften und Klimaschutz. Akteure für zukunftsfähige, solidarische Städte (pp. 257–283). Wiesbaden: VS Verlag.

Blandow, R., Knabe, J., & van Rießen, A. (Eds.). (2014). Städtische Quartiere gestalten. Kommunale Herausforderungen und Chancen im transformierten Wohlfahrtsstaat. Bielefeld: Transcript.

Blättel-Mink, B., & Hellmann, K.-U. (Eds.). (2010). Prosumer revisited. Zur Aktualität einer Debatte. Wiesbaden: VS Verlag.

Blätter für Deutsche und Internationale Politik (Eds.). (2015). Mehr geht nicht! Der Postwachstums-Reader. Berlin: Blätter Verlagsgesellschaft.

Blühdorn, I. (2000). Post-ecologist politics. Social theory and the abdication of the ecologist paradigm. London, New York: Routledge.

Blühdorn, I. (2011). Das postdemokratische Doppeldilemma. Politische Repräsentation in der simulativen Demokratie. In M. Linden & W. Thaa (Eds.), Krise und Reform politischer Repräsentation (pp. 45–74). Baden-Baden: Nomos.

Blühdorn, I. (2013). Simulative Demokratie. Neue Politik nach der postdemokratischen Wende. Berlin: Suhrkamp.

Bluhm, D. H., & Krause, D. S. (2012). Einleitung. Robert Michels' Soziologie des Parteiwesens. Oligarchien und Eliten – die Kehrseiten moderner Demokratie. In H. Bluhm & S. Krause (Eds.), Robert Michels' Soziologie des Parteiwesens (pp. 9–19). Wiesbaden: VS Verlag.

Blümle, M. A., Nehring, B., & Schmid, W. (2012). Gruppenarbeit und Co-Management. Einführung und Weiterentwicklung von Beteiligungsformen. In R. Schimweg, P. Fuchs-Frohnhofen & D. Brandt (Eds.), Partizipation und Führung. Erfolgsfaktoren quer zum Zeitgeist (pp. 147–159). Marburg: Tectum.

Bock und Polach, C. von, Kunze, C., Maaß, O., & Grundmann, P. (2015). Bioenergy as a socio-technical system. The nexus of rules, social capital and cooperation in the development of bioenergy villages in Germany. Energy Research & Social Science, 6, 128–135.

Bode, I. (2013). Die Infrastruktur des postindustriellen Wohlfahrtsstaats. Organisation, Wandel, gesellschaftliche Hintergründe. Wiesbaden: Springer VS.

Bode, M., & Schmidt, S. (2008). Off the grid. Göteborg: Valand School of Fine Arts, Faculty of Fine, Applied and Performing Arts, Univ. of Gothenburg.

Bödeker, S. (2011). Die soziale Frage der Demokratie. Einkommen und Bildung beeinflussen die Chancen politischer Teilhabe. Wissenschaftszentrum Berlin für Sozialforschung – Mitteilungen, 134, 26–29.

Boeser, C., & Schnebel, K. (2013). Über „dumme Bürger" und „feige Politiker". Streitschrift für mehr Niveau in politischen Alltagsgesprächen. Wiesbaden: VS Verlag.

Bogner, A. (2014). Emergierende Technologien und projektförmige Partizipation. Forschungsjournal Soziale Bewegungen, 27 (4), 82–91.

Bogner, A., Littig, B., & Menz, W. (Eds.). (2009). Experteninterviews. Theorien, Methoden, Anwendungsfelder (3rd ed.). Wiesbaden: VS Verlag.

Bogner, A., Littig, B., & Menz, W. (Eds.). (2014). Interviews mit Experten. Eine praxisorientierte Einführung. Wiesbaden: VS Verlag.

Bogumil, J. (1999). Alle Politik ist lokal. Kommunales Handeln in der Bürgergesellschaft. In U. von Alemann, R. G. Heinze, & U. Wehrhöfer (Eds.), Bürgergesellschaft und Gemeinwohl: Analyse, Diskussion, Praxis (pp. 159–168). Opladen: Leske + Budrich.

Bogumil, J., & Holtkamp, L. (2011). Bürgerkommune. In B. Blanke, F. Nullmeier, C. Reichard, & G. Wewer (Eds.), Handbuch zur Verwaltungsreform (pp. 177–185). Wiesbaden: VS Verlag.

Bogumil, J., & Holtkamp, L. (2013). Kommunalpolitik und Kommunalverwaltung. Eine praxisorientierte Einführung. Bonn: Bundeszentrale für politische Bildung.

Bogumil, J., Holtkamp, L., & Schwarz, G. (2003). Das Reformmodell Bürgerkommune. Leistungen, Grenzen, Perspektiven. Berlin: Edition Sigma.

Böhnke, P. (2011). Ungleiche Verteilung politischer und zivilgesellschaftlicher Partizipation. Aus Politik und Zeitgeschichte APuZ, 61 (1), 18–25.

Bohnsack, F. (2003). Demokratie als erfülltes Leben. Die Aufgabe von Schule und Erziehung. Ausgewählte und kommentierte Aufsätze unter Berücksichtigung der Pädagogik John Deweys. Bad Heilbrunn: Klinkhardt.

Bohnsack, R., Nentwig-Gesemann, I., & Nohl, A.-M. (Eds.). (2013). Die dokumentarische Methode und ihre Forschungspraxis. Grundlagen qualitativer Sozialforschung (3rd ed.). Wiesbaden: VS Verlag.

Boillat, S., Gerber, J.-F., & Funes-Monzote, F. R. (2012). What economic democracy for degrowth? Some comments on the contribution of socialist models and Cuban agroecology. Futures, 44 (6), 600–607.

Bolton, R., & Foxon, T. J. (2015a). A socio-technical perspective on low carbon investment challenges – Insights for UK energy policy. Environmental Innovation and Societal Transitions, 14, 165–181.

Bolton, R., & Foxon, T. J. (2015b). Infrastructure transformation as a socio-technical process – Implications for the governance of energy distribution networks in the UK. Technological Forecasting and Social Change, 90, Part B, 538–550.

Bolzendahl, C., & Coffé, H. (2013). Are "Good" Citizens "Good" Participants? Testing Citizenship Norms and Political Participation across 25 Nations. Political Studies, 61, 45–65.

Bomberg, E., & McEwen, N. (2012). Mobilizing community energy. Energy Policy, 51, 435–444.

Bonaiuti, M. (2012). Growth and democracy: Trade-offs and paradoxes. Futures, 44 (6), 524–534.

Bonar, P. A. J., Bryden, I. G., & Borthwick, A. G. L. (2015). Social and ecological impacts of marine energy development. Renewable and Sustainable Energy Reviews, 47, 486–495.

Bono, M. L. (2012). Wirkungsorientierung und organisationales Lernen. VM: Fachzeitschrift Für Verbands- und Nonprofit-Management, 38 (2), 14–20.

Booher, D. E. (2004). Collaborative governance practices and democracy. National Civic Review, 93 (4), 32–46.

Boon, F. P., & Dieperink, C. (2014). Local civil society based renewable energy organisations in the Netherlands: Exploring the factors that stimulate their emergence and development. Energy Policy, 69, 297–307.

Borell, N. (2015). disruption. Das Spiel mit Technologien und Paradigmen. Hamburg: tredition.

Bornemann, B. (2014). *Policy-Integration und Nachhaltigkeit: Integrative Politik in der Nachhaltigkeitsstrategie der deutschen Bundesregierung* (2nd ed.). Wiesbaden: Springer VS.

Bornemann, B., & Saretzki, T. (2018). Konfliktfeldanalyse – das Beispiel „Fracking" in Deutschland. In L. Holstenkamp & J. Radtke (Eds.), *Handbuch Energiewende und Partizipation* (pp. 563–581). Wiesbaden: Springer VS. https://doi.org/10.1007/978-3-658-09416-4_34

Bornemann, B., & Verlinden, J. (2002). Ökologische Modernisierung in Theorie und Politik. Forschungsjournal Soziale Bewegungen, 15 (4), 80–82.

Bornstein, D. (2007). How to change the world. Oxford: Oxford University Press.

Borras, S., & Edler, J. (2015). The Governance of Socio-Technical Systems: Explaining Change. Cheltenham: Edward Elgar.

Borrás, S., & Edler, J. (Eds.), 2014: The governance of socio-technical systems: explaining change, Cheltenham: Edward Elgar.

Bosch, S., & Peyke, G. (2011). Gegenwind für die Erneuerbaren – Räumliche Neuorientierung der Wind-, Solar- und Bioenergie vor dem Hintergrund einer verringerten Akzeptanz sowie zunehmender Flächennutzungskonflikte im ländlichen Raum. Raumforschung und Raumordnung, 69 (2), 105–118.

Böschen, S., & Pfersdorf, S. (2014). Partizipation von zivilgesellschaftlichen Organisationen in Innovationsentwicklung und Risikobewältigung. Forschungsjournal Soziale Bewegungen, 27 (4), 50–58.

Böschen, S., Gill, B., Kropp, C., & Vogel, K. (Eds.). (2014). Klima von unten. Regionale Governance und gesellschaftlicher Wandel. Frankfurt a. M., New York: Campus.

Boss-Stenner, H., Pufendorf, U. von, & Schade, F. K. (1970). Partizipation. Aspekte politischer Kultur. Opladen: Westdeutscher Verlag.

Bossel, H. (1978). Bürgerinitiativen entwerfen die Zukunft. Neue Leitbilder. Neue Werte. 30 Szenarien. Ein Alternativ-Bericht des Öko-Instituts Freiburg/Br. Frankfurt a. M.: Fischer Taschenbuch Verlag.

Bossy, S. (2014). The utopias of political consumerism. The search of alternatives to mass consumption. Journal of Consumer Culture, 14 (2), 179–198.

Bostrom, Nick, 2014: Superintelligence: paths, dangers, strategies. Oxford: Oxford University Press.

Bott, H., Grassl, G. C., Anders, S., & Altmann, M. (2013). Nachhaltige Stadtplanung. Konzepte für nachhaltige Quartiere. München: Detail, Inst. für Internat. Architektur-Dokumentation.

Bourdieu, P. (1979). Entwurf einer Theorie der Praxis. Auf der ethnologischen Grundlage der kabylischen Gesellschaft (3rd ed.). Frankfurt a. M.: Suhrkamp.

Bourdieu, P. (1983). Ökonomisches Kapital, kulturelles Kapital, soziales Kapital. In R. Kreckel (Ed.), Soziale Ungleichheiten (pp. 183–198). Göttingen: Schwartz.

Bourdieu, P. (2014). Über den Staat. Vorlesungen am Collège de France 1989–1992. Berlin: Suhrkamp.

Bovet, J., & Lienhoop. (2015). Trägt die wirtschaftliche Teilhabe an Flächen für die Windkraftnutzung zur Akzeptanz bei? Zum Gesetzesentwurf eines Bürger- und Gemeindebeteiligungsgesetzes in Mecklenburg-Vorpommern unter Berücksichtigung von empirischen Befragungen. Zeitschrift für Neues Energierecht, 16 (3), 227–234.

Box, R. C. (1997). Citizen Governance. Leading American Communities into the 21st Century. Los Angeles: Sage.

Boyle, G., & Open University (Eds.). (2012). Renewable energy: power for a sustainable future (3rd ed.). Oxford: Oxford University Press in association with the Open University.

Boyte, H. C. (Ed.). (2015). Democracy's Education. Public Work, Citizenship, and the Future of Colleges and Universities. Nashville: Vanderbilt University Press.

Brachmann, H. (2009). Gründung einer Genossenschaft im Quartier. In M. Drilling & O. Schnur (Eds.), Governance der Quartiersentwicklung. Theoretische und praktische Zugänge zu neuen Steuerungsformen (pp. 205–210). Wiesbaden: VS Verlag.

Bracken, L. J., Bulkeley, H. A., & Maynard, C. M. (2014). Micro-hydro power in the UK: The role of communities in an emerging energy resource. Energy Policy, 68, 92–101.

Brady, H. E., Verba, S., & Schlozman, K. L. (1995). Beyond SES: A Resource Model of Political Participation. The American Political Science Review, 89 (2), 271–294.

Brand, K.-W. (2010). Die Neuerfindung des Bürgers. In T. Olk, A. Klein, & B. Hartnuß (Eds.), Engagementpolitik (pp. 123–152). Wiesbaden: VS Verlag.

Braun, D. (1997). Handlungstheoretische Grundlagen in der empirisch-analytischen Politikwissenschaft. Eine kritische Übersicht. In A. Benz & W. Seibel (Eds.), Beiträge zur Theorieentwicklung in der Politik- und Verwaltungswissenschaft (pp. 45–74). Baden-Baden: Nomos.

Braun, S. (2003). Freiwillige Vereinigungen als Produzenten von Sozialkapital? VM: Fachzeitschrift für Verbands- und Nonprofit-Management, 29 (1), 28–37. Potsdam: Universitäts-Verlag.

Braun, S. (2004). Solidarität, Gemeinwesen, Gemeinwohl: das Assoziationswesen in aktuellen Diskussionen. In H. K. Anheier (Ed.), Zwischen Eigennutz und Gemeinwohl. Neue Formen und Wege der Gemeinnützigkeit (pp. 131–146). Gütersloh: Verl. Bertelsmann-Stiftung.

Braun, S. (2005). Bürgergesellschaft und sozialer Zusammenhalt. Theoretische Überlegungen und empirische Befunde zu den Integrationsleistungen von freiwilligen Vereinigungen im Dritten Sektor. In K. Birkhölzer, A. Klein, E. Priller, & A. Zimmer (Eds.), Dritter Sektor/Drittes System (pp. 131–159). Wiesbaden: VS Verlag.

Braun, S. (2006). Die Wiederentdeckung des Vereinswesens im Windschatten gesellschaftlicher Krisen. Konzepte, Kontroversen, Perspektiven. In J. Franzke (Ed.), Making civil societies work. Zivilgesellschaft und gesellschaftliche Praxis (pp. 26–40). Potsdam: Universitätsverlag Potsdam.

Braun, S. (2007). Freiwillige Vereinigungen als Katalysatoren von Sozialkapital? Ergebnisse einer repräsentativen Bevölkerungsbefragung in Deutschland. In J. Lüdicke &

M. Diewald (Eds.), Soziale Netzwerke und soziale Ungleichheit. Zur Rolle von Sozialkapital in modernen Gesellschaften (pp. 201–234). Wiesbaden: VS Verlag.

Braun, S. (2009). Assoziative Lebenswelt, bindendes Sozialkapital und Wahlgemeinschaften des Geschmacks. Forschungsjournal Soziale Bewegungen, 3, 76–87.

Braun, S., Hansen, S., & Ritter, S. (2007). Vereine als Katalysatoren sozialer und politischer Kompetenzen? In L. Schwalb & H. Walk (Eds.), Local Governance – mehr Transparenz und Bürgernähe? (pp. 109–130). Wiesbaden: VS Verlag.

Braungart, M., & McDonough, W. (2013). Intelligente Verschwendung: the Upcycle. Auf dem Weg in eine neue Überflussgesellschaft. München: Oekom.

Braungart, M., & McDonough, W. (Eds.). (2011). Die nächste industrielle Revolution: die Cradle to Cradle-Community (3rd ed.). Hamburg: Europ. Verl.-Anst.

Braunmühl, C. v. (2010). Demokratie, gleichberechtigte Bürgerschaft und Partizipation. In I. Seidl & A. Zahrnt (Eds.), Postwachstumsgesellschaft. Konzepte für die Zukunft (pp. 189–197). Marburg: Metropolis.

Braunmühl, C. v. (2011). Ein gutes Klima für und mit gleichberechtigter Bürgerschaft? In S. S. Schüttemeyer (Ed.), Politik im Klimawandel: keine Macht für gerechte Lösungen (pp. 113–126). Baden-Baden: Nomos.

Brazda, J., & Schediwy, R. (2013). Egoismus und Altruismus in der Genossenschaftswissenschaft. In J. Brazda, M. Dellinger, & D. Rößl (Eds.), Genossenschaften im Fokus einer neuen Wirtschaftspolitik. Bericht der XVII. Internationalen Genossenschaftswissenschaftlichen Tagung (IGT) 2012 in Wien. Teilband 3 (pp. 845–854). Wien: LIT.

Brazda, J., Dellinger, M., & Rößl, D. (Eds.). (2013). Genossenschaften im Fokus einer neuen Wirtschaftspolitik. Bericht der XVII. Internationalen Genossenschaftswissenschaftlichen Tagung (IGT) 2012 in Wien. 4 Teilbände. Wien: LIT.

Brennan, J. (2016). Against Democracy. Princeton: Princeton University Press.

Brennan, J., & Hill, L. (2014). Compulsory Voting. For and Against. New York: Cambridge University Press.

Brennecke, V. M. (2015). Frühe Öffentlichkeitsbeteiligung zwischen Rechtsvorschrift und Selbstregulierung. Die neue Richtlinie VDI 7000. Verwaltungsarchiv, 106 (1), 34–54.

Brenner, N., Marcuse, P., & Mayer, M. (Eds.). (2012). Cities for People, Not for Profit. Critical Urban Theory and the Right to the City. London; New York: Routledge.

Bretherton, L. (2014). Resurrecting Democracy: Faith, Citizenship, and the Politics of a Common Life. New York: Cambridge University Press.

Brettschneider, F., & Schuster, W. (Eds.). (2013). Stuttgart 21. Ein Großprojekt zwischen Protest und Akzeptanz. Wiesbaden: Springer VS.

Brettschneider, J. (2012). Die Welt als Shop. Konsum und Konsumenten. Braunschweig: Westermann.

Breukers, S., Mourik, R., & Heiskanen, E. (2013). Changing Energy Demand Behavior: Potential of Demand-Side Management. In J. Kauffman & K.-M. Lee (Eds.), Handbook of Sustainable Engineering. Volume 2 (pp. 773–792). Dordrecht u. a.: Springer.

Brewer, M. B. (1999). The Psychology of Prejudice: Ingroup Love and Outgroup Hate? Journal of Social Issues, 55 (3), 429–444.

Bridge, G., Barr, S., Bouzarovski, S., Bradshaw, M., Brown, E., Bulkeley, H., & Walker, G. (2018). *Energy and Society: A Critical Perspective*. Abingdon, New York: Routledge.

Bringenberg, L. (2013). Nothing about us, without us? – A comparative case study of "responsiveness" in two public participation processes at the German federal level. In

A. Römmele & H. Banthien (Eds.), Empowering Citizens. Studies in Collaborative Democracy (pp. 139–182). Baden-Baden: Nomos.

Bröchler, S., & Lauth, H.-J. (Eds.). (2014). Von Government zu Governance. Informelles Regieren im Vergleich. Wiesbaden: VS Verlag.

Bröchler, S., Grunden, T., & Deutsche Vereinigung für Politische Wissenschaft (Eds.). (2014). Informelle Politik. Konzepte, Akteure und Prozesse. Wiesbaden: Springer VS.

Brodocz, A., Llanque, M., & Schaal, G. S. (2009). Bedrohungen der Demokratie. Wiesbaden: VS Verlag.

Brooks, S., Leach, M., Lucas, H., & Millstone, E. (2009). Silver Bullets, Grand Challenges and the New Philanthropy. Brighton: STEPS Centre, University of Sussex.

Brown, L. R., & Brown, L. R. (2009). Plan B 4.0: mobilizing to save civilization. New York: W.W. Norton.

Brown, L. R., Larsen, J., Roney, J. M., & Adams, E. E. (2015). The great transition: shifting from fossil fuels to solar and wind energy. New York: W.W. Norton.

Browne, A., Medd, W., Anderson, B., & Pullinger, M. (2014). Method as intervention: intervening in practise through quantitative and mixed methodologies. In C. Maller & Y. Strengers (Eds.), Intervening in social practices for sustainability: Beyond behaviour change (pp. 1–21). New York: Routledge.

Brücher, W. (2009). Energiegeographie. Wechselwirkungen zwischen Ressourcen, Raum und Politik. Berlin: Borntraeger.

Bruckner, H., & Oswalt, P. (2015). Energielandschaften 3.0. Leipzig: Spector Books.

Brühne, T. (2015). Die Rückkehr zur Fläche – Postmoderne Energielandschaften als Zeichen sozialer Aushandlungsprozesse im Raum. In J. Lempp, G. van der Beek, & T. Korn (Eds.), Aktuelle Herausforderungen in der Wirtschaftsförderung (pp. 111–117). Wiesbaden: Springer Gabler.

Brühne, T., & Tempel, M. (2013). Postmoderne Energielandschaften in Rheinland-Pfalz. Geographische Rundschau, 65 (1), 28–35.

Bruninx, K., Madzharov, D., Delarue, E., & D'haeseleer, W. (2013). Impact of the German nuclear phase-out on Europe's electricity generation – A comprehensive study. Energy Policy, 60, 251–261.

Brunkhorst, H. (Ed.). (1998). Demokratischer Experimentalismus. Politik in der komplexen Gesellschaft. Frankfurt a. M.: Suhrkamp.

Brunnengräber, A., & Di Nucci, M. R. (Eds.). (2014). Im Hürdenlauf zur Energiewende. Von Transformationen, Reformen und Innovationen. Wiesbaden: Springer VS.

Bruns, A. (2009). „Produtzung: von medialer zu politischer Partizipation. In C. Bieber, M. Eifert, T. Groß, & J. Lamla (Eds.), Soziale Netze in der digitalen Welt. Das Internet zwischen egalitärer Teilhabe und ökonomischer Macht (pp. 65–85). Frankfurt a. M., New York: Campus.

Bruns, E., & Ohlhorst, D. (2011). Wind Power Generation in Germany-a transdisciplinary view on the innovation biography. *The Journal of Transdisciplinary Environmental Studies, 10*(1), 45–67.

Bruns, E., Ohlhorst, D., Wenzel, B., & Köppel, J. (2011). Renewable Energies in Germany's Electricity Market. Dordrecht u. a.: Springer Netherlands.

Bruns, E., Ohlhorst, D., Wenzel, B., & Köppel, J. (2009). Erneuerbare Energien in Deutschland: eine Biographie des Innovationsgeschehens. Berlin: TU Universitäts-Verlag.

Brynjolfsson, E., & McAfee, A. (2014). The Second Machine Age. Work, Progress, and Prosperity in a Time of Brilliant Technologies. New York: W. W. Norton.
Bscher, B., & Igoe, J. (2013). Prosuming conservation? Web 2.0, nature and the intensification of value-producing labour in late capitalism. Journal of Consumer Culture, 13 (3), 283–305.
Buchholz, F., & Huge, A. (2014). Beteiligung: ein Mittel, um die Bürger bei der Energiewende mitzunehmen? Ein aktueller Zwischenbericht zur Windenergieplanung in Baden-Württemberg. In S. Grotheer, A. Schwöbel & M. Stepper (Eds.), Nimm's sportlich: Planung als Hindernislauf. 16. Junges Forum der ARL, 29. bis 31. Mai 2013 in Kaiserslautern (pp. 4–17). Hannover: Akademie für Raumforschung und Landesplanung.
Buchstein, H. (Ed.). (2013). Die Versprechen der Demokratie. 25. wissenschaftlicher Kongress der Deutschen Vereinigung für Politische Wissenschaft. Baden-Baden: Nomos.
Buchstein, H. (2000). Bürgergesellschaft und Bürgerkompetenz. In G. Breit & P. Massing (Eds.), Bürgergesellschaft, Zivilgesellschaft, Dritter Sektor (pp. 8–18). Schwalbach: Wochenschau.
Budde, G., Conze, E. & Rauh, C. (2010). Bürgertum nach dem bürgerlichen Zeitalter. Leitbilder und Praxis seit 1945. Göttingen: Vandenhoeck & Ruprecht.
Bude, H., Fischer, J., & Kauffmann, B. (Eds.). (2010). Bürgerlichkeit ohne Bürgertum. In welchem Land leben wir? München: W. Fink.
Bühler, S. (2010). Determinanten Freiwilligen Engagements. Argumentation für den Nutzen einer handlungstheoretisch geleiteten Herangehensweise an eine theoretische Integration. Marburg: Tectum.
Bühler, T. (1997). Bürgerbeteiligung und Demokratie vor Ort. Bonn: Stiftung Mitarbeit.
Bühlmann, M. (2013). Verbundenheit mit der Gemeinde. In J. W. van Deth & M. Tausendpfund (Eds.), Politik im Kontext: Ist alle Politik lokale Politik? (pp. 329–358). Wiesbaden: Springer Fachmedien.
Bühlmann, M., & Freitag, M. (2004). Individuelle und kontextuelle Determinanten der Teilhabe an Sozialkapital. KZfSS Kölner Zeitschrift Für Soziologie Und Sozialpsychologie, 56 (2), 326–349.
Bühlmann, M., & Freitag, M. (2007). Freiwilligentätigkeit als Sozialkapital. Eine empirische Analyse zu den Rahmenbedingungen bürgerschaftlichen Vereinsengagements. In A. Franzen & M. Freitag (Eds.), Sozialkapital. Grundlagen und Anwendungen (pp. 163182). Wiesbaden: VS Verlag.
Bulgarian Academy of Sciences. (1900). Energy Planning, Management and Efficiency in Local Context. Summary of an American-Bulgarian-Romanian Workshop. Washington: National Academies Press.
Bull, R., Lemon, M., Everitt, D., & Stuart, G. (2015). Moving beyond feedback: Energy behaviour and local engagement in the United Kingdom. Energy Research & Social Science, 8, 32–40.
Bullwinkel, B., & Probst, L. (2014). Innerparteiliche Willensbildung und Entscheidungsprozesse durch digitale Partizipation. Ein Praxistext des Konzepts der Liquid Democracy. Zeitschrift Für Parlamentsfragen, 45 (2), 382–402.
Bulut, B., Çakmak, Z., & Kara, C. (2013). Global Citizenship in Technology Age from the Perspective of Social Sciences. Procedia – Social and Behavioral Sciences, 103, 442–448.
Bundesministerium für Umwelt, Naturschutz und Reaktorsicherheit (Eds.). (2008). Die Dritte Industrielle Revolution – Aufbruch in ein ökologisches Jahrhundert. Dimensionen

und Herausforderungen des industriellen und gesellschaftlichen Wandels. Berlin: Bundesministerium für Umwelt, Naturschutz und Reaktorsicherheit.

Bundesministerium für Wirtschaft und Technologie (BMWi). (2010). Energiekonzept für eine umweltschonende, zuverlässige und bezahlbare Energieversorgung. Stand: 28. September 2010. Berlin: BMWi.

Bundesministerium für Wirtschaft und Energie (BMWi). (2014). Die Energie der Zukunft. Ein gutes Stück Arbeit. Erster Fortschrittsbericht zur Energiewende. Berlin: BMWi. http://www.bmwi.de/BMWi/Redaktion/PDF/Publikationen/fort-schrittsbericht.pdf

Bundesministerium für Wirtschaft und Energie (BMWi). (2016). EEG-Novelle 2016 – Fortgeschriebenes Eckpunktepapier zum Vorschlag des BMWi für das neue EEG. Berlin. https://www.bmwi.de/BMWi/Redaktion/PDF/E/eeg-novel-le-2016-fortgeschriebenes-eckpunktepapier,property=pdf,bereich=bmwi2012,spra-che=de,rwb=true.pdf

Bundeszentrale für Politische Bildung. (2012). Digitale Demokratie. Bonn: Bundeszentrale für Politische Bildung.

Burch, J., Woods, J., Kozubal, E., & Boranian, A. (2012). Zero Energy Communities with Central Solar Plants using Liquid Desiccants and Local Storage. Energy Procedia, 30, 55–64.

Burchardt, S. (2008). Inszenierte Bürgerbeteiligung? Die lokalen Begleitausschüsse des Bundesprogramms „Lokales Kapital für Soziale Zwecke (LOS)". In A. Vetter (Ed.), Erfolgsbedingungen lokaler Bürgerbeteiligung (pp. 217–235). Wiesbaden: VS Verlag.

Burchell, K., Rettie, R., & Roberts, T. C. (2015). Community, the very idea! Perspectives of participants in a demand-side community energy project. People Place and Policy, 8 (3), 168–179.

Burchell, K., Rettie, R., & Roberts, T. C. (2016). Householder engagement with energy consumption feedback: the role of community action and communications. Energy Policy, 88, 178–186.

Bürgenmeier, B. (2006). Die Freiwilligenarbeit zwischen Geschenkökonomie und Markt. In P. Farago & H. Ammann (Eds.), Monetarisierung der Freiwilligkeit. Referate und Zusammenfassungen der 5. Tagung der Freiwilligenuniversität vom 30. bis 31.5.2005 in Luzern (pp. 44–62). Zürich: Seismo.

Burger, C., & Weinmann, J. (2014). Chapter 3 – Germany's Decentralized Energy Revolution. In F. P. Sioshansi (Ed.), Distributed Generation and its Implications for the Utility Industry (pp. 49–73). Boston: Academic Press.

Bürgisser, S. (2011). Zusammenarbeit zwischen Vorstand und Geschäftsführung. VM: Fachzeitschrift Für Verbands- und Nonprofit-Management, 37 (2), 38–45.

Bürgisser, S. (2012a). Konflikte zwischen Vorstand und Geschäftsführung in Nonprofit-Organisationen. Eine Analyse der Spannungsfelder und deren Ursachen. Wiesbaden: Springer VS.

Bürgisser, S. (2012b). Zusammenarbeit zwischen Vorstand und Geschäftsführung in Verbänden und anderen Nonprofit Organisationen. Fribourg/Suisse: Universität, FSES.

Bürgisser, S., & Helmig, B. (2009). Interessenskonflikte zwischen Ehrenamt und Hauptamt. VM: Fachzeitschrift für Verbands- und Nonprofit-Management, 35 (2), 36–45.

Burke, M. J., & Stephens, J. C. (2017). Energy democracy: Goals and policy instruments for sociotechnical transitions. *Energy Research & Social Science, 33*, 35–48. https://doi.org/10.1016/j.erss.2017.09.024

Burns, N., Schlozman, K. L., & Verba, S. (Eds.). (2001). The private roots of public action: gender, equality, and political participation. Cambridge, Mass.: Harvard University Press.

Buschle, D., & Talus, K. (2015). The Energy Community. A New Energy Governance System. Antwerp u. a.: Intersentia Uitgevers N V.

Buse, M., Hahn, R., Nelles, W., & Oppermann, R. (1978). Determinanten politischer Partizipation. Theorieansatz und empirische Überprüfung am Beispiel der Stadtsanierung Andernach. Meisenheim am Glan: Hain.

Bußjäger, P., & Gamper, A. (Eds.). (2015). Demokratische Innovation und Partizipation in der Europaregion. Wien: New Academic Press.

Butler, C., Demski, C., Parkhill, K., Pidgeon, N., & Spence, A. (2015). Public values for energy futures: Framing, indeterminacy and policy making. Energy Policy, 87, 665–672.

Butler, C., Parkhill, K. A., & Pidgeon, N. F. (2014). Energy consumption and everyday life. Choice, values and agency through a practice theoretical lens. Journal of Consumer Culture, 1–21.

Butzlaff, F. (2016). Die neuen Bürgerproteste in Deutschland. Organisatoren – Erwartungen – Demokratiebilder. Bielefeld: Transcript.

Byrne, J., & Toly, N. (2006). Energy as a social project: Recovering a discourse. In J. Byrne, N. Toly, & L. Glover (Eds.), Transforming Power: Energy, Environment and Society in Conflict (pp. 1–32). New Brunswick, N.J. u. a.: Transaction Publishers.

Byrnes, L., Brown, C., Foster, J., & Wagner, L. D. (2013). Australian renewable energy policy: Barriers and challenges. Renewable Energy, 60, 711–721.

C.A.R.M.E.N. e.V. (2014). Akzeptanz für Erneuerbare Energien. Ein Leitfaden. http://www.carmen-ev.de/files/Sonne_Wind_und_Co/Akzeptanz/Akzeptanzbroschuere.pdf

Cajaiba-Santana, G. (2014). Social innovation: Moving the field forward. A conceptual framework. Technological Forecasting and Social Change, 82, 42–51.

Calvert, K. (2015). Energy and Society. In J. D. Wright (Ed.), International Encyclopedia of the Social & Behavioral Sciences (2nd ed.) (pp. 615–620). Oxford: Elsevier.

Calvert, K. (2016). From "energy geography" to "energy geographies" Perspectives on a fertile academic borderland. Progress in Human Geography, 40 (1), 105–125.

Canzler, W., & Wittowsky, D. (2016). The impact of Germany's Energiewende on the transport sector – Unsolved problems and conflicts. *Utilities Policy, 41*, 246–251. https://doi.org/10.1016/j.jup.2016.02.011

Capener, P. (2009). People-powered Response to Climate Change. Mapping Community-led Proposals to NESTA's Big Green Challenge. London: NESTA (National Endowment for Science, Technology and the Arts).

Cass, N., & Walker, G. (2009). Emotion and rationality. The characterisation and evaluation of opposition to renewable energy projects. Emotion, Space and Society, 2 (1), 62–69.

Cass, N., Walker, G., & Devine-Wright, P. (2010). Good neighbours, public relations and bribes: the politics and perceptions of community benefit provision in renewable energy development in the UK. Journal of Environmental Policy & Planning, 12 (3), 255–275.

Cassell, J. (2013). The Ultimate Guide to Self-Reliant Living. New York: Skyhorse Publishing.

Castells, M. (1975). Kampf in den Städten. Gesellschaftliche Widersprüche und politische Macht. West-Berlin: VSA, Verlag für das Studium der Arbeiterbewegung.

Castiglione, D., Deth, J. W. van, & Wolleb, G. (Eds.). (2008). The handbook of social capital. Oxford: Oxford University Press.

Catney, P., MacGregor, S., Dobson, A., Hall, S. M., Royston, S., Robinson, Z., Ormerod, M., & Ross, S. (2014). Big society, little justice? Community renewable energy and the politics of localism. Local Environment, 19 (7), 715–730.

Cattacin, S. (2006). Wandel der traditionellen Freiwilligenarbeit. Überblick. In P. Farago & H. Ammann (Eds.), Monetarisierung der Freiwilligkeit. Referate und Zusammenfassungen der 5. Tagung der Freiwilligenuniversität vom 30. bis 31.5.2005 in Luzern (pp. 217–220). Zürich: Seismo.

Cattaneo, C., D'Alisa, G., Kallis, G., & Zografos, C. (2012). Degrowth futures and democracy. Futures, 44 (6), 515–523.

Challies, E., Newig, J., Thaler, T., Kochskämper, E., & Levin-Keitel, M. (2016). Participatory and collaborative governance for sustainable flood risk management: An emerging research agenda. Environmental Science & Policy, 55, Part 2, 275–280.

Chapple, K. (2015). Planning Sustainable Cities and Regions. Towards More Equitable Development. Abingdon, New York: Routledge.

Chatalova, L., & Valentinov, V. (2014). Energiewende: Die zwielichtige Rolle der Energie-Genossenschaften. Die Zeit Online v. 20.4.2014. http://www.zeit.de/wissen/umwelt/2014-04/energiegenossenschaften-rendite

Cheema, G. S., & Popovski, V. (Eds.). (2010). Engaging Civil Society. Emerging Trends in Democratic Governance. Tokyo, New York: United Nations University.

Chilvers, J. (2012a). Expertise, Technologies and Ecologies of Participation. Expertise, Technologies and Ecologies of Participation. 3S Working Paper 2012-17. Norwich: Science, Society and Sustainability Research Group.

Chilvers, J. (2012b). Reflexive Engagement: Actors, Learning and Reflexivity in Participatory Governance of Science and Technology. 3S Working Paper 2012-06. Norwich: Science, Society and Sustainability Research Group.

Chilvers, J., & Longhurst, N. (2014). Co-production and emergence of diverse public engagements in energy transitions. 3S Working Paper 201426. Norwich: Science, Society and Sustainability Research Group.

Chilvers, J., & Kearnes, M. (Eds.). (2016). Remaking Participation. Science, Environment and Emergent Publics. London, New York: Routledge.

Chisholm, L., Ostendorf, A., Thoma, M., & Weber, W. G. (2012). Introduction: Whither Democracy in Everyday Social Life? In W. G. Weber, M. Thoma, A. Ostendorf, & L. Chisholm (Eds.), Democratic Competences and Social Practices in Organizations (pp. 9–16). Wiesbaden: VS Verlag.

Chitewere, T. (2016). Sustainable Communities and Green Lifestyles Consumption and Environmentalism. New York: Routledge.

Chitewere, T., & Taylor, D. E. (2010). Sustainable living and community building in Ecovillage at Ithaca. The challenges of incorporating social justice concerns into the practices of an ecological cohousing community. In Environment and Social Justice: An International Perspective (Vol. 18, pp. 141–176). Emerald Group Publishing Limited.

Chmutina, K., & Goodier, C. I. (2014). Alternative future energy pathways. Assessment of the potential of innovative decentralised energy systems in the UK. Energy Policy, 66, 62–72.

Chmutina, K., Wiersma, B., Goodier, C. I., & Devine-Wright, P. (2014). Concern or compliance? Drivers of urban decentralised energy initiatives. Sustainable Cities and Society, 10, 122–129.

Christ, T., Gellrich, A., & Ide, T. (Eds.). (2012). Zugänge zur Klimadebatte in Politikwissenschaft, Soziologie und Psychologie. Marburg: Metropolis-Verlag.

Christensen, H. S. (2011). Political participation beyond the vote: how the institutional context shapes patterns of political participation in the 18 western European democracies. Åbo: Åbo Akad. Förl.

Chung, M., Park, C., Lee, S., Park, H.-C., Im, Y.-H., & Chang, Y. (2012). A decision support assessment of cogeneration plant for a community energy system in Korea. Energy Policy, 47, 365–383.

Clark, S. (2012). Slow Democracy: Rediscovering Community, Bringing Decision Making Back Home. White River Junction, Vt: Chelsea Green.

Clark, W. W. (2010). Sustainable Communities. New York: Springer.

Clark II, W. W., & Cooke, G. (2015a). Appendix 11 – Smart Green Energy Communities: A Definition and an Analysis of Their Economic Sustainability in Europe. In W. W. Clark, & G. Cooke (Eds.), The Green Industrial Revolution (pp. 377–391). Oxford, Waltham: Butterworth-Heinemann.

Clark II, W. W., & Cooke, G. (2015b). Chapter 13 – Smart Sustainable Communities. The Way We Will Live in the Future. In W. W. Clark, & G. Cooke (Eds.), The Green Industrial Revolution (pp. 253–274). Oxford, Waltham: Butterworth-Heinemann.

Clark II, W. W., & Cooke, G. (2015c). The Green Industrial Revolution. Energy, Engineering and Economics. Oxford, Waltham: Butterworth-Heinemann.

Clark II, W. W., & Cooke, G. (2016). *Smart Green Cities: Toward a Carbon Neutral World.* London: Routledge.

Clark II, W. W., & Eisenberg, L. (2008). Agile sustainable communities: On-site renewable energy generation. Utilities Policy, 16 (4), 262–274.

Clark II, W. W., & Li, X. (2010). "Social capitalism" in renewable energy generation: China and California comparisons. Utilities Policy, 18 (1), 53–61.

Clark II, W. W., & Li, X. (2014). Chapter 19 – Political-Economic Governance of Renewable Energy Systems: The Key to Creating Sustainable Communities. In W. W. Clark (Ed.), Global Sustainable Communities Handbook (pp. 469–494). Oxford, Waltham: Butterworth-Heinemann.

Clarke, N. (2008a). From ethical consumerism to political consumption. Geography Compass, 2 (6), 1870–1884.

Clarke, S. E. (2008b). Community and problematic citizenship. Political Geography, 27 (1), 22–28.

Clayton, S., Devine-Wright, P., Stern, P. C., Whitmarsh, L., Carrico, A., Steg, L., Swim, J., & Bonnes, M. (2015a). Psychological research and global climate change. Nature Climate Change, 5 (7), 640–646.

Clayton, S., Devine-Wright, P., Swim, J., Bonnes, M., Steg, L., Whitmarsh, L., & Carrico, A. (2015b). Expanding the Role for Psychology in Addressing Environmental Challenges. The American Psychologist v. 6. Juli 2015.

Clegg, S. R., Courpasson, D., & Phillips, N. X. (2006). Power and organizations. London u. a.: Sage.

Clifton, J., Fuentes, D. D., & Warner, M. (2016). The loss of public values when public shareholders go abroad. *Utilities Policy, 40*, 134–143. https://doi.org/10.1016/j.jup.2015.11.003

Cloke, K., & Goldsmith, J. (2002). The end of management and the rise of organizational democracy. San Francisco, Calif.: Jossey-Bass.
Coelho, V. S. P., & von Lieres, B. (Eds.). (2010). Mobilizing for democracy: citizen action and the politics of public participation. London: Zed Books.
Cohen, J. J., Reichl, J., & Schmidthaler, M. (2013a). Best Practices for Improving Public Acceptance of Energy Infrastructure. Working Paper. The Energy Institute at Johannes Kepler University. Linz: Johannes Kepler University.
Cohen, M. J., Brown, H. S., & Vergragt, P. (Eds.). (2013b). Innovations in Sustainable Consumption. New Economics, Socio-technical Transitions and Social Practices. Cheltenham: Edward Elgar.
Cohen, S., Eimicke, W. B., & Miller, A. (2015). Sustainability policy: hastening the transition to a cleaner economy. Hoboken, New Jersey: Jossey-Bass.
Coleman, J. S. (1979). Macht und Gesellschaftsstruktur. Tübingen: Mohr.
Coleman, J. S. (1988). Social Capital in the Creation of Human Capital. American Journal of Sociology, 94, 95–120.
Coleman, J. S. (1990). Foundations of social theory. Cambridge, Mass.: Harvard Univ. Press.
Coleman, S., & Freelon, D. (Eds.). (2015). Handbook of Digital Politics. Cheltenham: Edward Elgar.
Coles, R., & Millman, Z. (Eds.). 2014: Landscape, well-being and environment. London, New York: Routledge.
Collins, K., & Ison, R. (2009). Jumping off Arnstein's ladder: social learning as a new policy paradigm for climate change adaptation. Environmental Policy and Governance, 19 (6), 358–373.
Connolly, W. E. (2006). Then and now: participant-observation in political theory. In J. S. Dryzek (Ed.), The Oxford handbooks of political science: The Oxford handbook of political theory (pp. 827–843). Oxford: Oxford University Press.
Connor, D. M. (1988). A new ladder of citizen participation. National Civic Review, 77 (3), 249–257.
Conrad, J. (Ed.). (1996). Eco-villages and sustainable communities: models for the 21st century. Forres: Findhorn Press.
Cooke, B., & Kothari, U. (Eds.). (2001). Participation: the new tyranny? London: Zed Books.
Cordes, A. (2003). Stadt – Gemeinde – Genossenschaft. Festschrift für Gerhard Dilcher zum 70. Geburtstag. Berlin: Schmidt.
Cornwall, A. (2002). Locating citizen participation. IDS Bulletin, 33 (2), i-x.
Cornwall, A., & Coelho, V. S. (2007). Spaces for change? The politics of citizen participation in new democratic arenas (4. Auflage). London, New York: Zed Books.
Cosmi, C., Dvarionenė, J., Marques, I., Di Leo, S., Gecevičius, G., Gurauskienė, I., Mendes, G., & Selada, C. (2015). A holistic approach to sustainable energy development at regional level: The RENERGY self-assessment methodology. Renewable and Sustainable Energy Reviews, 49, 693–707.
Cotton, M., & Devine-Wright, P. (2011). Discourses of energy infrastructure development: a Q-method study of electricity transmission line siting in the UK. Environment and Planning A, 43 (4), 942–960.
Cotton, M., & Devine-Wright, P. (2012). Making electricity networks "visible": Industry actor representations of "publics" and public engagement in infrastructure planning. Public Understanding of Science, 21 (1), 17–35.

Cotton, M., & Devine-Wright, P. (2013). Putting pylons into place: a UK case study of public perspectives on the impacts of high voltage overhead transmission lines. Journal of Environmental Planning and Management, 56 (8), 1225–1245.

Couldry, N. (2004). The productive "consumer"and the dispersed "citizen". International Journal of Cultural Studies, 7 (1), 21–32.

Cowell, R. (2010). Wind power, landscape and strategic, spatial planning – The construction of "acceptable locations" in Wales. Land Use Policy, 27 (2), 222–232.

Cowell, R., Bristow, G., & Munday, M. (2011). Acceptance, acceptability and environmental justice: the role of community benefits in wind energy development. Journal of Environmental Planning and Management, 54 (4), 539–557.

Cox, J. R. (2012). Environmental Communication and the Public Sphere (3rd ed.). Los Angeles: Sage.

Cox, M., Villamayor-Tomas, S., & Arnold, G. (2016). Design principles in commons science: A response to "Ostrom, Hardin and the commons" (Araral). Environmental Science & Policy, 61, 238–242.

Crabtree, G., Kocs, E., & Aláan, T. (2014). Energy, society and science: The fifty-year scenario. Futures, 58, 53–65.

Craig, T. (2014). Citizen Forums against Technocracy? The Challenge of Science to Democratic Decision Making. Perspectives on Political Science, 43 (1), 31–40.

Creamer, E., Taylor Aiken, G., van Veelen, B., Walker, G., & Devine-Wright, P. (2019). Community renewable energy: What does it do? Walker and Devine-Wright (2008) ten years on. *Energy Research & Social Science, 57*, 101223. https://doi.org/10.1016/j.erss.2019.101223

Creighton, J. L. (2005). The Public Participation Handbook. Making Better Decisions Through Citizen Involvement. San Francisco: Jossey-Bass.

Creswell, J. W. (2013). Research design: Qualitative, quantitative, and mixed methods approaches. Los Angeles: Sage.

Creswell, J. W. (2015). A concise introduction to mixed methods research. Los Angeles: Sage.

Creswell, J. W., & Clark, V. L. P. (2011). Designing and conducting mixed methods research (2nd ed.). Los Angeles u. a.: Sage.

Cronin, T., Ram, B., Gannon, J., Clausen, N.-E., Thuesen, C., Maslesa, E., Kreye, M., & Geraldi, J. (2015). Public acceptance of wind farm development. Developer practices and review of scientific literature. Wind2050 WP3 Deliverable 1. Technical University of Denmark, Lyngby: DTU Wind Energy.

Crouch, C. (2004). *Post-democracy*. Cambridge: Polity Press.

Crouch, C., & Heller, F. A. (1983). Organizational democracy and political processes. Chichester: Wiley.

Curtis, J. A., & McConnell, K. E. (2002). The citizen versus consumer hypothesis: evidence from a contingent valuation survey. Australian Journal of Agricultural and Resource Economics, 46 (1), 69–83.

D'Alisa, G., De Maria, F., & Kallis, G. (Eds.). (2015). Degrowth: a vocabulary for a new era. New York: Routledge.

D'Souza, C., & Yiridoe, E. K. (2014). Social acceptance of wind energy development and planning in rural communities of Australia: A consumer analysis. Energy Policy, 74, 262–270.

Dachwitz, K. (2002). Bürgerinitiativen. Was wollen sie? Wie arbeiten sie? Was leisten sie für die Lebensqualität in der Großstadt? Projektberichte aus den 2-Jahres-Kursen X und XII „Sozialwissenschaftliche Grundbildung" der Akademie für Arbeit und Politik an der Universität Bremen. Bremen: Univ., Akademie für Arbeit und Politik.

Dahl, R. A. (1984). Polyarchy, Pluralism, and Scale. Scandinavian Political Studies, 7 (4), 225–240.

Dahl, R. A. (1992). The Problem of Civic Competence. Journal of Democracy, 3 (4), 45–59.

Dahl, R. A. (1994). A Democratic Dilemma: System Effectiveness versus Citizen Participation. Political Science Quarterly, 109 (1), 23–34.

Dahl, R. A. (2000). A Democratic Paradox? Political Science Quarterly, 115 (1), 35–40.

Dahl, R. A., & Tufte, E. R. (1973). Size and Democracy. Stanford, California: Stanford University Press.

Dahlgren, P. (2013). The political web: media, participation and alternative democracy. Basingstoke, New York: Palgrave Macmillan.

Dalton, R. J. (2004). Democratic Challenges, Democratic Choices: The Erosion of Political Support in Advanced Industrial Democracies. Oxford, New York: Oxford University Press.

Dalton, R. J. (2007). The Good Citizen. How a Younger Generation is Reshaping American Politics. Washington, D.C: CQ Press.

Dalton, R. J. (2008). Citizenship Norms and the Expansion of Political Participation. Political Studies, 56 (1), 76–98.

Dalton, R. J., & Welzel, C. (Eds.). (2014). The Civic Culture Transformed: From Allegiant to Assertive Citizens. New York: Cambridge University Press.

Dammayr, M., Graß, D., & Rothmüller, B. (Eds.). (2015). Legitimität. Gesellschaftliche, politische und wissenschaftliche Bruchlinien der Rechtfertigung. Bielefeld: Transcript.

Daniel, C., Bolen, M. H., Cross, J. A., & Neuringer-Benefiel, H. E. (1986). Where is the altruism in the altruistic personality? Journal of Personality and Social Psychology, 50 (1), 212–220.

Dannenberg, P., & Follmann, A. (2015). Ringen um Grün in der Stadt. Standort 39, 94–100.

Danner, M., Michelsen, G., & Godemann, J. (2007). Stadtteilorientierte Umweltkommunikation durch intermediäre Organisationen. In G. Michelsen & J. Godemann, Handbuch Nachhaltigkeitskommunikation. Grundlagen und Praxis (pp. 749–759). München: Oekom.

Dathe, D., & Kistler, E. (2002). Entwicklung und Strukturwandel bürgerschaftlichen Engagements. In Enquete-Kommission „Zukunft des Bürgerschaftlichen Engagements" des 14. Deutschen Bundestages, Bürgerschaftliches Engagement und Erwerbsarbeit (pp. 13–67). Opladen: Leske + Budrich.

David, M., & Schönborn, S. (2016). Die Energiewende als Bottom-up-Innovation. Wie Pionierprojekte das Energiesystem verändern. München: Oekom.

Davis, B. (2015). Living Off The Grid. The Ultimate Guide To Self-Sufficiency – How To Create A Self-Reliant Supply Of Energy, Storage, Water Treatment And Shelter! Kindle Edition.

De Vreese, C. H. (2007). Digital renaissance: Young consumer and citizen? The Annals of the American Academy of Political and Social Science, 611 (1), 207–216.

Dean, H. (2001). Green citizenship. Social Policy & Administration, 35 (5), 490–505.

De Boeck, L., Van Asch, S., De Bruecker, P., & Audenaert, A. (2016). Comparison of support policies for residential photovoltaic systems in the major EU markets through investment profitability. Renewable Energy, 87, Part 1, 42–53.
Debor, S. (2014). The socio-economic power of renewable energy production cooperatives in Germany: results of an empirical assessment. Wuppertal. http://epub.wupperinst.org/frontdoor/index/index/docId/5364
Decker, F. (2012). Welche Art der direkten Demokratie brauchen wir? In T. Mörschel & C. Krell (Eds.), Demokratie in Deutschland (pp. 175–198). Wiesbaden: VS Verlag.
deENet. (2009). Schriftliche Befragung von Erneuerbare-Energie-Regionen in Deutschland. Regionale Ziele, Aktivitäten und Einschätzungen in Bezug auf 100% Erneuerbare Energie in Regionen. http://www.100-ee.de/downloads/schriftenrei-he/?eID=dam_frontend_push&docID=1141
Defila, R., Giulio, A. D., & Kaufmann-Hayoz, R. (2011). Wesen und Wege nachhaltigen Konsums. Ergebnisse aus dem Themenschwerpunkt „Vom Wissen zum Handeln – Neue Wege zum Nachhaltigen Konsum". München: Oekom.
Degenhart, H., & Holstenkamp, L. (2010). Genossenschaftliche Beteiligungsfinanzierung von Investitionen für die Erzeugung und Verteilung erneuerbarer Energien. In W. George & M. Bonow (Eds.), Regionales Zukunftsmanagement, Bd. 4: Kommunale Kooperation (pp. 86–110). Lengerich u. a.: Pabst Science Publishers.
Degenhart, H., & Holstenkamp, L. (2011). Genossenschaftlich organisierte Bürgerbeteiligung als Finanzierungs- und Nachhaltigkeitsmodell. In W. George & T. Berg (Eds.), Energiegenossenschaften gründen und erfolgreich betreiben (pp. 47–55). Lengerich u. a.: Pabst Science Publ.
Degenhart, H., & Holstenkamp, L. (2013). Energiegenossenschaften als Bürgerbeteiligungen. Kommunalwirtschaft, Sonderausgabe Oktober, 76–79.
Degenhart, H., & Schomerus, T. (Eds.). (2014). Recht und Finanzierung von Erneuerbaren Energien: Bürgerbeteiligungsmodelle. Baden-Baden: Nomos.
Deicher, P. (2010). Leitung einer Nonprofit-Organisation im Kontext der Freiwilligenarbeit. VM: Fachzeitschrift für Verbands- und Nonprofit-Management, 36 (3), 38–45.
Deichmann, C. (2015). Der neue Bürger. Politische Ethik, politische Bildung und politische Kultur. Wiesbaden: Springer VS.
Dekker, P., & Uslaner, E. M. (Eds.). (2001). Social capital and participation in everyday life. London: Routledge.
Delanty, G. (2003). Community. London: Routledge.
Delina, L. L. (2012). Coherence in energy efficiency governance. Energy for Sustainable Development, 16 (4), 493–499.
Deline, M. B. (2015). Energizing organizational research: Advancing the energy field with group concepts and theories. Energy Research & Social Science, 8, 207–221.
Delli Carpini, M. X., & Shapiro, R. Y. (Eds.). (2002). Political decision-making, deliberation and participation. Amsterdam: Jai.
Delli Carpini, M. X., Cook, F. L., & Jacobs, L. R. (2004). Public deliberation, discursive participation, and citizen engagement: A review of the empirical literature. Annual Review of Political Science, 7, 315–344.
Demirović, A. (2007). Demokratie in der Wirtschaft. Positionen – Probleme – Perspektiven. Münster: Westfälisches Dampfboot.

de Moor, J. (2014). Reinterpreting the relation between external efficacy and political participation. Paper presented at the 5th ECPR General Conference. https://lirias.kuleuven.be/bitstream/123456789/472807/1/Joost+de+Moor_External+output+efficacy.pdf

de Moor, J. (2016). External Efficacy and Political Participation Revisited: The Role of Perceived Output Structures for State- and Non-State-Oriented Action Forms. *Parliamentary Affairs, 69*(3), 642–662. https://doi.org/10.1093/pa/gsv055

de Moor, J. (2017). Lifestyle politics and the concept of political participation. *Acta Politica, 52*(2), 179–197. https://doi.org/10.1057/ap.2015.27

de Moor, J. (2016). Practicing Openness: Investigating the Role of Everyday Decision Making in the Production of Squatted Space. *International Journal of Urban and Regional Research, 40*(2), 410–424. https://doi.org/10.1111/1468-2427.12305

de Moor, J., Marien, S., & Hooghe, M. (2013). Linking lifestyle politics and state-oriented action. Paper presented at the ECPR Summer School on Methods for the Study of Participation and Mobilization Florence, 16–27 September 2013. https://lirias.kuleuven.be/bitstream/123456789/448769/1/LINKING+LIFESTYLE+POLITICS+AND+STATE-ORIENTED+ACTION.pdf

Demski, C., Butler, C., Parkhill, K. A., Spence, A., & Pidgeon, N. F. (2015). Public values for energy system change. Global Environmental Change, 34, 59–69.

Denecke, M., Ganzert, A., Otto, I., & Stock, R. (Eds.). (2016). ReClaiming Participation. Technology – Mediation – Collectivity. Bielefeld: Transcript.

Denscombe, M. (2010). The good research guide: for small-scale social research projects. Maidenhead: McGraw-Hill/Open University Press.

Department of Energy and Climate Change (UK Government) (2014). Community Energy Strategy. Full Report. London. https://www.gov.uk/government/publications/community-energy-strategy

Deppermann, A. (2008). Gespräche analysieren. Eine Einführung (4th ed.). Wiesbaden: VS Verlag.

Deriu, M. (2012). Democracies with a future: Degrowth and the democratic tradition. Futures, 44 (6), 553–561.

Deth, J. W. van. (2001). Soziale und politische Beteiligung: Alternativen, Ergänzungen oder Zwillinge? In A. Koch, M. Wasmer, & P. Schmidt (Eds.), Politische Partizipation in der Bundesrepublik Deutschland. Empirische Befunde und theoretische Erklärungen (pp. 195–220). Opladen: Leske + Budrich.

Deth, J. W. van. (2004). Soziales Engagement und die Vertretung von Interessen. In C. H.C. A. Henning & C. Melbeck (Eds.), Interdisziplinäre Sozialforschung: Theorie und empirische Anwendungen. Festschrift für Franz Urban Pappi (pp. 285–303). Frankfurt a. M., New York: Campus.

Deth, J. W. van. (2007). Norms of Citizenship. In R. J. Dalton & H.-D. Klingemann (Eds.), *The Oxford Handbook of Political Behavior* (pp. 402–417). Oxford, New York: Oxford University Press.

Deth, J. W. van. (2009). Politische Partizipation. In V. Kaina & A. Römmele (Eds.), Politische Soziologie (pp. 141–161). Wiesbaden: VS Verlag.

Deth, J. W. van. (2011). Is creative participation good for democracy? In M. Micheletti & A. S. McFarland (Eds.), Creative participation: responsibility-taking in the political world (pp. 148–172). Boulder: Paradigm Publ.

Deth, J. W. van. (2012). Demokratische Bürgertugenden. In S. I. Keil & J. W. van Deth (Eds.), Deutschlands Metamorphosen: Ergebnisse des European Social Survey 2002 bis 2008 (pp. 363–390). Baden-Baden: Nomos.

Deth, J. W. van. (2013a). Citizenship and the Civic Realities of Everyday Life. In M. Print & D. Lange (Eds.), Civic Education and Competences for Engaging Citizens in Democracies (pp. 9–21). Rotterdam: SensePublishers.

Deth, J. W. van. (2013b). Sind Partizipierende die besseren Demokraten? In S. I. Keil & S. I. Thaidigsmann (Eds.), Zivile Bürgergesellschaft und Demokratie (pp. 35–52). Wiesbaden: Springer VS.

Deth, J. W. van (2014a). A conceptual map of political participation. Acta Politica, International Journal of Political Science, Ocial Journal of the Dutch Political Science Association, 49 (3), 349–367.

Deth, J. W. van. (2014b). Das schwierige Verhältnis zwischen Partizipation und Demokratie. In K. Pohl & P. Massing (Eds.), Mehr Partizipation – mehr Demokratie? (pp. 9–21). Schwalbach am Taunus: Wochenschau Verl.

Deth, J. W. van. (2015) (Ed.). Demokratie in der Großstadt. Ergebnisse des ersten Mannheimer Demokratie Audit. Wiesbaden: Springer VS.

Deth, J. W. van, & Maloney, W. A. (Eds.). (2012). New participatory dimensions in civil society: professionalization and individualized collective action. London: Routledge.

Deth, J. W. van, & Tausendpfund, M. (2013). Politik im Kontext: ist alle Politik lokale Politik? Individuelle und kontextuelle Determinanten politischer Orientierungen. Wiesbaden: VS Verlag.

Deth, J. W. van, & Zmerli, S. (2010). Introduction: Civicness, Equality, and Democracy – A "Dark Side" of Social Capital? American Behavioral Scientist, 53 (5), 631–639.

Deth, J. W. van, Montero, J. R., & Westholm, A. (2007). *Citizenship and Involvement in European Democracies: A Comparative Analysis*. Routledge.

Detjen, J. (1999). „Der demokratiekompetente Bürger" – politikwissenschaftliche Anmerkungen zu einer normativen Leitvorstellung Politischer Bildung. Wolnzach: Kastner.

Detjen, J. (2000). Die Demokratiekompetenz der Bürger. Aus Politik und Zeitgeschichte APuZ, 25, 11–20.

Dettling, W. (2000a). Die Bürgergesellschaft als Reformperspektive. Neue Chancen für das Ehrenamt. Forschungsjournal Soziale Bewegungen, 13 (2), 8–14.

Dettling, W. (2000b). Ehrenamt in der Bürgergesellschaft: Ein neues Leitbild für freiwilliges ehrenamtliches Engagemnet. Eine gesellschaftspolitische Standortbestimmung (2nd ed.). Stuttgart: Robert Bosch Stiftung.

Deutscher Genossenschafts- und Raiffeisenverband e.V. (DGRV), 2014: Energiegenossenschaften. Ergebnisse der Umfrage des DGRV und seiner Mitgliedsverbände. Frühjahr 2014. http://www.dgrv.de/de/dienstleistungen/energiegenos-senschaften/jahresumfrage

Deutscher Genossenschafts- und Raiffeisenverband e.V. (DGRV), 2015: Energiegenossenschaften. Ergebnisse der DGRV-Jahresumfrage (zum 31.12.2014). 16.7.2015. https://www.dgrv.de/webde.nsf/7d5e59ec98e72442c1256e5200432395/418a5acd4479ba4ec1257e8400272bec/$FILE/DGRV-Jahresumfrage.pdf

Deutsches Institut für Urbanistik (Ed.). (2005a). Zukunft von Stadt und Region. Band I: Integration und Ausgrenzung in der Stadtgesellschaft. Beiträge zum Forschungsverbund „Stadt 2030". Wiesbaden: VS Verlag.

Deutsches Institut für Urbanistik (Ed.). (2005b). Zukunft von Stadt und Region. Band II: Perspektiven der Regionalisierung. Beiträge zum Forschungsverbund „Stadt 2030". Wiesbaden: VS Verlag.

Devine-Wright, P. (2005a). Beyond NIMBYism: towards an integrated framework for understanding public perceptions of wind energy. Wind Energy, 8 (2), 125–139.

Devine-Wright, P. (2005b). Local aspects of UK renewable energy development: exploring public beliefs and policy implications. Local Environment, 10 (1), 57–69.

Devine-Wright, P. (2007). Energy Citizenship. Psychological Aspects of Evolution in Sustainable Energy Technologies. In J. Murphy (Ed.), Governing technology for sustainability (pp. 63–86). London: Earthscan.

Devine-Wright, P. (2008). Reconsidering Public Acceptance of Renewable Energy Technologies: a Critical Review. In M. Grubb, T. Jamasb, & M. G. Pollitt (Eds.), Delivering a low-carbon electricity system: technologies, economics and policy (pp. 443–461). Cambridge, New York: Cambridge University Press.

Devine-Wright, P. (2009). Rethinking NIMBYism. The role of place attachment and place identity in explaining place-protective action. Journal of Community & Applied Social Psychology, 19 (6), 426–441.

Devine-Wright, P. (2011a). Enhancing local distinctiveness fosters public acceptance of tidal energy: A UK case study. Energy Policy, 39 (1), 83–93.

Devine-Wright, H. (2011b). Envisioning public engagement with renewable energy: an empirical analysis of images within the UK National Press 2006/7. In P. Devine-Wright (Ed.), Renewable Energy and the Public: From NIMBY to Participation (pp. 101–114). London u. a.: Earthscan.

Devine-Wright, P. (2011c). From Backyards to Places. Public engagement and the emplacement of renewable energy technologies. In P. Devine-Wright (Ed.), Renewable Energy and the Public: From NIMBY to Participation (pp. 57–73). London u. a.: Earthscan.

Devine-Wright, P. (2011d). Place attachment and public acceptance of renewable energy. A tidal energy case study. Journal of Environmental Psychology, 31 (4), 336–343.

Devine-Wright, P. (2011e). Public engagement with large-scale renewable energy technologies: breaking the cycle of NIMBYism. Wiley Interdisciplinary Reviews: Climate Change, 2 (1), 19–26.

Devine-Wright, P. (Ed.) (2011f). Renewable Energy and the Public. From NIMBY to Participation. London u. a.: Earthscan.

Devine-Wright, P. (2013a). Explaining "NIMBY" Objections to a Power Line. The Role of Personal, Place Attachment and Project-Related Factors. Environment and Behavior, 45(6), 761–781.

Devine-Wright, P. (2013b). Think global, act local? The relevance of place attachments and place identities in a climate changed world. Global Environmental Change, 23 (1), 61–69.

Devine-Wright, P. (2014). Towards a comprehensive understanding of energy and communities. Advances, experiments, gaps and challenges. Präsentation Tagung 1st Symposium on Community Energy Systems. Lille, Frankreich.

Devine-Wright, P. (2015). Local attachments and identities. A theoretical and empirical project across disciplinary boundaries. Progress in Human Geography, 39 (4), 527–530.

Devine-Wright, P., & Batel, S. (2013). Explaining public preferences for high voltage pylon designs. An empirical study of perceived fit in a rural landscape. Land Use Policy, 31, 640–649.

Devine-Wright, P., & Clayton, S. (2010). Introduction to the special issue: Place, identity and environmental behaviour. Journal of Environmental Psychology, 30 (3), 267–270.

Devine-Wright, P., & Devine-Wright, H. (2009a). Public Engagement with Community-Based Energy Service Provision: An Exploratory Case Study. Energy & Environment, 20(3), 303–317.

Devine-Wright, H., & Devine-Wright, P. (2009b). Social representations of electricity network technologies: exploring processes of anchoring and objectification through the use of visual research methods. The British Journal of Social Psychology/the British Psychological Society, 48 (2), 357–373.

Devine-Wright, P., & Howes, Y. (2010). Disruption to place attachment and the protection of restorative environments: A wind energy case study. Journal of Environmental Psychology, 30 (3), 271–280.

Devine-Wright, P., & Wiersma, B. (2013). Opening up the "local" to analysis: exploring the spatiality of UK urban decentralised energy initiatives. Local Environment, 18 (10), 1099–1116.

Devine-Wright, P., Devine-Wright, H., & Sherry-Brennan, F. (2010). Visible technologies, invisible organisations: An empirical study of public beliefs about electricity supply networks. Energy Policy, 38 (8), 4127–4134.

Devine-Wright, P., McAlpine, G., & Batley-White, S. (2001). Wind turbines in the landscape: an evaluation of local community involvement and other considerations in UK wind farm development. EDRA 32 – 2001: Old World – New Ideas, 133–137.

Devinney, T. M., Auger, P., & Eckhardt, G. M. (2010). The Myth of the Ethical Consumer. New York: Cambridge University Press.

Dew, J. R. (1997). Empowerment and democracy in the workplace. Applying adult education theory and practice for cultivating empowerment. Westport, Conn.: Quorum Books.

Dewey, J. (1916). Democracy and education. An introduction to the philosophy of education. New York: Macmillan.

Dewey, J. (1988). *The later works, 1925–1953.* Carbondale Edwardsville: Southern Illinois University Press.

Dewey, J. (2008). Creative Democracy – The Task Before Us. In J. A. Boydston (Ed.), The collected works of John Dewey. Vol. 14: The later works, 1925–1953, 1939–1941. Carbondale: Southern Illinois Univ. Press.

Dhar Chakrabarti, P. G., & Energy and Resources Institute (Eds.). (2015). Global sustainable development report 2015: climate change and sustainable development: assessing progress of regions and countries. New Delhi: Oxford University Press.

Diebäcker, M. (2008). Governance und Demokratie. In A. Hamedinger, O. Frey, J. S. Dangschat, & A. Breitfuss (Eds.), Strategieorientierte Planung im kooperativen Staat (pp. 266–281). Wiesbaden: VS Verlag.

Dieckhoff, C., Leuschner, A., & Neuber, F. (Eds.). (2016). Die Energiewende und ihre Modelle. Was uns Energieszenarien sagen können – und was nicht. Bielefeld: Transcript.

Diefenbacher, H., Schasse, U., Kissler, L., Nutzinger, H. G., & Teichert, V. (1984). Mitbestimmung: Norm und Wirklichkeit. Fallstudie aus einem Großbetrieb der Automobilindustrie. Frankfurt a. M., New York: Campus.

Diekmann, A. (2007a). Dimensionen des Sozialkapitals. In A. Franzen & M. Freitag (Eds.), Sozialkapital: Grundlagen und Anwendungen (pp. 47–65). Wiesbaden: VS Verlag.

Diekmann, A. (2007b). Empirische Sozialforschung. Grundlagen, Methoden, Anwendungen. Reinbek bei Hamburg: Rowohlt.

Diendorfer, G., & Welan, M. (Eds.). (2016). Demokratie und Nachhaltigkeit. Verbindungslinien, Potenziale und Reformansätze. Innsbruck, Wien, Bozen: StudienVerlag.

Dienel, H.-L. (2011). Bürgerbeteiligung. In T. Olk & B. Hartnuß (Eds.), Handbuch Bürgerschaftliches Engagement (pp. 203–214). Weinheim u. a.: Beltz Juventa.

Dienel, H.-L., Franzl, K., Fuhrmann, R. D., Lietzmann, H. J., & Vergne, A. (2014). Die Qualität von Bürgerbeteiligungsverfahren: Evaluation und Sicherung von Standards am Beispiel von Planungszellen und Bürgergutachten. Stuttgart: Steiner.

Dienel, P. C. (1978). Die Planungszelle. Der Bürger plant seine Umwelt. Eine Alternative zur Establishment-Demokratie. Opladen: Westdeutscher Verl.

Dienel, P. C. (2005). Die Befreiung der Politik durch den Bürger. In P. C. Dienel (Ed.), Die Befreiung der Politik (pp. 9–12). Wiesbaden: VS Verlag.

Diewald, M., & Lüdicke, J. (2007). Akzentuierung oder Kompensation? Zum Zusammenhang von Sozialkapital, sozialer Ungleichheit und subjektiver Lebensqualität. In J. Lüdicke & M. Diewald (Eds.), Soziale Netzwerke und soziale Ungleichheit (pp. 11–51). Wiesbaden: VS Verlag.

Di Giulio, M., Galanti, M. T., & Moro, F. N. (2016). Political coalitions, local leaders and the internationalization of local public services in Italy. *Utilities Policy, 40*, 144–151. https://doi.org/10.1016/j.jup.2016.01.008

Dincer, I. (2012). EXERGY: Energy, Environment and Sustainable Development (2nd ed.). Oxford: Elsevier.

Ding, W., Wang, L., Chen, B., Xu, L., & Li, H. (2014). Impacts of renewable energy on gender in rural communities of north-west China. Renewable Energy, 69, 180–189.

Dobner, P. (2008). Nur zweite Reihe? – Staat und Regierung in der Global Governance of Water. In E. Holtmann & W. J. Patzelt (Eds.), Führen Regierungen tatsächlich? Zur Praxis gouvernementalen Handelns (pp. 155–170). Wiesbaden: VS Verlag.

Dobson, A. (2003). Citizenship and the environment. Oxford: Oxford University Press.

Dobson, A., & Bell, D. (Eds.). (2006). Environmental citizenship. London, Cambridge, Mass.: MIT Press.

Dóci, G., Vasileiadou, E., & Petersen, A. C. (2015). Exploring the transition potential of renewable energy communities. Futures, 66, 85–95.

Doherty, B., Haugh, H., & Huybrechts, B. (2014). Fair trade in the frame. A rhetorical analysis of new market creation and institutionalization. Academy of Management Proceedings, 2014 (1), Nr. 16179.

Dolata, U., & Schrape, J.-F. (Eds.). (2013a). Internet, Mobile Devices und die Transformation der Medien: radikaler Wandel als schrittweise Rekonfiguration. Berlin: Edition Sigma.

Dolata, U., & Schrape, J.-F. (2013b). Zwischen Individuum und Organisation. Neue kollektive Akteure und Handlungskonstellationen im Internet. SOI Discussion Paper 2013-02. Stuttgart: Universität Stuttgart. http://www.uni-stuttgart.de/soz/Foi/publikationen/soi_2013_2_Dolata_Schrape_Zwischen_Individuum_und_Organisation.pdf

Domenech, B., Ferrer-Martí, L., Lillo, P., Pastor, R., & Chiroque, J. (2014). A community electrification project. Combination of microgrids and household systems fed by wind, PV or micro-hydro energies according to micro-scale resource evaluation and social constraints. Energy for Sustainable Development, 23, 275–285.

Donahue, J. D., & Zeckhauser, R. (2011). Collaborative governance. Private roles for public goals in turbulent times. Princeton, NJ u. a.: Princeton University Press.

Donges, P. (2012). Politische Organisationen als Mikro-Meso-Makro-Link. In T. Quandt & B. Scheufele (Eds.), Ebenen der Kommunikation (pp. 217–231). Wiesbaden: VS Verlag.

Doppelt, B. (2010). The power of sustainable thinking: how to create a positive future for the climate, the planet, your organization and your life. London: Earthscan.

Dorniok, D. (2014). Energiegenossenschaften als Protestbewegung? Eine systemtheoretische Analyse aktueller Entwicklungen. In G. Birnkraut, R. Lisowski, & R. Wortmann (Eds.), Jahrbuch für Management in Nonprofit-Organisationen (pp. 81–101). Münster: LIT Verlag.

Dorniok, D. (2017). Energiegenossenschaften als soziale Innovation und Initiator sozialer Innovationen – Neo-Institutionalistische Untersuchung von Energiegenossenschaften und ihrer funktionalen Wirkungen. In M. Jaeger-Erben, J. Rückert-John, & M. Schäfer (Eds.), *Soziale Innovationen für nachhaltigen Konsum: Wissenschaftliche Perspektiven, Strategien der Förderung und gelebte Praxis* (pp. 149–167). Wiesbaden: Springer VS. https://doi.org/10.1007/978-3-658-16545-1_7

Dorniok, D., & Lautermann, C. (2016). Energiegenossenschaften als soziale Unternehmen in der dezentralen Energiewende. In A. Hildebrandt & W. Landhäußer (Eds.), CSR und Energiewirtschaft (pp. 173–184). Berlin, Heidelberg: Springer.

Drazkiewicz, A., Challies, E., & Newig, J. (2015). Public participation and local environmental planning. Testing factors influencing decision quality and implementation in four case studies from Germany. Land Use Policy, 46, 211–222.

Drewe, P., Klein, J.-L., & Hulsbergen, E. (2008). The challenge of social innovation in urban revitalization. Amsterdam: Techne Press.

Drilling, M., & Schnur, O. (Eds.). (2012). Nachhaltige Quartiersentwicklung. Positionen, Praxisbeispiele und Perspektiven. Wiesbaden: Springer VS.

Droege, P. (2014). Regenerative Region: Energie- und Klimaatlas Bodensee-Alpenrhein. München: Oekom.

Droß, P. J. (2013). Ökonomisierungstrends im Dritten Sektor. Verbreitung und Auswirkungen von Wettbewerb und finanzieller Planungsunsicherheit in gemeinnützigen Organisationen. Berlin: Wissenschaftszentrum Berlin für Sozialforschung.

Droubi, S., Heffron, R. J., & McCauley, D. (2022). A critical review of energy democracy: A failure to deliver justice? *Energy Research & Social Science, 86*, 102444. https://doi.org/10.1016/j.erss.2021.102444

Dryzek, J. S. (1990). Discursive democracy. Politics, policy, and political science. Cambridge: Cambridge University Press.

Dryzek, J. S. (2000). Deliberative democracy and beyond. Liberals, critics and contestations. Oxford u. a.: Oxford University Press.

Dryzek, J. S. (2012). Foundations and frontiers of deliberative governance. Oxford: Oxford University Press.

Dryzek, J. S. (Ed.). (2003). Green states and social movements. Environmentalism in the United States, United Kingdom, Germany, and Norway. Oxford, New York: Oxford University Press.

Düber, M., Rohrmann, A., & Windisch, M. (Eds.). (2015). Barrierefreie Partizipation. Entwicklungen, Herausforderungen und Lösungsansätze auf dem Weg zu einer neuen Kultur der Beteiligung. Weinheim: Beltz Juventa.

Dufays, F., & Huybrechts, B. (2014). Connecting the Dots for Social Value. A Review on Social Networks and Social Entrepreneurship. Journal of Social Entrepreneurship, 5 (2), 214–237.

Dumitru, A., De Gregorio, E., Bonnes, M., Bonaiuto, M., Carrus, G., Garcia-Mira, R., & Maricchiolo, F. (2016). Low carbon energy behaviors in the workplace: A qualitative study in Italy and Spain. *Energy Research & Social Science, 13*, 49–59. https://doi.org/10.1016/j.erss.2015.12.005

Dumitru, A., Lema-Blanco, I., García-Mira, R., Haxeltine, A., & France, A. (2015). Transformative Social Innovation Narrative of Credit Unions. TRANSIT Working Paper.2013.3.2-1. Rotterdam.

Dunker, R., & Mono, R. (2013). Bürgerbeteiligung und erneuerbare Energien. Kurz-Studie von Beteiligungsprojekten in Deutschland durch die 100 prozent erneuerbar stiftung. Berlin. http://100-prozent-erneuerbar.de/wp-content/uploads/2013/07/Buergerbeteiligung-und-Erneuerbare-Energien_100pes.pdf

Düx, W., Sass, E., & Prein, G. (2009). Kompetenzerwerb im freiwilligen Engagement. Eine empirische Studie zum informellen Lernen im Jugendalter (2nd ed.). Wiesbaden: VS Verlag.

Dvarioniene, J., Gurauskiene, I., Gecevicius, G., Trummer, D. R., Selada, C., Marques, I., & Cosmi, C. (2015). Stakeholders involvement for energy conscious communities: The Energy Labs experience in 10 European communities. Renewable Energy, 75, 512–518.

Dwyer, P. C., Maki, A., & Rothman, A. J. (2015). Promoting energy conservation behavior in public settings. The influence of social norms and personal responsibility. Journal of Environmental Psychology, 41, 30–34.

Eadson, W., & Foden. (2015). Editorial: critical perspectives on community energy. People Place and Policy, 8 (3), 145–148.

Ebbinghaus, B. (2009). Mehr oder weniger? Quantitativer versus qualitativer Vergleich. In S. Pickel, G. Pickel, H.-J. Lauth, & D. Jahn (Eds.), Methoden der vergleichenden Politik- und Sozialwissenschaft (pp. 197–212). Wiesbaden: VS Verlag.

Ebert, T. (1974). Bürgerinitiativen. In W. Pehnt (Ed.), Die Stadt in der Bundesrepublik Deutschland. Lebensbedingungen, Aufgaben, Planung (pp. 107–125). Stuttgart: Reclam.

Ebert, T., Kuckartz, U., Maschke, S., & Stecher, L. (2012). Online-Erhebung von Mixed Methods-Daten. Enzyklopädie Erziehungswissenschaft Online, 1–19.

Ebrecht, J., & Hillebrandt, F. (2004). Bourdieus Theorie der Praxis: Erklärungskraft – Anwendung – Perspektiven (2nd ed.). Wiesbaden: Wiesbaden: VS Verlag.

Edelstein, W., & Fauser, P. (2001). Demokratie lernen und leben. Gutachten für ein Modellversuchsprogramm der Bund-Länder-Kommission für Bildungsplanung und Forschungsförderung. Bonn: BLK.

Edwards, B., Foley, M. W., & Diani, M. (Eds.). (2001). Beyond Tocqueville: civil society and the social capital debate in comparative perspective. Hanover, NH: University Press of New England.

Ehrhardt, J. (2011). Ehrenamt. Formen, Dauer und kulturelle Grundlagen des Engagements. Frankfurt a. M., New York: Campus.

Eikeland, P. O., & Inderberg, T. H. J. (2016). Energy system transformation and long-term interest constellations in Denmark: can agency beat structure? Energy Research & Social Science, 11, 164–173.

Eiselt, J. (2012). Dezentrale Energiewende. Chancen und Herausforderungen. Wiesbaden: Vieweg+Teubner.

Ekardt, F. (2014). Jahrhundertaufgabe Energiewende. Ein Handbuch. Berlin: Ch. Links Verlag.

Ekardt, F., & Hennig, B. (2014). Chancen und Grenzen kommunaler Klimaschutzkonzepte. Grundprobleme und Beispiele. Marburg: Metropolis.

Ekardt, F., Hennig, B., & Unnerstall, H. (Eds.). (2012). Erneuerbare Energien. Ambivalenzen, Governance, Rechtsfragen. Marburg: Metropolis.

Eleftheriadis, I. M., & Anagnostopoulou, E. G. (2015). Identifying barriers in the diffusion of renewable energy sources. Energy Policy, 80, 153–164.

Ellis, G., Barry, J., & Robinson, C. (2007). Many ways to say "no", different ways to say "yes". Applying Q-Methodology to understand public acceptance of wind farm proposals. Journal of Environmental Planning and Management, 50 (4), 517–551.

Ellis, G., Cowell, R., Sherry-Brennan, F., Strachan, P., & Toke, D. (2013). Planning, energy and devolution in the UK. Town Planning Review, 84 (3), 397–410.

Elsen, S. (2004). Bürgerschaftliche Aneignung gegen die Enteignungsökonomie. Genossenschaften als Akteure im „Dritten Sektor". Sozial extra: Zeitschrift für soziale Arbeit, 28, 42–48.

Elsen, S. (2009). Soziale Arbeit und die Ökonomie des Gemeinwesens. *Soziale Arbeit in der Krise der Arbeitsgesellschaft, 287*, 9–14.

Elsen, S. (2012). Genossenschaften als Organisationen der sozialen Innovation und nachhaltigen Entwicklung. In G. Beck, C. Kropp, & I. Deppe (Eds.), Gesellschaft innovativ: wer sind die Akteure? (pp. 85–102). Wiesbaden: VS Verlag.

Elsen, S. (2014). Genossenschaften als transformative Kräfte auf dem Weg in die Postwachstumsgesellschaft. In C. Schröder & H. Walk (Eds.), Genossenschaften und Klimaschutz. Akteure für zukunftsfähige, solidarische Städte (pp. 31–47). Wiesbaden: Springer VS.

Elsen, S. (2015). Die Kunst des Wandels. Ansätze für die ökosoziale Transformation. München: Oekom.

Elzen, B., Geels, F. W., & Green, K. (2004). System innovation and the transition to sustainability: theory, evidence and policy. Cheltenham: Edward Elgar.

Embacher, S. (2015). Die Energiewende – eine partizipative Herausforderung. Betrifft: Bürgergesellschaft Nr. 39. Bonn: Friedrich-Ebert-Stiftung.

Emmelius, G., & Krönlein, N. (2012). Mitverantwortung: verantwortliches Unternehmertum genossenschaftlich interpretiert! In G. Ringle & H.-M. Münkner (Eds.), Genossenschaftliche Kooperation – anders wirtschaften (pp. 67–75). Baden-Baden: Nomos.

Energieagentur Rheinland-Pfalz, & Landesnetzwerk Bürgerenergiegenossenschaften Rheinland-Pfalz. (2015). Geschäftsmodelle für Bürger-Energiegenossenschaften. Markterfassung und Zukunftsperspektiven. Kaiserslautern. http://www.energieagentur.rlp.de/fileadmin/user_upload/Buergerenergiegenossenschaften_Broschuere_160210_Small.pdf

Enevoldsen, P., & Sovacool, B. K. (2016). Examining the social acceptance of wind energy. Practical guidelines for onshore wind project development in France. Renewable and Sustainable Energy Reviews, 53, 178–184.

Engerer, H. (2014). Energiegenossenschaften in der Energiewende. DIW Berlin Roundup. http://www.diw.de/de/diw_01.c.470180.de/presse/diw_roundup/energiegenossenschaften_in_der_energiewende.html

Enste, D., Neumann, M., & Schare, T. (2012). Erster Engagementbericht. Für eine Kultur der Mitverantwortung. Bericht der Sachverständigenkommission und Stellungnahme der Bundesregierung. Unterrichtung durch die Bundesregierung. http://www.bmfsfj.de/RedaktionBMFSFJ/Engagement/Pdf-Anlagen/engagementbe-richt-langfassung.pdf

Enzensberger, N., Fichtner, W., & Rentz, O. (2003). Financing renewable energy projects via closed-end funds – a German case study. Renewable Energy 28, 2023–2036.

Erhard, J., Lauwers, S., & Schmerz, S. (2013). Do unconventional forms of citizen participation add value to the quality of democracy in Germany? A case study of the Bürgerdialog Energietechnologien für die Zukunft. In A. Römmele & H. Banthien (Eds.), Empowering Citizens. Studies in Collaborative Democracy (pp. 17–105). Baden-Baden: Nomos.

Erlinghagen, M. (2003). Die individuellen Erträge ehrenamtlicher Arbeit. KZfSS Kölner Zeitschrift Für Soziologie und Sozialpsychologie, 55 (4), 737–757.

Erlinghagen, M. (2013). Ehrenamt. In S. Mau & N. M. Schöneck (Eds.), Handwörterbuch zur Gesellschaft Deutschlands (pp. 199–212). Wiesbaden: Springer VS.

Ernst, S. (2010). Prozesstheoretische Forschungs- und Methodenzugänge. In S. Ernst (Ed.), Prozessorientierte Methoden in der Arbeits- und Organisationsforschung (pp. 70–78). Wiesbaden: VS Verlag.

Etzioni, A. (1995). Die Entdeckung des Gemeinwesens. Ansprüche, Verantwortlichkeiten und das Programm des Kommunitarismus. Stuttgart: Schäffer-Poeschel.

Etzioni, A. (2009). Die aktive Gesellschaft. Eine Theorie gesellschaftlicher und politischer Prozesse (2nd ed.). Wiesbaden: VS Verlag.

European Economic and Social Committee. (2015). CHANGING THE FUTURE OF ENERGY: CIVIL SOCIETY AS A MAIN PLAYER IN RENEWABLE ENERGY GENERATION. EESC study on the role of civil society in the implementation of the EU Renewable Energy Directive. FINAL REPORT. http://www.eesc.europa.eu/?i=portal.en.sdo-observatory-red

European Institute for Public Participation. (2009). *Public Participation in Europe: An international perspective*. Berlin: European Institute for Public Participation.

Everett, B., & Open University (Eds.). (2012). Energy systems and sustainability. Power for a sustainable future (2nd ed.). Oxford, New York: Oxford University Press, in association with the Open University.

Evers, A. (2006). Wenn Welten durcheinander geraten. Monetarisierung, bezahlte Arbeit und freiwilliges Engagement. In P. Farago & H. Ammann (Eds.), Monetarisierung der Freiwilligkeit. Referate und Zusammenfassungen der 5. Tagung der Freiwilligenuniversität vom 30. bis 31.5.2005 in Luzern (pp. 63–74). Zürich: Seismo.

Evers, A. (2009). Bürgerschaftliches Engagement. Versuch, einem Allerweltsbegriff wieder Bedeutung zu geben. In I. Bode, A. Evers, & A. Klein (Eds.), Bürgergesellschaft als Projekt (pp. 66–79). Wiesbaden: VS Verlag.

Evers, A., & Roth, R. (2005). Kommunen und die Entdeckung des „unterschätzten Bürgers". Forschungsjournal Soziale Bewegungen, 3, 103–108.

Evers, A., & Zimmer, A. (2010). Third sector organizations facing turbulent environments. Baden-Baden: Nomos.

Faaij, A., Jager, D., & Kok, M. (2013). Global warming and social innovation. The challenge of a climate neutral society. London u. a.: Earthscan.

Fagerberg, J., Laestadius, S., & Martin, B. R. (Eds.). (2015). The Triple Challenge for Europe. Economic Development, Climate Change, and Governance. Oxford: Oxford University Press.

Fairtlough, G. (2005). The Three Ways of Getting Things Done. Hierarchy, Heterarchy & Responsible Autonomy in Organizations. Bridport, Dorset: Triarchy Press.

Farago, P., & Ammann, H. (Eds.) (2006). Monetarisierung der Freiwilligkeit. Referate und Zusammenfassungen der 5. Tagung der Freiwilligenuniversität vom 30. bis 31.5.2005 in Luzern. Zürich: Seismo.

Farmer, F. (2013). After the public turn. Composition, counterpublics, and the citizen bricoleur. Logan, Utah: Utah State University Press.

Farrell, J. (2008). Driving Our Way to Energy Independence. Minneapolis: New Rules Project.

Farrell, J. (2010). Energy Self-Reliant States (2nd ed.). Minneapolis: New Rules Project.

Farrell, J. (2011). Democratizing the Electricity System. A Vision for the 21st Century Grid. Minneapolis: New Rules Project.

Farrell, J., & Morris, D. (2008). Rural Power. Community-Scaled Renewable Energy and Rural Economic Development. Minneapolis: New Rules Project.

Fast, S. (2013). A Habermasian analysis of local renewable energy deliberations. Journal of Rural Studies, 30, 86–98.

Fast, S., & Mabee, W. (2015). Place-making and trust-building. The influence of policy on host community responses to wind farms. Energy Policy, 81, 27–37.

Fatheuer, T., Unmüßig, B., & Fuhr, L. (2015). Kritik der Grünen Ökonomie. München: Oekom.

Faust, H. (1977). Geschichte der Genossenschaftsbewegung. Ursprung und Aufbruch der Genossenschaftsbewegung in England, Frankreich und Deutschland sowie ihre weitere Entwicklung im deutschen Sprachraum (3rd ed.). Frankfurt a. M.: KnaS.

Fehr, E., & Fischbacher, U. (2002). Why Social Preferences Matter – the Impact of Non-Selfish Motives on Competition, Cooperation and Incentives. The Economic Journal, 112 (478), C1-C33.

Fehr, E., & Fischbacher, U. (2005). Altruists with green beards. Analyse und Kritik, 27, 73–84.

Fehren, O. (2008). Wer organisiert das Gemeinwesen? Zivilgesellschaftliche Perspektiven Sozialer Arbeit als intermediärer Instanz. Berlin: Edition Sigma.

Feindt, P. H. (2004). Motor der Demokratisierung oder der Exklusion? Zur Rolle und Bildung von Sozialkapital in Politiknetzwerken. In A. Klein, K. Kern, B. Geißel, & M. Berger (Eds.), Zivilgesellschaft und Sozialkapital (pp. 169–186). Wiesbaden: VS Verlag.

Feindt, P. H., & Saretzki, T. (Eds.) (2010). Umwelt- und Technikkonflikte. Wiesbaden: VS Verlag.

Felber, C. (2012). Die Gemeinwohl-Ökonomie: Aktualisierte und erweiterte Neuausgabe (6th ed.). Wien: Deuticke Verlag.

Feldman, S., & Turner, D. (2011). Why Not NIMBY? Ethics, Policy and Environment, 13 (3), 251–266.

Feldman, S., & Turner, D. (2014). Why Not NIMBY? Reply to Critics. Ethics, Policy & Environment, 17 (1), 105–115.

Fellner, R. (2015). *Nachhaltige Unternehmensführung erfolgreich umsetzen: Aktuelle Themen und Trends aus Wissenschaft und Unternehmenspraxis*. Freiburg: Haufe-Lexware.

Feola, G., & Nunes, R. (2014). Success and failure of grassroots innovations for addressing climate change. The case of the Transition Movement. Global Environmental Change, 24, 232–250.

Ferris, G. R., Treadway, D. C., Kolodinsky, R. W., Hochwarter, W. A., Kacmar, C. J., Douglas, C., & Frink, D. D. (2005). Development and Validation of the Political Skill Inventory. Journal of Management, 31 (1), 126–152.

Feurtey, E., Ilinca, A., Sakout, A., & Saucier, C. (2015). Lessons learned in France and Quebec regarding financial and legal mechanisms to develop renewable energy: A hybrid model as an acceptable solution for onshore wind? *Renewable and Sustainable Energy Reviews, 47*, 34–45. https://doi.org/10.1016/j.rser.2015.03.004

Findlay, I. M., & Findlay, L. (2013). Co-operatives. After the Crisis and Beyond the Binaries. In J. Brazda, M. Dellinger, & D. Rößl (Eds.), Genossenschaften im Fokus einer neuen Wirtschaftspolitik. Bericht der XVII. Internationalen Genossenschaftswissenschaftlichen Tagung (IGT) 2012 in Wien. Teilband 3 (pp. 809–820). Wien: LIT.

Finke, P., & Laszlo, E. (2014). Citizen Science. Das unterschätzte Wissen der Laien. München: Oekom.

Fiorina, M. P. (1999). Extreme Voices: A Dark Side of Civic Engagement. In T. Skocpol & M. P. Fiorina (Eds.), Civic participation and the equality problem (pp. 395–426). Washington, D.C: Brookings Inst. Press u. a.

Firestone, J., Bates, A., & Knapp, L. A. (2015). See me, Feel me, Touch me, Heal me. Wind turbines, culture, landscapes, and sound impressions. Land Use Policy, 46, 241–249.

Firestone, J., Kempton, W., & Krueger, A. (2009). Public acceptance of offshore wind power projects in the USA. Wind Energy, 12 (2), 183–202.

Fischedick, M., Leggewie, C., Engler, S., Pietzner, K., & Vallentin, D. (2014). Gemeinschaftswerk Energiewende in Nordrhein-Westfalen. Der wissenschaftliche Beitrag des Virtuellen Instituts „Transformation – Energiewende NRW". Essen/Wuppertal.

Fischer, D., Lüdecke, G., Godemann, J., Michelsen, G., Newig, J., Rieckmann, M., & Schulz, D. (2016). Sustainability Communication. In H. Heinrichs, P. Martens, G. Michelsen, & A. Wiek (Eds.), Sustainability Science (pp. 139–148). Dordrecht: Springer Netherlands.

Fischer, F. (1997). Öffentlichkeit und das Problem des Expertentums – Partizipatorische Forschung als demokratische Praxis. In K. M. Schmals & H. Heinelt (Eds.), Zivile Gesellschaft. Entwicklung, Defizite und Potentiale (pp. 261–270). Opladen: Leske + Budrich.

Fischer, M., Nackenoff, C., & Chmielewski, W. E. (Eds.). (2009). Jane Addams and the practice of democracy. Urbana: University of Illinois Press.

Fishkin, J. S. (2009). When the people speak. Deliberative democracy and public consultation. Oxford: Oxford University Press.

Fishkin, J. S., & Luskin, R. C. (2005). Experimenting with a democratic ideal. Deliberative polling and public opinion. Acta Politica, 40 (3), 284–298.

Fleiß, J. (2011). Paul Lazarsfelds typologische Methode und die Grounded Theory. Generierung und Qualität von Typologien. Österreichische Zeitschrift für Soziologie, 35 (3), 3–18.

Fleischer, T. (2013). Wandel des Systems der Elektrizitätsversorgung. Was Bürger darüber denken und dazu erwarten. In G. Banse & L.-G. Fleischer (Eds.), Energiewende. Produktivkraftentwicklung und Gesellschaftsvertrag. Berlin: Trafo.

Flick, U. (2004). Triangulation. Eine Einführung. Wiesbaden: VS Verlag.

Flieger, B. (1996). Produktivgenossenschaft als fortschrittsfähige Organisation. Theorie, Fallstudie, Handlungshilfen. Marburg: Metropolis.

Flieger, B. (2002). Terra incognita: konsequente Mitarbeiterbeteiligungsformen in Deutschland. In K. R. Wagner (Ed.), Mitarbeiterbeteiligung. Visionen für eine Gesellschaft von Teilhabern (pp. 271–286). Wiesbaden: Gabler.

Flieger, B. (2006). Genossenschaften in Deutschland. Teil der Solidarischen Ökonomie? In E. Altvater (Ed.), Solidarische Ökonomie. Reader des Wissenschaftlichen Beirats von Attac (pp. 47–61). Hamburg: VSA-Verl.

Flieger, B. (2008). Neue Genossenschaftstypen. Anzeichen einer Modernisierung des Genossenschaftswesens. In S. Giegold (Ed.), Solidarische Ökonomie im globalisierten Kapitalismus (pp. 34–38). Hamburg: VSA-Verl.

Flieger, B. (2010). Energische Bürger. Publik-Forum, 21, 14–15.

Flieger, B. (2011). Energiegenossenschaften – Eine klimaverantwortliche, bürgernahe Energiewirtschaft ist möglich. In S. Elsen (Ed.), Solidarische Ökonomie und die Gestaltung des Gemeinwesens. Perspektiven und Ansätze der ökosozialen Transformation von unten (pp. 315–338). Neu-Ulm: AG-SPAK-Bücher.

Flieger, B. (2012). Energiewende: Windige Zeiten? – Neue Energiegenossenschaften setzen soziale und ökonomische Maßstäbe. Contraste Monatszeitung für Selbstorganisation, 6, 7–10.

Flieger, B., Klemisch, H., & Radtke, J. (2015). Bürgerbeteiligung in und durch Energiegenossenschaften. eNewsletter Netzwerk Bürgerbeteiligung, 3, 1–12.

Floridi, Luciano, 2015: Die 4. Revolution. Wie die Infosphäre unser Leben verändert. Berlin: Suhrkamp.

Flügel-Martinsen, Oliver, Gaus, D., Hitzel-Cassagnes, Tanja, & Martinsen, F. (Eds.). (2014). Deliberative Kritik. Kritik der Deliberation. Wiesbaden: Springer VS.

Flynn, R., Bellaby, P., & Ricci, M. (2008). Environmental citizenship and public attitudes to hydrogen energy technologies. Environmental Politics, 17 (5), 766–783.

Foldvary, F. E. (2002). Small-group, multi-level democracy: implications of Austrian public choice for governance structure. The Review of Austrian Economics, 15 (2), 161–174.

Foljanty-Jost, G., Haufe, K., & Aoki, M. (2013). Bürger als Partner. Kooperative Demokratie in japanischen Kommunen. Wiesbaden: Springer VS.

Forndran, E. (2003). Staatsaufgaben und Bürgertugenden in Demokratien. In G. Lohmann (Ed.), Demokratische Zivilgesellschaft und Bürgertugenden in Ost und West (p. 3172). Frankfurt a. M.: Lang.

Forschungsgruppe Weltanschauungen in Deutschland. (2015). Religionszugehörigkeit Bevölkerung Deutschland. (Stand 01.01.2014). Berlin. http://fowid.de/fileadmin/datenarchiv/Religionszugehoerigkeit/Religionszugehoerigkeit_Bevoelkerung_Deutschland_2014.pdf

Forschungsjournal Soziale Bewegungen (Ed.). (2014). Technik und Protest. Von Stuttgart 21 über Atomkraftendlager bis Fracking und Nanotechnolgie. Sonderschwerpunkt: Migration, Protest und Partizipation in Europa. Stuttgart: Lucius & Lucius.

Fotopoulos, T. (1997). Towards an inclusive democracy. The crisis of the growth economy and the need for a new liberatory project. London: Cassell.

Fox, S. (2013). Is it Time to Update the Definition of Political Participation? Political Participation in Britain: The Decline and Revival of Civic Culture. Parliamentary Affairs, 66 (1), 1–11.

Fraenkel, E. (1974). Deutschland und die westlichen Demokratien (6th ed.). Stuttgart: Kohlhammer.

Frantz, C., & Fuchs, D. (2014). The Impact of Civil Society on Sustainable Development. In M. Freise & T. Hallmann (Eds.), Modernizing Democracy (pp. 83–96). New York: Springer.

Franzen, A., & Freitag, M. (Eds.) (2007). Sozialkapital. Grundlagen und Anwendungen. Wiesbaden: VS Verlag.

Franzen, A. (2014). Antwortskalen in standardisierten Befragungen. In N. Baur, & J. Blasius (Eds.), Handbuch Methoden der empirischen Sozialforschung (pp. 701–711). Wiesbaden: Springer VS.

Fratzscher, M. (2016). Verteilungskampf. Warum Deutschland immer ungleicher wird. München: Hanser.

Fraune, C. (2014). Energy policy and gender relations in industrialized countries. Evidence from Germany. Presented at the 72th Annual MPSA Conference, Chicago.

Fraune, C. (2015). Gender matters. Women, renewable energy, and citizen participation in Germany. Energy Research & Social Science, 7, 55–65.

Freise, M., & Hallmann, T. (2014). Modernizing Democracy. Associations and Associating in the 21st Century. New York: Springer.

Frey, B. S., & Jegen, R. (2002). Kontraproduktive Wirkung des Motivators „Geld"? VM: Fachzeitschrift Für Verbands- und Nonprofit-Management, 28 (3), 30–41.

Frey, M. (2013). Ausbau der Windkraft und Bürgerbeteiligung. Verwaltungsblätter für Baden-Württemberg (VBlBW), 34 (11), 417–421.

Fri, R. W., & Savitz, M. L. (2014). Rethinking energy innovation and social science. Energy Research & Social Science, 1, 183–187.

Frick, B. (1999). Die wirtschaftlichen Folgen der Mitbestimmung. Expertenberichte für die Kommission Mitbestimmung der Bertelsmann-Stiftung und Hans-Böckler-Stiftung. Frankfurt a. M., New York: Campus.

Fricke, W. (2012). Innovatory Qualifications at Work. In W. G. Weber, M. Thoma, A. Ostendorf, & L. Chisholm (Eds.), Democratic Competences and Social Practices in Organizations (pp. 162–182). Wiesbaden: VS Verlag.

Friedman, K., & Cooke, A. (2011). City Versus National Energy Use. Implications For Urban Energy Policy and Strategies. Procedia Engineering, 21, 464–472.

Friedrichs, J. (1987). Neue Technologien und Raumentwicklung. Eine Theorie der Technologie als Problemlösung. In B. Lutz (Ed.), Technik und sozialer Wandel. Verhandlungen des 23. Deutschen Soziologentages in Hamburg 1986 (pp. 332–356). Frankfurt a. M., New York: Campus

Friedrichs, W., & Lange, D. (2012). Bewusstlose Demokratie? Das Bürgerbewusstsein in der (post-)demokratischen Konstellation der Gegenwart. In T. Mörschel & C. Krell (Eds.), Demokratie in Deutschland (pp. 53–70). Wiesbaden: VS Verlag.

Friedrichsen, M., & Kohn, R. (2015). Digitale Politikvermittlung. Chancen und Risiken interaktiver Medien (2nd ed.). Wiesbaden: Springer VS.

Fries, R., Kalwar, T., & Pöttinger, I. (Eds.). (2016). Doing politics. Politisch agieren in der digitalen Gesellschaft. München: kopaed.

Frischmann, B. M. (2012). Infrastructure. The Social Value of Shared Resources. New York: Oxford University Press.

Fritsche, M. (2011). Mikropolitik im Quartier. Bewohnerbeteiligung im Stadtumbauprozess. Wiesbaden: VS Verlag.

Frolova, M., Prados, M.-J., & Nadaï, A. (Eds.). (2015). Renewable Energies and European Landscapes. Lessons from Southern European Cases. Dordrecht: Springer.

Fuchs, M. (2003). Ein Kompetenzstufenmodell für soziales Lernen. Oldenburg: Univ., Didaktisches Zentrum.

Fuhse, J. (2010). Netzwerke und soziale Ungleichheit. In C. Stegbauer (Ed.), *Netzwerkanalyse und Netzwerktheorie: Ein neues Paradigma in den Sozialwissenschaften* (pp. 79–90). Wiesbaden: VS Verlag.

Fuller, S., & McCauley, D. (2016). Framing energy justice: perspectives from activism and advocacy. Energy Research & Social Science, 11, 1–8.

Funcke, S., & Bauknecht, D. (2016). Typology of centralised and decentralised visions for electricity infrastructure. *Utilities Policy, 40*, 67–74. https://doi.org/10.1016/j.jup.2016.03.005.

Fung, A. (2006). Empowered Participation. Reinventing Urban Democracy (2nd ed.). Princeton, NJ u. a.: Princeton University Press.

Fung, A., & Wright, E. O. (2001). Deepening Democracy. Innovations in Empowered Participatory Governance. Politics & Society, 29 (1), 5–42.

Fürst, D., & Scholles, F. (2008). Handbuch Theorien und Methoden der Raum- und Umweltplanung (3rd ed.). Dortmund: Rohn.

Gabriel, O. W. (Ed.). (1983). Bürgerbeteiligung und kommunale Demokratie. München: Minerva.

Gabriel, O. W. (2000). Bürgerinitiativen. In E. Holtmann (Ed.), Politik-Lexikon (3rd ed., pp. 84–87). München: Oldenbourg.

Gabriel, O. W. (2010). Zwischen Markt und Staat. Sozialkapital und die Zukunft der Demokratie. In K. H. Schrenk & M. Soldner (Eds.), Analyse demokratischer Regierungssysteme (pp. 129–149). Wiesbaden: VS Verlag.

Gabriel, O. W. (2013a). Cognitive political engagement. In S. I. Keil & O. W. Gabriel (Eds.), Society and Democracy in Europe. London: Routledge.

Gabriel, O. W. (2013b). Politische Partizipation. In J. W. van Deth & M. Tausendpfund (Eds.), Politik im Kontext: Ist alle Politik lokale Politik? (pp. 381–411). Wiesbaden: Springer VS.

Gabriel, O. W. (2014). Bürgerbeteiligung in Deutschland. In K. Pohl & P. Massing (Eds.), Mehr Partizipation – mehr Demokratie? (pp. 27–45). Schwalbach am Taunus: Wochenschau Verl.

Gabriel, O. W. (2015). Politische Partizipation und sozio-ökonomische Ressourcenausstattung in europäischen Demokratien. In Landeszentrale für politische Bildung Baden-Württemberg (Ed.), Bricht Europa Auseinander? Reichtum und Armut in Europa (pp. 68–73). Stuttgart: Landeszentrale für politische Bildung Baden-Württemberg.

Gabriel, O. W., Kunz, V., Roßteutscher, S., & Deth, J. W. van (Eds.). (2002). Sozialkapital und Demokratie. Zivilgesellschaftliche Ressourcen im Vergleich. Wien: WUV-Universitäts-Verlag.

Gabriel, O. W., & Kersting, N. (2014). Politisches Engagement in deutschen Kommunen: Strukturen und Wirkungen auf die politischen Einstellungen von Bürgerschaft, Politik und Verwaltung. In Bertelsmann-Stiftung & Staatsministerium Baden-Württemberg (Eds.), Partizipation im Wandel. Unsere Demokratie zwischen Wählen, Mitmachen und Entscheiden (pp. 43–181). Gütersloh: Bertelsmann-Stiftung.

Gabriel, O. W., Schoen, H., & Faden-Kuhne, K. (2014). Der Volksentscheid über Stuttgart 21. Aufbruch zu neuen demokratischen Ufern? Opladen: Leske + Budrich.

Gabrielson, T. (2008). Green citizenship: a review and critique. Citizenship Studies, 12 (4), 429–446.

Gabrielson, T. (2016). Oxford handbook of environmental political theory. New York: Oxford University Press.

Gabrielson, T., & Parady, K. (2010). Corporeal citizenship: rethinking green citizenship through the body. Environmental Politics, 19 (3), 374–391.

Gadinger, F., Jarzebski, S., & Yildiz, T. (Eds.). (2014). Politische Narrative. Konzepte – Analysen – Forschungspraxis. Wiesbaden: Springer VS.

Gailing, L., & Leibenath, M. (Eds.). (2013). Neue Energielandschaften – Neue Perspektiven der Landschaftsforschung. Wiesbaden: Springer VS.

Gailing, L., & Röhring, A. (2014). Was ist dezentral an der Energiewende? Infrastrukturen erneuerbarer Energien als Herausforderungen und Chancen für ländliche Räume. Raumforschung und Raumordnung, 73, 31–43.

Gailing, L., Hüesker, F., Kern, K., & Röhring, A. (2013). Die räumliche Gestaltung der Energiewende zwischen Zentralität und Dezentralität. Explorative Anwendung einer Forschungsheuristik. Erkner: Leibniz-Institut für Regionalentwicklung und Strukturplanung.

Gailing, L., & Röhring, A. (2016). Is it all about collaborative governance? Alternative ways of understanding the success of energy regions. Utilities Policy, 1–9.

Galli, D., Elefanti, M., & Valotti, G. (2013). From Corporate To Shared Social Responsibility. Community Governance and Social Capital Creation Through Collaboration. Konferenz-Paper. 2013 APPAM International Conference. Shanghai. http://www.umdcipe.org/conferences/GovernmentCollaborationShanghai/Submitted_Papers/Galli_Elefanti_Valotti_Paper.pdf

Galvin, R., & Terry, N. (2016). Selling energy savings in the United Kingdom. A case study of top-down pro-environmental behaviour change in commercial office buildings. Energy Research & Social Science, 11, 155–163.

Gamel, J., Menrad, K., & Decker, T. (2016). Is it really all about the return on investment? Exploring private wind energy investors' preferences. Energy Research & Social Science, 14, 22–32.

Gangale, F., Mengolini, A., & Onyeji, I. (2013). Consumer engagement. An insight from smart grid projects in Europe. Energy Policy, 60, 621–628.

Gans, J. (2016). The Disruption Dilemma. Cambridge: The MIT Press.

Ganuza, E., & Francés, F. (2011a). The deliberative turn in participation: the problem of inclusion and deliberative opportunities in participatory budgeting. European Political Science Review, 4 (02), 283–302.

Ganuza, E. & Francés, F. (2011b). Rethinking the Sources of Participation in Europe (Second Part). IESA/CSIC Working Paper. http://digital.csic.es/bitstream/10261/76834/1/WP%20Rethinking%20the%20sources%20of%20particiap-tion%20_Second%20Part_.pdf

Ganuza, E., Nez, H., & Morales, E. (2014). The Struggle for a Voice. Tensions between Associations and Citizens in Participatory Budgeting: Conflict between associations and citizens in participatory budgeting. International Journal of Urban and Regional Research, 38 (6), 2274–2291.

Garnett Jr., Robert F., 2014: Commerce and Community. Ecologies of Social Cooperation Lewis, Paul/Ealy, Lenore T. (Eds.), Hoboken: Taylor and Francis.

Gastil, J. (1993). Democracy in small groups. Participation, decision making, and communication. Philadelphia, PA: New Society Publ.

Gatens, M. (2006). Politicizing the body. Property, contract, and rights. In J. S. Dryzek (Ed.), The Oxford handbooks of political science – The Oxford handbook of political theory (pp. 677–693). Oxford: Oxford University Press.

Herrmann, H., Gatzweiler, H. P., & Kaltenbrunner, R. (Eds.). (2015). Ausbaukontroverse Windenergie. Informationen zur Raumentwicklung vom Bundesinstitut für Bau-, Stadt- und Raumforschung (BBSR) im Bundesamt für Bauwesen und Raumordnung (BBR), Heft 6. Stuttgart: Franz Steiner Verlag.

Gawel, E., Korte, K., & Tews, K. (2016). Thesen zur Sozialverträglichkeit der Förderung erneuerbarer Energien durch das EEG – eine kritische Analyse. Sozialer Fortschritt, 65(3), 51–60. https://doi.org/10.3790/sfo.65.3.51.

Gawel, E., Lehmann, P., Korte, K., Strunz, S., Bovet, J., Köck, W., Massier, P., Löschel, A., Schober, D., Ohlhorst, D., Tews, K., Schreurs, M., Reeg, M., & Wassermann, S. (2014a). Die Zukunft der Energiewende in Deutschland. Policy-Brief Helmholtz Allianz ENERGY TRANS 02/24. http://www.energy-trans.de/downloads/ENERGY-TRANS-Policy_Brief-_Zukunft_Energiewende_in_Deutschland.pdf

Gawel, E., Strunz, S., & Lehmann, P. (2014b). Wie viel Europa braucht die Energiewende? Zeitschrift für Energiewirtschaft, 38 (3), 163–182.

Gaxie, D. (1978). Le cens caché: inégalités culturelles et ségrégation politique. Paris: Seuil.

Geels, F. W., & Schot, J. (2007). Typology of sociotechnical transition pathways. Research Policy, 36, 399–417.

Gehrau, V. (Ed.). (2014). Dynamiken der öffentlichen Problemwahrnehmung. Umwelt, Terrorismus, Rechtsextremismus und Konsumklima in der deutschen Öffentlichkeit. Wiesbaden: VS Verlag.

Gehring, A. R. (2012). The Ultimate Self-Sufficiency Handbook. A Complete Guide to Baking, Crafts, Gardening, Preserving Your Harvest, Raising Animals, and More. New York: Constable & Robinson.

Geiger, C. P. (2012). Bürger.Macht.Staat. Integration von Bürgern und Gesellschaft in den Staat. In S. A. Jansen, E. Schröter, & N. Stehr (Eds.), Bürger. Macht. Staat? (pp. 91–108). Wiesbaden: Springer VS.

Geißel, B. (2004a). Einleitung: Sozialkapital im demokratischen Prozess. Theorieangebote und empirische Befunde. In A. Klein, K. Kern, B. Geißel & M. Berger (Eds.), Zivilgesellschaft und Sozialkapital (pp. 103–107). Wiesbaden: VS Verlag.

Geißel, B. (2004b). Konflikte um Definitionen und Konzepte in der genderorientierten und Mainstream-Partizipationsforschung: Ein Literaturüberblick. Veröffentlichungsreihe der Arbeitsgruppe Politische Öffentlichkeit und Mobilisierung des Wissenschaftszentrums Berlin für Sozialforschung. Berlin.

Geißel, B. (2008a). Wozu Demokratisierung der Demokratie? – Kriterien zur Bewertung partizipativer Arrangements. In A. Vetter (Ed.), Erfolgsbedingungen lokaler Bürgerbeteiligung (pp. 29–48). Wiesbaden: VS Verlag.

Geißel, B. (2008b). Zur Evaluation demokratischer Innovationen – die lokale Ebene. In H. Heinelt & A. Vetter (Eds.), Lokale Politikforschung heute (pp. 227–248). Wiesbaden: VS Verlag.

Geißel, B. (2009). Participatory Governance: Hope or Danger for Democracy? A Case Study of Local Agenda 21. Local Government Studies, 35 (4), 401–414.

Geißel, B. (2011a). Kritische Bürger. Gefahr oder Ressource für die Demokratie? Frankfurt a. M., New York: Campus.

Geißel, B. (2011b). Partizipative Innovationen auf lokaler Ebene – Chance oder Gefahr für die politische Repräsentation von Armen und Fremden? In M. Linden & W. Thaa (Eds.), Krise und Reform politischer Repräsentation (pp. 195–216). Baden-Baden: Nomos.

Geißel, B., Kern, K., Klein, A., & Berger, M. (2004). Einleitung: Integration, Zivilgesellschaft und Sozialkapital. In A. Klein, K. Kern, B. Geißel, & M. Berger (Eds.), Zivilgesellschaft und Sozialkapital (pp. 7–18). Wiesbaden: VS Verlag.

Geißel, B., & Newton, K. (Eds.). (2012). Evaluating Democratic Innovations. Curing the democratic malaise? London: Routledge.
Geißel, B., & Joas, M. (2013). Participatory Democratic Innovations in Europe. Improving the Quality of Democracy? Opladen: Barbara Budrich.
Geißler, G. (2014a). The role of environmental assessment and planning in renewable energy diffusion in the US and Germany. Dissertation. Berlin: TU Berlin.
Geißler, R. (2014b). Die Sozialstruktur Deutschlands (7th ed.). Wiesbaden: VS Verlag.
Geis, A., Nullmeier, F., & Daase, C. (Eds.). (2012). Der Aufstieg der Legitimitätspolitik. Baden-Baden: Nomos.
Geisen, T., Kessl, F., Olk, T., & Schnurr, S. (Eds.). (2013). Soziale Arbeit und Demokratie. Wiesbaden: Springer VS.
Gensicke, T. (2010a). Freiwilligensurvey: Ein umfragegestütztes Informationssystem für die Bürgergesellschaft. In M. Bär, J. Borcherding, & B. Keller (Eds.), Fundraising im Non-Profit-Sektor (pp. 88–103). Wiesbaden: Gabler.
Gensicke, T. (2010b). Zivilgesellschaft und freiwilliges Engagement in Deutschland im Lichte des Freiwilligensurveys 1999, 2004 und 2009. Zeitschrift für Erziehungswissenschaft, 2, 215–232.
Gensicke, T., & Geiss, S. (2006). Bürgerschaftliches Engagement: Das politisch-soziale Beteiligungsmodell der Zukunft? In B. Hoecker (Ed.), Politische Partizipation zwischen Konvention und Protest: eine studienorientierte Einführung (pp. 308–328). Opladen: Budrich.
Gensicke, T., & Geiss, S. (2010). Hauptbericht des Freiwilligensurveys 2009. Zivilgesellschaft, soziales Kapital und freiwilliges Engagement in Deutschland 1999 – 2004 – 2009. Ergebnisse der repräsentativen Trenderhebung zu Ehrenamt, Freiwilligenarbeit und Bürgerschaftlichem Engagement (Okt. 2010.). Berlin: Bundesministerium für Familie, Senioren, Frauen und Jugend. http://www.bmfsfj.de/RedaktionBMFSFJ/Broschuerenstelle/Pdf-Anlagen/3._20Freiwilligensurvey-Hauptbericht,pro-perty=pdf,bereich=bmfsfj,sprache=de,rwb=true.pdf
Gensicke, T., & Geiss, S. (2015). Freiwilliges Engagement in Deutschland: Freiwilligensurvey 2009. Wiesbaden: Springer VS.
Gerhardt, V. (2007). Partizipation. Das Prinzip der Politik. München: Beck.
Gershon, D. (2011). Empowerment. The Art of Creating Your Life as You Want It (2nd ed.). New York: Sterling Ethos.
Gertenbach, L. (2014). Gemeinschaft versus Gesellschaft: in welchen Formen instituiert sich das Soziale? In Handbuch der Soziologie (pp. 131–145). Konstanz u. a.: UVK.
Gesang, B. (2014). Kann Demokratie Nachhaltigkeit? Wiesbaden: VS Verlag.
Gestring, N., Ruhne, R., & Wehrheim, J. (Eds.). (2014). Stadt und soziale Bewegungen. Wiesbaden: Springer VS.
Giessen, L. (2010). Regional Governance für ländliche Räume – innovativer Ansatz, politischer Gegenwind und der Weg vorwärts. Raumforschung und Raumordnung, 68 (1), 3–14.
Gilbert, A. Q., & Sovacool, B. K. (2016). Looking the wrong way: Bias, renewable electricity, and energy modelling in the United States. Energy, 94, 533–541.
Gilg, A., Barr, S., & Ford, N. (2005). Green consumption or sustainable lifestyles? Identifying the sustainable consumer. Futures, 37 (6), 481–504.

Ginsborg, P. (2005). The politics of everyday life: making choices, changing lives. New Haven, London: Yale University Press.

Girvitz, G., & Lipp, J. (2005). Community power Canadian style. WindShare and the Toronto renewable energy co-operative. Refocus, 6 (1), 28–30.

Gladwell, M. (2010). Small Change. The New Yorker v. 4.10.2010. http://www.newyorker.com/magazine/2010/10/04/small-change-malcolm-gladwell

Glaser, B. G., & Strauss, A. L. (2010). Grounded theory. Strategien qualitativer Forschung. (3rd ed.). Bern: Huber.

Gläser, J., & Laudel, G. (2010). Experteninterviews und qualitative Inhaltsanalyse als Instrumente rekonstruierender Untersuchungen (4th ed.). Wiesbaden: VS Verlag.

Gliedt, T., & Parker, P. (2007). Green community entrepreneurship. Creative destruction in the social economy. International Journal of Social Economics, 34 (8), 538–553.

Glöckner, R., Ehrlich, K., & Lang, T. (2013). Genossenschaften in der Neuen Sozialen Ökonomie. In J. Brazda, M. Dellinger, & D. Rößl (Eds.), Genossenschaften im Fokus einer neuen Wirtschaftspolitik. Bericht der XVII. Internationalen Genossenschaftswissenschaftlichen Tagung (IGT) 2012 in Wien. Teilband 4 (pp. 1127–1138). Wien: LIT.

Gluch, P., Johansson, K., & Räisänen, C. (2013). Knowledge sharing and learning across community boundaries in an arena for energy efficient buildings. Journal of Cleaner Production, 48, 232–240.

Gmür, M. (2011). Member Value jenseits von Moden und Mythen. Zeitschrift für das gesamte Genossenschaftswesen ZfgG, 61 (4), 259–260.

Gmür, M. (2013a). Die Krise als Chance – Genossenschaften aus der Perspektive des Freiburger Management-Modells für NPO. In J. Brazda, M. Dellinger, & D. Rößl (Eds.), Genossenschaften im Fokus einer neuen Wirtschaftspolitik. Bericht der XVII. Internationalen Genossenschaftswissenschaftlichen Tagung (IGT) 2012 in Wien. Teilband 1 (pp. 133–145). Wien: LIT.

Gmür, M. (2013b). Grenzen der Zivilgesellschaft – Ein polemischer Streifzug. VM: Fachzeitschrift für Verbands- und Nonprofit-Management, 2, 32–37.

Gmür, M., Lichtsteiner, H., & Purtschert, R. (2011). Herausforderungen an das Management von Nonprofit-Organisationen im Zeitalter von Individualisierung und Globalisierung. In A. Heilmair (Ed.), Perspektiven des Verbandsmanagements. Festschrift für Dieter Witt zum 70. Geburtstag (pp. 17–27). Wiesbaden: Gabler.

Goebel, J., & Haas, H. (2014). SOEP 2012: SOEPmonitor Person 1984 – 2012 (SOEP v29). Berlin: DIW.

Goeke, P., Lippuner, R., & Wirths, J. (2015). Konstruktion und Kontrolle. Zur Raumordnung sozialer Systeme. Wiesbaden: Springer VS.

Gohl, C., & Wüst, J. (2008). Beteiligung braucht Wissen – Beteiligung schafft Wissen. In A. Vetter (Ed.), Erfolgsbedingungen lokaler Bürgerbeteiligung (pp. 259–280). Wiesbaden: VS Verlag.

Goldblatt, D. L. (2005). Sustainable Energy Consumption and Society. Personal, Technological, or Social Change? Dordrecht: Springer.

Goldfarb, J. C. (2007). The Politics of Small Things. The Power of the Powerless in Dark Times. Chicago: Univ. of Chicago Press.

Golding, E. W., & Thacker, M. S. (1956). The utilization of wind, solar radiation and other local energy resources for the development of a community in an arid or semi-arid area. Wind and Solar Energy: Proceedings of the New Delhi Symposium, 7, 119–126.

Goldmann, S. (2013). Basisbildung Wirtschaft. Theoretische Grundlagen für Genossenschaften. In J. Brazda, M. Dellinger, & D. Rößl (Eds.), Genossenschaften im Fokus einer neuen Wirtschaftspolitik. Bericht der XVII. Internationalen Genossenschaftswissenschaftlichen Tagung (IGT) 2012 in Wien. Teilband 3 (pp. 855–860). Wien: LIT.

Goldsmith, S. (2010). The power of social innovation. How civic entrepreneurs ignite community networks for good. San Francisco: John Wiley & Sons.

Goldsmith, S., Georges, G., & Burke, T. G. (2010). The power of social innovation. San Francisco: Jossey Bass.

Goldthau, A. (2014). Rethinking the governance of energy infrastructure. Scale, decentralization and polycentrism. Energy Research & Social Science, 1, 134–140.

Göler von Ravensburg, N. (2012). Wirtschaftliche und soziale Elemente genossenschaftlicher Kooperation in Deutschland. In G. Ringle & H.-M. Münkner (Eds.), Genossenschaftliche Kooperation – anders wirtschaften (pp. 99–116). Baden-Baden: Nomos.

Göll, E., & Sie, L. T. (2004). *Nachhaltigkeitspolitik in EU-Staaten*. Baden-Baden: Nomos.

Goodin, R. E., & Dryzek, J. S. (2006). Deliberative impacts: the macro-political uptake of mini-publics. Politics & Society, 34 (2), 219–244.

Goshn, R. (2009). Landscapes of energy. New York: Harvard Univ. Press.

Gossen, M., Scholl, G., Holzhauer, B., & Schipperges, M. (2016). Umweltbewusstsein in Deutschland 2014. Vertiefungsstudie: Umweltbewusstsein und Umweltverhalten junger Menschen. Dessau-Roßlau: Umweltbundesamt.

Gottschalk, N., & Elstner, M. (1997). Technik und Politik. Überlegungen zu einer innovativen Technikgestaltung in partizipativen Verfahren. In M. Elstner & K. Bayertz (Eds.), Gentechnik, Ethik und Gesellschaft (pp. 143–180). Berlin u. a.: Springer.

Gottschick, M., & Ette, J. (2014). Etablierte Partizipationslandschaften. Hemmnis für Innovationen zur nachhaltigen regionalen Entwicklung und zur Anpassung an den Klimawandel? In A. Knierim, S. Baasch & M. Gottschick (Eds.), Partizipation und Klimawandel: Ansprüche, Konzepte und Umsetzung. München: Oekom.

Goetzke, F., & Rave, T. (2016). Exploring heterogeneous growth of wind energy across Germany. *Utilities Policy, 41*, 193–205. https://doi.org/10.1016/j.jup.2016.02.010.

Götzl, H. (2013). Die Genossenschaft – Kooperationsmodell in Wirtschaft und Gesellschaft. In J. Brazda, M. Dellinger, & D. Rößl (Eds.), Genossenschaften im Fokus einer neuen Wirtschaftspolitik. Bericht der XVII. Internationalen Genossenschaftswissenschaftlichen Tagung (IGT) 2012 in Wien. Teilband 1 (pp. 191–198). Wien: LIT.

Graeber, D. (2013). The Democracy Project: a history, a crisis, a movement. New York: Spiegel & Grau.

Graf, A., & Fuchs, D. (2015). Energiewende konkret – Lokale Transformationsprozesse und ihre normative Einbettung in Governance-Strukturen des Mehrebenensystems. Münster: Aschendorff.

Gramke, J. (1978). Praktizierte Bürgernähe. Aus Politik und Zeitgeschichte APuZ, 28 (15), 1–21.

Grant, J. A. (2003). Community, democracy, and the environment: learning to share the future. Lanham, Md.: Rowman & Littlefield.

Gräßer, L., & Hagedorn, F. (2012). Soziale und politische Teilhabe im Netz? E-Partizipation als Herausforderung. Düsseldorf: Kopaed.

Greffrath, M. (2010). Kultur und Kritik – Auf der Suche nach den Bürgertugenden für das 21. Jahrhundert. Neue Gesellschaft, Frankfurter Hefte, 57 (1), 82–85.

Grehn, K., & Kumpf, U. (2002). Einleitung. In Enquete-Kommission „Zukunft des Bürgerschaftlichen Engagements“ des 14. Deutschen Bundestages (Ed.), Bürgerschaftliches Engagement und Erwerbsarbeit (pp. 9–12). Opladen: Leske + Budrich.
Greifenstein, R., & Kißler, L. (2010). Mitbestimmung im Spiegel der Forschung: eine Bilanz der empirischen Untersuchungen 1952–2010. Berlin: Edition Sigma.
Greifenstein, R., Jansen, P., & Kißler, L. (1991). Neue Technologien und Mitbestimmung am Arbeitsplatz. Implementationsprobleme direkter Partizipation bei technischen Innovationen. Opladen: Westdeutscher Verlag.
Greifenstein, R., Jansen, P., & Kißler, L. (1993). Gemanagte Partizipation. Qualitätszirkel in der deutschen und der französischen Automobilindustrie. München u. a.: HamS.
Greven, M. T. (1997). Politisierung ohne Citoyens. Über die Kluft zwischen politischer Gesellschaft und gesellschaftlicher Individualisierung. In A. Klein & R. Schmalz-Bruns (Eds.), Politische Beteiligung und Bürgerengagement in Deutschland (pp. 231–251). Bonn: Bundeszentrale für Politische Bildung.
Greven, M. T. (2000). Kontingenz und Dezision: Beiträge zur Analyse der politischen Gesellschaft. Opladen: Leske + Budrich.
Greven, M. T. (2009). Die politische Gesellschaft. Kontingenz und Dezision als Probleme des Regierens und der Demokratie (2nd ed.). Wiesbaden: VS Verlag.
Griffin, M., Learmonth, M., & Elliott, C. (2015). Non-domination, contestation and freedom: the contribution of Philip Pettit to learning and democracy in organisations. Management Learning – The Journal for Managerial and Organizational Learning, 46 (3), 317–336.
Grin, J., Rotmans, J., & Schot, J. W. (2010). Transitions to sustainable development: new directions in the study of long term transformative change. New York: Routledge.
Grober, U. (2013). *Die Entdeckung der Nachhaltigkeit: Kulturgeschichte eines Begriffs*. München: Kunstmann.
Groddeck, V. von, & Wilz, S. M. (Eds.). (2015). Formalität und Informalität in Organisationen. Wiesbaden: VS Verlag.
Gross, C. (2007). Community perspectives of wind energy in Australia. The application of a justice and community fairness framework to increase social acceptance. Energy Policy, 35 (5), 2727–2736.
Groß, M. (2014). Experimentelles Nichtwissen. Umweltinnovationen und die Grenzen sozial-ökologischer Resilienz. Bielefeld: Transcript.
Groß, M., & Mautz, R. (Eds.) (2014). Renewable Energies. Hoboken: Taylor and Francis.
Großmann, K., Schaffrin, A., & Smigiel, C. (Eds.). (2016). Energie und soziale Ungleichheit. Zur gesellschaftlichen Dimension der Energiewende in Deutschland und Europa. Wiesbaden: Springer VS.
Grotz, F. (2009). Direkte Demokratie in Europa. Erträge, Probleme und Perspektiven der vergleichenden Forschung. Politische Vierteljahresschrift, 50 (2), 286–305.
Grundmann, P., & Ehlers, M.-H. (2016). Determinants of courses of action in bioenergy villages responding to changes in renewable heat utilization policy. *Utilities Policy, 41*, 183–192. https://doi.org/10.1016/j.jup.2016.02.012.
Grunwald, A. (2003). Technikgestaltung zwischen Wunsch und Wirklichkeit. Berlin: Springer.
Grunwald, A., & Kopfmüller, J. (2021). *Nachhaltigkeit* (3rd ed.). Frankfurt: Campus.
Grunwald, A. (2015a). Auf der Suche nach Orientierung: Technikzukünfte als interdisziplinärer Forschungs- und Reflexionsgegenstand. In E. Hilgendorf & S. Hötitzsch

(Eds.), Das Recht vor den Herausforderungen der modernen Technik (pp. 41–62). Baden-Baden: Nomos.
Grunwald, A. (2015b). Ökomodernismus ist verantwortungsethisch nicht haltbar. GAIA – Ecological Perspectives for Science and Society, 24 (4), 249–253.
Grunwald, A. (2016a). Gesellschaftliche Folgen des technischen Fortschritts: Anlass für interdisziplinäre Erforschung und Gestaltung. In G. Graube & I. Mammes (Eds.), Gesellschaft im Wandel: Konsequenzen für natur- und technikwissenschaftliche Bildung in der Schule. Bad Heilbrunn: Klinkhardt.
Grunwald, A. (2016). Wissenschaftliche Synthese bei der Forschung zur Entsorgung radioaktiver Reststoffe in der Forschungsplattform ENTRIA. In U. Smeddinck, S. Kuppler, & S. Chaudry (Eds.), *Inter- und Transdisziplinarität bei der Entsorgung radioaktiver Reststoffe* (pp. 111–119). Wiesbaden: Springer VS. https://doi.org/10.1007/978-3-658-12254-6_12.
Grunwald, A., & Wagner, F. (2015). Wissen, was wirkt: Reallabore in Baden-Württemberg. GAIA – Ecological Perspectives for Science and Society, 24 (4), 217–217.
Grunwald, W. (1980). Das „Eherne Gesetz der Oligarchie". Ein Grundproblem demokratischer Führung in Organisationen. In W. Grunwald & H.-G. Lilge (Eds.), Partizipative Führung. Betriebswirtschaftliche und sozialpsychologische Aspekte (pp. 245–285). Bern u. a.: Haupt.
Guggenberger, B. (2009). Bürgerinitiativen. In U. Andersen (Ed.), Handwörterbuch des politischen Systems der Bundesrepublik Deutschland (pp. 39–45). Wiesbaden: VS Verlag.
Guggenberger, B., & Kempf, U. (1984). Bürgerinitiativen und repräsentatives System (2nd ed.). Opladen: Westdeutscher Verlag
Gundersen, A. G. (1995). The environmental promise of democratic deliberation. Madison, Wis.: University of Wisconsin Press.
Güntert, S. T., & Wehner, T. (2006). Ist Freiwilligenarbeit mehr als unbezahlte Arbeit? Wird diese Qualität durch monetäre Anreize gefährdet? Überblick. In P. Farago & H. Ammann (Eds.), Monetarisierung der Freiwilligkeit. Referate und Zusammenfassungen der 5. Tagung der Freiwilligenuniversität vom 30. bis 31.5.2005 in Luzern (pp. 139–148). Zürich: Seismo.
Gusfield, J. R. (1975). Community: a critical response. Oxford: Blackwell.
Haan, G. de. (2001). Typenbildung in der sozialwissenschaftlichen Umweltforschung. Opladen: Leske + Budrich.
Habermann, F., Rosa, H., Paech, N., Habermann, F., Haug, F., Wittmann, F., & Kirschenmann, L. (2015). Zeitwohlstand. Wie wir anders arbeiten, nachhaltig wirtschaften und besser leben (2nd ed.). München: Oekom.
Habermas, J. (1977). Kultur und Kritik: verstreute Aufsätze (2nd ed.). Frankfurt a. M.: Suhrkamp.
Habermas, J. (1992). Drei normative Modelle der Demokratie: zum Begriff deliberativer Politik. In I. Fetscher & H. Münkler (Eds.), Die Chancen der Freiheit. Grundprobleme der Demokratie (pp. 11–24). München u. a.: Piper.
Habermas, J. (1998). Faktizität und Geltung. Beiträge zur Diskurstheorie des Rechts und des demokratischen Rechtsstaats. Frankfurt a. M.: Suhrkamp.
Habermas, J. (2011). Theorie des kommunikativen Handelns (8th ed.). Frankfurt a. M.: Suhrkamp.
Habermas, J. (2011a). Handlungsrationalität und gesellschaftliche Rationalisierung. Theorie des kommunikativen Handelns. Band 1 (Nachdr.). Frankfurt a. M.: Suhrkamp.

Habermas, J. (2011b). Zur Kritik der funktionalistischen Vernunft. Theorie des kommunikativen Handelns. Band 2 (Nachdr.). Frankfurt a. M.: Suhrkamp.

Hacker, J. S., & Pierson, P. P. (2006). Off Center. The Republican Revolution and the Erosion of American Democracy. New Haven: Yale University Press.

Haggett, C. (2010). A Call for Clarity and a Review of the Empirical Evidence: Comment on Felman and Turner's "Why Not NIMBY?". Ethics, Place & Environment, 13 (3), 313–316.

Haggett, C. (2011). Understanding public responses to offshore wind power. Energy Policy, 39 (2), 503–510.

Hain, J. J., Ault, G. W., Galloway, S. J., Cruden, A., & McDonald, J. R. (2005). Additional renewable energy growth through small-scale community orientated energy policies. Energy Policy, 33 (9), 1199–1212.

Hake, J.-F., Fischer, W., Venghaus, S., & Weckenbrock, C. (2015). The German Energiewende – History and status quo. Energy, 92, Part 3, 532–546.

Halff, A., Sovacool, B. K., & Rozhon, J. (Eds.). (2014). Energy poverty. Global challenges and local solutions. Oxford: Oxford University Press.

Hall, D., Lobina, E., & Terhorst, P. (2013a). Re-municipalisation in the early twenty-first century: water in France and energy in Germany. International Review of Applied Economics, 27 (2), 193–214.

Hall, N., Ashworth, P., & Devine-Wright, P. (2013b). Societal acceptance of wind farms. Analysis of four common themes across Australian case studies. Energy Policy, 58, 200–208.

Hall, S., Foxon, T. J., & Bolton, R. (2016). Financing the civic energy sector. How financial institutions affect ownership models in Germany and the United Kingdom. Energy Research & Social Science, 12, 5–15.

Hallmann, T. (2005). Vereine, lokale Politik und Demokratie. Forschungsjournal Soziale Bewegungen, 3, 97–103.

Hälterlein, J. (2015). Die Regierung des Konsums. Wiesbaden: Springer VS.

Hamdi, N. (2004). Small change. About the art of practice and the limits of planning in cities. London u. a.: Earthscan.

Hanekop, H., & Wittke, V. (2010). Kollaboration der Prosumenten. In B. Blättel-Mink & K.-U. Hellmann (Eds.), Prosumer Revisited (pp. 96–113). Wiesbaden: VS Verlag.

Hanel, K., & Marschall, S. (2012). Die Nutzung kollaborativer Online-Plattformen durch Parteien: "top down" oder "bottom up"? Zeitschrift für Politikwissenschaft, 22 (1), 5–34.

Hanesch, W., König, J., & Strube, A. (2014). Teilhabemöglichkeiten für benachteiligte ältere Menschen – Sozialraumbezogene Ansätze der Aktivierung und Beteiligung. Berichtszeitraum: 01.09.2011 – 31.08.2014. Darmstadt: Hochschule Darmstadt, Fachbereich Gesellschaftwiss. und Soziale Arbeit.

Hanh, T. N. (2012). Good Citizens. Creating Enlightened Society. Berkeley, California: Parallax Press.

Hansen, A. R. (2016). The social structure of heat consumption in Denmark: New interpretations from quantitative analysis. Energy Research & Social Science, 11, 109–118.

Hansen, S. (2008). Lernen durch freiwilliges Engagement. Eine empirische Studie zu Lernprozessen in Vereinen. Wiesbaden: VS Verlag.

Hardin, R. (2015). Collective Action. Florence: Taylor and Francis.

Hardtke, A. (2011). *Gesellschaftliche Verantwortung von Unternehmen: Von der Idee der Corporate Social Responsibility zur erfolgreichen Umsetzung*. Wiesbaden: Gabler.

Hargreaves, T., Hielscher, S., Seyfang, G., & Smith, A. (2012a). Exploring the role of intermediaries in UK community energy: grassroots innovations and niche development. 3S Working Paper 2012-12 (Norwich: Science, Society and Sustainability Research Group).
Hargreaves, T., Hielscher, S., Seyfang, G., & Smith, A. (2013). Grassroots innovations in community energy. The role of intermediaries in niche development. Global Environmental Change, 23 (5), 868–880.
Hargreaves, T., Longhurst, N., & Seyfang, G. (2012b). Understanding Sustainability Innovations. Points of Intersection between the Multi-Level Perspective and Social Practice Theory. 3S Working Paper 2012-03. Norwich: Science, Society and Sustainability Research Group.
Harles, L., & Lange, D. (Eds.). (2015). Zeitalter der Partizipation. Paradigmenwechsel in Politik und politischer Bildung? Schwalbach: Wochenschau.
Harrison, J. S., & Freeman, R. E. (2004). Special Topic: Democracy in and Around Organizations. Is organizational democracy worth the effort? The Academy of Management Executive, 18 (3), 49–53.
Hartmann, M. (2009). Sozialkapital in der Netzwerkgesellschaft. Forschungsjournal Soziale Bewegungen, 3, 46–54.
Hartmann, M., 2003: Die Kreativität der Gewohnheit. Grundzüge einer pragmatistischen Demokratietheorie. Frankfurt a. M., New York: Campus.
Hartmann, M., Liptow, J., & Willaschek, M. (Eds.). (2013). Die Gegenwart des Pragmatismus. Berlin: Suhrkamp.
Hartmann, P. H., & Lengerer, A. (2014). Verwaltungsdaten und Daten der amtlichen Statistik. In N. Baur & J. Blasius (Eds.), Handbuch Methoden der empirischen Sozialforschung (pp. 907–914). Wiesbaden: Springer VS.
Hartwig, J., & Kroneberg, D. W. (Eds.). (2014). Moderne Formen der Bürgerbeteiligung in Kommunen. Konzepte und Praxis. Berlin: LIT.
Harvey, D. (1996). Justice, nature and the geography of difference. Cambridge, Mass. u. a.: Blackwell Publ.
Harvey, D. (2012). Rebel Cities. From the Right to the City to the Urban Revolution. New York: Verso.
Hathway, K. (2010). Community Power Empowers. Making community, co-operative and municipal renewable energy happen – lessons from across Europe. London: Winston Churchill Memorial Trust. http://www.communitypathways.org.uk/files/docs/biblio/community_power_empowers_2010_07.pdf
Hättich, M. (1978). Gefahren und Chancen für die Freiheit. München: Bayer. Landeszentrale für Polit. Bildungsarbeit.
Hättich, M. (1984). Zornige Bürger. Vom Sinn und Unsinn des Demonstrierens. München: Olzog.
Häuberer, J. (2011). Social capital theory: towards a methodological foundation. Wiesbaden: VS Verlag.
Hauff, M. von (Ed.). (2014). Nachhaltige Entwicklung. Aus der Perspektive verschiedener Disziplinen. Baden-Baden: Nomos.
Haus, M. (2002). Theoretische Überlegungen zum Verhältnis von Bürgergesellschaft und lokaler Politik – zwischen deliberativer Demokratie und kommunitärer Solidarität. In M. Haus (Ed.), Bürgergesellschaft, soziales Kapital und lokale Politik (pp. 76–101). Opladen: Leske + Budrich.

Hauser, E., Weber, A., Zipp, A., Leprich, U., Hofmüller, S., & Kochems, J. (2014). Bewertung von Ausschreibungsverfahren als Finanzierungsmodell für Anlagen erneuerbarer Energienutzung. Endbericht. Auftraggeber: Bundesverband Erneuerbare Energie e.V. Auftragnehmer: IZES gGmbH. Saarbrücken.

Hauxwell-Baldwin, R. (2013). The Politics and Practice of "Community" in UK Government Funded Climate Change Initiatives. 3S Working Paper 2013-19. Norwich: Science, Society and Sustainability Research Group.

Haxeltine, A., Kemp, R., Dumitru, Adina, F., Avelino, Flor, R., Pel, Bonno, P., & Wittmayer, J. (2015). A first prototype of TSI theory. TRANSIT Working Paper. Rotterdam.

Haxeltine, A., Wittmayer, J., Avelino, F., Kemp, R., Weaver, P., Backhaus, J., & O'Riordan, T. (2013). Transformative social innovations. A sustainability transition perspective on social innovation. Paper presented at the international conference Social Frontiers: The next edge of social innovation research, at GCU's London Campus on 14th and 15th November 2013.

Hay, C. (2007). Why we hate politics. Cambridge: Polity Press.

Hay, C., & Stoker, G. (2009). Revitalising politics: have we lost the plot? Representation, 45 (3), 225–236.

Heap, J., Pot, F., & Vaas, F. (2008). Social innovation, the new challenge for Europe. International Journal of Productivity and Performance Management, 57 (6), 468–473.

Hebestreit, R. (2013). Partizipation in der Wissensgesellschaft. Funktion und Bedeutung diskursiver Beteiligungsverfahren. Wiesbaden: Springer VS.

Hehn, N. (2015). Postfossile Stadtentwicklung. Rechts- und Steuerungsprobleme einer Umsetzung kommunaler Energiewende- und Klimaschutzkonzepte im Rahmen der Stadtplanung. Marburg: Metropolis-Verl.

Heidbrink, L., Schmidt, I., & Ahaus, B. (2011). Die Verantwortung des Konsumenten. Über das Verhältnis von Markt, Moral und Konsum. Frankfurt a. M., New York: Campus.

Heigl, A., & Hacker, P. (2010). Politik 2.0: Demokratie im Netz. Wien: Czernin.

Heijden, H.-A. van der (2014). Handbook of Political Citizenship and Social Movements. Cheltenham: Edward Elgar.

Heinrich-Kaufmann-Stiftung. (2012). Ländliche Genossenschaften. Beiträge zur 5. Tagung zur Genossenschaftsgeschichte am 05. und 06. November 2010 im Warburg-Haus in Hamburg. Norderstedt: Books on Demand.

Heinrichs, H., Fischedick, M., Lechtenböhmer, S., Newig, J., Roßnagel, A., Ruck, W., Schomerus, T., & Thomas, S. (2011a). Die Energiewende als transdisziplinäre Herausforderung. Gaia, 20 (3), 202–204.

Heinrichs, H., Kuhn, K., & Newig, J. (Eds.). (2011b). Nachhaltige Gesellschaft. Welche Rolle für Partizipation und Kooperation?. Wiesbaden: Springer VS.

Heinrichs, H., & Biermann, F. (2016). Sustainability: Politics and Governance. In H. Heinrichs, P. Martens, G. Michelsen, & A. Wiek (Eds.), Sustainability Science (pp. 129–137). Dordrecht: Springer Netherlands.

Heinze, R. G., & Strünck, C. (1999). Individualismus und Engagement. Das Ehrenamt im Strukturwandel. In U. von Alemann, R. G. Heinze, & U. Wehrhöfer (Eds.), Bürgergesellschaft und Gemeinwohl. Analyse, Diskussion, Praxis (pp. 169–184). Opladen: Leske + Budrich.

Heiskanen, E., Jalas, M., Rinkinen, J., & Tainio, P. (2015). The local community as a "low-carbon lab": Promises and perils. Environmental Innovation and Societal Transitions, 14, 149–164.

Heiskanen, E., Johnson, M., & Vadovics, E. (2013). Learning about and involving users in energy saving on the local level. Journal of Cleaner Production, 48, 241–249.

Held, M., Kubon-Gilke, G. & Sturn, R. (2015). Die große Transformation. Jahrbuch normative und institutionelle Grundfragen der Ökonomik Nr. 15. Marburg: Metropolis-Verl.

Helfferich, C. (2011). Die Qualität qualitativer Daten. Manual für die Durchführung qualitativer Interviews (4th ed.). Wiesbaden: VS Verlag.

Helfferich, C. (2014). Leitfaden- und Experteninterviews. In N. Baur & J. Blasius (Eds.), Handbuch Methoden der empirischen Sozialforschung (pp. 559–574). Wiesbaden: Springer VS.

Helfrich, S. (2014). Commons. Für eine neue Politik jenseits von Markt und Staat. Bielefeld: Transcript.

Helfrich, S., & Bollier, D. (Eds.). (2015). Die Welt der Commons. Muster gemeinsamen Handelns. Bielefeld: Transcript.

Heller, F. A. (1998). Organizational participation: myth and reality. Oxford: Oxford University Press.

Heller, F. A. (Ed.). (2000). Managing democratic organizations. Aldershot u. a.: Ashgate.

Hellige, H. D. (2013). Transformationen und Transformationsblockaden im deutschen Energiesystem: eine strukturgenetische Betrachtung der aktuellen Energiewende. In J. Radtke & B. Hennig (Eds.), Die deutsche „Energiewende“ nach Fukushima. Der wissenschaftliche Diskurs zwischen Atomausstieg und Wachstumsdebatte (pp. 37–75). Marburg: Metropolis.

Hellmann, K.-U. (2004). Solidarität, Sozialkapital und Systemvertrauen Formen sozialer Integration. In A. Klein, K. Kern, B. Geißel & M. Berger (Eds.), Zivilgesellschaft und Sozialkapital (pp. 131–149). Wiesbaden: VS Verlag.

Hellmann, K.-U. (2013). Der Konsum der Gesellschaft. Studien zur Soziologie des Konsums. Wiesbaden: VS Verlag.

Hellmann, K.-U. (2018). Energiewende, Bürgerenergie und Prosumtion. Oder welchen Stellenwert hat das Konzept des mitarbeitenden Kunden für diesen Trend? In L. Holstenkamp & J. Radtke (Eds.), *Handbuch Energiewende und Partizipation* (pp. 507–526). Wiesbaden: Springer VS. https://doi.org/10.1007/978-3-658-09416-4_31.

Hemetsberger, A. (2012). The Democratization of Markets through Participative and Collaborative Practices. In W. G. Weber, M. Thoma, A. Ostendorf, & L. Chisholm (Eds.), Democratic Competences and Social Practices in Organizations (pp. 17–33). Wiesbaden: VS Verlag.

Henderson, H. (1993). Social innovation and citizen movements. Futures, 25 (3), 322–338.

Hendler, R. (1977). Die bürgerschaftliche Mitwirkung an der städtebaulichen Planung. Göttingen: Schwartz.

Hepp, A., & Pfadenhauer, M. (2014). Mediatisierte Partizipation? Kleine Formen der Beteiligung jenseits von Medienlogik. In A. F. Krotz, C. Despotovic & M.-M. Kruse (Eds.), Die Mediatisierung sozialer Welten. Synergien empirischer Forschung (pp. 253–262). Wiesbaden: VS Verlag.

Herbert, G. (2008). Demokratie praktizieren – auch in der Wirtschaft. Forum Wissenschaft, 2, 23–26.

Herbert, S. (2005). The Trapdoor of Community. Annals of the Association of American Geographers, 95 (4), 850–865.

Herbes, C. (2015). Marketing Erneuerbarer Energien. Grundlagen, Geschäftsmodelle, Fallbeispiele. Wiesbaden: Springer Gabler.

Hermwille, L. (2016). The role of narratives in socio-technical transitions – Fukushima and the energy regimes of Japan, Germany, and the United Kingdom. Energy Research & Social Science, 11, 237–246.

Herrmann, C. (2010). *Ganzheitliches Life Cycle Management: Nachhaltigkeit und Lebenszyklusorientierung in Unternehmen*. Berlin: Springer.

Herrmann, H., & Gatzweiler, H. P. (2012). Regionale Entwicklungsimpulse durch Bürgerinvestitionen in die Energiewende. Stuttgart: Steiner.

Hessel, S. (2011). Engagiert Euch! Im Gespräch mit Gilles Vanderpooten. Berlin: Ullstein.

Hessisches Sozialministerium. (2007). „Ohne Moos nix los?!“ Wie viel Bezahlung verträgt das bürgerschaftliche Engagement? Fachtagung, 14. Februar 2007 an der Johann Wolfgang Goethe-Universität Frankfurt a. M. Wiesbaden.

Hibbing, J. R., & Theiss-Morse, E. (2002). Stealth Democracy. Americans' Beliefs about How Government Should Work. Cambridge, New York: Cambridge University Press.

Hicks, J., & Ison, N. (2011). Community-owned renewable energy (CRE): Opportunities for rural Australia. *Rural Society, 20*(3), 244–255. https://doi.org/10.5172/rsj.20.3.244

Hicks, J., Ison, N., Gilding, J., & Mey, F. (2014). Community-owned renewable energy. A how to guide. Sydney: Community Power Agency. http://cpagency.org.au/wp-content/uploads/2014/06/CPAgency_HowtoGuide2014-web.pdf

Hielscher, S. (2011). Community Energy in the UK. A review of the research literature. Brighton: University of Sussex. https://grassrootsinnovations.files.wordpress.com/cise-literature-review.pdf

Hielscher, S., Seyfang, G., & Smith, A. (2011). Community Innovation for Sustainable Energy. CSERGE Working Paper Nr. 2011-03. http://www.cserge.ac.uk/sites/default/files/2011-03.pdf

Hielscher, S., Seyfang, G., & Smith, A. (2013a). Exploring niche development processes among community energy initiatives. In M. J. Cohen, H. Szejnwald Brown, & P. J. Vergragt (Eds.), Innovations in Sustainable Consumption: New Economics, Socio-technical Transitions, and Social Practices (pp. 133–158). Cheltenham: Edward Elgar Publishing.

Hielscher, S., Seyfang, G., & Smith, A. (2013b). Grassroots innovations for sustainable energy: exploring niche-development processes among community-energy initiatives. In M. J. Cohen (Ed.), Innovations in Sustainable Consumption. New Economics, Socio-technical Transitions and Social Practices (pp. 133–158). Cheltenham: Edward Elgar.

Hildebrand, J. (2015). Dezentralität und Bürgerbeteiligung. Die Energiewende im Förderalismus aus Sicht der Akzaptanzforschung. In T. Müller & H. Kahl (Eds.), Energiewende im Föderalismus (pp. 131–146). Baden-Baden: Nomos.

Hildebrand, J., Fechner, A., & Söldner, S. (2014). Maßnahmen zur Änderung der Energienutzung. Bürger als Energiekonsumierende. Ökologisches Wirtschaften, 29 (1), 18–19.

Hill, P. T. (2015). A democratic constitution for public education. Chicago, London: The University of Chicago Press.

Hillebrandt, F. (2014). Soziologische Praxistheorien. Eine Einführung. Wiesbaden: Springer VS.

Hilmer, J. D. (2010). The State of Participatory Democratic Theory. New Political Science, 32 (1), 43–63.

Hiremath, R. B., Shikha, S., & Ravindranath, N. H. (2007). Decentralized energy planning. Modeling and application – a review. Renewable and Sustainable Energy Reviews, 11 (5), 729–752.

Hirsch, J., Brüchert, O., Krampe, E.-M., Manzei, A., Resch, C., Sonnenfeld, C., & Steinert, H. (Eds.). (2013). Sozialpolitik anders gedacht: Soziale Infrastruktur. Hamburg: VSA-Verl.

Hirschl, B. (2008). Erneuerbare Energien-Politik. Eine Multi-Level Policy-Analyse mit Fokus auf den deutschen Strommarkt. Wiesbaden: VS Verlag.

Hirschman, A. O. (1982). Shifting Involvements. Private Interest and Public Action. Princeton, N.J.: Princeton University Press.

Hirst, P. (1997). From statism to pluralism. Democracy, civil society and global politics. London: UCL Press.

Hirst, P. (2013). Associative Democracy. New Forms of Economic and Social Governance. Elektronische Ausgabe der Original-Ausgabe v. 1994. Hoboken: Wiley.

Hirst, P., & Bader, V.-M. (2001). Associative democracy. The real third way. London u. a.: Cass.

Hitzeroth, M., & Megerle, A. (2013). Renewable Energy Projects: Acceptance Risks and Their Management. Renewable and Sustainable Energy Reviews, 27, 576–584.

Hjorth, D., & Bjerke, B. (2006). Public entrepreneurship. Moving from social/consumer to public/citizen. In C. Steyaert & D. Hjorth (Eds.), Entrepreneurship as social change (pp. 97–120). Cheltenham: Edward Elgar.

Hobman, E. V., & Frederiks, E. R. (2014). Barriers to green electricity subscription in Australia: "Love the environment, love renewable energy … but why should I pay more?" Energy Research & Social Science, 3, 78–88.

Hodbod, J., & Adger, W. N. (2014). Integrating social-ecological dynamics and resilience into energy systems research. Energy Research & Social Science, 1, 226–231.

Hoecker, B. (2006). Politische Partizipation. Systematische Einführung. In B. Hoecker (Ed.), Politische Partizipation zwischen Konvention und Protest. Eine studienorientierte Einführung (pp. 3–20). Opladen: Leske + Budrich.

Höfer, H.-H., & Rommel, J. (2015). Internal governance and member investment behavior in energy cooperatives: An experimental approach. Utilities Policy, 36, 52–56.

Hoffjann, O., Gusko, J., & Sliwa, A. (2013). Der Partizipationsmythos. Deutschlands Verbände wollen viel Beteiligung ermöglichen, bieten aber nur wenig an. Forschungsjournal Soziale Bewegungen, 26 (2), 88–99.

Hoffman, S. M., & High-Pippert, A. (2005). Community Energy. A Social Architecture for an Alternative Energy Future. Bulletin of Science, Technology & Society, 25 (5), 387–401.

Hoffman, S. M., & High-Pippert, A. (2010). From private lives to collective action. Recruitment and participation incentives for a community energy program. Energy Policy, 38 (12), 7567–7574.

Hoffmann, S.-L. (2003). Geselligkeit und Demokratie. Vereine und zivile Gesellschaft im transnationalen Vergleich 1750–1914. Göttingen: Vandenhoeck & Ruprecht.

Hoffmann, U. (Ed.). (2014). Bürgerpartizipation und Naturschutz. Schwerpunktheft Nr. 6 (2014). Natur und Landschaft. Zeitschrift für Naturschutz und Landschaftspflege.

Hoffmann-Axthelm, D. (2004). Lokale Selbstverwaltung. Möglichkeit und Grenzen direkter Demokratie. Wiesbaden: VS Verlag.

Hoffmeyer-Zlotnik, J. H. P., & Warner, U. (2014). Soziodemographische Standards. In N. Baur & J. Blasius (Eds.), Handbuch Methoden der empirischen Sozialforschung (pp. 733–743). Wiesbaden: Springer VS.

Hofmann, S. (Ed.). (2014). Partizipation macht Architektur. Die Baupiloten – Methode und Projekte. Berlin: Jovis.

Hogl, K. (Ed.). (2012). Environmental governance. The Challenge of Legitimacy and Effectiveness. Cheltenham: Edward Elgar.

Hohberg, B., Lübcke, D. M., & Hagedorn, H. (2014). Das BürgerForum – ein überregionales, nachhaltiges Beteiligungsformat. In K. Voss (Ed.), Internet und Partizipation (pp. 323–336). Wiesbaden: Springer VS.

Hohnsträter, D. (Ed.). (2015). Konsum und Kreativität. Bielefeld: Transcript.

Hoidn, B., Burdett, R., Burgdorff, F., Chin, S., Drake, S., Hoidn, B., Keen, A., Lüscher, R., Matzner, F., Muniz, C., Perrez, J. C., Polinna, C., Puntoni, A., Schneider, B., Stih, R., Uriarte, R., van Valkenburgh, M., Walter, J., Wang, W., Zúñiga, B., & Meerapfel, J. (2016). Demo: Polis. Das Recht auf öffentlichen Raum. Zürich: Park Books.

Holeschak, W. (2000). Vertrauen durch Partizipation. Strategien zum Umgang mit riskanten Technologien. Wiesbaden: Deutscher Universitäts-Verlag.

Hollstein, B. (2013). Gemeinsinn und Engagement. Ressourcen für die Soziale Marktwirtschaft? Zeitschrift für Wirtschafts- und Unternehmensethik, 14 (1), 45–61.

Holm, A. (2011). Ein ökosoziales Paradox. Stadtumbau und Gentrifizierung. politische ökologie, 124, 45–52.

Holm, A., & Gebhardt, D. (2011). Initiativen für ein Recht auf Stadt. Theorie und Praxis städtischer Aneignungen. Hamburg: VSA-Verl.

Holm, P., Goodsite, M. E., Cloetingh, S., Agnoletti, M., Moldan, B., Lang, D. J., Leemans, R., Moeller, J. O., Buendía, M. P., & Zondervan, R. (2013). Collaboration between the natural, social and human sciences in Global Change Research. Environmental Science & Policy, 28, 25–35.

Holmberg, J. (1995). Socio-Ecological Principles and Indicators for Sustainability. Chalmers University of Technology. http://publications.lib.chalmers.se/publication/1325-socio-ecological-principles-and-indicators-for-sustainability

Holstenkamp, L. (2012). Ansätze einer Systematisierung von Energiegenossenschaften. Arbeitspapierreihe Wirtschaft & Recht Nr. 11. Lüneburg: Leuphana Universität.

Holstenkamp, L. (2014). Zur Geschichte der Energiegenossenschaften in der Region Lüneburg. Arbeitspapierreihe Wirtschaft & Recht Nr. 19. Lüneburg: Leuphana Universität.

Holstenkamp, L. (2015). Local investment schemes for renewable energy. A financial perspective. In M. Peeters (Ed.), Renewable Energy Law in the Eu. Legal Perspectives on Bottom-up Approaches (pp. 232–255). Cheltenham: Edward Elgar.

Holstenkamp, L. (2018). Die Geschichte der Elektrizitätsgenossenschaften in Deutschland. In L. Holstenkamp & J. Radtke (Eds.), *Handbuch Energiewende und Partizipation* (pp. 403–419). Wiesbaden: Springer VS. https://doi.org/10.1007/978-3-658-09416-4_24.

Holstenkamp, L., & Degenhart, H. (2013). Bürgerbeteiligungsmodelle für erneuerbare Energien. Eine Begriffsbestimmung aus finanzwirtschaftlicher Perspektive. Arbeitspapierreihe Wirtschaft & Recht Nr. 13. Lüneburg: Leuphana Universität.

Holstenkamp, L. & Degenhart, H. (2014). Problemfelder und mögliche Lösungsansätze bei genossenschaftlichen Bürgerwindparks. Ressourcenmobilisierung und Projektaquise. Zeitschrift für das gesamte Genossenschaftswesen, 64 (3), 185–200.

Holstenkamp, L., & Müller, J. R. (2013). Zum Stand von Energiegenossenschaften in Deutschland. Ein statistischer Überblick zum 31.12.2012. Arbeitspapierreihe Wirtschaft & Recht Nr. 14. Lüneburg: Leuphana Universität.

Holstenkamp, L., & Rückheim, N. (2013). Zur Zusammenarbeit von Kommunen und Energiegenossenschaften – Stand, Perspektiven und Problemfelder. Arbeitspapierreihe Wirtschaft & Recht Nr. 16. Lüneburg: Leuphana Universität

Holstenkamp, L., Degenhart, H., & Bettinger, C. (2015). Anmerkungen zur Bestimmung der Finanzierbarkeit von Erneuerbare-Energien-Projekten als Bestandteil von Smart-Microgrid-Konzepten. Arbeitspapierreihe Wirtschaft & Recht Nr. 23. Lüneburg: Leuphana Universität

Holstenkamp, L., & Radtke, J. (Eds.). (2018). *Handbuch Energiewende und Partizipation*. Wiesbaden: Springer VS. https://doi.org/10.1007/978-3-658-09416-4.

Holstenkamp, L., & Stier, B. (2018). Dezentrale Energieversorgung in Deutschland in historischer Perspektive. In L. Holstenkamp & J. Radtke (Eds.), *Handbuch Energiewende und Partizipation* (pp. 387–401). Wiesbaden: Springer VS. https://doi.org/10.1007/978-3-658-09416-4_23.

Holstenkamp, L., & Kahla, F. (2016). What are community energy companies trying to accomplish? An empirical investigation of investment motives in the German case. *Energy Policy, 97*, 112–122. https://doi.org/10.1016/j.enpol.2016.07.010.

Holtkamp, L. (2001). Bürgerbeteiligung in Städten und Gemeinden. Ein Praxisleitfaden für die Bürgerkommune (2nd ed.). Berlin: Heinrich-Böll-Stiftung.

Holtkamp, L. (2010). Zur aktuellen Lage der kommunalen Selbstverwaltung. Demokratische Potentiale, einschneidende Haushaltskrisen und symbolische Politikangebote. In S. Stieren & T.-R. Bornholt (Eds.), Kommunalpolitik. Probleme und Potentiale der „Wiege der Demokratie". Eine Einführung (pp. 80–102). Schwalbach: Wochenschau.

Holtkamp, L. (2011). Der lokale Sozialstaat im Lichte kommunaler Governance-Trends: partizipative Wende oder das Ende der kommunalen Selbstverwaltung? In W. Hanesch (Ed.), Die Zukunft der „Sozialen Stadt". Strategien gegen soziale Spaltung und Armut in den Kommunen (pp. 157–180). Wiesbaden: VS Verlag.

Holtkamp, L. (2013). Kommunale Handlungsspielräume und demokratische Legitimation. In K. Harm (Ed.): Die subjektive Seite der Stadt. Neue politische Herausforderungen und die Bedeutung von Eliten im lokalen Bereich (pp. 131–149). Wiesbaden: Springer VS.

Holtkamp, L., & Bathge, T. (2012). Lokale Bürgerbeteiligung in der Haushaltskrise. der moderne staat – Zeitschrift für Public Policy, Recht und Management, 5 (1), 47–64.

Holtkamp, L., & Bathge, T. (2013). Kooperative und elektronische Demokratie in der Kulturpolitik. In N. Sievers (Ed.), Thema: Kulturpolitik und Planung (pp. 267–273). Essen: Klartext.

Holtkamp, L., Bogumil, J., & Kißler, L. (2006). Kooperative Demokratie. Das politische Potenzial von Bürgerengagement. Frankfurt a. M., New York: Campus.

Holtz, R. E. (1977). On the grid connection of an integrated community energy system. Energy Conversion, 17 (1), 41–44.

Hölzinger, O., Horst, D. van der, & Sadler, J. (2014). City-wide Ecosystem Assessments – Lessons from Birmingham. Ecosystem Services, 9, 98–105.

Honneth, Axel. (1999). Demokratie als reflexive Kooperation. John Dewey und die Demokratietheorie der Gegenwart. In H. Brunkhorst & P. Niesen (Eds.), Das Recht der Republik (pp. 37–65). Frankfurt a. M.: Suhrkamp.

Hooghe, M., & Quintelier, E. (2013). Political participation in Europe. In S. I. Keil & O. W. Gabriel (Eds.), Society and Democracy in Europe. London: Routledge.

Hooghe, M., & Quintelier, E. (2014). Political participation in European countries: The effect of authoritarian rule, corruption, lack of good governance and economic downturn. Comparative European Politics, 12 (2), 209–232.

Hooghe, M., Hosch-Dayican, B., & van Deth, J. W. (2014). Conceptualizing political participation. Acta Politica, 49 (3), 337–348.

Hooghe, M., & Oser, J. (2015). The rise of engaged citizenship. The evolution of citizenship norms among adolescents in 21 countries between 1999 and 2009. International Journal of Comparative Sociology, 1–24.

Hopkins, R. (2008). The transition handbook. From oil dependency to local resilience. White River Junction, Vt: Chelsea Green Pub.

Hoppe, T. (2012). Adoption of innovative energy systems in social housing. Lessons from eight large-scale renovation projects in The Netherlands. Energy Policy, 51, 791–801.

Hoppe, T., Bressers, J. T. A., & Lulofs, K. R. D. (2011). Local government influence on energy conservation ambitions in existing housing sites – Plucking the low-hanging fruit? Energy Policy, 39 (2), 916–925.

Hoppe, T., Graf, A., Warbroek, B., Lammers, I., & Lepping, I. (2015). Local Governments Supporting Local Energy Initiatives. Lessons from the Best Practices of Saerbeck (Germany) and Lochem (The Netherlands). Sustainability, 7 (2), 1900–1931.

Horch, H.-D. (1992). Geld, Macht und Engagement in freiwilligen Vereinigungen. Grundlagen einer Wirtschaftssoziologie von Non-Profit-Organisationen. Berlin: Duncker & Humblot.

Horst, D. van der (2007). NIMBY or not? Exploring the relevance of location and the politics of voiced opinions in renewable energy siting controversies. Energy Policy, 35 (5), 2705–2714.

Horst, D. van der (2008). Social enterprise and renewable energy: emerging initiatives and communities of practice. Social Enterprise Journal, 4 (3), 171–185.

Horst, D. van der (2015). Climate policy and the siting of renewable energy projects: towards common but differentiated responsibility. People Place and Policy, 8 (3), 222–234.

Horsthemke, A. (2002). Mitgliederbindung und Ökonomie – ein Widerspruch? VM: Fachzeitschrift für Verbands- und Nonprofit-Management, 28 (1), 38–45.

Houghton, T. (2010). Galvanising community-led responses to climate change. Studie im Auftrag von NESTA (National Endowment for Science, Technology and the Arts). London: NESTA. http://www.nesta.org.uk/sites/default/files/galvanising_community-led_responses_to_climate_change.pdf

Howaldt, J., & Jacobsen, H. (2010). Soziale Innovation. Auf dem Weg zu einem postindustriellen Innovationsparadigma. Wiesbaden: VS Verlag.

Howaldt, J., Kopp, R., & Beerheide, E. (2011). Innovationsmanagement 2.0. Handlungsorientierte Einführung und praxisbasierte Impulse. Wiesbaden: Gabler/Springer.

Howaldt, J., Kopp, R., & Schwarz, M. (2014). Zur Theorie sozialer Innovationen. Tardes vernachlässigter Beitrag zur Entwicklung einer soziologischen Innovationstheorie. Weinheim: Beltz Juventa.

Huang, Z., Yu, H., Peng, Z., & Zhao, M. (2015). Methods and tools for community energy planning: A review. Renewable and Sustainable Energy Reviews, 42, 1335–1348.

Hubbard, A., & Fong, C. (1995). Community energy workbook. A guide to building a sustainable economy. Snowmass, Colorado: Rocky Mountain Institute.

Hubert, M. (2015). Energiearmut bei Sozialleistungsempfängern. Eine Betrachtung der Ursachen und mögliche Lösungsansätze. Hamburg: Diplomica-Verl.

Hübner, G., & Löffler, E. (2013). Wirkungen von Windkraftanlagen auf Anwohner in der Schweiz: Einflussfaktoren und Empfehlungen. Abschlussbericht. Halle. http://www.bfe.admin.ch/php/modules/enet/streamfile.php?file=000000011121.pdf&name=000000290884

Hübner, J., Renz, G., & Boergen, I. (2015). *Gut - besser - zukunftsfähig: Nachhaltigkeit und Transformation als gesellschaftliche Herausforderung* (1st ed.). Stuttgart: Kohlhammer.

Hulme, M. (2012). What sorts of knowledge for what sort of politics? Science climate change and the challenges of democracy. 3S Working Paper 2012-15. Norwich: Science Society and Sustainability Research Group.

Hummel, K. (2015). Demokratie in den Städten. Neuvermessung der Bürgerbeteiligung – Stadtentwicklung und Konversion. Baden-Baden: Nomos.

Huning, S. (2014). Wer plant für wen? Partizipation im Kontext gesellschaftlicher Differenzierung. In P. Küpper, M. Levin-Keitel, F. Maus, P. Müller, S. Reimann, M. Sondermann, K. Stock & T. Wiegand (Eds.), Raumentwicklung 3.0 – Gemeinsam die Zukunft der räumlichen Planung gestalten 15. Junges Forum der ARL 6. bis 8. Juni 2012 in Hannover (pp. 33–43). Hannover: Akademie für Raumforschung und Landesplanung.

Hutter, G. (2016). Collaborative governance and rare floods in urban regions – Dealing with uncertainty and surprise. Environmental Science & Policy, 55 (2), 302–308.

Huybrechts, B. (2012). Fair trade organizations and social enterprise. Social innovation through hybrid organization models. New York u. a.: Routledge.

Huybrechts, B. (2013a). Social Enterprise, Social Innovation and Alternative Economies. Insights from Fair Trade and Renewable Energy. In H.-M. Zademach & S. Hillebrand (Eds.), Alternative Economies and Spaces. New Perspectives for a Sustainable Economy (pp. 113–130). Bielefeld: Transcript.

Huybrechts, B. (2013b). The role of networks in gaining legitimacy for hybrid organizations. The case of renewable energy source cooperatives (REScoops). In Belgique Université Louvain, Belgique Université libre Bruxelles, J.-P. van Ypersele & M. Hudon (Eds.), La Conférence environnementale pour la transition écologique. Transition Pour Nos Sociétés? Thème 6 Les Acteurs Non-Étatiques de La Transition (pp. 61–82). Namur. http://docplayer.fr/11862964-1er-congres-interdisciplinaire-du-developpement-durable-theme-6-les-acteurs-non-etatiques-de-la-transition-31-01-13-01-02-13-namur.html

Huybrechts, B., & Defourny, J. (2008). Are fair trade organisations necessarily social enterprises? Social Enterprise Journal, 4 (3), 186–201.

Huybrechts, B., & Mertens de Wilmars, S. (2011). Renewable Energy Source Cooperatives (REScoops). Assets, Obstacles and Diffusion Strategies. 3rd EMES Research Conference on Social Enterprise. Roskilde. http://orbi.ulg.ac.be/bitstre-am/2268/118878/1/Huybrechts%20Mertens%20REScoops.pdf

Huybrechts, B., & Mertens de Wilmars, S. (2014). The Relevance of the Cooperative Model in the Field of Renewable Energy. Annals of Public and Cooperative Economics, 85 (2), 193–212.

Huybrechts, B., & Nicholls, A. (2012). Social entrepreneurship: definitions, drivers and challenges. In C. K. Volkmann (Ed.), Social entrepreneurship and social business. An introduction and discussion with case studies (pp. 31–48). Wiesbaden: Springer Gabler.

Huybrechts, B., & Nicholls, A. (2013). The role of legitimacy in social enterprise-corporate collaboration. Social Enterprise Journal, 9 (2), 130–146.

Huybrechts, B., Mertens de Wilmars, S., & Rijpens, J. (2014). Explaining stakeholder involvement in social enterprise governance through resources and legitimacy. In J. Defourny, L. Hulgard, & V. Pestoff (Eds.), Social Enterprise and the Third Sector: Changing European Landscapes in a Comparative Perspective (pp. 157–175). New York: Routledge (Chapman & Hall).

Ichilov, O. (2009). The retreat from public education. Global and Israeli perspectives. New York: Springer.

Illing, F. (2012). Energiepolitik in Deutschland. Die energiepolitischen Maßnahmen der Bundesregierung 1949 – 2013. Baden-Baden: Nomos.

Imbusch, P. (Ed.) (2012). Macht und Herrschaft. Sozialwissenschaftliche Theorien und Konzeptionen (2nd ed.). Wiesbaden: Springer VS.

Imhof, K. (2015). Demokratisierung durch Social Media? In K. Imhof, R. Blum, H. Bonfadelli, O. Jarren, & V. Wyss (Eds.), *Demokratisierung durch Social Media? Mediensymposium 2012* (pp. 15–26). Wiesbaden: Springer VS. https://doi.org/10.1007/978-3-658-10140-4_2

Immerfall, S., Priller, E., & Delhey, J. (2010). Association and Community. In S. Immerfall & G. Therborn (Eds.), Handbook of European Societies (pp. 7–37). New York: Springer.

Innerarity, D. (2013). Demokratie des Wissens. Plädoyer für eine lernfähige Gesellschaft. Bielefeld: Transcript.

Irvine, K. N., Devine-Wright, P., Payne, S. R., Fuller, R. A., Painter, B., & Gaston, K. J. (2009). Green space, soundscape and urban sustainability. An interdisciplinary, empirical study. Local Environment, 14 (2), 155–172.

Irving, S., Harrison, R., & Rayner, M. (2002). Ethical consumerism. Democracy through the wallet. Journal of Research for Consumers, 3, 1–20.

Ison, N. (2010). Governance of Community Energy Projects. Independent Research Project. Lancaster Environment Centre. http://www.cpagency.org.au/files/GovernanceOfCommunityEnergyProjects.pdf

Izutsu, K., Takano, M., Furuya, S., & Iida, T. (2012). Driving actors to promote sustainable energy policies and businesses in local communities. A case study in Bizen city, Japan. Renewable Energy, 39 (1), 107–113.

Jaccard, M., Failing, L., & Berry, T. (1997). From equipment to infrastructure. Community energy management and greenhouse gas emission reduction. Energy Policy, 25 (13), 1065–1074.

Jackson, T. (2016). *Prosperity without Growth: Foundations for the Economy of Tomorrow* (2nd ed.). London ; New York: Routledge.

Jackson, T. (2021). *Post Growth: Life after Capitalism*. Cambridge, UK: Polity.

Jäckel, M. (2014). Innovation und Konsum. In M. Mai (Ed.), Handbuch Innovationen (pp. 141–155). Wiesbaden: Springer VS.

Jacob, K., Bär, H., & Graaf, L. (2015). Transformative Environmental Policy – An approach for the governance of sustainability trans-formation(s)? Berlin: Forschungszentrum für Umweltpolitik, Freie Universität Berlin.

Jacobs, L. R., Cook, F. L., & Delli Carpini, M. X. (Eds.). (2009). Talking together. Public deliberation and political participation in America. Chicago, Ill.: University of Chicago Press.

Jaeger-Erben, M., & Walk, H. (2014). Kollektives Handeln für den Klimaschutz. Zur Relevanz unterschiedlicher Erklärungsansätze aus der Lebensstil-, Milieu- und Bewegungsforschung. In C. Schröder & H. Walk (Eds.), Genossenschaften und Klimaschutz (pp. 229–256). Wiesbaden: Springer VS.

Jäger, W. (2011). Die Moral der Organisation. Beobachtungen in der Entscheidungsgesellschaft und Anschlussüberlegungen zu einer Theorie der Interaktionssysteme. Wiesbaden: VS Verlag.

Jahn, T. (2003). Sozial-ökologische Forschung. Ein neuer Forschungstyp in der Nachhaltigkeitsforschung. In G. Linne & M. Schwarz (Eds.), Handbuch Nachhaltige Entwicklung (pp. 545–555). Wiesbaden: VS Verlag.

Jähnke, P., Christmann, G. B., & Balgar, K. (2011). Zur Einführung: Social Entrepreneurship und Raumentwicklung. In P. Jähnke, G. B. Christmann, & K. Balgar (Eds.), Social Entrepreneurship (pp. 7–19). Wiesbaden: VS Verlag.

Jakes, C. (2015). Living Off The Grid. The Ultimate Guide to Creating a Self-Reliant Supply of Energy, Shelter, Water Harvesting, Water Treatment, and Storage. CreateSpace Independent Publishing Platform.

Jakob, G. (2001). Wenn Engagement zur Arbeit wird ... – Zur aktuellen Diskussion um freiwilliges Engagement im Wandel der Arbeitsgesellschaft. In R. G. Heinze & T. Olk (Eds.), Bürgerengagement in Deutschland. Bestandsaufnahme und Perspektiven (pp. 167–188). Opladen: Leske + Budrich.

Jakob, G. (2006). „Ohne Geld, aber nicht umsonst!" Freiwilligenarbeit braucht eine vielfältige Anerkennungskultur. Überblick. In P. Farago & H. Ammann (Eds.), Monetarisierung der Freiwilligkeit. Referate und Zusammenfassungen der 5. Tagung der Freiwilligenuniversität vom 30. bis 31.5.2005 in Luzern (pp. 266–273). Zürich: Seismo.

Jakob, M., & Edenhofer, O. (2015). Welfare with or without Growth? Do We Need to Reduce Economic Activity to Protect the Environment and Increase the Quality of Life? GAIA – Ecological Perspectives for Science and Society, 24 (4), 240–242.

Jamasb, T., & Pollitt, M. G. (Eds.). (2011). The future of electricity demand: customers, citizens, and loads. Cambridge, New York: Cambridge University Press.

Jami, A. A. N., & Walsh, P. R. (2014). The role of public participation in identifying stakeholder synergies in wind power project development. The case study of Ontario, Canada. Renewable Energy, 68, 194–202.

Jänicke, M. (2000). Ökologische Modernisierung als Innovation und Diffusion in Politik und Technik. Möglichkeiten und Grenzen eines Konzepts. Zeitschrift für Angewandte Umweltforschung, 13 (3), 281–297.

Jänicke, M., & Jacob, K. (2008). Die dritte industrielle Revolution – Am Ende der fossilen Ära. Nur das Solarzeitalter kann den Planeten retten. Internationale Politik, 63 (10), 32–40.

Jänicke, M., Kunig, P., & Stitzel, M. (2003). Lern- und Arbeitsbuch Umweltpolitik. Politik, Recht und Management des Umweltschutzes in Staat und Unternehmen (2nd ed.). Bonn: Dietz.

Janning, H., & Bartjes, H. (1999). Ehrenamt und Wirtschaft: internationale Beispiele bürgerschaftlichen Engagements der Wirtschaft. Stuttgart: Robert Bosch Stiftung.

Jefferson, M. (2014). Closing the gap between energy research and modelling, the social sciences, and modern realities. Energy Research & Social Science, 4, 42–52.

Jeffrey, A., McFarlane, C., & Vasudevan, A. (2012). Rethinking Enclosure: Space, Subjectivity and the Commons. Antipode, 44 (4), 1247–1267.

Jegou, F., & Manzini, E. (2008). Collaborative services: Social innovation and design for sustainability.

Jensen, C. L. (2013). Social Practices in Energy Related Transitions? The Complex Example of Electrical Lighting. 3S Working Paper 2013 Nr. 22. Norwich: Science, Society and Sustainability Research Group.

Joas, H. (1992). Die Kreativität des Handelns. Frankfurt a. M.: Suhrkamp.

Joas, H. (Ed.). (2000). Philosophie der Demokratie. Beiträge zum Werk von John Dewey. Frankfurt a. M.: Suhrkamp.

Jobert, A., Laborgne, P., & Mimler, S. (2007). Local acceptance of wind energy. Factors of success identified in French and German case studies. Energy Policy, 35 (5), 2751–2760.

Johanisova, N., & Wolf, S. (2012). Economic democracy. A path for the future? Futures, 44 (6), 562–570.

Johanisova, N., Crabtree, T., & Fraňková, E. (2013). Social enterprises and non-market capitals: a path to degrowth? Journal of Cleaner Production, 38, 7–16.

John-Rückert, J., John, R., & Jaeger-Erben, M. (2015). Neue Formen des Konsums aus Sicht der Politik. Forschungsjournal Soziale Bewegungen, 28 (2), 77–89.

Johnson, D. G., & Wetmore, J. M. (Eds.). (2009). Technology and society: building our sociotechnical future. Cambridge, Mass.: MIT Press.

Johnson, R. B., & Onwuegbuzie, A. J. (2004). Mixed methods research. A research paradigm whose time has come. Educational Researcher, 33 (7), 14–26.

Johnson, R. B., Onwuegbuzie, A. J., & Turner, L. A. (2007). Toward a Definition of Mixed Methods Research. Journal of Mixed Methods Research, 1 (2), 112–133.

Johnson, V. C. A., & Hall, S. (2015). Community energy and equity. The distributional implications of a transition to a decentralised electricity system. People Place and Policy, 8 (3), 149–167.

Jones, C. R., Orr, B. J., & Eiser, J. R. (2011). When is enough, enough? Identifying predictors of capacity estimates for onshore wind-power development in a region of the UK. Energy Policy, 39 (8), 4563–4577.

Jørgensen, M. S., Dorland, J., Pel, B., & Wittmayer, J. (2015). Characterisation and comparison of case study findings – Batch 1 cases. TRANSIT-Working Paper. Rotterdam.

Jörke, D. (2003). Demokratie als Erfahrung. John Dewey und die politische Philosophie der Gegenwart. Wiesbaden: VS Verlag.

Jörke, D. (2011). Bürgerbeteiligung in der Postdemokratie. Aus Politik und Zeitgeschichte: APuZ, 61 (1-2), 13–18.

Jörke, D. (2012). Eine Phänomenologie der Macht – zur Aktualität von Michels' mikropolitischen Beobachtungen. In H. Bluhm & S. Krause (Eds.), Robert Michels' Soziologie des Parteiwesens (pp. 229–240). Wiesbaden: VS Verlag.

Jun, U. (2009). Liegt die Zukunft politischer Partizipation wirklich bei der „Produtzung"? In C. Bieber, M. Eifert, T. Groß & J. Lamla (Eds.), Soziale Netze in der digitalen Welt. Das Internet zwischen egalitärer Teilhabe und ökonomischer Macht (pp. 87–98). Frankfurt a. M., New York: Campus.

Junginger, M., Sark, W. van, & Faaij, A. (2010). Technological Learning in the Energy Sector: Lessons for Policy, Industry and Science. Cheltenham: Edward Elgar Publishing.

Juntunen, J. K. (2014). Prosuming Energy – User Innovation and New Energy Communities in Renewable Micro-Generation. Helsinki: Aalto University.

Jürges, N., & Newig, J. (2015). What role for frames in scalar conflicts? Land Use Policy, 49, 426–434.

Jütting, D. H., Bentem, N. van, & Oshege, V. (2003). Vereine als sozialer Reichtum. Empirische Studien zu lokalen freiwilligen Vereinigungen. Münster, New York: Waxmann.

Kaase, M. (1992). Politische Beteiligung/Politische Partizipation. In D. U. Andersen & D. W. Woyke (Eds.), Handwörterbuch des politischen Systems der Bundesrepublik Deutschland (pp. 429–433). Wiesbaden: VS Verlag.

Kaase, M. (2000). Partizipation. In E. Holtmann (Ed.), Politik-Lexikon (3rd ed., pp. 466–470). München: Oldenbourg.

Kaase, M. (2011). Participation. In B. Badie, D. Berg-Schlosser, & L. Morlino (Eds.), International encyclopedia of political science. Vol. 6. Non-Pol (pp. 1777–1788). Los Angeles: Sage.

Kaase, M., Niedermayer, O., & Westle, B. (Eds.). (2000). Demokratie und Partizipation. Festschrift für Max Kaase. Wiesbaden: Westdeutscher Verlag.

Kadlec, A. (2007). Dewey's critical pragmatism. Lanham, MD: Lexington Books.

Kädtler, J., Sperling, H. J., Wittke, V., & Wolf, H. (2013). Mitbestimmte Innovationsarbeit. Konstellationen, Spielregeln und Partizipationspraktiken. Berlin: Edition Sigma.

Kaiser, R. (2014). Qualitative Experteninterviews. Wiesbaden: VS Verlag.

Kalkbrenner, B. J., & Roosen, J. (2016). Citizens' willingness to participate in local renewable energy projects. The role of community and trust in Germany. Energy Research & Social Science, 13, 60–70.

Kallis, G., De Maria, F., & D'Alisa, G. (2015). Degrowth. In J. D. Wright (Ed.), International Encyclopedia of the Social & Behavioral Sciences (2nd ed.) (pp. 24–30). Oxford: Elsevier.

Kallis, G., Kerschner, C., & Martinez-Alier, J. (2012). The economics of degrowth. *Ecological Economics, 84*, 172–180. https://doi.org/10.1016/j.ecolecon.2012.08.017

Kallis, G., Schneider, F., & Martinez-Alier, J. (2010). Growth, Recession or Degrowth for Sustainability and Equity? (Special Issue). Journal of Cleaner Production, 18 (6), 511–606.

Kallus, K. W. (2010). Erstellung von Fragebogen. Wien: facultas.wuv.

Kamlage, J.-H. (2013a). Der Dialog mit den Bürgern erhöht die politische Handlungsfähigkeit. Innovative Verwaltung, 35 (10), 10–13.

Kamlage, J.-H. (2013b). Dialogorientierte Verfahren der Bürgerbeteiligung in lokalen Konfliktfällen. Wirkungen des Tunneldialogs in Schwäbisch Gmünd. Planung neu denken online: Texte und Diskussionen zur Entwicklung von Stadt und Region, 2/3. http://duepublico.uni-duisburg-essen.de/servlets/DozBibEn-tryServlet?mode=show&id=43085

Kamlage, J.-H., & Fleischer, B. (2014). Kommunen und ihre Bürger als Träger der Energiewende. Innovative Verwaltung, 01, 35–38.

Kamlage, J.-H., & Nanz, P. (2015). Krise und Partizipation in der Europäischen Union: Für eine neue Politik der Bürgerbeteiligung am Beispiel der Energiepolitik. In W. Brömmel, H. König, & M. Sicking (Eds.), *Europäische Horizonte* (pp. 153–176). Bielefeld: transcript. https://doi.org/10.14361/9783839430101-008

Kamlage, J.-H., Nanz, P., & Fleischer, B. (2014). Dialogorientierte Bürgerbeteiligung im Netzausbau. Jahrbuch Nachhaltige Ökonomie, 4, 195–216.

Kandpal, T. C., & Broman, L. (2014). Renewable energy education: A global status review. Renewable and Sustainable Energy Reviews, 34, 300–324.

Kanter, R. M. (2000). When a thousand flowers bloom: Structural, collective, and social conditions for innovation in organization. In R. Swedberg (Ed.), Entrepreneurship. The Social Science View, 167–210. Oxford, New York: Oxford University Press.

Kaphengst, T., & Velten, E. K. (2014). Energy transition and behavioural change in rural areas – The role of energy cooperatives. WWWforEurope Working Papers series No. 60. http://econpapers.repec.org/paper/feuwfewop/y_3a2014_3am_3a4_3ad_3a0_3ai_3a60.htm

Karch, A. (2007). Democratic Laboratories. Policy Diffusion among the American States. Ann Arbor: University of Michigan Press.

Karl, F., Aner, K., Bettmer, F., & Olbermann, E. (2008). Perspektiven einer neuen Engagementkultur. Praxisbuch zur kooperativen Entwicklung von Projekten. Wiesbaden: VS Verlag.

Karlstrøm, H., & Ryghaug, M. (2014). Public attitudes towards renewable energy technologies in Norway. The role of party preferences. Energy Policy, 67, 656–663.

Karner, A., Rößl, D., & Weismeier-Sammer, D. (2010). Genossenschaftliche Erfüllung kommunaler Aufgaben in PCP-Modellen. Typen und Determinanten einer erfolgreichen Entwicklung. In H. H. Münker & G. Ringle (Eds.), Neue Genossenschaften und innovative Aktionsfelder – Grundlagen und Fallstudien (pp. 85–106). Baden-Baden: Nomos.

Kerschner, C., & Ehlers, M.-H. (2016). A framework of attitudes towards technology in theory and practice. Ecological Economics, 126, 139–151.

Kersten, J., Neu, C., & Vogel, B. (2012). Die demografische Provokation der Infrastrukturen. Leviathan, 40 (4), 563–590.

Kataki, R. (2012). Renewable energy and sustainable development. Guwahati: EBH Publishers.

Kaufman, M., & Dilla Alfonso, H. (Eds.). (1997). Community power and grassroots democracy: the transformation of social life. London: Zed Books.

Kegler, H. (2014). Resilienz: Strategien & Perspektiven für die widerstandsfähige und lernende Stadt. Basel: Birkhäuser.

Keil, S. I. (2012). Chapter Seven: Social Participation. In O. W. Gabriel, S. I. Keil, & E. Kerrouche (Eds.), Political participation in France and Germany (pp. 189–208). Colchester: ECPR Press.

Keil, S. I. (2013a). Soziale Partizipation. In J. W. van Deth & M. Tausendpfund (Eds.), Politik im Kontext: Ist alle Politik lokale Politik? (pp. 157–189). Wiesbaden: VS Verlag.

Keil, S. I. (2013b). Vereine und Ungleichheit. In S. I. Keil & S. I. Thaidigsmann (Eds.), Zivile Bürgergesellschaft und Demokratie (pp. 53–69). Wiesbaden: VS Verlag.

Keiner, M., & Kim, A. (2008). Chapter 8 – City Energy Networking in Europe. In P. Droege (Ed.), Urban Energy Transition (pp. 193–209). Amsterdam: Elsevier.

Kelle, U. (2008). Die Integration qualitativer und quantitativer Methoden in der empirischen Sozialforschung: Theoretische Grundlagen und methodologische Konzepte (2nd ed.). Wiesbaden: VS Verlag.

Kelle, U. (2014). Mixed Methods. In N. Baur & J. Blasius (Eds.), Handbuch Methoden der empirischen Sozialforschung (pp. 153–166). Wiesbaden: VS Verlag.

Kelle, U., & Kluge, S. (1999). Vom Einzelfall zum Typus. Fallvergleich und Fallkontrastierung in der qualitativen Sozialforschung. Opladen: Leske + Budrich.

Keller, R. (2012). Das Interpretative Paradigma. Eine Einführung. Wiesbaden: VS Verlag.

Kemp, R., Loorbach, D., & Rotmans, J. (2007). Transition management as a model for managing processes of co-evolution towards sustainable development. International Journal of Sustainable Development & World Ecology, 14 (1), 78–91.

Keppler, D. (Ed.). (2010). Forschungs- und Diskussionsstand „Regionale Beteiligung von Bürgern und Bürgerinnen. Theoretische Vorüberlegungen zu einer Untersuchung regionaler Beteiligungsprozesse im Bereich erneuerbare Energien. Berlin: Technische Universität Berlin Zentrum Technik und Gesellschaft. http://www.tu-berlin.de/fileadmin/PDFs/Sonstiges/Keppler_2010_Beteiligung_EE.pdf

Kern, A. (2006). The use of key figures and its impact on activity: the case of a hospital. Frankfurt a. M.: Lang.

Kern, K. (2004). Sozialkapital, Netzwerke und Demokratie. In In A. Klein, K. Kern, B. Geißel & M. Berger (Eds.), Zivilgesellschaft und Sozialkapital (pp. 109–129). Wiesbaden: VS Verlag.

Kerr, S., Colton, J., Johnson, K., & Wright, G. (2015). Rights and ownership in sea country: implications of marine renewable energy for indigenous and local communities. Marine Policy, 52, 108–115.

Kerr, S., Watts, L., Colton, J., Conway, F., Hull, A., Johnson, K., Jude, S., Kannen, A., MacDougall, S., McLachlan, C., Potts, T., & Vergunst, J. (2014). Establishing an agenda for social studies research in marine renewable energy. Energy Policy, 67, 694–702.

Kerschner, C., Wächter, P., Linda, N., & Ehlers, M.-H. (2015). Special volume: Technology and Degrowth. *Journal of Cleaner Production, 10*. https://doi.org/10.1016/j.jclepro.2015.06.107

Kersting, N. (2004). Die Zukunft der lokalen Demokratie. Modernisierungs- und Reformmodelle. Frankfurt a. M., New York: Campus.

Kersting, N. (2008). Politische Beteiligung. Einführung in dialogorientierte Instrumente politischer und gesellschaftlicher Partizipation. Wiesbaden: VS Verlag.

Kersting, N. (2014). Online Beteiligung – Elektronische Partizipation – Qualitätskriterien aus Sicht der Politik. In K. Voss (Ed.), Internet und Partizipation (pp. 53–87). Wiesbaden: VS Verlag.

Kersting, N. (Ed.). (2017). *Urbane Innovation*. Wiesbaden: Springer VS. https://doi.org/10.1007/978-3-658-07321-3

Kersting, N., & Woyke, W. (2012). Vom Musterwähler zum Wutbürger? Politische Beteiligung im Wandel. Münster: Aschendorff.

Kersting, N., Caulfield, J., Nickson, R. A., Olowu, D., & Wollmann, H. (Eds.). (2009). Local Governance Reform in Global Perspective. Wiesbaden: VS Verlag.

Kettner, M. (1998). John Deweys demokratische Experimentiergemeinschaft. In H. Brunkhorst (Ed.), Demokratischer Experimentalismus: Politik in der komplexen Gesellschaft. Frankfurt a. M.: Suhrkamp.

Keum, H., Devanathan, N., Deshpande, S., Nelson, M. R., & Shah, D. V. (2004). The citizen-consumer. Media effects at the intersection of consumer and civic culture. Political Communication, 21 (3), 369–391.

Keupp, H. (2010a). Kommunale Förderbedingungen für bürgerschaftliches Engagement. In A. P. Ortega, A. Felbinger, R. Mikula, & R. Egger (Eds.), Macht – Eigensinn – Engagement (pp. 137–150). Wiesbaden: VS Verlag.

Keupp, H. (2010b). Visionen der Zivilgesellschaft: Der aufmüpfige Citoyen oder eine Mittelschichtveranstaltung? In A. P. Ortega, A. Felbinger, R. Mikula, & R. Egger (Eds.), Macht – Eigensinn – Engagement (pp. 17–40). Wiesbaden: VS Verlag.

Kevenhörster, P. (1975). Das imperative Mandat. Seine gesellschaftspolitische Bedeutung. Frankfurt: Herder & Herder.

Khorsand, I., Kormos, C., MacDonald, E. G., & Crawford, C. (2015). Wind energy in the city. An interurban comparison of social acceptance of wind energy projects. Energy Research & Social Science, 8, 66–77.

Kim, Y. (2011). Understanding green purchase. The influence of collectivism, personal values and environmental attitudes, and the moderating effect of perceived consumer effectiveness. Seoul Journal of Business, 17 (1), 65–92.

Kim, Y., & Choi, S. M. (2005). Antecedents of green purchase behavior. An examination of collectivism, environmental concern, and PCE. Advances in Consumer Research, 32, 592–599.

Kinnear, T. C., Taylor, J. R., & Ahmed, S. A. (1974). Ecologically Concerned Consumers: Who are they? The Journal of Marketing, 38 (2), 20–24.

Kirchhoff, S., Kuhnt, S., Lipp, P., & Schlawin, S. (Eds.). (2010). Der Fragebogen. Datenbasis, Konstruktion und Auswertung (5th ed.). Wiesbaden: VS-Verl.

Kirwan, S., Dawney, L., & Brigstocke, J. (Eds.). (2016). Space, power and the commons: the struggle for alternative futures. New York: Routledge.

Kißler, L. (1989). Modernisierung der Arbeitsbeziehungen. Direkte Arbeitnehmerbeteiligung in deutschen und französischen Betrieben. Frankfurt a. M., New York: Campus.

Kißler, L., Greifenstein, R., & Schneider, K. (2011). Die Mitbestimmung in der Bundesrepublik Deutschland. Eine Einführung. Wiesbaden: VS Verlag.

Klages, H. (2000a). Die Deutschen – ein Volk von Ehrenämtlern. Forschungsjournal Soziale Bewegungen, 13 (02), 33–47.

Klages, H. (2000b). Gutachten: Motivation und Motivationswandel bürgerschaftlichen Engagements. Berlin: Deutscher Bundestag, 14. Legislaturperiode.

Klages, H. (2002). Wertewandel und bürgerschaftliches Engagement an der Schwelle zum 21. Jahrhundert (2nd ed.). Speyer: Forschungsinst. für öffentliche Verwaltung.

Klages, H. (2011). Bürgerhaushalte als Türöffner und Antrieb für eine neue Beteiligungskultur in den Kommunen. In M. Stock (Ed.), Die Zukunft der Bürgerbeteiligung. Herausforderungen, Trends, Projekte (pp. 124–134). Bonn: Stiftung Mitarbeit.

Klages, H. (2014). Stadt beteiligt. Wie gute Beteiligung verankert wird. Berlin: Heinrich-Böll-Stiftung.

Klages, H., & Vetter, A. (2013). Bürgerbeteiligung auf kommunaler Ebene. Perspektiven für eine systematische und verstetigte Gestaltung. Berlin: Edition Sigma.

Klagge, B., & Brocke, T. (Eds.). (2013). Energiewende vor Ort. Dezentrale Stromerzeugung und die Rolle von Stadtwerken und Regionalversorgern. Geographische Rundschau, 1, 12–18.

Klappstein, V. (2013). Verleiht die virtuelle Generalversammlung der deutschen Genossenschaft Konkurrenzfähigkeit im europäischen Wettbewerb der Rechtsformen? In J. Brazda, M. Dellinger, & D. Rößl (Eds.), Genossenschaften im Fokus einer neuen Wirtschaftspolitik. Bericht der XVII. Internationalen Genossenschaftswissenschaftlichen Tagung (IGT) 2012 in Wien. Teilband 3 (pp. 1041–1087). Wien: LIT.

Klatt, J., Walter, F., & Bebnowski, D. (2011). Entbehrliche der Bürgergesellschaft? Sozial Benachteiligte und Engagement. Bielefeld: Transcript.

Klausen, J. E., & Winsvold, M. (2012). Boosting involvement between elections – The case of Citizen's Initiative. In B. Egner, M. Haus, & G. Terizakis (Eds.), Regieren (pp. 493509). Wiesbaden: VS Verlag.

Klein, N. (2014). *This Changes Everything: Capitalism vs. the Climate*. New York: Simon & Schuster.

Klein, A., Heitmeyer, W., & Zick, A. (2012). Demokratie als Kitt einer gespaltenen Gesellschaft? In S. Braun & A. Geisler (Eds.), Die verstimmte Demokratie (pp. 69–76). Wiesbaden: VS Verlag.

Klein, A., Kern, K., Geißel, B., & Berger, M. (Eds.). (2004a). Zivilgesellschaft und Sozialkapital. Herausforderungen politischer und sozialer Integration. Wiesbaden: VS Verlag.

Klein, A., Liegrand, J., & Leif, T. (2004b). Zwischen Meier und Verein. Modernisierungspotentiale im Ehrenamt. Stuttgart: Lucius & Lucius.

Klein, A., & Olk, T. (2014). Transsektorale Vernetzung und assoziative Demokratie. In A. E. Zimmer & R. Simsa (Eds.), Forschung zu Zivilgesellschaft, NPOs und Engagement (pp. 431–448). Wiesbaden: Springer VS.

Klein, A., Sprengel, R., & Neuling, J. (2013). Jahrbuch Engagementpolitik 2013. Staat und Zivilgesellschaft. Schwalbach: Wochenschau.

Klemisch, H. (2014a). Chance für den Strukturwandel: Energiegenossenschaften. AKP - Fachzeitschrift für alternative Kommunalpolitik, 35 (1), 33–35.

Klemisch, H. (2014b). Die Rolle von Genossenschaften in der Energiewende. Die Transformation der Energiewirtschaft. Ökologisches Wirtschaften, 29 (1), 22–23.

Klemisch, H., (2014c). Energiegenossenschaften als regionale Antwort auf den Klimawandel. In C. Schröder, & H. Walk (Eds.), Genossenschaften und Klimaschutz (pp. 149–166). Wiesbaden: Springer VS.

Klemisch, H., & Boddenberg, M. (2013). Energiegenossenschaften und die Rekommunalisierung als Elemente Energiewirtschaftlicher Umbaumodelle. In J. Brazda (Ed.), Genossenschaften im Fokus einer neuen Wirtschaftspolitik. Bericht der XVII. Internationalen Genossenschaftswissenschaftlichen Tagung (IGT) 2012 in Wien. Teilband 3 (pp. 925–944). Wien u. a.: LIT.

Klemisch, H., & Boddenberg, M. (2016). Genossenschaftliche Prosumermodelle – Potenziale für eine verbraucherfreundliche Gestaltung der Energiewende. In C. Bala & W. Schuldzinski (Eds.), Prosuming und Sharing – neuer sozialer Konsum (pp. 153–172). Düsseldorf: Verbraucherzentrale NRW.

Klemisch, H., & Maron, H. (2010). Genossenschaftliche Lösungsansätze zur Sicherung der kommunalen Daseinsvorsorge. Zeitschrift für das gesamte Genossenschaftswesen, 60 (1), 3–13.

Klemisch, H., & Vogt, W. (2012). Genossenschaften und ihre Potenziale für eine sozial gerechte und nachhaltige Wirtschaftsweise. Bonn: Friedrich-Ebert-Stiftung, Abt. Wirtschafts- und Sozialpolitik.

Klie, T., & Stemmer, P. (2011a). Freiwilligkeit im Spannungsfeld ökonomischer Kalküle. Analyse und Kategorisierungskonzept zur Monetarisierung freiwilligen Engagements – Teil 1. Deutscher Verein für öffentliche und private Fürsorge: Nachrichtendienst des deutschen Vereins für öffentliche und private Fürsorge: NDV, 91 (1), 34–38.

Klie, T., & Stemmer, P. (2011b). Freiwilligkeit im Spannungsfeld ökonomischer Kalküle. Analyse und Kategorisierungskonzept zur Monetarisierung freiwilligen Engagements – Teil 2. Deutscher Verein für öffentliche und private Fürsorge: Nachrichtendienst des deutschen Vereins für öffentliche und private Fürsorge: NDV, 91 (2), 80–84.

Klie, T., Stemmer, P., & Wegner, M. (2010). Untersuchung zur Monetarisierung von Ehrenamt und Bürgerschaftlichen Engagement in Baden-Württemberg. Im Auftrag des

Ministeriums für Arbeit und Soziales Baden-Württemberg. Stuttgart. http://www.zze-freiburg.de/assets/pdf/Abschlussbericht-Monetarisierung-100226.pdf

Klintman, M. (2009). Participation in green consumer policies: deliberative democracy under wrong conditions? Journal of Consumer Policy, 32 (1), 43–57.

Klitgaard, K. A., & Krall, L. (2012). Ecological economics, degrowth, and institutional change. Ecological Economics, 84, 247–253.

Klöckner, J., & Friedrichs, J. (2014). Gesamtgestaltung des Fragebogens. In N. Baur & J. Blasius (Eds.), Handbuch Methoden der empirischen Sozialforschung (pp. 675–685). Wiesbaden: Springer VS.

Kluge, S. (1999). Empirisch begründete Typenbildung. Zur Konstruktion von Typen und Typologien in der qualitativen Sozialforschung. Opladen: Leske + Budrich.

Knaut, M. (2015). Nachhaltige Mobilität, Energiewende und Industrie 4.0. Beiträge und Positionen 2015. Berlin: Berliner Wissenschafts-Verl.

Kneip, V. (2010). Consumer Citizenship und Corporate Citizenship. Bürgerschaft als politische Dimension des Marktes. Baden-Baden: Nomos.

Kneuer, M. (2013). Das Internet: Bereicherung oder Stressfaktor für die Demokratie? Baden-Baden: Nomos.

Kneußel, H. (2014). Kooperation und Partizipation im Energiesektor Deutschlands. Eine Analyse von Energiegenossenschaften und sozialer Bewegung. Bremen: EKV Academicpress.

Knierim, A., Baasch, S., & Gottschick, M. (2013). Partizipation und Klimawandel. Ansprüche, Konzepte und Umsetzung. München: Oekom.

Knittlmayer, H. (2004). Zwischen Merkantilisierung und Bürokratisierung. VM: Fachzeitschrift für Verbands- und Nonprofit-Management, 30 (2), 60–67.

Knopf, D. (1983). Das Geld und das Ehrenamt. In R. Schmidt (Ed.), Ehrenamtliche Dienste in der Altenhilfe. Ein Reader. Diskussionsbeiträge anläßlich der gleichnamigen Tagung vom 12. bis 15. Mai 1982 in Lübeck-Travemünde (Bd. 44, pp. 99–108). Berlin: Deutsches Zentrum für Altersfragen.

Knudsen, J. K., Wold, L. C., Aas, Ø., Kielland Haug, J. J., Batel, S., Devine-Wright, P., Qvenild, M., & Jacobsen, G. B. (2015). Local perceptions of opportunities for engagement and procedural justice in electricity transmission grid projects in Norway and the UK. Land Use Policy, 48, 299–308.

Kober, R. (2010). Der „gemeinschaftliche Geschäftsbetrieb". Was bedeutet er für potenzielle Neugründer von Genossenschaften? In H.-H. Münkner (Ed.), Neue Genossenschaften und innovative Aktionsfelder. Grundlagen und Fallstudien (pp. 55–65). Baden-Baden: Nomos.

Koch-Baumgarten, S. (2014). Verbände zwischen Öffentlichkeit, Medien und Politik. Wiesbaden: Springer VS.

Kocka, J. (2002). Das Bürgertum als Träger von Zivilgesellschaft – Traditionslinien, Entwicklungen, Perspektiven. In Enquete-Kommission „Zukunft des Bürgerschaftlichen Engagements" des 14. Deutschen Bundestages (Eds.), Bürgerschaftliches Engagement und Zivilgesellschaft (pp. 15–22). Opladen: Leske + Budrich.

Kocka, J. (1993). Obrigkeitsstaat und Bürgerlichkeit. Zur Geschichte des deutschen Bürgertums im 19. Jahrhundert. In: W. Hardtwig & H.-H. Brandt (Eds.), Deutschlands Weg in die Moderne. Politik, Gesellschaft und Kultur im 19. Jahrhundert (pp. 107–121). München: Beck.

Kocka, J. (2012). Arbeiten an der Geschichte. Gesellschaftlicher Wandel im 19. und 20. Jahrhundert (2nd ed.). Göttingen: Vandenhoeck & Ruprecht.

Kocka, J., & Merkel, W. (2015). Kapitalismus und Demokratie. Kapitalismus ist nicht demokratisch und Demokratie nicht kapitalistisch. In W. Merkel (Ed.), Demokratie und Krise. Zum schwierigen Verhältnis von Theorie und Empirie (pp. 307–337). Wiesbaden: Springer VS.

Kohls, M., & Wustlich, G. (2015). Die Pilot-Ausschreibung für Photovoltaikanlagen. Eine Einführung in die Freiflächenausschreibungsverordnung. Neue Zeitschrift für Verwaltungsrecht, 34 (6), 313–321.

Kohout, F. (2002). Vom Wert der Partizipation. Eine Analyse partizipativ angelegter Entscheidungsfindung in der Umweltpolitik. Münster: Lit.

Koirala, B. P., Koliou, E., Friege, J., Hakvoort, R. A., & Herder, P. M. (2016). Energetic communities for community energy. A review of key issues and trends shaping integrated community energy systems. Renewable and Sustainable Energy Reviews, 56, 722–744.

Kolbe, S. (2013). Mitbestimmung und Demokratieprinzip. Tübingen: Mohr Siebeck.

Kommission Mitbestimmung. (1999). Mitbestimmung in Deutschland. Tradition und Effizienz. Expertenberichte für die Kommission Mitbestimmung, Bertelsmann Stiftung/ Hans-Böckler-Stiftung. Frankfurt a. M., New York: Campus.

König, B. (2004). Stadtgemeinschaften. Das Potenzial der Wohnungsgenossenschaften für die soziale Stadtentwicklung. Berlin: Edition Sigma.

König, T., Debus, M., & Tsebelis, G. (Eds.). (2010). Reform Processes and Policy Change. Veto Players and Decision-Making in Modern Democracies. New York: Springer.

Koontz, T. M., & Newig, J. (2014). From Planning to Implementation. Top-Down and Bottom-Up Approaches for Collaborative Watershed Management. Policy Studies Journal, 42 (3), 416–442.

Koopmann, K. (2012). Diskussion: Was ist Partizipation? Kongress der Bundeszentrale für Politische Bildung 2012. http://www.bundeskongress-partizipation.de/wiki/index.php/Diskussion:Was_ist_Partizipation%3F

Kooyman, R., & Smit, E. (2013). Creative Sustainable Urban Development – The Coop Model. A Dutch Example. In J. Brazda, M. Dellinger, & D. Rößl (Eds.), Genossenschaften im Fokus einer neuen Wirtschaftspolitik. Bericht der XVII. Internationalen Genossenschaftswissenschaftlichen Tagung (IGT) 2012 in Wien. Teilband 4 (pp. 1139–1150). Wien: LIT.

Kopatz, M., Kettler, C., Gundlach, K., Preute, M., & Schaller, S. (2013). Energiewende. Aber fair! Wie sich die Energiezukunft sozial tragfähig gestalten lässt. München: Oekom.

Kopf, H. (Ed.). (2015). Soziale Innovationen in Deutschland. Von der Idee zur gesellschaftlichen Wirkung. Wiesbaden: Springer VS.

Kopp, J., & Lois, D. (2014). Sozialwissenschaftliche Datenanalyse. Eine Einführung (2nd ed.). Wiesbaden: VS Verlag.

Kortsch, T., Hildebrand, J., & Schweizer-Ries, P. (2015). Acceptance of biomass plants – Results of a longitudinal study in the bioenergy-region Altmark. Renewable Energy, 83, 690–697.

Kost, A. (2013). Bürgerpartizipation in Kommunen. In M. Junkernheinrich & W. H. Lorig (Eds.), Kommunalreformen in Deutschland (pp. 191–205). Baden-Baden: Nomos.

Kraus, P. A. (2004). Die Begründung demokratischer Politik in Europa. Zur Unterscheidung von Input-und Output-Legitimation bei Fritz W. Scharpf. Leviathan, 32 (4), 558–567.

Kremer, J.-F. (2010). Das Führen leitfadengestützter Interviews. In N. Schöneck-Voß, W. Voß, & J.-F. Kremer (Eds.), Methodenintegrative Forschung. Darstellung am Beispiel einer Befragung von Studierenden zu Studienbeiträgen (pp. 7–14). Bochum: Universität Bochum, Fakultät. für Sozialwissenschaften.

Kreß, M., Rubik, F., & Müller, R. (2014a). Bürger als Träger der Energiewende – Einführung in das Schwerpunktthema. Ökologisches Wirtschaften, 1, 14–15.

Kreß, M., Rubik, F., Reinhard, J., Brandsch, S., & Bietz, S. (2014b). Rollen der Bürgerinnen und Bürger in der Energiewende in Heidelberg. Vorbereitungspapier für den Workshop am 24.11.2014 in Heidelberg. Rahmenbedingungen, Akteure und Aktivierungspotenziale der Bürgerinnen und Bürger in der Stadt Heidelberg. Berlin: Institut für ökologische Wirtschaftsforschung (IÖW). http://www.ioew.de/uploads/tx_ukioewdb/Klima-Citoyen_Workshop_Heidelberg.pdf

Kreß, M., Weber, J., & Scherb, A. (2011). Erneuerbare Energien im Landkreis Lüchow-Dannenberg. Ausgewählte Ergebnisse einer Bevölkerungsbefragung. Vorläufige Kurzauswertung. Institut für ökologische Wirtschaftsforschung (IÖW): Heidelberg.

Kriesi, H. (2007a). Sozialkapital. Eine Einführung. In A. Franzen & M. Freitag (Eds.), Sozialkapital. Grundlagen und Anwendungen (pp. 23–46). Wiesbaden: VS Verlag.

Kriesi, H. (2007b). The Participation of Swiss Direct-Democratic Votes. In C. H. de Vreese (Ed.), Dynamics of referendum campaigns. An international perspective (pp. 117–141). Basingstoke, New York: Palgrave Macmillan.

Kriesi, H. (2009). Sind Abstimmungen käuflich? In A. Vatter (Ed.), Demokratie als Leidenschaft. Planung, Entscheidung und Vollzug in der schweizerischen Demokratie. Festschrift für Prof. Dr. Wolf Linder zum 65. Geburtstag (pp. 83–104). Bern: Haupt.

Kristof, K. (2014). Bedingungen für erfolgreiche Veränderungsprozesse. Warum wir uns nicht nur mit dem „Was", sondern mit dem „Wie" der anstehenden Veränderungen beschäftigen müssen. Jahrbuch Nachhaltige Ökonomie, 4 (15), 217–233.

Krohn, S., & Damborg, S. (1999). On public attitudes towards wind power. Renewable Energy, 16 (1-4), 954–960.

Kronauer, M., & Siebel, W. (Eds.). (2013). Polarisierte Städte. Soziale Ungleichheit als Herausforderung für die Stadtpolitik. Frankfurt a.M.: Campus.

Krug, M. (2014). Umwelt- und sozialverträglicher Ausbau der erneuerbaren Energien. In A. Brunnengräber & M. R. Di Nucci (Eds.), Im Hürdenlauf zur Energiewende (pp. 225–246). Wiesbaden: Springer VS.

Krüger, T. (2015). Das Hegemonieprojekt der ökologischen Modernisierung. Die Konflikte um Carbon Capture and Storage (CCS) in der internationalen Klimapolitik. Bielefeld: Transcript.

Krumm, T. (2009). Grundlagen der qualitativen Datenanalyse. In B. Westle (Ed.), Methoden der Politikwissenschaft (pp. 297–324). Baden-Baden: Nomos.

Krumm, T., & Westle, B. (2009). Der Forschungsprozess im Überblick. In B. Westle (Ed.), Methoden der Politikwissenschaft (pp. 115–124). Baden-Baden: Nomos.

Kruse, J. (2014). Qualitative Interviewforschung. Ein integrativer Ansatz. Weinheim: Beltz Juventa.

Kubicek, H. (2014). Staatliche Beteiligungsangebote im Internet – Ein Überblick. In K. Voss (Ed.), Internet und Partizipation (pp. 263–298). Wiesbaden: Springer VS.

Kubicek, H., Lippa, B., & Westholm, H. (2009). Medienmix in der Bürgerbeteiligung. Die Integration von Online-Elementen in Beteiligungsverfahren auf lokaler Ebene. Berlin: Edition Sigma.

Kuckartz, U. (1988). Computer und verbale Daten. Chancen zur Innovation sozialwissenschaftlicher Forschungstechniken. Frankfurt a. M.: Lang.

Kuckartz, U. (1990). Computerunterstützte Suche nach Typologien in qualitativen Interviews. In F. Faulbaum, R. Haux, & K.-H. Jöckel (Eds.), Softstat '89. 5. Konferenz über die Wissenschaftliche Anwendung von Statistik-Software, Heidelberg, 1989 (pp. 495–502). Stuttgart: Fischer.

Kuckartz, U. (2001). Aggregation und Dis-Aggregation in der sozialwissenschaftlichen Umweltforschung. In G. de Haan, E.-D. Lantermann, V. Linneweber, & F. Reusswig (Eds.), Typenbildung in der sozialwissenschaftlichen Umweltforschung (pp. 17–38). Wiesbaden: VS Verlag.

Kuckartz, U. (2009). Methodenkombination. In B. Westle (Ed.), Methoden der Politikwissenschaft (pp. 352–362). Baden-Baden: Nomos.

Kuckartz, U. (2010a). Einführung in die computergestützte Analyse qualitativer Daten (3rd ed.). Wiesbaden: VS Verlag.

Kuckartz, U. (2010b). Typenbildung. In G. Mey & K. Mruck (Eds.), Handbuch qualitative Forschung in der Psychologie (pp. 553–568). Wiesbaden: VS Verlag.

Kuckartz, U. (2014a). Mixed Methods. Methodologie, Forschungsdesigns und Analyseverfahren. Wiesbaden: Springer VS.

Kuckartz, U. (2014b). Qualitative Inhaltsanalyse. Methoden, Praxis, Computerunterstützung (2nd ed.). Weinheim: Beltz Juventa.

Kuder, T., & Ritzi, C. (2013). Die Wirkung der Mitwirkung. Dialog im Stresstest. Forum Wohnen und Stadtentwicklung, 5, 215–220.

Kufeld, W. (Ed.). (2013). Klimawandel und Nutzung von regenerativen Energien als Herausforderungen für die Raumordnung. Hannover: Verlag der ARL.

Kühl, S. (2001). Über das erfolgreiche Scheitern von Gruppenarbeitsprojekten. Rezentralisierung und Rehierarchisierung in Vorreiterunternehmen der Dezentralisierung. Zeitschrift für Soziologie, 30 (3), 199–222.

Kühl, S., Strodtholz, P., & Taffertshofer, A. (Eds.) (2009). Handbuch Methoden der Organisationsforschung. Quantitative und Qualitative Methoden. Wiesbaden: VS Verlag.

Kühling, J. (2014). Nachhaltiger Konsum und individuelle Konsumwahl. Eine Analyse umweltfreundlichen Konsumverhaltens. Marburg: Metropolis.

Kuhlmann, S. (2010). Reformen lokaler Politik in Deutschland. Direkte und kooperative Demokratie. In S. Schieren & T.-R. Bornholt (Eds.), Kommunalpolitik. Probleme und Potentiale der „Wiege der Demokratie". Eine Einführung (pp. 55–79). Schwalbach: Wochenschau.

Kühnlein, I., & Böhle, F. (2002a). Das Verhältnis von Erwerbsarbeit und bürgerschaftlichem Engagement. Ersatz – Ergänzung – Konkurrenz? In Enquete-Kommission „Zukunft des Bürgerschaftlichen Engagements" des 14. Deutschen Bundestages (Eds.), Bürgerschaftliches Engagement und Erwerbsarbeit (pp. 87–109). Opladen: Leske + Budrich.

Kühnlein, I., & Böhle, F. (2002b). Motive und Motivationswandel des bürgerschaftlichen Engagements. In Enquete-Kommission „Zukunft des Bürgerschaftlichen Engagements" des 14. Deutschen Bundestages (Eds.), Bürgerschaftliches Engagement und Erwerbsarbeit (pp. 267–297). Opladen: Leske + Budrich.

Künneke, R., Mehos, D. C., Hillerbrand, R., & Hemmes, K. (2015). Understanding values embedded in offshore wind energy systems. Toward a purposeful institutional and technological design. Environmental Science & Policy, 53 (Part B), 118–129.

Kunze, C., & Becker, S. (2015a). Collective ownership in renewable energy and opportunities for sustainable degrowth. Sustainability Science, 10 (3), 425–437.
Kunze, C., & Becker, S. (2015b). Wege der Energiedemokratie. Emanzipatorische Energiewenden in Europa. Stuttgart: ibidem.
Kunze, C., & Hertel, M. (2015). Tiefe Geothermie – von hohen Erwartungen zur Risikotechnologie. GAIA – Ecological Perspectives for Science and Society, 24 (3), 169–173.
Kunze, C., & Lehmann, P. (2015). The Energiewende did not lead to more coal or CO2 emissions. EnergyPost.eu. http://www.energypost.eu/energiewende-dark-side/
Küpper, P., Levin-Keitel, M., Maus, F., Müller, P., Reimann, S., Sondermann, M., Stock, K, & Wiegand, T. (Eds.). (2014). Raumentwicklung 3.0 – Gemeinsam die Zukunft der räumlichen Planung gestalten. 15. Junges Forum der ARL 6. bis 8. Juni 2012 in Hannover. Hannover: ARL Akademie.
Küsters, I. (2014). Narratives Interview. In N. Baur & J. Blasius (Eds.), Handbuch Methoden der empirischen Sozialforschung (pp. 575–580). Wiesbaden: Springer VS.
Kuzemko, C., Lockwood, M., Mitchell, C., & Hoggett, R. (2016). Governing for sustainable energy system change. Politics, contexts and contingency. Energy Research & Social Science, 12, 96–105.
Ladenburg, J., & Dubgaard, A. (2007). Willingness to pay for reduced visual disamenities from offshore wind farms in Denmark. Energy Policy, 35 (8), 4059–4071.
Ladenburg, J., & Dubgaard, A. (2009). Preferences of coastal zone user groups regarding the siting of offshore wind farms. Ocean & Coastal Management, 52 (5), 233–242.
Ladenburg, J. (2015a). A note on the cumulative effects of daily wind power encounters on the relative acceptance of increasing the wind power capacity offshore and onshore. Copenhagen: KORA, Danish Institute for Local and Regional Government Research. http://www.wind2050.dk/-/media/Sites/Wind2050/publikationer/a%20note%20on%20the%20cumulative%20effects.ashx?la=da
Ladenburg, J. (2015b). Does more wind energy influence the choice of location for wind power development? Assessing the cumulative effects of daily wind turbine encounters in Denmark. Energy Research & Social Science, 10, 26–30.
Lamla, J. (2007). Die Autonomie des Verbrauchers und ihre politischen Formen. Bausteine einer Kulturtheorie des Consumer Citizen. In S. Baringhorst, V. Kneip, A. März, J. Niesyto (Eds.), Politik mit dem Einkaufswagen. Unternehmen und Konsumenten als Bürger in der globalen Mediengesellschaft (pp. 53–80). Bielefeld: Transcript.
Lamla, J. (2008). Consumer citizen. The constitution of consumer democracy in sociological perspective. German Policy Studies/Politikfeldanalyse, 4 (1), 131–65.
Lamla, J. (2012). „Netizenship" oder Alltagsökonomie? Typologische Betrachtungen über die Motivlagen und Beteiligungsmuster von Internetnutzern sowie die Zukunft digitaler Demokratie. In T. Beyreuther (Ed.), Consumers@work. Zum neuen Verhältnis von Unternehmen und Usern im Web 2.0 (pp. 152–179). Frankfurt a. M., New York: Campus.
Lamla, J. (2013). Verbraucherdemokratie. Politische Soziologie der Konsumgesellschaft. Berlin: Suhrkamp.
Lamla, J., & Neckel, S. (Eds.). (2006). Politisierter Konsum, konsumierte Politik. Wiesbaden: VS Verlag.
Lamnek, S. (2010). Qualitative Sozialforschung. Lehrbuch. Mit Online-Materialien (5th ed.). Weinheim, Basel: Beltz.

Landert, C. (2006). Normative Aspekte der Monetarisierung. Überblick. In P. Farago & H. Ammann (Eds.), Monetarisierung der Freiwilligkeit. Referate und Zusammenfassungen der 5. Tagung der Freiwilligenuniversität vom 30. bis 31.5.2005 in Luzern (pp. 299–302). Zürich: Seismo.

Landesverband Erneuerbare Energien NRW e.V., & World Wind Energy Association WWEA e.V. (2016). „Bürgerwind-Perspektiven aus NRW und der Welt". Zusammenfassung der vorläufigen Studienergebnisse. http://www.lee-nrw.de/wp-content/uploads/2016/01/Zwischenergebnisse-der-Studie-B%C3%BCrgerwind-Perspektiven-aus-NRW-und-der-Welt_WWEA_LEE-NRW.pdf

Landwehr, C., & Schmalz-Bruns, R. (2014). Deliberative Demokratie in der Diskussion. Herausforderungen, Bewährungsproben, Kritik. Baden-Baden: Nomos.

Lane, J. F., Floress, K., & Rickert, M. (2014). Development of school energy policy and energy education plans. A comparative case study in three Wisconsin school communities. Energy Policy, 65, 323–331.

Lang, R. (2013). Social Capital of Residents in Cooperative Housing. Empirical Evidence from Vienna. In J. Brazda, M. Dellinger, & D. Rößl (Eds.), Genossenschaften im Fokus einer neuen Wirtschaftspolitik. Bericht der XVII. Internationalen Genossenschaftswissenschaftlichen Tagung (IGT) 2012 in Wien. Teilband 2 (pp. 585–596). Wien: LIT.

Lang, R., Rößl, D., & Weismeier-Sammer, D. (2013). Co-operative Governance of Public-Citizen Partnerships. Two Diametrical Participation Modes. Studies in Public and Non-Profit Governance, 1, 227–246.

Lang, T., & Gabriel, Y. (2005). A brief history of consumer activism. In D. S. Shaw, R. Harrison & T. Newholm, The ethical consumer (pp. 39–53). Thousand Oaks, London: Sage.

Lange, H. (2008). *Nachhaltigkeit als radikaler Wandel: Die Quadratur des Kreises?* Wiesbaden: VS Verlag.

Langer, G. (2011). *Unternehmen und Nachhaltigkeit: Analyse und Weiterentwicklung aus der Perspektive der wissensbasierten Theorie der Unternehmung*. Wiesbaden: Gabler.

Larsen, A. K. (2013). Participation in Community Work. Hoboken: Taylor and Francis.

Larsen, A. K., Sewpaul, V., & Hole, G. O. (Eds.). (2013). *Participation in Community Work*. Hoboken: Taylor and Francis.

Latcheva, R., & Davidov, E. (2014). Skalen und Indizes. In N. Baur & J. Blasius (Eds.), Handbuch Methoden der empirischen Sozialforschung (pp. 745–756). Wiesbaden: Springer VS.

Latouche, S. (2010). Degrowth. Journal of Cleaner Production, 18 (6), 519–522.

Latouche, S. (2015). Es reicht! Abrechnung mit dem Wachstumswahn. München: Oekom.

Latour, B. (2001). Das Parlament der Dinge. Für eine politische Ökologie. Frankfurt a. M.: Suhrkamp.

Latour, B., & Weibel, P. (Eds.). (2005). Making things public: atmospheres of democracy. Cambridge, Mass.: MIT Press.

Lauber, V., & Jacobsson, S. (2016). The politics and economics of constructing, contesting and restricting socio-political space for renewables – The German Renewable Energy Act. Environmental Innovation and Societal Transitions, 18, 147–163.

Lawson, S. J., Gleim, M. R., Perren, R., & Hwang, J. (2016). Freedom from ownership: An exploration of access-based consumption. Journal of Business Research, 69 (8), 2615–2623.

Lave, J., & Wenger, E. (1991). Situated learning. Legitimate peripheral participation. Cambridge: Cambridge University Press.

Leach, M., Scoones, I., & Stirling, A. (2010). Governing epidemics in an age of complexity. Narratives, politics and pathways to sustainability. Global Environmental Change, 20 (3), 369–377.

Leach, M. (2007). Understanding governance. Pathways to sustainability. Brighton: STEPS Centre. http://steps-centre.org/wp-content/uploads/final_steps_governance.pdf

Leach, M., Rockström, J., Raskin, P., Scoones, I., Stirling, A. C., Smith, A., Thompson, J., Millstone, E., Ely, A., Arond, E., Folke, C., & Olsson, P. (2012). Transforming Innovation for Sustainability. Ecology and Society, 17 (2), 1–6.

Leach, W. D. (2004). Is Devolution Democratic? Assessing Collaborative Environmental Management. The Center for Collaborative Policy. Working Paper. University of Southern California, Sacramento. http://papers.ssrn.com/sol3/Delivery.cfm/SSRN_ID628122_code426661.pdf

Leadbeater, C. (2007). Social enterprise and social innovation. Strategies for the next ten years. A Social Enterprise Think Piece for the Cabinet Office of the Third Sector. London. http://www.peopleproject.eu/wiki/PEOPLE%20WIKIS/socialentrepreneurship/mainSpace/files/Social%20enterprise%20and%20social%20innovation.pdf

Ledec, G., Rapp, K. W., & Aiello, R. (2011). Greening the Wind. Environmental and Social Considerations for Wind Power Development. Washington, D.C.: World Bank.

Lee, C. W. (2015). Do-it-yourself democracy. The rise of the public engagement industry. New York: Oxford University Press.

Lee, C. W., McQuarrie, M., & Walker, E. T. (Eds.). (2015). Democratizing Inequalities. Dilemmas of the New Public Participation. New York: NYU Press.

Lefebvre, H., & Ronneberger, K. (2014). Die Revolution der Städte. Hamburg: CEP Europ. Verl.-Anst.

Lefebvre, H., & Schäfer, C. (2016). Das Recht auf Stadt. Hamburg: Edition Nautilus.

Leggewie, C. (2011). Mut statt Wut. Aufbruch in eine neue Demokratie. Hamburg: Körber-Stiftung.

Leggewie, C. & Sachße, C. (Eds.). (2008). Soziale Demokratie, Zivilgesellschaft und Bürgertugenden. Festschrift für Adalbert Evers. Frankfurt a. M., New York: Campus.

Leggewie, C., & Bieber, C. (2001). Interaktive Demokratie. Politische Online-Kommunikation und digitale Politikprozesse. Aus Politik und Zeitgeschichte APuZ, 41, 37–45.

Leggewie, C., & Bieber, C. (2003). Demokratie 2.0 – Wie tragen neue Medien zur demokratischen Erneuerung bei? In C. Offe (Ed.), Demokratisierung der Demokratie. Diagnosen und Reformvorschläge. Frankfurt a. M., New York: Campus.

Leggewie, C., & Welzer, H. (2011). Das Ende der Welt, wie wir sie kannten. Klima, Zukunft und die Chancen der Demokratie. Frankfurt a. M.: Fischer.

Leibenath, M., Wirth, P., & Lintz, G. (2016). Just a talking shop? – Informal participatory spatial planning for implementing state wind energy targets in Germany. *Utilities Policy, 41*, 206–213. https://doi.org/10.1016/j.jup.2016.02.008

Leibfried, S., & Zürn, M. (Eds.). (2006). Transformationen des Staates? Frankfurt a. M.: Suhrkamp.

Leibfried, S., Huber, E., Lange, M., Levy, J. D., Nullmeier, F., & Stephens (Eds.). (2015). The Oxford handbook of transformations of the state. Oxford: Oxford Univ. Press.

Leistner, A. (2013). Die Selbststabilisierung sozialer Bewegungen. Das analytische und theoretische Potential des Schlüsselfigurenansatzes. Forschungsjournal Soziale Bewegungen, 26, 14–23.
Lembcke, O., Ritzi, C., & Schaal, G. S. (Eds.) (2012). Zeitgenössische Demokratietheorie. Bd. 1. Normative Demokratietheorien. Wiesbaden: Springer VS.
Lembcke, O., Ritzi, C., & Schaal, G. S. (Eds.). (2015). Zeitgenössische Demokratietheorie. Bd. 2. Empirische Demokratietheorien. Wiesbaden: Springer VS.
Lemke, M. S. (2012). Die gerechte Stadt. Politische Gestaltbarkeit verdichteter Räume. Stuttgart: Steiner.
Lemke, M., Schwarz, O., Stark, T., & Weissenbach, K. (Eds.). (2015). Legitimitätspraxis. Politikwissenschaftliche und soziologische Perspektiven. Wiesbaden: Springer VS.
Lenhart, J., van Vliet, B., & Mol, A. P. J. (2015). New roles for local authorities in a time of climate change: the Rotterdam Energy Approach and Planning as a case of urban symbiosis. Journal of Cleaner Production, 107, 593–601.
Leprich, U. (2014). Transformation des bundesdeutschen Stromsystems. Jahrbuch Nachhaltige Ökonomie, 4 (15), 117–138.
Leprich, U., & Rogall, H. (2014). Die Energiewende als gesellschaftlicher Transformationsprozess. Jahrbuch Nachhaltige Ökonomie, 4 (15), 15–30.
Leser, C. (2011). Demokratie-Lernen durch Partizipation? Fallrekonstruktive Analysen zur Partizipation als pädagogischer Praxis. Opladen: Leske + Budrich.
Leshinsky, R., & Legacy, C. (Eds.). (2015). Instruments of planning. Tensions and challenges for more equitable and sustainable cities. Abingdon: Routledge.
Lessenich, S. (2013). Die Neuerfindung des Sozialen. Der Sozialstaat im flexiblen Kapitalismus (3rd ed.). Bielefeld: Transcript.
Letcher, M., Redgrove, Z., Roberts, S., Longstaff, B., & Inverarity, A. (2007). Mobilising individual behaviour change through community initiatives. Lessons for climate change. Report by the Centre for Sustainable Energy (CSE) and Community Development Xchange (CDX). Studie im Auftrag von: DEFRA, Communities and Local Government, DTI, DfT and HM Treasury. London: Department for Environment, Food and Rural Affairs Nobel House. http://www.cse.org.uk/pdf/pub1073.pdf
Lettice, F., & Parekh, M. (2010). The social innovation process. Themes, challenges and implications for practice. International Journal of Technology Management, 51 (1), 139–158.
Leuphana Universität Lüneburg, & Nestle, U. (2014). Marktrealität von Bürgerenergie und mögliche Auswirkungen von regulatorischen Eingriffen. Eine Studie für das Bündnis Bürgerenergie e.V. (BBEn) und dem Bund für Umwelt und Naturschutz Deutschland e.V. (BUND). http://www.leuphana.de/fileadmin/user_upload/Forschungseinrichtungen/professuren/finanzierung-finanzwirtschaft/files/Studie_Mark-trealitaet_von_Buergerenergie_Leuphana_FINAL_23042014.pdf
Lewinsohn-Zamir, D. (1998). Consumer Preferences, Citizen Preferences, and the Provision of Public Goods. The Yale Law Journal, 108 (2), 377–406.
Li, L. W., Birmele, J., Schaich, H., & Konold, W. (2013). Transitioning to Community-owned Renewable Energy. Lessons from Germany. Procedia Environmental Sciences, 17, 719–728.
Li, Y. (2015). Handbook of Research Methods and Applications in Social Capital. Cheltenham: Edward Elgar.

Liebig, R. (2011). Was bleibt für das Ehrenamt? Analysen und Forschungsbefunde zum Wandel der Führungsstrukturen im Sozialbereich. In T. Rauschenbach & A. Zimmer (Eds.), Bürgerschaftliches Engagement unter Druck? Analysen und Befunde aus den Bereichen Soziales, Kultur und Sport (pp. 29–163). Opladen: Leske + Budrich.

Lietzmann, H. J. (2012). Die Kontingenz der Repräsentation. Bürgerbeteiligung. In O. Asbach, R. Schäfer, V. Selk, A. Weiß, & K. Kock (Eds.), Zur kritischen Theorie der politischen Gesellschaft. Festschrift für Michael Th. Greven zum 65. Geburtstag (pp. 165–188). Wiesbaden: VS Verlag.

Lietzmann, H. J. (2013). Bürgerschaftliche Partizipation beim Netzausbau. Höhere Effizienz der Planung und Beschleunigung der Verfahren. In Bundesnetzagentur (Ed.), Wissenschaftsdialog 2013. Technologie, Kommunikation, Wirtschaft, Landschaft (pp. 79–94). Berlin. http://www.netzausbau.de/SharedDocs/Downloads/DE/.../Tagungsband.pdf

Lietzmann, H. J., & Mittendorf, V. (2011). Dialogische Local Governance. In P. Rohland (Ed.), Dialog. Zur Stärkung lokaler Demokratie (pp. 77–82). Bonn: vhw – Verlag Dienstleistung.

Lietzmann, H. J., Ehlers, A., & Ülpenich, B. (2013). Bürgerbeteiligung in den Kommunen. Die „neue Gewaltenteilung" in der lokalen Politik. Gutachten der Forschungsstelle Bürgerbeteiligung im Auftrag der GAR NRW. Düsseldorf. http://www.gar-nrw.de/files/GutachtenBürgerbeteiligungTelgteWeb.pdf

Lijphart, A. (1999). Patterns of Democracy. Government Forms and Performance in Thirty-Six Countries. New Haven, Conn.: Yale University Press.

Lilge, H.-G. (1980). Partizipative Führung. Betriebswirtschaftliche und sozialpsychologische Aspekte. Bern u. a.: Haupt.

Lind, G. (2012). Moral Competence and Democratic Ways of Life. In W. G. Weber, M. Thoma, A. Ostendorf, & L. Chisholm (Eds.), Democratic Competences and Social Practices in Organizations (pp. 62–85). Wiesbaden: VS Verlag.

Linden, M., & Thaa, W. (2014). Ungleichheit und politische Repräsentation. Baden-Baden: Nomos.

Lindner, R., Aichholzer, G., & Hennen, L. (Eds.). (2016). Electronic Democracy in Europe. New York: Springer.

Lindquist, H. (2014). Chapter 1 – The Journey of Reinventing the European Electricity Landscape – Challenges and Pioneers. In L. E. Jones (Ed.), Renewable Energy Integration (pp. 3–12). Boston: Academic Press.

List, C., & Pettit, P. (2013). Group agency. The possibility, design, and status of corporate agents. Oxford: Oxford Univ. Press.

Little, A. (2002). The politics of community. Theory and practice. Edinburgh: Edinburgh Univ. Press.

Livingstone, S., Lunt, P., & Miller, L. (2007). Citizens, consumers and the citizen-consumer. Articulating the citizen interest in media and communications regulation. Discourse & Communication, 1 (1), 63–89.

Lockie, S. (2009). Responsibility and agency within alternative food networks. Assembling the "citizen consumer". Agriculture and Human Values, 26 (3), 193–201.

Löhle, C. (2012). Direkte Demokratie – Motor oder Bremse für die Energiewende. eNewsletter Wegweiser Bürgergesellschaft, 10, 1–8.

Lohmann, G. (2003). Demokratische Zivilgesellschaft und Bürgertugenden in Ost und West. Frankfurt a. M.: Lang.

Loorbach, D. (2007). Transition Management: New mode of governance for sustainable development. Utrecht: International Books.

Loorbach, D. (2010). Transition Management for Sustainable Development. A Prescriptive, Complexity-Based Governance Framework. Governance, 23, 161–183.

Lopes, M. A. R., Antunes, C. H., & Martins, N. (2012). Energy behaviours as promoters of energy efficiency. A 21st century review. Renewable and Sustainable Energy Reviews, 16 (6), 4095–4104.

Löschel, A., Flues, F., Pothen, & Massier, P. (2015). Der deutsche Strommarkt im Umbruch. Zur Notwendigkeit einer neuen Marktordnung. In H. J. Ramser (Ed.), Entwicklung und Perspektiven der Wirtschaftswissenschaft. Wirtschaftswissenschaftliches Seminar Ottobeuren, Band 41. Tübingen: Mohr Siebeck.

Lotter, W. (2013). Zivilkapitalismus. Wir können auch anders. München: Pantheon.

Lövbrand, E., Beck, S., Chilvers, J., Forsyth, T., Hedrén, J., Hulme, M., Lidskog, R., & Vasileiadou, E. (2015). Who speaks for the future of Earth? How critical social science can extend the conversation on the Anthropocene. Global Environmental Change, 32, 211–218.

Lovins, A. B. (1977). Soft Energy Paths. Toward a Durable Peace. Hamondsworth: Penguin Books.

Lowitzsch, J., Hanisch, S., & Hans-Böckler-Stiftung (Eds.). (2014). Mitarbeiterbeteiligung unter Verwendung einer Beteiligungsgesellschaft – Gestaltung und Finanzierungsansätze. Düsseldorf: Hans-Böckler-Stiftung.

Luck, E., & Ginanti, A. (2013). Online environmental citizenship. Blogs, green marketing and consumer sentiment in the 21st century. Electronic Green Journal, 1 (35), 1–26.

Lüdeke-Freud, F., & Opel, O. (2014). Energie. In H. Heinrichs & G. Michelsen (Eds.), Nachhaltigkeitswissenschaften (pp. 429–453). Berlin: Springer Spektrum.

Lüdicke, J. (2007). Einleitung. In J. Lüdicke & M. Diewald (Eds.), Soziale Netzwerke und soziale Ungleichheit. Zur Rolle von Sozialkapital in modernen Gesellschaften (pp. 7–10). Wiesbaden: VS Verlag.

Luhmann, N. (1983). Legitimation durch Verfahren. Frankfurt a. M.: Suhrkamp.

Luhmann, N. (2008). Die Soziologie und der Mensch (3rd ed.). Wiesbaden: VS Verlag.

Luhmann, N. (2009). Beiträge zur funktionalen Differenzierung der Gesellschaft (4th ed.). Wiesbaden: VS Verlag.

Luhmann, N. (2014). Vertrauen. Ein Mechanismus der Reduktion sozialer Komplexität (5th ed.). Konstanz: UVK.

Luks, F., & Siebenhüner, B. (2007). Transdisciplinarity for social learning? The contribution of the German socio-ecological research initiative to sustainability governance. Ecological Economics, 63 (2-3), 418–426.

Lund, H. (Ed.). (2014). Renewable Energy Systems. A Smart Energy Systems Approach to the Choice and Modeling of 100% Renewable Solutions (2nd ed.). Amsterdam: Academic Press/Elsevier.

Lund, H., Hvelplund, F., Østergaard, P., Möller, B., Mathiesen, B. V., Connolly, D., & Andersen, A. N. (2014). Chapter 6 – Analysis: Smart Energy Systems and Infrastructures. In H. Lund (Ed.), Renewable Energy Systems (2nd ed.) (pp. 131–184). Boston: Academic Press.

Lüttringhaus, M. (2000). Stadtentwicklung und Partizipation. Fallstudien aus Essen Katernberg und der Dresdner äußeren Neustadt. Bonn: Stiftung Mitarbeit.

Lüttringhaus, M. (2003). Voraussetzungen für Aktivierung und Partizipation. In M. Lüttringhaus & H. Richers (Eds.), Handbuch aktivierende Befragung. Konzepte, Erfahrungen, Tipps für die Praxis. (pp. 66–72). Bonn: Stiftung Mitarbeit.

Lutz, K., Rösch, E., & Seitz, D. (Eds.). (2012). Partizipation und Engagement im Netz. Neue Chancen für Demokratie und Medienpädagogik. München: kopaed.

Maas, W., & Madrazo, F. (2013). City Shock. Planning the Unexpect. Rotterdam: nai010 Publishers.

Maaser, W. (2010). Reformpolitische Leitbilder des Engagementbegriffs. Systematischhistorische Dimensionen. In T. Olk, A. Klein, & B. Hartnuß (Eds.), Engagementpolitik (pp. 153–171). Wiesbaden: VS Verlag.

MacAskill, W. (2015). Doing Good Better. How Effective Altruism Can Help You Make a Difference. New York: Gotham Books.

Macdonald, T. (2012). Citizens or stakeholders? Exclusion equality and legitimacy in global stakeholder democracy. In D. Archibugi, M. Koenig-Archibugi, & R. Marchetti (Eds.), Global Democracy. Normative and Empirical Perspectives (pp. 47–68). Cambridge: Cambridge University Press.

Macedo, S. (2005). Democracy at risk. How political choices undermine citizen participation and what we can do about it. Washington, D.C.: Brookings Institution Press.

MacGillivray, B. H., & Franklin, A. (2015). Place as a boundary device for the sustainability sciences. Concepts of place, their value in characterising sustainability problems, and their role in fostering integrative research and action. Environmental Science & Policy, 53 (Part A), 1–7.

MacGregor, S. (2014). Ecological citizenship. In H.-A. van der Heijden (Ed.), Handbook of Political Citizenship and Social Movements (pp. 107–132). Northampton, MA: Edward Elgar.

Magnani, N., & Osti, G. (2016). Does civil society matter? Challenges and strategies of grassroots initiatives in Italy's energy transition. Energy Research & Social Science, 13, 148–157.

Magnani, N., & Vaona, A. (2016). Access to electricity and socio-economic characteristics: Panel data evidence at the country level. *Energy, 103*, 447–455. https://doi.org/10.1016/j.energy.2016.02.106

Majhanovich, S., & Malet, R. (Eds.). (2015). Building Democracy through Education on Diversity. Rotterdam: SensePublishers.

Maloney, W. A., & Roßteutscher, S. (Eds.). (2007). Social Capital and Associations in European Democracies. A comparative analysis. London: Routledge.

Maloney, W. A., & Deth, J. W. van. (2010). Civil society and activism in Europe. Contextualizing engagement and political orientations. London: Routledge.

Malowitz, K. (2002). Freiheit in Gemeinschaft. Zu Rezeption und Bedeutung der Gemeinwohlidee in der Genossenschaftstheorie Otto von Gierkes. In H. Münkler & K. Fischer (Eds.), Gemeinwohl und Gemeinsinn im Recht. Konkretisierung und Realisierung öffentlicher Interessen (pp. 141–165). Berlin: Akademie Verlag.

Mans, U., & Kayser, L. (2013). Bürgerschaft und dezentrale Energieversorgung. In K. Töpfer, D. Volkert, & Mans (Eds.), Verändern durch Wissen. Chancen und Herausforderungen demokratischer Beteiligung. Von „Stuttgart 21" bis zur Energiewende (pp. 159–171). München: Oekom.

Mansbridge, J. (1999). On the idea that participation makes better citizens. In S. L. Elkin & K. Edward (Eds.), Citizen Competence and Democratic Institutions (pp. 291–325). State College: The Pennsylvania State University Press.

Manske, A. (2007). Zum ungleichen Wert von Sozialkapital – Netzwerke aus einer Perspektive sozialer Praxis. In J. Lüdicke & M. Diewald (Eds.), Soziale Netzwerke und soziale Ungleichheit (pp. 135–161). Wiesbaden: VS Verlag.

Marg, S., Geiges, L., Butzlaff, F., & Walter, F. (2013). Die neue Macht der Bürger. Was motiviert die Protestbewegungen? BP-Gesellschaftsstudie. Reinbek bei Hamburg: Rowohlt.

Marie, T. T. (2016). Public values as essential criteria for public entrepreneurship: Water management in France. *Utilities Policy, 40*, 162–169. https://doi.org/10.1016/j.jup.2016.02.005

Markandya, A., Galarraga, I., & González-Eguino, M. (Eds.). (2011). Handbook of sustainable energy. Cheltenham: Edward Elgar.

Markard, J., Wirth, S., & Truffer, B. (2016). Institutional dynamics and technology legitimacy – A framework and a case study on biogas technology. Research Policy, 45 (1), 330–344.

Märker, O., & Wehner, J. (2011). Online-Bürgerbeteiligung in Kommunen. Anfänge – Aktuelle Verfahren – Weiterführende Fragen. Forum Wohnen und Stadtentwicklung, 3 (4), 201–207.

Maron, H., & Maron, B. (2012). Genossenschaftliche Unterstützungsstrukturen für eine sozialräumlich orientierte Energiewirtschaft. Machbarkeitsstudie. Köln: Klaus Novy Institut.

Maron, H., & Maron, B. (2013). Genossenschaften als sozialräumliches Phänomen energiewirtschaftlicher Neuausrichtungen. In J. Brazda, M. Dellinger, & D. Rößl (Eds.), Genossenschaften im Fokus einer neuen Wirtschaftspolitik. Bericht der XVII. Internationalen Genossenschaftswissenschaftlichen Tagung (IGT) 2012 in Wien. Teilband 3 (pp. 905–924). Wien: LIT.

Marquart-Pyatt, S. T. (2013). Participation. Public opinion and environmental action. In P. G. Harris (Ed.), Routledge Handbook of Global Environmental Politics (pp. 333–346). London: Routledge Chapman & Hall.

Marres, N. (2012). Material Participation. Technology, the Environment and Everyday Publics. Basingstoke, New York: Palgrave Macmillan.

Martin, C. J., Taylor, P. G., Upham, P., Ghiasi, G., Bale, C. S. E., James, H., Owen, A., Gale, W. F., Slack, R. J., & Helmer, S. (2014). Energy in low carbon cities and social learning. A process for defining priority research questions with UK stakeholders. Sustainable Cities and Society, 10, 149–160.

Martin, N. J., & Rice, J. L. (2012). Developing renewable energy supply in Queensland, Australia. A study of the barriers, targets, policies and actions. Renewable Energy, 44, 119–127.

Martin, R. L., & Osberg, S. (2007). Social entrepreneurship. The case for definition. Stanford Social Innovation Review, 5 (2), 28–39.

Martínez-Alier, J., Pascual, U., Vivien, F.-D., & Zaccai, E. (2010). Sustainable de-growth. Mapping the context, criticisms and future prospects of an emergent paradigm. Ecological Economics, 69 (9), 1741–1747.

Martinsen, R., & Simonis, G. (2000). Demokratie und Technik – (k)eine Wahlverwandtschaft? Opladen: Leske + Budrich.

Martinsson, J., & Lundqvist, L. J. (2010). Ecological citizenship. Coming out "clean" without turning "green"? Environmental Politics, 19 (4), 518–537.
Maruyama, Y., Nishikido, M., & Iida, T. (2007). The rise of community wind power in Japan. Enhanced acceptance through social innovation. Energy Policy, 35 (5), 2761–2769.
Mason, P. (2015). PostCapitalism. A Guide to Our Future. London: Allen Lane.
Masser, K., Pistoia, A., & Nitzsche, P. (2013). Bürgerbeteiligung und Web 2.0. Potentiale und Risiken webgestützter Bürgerhaushalte. Wiesbaden: VS Verlag.
Mather, C. (2009). Thriving during challenging times. The energy, food and financial independence handbook. Tamworth, Canada: Aztext Press.
Mathieu, P. (2005). Tactics of hope. The public turn in English composition. Portsmouth, NH: Boynton/Cook Publishers.
Mattes, J., Huber, A., & Koehrsen, J. (2015). Energy transitions in small-scale regions – What we can learn from a regional innovation systems perspective. Energy Policy, 78, 255–264.
Matthies, E. (2013). Nutzerverhalten im Energiesystem. Erkenntnisse und Forschungsfragen aus der Psychologie. Technikfolgenabschätzung, Theorie und Praxis, 22 (2), 36–42.
Maubach, K.-D. (2014). Energiewende. Wege zu einer bezahlbaren Energieversorgung (2nd ed.). Wiesbaden: Springer VS.
Mautz, R., Byzio, A., & Rosenbaum, W. (2008). Auf dem Weg zur Energiewende. Die Entwicklung der Stromproduktion aus erneuerbaren Energien in Deutschland. Eine Studie aus dem Soziologischen Forschungsinstitut Göttingen (SOFI). Göttingen: Univ.-Verl. Göttingen.
Mayer, A.-T., Schwehr, P., & Bürgin, M. (2011). Nachhaltige Quartiersentwicklung im Fokus flexibler Strukturen. Luzern: vdf Hochsch.-Vlg.
Mayer, H. O. (2012). Interview und schriftliche Befragung. Grundlagen und Methoden empirischer Sozialforschung. München: Oldenbourg.
Mayer, M. (2004). Vom Versprechen lokaler Kohäsion. In F. Kessl & H.-U. Otto (Eds.), Soziale Arbeit und Soziales Kapital (pp. 63–78). Wiesbaden: VS Verlag.
Mayntz, R. (1999). Individuelles Handeln und gesellschaftliche Ereignisse. Zur Mikro-Makro-Problematik in den Sozialwissenschaften. MPIfG Working Paper. Köln: Max-Planck-Institut für Gesellschaftsforschung.
Mayntz, R. (2002). Wohlfahrtsökonomische und systemtheoretische Ansätze zur Bestimmung von Gemeinwohl. In H. Münkler & K. Fischer (Eds.), Gemeinwohl und Gemeinsinn. Rhetoriken und Perspektiven sozial-moralischer Orientierung (pp. 111–127). Berlin: Akademie Verl.
Mayring, P. (2001). Combination and Integration of Qualitative and Quantitative Analysis. Forum Qualitative Sozialforschung/Forum: Qualitative Social Research, 2 (1). http://www.qualitative-research.net/index.php/fqs/article/view/967
Mayring, P. (2015). Qualitative Inhaltsanalyse. Grundlagen und Techniken (12th ed.). Weinheim: Beltz.
Mayring, P., & Fenzl, T. (2014). Qualitative Inhaltsanalyse. In N. Baur & J. Blasius (Eds.), Handbuch Methoden der empirischen Sozialforschung (pp. 543–556). Wiesbaden: Springer VS.
McAfee, A. (2013). Tools for Change. CityPlan Vancouver's Strategic Planning Process. Built Environment, 39 (4), 438–453.

Mc Morran, R., Scott, A. J., & Price, M. F. (2014). Reconstructing sustainability. Participant experiences of community land tenure in North West Scotland. Journal of Rural Studies, 33, 20–31.

McCloskey, D. N. (2006). The bourgeois virtues. Ethics for an age of commerce. Chicago, Ill.: Univ. of Chicago Press.

McCloskey, D. N. (2011). Bourgeois dignity. Why economics can't explain the modern world. Chicago, Ill.: Univ. of Chicago Press.

Mcclymont, K., & O'Hare, P. (2008). "We're not NIMBYs!" Contrasting local protest groups with idealised conceptions of sustainable communities. Local Environment, 13 (4), 321–335.

McComas, K. A., Stedman, R., & Sol Hart, P. (2011). Community support for campus approaches to sustainable energy use. The role of "town-gown" relationships. Energy Policy, 39 (5), 2310–2318.

McDonald, D. A. (2016). To corporatize or not to corporatize (and if so, how?). *Utilities Policy, 40*, 107–114. https://doi.org/10.1016/j.jup.2016.01.002

McDonough, W. J., & Braungart, M. (2009). Cradle to cradle. Remaking the way we make things. London: Vintage Books.

McElroy, M. W. (2002). Social innovation capital. Journal of Intellectual Capital, 3 (1), 30–39.

McKeever, E., Jack, S., & Anderson, A. (2015). Embedded entrepreneurship in the creative re-construction of place. *Journal of Business Venturing, 30*(1), 50–65. https://doi.org/10.1016/j.jbusvent.2014.07.002

McLaren Loring, J. (2007). Wind energy planning in England, Wales and Denmark. Factors influencing project success. Energy Policy, 35 (4), 2648–2660.

McMillan, D. W., & Chavis, D. M. (1986). Sense of community. A definition and theory. Journal of Community Psychology, 14 (1), 6–23.

Meadowcroft, J. (2002). Politics and scale. Some implications for environmental governance. Landscape and Urban Planning, 61 (2-4), 169–179.

Meadowcroft, J. (2009). What about the politics? Sustainable development, transition management, and long term energy transitions. Policy Sciences, 42, 323–340.

Meadows, D. L., Meadows, D. H., Zahn, E., Milling, P., & Heck, H.-D. (1972). Die Grenzen des Wachstums. Bericht des Club of Rome zur Lage der Menschheit. Stuttgart: Dt. Verl.-Anst.

Medjedović, I. (2014). Qualitative Daten für die Sekundäranalyse. In N. Baur & J. Blasius (Eds.), Handbuch Methoden der empirischen Sozialforschung (pp. 223–232). Wiesbaden: Springer VS.

Meinefeld, W. (1997). Ex-ante-Hypothesen in der Qualitativen Sozialforschung. Zwischen „fehl am Platz“ und „unverzichtbar“. Zeitschrift Für Soziologie, 26 (1), 22–34.

Mendonça, M., Lacey, S., & Hvelplund, F. (2009). Stability, participation and transparency in renewable energy policy. Lessons from Denmark and the United States. Policy and Society, 27 (4), 379–398.

Merkel, W., & Petring, A. (2012). Politische Partizipation und demokratische Inklusion. In T. Mörschel & C. Krell (Eds.), Demokratie in Deutschland (pp. 93–119). Wiesbaden: VS Verlag.

Merkel, W. (2015a). Demokratie und Krise. Zum schwierigen Verhältnis von Theorie und Empirie. Wiesbaden: Springer VS.

Merkel, W. (2015b). Nur schöner Schein? Demokratische Innovationen in Theorie und Praxis Frankfurt a.M.: Otto-Brenner-Stiftung.

Merritt, A., & Stubbs, T. (2012). Incentives to Promote Green Citizenship in UK Transition Towns. Development, 55 (1), 96–103.

Mertens, D. M. (2014). Research and evaluation in education and psychology. Integrating diversity with quantitative, qualitative, and mixed methods. Los Angeles: Sage.

Metlay, D. (1999). Institutional trust and confidence. A journey into a conceptual quagmire. In G. Cvetkovich & R. E. Löfstedt (Eds.), Social trust and the management of risk (pp. 100–116). London: Earthscan.

Meusel, S. (2016). *Freiwilliges Engagement und soziale Benachteiligung. Eine biografieanalytische Studie mit Akteuren in schwierigen Lebenslagen.* Bielefeld: Transcript.

Meuser, M., & Nagel, U. (1991). ExpertInneninterviews – vielfach erprobt, wenig bedacht. In D. Garz & K. Kraimer (Eds.), Qualitativ-empirische Sozialforschung (pp. 441–471). Opladen: Westdeutscher Verlag.

Meuser, M., & Nagel, U. (2009). Das Experteninterview – konzeptionelle Grundlagen und methodische Anlage. In S. Pickel, G. Pickel, H.-J. Lauth, & D. Jahn (Eds.), Methoden der vergleichenden Politik- und Sozialwissenschaft (pp. 465–479). Wiesbaden: VS Verlag.

Meuser, M., & Nagel, U. (2013). Experteninterviews. Wissenssoziologische Voraussetzungen und methodische Durchführung. In B. Friebertshäuser & H. Boller, Handbuch qualitative Forschungsmethoden in der Erziehungswissenschaft (4th ed., pp. 457–471). Weinheim u. a.: Beltz Juventa.

Mey, F., & Hicks, J. (2015). *Community renewable energy in Australia: Exploring its character & emergence in the context of climate change action.* 5th EMES International Research Conference on Social Enterprise, 30 June - 3 July 2015, Helsinki, Finland. (Australia). Retrieved from https://apo.org.au/node/233881

Mey, F., Diesendorf, M., & MacGill, I. (2016). Can local government play a greater role for community renewable energy? A case study from Australia. *Energy Research & Social Science, 21*, 33–43. https://doi.org/10.1016/j.erss.2016.06.019

Mey, G., & Mruck, K. (2011). Grounded theory reader. Wiesbaden: VS Verlag.

Meyer, J. M. (2015). Engaging the everyday. Environmental social criticism and the resonance dilemma. Cambridge, Mass.: The MIT Press.

Meyer, T. (2003). Die Bürgerrolle. Citizenship. In T. Meyer (Ed.), Was ist Politik? (pp. 165–170). Wiesbaden: VS Verlag.

Meyermann, A., Gebel, T., & Liebig, S. (2014). Organisationsdaten. In N. Baur & J. Blasius (Eds.), Handbuch Methoden der empirischen Sozialforschung (pp. 959–972). Wiesbaden: Springer VS.

Michael, F. A. (2015). Materials and sustainable development. Waltham, MS: Elsevier.

Micheletti, M. (2003). Political virtue and shopping. Individuals, consumerism and collective action. Basingstoke, New York: Palgrave Macmillan.

Micheletti, M., & McFarland, A. S. (Eds.). (2011). Creative participation. Responsibilitytaking in the political world. Boulder: Paradigm Publ.

Micheletti, M., Føllesdal, A., & Stolle, D. (Eds.). (2004). Politics, products, and markets. Exploring political consumerism past and present. New Brunswick, N.J.: Transaction Publishers.

Micheletti, M., Stolle, D., & Berlin, D. (2012). Habits of Sustainable Citizenship. The Example of Political Consumerism. In A. Warde & D. Southerton (Eds.), The Habits of Consumption. COLLeGIUM. Studies across Disciplines in the Humanities and Social Sciences 12 (pp. 141–163). Helsinki: Helsinki Collegium for Advanced Studies.

Michels, R. (1908). Die oligarchischen Tendenzen der Gesellschaft. Ein Beitrag zum Problem der Demokratie. Archiv Für Sozialwissenschaft und Sozialpolitik, 27, 73–135.

Michels, R. (1911). Zur Soziologie des Parteiwesens in der modernen Demokratie. Untersuchungen über die oligarchischen Tendenzen des Gruppenlebens. Leipzig: Klinkhardt.

Michelsen, D., & Walter, F. (2013). Unpolitische Demokratie. Zur Krise der Repräsentation. Berlin: Suhrkamp.

Michelsen, G., & Godemann, J. (2007). Handbuch Nachhaltigkeitskommunikation. Grundlagen und Praxis (2nd ed.). München: Oekom.

Michelsen, G., Grunenberg, H., Mader, C., & Barth, M. (2016). Nachhaltigkeit bewegt die jüngere Generation Greenpeace. Nachhaltigkeitsbarometer 2015. Bad Homburg: VAS.

Michie, J., Blassi, J., & Borzaga, C. (Eds.). (2015). The Oxford Handbook for Cooperative and Mutual Business. Oxford: Oxford University Press.

Micklethwait, J., & Wooldridge, A. (2014). The Fourth Revolution. The Global Race to Reinvent the State. New York: Allen Lane.

Middlemiss, L., & Parrish, B. D. (2010). Building capacity for low-carbon communities. The role of grassroots initiatives. Energy Policy, 38 (12), 7559–7566.

Miessen, M. (2012). Albtraum Partizipation. Berlin: Merve.

Milbrath, L. W. (1965). Political participation: How and why do people get involved in politics? Chicago: Rand McNally.

Miller, C. A., O'Leary, J., Graffy, E., Stechel, E. B., & Dirks, G. (2015a). Narrative futures and the governance of energy transitions. Futures, 70, 65–74.

Miller, C. A., Richter, J., & O'Leary, J. (2015b). Socio-energy systems design. A policy framework for energy transitions. Energy Research & Social Science, 6, 29–40.

Miller, M. (2015). *The Internet of Things: How Smart TVs, Smart Cars, Smart Homes, and Smart Cities Are Changing the World.* Que Publishing.

Mills, T. M. (1967). The sociology of small groups. Englewood Cliffs, NJ: Prentice-Hall.

Misztal, B. A. (1996). Trust in modern societies. The search for the bases of social order. Cambridge: Polity Press.

Mitchell, D. (2003). The Right to the City. Social Justice and the Fight for Public Space. New York: Guilford Press.

Mitchell, T. (2013). Carbon Democracy. Political Power in the Age of Oil. London: Verso.

Mitschke-Collande, T. von. (1977). Der Einfluß der Mitbestimmung. Ein Konzept zur empirischen Messung. München: Universität München.

Mittelbach, G. G., & Schemske, D. W. (2015). Ecological and evolutionary perspectives on community assembly. Trends in Ecology & Evolution, 30 (5), 241–247.

Mittler, D. (2015). Die Klimapolitik ist in – und braucht – Bewegung. Reaktion auf vier Beiträge zum Thema Klimaschutz als Weltbürgerbewegung in GAIA: A. Brunnengräber (2014), C. Leggewie et al. (2015), S. Bauriedl (2015), B. Unmüßig (2015). GAIA – Ecological Perspectives for Science and Society, 24 (4), 228–231.

Mol, A. (2009). Good taste. The embodied normativity of the consumer-citizen. Journal of Cultural Economy, 2 (3), 269–283.

Moldaschl, M. (2004). Partizipation und/als/statt Demokratie. Zum Entwicklungsverhältnis von gesellschaftlicher Demokratisierung und organisationaler Partizipation. Weber et al. (2004), 216–245.

Moldaschl, M. F., & Weber, W. G. (2009). Trägt organisationale Partizipation zur gesellschaftlichen Demokratisierung bei? Journal Für Entwicklungspolitik, 25 (3), 87–112.

Montag, T. (2011). „Direkte Demokratie" und Parlamentarismus. Argumente und Positionen. Sankt Augustin/Berlin: Konrad-Adenauer-Stiftung.

Montefrio, M. J. F., Sonnenfeld, D. A., & Luzadis, V. A. (2015). Social construction of the environment and smallholder farmers' participation in 'low-carbon', agro-industrial crop production contracts in the Philippines. *Ecological Economics, 116*, 70–77. https://doi.org/10.1016/j.ecolecon.2015.04.017

Moore, M.-L., & Westley, F. (2011). Surmountable chasms. Networks and social innovation for resilient systems. Ecology and Society, 16 (1), 1–13.

Moore, S., & Hackett, E. J. (2016). The construction of technology and place. Concentrating solar power conflicts in the United States. Energy Research & Social Science, 11, 67–78.

Moretti, F. (2014). Der Bourgeois. Eine Schlüsselfigur der Moderne. Berlin: Suhrkamp.

Mori, P. A. (2014). Community and Cooperation. The Evolution of Cooperatives Towards New Models of Citizens' Democratic Participation in Public Services Provision. Annals of Public and Cooperative Economics, 85 (3), 327–352.

Morris, D. (1982). Self-reliant cities. Energy and the transformation of urban America. San Francisco, Calif.: Sierra Club Books.

Morris, D. (2001). Seeing the light. Regaining control of our electricity system. Minneapolis, MN: Institute for Local Self-Reliance.

Moser, C., Rösch, A., & Stauffacher, M. (2015). Exploring Societal Preferences for Energy Sufficiency Measures in Switzerland. Frontiers in Energy Research, 3, 1–12.

Moser, P. (2011). Wegweiser für eine dezentrale Energieversorgung. 100% Erneuerbare-Energie-Regionen in Deutschland. Ökologisches Wirtschaften, 3, 16–18.

Moss, T., & Francesch-Huidobro, M. (2016). Realigning the electric city. Legacies of energy autarky in Berlin and Hong Kong. Energy Research & Social Science, 11, 225–236.

Moss, T., & Newig, J. (2010). Multilevel Water Governance and Problems of Scale. Setting the Stage for a Broader Debate. Environmental Management, 46 (1), 1–6.

Moss, T., Becker, S., & Naumann, M. (2015). Whose energy transition is it, anyway? Organisation and ownership of the „Energiewende" in villages, cities and regions. Local Environment, 20, 1547–1563.

Mouffe, C. (2011). „Postdemokratie" und die zunehmende Entpolitisierung. Aus Politik Und Zeitgeschichte APuZ, 1-2, 3–5.

Moulaert, F., Swyngedouw, E., Martinelli, F., & Gonzalez, S. (Eds.). (2010a). Can neighbourhoods save the city? Community Development and Social Innovation. Abdingdon, New York: Routledge.

Moulaert, F. (2010). Social innovation and community development: Concepts, theories and challenges. In F. Moulaert, E. Swyngedouw, F. Martinelli, & S. Gonzalez (Eds.), *Can Neighbourhoods Save the City?* (pp. 20–32). London: Routledge. https://doi.org/10.4324/9780203849132

Moulaert, F. (2013). The international handbook on social innovation. Collective action, social learning and transdisciplinary research. Cheltenham: Edward Elgar.

Moulaert, F., & MacCallum, D. (2009). Social innovation. Institutionally embedded, territorially (re) produced. In D. MacCallum, F. Moulaert, J. Hillier & S. V. Haddock, Social Innovation and Territorial Development (pp. 11–23). Farnham: Ashgate.

Moulaert, F., Martinelli, F., González, S., & Swyngedouw, E. (2007). Introduction. Social innovation and governance in european cities urban development between path dependency and radical innovation. European Urban and Regional Studies, 14 (3), 195–209.

Moulaert, F., Swyngedouw, E., Martinelli, F., & Gonzalez, S. (2010b). Can neighbourhoods save the city? Community development and social innovation. Abingdon, New York: Routledge.

Mudasser, M., Yiridoe, E. K., & Corscadden, K. (2013). Economic feasibility of large community feed-in tariff-eligible wind energy production in Nova Scotia. Energy Policy, 62, 966–977.

Mulder, M. (1977). The daily power game. Leiden: Nijhoff.

Mulgan, G. (2006). The process of social innovation. Innovations, 1 (2), 145–162.

Mulgan, G., Tucker, S., Ali, R., & Sanders, B. (2007). Social innovation. What it is, why it matters and how it can be accelerated. London: The Young Foundation. http://youngfoundation.org/publications/social-innovation-what-it-is-why-it-matters-how-it-can-be-accelerated/

Müller-Christ, G. (2012). Nachhaltiges Management aus der Entscheidungsperspektive. Restitutionskosten, Jetzt-für-dann-Entscheidungen und Trade-offs. In H. Corsten & S. Roth (Eds.), Nachhaltigkeit (pp. 51–66). Wiesbaden: Springer Gabler.

Müller, C., & Szynka, P. (2010). Community Organizing. Enzyklopädie Erziehungswissenschaft Online. Weinheim: Beltz.

Müller, J. R., & Holstenkamp, L. (2015). Zum Stand von Energiegenossenschaften in Deutschland. Aktualisierter Überblick über Zahlen und Entwicklungen zum 31.12.2014. Arbeitspapierreihe Wirtschaft & Recht Nr. 20. Lüneburg: Leuphana Universität.

Müller, J. R., Dorniok, D., Flieger, B., Holstenkamp, L., Mey, F., & Radtke, J. (2015). Energiegenossenschaften in Deutschland – ein Modell mit Zukunft? Beobachtungen, Erklärungen, Prognosen. GAIA – Ecological Perspectives for Science and Society, 24 (2), 96–101.

Müller, J., Rommel, J. (2011). Is There a Future Role for Urban Electricity Cooperatives? The case of Greenpeace Energy. In J. Ramos-Martín, M. Giampietro, S. Ulgiati, S. G. F. Bukkens (2011) (Eds.), Can We Break the Addiction to Fossil Energy? Proceedings of the 7th Biennial International Workshop Advances in Energy Studies Barcelona, Spain, 19–21 October 2010 (pp. 185–195). Barcelona: Universitat Autònoma de Barcelona. http://www.societalmetabolism.org/aes2010/Proceeds/DIGITALPROCEEDINGS_files/PAPERS/O_144_Mueller_Rommel.pdf

Müller, J. R., & Sagebiel, J. (2015). Machen Genossenschaften Ökostrom wertvoller? Zeitschrift für öffentliche und gemeinwirtschaftliche Unternehmen, 38, 226–237.

Müller, K. (2014). Regionale Energiewende. Akteure und Prozesse in Erneuerbare-Energie-Regionen. Frankfurt a. M.: PL Academic Research.

Müller, M. O., Stämpfli, A., Dold, U., & Hammer, T. (2011). Energy autarky. A conceptual framework for sustainable regional development. Energy Policy, 39 (10), 5800–5810.

Müller, T., & Kahl, H. (Eds.). (2015). Energiewende im Föderalismus. Baden-Baden: Nomos.

Müller, C. von, & Zinth, C.-P. (Eds.). (2014). *Managementperspektiven für die Zivilgesellschaft des 21. Jahrhunderts: Management als Liberal Art*. Wiesbaden: Springer Gabler.
Mullis, D. (2014). Recht auf die Stadt. Von Selbstverwaltung und radikaler Demokratie. Münster: Unrast.
Mumford, M. D., & Moertl, P. (2003). Cases of social innovation. Lessons from two innovations in the 20th century. Creativity Research Journal, 15 (2-3), 261–266.
Münch, S. (2015). Interpretative Policy-Analyse. Eine Einführung. Wiesbaden: Springer VS.
Müngersdorff, M., Hanusch, F., Schad, M., Voss, E., Schönborn, S., Schmitt, L., & Siepmann, M. (2015). Building Europe's (Energy) Future. A manifesto for an European Community for Energy Transition. Essen: Kulturwissenschaftliches Institut (KWI). http://www.kulturwissenschaften.de/images/text_material-3005.img
Münkler, H. (1994). Zivilgesellschaft und Bürgertugend – Bedürfen demokratisch verfasste Gemeinwesen einer sozio-moralischen Fundierung? Antrittsvorlesung 10. Mai 1993. Berlin: Humboldt-Universität zu Berlin.
Münkler, H. (1997). Der kompetente Bürger. In A. Klein & R. Schmalz-Bruns (Eds.), Politische Beteiligung und Bürgerengagement in Deutschland (pp. 153–172). Bonn: Bundeszentrale für Politische Bildung.
Münkler, H. (2000). Ehre, Amt und Engagement. Wie kann die knappe Ressource Bürgersinn gesichert werden? Forschungsjournal Soziale Bewegungen, 13 (2), 22–32.
Münkler, H. (2001). Bürgersinn und Bürgerehre. Warum die Zivilgesellschaft engagierte Bürger braucht. Universitas. Orientierung in der Wissenswelt, 56, 1220–1233.
Münkler, H. (2002). Neue Oligarchien? Über den jüngsten Wandel der Demokratie unter dem Einfluß von neuen Medien und veränderter Bürgerpartizipation. In H. Münkler & I. Fetscher (Eds.), Der demokratische Nationalstaat in den Zeiten der Globalisierung. Politische Leitideen für das 21. Jahrhundert. Festschrift zum 80. Geburtstag von Iring Fetscher (pp. 163–174). Berlin: Akad.-Verl.
Münkler, H., & Krause, S. (2001). Der aktive Bürger – Eine Gestalt der politischen Theorie im Wandel. In C. Leggewie & R. Münch (Eds.), Politik im 21. Jahrhundert (pp. 299–320). Frankfurt a. M.: Suhrkamp.
Münkler, H., & Loll, A. (2005). Das Dilemma von Tugend und Freiheit. Die Notwendigkeit von Eigenverantwortung in einer funktionierenden Bürgergesellschaft. Bonn: Friedrich-Ebert-Stiftung.
Münkner, H.-H. (2012). Potenziale des Genossenschaftswesens für eine nachhaltigere und sozial gerechtere Wirtschaftsweise. Fachgespräch Friedrich Ebert Stiftung, Arbeitskreis Mittelstand. Berlin. http://www.fes.de/wiso/pdf/mittel-stand/2012/300312/Muenkner.pdf
Muno, W. (2009). Fallstudien und die vergleichende Methode. In S. Pickel, G. Pickel, H.-J. Lauth, & D. Jahn (Eds.), Methoden der vergleichenden Politik- und Sozialwissenschaft (pp. 113–131). Wiesbaden: VS Verlag.
Munsch, C. (2005). Wie Engagement soziale Ausgrenzung reproduziert. Forschungsjournal Soziale Bewegungen, 3, 108–114.
Murphy, J. (Ed.). (2007). Governing technology for sustainability. London, Sterling, VA: Earthscan.
Murray, R., Caulier-Grice, J., & Mulgan, G. (2010). The open book of social innovation. National endowment for science, technology and the art. London: NESTA. https://www.nesta.org.uk/sites/default/files/the_open_book_of_social_innovation.pdf

Musall, F. D., & Kuik, O. (2011). Local acceptance of renewable energy – A case study from southeast Germany. Energy Policy, 39 (6), 3252–3260.

Mutz, D. C. (2008). Is Deliberative Democracy a Falsifiable Theory? Annual Review of Political Science, 11 (1), 521–538.

Nabatchi, T., & Leighninger, M. (2015). Public Participation for 21st Century Democracy. Hoboken: Wiley.

Nabil, N. A., & Eldayem, G. E. A. (2015). Influence of mixed land-use on realizing the social capital. HBRC Journal, 11 (2), 285–298.

Nachreiner, M., & Matthies, E. (2016). Enhancing informational strategies for supporting residential electricity saving. Identifying potential and household characteristics in Germany. Energy Research & Social Science, 11, 276–287.

Nanz, P., & Fritsche, M. (Eds.) (2012). Handbuch Bürgerbeteiligung. Verfahren und Akteure, Chancen und Grenzen. Bonn: Bundeszentrale für Politische Bildung.

Nanz, P., & Leggewie, C. (2016). Die Konsultative. Mehr Demokratie durch Bürgerbeteiligung. Berlin: Verlag Klaus Wagenbach.

Nash, N., Lewis, A., & Griffin, C. (2010). "Not in our front garden". Land use conflict, spatial meaning and the politics of naming place. Journal of Community & Applied Social Psychology, 20 (1), 44–56.

National Democratic Institute (Ed.). (2014). *Citizen Participation and Technology: An NDI Study*. Washington, D.C. https://www.ndi.org/files/Citizen-Participation-and-Technology-an-NDI-Study.pdf

Naumann, S. (2010). Bildungsprozesse in bürgerschaftlichen Initiativen. Eine empirische Studie zur Transformation konjunktiver Orientierungen. Wiesbaden: VS Verlag.

Naus, J., Spaargaren, G., van Vliet, B. J. M., & van der Horst, H. M. (2014). Smart grids, information flows and emerging domestic energy practices. Energy Policy, 68, 436–446.

Navis, C., & Glynn, M. A. (2010). How New Market Categories Emerge. Temporal Dynamics of Legitimacy, Identity, and Entrepreneurship in Satellite Radio, 1990–2005. Administrative Science Quarterly, 55 (3), 439–471.

Navis, C., & Glynn, M. A. (2011). Legitimate Distinctiveness and The Entrepreneurial Identity. Influence on Investor Judgments of New Venture Plausibility. Academy of Management Review, 36 (3), 479–499.

Nelson, M. R., Rademacher, M. A., & Paek, H.-J. (2007). Downshifting consumer = upshifting citizen? An examination of a local freecycle community. The Annals of the American Academy of Political and Social Science, 611 (1), 141–156.

Nelson, T., Nelson, D., Huybrechts, B., Dufays, F., O'shea, N., & Trasciani, G. (2019). Emergent identity formation and the co-operative: Theory building in relation to alternative organizational forms. In C. M. Leitch & R. T. Harrison (Eds.), *Entrepreneurial Identity and Identity Work* (pp. 110–134). London: Routledge. https://doi.org/10.4324/9781315193069-6

Neuberger, O., Conradi, W., & Maier, W. (1985). Individuelles Handeln und sozialer Einfluss. Einführung in die Sozialpsychologie. Opladen: Westdeutscher Verlag.

Neuhoff, K., Diekmann, J., Kunz, F., Rüster, S., Schill, W.-P., & Schwenen, S. (2016). A coordinated strategic reserve to safeguard the European energy transition. *Utilities Policy, 41*, 252–263. https://doi.org/10.1016/j.jup.2016.02.002

Neunecker, M. (2016). Partizipation trifft Repräsentation. Die Wirkungen konsultativer Bürgerbeteiligung auf politische Entscheidungen. Wiesbaden: Springer VS.

Nève, D. de. (2013). Politische Partizipation jenseits der Konventionen. Opladen: Leske + Budrich.

Neves, A. R., Leal, V., & Lourenço, J. C. (2015). A methodology for sustainable and inclusive local energy planning. Sustainable Cities and Society, 17, 110–121.

Newig, J. (2011). Partizipation und neue Formen der Governance. In M. Groß (Ed.), Handbuch Umweltsoziologie (pp. 485–502). Wiesbaden: VS Verlag.

Newig, J. (2013). Produktive Funktionen von Kollaps und Zerstörung für gesellschaftliche Transformationsprozesse in Richtung Nachhaltigkeit. In J. Rückert-John (Ed.), Soziale Innovation und Nachhaltigkeit (pp. 133–149). Wiesbaden: Springer VS.

Newig, J. (2014). Kommunikation, Partizipation und digitale Medien. In H. Heinrichs & G. Michelsen (Eds.), Nachhaltigkeitswissenschaften (pp. 381–397). Berlin: Springer Spektrum.

Newig, J., & Fritsch, O. (2009). More input, better output. Does citizen involvement improve environmental governance? In I. Blühdorn (Ed.), In search of legitimacy. Policy making in Europe and the challenge of complexity (pp. 205–224). Opladen u. a.: Barbara Budrich.

Newig, J., Jager, N. W., & Challies, E. (2012). Führt Bürgerbeteiligung in umweltpolitischen Entscheidungsprozessen zu mehr Effektivität und Legitimität? Zeitschrift für Politikwissenschaft, 22 (4), 527–564.

Newig, J., Kochskämper, E., Challies, E., & Jager, N. W. (2016). Exploring governance learning. How policymakers draw on evidence, experience and intuition in designing participatory flood risk planning. Environmental Science & Policy, 55 (2), 353–360.

Newig, J., Kuhn, K., & Heinrichs, H. (2011). Nachhaltige Entwicklung durch gesellschaftliche Partizipation und Kooperation? – eine kritische Revision zentraler Theorien und Konzepte. In H. Heinrichs, K. Kuhn, & J. Newig (Eds.), Nachhaltige Gesellschaft (pp. 27–45). Wiesbaden: VS Verlag.

Newsham, G. R., & Donnelly, C. L. (2013). A model of residential energy end-use in Canada. Using conditional demand analysis to suggest policy options for community energy planners. Energy Policy, 59, 133–142.

Nicholls, A., & Murdock, A. (2011). Social innovation. Blurring boundaries to reconfigure markets. Basingstoke, New York: Palgrave Macmillan.

Nida-Rümelin, J. (2013). Was ist Demokratie? In U. Davy (Ed.), Demokratie morgen. Überlegungen aus Wissenschaft und Politik (pp. 17–35). Bielefeld: Transcript.

Nie, N. H., Powell, G. B., & Prewitt, K. (1969a). Social Structure and Political Participation: Developmental Relationships, Part I. The American Political Science Review, 63 (2), 361–378.

Nie, N. H., Powell, G. B., & Prewitt, K. (1969b). Social Structure and Political Participation: Developmental Relationships, Part II. The American Political Science Review, 63 (3), 808–832.

Niedenhoff, H.-U. (2005). Mitbestimmung in der Bundesrepublik Deutschland: Aufsichtsrat, Aufsichtsratswahl, Betriebsrat, Betriebsratswahl, Beratung, Betriebspartner, Betriebsvereinbarung, Betriebsversammlung, Einigungsstelle, Europäischer Betriebsrat, Gesetze, Information, Interessenausgleich, Jugend- und Auszubildendenvertretung, Konfliktlösung, Kosten, Qualifikation, Sozialpartner, Sprecherausschuss, Sprecherausschusswahlen, Verhandlungen, Verhaltensregeln, Wahlen, Wirtschaftsausschuss, Zusammenarbeit (14th ed.). Köln: Deutscher Instituts-Verlag.

Niedermayer, O. (2014a). Parteimitglieder in Deutschland. Version 2014. Berlin: Freie Universität Berlin.
Niedermayer, O. (2014b). Parteimitgliedschaften im Jahre 2013. Zeitschrift für Parlamentsfragen, 2, 416–439.
Niedermayer, O., Höhne, B., & Jun, U. (Eds.). (2013). Abkehr von den Parteien? Parteiendemokratie und Bürgerprotest. Wiesbaden: Springer VS.
Nitschke, P. (Ed.). (2005). Die freiwillige Gesellschaft. Über das Ehrenamt in Deutschland. Frankfurt a. M.: Lang.
Nobis, T. (2012). Politische Sozialisationsleistungen von Freiwilligenvereinigungen. Berlin: Humboldt Universität zu Berlin, Philosophische Fakultät III.
Noetzel, T., Krumm, T., & Westle, B. (2009). Dokumentenanalyse. In B. Westle (Ed.), Methoden der Politikwissenschaft (pp. 325–333). Baden-Baden: Nomos.
Nohl, A.-M. (2012). Interview und dokumentarische Methode. Anleitungen für die Forschungspraxis (4th ed.). Wiesbaden: VS Verlag.
Nolden, C. (2013). Governing community energy – Feed-in tariffs and the development of community wind energy schemes in the United Kingdom and Germany. Energy Policy, 63, 543–552.
Nolte, C. (2013). Die genossenschaftliche Governance als Marke. In J. Brazda, M. Dellinger, & D. Rößl (Eds.), Genossenschaften im Fokus einer neuen Wirtschaftspolitik. Bericht der XVII. Internationalen Genossenschaftswissenschaftlichen Tagung (IGT) 2012 in Wien. Teilband 2 (pp. 431–448). Wien: LIT.
Nolte, P. (2003). Zivilgesellschaft und soziale Ungleichheit. Forschungsjournal Soziale Bewegungen, 2, 38–46.
Nolte, P. (2011). Von der repräsentativen zur multiplen Demokratie. Aus Politik und Zeitgeschichte APuZ, 61 (1-2), 5–12.
Nolte, P., Darbishire, H., & Möllers, C. (Eds.). (2014). Weil Demokratie sich ändern muss: im Gespräch mit Paul Nolte, Helen Darbishire, Christoph Möllers. Wiesbaden: Springer VS.
Nonn, T. (2012). Mitgliederorientierung in Großgenossenschaften. Gelebtes Selbstverständnis am Beispiel der REWE-Group. In G. Ringle & H.-M. Münkner (Eds.), Genossenschaftliche Kooperation – anders wirtschaften (pp. 175–186). Baden-Baden: Nomos.
Nordic Council of Ministers, Nordic Council of Ministers Secretariat. (2015). Social entrepreneurship and social innovation in the Nordic countries. Initiatives to promote social entrepreneurship and social innovation. Copenhagen.
Norris, P. (2011). Democratic Deficit. Cambridge u. a.: Cambridge University Press.
North, P. (2015). The business of the Anthropocene? Substantivist and diverse economies perspectives on SME engagement in local low carbon transitions. Progress in Human Geography, 17. Mai 2015, 1–18.
North, P., & Longhurst, N. (2012). Beyond the rural idyll. Political strategies of urban "Transition" initiatives. 3S Working Paper 2012-07. Norwich: Science, Society and Sustainability Research Group.
Notz, G. (2000). Ehre(n)Amt und Arbeit. Wer ist der Engagierteste im Land? Forschungsjournal Soziale Bewegungen, 2, 48–58.
Nowak, E., Schrader, D. E., & Zizek, B. (Eds.). (2013). Educating Competencies for Democracy. Frankfurt a. M.: Lang.
Nullmeier, F. (2002). Vergesst die Bürgergesellschaft?! Forschungsjournal Soziale Bewegungen, 4, 13–20.

Nulman, E. (2015). Climate change and social movements. Civil society and the development of national climate change policy. Basingstoke, New York: Palgrave Macmillan.
Nunes, J. A., & de Sousa Santos, B. (Eds.) (2006). Reinventing Democracy. Grassroots Movements in Portugal. Abingdon, New York: Routledge.
Obinger, H., Starke, P., Moser, J., Bogedan, C., Gindulis, E., & Leibfried, S. (2010). Transformations of the welfare state. Small states, big lessons. Oxford: Oxford Univ. Press.
Obst, P. L., & White, K. M. (2005). An exploration of the interplay between psychological sense of community, social identification and salience. Journal of Community & Applied Social Psychology, 15 (2), 127–135.
Offe, C. (Ed.) (2003a). Demokratisierung der Demokratie. Diagnosen und Reformvorschläge. Frankfurt a. M., New York: Campus.
Offe, C. (2003b). Herausforderungen der Demokratie. Zur Integrations- und Leistungsfähigkeit politischer Institutionen. Frankfurt a. M., New York: Campus.
Offe, C. (2006). Strukturprobleme des kapitalistischen Staates. Aufsätze zur Politischen Soziologie. Frankfurt a. M., New York: Campus.
Offe, C. (2014). Participatory inequality in the austerity state. A supply side approach. Working Paper 1/2014 der DFG-KollegforscherInnengruppe Postwachstumsgesellschaften.
Ohlhorst, D. (2009). *Windenergie in Deutschland: Konstellationen, Dynamiken und Regulierungspotenziale im Innovationsprozess* (1. Aufl.). Wiesbaden: VS, Verl. für Sozialwiss.
Ohlhorst, D. D., Tews, K., & Schreurs, P. D. M. (2014). Energiewende als Herausforderung der Koordination im Mehrebenensystem. In A. Brunnengräber & M. R. Di Nucci (Eds.), Im Hürdenlauf zur Energiewende (pp. 93–104). Wiesbaden: Springer VS.
Öhlinger, T., & Poier, K. (2015). Direkte Demokratie und Parlamentarismus. Wie kommen wir zu den besten Entscheidungen? Wien: Böhlau.
Ohlmeier, B., & Brunold, A. (2015). Politische Bildung für nachhaltige Entwicklung. Eine Evaluationsstudie. Wiesbaden: Springer VS.
Okkonen, L., & Lehtonen, O. (2016). Socio-economic impacts of community wind power projects in Northern Scotland. Renewable Energy, 85, 826–833.
Oliver, J. E. (2000). City Size and Civic Involvement in Metropolitan America. American Political Science Review, 94 (02), 361–373.
Oliver, J. E., Ha, S. E., & Callen, Z. (Eds.). (2012). Local elections and the politics of small-scale democracy. Princeton, N.J.: Princeton University Press.
Olk, T., & Gensicke, T. (Eds.). (2014). Bürgerschaftliches Engagement in Ostdeutschland. Stand und Perspektiven. Wiesbaden: VS Verlag.
Olk, T., & Hartnuß, B. (2011). Bürgerschaftliches Engagement. In T. Olk & B. Hartnuß (Eds.), Handbuch Bürgerschaftliches Engagement (pp. 145–161). Weinheim u. a.: Beltz Juventa.
Olk, T., Klein, A., & Hartnuß, B. (Eds.). (2010). Engagementpolitik. Die Entwicklung der Zivilgesellschaft als politische Aufgabe. Wiesbaden: VS Verlag.
Olsen, B. E., & Anker, H. T. (2014). Local acceptance and the legal framework – the Danish wind energy case. In L. Squitani, H. H. B. Vedder, M. Reese, & B. Elyakime (Eds.), Sustainable Energy United in Diversity. Challenges and Approaches in Energy Transition in the EU (pp. 137–155). Leipzig: European Environmental Law Forum.
Olson, M. (1992). Die Logik des kollektiven Handelns. Kollektivgüter und die Theorie der Gruppen. Tübingen: Mohr.

Ortega, A. P. (2010). Biographisierte Wir-Bezüge und ihre Relevanz für soziales Engagement. Eine kritische Momentaufnahme. In A. P. Ortega, A. Felbinger, R. Mikula, & R. Egger (Eds.), Macht – Eigensinn – Engagement (pp. 81–97). Wiesbaden: VS Verlag.

Oshege, V. (2002). Freiwillige. Produzenten und Träger sozialen Kapitals. Eine empirisch-qualitative Untersuchung zum Engagement in freiwilligen Vereinigungen. Münster: Waxmann.

Ostendorf, A., & Thoma, M. (2012). Images of Corporate Participation and Democratic Structures in Business Administration Textbooks used in Higher Vocational Schools in Austria, Switzerland and Germany. In W. G. Weber, M. Thoma, A. Ostendorf, & L. Chisholm (Eds.), Democratic Competences and Social Practices in Organizations (pp. 86–101). Wiesbaden: VS Verlag.

Österberg, P., & Nilsson, J. (2009). Members' perception of their participation in the governance of cooperatives. The key to trust and commitment in agricultural cooperatives. Agribusiness, 25 (2), 181–197.

Ostrom, E. (1990). Governing the commons. The evolution of institutions for collective action. Cambridge: Cambridge University Press.

Ott, K. (2012). Variants of de-growth and deliberative democracy. A Habermasian proposal. Futures, 44 (6), 571–581.

Otto, S., Arnold, O., & Kaiser, F. (2014). Rebound. Wieso Energieeffizienz ohne suffiziente Lebensstile nicht zur Reduktion des gesellschaftlichen Energieverbrauchs führt. In F. Steger (Ed.), Bedroht Entscheidungsfreiheit Gesundheit und Nachhaltigkeit? Zwischen notwendigen Grenzen und Bevormundung (pp. 117–138). Münster: mentis-Verl.

Owetschkin, D. (2016). *Vom Verteilen zum Gestalten. Geschichte der betrieblichen Mitbestimmung in der westdeutschen Automobilindustrie nach 1945*. Bielefeld: Transcript.

Oxenfarth, A., & Obermayr, H. (2011). Bürgerbeteiligung 3.0. Zwischen Volksbegehren und Occupy-Bewegung. München: Oekom.

Paech, N. (2013). Befreiung vom Überfluss. Auf dem Weg in die Postwachstumsökonomie (4th ed.). München: Oekom.

Pahl, G. (2007). The citizen-powered energy handbook. Community solutions to a global crisis. White River Junction, Vt.: Green.

Pahl, G. (2012). Power from the people. How to organize, finance, and launch local energy projects. White River Junction, Vt: Chelsea Green Pub.

Painuly, J. (2001). Barriers to renewable energy penetration. A framework for analysis. Renewable Energy, 24 (1), 73–89.

Pállinger, Z. T. (2014). Das Konzept des (Staats-)Bürgers. Analysen aus politik-, rechts- und wirtschaftswissenschaftlicher Perspektive. Baden-Baden: Nomos.

Palm, A. (2016). Local factors driving the diffusion of solar photovoltaics in Sweden. A case study of five municipalities in an early market. Energy Research & Social Science, 14, 1–12.

Pankow, S. (2014). Die Weiterentwicklung des Erneuerbare-Energien-Gesetzes (EEG) für die zweite Phase der Energiewende: Ausschreibungsmodell vs. Quotenmodell. Berlin: wvb.

Pant, L. P., Adhikari, B., & Bhattarai, K. K. (2015). Adaptive transition for transformations to sustainability in developing countries. Current Opinion in Environmental Sustainability, 14, 206–212.

Papacharissi, Z. A. (2010). A Private Sphere. Democracy in a Digital Age. Cambridge: Polity Press.
Papadopoulos, Y. (2003). Cooperative forms of governance. Problems of democratic accountability in complex environments. European Journal of Political Research, 42 (4), 473–501.
Papadopoulos, Y. (2004). Governance und Demokratie. In A. Benz (Ed.), Governance – Regieren in komplexen Regelsystemen (pp. 215–237). Wiesbaden: VS Verlag.
Papadopoulos, Y. (2013). Democracy in Crisis? Politics, Governance and Policy. Basingstoke, New York: Palgrave Macmillan.
Pappi, F. U. (2004). Bürgerinitiativen. In D. Nohlen (Ed.), Lexikon der Politikwissenschaft. Theorien – Methoden – Begriffe. Bd. 1 (pp. 88–89). München: Beck.
Parag, Y., Hamilton, J., White, V., & Hogan, B. (2013). Network approach for local and community governance of energy. The case of Oxfordshire. Energy Policy, 62, 1064–1077.
Park, J. J. (2012). Fostering community energy and equal opportunities between communities. Local Environment, 17 (4), 387–408.
Parker, G. (1999). The role of the consumer-citizen in environmental protest in the 1990s. Space & Polity, 3 (1), 67–83.
Parkhill, K. A., Shirani, F., Butler, C., Henwood, K. L., Groves, C., & Pidgeon, N. F. (2015). "We are a community [but] that takes a certain amount of energy". Exploring shared visions, social action, and resilience in place-based community-led energy initiatives. Environmental Science & Policy, 53, Part A, 60–69.
Parsons, T., Shils, E. A., & Smelser, N. J. (Eds.) (1965). Toward a General Theory of Action. Theoretical Foundations for the Social Sciences. Transaction Publishers. New York: Harper and Row.
Pasqualoni, P. P., & Treichl, H. M. (2012). Post-democracy and Engaged Citizenship – The Case of Attac. In W. G. Weber, M. Thoma, A. Ostendorf, & L. Chisholm (Eds.), Democratic Competences and Social Practices in Organizations (pp. 183–192). Wiesbaden: VS Verlag.
Passoth, J.-H. (2008). Technik und Gesellschaft. Sozialwissenschaftliche Techniktheorien und die Transformationen der Moderne. Wiesbaden: VS Verlag.
Passy, F. (1993). Compétence et décision politique. In H. Kriesi (Ed.), Citoyenneté et démocratie directe. Compétence, participation et décision des citoyens et citoyennes suisses (pp. 213–232). Zürich: Seismo.
Pateman, C. (1970). Participation and democratic theory. Cambridge: Cambridge University Press.
Pateman, C. (1975). A Contribution to the Political Theory of Organizational Democracy. Administration and Society, 7 (1), 5–26.
Pateman, C. (2012). Participatory Democracy Revisited. Perspectives on Politics. A Political Science Public Sphere, 10 (1), 7–20.
Patzelt, W. J. (2012). Politikwissenschaft. In U. Flick (Ed.), Handbuch qualitative Sozialforschung. Grundlagen, Konzepte, Methoden und Anwendungen (pp. 53–55). Weinheim: Beltz.
Paulsen, F., Stallmann, F., & Zimmer, A. (2008). Schach dem Parlament – Lokalvereine machen Ratsentscheidung rückgängig. In A. Vetter (Ed.), Erfolgsbedingungen lokaler Bürgerbeteiligung (pp. 149–170). Wiesbaden: VS Verlag.

Pel, B., Bauler, T., Kemp, R., Wittmayer, J., Avelino, F., & Dorland, J. (2015). From research design to meta analysis guidelines. TRANSIT Working Paper. Rotterdam.

Pellizzone, A., Allansdottir, A., De Franco, R., Muttoni, G., & Manzella, A. (2015). Exploring public engagement with geothermal energy in southern Italy. A case study. Energy Policy, 85, 1–11.

Perlaviciute, G., & Steg, L. (2014). Contextual and psychological factors shaping evaluations and acceptability of energy alternatives. Integrated review and research agenda. Renewable and Sustainable Energy Reviews, 35, 361–381.

Perreault, T., Bridge, G., & McCarthy, J. (Eds.). (2015). The Routledge Handbook of Political Ecology. Abingdon, New York: Routledge.

Pesendorfer, D. (2007). *Paradigmenwechsel in der Umweltpolitik: Von den Anfängen der Umwelt- zu einer Nachhaltigkeitspolitik: Modellfall Österreich?* Wiesbaden: VS Verlag.

Peters, M. (Ed.). (2010). Low carbon communities. Imaginative approaches to combating climate change locally. Cheltenham: Edward Elgar.

Peters, M., & Roberts, S. (Eds.). (2010). The role of local authorities in galvanizing action to tackle climate change. A practitioner's perspective. In M. Peters (Ed.), Low carbon communities. Imaginative approaches to combating climate change locally (pp. 47–60). Cheltenham: Edward Elgar.

Peters, M., Fudge, S., & Sinclair, P. (2010). Mobilising community action towards a low-carbon future. Opportunities and challenges for local government in the UK. Energy Policy, 38 (12), 7596–7603.

Petersen, T., & Klauer, B. (2014). Öffentlichkeitsbeteiligung, Partizipation und die Verantwortung des Staates in der Umweltpolitik. Leipzig: UFZ.

Peterson, A. L. (2009). Everyday Ethics and Social Change. The Education of Desire. New York: Columbia University Press.

Peterson, S. A. (1990). Political behavior. Patterns in everyday life. Los Angeles: Sage.

Petrova, M. A. (2016). From NIMBY to acceptance. Toward a novel framework – VESPA – For organizing and interpreting community concerns. Renewable Energy, 86, 1280–1294.

Pettit, P. (2008a). Participation, Deliberation, and We-thinking. In D. I. O'Neill, M. L. Shanley, & I. M. Young (Eds.), Illusion of consent. Engaging with Carole Pateman (pp. 185–204). University Park, Pa.: Pennsylvania State University Press.

Pettit, P. (2008b). Three conceptions of democratic control. Constellations, 15 (1), 46–55.

Pettit, P. (2012). On the People's Terms. A Republican Theory and Model of Democracy. Cambridge: Cambridge University Press.

Pfaff, M., & Blivice, S. (1977). Socioeconomic correlates of consumer and citizen dissatisfaction and activism. In R. L. Day (Ed.), Consumer Satisfaction, Dissatisfaction, and Complaining Behavior (pp. 115–123). Bloomington: Dept. of Marketing, School of Business, Indiana University.

Pfenning, U., & Benighaus, C. (2008). Partizipativer Wandel – methodischer Wandel. Neue und klassische Formen der Bürgerbeteiligung im Vergleich. In A. Vetter (Ed.), Erfolgsbedingungen lokaler Bürgerbeteiligung (pp. 195–216). Wiesbaden: VS Verlag.

Pfriem, R., Lautermann, C., Antoni-Komar, I., Paech, N., & Dorniok, D. (2014). Bürgerbeteiligung, Energiedemokratie, Dezentralität? – Kernziele der Energiewende in Gefahr! Ein Positionspapier des Forschungsprojektes EnGeno zur aktuellen energiepolitischen Entwicklung. Langfassung. Oldenburg.

Phills, J. A., Deiglmeier, K., & Miller, D. T. (2008). Rediscovering social innovation. Stanford Social Innovation Review, 6 (4), 34–43.

Pias, C. (2016). Collectives, Connectives, and the „Nonsense“ of Participation. In M. Denecke, A. Ganzert, I. Otto, & R. Stock (Eds.), ReClaiming Participation. Technology – Mediation – Collectivity (pp. 23–38). Bielefeld: Transcript.

Pickel, G. (2010). Politische Kultur und Demokratieforschung. In K. H. Schrenk & M. Soldner (Eds.), Analyse demokratischer Regierungssysteme (pp. 611–626). Wiesbaden: VS Verlag.

Pickel, G., & Pickel, S. (2006). Demokratisierung im internationalen Vergleich. Neue Erkenntnisse und Perspektiven. Wiesbaden: VS Verlag.

Pickel, S. (2009). Die Triangulation als Methode in der Politikwissenschaft. In S. Pickel (Ed.), Methoden der vergleichenden Politik- und Sozialwissenschaft. Neue Entwicklungen und Anwendungen (pp. 517–542). Wiesbaden: VS Verlag.

Pickel, S. (2012). Das politische Handeln der Bürgerinnen und Bürger – ein Blick auf die Empirie. In G. Weißeno & H. Buchstein (Eds.), Politisch Handeln. Modelle, Möglichkeiten, Kompetenzen (pp. 39–57). Bonn: Bundeszentrale für politische Bildung.

Pietschmann, H. (2009). Die Atomisierung der Gesellschaft. Wien: Ibera.

Pinzani, A. (2003). Brauchen wir Bürgertugenden oder demokratischere Institutionen? Gegen einige Irrtümer des Republikanismus. Berliner Debatte Initial. Sozial- Und Geisteswissenschaftliches Journal, 34 (1), 34–44.

Pinzani, A. (2009). An den Wurzeln moderner Demokratie. Bürger und Staat in der Neuzeit. Berlin: Akademie-Verlag.

Plasser, F., & Ulram, P. A. (Eds.). (1993). Staatsbürger oder Untertanen? Politische Kultur Deutschlands, Österreichs und der Schweiz im Vergleich. Frankfurt a. M.: Lang.

Plenz, M., Holstenkamp, L., & Grumm, F. (2015). Umbau des Energiesystems, virtuelle Kraftwerke und Kanalpumpspeicher. In H. Degenhart, T. Schomerus, & D. Schulz (Eds.), Pumpspeicher an Bundeswasserstraßen (pp. 1–6). Wiesbaden: Springer VS.

Poguntke, T. (Ed.). (2015). Citizenship and Democracy in an Era of Crisis. Essays in honour of Jan W. van Deth. London, New York: Routledge.

Pohl, K., Massing, P., & Deth, J. W. van (Eds.). (2014). Mehr Partizipation – mehr Demokratie? Schwalbach: Wochenschau.

Poisat, J., Goujon, D., & Mieszczak, J.-L. (2013). How co-ops can contribute to the social and economic redevelopment of local areas. In J. Brazda, M. Dellinger, & D. Rößl (Eds.), Genossenschaften im Fokus einer neuen Wirtschaftspolitik. Bericht der XVII. Internationalen Genossenschaftswissenschaftlichen Tagung (IGT) 2012 in Wien. Teilband 4 (pp. 1165–1173). Wien: LIT.

Pol, E., & Ville, S. (2009). Social innovation. Buzz word or enduring term? The Journal of Socio-Economics, 38 (6), 878–885.

Pollet, B. G., Staffell, I., & Adamson, K.-A. (2016). The Energy Landscape in the Republic of South Africa. Cham: Springer.

Pollin, R. (2015). Greening the Global Economy. Cambridge: MIT Press.

Pollitt, M. G. (2012). The role of policy in energy transitions. Lessons from the energy liberalisation era. Energy Policy, 50, 128–137.

Poocharoen, O., & Sovacool, B. K. (2012). Exploring the challenges of energy and resources network governance. Energy Policy, 42, 409–418.

Poppen, S. (2015). Energiegenossenschaften und deren Mitglieder – Erste Ergebnisse einer empirischen Untersuchung. Arbeitspapiere des Instituts für Genossenschaftswesen der Westfälischen Wilhelms-Universität Münster, Nr. 157.

Porst, R. (2014a). Fragebogen. Ein Arbeitsbuch (4th ed.). Wiesbaden: VS Verlag.

Porst, R. (2014b). Frageformulierung. In N. Baur & J. Blasius (Eds.), Handbuch Methoden der empirischen Sozialforschung (pp. 687–699). Wiesbaden: Springer VS.

Porta, D. della (2013). Can Democracy Be Saved? Participation, Deliberation and Social Movements. Cambridge: Polity Press.

Posner, R. A. (2011). The Crisis of Capitalist Democracy. Cambridge, Mass.: Harvard University Press.

Pratchett, L., Durose, C., Lowndes, V., Smith, G., Stoker, G., & Wales, C. (2009). Empowering communities to influence local decision making. A systematic review of the evidence. London: Dept. for Communities and Local Government.

Pratt, J. C., & Luetchford, P. (2014). Food for change. The politics and values of social movements. London: PlutoPress.

Preisendörfer, M. (2007). Sozialkapital und unternehmerisches Handeln. Das soziale Netzwerk von Unternehmensgründern als Erfolgskapital. In A. Franzen & M. Freitag (Eds.), Sozialkapital. Grundlagen und Anwendungen (pp. 272–293). Wiesbaden: VS Verlag.

Prexl, A. (2010). *Nachhaltigkeit kommunizieren - nachhaltig kommunizieren: Analyse des Potenzials der Public Relations für eine nachhaltige Unternehmens- und Gesellschaftsentwicklung*. Wiesbaden: VS Verlag.

Priller, E. (2010). Stichwort: Vom Ehrenamt zum zivilgesellschaftlichen Engagement. Zeitschrift für Erziehungswissenschaft, 13 (2), 195–213.

Priller, E., Alscher, M., Dathe, D., & Speth, R. (Eds.). (2011). Zivilengagement. Herausforderungen für Gesellschaft, Politik und Wissenschaft. Berlin: LIT.

Priller, E., Alscher, M., Droß, P. J., Paul, F., Poldrack, C. J., Schmeißer, C., & Waitkus, N. (2013). Dritte-Sektor-Organisationen heute. Eigene Ansprüche und ökonomische Herausforderungen. Ergebnisse einer Organisationsbefragung. Berlin: Wissenschaftszentrum Berlin für Sozialforschung.

Projektgruppe Neue Mitleidsökonomie. (2016). Die neue Mitleidsökonomie Armutsbekämpfung jenseits des Wohlfahrtsstaats? Bielefeld: Transcript.

Przyborski, A. (2004). Gesprächsanalyse und dokumentarische Methode. Qualitative Auswertung von Gesprächen, Gruppendiskussionen und anderen Diskursen. Wiesbaden: VS Verlag.

Przyborski, A., & Wohlrab-Sahr, M. (2008). Qualitative Sozialforschung. Ein Arbeitsbuch. München: Oldenbourg.

Przyborski, A., & Wohlrab-Sahr, M. (2014). Forschungsdesigns für die qualitative Sozialforschung. In N. Baur & J. Blasius (Eds.), Handbuch Methoden der empirischen Sozialforschung (pp. 117–133). Wiesbaden: Springer VS.

Pufé, I. (2014). *Nachhaltigkeit* (2nd ed.). Konstanz: UVK-Verl.-Ges.

Purkus, A., Gawel, E., Deissenroth, M., Nienhaus, K., & Wassermann, S. (2014). Beitrag der Marktprämie zur Marktintegration Erneuerbarer – Erfahrungen aus dem EEG 2012 und Perspektiven der verpflichtenden Direktvermarktung. Energiewirtschaftliche Tagesfragen, 12 (64).

Purtschert, R. (2013). Keine Unternehmensform für Abzocker. Akzent Magazin, Oktober/November, 32–34.

Putnam, R. (2002). Soziales Kapital in der Bundesrepublik Deutschland und in den USA. In Enquete-Kommission Zukunft des Bürgerschaftlichen Engagements des Deutschen Bundestages (Eds.), Bürgerschaftliches Engagement und Zivilgesellschaft (pp. 257–271). Opladen: Leske + Budrich.

Putnam, R. D. (2000). Bowling Alone. The Collapse and Revival of American Community. New York: Simon & Schuster.

Putnam, R. D. (Ed.). (2001). Gesellschaft und Gemeinsinn. Sozialkapital im internationalen Vergleich. Gütersloh: Verl. Bertelsmann-Stiftung.

Putnam, R. D., Leonardi, R., & Nanetti, R. Y. (1993). Making Democracy Work. Civic Traditions in Modern Italy. Princeton, NJ: Princeton University Press.

Quitzow, L., Canzler, W., Grundmann, P., Leibenath, M., Moss, T., & Rave, T. (2016). The German Energiewende – What's happening? Introducing the special issue. *Utilities Policy, 41*, 163–171. https://doi.org/10.1016/j.jup.2016.03.002

Raab-Steiner, E., & Benesch, M. (2012). Der Fragebogen. Von der Forschungsidee zur SPSS-Auswertung (3rd ed.). Wien: Facultas.

Rademacher, L., & Lintemeier, K. (2015). Smarte Partizipation?! Warum es noch kein Erfolgsmodell für Beteiligung und Dialog gibt. Wie deutsche Politiker über frühe Öffentlichkeitsbeteiligung bei Bau- und Infrastrukturprojekten denken. Berlin: DialogGesellschaft.

Radinger-Peer, V., Penker, M., Chiari, S., Danzinger, G., Enengel, B., Kühnel, F., & Sammer, K. (2015). Regional Vulnerability to the Challenges of Climate Change and Energy Provision. Lessons Learned from Transdisciplinary Assessments in Austria and Germany. GAIA – Ecological Perspectives for Science and Society, 24 (4), 261–270.

Radke, V. (1999). *Nachhaltige Entwicklung: Konzept und Indikatoren aus wirtschaftstheoretischer Sicht ; mit 2 Tabellen*. Heidelberg: Physica-Verl.

Radtke, J. (2013). Bürgerenergie in Deutschland – ein Modell für Partizipation? In J. Radtke & B. Hennig (Eds.), Die deutsche „Energiewende" nach Fukushima. Der wissenschaftliche Diskurs zwischen Atomausstieg und Wachstumsdebatte (pp. 139–182). Marburg: Metropolis.

Radtke, J. (2014). A closer look inside collaborative action: Civic engagement and participation in community energy initiatives. *People, Place and Policy Online, 8*(3), 235–248. https://doi.org/10.3351/ppp.0008.0003.0008

Radtke, J. (2015). Das Zusammenspiel von Raum und Technik bei der Etablierung Erneuerbarer Energien. Transformationen in der Energiewende. Raumforschung und Raumordnung, 73 (6), 389–405.

Radtke, J. (2018a). Die Mehrebenen-Architektur der Energiewende: Drei Modelle im Vergleich. In L. Holstenkamp & J. Radtke (Eds.), *Handbuch Energiewende und Partizipation* (pp. 793–814). Wiesbaden: Springer Fachmedien Wiesbaden. https://doi.org/10.1007/978-3-658-09416-4_47

Radtke, J., & Hennig, B. (2013). Die deutsche „Energiewende" nach Fukushima: *Der wissenschaftliche Diskurs zwischen Atomausstieg und Wachstumsdebatte*. Marburg: Metropolis-Verl.

Radtke, J., & Schaal, G. S. (2018b). Die Energiewende in Deutschland. Versuch einer demokratietheoretischen Systematisierung. In L. Holstenkamp & J. Radtke (Eds.), *Handbuch Energiewende und Partizipation* (pp. 143–155). Wiesbaden: Springer VS. https://doi.org/10.1007/978-3-658-09416-4_9

Radtke, J., & Schaal, G. S. (2016). (i. E.). Die Energiewende in Deutschland. Versuch einer demokratietheoretischen Systematisierung. In L. Holstenkamp & J. Radtke (Eds.), Handbuch Energiewende und Partizipation. Wiesbaden: Springer VS.

Rae, C., & Bradley, F. (2012). Energy autonomy in sustainable communities – A review of key issues. Renewable and Sustainable Energy Reviews, 16 (9), 6497–6506.

Raimi, K. T., & Carrico, A. R. (2016). Understanding and beliefs about smart energy technology. Energy Research & Social Science, 12, 68–74.

Rammert, W. (1982). Soziotechnische Revolution. Sozialstruktureller Wandel und Strategien der Technisierung. Analytische Perspektiven einer Soziologie der Technik. In R. Jokisch (Ed.), Techniksoziologie (pp. 32–81). Frankfurt a. M.: Suhrkamp.

Rammert, W. (1993). Forschungsstand, Theorieansätze, Fallbeispiele – ein Überblick. Opladen: Westdeutscher Verlag.

Rammert, W. (2007). Technik und Gesellschaft. In H. Joas (Ed.), Lehrbuch der Soziologie (3rd ed., pp. 481–504). Frankfurt a. M., New York: Campus.

Ramos, A., De Jonghe, C., Gómez, V., & Belmans, R. (2016). Realizing the smart grid's potential: Defining local markets for flexibility. *Utilities Policy, 40*, 26–35. https://doi.org/10.1016/j.jup.2016.03.006

Ranaboldo, M., Domenech, B., Reyes, G. A., Ferrer-Martí, L., Pastor Moreno, R., & García-Villoria, A. (2015). Off-grid community electrification projects based on wind and solar energies. A case study in Nicaragua. Solar Energy, 117, 268–281.

Ranaboldo, M., Ferrer-Martí, L., García-Villoria, A., & Pastor Moreno, R. (2013). Heuristic indicators for the design of community off-grid electrification systems based on multiple renewable energies. Energy, 50, 501–512.

Randers, J. (2014). 2052. Der neue Bericht an den Club of Rome. Eine globale Prognose für die nächsten 40 Jahre. München: Oekom.

Rathnayaka, A. J. D., Potdar, V. M., Dillon, T., & Kuruppu, S. (2015). Framework to manage multiple goals in community-based energy sharing network in smart grid. International Journal of Electrical Power & Energy Systems, 73, 615–624.

Ratinen, M., & Lund, P. (2015). Policy inclusiveness and niche development. Examples from wind energy and photovoltaics in Denmark, Germany, Finland, and Spain. Energy Research & Social Science, 6, 136–145.

Ratto, M., & Boler, M. (Eds.). (2014). DIY citizenship. Critical making and social media. Cambridge, Mass.: MIT Press.

Rau, I., & Zöllner, J. (2011). Aktivität und Teilhabe – Akzeptanz Erneuerbarer Energien durch Beteiligung steigern. Projektabschlussbericht. Laufzeit: 01.07.2008 – 30.06.2010. Magdeburg u. a. http://www.fg-umwelt.de/assets/files/Aktivi-taet_und_Teilhabe/Abschlussbericht_Aktivitaet_Teilhabe_FKZ_0325052.pdf

Rau, I., Schweizer-Ries, P., & Hildebrand, J. (2012). Participation. The Silver Bullet for the Acceptance of Renewable Energies? In S. Kabisch, International Association for People-Environment Studies, & Conference (Ed.), Vulnerability, risks, and complexity. Impacts of global change on human habitats (pp. 177–192). Göttingen: Hogrefe.

Rauschenbach, T., & Zimmer, A. (2011). Bürgerschaftliches Engagement unter Druck? Eine Einleitung. In T. Rauschenbach & A. Zimmer (Eds.), Bürgerschaftliches Engagement unter Druck? Analysen und Befunde aus den Bereichen Soziales, Kultur und Sport (pp. 11–28). Opladen: Leske + Budrich.

Rauschmayer, F. (2015). Mutbürger oder Wutbürger? Wie das Menschenbild auf die Energiewende wirkt. *Frankfurter Rundschau, 71*(66), 18.

Rauschmayer, F., & Omann, I. (2015). Well-being in sustainability transitions: Making use of needs. In K. Lykke Syse & M. L. Mueller (Eds.), *Sustainable consumption and the good life: Interdisciplinary perspectives* (pp. 111–125). Abingdon; New York: Routledge.

Rauschmayer, F., Centgraf, S., & Masson, T. (2015). Ergebnisse der EnGeno Mitgliederbefragung von Energiegenossenschaften. Forschungsprojekt EnGeno – Transformationspotenzial von Energiegenossenschaften. Mit postfossilen Dezentralisierungsstrategien zur Energiewende. Leipzig: Helmholtz-Zentrum für Umweltforschung GmbH – UFZ.

Rauterberg, H. (2013). Wir sind die Stadt! Urbanes Leben in der Digitalmoderne. Berlin: Suhrkamp.

Raven, R. P. J. M., Jolivet, E., Mourik, R. M., & Feenstra, Y. C. F. J. (2009). ESTEEM. Managing societal acceptance in new energy projects. A toolbox method for project managers. Technological Forecasting and Social Change, 76 (7), 963–977.

Ravindra, K., & Iyer, P. P. (2014). Decentralized demand-supply matching using community microgrids and consumer demand response. A scenario analysis. Energy, 76, 32–41.

Raymond, C. M., Brown, G., & Weber, D. (2010). The measurement of place attachment. Personal, community, and environmental connections. Journal of Environmental Psychology, 30 (4), 422–434.

Raymond, L. (2002). Localism in environmental policy. New insights from an old case. Policy Sciences, 35 (2), 179–201.

Reder, M., Cojocaru, M.-D., Brieskorn, N., Enderle, G., & Magnis-Suseno, F. (2014). Zukunft der Demokratie. Ende einer Illusion oder Aufbruch zu neuen Formen? Stuttgart: Kohlhammer.

Regalia, I. (2006). Regulating new forms of employment. Local experiments and social innovation in Europe. Abingdon, New York: Routledge.

Rehbein, B., Baumann, B., Costa, L., & Fadaee, S. (Eds.). (2015). Reproduktion sozialer Ungleichheit in Deutschland. Konstanz, München: UVK.

Reiche, K. (Ed.). (2009). Energiegeladen. Koordinaten einer zukunftsfähigen Klima- und Energiepolitik. Potsdam: Ch. Goetz Verlag.

Reichert-Garschhammer, E., Kieferle, C., Wertfein, M., & Becker-Stoll, F. (2015). Inklusion und Partizipation. Vielfalt als Chance und Anspruch. Göttingen: Vandenhoeck & Ruprecht.

Reichertz, J. (2014). Empirische Sozialforschung und soziologische Theorie. In N. Baur & J. Blasius (Eds.), Handbuch Methoden der empirischen Sozialforschung (pp. 65–80). Wiesbaden: Springer VS.

Reid, T. (2011). The Everything Guide to Living Off the Grid. A back-to-basics manual for independent living. Avon: Adams Media (F+W Media).

Reinhardt, S. (2004). Demokratie-Kompetenzen. Berlin: Bundesministerium für Bildung und Forschung. http://edoc.bibliothek.uni-halle.de/servlets/MCRFileNodeServlet/HAL-CoRe_derivate_00000676/Reinhardt.pdf

Reinhardt, S. (2011). Die Demokratie-Kompetenz der Konfliktfähigkeit – lässt sie sich messen? In A. Rüdiger & E.-M. Seng (Eds.), Dimensionen der Politik: Festschrift für Richard Saage zum 65. Geburtstag (pp. 501–520). Berlin: Duncker & Humblot.

Reinsberger, K., Brudermann, T., Hatzl, S., Fleiß, E., & Posch, A. (2015). Photovoltaic diffusion from the bottom-up: Analytical investigation of critical factors. Applied Energy, 159, 178–187.

Reis, S. H. D., Janke, M., & Wagner, C. (2005). Laien erleben die Bürgerrolle. In P. C. Dienel (Ed.), Die Befreiung der Politik (pp. 38–39). Wiesbaden: VS Verlag.

Ren, J., Goodsite, M. E., & Sovacool, B. K. (2015). Climate change: Climate justice more vital than democracy. Nature, 526 (7573), 323–323.

Renewable Energies Agency (Agentur für Erneuerbare Energien). (2015). *Jahresreport Föderal Erneuerbar 2015*. Berlin: Agentur für Erneuerbare Energien.

Renn, O. (1999). Kooperativer Diskurs – Kommunikation und Konfliktschlichtung in der Umweltpolitik. In H. Bartmann & K. D. John (Eds.), Kooperative Umweltpolitik. Beiträge zum 8. Mainzer Umweltsymposium (pp. 89–108). Aachen: Shaker Verlag.

Renn, O. (2001). The role of social science in environmental policy making: experiences and outlook. Science and Public Policy, 28 (6), 427–437.

Renn, O. (2012). Öffentlichkeitsbeteiligung – Aktueller Forschungsstand und Folgerungen für die praktische Umsetzung. In U. Grünewald (Ed.), Wasserbezogene Anpassungsmaßnahmen an den Landschafts- und Klimawandel (pp. 184–193). Stuttgart: Schweizerbart.

Renn, O. (2013a). Bürgerbeteiligung bei öffentlichen Vorhaben. Aktueller Forschungs-stand und Folgerungen für die praktische Umsetzung. One Stop Europe Angewandte Bürgerbeteiligung, 6.

Renn, O. (2013b). Partizipation bei öffentlichen Planungen. Möglichkeiten, Grenzen, Reformbedarf. In S. I. Keil & S. I. Thaidigsmann (Eds.), Zivile Bürgergesellschaft und Demokratie (pp. 71–96). Wiesbaden: Springer VS.

Renn, O. (2014). *Stakeholder involvement in risk governance*. Ark Group London.

Renn, O., & Schweizer, P.-J. (2009). Inclusive risk governance: Concepts and application to environmental policy making. *Environmental Policy and Governance, 19*(3), 174–185. https://doi.org/10.1002/eet.507

Renn, O., Köck, W., Schweizer, P.-J., Bovet, J., Benighaus, C., Scheel, O., & Schröter, K. (2014). Öffentlichkeitsbeteiligung bei Planungsvorhaben der Energiewende. Policy-Brief Helmholtz Allianz ENERGY TRANS 1/2014. http://www.energy-trans.de/downloads/ENERGY-TRANS-Policy_Brief-Oeffentlichkeitsbeteili-gung_bei_Planungsvorhaben_der_Energiewende.pdf

Renn, O., Webler, T., & Wiedemann, P. (Eds.). (1995). Fairness and Competence in Citizen Participation. Dordrecht u. a.: Kluwer Academic.

Reuter, C. (2015). Emergent collaboration infrastructures. Technology design for interorganizational crisis management. Wiesbaden: Springer Gabler.

Rhodius, R. (2012). Mehr Legitimität? Zur Wirksamkeit partizipativer Verfahren in räumlichen Planungsprozessen. Dissertation. Freiburg i. Br. http://www.freidok.uni-freiburg.de

Ricci, M., Bellaby, P., & Flynn, R. (2010). Engaging the public on paths to sustainable energy. Who has to trust whom? Energy Policy, 38 (6), 2633–2640.

Richards, G., Noble, B., & Belcher, K. (2012). Barriers to renewable energy development: A case study of large-scale wind energy in Saskatchewan, Canada. Energy Policy, 42, 691–698.

Richter, N. (2013). Organisation, Macht, Subjekt. Zur Genealogie des modernen Managements. Bielefeld: Transcript.

Riehm, U. (2009). Bürgerbeteiligung durch E-Petitionen. Analysen von Kontinuität und Wandel im Petitionswesen. Berlin: Edition Sigma.

Rießen, A. van, Bleck, C., & Knopp, R. (Eds.). (2015). Sozialer Raum und Alter(n). Zugänge, Verläufe und Übergänge sozialräumlicher Handlungsforschung. Wiesbaden: Springer VS.

Rifkin, J. (2011). Die dritte industrielle Revolution. Die Zukunft der Wirtschaft nach dem Atomzeitalter. Frankfurt a. M., New York: Campus.

Rifkin, J. (2014). The Zero Marginal Cost Society. The Internet of Things, the Collaborative Commons, and the Eclipse of Capitalism. New York: Palgrave Macmillan.

Ringle, G. (2003). Mitgliedschaft als strategischer Vorteil der Genossenschaften. VM: Fachzeitschrift für Verbands- und Nonprofit-Management, 29 (2), 6–15.

Ringle, G. (2005). Management der Mitgliederbindung in Genossenschaften. Fachzeitschrift für Verbands- und Nonprofit-Management, 31 (2), 38–49.

Ringle, G. (2006). Aktive Mitgliedschaft – eine strategische Notwendigkeit. VM: Fachzeitschrift für Verbands- und Nonprofit-Management, 32 (3), 50–59.

Ringle, G. (2007). Der Faktor „Vertrauen" in Genossenschaften. Zeitschrift für das gesamte Genossenschaftswesen, 57 (4), 284–298.

Ringle, G. (2010). Der genossenschaftliche Förderauftrag. Missverständnisse und Präzisierungsversuche. Zeitschrift für das gesamte Genossenschaftswesen, 60 (3), 176–190.

Ringle, G. (2012a). Kommunikationsmanagement im Mitgliedergeschäft von Genossenschaften. Zeitschrift für das gesamte Genossenschaftswesen, 62 (1), 3–18.

Ringle, G. (2012b). „Management of Change" in Genossenschaftsunternehmen. In G. Ringle & H.-M. Münkner (Eds.), Genossenschaftliche Kooperation – anders wirtschaften (pp. 251–267). Baden-Baden: Nomos.

Ringle, G. (2012c). Neuere „Werte der Genossenschaften" auf dem Prüfstand – auch Transparenz. VM: Fachzeitschrift für Verbands- und Nonprofit-Management, 38 (3), 22–31.

Ringle, G. (2012d). Shareholder Value und Member Value: zur Frage der Vereinbarkeit. In G. Ringle & H.-M. Münkner (Eds.), Genossenschaftliche Kooperation – anders wirtschaften (pp. 211–228). Baden-Baden: Nomos.

Ringle, G. (2012e). Werte der Genossenschaftsunternehmen: „Kultureller Kern" und neue Werte-Vorstellungen. Wismarer Diskussionspapiere 07/2012. Wismar: Hochschule Wismar, Fakultät. für Wirtschaftswissenschaften.

Ringle, G. (2013a). Genossenschaftliche Werte und deren Nutzen. Zeitschrift für das gesamte Genossenschaftswesen, 63 (2), 79–80.

Ringle, G. (2013b). Auf der Suche nach der „richtigen" Mitgliederförderung. Wismarer Diskussionspapiere 03/2013. Wismar: Hochschule Wismar, Fakultät für Wirtschaftswissenschaften.

Ringle, G., & Göler von Ravensburg, N. (2010). Der genossenschaftliche Förderauftrag. Wismar: Hochschule Wismar, Fachbereich Wirtschaft.

Ritter, Martina. (2008). *Die Dynamik von Privatheit und Öffentlichkeit in modernen Gesellschaften*. Wiesbaden: VS Verlag.

Ritzi, C. (2014). Die Postdemokratisierung politischer Öffentlichkeit. Kritik zeitgenössischer Demokratie. Theoretische Grundlagen und analytische Perspektiven. Wiesbaden: Springer VS.

Rixen, S., & Welskop-Deffaa, E. M. (Eds.). (2015). Zukunft der Selbstverwaltung. Responsivität und Reformbedarf. Wiesbaden: Springer VS.

Röber, J. (2015). Zukunftsfähig durch Regionsbildung? Institutionenbildung in politischadministrativen Verflechtungsräumen. Opladen: Budrich.

Roberts, J. A. (1996). Green consumers in the 1990s: profile and implications for advertising. Journal of Business Research, 36 (3), 217–231.

Roberts, N. C. (Ed.). (2015). The age of direct citizen participation. London: Routledge.

Rochlin, G. I. (2014). Energy research and the contributions of the social sciences: A retrospective examination. Energy Research & Social Science, 3, 178–185.

Rodger, E. (2008). Building a green community. New York: Crabtree.
Rodprasert, R., Chandarasupsang, T., Chakpitak, N., & Yupapin, P. P. (2014). Green Energy Community with Smart Society for Sustainable Living. Energy Procedia, 56, 678–689.
Rogall, H., Binswanger, H.-C., Ekardt, F., Grothe, A., Hasenclever, W.-D., Hauchler, I., Jänicke, M., Kollmann, K., Michaelis, N. V., Nutzinger, H. G., & Scherhorn, G. (2014). Jahrbuch Nachhaltige Ökonomie 2014/2015. Im Brennpunkt: Die Energiewende als gesellschaftlicher Transformationprozess. Marburg: Metropolis.
Rogers, J. C., Simmons, E. A., Convery, I., & Weatherall, A. (2008). Public perceptions of opportunities for community-based renewable energy projects. Energy Policy, 36 (11), 4217–4226.
Rohland, P. (2011). Dialog. Zur Stärkung lokaler Demokratie. Bonn: vhw – Verlag Dienstleistung.
Romano, O. (2012). How to rebuild democracy, re-thinking degrowth. Futures, 44 (6), 582–589.
Romero-Rubio, C., & de Andrés Díaz, J. R. (2015). Sustainable energy communities: a study contrasting Spain and Germany. Energy Policy, 85, 397–409.
Rommel, J., Buttmann, V., Liebig, G., Schönwetter, S., & Svart-Gröger, V. (2015). Motivation crowding theory and pro-environmental behavior: Experimental evidence. Economics Letters, 129, 42–44.
Rommel, J., Sagebiel, J., & Müller, J. R. (2016a). Quality uncertainty and the market for renewable energy: Evidence from German consumers. Renewable Energy, 94, 106–113.
Rommel, J., Radtke, J., von Jorck, G., Mey, F., & Yildiz, Ö. (2018). Community renewable energy at a crossroads: A think piece on degrowth, technology, and the democratization of the German energy system. *Journal of Cleaner Production, 197*, 1746–1753. https://doi.org/10.1016/j.jclepro.2016.11.114
Römmele, A. (2013). Empowering Citizens. Studies in Collaborative Democracy. Baden-Baden: Nomos.
Römmele, A., & Schober, H. (Eds.). (2013). The Governance of Large-Scale Projects. Linking Citizens and the State. Baden-Baden: Nomos.
Rorty, R. (1982). Consequences of pragmatism. Essays 1972–1980. Brighton: The Harvester Pr.
Roß, P.-S. (2008). Alles Arbeit, oder was?! Bezahlte Arbeit und freiwilliges Engagement im Tätigkeits-Mix. In K. Maier (Ed.), Soziale Arbeit in der Krise der Arbeitsgesellschaft (pp. 203–227). Freiburg, Br.: FEL.
Roß, P.-S. (2012). Demokratie weiter denken. Reflexionen zur Förderung bürgerschaftlichen Engagements in der Bürgerkommune. Baden-Baden: Nomos.
Roß, P.-S., Harhues, O., & Terhorst, T. (2006). „Wir müssen uns neu erfinden!“ Bürgergesellschaft: Ein „neuer“ Blick auf „alte“ Verbände. Forschungsjournal Soziale Bewegungen, 1, 94–101.
Roßteutscher, S. (2004). Von Realisten und Konformisten – Wider die Theorie der Wertsynthese. KZfSS Kölner Zeitschrift für Soziologie und Sozialpsychologie, 56 (3), 407–431.
Roßteutscher, S. (2009a). Undemokratische Assoziationen. In A. Brodocz, M. Llanque, & G. S. Schaal (Eds.), Bedrohungen der Demokratie (pp. 61–76). Wiesbaden: VS Verlag.
Roßteutscher, S. (2009b). Soziale Partizipation und Soziales Kapital. In V. Kaina & A. Römmele (Eds.), Politische Soziologie (pp. 163–180). Wiesbaden: VS Verlag.

Roßteutscher, S., & Deth, J. W. van. (2002). Associations between associations: the structure of the voluntary association sector. Mannheim: Mannheimer Zentrum für Europäische Sozialforschung.

Rosa, E. A., Machlis, G. E., & Keating, K. M. (1988). Energy and Society. Annual Review of Sociology, 14, 149–172.

Rosa, H. (2005). Beschleunigung. Die Veränderung der Zeitstrukturen in der Moderne (10th ed.). Frankfurt a. M.: Suhrkamp.

Rosa, H. (2012a). Leiharbeiter und Aktivbürger: Was stimmt nicht mit dem spätmodernen Kapitalismus? In Soziologie – Kapitalismus – Kritik. Eine Debatte (pp. 205–223). Frankfurt a. M.: Suhrkamp.

Rosa, H. (2012b). Politisches Handeln und die Entstehung des Neuen in der Politik. In G. Weißeno & H. Buchstein (Eds.), Politisch Handeln. Modelle, Möglichkeiten, Kompetenzen (pp. 133–154). Bonn: Bundeszentrale für politische Bildung.

Rosa, H. (2013a). Beschleunigung und Entfremdung. Entwurf einer kritischen Theorie spätmoderner Zeitlichkeit (3rd ed.). Berlin: Suhrkamp.

Rosa, H. (2013b). Social acceleration. A new theory of modernity. New York: Columbia University Press.

Rosa, H., Lessenich, S., Kennedy, M., & Waigel, T. (2014). Weil Kapitalismus sich ändern muss. Im Gespräch mit Hartmut Rosa, Stephan Lessenich, Margrit Kennedy, Theo Waigel. Wiesbaden: Springer VS.

Rosanvallon, P. (2010). Demokratische Legitimität: Unparteilichkeit – Reflexivität – Nähe. Hamburg: Hamburger Edition.

Rösch, C., Bräutigam, K.-R., Kopfmüller, J., Lichtner, P., & Stelzer, V. (2016). Nachhaltigkeitsindikatoren zur Bewertung des deutschen Energiesystems. GAIA, 25 (1), 69–70.

Rosen, N. (2010). Off the grid: inside the movement for more space, less government, and true independence in modern America. New York: Penguin Books.

Rosenau, P. M. (1991). Post-Modernism and the Social Sciences: Insights, Inroads, and Intrusions. Princeton: Princeton University Press.

Rosenkranz, G. (2014). Energiewende 2.0: aus der Nische zum Mainstream. Berlin: Heinrich-Böll-Stiftung. http://www.boell.de/sites/default/files/energiewende2.0_1.pdf

Rösler, C. (2004). Kommunen auf dem Weg zur Nachhaltigkeit. Kongressdokumentation. Berlin: Dt. Inst. für Urbanistik.

Roth, R. (1997). Die Kommune als Ort der Bürgerbeteiligung. In A. Klein & R. Schmalz-Bruns (Eds.), Politische Beteiligung und Bürgerengagement in Deutschland (pp. 404–447). Bonn: Bundeszentrale für Politische Bildung.

Roth, R. (2000). Bürgerschaftliches Engagement – Formen, Bedingungen, Perspektiven. In A. Zimmer & S. Nährlich (Eds.), Engagierte Bürgerschaft. Traditionen und Perspektiven (pp. 25–48). Opladen: Leske + Budrich.

Roth, R. (2003). Die dunklen Seiten der Zivilgesellschaft. Forschungsjournal Soziale Bewegungen, 2, 59–74.

Roth, R. (2004). Die dunklen Seiten der Zivilgesellschaft. Grenzen einer zivilgesellschaftlichen Fundierung von Demokratie. In A. Klein, K. Kern, B. Geißel, & M. Berger (Eds.), Zivilgesellschaft und Sozialkapital (pp. 41–64). Wiesbaden: VS Verlag.

Roth, R. (2008). Exkurs. Die unzivile Zivilgesellschaft. In S. Embacher (Ed.), Lern- und Arbeitsbuch Bürgergesellschaft (pp. 68–88). Bonn: Dietz.

Roth, R. (2010). Engagementförderung als Demokratiepolitik: Besichtigung einer Reformbaustelle. In T. Olk, A. Klein, & B. Hartnuß (Eds.), Engagementpolitik (pp. 611–636). Wiesbaden: VS Verlag.

Roth, R. (2011a). Bürgermacht. Eine Streitschrift für mehr Partizipation. Hamburg: Körber-Stiftung.

Roth, R. (2011b). Die Blockade zwischen Staat und Bürgern – Demokratie im Wandel. Forschungsjournal Soziale Bewegungen, 24 (1), 83–87.

Roth, R. (2011c). Durch Beteiligung zur Bürgerdemokratie. In K. Beck & J. Ziekow (Eds.), Mehr Bürgerbeteiligung wagen. Wege zur Vitalisierung der Demokratie (pp. 45–55). Wiesbaden: VS Verlag.

Roth, R. (2011d). Lokale Politik auf dem Rückzug? Forschungsjournal Soziale Bewegungen, 26 (2), 177–179.

Roth, R. (2011e). Partizipation. In T. Olk & B. Hartnuß (Eds.), Handbuch Bürgerschaftliches Engagement (pp. 77–90). Weinheim: Beltz Juventa.

Roth, R. (2013a). 50 Jahre Stärkung der Demokratie und der politischen Partizipation in Deutschland – einige Streiflichter. In Stiftung Mitarbeit (Ed.), 50 Jahre Stiftung Mitarbeit. Bonn: Stiftung Mitarbeit.

Roth, R. (2013b). Bürgerbeteiligung und direkte Demokratie – das Stuttgarter Vermächtnis. In E. Kiderlen (Ed.), Experiment Bürgerbeteiligung. Das Beispiel Baden-Württemberg (pp. 141–149). Berlin: Heinrich-Böll-Stiftung.

Roth, R. (2013c). Für mehr Partizipation und Engagement. Erfolgsbedingungen, Perspektiven und Grenzen. In J. Hasse & G. Rosenthal (Eds.), Wider die Gleichgültigkeit! Aktiv gegen Rechtsextremismus. Perspektiven, Projekte, Tipps (pp. 47–63). Bonn: Bundeszentrale für politische Bildung.

Roth, R. (2013d). Wieso ist Partizipation notwendig für die Zukunftsfähigkeit der Kommunen? In A. Klein, R. Sprengel, & J. Neuling (Eds.), Jahrbuch Engagementpolitik 2013: Staat und Zivilgesellschaft (pp. 49–54). Schwalbach: Wochenschau.

Roth, R. (Ed.). (1994). Kommunalpolitik. Politisches Handeln in den Gemeinden. Opladen: Leske + Budrich.

Roth, R., & Olk, T. (2010). Vereine als bürgerschaftliche Lernorte. In Bertelsmann Stiftung (Ed.), Kinder- und Jugendbeteiligung in Deutschland. Entwicklungsstand und Handlungsansätze (pp. 205–220). Gütersloh: Verlag Bertelsmann Stiftung.

Rothfuß, E., & Dörfler, T. (2013). Prolog – Raumbezogene Qualitative Sozialforschung. Konzeptionelle Überlegungen zwischen Geographie und Soziologie. In E. Rothfuß & T. Dörfler (Eds.), Raumbezogene qualitative Sozialforschung (pp. 7–31). Wiesbaden: Springer VS.

Rothschild, J., & Whitt, J. A. (1986). The cooperative workplace: potentials and dilemmas of organizational democracy and participation. Cambridge, Mass.: Cambridge University Press.

Rowe, G., & Frewer, L. J. (2005). A Typology of Public Engagement Mechanisms. Science, Technology & Human Values, 30 (2), 251–290.

Roy, J. (2013). From Machinery to Mobility. Government and Democracy in a Participative Age. New York: Springer.

Rubik, F., & Kreß, M. (2014). Climate Citizens – Analysis of roles, experiences, challenges and opportunities using the example of the citizens of Heidelberg/Germany. Heidelberg: Institut für ökologische Wirtschaftsforschung. http://www.ioew.de/uploads/tx_ukioewdb/Rubik_Kress_Climate_Citizens_01.pdf

Rubik, F., Müller, R., Kim, T., Reinhard, J., Brandsch, S., Kreß, M., & Bietz, S. (2014). Rollen der Bürgerinnen und Bürger in der Energiewende im Kreis Steinfurt. Vorbereitungspapier für den Workshop am 19.11.2014 in Steinfurt. Rahmenbedingungen, Akteurskonstellationen, Aktivierungspotenziale der Bürger im Kreis Steinfurt. Berlin: Institut für ökologische Wirtschaftsforschung (IÖW). http://www.ioew.de/uploads/tx_ukioewdb/Workshop_Steinfurt_Vorbereitungspapier.pdf

Rucht, D. (1997). Soziale Bewegungen als demokratische Produktivkraft. In A. Klein & R. Schmalz-Bruns (Eds.), Politische Beteiligung und Bürgerengagement in Deutschland (pp. 382–403). Bonn: Bundeszentrale für Politische Bildung.

Rucht, D. (2010). Engagement im Wandel. Politische Partizipation in Deutschland. WZ-Brief Zivilengagement. Berlin: Wissenschaftszentrum Berlin für Sozialforschung.

Rucht, D., Yang, M., & Zimmermann, A. (2008). Politische Diskurse im Internet und in Zeitungen. Das Beispiel Genfood. Wiesbaden: VS Verlag.

Rückert-John, J. (Ed.). (2013). Soziale Innovation und Nachhaltigkeit. Perspektiven sozialen Wandels. Wiesbaden: Springer VS.

Rückert-John, J., & Schäfer, M. (Eds.). (2015). Nachhaltiger Konsum durch soziale Innovationen. Wiesbaden: VS Verlag.

Rückert-John, J., Bormann, I., & John, R. (2013). Repräsentativumfrage zu Umweltbewusstsein und Umweltverhalten im Jahr 2012. Umweltforschungsplan des Bundesministeriums für Umwelt, Naturschutz und Reaktorsicherheit. Forschungsprojekt. Berlin: Bundesministerium für Umwelt, Naturschutz, Bau und Reaktorsicherheit.

Rückert-John, J., Jaeger-Erben, M., & Schäfer, M. (2014). Soziale Innovationen im Aufwind. Ein Leitfaden zur Förderung sozialer Innovationen für nachhaltigen Konsum. Dessau-Roßlau: Umweltbundesamt.

Rückert-John, J., Jaeger-Erben, M., Schäfer, M., Scholl, G., & Gossen, M. (2016). *Nachhaltiger Konsum durch soziale Innovationen – Konzepte und Praxis*. Dessau-Roßlau: Umweltbundesamt. https://www.umweltbundesamt.de/publikationen/nachhaltiger-konsum-durch-soziale-innovationen

Ruddat, M., & Sonnberger, M. (2015). Wie die Bürgerinnen und Bürger ihre Rolle bei der Energiewende sehen. Energiewirtschaftliche Tagesfragen, 65 (1/2), 121–125.

Rudzio, W. (2015). Politische Kultur der gelockerten Bindungen. In W. Rudzio (Ed.), Das politische System der Bundesrepublik Deutschland (pp. 501–531). Wiesbaden: Springer VS.

Ruepert, A., Keizer, K., Steg, L., Maricchiolo, F., Carrus, G., Dumitru, A., García Mira, R., Stancu, A., & Moza, D. (2016). Environmental considerations in the organizational context: A pathway to pro-environmental behaviour at work. *Energy Research & Social Science, 17*, 59–70. https://doi.org/10.1016/j.erss.2016.04.004

Rügenhagen, J. U. (2013). Die betriebliche Mitbestimmung im Konzern. Baden-Baden: Nomos.

Ruggiero, S., Onkila, T., & Kuittinen, V. (2014). Realizing the social acceptance of community renewable energy: A process-outcome analysis of stakeholder influence. Energy Research & Social Science, 4, 53–63.

Ruiz-Romero, S., Colmenar-Santos, A., Mur-Pérez, F., & López-Rey, Á. (2014). Integration of distributed generation in the power distribution network: The need for smart grid control systems, communication and equipment for a smart city – Use cases. Renewable and Sustainable Energy Reviews, 38, 223–234.

Rule, T. A. (2014). Solar, Wind and Land. Conflicts in Renewable Energy Development. London, New York: Routledge.

Ruppert-Winkel, C., & Hauber, J. (2014). Changing the Energy System towards Renewable Energy Self-Sufficiency – Towards a multi-perspective and Interdisciplinary Framework. Sustainability, 6 (5), 2822–2831.

Ruppert-Winkel, C., Hauber, J., Aretz, A., Funcke, S., Kress, M., Noz, S., Salecki, S., Schlager, P., & Stablo, J. (2013). Die Energiewende gemeinsam vor Ort gestalten. Ein Wegweiser für eine sozial gerechte und naturverträgliche Selbstversorgung aus Erneuerbaren Energien-Schwerpunkt Bioenergie. ZEE Working Paper 06. Freiburg: Zentrum für Erneuerbare Energien (ZEE). http://www.zee-uni-freiburg.de/fileadmin/PDF2013/EE-Regionen_Wegweiser_2013.pdf

Russell, P. H., & Sossin, L. (Eds.). (2009). Parliamentary Democracy in Crisis. Toronto, Buffalo: University of Toronto Press.

Ryan, S. E., Hebdon, C., & Dafoe, J. (2014). Energy research and the contributions of the social sciences: A contemporary examination. Energy Research & Social Science, 3, 186–197.

Rydin, Y., Guy, S., Goodier, C., Chmutina, K., Devine-Wright, P., & Wiersma, B. (2015). The financial entanglements of local energy projects. Geoforum, 59, 1–11.

Rydin, Y., Turcu, C., Chmutina, K., Devine-Wright, P., Goodier, C., Guy, S., Hunt, L., Milne, S., Rynikiewicz, C., Sheriff, G., Watson, J., & Wiersma, B. (2012). Urban energy initiatives: the implications of new urban energy pathways for the UK. Network Industries Quarterly, 14 (2 & 3), 20–23.

Rydzy, E., & Griefahn, M. (2014). *Natürlich wachsen*. Wiesbaden: Springer VS. https://doi.org/10.1007/978-3-658-02850-3

Ryker, L. (2007). Off the grid homes: case studies for sustainable living. Salt Lake City, Utah: Gibbs Smith.

Sack, D. (2013). Regieren und Governance in der BRD. Ein Studienbuch. München: Oldenbourg.

Sack, D. (2014). Governance und Gouvernementalität. Komplementäres und Distinktes zweier Regierungslehren. In: A. Vasilache (Ed.): Gouvernementalität, Staat und Weltgesellschaft. Studien zum Regieren im Anschluss an Foucault. Wiesbaden: Springer Fachmedien, pp. 101–135.

Sack, D. (2018). Zwischen europäischer Liberalisierung und Energiewende – Der Wandel der Governanceregime im Energiesektor (1990 – 2016). In L. Holstenkamp & J. Radtke (Eds.), *Handbuch Energiewende und Partizipation* (pp. 81–99). Wiesbaden: Springer VS. https://doi.org/10.1007/978-3-658-09416-4_6

Sagebiel, J., Müller, J. R., & Rommel, J. (2014). Are consumers willing to pay more for electricity from cooperatives? Results from an online Choice Experiment in Germany. Energy Research & Social Science, 2, 90–101.

Salamon, L. M. (2010). The changing context of nonprofit leadership and management. In D. O. Renz (Ed.), The Jossey-Bass handbook of nonprofit leadership and management (pp. 77–100). San Francisco, Calif.: Jossey-Bass.

Salheiser, A. (2014). Natürliche Daten: Dokumente. In N. Baur & J. Blasius (Eds.), Handbuch Methoden der empirischen Sozialforschung (pp. 813–827). Wiesbaden: Springer VS.

Salomon, D. (2010). Elemente neuer Bürgerlichkeit. Bourgeois und Citoyen in der postdemokratischen Elitenherrschaft. Prokla: Zeitschrift für kritische Sozialwissenschaft, 160 (325), 311–325.

Sandberg, B. (2011). *Corporate Social Responsibility in kommunalen Unternehmen: Wirtschaftliche Betätigung zwischen öffentlichem Auftrag und gesellschaftlicher Verantwortung*. Wiesbaden: VS Verlag.

Sandberg, B., & Embacher, S. (2014). Auf dem Weg zum De-Aktivierenden Staat? Zum Widerspruch von Leitbildrhetorik und engagementpolitischem Handeln. Verwaltung & Management, 20 (1), 30–38.

Sandel, M. J. (1982). Liberalism and the limits of justice. Cambridge: Cambridge University Press.

Sandner, K. (1993). Prozesse der Macht. Zur Entstehung, Stabilisierung und Veränderung der Macht von Akteuren in Unternehmen (2nd ed.). Heidelberg: Physica.

Santoyo-Castelazo, E., & Azapagic, A. (2014). Sustainability assessment of energy systems: integrating environmental, economic and social aspects. Journal of Cleaner Production, 80, 119–138.

Saretzki, T. (2001). Energiepolitik in der Bundesrepublik Deutschland 1949–1999. In U. Willems (Ed.), Demokratie und Politik in der Bundesrepublik 1949–1999 (pp. 195–221). Wiesbaden: VS Verlag.

Saretzki, T. (2010). Umwelt- und Technikkonflikte: Theorien, Fragestellungen, Forschungsperspektiven. In P. H. Feindt & T. Saretzki (Eds.), Umwelt- und Technikkonflikte (pp. 33–53). Wiesbaden: VS Verlag.

Saretzki, T. (2011). Der Klimawandel und die Problemlösungsfähigkeit der Demokratie. In S. S. Schüttemeyer (Ed.), Politik im Klimawandel. Keine Macht für gerechte Lösungen (pp. 41–63). Baden-Baden: Nomos.

Saretzki, T., & Bornemann, B. (2014). Die Rolle von Unternehmensdialogen im gesellschaftlichen Diskurs über umstrittene Technikentwicklungen. Der "InfoDialogFracking." Forschungsjournal Soziale Bewegungen, 27 (4), 70–82.

Sarrica, M., Brondi, S., Cottone, P., & Mazzara, B. M. (2016). One, no one, one hundred thousand energy transitions in Europe: The quest for a cultural approach. *Energy Research & Social Science, 13*, 1–14. https://doi.org/10.1016/j.erss.2015.12.019

Sartori, G. (1994). Compare why and how. Comparing, miscomparing and the comparative method. In M. Dogan & A. Kazancigil (Eds.), Comparing nations: concepts, strategies, substance (pp. 14–34). Oxford: Blackwell.

Sauer, B. (1994). Was heißt und zu welchem Zweck partizipieren wir? Kritische Anmerkungen zur Partizipationsforschung. In E. Biester, B. Holland-Cunz, & B. Sauer (Eds.), Demokratie oder Androkratie?: Theorie und Praxis demokratischer Herrschaft in der feministischen Diskussion (pp. 99–130). Frankfurt a. M., New York: Campus.

Sauer, T., Barnebeck, S., Kalff, Y., Schicklinski, J., Elsen, S., Garzillo, C., Hopp, J., & Kuhn, S. (2015a). The Role of Cities in the Socio-Ecological Transition of Europe (ROCSET). WWWforEurope Working Paper No. 93.

Sauer, T., Elsen, S., Kuhn, S., Barnebeck, S., Garzillo, C., Kalff, Y., & Schicklinski, J. (2015b). Cities: Places of new European prosperity. Compendium of case studies on the socioecological transition of urban commons. WWWforEurope Working Paper No. 6.

Saunders, R. W., Gross, R. J. K., & Wade, J. (2012). Can premium tariffs for micro-generation and small scale renewable heat help the fuel poor, and if so, how? Case studies of innovative finance for community energy schemes in the UK. Energy Policy, 42, 78–88.

Saward, M. (Ed.). (2000). Democratic Innovation. Deliberation, representation and association. London: Routledge.

Saward, M. (2006). Democracy and citizenship: expanding domains. In J. S. Dryzek (Ed.), The Oxford handbooks of political science: The Oxford handbook of political theory (pp. 400–419). Oxford: Oxford University Press.

Scammell, M. (2000). The internet and civic engagement. The age of the citizen-consumer. Political Communication, 17 (4), 351–355.

Scerri, A. (2012). Greening citizenship: sustainable development, the state and ideology. Basingstoke, New York: Palgrave Macmillan.

Scerri, A., & Magee, L. (2012). Green householders, stakeholder citizenship and sustainability. Environmental Politics, 21 (3), 387–411.

Schaal, G. S. (2012). Oligarchie als bessere Demokratie. In O. W. Lembcke, C. Ritzi, & G. S. Schaal (Eds.), Zeitgenössische Demokratietheorie (pp. 445–472). Wiesbaden: Springer VS.

Schaal, G. S., & Ritzi, C. (2009). Empirische Deliberationsforschung. Köln: MPIfG. MPIfG Working Paper. http://www.mpifg.de/pu/workpap/wp09-9.pdf

Schaal, G. S., Lemke, M., & Ritzi, C. (2014). Die Ökonomisierung der Politik in Deutschland: eine vergleichende Politikfeldanalyse. Wiesbaden: Springer VS.

Schack, K., & Gellrich, A. (2015). *Umweltbewusstsein in Deutschland 2014. Ergebnisse einer repräsentativen Bevölkerungsumfrage*. Berlin: Bundesmin. für Umwelt, Naturschutz, Bau und Reaktorsicherheit.

Schaefers, K. (2014). Nachhaltiges Investieren: ein wirtschaftsethisches Beratungskonzept. Bern: Haupt.

Schäfer, A. (2006a). Die demokratische Grenze output-orientierter Legitimation. Integration, 29 (3), 187–200.

Schäfer, A. (2006b). Nach dem permissiven Konsens: das Demokratiedefizit der Europäischen Union. Leviathan, 34, 350–376.

Schäfer, A. (2011). Mehr Mitsprache, aber nur für wenige? Direkte Demokratie und politische Gleichheit. Max-Planck-Institut für Gesellschaftsforschung: MPIfG-Jahrbuch, 1 (1), 53–61.

Schäfer, A. (2013a). Der Verlust politischer Gleichheit: warum ungleiche Beteiligung der Demokratie schadet. In K. Armingeon (Ed.), Staatstätigkeiten, Parteien und Demokratie: Festschrift für Manfred G. Schmidt (pp. 547–566). Wiesbaden: VS Verlag.

Schäfer, A., & Schoen, H. (2013). Mehr Demokratie, aber nur für wenige? Der Zielkonflikt zwischen mehr Beteiligung und politischer Gleichheit. Leviathan, 41 (1), 94–120.

Schäfer, F., Daniel, A., & Hillebrandt, F. (Eds.). (2014). Methoden einer Soziologie der Praxis. Bielefeld: Transcript.

Schäfer, H. (2013b). Die Instabilität der Praxis. Reproduktion und Transformation des Sozialen in der Praxistheorie. Weilerswist: Velbrück.

Schaffer, G., & Eidherr, W. (1973). Ideen und Probleme der Mitbestimmung. Wien: Jupiter.

Schaffer, A., Lang, E., & Hartard, S. (Eds.). (2014). Systeme in der Krise im Fokus von Resilienz und Nachhaltigkeit. Marburg: Metropolis.

Schaper, D. M. (2010). Making ecopreneurs: developing sustainable entrepreneurship. Farnham: Gower Publishing.

Schäpke, N., & Rauschmayer, F. (2014). Going beyond efficiency: Including altruistic motives in behavioral models for sustainability transitions to address sufficiency. *Sustainability: Science, Practice and Policy, 10*(1), 29–44. https://doi.org/10.1080/15487733.2014.11908123

Schäpke, N., Singer-Brodowski, M., Stelzer, F., Bergmann, M., & Lang, D. J. (2015). Creating Space for Change. Real-world Laboratories for Sustainability Transformations – The Case of Baden-Württemberg. GAIA – Ecological Perspectives for Science and Society, 24 (4), 281–283.

Scharpf, F. W. (1994). Optionen des Föderalismus in Deutschland und Europa. Frankfurt a. M., New York: Campus.

Scharpf, F. W. (1999). Regieren in Europa: effektiv und demokratisch? Frankfurt a. M., New York: Campus.

Scharpf, F. W. (2005). Legitimationskonzepte jenseits des Nationalstaats. In G. F. Schuppert & M. Bach (Eds.), Europawissenschaft (pp. 705–741). Baden-Baden: Nomos.

Schaumann, G. K. (2011). Genossenschaften benötigen eine Unternehmenskultur mit großer „SOG-Kraft". In Verein zur Förderung der Solidarischen Ökonomie e. V. (Eds.), Schritte auf dem Weg zur solidarischen Ökonomie. Workshop (pp. 129–134). Kassel: Kassel University Press.

Scheer, H. (2010). Der energethische Imperativ. 100 Prozent jetzt: wie der vollständige Wechsel zu erneuerbaren Energien zu realisieren ist. München: Kunstmann.

Schein, E. H., Schneier, I., & Barker, C. H. (1961). Coercive persuasion: a socio-psychological analysis of the "brainwashing" of american civilian prisoners by the chinese communists. New York: Norton.

Scheiner, K., Graf, A., & Härdtlein, M. (2015). Intelligente Infrastrukturen im Kontext der deutschen Energiewende. Eine Analyse des sozio-technischen Innovationsfeldes. LI-TRES Discussion Paper 2014-04. Universität Stuttgart, Institut für Sozialwissenschaften, Abteilung für Organisations- und Innovationssoziologie.

Schelisch, L. (2013). Nachhaltiges Wohnen auf höchstem Niveau. Vernetzte Technik und Dienstleistungen in Wohnungsgenossenschaften. In J. Blazda, M. Dellinger, & D. Rößl (Eds.), Genossenschaften im Fokus einer neuen Wirtschaftspolitik. Bericht der XVII. Internationalen Genossenschaftswissenschaftlichen Tagung (IGT) 2012 in Wien. Teilband 3 (pp. 945–950). Wien: LIT.

Scherb, A. (2008). Der Bürger in der Streitbaren Demokratie. Über die normativen Grundlagen Politischer Bildung. Wiesbaden: VS Verlag.

Schiller, T. (2012). Direkte Demokratie – die mühsame Öffnung zum Volksentscheid. In S. Braun & A. Geisler (Eds.), Die verstimmte Demokratie (pp. 199–207). Wiesbaden: VS Verlag.

Schimank, U., & Volkmann, U. (2008). Ökonomisierung der Gesellschaft. In A. Maurer (Ed.), Handbuch der Wirtschaftssoziologie (pp. 382–393). Wiesbaden: VS Verlag.

Schippl, J., & Grunwald, A. (2013). Energiewende 2.0 – vom technischen zum soziotechnischen System? Einführung in den Schwerpunkt. TATuP – Zeitschrift des ITAS zur Technikfolgenabschätzung, 2, 4–10.

Schlozman, K. L., Brady, H. E., & Verba, S. (Eds.). (2012). The unheavenly chorus: unequal political voice and the broken promise of American democracy. Princeton: Princeton University Press.

Schlozman, K. L., Verba, S., & Brady, H. E. (1999). Civic participation and the equality problem. In T. Skocpol & M. P. Fiorina (Eds.), Civic participation and the equality problem (pp. 427–459). Washington, D.C: Brookings Inst. Press u. a.

Schlozman, K. L., Verba, S., & Brady, H. E. (2010). Weapon of the strong? Participatory inequality and the Internet. Perspectives on Politics, 8 (2), 487–509.

Schluchter, W. (2002). Stadtentwicklung und Partizipation. In E. Riehle (Ed.), Stadtentwicklung, Gemeinwesen und Mediation (pp. 45–61). Münster: LIT.

Schmale, I. (2012). Genossenschaften und soziale Marktwirtschaft in einer pluralistischen Gesellschaft: Wege zu einer gerechteren und leistungsfähigeren Entwicklung. In Genossenschaftliche Kooperation – anders wirtschaften (pp. 19–35). Baden-Baden: Nomos.

Schmale, I., & Degens, P. (2013). Selbstbestimmung, Lebenslage und Fähigkeiten: Beiträge von Genossenschaften zur wirtschaftlichen und sozialen Entwicklung. In J. Brazda, M. Dellinger, & D. Rößl (Eds.), Genossenschaften im Fokus einer neuen Wirtschaftspolitik. Bericht der XVII. Internationalen Genossenschaftswissenschaftlichen Tagung (IGT) 2012 in Wien. Teilband 3 (pp. 775–794). Wien: LIT.

Schmalz-Bruns, R. (1995). Reflexive Demokratie. Die demokratische Transformation moderner Politik. Baden-Baden: Nomos.

Schmid, B. E. (2009). Beteiligungsorientierung in Unternehmen. Eine Studie zum Einfluss von partizipativen Strukturen und Verfahren auf die psychologische Bindung von Unternehmensmitgliedern. Innsbruck: University Press.

Schmid, E., Knopf, B., & Pechan, A. (2016). Putting an energy system transformation into practice: The case of the German Energiewende. Energy Research & Social Science, 11, 263–275.

Schmid, S. I., & Zimmer, R. (2012). Akzeptanz von Windkraftanlagen in Baden-Württemberg. Studie im Rahmen des UfU-Schwerpunktes „Erneuerbare Energien im Konflikt". Berlin. http://www.ufu.de/media/content/files/Fachgebiete/Ressourcenschutz/UfU%20Paper%201-13%20Akzeptanz%20von%20Windkraftanla-gen%20in%20Baden%20Wuerttemberg.pdf

Schmidt, G. (2014). Urban Governance zwischen Inklusion und Effektivität. Lokale Partnerschaften in New Labours integrierter Stadtteilentwicklung. Wiesbaden: VS Verlag.

Schmitt-Egner, P. (2015). Gemeinwohl. Konzeptionelle Grundlinien zur Legitimität und Zielsetzung von Politik im 21. Jahrhundert. Baden-Baden: Nomos.

Schneider-Wilkes, R. E. (2001). Engagement und Misserfolg in Bürgerinitiativen. Politische Lernprozesse von Berliner Verkehrsbürgerinitiativen. Berlin: Freie Universität.

Schnelle, K., & Voigt, M. (2012). Energiewende und Bürgerbeteiligung. Öffentliche Akzeptanz von Infrastruktur-Projekten am Beispiel der „Thüringer Strombrücke". Studie im Auftrag von Germanwatch e. V., DAKT e.V. und Heinrich-Böll-Stiftung Thüringen. Erfurt: Heinrich-Böll-Stiftung Thüringen.

Schneidewind, U., & Zahrnt, A. (2013). *Damit gutes Leben einfacher wird.* oekom verlag. https://doi.org/10.14512/9783865816481

Schneidewind, U., Santarius, T., & Humburg, A. (Eds.). (2013). *Economy of sufficiency: Essays on wealth in diversity, enjoyable limits and creating commons*. Wuppertal: Wuppertal Inst. for Climate, Environment and Energy.

Schoene, H. (2011). Civic Engagement. In B. Badie, D. Berg-Schlosser, & L. Morlino (Eds.), International encyclopedia of political science. Vol. 1. A-Coh (pp. 250–251). Los Angeles: Sage.

Scholl, W., Breitling, K., & Janetzke, H. (2013). Innovationserfolg durch aktive Mitbestimmung. Die Auswirkungen von Betriebsratsbeteiligung, Vertrauen und Arbeitnehmerpartizipation auf Prozessinnovationen. Berlin: Edition Sigma.

Schönberg, T., & Jost, T. (2011). Stadtwerke als „gute Bürger". In B. Sandberg & K. Lederer (Eds.), Corporate Social Responsibility in kommunalen Unternehmen (pp. 309–321). Wiesbaden: VS Verlag.

Schoor, T. van der & Scholtens, B. (2015). Power to the people. Local community initiatives and the transition to sustainable energy. Renewable and Sustainable Energy Reviews 43, 666–675.

Schrape, J.-F. (2010). Neue Demokratie im Netz? Eine Kritik an den Visionen der Informationsgesellschaft. Bielefeld: Transcript.

Schreuer, A. (2016). The establishment of citizen power plants in Austria: A process of empowerment? Energy Research & Social Science, 13, 126–135.

Schreuer, A., & Weismeier-Sammer, D. (2010). Energy cooperatives and local ownership in the field of renewable energy technologies: A literature review. RiCC-Research Report, 4.

Schreurs, M. A., & Steuwer, S. (2015). Der Koordinierungsbedarf zwischen Bund und Ländern bei der Umsetzung der Energiewende aus politikwissenschaftlicher Sicht. In T. Müller & H. Kahl (Eds.), Energiewende im Föderalismus (pp. 45–67). Baden-Baden: Nomos.

Schröder, C., & Walk, H. (2013). Genossenschaftliche Handlungsmöglichkeiten in Zeiten des Klimawandels. In J. Brazda, M. Dellinger, & D. Rößl (Eds.), Genossenschaften im Fokus einer neuen Wirtschaftspolitik. Bericht der XVII. Internationalen Genossenschaftswissenschaftlichen Tagung (IGT) 2012 in Wien. Teilband 3 (pp. 883–892). Wien: LIT.

Schröder, C., & Walk, H. (Eds.). (2014). Genossenschaften und Klimaschutz. Akteure für zukunftsfähige, solidarische Städte. Wiesbaden: Springer VS.

Schröter, R., & Scheel, O. (2015). Bürgerbeteiligung bei großen Infrastrukturprojekten. Erfahrungsaustausch in Westkanada. GAIA – Ecological Perspectives for Science and Society, 24 (4), 284–285.

Schroeter, R., Scheel, O., Renn, O., & Schweizer, P.-J. (2016). Testing the value of public participation in Germany: Theory, operationalization and a case study on the evaluation of participation. *Energy Research & Social Science, 13*, 116–125. https://doi.org/10.1016/j.erss.2015.12.013

Schubert, H.-J. (2005). Fünf soziologische Theorien der Demokratie. Eine Typologie handlungstheoretisch begründeter Demokratietheorien als Ausgangspunkt komparativer Demokratieforschung. European Journal of Sociology, 46 (01), 3–43.

Schubert, S. (2014). The Need for Local Thermal Energy Planning. *Journal of Urban Technology, 21*(3), 21–36. https://doi.org/10.1080/10630732.2014.940700

Schubert, S. (2017). Mini-/Mikro-KWK als Innovationsimpuls an den Schnittstellen städtischer Energiesysteme. In G. Fuchs (Ed.), *Lokale Impulse für Energieinnovationen: Bürgerwind, Contracting, Kraft-Wärme-Kopplung, Smart Grid* (pp. 101–121). Wiesbaden: Springer VS. https://doi.org/10.1007/978-3-658-14801-0_5

Schudson, M. (2006). The troubling equivalence of citizen and consumer. The ANNALS of the American Academy of Political and Social Science, 608 (1), 193–204.

Schultze, R.-O. (2005). Partizipation. In D. Nohlen (Ed.), Lexikon der Politikwissenschaft. Theorien, Methoden, Begriffe (pp. 675–677). München: Beck.

Schulz, T., & Möller, B. (2015). Pilot des EEG-Systemwechsels – die FFAV: Die Ausschreibung der finanziellen Förderung für Solar-Freiflächenanlagen. Energierecht, 4 (3), 87–95.

Schumacher, E. F. (1973). Small Is Beautiful. Economics as if People Mattered. New York: Harper & Row.

Schumacher, U. (2003). Lohn und Sinn. Individuelle Kombinationen von Erwerbsarbeit und freiwilligem Engagement. Opladen: Leske + Budrich.

Schuppert, G. F. (1997). Assoziate Demokratie. Zum Platz des organisierten Menschen in der Demokratietheorie. In A. Klein & R. Schmalz-Bruns (Eds.), Politische Beteiligung und Bürgerengagement in Deutschland (pp. 114–152). Bonn: Bundeszentrale für Politische Bildung.

Schürmann, L. K. (2013). Motivation und Anerkennung im freiwilligen Engagement. Kampagnen und ihre Umsetzung in Internet und Social Media. Wiesbaden: Springer VS.

Schüssler, F. (Ed.). (2014). Geographische Energieforschung. Strukturen und Prozesse im Spannungsfeld zwischen Ökonomie, Ökologie und sozialer Sicherheit. Frankfurt: Peter Lang.

Schüttpelz, E., & Gießmann, S. (2015). Medien der Kooperation. Überlegungen zum Forschungsstand. In AG Medien der Kooperation (Ed.), Medien der Kooperation (pp. 7–54). Siegen: Universi, Univ.-Verl.

Schwalb, L. (2011). Kreative Governance? Public Private Partnerships in der lokalpolitischen Steuerung. Wiesbaden: VS Verlag.

Schwalb, L., & Walk, H. (Eds.). (2007). Local Governance. Mehr Transparenz und Bürgernähe? Wiesbaden: VS Verlag.

Schweizer, P.-J., Renn, O., Köck, W., Bovet, J., Benighaus, C., Scheel, O., & Schröter, R. (2016). Public participation for infrastructure planning in the context of the German "Energiewende." *Utilities Policy, 43*, 206–209. https://doi.org/10.1016/j.jup.2014.07.005

Schweizer-Ries, P. (2008). Energy sustainable communities. Environmental psychological investigations. Energy Policy, 36 (11), 4126–4135.

Schweizer-Ries, P. (2011). Socio-Environmental Research on Energy Sustainable Communities. Participation Experiences of Two Decades. In P. Devine-Wright (Ed.), Renewable Energy and the Public: From NIMBY to Participation (pp. 187–202). London u. a.: Earthscan.

Schweizer-Ries, P., Hildebrand, J., & Rau, I. (Eds.). (2013). Klimaschutz & Energienachhaltigkeit. Die Energiewende als sozialwissenschaftliche Herausforderung. Saarbrücken: Universaar.

Schweizer-Ries, P., Rau, I., & Zöllner, J. (2008). Projektabschlussbericht „Akzeptanz erneuerbarer Energien und sozialwissenschaftliche Fragen". Forschungsprojekt der Forschungsgruppe Umweltpsychologie. Projektlaufzeit: 01.07.2005–30.09.2008. Magdeburg: Otto-von-Guericke-Univ., Inst. f. Psychologie I, Forschungsgruppe Umweltpsychologie. http://edok01.tib.uni-hannover.de/edoks/e01fb09/612638286.pdf

Schweizer-Ries, P., Zöllner, J., & Rau, I. (2010). Akzeptanz neuer Netze. Die Psychologie der Energiewende. In Agentur für Erneuerbare Energien (Ed.), Kraftwerke für Jedermann: Chancen und Herausforderungen einer dezentralen erneuerbaren Energieversorgung. Sammelband Dezentralität (pp. 60–63). Reinheim: LokayDruck.

Schweizer-Ries, P., Zöllner, J., & Rau, I. (2016). Soziale Aspekte einer nachhaltigen Energieerzeugung. In L. Kruse (Ed.), Natur, Naturwahrnehmung, Naturschutz. Nachhaltige Entwicklung aus Sicht der Psychologie. Sankt Augustin: Academia.

Schweizer, P.-J. (2015). Partizipation bei der Energiewende und beim Ausbau der Stromnetze: Philosophische Fundierung. TAB-Brief Nr. 45. Berlin.

Schweizer, P.-J., & Renn, O. (2013). Partizipation in Technikkontroversen: Panakeia für die Energiewende? Technikfolgenabschätzung, 22, 42–47.

Scoones, I., Leach, M., & Newell, P. (Eds.). (2015). The Politics of Green Transformations. London, New York: Routledge.

Scott-Cato, M., & Hillier, J. (2010). How could we study climate-related social innovation? Applying Deleuzean philosophy to Transition Towns. Environmental Politics, 19 (6), 869–887.

Sebaldt, M. (2015). Pathologie der Demokratie. Defekte, Ursachen und Therapie des modernen Staates. Wiesbaden: Springer VS.

Seckelmann, M. (2014). Wohin schwimmt die Demokratie? „Liquid Democracy" auf dem Prüfstand. Die Öffentliche Verwaltung, 67 (1), 1–10.

Seibel, W. (2003). Das Spannungsfeld zwischen Mission und Ökonomie. VM: Fachzeitschrift für Verbands- und Nonprofit-Management, 29 (1), 48–50.

Seidl, I., & Zahrnt, A. (2010). *Postwachstumsgesellschaft: Konzepte für die Zukunft*. Marburg: Metropolis.

Sekulova, F., Kallis, G., Rodríguez-Labajos, B., & Schneider, F. (2013). Degrowth: from theory to practice. Journal of Cleaner Production, 38, 1–6.

Selle, K. (2000). Nachhaltige Kommunikation? Stadtentwicklung als Verständigungsarbeit: Entwicklungslinien, Stärken, Schwächen und Folgerungen. Informationen zur Raumentwicklung, (1), 9–19.

Selle, K. (2013). Über Bürgerbeteiligung hinaus. Stadtentwicklung als Gemeinschaftsaufgabe? Analysen und Konzepte. Detmold: Rohn.

Selle, K., & Beneke, G. (Eds.). (2000). Verständigungen über Planung und Kooperation. Erörterungen und Erfahrungsberichte. Dortmund: Dortmunder Vertrieb für Bau- und Planungsliteratur.

Selle, K., Rösener, B., & Rössig, M. (Eds.). (1996). Planung und Kommunikation. Gestaltung von Planungsprozessen in Quartier, Stadt und Landschaft. Grundlagen, Methoden, Praxiserfahrungen. Wiesbaden: Bauverl.

Send, H., Ebert, J., & Friesike, S. (2014). Online mitmachen und entscheiden: Partizipationsstudie 2014. Berlin: Alexander von Humboldt Institut für Internet und Gesellschaft.

Sennett, R. (2012). Zusammenarbeit. Was unsere Gesellschaft zusammenhält. München: Hanser.

Sennett, R. (2014). Verfall und Ende des öffentlichen Lebens. Die Tyrannei der Intimität (2nd ed.). Berlin: Berliner Taschenbuch-Verl.

Servatius, H.-G., Schneidewind, U., & Rohlfing, D. (2012). Smart Energy. Wandel zu einem nachhaltigen Energiesystem. Berlin: Springer.

Seubert, S. (2009). Das Konzept des Sozialkapitals: eine demokratietheoretische Analyse. Frankfurt a. M., New York: Campus.

Seyfang, G. (2005). Shopping for sustainability: can sustainable consumption promote ecological citizenship? Environmental Politics, 14 (2), 290–306.

Seyfang, G. (2006). Ecological citizenship and sustainable consumption: Examining local organic food networks. Journal of Rural Studies, 22 (4), 383–395.

Seyfang, G., & Haxeltine, A. (2010). Growing grassroots innovations: exploring the role of community-based initiatives in governing sustainable energy transitions. Working Paper. Centre for Social and Economic Research on the Global Environment. http://www.envplan.com/openaccess/c10222.pdf

Seyfang, G., & Haxeltine, A. (2012). Growing grassroots innovations: exploring the role of community-based initiatives in governing sustainable energy transitions. Environment and Planning-Part C: Government and Policy, 30, 381–400.

Seyfang, G., & Longhurst, N. (2012a). Grassroots innovation for sustainability: A niche analysis of community currencies. 3S Working Paper 2012-10. Norwich: Science, Society and Sustainability Research Group.

Seyfang, G., & Longhurst, N. (2012b). Money, Money, Money? A Scoping Study of Grassroots Complementary Currencies for Sustainability. 3S Working Paper 2012-02. Norwich: Science, Society and Sustainability Research Group.

Seyfang, G., & Longhurst, N. (2013). Growing green money? Mapping community currencies for sustainable development. Ecological Economics, 86, 65–77.

Seyfang, G., & Longhurst, N. (2016). What influences the diffusion of grassroots innovations for sustainability? Investigating community currency niches. Technology Analysis & Strategic Management, 28 (1), 1–23.

Seyfang, G., Haxeltine, A., Hargreaves, T., & Longhurst, N. (2010). Energy and communities in transition: Towards a new research agenda on agency and civil society in sustainability transitions. CSERGE working paper EDM No. 10-13.

Seyfang, G., Hielscher, S., Hargreaves, T., Martiskainen, M., & Smith, A. (2014). A grassroots sustainable energy niche? Reflections on community energy in the UK. Environmental Innovation and Societal Transitions, 13, 21–44.

Seyfang, G., Park, J. J., & Smith, A. (2012). Community energy in the UK. 3S Working Paper 2012-11. Norwich: Science, Society and Sustainability Research Group.

Seyfang, G., Park, J. J., & Smith, A. (2013). A thousand flowers blooming? An examination of community energy in the UK. Energy Policy, 61, 977–989.

Shaw, D., Newholm, T., & Dickinson, R. (2006). Consumption as voting: an exploration of consumer empowerment. European Journal of Marketing, 40 (9/10), 1049–1067.

Shenhav, S. R. (2005). Thin and thick narrative analysis: On the question of defining and analyzing political narratives. Narrative Inquiry, 15 (1), 75–99.

Shenhav, S. R. (2006). Political Narratives and Political Reality. International Political Science Review, 27 (3), 245–262.

Sherry, J. F. (2000). Place, Technology, and Representation. Journal of Consumer Research, 27 (2), 273–278.

Sherry-Brennan, F., Devine-Wright, H., & Devine-Wright, P. (2010). Public understanding of hydrogen energy: A theoretical approach. Energy Policy, 38 (10), 5311–5319.

Shippee, G. (1981). Energy conservation and the role of the social sciences. Energy Policy, 9 (1), 32–38.

Shirky, C. (2008). Here comes everybody: the power of organizing without organizations. New York: Penguin Press.

Shivakumar, A. R. (1996). Attempting to fulfil rural energy needs with community participation. Energy for Sustainable Development, 3 (1), 5–6.

Shove, E., & Spurling, N. (Eds.). (2012). Sustainable Practices. Social theory and climate change. Abingdon, New York: Routledge.

Shove, E., Walker, G., & Brown, S. (2014). Material culture, room temperature and the social organisation of thermal energy. Journal of Material Culture, 19 (2), 113–124.

Sidhu, I. (2015). The Digital Revolution. How Connected Digital Innovations Are Transforming Your Industry, Company & Career. Old Tappan, New Jersey: Pearson.

Siegenthaler, H. (2006). Unentgeltliche Arbeit in einer monetarisierten Welt. In P. Farago & H. Ammann (Eds.), Monetarisierung der Freiwilligkeit. Referate und Zusammenfassungen der 5. Tagung der Freiwilligenuniversität vom 30. bis 31.5.2005 in Luzern (pp. 29–43). Zürich: Seismo.

Simmons, P., & Walker, G. P. (2004). Living with technological risk. Industrial encroachment on sense of place. In A. Boholm & R. E. Lofstedt (Eds.), Facility Siting. Risk, Power and Identity in Land Use Planning (pp. 90–106). London: Earthscan.

Simon, K. (1983a). Lokale Vereine – Schule der Demokratie? Zum Einfluss lokaler Freizeitvereinigungen auf die politische Beteiligung der Bürger in der Gemeinde. In O. W. Gabriel (Ed.), Bürgerbeteiligung und kommunale Demokratie (pp. 241–270). München: Minerva.

Simon, K. (1983b). Von der Ein-Punkt-Aktion zur sozialen Bewegung? Bürgerinitiativen in der Kommunalpolitik. In O. W. Gabriel (Ed.), Bürgerbeteiligung und kommunale Demokratie (pp. 271–304). München: Minerva.

Simonis, G. (Ed.). (2013). Konzepte und Verfahren der Technikfolgenabschätzung. Wiesbaden: Springer VS.

Simonis, G., & Saretzki, T. (2001). Politik und Technik. Analysen zum Verhältnis von technologischem, politischem und staatlichem Wandel am Anfang des 21. Jahrhunderts. Wiesbaden: Westdeutscher Verlag.

Simsa, R., & Zimmer, A. (2014). Quo vadis? In A. Zimmer & R. Simsa (Eds.), Forschung zu Zivilgesellschaft, NPOs und Engagement (pp. 11–37). Wiesbaden: Springer VS.

Sintomer, Y., Herzberg, C., & Röcke, A. (2010). Der Bürgerhaushalt in Europa – eine realistische Utopie? Zwischen partizipativer Demokratie, Verwaltungsmodernisierung und sozialer Gerechtigkeit. Wiesbaden: VS Verlag.

Sircar, I., Sage, D., Goodier, C., Fussey, P., & Dainty, A. (2013). Constructing Resilient Futures. Integrating UK multi-stakeholder transport and energy resilience for 2050. Futures, 49, 49–63.

Skelcher, C., Mathur, N., & Smith, M. (2005). The public governance of collaborative spaces: Discourse, design and democracy. Public Administration, 83 (3), 573–596.

Skerratt, S. (2013). Enhancing the analysis of rural community resilience: Evidence from community land ownership. Journal of Rural Studies, 31, 36–46.

Skocpol, T. (1997). The Tocqueville Problem. Civic Engagement in American Democracy. Social Science History, 21 (4), 455–479.

Skocpol, T. (1999). Advocates without Members. The Recent Transformation of American Civic Life. In T. Skocpol & M. P. Fiorina (Eds.), Civic participation and the equality problem (pp. 461–509). Washington, D.C: Brookings Inst. Press u. a.

Skocpol, T. (2003). Diminished Democracy. From Membership to Management in American Civic Life. Norman: Univ. of Oklahoma Press.

Skocpol, T., & Fiorina, M. P. (1999). Civic engagement in American democracy. Washington, DC: Brookings Inst. Press.

Skopik, F. (2014). The social smart grid. Dealing with constrained energy resources through social coordination. Journal of Systems and Software, 89, 3–18.

Sladek, S. (2015). EWS Schönau: die Schönauer Stromrebellen. Energiewende in Bürgerhand. In H. Kopf (Ed.), Soziale Innovationen in Deutschland. Von der Idee zur gesellschaftlichen Wirkung (pp. 277–289). Wiesbaden: Springer VS.

Slee, B. (2015). Is there a case for community-based equity participation in Scottish on-shore wind energy production? Gaps in evidence and research needs. Renewable and Sustainable Energy Reviews, 41, 540–549.

Sliep, K. (2010). Bürgerkompetenzen von Vereinsmitgliedern. Eine empirische Untersuchung zu Bürgertypen in Vereinen. Dissertation. Paderborn: Universität Paderborn.

Slocum, R. (2004). Consumer citizens and the Cities for Climate Protection campaign. Environment and Planning A, 36 (5), 763–782.

Smith, A. (2007). Emerging in between: The multi-level governance of renewable energy in the English regions. Energy Policy, 35 (12), 6266–6280.

Smith, A. (2012). Civil Society in Sustainable Energy Transitions. In G. Verbong & D. Loorbach (Eds.), Governing the energy transition: reality, illusion or necessity? (pp. 180–202). New York: Routledge.

Smith, A., & Seyfang, G. (2013). Constructing grassroots innovations for sustainability. Global Environmental Change, 23 (5), 827–829.

Smith, A., & Stirling, A. (2007). Moving Outside or Inside? Objectification and Reflexivity in the Governance of Socio-Technical Systems. Journal of Environmental Policy & Planning, 9 (3–4), 351–373.

Smith, A., Hargreaves, T., Hielscher, S., Martiskainen, M., & Seyfang, G. (2015). Making the most of community energies: Three perspectives on grassroots innovation. Environment and Planning A, 48 (2), 407–432.

Smith, A., & Stirling, A. (2010a). Social-ecological resilience and socio- technical transitions: critical issues for sustainability governance. Brighton: STEPS Centre, University of Sussex.

Smith, A., & Stirling, A. (2010b). The politics of social-ecological resilience and sustainable socio-technical transitions. Ecology and Society, 15 (1), 1–13.

Smith, G. (2005a). Green citizenship and the social economy. Environmental Politics, 14 (2), 273–289.

Smith, G. (2005b). Power Beyond the Ballot: 57 Democratic Innovations from Around the World. A report for the Power Inquiry. London: The Power Inquiry.

Smith, G. (2009). Democratic Innovations. Designing Institutions for Citizen Participation. Cambridge, New York: Cambridge University Press.

Smith, G., Maloney, W., & Stoker, G. (2004). Building Social Capital in City Politics: Scope and Limitations at the Inter-organisational Level. Political Studies, 52 (3), 508–530.

Smith, G., & Stephenson, S. (2005). The Theory and Practice of Group Representation: Reflections on the Governance of Race Equality in Birmingham. Public Administration, 83 (2), 323–343.

Smith Stegen, K., & Seel, M. (2013). The winds of change: How wind firms assess Germany's energy transition. Energy Policy, 61, 1481–1489.

Sohre, A. (2014). Strategien in der Energie- und Klimapolitik. Bedingungen strategischer Steuerung der Energiewende in Deutschland und Grossbritannien. Wiesbaden: Springer VS.

Solar, M. (2016). Regieren im Schatten der Volksrechte. Direkte Demokratie in Berlin und Hamburg. Wiesbaden: Springer VS.

Soler, L. (Ed.). (2014). Science after the practice turn in the philosophy, history, and social studies of science. New York: Routledge.

Sommer, J. (Ed.). (2015). Kursbuch Bürgerbeteiligung. Berlin: Deutsche Umweltstiftung.

Sommer, J. (Ed.). (2017). Kursbuch Bürgerbeteiligung 2.0. Berlin: Deutsche Umweltstiftung.

Sommer, B., & Welzer, H. (2014). Transformationsdesign. Wege in eine zukunftsfähige Moderne. München: Oekom.

Songsore, E., & Buzzelli, M. (2014). Social responses to wind energy development in Ontario: The influence of health risk perceptions and associated concerns. Energy Policy, 69, 285–296.

Sonnberger, Marco, 2015: Der Erwerb von Photovoltaikanlagen in Privathaushalten, Wiesbaden: Springer VS.

Soper, K. (2004). Rethinking the "Good Life". The consumer as citizen. Capitalism Nature Socialism, 15 (3), 111–116.

Soper, K. (2007). Re-thinking the Good Life. The citizenship dimension of consumer disaffection with consumerism. Journal of Consumer Culture, 7 (2), 205–229.

Soper, K. (Ed.). (2008). Citizenship and consumption. Basingstoke, New York: Palgrave Macmillan.

Sørensen, H. C., Hansen, L. K., & Hammarlund, K. (2001). Social Acceptance, Environmental Impact and Politics: Final Report. Copenhagen.

Sørensen, H. C., Hansen, L. K., Hammarlund, K., & Larsen, J. H. (2002). Experience with and strategies for public involvement in offshore wind projects. International Journal of Environment and Sustainable Development, 1 (4), 327.

Southwell, B., Ronneberg, K., Shen, K., Jorgens, E., Hazel, J., Alemu, R., Ross, J., Richman, L., & Vermeer, D. (2014). Energy information engagement among the poor. Predicting participation in a free workshop. Energy Research & Social Science, 4, 21–22.

Sovacool, B. K. (2009). The cultural barriers to renewable energy and energy efficiency in the United States. Technology in Society, 31 (4), 365–373.

Sovacool, B. K. (2011). An international comparison of four polycentric approaches to climate and energy governance. Energy Policy, 39 (6), 3832–3844.

Sovacool, B. K. (2013). Energy policymaking in Denmark. Implications for global energy security and sustainability. Energy Policy, 61, 829–839.

Sovacool, B. K. (2014). What are we doing here? Analyzing fifteen years of energy scholarship and proposing a social science research agenda. Energy Research & Social Science, 1, 1–29.

Sovacool, B. K. (2016). How long will it take? Conceptualizing the temporal dynamics of energy transitions. Energy Research & Social Science, 13, 202–215.

Sovacool, B. K., & Brown, M. A. (2015). Deconstructing facts and frames in energy research. Maxims for evaluating contentious problems. Energy Policy, 86, 36–42.

Sovacool, B. K., & Dworkin, M. (2012). Overcoming the Global Injustices of Energy Poverty. Environment. Science and Policy for Sustainable Development, 54 (5), 14–28.

Sovacool, B. K., & Dworkin, M. H. (2015). Energy justice. Conceptual insights and practical applications. Applied Energy, 142, 435–444.

Sovacool, B. K., & Linnér, B.-O. (2015). The political economy of climate change adaptation. Basingstoke, New York: Palgrave Macmillan.

Sovacool, B. K., & Ryan, S. E. (2016). The geography of energy and education. Leaders, laggards, and lessons for achieving primary and secondary school electrification. Renewable and Sustainable Energy Reviews, 58, 107–123.

Sovacool, B. K., Brown, M. A., & Valentine, S. V. (2016). Fact and fiction in global energy policy: fifteen contentious questions. Baltimore: Johns Hopkins University Press.

Sovacool, B. K., Clarke, S., Johnson, K., Crafton, M., Eidsness, J., & Zoppo, D. (2013). The energy-enterprise-gender nexus: Lessons from the Multifunctional Platform (MFP) in Mali. Renewable Energy, 50, 115–125.

Sovacool, B. K., Linnér, B.-O., & Goodsite, M. E. (2015a). The political economy of climate adaptation. Nature Climate Change, 5 (7), 616–618.

Sovacool, B. K., Munoz Perea, M. A., Matamoros, A. V., & Enevoldsen, P. (2015b). Valuing the manufacturing externalities of wind energy. Assessing the environmental profit and loss of wind turbines in Northern Europe. Valuing the externalities of wind energy. Wind Energy, 1–25.

Sovacool, B. K., Ryan, S. E., Stern, P. C., Janda, K., Rochlin, G., Spreng, D., Pasqualetti, M. J., Wilhite, H., & Lutzenhiser, L. (2015c). Integrating social science in energy research. Energy Research & Social Science, 6, 95–99.

Sovacool, B. K., Sidortsov, R. V., & Jones, B. R. (2014). *Energy security, equality and justice*. Abingdon, Oxon: Routledge, Taylor & Frances Group.

Sozialministerium des Landes Baden-Württemberg. (2000a). Lebenswelt und Bürgerschaftliches Engagement. Stuttgart.

Sozialministerium des Landes Baden-Württemberg. (2000b). Ökonomie und Bürgerengagement. Beiträge zum 3. Sektor, zur Sozialwirtschaft und zur Bedeutung Bürgerschaftlichen Engagements in Baden-Württemberg. Stuttgart.

Späth, R. (2015. Forest Commons – Gemeinschaftswälder in Europa. Siegerland. Blätter des Siegerländer Heimat- und Geschichtsvereins e. V., 92 (2), 288–304.

Spennemann, F., & Stempka, S. (2010). Die Typologische Analyse nach Udo Kuckartz. In N. Schöneck-Voß, W. Voß, & J.-F. Kremer (Eds.), Methodenintegrative Forschung: Darstellung am Beispiel einer Befragung von Studierenden zu Studienbeiträgen (pp. 31–42). Bochum: Univ., Fak. für Sozialwiss.

Speth, R. (Ed.). (2013). Grassroots-Campaigning. Wiesbaden: Springer VS.

Spieß, E., & Nerdinger, F. W. (1998). Kooperation in Unternehmen. München u. a.: HamS.

Sprengel, R. (2007). Bürgerschaftliches Engagement und Organisationsentwicklung der Verbände: Gutachten erstellt für den Arbeitskreis „Bürgergesellschaft und Aktivierender Staat“ der Friedrich-Ebert-Stiftung. Bonn: Friedrich-Ebert-Stiftung.

Spring, J. (2003). Educating the consumer-citizen. A history of the marriage of schools, advertising, and media. Mahwah, NJ: Erlbaum.

Squitani, L., Vedder, H. H. B., Reese, M., & Elyakime, B. (Eds.). (2014). Sustainable Energy United in Diversity – Challenges and Approaches in Energy Transition in the European Union. Leipzig: European Environmental Law Forum.

Sreejesh, S., & Mohapatra, S. (2014). Mixed method research design: an application in consumer-brand relationships (CBR). New York: Springer.

St. Denis, G., & Parker, P. (2009). Community energy planning in Canada: The role of renewable energy. Renewable and Sustainable Energy Reviews, 13 (8), 2088–2095.

Staab, J. (2016). Erneuerbare Energien in Kommunen. Energiegenossenschaften gründen, führen und beraten (3rd ed.). Wiesbaden: Springer Gabler.

Stadelmann-Steffen, I., & Traunmüller, R. (2010). Scheckbuch-Partizipation als moderne Form des Engagements: die Spendenkulturen in den deutschen Kreisen. In M. Freitag & A. Vatter (Eds.), Vergleichende subnationale Analysen für Deutschland. Institutionen, Staatstätigkeiten und politische Kulturen (pp. 345–368). Münster: LIT.

Städler, A. (1984). Hierarchie in Unternehmungen. Eine Analyse der theoretischen Grundlagen sowie der Möglichkeiten und Grenzen einer Enthierarchisierung durch Organisation und Partizipation. Münster: Universität Münster.

Stadt Frankfurt a. M. (2007). „Ohne Moos nix los“ – Wie viel Bezahlung verträgt das Bürgerschaftliche Engagement? Dokumentation der Fachtagung vom 14. Februar 2007 in Frankfurt a. M. http://www.gemeinsam-aktiv.de/mm/ohnemoos_dokumentation.pdf

Staeheli, L. A. (2008). Citizenship and the problem of community. Political Geography, 27 (1), 5–21.

Stark, S. (2006). Nachhaltigkeitspolitik. *Die zukünftige Umweltpolitik oder das Stiefkind der Nationen? Eine vergleichende Studie vier europäischer Länder*. Dortmund: Rohn.

Stark, T. (2015). Determinanten politischen Verhaltens – (Un)konventionelle Partizipation und verhaltensprägende Einstellungen, „Determinants of Political Behavior – (Un) conventional Participation and Attitudes that Affect Behavior". Dissertation. Universität Duisburg-Essen: Fakultät für Gesellschaftswissenschaften, Institut für Politikwissenschaft. http://duepublico.uni-duisburg-essen.de/servlets/DocumentServlet?id=39171

Statistisches Bundesamt (2013). Statistisches Jahrbuch Deutschland und Internationales. Wiesbaden: Statistisches Bundesamt. https://www.destatis.de/DE/Publikationen/StatistischesJahrbuch/StatistischesJahrbuch2013.pdf

Statistisches Bundesamt. (2015). Statistisches Jahrbuch Deutschland 2015. Wiesbaden: Statistisches Bundesamt.

Statistisches Bundesamt (Destatis), & Wissenschaftszentrum Berlin für Sozialforschung (WZB) (Eds.). (2013). Datenreport 2013. Ein Sozialbericht für die Bundesrepublik Deutschland. Bonn: Bundeszentrale für politische Bildung.

Stecker, C. (2005). Nonprofit-Sektor, Sozialkapital und Zivilgesellschaft – Konzepte, Funktionen und Wirkungen. In P. Nitschke (Ed.), Die freiwillige Gesellschaft: über das Ehrenamt in Deutschland (pp. 17–40). Frankfurt a. M.: Lang.

Stecker, C., & Nährlich, S. (2005). Die „dunkle Seite“ von Dritte-Sektor-Organisationen. Funktionen, Effekte und Konsequenzen. In K. Birkhölzer, A. Klein, & A. Zimmer (Eds.), Dritter Sektor/Drittes System. Theorie, Funktionswandel und zivilgesellschaftliche Perspektiven (pp. 177–189). Wiesbaden: VS Verlag.

Steger, T., & Kranz, O. (2014). Zwischen Instrumentalisierung und Bedeutungslosigkeit. Mitarbeiter-Partizipation im organisationalen Kontext in Mittel- und Osteuropa. München u. a.: HamS.

Stehr, N. (Ed.). (2015). Der zündende Funke. Innovationen fördern als Weg zu sauberer und bezahlbarer Energie für alle. Wiesbaden: Springer VS.

Stein, T. (2015). Neue politische Engagementformen: Bürgerinnen und Bürger als civil entrepreneurs für die Transformation. In M. Tauschek & M. Grewe (Eds.), Knappheit, Mangel, Überfluss. Kulturwissenschaftliche Positionen zum Umgang mit begrenzten Ressourcen (pp. 103–123). Frankfurt a.M., New York: Campus.

Steinberg, R. (2014a). Die Bürgerbeteiligung bei Infrastrukturvorhaben. Entwicklung, Funktionen, Grenzen. In W. Ewer, U. Ramsauer, M. Reese, R. Rubel, H.-J. Koch (Eds.), Methodik – Ordnung – Umwelt: Festschrift für Hans-Joachim Koch aus Anlass seines siebzigsten Geburtstags (pp. 253–267). Berlin: Duncker & Humblot.

Steinberg, R. (2014b). Direkte Demokratie in politischen Parteien. Überlegungen anlässlich des Mitgliederentscheids der SPD. Zeitschrift Für Parlamentsfragen, 45 (2), 402–415.

Steiner, G., & Schütt, A. (2011). „Vertrauen in Deutschland“ und genossenschaftliche Werte. Zeitschrift für das gesamte Genossenschaftswesen, 61 (3), 201–216.

Steinfort, J. (2010). Identität und Engagement im Alter. Eine empirische Untersuchung. Wiesbaden: VS Verlag.

Steinkellner, V. (Ed.). (2015). CSR und Kultur. Berlin, Heidelberg: Springer.

Stephens, J. C. (2019). Energy Democracy: Redistributing Power to the People Through Renewable Transformation. *Environment: Science and Policy for Sustainable Development, 61*(2), 4–13. https://doi.org/10.1080/00139157.2019.1564212

Stephenson, J., Barton, B., Carrington, G., Gnoth, D., Lawson, R., & Thorsnes, P. (2010). Energy cultures: A framework for understanding energy behaviours. Energy Policy, 38 (10), 6120–6129.

Stern, P. C. (2014). Individual and household interactions with energy systems. Toward integrated understanding. Energy Research & Social Science, 1, 41–48.

Stern, R. N., & McCarthy, S. M. (Eds.). (1986). The organizational practice of democracy. Chichester u. a.: Wiley.

Stevens, G. L. (1994). Linking consumer rights with citizen roles. An opportunity for consumer educators. Journal of Consumer Education, 12, 1–8.

Steward, F., Liff, S., & Dunkelan, M. (2009). Mapping the Big Green Challenge: an analysis of 355 community proposals for low carbon innovation. Project Report. NESTA (National Endowment for Science, Technology and the Arts). http://www.swslim.org.uk/documents/themes/lt18-resource48.pdf

Stier, B. (1999). Staat und Strom. Ubstadt-Weiher: verlag regionalkultur.

stiftung 100 prozent erneuerbar, Haug, S., & Mono, R. (2012). Akzeptanz für Erneuerbare Energien: Akzeptanz planen, Bürgerbeteiligung gestalten, Legitimität gewinnen. Norderstedt: Books on Demand.

Stigka, E. K., Paravantis, J. A., & Mihalakakou, G. K. (2014). Social acceptance of renewable energy sources. A review of contingent valuation applications. Renewable and Sustainable Energy Reviews, 32, 100–106.

Stirling, A. (2011). Pluralising progress: From integrative transitions to transformative diversity. Environmental Innovation and Societal Transitions, 1 (1), 82–88.

Stirling, A. (2014). Transforming power: Social science and the politics of energy choices. Energy Research & Social Science, 1, 83–95.

Stirling, A. (2015a). Does the Anthropocene mean we have to „put Democracy on Hold"?, STEPS Centre Blog, 3. August 2015. http://steps-centre.org/2015/blog/does-the-anthropocene-mean-we-have-to-put-democracy-on-hold

Stirling, A. (2015b). From Knowledge Economy to Innovation Democracy. Blog for STEPS Centre 'the Crossing', 28. Januar 2015. http://steps-centre.org/2015/blog/stirlinginnovdemo

Stirling, A. (2016). Knowing Doing Governing: Realising Heterodyne Democracies. In J.-P. Voss & R. Freeman (Eds.), Knowing governance: the epistemic construction of political order (pp. 259–286). Basingstoke, New York: Palgrave.

Stirling, A., Leach, M., Mehta, L., Scoones, I., Smith, A., Stagl, S. & Thompson, J. (2007). Empowering Designs: towards more progressive appraisal of sustainability. STEPS Working Paper 3, Brighton: STEPS Centre, University of Sussex.

Stohl, C., & Cheney, G. (2001). Participatory Processes/Paradoxical Practices Communication and the Dilemmas of Organizational Democracy. Management Communication Quarterly, 14 (3), 349–407.

Stoker, G. (1998). Governance as theory: five propositions. International Social Science Journal, 50 (155), 17–28.

Stolle, D., Hooghe, M., & Micheletti, M. (2004). Zwischen Markt und Zivilgesellschaft. Politischer Konsum als bürgerliches Engagement. In D. Gosewinkel, D. Rucht, W. van der Daele, J. Kocka (Eds.), Zivilgesellschaft – national und transnational (pp. 151–172). Berlin: Edition Sigma.

Stolle, D., Hooghe, M., & Micheletti, M. (2005). Politics in the Supermarket. Political Consumerism as a Form of Political Participation. International Political Science Review, 26 (3), 245–269.

Stolle, D., & Micheletti, M. (2013). Political consumerism: global responsibility in action. New York: Cambridge University Press.

Stolze, F., & Petrlic, A. (2016). Nachhaltigkeit für Einsteiger. München: Oekom.

Stout, J. (2013). Blessed Are the Organized. Grassroots Democracy in America (3rd ed.). Princeton, NJ: Princeton Univ. Press.

Straka, G. A., & Macke, G. (2002). Lern-lehr-theoretische Didaktik. Münster: Waxmann.

Strasser, D. H., Dorfinger, M. N., & Mahler, B. (2012). Stadtwerk: Lehen. Solar energy in urban community in City of Salzburg, Austria. Energy Procedia, 30, 866–874.

Straßburger, G., & Rieger, J. (2014). Partizipation kompakt. Für Studium, Lehre und Praxis sozialer Berufe. Weinheim: Beltz Juventa.

Straughan, R. D., & Roberts, J. A. (1999). Environmental segmentation alternatives: a look at green consumer behavior in the new millennium. Journal of Consumer Marketing, 16 (6), 558–575.

Straughn, J. B., & Andriot, A. L. (2011). Education, Civic Patriotism, and Democratic Citizenship: Unpacking the Education Effect on Political Involvement. Sociological Forum, 26 (3), 556–580.

Streeck, W. (2013). Gekaufte Zeit. Die vertagte Krise des demokratischen Kapitalismus. Frankfurter Adorno-Vorlesungen 2012 (4th ed.). Berlin: Suhrkamp.

Stremke, S., & Dobbelsteen, A. van den (Eds.). (2013). Sustainable energy landscapes: designing, planning, and development. Boca Raton, FL: Taylor & Francis.

Stricker, M. (2007). Ehrenamt als soziales Kapital. Partizipation und Professionalität in der Bürgergesellschaft. Berlin: Köster.

Stricker, M. (2011). Ehrenamt. In T. Olk & B. Hartnuß (Eds.), Handbuch Bürgerschaftliches Engagement (pp. 163–171). Weinheim u. a.: Beltz Juventa.

Strømsnes, K. (2009). Political Consumerism: A Substitute for or Supplement to Conventional Political Participation? Journal of Civil Society, 5 (3), 303–314.

Struber, C. (2013). Wohnbau und E-Mobilität aus der Sicht eines gemeinnützigen Unternehmens. In J. Brazda, M. Dellinger, & D. Rößl (Eds.), Genossenschaften im Fokus einer neuen Wirtschaftspolitik. Bericht der XVII. Internationalen Genossenschaftswissenschaftlichen Tagung (IGT) 2012 in Wien. Teilband 3 (pp. 951–955). Wien: LIT.

Strübing, J. (2014a). Grounded Theory. Zur sozialtheoretischen und epistemologischen Fundierung des Verfahrens der empirisch begründeten Theoriebildung (3rd ed.). Wiesbaden: Springer VS.

Strübing, J. (2014b). Grounded Theory und Theoretical Sampling. In N. Baur & J. Blasius, Handbuch Methoden der empirischen Sozialforschung (pp. 457–472). Wiesbaden: Springer VS.

Strünck, C. (2011a). Der Mythos vom mündigen Verbraucher. Orientierungen zur Wirtschaftsund Gesellschaftspolitik, 129, 6–9.

Strünck, C. (2011b). Die Verbraucherpolitik braucht Pragmatismus statt wirklichkeitsferner Leitbilder. Wirtschaftsdienst, 91 (3), 165–168.

Strünck, C. (2014). Gibt es ein Recht auf Gemeinwohl? Öffentliche Interessen im Blickwinkel von Rechts- und Politikwissenschaft. Wiesbaden: Springer VS.

Strunz, S. (2013). The German energy transition as a regime shift. UFZ Discussion Papers No. 10/2013.

Strunz, S., Gawel, E., & Lehmann, P. (2016). The political economy of renewable energy policies in Germany and the EU. *Utilities Policy, 42*, 33–41. https://doi.org/10.1016/j.jup.2016.04.005

Strupeit, L., & Palm, A. (2016). Overcoming barriers to renewable energy diffusion: business models for customer-sited solar photovoltaics in Japan, Germany and the United States. Journal of Cleaner Production, 123, 124–136.

Stuart Wabe, J. (1988). The weak links in community energy policy. Energy Policy, 16 (3), 305–307.

Sundström, A., & McCright, A. M. (2016). Women and nuclear energy. Examining the gender divide in opposition to nuclear power among swedish citizens and politicians. Energy Research & Social Science, 11, 29–39.

Sunikka-Blank, M., & Galvin, R. (2016). Irrational homeowners? How aesthetics and heritage values influence thermal retrofit decisions in the United Kingdom. Energy Research & Social Science, 11, 97–108.

Suter, P. (2013). Member Value in Genossenschaften – ein multidimensionales Konstrukt. In M. Gmür (Ed.), Performance Management in Nonprofit-Organisationen. Theoretische Grundlagen, empirische Ergebnisse und Anwendungsbeispiele. Dokumentation zum 10. Internationalen NPO-Forschungscolloquium 2012 an der Universität Fribourg (pp. 326–334). Bern: Haupt.

Swyngedouw, E. (2010). Apocalypse Forever? Post-political Populism and the Spectre of Climate Change. Theory, Culture & Society, 27 (2–3), 213–232.

Szarka, J., Cowell, R., Ellis, G., Strachan, P. A., & Warren, C. (2012). Learning from Wind Power. Governance, Societal and Policy Perspectives on Sustainable Energy. Basingstoke, New York: Palgrave Macmillan.

Szatow, A., Quezada, G., & Lilley, B. (2012). New light on an old problem. Reflections on barriers and enablers of distributed energy. Energy Policy, 43, 1–5.

Szulecki, K. (2018). Conceptualizing energy democracy. *Environmental Politics, 27*(1), 21–41. https://doi.org/10.1080/09644016.2017.1387294

Szulecki, K., & Overland, I. (2020). Energy democracy as a process, an outcome and a goal: A conceptual review. *Energy Research & Social Science, 69*, 101768. https://doi.org/10.1016/j.erss.2020.101768

Taatila, V. P., Suomala, J., Siltala, R., & Keskinen, S. (2006). Framework to study the social innovation networks. European Journal of Innovation Management, 9 (3), 312–326.

Tan, B.-C., & Lau, T.-C. (2011). Green Purchase Behavior. Examining the Influence of Green Environmental Attitude, Perceived Consumer Effectiveness and Specific Green Purchase Attitude. Australian Journal of Basic and Applied Sciences, 5 (8), 559–567.

Tänzler, D., & Müller, A. (2014). Neue Handlungsspielräume erschließen: die Notwendigkeit einer Außenpolitik für die Energiewende. Jahrbuch Nachhaltige Ökonomie, 4 (15), 293–314.

Tarhan, M. D. (2015). Renewable Energy Cooperatives. A Review of Demonstrated Impacts and Limitations. The Journal of Entrepreneurial and Organizational Diversity 4, 104–120.

Tashakkori, A., & Teddlie, C. (Eds.). (2010). Sage handbook of mixed methods in social & behavioral research (2nd ed.). Los Angeles: Sage.

Tauschek, M., & Grewe, M. (Eds.). (2015). Knappheit, Mangel, Überfluss. Kulturwissenschaftliche Positionen zum Umgang mit begrenzten Ressourcen. Frankfurt a.M., New York: Campus.

Taylor, C. (2002). Wieviel Gemeinschaft braucht die Demokratie? Aufsätze zur politischen Philosophie. Frankfurt a. M.: Suhrkamp.

Taylor, J. B. (1970). Introducing social innovation. The Journal of Applied Behavioral Science, 6 (1), 69–77.

Telesiene, A., & Groß, M. (Eds.). (2016). Green European. Environmental Behaviour and Attitudes in Europe in a Historical and Cross-cultural Comparative Perspective. Abingdon, New York: Routledge.

Tenfelde, K. (2012). Arbeiter, Bürger, Städte. Zur Sozialgeschichte des 19. und 20. Jahrhunderts. Göttingen: Vandenhoeck & Ruprecht.

Teske, S. (2005). Energy (R)evolution. A sustainable world energy outlook. Report. Amsterdam: Greenpeace International. http://www.greenpeace.org/international/en/campaigns/climate-change/energyrevolution

Tester, J. W. (Ed.). (2012). Sustainable energy: choosing among options (2nd ed.). Cambridge, MA: MIT Press.

Tews, K. (2014). Energiearmut – vom politischen Schlagwort zur handlungsleitenden Definition. In A. Brunnengräber & M. R. Di Nucci (Eds.), Im Hürdenlauf zur Energiewende (pp. 441–449). Wiesbaden: Springer VS.

Thaa, W. (2009). Das ungelöste Inklusionsproblem in den partizipatorischen Neubewertungen politischer Repräsentation. In M. Linden & W. Thaa (Eds.), Die politische Repräsentation von Fremden und Armen (pp. 61–78). Baden-Baden: Nomos.

Thaa, W. (2011). Politisches Handeln. Demokratietheoretische Überlegungen im Anschluss an Hannah Arendt. Baden-Baden: Nomos.

The European Wind Energy Association (2012). Wind Energy – The Facts: A Guide to the Technology, Economics and Future of Wind Power. London: Earthscan.

The Scottish Government (2013). 2020 Routemap For Renewable Energy In Scotland – Update. Edinburgh. http://www.gov.scot/Resource/0044/00441628.pdf

Theocharis, Y., & van Deth, J. W. (2018). *Political Participation in a Changing World. Conceptual and Empirical Challenges in the Study of Citizen Engagement*. New York: Routledge.

Theurl, T. (2013). Genossenschaftliches MemberValue-Management. In M. Gmür (Ed.), Performance Management in Nonprofit-Organisationen. Theoretische Grundlagen, empirische Ergebnisse und Anwendungsbeispiele. Dokumentation zum 10. Internationalen NPO-Forschungscolloquium 2012 an der Universität Fribourg (pp. 316–325). Bern: Haupt.

Theuvsen, L. (2013). Nonprofit-Organisationen als Treiber der Nachhaltigkeitsdebatte. In M. Gmür (Ed.), Performance Management in Nonprofit-Organisationen. Theoretische Grundlagen, empirische Ergebnisse und Anwendungsbeispiele. Dokumentation zum 10. Internationalen NPO-Forschungscolloquium 2012 an der Universität Fribourg (pp. 403–411). Bern: Haupt.

Thiemann, B., & Armbruster, P. G. (2000). Die Genossenschaften an der Jahrtausendwende. Sicherung des Genossenschaftsgedankens zwischen Tradition und Moderne. Frankfurt a. M.: KnaS.

Thierbach, C., & Petschick, G. (2014). Beobachtung. In N. Baur & J. Blasius (Eds.), Handbuch Methoden der empirischen Sozialforschung (pp. 855–866). Wiesbaden: Springer VS.

Thießen, F. (2012). Grenzen der Demokratie. Die gesellschaftliche Auseinandersetzung bei Großprojekten (2nd ed.). Wiesbaden: Springer VS.

Thimm, C., & Bürger, T. (2012). Digitale Citoyens. Politische Partizipation in Zeiten von Social Media. Fallanalysen zur politischen Beteiligung in Deutschland, Ägypten und China. http://www.bapp-bonn.de/medien/downloads/publikation_forschungsergebnisse/publikation_forschungsergebnisse_kurz.pdf

Thompson, G., & Laufman, J. (1996). Civility and village power: renewable energy and playground politics. Energy for Sustainable Development, 3 (2), 29–33.

Thorson, K. (2012). What Does It Mean to Be a Good Citizen? Citizenship Vocabularies as Resources for Action. The ANNALS of the American Academy of Political and Social Science, 644 (1), 70–85.

Thüringer Energie- und GreenTech-Agentur (ThEGA). (2012). Energie von Bürgern für Bürger. Wie Bürger und Kommunen von der Energiewende profitieren. Erfurt. http://www.thega.de/service/publikationen/dokument/03-ener-gie-von-buergern-fuer-buerger

Tils, R. (2005). *Politische Strategieanalyse: Konzeptionelle Grundlagen und Anwendung in der Umwelt- und Nachhaltigkeitspolitik* (1st ed.). Wiesbaden: VS, Verl. für Sozialwiss.

Tiwary, A., Namdeo, A., Fuentes, J., Dore, A., Hu, X.-M., & Bell, M. (2013). Systems scale assessment of the sustainability implications of emerging green initiatives. Environmental Pollution, 183, 213–223.

Toffler, A. (1980). Die dritte Welle: Zukunftschancen. Perspektiven für die Gesellschaft des 21. Jahrhunderts. München: Goldmann.

Toke, D. (2005). Explaining wind power planning outcomes: some findings from a study in England and Wales. Energy Policy, 33 (12), 1527–1539.

Töller, A. E., & Vollmer, A. (2013). Wem nützt direkte Demokratie? Policy-Effekte direkter Demokratie und Folgerungen für die Forschung zu Deutschland. Zeitschrift für Vergleichende Politikwissenschaft, 7 (4), 299–320.

Tönnies, F. (1991). Gemeinschaft und Gesellschaft. Grundbegriffe der reinen Soziologie (8th ed.). Darmstadt: Wissenschaftliche Buchgesellschaft.

Ethik-Kommission Sichere Energieversorgung (2011). Deutschlands Energiewende. Ein Gemeinschaftswerk für die Zukunft. Rostock: Publikationsversand der Bundesregierung. http://www.bundesregierung.de/ContentArchiv/DE/Archiv17/_Anlagen/2011/07/2011-07-28-abschlussbericht-ethikkommission.pdf

Töpfer, K., Volkert, D., & Mans, U. (2013). Verändern durch Wissen. Chancen und Herausforderungen demokratischer Beteiligung: von „Stuttgart 21" bis zur Energiewende. München: Oekom.

Trachtenberg, Z. (2010). Complex green citizenship and the necessity of judgement. Environmental Politics, 19 (3), 339–355.

Trachtenberg, Z. (2015a). Anticipating the Anthropocene. Earth's Future, 3 (9), 313–316.

Trachtenberg, Z. (2015b). The Anthropocene, Ethics, and the Nature of Nature. Telos, 2015 (172), 38–58.

Tremmel, J., & Rutsche, M. (Eds.). (2015). Politische Beteiligung junger Menschen. Grundlagen – Perspektiven – Fallstudien. Wiesbaden: Springer VS.

trend:research GmbH, & Leuphana Universität Lüneburg. (2013). Definition und Marktanalyse von Bürgerenergie in Deutschland. Bremen, Lüneburg. http://www.leuphana.

de/fileadmin/user_upload/Forschungseinrichtungen/professuren/finanzierung-finanz-wirtschaft/files/Definition-und-Marktanalyse-von-Buergerenergie-in-Deutschland.pdf
Troglio, E., & Haas, T. (2013). Sustainable Urban Cells and the Energy Transect Modeling. Reconciling the Green and the Urban. ERSA Conference Paper. http://www-sre.wu.ac.at/ersa/ersaconfs/ersa13/ERSA2013_paper_00377.pdf
Trott zu Solz, L. (1999). „Big and Small Democracy". Zur Verbindung von Bürgergesellschaft und Demokratie. In U. von Alemann, R. G. Heinze, & U. Wehrhöfer (Eds.), Bürgergesellschaft und Gemeinwohl: Analyse, Diskussion, Praxis (pp. 69–82). Opladen: Leske + Budrich.
Trottier, D. (Ed.). (2015). Social media, politics and the state. Protests, revolutions, riots, crime and policing in the age of Facebook, Twitter and YouTube. New York: Routledge.
Trumann, J. (2013). Lernen in Bewegung(en). Politische Partizipation und Bildung in Bürgerinitiativen. Bielefeld: Transcript.
Trutnevyte, E., & Stauffacher, M. (2012). Opening up to a critical review of ambitious energy goals. Perspectives of academics and practitioners in a rural Swiss community. Environmental Development, 2, 101–116.
Trutnevyte, E., Stauffacher, M., & Scholz, R. W. (2011). Supporting energy initiatives in small communities by linking visions with energy scenarios and multi-criteria assessment. Energy Policy, 39 (12), 7884–7895.
Tsebelis, G. (2002). Veto Players. How Political Institutions Work. New York: Russell Sage Foundation.
Turner, M. D. (2015). Political ecology II. Engagements with ecology. Progress in Human Geography, 6. April 2015, 1–9.
Tveten, Å. G., Bolkesjø, T. F., Martinsen, T., & Hvarnes, H. (2013). Solar feed-in tariffs and the merit order effect: A study of the German electricity market. Energy Policy, 61, 761–770.
Tweed, J. (2015). Practitioner Comment – Local Energy Collaboration. The role of local authorities in community energy. People Place and Policy, 8 (3), 249–254.
Uhlendahl, T. (2013). Untersuchung von Beteiligungsprozessen in der Raum- und Umweltplanung – Ein methodischer Beitrag am Beispiel des Gewässermanagements. In E. Rothfuß & T. Dörfler (Eds.), Raumbezogene qualitative Sozialforschung (pp. 147–173). Wiesbaden: Springer VS.
Ullrich, A., Pogrebinschi, T., & Thaa, W. (2014). Repräsentation trifft Beteiligung. Berlin: Heinrich-Böll-Stiftung.
Ulrich, P. (2008). Integrative Wirtschaftsethik. Grundlagen einer lebensdienlichen Ökonomie. Bern: Haupt.
Umweltbundesamt. (2014). Reform des Erneuerbare-Energien-Gesetzes. Schriftliche Stellungnahme zur BT-Drucksache 18/1304. Anhörung im Bundestag am 4. Juni 2014. Dessau-Roßlau: UBA.
Unterrainer, C., Palgi, M., Weber, W. G., Iwanowa, A., & Oesterreich, R. (2011). Structurally anchored organizational democracy: does it reach the employee? Journal of Personnel Psychology, 10 (3), 118–132.
Upham, P., Oltra, C., & Boso, À. (2015). Towards a cross-paradigmatic framework of the social acceptance of energy systems. Energy Research & Social Science, 8, 100–112.
Urquhart, R. (2005). Ordinary Choices. Individuals, Incommensurability, and democracy. London, New York: Routledge.
Vahsen, F. G. (2014). Die erstarrte Gesellschaft. Zum Verlust des Gemeinsinns. Berlin: LIT.

van Veelen, B., & van der Horst, D. (2018). What is energy democracy? Connecting social science energy research and political theory. *Energy Research & Social Science, 46*, 19–28. https://doi.org/10.1016/j.erss.2018.06.010

Vannini, P., & Taggart, J. (2015). Off the grid. Re-assembling domestic life. New York: Routledge.

Varnelis, K., & Baer, W. (2008). Networked publics. Cambridge, Mass.: MIT Press.

Vasileiadou, E., Huijben, J. C. C. M., & Raven, R. P. J. M. (2016). Three is a crowd? Exploring the potential of crowdfunding for renewable energy in the Netherlands. *Journal of Cleaner Production, 128*, 142–155. https://doi.org/10.1016/j.jclepro.2015.06.028

Vaze, P., & Tindale, S. (Eds.). (2011). Repowering communities: small-scale solutions for large-scale energy problems. London: Earthscan.

Verba, S., & Nie, N. H. (1972). Participation in America. New York u. a.: Harper & Row.

Verba, S., Nie, N. H., & Kim, J.-O. (1978). Participation and political equality. A seven-nation comparison. Cambridge: Cambridge University Press.

Verba, S., Schlozman, K. L., & Brady, H. E. (1995). Voice and equality. Civic voluntarism in American politics. Cambridge, Mass.: Harvard University Press.

Verein Deutscher Ingenieure (VDI) (2013) VDI-Richtlinie: VDI 7000. Frühe Öffentlichkeitsbeteiligung bei Industrie- und Infrastrukturprojekten. Berlin: Beuth.

Verein Deutscher Ingenieure (VDI) (2014). VDI-Richtlinie: VDI 7001. Kommunikation und Öffentlichkeitsbeteiligung bei Planung und Bau von Infrastrukturprojekten. Standards für die Leistungsphasen der Ingenieure. Düsseldorf: VDI-Verl.

Verbong, G. P. J., Beemsterboer, S., & Sengers, F. (2013). Smart grids or smart users? Involving users in developing a low carbon electricity economy. Energy Policy, 52, 117–125.

Verbong, G., & Geels, F. (2007). The ongoing energy transition. Lessons from a socio-technical, multi-level analysis of the Dutch electricity system (1960–2004). Energy Policy, 35 (2), 1025–1037.

Verbong, G., & Loorbach, D. (Eds.). (2012). Governing the energy transition: reality, illusion or necessity? New York: Routledge.

Verdorfer, A. P., Weber, W. G., Unterrainer, C., & Seyr, S. (2013). The relationship between organizational democracy and socio-moral climate. Exploring effects of the ethical context in organizations. Economic and Industrial Democracy: EID, an International Journal, 34 (3), 423–449.

Vesnic-Alujevic, L., Breitegger, M., & Pereira, Â. G. (2016). What smart grids tell about innovation narratives in the European Union: Hopes, imaginaries and policy. Energy Research & Social Science, 12, 16–26.

Vetter, A. (2013). Zufriedenheit der Bürger mit politischen Institutionen und der Demokratie. In J. W. van Deth & M. Tausendpfund (Eds.), Politik im Kontext: Ist alle Politik lokale Politik? (pp. 359–380). Wiesbaden: VS Verlag.

Vetter, A. (Ed.) (2008). Erfolgsbedingungen lokaler Bürgerbeteiligung. Wiesbaden: VS Verlag.

Vetter, A., Klages, H., & Ulmer, F. (2013). Bürgerbeteiligung braucht Verstetigung und Verlässlichkeit. Gestaltungselemente einer dauerhaften und systematischen Bürgerbeteiligung in Städten und Gemeinden. Der Moderne Staat, 6 (1), 253–271.

Viardot, E. (2013). The role of cooperatives in overcoming the barriers to adoption of renewable energy. Energy Policy, 63, 756–764.

Vilmar, F. (1973). Strategien der Demokratisierung. Darmstadt: Luchterhand.

Vilmar, F. (1977). Elemente einer integralen Theorien der Partizipation. In O. Rammstedt (Ed.), Bürgerbeteiligung und Bürgerinitiativen. Legitimation und Partizipation in der

Demokratie angesichts gesellschaftlicher Konfliktsituationen (pp. 294–315). Villingen-Schwenningen: Neckar-Verl.
Vilmar, F., & Weber, W. G. (2004). Demokratisierung und Humanisierung der Arbeit – ein Überblick. In W. G. Weber (Ed.), Wirtschaft, Demokratie und Soziale Verantwortung (pp. 105–143). Göttingen: Vandenhoeck & Ruprecht.
Vogt, L. (2005). Das Kapital der Bürger. Theorie und Praxis zivilgesellschaftlichen Engagements. Frankfurt a. M., New York: Campus.
Vogt, L. (2009). Geschlossene Gesellschaft. Zur exklusiven Wirkung des Sozialkapitals am Beispiel einer deutschen Bürgerstiftung. Forschungsjournal Soziale Bewegungen, 3, 66–75.
Voigt, R. (2014). Den Staat denken. Der Leviathan im Zeichen der Krise (3rd ed.). Baden-Baden: Nomos.
Voigt, R. (Ed.). (2016). Staatsdenken. Zum Stand der Staatstheorie heute. Baden-Baden: Nomos.
Voigtländer, L. E. (2015). Armut und Engagement. Zur zivilgesellschaftlichen Partizipation von Menschen in prekären Lebenslagen. Bielefeld: Transcript.
Volz, R. (2011a). Strukturen und Merkmale von Energiegenossenschaften in Deutschland – Ausgewählte Ergebnisse einer bundesweit durchgeführten Vollerhebung. In R. Doluschitz (Ed.), Hohenheimer Genossenschaftsforschung 2011 (pp. 65–88). Filderstadt: F. und T. Müllerbader.
Volz, R. (2011b). Zur Umsetzung des Förderauftrags in Energiegenossenschaften. Zeitschrift für das gesamte Genossenschaftswesen, 61 (4), 289–304.
Volz, R. (2012a). Genossenschaften im Bereich erneuerbarer Energien. Status quo und Entwicklungsmöglichkeiten eines neuen Betätigungsfeldes. Stuttgart-Hohenheim: Forschungsstelle für Genossenschaftswesen an der Univ. Hohenheim.
Volz, R. (2012b). Bedeutung und Potenziale von Energiegenossenschaften in Deutschland. Eine empirische Aufbereitung. Informationen zur Raumentwicklung, 2012 (9–10), 515–524.
Vonken, M. (2005). Handlung und Kompetenz. Theoretische Perspektiven für die Erwachsenenund Berufspädagogik. Wiesbaden: VS Verlag.
Vorkinn, M., & Riese, H. (2001). Environmental Concern in a Local Context. The Significance of Place Attachment. Environment and Behavior, 33 (2), 249–263.
Vortkamp, W. (2003). Partizipation und soziale Integration in heterogenen Gesellschaften. Louis Wirths Konzeption sozialer Organisation in der Tradition der Chicagoer Schule. Wiesbaden: VS Verlag.
Vortkamp, W. (2005). Integration durch Partizipation. Aktives Bürgerengagement und die Rolle von Vereinen in Ostdeutschland. Forschungsjournal Soziale Bewegungen, 18 (3), 69–84.
Vortkamp, W. (2008). Integration durch Teilhabe. Das zivilgesellschaftliche Potenzial von Vereinen. Frankfurt a. M., New York: Campus.
Vortkamp, W. (2013). Wozu braucht die repräsentative Demokratie die Bürger? Forschungsjournal Soziale Bewegungen, 1, 10–18.
Voß, J.-P., Bauknecht, D., & Kemp, R. (Eds.). (2006). Reflexive Governance for Sustainable Development. Cheltenham: Edward Elgar.
Voss, K. (2014). Internet und Partizipation: Bottom-up oder Top-down? Politische Beteiligungsmöglichkeiten im Internet. Wiesbaden: Springer VS.

Voß, W., & Studierende. (2010). Clusteranalytische Klassfikation. In N. Schöneck-Voß, W. Voß, & J.-F. Kremer (Eds.), Methodenintegrative Forschung. Darstellung am Beispiel einer Befragung von Studierenden zu Studienbeiträgen (pp. 43–54). Bochum: Universität Bochum, Fak. für Sozialwiss.

Voßkuhle, A., Bumke, C., & Meinel, F. (Eds.). (2013). Verabschiedung und Wiederentdeckung des Staates im Spannungsfeld der Disziplinen. Berlin: Duncker & Humblot.

Vowe, G. (2014). Digital Citizens und Schweigende Mehrheit: Wie verändert sich die politische Beteiligung der Bürger durch das Internet? Ergebnisse einer kommunikationswissenschaftlichen Langzeitstudie. In K. Voss (Ed.), Internet und Partizipation (pp. 25–52). Wiesbaden: Springer VS.

Wade, M. (2015). Mikrokosmos Stadtviertel. Lokale Partizipation und Raumpolitik. Bielefeld: Transcript.

Wagner, F., & Ertner, S. (2016). Reallabore für nachhaltiges Wissen – Forschung für und mit Zukunft. GAIA, 25 (1), 57–58.

Wagner, P., Hering, L. (2014). Online-Befragung. In: N. Baur & J. Blasius (Eds.), Handbuch Methoden der empirischen Sozialforschung (pp. 661–673). Wiesbaden: Springer VS.

Wagner, T. (2013). Die Mitmachfalle. Bürgerbeteiligung als Herrschaftsinstrument. Köln: Papyrossa Verlagsgesellschaft.

Wahlund, M., & Palm, J. (2022). The role of energy democracy and energy citizenship for participatory energy transitions: A comprehensive review. *Energy Research & Social Science, 87*, 102482. https://doi.org/10.1016/j.erss.2021.102482

Wakefield, J. C. (1993). Is Altruism Part of Human Nature? Toward a Theoretical Foundation for the Helping Professions. Social Service Review, 67 (3), 406–458.

Walk, H. (2008). Partizipative Governance. Beteiligungsformen und Beteiligungsrechte im Mehrebenensystem der Klimapolitik. Wiesbaden: VS Verlag.

Walk, H. (2011). Kommentar zum Handbuch Partizipation, herausgegeben von der Senatsverwaltung für Stadtentwicklung Berlin. Bundesnetzwerk Bürgerschaftliches Engagement: BBE-Newsletter, 12, 3.

Walk, H. (2014). Energiegenossenschaften. Neue Akteure einer nachhaltigen und demokratischen Energiewende? In A. Brunnengräber & M. R. Di Nucci (Eds.), Im Hürdenlauf zur Energiewende (pp. 451–464). Wiesbaden: Springer VS.

Walker, B. J. A., Wiersma, B., & Bailey, E. (2014). Community benefits, framing and the social acceptance of offshore wind farms: An experimental study in England. Energy Research & Social Science, 3, 46–54.

Walker, G. (2008). What are the barriers and incentives for community-owned means of energy production and use? Energy Policy, 36 (12), 4401–4405.

Walker, G. (2011). The role for "community" in carbon governance. Wiley Interdisciplinary Reviews: Climate Change, 2 (5), 777–782.

Walker, G. P. (2012). Environmental justice. London, New York: Routledge.

Walker, G., & Cass, N. (2007). Carbon reduction, "the public" and renewable energy: engaging with socio-technical configurations. Area, 39 (4), 458–469.

Walker, G., & Day, R. (2012). Fuel poverty as injustice. Integrating distribution, recognition and procedure in the struggle for affordable warmth. Energy Policy, 49, 69–75.

Walker, G., & Devine-Wright, P. (2008). Community renewable energy: What should it mean? Energy Policy, 36 (2), 497–500.

Walker, G., & Shove, E. (2007). Ambivalence, Sustainability and the Governance of Socio-Technical Transitions. Journal of Environmental Policy & Planning, 9 (3–4), 213–225.

Walker, G., & Simcock, N. (2012). Community Energy Systems. In S. J. Smith (Ed.), International Encyclopedia of Housing and Home (pp. 194–198). San Diego: Elsevier.

Walker, G., Devine-Wright, P., & Evans, B. (2006). Community Energy Initiatives: Embedding Sustainable Technology at a Local Level. Report to the Economic and Social Research Council (UK). http://www.esrc.ac.uk/my-esrc/grants/RES-338-25-0010-A/outputs/Download/f102224a-dffd-4954-b234-a00d57863890

Walker, G., Devine-Wright, P., Barnett, J., Burningham, K., Cass, N., Devine-Wright, H., Speller, G., Barton, J., Evans, B., Heath, Y., Infield, D., Parks, J., & Theobald, K. (2011). Symmetries, expectations, dynamics and contexts: a framework for understanding public engagement with renewable energy projects. In P. Devine-Wright (Ed.), Renewable Energy and the Public: From NIMBY to Participation (pp. 1–14). London u. a.: Earthscan.

Walker, G., Devine-Wright, P., Hunter, S., High, H., & Evans, B. (2010). Trust and community: Exploring the meanings, contexts and dynamics of community renewable energy. Energy Policy, 38 (6), 2655–2663.

Walker, G., Hunter, S., Devine-Wright, P., Evans, B., & Fay, H. (2007). Harnessing Community Energies: Explaining and Evaluating Community-Based Localism in Renewable Energy Policy in the UK. Global Environmental Politics, 7 (2), 64–82.

Walker, G., Karvonen, A., & Guy, S. (2015a). Zero carbon homes and zero carbon living: sociomaterial interdependencies in carbon governance. Transactions of the Institute of British Geographers, 40 (4), 494–506.

Walker, I., Leviston, Z., Price, J., & Devine-Wright, P. (2015b). Responses to a worsening environment: relative deprivation mediates between place attachments and behaviour. European Journal of Social Psychology, 45 (7), 833–846.

Wall, R., Devine-Wright, P., & Mill, G. A. (2007). Comparing and Combining Theories to Explain Proenvironmental Intentions. The Case of Commuting-Mode Choice. Environment and Behavior, 39 (6), 731–753.

Wallenborn, G., & Wilhite, H. (2014). Rethinking embodied knowledge and household consumption. Energy Research & Social Science, 1, 56–64.

Walter, F. (2009). Im Herbst der Volksparteien? Eine kleine Geschichte von Aufstieg und Rückgang politischer Massenintegration (2nd ed.). Bielefeld: Transcript.

Walter, F. (2013). Zivilgesellschaft und Partizipationsdemokratie – ein Albtraum? Blog des Göttinger Instituts für Demokratieforschung. Ausgabe v. 7. Februar 2013. http://www.demokratie-goettingen.de/blog/zivilgesellschaft-und-partizipationsdemokratie-ein-albtraum

Walter, G. (2014). Determining the local acceptance of wind energy projects in Switzerland. The importance of general attitudes and project characteristics. Energy Research & Social Science, 4, 78–88.

Walzer, M. (1992). Zivile Gesellschaft und amerikanische Demokratie. Berlin: Rotbuch.

Warbasse, J. P. (1926). Genossenschaftliche Demokratie erzielt durch freiwillige Vereinigung der Menschen als Verbraucher. Eine Erörterung der Genossenschaftsbewegung, ihrer Philosophie, Methoden, Leistungen und Möglichkeiten und ihrer Beziehung zu Staat, Wissenschaft, Kunst und Handel und anderen Systemen wirtschaftlicher Organisation. Hamburg: Verlagsgesellschaft Deutscher Konsumvereine.

Ward, H. (2012). The Future of Democracy in the Face of Climate Change. Paper Five. London: Foundation for Democracy and Sustainable Development. http://www.fdsd.org/site/wp-content/uploads/2014/11/Democracy-and-climate-change-scenarios-final-with-foreword.pdf

Ward, J. (2011). Political Consumerism as Political Participation? In K. Brants & K. Voltmer (Eds.), Political Communication in Postmodern Democracy (pp. 167–182). Basingstoke, New York: Palgrave Macmillan.

Warren, C. R., & McFadyen, M. (2010). Does community ownership affect public attitudes to wind energy? A case study from south-west Scotland. Land Use Policy, 27 (2), 204–213.

Watson, J., & Devine-Wright, P. (2011). Centralisation, decentralisation and the scales in between. In M. Pollitt & T. Jamasb (Eds.), The Future of Electricity Demand. Customers, Citizens and Loads (pp. 542–577). Cambridge: Cambridge University Press.

Weber, W. G. (1998). Kooperation in Organisationen unter arbeits- und sozialpsychologischen Gesichtspunkten – vom individual-utilitaristischen zum prosozialen Handeln? In E. Spieß & F. W. Nerdinger (Eds.), Kooperation in Unternehmen (pp. 33–60). München: HamS.

Weber, W. G. (1999). Organisationale Demokratie – Anregungen für innovative Arbeitsformen jenseits bloßer Partizipation? Zeitschrift für Arbeitswissenschaft, 53 (4), 270–281.

Weber, W. G. (2004a). Entscheidungsbeteiligung, Commitment und prosoziale Orientierung in selbstverwalteten und Genossenschaftsunternehmen. In C. Liebig (Ed.), Psychologie und Wirtschaft leben. Aktuelle Themen der Wirtschaftspsychologie in Forschung und Praxis (pp. 428–433). München: HamS.

Weber, W. G. (2004b). Wirtschaft, Demokratie und soziale Verantwortung. Kontinuitäten und Brüche. Göttingen: Vandenhoeck & Ruprecht.

Weber, W. G., & Höge, T. (2009). Demokratie im Unternehmen. Terra Incognita der Organisationspsychologie? Wirtschaftspsychologie, 11 (4), 3–8.

Weber, W. G., & Lampert, B. (2010). Analysis o collective action regulation and cooperation-relevant attitudes in industrial group work. Psychologie des Alltagshandelns: Journal, 3 (1), 19–38.

Weber, W. G., & Moldaschl, M. F. (2012). Beyond the selfishness paradigm and "organizational citizenship": Work-related prosocial orientations and organizational democracy. Wirtschaftspsychologie, 14 (1), 100–112.

Weber, W. G., & Unterrainer, C. (2012). The Analysis of Preconditions for the Fostering of Democratic Behavioural Orientations in Business Organizations – The ODEM Questionnaire (POPD). In W. G. Weber, M. Thoma, A. Ostendorf, & L. Chisholm (Eds.), Democratic Competences and Social Practices in Organizations (pp. 118–143). Wiesbaden: Springer VS.

Weber, W. G., Ostendorp, C., & Wehner, T. (2003). Soziale Handlungsorientierungen und soziale Kompetenzen in interorganisationalen Netzwerken. Zeitschrift für Arbeitswissenschaft, 57 (5), 198–213.

Weber, W. G., Thoma, M., Ostendorf, A., & Chisholm, L. (Eds.). (2012). Democratic Competences and Social Practices in Organizations. Wiesbaden: Springer VS.

Weber, W. G., Unterrainer, C., & Höge, T. (2008). Sociomoral atmosphere and prosocial and democratic value orientations in enterprises with different levels of structurally anchored participation. Zeitschrift Für Personalforschung (ZfP), 22(2), 171–194.

Weber, W. G., Unterrainer, C., & Schmid, B. E. (2009). The influence of organizational democracy on employees' socio-moral climate and prosocial behavioral orientations. Journal of Organizational Behavior, 30(8), 1127–1149.

Weber, W. G., Unterrainer, C., Schmid, B. E., & Iwanowa, A. N. (2007). Solidarisches Handeln in demokratischen Betrieben – Illusion oder Realität? Zeitschrift für Sozialpsychologie und Gruppendynamik in Wirtschaft und Gesellschaft, 32 (1), 22–37.
Weg, M. (2005). Going Gender für die BürgerInnengesellschaft. Gender-Mainstreaming in zivilgesellschaftlichen Organisationen Studie für den Arbeitskreis „Bürgergesellschaft und Aktivierender Staat" der Friedrich-Ebert-Stiftung. Bonn: Friedrich-Ebert-Stiftung.
Wegge, J., Jeppesen, H. J., Weber, W. G., Pearce, C. L., Silva, S. A., Pundt, A., Jonsson, T., Wolf, S., Wassenaar, C., Unterrainer, C., & Piecha, A. (2010). Promoting Work Motivation in Organizations: Should Employee Involvement in Organizational Leadership Become a New Tool in the Organizational Psychologist's Kit? Journal of Personnel Psychology, 9 (4), 154–171.
Wegner, G. (Ed.). (2013). Wohlstand, Wachstum, gutes Leben. Wege zu einer Transformation der Ökonomie. Marburg: Metropolis Verlag.
Weingart, P. (1982). Strukturen technologischen Wandels. Zu einer soziologischen Analyse der Technik. In R. Jokisch (Ed.), Techniksoziologie (pp. 112–140). Frankfurt a. M.: Suhrkamp.
Weingart, P. (Ed.). (1989). Technik als sozialer Prozeß. Frankfurt a. M.: Suhrkamp.
Weis, L., Becker, S., & Naumann, M. (2015). Energiedemokratie. Grundlage und Perspektive einer kritischen Energieforschung. Berlin: Rosa-Luxemburg-Stiftung.
Weißeno, G. (Ed.). (2010a). Bürgerrolle heute. Migrationshintergrund und politisches Lernen. Opladen: Leske + Budrich.
Weißeno, G. (2010b). Konzepte der Politik – ein Kompetenzmodell. Schwalbach: Wochenschau.
Weißeno, G., & Buchstein, H. (Eds.). (2012). Politisch Handeln. Modelle, Möglichkeiten, Kompetenzen. Opladen: Leske + Budrich.
Weisel, O., & Böhm, R. (2015). "Ingroup love" and "outgroup hate" in intergroup conflict between natural groups. Journal of Experimental Social Psychology, 60, 110–120.
Weismeier-Sammer, D., & Reiner, E. (2011). Cooperative Solutions for Renewable Energy Production. Working Papers/RICC, 2011/02. Wien: WU Vienna University of Economics and Business.
Weizsäcker, C. C. von, Lindenberger, D., & Höffler (Eds.). (2016). Interdisziplinäre Aspekte der Energiewirtschaft. Heidelberg: Springer Vieweg.
Weller, I. (2014). Nachhaltiger Konsum in Zeiten des Klimawandels. In M. v. Hauff (Ed.), Nachhaltige Entwicklung. Aus der Perspektive verschiedener Disziplinen (pp. 75–90). Baden-Baden: Nomos.
Weller, I., & Funk, M. (2014). Ein Stadtwerk stemmt die Energiewende. Standortbestimmung, Strategieentwicklung und Umsetzung. Wiesbaden: Springer Gabler.
Welzer, H. (2013). Selbst denken. Eine Anleitung zum Widerstand. Frankfurt a. M.: Fischer.
Welzer, H. (2016). Die smarte Diktatur. Der Angriff auf unsere Freiheit. Frankfurt a.M.: S. Fischer.
Welzer, H., & Wiegandt, K. (Eds.). (2011). *Perspektiven einer nachhaltigen Entwicklung: Wie sieht die Welt im Jahr 2050 aus?* Frankfurt am Main: Fischer-Taschenbuch-Verl.
Welzer, H., & Wiegandt, K. (Eds.). (2013). Wege aus der Wachstumsgesellschaft. Frankfurt a. M.: Fischer.
Welzer, H., Giesecke, D., & Tremel, L. (2014). FUTURZWEI Zukunftsalmanach 2015/16. Frankfurt a. M.: Fischer.

Welzer, H., Soeffner, H.-G., & Giesecke, D. (Eds.). (2010). KlimaKulturen. Soziale Wirklichkeiten im Klimawandel. Frankfurt a. M., New York: Campus.

Weng, T. V. (2003). Werte und Wertewandel im Ehrenamt und bei Freiwilligen. VM: Fachzeitschrift für Verbands- und Nonprofit-Management, 29 (1), 6–19.

Weninger, H. (2011). Mitbestimmungsspezifische Interessenkonflikte von Arbeitnehmervertretern im Aufsichtsrat. Köln: Heymann.

Wenzelburger, G., & Zohlnhöfer, R. (Eds.). (2015). Handbuch Policy-Forschung. Wiesbaden: Springer VS.

Werber, N. (2011). Raumvergessenheit oder Raumontologie, Latour oder Luhmann? Zur Rolle der Systemtheorie in einer (medien)geographischen Kontroverse. Soziale Systeme. Zeitschrift Für Soziologische Theorie, 17 (2), 361–372.

Wesselink, A., Paavola, J., Fritsch, O., & Renn, O. (2011). Rationales for public participation in environmental policy and governance: practitioners' perspectives. Environment and Planning A, 43 (11), 2688–2704.

Wesselmann, C. (2002). Internet und Partizipation in Kommunen. Strategien des optimalen Kommunikations-Mix. Wiesbaden: Dt. Universitäts-Verlag.

Weßels, B. (2013). 13.2 Politische Integration und politisches Engagement. In Statistisches Bundesamt (Destatis) & Wissenschaftszentrum Berlin für Sozialforschung (WZB) (Eds.), Datenreport 2013: ein Sozialbericht für die Bundesrepublik Deutschland (pp. 363–369). Bonn: Bundeszentrale für politische Bildung.

West, J., Bailey, I., & Winter, M. (2010). Renewable energy policy and public perceptions of renewable energy: A cultural theory approach. Energy Policy, 38 (10), 5739–5748.

Westholm, E., & Beland Lindahl, K. (2012). The Nordic welfare model providing energy transition? A political geography approach to the EU RES directive. Energy Policy, 50, 328–335.

Westle, B. (2012). Souveräne Teilhabe unter Unsicherheit und Halbwissen. Politisches Wissen und politische Partizipation. In S. Braun & A. Geisler (Eds.), Die verstimmte Demokratie (pp. 51–68). Wiesbaden: Springer VS.

Westle, B., & Gabriel, O. W. (2008). Sozialkapital. Eine Einführung. Baden-Baden: Nomos.

Westle, B., & Krumm, T. (2009). Ausgewählte Verfahren der Datenerhebung. In B. Westle (Eds.), Methoden der Politikwissenschaft (pp. 207–272). Baden-Baden: Nomos.

Westley, F., & Antadze, N. (2009). Making a difference: strategies for scaling social innovation for greater impact. The Innovation Journal: The Public Sector Innovation Journal, 15 (2), Artikel 2. University of Waterloo, Canada.

Wex, T. (2004). Der Nonprofit-Sektor der Organisationsgesellschaft. Wiesbaden: Deutscher Universitäts-Verlag.

Whiteley, P. F. (2012). Political participation in Britain. The decline and revival of civic culture. Basingstoke, New York: Palgrave Macmillan.

Whitton, J., Parry, I. M., Akiyoshi, M., & Lawless, W. (2015). Conceptualizing a social sustainability framework for energy infrastructure decisions. Energy Research & Social Science, 8, 127–138.

Widmaier, B. (Ed.). (2011). Politische Bildung – Formal, non-formal, informell. Eine Begriffsannäherung. Journal für Politische Bildung, Heft 3.

Widmaier, U. (1978). Politische Gewaltanwendung als Problem der Organisation von Interessen. Eine Querschnittsstudie der soziopolitischen Ursachen gewaltsamer Konfliktsaustragung innerhalb von Nationalstaaten. Meisenheim am Glan: Hain.

Wiedenhofer, D., Lenzen, M., & Steinberger, J. K. (2013). Energy requirements of consumption: Urban form, climatic and socio-economic factors, rebounds and their policy implications. Energy Policy, 63, 696–707.

Wieg, A. (2011). Energiegenossenschaften. Bürger, Kommunen und lokale Wirtschaft in guter Gesellschaft. Berlin: Agentur für Erneuerbare Energien. http://www.kommunal-erneuerbar.de/fileadmin/content/PDF/AEE_DGRV_Energie-genossenschaften_2013_web.pdf

Wiersma, B., & Devine-Wright, P. (2014a). Decentralising energy: comparing the drivers and influencers of projects led by public, private, community and third sector actors. Contemporary Social Science 9, 456–470.

Wiersma, B., & Devine-Wright, P. (2014b). Public engagement with offshore renewable energy: a critical review. Wiley Interdisciplinary Reviews: Climate Change, 5(4), 493–507.

Wilde, G. (2014). Zivilgesellschaftsforschung aus Geschlechterperspektive. In A. E. Zimmer & R. Simsa (Eds.), Forschung zu Zivilgesellschaft, NPOs und Engagement (pp. 209–227). Wiesbaden: Springer VS.

Wilkesmann, U. (2007). Einzelinteressen und kollektives Handeln in Organisationen. Das Dilemma der Steuerung wissensintensiver Arbeit. In N. C. Bandelow & W. Bleek (Eds.), Einzelinteressen und kollektives Handeln in modernen Demokratien (pp. 163–185). Wiesbaden: VS Verlag.

Wilkinson, A. (Ed.). (2014). Handbook of research on employee voice. Cheltenham u. a.: Edward Elgar.

Wilkinson, A., Gollan, P. J., Marchington, M., & Lewin, D. (2012). The Oxford Handbook of Participation in Organizations. Oxford, New York: Oxford University Press.

Williams, B. (1988). Formal structures and social reality. In D. Gambetta (Ed.), Trust: making and breaking cooperative relations (pp. 3–13). New York: Blackwell.

Williams, B. (2010). Greening the Economy. Integrating Economics and Ecology to Make Effective Change. London, New York: Routledge.

Williams, R. (1976). Keywords: a vocabulary of culture and society. London: Fontana/Croom Helm.

Willis, M. M., & Schor, J. B. (2012). Does Changing a Light Bulb Lead to Changing the World? Political Action and the Conscious Consumer. The ANNALS of the American Academy of Political and Social Science, 644 (1), 160–190.

Willmott, P. (1987). Friendship networks and social support. London: Policy Studies Institute.

Wilpert, B. (1994). Chapter Fourteen: Participation Research in Organisational Psychology. In P. Bertelson, P. Eelen, & G. d' Ydewalle (Eds.), International Perspectives On Psychological Science, II: The State of the Art (pp. 293–310). Hove u. a.: Erlbaum.

Wilpert, B. (1997). Mitbestimmung. In S. Greif, H. Holling & N. Nicholson, Arbeits-Und Organisationspsychologie. Internationales Handbuch in Schlüsselbegriffen (3rd ed., pp. 324–328). Weinheim: Beltz.

Wilpert, B., & Rayley, J. (1983). Anspruch und Wirklichkeit der Mitbestimmung. Frankfurt a. M., New York: Campus.

Wilpert, B., & Sorge, A. (Eds.). (1984). International perspectives on organizational democracy. Chichester u. a.: Wiley.

Wilson, J., & Swyngedouw, E. (Eds.). (2014). The post-political and its discontents: spaces of depoliticisation, spectres of radical politics. Edinburgh: Edinburgh University Press.

Winkler, J., Gaio, A., Pfluger, B., & Ragwitz, M. (2016). Impact of renewables on electricity markets – Do support schemes matter? Energy Policy, 93, 157–167.

Wirth, S. (2014). Communities matter: Institutional preconditions for community renewable energy. Energy Policy, 70, 236–246.

Wissenschaftlicher Beirat der Bundesregierung Globale Umweltveränderungen (WBGU) (Ed.). (2012). Finanzierung der globalen Energiewende. Berlin: Wissenschaftlicher Beirat der Bundesregierung Globale Umweltveränderungen (WBGU).

Wissenschaftlicher Beirat der Bundesregierung Globale Umweltveränderungen (WBGU). (2014). Klimaschutz als Weltbürgerbewegung. Sondergutachten. Berlin: Wissenschaftlicher Beirat der Bundesregierung Globale Umweltveränderungen (WBGU).

Witte, U. (2014). Nachhaltigkeit gestalten. Trends und Entwicklungen in der Umweltkommunikation. München: Oekom.

Wittmayer, J., Avelino, F., Dorland, J., Pel, B., Jørgensen, M. S., & Wittmayer, J. (2015a). Methodological Guidelines for Batch 2. TRANSIT Working Paper Deliverable 4.3. Rotterdam.

Wittmayer, J., Backhaus, J., Avelino, F., Pel, B., Strasser, T., & Kunze, I. (2015b). Narratives of change: How Social Innovation Initiatives engage with their transformative ambitions. TRANSIT Working Paper #4, October 2015. Rotterdam.

Witzel, A. (2000). The Problem-centered Interview. Forum Qualitative Sozialforschung/Forum: Qualitative Social Research, 1 (1). http://www.qualitative-research.net/index.php/fqs/article/view/1132

Witzel, A., & Reiter, H. (2012). The problem-centred interview: principles and practice. Los Angeles: Sage.

Wöhl, S. (2013). Die „Krise" der repräsentativen Demokratie in Europa. Demokratietheoretische und politikfeldbezogene Reflexionen. Forschungsjournal Soziale Bewegungen, 26 (1), 42–50.

Wöhler, C. (2015). Verbandsmanagement mit Zukunft. Non-Profit-Organisationen professionell und erfolgreich führen. Wiesbaden: Springer Gabler.

Wolf, A. C. (2012). Lokale Engagementförderung. Kritik und Perspektiven. Wiesbaden: Springer VS.

Wolf, A. C., & Zimmer, A. (2010). Besetzung ehrenamtlicher Vereinsvorstände – Vorstände verzweifelt gesucht. VM: Fachzeitschrift für Verbands- und Nonprofit-Management, 36 (3), 28–37.

Wolf, F., & Pfohl, T. (2014). Protecting the population in a multilevel system: horizontal and vertical informal governance patterns in Germany. Zeitschrift für vergleichende Politikwissenschaft, 8 (1), 259–285.

Wolin, S. S. (1994). "Fugitive Democracy". Constellations, 1 (1), 11–25.

Wolling, J., & Arlt, D. (2011). Energiebewusstsein 2011. Ergebnisse einer repräsentativen Bevölkerungsumfrage in Thüringen zu energiebezogenen Einstellungen und Verhaltensweisen. Ilmenau: Techn. Univ. http://www.db-thueringen.de/servlets/DerivateServlet/Derivate-24315/ilm1-2011200540.pdf

Wolling, J., & Bräuer, M. (2010). Bürgerinitiativen. Ihre Funktion aus Sicht der Bevölkerung und ihre kommunikativen Aktivitäten. Ilmenau: Ilmedia.

Wollmann, H. (2002). Die Entwicklung der politischen Partizipationsmöglichkeiten auf kommunaler Ebene. In Enquete-Kommission „Zukunft des Bürgerschaftlichen Engagements" des 14. Deutschen Bundestages (Eds.), Bürgerschaftliches Engagement und Zivilgesellschaft (pp. 101–119). Opladen: Leske + Budrich.

Wolsink, M. (2000). Wind power and the NIMBY-myth: institutional capacity and the limited significance of public support. Renewable Energy, 21 (1), 49–64.

Wolsink, M. (2002). Der „Infrastrukturansatz" und der Versuch zur Neugestaltung des Niederländischen Planungssystems. Planungsrundschau, 6, 42–67. http://www.planungsrundschau.de/planungsrundschau06/frameset.htm

Wolsink, M. (2010). Contested environmental policy infrastructure: Socio-political acceptance of renewable energy, water, and waste facilities. Environmental Impact Assessment Review, 30 (5), 302–311.

Wolsink, M. (2012a). The research agenda on social acceptance of distributed generation in smart grids: Renewable as common pool resources. Renewable and Sustainable Energy Reviews, 16 (1), 822–835.

Wolsink, M. (2012b). Undesired reinforcement of harmful "self-evident truths" concerning the implementation of wind power. Energy Policy, 48, 83–87.

Wolsink, M. (2012c). Wind Power: Basic Challenge Concerning Social Acceptance. In R. A. Meyers (Ed.), Encyclopedia of Sustainability Science and Technology (pp. 1785–1821). New York: Springer.

Wolterstorff, A. (1919). Gründung und Finanzierung von Elektrizitätsgenossenschaften. Berlin: Springer.

Wong, C. M. L. (2016). Assembling Interdisciplinary Energy Research through an Actor Network Theory (ANT) frame. Energy Research & Social Science, 12, 106–110.

Woodin, T., Crook, D., Carpentier, V., & Joseph Rowntree Foundation. (2010). Community and mutual ownership: a historical overview. York: Joseph Rowntree Foundation.

Woods, E. (2016). Living Off The Grid. A Step-By-Step Guide to a More Self-Sufficient, Self Reliant, Sustainable Life. CreateSpace Independent Publishing Platform.

Woyke, W. (2009). Politische Beteiligung/Politische Partizipation. In U. Andersen (Ed.), Handwörterbuch des politischen Systems der Bundesrepublik Deutschland (pp. 549–553). Wiesbaden: VS Verlag.

Wray, K. B. (2015). Epistemic Communities and Collaborative Research, History of. In J. D. Wright (Ed.), International Encyclopedia of the Social & Behavioral Sciences (2nd ed.) (pp. 867–872). Oxford: Elsevier.

Wright, Z. M. (2012). A Voice for the Community: Public Participation in Wind Energy Development. Dalhousie Journal of Interdisciplinary Management, 8 (1), 1–17.

Wunderlich, C., & Vohrer, P. (2012). Akzeptanz Erneuerbarer Energien in der deutschen Bevölkerung. Bundesländergenaue Ergebnisse einer repräsentativen Umfrage von TNS Infratest im Auftrag der Agentur für Erneuerbare Energien. Renews Spezial. http://www.unendlich-viel-energie.de/media/file/170.60_Renews_Spe-zial_Akzeptanz_online_final.pdf

Wüstenhagen, R., Wolsink, M., & Bürer, M. J. (2007). Social acceptance of renewable energy innovation: An introduction to the concept. Energy Policy, 35 (5), 2683–2691.

Wynsberghe, R. van. (2001). Organizing a community response to environmental injustice: Walpole island's heritage centre as a social movement organization. In R. K. Schutt & S. W. Hartwell (Eds.), The organizational response to social problems (pp. 221–243). Amsterdam: JAI Press.

Xu, X., Taylor, J. E., Pisello, A. L., & Culligan, P. J. (2012). The impact of place-based affiliation networks on energy conservation: An holistic model that integrates the influence of buildings, residents and the neighborhood context. Energy and Buildings, 55, 637–646.

Yang, M. (2012). Deliberative Politik von unten. Eine diskursanalytische Feldstudie dreier politischer Kleingruppen. Baden-Baden: Nomos.

Yang, M., & Baringhorst, S. (2014). Reintermediation durch Social-Web? Eine Analyse von Social-Web-Projekten im Bereich des politischen Konsums. In F. Oehmer (Ed.), Politische Interessenvermittlung und Medien. Funktionen, Formen und Folgen medialer Kommunikation von Parteien, Verbänden und sozialen Bewegungen (pp. 399–423). Baden-Baden: Nomos.

Yang, M., Baringhorst, S., & Quednau, T. (Eds.). (2015). Das Private ist politisch – Konsum und Lebensstile. Forschungsjournal Soziale Bewegungen. Jahrgang 28, Heft 2. Stuttgart: Lucius & Lucius.

Yankov, A. (2010). Auswertungsmethoden leitfadengestützter Interviews. In N. Schöneck-Voß, W. Voß, & J.-F. Kremer (Eds.), Methodenintegrative Forschung: Darstellung am Beispiel einer Befragung von Studierenden zu Studienbeiträgen (pp. 15–30). Bochum: Universität Bochum, Fak. für Sozialwiss.

Yildiz, Ö. (2013). Energiegenossenschaften in Deutschland. Bestandsentwicklung und institutionenökonomische Analyse. Zeitschrift für das gesamte Genossenschaftswesen, 63 (3), 173–185.

Yildiz, Ö. (2014). Financing renewable energy infrastructures via financial citizen participation – The case of Germany. Renewable Energy, 68, 677–685.

Yildiz, Ö., Rommel, J., Debor, S., Holstenkamp, L., Mey, F., Müller, J. R., Radtke, J., Rognli, J. (2015). Renewable energy cooperatives as gatekeepers or facilitators? Recent developments in Germany and a multidisciplinary research agenda. Energy Research & Social Science, 6, 59–73.

Yin, Y. (2012). A socio-political analysis of policies and incentives applicable to community wind in Oregon. Energy Policy, 42, 442–449.

Young, H. P. (2011). The dynamics of social innovation. Proceedings of the National Academy of Sciences, 108 (Supplement 4), 21285–21291.

Young, I. M. (1990). Justice and the politics of difference. Princeton, NJ: Princeton University Press.

Young, O. R., Berkhout, F., Gallopin, G. C., Janssen, M. A., Ostrom, E., & van der Leeuw, S. (2006). The globalization of socio-ecological systems: An agenda for scientific research. Global Environmental Change, 16 (3), 304–316.

Zarnikau, J. (2003). Consumer demand for "green power" and energy efficiency. Energy Policy, 31 (15), 1661–1672.

Zentrum für zivilgesellschaftliche Entwicklung. (2016). Zweiter Engagementbericht der Bundesregierung. Berlin: Bundesministerium für Familie, Senioren, Frauen und Jugend.

Zeuch, M. (2012). Nähe zum Mitglied und Mitgliederorientierung: gelebtes Selbstverständnis am Beispiel der Raiffeisenbank Lohr am Main eG. In G. Ringle & H.-M. Münkner (Eds.), Genossenschaftliche Kooperation – anders wirtschaften (pp. 151–173). Baden-Baden: Nomos.

Ziekow, J., Barth, R., Schütte, S., & Ewen, C. (2014). Konfliktdialog bei der Zulassung von Vorhaben der Energiewende. Leitfaden für Behörden. Sechsteilige Studie im Auftrag des Umweltbundesamtes. Dessau-Roßlau: Umweltbundesamt.

Ziekow, J., Ewen, C., Barth, R., & Schütte, S. (2015). Neuartiger Öffentlichkeitsdialog in Verfahren mit Umweltprüfung am Beispiel bestimmter Vorhabentypen/Vorhabeneigenschaften. Leitfäden für Behörden und rechtliche Verankerung. Speyer: Deutsches Forschungsinstitut für Öffentliche Verwaltung.

Ziesenіß, R., & Ernst, T. (2013). Ökonomische Laborexperimente als Instrument der Politikanalyse. In J. Brazda, M. Dellinger, & D. Rößl (Eds.), Genossenschaften im Fokus einer neuen Wirtschaftspolitik. Bericht der XVII. Internationalen Genossenschaftswissenschaftlichen Tagung (IGT) 2012 in Wien. Teilband 2 (pp. 449–477). Wien: LIT.

Zimmer, A. (2000). Engagierte Bürgerschaft. Traditionen und Perspektiven. Opladen: Leske + Budrich.

Zimmer, A. (2003). Über Macht und Ehre in Vereinen und Verbänden. Ein Rückblick auf Forschung und Politik. Gruppendynamik und Organisationsberatung, 34 (4), 331–345.

Zimmer, A. (2005a). Führungskräfte in gemeinnützigen Organisationen. Bürgerschaftliches Engagement und Management. Bramsche: Rasch. http://www.forschungsverbund.tu-dortmund.de/fileadmin/Files/Texte_Reinhard/BE_M-Broschuere_1._Phase__2005_.pdf

Zimmer, A. (2005b). Vom Ehrenamt zum Bürgerschaftlichen Engagement – Einführung in den Stand der Debatte. Forschungsjournal Soziale Bewegungen, 3, 29–39.

Zimmer, A. (2007). Vereine – Zivilgesellschaft konkret (2nd ed.). Wiesbaden: VS Verlag.

Zimmer, A. (2011). Vereine. In T. Olk & B. Hartnuß (Eds.), Handbuch Bürgerschaftliches Engagement (pp. 453–464). Weinheim u. a.: Beltz Juventa.

Zimmer, A., & Priller, E. (2007). Gemeinnützige Organisationen im gesellschaftlichen Wandel. Ergebnisse der Dritte-Sektor-Forschung (2nd ed.). Wiesbaden: VS Verlag.

Zimmer, A., & Simsa, R. (2014). Forschung zu Zivilgesellschaft, NPOs und Engagement: Quo vadis? Wiesbaden: Springer VS.

Zimmer, A., & Speth, R. (2009). Verbändeforschung. In V. Kaina & A. Römmele (Eds.), Politische Soziologie (pp. 267–309). Wiesbaden: VS Verlag.

Zimmerer, K. (Ed.). (2013). The new geographies of energy: assessment and analysis of critical landscapes. London: Routledge.

Zipp, J. F., Landerman, R., & Luebke, P. (1982). Political Parties and Political Participation: A Reexamination of the Standard Socioeconomic Model. Social Forces, 60 (4), 1140–1153.

Zmerli, S., & Feldman, O. (Eds.). (2015). Politische Psychologie. Handbuch für Studium und Wissenschaft. Baden-Baden: Nomos.

Zöllner, J., Ittner, H., & Schweizer-Ries, P. (2005). Perceived procedural justice as a conflict factor in wind energy plants planning processes. Präsentation: Fifth BIEE Academic Conference: "European Energy-Synergies and Conflicts", Oxford. http://www.fachagentur-windenergie.de/fileadmin/files/Akzeptanz/204_ProceduralJustice_Oxford_Zoellner.pdf

Zöllner, J., Rau, I., & Schweizer-Ries, P. (2011). Beteiligungsprozesse und Entwicklungschancen für Kommunen und Regionen. Zur Akzeptanz von erneuerbaren Energien. Ökologisches Wirtschaften, 3, 25–27.

Zöllner, J., Schweizer-Ries, P., & Rau, I. (2012). Akzeptanz Erneuerbarer Energien. In T. Müller (Ed.), 20 Jahre Recht der Erneuerbaren Energien. Baden-Baden: Nomos.

Zöllner, J., Schweizer-Ries, P., & Wemheuer, C. (2008). Public acceptance of renewable energies. Results from case studies in Germany. Energy Policy, 36 (11), 4136–4141.

Zöllner, J., Wemheuer, C., & Schweizer-Ries, P. (2007). Akzeptanz erneuerbarer Energien am Beispiel von PV-Freiflächenanlagen. In Ostbayerisches Energie-Kolleg (Eds.), 22. Symposium Photovoltaische Solarenergie (pp. 157–164). Regensburg: Ostbayerisches Technologie-Transfer-Institut e.V. (OTTI).

Zschocke, D. (2007). Regionalisierung und Partizipation. Eine Untersuchung am Beispiel der Städteregion Ruhr und der Region Braunschweig. Bonn: Stiftung Mitarbeit.

Zukin, C., Keeter, S., Andolina, M., Jenkins, K, & Delli Carpini, M. X. (2006). A new engagement? Political Participation, Civic Life, and the Changing American Citizen. New York u. a.: Oxford University Press.

Zürn, M. (1998). Regieren jenseits des Nationalstaates. Globalisierung und Denationalisierung als Chance. Frankfurt a. M.: Suhrkamp.

Zürn, M. (2005). Introduction: Law and compliance at different levels. In M. Zürn & C. Joerges (Eds.), Law and Governance in Postnational Europe: Compliance beyond the Nation-State (pp. 1–38). Cambridge u. a.: Cambridge University Press.

Zürn, M. (2013). „Critical Citizens" oder „Critical Decisions" – Eine Erwiderung. Politische Vierteljahresschrift, 54, 173–185.

Zürn, M., & Weidner, H. (2009). Die Politisierung der Ökonomisierung? Zum gegenwärtigen Verhältnis von Politik und Ökonomie. In J. Wieland (Ed.), CSR als Netzwerkgovernance – theoretische Herausforderungen und praktische Antworten. Über das Netzwerk von Wirtschaft, Politik und Zivilgesellschaft (pp. 155–184). Marburg: Metropolis.